# Lecture Notes in Computer Science 14100



## Advanced Research in Computing and Software Science

Subline of Lecture Notes in Computer Science

More information about this series at https://link.springer.com/bookseries/558

José Cano · Marios D. Dikaiakos ·
George A. Papadopoulos ·
Miquel Pericàs · Rizos Sakellariou
Editors

# Euro-Par 2023: Parallel Processing

29th International Conference on Parallel and Distributed Computing
Limassol, Cyprus, August 28 – September 1, 2023
Proceedings

*Editors*
José Cano
University of Glasgow
Glasgow, UK

Marios D. Dikaiakos
University of Cyprus
Nicosia, Cyprus

George A. Papadopoulos
University of Cyprus
Nicosia, Cyprus

Miquel Pericàs
Chalmers University of Technology
Gothenburg, Sweden

Rizos Sakellariou
University of Manchester
Manchester, UK

ISSN 0302-9743 ISSN 1611-3349 (electronic)
Lecture Notes in Computer Science
ISBN 978-3-031-39697-7 ISBN 978-3-031-39698-4 (eBook)
https://doi.org/10.1007/978-3-031-39698-4



This Springer imprint is published by the registered company Springer Nature Switzerland AG
The registered company address is: Gewerbestrasse 11, 6330 Cham, Switzerland

# Preface

This volume contains the papers presented at Euro-Par 2023, the 29th International European Conference on Parallel and Distributed Computing, held in Limassol, Cyprus between August 28th and September 1st, 2023.

For over 25 years, Euro-Par has consistently brought together researchers in parallel and distributed computing. Founded by pioneers as a merger of the three thematically related European conference series PARLE and CONPAR-VAPP, Euro-Par started with the aim to create the main annual scientific event on parallel and distributed computing in Europe and to be the primary choice of professionals for the presentation of their latest results. Since its inception, Euro-Par has covered all aspects of parallel and distributed computing, ranging from theory to practice, scaling from the smallest to the largest parallel and distributed systems, from fundamental computational problems and models to full-fledged applications, from architecture and interface design and implementation to tools, infrastructures and applications. Over time, Euro-Par has forged a community that follows the latest developments in the field, at the same time bringing together a broad and diverse audience, supporting young researchers and promoting networking across borders.

Previous conference editions took place in Stockholm, Lyon, Passau, Southampton, Toulouse, Munich, Manchester, Paderborn, Klagenfurt, Pisa, Lisbon, Dresden, Rennes, Las Palmas, Delft, Ischia, Bordeaux, Rhodes, Aachen, Porto, Vienna, Grenoble, Santiago de Compostela, Turin, Göttingen, Warsaw, Lisbon and Glasgow.

The 29th edition of Euro-Par was organized by the Department of Computer Science at the University of Cyprus.

Euro-Par 2023 accepted papers in the following 6 tracks:

- Programming, Compilers and Performance
- Scheduling, Resource Management, Cloud, Edge Computing and Workflows
- Architectures and Accelerators
- Data Analytics, AI and Computational Science
- Theory and Algorithms
- Multidisciplinary, Domain-Specific and Applied Parallel and Distributed Computing

A total of 164 full papers were submitted by authors from 37 different countries. The number of submitted papers, the range of topics, and the requirement to obtain high-quality reviews mandated careful selection using a large pool of experts. The chairs along with 164 members of the program committee and 90 external reviewers produced a total of 654 single-blind reviews, an average of about 3.98 reviews per paper. The accepted papers were selected in a two-phase process. Following initial discussion, each track proposed sets of papers for acceptance, further discussion or rejection. The papers from all tracks were reviewed and discussed in an online selection meeting on 26th April 2023. The outcome was to select 49 papers to be presented at the conference and published in these proceedings, a 29.9% acceptance rate.

Four of the accepted papers were selected to be presented in a plenary session and compete for the Euro-Par 2023 best paper award, which was generously sponsored by Springer. The four papers were:

"MMExit: Enabling Fast and Efficient Multi-modal DNN Inference with Adaptive Network Exits", *Xiaofeng Hou, Jiacheng Liu, Xuehan Tang, Chao Li, Kwang-Ting Cheng, Li Li and Minyi Guo*

"Optimizing Data Movement for GPU-Based In-Situ Workflow Using GPUDirect RDMA", *Bo Zhang, Philip E Davis, Nicolas Morales, Zhao Zhang, Keita Teranishi and Manish Parashar*

"Distributed k-Means with Outliers in General Metrics", *Enrico Dandolo, Andrea Pietracaprina and Geppino Pucci*

"An Efficient Parallel Adaptive GMG Solver for Large-Scale StokesProblems", *S. Saberi, G. Meschke and A. Vogel*

To increase reproducibility of the research appearing at Euro-Par, the conference encourages authors to submit artifacts, such as source code, data sets and reproducibility instructions. In the notification of acceptance authors were encouraged to submit artifacts for evaluation. A total of 16 artifacts were submitted in support of accepted papers and evaluated by the Artifact Evaluation Committee (AEC). The AEC successfully reproduced results for 14 artifacts, or 28.5% of accepted papers. These papers are marked in the proceedings by a special stamp and the artifacts are available online in the Figshare repository (https://springernature.figshare.com/europar). Selected artifacts will also be published in a Euro-Par special issue of the Journal of Open Source Software.

In addition to the technical program, we had the pleasure of hosting three distinguished keynote talks by:

- Schahram Dustdar, Vienna University of Technology, Austria
- Enrique S. Quintana-Orti, Universitat Politècnica de València, Spain
- Jahna Otterbacher, Open University of Cyprus, Cyprus

Euro-Par 2023 started with two days of workshops, a tutorial and a PhD Symposium, and was followed by three days dedicated to the main conference sessions. A poster and demo session ran alongside the main conference. Dora Blanco Heras and Demetris Zeinalipour coordinated the workshops as workshop co-chairs. Herodotos Herodotou and Demetris Trihinas coordinated the PhD Symposium. George Pallis coordinated the poster and demo session. A selection of the papers presented at the workshops are published in a separate Springer LNCS volume. Contributions presented at the PhD symposium and the poster session are also published in the same volume.

We would like to thank the authors, chairs, PC members and reviewers for contributing to the success of Euro-Par 2023. Similarly, we would like to extend our appreciation to the Euro-Par Steering Committee for its support.

August 2023

José Cano
Marios D. Dikaiakos
George A. Papadopoulos
Miquel Pericàs
Rizos Sakellariou

# Organization

## Steering Committee

### Full Members

| | |
|---|---|
| Fernando Silva (SC Chair) | University of Porto, Portugal |
| Dora Blanco Heras (Workshops Chair) | University of Santiago de Compostela, Spain |
| Maciej Malawski (Virtualization Chair) | AGH University of Science and Technology, Poland |
| Henk Sips (Finance chair) | Delft University of Technology, The Netherlands |
| Massimo Torquati (Artifacts Chair) | University of Pisa, Italy |
| Marco Aldinucci | University of Turin, Italy |
| Luc Bougé | ENS Rennes, France |
| Jesus Carretero | Carlos III University of Madrid, Spain |
| Christos Kaklamanis | Computer Technology Institute and University of Patras, Greece |
| Paul Kelly | Imperial College London, UK |
| Thomas Ludwig | University of Hamburg, Germany |
| Tomàs Margalef | Autonomous University of Barcelona, Spain |
| Wolfgang Nagel | Dresden University of Technology, Germany |
| George Papadopoulos | University of Cyprus, Cyprus |
| Francisco Fernández Rivera | University of Santiago de Compostela, Spain |
| Krzysztof Rządca | University of Warsaw, Poland |
| Rizos Sakellariou | University of Manchester, UK |
| Leonel Sousa | University of Lisbon, Portugal |
| Phil Trinder | University of Glasgow, UK |
| Felix Wolf | Technical University of Darmstadt, Germany |
| Ramin Yahyapour | GWDG and University of Göttingen, Germany |

### Honorary Members

| | |
|---|---|
| Christian Lengauer | University of Passau, Germany |
| Ron Perrott | Oxford e-Research Centre, UK |
| Karl Dieter Reinartz | University of Erlangen-Nürnberg, Germany |

## General Chair

| | |
|---|---|
| George Papadopoulos | University of Cyprus, Cyprus |

**Program Chairs**

| | |
|---|---|
| Marios Dikaiakos | University of Cyprus, Cyprus |
| Rizos Sakellariou | University of Manchester, UK |

**Workshop Chairs**

| | |
|---|---|
| Dora Blanco Heras | University of Santiago de Compostela, Spain |
| Demetris Zeinalipour | University of Cyprus, Cyprus |

**Publication Chairs**

| | |
|---|---|
| José Cano | University of Glasgow, UK |
| Miquel Pericàs | Chalmers University of Technology, Sweden |

**Local Chairs**

| | |
|---|---|
| Chryssis Georgiou | University of Cyprus, Cyprus |
| George Pallis | University of Cyprus, Cyprus |

## Scientific Organization

## Track 1: Programming, Compilers and Performance

**Chairs**

| | |
|---|---|
| Biagio Cosenza | University of Salerno, Italy |
| Thomas Fahringer | University of Innsbruck, Austria |

**Program Committee**

| | |
|---|---|
| Siegfried Benkner | University of Vienna, Austria |
| Walter Binder | Università della Svizzera italiana, Switzerland |
| Bruno Loic Alexandre Bodin | Yale-NUS College, Singapore |
| Jeronimo Castrillon | TU Dresden, Germany |
| Stefano Cherubin | Edinburgh Napier University, UK |
| Tom Deakin | University of Bristol, UK |
| Juan Durillo Barrionuevo | Leibniz Supercomputing Centre, Germany |
| Bernhard Egger | Seoul National University, South Korea |
| Juan Fumero | University of Manchester, UK |
| Sergei Gorlatch | University of Münster, Germany |
| Ramaswamy Govindarajan | Indian Institute of Science, India |
| Giulia Guidi | Cornell University, USA |
| Adrian Jackson | University of Edinburgh, UK |
| Abhinav Jangda | Microsoft Research, USA |
| Sohan Lal | TU Hamburg, Germany |
| Partick McCormick | Los Alamos National Laboratory, USA |

| | |
|---|---|
| Gihan Mudalige | University of Warwick, UK |
| Fernando Magno Quintão Pereira | Federal University of Minas Gerais, Brazil |
| Pablo de Oliveira Castro | University of Versailles, France |
| Polyvios Pratikakis | FORTH, Greece |
| István Reguly | Pázmány Péter Catholic University, Hungary |
| Ruymán Reyes | Codeplay Software/Intel, UK |
| Bernhard Scholz | University of Sydney, Australia |
| Michel Steuwer | University of Edinburgh, UK |
| Giuseppe Tagliavini | University of Bologna, Italy |
| Peter Thoman | University of Innsbruck, Austria |
| Massimo Torquati | University of Pisa, Italy |
| Miwako Tsuji | RIKEN Center for Computational Science, Japan |
| Antonino Tumeo | Pacific Northwest National Laboratory, USA |
| Didem Unat | Koç University, Turkey |
| Hans Vandierendonck | Queen's University Belfast, UK |

## Track 2: Scheduling, Resource Management, Cloud, Edge Computing, and Workflows

### Chairs

| | |
|---|---|
| Marco Aldinucci | University of Torino, Italy |
| Ivona Brandic | Vienna University of Technology, Austria |

### Program Committee

| | |
|---|---|
| Christos Anagnostopoulos | University of Glasgow, UK |
| Atakan Aral | University of Vienna, Austria |
| Anne Benoit | ENS Lyon, France |
| Silvina Caíno-Lores | University of Tennessee, USA |
| Valeria Cardellini | University of Roma "Tor Vergata", Italy |
| Iacopo Colonnelli | Università di Torino, Italy |
| Patrizio Dazzi | University of Pisa, Italy |
| Vincenzo De Maio | TU Vienna, Austria |
| Rafael Ferreira da Silva | Oak Ridge National Laboratory, USA |
| Sukhpal Gill | Queen Mary University of London, UK |
| Anastasios Gounaris | Aristotle University of Thessaloniki, Greece |
| Ioannis Konstantinou | University of Thessaly, Greece |
| Marco Lapegna | Università degli Studi di Napoli Federico II, Italy |
| Simone Leo | CRS4, Italy |
| Anirban Mandal | Renaissance Computing Institute, USA |
| Loris Marchal | CNRS, France |
| Alberto Riccardo Martinelli | University of Torino, Italy |
| Doriana Medic | University of Torino, Italy |
| Raffaele Montella | University of Naples Parthenope, Italy |
| Grégory Mounié | Université Grenoble-Alpes, France |

| | |
|---|---|
| Dimitrios Nikolopoulos | Virginia Tech, USA |
| Maria S. Perez | Universidad Politécnica de Madrid, Spain |
| Artur Podobas | KTH Royal Institute of Technology, Sweden |
| Krzysztof Rzadca | University of Warsaw, Poland |
| Uwe Schwiegelshohn | TU Dortmund, Germany |
| Jeremy Singer | University of Glasgow, UK |
| Oliver Sinnen | University of Auckland, New Zealand |
| Athanasios Stratikopoulos | University of Manchester, UK |
| Moysis Symeonidis | University of Cyprus, Cyprus |
| Nguyen Kim Thang | University Grenoble-Alpes, France |
| Frédéric Vivien | Inria, France |
| Ramin Yahyapour | University of Göttingen, Germany |

## Track 3: Architectures and Accelerators

### Chairs

| | |
|---|---|
| Jesus Carretero | Carlos III University of Madrid, Spain |
| Leonel Sousa | University of Lisbon, Portugal |

### Program Committee

| | |
|---|---|
| Jean-Thomas Acquaviva | DDN, France |
| Giovanni Agosta | Politecnico di Milano, Italy |
| Hartwig Anzt | University of Tennessee, USA |
| Raja Appuswamy | EURECOM, France |
| Jean-Baptiste Besnard | ParaTools SAS, France |
| Jorge G. Barbosa | University of Porto, Portugal |
| George Bosilca | University of Tennessee, USA |
| Xing Cai | Simula Research Laboratory, Norway |
| Toshio Endo | Tokyo Institute of Technology, Japan |
| Javier Garcia Blas | Carlos III University of Madrid, Spain |
| Brice Goglin | Inria, France |
| Alfredo Goldman | University of São Paulo, Brazil |
| Akihiro Hayashi | Georgia Institute of Technology, USA |
| Francisco D. Igual | Universidad Complutense de Madrid, Spain |
| Emmanuel Jeannot | Inria, France |
| Hatem Ltaief | King Abdullah University of Science and Technology, Saudi Arabia |
| Ravi Reddy Manumachu | UCD, Ireland |
| Dejan Milojicic | Hewlett Packard Enterprise, USA |
| Francesca Palumbo | University of Sassari, Italy |
| Oscar Plata | University of Malaga, Spain |
| Loïc Pottier | Lawrence Livermore National Laboratory, USA |
| Matei Ripeanu | University of British Columbia, Canada |
| Nuno Roma | Universidade de Lisboa, Portugal |
| Martin Schreiber | Université Grenoble-Alpes, France |

| | |
|---|---|
| Estela Suarez | Forschungszentrum Jülich, Germany |
| Samuel Thibaul | Université Bordeaux 1, France |
| Juan Tourino | University of A Coruña, Spain |
| Pedro Trancoso | Chalmers University of Technology, Sweden |
| Marc-André Vef | Johannes Gutenberg University Mainz, Germany |
| Chao Wang | University of Southern California, USA |
| Roman Wyrzykowski | Czestochowa University of Technology, Poland |

## Track 4: Data Analytics, AI, and Computational Science

### Chairs

| | |
|---|---|
| Maciej Malawski | AGH University of Science and Technology, Poland |
| Radu Prodan | University of Klagenfurt, Austria |

### Program Committee

| | |
|---|---|
| Ashiq Anjum | University of Leicester, UK |
| Bartosz Balis | AGH University of Science and Technology, Poland |
| Daniel Balouek-Thomert | University of Utah, USA |
| Christos Baloukas | National Technical University of Athens, Greece |
| Luiz F. Bittencourt | University of Campinas, Brazil |
| Pascal Bouvry | University of Luxembourg, Luxembourg |
| Carmela Comito | ICAR CNR, Italy |
| Haleh Dijazi | University of Klagenfurt, Austria |
| Pedro Diniz | INESC-ID, Portugal |
| Reza Farahani | University of Klagenfurt, Austria |
| Philipp Gschwandtner | University of Innsbruck, Austria |
| Shadi Ibrahim | Inria Rennes, France |
| Dalibor Klusacek | CESNET Brno, Czech Republic |
| Young Choon Lee | Macquarie University, Australia |
| Jože Rožanec | Jožef Stefan Institute, Slovenia |
| Rabia Saleem | University of Derby, UK |
| Josef Spillner | Zurich University of Applied Sciences, Switzerland |
| Dingwen Tao | Indiana University, USA |
| Douglas Thain | University of Notre Dame, USA |
| Rafael Tolosana-Calasanz | Universidad de Zaragoza, Spain |
| Jidong Zhai | Tsinghua University, China |

## Track 5: Theory and Algorithms

### Chairs

| | |
|---|---|
| Chryssis Georgiou | University of Cyprus, Cyprus |
| Christos Kaklamanis | Computer Technology Institute and University of Patras, Greece |

### Program Committee

| | |
|---|---|
| Vittorio Bilo | University of Salento, Italy |
| Costas Busch | Augusta University, USA |
| Thomas Erlebach | Durham University, UK |
| Lionel Eyraud-Dubois | Inria Bordeaux Sud-Ouest, France |
| Panagiota Fatourou | University of Crete, Greece |
| Antonio Fernandez Anta | IMDEA Networks Institute, Spain |
| Paola Flocchini | University of Ottawa, Canada |
| Pierre Fraigniaud | Université Paris Cité and CNRS, France |
| Maurice Herlihy | Brown University, USA |
| Sayaka Kamei | Hiroshima University, Japan |
| Panagiotis Kanellopoulos | University of Essex, UK |
| Danny Krizanc | Wesleyan University, USA |
| Othon Michail | University of Liverpool, UK |
| Achour Mostéfaoui | Université de Nantes, France |
| Lata Narayanan | Concordia University, Canada |
| Vicky Papadopoulou | European University Cyprus, Cyprus |
| Giuseppe Persiano | Università degli Studi di Salerno, Italy |
| Maria Potop-Butucaru | Sorbonne University, France |
| Geppino Pucci | Università di Padova, Italy |
| Peter Sanders | Karlsruhe Institute of Technology, Germany |
| Thomas Sauerwald | University of Cambridge, UK |
| Christian Scheideler | University of Paderborn, Germany |
| Maria Serna | Universitat Politècnica de Catalunya, Spain |
| Gadi Taubenfeld | Reichman University, Israel |

## Track 6: Multidisciplinary, Domain-Specific and Applied Parallel and Distributed Computing

### Chairs

| | |
|---|---|
| Francisco F. Rivera | University of Santiago de Compostela, Spain |
| Domenico Talia | University of Calabria, Italy |

### Program Committee

| | |
|---|---|
| Salvador Abreu | University of Évora, Portugal |
| Michael Bane | Manchester Metropolitan University, UK |
| Loris Belcastro | University of Calabria, Italy |
| Cristiana Bentes | State University of Rio de Janeiro, Brazil |
| Paolo Bientinesi | Umeå University, Sweden |
| Vicente Blanco | University of La Laguna, Spain |
| Cristina Boeres | Universidade Federal Fluminense, Brazil |
| Alvaro L. Coutinho | Federal University of Rio de Janeiro, Brazil |
| Pasqua D'Ambra | IAC-CNR, Italy |
| Begüm Demir | TU Berlin, Germany |
| David Expósito Singh | Carlos III University of Madrid, Spain |

| | |
|---|---|
| Maria Fazio | University of Messina, Italy |
| Stefka Fidanova | Bulgarian Academy of Sciences, Bulgaria |
| Patricia González | University of A Coruña, Spain |
| Nicolás Guil | University of Málaga, Spain |
| Juan Angel Lorenzo del Castillo | CY Cergy Paris Université, France |
| Stefano Markidis | KTH Royal Institute of Technology, Sweden |
| Sreeja S. Nair | ZettaScale Technology, France |
| Enrique S. Quintana-Orti | Universitat Politècnica de València, Spain |
| Pedro Ribeiro | University of Porto, Portugal |
| Tuomo Rossi | University of Jyväskylä, Finland |
| Natalia Seoane | University of Santiago de Compostela, Spain |
| Paolo Trunfio | University of Calabria, Italy |
| Petr Tuma | Charles University, Czech Republic |
| David L. Vilariño | University of Santiago de Compostela, Spain |

## Artifact Evaluation

### Chairs

| | |
|---|---|
| Harald Gjermundrod | University of Nicosia, Cyprus |
| Georgia Kapitsaki | University of Cyprus, Cyprus |
| Massimo Torquati | University of Pisa, Italy |
| Haris Volos | University of Cyprus, Cyprus |

### Artifact Evaluation Committee

| | |
|---|---|
| Pandelis Agathangelou | University of Nicosia, Cyprus |
| Iacopo Colonnelli | University of Turin, Italy |
| Ioannis Constantinou | University of Cyprus, Cyprus |
| Daniele De Sensi | Sapienza University of Rome, Italy |
| Antreas Dionysiou | University of Cyprus, Cyprus |
| Joanna Georgiou | University of Cyprus, Cyprus |
| Marios Kyriakou | University of Cyprus, Cyprus |
| Frank Loots | University of Nicosia, Cyprus |
| Alberto R. Martinelli | University of Turin, Italy |
| Markos Othonos | University of Cyprus, Cyprus |
| Moysis Symeonides | University of Cyprus, Cyprus |
| Nicolò Tonci | University of Pisa, Italy |
| Paolo Viviani | LINKS Foundation, Italy |

## Additional Reviewers

Samira Afzal
Sabtain Ahmad
José Ignacio Aliaga
Francisco Almeida
Francisco Arguello
Eishi Arima
Hamza Baniata
Sergio Barrachina Mir
Matteo Basso
Alfredo Buttari
José Carlos Cabaleiro
Alberto Cabrera
Riccardo Cantini
Rocío Carratalá-Sáez
Adrián Castelló
Francisco Manuel Castro
Sandra Catalan
Dominika Ciupek
Enrique Comesaña Figueroa
Luís Crespo
Michael Davis
Charlotte Debus
Alberto Antonio Del Barrio García
Alexandre Denis
Manuel F. Dolz
Fabio Durastante
Hao Feng
Salvatore Filippone
Yuankun Fu
Anirban Ghose
Mehdi Goli
Jose González
Thomas Grützmacher
Thomas Guignon
Markus Götz
Josef Hammer
Hermann Hellwagner
Kurt Horvath
Tianjin Huang
Dominik Huber
Sian Jin
Pierre Jolivet
Pascal Jungblut
Lars Karlsson
Eniko Kevi
Fabian Knorr
Marcin Kurdziel
Bastian Köpcke
Martin Kühn
Ruben Laso
Johannes Lenfers
Felix Liu
Tim Luehnen
Daniel Luger
Fabrizio Marozzo
Theo Mary
Narges Mehran
Jan Meizner
Facundo Molina Heredia
Zahra Najafabadi Samani
Nuno Neves
Anh Nguyen
Pedro Ojeda
Alessio Orsino
John Owens
Amirmohammad Pasdar
Maciej Pawlik
Tomas Pena
James Phung
Doru Thom Popovici
Ricardo Quislant
Julián Ramos Cózar
Vinod Rebello
Manuel Renz
Eduardo Rosales
Andrea Rosà
Daniel Ruprecht
Katarzyna Rycerz
Philip Salzmann
Martin Schatz
Richard Schulze
Baixi Sun

Frederic Suter
Syed Ibtisam Tauhidi
Yu-Hsiang Tsai
Julio Villalba
Daoce Wang
Huijun Wang
Binqi Zhang
Chengming Zhang

# Euro-Par 2023 Invited Talks

# Distributed Intelligence in the Computing Continuum

Schahram Dustdar

Vienna University of Technology, Austria

Modern distributed systems also deal with uncertain scenarios, where environments, infrastructures, and applications are widely diverse. In the scope of IoT-Edge-Fog-Cloud computing, leveraging these neuroscience-inspired principles and mechanisms could aid in building more flexible solutions able to generalize over different environments. A captivating set of hypotheses from the field of neuroscience suggests that human and animal brain mechanisms result from a few powerful principles. If proved to be accurate, these assumptions could open a deep understanding of the way humans and animals manage to cope with the unpredictability of events and imagination.

# A Continuum of Matrix Multiplications: From Scientific Computing to Deep Learning

Enrique S. Quintana-Orti

Universitat Politècnica de València, Spain

Matrix multiplication (GEMM) is a key, pervasive computational kernel that spans across multiple domains. On the one hand, many applications arising in scientific computing require the solution of linear systems of equations, least-square problems, and eigenvalue problems. For portability, these applications often rely on linear algebra routines from LAPACK (linear algebra package). In turn, in order to deliver high performance, LAPACK heavily relies on GEMM and other Basic Linear algebra subroutines (BLAS). On the other hand, to a large extent, the computational cost for the convolutional neural networks (CNNs) that dominate machine learning algorithms for signal processing and computer vision tasks, as well as the transformers behind recent deep learning (DL) applications, such as ChatGPT, is largely determined by the performance of GEMM.

In this talk we will first expose caveats of current instances of GEMM in linear algebra libraries for conventional multicore architectures: suboptimal performance and missing support for DL-oriented data types. Starting from that point, we will then demonstrate how these problems can be overcome via tools for the (semi-)automatic generation of the only architecture-specific piece of GEMM, known as the micro-kernel, together with an analytical-based model to capture the cache hierarchy configuration. In addition, we will show that this approach carries over to more "exotic" architectures, from high-end vector accelerators and the Xilinx artificial intelligence engine (AIE) to low-power designs such as RISC-V processors and ARM-based (Arduino) micro-controllers.

# Bias in Data and Algorithms: Problems, Solutions and Stakeholders

Jahna Otterbacher

Open University of Cyprus, Cyprus

Mitigating bias in algorithmic processes and systems is a critical issue drawing increasing attention across research communities within the computer and information sciences. Given the complexity of the problem and the involvement of multiple stakeholders – not only developers, but also end-users and third parties – there is a need to understand the landscape of the sources of bias, as well as the solutions being proposed to address them. In this talk, I present insights from a survey of 300+ articles across four domains (Machine Learning, Information Retrieval, Human-Computer Interaction, and Recommender Systems) in which a critical mass of work relating to algorithmic bias has been produced, with the aim of providing a "fish-eye view" of the field. In the second part of the talk, I will discuss examples of our ongoing work on auditing proprietary computer vision systems for social biases, positioning this work vis-à-vis the aforementioned framework as well as the emerging science of *machine behavior*.

# Euro-Par 2023 Track Overviews

# Track 1: Programming, Compilers and Performance

Biagio Cosenza and Thomas Fahringer

This track encompasses a broad range of topics related to programming tools and system software for modern parallel and distributed computing systems. The track emphasizes traditional subjects like compilation techniques and programming models and tools for multi-/many-core and heterogeneous architectures. It also focuses on contemporary approaches targeting emerging architectures, including low-power accelerator hardware, reconfigurable hardware, processors-in-memory and emerging exascale systems. Additionally, the track explores methods and tools for optimizing non-functional properties such as performance, power and energy efficiency, reliability, scalability, productivity, and performance portability. Among other topics, the track sought papers in relation to the following:

- High-level programming models and tools for multi-/many-core and heterogeneous architectures
- Programming environments, interoperable tool environments
- Productivity and performance portability
- Compiling for multithreaded/multi-core and heterogeneous processors/architectures
- Compiling for emerging architectures (low-power accelerator hardware, reconfigurable hardware, processors in memory)
- Iterative, just-in-time, feedback-oriented, dynamic, and machine-learning-based compilation
- Static and dynamic program analysis
- Program transformation systems
- Interaction between compiler, runtime system, hardware, and operating system
- Compiler, run-time, and architectural support for dynamic adaptation
- Compilers for domain-specific languages
- Instrumentation, monitoring, evaluation and prediction of non-functional program behaviour
- Auto-tuning and multi-objective code optimization
- Verification and validation of performance models
- Power consumption modelling and prediction
- Performance modelling and simulation of emerging exascale systems

# Track 2: Scheduling, Resource Management, Cloud, Edge Computing, and Workflows

Marco Aldinucci and Ivona Brandic

This track invited papers in a range of topics related to resource management, which remains a core topic in parallel and distributed systems. Not surprisingly, this became the track with the highest number of submissions. Among other topics, the track sought papers in relation to the following:

- High-level programming models and tools for multi-/many-core and heterogeneous architectures
- Scheduling algorithms for homogeneous and heterogeneous platforms
- Theoretical foundations of scheduling algorithms
- Real-time scheduling on parallel and distributed machines
- Scheduling, coordination and overhead at extreme scales
- Energy and temperature awareness in scheduling and load balancing
- Resource management for HPC and Clouds
- Workload characterization and modelling
- Workflow and job scheduling
- Performance models for scheduling and load balancing
- Heterogeneous parallel programming models for the computing continuum
- Workflow environments for the computing continuum
- Parallel programming in the edge and in the computing continuum

# Track 3: Architectures and Accelerators

Jesus Carretero and Leonel Sousa

This track invited papers in all topics related to parallel and distributed computing architectures. Among other topics, the track sought papers in relation to the following:

- Architectures for instruction-level and thread-level parallelism
- Manycores, multicores, accelerators, domain-specific and special-purpose architectures, reconfigurable architectures
- Cloud and HPC storage architectures and systems
- Memory technologies and hierarchies
- Exascale system designs; data center and warehouse-scale architectures
- Novel big data architectures
- Parallel I/O and storage systems
- Power-efficient and green computing systems
- Resilience, security, and dependable architectures
- Software architectures spanning IoT/Edge, Fog, Cloud, 5G and HPC computing
- Processing in Memory and Near-Memory Processing
- Interconnect/memory architectures

# Track 4: Data Analytics, AI, and Computational Science

Maciej Malawski and Radu Prodan

This track attracted papers covering timely areas of data analytics and AI, as these topics are increasingly important in parallel and distributed processing applications. The papers show the interest of the community in both traditional computer systems research and in new developments of distributed processing for AI, including federated learning. Among other topics, the track sought papers in relation to the following:

- Artificial Intelligence in the IoT-Edge-Cloud continuum
- Data management in Edge devices and the computing continuum
- Innovative applications and case studies
- Large-scale data processing applications in science, engineering, business and healthcare
- Emerging trends for computing, machine learning, approximate computing, and quantum computing.
- Parallel, replicated, and highly available distributed databases
- Scientific data analytics (Big Data or HPC-based approaches)
- Middleware for processing large-scale data
- Programming models for parallel and distributed data analytics
- Workflow management for data analytics
- Coupling HPC simulations with in situ data analysis
- Parallel data visualization
- Distributed and parallel transaction, query processing and information retrieval
- Internet-scale data-intensive applications
- Sensor network data management
- Data-intensive computing infrastructures
- Parallel data streaming and data stream mining
- New storage hierarchies in distributed data systems
- Parallel and distributed machine learning, knowledge discovery and data mining
- Privacy and trust in parallel and distributed data management and analytics systems
- IoT data management and analytics
- Parallel and distributed data science applications
- Data analysis in cloud and serverless models

# Track 5: Theory and Algorithms

Chryssis Georgiou and Christos Kaklamanis

This track attracted papers spanning several topics from theory and algorithms, such as parallel processing, networking, distributed learning and clustering, consensus and blockchains, as well as graph partitioning and atomic storage. Among other topics, the track sought papers in relation to the following:

- Theoretical foundations, models, and complexity issues
- Emerging paradigms for parallel and distributed computation
- Lower bounds
- Approximation and randomized algorithms
- Design, analysis and engineering of distributed and parallel algorithms
- Data structures for parallel and distributed algorithms
- Algorithms for combinatorial and graph problems
- Algorithms and models for big Data/Data-intensive computing
- Learning and mining algorithms
- Algorithms for routing and information dissemination in communication networks
- Algorithms for social networks
- Fault tolerant and self-stabilizing algorithms
- Power/energy-efficient algorithms
- Algorithms for distributed computing
- Algorithms and principles of distributed ledgers (blockchains)
- Algorithms for cloud and edge computing
- Algorithmic game theory related to parallel and distributed systems
- Theoretical aspects of dependable, secure and privacy-preserving distributed systems

# Track 6: Multidisciplinary, Domain-Specific and Applied Parallel and Distributed Computing

Francisco F. Rivera and Domenico Talia

This track invited papers in relation to all topics pertaining to parallel and distributed applications. The track was particularly successful, with several papers considering the use of HPC strategies in different applications with different requirements, particularly those related to the use of GPUs. Among other topics, the track sought papers in relation to the following:

– Applications of numerical algorithms in science and engineering
– Domain-specific libraries and languages in parallel and distributed computing
– Application case studies for benchmarking and comparative studies of parallel programming models
– Numerical methods for large-scale data analysis
– High-dimensional problems and reduction methods
– Implementation and analysis of parallel numerical algorithms
– Optimization and non-linear problems in parallel and distributed computing
– Parallel numerical linear algebra for dense and sparse matrices
– Partial/ordinary and differential algebraic equations in parallel and distributed computing
– Discrete and combinatorial parallel algorithms
– Parallel metaheuristics and hyperheuristics
– Innovative paradigms, programming models, languages, and libraries for parallel and distributed applications
– Parallel and distributed programming productivity, usability, and component-based parallel programming
– Tensor operations, low-rank approximations
– Data-centric parallel and distributed algorithms for exascale computing

# Contents

**Programming, Compilers and Performance**



**Scheduling, Resource Management, Cloud, Edge Computing, and Workflows**

**Theory and Algorithms**



**Multidisciplinary, Domain-Specific and Applied Parallel and Distributed Computing**

# Programming, Compilers and Performance

# DIPPM: A Deep Learning Inference Performance Predictive Model Using Graph Neural Networks

Karthick Panner Selvam(✉) and Mats Brorsson

SnT, University of Luxembourg, Kirchberg, Luxembourg
{karthick.pannerselvam,mats.brorsson}@uni.lu

**Abstract.** Deep Learning (DL) has developed to become a corner-stone in many everyday applications that we are now relying on. However, making sure that the DL model uses the underlying hardware efficiently takes a lot of effort. Knowledge about inference characteristics can help to find the right match so that enough resources are given to the model, but not too much. We have developed a DL Inference Performance Predictive Model (DIPPM) that predicts the inference *latency*, *energy*, and *memory usage* of a given input DL model on the NVIDIA A100 GPU. We also devised an algorithm to suggest the appropriate A100 Multi-Instance GPU profile from the output of DIPPM. We developed a methodology to convert DL models expressed in multiple frameworks to a generalized graph structure that is used in DIPPM. It means DIPPM can parse input DL models from various frameworks. Our DIPPM can be used not only helps to find suitable hardware configurations but also helps to perform rapid design-space exploration for the inference performance of a model. We constructed a graph multi-regression dataset consisting of 10,508 different DL models to train and evaluate the performance of DIPPM, and reached a resulting Mean Absolute Percentage Error (MAPE) as low as 1.9%.

**Keywords:** Performance Prediction · Multi Instance GPU · Deep Learning Inference

## 1 Introduction

Many important tasks a now relying on Deep learning models, for instance in computer vision and natural language processing domains [3,14]. In recent years, researchers have focused on improving the efficiency of deep learning models to reduce the computation cost, energy consumption and increase the throughput of them without losing their accuracy. At the same time, hardware manufacturers like NVIDIA increase their computing power. For example, the NVIDIA A100[1] GPU half-precision Tensor Core can perform matrix operations at 312 TFLOPS. But all deep learning models will not fully utilize the GPU because the workload

[1] https://www.nvidia.com/en-us/data-center/a100/.


J. Cano et al. (Eds.): Euro-Par 2023, LNCS 14100, pp. 3–16, 2023.
https://doi.org/10.1007/978-3-031-39698-4_1

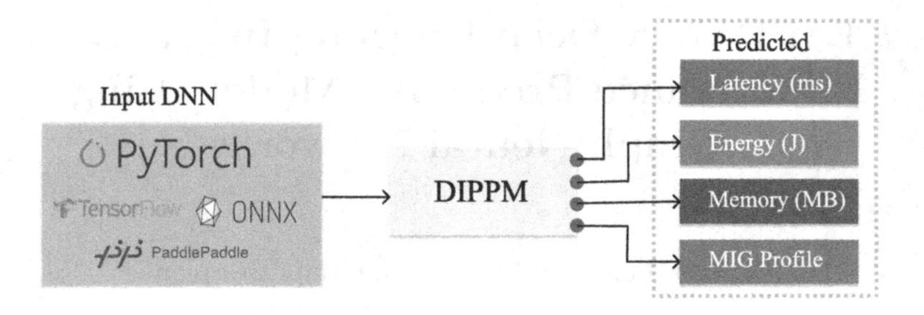


**Fig. 1.** DIPPM can predict the Latency, Energy, Memory requirement, and MIG Profile for inference on an NVIDIA A100 GPU without actually running on it.

and number of matrix operations will vary according to the problem domain. For this reason, NVIDIA created the Multi-Instance GPU (MIG[2]) technology starting from the Ampere architecture; they split the single physical GPU into multi-isolated GPU instances, so multiple applications can simultaneously run on different partitions of the same GPU, which then can be used more efficiently.

However, determining the DL model's efficiency on a GPU is not straightforward. If we could predict parameters such as inference latency, energy consumption, and memory usage, we would not need to measure them on deployed models which is a tedious and costly process. The predicted parameters could then also support efficient Neural Architecture Search (NAS) [5], efficient DL model design during development, and avoid job scheduling failures in data centers. According to Gao et al. [7], most failed deep learning jobs in data centers are due to out-of-memory errors.

In order to meet this need, we have developed a novel *Deep Learning Inference Performance Predictive Model* (DIPPM) to support DL model developers in matching their models to the underlying hardware for inference. As shown in Fig. 1, DIPPM takes a deep learning model expressed in any of the frameworks: PyTorch, PaddlePaddle, Tensorflow, or ONNX, and will predict the latency (ms), energy (J), memory requirement (MB), and MIG profile for inference on an Nvidia A100 GPU without running on it. At the moment, the model is restricted to inference and the Nvidia A100 architecture, but we aim to relax these restrictions in future work. As far as we are aware, this is the first predictive model that can take input from any of the mentioned frameworks and to predict all of the metrics above.

Our contributions include the following:

- We have developed, trained and evaluated a performance predictive model which predicts inference latency, energy, memory, and MIG profile for A100 GPU with high accuracy.
- We have developed a methodology to convert deep learning models from various deep learning frameworks into generalized graph structures for graph learning tasks in our performance predictive model.

[2] https://docs.nvidia.com/datacenter/tesla/mig-user-guide/.

- We have devised an algorithm to suggest the MIG profile from predicted Memory for the given input DL model.
- We have created an open-sourced performance predictive model dataset containing 10,508 graphs for graph-level multi-regression problems.

Next, we discuss our work in relation to previous work in this area before presenting our methodology, experiments, and results.

## 2 Related Work

Performance prediction of deep learning models on modern architecture is a rather new research field being attended to only since a couple of years back. Bouhali et al. [2] and Lu et al. [15] have carried out similar studies where a classical Multi-Layer Perceptron (MLP) is used to predict the inference latency of a given input DL model. Their approach was to collect high-level DL model features such as batch size, number of layers, and the total number of floating point operations (FLOPS) needed. They then fed these features into an MLP regressor as input to predict the latency of the given model. Bai et al. [1] used the same MLP method but predicted both the latency and memory. However, the classical MLP approach did not work very well due to the inability to capture a detailed view of the given input DL model.

To solve the above problems, some researchers came up with a kernel additive method; they predict each kernel operation, such as convolution, dense, and LSTM, individually and sum up all kernel values to predict the overall performance of the DL model [9,16,19,21,23,25]. Yu et al. [24] used the wave-scaling technique to predict the inference latency of the DL model on GPU, but this technique requires access to a GPU in order to make the prediction.

Kaufman et al. and Dudziak et al. [4,10] used graph learning instead of MLP to predict each kernel value. Still, they used the kernel additive method for inference latency prediction. However, this kernel additive method did not capture the overall network topology of the model, and instead it will affect the accuracy of the prediction. To solve the above problem, Liu et al. [13] used a Graph level task to generalize the entire DL model into node embeddings and predicted the inference latency of the given DL model. However, they did not predict other parameters, such as memory usage and energy consumption. Gao et al. [6] used the same graph-level task to predict the single iteration time and memory consumption for deep learning training but not for inference.

Li et al. [12] tried to predict the MIG profiles on A100 GPU for the DL models. However, their methodology is not straightforward; they used CUDA Multi-Process Service (MPS) values to predict the MIG, So the model must run at least on the target hardware once to predict the MIG Profile.

Most of the previous research work concentrated on parsing the input DL model from only one of the following frameworks (PyTorch, TensorFlow, PaddlePaddle, ONNX). As far as we are aware, none of the previous performance prediction models predicted Memory usage, Latency, Energy, and MIG profile simultaneously.

**Table 1.** Related Work comparison

| Related Works | A100 | MIG | GNN[a] | Multi-SF[b] | Latency | Power | Memory |
|---|---|---|---|---|---|---|---|
| Ours (**DIPPM**) | ✓ | ✓ | ✓ | ✓ | ✓ | ✓ | ✓ |
| Bai et al. [1] | – | – | – | – | ✓ | – | ✓ |
| Bouhali et al. [2] | – | – | – | – | ✓ | – | – |
| Dudziak et al. [4] | – | – | ✓ | – | ✓ | – | – |
| Gao et al. [6] | – | – | ✓ | – | ✓ | – | ✓ |
| Justus et al. [9] | – | – | – | – | ✓ | – | – |
| Kaufman et al. [10] | – | – | ✓ | – | ✓ | – | – |
| Li et al. [12] | ✓ | ✓ | – | – | – | – | – |
| Liu et al. [13] | – | – | ✓ | – | ✓ | – | – |
| Lu et al. [15] | – | – | – | – | ✓ | ✓ | ✓ |
| Qi et al. [16] | – | – | – | – | ✓ | – | – |
| Sponner et al. [19] | ✓ | – | – | – | ✓ | ✓ | ✓ |
| Wang et al. [21] | – | – | – | – | ✓ | – | – |
| Yang et al. [23] | – | – | – | – | ✓ | – | – |
| Yu et. al. [24] | ✓ | – | – | – | ✓ | – | – |
| Zhang et al. [25] | – | – | – | – | ✓ | – | – |

[a] Using Graph Neural Network for performance prediction
[b] Able to parse DL model expressed in Multiple DL Software Framework

Our novel Deep Learning Inference Performance Predictive Model (DIPPM) fills a gap in previous work; a detailed comparison is shown in Table 1. DIPPM takes a deep learning model as input from various deep learning frameworks such as PyTorch, PaddlePaddle, TensorFlow, or ONNX and converts it to generalize graph with node features. We used a graph neural network and MIG predictor to predict the inference latency (ms), energy (J), memory (MB), and MIG profile for A100 GPU without actually running on it.

## 3 Methodology

The architecture of DIPPM consists of five main components: Deep Learning Model into Relay IR, Node Feature Generator, Static Feature Generator, Performance Model Graph Network Structure (PMGNS), and MIG Predictor, as shown in Fig. 2. We will explain each component individually in this section.

### 3.1 Deep Learning Model into Relay IR

The Relay Parser takes as input a DL model expressed in one of several supported DL frameworks, converts it to an Intermediate Representation (IR), and passes this IR into the Node Feature Generator and the Static Feature Generator components.

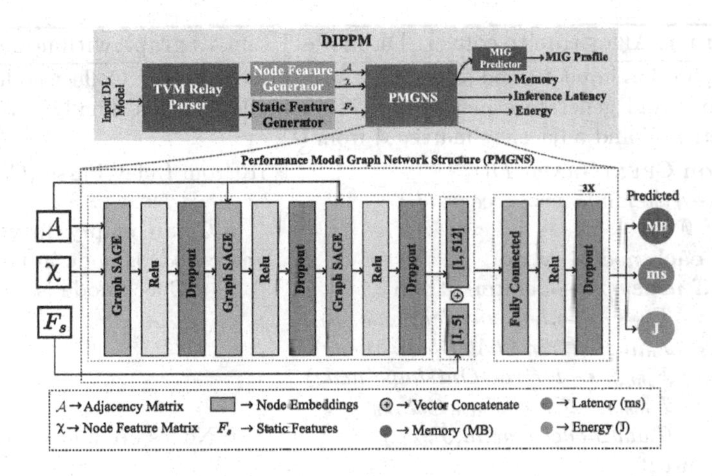


**Fig. 2.** Overview of DIPPM Architecture

Most of the previously proposed performance models are able to parse the given input DL model from a single DL framework, not from several, as we already discussed in Sect. 2. To enable the use of multiple frameworks, we used a relay, which is a high-level IR for DL models [17]. It has been used to compile DL models for inference in the TVM[3] framework.

We are inspired by the approach of converting DL models from different frameworks into a high-level intermediate representation (IR), so we incorporated their techniques into our architecture. However, we couldn't directly employ relay IR in DIPPM. To overcome this, we developed a method explained in Sect. 3.2. It involves parsing the Relay IR and transforming it into a graph representation with node features.

It allows parsing given input DL models from various frameworks, including PyTorch, TensorFlow, ONNX, and PaddlePaddle. However, for the purposes of this study, we have focused on the implementation and evaluation of the framework specifically within the PyTorch environment. We pass this DL IR to the subsequent components in our DIPPM architecture.

### 3.2 Node Feature Generator

The Node Feature Generator (NFG) converts the DL IR into an Adjacency Matrix ($\mathcal{A}$) and a Node feature matrix ($\mathcal{X}$) and passes this data to the PMGNS component.

The NFG takes the IR from the relay parser component. The IR is itself a computational data flow graph containing more information than is needed for our performance prediction. Therefore we filter and pre-process the graph by post-order graph traversal to collect necessary node information. The nodes in the IR contain useful features such as operator name, attributes, and output

[3] https://tvm.apache.org/.

**Algorithm 1.** Algorithm to convert DL model IR into a graph with node features

CreateGraph takes input IR and filters it by post-order traversal. Collect node features for each node and generate a new graph $\mathcal{G}$ with node features, finally extract node feature matrix $\mathcal{X}$ and adjacency matrix $\mathcal{A}$ from $\mathcal{G}$.

```
1: function CREATGRAPH(IR)                              ▷ IR from Relay Parser Component
2:     N ← filter_and_preprocess(IR)
3:     G ← ∅                                            ▷ Create empty directed graph
4:     for each node ∈ N do                             ▷ where node is node in node_list N
5:         if node.op ∈ [operators] then                ▷ Check node is an operator
6:             F_oh ← one_hot_encoder(node.op)
7:             F_attr ← ExtractAttributes(node)
8:             F_shape ← ExtractOutshape(node)
9:             F_node ← F_oh ⊕ F_attr ⊕ F_shape
10:            G.add_node(node.id, F_node)              ▷ Nodes are added in sequence
11:        end if
12:    end for
13:    A ← GetAdjacencyMatrix(G)
14:    X ← GetNodeFeatureMatrix(G)
15:    return A, X
16: end function
```

shape of the operator, which after this first filtering step are converted into a suitable data format for our performance prediction. In the subsequent step, we loop through the nodes and, for each operator node, generate node features Fnode with a fixed length of 32 as discussed on line 9 in Algorithm 1.

The central part of the NFG is to generate an **Adjacency Matrix** ($\mathcal{A}$) and a **Node feature matrix** ($\mathcal{X}$) as expressed in Algorithm 1. $\mathcal{X}$ has the shape of $[N_{op}, N_{features}]$, where $N_{op}$ is the number of operator nodes in the IR and $N_{features}$ is the number of features. In order to create node features $\mathcal{F}_n$ for each *node*, first, we need to encode the node operator name into a one hot encoding as can be seen on line 6 in Algorithm 1. Then extract the node attributes $\mathcal{F}_{attr}$ and output shape $\mathcal{F}_{shape}$ into vectors. Finally, perform vector concatenation to generate $\mathcal{F}_n$ for a node. We repeat this operation for each node and create the $\mathcal{G}$. From the $\mathcal{G}$, we extract $\mathcal{A}$, $\mathcal{X}$ that are passed to the main part of our model, the Performance Model Graph Network Structure.

### 3.3 Static Feature Generator

The Static Feature Generator (SFG) takes the IR from the relay parser component and generates static features $\mathcal{F}_s$ for a given DL model and passes them into the graph network structure.

For this experiment, we limited ourselves to five static features. First, we calculate the $\mathcal{F}_{mac}$ total multiply-accumulate (MACs) of the given DL model. We used the TVM relay analysis API to calculate total MACs, but it is limited to calculating MACs for the following operators (in TVM notation): Conv2D, Conv2D transpose, dense, and batch matmul. Then we calculate the total number of convolutions $F_{Tconv}$, Dense $F_{Tdense}$, and Relu $F_{Trelu}$ operators from the IR. We included batch size $F_{batch}$ as one of the static features because it gives the ability to predict values for various batch sizes of a given model. Finally, we concatenate all the features into a vector $\mathcal{F}_s$ as expressed in Eq. 1. The feature set $\mathcal{F}_s$ is subsequently passed to the following graph network structure.

$$\mathcal{F}_s \leftarrow \mathcal{F}_{mac} \oplus \mathcal{F}_{batch} \oplus \mathcal{F}_{Tconv} \oplus \mathcal{F}_{Tdense} \oplus \mathcal{F}_{Trelu} \quad (1)$$

### 3.4 Performance Model Graph Network Structure (PMGNS)

The PMGNS takes the node feature matrix ($\mathcal{X}$), the adjacency matrix ($\mathcal{A}$) from the Node Feature Generator component, and the feature set ($\mathcal{F}_s$) from the Static feature generator and predicts the given input DL model's memory, latency, and energy, as shown in Fig. 2.

The PMGNS must be trained before prediction, as explained in Sect. 4. The core idea of the PMGNS is to generate the node embedding $z$ from $\mathcal{X}$ and $\mathcal{A}$ and then to perform vector concatenation of $z$ with $\mathcal{F}_s$. Finally, we pass the concatenated vector into a Fully Connected layer for prediction, as shown in Fig. 2. In order to generate $z$, we used the graphSAGE algorithm suggested by Hamilton et al. [8], because of its inductive node embedding, which means it can generate embedding for unseen nodes without pretraining. GraphSAGE is a graph neural network framework that learns node embeddings in large-scale graphs. It performs inductive learning, generalizing to unseen nodes by aggregating information from nodes and neighbors. It generates fixed-size embeddings, capturing features and local graph structure. With a neighborhood aggregation scheme, it creates node embeddings sensitive to their local neighborhood, even for new, unobserved nodes.

We already discussed that we generate node features of each node in the Sect. 3.2. The graphSAGE algorithm will convert node features into a node embedding $z$ which is more amenable for model training. The PMGNS contains three sequential graphSAGE blocks and three sequential Fully connected (FC) blocks as shown in Fig. 2. At the end of the final graphSAGE block, we get the generalized node embedding of given $\mathcal{X}$ and $\mathcal{A}$, which we concatenate with $\mathcal{F}_s$. Then we pass the concatenated vector into FC to predict the memory (MB), latency (ms), and energy (J).

### 3.5 MIG Predictor

The MIG predictor takes the memory prediction from PMGNS and predicts the appropriate MIG profile for a given DL model, as shown in Fig. 2.

As mentioned in the introduction, the Multi-instance GPU (MIG) technology allows to split an A100 GPU into multiple instances so that multiple applications can use the GPU simultaneously. The different instances differ in their compute capability and, most importantly, in the maximum memory limit that is allowed to be used. The four MIG profiles of the A100 GPU that we consider here are: 1g.5gb, 2g.10gb, 3g.20gb, and 7g.40gb, where the number in front of "gb"

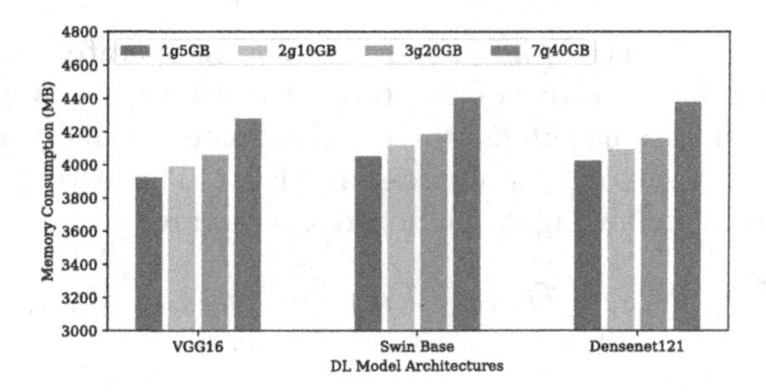


**Fig. 3.** MIG Profile comparison of three different DL models memory consumption on A100 GPU. We used batch size 16 for VGG16 and Densenet121 model and batch size 8 for Swin base model

denotes the maximum amount of memory in GB that the application can use on that instance. For example, the maximum memory limit of 1g.5gb is 5 GB, and 7g.40gb is 40GB. For a given input DL model, PMGNS predicts memory for 7g.40gb MIG profile, which is the full GPU. We found that this prediction can be used as a pessimistic value to guide the choice of MIG profile. Figure 3 shows manual memory consumption measurements of the same DL model inference on different profiles. The results show no significant difference in the memory allocation of DL in the different MIG profiles even though the consumption slightly increases with the capacity of the MIG profile. The memory consumption is always the highest when running on the 7g.40gb MIG profile.

As mentioned, PMGNS predicts memory for 7g.40gb, so we claim that predicted memory will be an upper bound. Then we perform a rule-based prediction to predict the MIG profile for the given input DL model, as shown in Eq. 2. Where $\alpha$ is predicted memory from PMGNS.

$$\mathrm{MIG}(\alpha) = \begin{cases} \text{1g.5gb}, & \text{if } 0gb < \alpha < \text{5gb} \\ \text{2g.10gb}, & \text{if 5gb} < \alpha < \text{10gb} \\ \text{3g.20gb}, & \text{if 10gb} < \alpha < \text{20gb} \\ \text{7g.40gb}, & \text{if 20gb} < \alpha < \text{40gb} \\ \text{None}, & \text{otherwise} \end{cases} \tag{2}$$

# 4 Experiments and Results

## 4.1 The DIPPM Dataset

We constructed a graph-level multi-regression dataset containing 10,508 DL models from different model families to train and evaluate our DIPPM. The dataset distribution is shown in Table 2. To the best of our knowledge, the previous predictive performance model dataset doesn't capture memory consumption, inference latency, and energy consumption parameters for wide-range DL models on A100 GPU so we created our own dataset for performance prediction of DL models.

**Table 2.** DIPPM Graph dataset distribution

| Model Family | # of Graphs | Percentage (%) |
|---|---|---|
| Efficientnet | 1729 | 16.45 |
| Mnasnet | 1001 | 9.53 |
| Mobilenet | 1591 | 15.14 |
| Resnet | 1152 | 10.96 |
| Vgg | 1536 | 14.62 |
| Swin | 547 | 5.21 |
| Vit | 520 | 4.95 |
| Densenet | 768 | 7.31 |
| Visformer | 768 | 7.31 |
| Poolformer | 896 | 8.53 |
| **Total** | **10508** | 100% |

Our dataset consists of DL models represented in graph structure, as generated by the Relay parser described in Sect. 3.1. Each data point consists of four variables: $\mathcal{X}$, $\mathcal{A}$, $\mathcal{Y}$, and $\mathcal{F}_s$, where $\mathcal{X}$ and $\mathcal{A}$ are the Node feature matrix and Adjacency Matrix, respectively, as discussed in Sect. 3.2, and $\mathcal{F}_s$ is the static features of the DL model as discussed in Sect. 3.3. We used the Nvidia Management Library[4] and the CUDA toolkit[5] to measure the energy, memory, and inference latency of each given model in the dataset. For each model, we ran the inference five times to warm up the architecture and then the inference 30 times, and then took the arithmetic mean of those 30 values to derive the $\mathcal{Y}$, where $\mathcal{Y}$ consists of inference latency (ms), memory usage (MB), and energy (J) for a given DL on A100 GPU. We used a full A100 40 GB GPU, or it is equivalent to using 7g.40gb MIG profile to collect all the metrics.

### 4.2 Enviroment Setup

We used an HPC cluster at the Jülich research centre in Germany called JUWELS Booster for our experiments[6]. It is equipped with 936 nodes, each with AMD EPYC 7402 processors, 2 sockets per node, 24 cores per socket, 512 GB DDR4-3200 RAM and 4 NVIDIA A100 Tensor Core GPUs with 40 GB HBM.

The main software packages used in the experiments are: Python 3.10, CUDA 11.7 torch 1.13.1, torch-geometric 2.2.0, torch-scatter 2.1.0, and torch-sparse 0.6.16.

### 4.3 Evaluation

The Performance Model Graph Network Structure is the main component in DIPPM, and we used the PyTorch geometric library to create our model, as

[4] https://developer.nvidia.com/nvidia-management-library-nvml.
[5] https://developer.nvidia.com/cuda-toolkit.
[6] https://apps.fz-juelich.de/jsc/hps/juwels/booster-overview.html.

**Table 3.** Settings in GNN comparison.

| Setting | Value |
|---|---|
| Dataset partition | Train (70%) / Validation (15%) / Test (15%) |
| Nr hidden layers | 512 |
| Dropout probability | 0.05 |
| Optimizer | Adam |
| Learning rate | $2.754 \cdot 10^{-5}$ |
| Loss function | Huber |

**Table 4.** Comparison with different GNN algorithms and MLP with graphSAGE, we trained all the models for 10 epochs and used Mean Average Percentage Error for validation. The results indicate that DIPPM with graphSAGE performs significantly better than other variants.

| Model | Training | Validation | Test |
|---|---|---|---|
| GAT | 0.497 | 0.379 | 0.367 |
| GCN | 0.212 | 0.178 | 0.175 |
| GIN | 0.488 | 0.394 | 0.382 |
| MLP | 0.371 | 0.387 | 0.366 |
| **(Ours) GraphSAGE** | **0.182** | **0.159** | **0.160** |

shown in Fig. 2. We split our constructed dataset into three parts randomly: training set 70%, validation set 15%, and a test set 15%.

In order to validate that graphSAGE performs better than other GNN algorithms and plain MLP, we compared graphSAGE with the following other algorithms:, GAT [20], GCN [11], GIN [22], and finally, plain MLP without GNN. Table 3 summarizes the settings used. The learning rate was determined using a learning rate finder as suggested by Smith [18]. The Huber loss function achieved a higher accuracy than mean square error, which is why we chose that one. For the initial experiment, we trained for 10 epochs and used Mean Average Percentage Error (MAPE) as an accuracy metric to validate DIPPM. A MAPE value close to zero indicates good performance on regression prediction. Table 4 shows that graphSAGE gives a lower MAPE value in all of the training, validation, and test datasets. Without using a GNN, MLP gives 0.366 of MAPE. With graphSAGE, MAPE is 0.160 on the test dataset which is a significant improvement on a multi-regression problem. We conclude that graphSAGE outperforms other GNN algorithms, and MLP because of its inductive learning, as discussed in Sect. 3.4. After this encouraging result we increased the number of epochs for training our DIPPM with graphSAGE to increase the prediction accuracy. After 500 epochs, we attained MAPE of 0.041 on training and 0.023 on the validation dataset. In the end, we attained 1.9% MAPE on the test dataset. Some of the DIPPM predictions on the test dataset are shown in Fig. 4.

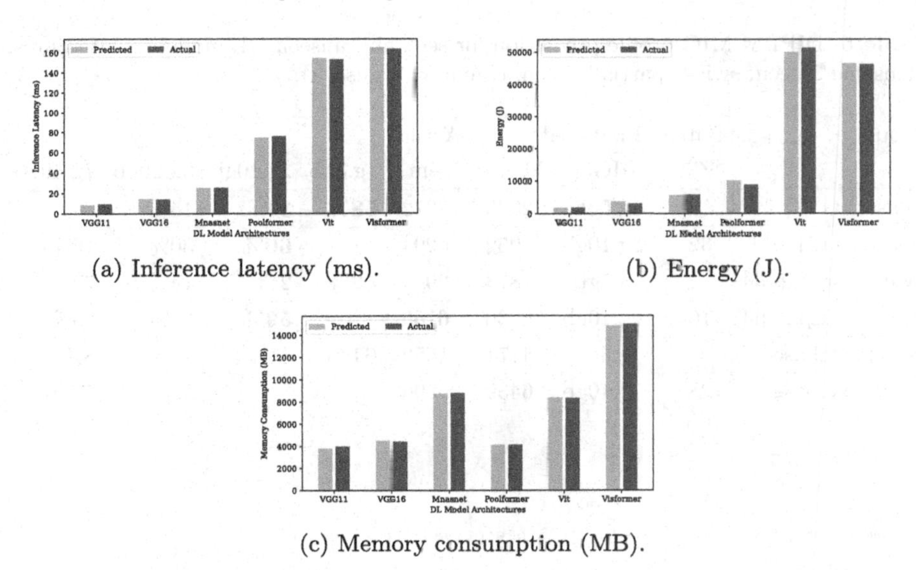


(a) Inference latency (ms).

(b) Energy (J).

(c) Memory consumption (MB).

**Fig. 4.** Comparison of actual value with DIPPM predicted values on the test dataset. Results show that DIPPM predictions are close to the actual predictions.

### 4.4 Prediction of MIG Profiles

In order to verify the MIG profile prediction for a given DL model, we compared the actual MIG profile value with the predicted MIG profile from the DIPPM, as shown in Table 5. To calculate the actual suitable MIG profile, we divide actual memory consumption by the maximum memory limit of the MIG profiles. The higher the value is, the more appropriate profile for the given DL model. For example, the predicted memory consumption for densenet121 at batch size 8 is 2865 MB. The actual memory consumption for the 7g.40gb MIG profile is 3272 MB. The actual memory consumption of 1g.5GB is 2918 MB, the percentage is 58%. Which is higher than other MIG profiles. Results show that DIPPM correctly predicted the MIG profile 1g.5gb for densenet121. It is interesting to note that the densent121 models are from our test dataset and the swin base patch4 model is not in our DIPPM dataset but a similar swin base model family was used to train DIPPM. The convnext models are completely unseen to our DIPPM, but it's still predicting the MIG profile correctly.

### 4.5 DIPPM Usability Aspects

DIPPM takes basic parameters like frameworks, model path, batch, and input size, and finally, device type. As of now, we only considered A100 GPU; we are working to extend DIPPM to various hardware platforms. With a simple python API call, DIPPM predicts memory, latency, energy, and MIG profile for the given model, as can be seen in Fig. 5.

**Table 5.** DIPPM MIG profile prediction for seen and unseen DL model architectures. (densenet*: seen, swin*: partially seen, convnext*: unseen).

| Model | Batch size | Predicted | | Actual | | | | |
|---|---|---|---|---|---|---|---|---|
| | | MIG | Mem | Mem | 1g.5gb | 2g.10gb | 3g.20gb | 7g.40gb |
| densenet121 | 8 | 1g.5gb | 2865 | 3272 | **58%** | 30% | 15% | 8% |
| densenet121 | 32 | 2g.10gb | 5952 | 6294 | | **60%** | 30% | 16% |
| swin_base_patch4 | 2 | 1g.5gb | 2873 | 2944 | **52%** | 27% | 14% | 7% |
| swin_base_patch4 | 16 | 2g.10gb | 6736 | 6156 | | **59%** | 30% | 15% |
| convnext_base | 4 | 1g.5gb | 4771 | 1652 | **61%** | 31% | 16% | 8% |
| convnext_base | 128 | 7g.40gb | 26439 | 30996 | | | | **77%** |

```
import dippm
import torchvision

model = (torchvision.models.vgg16(pretrained=True)).eval()

predicted = dippm.predict(model, batch=8, input="3,244,244", device="A100")
print("Memory {0} MB, Energy {1} J, Latency {2} ms, MIG{3}".format(*predicted))
```

**Fig. 5.** An example code demonstrating the utilization of DIPPM for performance prediction of a VGG16 deep learning model with a batch size of 8.

# 5 Conclusion

We have developed a novel Deep Learning (DL) Inference Performance Predictive Model (DIPPM) to predict the inference latency, energy, and memory consumption of a given input DL model on an A100 GPU without running on it. Furthermore, We devised an algorithm to select the appropriate MIG profile from the memory consumption predicted by DIPPM. The model includes a methodology to convert the DL model represented in various frameworks to a generalized graph structure for performance prediction. To the best of our knowledge, DIPPM can help to develop an efficient DL model to utilize the underlying GPU effectively. Furthermore, we constructed and open-sourced[7] a multi-regression graph dataset containing 10,508 DL models for performance prediction. It can even be used to evaluate other graph-based multi-regression GNN algorithms. Finally, we achieved 1.9% MAPE on our dataset.

**Acknowledgment.** This work has been done in the context of the MAELSTROM project, which has received funding from the European High-Performance Computing Joint Undertaking (JU) under grant agreement No 955513. The JU receives support from the European Union's Horizon 2020 research and innovation program and United Kingdom, Germany, Italy, Switzerland, Norway, and in Luxembourg by the Luxembourg National Research Fund (FNR) under contract number 15092355.

[7] https://github.com/karthickai/dippm.

## References


1. Bai, L., Ji, W., Li, Q., Yao, X., Xin, W., Zhu, W.: Dnnabacus: toward accurate computational cost prediction for deep neural networks (2022)
2. Bouhali, N., Ouarnoughi, H., Niar, S., El Cadi, A.A.: Execution time modeling for CNN inference on embedded GPUs. In: Proceedings of the 2021 Drone Systems Engineering and Rapid Simulation and Performance Evaluation: Methods and Tools Proceedings, DroneSE and RAPIDO 2021, pp. 59–65. Association for Computing Machinery, New York, NY, USA (2021)
3. Brown, T.B., et al.: Language models are few-shot learners. In: Proceedings of the 34th International Conference on Neural Information Processing Systems, NIPS 2020, Curran Associates Inc., Red Hook, NY, USA (2020)
4. Dudziak, L., Chau, T., Abdelfattah, M.S., Lee, R., Kim, H., Lane, N.D.: BRP-NAS: prediction-based NAS using GCNs. In: Proceedings of the 34th International Conference on Neural Information Processing Systems, NIPS 2020, Curran Associates Inc., Red Hook, NY, USA (2020)
5. Elsken, T., Metzen, J.H., Hutter, F.: Neural architecture search: a survey. J. Mach. Learn. Res. **20**(1), 1997–2017 (2021)
6. Gao, Y., Gu, X., Zhang, H., Lin, H., Yang, M.: Runtime performance prediction for deep learning models with graph neural network. In: Proceedings of the 45th International Conference on Software Engineering, Software Engineering in Practice (SEIP) Track, ICSE 2023. IEEE/ACM (2023)
7. Gao, Y., et al.: Estimating GPU memory consumption of deep learning models. In: Proceedings of the 28th ACM Joint Meeting on European Software Engineering Conference and Symposium on the Foundations of Software Engineering, pp. 1342–1352. ESEC/FSE 2020, Association for Computing Machinery, New York, NY, USA (2020)
8. Hamilton, W.L., Ying, R., Leskovec, J.: Inductive representation learning on large graphs. In: Proceedings of the 31st International Conference on Neural Information Processing Systems, NIPS 2017, pp. 1025–1035. Curran Associates Inc., Red Hook, NY, USA (2017)
9. Justus, D., Brennan, J., Bonner, S., McGough, A.: Predicting the computational cost of deep learning models. In: 2018 IEEE International Conference on Big Data (Big Data), pp. 3873–3882. IEEE Computer Society, Los Alamitos, CA, USA (2018)
10. Kaufman, S., et al.: A learned performance model for tensor processing units. In: Smola, A., Dimakis, A., Stoica, I. (eds.) Proceedings of Machine Learning and Systems, vol. 3, pp. 387–400 (2021)
11. Kipf, T.N., Welling, M.: Semi-supervised classification with graph convolutional networks. In: International Conference on Learning Representations (ICLR) (2017)
12. Li, B., Patel, T., Samsi, S., Gadepally, V., Tiwari, D.: Miso: exploiting multi-instance GPU capability on multi-tenant GPU clusters. In: Proceedings of the 13th Symposium on Cloud Computing, SoCC 2022, pp. 173–189. Association for Computing Machinery, New York, NY, USA (2022)
13. Liu, L., Shen, M., Gong, R., Yu, F., Yang, H.: Nnlqp: a multi-platform neural network latency query and prediction system with an evolving database. In: Proceedings of the 51st International Conference on Parallel Processing, ICPP 2022. Association for Computing Machinery, New York, NY, USA (2023)
14. Liu, Z., et al.: Swin transformer: hierarchical vision transformer using shifted windows. In: 2021 IEEE/CVF International Conference on Computer Vision (ICCV), pp. 9992–10002. IEEE Computer Society, Los Alamitos, CA, USA (2021)

15. Lu, Z., Rallapalli, S., Chan, K., Pu, S., Porta, T.L.: Augur: modeling the resource requirements of convnets on mobile devices. IEEE Trans. Mob. Comput. **20**(2), 352–365 (2021)
16. Qi, H., Sparks, E.R., Talwalkar, A.: Paleo: a performance model for deep neural networks. In: 5th International Conference on Learning Representations, Conference Track Proceedings, ICLR 2017, Toulon, France, 24–26 April 2017. OpenReview.net (2017)
17. Roesch, J., et al.: Relay: a new IR for machine learning frameworks. In: Proceedings of the 2nd ACM SIGPLAN International Workshop on Machine Learning and Programming Languages, MAPL 2018, pp. 58–68. Association for Computing Machinery, New York, NY, USA (2018)
18. Smith, L.N.: Cyclical learning rates for training neural networks. In: 2017 IEEE Winter Conference on Applications of Computer Vision (WACV), pp. 464–472 (2017)
19. Sponner, M., Waschneck, B., Kumar, A.: Ai-driven performance modeling for AI inference workloads. Electronics **11**(15) (2022)
20. Veličković, P., Cucurull, G., Casanova, A., Romero, A., Liò, P., Bengio, Y.: Graph attention networks. In: International Conference on Learning Representations (2018). Accepted as poster
21. Wang, C.C., Liao, Y.C., Kao, M.C., Liang, W.Y., Hung, S.H.: Toward accurate platform-aware performance modeling for deep neural networks. SIGAPP Appl. Comput. Rev. **21**(1), 50–61 (2021)
22. Xu, K., Hu, W., Leskovec, J., Jegelka, S.: How powerful are graph neural networks? In: International Conference on Learning Representations (2019)
23. Yang, C., Li, Z., Ruan, C., Xu, G., Li, C., Chen, R., Yan, F.: PerfEstimator: a generic and extensible performance estimator for data parallel DNN training. In: 2021 IEEE/ACM International Workshop on Cloud Intelligence (CloudIntelligence), pp. 13–18 (2021)
24. Yu, G.X., Gao, Y., Golikov, P., Pekhimenko, G.: Habitat: a runtime-based computational performance predictor for deep neural network training. In: Proceedings of the 2021 USENIX Annual Technical Conference (USENIX ATC 2021) (2021)
25. Zhang, L.L., et al.: Nn-meter: towards accurate latency prediction of deep-learning model inference on diverse edge devices. In: Proceedings of the 19th Annual International Conference on Mobile Systems, Applications and Services, MobiSys 2021, pp. 81–93. Association for Computing Machinery, New York, NY, USA (2021)

# *perun*: Benchmarking Energy Consumption of High-Performance Computing Applications

Juan Pedro Gutiérrez Hermosillo Muriedas[1(✉)], Katharina Flügel[1,2], Charlotte Debus[1,2], Holger Obermaier[1], Achim Streit[1], and Markus Götz[1,2]

[1] Steinbuch Centre for Computing (SCC), Karlsruhe Institute for Technology (KIT), Hermann-von-Helmholtz Platz 1, 76344 Eggenstein-Leopoldshafen, Germany
{juan.muriedas,katharina.fluegel,charlotte.debus,holger.obermaier, achim.streit,markus.goetz}@kit.edu
[2] Helmholtz AI, Karlsruhe, Germany

**Abstract.** Looking closely at the Top500 list of high-performance computers (HPC) in the world, it becomes clear that computing power is not the only number that has been growing in the last three decades. The amount of power required to operate such massive computing machines has been steadily increasing, earning HPC users a higher than usual carbon footprint. While the problem is well known in academia, the exact energy requirements of hardware, software and how to optimize it are hard to quantify. To tackle this issue, we need tools to understand the software and its relationship with power consumption in today's high performance computers. With that in mind, we present *perun*, a Python package and command line interface to measure energy consumption based on hardware performance counters and selected physical measurement sensors. This enables accurate energy measurements on various scales of computing, from a single laptop to an MPI-distributed HPC application. We include an analysis of the discrepancies between these sensor readings and hardware performance counters, with particular focus on the power draw of the usually overlooked non-compute components such as memory. One of our major insights is their significant share of the total energy consumption. We have equally analyzed the runtime and energy overhead *perun* generates when monitoring common HPC applications, and found it to be minimal. Finally, an analysis on the accuracy of different measuring methodologies when applied at large scales is presented.

**Keywords:** Energy Benchmarking · High-performance Computing · Artificial Intelligence · Distributed Memory System

## 1 Introduction

High-performance computing (HPC) is a key technology to tackle an increasing amount of complex computational problems in science and industry. Example


J. Cano et al. (Eds.): Euro-Par 2023, LNCS 14100, pp. 17–31, 2023.
https://doi.org/10.1007/978-3-031-39698-4_2

applications include fluid dynamics [1], molecular biology [2], and quantum chromodynamics [3]. Recently, HPC has accrued particular interest due to the large computational demands and data quantities of artificial intelligence workloads. With this paradigm shift, the utilized hardware has simultaneously changed towards heterogeneous architectures with local storage, significant main memory, and accelerators like GPUs.

A commonly neglected conundrum of using such heterogeneous HPC systems is their massive energy consumption. Modern supercomputers have a power draw of up to 30 MW [4]. While the efficiency of individual hardware components has improved over time, it has enabled manufacturers to pack transistors and components more densely, to increase the number of computational processing units and nodes as well as to expand auxiliary infrastructure. In turn, the increased power consumption for large-scale computational tasks on HPC systems are outpacing individual hardware efficiency gains [5].

Due to the environmental impact of the corresponding energy generation technologies, recent research has focused on estimating the carbon footprint of compute-intensive workloads. A strong emphasis has been put on training and inference with deep learning models on single nodes with multiple accelerators. The overall conclusion: the utilized hardware, training time, and location are the main factors contributing to carbon dioxide and equivalent gas emission ($CO_2e$).

Yet, several unexplored research questions remain. How reliable are hardware performance counters when estimating application power draw compared to the actual consumption? Are non-compute components like memory, storage, and network sufficiently taken into account? How reliable are current estimation techniques when applied to distributed applications?

In an attempt to provide answers to the above questions, our contributions are as follows:

- A novel MPI-parallelized Python package called *perun*[1] facilitating energy benchmarking on HPC systems. *perun* can utilize both estimates based on sampling hardware performance counters and precise read-outs from energy sensors.
- The assessment of the power estimation and measurement gap.
- An analysis of the power consumption of multi-node applications based on different estimation methodologies, including scaling artifacts for selected benchmark programs with an emphasis on data-intensive deep learning workflows.
- A quantification of the measuring overhead created by *perun*.

## 2 Related Work

Interest in energy-efficient computing is not novel. For example, the Green500 list [6] ranks the most energy-efficient supercomputers and HPC systems. Its goal was to discourage the performance-at-any-cost design of supercomputing systems by introducing the FLOPs-per-Watt (FLOPs $W^{-1}$) metric. Yet, the

[1] https://github.com/Helmholtz-AI-Energy/perun.

determination of the energy consumption is non-standardized and may vary significantly based on the tooling used.

In recent years, several tools have appeared to aid researchers in compiling carbon footprint statements. Carbontracker [7], one of the most widely used, is a Python package primarily aimed at machine learning. It samples energy data from hardware libraries for a single training epoch to extrapolate the energy consumption during actual training, but is limited to a single device. Similar tools include *experiment-impact-tracker* [8] and *CodeCarbon* [9], collecting information using the same API endpoints. However, they do not predict the expected total consumption but are meant to monitor the application throughout its execution.

Outside the Python ecosystem is the *Machine Learning Emissions Calculator* [10], which targets users of Cloud Service Providers (CSP) such as AWS or Google Cloud. Users may input the training wallclock time, the used CSP, hardware, and geolocation. In turn, this data is used to gather information from public APIs to provide the estimated $CO_2e$ emissions. *Green algorithms* [11] is a similar website targeted to both CSP and personal computer users, with a more extensive set of configuration options.

Caspart *et al.* [12] collected energy measurements with physical sensors. The data was used to compare the efficiency of CPUs and GPUs for single-node, multi-accelerator machine learning applications. Hodak *et al.* [13] used a similar setup, but instead focused on which hardware settings significantly reduce the power draw without meaningfully increasing training time.

In the context of machine learning (ML), Strubell *et al.* [14] are among the first to look at the environmental impact of natural language processing (NLP) models. $CO_2e$ emissions are calculated as the sum of the energy consumption of all CPUs and GPUs throughout training, multiplied by the data center's power usage effectiveness (PUE) and carbon efficiency in the data center location. In that, the PUE is the ratio between the energy used by compute components and the energy used for the entire data center infrastructure [15], and carbon efficiency is the ratio of carbon and equivalent gas emissions in tonnes per kilo Watt hour ($\mathrm{t\ CO_2e/(kW\ h)}$). While PUE has widespread use in the industry, it has been critiqued because of the lack of data supporting published numbers, working more as a publicity stunt than a relevant metric [16]. Patterson *et al.* [17] analyzed modern NLP models based on the reported training time, hardware, data center power efficiency, and energy supply mix. They highlighted the importance of hardware and data center choice, as they have the highest impact on $CO_2e$ emissions. At the same time, it showcased the energy efficiency of sparse large-scale models like switch-transformers [18] when compared to a densely activated model such as GPT-3 [19]. PaLM 540B [20], another representative of large language models, is one of the first and few works that includes a carbon footprint statement, thou it lacks a clear electrical footprint report.

# 3 Energy Benchmarking in High-Performance Computing

## 3.1 Background: Determining Energy Consumption

In the following, we will provide a brief overview of common methods used to obtain energy consumption readings. Generally, we distinguish between *measuring* energy, i.e., the process of using physical sensors connected to the compute nodes or other components to monitor the hardware, and *estimating* energy, i.e., using indirect methods to approximate the energy consumption. Leveraging sensors to measure power draw has the highest accuracy, but requires the hardware to be either equipped with additional monitoring devices or manually tapped. Practically, this may hinder sensor use due to additional costs or access restrictions. Which components may be monitored depends on the computing hardware. Past works have focused on individual components like power source, CPU, cooling and memory [13], the individual components of internode communication switches [21], or the consumption of entire nodes [12].

In contrast, energy estimation utilizes indirect, albeit more accessible, tools. An increasingly common way is using the software interfaces provided by hardware manufacturers. The data made available through these interfaces maps to hardware performance counters, special registers embedded in the hardware with the specific purpose of monitoring the device. The energy consumption of hardware components is then estimated by regularly sampling the hardware counters while the monitored device or application is running. These data samples are then aggregated in a post-processing step. Overall, the accuracy of the complete estimation is bound by the registers' resolutions.

An example of such a hardware monitoring interface is `Nvidia Management Library` (NVML) [22], making the power draw of their GPUs available. Figure 1 illustrates an example of the data obtained through its management interface. Similarly, Intel provides access to the accumulated energy usage through the `Running Average Power Limit`[2] (RAPL) interface. It keeps track of the total energy used on a socket granularity for CPU and DRAM, which can be used to calculate the power draw. Which components may be monitored depends on the individual hardware manufacturers and their interfaces. Additionally, access to these interfaces is usually restricted to privileged users.

If no hardware monitoring interfaces are accessible, a rough estimate can be made using the specifications of the utilized hardware. This method assumes that each component requires the same amount of power throughout the runtime of an application. Practically, the constant power draw is an unrealistic assumption, leading to significant over- or underestimation and should be avoided if possible.

Regardless of the method used to obtain the power draw of individual components, the energy consumption of the application running on a single node can then be calculated by integrating the power draw $P$ over the total runtime $T$ for each component in a computational node and summing up all of them up to obtain the total energy of the node:

[2] https://github.com/powercap/raplcap.

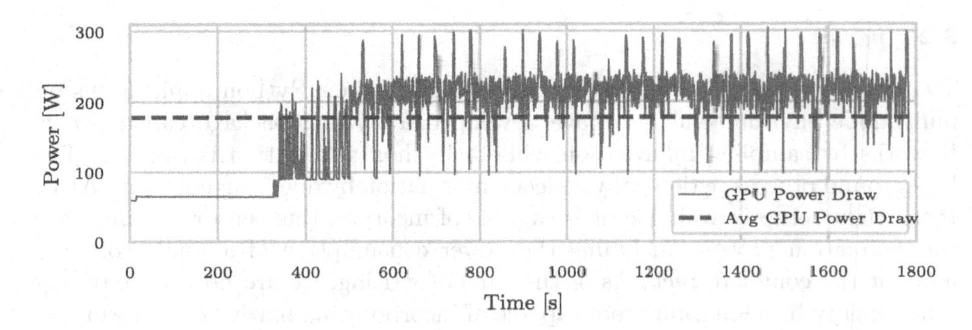


**Fig. 1.** Energy consumption of a single Nvidia A100 gathered from Nvidia-SMI running the OC20 [23] MLPerf benchmark.

$$E_{\text{node}} = \int_0^T P_{\text{cpu}}(t) + P_{\text{gpu}}(t) + P_{\text{ram}}(t) + P_{\text{others}}(t)dt, \tag{1}$$

where $E_{\text{node}}$ is the consumed energy of the subscript components. When running on multi-node applications, the energy of all the individual nodes has to be aggregated and multiplied by the power usage effectiveness (PUE) of the system to obtain the energy consumed of the application:

$$E_{\text{total}} = PUE \cdot \sum_{i}^{\#\text{nodes}} E_{\text{node}}^{(i)}. \tag{2}$$

PUE is a factor obtained by dividing the total equipment consumption of the data center by the power consumption of the compute equipment. This is a common metric used to compare the efficiency of data centers around the world, with the global average in 2020 being 1.58 [24] and some of the most efficient centers having a 1.02 $PUE$ [25].

For the purpose of this work, Eq. (2) is exhaustive to determine the energy consumption of software running on HPC systems. If needed, the corresponding carbon footprint can be derived by multiplying the resulting total energy $E_{\text{total}}$ with an energy-to-$CO_2$e conversion factor $r_e$. $r_e$ signifies the emission rate of the energy generation technologies. Just like $PUE$, this number depends on the location where the software is being run, but additionally changes over time depending on weather, seasons, and energy grid usage, as those factors have a great effect on the available energy sources. The total monetary cost may be derived similarly by replacing $r_e$ with the energy-to-cost conversion ratio.

Both emissions and price fluctuate continuously, whereas it is reasonable to expect that an algorithm would require a (close to) constant amount of power if executed on the same or similar hardware.

### 3.2 *perun*

To allow users to gather energy measurements of their Python applications on multi-node environments, we have developed a Python package called *perun*. It works by sampling information while a Python application is running. The background process periodically collects information by querying hardware APIs. If the right setup is available, it is capable of incorporating sensor readings into the estimation process, including the power consumption of a single compute node or the complete rack. As of the time of writing, we are not aware of any other energy benchmarking tool capable of incorporating hardware performance counters and sensor measurements of MPI distributed Python applications.

Currently, *perun* supports `Intel-RAPL` to sample CPU and DRAM information, `NVML` for GPU information, and `psutil`[3] to sample information on network and filesystem I/O. Sensor data may be additionally collected using Lenovo XClarityController[4], a hardware management system provided by the manufacturer. `psutil`, `Intel-RAPL` and the hardware sensors report the energy consumption of the whole system. To get more representative results, *perun* works best when there are no other programs running in the system.

To handle distributed Python applications, *perun* makes use of the Message Passing Interface (MPI). MPI defines a communication protocol standard for parallel computers. When using MPI applications, *perun* has a coordination step where each individual rank communicates its host name and the visible devices to all other ranks. Based on this information, the first rank in each host is selected to spawn the process and monitor the visible devices. This coordination step ensures that only one monitoring process is spawned per host and that each device is only accounted for once, keeping the overall overhead of *perun* low. Synchronization between the main and monitoring process is handled by using the `multiprocessing` events from the standard library.

All the raw data gathered during the execution of the monitored application is saved in a HDF5 file, along with metadata about the individual devices, nodes, and environment. *perun* then processes the data using Eqs. (1) and (2) and returns a summarized report. All the results can be exported to human as well as machine-readable formats, like JSON and YAML.

To facilitate usage in different environments, *perun* provides a command line interface as a replacement for the Python command. Alternatively, a `monitor` decorator can be used to target specific functions, as shown in Listing 1. *perun*'s behavior can be modified using a configuration file, command line arguments, decorator arguments, or environmental variables.

While most of the interfaces and software features described during this and previous sections can be applied similarly to other programming languages, due to the way *perun* manages the primary Python process when started from the command line, its functionality is as of the time of writing limited to Python applications.

---

[3] https://github.com/giampaolo/psutil.

[4] https://www.lenovo.com/in/en/data-center/software/systems-management/XClarity-Controller/p/WMD00000367.

```
import perun

@perun.monitor(data_out="results/", format="json")
def expensive_computation(input_args):
    pass
```

Listing 1: Example decorator usage

# 4 Experimental Evaluation

The goal of the following experiments, as described in Sect. 1, are the following: quantify the runtime and power overhead caused by sampling performance counters using *perun*, determine the accuracy of the available performance counters when compared to measurements provided by hardware sensors embedded in the system, observe the power consumption of non-compute components and the impact they have on the overall system consumption, and compare different energy estimation methodologies when applied at scale.

The following sections describe the different use cases used for the analysis, and the system where the experiments were implemented.

## 4.1 Application Use Cases

As a calibration measure, the energy consumption of an idle node with and without the monitoring software is compared. Based on sensor data obtained during both types of execution, the runtime, and average power usage difference between monitored and non-monitored applications can be used to get an estimate on the overhead caused by *perun*.

Two single-node use cases are considered, one running on CPU and the other running on four GPUs. First, we apply *perun* to monitor *Black-Scholes* [26] option pricing, an operation commonly used in finance, that can be computed in an embarrassingly parallel way, as a common benchmark in the HPC community. We monitor the energy consumption of solving one billion *Black-Scholes* operations using 76 CPU threads as a single-node high resource utilization example. As a second example, we fine-tune the NLP model BERT [27] on the QUAD 1.2 question-answering dataset using a multi-GPU implementation based on the *huggingface*[5] libraries.

As a large-scale, multi-node example, we evaluate *perun* on two tasks from the MLPerf HPC benchmark suite [28]. The BERT use case was also scaled to two nodes, i.e. eight GPUs. *DeepCam* [29] is an image segmentation model trained on the CAM 5 weather simulation dataset. OpenCatalyst 2020 (OC20) [23] dataset consists of molecular simulation data and defines three supervised learning tasks, where attributes of individual molecules are recreated based on the initial structure. Both models are trained to a pre-defined performance threshold. The imple-

[5] https://huggingface.co.

mentation used is based on the closed submission by the Helmholtz AI group[6]. The OC20 benchmark was run using up to 128 nodes, each one with four GPUs, to observe how scaling affects the overall energy consumption of the application. DeepCam was run using the same hardware setup. All single node programs were run a total of 20 times, half using *perun*, and the other half without. MLPerf programs were run only six times, five times using *perun* and once without.

### 4.2 Hardware Environment

The use cases were run using two different hardware configurations of the HoreKa supercomputer at the Karlsruhe Institute for Technology: CPU-only nodes, which have no accelerated hardware, and GPU nodes, which include four Nvidia A100-40 GB GPUs. Each node in both partitions has two Intel Xeon Platinum 8368 processors, a 960 GB SSD, and is interconnected with an InfiniBand HDR fabric. The CPU-only nodes have 256 GB, while the accelerated nodes have 512 GB of main memory.

Each node includes special hardware that gathers power measurements from different components, including the CPU, GPU, and the entire node. This information is consistently being collected via the Lenovo XClarity Controllers Redfish REST API and is transferred to an InfluxDB time series database. According to the server documentation[7], XClarity Controller measurements for GPU and CPU has an 97% accuracy at a 100 Hz sampling rate. The system uses an energy-efficient hot water cooling system, making it a highly efficient HPC system with a PUE of 1.05.

### 4.3 Software

Two different stacks were used to run the different use cases: a container-based environment, used for both MLPerf use cases, and a *native* environment, which was used for the rest. The native environment makes use of Python 3.8.6, `OpenMPI` 4.1.3, `mip4py` 3.1.4, and `pytorch` 1.12.1 with `CUDA` 11.6. The base container used for the MLPerf Benchmarks is `pytorch:22.08-py3-devel` from the Nvidia Container Registry. It contains Python 3.8.12, `OpenMPI` 4.1.2, `mpi4py` 1.13 and `pytorch` 1.13 with `CUDA` 11.7. The *perun* version used at the time of the experiments is 0.1.0b16. All jobs were scheduled using SLURM[8].

## 5 Results

### 5.1 Monitoring Overhead

First, we measured the overhead that running an application with *perun* entails using hardware sensor data. Table 1 shows differences in runtime, average power draw per node, and the total energy consumption for runs with and without *perun*. Column N indicates the number of nodes used for each use case.

[6] https://mlcommons.org/en/training-hpc-20/.
[7] https://lenovopress.lenovo.com/lp1395-thinksystem-sd650-v2-server.
[8] https://slurm.schedmd.com/overview.html.

**Table 1.** Runtime and average node power consumption comparison between software run with and without monitoring software, aggregated over multiple runs.

| Name | N | Runtime | | | | | $\overline{P}_{node}$ | | | | |
|---|---|---|---|---|---|---|---|---|---|---|---|
| | | Unmonitored | | Monitored | | Δ | Unmonitored | | Monitored | | Δ |
| | | [s] | ± | [s] | ± | Δ | [W] | ± | [W] | ± | Δ |
| idle | 1 | 78.58 | 1.73 | 81.71 | 1.64 | 3.13 | 293.67 | 12.53 | 292.26 | 13.34 | −1.42 |
| idle gpu | 1 | 81.10 | 0.57 | 86.92 | 2.07 | 5.82 | 571.20 | 15.36 | 564.75 | 13.20 | −6.45 |
| black-scholes | 1 | 1998.00 | 29.36 | 2085.56 | 150.11 | 87.56 | 618.55 | 18.44 | 634.35 | 31.27 | 15.80 |
| BERT | 1 | 1180.27 | 3.93 | 1190.15 | 18.10 | 9.88 | 1319.53 | 29.97 | 1301.74 | 43.31 | −17.79 |
| BERT | 2 | 970.60 | 12.40 | 975.75 | 7.07 | 5.15 | 1058.19 | 58.22 | 1079.33 | 51.90 | 21.14 |
| OC20 | 64 | 2542.00 | – | 2428.51 | 84.16 | −113.49 | 1305.48 | 25.71 | 1300.41 | 31.74 | −5.06 |
| OC20 | 128 | 1752.00 | – | 1785.00 | 53.60 | 33.00 | 1096.76 | 33.16 | 1106.29 | 31.09 | 9.53 |
| DeepCam | 128 | 526.00 | – | 484.60 | 33.03 | −41.40 | 1030.50 | 120.24 | 995.39 | 116.58 | −35.11 |

The high variance makes identifying a clear trend from these results difficult, as the overhead caused by *perun* is often in the same order of magnitude as the variance. The variance in the software's runtime seems to have the biggest impact and makes it difficult to discern the effect running *perun* has on the monitored software runtime and power consumption. From the execution time of the use cases idle and BERT, we can expect an increase of 5 s to 10 s of execution time on average. The results of OC20 and DeepCamp have low statistical relevance, as those use cases were run only once without *perun*. Even then, *perun* seems to have a small enough impact that some monitored applications had shorter execution times than the monitored ones.

*perun* has the biggest impact on the runtime of the *Black-Scholes* use case. As it is a CPU-intensive benchmark compared to the others, the extra processing load from the monitoring process hurts the overall performance. Like the runtime, the average power draw per node has a similarly high variance, often larger than the difference between monitored and unmonitored runs. The high variance can be explained in part by small changes in the hardware itself, as the software was run on different nodes with the same hardware, and there were no warm-up runs before running the use cases, putting the nodes in different stages of idleness/activity when the software started.

Given that the difference in power draw between monitored and unmonitored applications is close to zero, it is fair to assume that the background sampling process does not meaningfully raise the power consumption.

### 5.2 Monitoring Accuracy and Missing Power Consumption

In order to assess the accuracy of *perun*'s estimates based on hardware performance counters, we compare the difference between the power reported by hardware libraries and sensor data for individual devices. Based on the power consumption of the compute components and sensor data from the entire node, the power draw of difficult to access components, e.g., internal fan, storage, networking cards, can be quantified as a group.

**Table 2.** Average power draw for component $x$ as reported by performance counters $\overline{P}_{x,p}$ and the hardware sensors $\overline{P}_{x,s}$ for each use case.

| Name | N | $\overline{P}_{\text{dram},p}$ | | $\overline{P}_{\text{dram},s}$ | | $\overline{P}_{\text{cpu},p}$ | | $\overline{P}_{\text{cpu},s}$ | | $\overline{P}_{\text{gpu},p}$ | | $\overline{P}_{\text{gpu},s}$ | | $\overline{P}_{\text{node},p}$ | | $\overline{P}_{\text{node},s}$ | |
|---|---|---|---|---|---|---|---|---|---|---|---|---|---|---|---|---|---|
| | | [W] | ± | [W] | ± | [W] | ± | [W] | ± | [W] | ± | [W] | ± | [W] | ± | [W] | ± |
| idle | 1 | 16.8 | 1.3 | 16.4 | 1.2 | 195.5 | 11.1 | 198.0 | 12.2 | – | – | – | – | 212.4 | 11.8 | 289.4 | 14.2 |
| idle gpu | 1 | 24.6 | 0.8 | 24.5 | 1.1 | 210.5 | 5.3 | 208.2 | 9.2 | 218.6 | 3.3 | 218.6 | 3.4 | 453.6 | 5.8 | 560.4 | 13.8 |
| black-scholes | 1 | 17.8 | 0.8 | 17.7 | 0.8 | 529.4 | 28.2 | 531.5 | 28.4 | – | – | – | – | 547.1 | 27.8 | 642.7 | 31.4 |
| BERT | 1 | 26.3 | 1.1 | 26.2 | 1.1 | 231.7 | 5.1 | 232.1 | 5.4 | 970.7 | 24.6 | 941.6 | 33.0 | 1228.7 | 24.1 | 1338.5 | 57.4 |
| BERT | 2 | 27.6 | 1.0 | 27.5 | 1.1 | 240.4 | 5.9 | 240.0 | 5.8 | 712.6 | 19.0 | 698.2 | 24.1 | 980.6 | 19.3 | 1115.6 | 63.6 |
| OC20 | 16 | 26.2 | 1.2 | 26.1 | 1.2 | 256.7 | 6.8 | 257.3 | 6.8 | 1035.4 | 14.8 | 1031.4 | 15.5 | 1318.3 | 18.0 | 1473.7 | 22.7 |
| OC20 | 32 | 26.4 | 1.2 | 26.3 | 1.2 | 258.8 | 7.2 | 259.3 | 7.0 | 1027.5 | 18.5 | 1022.4 | 19.6 | 1312.7 | 21.3 | 1465.3 | 29.3 |
| OC20 | 64 | 26.6 | 1.2 | 26.6 | 1.2 | 266.9 | 7.2 | 267.1 | 7.4 | 882.8 | 16.5 | 874.6 | 19.2 | 1176.3 | 18.8 | 1316.2 | 29.5 |
| OC20 | 128 | 26.8 | 1.2 | 27.5 | 23.1 | 268.4 | 7.7 | 269.0 | 8.0 | 692.1 | 13.7 | 686.1 | 19.1 | 987.3 | 17.3 | 1119.4 | 31.9 |
| DeepCam | 16 | 31.1 | 1.2 | 30.6 | 1.3 | 261.4 | 6.6 | 259.6 | 7.7 | 640.0 | 15.5 | 645.2 | 43.0 | 932.5 | 16.9 | 1032.9 | 74.6 |
| DeepCam | 128 | 30.3 | 1.3 | 30.1 | 1.8 | 246.6 | 7.0 | 251.1 | 11.5 | 681.8 | 12.6 | 692.0 | 83.6 | 958.7 | 15.7 | 1026.1 | 124.5 |

Table 2 shows the average power draw measured by each device throughout the execution of the software, averaged over multiple runs. All DRAM, CPUs, and GPUs in a node are grouped and summed together. $\overline{P}$ indicates the average power draw from the compute nodes while the software was executed. The subscript indicates the hardware component and the data source, $p$ for performance counters and $s$ for sensor data.

For DRAM and CPU, we observe almost no difference between the sensor data and performance counters, with a maximum difference of 1 W for DRAM and 0 W to 2 W for CPU power draw. This difference is more pronounced for GPU devices, averaging at 5.68 ± 10.35 W overestimation from performance counters. Data from performance counters and sensors have a higher variance for GPUs than other hardware components, making it harder to approximate. According to the official Nvidia System Management Library documentation [22], the power values returned by the performance counters have an accuracy of ±5 W. Additionally, the measured sensor includes the power consumption of all components on the GPU board at a higher sampling frequency, not only the GPU and High Bandwidth Memory (HBM) that are measured by the performance counters.

When looking at the aggregated power consumption for the entire node, there is a clear difference between what can be estimated using performance counters and full node sensor data, providing a clearer picture on the power draw of components lacking monitoring support. In this particular setup, this means networking, storage, cooling systems, power supply and motherboard. The power consumption of these components are also application dependent and come with their own variance, adding uncertainty to the estimation process. For nodes without GPUs, we have measured their required power draw to be 78.93 ± 8.39 W, and for nodes with GPUs, the unaccounted power draw is on average 109.37 ± 30.51 W. The previous values can be inserted into Eq. (1) alongside the estimates for CPU, GPU, and DRAM to correct the energy estimation of individual nodes, thus closing the gap between estimated and measured total energy consumption seen in the last two columns.

In conclusion, the usage of performance counters provide a good estimation of the energy consumption for individual components, reducing the need of dedicated hardware unless precision is of utmost importance. Estimations of the total node power draw can be improved by adding a constant power draw throughout the runtime of the application. Finding an optimal value is difficult without measuring equipment, and will need to be chosen carefully based on the system.

### 5.3 Impact of Non-compute Devices on the Overall Energy Consumption

**Table 3.** Power draw percentage per device.

| Name | N | $\overline{P}_{\text{dram}}$ | | $\overline{P}_{\text{cpu}}$ | | $\overline{P}_{\text{gpu}}$ | | $\overline{P}_{\text{rest}}$ | | $\overline{P}_{\text{node}}$ [W] |
|---|---|---|---|---|---|---|---|---|---|---|
| | | [W] | [%] | [W] | [%] | [W] | [%] | [W] | [%] | |
| idle | 1 | 16.4 | 5.7 | 198.0 | 68.4 | – | 0.0 | 75.1 | 25.9 | 289.4 |
| idle gpu | 1 | 24.5 | 4.4 | 208.2 | 37.1 | 218.6 | 39.0 | 109.1 | 19.5 | 560.4 |
| black-scholes | 1 | 17.7 | 2.7 | 531.5 | 82.7 | – | 0.0 | 93.6 | 14.6 | 642.7 |
| BERT | 1 | 26.2 | 2.0 | 232.1 | 17.3 | 941.6 | 70.3 | 138.7 | 10.4 | 1338.5 |
| BERT | 2 | 27.5 | 2.5 | 240.0 | 21.5 | 698.2 | 62.6 | 149.9 | 13.4 | 1115.6 |
| OC20 | 16 | 26.1 | 1.8 | 257.3 | 17.5 | 1031.4 | 70.0 | 158.9 | 10.8 | 1473.7 |
| OC20 | 32 | 26.3 | 1.8 | 259.3 | 17.7 | 1022.4 | 69.8 | 157.4 | 10.7 | 1465.3 |
| OC20 | 64 | 26.6 | 2.0 | 267.1 | 20.3 | 874.6 | 66.4 | 147.9 | 11.2 | 1316.2 |
| OC20 | 128 | 27.5 | 2.5 | 269.0 | 24.0 | 686.1 | 61.3 | 136.7 | 12.2 | 1119.4 |
| DeepCam | 16 | 30.6 | 3.0 | 259.6 | 25.1 | 645.2 | 62.5 | 97.5 | 9.4 | 1032.9 |
| DeepCam | 128 | 30.1 | 2.9 | 251.1 | 24.5 | 692.0 | 67.4 | 52.8 | 5.2 | 1026.1 |

As shown in the previous section, the power draw of non-compute components is not negligible, contributing to a high percentage of the overall energy consumption. Table 3 breaks up the total energy consumption by devices, assigning the remainder to the non-compute components.

We observe that as the CPU and GPU utilization, and with it their power draw, increases, the share of non-compute components in the total energy consumption decreases. However, even under high utilization, non-compute components make up about 15% of the energy consumption of CPU-only nodes and more than 5% of GPU nodes.

### 5.4 Scaling Behavior for Multi-Node Applications

Using the OC20 use case, we compare the accuracy of different energy consumption estimation methods on massively parallel applications. We consider

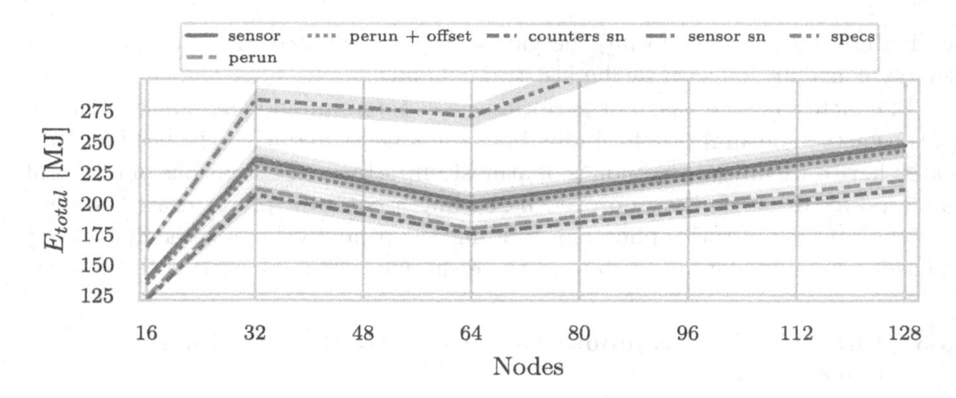


**Fig. 2.** Reported total energy consumption of different estimation methods on the OC20 tasks as a function of number of compute nodes.

performance counters (*perun*), performance counters including a "correction offset" of 110 W based on the analysis done in Sect. 5.2 (*perun*+offset), hardware measurements (sensors), and a simpler estimation based on the hardware specifications (specs) of the CPU and GPU. The analysis will also include estimations based on the data of a single node (sn) for both sensors and performance counters, following the methodology described in Green500 benchmark tutorial [30] from 2007.

Figure 2 displays the total energy calculated by the different estimations methods. The transparent area around each line represents the standard deviation. At a first glance, it becomes clear that using the specified Thermal Design Power from the components leads to an overestimation of the consumed energy, with the difference becoming bigger as the number of nodes increases and the utilization of each component decrease. It can work as an upper bound if no other source of information is available.

The results show, that for this particular use case, measuring a single full node and multiplying by the number of nodes provides an accurate approximation of the total energy usage during the application runtime. This might change for different applications, if the load distribution is drastically different in the individual compute nodes. A close second is *perun*+offset, which managed to close the gap between sensors and performance counters by adding a flat offset to the original estimation of *perun*. Estimations based on performance counters (*perun* and sensor sn) slowly diverge as the number of nodes increases, with a difference of around 25 MJ on the 128 node configuration. Still, performance counter based estimations provide better results when run on all nodes, with a difference in the order of MJ between multi-node and single-node estimations on all node configurations. This supports the need for a distributed monitoring tool when hardware sensors are not an option.

# 6 Conclusion

In this study, we introduce *perun*, a novel Python package to facilitate energy benchmarking of MPI-distributed workloads. We analyzed the impact such a tool has on the overall runtime and energy consumption and found that the overhead is negligible.

Making use of *perun*, an analysis of the energy estimations based on hardware performance counters was presented alongside sensor data from those same components and the entire node. The difference in reported power draw from the two sources indicates that CPU and DRAM data matches the sensor readings adequately. A larger distance is observed between power draw estimations and measurements for GPUs.

From these results, an approximation could be made on the power draw of often unaccounted hardware components, which can later be used to correct any power estimations made using only CPUs, GPUs, and DRAM. The data shows that the power of those components entails a non-minuscule percentage of the total power consumption of each node, and its impact should be considered when writing impact statements.

Finally, the difference between different energy estimation methodologies is highlighted using the OC20 benchmark on different hardware configurations. The results highlight the importance of making use of distributed monitoring tools like *perun* and the need to account the power draw of non-compute components, as their impact increases with the number of nodes.

## 6.1 Limitations

While the individual hardware components and software interfaces are common in other HPC systems, the power measuring equipment is not so, complicating the evaluation of the presented approach in other systems. Similar studies with different hardware and workloads will further aid in understanding the energy consumption of applications with high levels of parallelism.

In the making of this paper, a total of 2136.42 kWh were used, which based on the location and time of our experiments, generated 841.75 kg $CO_2$e.

**Acknowledgments.** This work is supported by the Helmholtz project HiRSE_PS, the Helmholtz AI platform and the HAICORE@KIT grant.

# References

1. Zhang, F., Bonart, H., Zirwes, T., Habisreuther, P., Bockhorn, H., Zarzalis, N.: Direct numerical simulation of chemically reacting flows with the public domain code OpenFOAM. In: Nagel, W.E., Kröner, D.H., Resch, M.M. (eds.) High Performance Computing in Science and Engineering 2014, pp. 221–236. Springer, Cham (2015). https://doi.org/10.1007/978-3-319-10810-0_16 ISBN: 978-3-319-10810-0

2. Weiel, M., Götz, M., Klein, A., et al.: Dynamic particle swarm optimization of biomolecular simulation parameters with flexible objective functions. Nat. Mach. Intell. **3**(8), 727–734 (2021). https://doi.org/10.1038/s42256-021-00366-3. ISSN: 2522-5839
3. Durr, S., Fodor, Z., Frison, J., et al.: Ab initio determination of light hadron masses. Science **322**(5905), 1224–1227 (2008)
4. Strohmaier, E., Dongarra, J., Simon, H., et al.: TOP500 (1993). https://www.top500.org/. Accessed 20 Feb 2023
5. Patterson, D., Gonzalez, J., Hülzle, U., et al.: The carbon footprint of machine learning training will plateau, then shrink. Computer **55**(7), 18–28 (2022). https://doi.org/10.1109/MC.2022.3148714. Conference Name: Computer, ISSN: 1558-0814
6. Feng, W.-C., Cameron, K.: The Green500 list: encouraging sustainable supercomputing. Computer **40**(12), 50–55 (2007). https://doi.org/10.1109/MC.2007.445. Conference Name: Computer, ISSN: 1558-0814
7. Anthony, L.F.W., Kanding, B., Selvan, R.: Carbontracker: tracking and predicting the carbon footprint of training deep learning models (2020). arXiv: 2007.03051 [cs, eess, stat]
8. Henderson, P., Hu, J., Romoff, J., et al.: Towards the systematic reporting of the energy and carbon footprints of machine learning. J. Mach. Learn. Res. **21**(248), 1–43 (2020). ISSN: 1533-7928
9. Schmidt, V., Goyal-Kamal, Courty, B., et al.: mlco2/codecarbon: v2.1.4 (2022). https://doi.org/10.5281/zenodo.7049269
10. Lacoste, A., Luccioni, A., Schmidt, V., et al.: Quantifying the carbon emissions of machine learning. arXiv preprint arXiv:1910.09700 (2019)
11. Lannelongue, L., Grealey, J., Inouye, M.: Green algorithms: quantifying the carbon footprint of computation. Adv. Sci. **8**(12), 2100707 (2021). https://doi.org/10.1002/advs.202100707. ISSN: 2198-3844, 2198-3844
12. Caspart, R., et al.: Precise energy consumption measurements of heterogeneous artificial intelligence workloads. In: Anzt, H., Bienz, A., Luszczek, P., Baboulin, M. (eds.) ISC High Performance 2022. LNCS, vol. 13387, pp. 108–121. Springer, Cham (2022). https://doi.org/10.1007/978-3-031-23220-6_8 ISBN: 978-3-031-23220-6
13. Hodak, M., Dholakia, A.: Recent efficiency gains in deep learning: performance, power, and sustainability. In: 2021 IEEE International Conference on Big Data (Big Data), pp. 2040–2045 (2021). https://doi.org/10.1109/BigData52589.2021.9671762
14. Strubell, E., Ganesh, A., McCallum, A.: Energy and policy considerations for deep learning in NLP (2019). https://doi.org/10.48550/arXiv.1906.02243. arXiv:1906.02243 [cs]
15. ISO/IEC 30134-2:2016. ISO (2016). https://www.iso.org/standard/63451.html. Accessed 09 Feb 2023
16. Brady, G.A., Kapur, N., Summers, J.L., et al.: A case study and critical assessment in calculating power usage effectiveness for a data centre. Energy Convers. Manag. **76**, 155–161 (2013). https://doi.org/10.1016/J.ENCONMAN.2013.07.035
17. Patterson, D., Gonzalez, J., Le, Q., et al.: Carbon emissions and large neural network training (2021). https://doi.org/10.48550/arXiv.2104.10350. http://arxiv.org/abs/2104.10350 [cs]
18. Fedus, W., Zoph, B., Shazeer, N.: Switch transformers: scaling to trillion parameter models with simple and efficient sparsity (2022). arXiv:2101.03961 [cs]
19. Brown, T.B., Mann, B., Ryder, N., et al.: Language models are few-shot learners (2020). arXiv:2005.14165 [cs]
20. Chowdhery, A., Narang, S., Devlin, J., et al.: PaLM: scaling language modeling with pathways (2022). arXiv:2204.02311 [cs]

21. Wang, H., Li, Z., Zhao, X., He, Q., Sun, J.: Evaluating the energy consumption of InfiniBand switch based on time series. In: Wong, W.E., Zhu, T. (eds.) Computer Engineering and Networking. LNEE, vol. 277, pp. 963–970. Springer, Cham (2014). https://doi.org/10.1007/978-3-319-01766-2_110 ISBN: 978-3-319-01766-2
22. NVIDIA system management interface, NVIDIA Developer (2012). https://developer.nvidia.com/nvidia-system-management-interface. Accessed 14 Feb 2023
23. Chanussot, L., Das, A., Goyal, S., et al.: The open catalyst 2020 (OC20) dataset and community challenges. ACS Catal. **11**(10), 6059–6072 (2021). https://doi.org/10.1021/acscatal.0c04525. arXiv: 2010.09990 [cond-mat]. ISSN: 2155-5435, 2155-5435
24. Lawrence, A.: Data center PUEs flat since 2013. Uptime Institute Blog (2020). https://journal.uptimeinstitute.com/data-center-pues-flat-since-2013/. Accessed 31 Jan 2023
25. Miller, R.: Immersion cooling at scale: BitFury pushes density to 250kw per rack. Data Center Frontier (2015). https://www.datacenterfrontier.com/featured/article/11431449/immersion-cooling-at-scale-bitfury-pushes-density-to-250kw-per-rack. Accessed 31 Jan 2023
26. Black, F., Scholes, M.S.: The pricing of options and corporate liabilities. J. Polit. Econ. **81**, 637–654 (1973)
27. Devlin, J., Chang, M.-W., Lee, K., et al.: BERT: pre-training of deep bidirectional transformers for language understanding (2019). http://arxiv.org/abs/1810.04805 [cs]
28. Farrell, S., Emani, M., Balma, J., et al.: MLPerf HPC: a holistic benchmark suite for scientific machine learning on HPC systems (2021). arXiv:2110.11466 [cs]
29. Kurth, T., Treichler, S., Romero, J., et al.: Exascale deep learning for climate analytics. In: SC 2018: International Conference for High Performance Computing, Networking, Storage and Analysis, pp. 649–660 (2018). https://doi.org/10.1109/SC.2018.00054
30. Ge, R., Feng, X., Pyla, H., et al.: Power measurement tutorial for the Green500 list (2007)

# Extending OpenSHMEM with Aggregation Support for Improved Message Rate Performance

Aaron Welch[1(✉)], Oscar Hernandez[2], and Stephen Poole[3]

[1] University of Houston, Houston, TX 77004, USA
dawelch@uh.edu
[2] Oak Ridge National Laboratory, Oak Ridge, TN 37830, USA
oscar@ornl.gov
[3] Los Alamos National Laboratory, Los Alamos, NM 87545, USA
swpoole@lanl.gov

**Abstract.** OpenSHMEM is a highly efficient one-sided communication API that implements the PGAS parallel programming model, and is known for its low latency communication operations that can be mapped efficiently to RDMA capabilities of network interconnects. However, applications that use OpenSHMEM can be sensitive to point-to-point message rates, as many-to-many communication patterns can generate large amounts of small messages which tend to overwhelm network hardware that has predominantly been optimised for bandwidth over message rate. Additionally, many important emerging classes of problems such as data analytics are similarly troublesome for the irregular access patterns they employ. Message aggregation strategies have been proven to significantly enhance network performance, but their implementation often involves complex restructuring of user code, making them unwieldy. This paper shows how to combine the best qualities of message aggregation within the communication model of OpenSHMEM such that applications with small and irregular access patterns can improve network performance while maintaining their algorithmic simplicity. We do this by providing a path to a message aggregation framework called conveyors through a minimally intrusive OpenSHMEM extension introducing *aggregation contexts* that fit more naturally to the OpenSHMEM atomics, gets, and puts model. We test these extensions using four of the bale 3.0 applications which contain essential many-to-many access patterns to show how they can produce performance improvements of up to 65×.

**Keywords:** OpenSHMEM · PGAS · Conveyors · Message Aggregation · High Performance Computing

## 1 Introduction

OpenSHMEM [15] is a community-based specification for a one-sided communication API that implements the partitioned global address space (PGAS) parallel


J. Cano et al. (Eds.): Euro-Par 2023, LNCS 14100, pp. 32–46, 2023.
https://doi.org/10.1007/978-3-031-39698-4_3

programming model and is known for providing a thin layer of abstraction over remote direct memory access (RDMA) hardware resulting in extremely low small message latencies. However, as modern systems have been primarily optimised for bandwidth over larger and contiguous accesses, many OpenSHMEM applications can quickly overwhelm networks with large amounts of small messages on common irregular and many-to-many communication patterns [6], limiting performance scalability as the network reaches its maximum message rate capacity. Given that the performance implications and relevant solutions for applications with regular access patterns is already well-understood by the PGAS community, we aim to focus particularly on improving the performance rate of small messages in irregular access patterns.

The problem of small message rate performance is a result of hardware and software limitations, and has typically been approached with message aggregation strategies [3,5,13,16]. This relies on intelligently deferring and grouping together many small messages into much bigger operations to be executed later. Such strategies have been shown to be very effective at overcoming message rate performance issues, however they can often require significant and cumbersome restructuring of user code that is difficult to maintain and is unintuitive to work into application design. In particular, they may necessitate more complex synchronisation models and memory access patterns, and can often constrain applications to a particular aggregation strategy or library. These characteristics detract from a clear representation of algorithmic intent and contribute to productivity challenges when implementing them in application source code, which serves to impede their widespread adoption.

This paper shows that it is possible to take advantage of message aggregation while making minimal changes to application code and maintaining the simple atomics, gets, and puts (AGP) operation that OpenSHMEM provides. To that end, we will focus on the bale effort [10] and its message aggregation library called *conveyors*, along with an associated series of applications demonstrating access patterns that benefit from it. The conveyor interface is a low level API for aggregation that aims to address message rate performance bottlenecks in applications by providing a mechanism for packing and unpacking many small messages into larger buffers for remote transfer and processing, along with a contract for their use that promises particular behaviours and guarantees when followed. However, its main purpose was to demonstrate that aggregation strategies can be highly performant, and their more complex aggregation model was developed out of a necessity rather than with the intention of replacing a simple communication model in an application.

As a result, we aim to combine the benefits of conveyors with the simplicity and natural use of OpenSHMEM through a minimally intrusive extension to the latter that we call *aggregation contexts*. This extension builds upon the existing OpenSHMEM 1.5 feature of communication contexts and extends it with the option to support deferred execution of operations facilitated by conveyors in a way that largely fits into its preexisting usage model.

Our paper demonstrates that our aggregation contexts extension is simple to use, preserves the AGP model, and delivers good performance when used in applications. We demonstrate the benefits of our approach by comparing its simplicity of use and performance to the use of conveyors directly in four of the bale 3.0 applications.

The rest of this paper is organised as follows. Section 2 delves into the basic history of OpenSHMEM and its memory/communication model along with some background on the bale effort. Section 3 describes the design of our proposed contexts extension to OpenSHMEM, while Sect. 4 applies this design to a number of critical many-to-many access patterns and compares the result against what is achievable with either a pure AGP approach or direct use of conveyors. Section 5 describes related work to the small message problem, aggregation strategies, and their application to other PGAS programming models. Finally, Sect. 6 offers some conclusions on the work and its utility and provides some insight into its remaining deficits and how they may be improved upon in the future.

## 2 Background

This section provides a brief overview of OpenSHMEM and the bale effort that is sufficient to be able to understand our work. For a more in-depth description of either, see [10] and [15].

### 2.1 OpenSHMEM

OpenSHMEM is a community-based specification that builds upon Cray's SHMEM PGAS library, from which it originated. The specification has seen rapid advancement in recent years to modernise it with new features intended to better adapt to applications' needs and new state-of-the-art network interconnect capabilities. At the time of this writing, the latest OpenSHMEM version is 1.5. OpenSHMEM follows an SPMD model with an emphasis on one-sided AGP operations on remotely accessible data objects, along with a set of collective operations for synchronisation and data transfer (e.g. broadcast/reduction).

A distinguishing feature of the OpenSHMEM library is its use of *symmetric* memory, which means that allocation within this memory is a collective operation and results in each participating processing element (PE) allocating an equal portion of a remotely accessible distributed shared variable. All remote communication operations exclusively access memory in this symmetric space.

Since communication in OpenSHMEM is one-sided, there is no direct way to query completion of individual remote operations. Instead, its synchronisation model requires use of barriers for process synchronisation, fences for ordering, and *quiet* for ensuring all outstanding operations issued by a PE are complete.

To demonstrate what OpenSHMEM code looks like, we show a simple example from the bale applications employing a pattern called histogram in Listing 1. Histogram represents a communication pattern where PEs are updating random locations of a distributed table accessible by all of the PEs (e.g. counting the elements for each bin on a given data set). To simulate this in the histogram application, each PE generates a uniform list of random indices in the table and then proceeds to update each location by incrementing its value. The OpenSHMEM portion of the code contains a single atomic increment operation for each such index followed by a barrier at the end.

```
for (int64_t i = 0; i < data->l_num_ups; i++) {
    shmem_atomic_inc(&data->counts[data->pckindx[i] >> 20],
        data->pckindx[i] & 0xfffff);
}
shmem_barrier_all();
```

**Listing 1.** An OpenSHMEM Implementation of Histogram

### 2.2 Bale

The bale effort aims to address the many-to-many communication access patterns that often arise in distributed applications using the PGAS paradigm by providing message aggregation libraries along with a set of applications that employ them for comparison. While our focus will be on its *conveyor* library, it also provides two older libraries upon which it was partially based called exstack and exstack2. Conveyors have been proven to be highly efficient and scalable while also maintaining a high degree of modularity and portability, which makes it well suited for addressing the discussion of aggregation in OpenSHMEM across the wide variety of implmentations and system architectures its specification spans. They are akin to stateful message queues, with operations to *push*/*pull* messages to/from them along with a set of methods to manage them and their completion. Thus, conveyors implicitly employ a two-sided execution model. To efficiently aggregate messages, these queues generally contain a given number of fixed-size items, though optionally *elastic* conveyors can be used to transmit variable-sized items by adding size information to its internal packet structure and employing *epush*/*epull* alternatives. Operation of conveyors is based on a *contract* between them and the application, such that so long as the application obeys its end of the contract, the conveyors will guarantee that all operations are eventually completed without developers needing to be concerned about the manner or timing of their execution. Conveyors are available in different types that differ in their characteristics or how they are implemented (e.g. hops in the network topology) to meet different application requirements on a given system. This modularity allows for multiple conveyors of different qualities to be dynamically selected or configured at run-time.

General use of conveyors involves worker threads pushing messages onto their queues until they fail, then alternately advancing and pulling received messages until they can push again, optionally "unpulling" the most recent item if it is unable to be processed immediately. These messages are encoded and supplied by the application developer through user-defined item structures and their sizes. To properly use conveyors, however, the developer must carefully manage their progress and the different states they transition between. Upon creation, conveyors begin in a *dormant* state, where they may either be freed or moved to their *working* state via the `convey_begin` operation. While within this working state, data can be pushed and pulled freely, but must be manually progressed with calls to `convey_advance` to ensure progress, typically when pushing an item fails. The timing of when messages are sent is not guaranteed, but will happen dynamically as buffers fill or if the conveyor is advanced to its *endgame* state by indicating so via an argument to subsequent advance operations. Optionally, *steady* conveyors can be used to ensure that no messages are withheld indefinitely, even without filling output buffers. Once a process is done pushing data to a conveyor, it advances it to its endgame, after which it must continue progressing and pulling data until all other processes have also reached their endgame, at which point it moves to its *complete* state and can be freed or reset.

## 3 Design

Implementing message aggregation in a parallel programming model requires extensions to its memory and synchronisation model in order to manage the completion semantics of communication operations. This includes a deferred execution model that implicitly relaxes the guarantees of these operations. In our case, making changes to OpenSHMEM's semantics is unavoidable, but it's crucial to make sure that any extensions are implemented in a way that is both contained and backward compatible with the existing memory and synchronisation model, so that they do not have any negative impact on existing code.

OpenSHMEM 1.4 introduced *communication contexts* which we extended to introduce message aggregation. Communication contexts allow for arbitrary subsets of communication operations to be provided with ordering and completion semantics that are independent from those outside the context. This feature is particularly useful in avoiding contention, such as locks, in multithreaded executions of network operations. While the completion semantics within an individual context remain the same as outside of them, their abstraction provides a clear opportunity to introduce an option to change them. That is what we propose doing here—adding a `SHMEM_CTX_AGGREGATE` option to context creation to change these semantics and implicitly aggregate communication performed within them.

The completion semantics within these aggregation contexts are kept as loose as possible—while local input buffers are reusable upon return, no level of local or remote completion is guaranteed until the user requests a quiet operation on the context. These quiet operations implicitly advance the conveyors to their endgame and continues progressing until complete, then reset them before returning, effectively delineating communication epochs. This allows the implementation to employ conveyors (or any alternative aggregation libraries or strategies) without publicly exposing any of its details or usage requirements. Thus, aggregation contexts are continuously available for use without any state management until intentionally freed.

To implement conveyors within these contexts, we create a generic packet structure for messages containing the operation type, local and remote addresses, and value, as applicable. This has the implication that messages that require less than the maximum storage size of the packet incur a communication overhead for it, which could limit the potential for performance improvement relative to conveyors. To counteract this, we added a second level of internal deferment in the contexts extension to allow for multiple messages with small encoding requirements to fit into the same packet. For instance, since increment operations only require a target address, up to three of them can be packed into a single conveyor message for a given PE, thus leaving only the overhead of communicating the message type.

Conveyors are created and put into working state upon context creation, and progress is internally managed based on when local output buffers fill. They can be forced to advance until complete upon a call to `shmem_ctx_quiet()`. Implementing communication calls is quite simple since the only requirement for completion is that the operation is encoded into the previously described packet structure and pushed onto the conveyor. See Listing 2 for an example demonstrating this on a put call.

```
void shmem_ctx_int64_p(shmem_ctx_t ctx, int64_t *dest, int64_t value, int
     pe) {
    if (pe == shmem_my_pe()) {
        *dest = value;
        return;
    }
    int64_message_packet_t item;
    item.type = OP_PUT | SZ_INT64;
    item.remote = dest;
    item.value = value;
    while (convey_push(ctx->conveyor, &item, pe) != convey_OK)
        ctx_progress(ctx, false);
}
```

**Listing 2.** Implementation of an Aggregated Put

The most important part at the core of implementing aggregation contexts is in managing their progress. Progress is initiated either by a quiet operation or upon failing to push a message onto the conveyor. Each progress call starts by pulling all items waiting in the conveyor's inbound buffer, checking the operation types and applying them (e.g. adding a value to its local destination). For operations that require fetching data, this results in new items being pushed onto the conveyor's outbound buffer in response. To support variable-sized put/get operations, we use an additional elastic conveyor for better performance. If the context is servicing a fetching operation and fails to push its response, it unpulls the request and ceases further processing of its inbound queue. Finally, it finishes with a call to advance the conveyors and directs them to transition to their endgame state if the progress was called as part of a quiet operation, which must repeatedly restart the progress function until the conveyors reach their complete state.

## 4 Results

To evaluate the performance of aggregation contexts, we implemented four of the bale applications with them and compared their code and performance to both OpenSHMEM AGP and conveyors versions. The evaluation was conducted on the HPC Advisory Council's Iris system, a Dell C6400 32-node cluster with dual socket Intel Xeon 8280 CPUs, 192 GB of 2666 MHz DDR4 memory, and NVIDIA ConnectX-6 HDR100 100 Gb/s InfiniBand/VPI NICs connected via an NVIDIA HDR Quantum QM7800 switch. We used OpenSHMEM 1.4 from OpenMPI 4.1.3 that uses UCX 1.12.1, and compiled the software with GCC 8.5.0. The tests were performed on 32 nodes with 1, 2, 4, 8, 16, 32, and 56 processes per node using weak scaling, with the exception of triangles that uses strong scaling due to the nature of its graph generation making it nontrivial to scale up by arbitrary factors. In our evaluation, we compare the performance of using either the contexts extension or direct use of conveyors against the OpenSHMEM AGP timings as a baseline. The results are reported as relative performance improvements against this baseline as the goal of this work was to achieve good performance while maintaining the simplicity of the AGP model in applications.

### 4.1 Histogram

We modified the OpenSHMEM AGP version of histogram from Listing 1 by incorporating the aggregation contexts extension. The modifications required to use aggregation contexts were minimal, as shown in Listing 3. The first step was to create the context, after which we replaced the atomic increment operation used in the AGP version with its context-based counterpart. To ensure all communication completes, we also performed a quiet on the context before the final barrier.

```
shmem_ctx_t ctx;
if (shmem_ctx_create(SHMEM_CTX_AGGREGATE | SHMEM_CTX_PRIVATE, &ctx) != 0)
    {
    FAIL();
}
for (int64_t i = 0; i < data->l_num_ups; i++) {
    shmem_ctx_int64_atomic_inc(ctx, &data->counts[data->pckindx[i] >>
        20], data->pckindx[i] & 0xfffff);
}
shmem_ctx_quiet(ctx);
shmem_barrier_all();
```

**Listing 3.** Histogram Using Aggregation Contexts

In contrast, Listing 4 shows how the implementation using conveyors appears. The code begins by creating the conveyor and starting it in its working state by invoking `convey_begin` with the desired message item size if successful. Next, it performs a barrier to ensure all PEs are ready to begin before proceeding with its primary progress loop. The first part of the loop is responsible for pushing requests onto the conveyor, and it proceeds to the second part when it fails, which pulls any data it has received and performs the actual increment operation. As can be seen here, in the conveyor model the messages' nature/operation is defined solely by the receiver rather than the sender. Each loop iteration starts with a call to `convey_advance`, with the second argument determining when the sending PE is done sending its share of messages and communicating that to the conveyor. It exits out of the loop for the final barrier after the advance determines that the conveyor has also finished receiving and processing all of its messages. This illustrates how even such a simple communication pattern can become significantly more complex to develop using message aggregation with conveyors.

```
convey_t* conveyor = convey_new(SIZE_MAX, 0, NULL, convey_opt_SCATTER);
if (!conveyor || convey_begin(conveyor, sizeof(int64_t), 0) < 0) {
    FAIL();
}
shmem_barrier_all();
i = 0;
while (convey_advance(conveyor, i == data->l_num_ups)) {
    for (; i < data->l_num_ups; i++) {
        col = data->pckindx[i] >> 20;
        if(!convey_push(conveyor, &col, data->pckindx[i] & 0xfffff))
            break;
    }
    while (convey_pull(conveyor, &pop_col, NULL) == convey_OK) {
        data->lcounts[pop_col] += 1;
    }
}
shmem_barrier_all();
```

**Listing 4.** Histogram Using Conveyors

The results comparing the different versions against each other across 2,000,000 updates per PE can be seen in Fig. 1. The contexts version significantly outperformed the original AGP version with performance improvements of up to 65× achieved with only minimal changes to the application. The conveyors version achieved even greater performance improvements of up to 85×.

To provide some perspective, we also compared our results with the network utilisation numbers derived from the Ohio State University (OSU) microbenchmarks version 7.1 [1]. Specifically, we were interested in determining the efficiency of our utilisation of the available network bandwidth compared to regular accesses. To that end, we ran the message rate test for non-blocking OpenSHMEM put routines on 56 processes per node. We adjusted the highest performing message size to account for how quickly we could send the same amount of data as in our histogram tests if we were able to maintain this level of throughput. After normalising these results to the AGP histogram baseline, we found that this would have accounted for an 82× speedup.

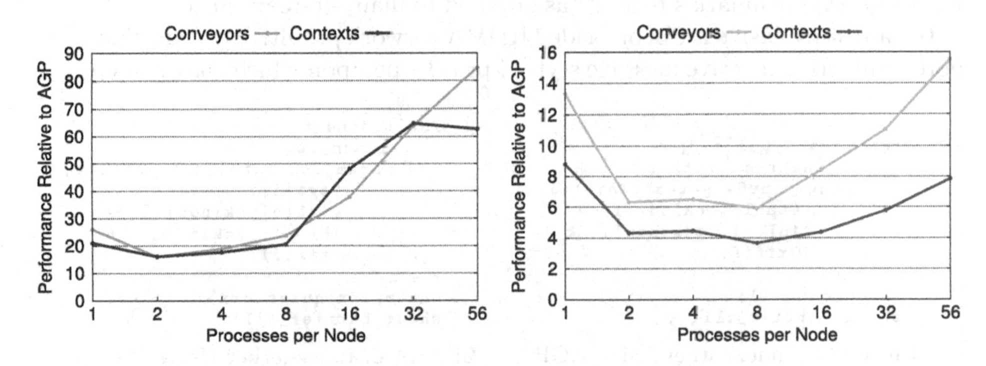


**Fig. 1.** Histogram Results

**Fig. 2.** Indexgather Results

### 4.2 Indexgather

Indexgather is similar to histogram but in the reverse direction, in that it represents a pattern where PEs are gathering data from random locations in a distributed array into a local array. Each PE generates a list of random elements and then performs back-to-back remote read operations to fetch all of them. The bale version of the classic AGP code was modified to use non-blocking get operations added to the more recent 1.4 OpenSHMEM specification for better comparison. Without this modification, the performance of the AGP baseline would be significantly worse and arguably less interesting. As a result, the AGP version now also requires a quiet operation to ensure that its non-blocking operations are complete. A side-by-side comparison between the AGP and contexts versions can be seen in Listing 5 and Listing 6. The listing again shows that minimal modifications are necessary to the AGP version to adapt it to aggregation contexts. The conveyors version of indexgather, which is much more complex due to requiring nested conveyors for read responses, can be found in [10].

Figure 2 shows the results across 8,000,000 requests per PE, and we can see that even compared to OpenSHMEM's non-blocking gets, aggregation contexts provides substantial performance improvements of up to 9× compared to a maximum improvement of up to 16× for the conveyors version. Compared to histogram, indexgather has a bit of additional headroom, much of which is due to not achieving quite as of a high packet efficiency, roughly half of which is lost compared to the conveyors version (i.e., the overhead for type and the unused value member). This is clearly reflected in the results as pressure is increased on the network, as it converges to about half the potential performance increase. It may be possible to optimise the packet encoding further for operations like these, but this is left for future work.

We conducted a similar comparison to the one described in Sect. 4.1, this time using the OSU message rate test for non-blocking OpenSHMEM get routines, which utilises a regular accesses. When comparing this to the AGP indexgather results, we found that the OSU benchmark achieved a message rate improvement of up to 47×. The relatively higher gains compared to what could be achieved with conveyors or aggregation contexts are likely due to a combination of factors including the OSU benchmark's regular (as opposed to many-to-many) access pattern, as well as the exclusive use of one-sided RDMA network primitives rather than the more bidirectional active message style of processing upon which conveyors rely.

```
for (int64_t i = 0; i <
     l_num_req; i++) {
    shmem_int64_get_nbi(&tgt[i],
        &table[pckindx[i] >>
        16], 1, pckindx[i] &
        0xffff);
}
shmem_quiet();
shmem_barrier_all();
```

**Listing 5.** Indexgather Using AGP

```
for (int64_t i = 0; i <
     l_num_req; i++) {
    shmem_ctx_int64_get_nbi(ctx,
        &tgt[i],
        &table[pckindx[i] >>
        16], 1, pckindx[i] &
        0xffff);
}
shmem_ctx_quiet(ctx);
shmem_barrier_all();
```

**Listing 6.** Indexgather Using Contexts

### 4.3 Sparse Matrix Transpose

This application transposes a distributed sparse matrix, which is especially useful in linear algebra and popular in machine learning algorithms (e.g. convolutional neural networks). The input matrix is encoded in compressed sparse row (CSR) format, which makes it difficult to aggregate since PEs need to synchronise in order to find the appropriate target locations before writing data. The first phase uses a histogram pattern to determine the number of nonzeroes in each column, followed by a second phase that acquires the new locations for each value and writes them to the destination PEs. An abbreviated snippet of the AGP version of this second phase is shown in Listing 7.

```
for (int64_t row = 0; row < A->lnumrows; row++) {
    for (int64_t j = A->loffset[row]; j < A->loffset[row + 1]; j++) {
        int64_t pos = shmem_atomic_fetch_add(&shtmp[A->lnonzero[j] /
            npes], npes, A->lnonzero[j] % npes);
        shmem_int64_p(&(*At)->nonzero[pos / npes], row * npes + me, pos %
            npes);
        if (A->value != NULL)
            shmem_double_p(&(*At)->value[pos / npes], A->lvalue[j], pos %
                npes);
    }
}
shmem_barrier_all();
```

**Listing 7.** Transpose Phase 2 Using AGP

The contexts version of sparse matrix transpose divides the second phase into two steps. It first prefetches all the required locations into a buffer, and then uses this buffer to perform the necessary writes. The result of this transformation can be seen in Listing 8.

The performance of these compared against AGP is an improvement of up to 17× for the contexts version and 72× for the conveyors version when run on a matrix with 1,000,000 rows with an average of 4 non-zeroes per row per PE, as shown in Fig. 3. While the contexts version demonstrates significant improvement over AGP, its performance is still limited by the prefetch size/granularity step, which significant stresses the memory subsystem capacity. We will look at this problem further in Sect. 4.4.

```
int64_t *pos[A->lnumrows];
for (int64_t row = 0; row < A->lnumrows; row++) {
    pos[row] = (int64_t *)malloc((A->loffset[row + 1] - A->loffset[row])
        * sizeof(int64_t));
    if (pos[row] == NULL) {
        FAIL();
    }
    for (int64_t j = 0, col = A->loffset[row]; col + j < A->loffset[row +
        1]; j++)
        shmem_ctx_int64_atomic_fetch_add_nbi(ctx, &pos[row][j],
            &shtmp[A->lnonzero[col + j] / npes], npes, A->lnonzero[col +
            j] % npes);
}
shmem_ctx_quiet(ctx);
shmem_barrier_all();
for (int64_t row = 0; row < A->lnumrows; row++) {
    for (int64_t j = 0, col = A->loffset[row]; col + j < A->loffset[row +
        1]; j++) {
        shmem_ctx_int64_p_nbi(ctx, &(*At)->nonzero[pos[row][j] / npes],
            row * npes + me, pos[row][j] % npes);
```

```
            if (A->value != NULL)
                shmem_double_p(&(*At)->value[pos[row][j] / npes],
                    A->lvalue[col + j], pos[row][j] % npes);
        }
        free(pos[row]);
    }
    shmem_ctx_quiet(ctx);
    shmem_barrier_all();
```

**Listing 8.** Transpose Phase 2 Using Contexts

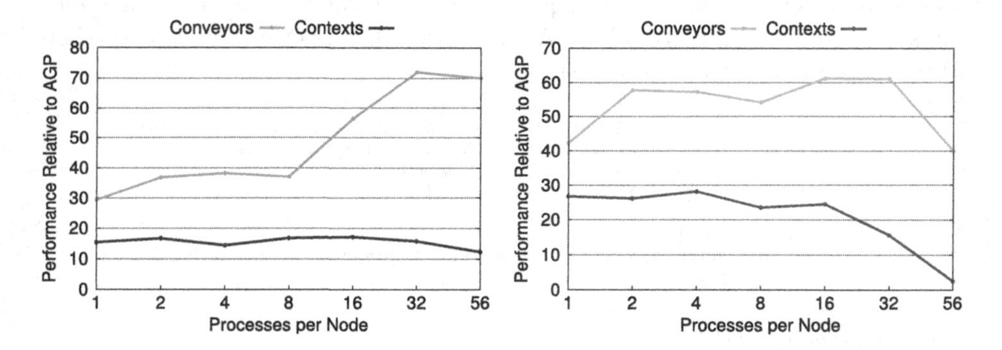


**Fig. 3.** Transpose Results

**Fig. 4.** Triangles Results

### 4.4 Triangle Counting

The final application counts triangles in undirected graphs by computing either $L \odot L \times U$ or $L \odot U \times L$, where $L$ and $U$ represent the lower and upper triangular matrices of its sparse input. This is an interesting application since it has two very different ways to implement its algorithm based on whether PEs can put their nonzeroes to other rows or PEs, which maps well to aggregation, or get their data from other PEs for computing itself, which fits the AGP model better.

Similar to the transpose algorithm, the aggregation contexts version prefetches future values in advance. However, the triangles algorithm requires multiple levels of get operations to perform the calculation, meaning that prefetching must similarly be implemented in a nested fashion. Despite this limitation, our approach achieved up to 28× performance improvement over the AGP version while maintaining its algorithmic intent. The conveyors version achieved a performance improvement up to 61×. The results for both versions are shown in Fig. 4, which was run on a matrix with 200,000 rows with an average of 48 non-zeroes per row.

From a user's perspective, our prefetching approach is convenient and intuitive, but it applies unnecessary memory pressure and can result in redundant loop overhead as a result of the loop fission. This can become more pronounced in nested scenarios as found in the triangles application. Although performance can be improved by prefetching data in fixed-size chunks, this approach decreases code readability and maintainability. Addressing these issues requires additional extensions to our contexts approach, which we discuss as future work in Sect. 6.

## 5 Related Work

There have been a number of diverse approaches to aggregation that are worth consideration depending upon user requirements or preferences. Early aggregation studies [14] show that message aggregation optimisations can be done either at the lowest level of communication in a programming model or at the application level. The benefits of such optimisations are also dependent on the behavior of low-level communication protocols, which may change their strategies at certain thresholds to move from handling small to large messages. The study suggests that aggregation can be initiated by either the sender or receiver, but that sender-initiated aggregation strategies are more efficient.

For a look at hardware-based aggregation, Scalable Hierarchical Aggregation and Reduction Protocol (SHARP) [7] focuses on streaming-aggregation at the network switch level and has been shown to improve performance by 2–5 times for collective operations such as reductions. However, the benefits of this approach can be offset by late arrivals to collective operations. Ozog [12] proposed addressing the message rate problem in OpenSHMEM via the *chaining* of network operations which is available on several interconnects. The approach combines chainable calls to execute them in bulk later. However, this may increase the overall message latency to that of the completion for the last operation added to the chain. Another work [2] explores an optimisation that combines static coalescing and the inspector-executor approach to reduce the latency of fine-grained shared accesses for Unified Parallel C (UPC) applications by prefetching shared data. It shows that the combination of these optimisations is effective in increasing network efficiency, but is bounded by the overhead of the inspector loops, which could benefit from data access summarisation. However, this can be challenging when accessing scattered or random data.

LAPPS [9] uses an access pattern prefetching technique introduced for Chapel before execution of loops with specific patterns such as transpose, stencil, etc. However, this technique requires application programmers to explicitly identify the access patterns as such in hints they provide to the system. Ferguson [4] introduces a cache for put and get operations in the Chapel runtime which can double application performance while being agnostic of the access patterns. The Chapel Aggregation Library (CAL) [8] provides more general high level abstractions for aggregation in the Chapel programming language and supports maps, scans, and reductions. These approaches require the introduction of cache or aggregator objects to Chapel applications and increases code complexity accordingly. The Berkeley Container Library (BCL) [3] takes a different approach in that rather than a general communication model, it provides a library for distributed data structures with aggregation abilities hidden within. It uses a structure for buffering hash table insertions that works similarly to other aggregation strategies like conveyors by deferring remote insertions until internal buffers reach a certain size or the user has finished insertion and performs a flush.

In contrast to our work, [13] shifts away from the classical AGP model OpenSHMEM represents and introduces conveyor-style aggregation to the PGAS paradigm by proposing an extension to the task-parallel Habanero-C Library (HCLib) using the actor model. In it, actors can have an arbitrary number of *mailboxes* with which they can send/receive fine-grained active messages to each other that are backed by conveyor aggregation. Although the abstraction around the conveyor API is very thin, it does still remove the requirement for users to explicitly manage conveyor state and progress along with the failure conditions of push/pull operations due to buffer considerations. Nonetheless, users still must design their communication around a conveyor-style active message system, increasing flexibility but removing the ability to express simple one-sided operations as such and making some operations such as remote reads complicated.

Global Memory and Threading (GMT) [11] takes a similar approach to aggregation but adds a programming model around it based on tasking and parallel loop constructs, with a targeted focus on in-memory procesing of data from domains with highly irregular memory accesses such as data analytics and pattern recognition. It employs a hierarchy of worker/helper and communication threads to hide latency, with workers taking up lightweight user-generated tasks as their dependent requests are satisfied, including additional context switching upon encountering blocking operations. These workers employ a two-stage aggregation scheme where communication commands for given destinations are first collected in local blocks before being copied in bulk the aggregation queue, the contents of which eventually get dispatched by the communication thread when either filled or a predetermined set of time has passed. While GMT does not provide the generality of a complete PGAS programming model, it was shown to be very performant at addressing the in-memory processing requirements of its target domains, able to compete even with custom system architectures.

## 6 Conclusion and Future Work

In this paper, we have demonstrated how our aggregation contexts extension to the OpenSHMEM AGP model can significantly improve small message rate performance with minimal changes to the application code. Although our extension may sacrifice some potential performance gains when compared to the direct use of conveyors, it is able to retain an application's algorithmic intent. Nevertheless, there is still considerable room for further improvements. For example, there is potential to reduce communication overhead for some operation types, particularly the commonly used put operation.

The transpose and triangle applications showed the limitations of our contexts approach and that additional extensions could be useful for not only deferring and aggregating communication operations, but also for their associated computations. Such an extension would reduce the complexity introduced by the prefetching issues described in Sect. 4.4. In this case, a user could simply "push" the relevant computations to the context associated with the communication primitives. This may require a feature akin to a rudimentary tasking and futures design, where the completion of certain communication operations could be made to predicate the execution of a computation that could in turn generate more communication or nested tasks. Further investigation into providing this additional extension to the model has the potential to greatly enhance the power and natural expressivity of OpenSHMEM code, while also achieving better message rate performance.

**Acknowledgments.** Notice: This manuscript has been authored by UT-Battelle, LLC under Contract No. DE-AC05-00OR22725 with the U.S. Department of Energy. The United States Government retains and the publisher, by accepting the article for publication, acknowledges that the United States Government retains a non-exclusive, paid-up, irrevocable, worldwide license to publish or reproduce the published form of this manuscript, or allow others to do so, for United States Government purposes. The Department of Energy will provide public access to these results of federally sponsored research in accordance with the DOE Public Access Plan (http://energy.gov/downloads/doe-public-access-plan).

## References

1. OSU micro-benchmarks. https://mvapich.cse.ohio-state.edu/benchmarks/. Accessed 31 May 2023
2. Alvanos, M., Farreras, M., Tiotto, E., Amaral, J.N., Martorell, X.: Improving communication in PGAS environments: static and dynamic coalescing in UPC. In: Proceedings of the 27th International ACM Conference on International Conference on Supercomputing, ICS 2013, pp. 129–138. Association for Computing Machinery, New York (2013). https://doi.org/10.1145/2464996.2465006
3. Brock, B., Buluç, A., Yelick, K.A.: BCL: a cross-platform distributed container library. CoRR abs/1810.13029 (2018). http://arxiv.org/abs/1810.13029
4. Ferguson, M.P., Buettner, D.: Caching puts and gets in a PGAS language runtime. In: 2015 9th International Conference on Partitioned Global Address Space Programming Models, pp. 13–24 (2015). https://doi.org/10.1109/PGAS.2015.10
5. Garg, R., Sabharwal, Y.: Software routing and aggregation of messages to optimize the performance of HPCC randomaccess benchmark. In: SC 2006: Proceedings of the 2006 ACM/IEEE Conference on Supercomputing, p. 15 (2006). https://doi.org/10.1109/SC.2006.56
6. Geng, H., Jamali, N.: Supporting many-to-many communication. In: Proceedings of the 2013 Workshop on Programming Based on Actors, Agents, and Decentralized Control, AGERE! 2013, pp. 81–86. Association for Computing Machinery, New York (2013). https://doi.org/10.1145/2541329.2541343
7. Graham, R.L., et al.: Scalable hierarchical aggregation and reduction protocol (SHARP)$^{TM}$ streaming-aggregation hardware design and evaluation. In: Sadayappan, P., Chamberlain, B.L., Juckeland, G., Ltaief, H. (eds.) ISC High Performance 2020. LNCS, vol. 12151, pp. 41–59. Springer, Cham (2020). https://doi.org/10.1007/978-3-030-50743-5_3
8. Jenkins, L., Zalewski, M., Ferguson, M.: Chapel aggregation library (CAL). In: 2018 IEEE/ACM Parallel Applications Workshop, Alternatives To MPI (PAW-ATM), pp. 34–43 (2018). https://doi.org/10.1109/PAW-ATM.2018.00009
9. Kayraklioglu, E., Ferguson, M.P., El-Ghazawi, T.: LAPPS: locality-aware productive prefetching support for PGAS. ACM Trans. Archit. Code Optim. **15**(3), 1–26 (2018). https://doi.org/10.1145/3233299

10. Maley, F.M., DeVinney, J.G.: Conveyors for streaming many-to-many communication. In: 2019 IEEE/ACM 9th Workshop on Irregular Applications: Architectures and Algorithms (IA3), pp. 1–8 (2019). https://doi.org/10.1109/IA349570.2019.00007
11. Morari, A., Tumeo, A., Chavarría-Miranda, D., Villa, O., Valero, M.: Scaling irregular applications through data aggregation and software multithreading. In: 2014 IEEE 28th International Parallel and Distributed Processing Symposium, pp. 1126–1135 (2014). https://doi.org/10.1109/IPDPS.2014.117
12. Ozog, D., Wasi-ur-Rahman, M., Holland, K.: Can deferring small messages enhance the performance of OpenSHMEM applications? In: Poole, S.W., Hernandez, O., Baker, M.B., Curtis, T. (eds.) OpenSHMEM 2021. LNCS, vol. 13159, pp. 160–177. Springer, Cham (2021). https://doi.org/10.1007/978-3-031-04888-3_10
13. Paul, S.R., Hayashi, A., Chen, K., Sarkar, V.: A scalable actor-based programming system for PGAS runtimes (2021). https://doi.org/10.48550/ARXIV.2107.05516, https://arxiv.org/abs/2107.05516
14. Pham, C.: Comparison of message aggregation strategies for parallel simulations on a high performance cluster. In: Proceedings 8th International Symposium on Modeling, Analysis and Simulation of Computer and Telecommunication Systems (Cat. No.PR00728), pp. 358–365 (2000). https://doi.org/10.1109/MASCOT.2000.876559
15. Poole, S.W., Curtis, A.R., Hernandez, O.R., Feind, K., Kuehn, J.A., Shipman, G.M.: OpenSHMEM: Towards a Unified RMA Model. Springer, New York (2011). https://www.osti.gov/biblio/1050391
16. Wesolowski, L., et al.: TRAM: optimizing fine-grained communication with topological routing and aggregation of messages. In: 2014 43rd International Conference on Parallel Processing, pp. 211–220 (2014). https://doi.org/10.1109/ICPP.2014.30

# Fault-Aware Group-Collective Communication Creation and Repair in MPI

Roberto Rocco(✉) and Gianluca Palermo

Dipartimento di Elettronica e Informazione, Politecnico di Milano, Milan, Italy
{Roberto.Rocco,Gianluca.Palermo}@polimi.it

**Abstract.** The increasing size of HPC systems indicates that executions involve more nodes and processes, making the faults' presence a more frequent eventuality. This issue becomes especially relevant since MPI, the de-facto standard for inter-process communication, lacks proper fault management functionalities. Past efforts produced extensions to the MPI standard enabling fault management, including ULFM. While providing powerful tools to handle faults, ULFM still faces limitations like the collectiveness of the repair procedure. With this paper, we overcome those limitations and achieve fault-aware group-collective communicator creation and repair. We integrate our solution into an existing fault-resiliency framework and measure the overhead in the application code. The experimental campaign shows that our solution is scalable and introduces a limited overhead, and the group-collective repair is a viable opportunity for ULFM-based applications.

**Keywords:** Fault Management · MPI · ULFM

## 1 Introduction

Computational science applications require more and more resources for their computation, leading to the growth of current HPC systems in terms of performance, energy efficiency and complexity. HPC systems have recently reached the exascale boundary ($10^{18}$ FLOPS)[1], but the additional performance brings new issues. The increase in the number of nodes brought a greater probability of transient and persistent faults, and HPC systems (and their applications) must be able to handle them. Studies [6,7,12] show that the impact of faults is already relevant in HPC. This result also comes from the absence of fault management techniques in the Message Passing Interface (MPI) [4], the de-facto standard for inter-process communication. The latest version of the MPI standard (4.0) tried to reduce the possible sources of faults, isolating them into single processes when possible. While removing the faults' impact on local functions, it neither avoids their propagation with communication nor overcomes their effect.

[1] https://www.top500.org/lists/top500/2023/06/.


J. Cano et al. (Eds.): Euro-Par 2023, LNCS 14100, pp. 47–61, 2023.
https://doi.org/10.1007/978-3-031-39698-4_4

The issue of fault tolerance in MPI is not new to the field and led to the production of fault-aware MPI implementations [3,8,9]. Most of these works received limited support and did not solve the problem entirely and efficiently. The User-Level Fault Mitigation (ULFM) MPI extension [1] is currently one of the most relevant works in this direction. ULFM features a collection of functions for fault detection and notification, structure repair, and execution resiliency. Among the added functionalities of ULFM, the *shrink*, *agree*, and *revoke* functions enable communicator repair, resilient agreement, and fault propagation, respectively. From the point of view of ULFM, faults are sudden terminations of computation, while other fault types, like timing errors and silent data corruption, are excluded from the analysis. ULFM is currently integrated directly into the latest versions of OpenMPI and MPICH, the most relevant MPI implementations.

While ULFM provides users with powerful new possibilities for fault management, it still faces limitations, like its repair procedure's collectiveness. In this effort, we overcome the ULFM repair collectiveness constraint to introduce fault handling in applications using group-collective calls. In particular, we focus on applications using the group-collective communicator creation functions (`MPI_Comm_create_group` and `MPI_Comm_create_from_group`). These functions do not involve all the processes inside a communicator (like their collective counterparts), but only some of them. Previous works [5] have shown the relevance of the first group-collective call, which has been included in the MPI standard since version 3.0. The other function is a recent addition (version 4.0) fundamental to the session execution model [13]. We propose a Liveness Discovery Algorithm (LDA) to overcome the collectiveness constraint of the repair, avoiding unnecessary synchronisations and allowing group-collective communicator creation, even with faults among the caller processes. We integrate this solution in the ULFM-based Legio fault resiliency framework [18] that transparently manages the absence of failed processes in the application and enables execution continuation.

The contributions of this paper are the following:

- We analyse the effects of faults considered by ULFM on the two group-collective communicator creation calls;
- We design and implement a LDA to group-collectively detect the failed processes and limit their impact on the analysed functions;
- We use the LDA to reimplement two of the most important ULFM functionalities with group-collective behaviour.
- We integrate the solution into an existing fault resiliency framework to simplify its usage inside the user code and evaluate the introduced overhead.

The paper is structured as follows: Sect. 2 discusses previous efforts on the MPI fault management topic, focusing on ULFM and the frameworks using it. Section 3 illustrates the behaviour of the two group-collective operations analysed. Section 4 discusses the Liveness Discovery Algorithm, its integration and the possibilities it enables. Section 5 covers the experimental campaign done to evaluate the proposed solution overhead and scalability. Lastly, Sect. 6 concludes the paper.

## 2 Background and Previous Work

The failure of an MPI process can impact an application execution since the MPI standard does not specify the behaviour of the survivor processes. The latest MPI standard (4.0) version introduced new functionalities to simplify fault handling, limiting their impact when possible. While providing ways to represent and react to faults, the standard still does not contain a defined method to recover the execution. After a fault occurrence, the best outcome planned by the MPI standard is the graceful termination of the application.

Many efforts proposed solutions to circumvent this limitation. The authors of [11] proposed a transaction model to coordinate the fault management actions needed. In [20], the authors designed the Stages model leveraging checkpoint and restart functionalities. The Reinit solution proposed in [14] allowed the execution to reinitialise itself, removing the fault impact from the execution. Besides these efforts, the one receiving the most attention is ULFM [1], providing tools for execution continuation after the incurrence of a fault. It is an MPI standard extension proposal focusing on fault detection, propagation and repair. While still under development, the ULFM extension got included in the latest versions of OpenMPI and MPICH, the principal MPI implementations. The idea behind ULFM is to allow application developers to manage faults by themselves, changing the application code by introducing ULFM functions directly. This approach allows maximum control of the fault management functionalities at the cost of additional integration complexity: the programmer must know how and when to handle faults, which is non-trivial.

The latest developments of the ULFM extension [2] introduced new functionalities that can simplify the interaction between the application and the fault tolerance functionalities. With the use of `MPI_Info` structures, the user can specify the error propagation policy and automate the failure notification phase after fault detection. The authors also included the non-blocking communicator repair functionality: it removes the need for coordination for multiple repairs and enables overlaps between application-level recovery and communicator repair.

While introducing new functionalities to allow the execution past the rise of a fault, ULFM does not provide any mechanism to recover the execution. This decision comes from the fact that different applications may require different types of recovery, while some do not even require any. The user should choose the best recovery mechanism and integrate it directly into its code. This approach gives maximum flexibility to the user but introduces unneeded complexity in its code. For this reason, many efforts produced all-in-one frameworks that combine ULFM with a recovery mechanism to simplify fault management integration inside user code [10,16,18,19,21,22].

The principal research efforts in this direction are towards ULFM and Checkpoint/Restart (C/R) functionalities integration [10,16,19,21,22]. This approach introduces fault tolerance (the ability to nullify the effect of a fault) in generic MPI applications. All these efforts came to similar solutions, with the execution restarting from the last consistent state, removing the fault impact. This approach simplifies the introduction of fault tolerance in MPI applications since it hides the complexity within the framework. Moreover, some efforts [16] removed the need for code changes in the application by leveraging a heuristic code analysis to choose the best integration with their framework.

The solution adopted in Legio [18] is slightly different: the effort produced a library that introduces fault resiliency (the ability to overcome a fault without nullifying its effect) in embarrassingly parallel applications. Applications using Legio continue after the fault detection, but the failed processes will not resume: the execution proceeds only with the survivor processes, causing a loss of correctness but resuming the execution faster. The authors claim that these characteristics make Legio ideal for approximate computing applications, where the algorithms already trade correctness for speed. Legio follows the policy of transparent integration with the application: it does not require any code change.

While ULFM is evolving with its latest introductions [2], the repair procedure still requires eventual participation from all the processes and is thus orthogonal to group collectiveness. This assumption blocks the users from gaining the benefits of group-collective communication creation, resulting in a potential loss of efficiency. With this work, we contribute to the development of ULFM, removing the collectiveness constraint and enabling group-collective fault handling.

## 3 Group-Collective Operations

A group-collective operation involves many processes inside an MPI communicator, but not all need to participate. In the MPI standard, it is possible to find two group-collective communicator creation calls, the `MPI_Comm_create_group` and `MPI_Comm_create_from_group` functions. The first was proposed in [5], and it got introduced with version 3.0 of the standard. The function creates a communicator containing only the processes part of the group structure passed as a parameter. This function must be called only by the group participants, not by all the processes in the communicator (differently from the `MPI_Comm_create` function). The second function behaves similarly but does not require a starting communicator. Introduced with version 4.0 of the standard, it is part of the functions that handle the Session execution model [13]. It allows the creation of a communicator starting only from a group of processes. The absence of a parent communicator makes this call unique and potentially problematic in case of faults. While dealing with faults in group-collective calls, we encountered two problems: the eventuality that the execution enters a state from which no repair is possible and the need for collectiveness within the repair procedure.

**Impossibility of Repair.** To detect the first problem, we conducted preliminary experiments injecting faults in MPI code with group-collective calls. To better represent the fault occurrence in a communicator, we describe it as either *faulty* or *failed*. In particular, *faulty* communicators contain some failed processes with no process acknowledging them. When a process discovers the failure, the communicator becomes *failed*, and the failure propagation begins. We ran those experiments using the latest version of OpenMPI featuring ULFM (v5.0.0) and implementing the standard MPI 4.0. ULFM use is mandatory since the fault presence would otherwise cause the crash of the application, nullifying any fault resilience effort. Our tests on the function `MPI_Comm_create_group` proved that:

- The call works if the communicator passed as a parameter is *faulty* as long as no process that is part of the group has itself failed;
- The call deadlocks with a *faulty* communicator parameter if one process that is part of the group has itself failed;
- The function fails with a *failed* communicator as a parameter, returning the ULFM-defined error code `MPIX_ERR_PROC_FAILED`, regardless of the presence of failed processes inside the group.

While the deadlock eventuality may be an implementation flaw of the current OpenMPI version, its removal is still non-trivial. ULFM should control the presence of failed processes within the group, even the ones with unacknowledged failures. ULFM provides a function to get the group of failed processes inside a communicator (the `MPIX_Comm_get_failed`), but it gives no guarantees on whether the output is up to date. This limitation comes from the fact that the function above is local, thus requiring no communication between the processes. It does not actively check the presence of new faults inside the communicator (proactively), but it just recalls the ones whose failure is known.

Our tests on the function `MPI_Comm_create_from_group` produced similar results: the call works if failed processes are not part of the group passed as a parameter and deadlocks otherwise. A fix for the first function can also solve the deadlock eventuality on this one. Therefore, the approach described in this paper aims to create an algorithm for removing failed processes from the group parameters of the group-collective functions.

**Collectiveness of Repair.** This is a known limitation of the ULFM extension. The standard ULFM solution to fault presence consists of letting the MPI call raise an error, eventually propagating it to processes not involved (with the *revoke* function). For collective calls, all the processes must agree on the correctness of the operation (with the *agree* function) and, if an error is present, repair the communicator (with the *shrink* function) and retry. The agreement and repair procedure cannot happen without the participation of all the processes inside a communicator and are mandatory to complete the communication creation calls since we cannot use failed communicators. This constraint invalidates the benefits that come from the adoption of group-collective communicator creation functions (less synchronisation). To introduce fault management in the group-collective call, we would ideally not use any collective operation, including the standard ULFM *shrink* and *agree* functions.

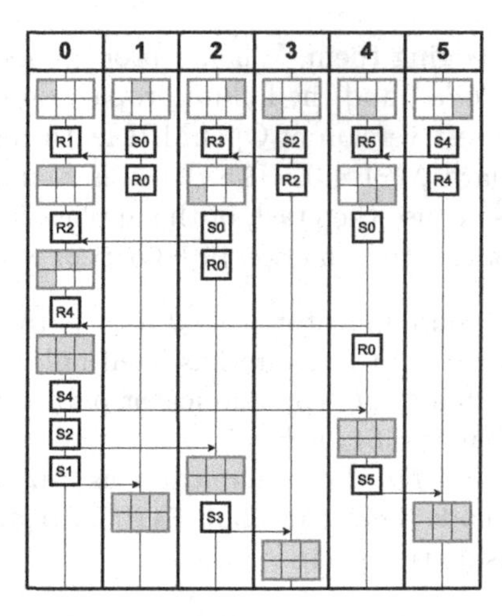


**Fig. 1.** A representation of the LDA. Each column represents a process, while green rectangles contain the data on the liveness of each participant. Black boxes represent MPI operations, with the first character showing the type (**S**end/**R**ecv) and the second the rank of the other process. (Color figure online)

## 4 Liveness Discovery Algorithm

The problem of finding which processes failed within a group is dual to the one of discovering the ones alive. In a collective scenario, we can solve the latter using the `MPI_Allgather` function: each process can share its rank with the others and obtain data about all the processes sharing. If an error arises, all the participants can share a communal view using the *agree* functionality and then proceed to remove the failures from the communication with the *shrink* call. The execution can repeat these steps until the function `MPI_Allgather` completes correctly: after the completion, each process has the list of survivor ranks since only the survivors can communicate with no errors in a collective call.

This solution faces many problems when moving to the group-collective scenario. All the needed functions are collective and not usable for fault-checking group-collective calls without introducing unnecessary synchronisation. Another possible solution comes from the authors of [17], who proposed a method to avoid the repair and perform operations in a failed communicator. In their solution, they reproduce collective functions using point-to-point communication in a fault-resilient way, using a series of messages to detect the failures of neighbour processes. Their solution is compatible with our problem since we need to perform the `MPI_Allgather` function in a possibly failed communicator. However, the complete replacement of collective calls with point-to-point ones significantly impacts the failure-free execution time, even for applications not using group-collective calls. Moreover, the above solution includes its mechanisms to detect faults in MPI communication introducing a series of messages like acknowledgements and heartbeats, already covered by ULFM functionalities. In this work, we took inspiration from this latter solution, designing an ad-hoc Liveness Discovery Algorithm (LDA), which proactively detects failed processes in a group and uses ULFM fault detection functionalities.

Algorithm 1 contains the pseudo-code of our first naive design, while Fig. 1 shows a sample execution with six processes. The naive solution consists of the recreation of the `MPI_Allgather` function as a combination of gather and broadcast operations. The algorithm follows a tree structure and implements communication using point-to-point send and receive routines. While this naive solution works in a fault-free scenario, failed processes' presence can compromise the result's correctness. This eventuality is not due to error propagation, MPI fault management or additional ULFM functionalities but rather an algorithmic issue. Each rank value has a single path towards all the other nodes: if it breaks, the information will not arrive since no fallback strategy is present. Figure 2a shows the erroneous behaviour in execution with two faults: the algorithm produces a wrong result since processes agree on different sets. While the fault on the rank 5 process does not affect the result correctness, the one on rank 2 separates the rank 3 one from the rest. We could prevent this behaviour by re-assigning the duties of the failed process to another non-failed one.

Following the above concept, we update Algorithm 1 into Algorithm 2 to consider the duties re-assignment. We use ULFM functionalities to test whether a process failed. The call `MPI_Recv` can manifest a `MPIX_ERR_PROC_FAILED` error, detecting the failure of the process sending information. Moreover, we already use the receive function in the algorithm, thus removing the need for ad-hoc fault detection mechanisms like message acknowledgement. After the fault detection, the failed process duties move to the next non-failed one.

**Algorithm 1:** Naive version of the LDA

```
Input: A processes' group of size s, each process with rank r (from 0 to s-1)
Output: A processes' group containing only non-failed processes
// all ranks are encoded using the minimum number of bits
1  data.append(r); // data contains only own rank
2  root_level = number of trailing zeros of r;
3  root_index = 1;
4  while root_index ≤ root_level do
5      partner = r + (1 << root_index); // receive from rank far from root
6      if partner < s then
7          receive data from partner and append to known
8      root_index++;
9  partner = r - (1 << root_index); // send data to rank closet to root
10 if root_index < bits used for encoding then
11     send all data to partner
12     receive full data from partner, substitute own data with the received one
   // Start the propagation towards leaves
13 root_index–;
14 while root_index > 0 do
15     partner = r + (1 << root_index);
16     if partner < s then
17         send full data to partner
   // Now all the processes' data contains all the non-failed ranks
```

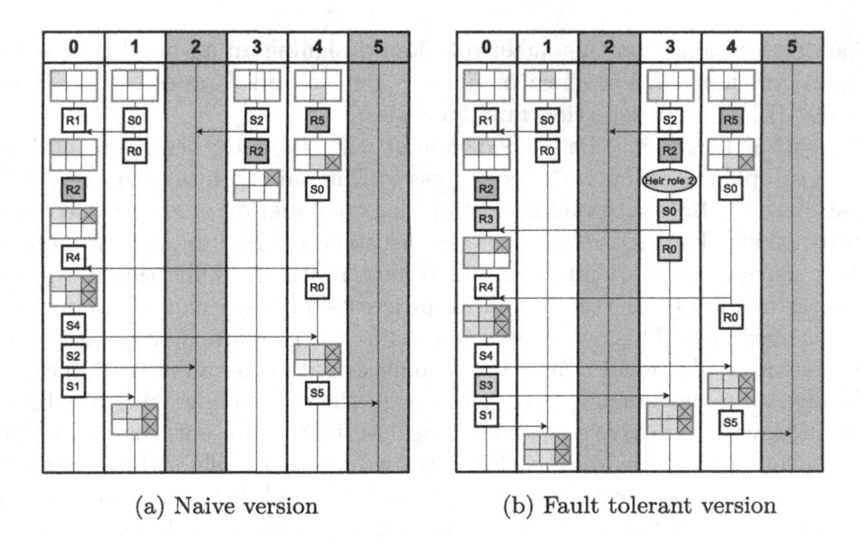


(a) Naive version (b) Fault tolerant version

**Fig. 2.** The figure shows the algorithm adaptation in the presence of faults. Red rectangles represent failed processes and MPI calls. Crossed red squares indicate processes known to have failed. Blue shapes represent additional or different calls due to processes inheriting roles. (Color figure online)

The last assumption ensures that fallback routes exist in our algorithm, preventing partitions. The fallback selection is also unequivocal, meaning that it is unique, and all the processes agree on the same without communicating with each other. Using these remarks, we can define the behaviour upon noticing a fault. In particular, a process would try to contact the successors of the failed one individually until receiving a response without errors. If all the successors between the process and the failed one produce errors, it assumes to be the closest live successor, so it inherits the failed process duties.

Figure 2b shows the behaviour of the updated algorithm in the presence of faults. It is possible to see that the execution outcome is correct despite failed processes because rank 3 gets the failed rank duties. Our changes affect the algorithm complexity: the worst case goes from logarithmic to linear complexity due to the single checks of all the failed process successors. Moreover, the changes above do not deal with faults occurring during the algorithm execution, which can compromise its correct execution. To solve this latter possibility, we must introduce additional messages and follow approaches similar to the ones proposed in [15]. While it is possible to consider faults happening during the algorithm, the LDA should introduce limited overhead and thus run for a short time, making a fault occurring during its execution improbable. In the end, we decided not to cover that case.

With this algorithm, all the processes can adjust the group parameter to remove failed ones. If we use this algorithm, the two group-collective calls do not manifest the deadlock eventuality. In particular, the `MPI_Comm_create_group` function exposes an error while the `MPI_Comm_create_from_group` completes correctly. This result has some remarkable implications for ULFM: *the existence of a call able to create a communicator despite faults' presence and without collectiveness opens the possibility for group-collective repair.* Upon detecting a failure, processes can substitute the communicator with a new one or partition it asynchronously. This possibility overcomes one of the main limitations of ULFM and opens new research directions in the field. The proposed method can also remove the collectiveness constraint of the ULFM *agree* call. We can use the LDA to group-collectively perform an all-reduce operation alongside the usual calls, achieving agreement even with faults.

While the LDA solves the problems of deadlocks in group-collective communicator creation and improves the ULFM functionalities, its complexity makes it unfeasible for user-level code. Being a distributed fault-aware algorithm, we think encapsulating its structure in an existing framework makes it easier to leverage by the users. For this reason, we integrated the LDA inside the state-of-the-art

**Algorithm 2:** Fault resilient version of the LDA

```
   Input: A processes' group of size s, each process with rank r (from 0 to s-1)
   Output: A processes' group containing only non-failed processes
 1 get_range(n,point)→ Adjusts global variables low and high to the value of point setting
                        the last n bits to 0 and 1 respectively.;
 2 effective = r; data.append(r);
 3 max_level = number of trailing zeros of s' next power of 2;
 4 forall the level ∈ [1,max_level] do
 5   | r_level = number of trailing zeros of effective;
 6   | if r_level < level then
 7   |   | get_range(level, effective);
 8   |   | forall the root ∈ [low,high] do
 9   |   |   | if root == effective then break else
10   |   |   |   | send data to root;
11   |   |   |   | receive full data from root, substitute own data with the received one, if
     |   |   |   L no error break
12   |   | if root == effective then
13   |   |   L effective = low; level -= 1; continue; // We inherited the root role
14   |   L else break
15   | else
16   |   | get_range(level-1, effective - (1 << level-1));
17   |   | forall the sender ∈ [low,high] do
18   |   |   | if sender == r then break receive data from sender, append to own, if no
     L   L   L error break.
19 level_root = number of trailing zeros of effective.;
20 r_level = number of trailing zeros of r.;
21 for level = level_root; level ≥ 1; level -= 1 do
22   | if level == r_level then
23   |   L effective = r
24   | get_range(level-1, effective + (1 << level-1);
25   | forall the searched ∈ [low,high] do
26   |   L if searched ∈ data then break
27   L send all data to searched if different from r.
   // Now all the processes' data contains all the non-failed ranks
```

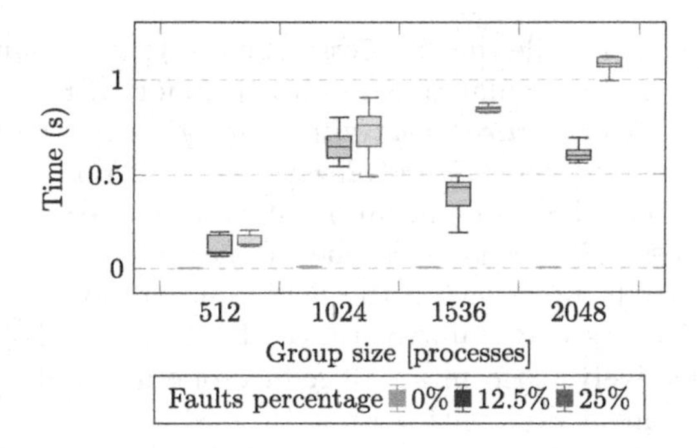


**Fig. 3.** Execution time distribution of the LDA over different group size and failure percentage scenarios.

Legio framework[2] [18] to introduce fault management support without changes in the application code through the use of the PMPI layer. The integration with Legio allows us to call the LDA before any group-collective communicator creation call, remove failed processes from the groups passed as parameters and complete the functions correctly, even in a faulty scenario. We do not use Legio functionalities to implement our solution but leverage it only as an encapsulation medium.

## 5 Experimental Campaign

The experimental campaign we propose evaluates the scalability and overhead of our solutions, both in the presence and absence of faults. We execute our experiments on the IT4Innovations Karolina cluster, featuring nodes with 2 x AMD Zen 2 EPYC$^{TM}$ 7H12, 2.6 GHz processors and 256 GB of RAM. Each node can run up to 128 processes without overloading. We use the latest version of OpenMPI featuring ULFM (v5.0.0), which implements MPI standard 4.0. In this experimental campaign, we first measure the proposed algorithm scalability and then evaluate the cost of fault management (fault discovery and removal) in group-collective communicator creation calls. Finally, we compare the group-collective versions of the *shrink* and *agree* functions with their ULFM counterparts. For all those tests, we designed simple ad-hoc applications that allow us to selectively stress the aspects we want to measure without the effect of other computations or synchronisations.

With the first experiment, we evaluate the time needed to complete the LDA with different group sizes and different amounts of faults inside the system. We run all the experiments using 16 nodes, each with 128 processes. We randomly choose the processes to fail since their position affects the time needed to complete the algorithm. This aspect comes from the tree topology of the algorithm: a leaf process interacts with only one other while the root communicates with

[2] Source code available here: https://github.com/Robyroc/Legio.

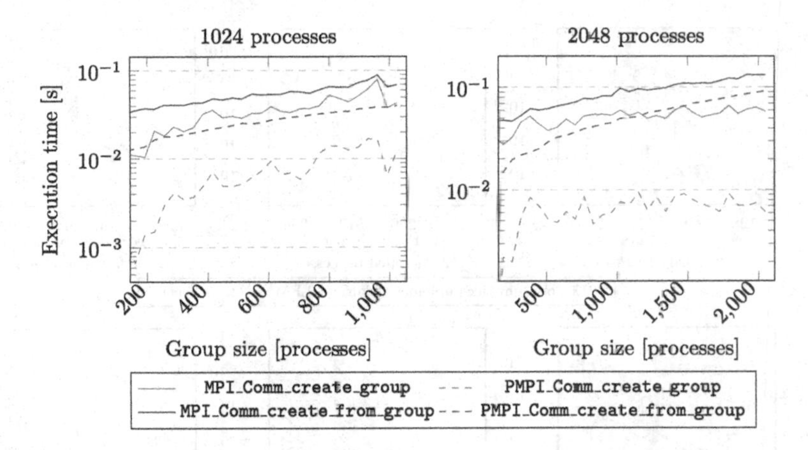


**Fig. 4.** Mean execution time of the Legio-integrated group-collective operations (MPI_*) compared to the original fault unaware versions (PMPI_*).

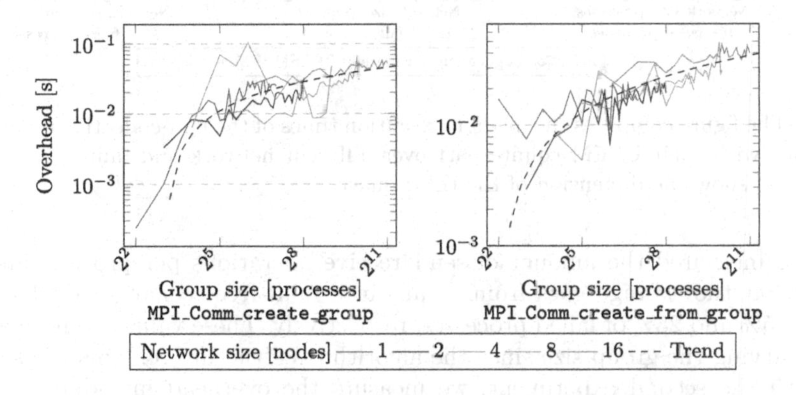


**Fig. 5.** The figure shows the correlation of the group-collective function mean overhead with the group size and number of nodes. The dashed black line represents the logarithmic trend followed by the measurements.

many more. This consideration implies that a failure in the root process causes many more communication errors than one in a leaf one, significantly changing the execution time and causing result variability.

We execute this test ten times for each group size and fault amount to better evaluate the results' variability. Figure 3 shows the results of this evaluation. From the results, it is possible to see that the dimension of the group does not significantly affect the time needed to complete the algorithm in a fault-free scenario. Faults' presence heavily impacts the time to complete the algorithm due to the gradual shift towards linear complexity and the time to manage errors at the ULFM level. In case of no faults, the execution completes in milliseconds, showing reduced time variability. In the case of applications not using frequent communicator creation functions, we think the observed overhead is negligible.

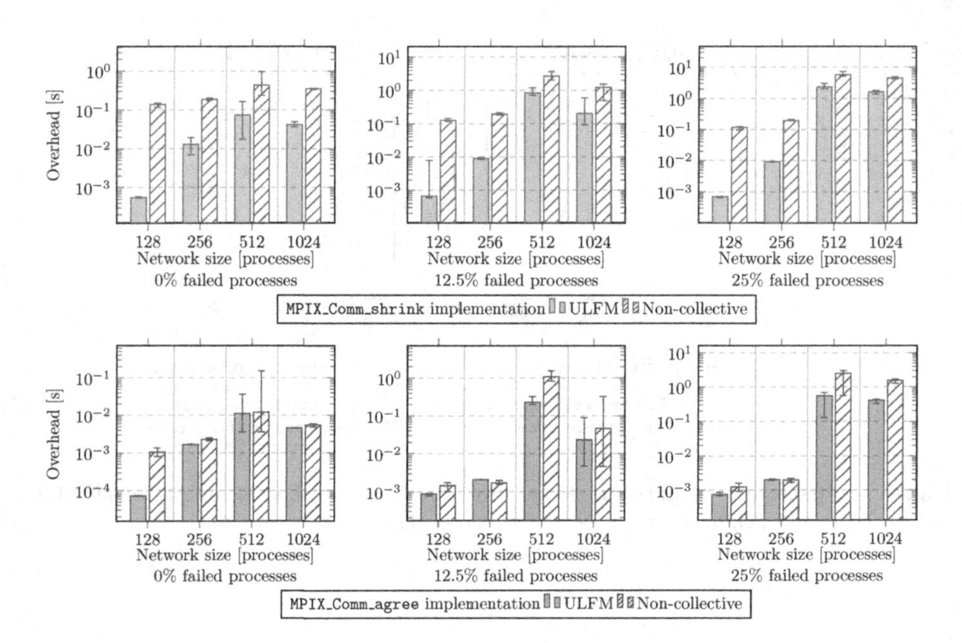


**Fig. 6.** The figure compares the median execution times of the non-collective reparation functions with their ULFM counterpart over different network and failure sizes. The range bars show the dimension of the third quartile.

We also measured the amount of send/receive operations per process, and we found that the average goes from 4 calls in a fault-free scenario to 4.4 and 5, with 12.5% and 25% of failed processes, respectively. These values do not change when varying the group size since the algorithm's structure remains the same.

With the second experiment, we measure the overhead introduced in the group-collective communicator creation calls in a fault-free scenario. We execute the benchmark ten times, measuring the average time needed to complete the calls. We compare the results with the time to complete the function without the additional fault discovery and removal functionalities. We repeat the experiment over networks of different sizes and with variable group dimensions to evaluate the scalability of our proposed integration. We distribute the processes inside the groups equally across the computing nodes. Figure 4 shows the evolution of execution times with networks of 1024 and 2048 processes (8 and 16 nodes), while Fig. 5 compares the overhead observed per function over different network sizes. The results show that the group size influences the overhead more than the network size, and the overhead follows a logarithmic trend. These considerations prove the scalability of the proposed integration in a fault-free scenario.

With the last experiment, we evaluate the performance of the proposed group-collective alternatives of the ULFM functions *shrink* and *agree*. We compare the execution times over networks of different sizes (from 1 to 16 nodes) and with various amounts of faults. We repeat each experiment ten times and extract the times to complete the functions. Figure 6 shows the execution time comparison. The proposed group-collective alternatives require a little more execution time than their ULFM counterparts. The additional time is noticeable in the *shrink* operation, while the *agree* call performs similarly to its ULFM counterpart. These experiments compare the performance in a collective scenario, which should further benefit the ULFM approach. The results validate the proposed group-collective ULFM alternatives, making them a promising addition to the ULFM proposal.

## 6 Conclusions

This paper presented a methodology to manage faults in a group-collective way. The proposed solution is helpful for applications leveraging group-collective communicator creation functions, which would incur unnecessary synchronisations using only ULFM functionalities. The designed LDA proactively detects failed processes, allowing their removal from the communicator creation and the subsequent completion of the call.

The experimental campaign showed the effectiveness of the LDA design, development and integration with low overhead. Its usage with ULFM enables group-collective communication creation and opens for group-collective communicator repair. We also showed that the group-collective variants of the ULFM *shrink* and *agree* have a manageable overhead compared to the collective ones. This result is relevant since it removes one of the weaknesses of ULFM, expanding its possible usage.

Nonetheless, we think integrating our proposed LDA directly with user application code introduces excessive complexity, making the code difficult to read and maintain. Moreover, the algorithm must execute before the group-collective call, unlike most ULFM functions. This fact implies that the usual packaging of ULFM functionalities inside error handlers is not feasible for this case. We integrated the algorithm inside the Legio library to leverage it transparently in our applications, but we think a ULFM extension is also possible.

**Acknowledgements.** This work was supported by the Italian Ministry of University and Research (MUR) under the PON/REACT project.

## References

1. Bland, W., Bouteiller, A., et al.: Post-failure recovery of MPI communication capability: design and rationale. Int. J. High Perform. Comput. Appl. **27**(3), 244–254 (2013)
2. Bouteiller, A., Bosilca, G.: Implicit actions and non-blocking failure recovery with MPI. arXiv preprint arXiv:2212.08755 (2022)
3. Bouteiller, A., Herault, T., et al.: Mpich-v project: a multiprotocol automatic fault-tolerant MPI. Int. J. High Perform. Comput. Appl. **20**(3), 319–333 (2006)
4. Clarke, L., Glendinning, I., et al.: The MPI message passing interface standard. In: Decker, K.M., Rehmann, R.M. (eds.) Programming environments for massively parallel distributed systems, pp. 213–218. Springer, Cham (1994). https://doi.org/10.1007/978-3-0348-8534-8_21

5. Dinan, J., et al.: Noncollective communicator creation in MPI. In: Cotronis, Y., Danalis, A., Nikolopoulos, D.S., Dongarra, J. (eds.) EuroMPI 2011. LNCS, vol. 6960, pp. 282–291. Springer, Heidelberg (2011). https://doi.org/10.1007/978-3-642-24449-0_32
6. Dixit, H.D., Pendharkar, S., et al.: Silent data corruptions at scale. arXiv preprint arXiv:2102.11245 (2021)
7. Egwutuoha, I.P., Levy, D., et al.: A survey of fault tolerance mechanisms and checkpoint/restart implementations for high performance computing systems. J. Supercomput. **65**(3), 1302–1326 (2013)
8. Fagg, G.E., Dongarra, J.J.: FT-MPI: fault tolerant MPI, supporting dynamic applications in a dynamic world. In: Dongarra, J., Kacsuk, P., Podhorszki, N. (eds.) EuroPVM/MPI 2000. LNCS, vol. 1908, pp. 346–353. Springer, Heidelberg (2000). https://doi.org/10.1007/3-540-45255-9_47
9. Ferreira, K., Riesen, R., et al.: rMPI: increasing fault resiliency in a message-passing environment. Sandia National Laboratories, Albuquerque, NM, Technical report SAND2011-2488 (2011)
10. Gamell, M., Katz, D.S., et al.: Exploring automatic, online failure recovery for scientific applications at extreme scales. In: Proceedings of the International Conference for High Performance Computing, Networking, Storage and Analysis, SC 2014. pp. 895–906. IEEE (2014)
11. Hassani, A., Skjellum, A., et al.: Design and evaluation of FA-MPI, a transactional resilience scheme for non-blocking MPI. In: 2014 44th Annual IEEE/IFIP International Conference on Dependable Systems and Networks, pp. 750–755. IEEE (2014)
12. Hochschild, P.H., Turner, P., et al.: Cores that don't count. In: Proceedings of the Workshop on Hot Topics in Operating Systems, pp. 9–16 (2021)
13. Holmes, D., Mohror, K., et al.: MPI sessions: leveraging runtime infrastructure to increase scalability of applications at exascale. In: Proceedings of the 23rd European MPI Users' Group Meeting, pp. 121–129 (2016)
14. Laguna, I., Richards, D.F., et al.: Evaluating and extending user-level fault tolerance in MPI applications. Int. J. High Perform. Comput. Appl. **30**(3), 305–319 (2016)
15. Lamport, L., Melliar-Smith, P.M.: Byzantine clock synchronization. In: Proceedings of the Third Annual ACM Symposium on Principles of Distributed Computing, pp. 68–74 (1984)
16. Losada, N., Cores, I., et al.: Resilient MPI applications using an application-level checkpointing framework and ULFM. J. Supercomput, **73**(1), 100–113 (2017)
17. Margolin, A., Barak, A.: Tree-based fault-tolerant collective operations for MPI. Concurr. Comput.: Pract. Exp. **33**(14), e5826 (2021)
18. Rocco, R., Gadioli, D., et al.: Legio: fault resiliency for embarrassingly parallel MPI applications. J. Supercomput. **78**, 1–21 (2021)
19. Shahzad, F., Thies, J., et al.: Craft: a library for easier application-level checkpoint/restart and automatic fault tolerance. IEEE Trans. Parallel Distrib. Syst. **30**(3), 501–514 (2018)
20. Sultana, N., Skjellum, A., et al.: MPI stages: checkpointing MPI state for bulk synchronous applications. In: Proceedings of the 25th European MPI Users' Group Meeting, pp. 1–11 (2018)

21. Suo, G., Lu, Y., et al.: NR-MPI: a non-stop and fault resilient MPI. In: 2013 International Conference on Parallel and Distributed Systems, pp. 190–199. IEEE (2013)
22. Teranishi, K., Heroux, M.A.: Toward local failure local recovery resilience model using MPI-ULFM. In: Proceedings of the 21st European MPI users' group meeting, pp. 51–56 (2014)

# Scheduling, Resource Management, Cloud, Edge Computing, and Workflows

# MetaLive: Meta-Reinforcement Learning Based Collective Bitrate Adaptation for Multi-Party Live Streaming

Yi Yang[1], Xiang Li[1], Yeting Xu[1], Wenzhong Li[1](✉), Jiangyi Hu[2], Taishan Xu[3], Xiancheng Ren[3], and Sanglu Lu[1]

[1] Nanjing University, Nanjing 210023, Jiangsu, China
{yiyang,mf1933051,mf20330097}@smail.nju.edu.cn,
{wenzhong.li,sanglu}@nju.edu.cn

[2] State Grid Chongqing Electric Power Company, Chongqing 400014, China
liyan2@sgepri.sgcc.com.cn

[3] Nari Technology Co., Ltd., Nanjing 210023, Jiangsu, China
{xutaishan,renxiancheng}@sgepri.sgcc.com.cn

**Abstract.** Multi-party interactive live video streaming applications have attracted millions of daily active users and are anticipated a blooming market in the next few years. A fundamental research problem in live streaming is bitrate coordination, which selects the proper upload/download bitrate for multiple participants in the system to maximize the users' quality of experience (QoE). The existing bitrate adaptation methods fail to achieve optimal performance across a broad set of network conditions with conflict QoE objectives, and lack of the ability of adaptation to dynamic user requirements. In this paper, we proposed a novel meta-reinforcement learning based solution called MetaLive for multi-party live video streaming bitrate adaptation. The proposed framework formulates the bitrate coordination problem as a reinforcement learning task, and introduces a meta-training method to train an agent to learn to carry out various complex tasks from historical experience, and generate bitrate adaptation policies to maximize expected QoEs in diverse environments. We implement MetaLive based on an emulation platform, and use real-world network traces to evaluate its performance. Extensive experiments show that MetaLive achieves the best comprehensive QoE compared with the state-of-the-arts in a variety of network scenarios.

**Keywords:** Video Streaming · Adaptive Bitrate · Meta Learning · Multi-Party Live Streaming

## 1 Introduction

Live streaming applications have experienced rapid growth in the past 5 years. According to the report[1], online video conferencing market size exceeded USD 15 billion in 2020, and it is predicted to reach 75 billion in 2027, expanding

[1] https://www.gminsights.com/industry-analysis/video-conferencing-market.


J. Cano et al. (Eds.): Euro-Par 2023, LNCS 14100, pp. 65–80, 2023.
https://doi.org/10.1007/978-3-031-39698-4_5

at around 23% compound annual growth rate from 2021 to 2027. The global live streaming market[2] is projected to reach USD 534.37 billion by 2030, growing continually at 29.3% compound annual growth rate throughout the forecast period. Live streaming platforms such as YouTube Live and Twitter Periscope have attracted more and more daily active users with emerging new applications such as online talent shows. In the multi-party interactive live video streaming [19] applications, the users perform conference meeting, singing, acting, and other activities together interactively by exchanging streams [14], where each user acts as both a sender to upload his own video and a receiver to download the composite videos from the server. In such applications, it is important for the streaming server to coordinate the upload/download bitrates of the participants to optimized the quality of experience (QoE) of the system.

Adaptive bitrate selection has been extensively studied in the past [9,18], but in the context of multi-party live video streaming, both uplink and downlink bitrates should be coordinated to optimize users' various QoE goals, which has not been addressed by the above methods. A pioneer work addressing multi-party live video streaming is MultiLive [19], which proposed a non-linear programming solution to the many-to-many bitrate selection problem.

However, MultiLive has drawbacks as a model-based solution. Firstly, the mathematical model may not fit the real deployment environment, requiring constant re-running of the bitrate coordination algorithm. Secondly, it fails to achieve optimal performance across network conditions and QoE objectives. Finally, it lacks the ability to adapt to dynamic user requirements.

To address these challenges, we proposed MetaLive. It is a meta-reinforcement-learning-based solution for multi-party live video streaming bitrate adaptation. It formulates the bitrate coordination problem as a reinforcement learning task and trains an AI model to maximize expected QoEs by selecting the best upload and download bitrates. Unlike conventional client-side bitrate selection methods, MetaLive introduces a novel meta-learning framework that leverages prior learning experience to generate bitrate adaptation policies that can adapt flexibly to dynamic environments. The contribution of our work are summarized as follows.

- We address the novel research problem of collaborative upload/download bitrate selection for multi-party live video streaming, which is important for the emerging interactive live streaming applications. We discuss challenges of multi-party bitrate coordination in coping with network heterogeneities, achieving conflicting QoE goals, and dealing with dynamic network.
- We propose a novel meta-learning based framework called MetaLive for solving the collaborative bitrate adaptation problem. The proposed framework formulates the bitrate coordination problem as a reinforcement learning task, and introduces a meta-training method to train an agent to learn to carry out various complex tasks from prior experience, and generate bitrate adaptation policies to maximize expected QoEs in diverse environments.

[2] https://www.marketresearchfuture.com/reports/live-streaming-market-10134.

- We implement the proposed MetaLive framework based on an emulation and use real-world network traces to evaluate its performance. Extensive experiments show that MetaLive achieves the best comprehensive QoE compared with the state-of-the-art bitrate adaptation algorithms in a variety of network scenarios.

## 2 Related Work

In this section, we summarize the related works on adaptive streaming bitrate selection in three aspects: model-based methods, learning-based methods and live streaming optimization methods.

The model-based methods model the network environment via a mathematical model. The model is used to estimate upcoming network conditions and make change to the bitrate. Many previous works have been done about model-based bitrate adaptation algorithms [8,17]. BBA [8] is a buffer-based method. It collects historical buffer occupancy information and makes decisions to adjust bitrate. BOLA [17] transforms the bitrate selection problem into a utility-maximization problem, which can be solved by using the Lyapunov function [11].

Networks are usually dynamic and changeable, making heuristic algorithms based on fixed simple rules unable to meet the demand for network resources for future applications and difficult to guarantee QoS/QoE. To address this situation, researchers have attempted to use machine learning to adjust network parameters in real time based on the current network state to maximize QoS/QoE.

Reinforcement learning techniques have gained popularity in recent years for learning-based bitrate adaptive algorithms. CS2P [18] analyzed real datasets and found that sessions with similar characteristics have similar throughput patterns, which can be used to cluster sessions and predict throughput evolution using a hidden Markov model. Pensieve [9] and Deep Q-Learning DASH (D-DASH) [5] use deep reinforcement learning to improve bitrate decisions. Pensieve does not rely on assumptions and uses neural networks to adapt to different buffering scenarios and network rates. D-DASH combines deep learning and reinforcement learning to improve DASH's QoE and achieve a good tradeoff between policy optimality and convergence speed.

With the popularity of video conferencing, the optimization of live video streaming, especially multi-party live streaming, is becoming increasingly important. While the above model-based methods and learning-based methods mainly focus on client side bitrate selection to optimize downlink QoEs, they seldom study the problem of multi-party live video streaming. Prior works such as [6,7] mainly focused on optimizing server selection and user-to-agent assignment. The coordination of uplink and downlink bitrates of multiple clients to optimize overall QoEs has yet been explored. Multilive [19] is a model-based method for multi-party live streaming bitrate selection. It uses non-linear programming to determine the target bitrate for each sender-receiver pair. The target bitrate is updated periodically based on buffer feedback to reducing modeling and measurement errors.

Different from the existing works, we propose MetaLive that applies a novel meta-learning approach to optimize QoEs for multi-party live streaming. To the best of our knowledge, MetaLive is the first meta-reinforcement learning method that coordinates uplink and downlink bitrates to achieve QoE maximization in multi-party live streaming systems.

# 3 Problem Formulation

## 3.1 System Model

We consider a multi-party live streaming system as illustrated in Fig. 1, where each client uploads their video frames to the server and downloads the live stream from the server. Due to the differences in network capacities, clients have varying link capacities. The streaming server periodically evaluates the QoE of each client and collaboratively adjusts the upload and download bitrates of each client to optimize the overall QoE of the system.

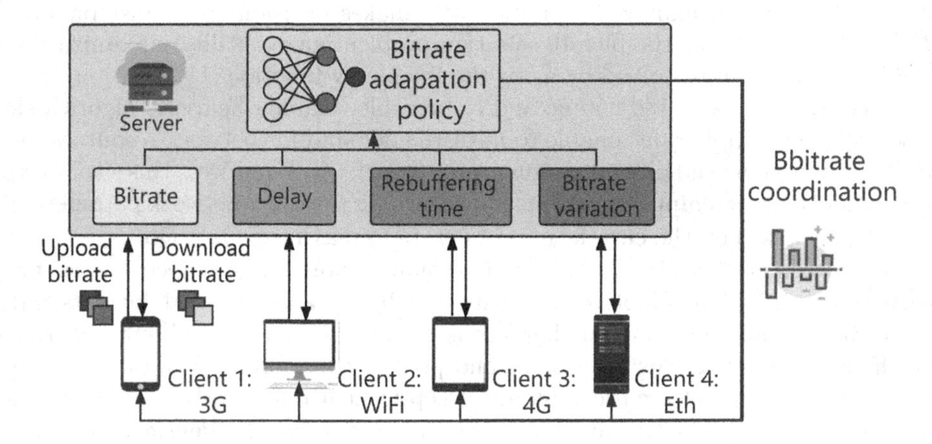


**Fig. 1.** The model of multi-party live streaming system.

Similar to the work of [19], we assume the Scalable Video Coding (SVC) [12] is used for aggregating the streams with different bitrate sent from the sender, and then the server can distribute the different layers among different receivers.

After receiving a frame, the server will cache it and relay the appropriate SVC layer of the frame to each receiver to fulfill their quality requirement. In the proposed scheme, the streaming server adopts a meta-reinforcement learning method called MetaLive to generate bitrate adaptation policies that can cope with dynamic varying network conditions.

## 3.2 QoE Metrics

To improve users' experience, media streaming should consider goals such as video quality, rebuffering time, and smoothness. The algorithm needs to optimize conflicting goals, e.g., increasing bitrate may lead to longer rebuffering and delay.

To quantify the QoE goals, we introduce several QoE metrics. The server evaluate the QoEs periodically, and each period consists of the transmission of $k$ frames from the sender to the receivers.

For $k$ frames transmitting from sender $i$ to receiver $j$, we denote the *video quality* that influences users' experience as $QoE_{hd}^{ij}$, which is calculated by:

$$QoE_{hd}^{ij} = \sum_{n=1}^{k} q(R_n^{ij}), \tag{1}$$

where $R_n^{ij}$ is the bitrate of the $n$-th frame from sender i to receiver j, and $q(\cdot)$ is a non-decreasing function which maps the selected bitrate to the video quality perceived by user. To describe the fluency of playback, we represent the *rebuffering time* as $QoE_{reb}^{ij}$, which is computed by:

$$QoE_{reb}^{ij} = \sum_{n=1}^{k} T_n^{ij}, \tag{2}$$

where $T_n^{ij} = \frac{size\ of\ frame_n}{R_n^{ij}}$ is the time required by downloading the $n$-th frame at the rate $R_n^{ij}$.

To consider the frequent quality variations in streaming, we define the *variation of quality* as $QoE_{var}^{ij}$, which is calculated by:

$$QoE_{var}^{ij} = \sum_{n=1}^{k-1} |q(R_{n+1}^{ij}) - q(R_n^{ij})|, \tag{3}$$

which represents the changes in video quality to influence smoothness.

We further define the *latency* of k continuous frames from sender $i$ to receiver $j$ as $QoE_{del}^{ij}$, which is computed by:

$$QoE_{del}^{ij} = T_k^{down(ij)} - T_k^{up(i)} + B_k^{down(ij)}, \tag{4}$$

where $T_k^{down(ij)}$ is the time when the receiver $j$ received all $k$ frames from $i$, $T_k^{up(i)}$ is the time when the sender $i$ sent the first frame, and $B_k^{down(ij)}$ is the buffer usage when the last frame is received.

With the above notations, the server can form a comprehensive QoE evaluation from sender $i$ to receiver $j$ representing by a weighted sum of the four QoE metrics (i.e. video quality, smoothness, rebuffering time and latency), which is written as

$$QoE^{ij} = \mu_1^{i,j} QoE_{hd}^{ij} - \mu_2^{i,j} QoE_{reb}^{ij} - \mu_3^{i,j} QoE_{var}^{ij} - \mu_4^{i,j} QoE_{del}^{ij}, \tag{5}$$

where $\mathcal{W} = (\mu_1^{i,j}, \mu_2^{i,j}, \mu_3^{i,j}, \mu_4^{i,j})$ is a set of non-negative weights corresponding to users' preferences on the video stream (from sender $i$ to receiver $j$) quality, rebuffering time, variation, and latancy, respectively.

### 3.3 Optimization Objective

The overall optimization objective of the multi-party live streaming system intends to maximize the sum of QoEs of all of the senders and receivers in the system:

$$\max \sum_{i} \sum_{j} QoE_{ij}, \tag{6}$$

**Table 1.** Notations in MetaLive

| Notation | Description |
|---|---|
| $\boldsymbol{R}_t$ | Bitrate of each link at time $t$ |
| $\boldsymbol{J}_t$ | Bitrate variation of each link between $t$ and $t-1$ |
| $\boldsymbol{B}_t$ | Buffer occupancy of each receiver relative to each sender at time $t$ |
| $\boldsymbol{D}_t$ | Delay of each link at time $t$ |
| $\boldsymbol{M}_t$ | QoE weights of each receiver relative to each sender at time $t$ |
| $\omega$ | Task potential variable |
| $\tau$ | State-action trajectory |
| $q_\phi$ | Variational inference network |
| $\pi_\theta$ | Policy network |

with regards to the following bandwidth constraints:

- The bitrate of an uploading frame is limited by the sender's uplink bendwidth. If we denote the uplink bandwidth of sender $i$ for sending the $n$-th frame as $C^{up(i,n)}$, it requires

$$\max_{j}\{R_n^{ij}\} \leq C^{up(i,n)}. \tag{7}$$

- The sum of bitrates of all received frames is limited by the receiver's downlink bandwidth. If we denote the downlink bandwidth of receiver $j$ when receiving the $n$-th frame as $C^{down(j,n)}$, it requires

$$\sum_{i} R_n^{ij} \leq C^{down(j,n)}. \tag{8}$$

The above problem is a non-linear programming problem which can be solved by convex optimization or heuristics [19]. However, such a model-based solution may encounter several drawbacks, e.g., failing to achieve optimal performance across a broad set of network conditions with conflict QoE objectives, and lacking of the ability of adaptation to dynamic user requirements. Therefore we consider a learning-based bitrate adaptation approcah in our solution, which is introduced in the following section.

# 4 MetaLive Solution

## 4.1 Collaborative Bitrate Adaptation with Reinforcement Learning

In this section, we propose a novel meta-reinforcement learning (MRL) based method called MetaLive for adaptive bitrate coordination for multi-party live streaming, and ultimately improve the performance of learning new tasks.

The collaborative bitrate adaptation problem for multi-party live streaming can be formulated with a deep reinforcement learning (DRL) framework, where learner observes the network environment individually and take actions select the best upload and download bitrates to maximize the expected QoE of the system. The notations used in problem formulation are summarized in Table 1.

Specifically, the DRL framework consists of the following basic elements.

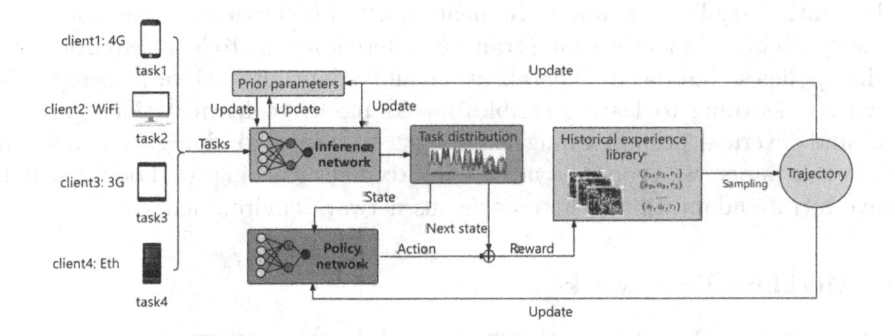


**Fig. 2.** The MetaLive Framework.

- **Agent:** In each decision period (i.e., transmitting $k$ frames), an agent is triggered to choose upload/download bitrates for each client in the live streaming application.
- **State:** The state observed by the agent consists of a number of network parameters that is used for QoE evaluations. In the $t$-th time period, the state observed by the DRL agent is denoted by

$$s_t = (\boldsymbol{R}_t, \boldsymbol{J}_t, \boldsymbol{D}_t, \boldsymbol{B}_t, \boldsymbol{M}_t), \tag{9}$$

where $\boldsymbol{R}_t$ is the set of download bitrates of video streams in period $t$ representing the quality of video; $\boldsymbol{J}_t$ is the set of bitrate differences of each stream between period $t$ and $t-1$ representing the variation of quality; $\boldsymbol{D}_t$ is the set of average latencies of each stream in period $t$, $\boldsymbol{B}_t$ is the set of buffer usages of each stream in period $t$, and $\boldsymbol{M}_t$ is the set of weights of each stream for a receiver in period $t$ representing the client's quality preferences on different upload streams during the live streaming session.
- **Action:** Upon observing a state $s_t$, the agent takes an action $a_t$ to coordinate the bitrates for the clients. The agent is typically deployed in the server side, and it selects upload bitrate for each sender and receive bitrate for each

receiver based on the policy learned by the DRL model. In deep reinforcement learning, the agent's bitrate coordination policy is generated by a deep neural network (DNN) model with parameters $\theta$. Using $\theta$, we can denote the generated policy by $\pi_\theta(s_t, a_t)$.

- **Reward:** In each time period $t$, the agent observes the state $s_t$, and chooses an action $a_t$. After applying the action, the state of the environment transitions to $s_{t+1}$ and the agent receives a reward $r_t$ representing by the overall QoE metric. The goal of the learning agent is to maximize the expected cumulative discounted reward:

$$\mathbb{E}[\sum_{t=0}^{\infty} \gamma^t r_t], \tag{10}$$

where $\gamma \in (0, 1]$ is a factor discounting future rewards.

In multi-party live streaming, N clients work in heterogeneous network environments. Reinforcement learning trains N different agents to learn environment-specific policies, but lacks generalization and adaptivity. Meta-learning, also known as "learning to learn", enables an AI model to learn various complex tasks and leverage prior learning experience to adapt to changing conditions [10]. In this paper, we propose a meta-reinforcement learning method for collaborative bitrate adaptation in heterogeneous network environments.

### 4.2 MetaLive Framework

The framework of MetaLive is shown in Fig. 2. In this framework, it consists of two neural networks for meta-training: an inference network and a policy network. The inference network collects the information from different clients in live streaming, and infers the latent distribution of the learning tasks. The inference network collects information from different clients and infers the latent distribution of learning tasks, while the policy network samples states from the task distribution, takes actions to the environment, and obtains rewards to maximize QoE. The state, action, and reward data are stored in a historical experiences library, and used to update both the inference and policy networks through an updatable prior knowledge. The process is repeated until convergence.

With the meta-learning framework, MetaLive is expected to better adapt and perform system-level bitrate adaptation for QoE requirements with dynamic requirements for different numbers of participants in diverse network conditions.

### 4.3 Meta-Training Algorithms

To cope with the diverse scenarios of multi-party online streaming, we train a meta-reinforcement learning agent with complex historically relevant tasks to generate flexible bitrate adaptation policies. To this end, we refer to the ideas of TRIO (Tracking, Inference, and policy Optimization) [13] for meta-training the proposed reinforcement learning model. Specifically, we train the DRL model based on a given family of tasks from different prior distributions to infer the correct prior distribution for future tasks in the test environment.

We model the learning task as a Markov decision process [2]: $\mathcal{M} = (\mathcal{S}, \mathcal{A}, \mathcal{R}, \mathcal{P}, s_0, \gamma)$, where $\mathcal{S}$ is the state space, $\mathcal{A}$ is the action space, $\mathcal{R}$ is the reward function, $\mathcal{P}$ is the policy, $s_0$ is state distribution, and $\gamma$ is the discount factor.

The goal of the agent is to find a policy that:

$$\arg\max_{\pi} \mathbb{E}_{\omega_t \sim \rho}[\sum_{t=0}^{T-1} \mathbb{E}[\sum_{h=0}^{H_t-1} \gamma^h r_{t,h} | \mathcal{M}_{\omega_t}, \pi]], \tag{11}$$

i.e., maximize the cumulative reward. We follows the settings similar to [13].

More precisely, the proposed meta-training process consists two parts:

- A variational inference module $q_\phi(\tau, z)$, which can fast infer the potential distribution of parameters from an empirical sample of a given task sequence, where $\phi$ represents the parameter of the model.
- A policy network module that acts on exploration and policy generation $\pi_\theta(s, q_\phi)$, where $\theta$ represents the parameter of the model. It selects the action on the potential parameters of a given state and distribution. During testing, we use curve fitting to track the evolution of potential parameters.

The inference module is used to infer the latent task distribution from the clients in live streaming using trajectory from historical experience and prior parameter $z$. Here we adopt the variational inference technique [3] to minimize the expected Kullback-Leibler (KL) divergence between the output of the inference module and the real posterior distribution to train the inference network:

$$\arg\min_{\phi} \mathbb{E}[\mathbb{E}_{\hat{\omega} \sim q_\phi}[logp(\tau|\hat{\omega}, z)] + KL(q_\phi(\tau, z) \| p_z)]. \tag{12}$$

This could be done by Monte Carlo sampling: the prior parameter $z$ is sampled from $p(z)$ and the latent variable is sampled from $p(z)$. Thus we get the optimization objective [13]:

$$\begin{aligned} \arg\min_{\phi} \sum_{i=1}^{n} (\|\mu_\phi(\tau_i, z_i) - \omega_i\|^2 + Tr(\sum_{\phi}(\tau_i, z_i)) \\ + \frac{\lambda}{H_i} KL(q_\phi(\tau_i, z_i) \| p_{z_i})). \end{aligned} \tag{13}$$

The policy network aims to make its action for the highest reward while considering exploration. We adopt a Bayesian optimization strategy to achieve this goal. The strategy is meta-trained to directly maximize the rewards on the observed state by proximal strategy optimization [13,16]:

$$\arg\min_{\theta} \sum_{i=1}^{n} \sum_{h=0}^{H_i-1} \gamma^h r_{h,i} \tag{14}$$

## 5 Experiments

In this section, we conducted extensive experiments based on real-world network traces to evaluate the performance of MetaLive. The evaluation mainly focuses on answering the following questions.

1. How does MetaLive perform compared to the previous bitrate adaptations algorithms in terms of QoEs? We found that MetaLive outperforms the best available solutions in terms of QoE in all test scenarios, where up to 13.12% QoE improvement was observed in the WiFi networks.
2. Whether MetaLive can adapt to more complex network environments and user needs? We found that MetaLive can also achieve better QoE performance than existing methods when user preferences are constantly changing.

The details of the experiments are discussed in the following.

### 5.1 Implementation

In our implementation of the proposed MetaLive scheme, the variational inference network $q_\phi(\tau, z)$ and the policy network $\pi_\theta(s, q_\phi)$ are three-layer fully connected neural networks using rectified linear units (ReLU) as the activation function for each neuron. We used RMSPropOptimizer to train the neural network on TensorFlow 1.13.1 with learning rates of 0.01 ($q_\phi$) and 0.0001 ($\pi_\theta$), respectively. By default, the reward discount factor $\gamma = 0.99$. The network structure of MetaLive is shown in Table 2. We use the simulated multimedia real-time streaming environment provided in [19], the number of clients in the system is set to 5 by default. We also follow the paper of [19] to set the default parameters for the simulations.

**Table 2.** Network Parameters of MetaLive.

| Network | Layers | Parameters | Layer hyper-parameter |
|---|---|---|---|
| $q_\phi$ | FC + Conv1d | 128*5 + 128*4*1*3 | bias = True; stride = 1 |
| | FC | 128*1 | bias = True |
| | LSTM | 128*1 | dropout = 0.8 |
| $\pi_\theta$ | FC + Conv1d | 128*4 + 128*4*1*3 | bias = True; stride = 1 |
| | FC | 128*1 | bias = True |
| | FC | 1*1 | bias = True |

### 5.2 QoE Parameters

In the experiments, we set the mapping function in Eq. (1) as $q(R_{n,v}) = R_n$. We use different combinations of $\mathcal{W}$ to simulate different scenarios, where $\mathcal{W} = (\mu_1^{ij}, \mu_2^{ij}, \mu_3^{ij}, \mu_4^{ij})$ is non-negative weighting parameters corresponding to users' preference on the video quality, rebuffering time, variation, and latency, respectively. Same as [19], we set $\mu_1^{ij} = 1$, $\mu_2^{ij} = 1$, $\mu_3^{ij} = 1$ and $\mu_4^{ij} = 20$ to show the importance of latency, except for $\mu_1^{0,2} = 0.6$, $\mu_4^{0,2} = 28$ (indicating a preference to sacrifice bitrate for reducing latency) and $\mu_1^{1,3} = 1.2$, $\mu_4^{1,3} = 16$ (indicating a preference to sacrifice latency for reducing bitrate).

### 5.3 Network Traces

To evaluate the algorithms on realistic network conditions, we generate several network trace scenarios using three real-world network communication datasets.

1. *3G Scenario*: We generate this trace using a 3G/HSDPA mobile dataset collected in Norway [15].
2. *WiFi Scenario*: We generate this trace using the broadband dataset provided by the FCC [1].
3. *4G Scenario*: We generated this trace from a 4G network dataset collected in Sydney [4].

We assign each of the three types of traces to a stream in the simulator and generate frame sequences at a rate of 30 frames per second.

### 5.4 Baseline Algorithms

We compare MetaLive with three state-of-the-art bitrate adaptation algorithms for multi-party live streaming coordination problem:

1. *BBA* [8]: is a buffer-based method that estimates future capacity based on the playback buffer occupancy from past observations to select the bitrate.
2. *MultiLive* [19]: A model-based bitrate adaptation algorithm, which calculate the bitrate for each pair of live streaming participants based on non-linear programming, and then adjusts the bitrate based on buffering feedback to avoid the accumulation of systematic errors.
3. *MultiLive_NLP* [19]: A simpler version of MultiLive where buffering feedback adjustment is not performed.

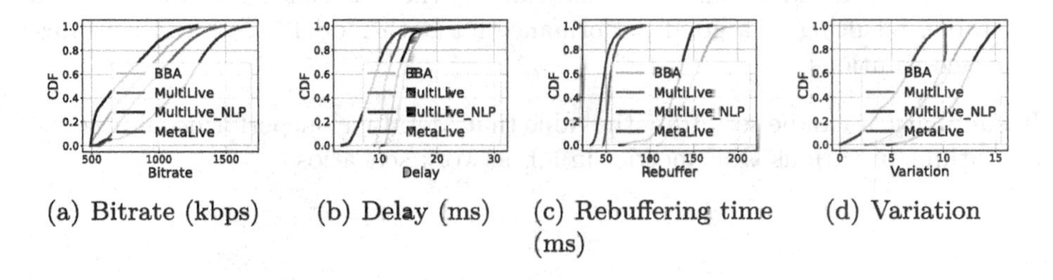


(a) Bitrate (kbps) (b) Delay (ms) (c) Rebuffering time (ms) (d) Variation

**Fig. 3.** CDFs of QoEs of different algorithms on the WiFi scenario.

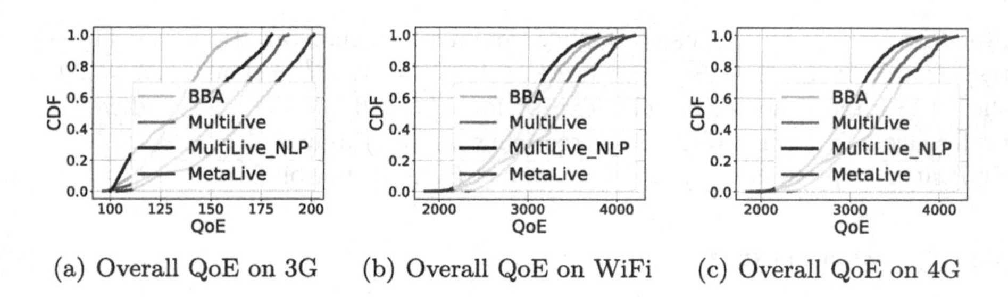


(a) Overall QoE on 3G (b) Overall QoE on WiFi (c) Overall QoE on 4G

**Fig. 4.** CDFs of QoEs of different algorithms on the 3G, WiFi and 4G scenario.

### 5.5 Comparison of Performance on Three Network Scenarios

We compared the performance of MetaLive with the baseline algorithms on three network scenarios. The Cumulative Distribution Functions (CDFs) of the algorithms on different QoE metrics (on WiFi network) are illustrated in Fig. 3. The overall QoE results are shown in Fig. 4, and the average results in all traces are shown in Table 3.

We obtained the following results from the figures and table.

1. In the 3G scenario, MetaLive improves the overall QoE by 5.04% compared to MultiLive, the best-performing algorithm in the baseline. This improvement is mainly due to the improvement in average rebuffering time, average bitrate variation and average latency improvement after sacrificing some of the average bitrate.
2. In the WiFi scenario, compared with MultiLive, the SOTA algorithm for multi-party live streaming, MetaLive improved 13.12% in average QoE, which is the most among the three scenarios. The reason lies in that the baseline algorithms cannot adapt to the network fluctuation caused by the dynamic change of bandwidth in WiFi network, whereas the meta-reinforcement learning approach can effectively reduce the average rebuffering time, average bitrate variation and average latency due to the power of meta-training.
3. In the 4G scenario, compared with MultiLive, MetaLive improved the average QoE by 3.29%, which is not as significant as that of WiFi and 3G scenarios. The reason could be that the bandwidth in the 4G scenario is sufficient and stable, resulting in a good performance for both model-based and learning-based solutions.

In summary, it can be seen from the table that MetaLive outperforms all baseline algorithms in various QoE metrics in all network scenarios.

**Table 3.** Comparison of average bitrate (kbps), rebuffering time (ms), variations, delay (ms) and their corresponding QoE metrics on different network scenarios.

| Trace | Method | Bitrate | Reb. | Variation | Delay | QoE |
|---|---|---|---|---|---|---|
| 3G | BBA | 109.987 | 152.939 | 26.207 | 19.258 | 510.144 |
| | MultiLive | **224.44** | 62.057 | 1.386 | 12.7 | 152.532 |
| | MultiLive_NLP | 107.138 | 137.765 | 2.691 | 26.207 | 507.739 |
| | MetaLive | 206.817 | **53.592** | **1.200** | **11.444** | **542.425** |
| WiFi | BBA | 825.792 | 146.833 | 8.966 | 14.475 | 721.003 |
| | MultiLive | 938.246 | 56.458 | 8.370 | 11.5833 | 865.697 |
| | MultiLive_NLP | 728.368 | 127.551 | 11.560 | 13.383 | 644.557 |
| | MetaLive | **1136.825** | **47.867** | **5.534** | **9.014** | **982.489** |
| 4G | BBA | 3254.97 | 233.200 | 20.884 | 15.231 | 3033.114 |
| | MultiLive | 3370.257 | 143.56 | 19.748 | 15.096 | 3196.874 |
| | MultiLive_NLP | 3137.287 | 213.955 | 22.923 | 15.3980 | 2918.196 |
| | MetaLive | **3543.39** | **134.575** | **16.898** | **15.493** | **3325.908** |

### 5.6 Comparison of Performance Adaptive Capability

We further explore the performance of different algorithms with dynamic changing of user preferences during the live streaming. We set the clients' preference weights $\mathcal{W} = (\mu_1^{ij}, \mu_2^{ij}, \mu_3^{ij}, \mu_4^{ij})$ within a predefined range, where $\mu_1^{ij} \in \{0.6, 1.2, 1.8\}$, $\mu_2^{ij} \in \{0.7, 1, 2\}$, $\mu_3^{ij} \in \{0.5, 1.2, 3\}$, and $\mu_4^{ij} \in \{16, 22, 28\}$. The preference weights are dynamically changing every 5 s with random values from the above ranges. This will test the adaptive capability of the algorithms.

**Table 4.** Comparison of average bitrate (kbps), rebuffering time (ms), variations, delay (ms) and their corresponding QoE metrics on WiFi Scenario.

| Method | Bitrate | Reb. | Variation | Delay | QoE |
|---|---|---|---|---|---|
| BBA | 745.92 | 160.723 | 9.876 | 15.662 | 648.927 |
| MultiLive | 934.322 | 50.501 | 8.801 | 9.844 | 809.947 |
| MultiLive_NLP | 642.413 | 140.306 | 13.065 | 13.383 | 644.557 |
| MetaLive | **1035.510** | **48.628** | **6.654** | **8.962** | **961.844** |

The experiment is conduct on the WiFi scenario, and the results are compared in Table 4. As shown in Table 4, MetaLive reveals an advantage due to meta-learning, and its QoE improves by 18.76% compared to MultiLive.

Specifically, comparing to the second-best algorithm, MetaLive improves the bitrate by 8.23%, reduces the rebuffering time by 3.71%, significantly reduced the average variation in bitrate by 24.4%, and in terms of latency, it manages to reduce it by 8.96%. This confirms the adaptive capability of MetaLive in the conditions of dynamic changing users' preferences.

### 5.7 Trade-Off Between QoE Metrics

We also studied the trade-off between bitrate, rebuffering time, variance of bitrate, and delay. The normalized results are visualized in Fig. 5. As shown in the figure, BBA and MultiLive_NLP yields much lower comprehensive QoEs than the other algorithms. In the 3G scenario, MultiLive has higher Bitrate, but its rebuffering time, variance, and delay are worse than MetaLive. MetaLive outperforms all baselines in WiFi and 4G scenarios, achieves the best trade-off between conflict QoE goals.

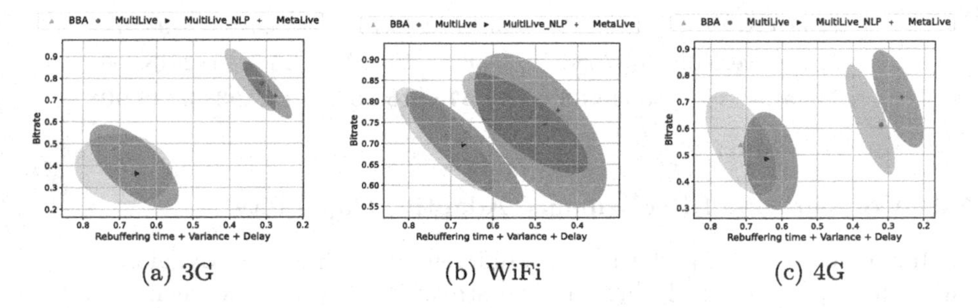


(a) 3G (b) WiFi (c) 4G

**Fig. 5.** Trade-off between bitrate, delay, rebuffering time, and variance.

## 6 Conclusion

In this paper, we addressed the challenging problem of collaborative bitrate adaptation in multi-party live streaming, and proposed a novel meta-reinforcement learning based solution called MetaLive to solve the problem. MetaLive formulated the bitrate coordination problem as a reinforcement learning task, where a learner observes the environment to learn from the historical experiences, and takes actions to interact with environment and select the best upload and download bitrates for individual participants. We introduced a meta-training method to train an agent to learn to carry out various complex tasks and generate bitrate adaptation policies to maximize expected QoEs in diverse environments. Extensive experiments based on real-world traces showed that MetaLive can provide better QoEs when compared to the state-of-the-art methods in all test scenarios. Moreover, MetaLive was able to achieve good performance in various dynamic environments, demonstrating the superiority and adaptivity of the meta-learning based solution.

**Acknowledgments.** This work was partially supported by the Natural Science Foundation of Jiangsu Province (Project "Research on Frontier Basic Theory and Method of Security Defense for Power Systems with High-dimensional Uncertain Factors", Grant No.BK20222003), the National Natural Science Foundation of China (Grant Nos. 61972196, 61832008, 61832005), the Collaborative Innovation Center of Novel Software Technology and Industrialization, and the Sino-German Institutes of Social Computing.

## References

1. Raw data - measuring broadband America (2016). https://www.fcc.gov/reports-research/reports/ (2021)
2. Al-Shedivat, M., Bansal, T., Burda, Y., Sutskever, I., Mordatch, I., Abbeel, P.: Continuous adaptation via meta-learning in nonstationary and competitive environments. In: 6th International Conference on Learning Representations, (ICLR 2018) (2018)
3. Blei, D.M., Kucukelbir, A., McAuliffe, J.D.: Variational inference: a review for statisticians. CoRR abs/1601.00670 (2016)
4. Bokani, A., Hassan, M., Kanhere, S.S., Yao, J., Zhong, G.: Comprehensive mobile bandwidth traces from vehicular networks. In: Proceedings of the 7th International Conference on Multimedia Systems, pp. 1–6 (2016)
5. Gadaleta, M., Chiariotti, F., Rossi, M., Zanella, A.: D-dash: a deep q-learning framework for dash video streaming. IEEE Trans. Cogn. Commun. Netw. **3**(4), 703–718 (2017)
6. Hajiesmaili, M.H., Mak, L.T., Wang, Z., Wu, C., Chen, M., Khonsari, A.: Cost-effective low-delay design for multiparty cloud video conferencing. IEEE Trans. Multimed. **19**(12), 2760–2774 (2017)
7. Hu, Y., Niu, D., Li, Z.: A geometric approach to server selection for interactive video streaming. IEEE Trans. Multimed. **18**(5), 840–851 (2016)
8. Huang, T.Y., Johari, R., McKeown, N., Trunnell, M., Watson, M.: A buffer-based approach to rate adaptation: evidence from a large video streaming service. In: Proceedings of the ACM Special Interest Group on Data Communication, SIGCOMM 2014, pp. 187–198 (2014)
9. Mao, H., Netravali, R., Alizadeh, M.: Neural adaptive video streaming with pensieve. In: Proceedings of the Conference of the ACM Special Interest Group on Data Communication, pp. 197–210 (2017)
10. McMahan, B., Moore, E., Ramage, D., Hampson, S., Arcas, B.A.: Communication-efficient learning of deep networks from decentralized data. In: Artificial Intelligence and Statistics, pp. 1273–1282. PMLR (2017)
11. Neely, M.J.: Stochastic Network Optimization with Application to Communication and Queueing Systems. Synthesis Lectures on Communication Networks. Morgan & Claypool Publishers, California (2010)
12. Ohm, J.R.: Advances in scalable video coding. Proc. IEEE **93**(1), 42–56 (2005)
13. Poiani, R., Tirinzoni, A., Restelli, M.: Meta-reinforcement learning by tracking task non-stationarity. In: Zhou, Z. (ed.) Proceedings of the Thirtieth International Joint Conference on Artificial Intelligence, IJCAI 2021, Virtual Event / Montreal, Canada 19–27 August 2021, pp. 2899–2905 (2021). https://www.ijcai.org/
14. Provensi, L., Singh, A., Eliassen, F., Vitenberg, R.: Maelstream: self-organizing media streaming for many-to-many interaction. IEEE Trans. Parallel Distrib. Syst. **29**(6), 1342–1356 (2018)

15. Riiser, H., Vigmostad, P., Griwodz, C., Halvorsen, P.: Commute path bandwidth traces from 3G networks: analysis and applications. In: Proceedings of the 4th ACM Multimedia Systems Conference, pp. 114–118 (2013)
16. Schulman, J., Wolski, F., Dhariwal, P., Radford, A., Klimov, O.: Proximal policy optimization algorithms. CoRR abs/1707.06347 (2017)
17. Spiteri, K., Urgaonkar, R., Sitaraman, R.K.: BOLA: near-optimal bitrate adaptation for online videos. IEEE/ACM Trans. Netw. **28**(4), 1698–1711 (2020)
18. Sun, Y., et al.: CS2P: improving video bitrate selection and adaptation with data-driven throughput prediction. In: Proceedings of the ACM Special Interest Group on Data Communication, SIGCOMM 2016, pp. 272–285 (2016)
19. Wang, Z., Cui, Y., Hu, X., Wang, X., Ooi, W.T., Li, Y.: MultiLive: adaptive bitrate control for low-delay multi-party interactive live streaming. In: 39th IEEE Conference on Computer Communications, (INFOCOM 2020), Toronto, ON, Canada, 6–9 July 2020, pp. 1093–1102. IEEE (2020)

# Asymptotic Performance and Energy Consumption of SLACK

A. Benoit[1], Louis-Claude Canon[2], R. Elghazi[2](✉), and P.-C. Héam[2]

[1] LIP, ENS Lyon, Lyon, France
[2] FEMTO-ST, U. Franche-Comté, Besançon, France
redouane.elghazi@gmail.com

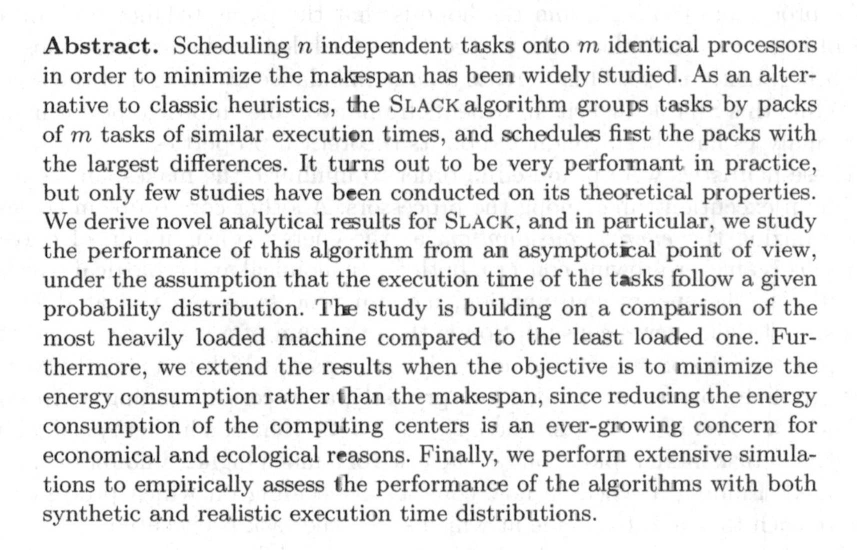

**Abstract.** Scheduling $n$ independent tasks onto $m$ identical processors in order to minimize the makespan has been widely studied. As an alternative to classic heuristics, the SLACK algorithm groups tasks by packs of $m$ tasks of similar execution times, and schedules first the packs with the largest differences. It turns out to be very performant in practice, but only few studies have been conducted on its theoretical properties. We derive novel analytical results for SLACK, and in particular, we study the performance of this algorithm from an asymptotical point of view, under the assumption that the execution time of the tasks follow a given probability distribution. The study is building on a comparison of the most heavily loaded machine compared to the least loaded one. Furthermore, we extend the results when the objective is to minimize the energy consumption rather than the makespan, since reducing the energy consumption of the computing centers is an ever-growing concern for economical and ecological reasons. Finally, we perform extensive simulations to empirically assess the performance of the algorithms with both synthetic and realistic execution time distributions.

## 1 Introduction

The problem of minimizing the computation time when scheduling $n$ independent tasks on $m$ identical processors is at the basis of scheduling theory, and a building block for solving many more complicated problems, hence it remains very important even though it has already been widely studied. Using Graham's notation [15], this problem is denoted $P||C_{\max}$.

While the problem is NP-complete (equivalent to 2-partition with two processors, or 3-partition when the number of processors $m$ is part of the input), an easy way to get efficient solutions consist in ordering the $n$ tasks according to some criterion, and then perform a list schedule, i.e., schedule the next task of the list on the least loaded processor, hence never leaving a processor idle. A classic ordering is the one of LPT (Longest Processing Time), which orders

*This work has been supported by the EIPHI Graduate School (contract ANR-17-EURE-0002).


J. Cano et al. (Eds.): Euro-Par 2023, LNCS 14100, pp. 81–95, 2023.
https://doi.org/10.1007/978-3-031-39698-4_6

tasks from the longest to the smallest [16]. This algorithm has proven to have good theoretical and even better practical performance. In particular, its rate of convergence has been studied, and new results were recently established when the distribution of task costs is generated using uniform integer compositions [5].

More recently, the SLACK heuristic was proposed in [9], showing promising empirical performance compared to LPT. Its principle is based on grouping tasks of similar execution times into packs, sorting the resulting packs by non-decreasing similarity (the similarity of a pack denoting the maximum difference of execution times between its tasks), and then scheduling the tasks in the order determined by the packs, following a list schedule (assign the next task to the least loaded processor). The idea is that a single pack cannot bring the imbalance of the processors too high, and the hope is that the packs balance each other. The objective is that the tasks in the last scheduled packs are very close to each other, hence they will not create a large imbalance at the end of the schedule. While this SLACK algorithm benefits from favorable empirical performance, fewer analyses have been conducted on its theoretical properties.

These heuristics were proposed in order to minimize the makespan, i.e., the maximum execution time among the processors. Another core problem consists in minimizing the *energy consumption*, as the energy consumption of current platforms is an ever-growing concern, both for economical and ecological reasons. To optimize the energy consumption, modern processors can run at different speeds, and their power consumption is then the sum of a static part (the cost for a processor to be turned on) and a dynamic part, which is a strictly convex function of the processor speed. More precisely, a processor running at speed $s$ dissipates a power of $s^\alpha$ Watts, where $2 \leq \alpha \leq 3$ [2]. Hence, a higher speed allows executing a task more rapidly, but at the price of a much higher amount of energy consumed. Finding a schedule now consists in deciding on which processor to execute each task and to decide at which speed the task is executed.

Therefore, we revisit this classic problem of scheduling $n$ independent tasks onto $m$ identical processors, with the aim of deriving analytical results for SLACK, when the goal is to minimize the makespan or the energy consumption. We study the performance of SLACK from an asymptotical point of view, under the assumption that the execution times of the tasks follow a given probability distribution. The study is building on a comparison of the most heavily loaded machine compared to the least loaded one, and hence it provides interesting insights both for the study of the classic makespan objective function, and its translation to the energy consumption. The goal of this paper is therefore to answer two main questions left unresolved in the literature so far: (i) provide a theoretical study to analyze the performance of SLACK, and (ii) consider the energy consumption in the theoretical and empirical analysis of the algorithms. Our main contributions are the following:

- A fundamental bound related to the result of SLACK (Sect. 4);
- A convergence rate for the makespan of SLACK when using uniform and exponential distributions, by applying the bound of Sect. 4 (Sect. 5.1);

- A general result for bounding the energy consumption (agnostic of the algorithm and the task distribution) and its application to SLACK, by applying the bound of Sect. 4 (Sect. 5.2);
- Simulations for comparison with the theoretical bounds that were computed for SLACK and LPT (Sect. 6).

First, Sect. 2 summarizes the existing contributions related to either the energy minimization problem or LPT and SLACK. Section 3 presents the problems and algorithms (LPT and SLACK). Then, Sect. 4 presents a useful bound on the result given by SLACK. Section 5 proposes applications of this bound: theoretical asymptotic results related to the minimization of the makespan and the energy with SLACK. In the case of the energy, Sect. 5.2 also gives a method to derive energy related guarantees for any algorithm bounded similarly to SLACK in Sect. 4. Section 6 presents the experimental results of the empirical study of LPT and SLACK. Finally, Sect. 7 concludes.

## 2 Related Work

Lowering the energy consumption of computational tasks has been widely studied in the last decades, be it in the context of High Performance Computing or in other contexts, such as Cloud Computing. Many models have been proposed for the energy consumption of CPUs. For instance, the energy consumption is scaling quadratically with the speed of the CPU in [22], and there is a focus on the online evaluation of the expected idle time. In [23], the only assumption is that the energy consumption is a convex function of the speed of the CPU, and clairvoyant online and offline solutions are proposed to the problem. The heuristics presented in these two articles are then evaluated, either empirically in [22], or with approximation ratios in [23]. In our work, we explore another way of evaluating algorithms, following the remark that with large systems, stochastic asymptotic results should be relevant.

Recent surveys such as [10] and [21] compile various techniques used for energy-efficient computing, including scheduling techniques. These techniques may use either Dynamic Voltage and Frequency Scaling (DVFS), as in [17], where the frequency (and hence the speed) of processors may be chosen, or Dynamic Power Management (DPM) as in [4]. These studies propose algorithms, but they mainly focus on an empirical evaluation of these algorithms, without theoretical study.

As for scheduling algorithms that have low complexities (and therefore low energy consumption), LPT has been a well known algorithm for decades and is known to provide good theoretical and practical performance while keeping a low time complexity in $O(n \log n)$ [16]. A more recent algorithm, SLACK, also remains with an $O(n \log n)$ time complexity, while providing results that are sometimes better than LPT [5,9].

There are multiple results about the asymptotic behavior of LPT under different assumptions. Frenk and Rhinnooy Kan [14] and Coffman et al. [8] study the difference between LPT and the optimal solution in the case where the execution times of the tasks follow a probability distribution of cumulative distribution function of the form $F(x) = x^\alpha$, where $0 < \alpha < +\infty$. Loulou [18] and Piersma and Romeijn [19] do not look at specific distributions, but instead they study LPT under the assumption that the execution times are independent and identically distributed random variables. More recently, Benoit et al. [5] studied the asymptotic optimality of SLACK and LPT under the assumption that the execution times are generated using a distribution called the uniform integer composition.

## 3 Framework

The $P||C_{\max}$ problem is a classic scheduling problem, where $n$ tasks have to be scheduled on $m$ identical machines, with the objective function of makespan minimization, i.e., minimize the execution time of the machine that completes last ($C_{\max}$). There are no constraints on tasks, which can be assigned to any machine in any order. Each task has a number of operations to perform, that we call its work and denote by $w_i$, and the time to execute the task is usually $t_i = w_i$, assuming that the machine executes one operation per time unit (speed $s = 1$). The problem complexity is well known, and in particular the associated decision problem is NP-complete as soon as $m \geq 2$.

**List Scheduling and LPT.** In order to solve this $P||C_{\max}$ problem, a simple but effective heuristic algorithm consists in never letting a machine idle, i.e., as soon as a task completes on a machine, a new task is assigned to this machine. This is called *list scheduling*, and it can be implemented as in Algorithm 1, by keeping the load of each machine in a vector $\overrightarrow{W}$ of length $m$ initialized to $(0, 0, \ldots, 0)$. For each task, we assign it to the currently least loaded machine, and the makespan is the maximum value of the vector $\overrightarrow{W}$ at the end of the execution. Any list schedule (whatever the order of tasks) is know to be a $(2 - \frac{1}{m})$-approximation algorithm [16]. A variant of the List Scheduling heuristic consists in first sorting the list $L$ by non-increasing task works, and it is called *Longest-Processing-Time-first* (LPT for short). This can be used if all tasks are known beforehand (offline scheduling), and it improves the approximation ratio of the algorithm to $(\frac{4}{3} - \frac{1}{3m})$ [16].

**Slack.** In this paper, we mainly focus on the SLACK algorithm, that was introduced in [9] and consists in applying the List Scheduling heuristic with a particular pretreatment on the list of tasks, as detailed in Algorithm 2. We first fill the

**Algorithm 1.** ListScheduling($L, m$)

**Require:** List $L$ of $n$ positive floats (task works); Number of processors $m$.
1: Let $\overrightarrow{W}$ be a vector of length $m$ initialized to $\overrightarrow{W} = (0, 0, \ldots, 0)$;
2: **for** $w \in L$ in the order they appear in the list **do**
3:     Let $j$ be the index of a minimal element of $\overrightarrow{W}$;
4:     $\overrightarrow{W}[j] = \overrightarrow{W}[j] + w$;
5: **end for**
6: **return** $\overrightarrow{W}$;

**Algorithm 2.** SLACK $(L, m)$

**Require:** List $L$ of $n$ positive floats (task works); Number of processors $m \leq n$.
1: Add $(-n \mod m)$ elements of work 0 at the end of $L$;
2: $r = n + (-n \mod m)$;
3: $L' = [x_1, \ldots, x_r]$ is obtained by sorting $L$ non-increasingly;
4: **for** $0 \leq i \leq \frac{r}{m} - 1$ **do**
5: $K_i = [x_{im+1}, x_{im+2}, \ldots, x_{im+m}]$;
6: $\alpha_i = x_{im+1} - x_{im+m}$;
7: **end for**
8: Let $H = [\alpha_{i_1}, \ldots, \alpha_{i_{\frac{r}{m}}}] = [\beta_1, \ldots, \beta_{\frac{r}{m}}]$ be a non-increasing sequencing of the $\alpha_i$'s; $L_{\text{SLACK}}$ is obtained by concatenating the $K_i$'s in the same order as the $\alpha$'s in $H$.
9: $\overrightarrow{W}$ =ListScheduling($L_{\text{SLACK}}, m$);

list $L$ to have a number of elements $r$ that is a multiple of $m$, by adding dummy tasks of work 0. Then, tasks are sorted by non-increasing works and grouped by packs of $m$ tasks, and then the packs are themselves sorted by non-increasing difference between the work of the longest task of the pack and the smallest one ($\alpha_i$'s). These differences are denoted $\beta_k$, where $\beta_1 \geq \beta_2 \ldots \geq \beta_{r/m}$. They correspond to the sorted $\alpha_i$'s.

Let us denote by $c_i(j)$ the load of processor $j$ after $i \times m$ tasks (i.e., the $i$ first packs) have been scheduled. Hence, $c_i(j) = \overrightarrow{W}[j]$ after $i \times m$ steps of the loop line 2 of Algorithm 1. One has for instance $c_0(j) = 0$ for all $j$ (initial load), and then at each iteration $i$, we schedule one more pack with $m$ tasks. We then define $\delta_i = \max_{0 \leq j,j' < m}(|c_i(j) - c_i(j')|)$, which is the maximum difference of load between two processors after iteration $i$.

Note that these values $\beta_i$ and $\delta_i$ can be extended to any list algorithm, in particular LPT, by simply considering the list of a tasks as a succession of $\frac{n}{m}$ packs.

**From Makespan to Energy Consumption.** When the goal is to minimize the energy consumption, we further consider that the frequency of the processors can be scaled using DVFS (Dynamic Voltage and Frequency Scaling). Hence, these processors have a static power $P_{stat}$, and can be operated at any speed (or frequency) $s \in \mathbb{R}_+^*$ [3], while we assumed so far that $s = 1$.

The execution time of task $T_i$ at speed $s$ then becomes $t_{i,s} = \frac{w_i}{s}$. In terms of energy consumption, there is a static part, which corresponds to the power consumed when the $m$ processors are turned on, during a time $C_{\max}$, hence a total of $m \times C_{\max} \times P_{stat}$. For each task $T_i$, there is also a dynamic energy consumption, directly related to the speed $s$ at which the processor operates the task. Using a general model, the dynamic energy consumption is $t_{i,s} \times s^\alpha$ [2], where $\alpha > 1$ (in general, $2 \leq \alpha \leq 3$). Finally, the total energy consumption of a schedule of length $C_{\max}$, where $T_i$ is operated at speed $s_i$, is:

$$E = m \times C_{\max} \times P_{stat} + \sum_{i=1}^{n} t_{i,s_i} \times s_i^\alpha.$$

**Table 1.** Main Notations

| Symbol | Definition |
|---|---|
| $m$ | number of processor |
| $n$ | number of tasks |
| $\{T_1, \ldots, T_n\}$ | the $n$ tasks |
| $w_i$ | work of $T_i$ (corresponding to the number of operations required by the task) |
| $t_i = w_i$ | the execution time of $T_i$ at speed 1 |
| $t_{i,s} = \frac{w_i}{s}$ | execution time of $T_i$ at speed $s$ |
| $m \times C_{\max} \times P_{stat}$ | static energy consumption for a duration $C_{\max}$ |
| $t_{i,s} \times s^{\alpha}$ | dynamic energy consumption of $T_i$ at speed $s$ |
| $\delta_i$ | largest difference between the total execution times of two processors after having processed $i \times m$ tasks (first $i$ packs) |
| $\beta_i$ | largest difference between the execution time of any two tasks in pack $i$ |
| $c_i(j)$ | total execution time of processor $j$ after $i \times m$ tasks have been scheduled (first $i$ packs) |
| $W_j = \sum_{alloc(i)=j} w_i$ | total work (number of operations) on processor $j$; $alloc(i)$ is the processor on which $T_i$ is allocated |
| $W_{\max} = \max_{1 \le j \le m} W_j$ | maximal number of operations allocated to a processor |
| $W = \sum_{1 \le i \le n} w_i$ | total number of operations to perform |
| $\overrightarrow{W} = (W_1, \ldots, W_m)$ | the $\rightarrow$ notation is used for $m$-length vectors (not only for $W$) |
| $\lVert \overrightarrow{x} \rVert_{\alpha} = \sqrt[\alpha]{\sum x_i^{\alpha}}$ | classic $\alpha$-norm of a vector |

For convenience, the main notations are summarized in Table 1.

## 4 A Bound for SLACK

This section is dedicated to proving a fundamental bound related to SLACK.

Let $\mathcal{X}$ be a distribution with positive values. We denote by $C(n, m, \mathcal{X})$ the random variable of the makespan returned by the SLACK algorithm on $m$ processors on a list of $n$ tasks that are independent random variables of distribution $\mathcal{X}$. Let $X_1, \ldots, X_n$ be $n$ independent random variables distributed according to $\mathcal{X}$. Let $X_{1:n} \le X_{2:n} \le \ldots \le X_{n:n}$ be associated order statistics. Particularly $X_{1:n}$ is the minimum of the $X_i$'s and $X_{n:n}$ the maximum. Let $D_i = (X_{i:n} - X_{i-1:n})$ for every $1 \le i \le n$, with the convention $X_{0:n} = 0$. The $D_i$'s are classically called spacings of adjacent order statistics. Let $\Delta_{\mathcal{X},n}$ be the random variable of the maximal value of $D_i$'s, that is the maximal difference between two consecutive $X_{i:n}$ (and between 0 and $X_{1:n}$).

**Theorem 1.** *When using* SLACK *(Algorithm 2),* $\max_{1 \le i,j \le m} (W_i - W_j) \le m\Delta_{\mathcal{X},n}$.

We provide here a sketch of the proof (see the companion research report [6] for all the complete proofs).

*Proof (Sketch of proof).* The proof is decomposed into a sequence of lemmas, aiming at proving that for every $j$, $\delta_{j+1} \leq \max(\beta_{j+1}, \delta_j)$. This inequality means that the difference between the most loaded processor and the least loaded processor after $j$ rounds of task affectation is bounded by either the difference after the previous round, or the maximum difference between the tasks handled at this round of affectation. It is proved by disjunctive elimination depending on the number of tasks allocated at the current step to the processor maximizing $c_{j+1}$ (i.e., maximizing the total execution time after step $j$).

This result is then used for an induction on $j$ to prove that $\max_{1 \leq i,j \leq m} (W_i - W_j) \leq \beta_1$. This result means that at the end of the execution of SLACK, the load difference between the most and the least loaded processors is bounded by $\beta_1$, the difference between the largest and the smallest tasks of the first round of task affectation. Finally, we use the fact that $\beta_1 \leq (m-1) \times \Delta_{\mathcal{X},n}$ to derive the desired result. □

## 5 Convergence Speed of SLACK

In this section, we use the fundamental bound found in Sect. 4 to derive asymptotic results on the optimality of SLACK, first in terms of makespan in Sect. 5.1, and then in terms of energy consumption in Sect. 5.2.

### 5.1 Convergence of the Makespan

This section is dedicated to prove asymptotic results on the optimality of SLACK. The following main result is a direct application of Theorem 1:

**Proposition 1.** *The makespan of* SLACK *differs from the optimal one by at most* $m\Delta_{\mathcal{X},n}$*:*

$$0 \leq C(n, m, \mathcal{X}) - OPT \leq m\Delta_{\mathcal{X},n}.$$

Now, we will use known results on order spacings to obtain convergence results for SLACK. It is proved in [20, corollary 1.4], [1, Section 3] that

$$\mathbb{E}\left(\Delta_{\mathcal{U}[0,1],n}\right) \sim \frac{\ln n}{n+1}, \tag{1}$$

where $\mathcal{U}[0,1]$ is the uniform distribution between 0 and 1.

From Proposition 1 and Eq. (1), one has the following result, proving that for a fixed $m$, the SLACK algorithm provides a scheduling that converges in expectation to the optimal (for the makespan):

**Corollary 1.** *For any fixed* $m \geq 2$,

$$0 \leq \mathbb{E}\left(C(n, m, \mathcal{U}[0,1])\right) - \mathbb{E}\left(OPT\right) = O\left(m\frac{\ln n}{n+1}\right).$$

As for the exponential distribution, it is shown in [12] that, almost surely,

$$\limsup_{n\to+\infty}\left(\frac{\Delta_{\mathcal{E}_1,n}}{\ln\ln n}\right)=1, \tag{2}$$

where $\mathcal{E}_1$ is the exponential distribution (with rate 1).

Using Proposition 1 and Eq. (2), we then have the following result:

**Corollary 2.** *For any fixed $m \geq 2$, one has almost surely*

$$0 \leq \limsup_{n\to+\infty}\left(\frac{C(n,m,\mathcal{E}_1)-OPT}{m\ln\ln n}\right)\leq 1.$$

Corollary 2 does not show a convergence of the makespan of SLACK to the optimal, but that, almost surely, the gap between their difference is under control since $\ln\ln n$ has a very slow growing speed.

### 5.2 Convergence of the Energy Consumption

Building upon the previous results bounding the $\delta_i$'s for SLACK and analyzing its impact on the makespan, we now move to the problem of minimizing the total energy consumption $E$, where the speed of each processor can take any value in $\mathbb{R}_+^*$. The main result, stated in Theorem 2, shows how to adapt a classic scheduling algorithm (without speed and energy consideration) into an energy-oriented one. The quality of the solution is bounded by a factor depending on the maximal difference $\delta$ between the execution times of the last finishing processor and the first finishing processor.

We show in the companion research report [6] that a better solution can always be achieved by using a constant speed per processor, and by modifying the speeds so that all processors finish at the same time.

**Theorem 2.** *If an algorithm without speeds outputs a schedule with* $\max(W_i - W_j) = \delta$, *then we can transform it in polynomial time, with the optimal choice of speeds, into a schedule with* $E \leq (1+\frac{m\delta}{W})\text{OPT}$, *where* OPT*is the minimal energy consumption that could be attained.*

*Proof (Sketch of proof).* We assume that the tasks are already assigned to the processors, with processor $j$ having a total work of $W_j$. We write $\vec{W}$ the vector containing every $W_j$. In this case, we can choose optimally the speed of processor $j$ as $s_j = \frac{W_j\sqrt[\alpha]{m\times P_{stat}}}{\left\|\vec{W}\right\|_\alpha\sqrt[\alpha]{\alpha-1}}$.

We then bound the optimal energy $E_{\text{OPT}}$ by induction over $m$ to show that:

$$P_{stat}^{\frac{\alpha-1}{\alpha}}\times\left[(\alpha-1)^{\frac{1}{\alpha}}+(\alpha-1)^{\frac{1-\alpha}{\alpha}}\right]\times W\leq E_{\text{OPT}}.$$

We also bound the worst case for the energy of the algorithm $E_{\mathcal{A}}$:

$$E_{\mathcal{A}}\leq P_{stat}^{\frac{\alpha-1}{\alpha}}\times\left[(\alpha-1)^{\frac{1}{\alpha}}+(\alpha-1)^{\frac{1-\alpha}{\alpha}}\right]\times(W+m\delta).$$

Finally, from these two bounds, we derive the desired result. □

**Proposition 2.** *The energy consumption of* SLACK *differs from the optimal one by at most* $m^2 \Delta_{\mathcal{X},n} \frac{\text{OPT}}{W}$*:*

$$0 \leq \frac{E(n,m,\mathcal{X}) - \text{OPT}}{\text{OPT}} \leq \frac{m^2 \Delta_{\mathcal{X},n}}{W}.$$

Analogously to Proposition 1, Proposition 2 provides asymptotic results on SLACK used for optimizing the energy consumption. It is derived directly from Theorems 1 and 2. Further results can be obtained both for the uniform distribution in Corollary 3 and for the exponential distribution in Corollary 4. Intuitively, the result shows that the relative difference between the energy provided by the adapted SLACK algorithm and the optimal energy consumption converges to 0 almost surely, when $n \to +\infty$, with a speed at least $\frac{m^2 \log n}{n^2}$ for the uniform distribution and $\frac{m^2 \log \log n}{n}$ for an exponential distribution.

It is proved in [11] that, almost surely,

$$\limsup_{n \to +\infty} \left( \frac{n \Delta_{\mathcal{U}[0,1],n} - \ln n}{2 \log n} \right) = 1.$$

**Corollary 3.** *When using* SLACK *as a base scheduling algorithm with uniform distribution for the tasks, one has almost surely*

$$\limsup_{n \to +\infty} \left( \frac{E_{\text{SLACK}}(n,m,\mathcal{U}[0,1]) - \text{OPT}}{\text{OPT}} \times \frac{n^2}{2(2+\ln 2)m^2 \log n} \right) \leq 1.$$

The proof is available in the companion research report [6].

As proved in [12], with $\mathcal{E}_1$ the exponential distribution of rate 1, almost surely,

$$\limsup_{n \to +\infty} \left( \frac{\Delta_{\mathcal{E}_1,n}}{\ln \ln n} \right) = 1.$$

The rate $\lambda$ of an exponential distribution is a scaling parameter, so almost surely

$$\limsup_{n \to +\infty} \left( \frac{\lambda \Delta_{\mathcal{E}_\lambda,n}}{\ln \ln n} \right) = 1.$$

**Corollary 4.** *With* SLACK *as a base scheduling algorithm with exponential distribution of rate* $\lambda$ *for the tasks, for any fixed* $m \geq 2$*, one has almost surely*

$$\limsup_{n \to +\infty} \left( \frac{E_{\text{SLACK}}(n,m,\mathcal{E}_\lambda) - \text{OPT}}{\text{OPT}} \times \frac{n}{m^2 \ln \ln n} \right) \leq 1.$$

## 6 Simulations

We first present the simulation setting in Sect. 6.1, before studying the $\delta_j$'s and $\beta_j$'s in Sect. 6.2, and the energy consumption in Sect. 6.3.

### 6.1 Experimental Setting

All the following experiments have been conducted on Python 3.8.10. Two types of instances have been used. Both instances have in common that the platform is composed of $m = 100$ processors.

*Theoretical instances* have been generated using the *random* package. These instances have been generated following commonly used random distributions: the uniform distribution, $\mathcal{U}[0,1]$; the exponential distribution of rate 1, $\mathcal{E}_1$; the distribution of cumulative distribution function $F(x) = x^\alpha$ where $0 < \alpha < \infty$ [14]. These simple distributions correspond to the ones for which there exist convergence results in the literature and they cover a wide range of situations.

*Realistic instances* have been generated using the experimental cumulative distribution functions of actual workloads [13]. These real workloads can be found on the Parallel Workload Archive from the website https://www.cs.huji.ac.il/labs/parallel/workload/. We used 3 specific instances: KIT ForHLR II with 114,355 tasks; NASA Ames iPSC/860 with 18066 tasks; and San Diego Supercomputer Center (SDSC) DataStar with 84907 tasks.

### 6.2 Simulations: Study of $\delta_j$ and $\beta_j$

In this section, we describe the results of our simulations comparing the values of $\delta_j$ and $\beta_j$ (the largest differences between the execution times of the processors and the tasks, as defined in Sect. 3) over the execution of Slack and Lpt.

In Figs. 1 and 2, we can see the evolution of the quantities studied in Sect. 4 when bounding the performance of Slack. The quantities are:

- $\beta_j$ the difference between the largest and the shortest task of pack $j$ (i.e., at step $j$ of the algorithm), it describes the imbalance between consecutive tasks during the execution of the algorithms;
- $\delta_j$ the difference between the largest processor and the shortest processor after step $j$ of the algorithm (i.e., after allocating $j \times m$ tasks), it describes the imbalance between processors during the execution of the algorithms.

With these experiments, we can both investigate the relation we stated in Sect. 4, and investigate the unexplained "wave pattern" presented in [5].

In the case of tasks drawn through a uniform distribution with Fig. 1, we observe that $\delta_j$, the imbalance between processors, alternates between high and low values, in a sort of wave pattern. With a new representation of the pattern, we now present more elements explaining it. This pattern can be explained by the fact that the imbalance created by $m$ consecutive tasks is then canceled by the $m$ following tasks, as they have similar relative differences. Once the imbalance on the processors have decreased, the next $m$ tasks will restore a new but smaller imbalance.

For most other distributions, on Fig. 2, Slack and Lpt perform similarly in terms of makespan, which is characterized by the last value $\delta_{\frac{n}{m}}$. Out of our six

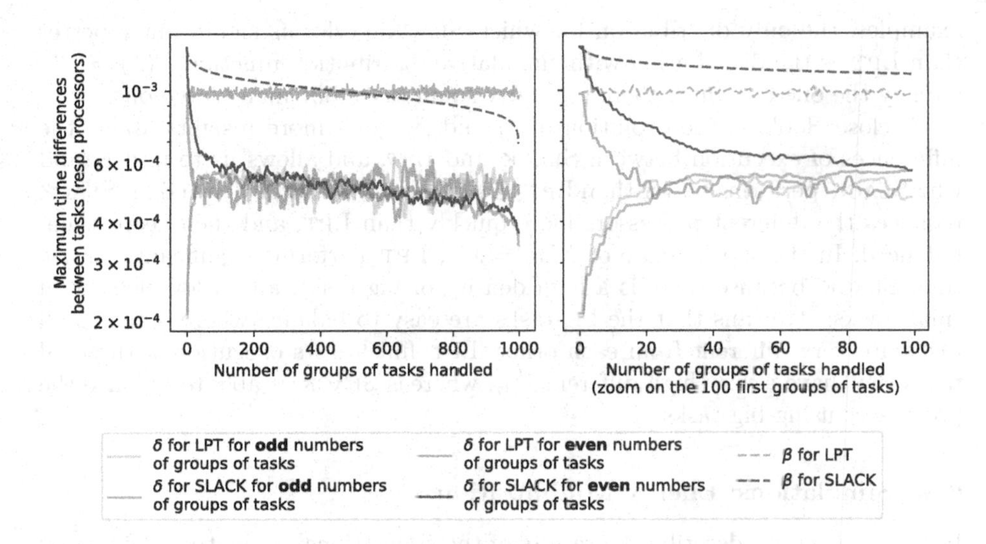


**Fig. 1.** Evolution of $\delta_j$ and $\beta_j$ (as defined in Sect. 3) during the execution of SLACK and LPT with the uniform distribution $\mathcal{U}[0,1]$ for the tasks. Each execution is done with $m = 100$ processors and $n = 100\,000$ tasks. The right graph is a zoomed version of the 100 first values of $\delta_j$ and $\beta_j$. Each point represents the average value of $\delta_j$ (resp. $\beta_j$) over 30 executions.

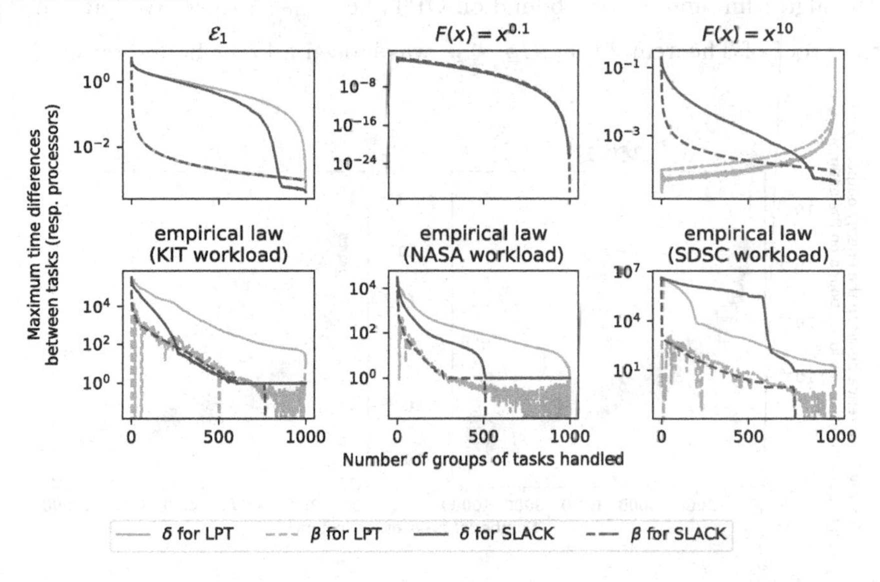


**Fig. 2.** Evolution of $\delta_j$ and $\beta_j$ (as defined in Sect. 3) during the execution of SLACK and LPT with various probability distributions for the tasks. Each execution is done with $m = 100$ processors and $n = 100\,000$ tasks. Each point represents the average value of $\delta_j$ (resp. $\beta_j$) over 30 executions.

examples, the only distribution for which SLACK performs significantly better than LPT is the distribution with cumulative distribution function $F(x) = x^{10}$, namely the one for which there are a few small tasks but many large ones.

A closer look at the evolution of $\delta_j$ and $\beta_j$ gives more insights about the differences of execution between SLACK and LPT, and allows us to understand why SLACK performs better than LPT in some cases. Generally speaking, SLACK balances the different processors more quickly than LPT, and then keeps them balanced. In the specific case of $F(x) = x^{10}$, LPT performs significantly worse than SLACK because there is a high density of big tasks, and a low density of small tasks. It means that the big tasks are easy to balance whereas the small tasks are very different from each other. LPT finishes its execution with small tasks that have a very high difference $\beta_j$, whereas SLACK is able to balance the processors using big tasks.

### 6.3 Simulations: Energy Minimization

In this section, we describe the results of the simulations, evaluating the energy consumed by the schedules of the algorithms derived from LPT and SLACK (as defined in Sect. 3).

We normalize the energy $E$ because the value of $W$ can vary depending on the instance. Instead, we consider the relative difference between the energy found by the algorithm and a lower bound on OPT, i.e., $\frac{E - E_{\frac{W}{m},\dots,\frac{W}{m}}}{E_{\frac{W}{m},\dots,\frac{W}{m}}}$. We have shown in the proof of Theorem 2 that $E_{\frac{W}{m},\dots,\frac{W}{m}}$ was indeed a lower bound on OPT.

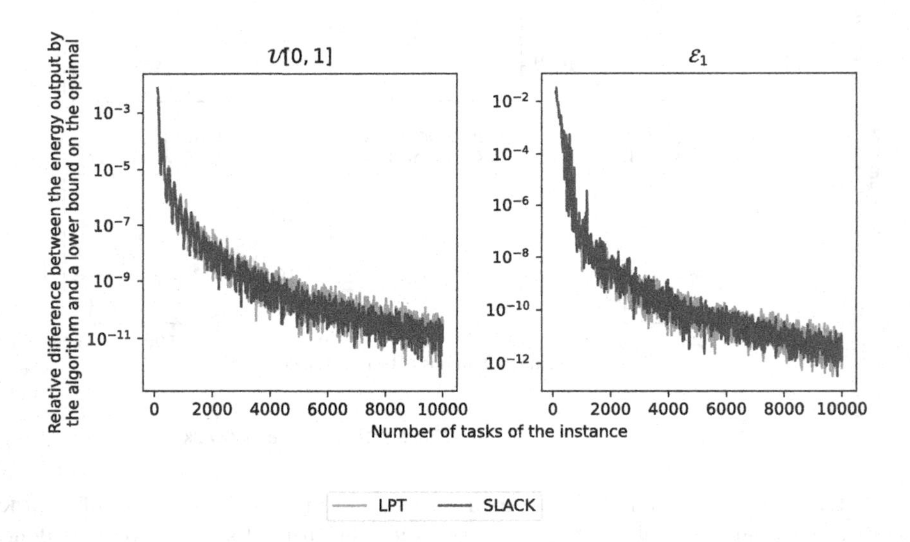


**Fig. 3.** Relative difference between the energy found by SLACK or LPT with the speed strategy described in Theorem 2 and a lower bound on OPT, with various theoretical probability distributions for the tasks. Each execution is done with $m = 100$ processors. Each point represents the average value of energy over 30 executions.

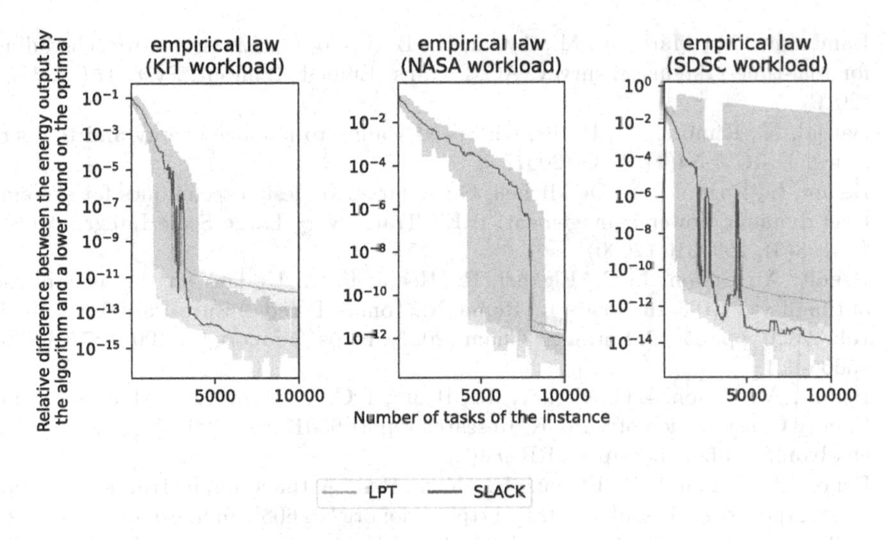


**Fig. 4.** Relative difference between the energy found by SLACK or LPT with the speed strategy described in Theorem 2 and a lower bound on OPT, with various empirical probability distributions for the tasks. For each number of tasks, the execution is repeated 30 times with $m = 100$ processors. The thick lines represent the moving median, while the ribbons extend to the moving minimum and maximum over 45 values.

The main conclusion that we can get from Figs. 3 and 4 is that LPT and SLACK both perform very well on all created instances, both theoretical and realistic. The schedule that the two algorithms output is at most a few percents away from the optimal for very small instances, and the room for improvement rapidly decreases to less than $10^{-8}\%$ for larger instances. It can be noted that SLACK performs better than LPT on average, even if they are both near optimal.

## 7 Conclusion

This paper proposes a bound for SLACK, a recent and efficient heuristic for scheduling independent tasks on homogeneous machines, from which two asymptotic results are derived: on the makespan, with either uniformly or exponentially distributed task costs; and on the energy consumption, thanks to a general mechanism that can adapt algorithms for the makespan to this criterion.

**Data Availibility Statement.** The data that support the findings of this study are openly available in figshare [7].

## References

1. Bairamov, I., Berred, A., Stepanov, A.: Limit results for ordered uniform spacings. Stat. Pap. **51**(1), 227–240 (2010)

2. Bambagini, M., Marinoni, M., Aydin, H., Buttazzo, G.: Energy-aware scheduling for real-time systems: a survey. ACM Trans. Embed. Comput. Syst. **15**(1), 1–34 (2016)
3. Bansal, N., Kimbrel, T., Pruhs, K.: Speed scaling to manage energy and temperature. J. ACM **54**(1), 1–39 (2007)
4. Benini, L., Bogliolo, A., De Micheli, G.: A survey of design techniques for system-level dynamic power management. IEEE Trans. Very Large Scale Integr. (VLSI) Syst. **8**(3), 299–316 (2000)
5. Benoit, A., Canon, L.-C., Elghazi, R., Héam, P.-C.: Update on the asymptotic optimality of LPT. In: Sousa, L., Roma, N., Tomás, P. (eds.) Euro-Par 2021. LNCS, vol. 12820, pp. 55–69. Springer, Cham (2021). https://doi.org/10.1007/978-3-030-85665-6_4
6. Benoit, A., Canon, L.C., Elghazi, R., Héam, P.C.: Asymptotic Performance and Energy Consumption of SLACK. Research report 9501, Inria (2023). https://graal.ens-lyon.fr/~abenoit/papers/RR-9501.pdf
7. Benoit, A., Canon, L-C., Elghazi, R., Héam, P-C.: Artifact and instructions to generate experimental results (2023). https://doi.org/10.6084/m9.figshare.23579472
8. Coffman, E.G., Jr., Lueker, G.S., Kan, R.A.H.G.: Asymptotic methods in the probabilistic analysis of sequencing and packing heuristics. Manage. Sci. **34**(3), 266–290 (1988)
9. Della Croce, F., Scatamacchia, R.: The longest processing time rule for identical parallel machines revisited. J. Schedul. **23**(2), 163–176 (2018). https://doi.org/10.1007/s10951-018-0597-6
10. Czarnul, P., Proficz, J., Krzywaniak, A.: Energy-aware high-performance computing: survey of state-of-the-art tools, techniques, and environments. Sci. Prog. **2019** (2019)
11. Devroye, L.: Laws of the iterated logarithm for order statistics of uniform spacings. Ann. Probab. **9**(5), 860–867 (1981)
12. Devroye, L.: The largest exponential spacing. Utilitas Math. **25**, 303–313 (1984)
13. Feitelson, D.G., Tsafrir, D., Krakov, D.: Experience with using the parallel workloads archive. J. Parallel Distrib. Comp. **74**(10), 2967–2982 (2014)
14. Frenk, J.B.G., Kan, A.H.G.R.: The rate of convergence to optimality of the LPT rule. Discr. Appl. Math. **14**(2), 187–197 (1986)
15. Graham, R.L., Lawler, E.L., Lenstra, J.K., Kan, A.H.G.R.: Optimization and approximation in deterministic sequencing and scheduling: a survey. Ann. Discr. Math. **5**, 287–326 (1979)
16. Graham, R.L.: Bounds on multiprocessing timing anomalies. SIAM J. Appl. Math. **17**(2), 416–429 (1969)
17. Lin, X., Wang, Y., Xie, Q., Pedram, M.: Task scheduling with dynamic voltage and frequency scaling for energy minimization in the mobile cloud computing environment. IEEE Trans. Serv. Comput. **8**(2), 175–186 (2014)
18. Loulou, R.: Tight bounds and probabilistic analysis of two heuristics for parallel processor scheduling. Math. Oper. Res. **9**(1), 142–150 (1984)
19. Piersma, N., Romeijn, H.E.: Parallel machine scheduling: a probabilistic analysis. Naval Res. Logistics (NRL) **43**(6), 897–916 (1996)
20. Pinelis, I.: Order statistics on the spacings between order statistics for the uniform distribution. arXiv preprint arXiv:1909.06406 (2019)
21. Thakkar, A., Chaudhari, K., Shah, M.: A comprehensive survey on energy-efficient power management techniques. Procedia Comput. Sci. **167**, 1189–1199 (2020)

22. Weiser, M., Welch, B., Demers, A., Shenker, S.: Scheduling for reduced CPU energy. In: Imielinski, T., Korth, H.F. (eds.) Mobile Computing. The Kluwer International Series in Engineering and Computer Science, vol. 353, pp. 449–471. Springer, Boston (1994). https://doi.org/10.1007/978-0-585-29603-6_17
23. Yao, F., Demers, A., Shenker, S.: A scheduling model for reduced CPU energy. In: Proceedings of the IEEE 36th Annual Foundations of Computer Science, pp. 374–382 (1995)

# A Poisson-Based Approximation Algorithm for Stochastic Bin Packing of Bernoulli Items

Tomasz Kanas(✉) and Krzysztof Rzadca

Institute of Informatics,
University of Warsaw, Warsaw, Poland
{t.kanas,krzadca}@mimuw.edu.pl

**Abstract.** A cloud scheduler packs tasks onto machines with contradictory goals of (1) using the machines as efficiently as possible while (2) avoiding overloading that might result in CPU throttling or out-of-memory errors. We take a stochastic approach that models the uncertainty of tasks' resource requirements by random variables. We focus on a little-explored case of items, each having a Bernoulli distribution that corresponds to tasks that are either idle or need a certain CPU share. RPAP, our online approximation algorithm, upper-bounds a subset of items by Poisson distributions. Unlike existing algorithms for Bernoulli items that prove the approximation ratio only up to a multiplicative constant, we provide a closed-form expression. We derive RPAPC, a combined approach having the same theoretical guarantees as RPAP. In simulations, RPAPC's results are close to FFR, a greedy heuristic with no worst-case guarantees; RPAPC slightly outperforms FFR on datasets with small items.

**Keywords:** cloud scheduling · stochastic bin packing · stochastic optimization · approximation algorithms

## 1 Introduction

Modern virtualization technologies—virtual machines (VMs) and Linux containers—allow execution in parallel of dozens of independent tasks on a single physical machine. Given the planet-wide scale [2] of the largest public (AWS, Azure, GCP) and private (e.g. Google) clouds, even small improvements in resource utilization slow the growth rate of the hardware fleets and thus save equipment and electricity [2,3,20].

Bin Packing (BP) [13] is perhaps the most fundamental model of datacenter allocation [19,21,22]. In BP, the goal is to pack the given items into as few equally-sized bins as only possible, without exceeding the capacity of any bin. In cloud computing, bins correspond to machines, items to *tasks* (VMs or containers) to allocate and items' sizes—to CPU or memory requirements.

However, there is a fundamental difference between packing boxes onto a truck and Linux containers onto a machine. Boxes' sizes are easy to measure and, barring


J. Cano et al. (Eds.): Euro-Par 2023, LNCS 14100, pp. 96–110, 2023.
https://doi.org/10.1007/978-3-031-39698-4_7

extreme events, unchanging. In contrast, the resource requirements of a task are more difficult to estimate. Tasks are commonly packed by *limits* [6,21,22]: essentially, the to-be-scheduled task declares (sometimes through automation [20]) to the scheduler an upper bound on the resources it might request. Yet, packing by limits is fundamentally inefficient [3]. Even if limits were clairvoyant (set to each task's exact maximal usage), using limits, the scheduler effectively assumes that every task will always consume exactly its maximal usage—which is rarely the case [12]. Even with overcommit [3], utilization remains low [16].

Stochastic Bin Packing (SBP) [11,15] models the uncertainty of tasks' resource requirements by using random variables as items' sizes. Accordingly, the constraint of never overpacking any bin is generalized to a probabilistic one—an upper bound $\alpha$ on the probability that each bin's capacity is exceeded. SBP can represent the cloud allocation problem [5,10,12]: the random variables map to observed or estimated tasks' resource usage; and $\alpha$ maps to a probabilistic Service Level Objective, SLO. Notably, [3] combines declared limits (for new tasks) with estimations of a machine's predicted total usage (for long-running ones); a prototype improved efficiency by 2% on 11,000 production machines in the internal Google cloud. While SBP models have limitations (e.g.: not explicitly modeling variability over time [17], dynamic arrivals and departures [8], or correlations between tasks [4]), we claim that solving a more general problem usually requires at some point solving its more fundamental version.

Perhaps the most restrictive assumption we take is that all the items follow scaled Bernoulli distributions. Such items correspond to tasks that for some fraction of time compute with (approximately) constant intensity, and then idle e.g. waiting for the next request. We claim that Bernoulli items are a reasonable model: e.g., in the Google Cluster Trace [12,23] shows a large task group with CPU requirements resembling the scaled Bernoulli distribution. One can argue that if there were enough tasks in one bin, then, from the Central Limit Theorem, the cumulative distribution of that bin would be close to normal. However, if the tasks are large, few of them fit into a machine, which makes the normal distribution inadequate [12]. Additionally, solving the special case of Bernoulli items could bring us closer to a distributionally-robust solution. From the theoretical perspective, Bernoulli items seem to pose more difficulties than other distributions like Poisson [11] or Gaussian [5,10] (Sect. 2).

**The Contribution of this Paper is the Following:**

- We design Refined Poisson Approximation Packing (RPAP), an online algorithm that finds a viable packing of Bernoulli variables to bins while keeping the overload probability of any bin below $\alpha$. Our algorithm is easy to implement and schedules one item in $\mathcal{O}(\log n)$ time (Sect. 4).
- We prove a closed-form formula of the RPAP approximation ratio, which depends only on the (given) overload probability $\alpha$ (Sect. 6, Eq. 6).
- In simulations, we compare RPAP with [15] and FFR, a heuristic with no worst-case guarantees. We propose RPAPC that combines RPAP with a heuristic, maintaining RPAP's guarantees. Our approaches outperform [15] and are close to FFR; slightly improving upon FFR on datasets with small items.

To the best of our knowledge, our paper shows the first proof of a closed-form formula for the approximation ratio of an algorithm for Stochastic Bin Packing with Bernoulli items ([15] shows only asymptotics) and the first experimental evaluation of SBP algorithms on Bernoulli items.

## 2 Related Work

We focus below on theoretical approaches to stochastic bin packing. SBP is a stochastic extension of a classic combinatorial optimization problem, an approach called stochastic optimization [11]. Works on SBP usually assume that all items' sizes follow a known distribution. When items have *normal* distribution, Breitgand and Epstein [5] show a $(2+\epsilon)$-approximation algorithm, and an offline 2-approximation; Cohen et al. [10] show that First Fit is 9/4-approximation; Martinovic and Selch [18] show improved lower bounds and discuss linearization techniques; Yan et al. [25] propose a new metric of bin load, develop algorithms and perform experiments on synthetic and real data. Other item distributions are also considered, for example, Goel and Indyk [11] propose a PTAS for *Poisson* and *exponential* items.

The *Bernoulli* distribution seems to be more difficult to work with. For a bin, computing the overflow probability is $\mathcal{O}(n)$ for Poisson and Gaussian distributions; yet it is #P hard for Bernoulli [15], i.e. as hard as counting the number of solutions of an NP-complete problem (which is hypothesized to be harder than finding any solution). Furthermore, a standard approach to stochastic bin packing is to calculate each stochastic item's *effective size*, which is then used by a deterministic packing algorithm. For Poisson and normal items, one can find an effective size that gives an $\mathcal{O}(1)$-approximation algorithm [7]. However, for Bernoulli items, any effective size-based algorithm has an $\Omega(\alpha^{-1/2})$ approximation ratio, where $\alpha$ is the maximal overflow probability [15]. [11] shows a QPTAS for *Bernoulli* items. [15] shows an $\mathcal{O}\left(\sqrt{\frac{\log \alpha^{-1}}{\log \log \alpha^{-1}}}\right)$-approximation and $\mathcal{O}(\epsilon^{-1})$-approximation for an $\epsilon$-relaxed problem.

**Our Approach Compared to Kleinberg et al.** [15]**:** Like [15], our algorithm also splits items into subgroups and similarly packs the small items (Sect. 5.1). In contrast, for the most complex case of the standard items we use a Poisson approximation (Sect. 5.2), while they use effective bandwidth and probabilistic inequalities. Moreover, there is only asymptotic analysis of the approximation factor in [15], which allows them to hide in the $\mathcal{O}$ notation the multiplicative constant arising from splitting items into subgroups. We managed to avoid such multiplicative constant by proving the upper bound of the expected value of any correctly packed bin (Lemma 6). Moreover, to bound the approximation constant, we proved a technical inequality on the inverse of Poisson CDF (Lemma 11). In contrast, [15] used results on antichains to optimize the asymptotic approximation factor of their algorithm.

## 3 Problem Formulation and Notation

We are given a sequence of items $X_1, \ldots, X_n$ and an infinite sequence of identical bins of capacity 1. The goal is to find a *viable* assignment of items to bins that uses the minimal number of bins. We assume that all items are random variables that follow *scaled Bernoulli* distributions. As in [11,15], we assume that random variables are independent. Our problem is thus clairvoyant, as we receive full information about an item on submission, although the sizes remain stochastic, in contrast to an alternative model in which a size is drawn from a certain distribution and then does not change.

We denote the Bernoulli distribution by $\text{Ber}(p)$ and the Poisson distribution by $\text{Poi}(\lambda)$. We define *scaled* Bernoulli $\text{Ber}(p, s)$ and Poisson $\text{Poi}(\lambda, s)$ distributions, where $s > 0$ is the *size*: $sX$ is scaled-Bernoulli distributed ($sX \sim \text{Ber}(p, s)$) when $X \sim \text{Ber}(p)$ (Poisson is defined analogically). For example, if an item $X_i \sim Ber(p, \frac{1}{3})$ then the item's size is equal to $\frac{1}{3}$ with probability $p$ and 0 with probability $1 - p$.

For a random variable $X$, $F_X$ denotes its cumulative distribution function (CDF), $F_X(t) = \mathbb{P}(X \leq t)$. We denote $Q$ as the Poisson CDF: $\mathbb{P}(\text{Poi}(\lambda) \leq x) = Q(x, \lambda)$; and $Q^{-1}(x, \gamma)$ as its inverse with respect to the second argument.

We assume that items $X_i \sim \text{Ber}(p_i, s_i)$, where $p_i \in (0, 1]$, and $s_i \leq s_{\max}$. $s_{\max} \in (0, 1]$ is an additional parameter that increases the versatility of our results. In the general case, $s_{\max} = 1$ (an item always fits in a single bin).

We denote the set of items in $j$-th bin by $\mathcal{B}_j$, their sum by $B_j$ and by $\alpha > 0$ the *maximal overflow probability*. An assignment is *viable* if for every bin $j$ the probability of exceeding the bin's capacity is at most $\alpha$, $\mathbb{P}(\sum_{i \in \mathcal{B}_j} X_i > 1) \leq \alpha$.

We argue that $\alpha$ should be treated as a constant in the context of the data center allocation, where $\alpha$ corresponds to the service level objective (SLO) negotiated between the provider and their clients. As only very rarely can the machine be overloaded, usually, there are only a few groups of items with fixed and small SLO values (e.g., $0.01, 0.005, 0.001$). We thus also assume that $0 < \alpha \leq \frac{1}{2}$.

We call a BP algorithm Any-Fit if it does not open a new bin if the current item fits in any already opened bin [9] (e.g. First Fit or Best Fit). We use Any-Fit algorithms as a building block for RPAP, but RPAP *is not* Any-Fit.

## 4 Refined Poisson Approximation Packing Algorithm

Refined Poisson Approximation Packing (RPAP, Algorithm 1), separates items into three disjoint groups. Each group is packed separately into a disjoint set of bins. We reduce the packing of each group to BP and pack with an Any-Fit algorithm. In this section, we describe the algorithm; the following Sect. 5 proves the viability of the allocation; and Sect. 6 proves the approximation ratio.

To separate items into three groups, we introduce two additional parameters: $p_{\max} \in (0, 1)$, $s_{\min} \in (0, s_{\max})$ (we show in Sect. 6.2 how to choose the values that minimize the approximation ratio). The groups are defined as follows:

**Algorithm 1:** Refined Poisson Approximation Packing (RPAP)

**Using** : PackAnyFit(*id, size*) method that packs item id with an Any-Fit algorithm to a bin of size 1.

1 ConfidentBins := EmptyPacking;
2 MinorBins := EmptyPacking;
3 $k_{\min} := \lfloor 1/s_{\max} \rfloor$;
4 $k_{\max} := \lceil 1/s_{\min} \rceil - 1$;
5 **for each** $k \in \{k_{\min}, \ldots, k_{\max}\}$ **:**
6 | $\lambda_k := Q^{-1}(k+1, 1-\alpha)$;
7 | StandardBins[$k$] := EmptyPacking;
8 $\mu_0 := (2\alpha + s_{\min} - \sqrt{s_{\min}^2 + 4\alpha s_{\min}})/2\alpha$;
9 **for each** *item i* **:**
10 | **if** $p_i > p_{\max}$ **then**
11 | | ConfidentBins.PackAnyFit($i, s_i$);
12 | **else if** $s_i \leq s_{\min}$ **then**
13 | | MinorBins.PackAnyFit($i, p_i s_i/\mu_0$);
14 | **else**
15 | | $k := \lfloor 1/s_i \rfloor$;
16 | | StandardBins[$k$].PackAnyFit($i, \log(1/(1-p_i))/\lambda_k$);
17 **return**: (ConfidentBins, MinorBins, StandardBins[$k_{\min}$], ..., StandardBins[$k_{\max}$])

- *Confident* items have non-zero load with high probability: $p > p_{\max}$.
- *Minor* items are small: $s \leq s_{\min}$, $p \leq p_{\max}$.
- *Standard* items are the remaining items: $s_{\min} < s \leq s_{\max}$, $p \leq p_{\max}$.

The algorithm proceeds as follows. Confident items have large probabilities, so we round their probabilities up to 1 and pack them by their sizes (line 11). Minor items are small, so they have small variances because the variance of $X \sim \mathrm{Ber}(p, s)$ is $s^2 p(1-p)$. Intuitively it means that with high probability small items are close to their mean. Thus, we pack them (line 13) by their means scaled by some factor $\mu_0$ (defined in line 8).

The core idea of our algorithm is to approximate the remaining, *standard*, items by Poisson variables. The problem of packing Poisson variables turns out to be equivalent to BP. We later prove that we can upper bound a Ber($p$) variable by a Poi($\log(1/(1-p))$) variable. As the items are *scaled* Bernoulli variables, we also use scaled Poisson variables, but to reduce the problem to BP, we need these sizes to be equal. Thus, we additionally group standard items into subgroups with similar sizes and round their sizes up to the upper bound of such subgroup (line 16: $k$ is the subgroup and $\lambda_k$ scales all items' sizes in that group).

## 5 Proof of Correctness

As RPAP packs the three groups into three disjoint sets of bins, we prove the correctness of the allocation case by case: confident and minor items in Sect. 5.1; and standard items in Sect. 5.2.

### 5.1 Confident and Minor Items

**Lemma 1.** *The packing of confident and minor items is viable.*

*Proof.* Confident items are packed by their sizes $s_i$, so the sum of sizes in any bin $\mathcal{B}$ is $\sum_i s_i \leq 1$, and the probability of overflow is $\mathbb{P}(B > 1) = 0 < \alpha$.

For minor items we have $\forall_i s_i \leq s_{\min}$ and we are packing them by their expected value $s_i p_i$, so if $\mathbb{E}(B) = \sum_i s_i p_i \leq \mu_0 < 1$, then from Chebyshev inequality:

$$\mathbb{P}(B > 1) \leq \frac{\mathrm{Var}(B)}{(1 - \mathbb{E}(B))^2} = \frac{\sum_i s_i^2 p_i (1 - p_i)}{(1 - \mathbb{E}(B))^2} < \frac{s_{\min} \sum_i s_i p_i}{(1 - \mathbb{E}(B))^2} \leq s_{\min} \frac{\mu_0}{(1 - \mu_0)^2}.$$

The viability of the packing follows from $\mu_0$ (Algorithm 1, line 8) being a solution of the equation: $\frac{(1-\mu_0)^2}{\mu_0} = \frac{s_{\min}}{\alpha}$. □

### 5.2 Standard Items

To pack standard items, we upper-bound the probability of overflow by the tail of the Poisson distribution. First, we separate items into subgroups, such that the $k$-th group consists of items whose sizes are in the interval $s_i \in \left(\frac{1}{k+1}, \frac{1}{k}\right]$, $k \in \{k_{\min}, \ldots, k_{\max}\}$ (Algorithm 1, lines 3–4). Inside a single subgroup, we round items' sizes up to the upper bound of the interval. Every subgroup is packed into a separate set of bins.

The proof uses the following two lemmas (all proofs are in the appendix [1]):

**Lemma 2.** *If $X \sim \mathrm{Ber}(p)$, $Y \sim \mathrm{Poi}(\lambda)$, and $\lambda \geq \ln\left(\frac{1}{1-p}\right)$, then $\forall_t F_X(t) \geq F_Y(t)$.*

**Lemma 3.** *If $X_1, X_2, Y_1, Y_2$ are discrete independent random variables with countable support and $\forall_t F_{X_i}(t) \geq F_{Y_i}(t)$ for $i \in \{1, 2\}$, then $\forall_t F_{X_1+X_2}(t) \geq F_{Y_1+Y_2}(t)$.*

The following lemma shows that a viable packing of Poisson variables is also a viable packing of the original Bernoulli variables and is a direct consequence of the above lemmas.

**Lemma 4.** *Let $X_i \sim \mathrm{Ber}(p_i, s_i)$, $P_i \sim \mathrm{Poi}\left(\ln\left(\frac{1}{1-p_i}\right), \bar{s}_i\right)$ for $i \in \{1, \ldots, m\}$ be independent and $\forall_i \bar{s}_i \geq s_i$. Moreover let $P = \sum_{i=1}^m P_i$ and $B = \sum_{i=1}^m X_i$. Then $\mathbb{P}(B > 1) \leq \mathbb{P}(P > 1)$.*

The following lemma shows that BP of scaled Poisson variables by their means is viable:

**Lemma 5.** *Packing of scaled Poisson variables $P_i \sim \mathrm{Poi}(\lambda_i, s)$ is viable if and only if it is correct packing of their means $\lambda_i$ with bin size $Q^{-1}(\lfloor \frac{1}{s} \rfloor + 1, 1 - \alpha)$, i.e. for every $\mathcal{B}_j$: $\mathbb{P}\left(\sum_{i \in \mathcal{B}_j} P_i > 1\right) \leq \alpha \iff \sum_{i \in \mathcal{B}_j} \lambda_i \leq Q^{-1}\left(\lfloor \frac{1}{s} \rfloor + 1, 1 - \alpha\right)$.*

*Proof.* As variables $P_i$ are independent, the load of any bin $P = \sum_{i \in \mathcal{B}} P_i$ is also a scaled Poisson variable $P \sim \text{Poi}(\lambda, s)$, where $\lambda = \sum_{i \in \mathcal{B}} \lambda_i$. We have $\frac{1}{s}P \sim \text{Poi}(\lambda)$, so $\mathbb{P}(P \leq 1) = \mathbb{P}\left(\frac{1}{s}P \leq \lfloor \frac{1}{s} \rfloor\right) = Q\left(\lfloor \frac{1}{s} \rfloor + 1, \lambda\right)$ and the thesis follows from applying $Q^{-1}\left(\lfloor \frac{1}{s} \rfloor + 1, \cdot\right)$. □

# 6 Approximation Ratio

We start in Sect. 6.1 by a formula for the approximation ratio of RPAP. Then, in Sect. 6.2, we optimize the approximation ratio by adjusting parameters: the least-probable confident item $p_{\max}$ and the largest minor item $s_{\min}$.

## 6.1 Proof of the Approximation Ratio

We prove the approximation factor by lower bounding the expected value of an average bin for any packing produced by RPAP, and upper bounding this average bin expected value for any viable packing, in particular the optimal one.

We will prove the upper bound by induction over the number of items in a bin. We need a stronger induction assumption: we want to reward adding items that increase the expected load of a bin *without increasing the overflow probability.* We model that by introducing a *discount function*: $C(X) = \sum_{x \in [0,1]} (1-x)\mathbb{P}(X = x)$ ($X$ has finite support, so the sum is well-defined).

**Lemma 6.** *Assume that* $\forall_{i \in \mathcal{B}} X_i \sim \text{Ber}(p_i, s_i)$, $s_i \leq 1$ *are independent random variables. If* $B = \sum_{i \in \mathcal{B}} X_i$, *satisfies* $\mathbb{P}(B > 1) \leq \alpha < 1$, *then* $\mathbb{E}(B) \leq \frac{1+\alpha}{1-\alpha}$.

*Proof.* Without loss of generality, assume that $\mathcal{B} = \{1, \ldots, N\}$, and denote $S_n = \sum_{i=1}^{n} X_i$. We proceed by induction over $n$, with the following assumption:

$$\mathbb{E}(S_n) \leq \frac{1}{1-\alpha}\Bigg(1 + \mathbb{P}(S_n > 1) - C(S_n)\Bigg).$$

Notice that it is enough to prove the induction, as $C(S_n) \geq 0$.

**Basis of Induction:** for $n = 0$ we have $\mathbb{P}(S_0 = 0) = 1$ so $\mathbb{P}(S_0 > 1) = 0$, $C(S_0) = 1$ and the thesis follows.

**Inductive Step:** Let us denote $S_{n+1} = S_n + X$, $X \sim \text{Ber}(p, s)$. From the induction assumption

$$\mathbb{E}(S_{n+1}) = \mathbb{E}(S_n) + ps \leq \frac{1}{1-\alpha}\Bigg(1 + \mathbb{P}(S_n > 1) - C(S_n)\Bigg) + ps,$$

so it suffices to show that

$$\mathbb{P}(S_n > 1) - C(S_n) + (1-\alpha)ps \leq \mathbb{P}(S_{n+1} > 1) - C(S_{n+1}).$$

We have recursive formulas:

$$\mathbb{P}(S_{n+1} > 1) = \mathbb{P}(S_n + X > 1) = \mathbb{P}(S_n > 1) + p\mathbb{P}(S_n \in (1-s, 1]);$$

$$C(S_{n+1}) = (1-p)C(S_n) + p \sum_{x \in [0,1]} (1-x)\mathbb{P}(S_n = x - s)$$

$$= C(S_n) - p \sum_{x \in (1-s,1]} (1-x)\mathbb{P}(S_n = x) - ps\mathbb{P}(S_n \in [0, 1-s]).$$

So after simplifications, we arrive at the inequality:

$$(1-\alpha)s \leq \mathbb{P}(S_n \in (1-s, 1]) + s\mathbb{P}(S_n \in [0, 1-s]) + \sum_{x \in (1-s,1]} (1-x)\mathbb{P}(S_n = x) = s\mathbb{P}(S_n \in [0, 1]) + A$$

where

$$A = (1-s)\mathbb{P}(S_n \in (1-s, 1]) + \sum_{x \in (1-s,1]} (1-x)\mathbb{P}(S_n = x) \geq 0$$

what completes the induction step, as $\mathbb{P}(S_n \in [0, 1]) \geq 1 - \alpha$. □

Next, we will prove the lower bound on the average expected value of all bins in packing produced by RPAP. Recall that in all item groups, we used at some point an Any-Fit algorithm, so we will need this slightly stronger version of the classic lemma [9]:

**Lemma 7.** *Assume that an Any-Fit algorithm packed real values $x_1, \ldots, x_n$ into bins $\mathcal{B}_1, \ldots, \mathcal{B}_m$ where $m \geq 2$. Then $\frac{1}{m}\sum_{j=1}^{m}\sum_{i \in \mathcal{B}_j} x_i > \frac{1}{2}$*

*Proof.* Denote $B_j := \sum_{i \in \mathcal{B}_j} x_i$. An Any-Fit algorithm opens a new bin only if the current item does not fit into any already open bin, so $\forall_j \forall_{l \neq j} B_j + B_l > 1$. If $m$ is even then $\sum_{j=1}^{m} B_j > \frac{m}{2}$, and the lemma is proved. If $m$ is odd then

$$2\sum_{j=1}^{m} B_j = \sum_{j=1}^{m-1} B_j + \sum_{j=2}^{m} B_j + B_1 + B_m > 2\frac{m-1}{2} + 1 = m.$$

□

As the lemma above does not hold for the special case with a single bin, we proceed with the proof for the typical case of at least two bins and deal with the special case directly in the proof of Theorem 1. We denote the average expected value of bins $\mathcal{B}_1, \ldots, \mathcal{B}_m$ by $\mathrm{AE}(\mathcal{B}) = \frac{1}{m}\sum_{j=1}^{m}\sum_{i \in \mathcal{B}_j} p_i s_i$. The following three lemmas are very similar and follow easily from the Lemma 7, so we will prove only the last (most complex) one.

**Lemma 8.** *If $\mathcal{B}_1, \ldots, \mathcal{B}_m$, $m \geq 2$ are bins with the confident items, then their average expected value fulfills $\mathrm{AE}(\mathcal{B}) > \frac{p_{\max}}{2}$.*

**Lemma 9.** *If $\mathcal{B}_1, \ldots, \mathcal{B}_m$, $m \geq 2$ are bins with the minor items, then their average expected value fulfills* $\mathrm{AE}(\mathcal{B}) > \frac{\mu_0}{2}$.

**Lemma 10.** *If $\mathcal{B}_1, \ldots, \mathcal{B}_m$, $m \geq 2$ are bins with the standard items of the $k$-th subgroup, then their average expected value fulfills* $\mathrm{AE}(\mathcal{B}) > \frac{\lambda_k(1-p_{\max})}{2(k+1)}$.

*Proof.* We packed the standard items of the $k$-th subgroup by $\frac{1}{\lambda_k}\ln\left(\frac{1}{1-p_i}\right)$ (Algorithm 1, line 16). For any such item $X_i \sim \mathrm{Ber}(p_i, s_i)$ we have $s_i > \frac{1}{k+1}$ and $\ln\left(\frac{1}{1-p_i}\right) \leq \frac{p_i}{1-p_i} \leq \frac{k+1}{1-p_{\max}} p_i s_i$. So from Lemma 7:

$$\frac{m}{2} < \frac{1}{\lambda_k} \sum_{j=1}^{m} \sum_{i \in \mathcal{B}_j} \ln\left(\frac{1}{1-p_i}\right) \leq \frac{k+1}{\lambda_k(1-p_{\max})} \sum_{j=1}^{m} \sum_{i \in \mathcal{B}_j} p_i s_i.$$

□

Additionally, we need the following result (proof in [1]) to find $k$ for which $\frac{\lambda_k}{k+1}$ is minimal:

**Lemma 11.** *For $\beta \in \left[\frac{1}{2}, 1\right)$ and $k \in \mathbb{N}$, $k \geq 2$: $Q^{-1}(k, \beta) \leq \frac{k}{k+1} Q^{-1}(k+1, \beta)$.*

Summing up Lemmas 8, 9, 10, 11 and using the expression for $\lambda_k$ (Algorithm 1 line 6) we get:

**Corollary 1.** *The average expected value of the bins in the subgroups having at least 2 bins is lower bounded by*

$$\mu_{\min} := \frac{1}{2} \min\left(p_{\max}, \mu_0, (1-p_{\max})\lambda_{\min}\right) \tag{1}$$

*where*

$$\lambda_{\min} = \frac{1}{\left\lfloor \frac{1}{s_{\max}} \right\rfloor + 1} Q^{-1}\left(\left\lfloor \frac{1}{s_{\max}} \right\rfloor + 1, 1-\alpha\right) \tag{2}$$

**Theorem 1.** *If RPAP packed items $X_1, \ldots, X_n$ to $M$ bins, and the optimal packing uses $OPT$ bins then $M \leq C \cdot OPT + k_{\max} - k_{\min} + 3$, where $C$ is the (asymptotic) approximation constant and equals $C = \frac{1+\alpha}{(1-\alpha)\mu_{\min}}$.*

*Proof.* First, let us consider only the items that belong to the subgroups that were packed into at least 2 bins by RPAP. Without loss of generality let us assume that those are the items $X_1, \ldots, X_m$. Let us denote the number of bins those items were packed to by $M'$, the number of bins in the optimal packing of those items by $OPT'$, and their total expected value by $S = \sum_{i=1}^{m} p_i s_i$. Then from the Lemma 6 and Corollary 1:

$$\frac{1}{OPT'} S \leq \frac{1+\alpha}{(1-\alpha)}, \quad \frac{1}{M'} S \geq \mu_{\min}, \quad M' \leq \frac{1+\alpha}{(1-\alpha)\mu_{\min}} OPT' \leq C \cdot OPT.$$

Finally, notice that we divided the items into $k_{\max} - k_{\min} + 3$ subgroups, so $M - M' \leq k_{\max} - k_{\min} + 3$, which is a constant and thus $M'$ is asymptotically equivalent to $M$. □

### 6.2 Optimization of the Approximation Ratio

Recall that the approximation constant depends on the values of parameters $p_{\max}$ and $s_{\min}$. To minimize the approximation constant $C = \frac{1+\alpha}{(1-\alpha)\mu_{\min}}$, we need to maximize the formula for $\mu_{\min}$ (Eq. 1). In case of $p_{\max}$, it comes down to solving the equation: $p_{\max} = (1 - p_{\max})\lambda_{\min}$, thus the optimal value is

$$p_{\max} = \frac{\lambda_{\min}}{1 + \lambda_{\min}} \tag{3}$$

To optimize $s_{\min}$, notice that the expression for $\lambda_{\min}$ (2) does not depend on $s_{\min}$, so we can take arbitrarily small $s_{\min}$ so that

$$\mu_0 = \frac{2\alpha + s_{\min} - \sqrt{s_{\min}^2 + 4\alpha s_{\min}}}{2\alpha} \xrightarrow{s_{\min}\to 0} 1.$$

In particular, it is enough to take $s_{\min}$ small enough to make $\mu_0 \geq p_{\max}$. Solving this inequality for $s_{\min}$ results in:

$$s_{\min} \leq \frac{\alpha(1 - p_{\max})^2}{p_{\max}}. \tag{4}$$

After such optimizations, we get the approximation constant:

$$C = 2\frac{1+\alpha}{1-\alpha}\frac{1+\lambda_{\min}}{\lambda_{\min}} \tag{5}$$

We recall that $C$ depends only on $\alpha$, as $\lambda_{\min}$ (Eq. 2) depends on $\alpha$ and $s_{\max}$, but $s_{\max} \leq 1$. In the general case with $s_{\max} = 1$, we get

$$C = 2\frac{1+\alpha}{1-\alpha}\left(1 + \frac{2}{Q^{-1}(2, 1-\alpha)}\right). \tag{6}$$

Values of $C$ vary considerably depending on the values of $\alpha$ and $s_{\max}$. For example for $\alpha = 0.1$ and $s_{\max} = 0.25$: $C \approx 7.47$, for $\alpha = 0.01$ and $s_{\max} = 1$: $C \approx 29.52$, while for $s_{\max} = 1$ and $\alpha = 0.001$: $C \approx 90.29$.

To investigate asymptotics of $C$ as $\alpha \to 0$, we need to investigate the asymptotic behavior of $\frac{1}{\lambda_{\min}}$. Expanding $Q^{-1}(a, z)$ near $z = 1$ with $Q^{-1}(a, z) = (-(z-1)\Gamma(a+1))^{1/a} + \mathcal{O}((z-1)^{2/a})$ [24],

$$C \sim \frac{1}{\lambda_{\min}} \sim \frac{1}{Q^{-1}\left(\left\lfloor \frac{1}{s_{\max}} \right\rfloor + 1, 1-\alpha\right)} = \mathcal{O}\left(\alpha^{-\frac{1}{\left\lfloor \frac{1}{s_{\max}} \right\rfloor + 1}}\right) = \mathcal{O}\left(\sqrt[\lfloor 1/s_{\max} \rfloor + 1]{1/\alpha}\right)$$

and in the general case with $s_{\max} = 1$, we get $C = \mathcal{O}\left(\sqrt{1/\alpha}\right)$.

The resulting asymptotics is worse than Kleinberg's [15] $\mathcal{O}\left(\sqrt{\frac{\log(1/\alpha)}{\log\log(1/\alpha)}}\right)$. However, we recall that the asymptotic analysis in [15] hides the multiplicative constant arising from splitting items into subgroups. Thus, the exact approximation ratio of their algorithm is better than ours most likely only for very small $\alpha$ values. In cloud computing, the SLOs are usually not greater than 4 nines (corresponding to $\alpha \geq 0.0001$) thus our analysis most likely results in a better approximation constant for $\alpha$ relevant to the field.

## 7 Dependence on the Maximal Overflow Probability

From the theoretical perspective, the dependence of the approximation constant on $\alpha$ is not perfect, especially when for other distributions, like Poisson or normal, there are approximation algorithms whose constant does not depend on $\alpha$ [5,10] (for the Bernoulli distribution no such algorithm is known). [15] prove that any algorithm based on a single *effective size* cannot achieve a better approximation constant than $\Omega(\alpha^{-1/2})$. The following theorem shows that the family of Any-Fit algorithms (not using the effective size approach) has the same upper bound. We start with a technical lemma (proof in [1]).

**Lemma 12.** *If* $X_1, X_2, \ldots, X_n \sim \mathrm{Ber}(2\alpha)$ *independent, then there exists* $n = \Omega(\alpha^{-1/2})$ *for which* $\mathbb{P}(\sum_{i=1}^{n} X_i \leq 1) \geq 1 - \alpha$.

**Theorem 2.** *Every Any-Fit for scaled Bernoulli trials has* $\Omega(\alpha^{-1/2})$ *approximation ratio.*

*Proof.* Let us fix the value of $\alpha' = \alpha + \epsilon$ for an arbitrarily small $\epsilon$. We consider the variables $X_i \sim \mathrm{Ber}(\alpha', 1 - \epsilon_{2i-1})$, $Y_i \sim \mathrm{Ber}(1, \epsilon_{2i})$, where $\epsilon_1 = \sqrt{\alpha}$, $\epsilon_i = \epsilon_{i-1} - \frac{\sqrt{\alpha}}{2^{i+2}}$. Then, we can pack $\Omega(\alpha^{-1/2})$ items $Y_i$ to a single bin, as taking the first $\alpha^{-1/2}$ of such items requires the capacity of at most $\alpha^{-1/2} \cdot \sqrt{\alpha} = 1$. Similarly, from the Lemma 12 we can pack $\Omega(\alpha^{-1/2})$ items $X_i$ to a single bin.

Let us now consider the case when those items appear on the input in the order $X_1, Y_1, X_2, Y_2, \ldots$. Using induction, we prove that every Any-Fit algorithm packs into the $i$-th bin just two items, $X_i, Y_i$. First, for every $i$, $X_i$ and $Y_i$ fit into one bin, because $1 - \epsilon_{2i-1} + \epsilon_{2i} < 1$. It is easy to calculate that no further item fits into the bin with items $X_i$ and $Y_i$. □

## 8 Evaluation by Simulations

We study RPAP and derived algorithms in the average case by comparing it with our modification of FF: First Fit Rounded (FFR), and our implementation of Kleinberg et al. [15].

FFR rounds up items' sizes to the integer multiple of $\epsilon > 0$, i.e. finds the smallest $k$ such that $\hat{s} := k\epsilon \geq s$ and packs the rounded items using FF. We cannot compare RPAP with First Fit, because First Fit computes overflow probabilities, which is #P-hard for sums of scaled Bernoulli variables [15]. Yet, for instances with few very small items (i.e. comparable to $\epsilon$), the results of FFR should be close to the results of FF. In our experiments, we take $\epsilon = 10^{-4}$.

We do not suspect RPAP to perform well compared to FFR, as RPAP was designed for theoretical purposes, so we also analyze a derived algorithm, the RPAP Combined (RPAPC). RPAPC separates the items into the same groups as RPAP, but within each group, it packs an item into the first bin according to RPAP or FFR. RPAPC in principle works like RPAP with First-Fit as an Any-Fit algorithm. However, when an item does not fit into a bin, RPAPC, just like FFR, approximates the probability of the overflow by rounding up items'

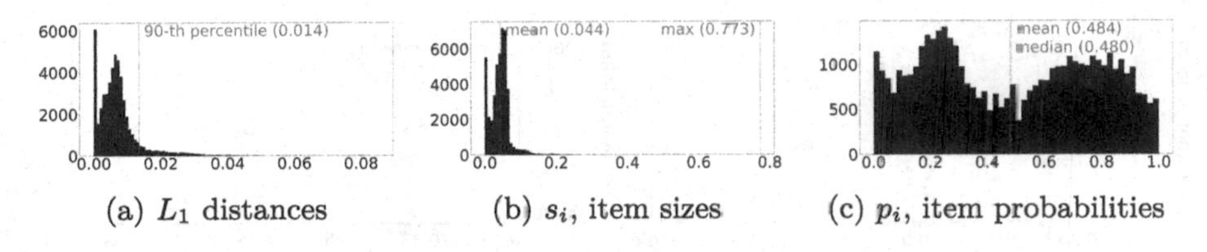


(a) $L_1$ distances (b) $s_i$, item sizes (c) $p_i$, item probabilities

**Fig. 1.** PDFs of items' metrics in *Google* dataset. (a) is a PDF of pair-wise $L_1$ distances between the CDFs of the derived Bernoulli items and the original data.

sizes to the integer multiple of $\epsilon$. This allows us to pack some items that RPAP would not pack because of the upper bounds we made for the proofs. Notice, that this means that RPAPC opens a new bin only if the current item does not fit into any already open bin in its group, so the Lemma 7 holds and from it follows the rest of the Sect. 6.1 and the following corollary:

**Corollary 2.** *RPAPC is an approximation algorithm with an approximation constant not greater than RPAP's.*

We also compare our algorithms against Kleinberg et.al. [15] and against its combined version (KleinbergC)—designed analogically as RPAPC.

As cloud schedulers work with large volumes of tasks, we are interested in analyzing performance on large instances: we performed experiments with $n = 5000$ items. The values of parameters $s_{\min}$ and $p_{\max}$ for RPAP were set according to the formulas (3) and (4) to show how RPAP performs without optimizing for a particular dataset. Kleinberg's algorithm does not have any parameters that could be optimized. For RPAPC we tuned $s_{\min}$ and $p_{\max}$ with respect to $\alpha$, $s_{\max}$ and a dataset (as cloud workload is generally stable over time, schedulers are typically tuned for the standard workload). To tune, we created new (smaller) instances for every combination of $\alpha$ and $s_{\max}$ and then did a grid search.

We tested $\alpha \in \{0.1, 0.01, 0.001\}$ and $s_{\max} \in \{1, 0.75, 0.5, 0.33, 0.25\}$. Each dot on a plot is a median from 10 experiments (each having the same parameter values but a different instance), then normalized by dividing by the average expected value of an item in the dataset. The (very short) vertical lines are the minimum and maximum of those 10 experiments—results are stable over instances. The lines connecting the dots are introduced for readability.

We generated 3 datasets. The *uniform* dataset is sampled from the uniform distribution: the sizes are sampled from the $(0, s_{\max}]$ interval, and the probabilities from $(0, 1]$. In the *normal* dataset, sizes are sampled from the normal distribution $N(0.1, 1)$, truncated to the $(0, s_{\max}]$ interval, while the probabilities are sampled from the uniform distribution on the $(0, 1]$ interval. Its results were very similar to the results for the uniform dataset, so we omit them. The *Google* dataset is derived from [23]. We started with the instantaneous CPU usage dataset [12]. For every task, we calculated the scaled Bernoulli distribution that is the closest to the task's empirical CPU usage (as measured by the $L_1$ distance between CDFs). Finally, we filtered out the 10% of items that had the highest distance from the original data (Fig. 1a), in order not to experiment

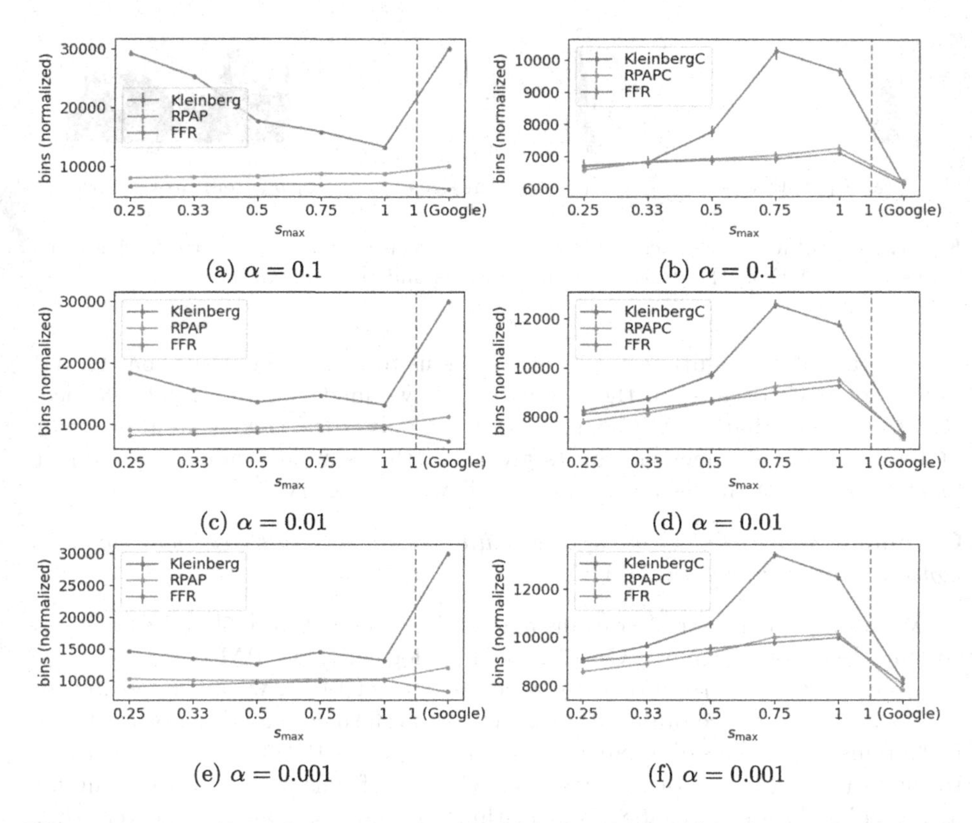


**Fig. 2.** Number of bins the items were packed into for *Uniform* (the first 5 columns) and *Google* (last column) instances, by the original (left) and combined (right) algorithms. Each point is a median of 10 instances. Bars show a minimum and maximum of 10 instances.

on tasks for which the Bernoulli approximation is the least exact. As on *Google*, a vast majority of items is small (Fig. 1b), results for different $s_{\max}$ are very similar, we only show $s_{\max} = 1$. Figure 2 shows results.

As expected, both RPAP and Kleinberg algorithms produce significantly worse results than FFR for all datasets (with *Google* being particularly unsatisfactory). In contrast, RPAPC achieves even over 4% better results than FFR on the *Google* dataset for small $\alpha$ values, and on the *uniform* dataset for small $s_{\max}$ values. Moreover, the overflow probabilities in bins packed by RPAPC are on average lower than those in bins packed by FFR (Fig. 3 in the appendix [1]): a good packing algorithm can result in both a lower number of bins and a lower overflow probability. On the other side, the KleinbergC algorithm performs worse than both FFR and RPAPC for all datasets, although for *Google* the difference is small. There are significant differences between results on the *uniform* and the *Google* datasets. A possible reason is that the *Google* dataset has a skewed distribution of sizes of items (Fig. 1b) with mean 0.044 and maximal size 0.773, although probabilities are distributed reasonably uniformly (Fig. 1c).

## 9 Conclusions

We propose RPAP, an online algorithm for Stochastic Bin Packing with scaled Bernoulli items. RPAP produces a viable packing that keeps the overflow probability of any bin below the requested parameter $\alpha$. We also prove that RPAP is an approximation algorithm with an approximation factor that depends only on the maximal overflow probability $\alpha$. We derive a combined approach, RPAPC, that has the same guarantees as RPAP. In simulations, we compare RPAP and RPAPC with [15], a state-of-the-art algorithm with proven worst-case guarantees, and FFR, a heuristic with no guarantees. Our approaches consistently surpass [15]. Additionally, RPAPC is close to FFR, outperforming it on *Google* by 4% and on *Uniform* datasets with small items.

**Acknowledgements and Data Availability.** Authors thank Arif Merchant for his comments on the manuscript. This research is supported by a Polish National Science Center grant Opus (UMO-2017/25/B/ST6/00116). Data supporting this study and the code used to perform the simulations and generate the plots will be available from [14].

## References

1. Appendix (online). www.mimuw.edu.pl/~krzadca/SBP-article-appendix.pdf
2. Barroso, L.A., Clidaras, J., Hölzle, U.: The Datacenter as a Computer: An Introduction to the Design of Warehouse-scale Machines. Synthesis Lectures on Computer Architecture, vol. 8. Morgan & Claypool Publishers (2013)
3. Bashir, N., Deng, N., Rzadca, K., Irwin, D.E., Kodak, S., Jnagal, R.: Take it to the limit: peak prediction-driven resource overcommitment in datacenters. In: EuroSys, pp. 556–573. ACM (2021)
4. Beaumont, O., Eyraud-Dubois, L., del Castillo, J.A.L.: Analyzing real cluster data for formulating allocation algorithms in cloud platforms. Parallel Comput. **54**, 83–96 (2016)
5. Breitgand, D., Epstein, A.: Improving consolidation of virtual machines with risk-aware bandwidth oversubscription in compute clouds. In: IEEE INFOCOM, pp. 2861–2865 (2012)
6. Burns, B., Grant, B., Oppenheimer, D., Brewer, E., Wilkes, J.: Borg, omega, and kubernetes. CACM **59**(5), 50–57 (2016)
7. Chen, M., Zhang, H., Su, Y.Y., Wang, X., Jiang, G., Yoshihira, K.: Effective VM sizing in virtualized data centers. In: IFIP/IEEE IM, pp. 594–601 (2011)
8. Coffman, E.G., Jr., Garey, M.R., Johnson, D.S.: Dynamic bin packing. SIAM J. Comput. **12**(2), 227–258 (1983)
9. Coffman, E.G., Csirik, J., Galambos, G., Martello, S., Vigo, D.: Bin packing approximation algorithms: survey and classification. In: Pardalos, P.M., Du, D.-Z., Graham, R.L. (eds.) Handbook of Combinatorial Optimization, pp. 455–531. Springer, New York (2013). https://doi.org/10.1007/978-1-4419-7997-1_35

10. Cohen, M.C., Zadimoghaddam, M., Keller, P., Mirrokni, V.: Overcommitment in cloud services - bin packing with chance constraints. Manage. Sci. **65**, 3255–3271 (2019)
11. Goel, A., Indyk, P.: Stochastic load balancing and related problems. In: FoCS, pp. 579–586 (1999)
12. Janus, P., Rzadca, K.: SLO-aware colocation of data center tasks based on instantaneous processor requirements. In: SoCC, ACM (2017)
13. Johnson, D.S.: Near-optimal bin packing algorithms. Ph.D. thesis, Massachusetts Institute of Technology (1973)
14. Kanas, T., Rzadca, K.: Artifact and instructions to generate experimental results for conference proceeding paper: a Poisson-based approximation algorithm for stochastic bin packing of Bernoulli items (2023). https://doi.org/10.6084/m9.figshare.23548263
15. Kleinberg, J., Rabani, Y., Tardos, É.: Allocating bandwidth for bursty connections. SIAM J. Comput. **30**(1), 191–217 (2000)
16. Lu, C., Ye, K., Xu, G., Xu, C.Z., Bai, T.: Imbalance in the cloud: an analysis on Alibaba cluster trace. In: Big Data, pp. 2884–2892. IEEE (2017)
17. Luo, Z., Qian, Z.: Burstiness-aware server consolidation via queuing theory approach in a computing cloud. In: IPDPS, pp. 332–341. IEEE (2013)
18. Martinovic, J., Selch, M.: Mathematical models and approximate solution approaches for the stochastic bin packing problem. COR **135**, 105439 (2021)
19. Pietri, I., Sakellariou, R.: Mapping virtual machines onto physical machines in cloud computing: a survey. CSUR **49**(3), 1–30 (2016)
20. Rzadca, K., et al.: Autopilot: workload autoscaling at Google scale. In: EuroSys. ACM (2020)
21. Tirmazi, M., et al.: Borg: the next generation. In: EuroSys. ACM (2020)
22. Verma, A., Pedrosa, L., Korupolu, M., Oppenheimer, D., Tune, E., Wilkes, J.: Large-scale cluster management at Google with Borg. In: EuroSys. ACM (2015)
23. Wilkes, J.: Google cluster-usage traces v3. Technical report, Google Inc., Mountain View, CA, USA (2020)
24. Wolfram Research Inc: Introduction to the gamma functions. https://functions.wolfram.com/GammaBetaErf/InverseGammaRegularized3/introductions/Gammas/05/
25. Yan, J., et al.: Solving the batch stochastic bin packing problem in cloud. In: SIGKDD. ACM (2022)

# Hierarchical Management of Extreme-Scale Task-Based Applications

Francesc Lordan[1](✉), Gabriel Puigdemunt[1], Pere Vergés[1,2], Javier Conejero[1], Jorge Ejarque[1], and Rosa M. Badia[1]

[1] Barcelona Supercomputing Center, Barcelona, Spain
{francesc.lordan,gabriel.puigdemunt, pere.verges,javier.conejero, jorge.ejarque,rosa.m.badia}@bsc.es

[2] University of California Irvine, Irvine, USA
pvergesb@uci.edu

**Abstract.** The scale and heterogeneity of exascale systems increment the complexity of programming applications exploiting them. Task-based approaches with support for nested tasks are a good-fitting model for them because of the flexibility lying in the task concept. Resembling the hierarchical organization of the hardware, this paper proposes establishing a hierarchy in the application workflow for mapping coarse-grain tasks to the broader hardware components and finer-grain tasks to the lowest levels of the resource hierarchy to benefit from lower-latency and higher-bandwidth communications and exploiting locality. Building on a proposed mechanism to encapsulate within the task the management of its finer-grain parallelism, the paper presents a hierarchical peer-to-peer engine orchestrating the execution of workflow hierarchies with fully-decentralized management. The tests conducted on the MareNostrum 4 supercomputer using a prototype implementation prove the validity of the proposal supporting the execution of up to 707,653 tasks using 2,400 cores and achieving speedups of up to 106 times faster than executions of a single workflow and centralized management.

**Keywords:** distributed systems · exascale · task-based · programming model · workflow · hierarchy · runtime system · peer-to-peer · decentralized management

## 1 Introduction

Systems targeting exascale computing are becoming more and more powerful by interconnecting a growing number of nodes equipping processors and accelerators with an increasing number of physical cores and novel memory hierarchies. The extreme scale and the heterogeneity of these systems increment the overall complexity of programming applications while exploiting them efficiently. On the one hand, developers have to identify enough parallelism inherent in the application to employ all the compute devices; on the other hand, they have to


J. Cano et al. (Eds.): Euro-Par 2023, LNCS 14100, pp. 111–124, 2023.
https://doi.org/10.1007/978-3-031-39698-4_8

face the heterogeneity of the system and deal with the specifics of each device (i.e. architectures with a different number of physical cores, memory sizes and hierarchies, network latency and bandwidth, and different programming models to interact with the device). This results in system-tailored applications that can not be ported to other systems without a significant performance loss.

Programming models overcome this development difficulty by providing an infrastructure- and parallelism-agnostic mechanism to describe the logic of an application. Then, at execution time, a runtime engine automatically handles the inherent parallelism to exploit the host infrastructure. Task-based programming models are a popular approach because of their high development productivity and their flexibility to adapt to the infrastructure. They build on the concept of task: an asynchronous operation processing a collection of input values to generate a set of output values. Tasks can take values generated by other tasks as input; hence, establishing data-dependency relationships among them. These dependencies define the workflow of the application and determine its inherent task-level parallelism; runtime engines orchestrate the parallel execution of all the tasks of an application guaranteeing the fulfilment of these dependencies.

Tasks encapsulate logic operations; however, the actual implementation carrying them out can change depending on the available hardware or the current workload of the system. Thus, the runtime engine can select an implementation leveraging a specific accelerator, running a multi-threaded implementation on multi-core processors, or a distributed version using several nodes. Runtime engines usually centralize the parallelism and resource management in one single node of the infrastructure (the orchestrator); on extreme-scale computers, the large number of tasks and nodes converts this management into a bottleneck.

Leveraging this task implementation versatility, applications can organize their parallelism hierarchically embedding finer-grain tasks within intermediate tasks to distribute the parallelism management overhead. Hence, the orchestrator node handles only the coarsest-grain parallelism and passes on the burden of managing the finer-grain parallelism along with the execution of the task. The node running a task decides whether to execute the tasks composing the inner workflow locally or offload them onto other nodes distributing the management workload in a recursive manner. For that to succeed, each node of the infrastructure must be aware of the computing devices equipped on the node and the amount of resources available on the other nodes of the infrastructure. This deprecates the orchestrator node approach in favour of a peer-to-peer model.

This paper contributes with an analysis of what are the requirements to bundle the fine-grain parallelism management within a task and the description of the necessary mechanisms to implement in a runtime system to support it. Besides, the article presents the results of evaluation tests using a prototype implementation conducted on the MareNostrum 4 supercomputer running two different applications (GridSearch and Random Forest) achieving higher degrees of parallelism and reducing the management overhead drastically.

The article continues by casting a glance over related work that can be found in the literature. Section 3 introduces the concepts of the proposed solution and

Sect. 4 describes how runtime systems must handle data, resources and tasks to adopt it. To validate the proposal, Sect. 5 contains the results of the evaluation of a prototype implementation in two use cases. The last section concludes the article and identifies potential lines for future work.

## 2 Related Work

Previous work has addressed the support for hierarchical or nested parallel regions, especially in shared memory systems such as multi-core architectures. Most of the widely-adopted shared memory programming models – e.g., OmpSs [5], Cilk [19] or OneAPI TBB [10] – support nested parallel regions or tasks, and the OpenMP standard also supports nested tasks since version 4.5 [16]. The management of nested parallelism focuses on handling dependencies between different nested parallel regions to allow their correct concurrent processing. Having shared memory simplifies this management since data regions can be directly identified by their memory addresses, and the different threads processing these regions have shared access to the control data. The solution presented in this article targets distributed systems where application and control data are spread across the infrastructure; thus, memory addresses no longer uniquely identify data regions and control data is not shared among all the computing nodes or devices making the parallelism management more complex.

In distributed systems, nested parallelism is typically achieved by combining different programming models, one supporting the distributed system part and another dealing with the execution within each shared memory system. This is the case of the hybrid MPI + OpenMP model [18], StarSs [17] or the COMPSs + OmpSs combination [6]. Since the runtime systems supporting these models do not share information, developers must master several models and manage the coordination of different levels of parallelism. The proposal of this article uses a single programming model to support parallelism at all granularity levels.

Current state-of-the-art workflow managers have done some efforts to enable nested parallelism. Most of them allow the explicit sub-workflow definition (e.g. Snakemake [15], NextFlow [4] and Galaxy [1]), or even allow the definition of external workflows as modules (e.g. Snakemake), to enable the composition of larger workflows. However, they rely on the dependency management of the underlying queuing system (e.g., Slurm [21]) and submit each task as an individual job with the required job dependencies. These systems are centralised and this methodology leads to floods of jobs. Alternatively, Dask [3] allows launching nested tasks within the same job by allowing the creation of clients that connect to the main Dask scheduler to spawn a child task. Unfortunately, this approach has the same essence as previous workflow managers since it also relies on a centralized scheduling system; besides, it is considered an experimental feature. The methodology described in this work differentiates from these solutions by following a decentralized approach to deal with this management. This feature has also been explored by dataflow managers (e.g., Swift/T [20] and TTG [8]); however, their management approach cannot be applied onto workflow managers.

## 3 Workflow Management Encapsulation

Task-based approaches with support for nested tasks are a good-fitting model for extreme-scale systems because of the flexibility of the task concept. Tasks are asynchronous operations with a defined set of input and output data – in the context of this article, the term data refers to individual files and objects. The definition of a task establishes an operation to carry out but specifies nothing about its implementation. Thus, a task can run sequentially or create new tasks to open additional parallelism (nested task detection). This establishes relationships among tasks. All the tasks created by the same task are child or nested tasks of the creating task; inversely, the creating task is the parent of all the tasks created by it. Tasks sharing the same parent are siblings.

It is during a task execution that nested tasks are discovered; thus, tasks never start executing earlier than their parent. When it comes to finishing a task, a parent task must wait until all of its nested tasks have been completed before it can finish its execution. This is because the output of the parent task relies on the outputs of its child tasks.

Task-based programming models build on data access atomicity to convert an application into a workflow by establishing dependency relations among tasks where the outputs of a task (task predecessor or value producer) are the inputs of another (task successor or value consumer). By detecting nested tasks, each task has the potential to become a new workflow, and thus, applications evolve from being a single workflow into a hierarchy of workflows. The workflow of a task can define data dependencies among its nested tasks based on the access to its input data or newly created intermediate data. However, beyond the scope of the task, only those values belonging to the output on the task definition are significant; hence, all intermediate data is negligible and can be removed.

As with the implementation, the task definition does not specify which resources should host its execution. Any node with access to such values can host the execution of the task; thus, by transferring the necessary input data, the workload of a task-based application can be distributed across large systems and run the tasks in parallel.

Ensuring that data has the expected value when passed in as a task input is crucial to guarantee that applications produce their expected results while making the most of the underlying infrastructure. To identify more parallelism between tasks, it is possible to maintain a duplicate of every value the data holds throughout the execution. These replicas allow any task to read the expected value even if another task has already updated it; thus, false dependencies are no longer considered. The counterpoint of this method is the additional storage. To orchestrate the parallel execution of tasks, it is crucial to keep track of the values held by a data, the location of their duplicate copies, and the pending-execution tasks reading each value. This tracking enables not only identifying dependency-free tasks but also detecting obsolete values – i.e., old values with no tasks reading them – that can be removed to free storage capacity.

Figure 1a illustrates the different values held by a data (*data X*) that enters as an input value of a task and is updated by three nested workflows. *Data X*

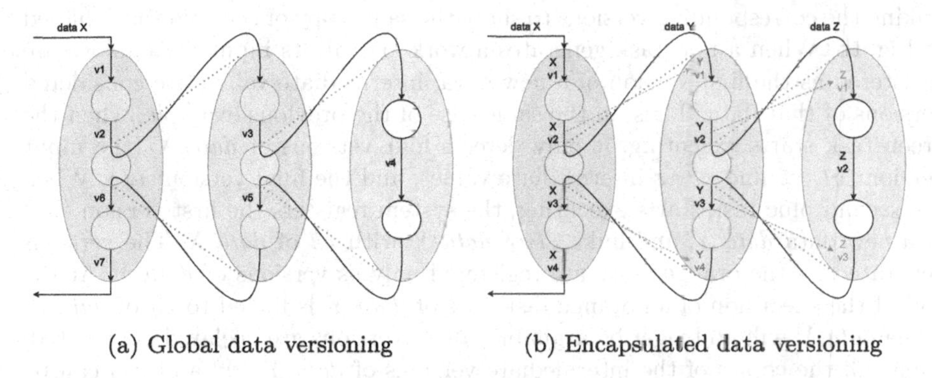


(a) Global data versioning (b) Encapsulated data versioning

**Fig. 1.** Example of data versioning where all tasks belonging to a three-level hierarchy of nested workflows update one data.

enters the coarsest-grain task (green oval) as an input value (*v1*) and is updated by the three-task workflow nested in the task (tasks within this workflow are blue). The first blue task reads and updates the input value by generating a new version (*v2*). This new version is passed in as the input of the second blue task, and, during the execution, another three-task nested workflow is detected (tasks within this workflow are depicted in orange). The first task of this finer-grain workflow updates the data (*v3*), and the second task gets it as input. Again, at run time, this second task becomes a workflow with two inner tasks (white) modifying the data and, thus, generating two subsequent versions (*v4* and *v5*). Upon completing the second white task, the whole workflow in the second orange task is completed; *v5* becomes the output value of the second orange task, and *v4* becomes an irrelevant intermediate value. The third orange task takes the *v5* value and updates the data generating *v6*. At this point, the whole workflow within the second blue task is completed; *v6* becomes the output value of the data for the blue task, and *v3* and *v5* become deprecated because they are intermediate values within the second blue task. Finally, the third blue task can be executed taking *v6* as input value to generate *v7*, which becomes the output value of the green task deprecating *v2* and *v6*.

Determining an incremental version number at task discovery time, as done in the previous example, is unfeasible. On the one hand, the execution of the different tasks is distributed across the whole system; maintaining this version record to ensure the proper handling of the dependencies requires a centralized entity or implementing consensus. Both solutions entail a significant communication overhead. On the other hand, versions generated by a nested workflow are detected at task execution time and not while the coarser-grain workflow is detected. Thus, data versions generated by tasks in a parent workflow would be detected earlier than the versions from its nested tasks. Hence, the data value discovery would not match the incremental order of the versions.

To workaround these difficulties and overcome both problems, this work proposes registering the intermediate values as versions from a different data and linking the corresponding versions to share the same copy of the value as depicted in Fig. 1b. When a new task generates a workflow, all its input data values are registered as the first version of a new data; intermediate values are considered versions of that data. Thus, in the same case of the previous example, when the green task starts executing, it only detects four versions of *data X* (the input version: *v1*, *v2* and *v3* as intermediate values, and the final version: *v4*). When the second blue task starts executing, the system registers the first version (*v1*) of a new data *data Y*, and links *v1* of *data Y* with *v2* of *data X*. The versions generated by the orange tasks are registered only as versions of *data Y*. At the end of the execution of all orange tasks, *v4* of *data Y* is linked to *v3* of *data X*. Since *data Y* will no longer be available, all its versions are declared deprecated. Thus, all the copies of the intermediate versions of *data Y* (*v2* and *v3*) can be removed. Still, the input and output versions (*v1* and *v4*) are kept because they are accessible through the versions of *data X*.

Following this proposal, the nested workflow management is encapsulated within the task creating it. Once a node starts running a task, it can spawn the nested tasks and orchestrate their execution independently from the execution of other workflows. As with the computational workload, the management overhead gets distributed to reduce the management bottleneck of centralized approaches.

## 4 Runtime System Architecture

The hardware of Exascale computers is already organized hierarchically. Systems are composed of thousands of nodes physically in racks interconnected by switches; internally, each node can have several processors with multiple cores and accelerators attached. This hierarchy can be put to use and define the different domain levels described to distribute the resource management. Thus, coarser-grained tasks can be mapped to the broader domains of the infrastructure, and finer-grain tasks, where the bulk of parallelism is, achieve higher performance by exploiting data locality and lower-latency and higher-bandwidth communications offered within the lowest levels of the resource hierarchy.

To fully achieve their potential performance, task computations require exclusive access to the resources running their logic to reduce the issues of concurrent execution on shared resources such as increasing the number of cache misses or memory swapping. Runtime systems monitor the resource occupation to orchestrate the task executions and grant this exclusivity. An orchestrator node handling a large number of task executions on many workers becomes a management bottleneck in extreme-scale infrastructures. Given the management independence provided by workflow hierarchies, peer-to-peer architectures arise as a promising architecture to efficiently support the detection of nested tasks and distribute the management overhead. In this approach, each node hosts an autonomous process (Agent) that establishes a collaborative data space with other nodes and handles the execution of tasks.

Each Agent controls the computing devices equipped on the node to allocate task executions and monitors the resources from neighbouring nodes with the

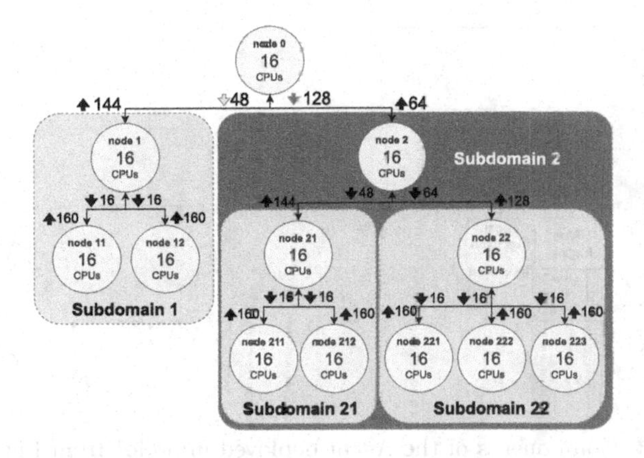


**Fig. 2.** 12-node cluster with a total of 176 cores divided into a hierarchy of domains. From the point of view of node0, the infrastructure is composed of two domains accessible via node1 (subdomain1) and node2 (subdomain2).

purpose of offloading tasks onto them. Despite not being a limit on the number of remote nodes, the more nodes being monitored, the larger the management overhead and the complexity of scheduling task executions. To distribute the management, the resources can be grouped into disjoint domains, each managed by one of the nodes within it. Instead of monitoring the state of many nodes, The orchestrator node only distributes the workload among a few resource-rich domains interacting with the manager node within each. In the example depicted in Fig. 2, a cluster is divided into two domains. The orchestrator node (node0) considers only 3 options to host the execution: its 16 local CPU cores, 48 CPU cores available in Domain1 through node1, or 128 CPU cores in Domain2 through node2. The resources within a domain can still be too many to be handled by a single node. To that end, domains can be subsequently divided into several subdomains establishing a resource hierarchy as depicted in Domain2 of Fig. 2 where node2 considers 3 options: hosting it in its local 16 CPU cores, delegating it to one of its subdomains (Subdomain21 with 48 cores or Subdomain22 with 64 cores) pushing it down the hierarchy, or offloading out from the domain ascending through the hierarchy (64 cores available through node0).

Agents comprise five main components as illustrated in Fig. 3. The *Agent API* offers users and other Agents an interaction interface to submit task execution requests and notify task completions. The *Data Manager* establishes a distributed key-value store used by Agents to register data values and share their values. The *Task Scheduler* monitors the data dependencies of the workflows generated by the tasks running on the node and decides the best moment to start a task execution or offload it onto a domain. The *Local Execution* and *Offloading Engine* respectively handle the execution of tasks on the local devices and their offloading onto remote Agents. An internal API allows tasks implemented with *task-based programming models* to notify the detection of nested workflows and request the execution of their child tasks.

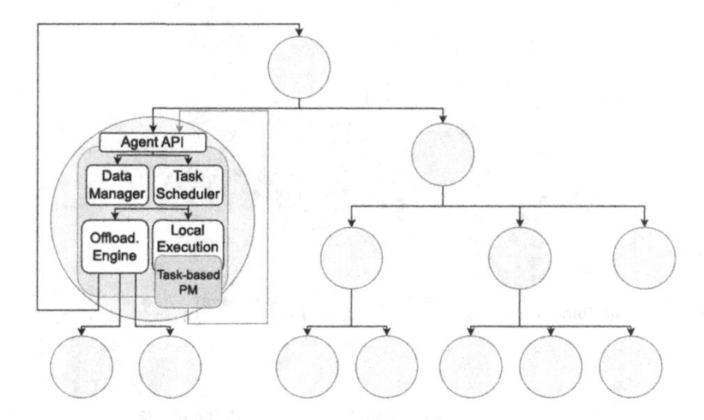


**Fig. 3.** Components of the Agent deployed in node1 from Fig. 2.

Tasks arrive to the Agent through an API indicating the operation to perform and its parameters (input data values and the expected results). Upon reception, the Agent registers each parameter as a new piece of data and binds the first version of all the input values with the corresponding version, as described in Sect. 3. Then, the task becomes part of a pool of pending workload; the Agent schedules the execution of these pending tasks considering the availability of the local or remote resources, aiming for an optimal distribution while providing resource exclusivity to the tasks. Arrived the time if the Agent decides to offload the task onto a remote node, it reserves the resources required by the task in the corresponding subdomain, submits via the API of the main Agent of the subdomain, and waits asynchronously for its completion to release the resources.

Otherwise, if the Agent decides to host the execution locally, it allocates the corresponding local resources, fetches all the missing input values and launches its execution. If implemented following a task-based programming model, the task becomes a workflow and spawns nested tasks with dependencies among them, creating new pieces of data and new versions of the already existing parameters. As explained in the previous section, this data management, as well as the parallelism among nested tasks, can be handled within the node with no need to interact with other peers. Hence, the programming model notifies the newly detected nested tasks and their dependencies to the local Agent. It manages their execution with the parent task running them locally or offloading them onto other nodes.

Workflow executions reach synchronization points where they wait for some of their nested tasks to end producing data values. Every task that becomes a workflow reaches at least one synchronization point at its end to wait for the completion of all its nested tasks. During these waits, the resources allocated for the parent task remain idle. For better exploitation of the infrastructure, the task can release these resources so they can host another task execution; for instance, one of its nested tasks. When the synchronization condition is met and the nested task being waited for ends its execution, the execution of the parent task can continue. At this point, the runtime system has to ensure that there are enough idle resources to host the parent task execution exclusively. If there are, the task resumes its execution; otherwise, the runtime will hold the execution until other tasks release their resources because they complete their execution or they reach a synchronization point.

Regardless of whether a task has become a workflow or not, upon finishing its execution (including its nested tasks), the Agent collects all the output values, binds them to the corresponding version of its parent task data (passed in as parameters) and removes all the references to the pieces of data created for the task. At this point, the runtime system considers the task completed, releasing its resources and dependencies. If the task was detected by a parent task running in the same node, the Agent releases the local resources allocated for its execution and any data dependency with its successors. Otherwise, if the task was offloaded from another node, the Agent notifies the completion of the task to the Agent from where it was submitted to release the resources of the corresponding domain. If the notified node is the Agent where the task was detected, it also releases the dependencies; otherwise, the notification is forwarded to the Agent that sent it, repeating the process until it reaches the source Agent to release the data dependencies and continue with the execution of the parent workflow.

## 5 Evaluation

To validate the proposed idea, several tests have been conducted using a prototype implementation building on Colony [14]: a framework to handle task executions on distributed infrastructures organizing the resources as a hierarchical peer-to-peer network. The task-based programming model selected for defining the nested workflows is COMPSs [13], for which Colony provides native support.

All the experiments have been run on the MareNostrum 4 supercomputer: a 3,456-node (48 servers of 72 nodes) supercomputer where each node has two 24-core Intel Xeon Platinum 8160 and 96 GB of main memory. A Full-fat tree 100Gb Intel Omni-Path network interconnects the nodes which also have access to a 14PB shared disk. Each node hosts the execution of an Agent managing its 48 cores. All the Agents within the same server join together as a domain and one becomes the interconnection node for the domain; in turn, one of these nodes interconnects all the domains and receives the main task of the application.

The scheduler within each Agent is the default Colony scheduler. Upon the arrival of a dependency-free task, it attempts to assign it to an idle resource considering the locality of its input values. If there are no available resources, the scheduler adds the task to a set of pending tasks. When a task completes, the scheduler releases the used resources and the successors and tries to employ any idle resources with one of the just dependency-freed tasks or one from the pending set computing a locality score for all the combinations and iteratively selecting the one with a higher value until no task can be assigned. To avoid loops where a task is being submitted between two Agents back and forth, the scheduler dismisses offloading the task onto the Agent detecting it or any of its parents; offloading is always down the hierarchy.

### 5.1 GridSearch

The first test evaluates the performance of GridSearch [11] with cross-validation: an algorithm that exhaustively looks for all the different combinations of hyper-parameters for a particular estimator. With cross-validation, it trains and evaluates several estimators for each combination (splits), and the final score obtained for a combination is the average of the scoring of the corresponding splits. GridSearch is one of the algorithms offered within dislib [2], a Python library built on top of COMPSs providing distributed mathematical and machine learning algorithms. The conducted test finds the optimal solution among 25 combinations of values for the *Gamma* (5 values from 0.1 to 0.5 ) and *C* (5 values from 0.1 to 0.5) hyper-parameters to train a Cascade-SVM classification model (CSVM) [7].

The implementation of GridSearch provided within dislib – Flat – delegates the detection of the tasks to the implementation of the estimator and invokes them sequentially expecting them to create all the finer-grain tasks at a time. CSVM is an iterative algorithm that checks the convergence of the model at the end of every iteration; hence, it stops the generation of tasks at the end of each iteration. This affects the parallelism of GridSearch; it does not detect tasks from a CSVM until the previous one converges. The Nested version of the GridSearch algorithm encapsulates the fitting and evaluation of each estimator within a coarse-grain task that generates the corresponding finer-grain tasks achieving higher degrees of parallelism. Albeit both versions reach the same task granularity, the Nested version overcomes the task generation blockage enabling parallel convergence checks by encapsulating them within nested workflows.

The first test studies the behaviour when training a small dataset (the IRIS dataset) using 4 Marenostrum nodes. Figure 4 depicts an execution trace with the 192 cores when executing the Flat (Fig. 4a) and Nested (Fig. 4b) implementations. Given the small size of the dataset, the corresponding CSVM implementation does not detect many tasks to run in parallel. In the Flat version case, where CSVMs run sequentially, the infrastructure is under-utilized and takes 116.27 s to run. Enabling nested task detection allows running several CSVMs simultaneously; this increases the number of finer-grain tasks detected at a time, and the infrastructure hosts more executions in parallel. The overall execution time is reduced to 9.33 s (12× speedup).

When CSVM processes larger datasets (e.g., the Atrial Fibrillation (AT) composed of 7,500 samples with 100 features characterizing an ECG), it can detect enough parallelism to fully use the 4 nodes simultaneously as shown in Fig. 5a. However, convergence checks reduce the parallelism in every iteration and a large part of the infrastructure is under-used. By overlapping several CSVMs, the Nested version employs these idle resources to compute tasks from other CSVMs as depicted in Fig. 5b. For this experiment, the Nested version reduces the time to find the optimal solution among 25 combinations from 27,887 s to 5,687 (4.9x speedup). Aiming at verifying the scalability of the solution, we run a GridSearch to find the optimal solution among 50 combinations: 250 CSVMs and 707,653 tasks. When processing the AT dataset, a CSVM generates parallelism to employ up to 4 nodes. With the FLAT version, the estimated shortest

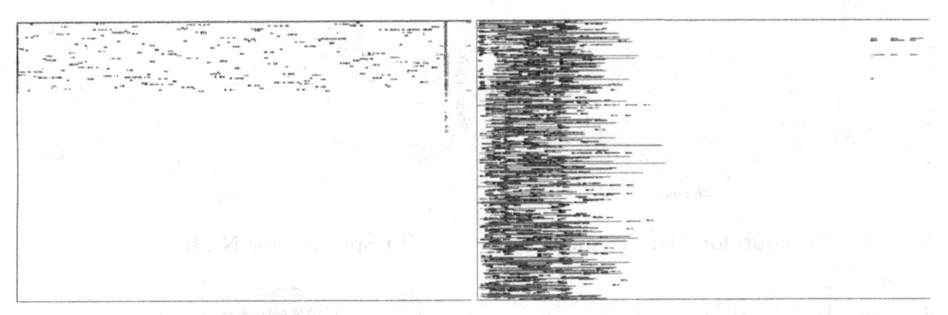

(a) Flat: 25 combinations - 118 seconds (b) Nested: 25 combinations - 10 seconds

**Fig. 4.** Execution trace of an IRIS model training with 4 nodes of 48 cores

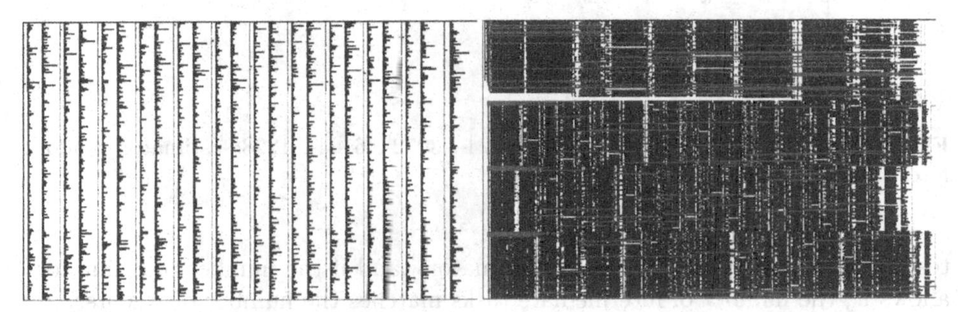

(a) Flat: 2 combinations - 2,500 seconds (b) Nested: 25 combinations - 5,700 seconds

**Fig. 5.** Execution trace of an AT model training with 4 nodes of 48 cores

execution time is 55,774 s. The Nested version expands this parallelism enabling the usage of more nodes. With 16 nodes, it lasts 4,315 s (13x). With 50, the execution already shows some workload imbalance due to the variability between CSVMs; it takes 1,824 s (30x).

### 5.2 Random Forest

The second experiment consists in training a classification model using the RandomForest algorithm [9], which constructs a set of individual decision-trees – estimators –, each classifying a given input into classes based on decisions taken in random order. The model aggregates the classification of all the estimators; thus, its accuracy depends on the number of estimators composing it. The training of an estimator has two tasks: the first one selects 30,000 random samples from the training set, and the second one builds the decision tree. The training of an estimator is independent of other estimators. The test uses two versions of the algorithm: one – Flat – where the main task directly generates all the tasks to train the estimators and the other – Nested – where the main task generates intermediate tasks grouping the training of several estimators. In the conducted

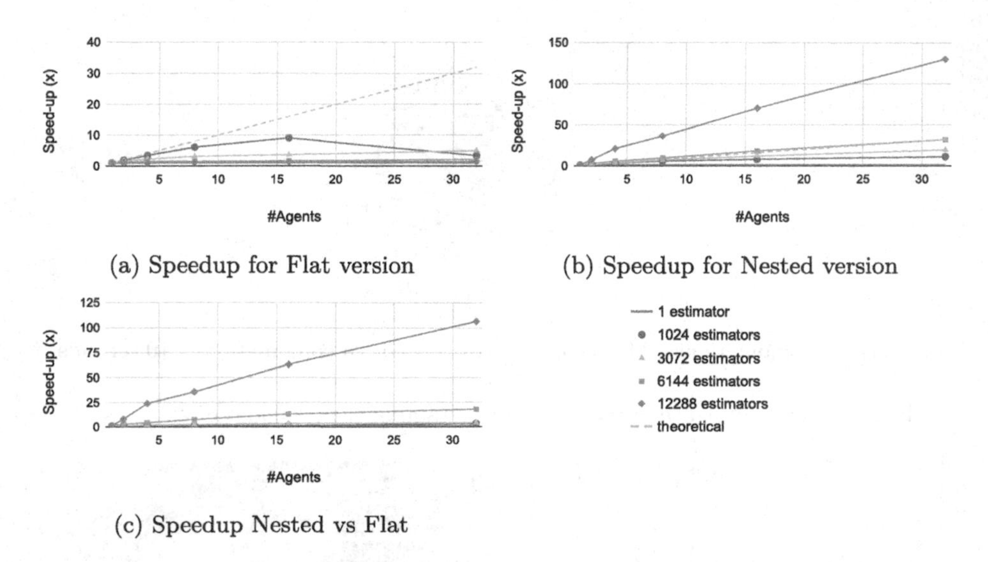


(a) Speedup for Flat version

(b) Speedup for Nested version

(c) Speedup Nested vs Flat

**Fig. 6.** Strong scaling results for a 1-, 1024-, 3072-, 6144-, 12288-estimator random forest model training

tests, each batch trains at least 48 estimators, and if the number of estimators allows it, the number of intermediate tasks matches the number of Agents.

Figure 6 depicts the speedup obtained when running a strong scaling test with each of the versions when training 1, 1024, 3072, 6144 and 12288 estimators. The results for the flat version (Fig. 6a) show the scalability limitation due to the workload imbalance when a parallelism hierarchy is not established (seen in the 1024-estimator case with not enough parallelism to exploit the 1536 cores in 32 agents). In addition, this alternative suffers from the delay produced by generating the tasks sequentially and from a scheduling overhead that grows exponentially with the number of pending tasks.

Nested tasks diminish the impact of the latter two. Several coarse-grained tasks can run at a time and generate finer-grain tasks in parallel; the faster tasks are detected, the faster the runtime system can submit their execution and better exploit the resources. Besides, the runtime system can distribute the scheduling of these tasks; hence, its overhead is drastically reduced as the infrastructure grows. As shown in Fig. 6b, mitigating these two issues allows a 130 times faster training of a 12,288-estimator model when using 32 times more resources.

Figure 6c compares the execution times obtained with both algorithms when training the same model using the same amount of resources. The larger the model and the infrastructure are, the higher the benefit of establishing a parallelism hierarchy is. In the largest test case, training a 12,288-estimator model using 32 nodes, the Nested algorithm achieves an execution time 106 times faster than the Flat. The experiments using a single node, where tasks are detected sequentially and the scheduler handles the same amount of tasks, do not reveal any significant overhead due to the handling of the additional parent task.

## 6 Conclusion

This manuscript describes a mechanism to organize the parallelism of task-based applications in a hierarchical manner and proposes a mechanism to encapsulate the management of the nested workflow along with the task to enable the distribution of the management overhead along the infrastructure. Matching the application parallelism, the article also proposes a hierarchical approach for organizing the resources of the infrastructure; thus, the scheduling problem reduces its complexity by handling fewer tasks and resources. The article also describes the architecture of a runtime system supporting it.

The paper validates the proposal with two tests on a prototype implementation running on the MareNostrum 4 supercomputer. The results reveal that, by establishing a task hierarchy, applications can achieve a higher degree of parallelism without undergoing an in-depth refactoring of the code. Encapsulating the finer-grain parallelism management within tasks to distribute the corresponding overhead is beneficial for the application performance; results achieve a speedup of up to 106 times faster than executions with centralized workflow management.

The tests also reveal some shortcomings of the prototype. The biggest concern is the limitation of the task scheduler to request task executions to higher layers of the resource hierarchy. Developing peer-to-peer scheduling strategies based on task-stealing, reactive offloading or game theory are future lines of research to improve. Also, the described work considers that the output of the task is available only at the end of its execution. However, a nested task can compute an output value of the parent task before its completion. Currently, other tasks depending on the value must wait for the parent task to end even if the value is already available. Enabling fine-grain dependency management that releases the dependency upon the completion of the nested task is also future work.

**Acknowledgements and Data Availability.** This work has been supported by the Spanish Government (PID2019-107255GB), by MCIN/AEI /10.13039/501100011033 (CEX2021-001148-S), by the Departament de Recerca i Universitats de la Generalitat de Catalunya to the Research Group MPiEDist (2021 SGR 00412), and by the European Commission through the Horizon Europe Research and Innovation program under Grant Agreements 101070177 (ICOS project) and 101016577 (AI-Sprint project). The data and code that support this study are openly available in figshare [12].

## References

1. Afgan, E., et al.: The galaxy platform for accessible, reproducible and collaborative biomedical analyses: 2018 update. Nucleic Acids Res. **46**(1), 537–544 (2018)
2. Cid-Fuentes, J.Á., et al.: dislib: Large scale high performance machine learning in python. In: Proceedings of the 15th International Conference on eScience, pp. 96–105 (2019)
3. Dask Development Team: Dask: Library for dynamic task scheduling (2016). https://dask.org
4. Di Tommaso, P., et al.: Nextflow enables reproducible computational workflows. Nat. Biotechnol. **35**(4), 316–319 (2017)

5. Duran, A., et al.: OmpSs: a proposal for programming heterogeneous multi-core architectures. Parallel Process. Lett. **21**(02), 173–193 (2011)
6. Ejarque, J., et al.: A hierarchic task-based programming model for distributed heterogeneous computing. Int. J. High Perform. Comput. Appl. **33**(5), 987–997 (2019)
7. Graf, H., et al.: Parallel support vector machines: the cascade SVM. In: Advances in Neural Information Processing Systems, vol. 17 (2004)
8. Herault, T., et al.: Composition of algorithmic building blocks in template task graphs. In: 2022 IEEE/ACM Parallel Applications Workshop: Alternatives To MPI+ X (PAW-ATM), pp. 26–38 (2022)
9. Ho, T.K.: Random decision forests. In: Proceedings of 3rd International Conference on Document Analysis and Recognition, vol. 1, pp. 278–282 (1995)
10. Intel Corporation: OneAPI TBB Nested parallelism (2022). https://oneapi-src.github.io/oneTBB/main/tbb_userguide/Cancellation_and_Nested_Parallelism.html
11. Lerman, P.: Fitting segmented regression models by grid search. J. R. Stat. Soc.: Ser. C: Appl. Stat. **29**(1), 77–84 (1980)
12. Lordan, F., et al.: Artifact and instructions to generate experimental results for the Euro-Par 2023 proceedings paper: hierarchical management of extreme-scale task-based applications. https://doi.org/10.6084/m9.figshare.23552229
13. Lordan, F., et al.: ServiceSs: an interoperable programming framework for the cloud. J. Grid Comput. **12**(1), 67–91 (2014)
14. Lordan, F., Lezzi, D., Badia, R.M.: Colony: parallel functions as a service on the cloud-edge continuum. In: Sousa, L., Roma, N., Tomás, P. (eds.) Euro-Par 2021. LNCS, vol. 12820, pp. 269–284. Springer, Cham (2021). https://doi.org/10.1007/978-3-030-85665-6_17
15. Mölder, F., et al.: Sustainable data analysis with snakemake. F1000Research **10**(33) (2021)
16. Perez, J.M., et al.: Improving the integration of task nesting and dependencies in OpenMP. In: 2017 IEEE International Parallel and Distributed Processing Symposium (IPDPS), pp. 809–818 (2017)
17. Planas, J., et al.: Hierarchical task-based programming with StarSs. Int J. High Perform. Comput. Appl. **23**(3), 284–299 (2009)
18. Rabenseifner, R., et al.: Hybrid MPI/OpenMP parallel programming on clusters of multi-core SMP nodes. In: 2009 17th Euromicro International Conference on Parallel, Distributed and Network-based Processing, pp. 427–436 (2009)
19. Vandierendonck, H., et al.: Parallel programming of general-purpose programs using task-based programming models. In: 3rd USENIX Workshop on Hot Topics in Parallelism (HotPar 11) (2011)
20. Wozniak, J.M., et al.: Swift/t: large-scale application composition via distributed-memory dataflow processing. In: 2013 13th IEEE/ACM International Symposium on Cluster, Cloud, and Grid Computing, pp. 95–102 (2013)
21. Yoo, A.B., et al.: SLURM: simple Linux utility for resource management. In: Job Scheduling Strategies for Parallel Processing, pp. 44–60 (2003)

# MESDD: A Distributed Geofence-Based Discovery Method for the Computing Continuum

Kurt Horvath[1], Dragi Kimovski[1(✉)], Christoph Uran[1,2], Helmut Wöllik[2], and Radu Prodan[1]

[1] Institute of Information Technology, University Klagenfurt, Klagenfurt, Austria
{kurt.horvath,dragi.kimovski,christoph.uran,radu.prodan}@aau.at

[2] Faculty of Engineering and IT, Carinthian University of Applied Science, Klagenfurt, Austria
{uran,wollik}@fh-kaernten.at

**Abstract.** Service discovery is a vital process that enables low latency provisioning of Internet of Things (IoT) applications across the computing continuum. Unfortunately, it becomes increasingly difficult to identify a proper service within strict time constraints due to the high heterogeneity of the computing continuum. Moreover, the plethora of network technologies and protocols commonly used by IoT applications further hinders service discovery. To address these issues, we introduce a novel *Mobile Edge Service Discovery using the DNS (MESDD)* algorithm, which uses a so-called Intermediate Discovery Code to identify suitable service instances. MESDD uses geofences for fine-grained service segmentation based on a naming scheme that identifies users' locations across the computing continuum. We deployed a real-life distributed computing continuum testbed and compared MESDD with three related methods, outperformed by 60 % after eight update iterations.

**Keywords:** Fog and Edge computing · service discovery · geofence · DNS

## 1 Introduction

The computing continuum, encompassing Cloud and Edge infrastructures, provides compute services close to end users to reduce communication latency and improve response time for various applications in the Internet of Things (IoT) [13]. It contains a heterogeneous set of computing nodes ranging from energy-efficient single-board devices to powerful cloud computing instances.

The heterogeneity of the computing continuum enables efficient support of applications with conflicting requirements, such as low execution time and high computing performance. These applications rely on various services, including low-energy data exchange and massive multi-media-content streaming, which further increases the requirements for computing infrastructures. To address


J. Cano et al. (Eds.): Euro-Par 2023, LNCS 14100, pp. 125–138, 2023.
https://doi.org/10.1007/978-3-031-39698-4_9

this issue, the computing continuum enables the geographical distribution and organization of services depending on the users' location.

Unfortunately, managing the services across the computing continuum is difficult and limited by the plethora of computing infrastructures, network technologies, and protocols. The most critical step in the process of services management is service discovery, which includes identifying available services for a given application distributed across the computing continuum. We, therefore, identify two main service discovery and management challenges across the computing continuum. Firstly, it is burdensome to orchestrate the services within the computing continuum concerning predicting the users' demand, primarily due to the need for geographical awareness and the persisting interoperability issues with the utilization of specific domain name (DNS) services [24]. The second challenge pertains to the accessibility and discovery of services, which recently moved towards using wireless technologies, such as 5G networks [3,16].

To address these issues, we propose a *Mobile Edge Service Discovery using the DNS (MESDD)* method, which uses DNS to build a multi-access Edge computing network [4] and exploits the geographical awareness of the Edge devices in the computing continuum. MESDD uses a so-called *Intermediate Discovery Code (IDC)* on the user side to analyze the network topology (i.e., within a state, city, or district) and discover IoT services [10] while maintaining the structure of their naming scheme with high geographical granularity. Furthermore, MESDD uses *geofences* to define a custom overlay over the network topology, representing user-defined areas defined around a geographical location [18]. Geofences can overlap, assign a particular position, or belong to a specific area but introduce additional lookup overheads from the current user location for service discovery.

Therefore, the main contributions of this work are:

- *Geofence-based service discovery model* tailored to IoT applications;
- *Client-oriented discovery* based on an IDC representation that identifies the nearest service instance;
- *Real-life implementation and evaluation* of a testbed and representative traffic warning IoT application.

We evaluate MESDD through extensive experiments with a real-world network environment using a traffic warning application with service instances widely distributed over three locations. We conducted an experimental study comprising 100 sequential requests, revealing an improved MESDD service discovery and update round-trip time after five service update iterations and outperforming state-of-the-art solutions by 30% to 40% after 15 iterations. The advantage of MESDD stems from its low discovery time within a specific geographical location, with a low 59.23 ms update round-trip time on Edge services.

The paper has seven sections. Section 2 reviews the related work. We describe the formal model for the geofence-based service discovery in Sect. 3 and explain the discovery method in Sect. 4. Section 5 describes the experimental setup, followed by the evaluation results in Sect. 6. Section 7 concludes the paper.

## 2 Related Work

This section revisits the centralized and decentralized related work on service discovery on the computing continuum.

### 2.1 Centralized Service Discovery

Centralized discovery mechanisms rely on atomic functionalities, such as query and register, and are accessible through traditional unsecured REpresentational State Transfer (REST) interfaces [23] as an underlying low overhead protocol.

Recent research in centralized service discovery also addresses the naming schemes using named data networking [14]. The work in [20] focuses on applications for semantic matching on information-centric networking. Similarly, [11] presents a novel approach for services discovery, designed around a novel communication network, such as 5G, as its native environment.

A discovery scheme designed for IoT applications is DisGB [7], which evaluates various methods to identify rendezvous points, such as nominal, flooding events, flooding subscriptions, consistent hashing or grid quorum, for exchange information among the brokers. DisGB aims to make services and information discoverable but does not address the latency benefit of Edge computing.

Centralized service discovery solutions are relatively easy to implement and deploy, suitable for various applications and services, such as DNS hierarchies which are the foundation of service localization on the Internet today. However, they suffer from a single point of failure and rely on deterministic static hierarchical algorithms unsuitable for the computing continuum.

### 2.2 Decentralized Service Discovery

Recently, decentralized solutions became popular for service discovery in the computing continuum. The authors in [23] developed a constrained REST environment, resource directory interface, and application protocol for decentralized service discovery. Another example [16] elaborates on the capabilities of wireless networks for peer-to-peer communication for decentralized discovery.

A more recent work [17] uses the Kademlia network to establish a hierarchy of nodes differentiating between Edge devices and cluster and global coordinators.

Furthermore, [26] uses Web Service Description Language to improve service description using multiple random walks and constrained flooding to enable hybrid service discovery. Besides, the authors in [6] present a hybrid decentralized system with an ontology-based naming scheme to discover services. Lastly, [22] presents a decentralized approach defined by the Internet Engineering Task Force [2] that sends a multicast DNS request to a local network group expecting a suitable service to respond. This approach does not require a separate server to manage the request, leading to multiple possible responses due to the vast undirected broadcast traffic, which is impractical for open networks.

In general, decentralized approaches are resilient to failures and scale well but suffer from interoperability issues, complex deployment, and high complexity, as the protocol among the nodes might alter over time to different versions.

# 3 Model

This section presents a formal model for the MESDD service discovery consisting of four sections.

## 3.1 Service Model

We first define a *service* $\omega$ as a tuple:

$$\omega = \{In_\omega, Out_\omega\},$$

where $In_\omega$ is a set of *inputs* required to invoke $\omega$ and $Out_\omega$ is the set of *outputs* returned by $\omega$ after its execution. A service exists globally and is accessible by its instances. For example, a traffic warning service provided to a mobile user has the location and current traffic in a certain area as output. We define a user as a person who consumes a service.

We define a *service instance* $\iota$ as a set of $n$ *Location Descriptors (LD)*:

$$\iota = \{\lambda_1 \ldots \lambda_n\}.$$

An LD consists of $m$ `tags` representing DNS records defined according to the RFC 1034 domain concepts standard [15].

$$\lambda = \{\texttt{tag}_1 \ldots \texttt{tag}_m\},$$

Figure 1 presents the structure of an LD consisting of four hierarchical stages explained in Table 1. A higher stage level indicates a more precise service instance selection accuracy.

- *Stage 1* is the shortest `tag` corresponding to the largest area, such as major cities or federal states (e.g., `kaernten.app.domain` in the Austrian region of Carinthia). Remote Cloud data centers host the services at this stage.
- *Stage 2* refines the granularity to a district or a state capital. For example, `klagenfurt.kaernten.app.domain` increases the detail level of the assigned service to the city of Klagenfurt in Carinthia, Austria. Local Fog data centers host the services at this stage.
- *Stage 3* further zooms the level of detail to an urban area, such as a city center. In our example, the `tag IS44.klagenfurt.kaernten.app.domain` addresses a busy intersection with the index 44. Edge devices in the user's proximity host the services at this stage.
- *Stage 4* provides the ability to enhance the geographical assignment of services with context-specific information. For example, Fig. 3 splits the intersection into four additional zones, including direction information (e.g., `D3.IS43.klagenfurt.kaernten.app.domain`)

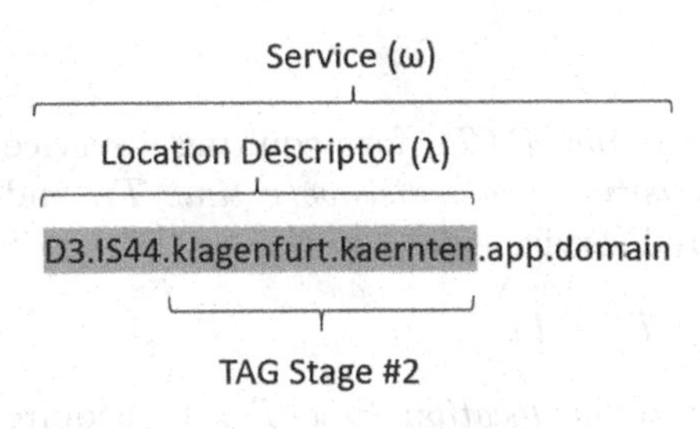


**Fig. 1.** Location Descriptor structure.

**Table 1.** Hierarchical LD stages and associated data centers.

| Stage | Location Descriptor | Data center |
|---|---|---|
| 4 | D4.IS43.klagenfurt.kaernten | Edge |
| 3 | IS43.klagenfurt.kaernten | Edge |
| 2 | klagenfurt.kaernten | Fog |
| 1 | kaernten | Cloud |

### 3.2 Geofence Model

Geofences build the foundation for flexible zone definition and service instance assignment. We define a *geofence* $\gamma$ as a cyclic graph:

$$\gamma = (V, E),$$

where $V = \{v_1 \dots v_o\}$ is a set of vertices representing locations and

$$E = \bigcup_{i \in [1, o-1]} (l_i, l_{i+1}) \cup (l_o, l_1)$$

is the set of edges representing the geofence boundaries. A *location* $l_i \in V$ is a tuple identified by its GPS latitude and longitude coordinates.

We further define a hierarchical set of *geofence levels*:

$$\Gamma^{(k)} \subset \dots \subset \Gamma^{(1)},$$

where each level consists of several overlapping geofences: $\Gamma^{(k)} = \left\{\gamma_1^{(k)}, \dots, \gamma_{l_k}^{(k)}\right\}$. A level $k$ geofence surrounds and contains the level $k-1$ geofence.

Each geofence $\gamma_l^{(k)} \in \Gamma^{(k)}$ has an associated LD $\lambda$ consisting of $k$ hierarchical stages, as defined in Sect. 3.1 and exemplified in Table 1.

We define $\Gamma_l = \{\gamma_1, \dots, \gamma_n\}$ as the geofences surrounding a service consumer's location $l$. A location $l \in \Gamma_l$ identified by the GPS position of a user device is the set of their geofences' LDs:

$$l = \{\lambda_1 \dots \lambda_n\},$$

where $\lambda_i$ is the LD of the geofence $\gamma_i$, where $i \in [1, n]$.

Let $\Gamma_\omega$ be the set of geofences associated with a service $\omega$ and $I_\omega$ its service instances. We define *service provisioning* as a function $P : I_\omega \rightarrow \Gamma_\omega$ that maps each instance $\iota \in I_\omega$ to a geofence $\gamma \in \Gamma_\omega$. The service provisioning is:

1. *balanced*, if the function is bijective and provisions exactly one service in each geofence, responsible for serving it with low latency: $|I_\omega| = |\Gamma_\omega|$;
2. *overprovisioned*, if the provisioning function is surjective and provisions more redundant services in each geofence: $|I_\omega| > |\Gamma_\omega|$;
3. *underprovisioned*, if the function is injective, indicating service scarcity with geofences lacking any provisioned instances and generating high latency to the users by unnecessary geofance transitions: $|I_\omega| < |\Gamma_\omega|$.

### 3.3 Service Discovery

We define the complete *discovery round-trip time* $RTT_D$ for acquiring a service as the sum between the service *IDC acquisition time*, *discovery time* $T_D$ and *forwarding time* $T_F$ for accessing the desired service as:

$$RTT_D = T_{IDC} + T_D + T_F.$$

We further split the discovery time into the *location time* $T_{loc}$ to acquire the user GPS position, *lookup time* $T_{lookup}$ to identify all geofences surrounding a user and its relevant service instances and *selection time* $T_{select}$ to validate the instances using an `nslookup` operation and sort their LD tags based on proximity:

$$T_D = T_{loc} + T_{lookup} + T_{select}.$$

A mobile user $u$ travelling across geofences $\gamma_u$ at an average speed $v_u$ must repeat the discovery process at a certain *discovery frequency* $f_d(u)$ to ensure an optimized service instance selection:

$$f_d = \frac{v_u}{d(\gamma_u)}.$$

where $d(\gamma_u)$ describes the average distance of the user to the geofence border.

For example, a user with an average speed of 10 m/s traversing a cyclic geofence with a diameter of 1000 m should run the discovery process every 500 m with a discovery frequency of $f_d = \frac{10}{500} = 0.02\,\text{Hz}$. Considering the geofence radius ensures sampling of each geozone at least once.

### 3.4 Service Runtime Update

Inside the geozone, a user must update the service information at a specific use case-dependent *update frequency* $f_u$. For example, critical safety-relevant services need high frequency and low latency updates, while IoT services with soft time constraints need fewer updates.

We define the *update round-trip time* $RTT_U$ as the forwarding time $T_F$ and the service-specific *information update time* $T_F$:

$$RTT_U = T_F + T_U.$$

Discovery is unnecessary if a user remains inside a geofence since no better service instance exists.

We quantify the accessibility of a service instance though the *cumulative discovery and update time* $T_C$, impacted by the update frequency $f_u$:

$$T_C = RTT_D + \sum_{j=1}^{f_u} RTT_U^j,$$

where $RTT_U^j$ is the update round-trip time in the $j^{th}$ update. Instances with a lower $T_C$ and similar update frequency provide a lower risk of violating $f_u$.

Let us assume a service that requires an update frequency $f_u = 10\,\text{Hz}$ for smooth user interaction. We further assume the existence of a global Cloud service instance that is easy to discover using conventional DNS approaches with $RTT_{DC} = 100\,\text{ms}$. The Cloud instance offers a slow runtime update of $RTT_{UC} = 120\,\text{ms}$ due to its far location away from the user, leading to a cumulative service discovery and update time of $T_{CC} = 100\,\text{ms} + 10 \cdot 120\,\text{ms} = 1300\,\text{ms}$. On the other hand, an Edge instance of the service, while harder to discover using MESDD in $RTT_{DE} = 400\,\text{ms}$, would offer a lower update latency of $RTT_{UE} = 50\,\text{ms}$ due to its proximity and a lower cumulative discovery and runtime update overhead of $T_{CE} = 400\,\text{ms} + 10 \cdot 50\,\text{ms} = 900\,\text{ms} < T_{CC}$.

### 3.5 Objective

We minimize the physical distance between the user location $l$ and an instance $\iota$ of a service $\omega$ located in a geofence $\gamma^{(k)} \in \Gamma_\omega$, assuming that a shorter physical distance leads to a lower cumulative discovery and update round-trip time, as described in Sect. 3.4).

$$\min_{\gamma^{(k)} \in \Gamma_\omega} d\left(l, \gamma^{(k)}\right).$$

To optimize the efficiency of our search, we must traverse the geofences ranked by their level and return the one with the lowest level: $\nexists \gamma^{(k)} \in \gamma^{(k')} \in \Gamma_\omega, k' < k$. The precision of the localization increases with the stage levels of an LD, as described in Sect. 3.1. Thus, minimizing the geofence level leads to a more accurate and better-performing service instance selection.

There are a range of algorithms to identify if a user location is within a geofence [25], such as based on geofence hierarchies [12].

## 4 Methodology

MESDD uses the concept of geofences that consider users' location for fine-grained service discovery. Figure 2 represents the discovery process structured in three phases: IDC acquisition, service instance discovery, and user forwarding to the service instance, described in the next sections.

*IDC acquisition:* The first phase in the discovery requires the user to download the IDC of a service hosted by the service provider on a Web server in the cloud. This phase requires a DNS lookup, for example, `idc.service.domain`, followed by an IDC download and execution in the user domain. In our reference implementation released on GitHub [9], the IDC uses JavaScript and executes in the user browser. The generic implementation applies to other services by changing the domain and service name.

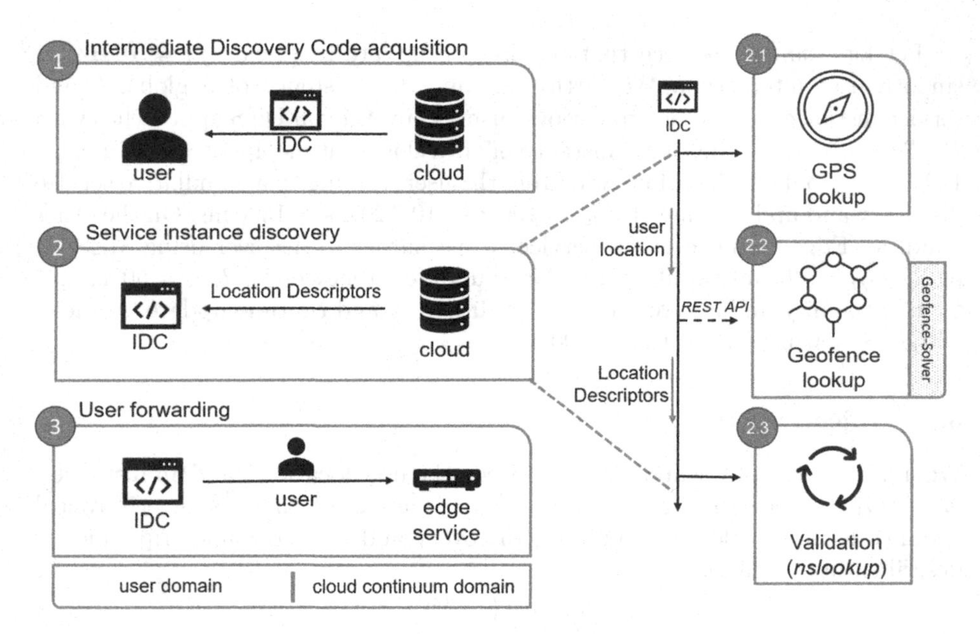


**Fig. 2.** MESDD architecture overview.

*Service instance discovery:* The actual discovery process is the core phase implemented in the IDC. This step aims to generate a valid *service instance URL* using the LD provided to the user for access. For this purpose, it needs to identify all LDs of the geofences surrounding a user and which contain valid service instances in three steps.

1. *GPS lookup* is the first step of the IDC that acquires the user (device) location, such as the `navigator.geolocation` JavaScript object used in our implementation. The output of this step is the location.
2. *Geofence lookup* uses an external interface provided by the `Geofence-Solver` service that returns a list of geofences surrounding the user's input location. We implemented the solver as a geofence application hosted on the same Web server as the IDC, accessed using a REST interface, and used a third-party implementation to validate if a user is in a geofence [8]. The service provider provisions the geozones in a GeoJson standard format [1] accessible to the service. The localization problem solved by the geofence application is a *point-in-polygon* with a vast number of algorithms [25] solving it. The geofence application uses an R-tree representation and follows the search method proposed in [5] (see Sect. 3.5).
3. *Validation* avoids selecting and forwarding the user to an invalid service instance if the geofences provided to the `Geofence-Solver` do not match the records maintained by the DNS server. The DNS server performs health checks that avoid resolving invalid services. The validation uses the hierarchies established in Sect. 3.1 and stops after finding a valid DNS address verified by an `nslookup` operation.

*User forwarding:* The last phase in the discovery process uses the URL the service instance discovery provides. The IDC forwards the user to the selected Edge service instance (e.g., `IS44.klagenfurt.kaernten.app.domain`). If the discovery could assemble no service instance URL based on the user location, the forwarding will target a global service instance (e.g., in the `app.domain`). There is no validation for the global instance because it acts as a last resort. The discovery process ends with the termination of the IDC in the user's browser.

## 5 Experimental Setup

We describe in this section the experimental testbed and evaluation scenarios involving three related methods and a real application.

### 5.1 Testbed

We deployed an experimental testbed using four servers in different geographical locations hosting different services, which are either instances of the desired service or are part of the discovery process.

*Global Cloud server* resides in the Google Cloud data center in Iowa, USA, and hosts a worldwide instance of the target service used as a fallback if MESDD cannot identify a closer service instance.

*Service Cloud server* resides in a data center in Vienna, Austria, and hosts an instance of the target service and other components required by the discovery.

- `Apache Web server` provides the IDC via HTTP or HTTPS and addressed using a static URL tag (e.g., `idc.app.domain`), and implementing the discovery process to the user, as described in Sect. 4. The IDC is a static JavaScript that requires no persistence (cookies) or personal data despite the interface call to the `Geofence-Solver`;
- `Geofence-Solver` *service* addressed by a static URL (e.g., `geo.app.domain`) manages the geofence application and performs a geofence lookup for a given user location using a REST interface (see Sect. 3.2). The service provisions geofences in a distinct directory as GeoJSON files (see Sect. 4).

*DNS server* resides in a different data center in Vienna and hosts the Consul [21] service that provides name resolution [15] and health check monitoring capabilities. The service provider is responsible for representing all geofences using an LD registered with the service instances managed by Consul.

*Edge server* hosted in Klagenfurt, Austria, provides the Edge instances of the service instances at the same location with the user and addressed according to the scheme introduced in Sect. 3 (e.g., `IS43.klagenfurt.kaernten.app.domain`).

*Local personal computer* at the university campus in Klagenfurt, Austria, represents the reference client that downloads the IDC and executes the discovery.

### 5.2 Related Work Comparison

We evaluate MESDD compared with three related methods.

*Consul* [19] is a DNS-based discovery registry that resolves the services addressed in DNS syntax. Its architecture includes a master DNS server and slave service instances that monitor the discoverable services. This state-of-the-art method does not incorporate any information on the users' location.

*DNS Service Discovery (DNS-SD)* [22], similar to Consul, uses the DNS protocol for resolving services but relies on broadcasting instead of direct communication. Instances providing a certain service listen to requests from any user consuming this service. The benefit is zero configuration and simple selection of the instance answering first on the broadcast with the lowest latency. The biggest limitation is that the broadcast in public networks fails or gives insufficient results.

*Discovery Geo-Broker (DisGB)* [7] is a publish/subscribe service discovery and data exchange approach that relies on a geographically distributed broker in the Cloud and at the Edge. Users can subscribe to services in certain areas, and publishers share their data on certain topics. A hierarchy of brokers effectively exchanges data and propagates information at the expense of long delays. Moreover, the overall publish/subscribe scheme is incompatible with most applications like video streaming or gaming.

### 5.3 Traffic Warning Application

We use a traffic warning application that requires low-latency communication and location awareness to manage essential health and traffic services. A camera-based emergency vehicle detection enables a local service at a specific intersection to warn other vehicles of incoming emergency vehicles. Figure 3 depicts an example of using geofences to segment an intersection and the four connecting alleys denoted as `D1`, `D2`, `D3`, and `D4`. Sensors connected to an Edge server on the roadside detect incoming emergency vehicles in the distance. User applications can register on an Edge server assigned to the intersection for alleys. An emergency vehicle entering from the north and traversing the geofence `D1` triggers a callback indicating an imminent danger or additional attention. The alignment of the geofences aids in informing drivers and pedestrians affected by the emergency vehicle. For example, a driver traversing the intersection `IS43` from geofence `D2` to `D3` and leaving the area might not be relevant. However, if another vehicle enters `D2`, the emergency vehicle in `D4` interferes with it. Nevertheless, informing all drivers in this intersection area on their mobile devices is a recommendation.

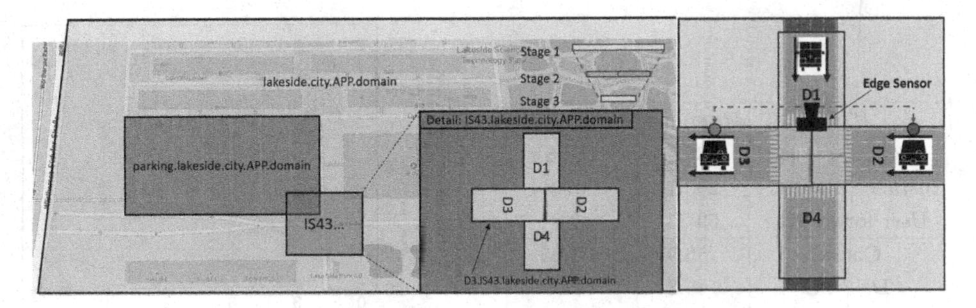


**Fig. 3.** Illistrative traffic warning application scenario.

We assume an emergency vehicle moving between geofences describing intersections and designated directions. A single service instance using the service in the fourth Edge geofence level (see Table 1) operates the intersection (`IS43`). This constraint shows that customization on the IDC can provide additional functionality in our scheme. To identify the transit between geofences, we distinguish between the initial service discovery and the runtime service update, as presented in Sect. 4. In this example, the discovery executes on all geofence levels, but the validation step will stop at the third level, beyond which there are no more service instances.

## 6 Results

We evaluate the performance of MESDD in terms of the discovery round-trip and runtime update performance compared to the three related approaches.

### 6.1 Service Discovery

The first evaluation focuses on the discovery round-trip time (see Sect. 3.3), assuming no previous service discovery. We assume a local user at the University of Klagenfurt and repeated the service discovery 100 times in sequence to assess the stability of the measurements.

We observe in (Fig. 4) that MESDD shows a round trip discovery time of 545.23 ms, split among the IDC acquisition, instance discovery, and user forwarding phases.

MESDD has 24 % longer discovery round-trip time than Consul and DNS-SD, which use simple lookups without acquiring the IDC or considering the user's location. Consul benefits from direct access to cloud instances using DNS. Still, there is no particular distribution of the users in this approach. DNS-SD's mean discovery time of 145.57 ms is more than three times longer than Consul. DisGB exhibits very high discovery times of more than 1055 ms in 95 % of the cases due to latency assumptions from the original simulation [7] based on a publish/subscribe implementation using the message queuing telemetry transport.

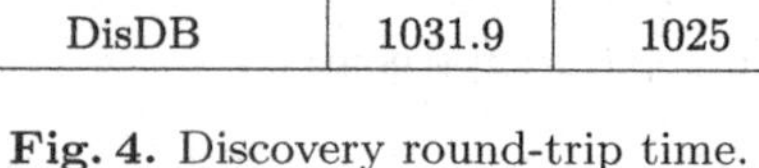

| *RTT* | *Mean* [ms] | *Median* [ms] |
|---|---|---|
| IDC acquisition | 280.9 | 302.8 |
| Instance discovery | 205.1 | 207.8 |
| User forwarding | 59.23 | 49.8 |
| Consul | 156.9 | 153.05 |
| DNS-SD | 145.3 | 142.3 |
| DisDB | 1031.9 | 1025 |

**Fig. 4.** Discovery round-trip time.

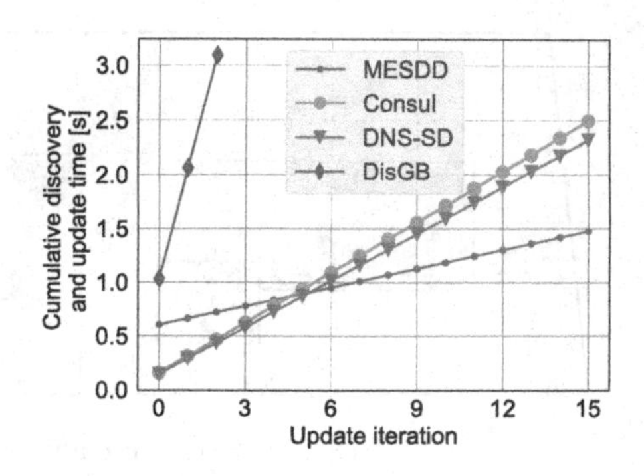


**Fig. 5.** Runtime service update.

### 6.2 Cumulative Service Discovery and Runtime Update

The second evaluation focuses on the runtime service update of a user remaining inside a geofence after performing an initial service discovery on the testbed described in Sect. 5.1.

The results in Fig. 5 extend the initial service discovery measurements from Table 4 (replicated as the iteration 0) with 14 iterative updates, as described in Sect. 3.4. MESDD geofence-aware method discovered service instances at the Edge server, which provides a low average update round-trip time of 59 ms to acquire service information. All the other approaches discovered services in the Cloud and require a higher update duration of 145 ms is average. While Consul and DNS-SD outperformed MESDD in the discovery round-trip time due to the much simpler protocol as covered in Sect. 4, MESDD catches and outperforms their cumulative service discovery and runtime update after only four update iterations.

## 7 Conclusion

Service discovery and management are essential to operating low-latency IoT applications on the computing continuum. Moving services from the Cloud to the Edge enables service discovery and instantiation close to the users.

This paper introduced MESDD, a service discovery method that uses IDC to identify suitable service instances based on users' location in the computing continuum. MESDD addresses services with their LD based on a naming scheme used to determine their corresponding geofences. We deployed a testbed and compared MESDD with three related discovery methods over a real-life traffic warning application. Evaluation results show that the MESDD discovery of Edge services close to the users compensates for its increased complexity after five runtime update iterations and even improves the cumulative service discovery and update time by 40 % after 17 iterations.

In the future, we plan to improve service discovery by restricting the validity of results based on user mobility patterns to avoid unnecessary initial discovery operations with high latency.

**Acknowledgement.** This work received funding from the European Commission's Horizon 2020 program (grant 101016835, DataCloud) and Austrian Research Promotion Agency (FFG) (grant 888098, Kärntner Fog).

## References

1. Butler, H., Daly, M., Doyle, A., Gillies, S., Schaub, T., Hagen, S.: The GeoJSON Format, RFC 7946 (2016)
2. Cheshire, S., Krochmal, M.: RFC 6763: DNS-based service discovery (2013)
3. Dharanyadevi, P., et al.: Internet of things-based service discovery for the 5G-VANET Milieu. In: Cloud and IoT-Based Vehicular Ad Hoc Networks, pp. 31–45 (2021)
4. ETSI. Enhanced DNS support towards distributed MEC environment, WP, 39 (2020)
5. Guttman, A.: R-trees: a dynamic index structure for spatial searching. In: Proceedings of the 1984 ACM SIGMOD International Conference on Management of Data (New York, NY, USA), SIGMOD 1984. Associate for Computing Machinery, pp. 47–57 (1984)
6. Han, T., Sim, K.M.: An ontology-enhanced cloud service discovery system. In: Proceedings of the International MultiConference of Engineers and Computer Scientists, vol. 1, pp. 17–19 (2010)
7. Hasenburg, J., Bermbach, D.: DisGB: using geo-context information for efficient routing in geo-distributed pub/sub systems. In: 2020 IEEE/ACM 13th International Conference on Utility and Cloud Computing, pp. 67–78 (2020)
8. Heroux, B.: Geofence service (2023)
9. Horvath, K.: MESDD reference implementation (2023)
10. Horvath, K., Wöllik, H., Christoph, U., Egger, V.: Location-based service discovery for mobile-edge computing using DNS. In: Yang, X.S., Sherratt, S., Dey, N., Joshi, A. (eds.) Proceedings of Seventh International Congress on Information and Communication Technology. LNCS, vol. 447, pp. 379–388. Springer, Singapore (2023). https://doi.org/10.1007/978-981-19-1607-6_33
11. Hsu, K.J., Choncholas, J., Bhardwaj, K., Gavrilovska, A.: DNS does not suffice for MEC-CDN. In: Proceedings of the 19th ACM Workshop on Hot Topics in Networks, HotNets 2020, Association for Computing Machinery, pp. 212–218 (2020)
12. Jawade, B., Goyal, K.: Low computation in-device geofencing algorithm using hierarchy-based searching for offline usage. In: 2018 3rd International Conference on Inventive Computation Technologies, pp. 591–596. IEEE (2018)
13. Kimovski, D., Mehran, N., Kerth, C.E., Prodan, R.: Mobility-aware IoT applications placement in the cloud edge continuum. IEEE Trans. Serv. Comput. **15**, 3358–3371 (2021)
14. Mastorakis, S., Mtibaa, A.: Towards service discovery and invocation in data-centric edge networks. In: 2019 IEEE 27th ICNP, pp. 1–6 (2019)
15. Mockapetris, P. : Domain names - concepts and facilities, RFC 1034 (1987)
16. Mumtaz, S., Huq, K.M.S., Rodriguez, J.: Direct mobile-to-mobile communication: paradigm for 5G. IEEE Wirel. Commun. **21**(5), 14–23 (2014)
17. Murturi, I., Dustdar, S.: A decentralized approach for resource discovery using metadata replication in edge networks. IEEE Trans. Serv. Comput. **15**, 2526–2537 (2021)

18. Namiot, D., Sneps-Sneppe, M.: Geofence and network proximity. In: Balandin, S., Andreev, S., Koucheryavy, Y. (eds.) NEW2AN/ruSMART -2013. LNCS, vol. 8121, pp. 117–127. Springer, Heidelberg (2013). https://doi.org/10.1007/978-3-642-40316-3_11
19. Paliwal, A., Shafiq, B., Vaidya, J., Xiong, H., Adam, N.: Semantics-based automated service discovery. IEEE Trans. Serv. Comput. **5**(2), 260–275 (2011)
20. Quevedo, J., Antunes, M., Corujo, D., Gomes, D., Aguiar, R.L.: On the application of contextual IoT service discovery in information centric networks. Comput. Commun. **89**, 117–127 (2016)
21. Sabharwal, N., Pandey, S., Pandey, P.: Getting started with HashiCorp consul. In: Infrastructure-as-Code Automation Using Terraform, Packer, Vault, Nomad and Consul, pp. 167–199. Apress, Berkeley, CA (2021). https://doi.org/10.1007/978-1-4842-7129-2_7
22. Stolikj, M., Cuijpers, P., Lukkien, J., Buchina, N.: Context based service discovery in unmanaged networks using MDNS/DNS-SD. In: 2016 IEEE International Conference on Consumer Electronics (ICCE), pp. 163–165 (2016)
23. Tanganelli, G., Vallati, C., Mingozzi, E.: Edge-centric distributed discovery and access in the internet of things. IEEE IoT J. **5**, 425–438 (2017)
24. Teranishi, Y., et al.: Demo abstract: LASK: a distributed service discovery platform on edge computing environments. In: 2019 IEEE 27th International Conference on Network Protocols (ICNP), pp. 1–2 (2019)
25. Xiao, N.: GIS algorithms. SAGE Advances in Geographic Information Science and Technology Series, SAGE Publications (2015)
26. Zhou, J., Abdullah, N.A., Shi, Z.: A hybrid P2P approach to service discovery in the cloud. Int. J. Inf. Technol. Comput. Sci. **3**(1), 1–9 (2011)

# Parameterized Analysis of a Dynamic Programming Algorithm for a Parallel Machine Scheduling Problem

Istenc Tarhan[1,2(✉)], Jacques Carlier[2], Claire Hanen[1,3], Antoine Jouglet[2], and Alix Munier Kordon[1]

[1] Sorbonne Université, CNRS, LIP6, 75005 Paris, France
{Istenc.Tarhan,Claire.Hanen,Alix.Munier}@lip6.fr
[2] UTC Heudiasyc, Compiègne, France
{Istenc.Tarhan,Jacques.Carlier,Antoine.Jouglet}@hds.utc.fr
[3] UPL, Université Paris Nanterre, 92000 Nanterre, France
http://www.lip6.fr

**Abstract.** We consider in this paper the scheduling problem defined by a set of dependent jobs with release times and deadlines to be processed by identical parallel machines. This problem is denoted by $P|prec, r_i, d_i|\star$ in the literature. Starting from an extension of the Branch-and-Bound algorithm of Demeulemeester and Herroelen to take into account release times and deadlines, we build a state graph of which longest paths represent all active schedule. New dominance rules are also proposed.

We establish that our state graph construction algorithm is fixed-parameter tractable. The two parameters are the pathwidth, which corresponds to the maximum number of overlapping jobs time windows and the maximum execution time of a job. The algorithm is experimented on random instances. These experiments show that the pathwidth is also a key factor of the practical complexity of the algorithm.

**Keywords:** Scheduling · Parallel machines · Release times and deadlines · Branch-and-Bound · Fixed-parameter tractable

## 1 Introduction

Scheduling problems with resource limitation and precedence constraints have many applications in various fields, such as production systems, the use of multi-core parallel machines, or the design of embedded systems. Also, many authors have developed exact or approximate algorithms to efficiently solve these problems since the beginning of the sixties. Several books and surveys are dedicated to this class of combinatorial optimization problems [3,5,13].

This paper considers the basic scheduling problem defined by a set of $n$ non-preemptive jobs $\mathcal{T}$ to be executed by $m$ identical machines. Each job $i \in \mathcal{T}$

Supported by EASI project, Sorbonne Universités.


J. Cano et al. (Eds.): Euro-Par 2023, LNCS 14100, pp. 139–153, 2023.
https://doi.org/10.1007/978-3-031-39698-4_10

has a positive processing time $p_i$, a release time $r_i$ and a deadline $d_i$; all these values are supposed to be integers. The starting time $s(i)$ of any job $i$ verifies $r_i \le s(i) \le d_i - p_i$. Each job $i \in \mathcal{T}$ has to be scheduled on one machine, each of which can process at most one job at a time. Lastly, a directed acyclic graph $G = (\mathcal{T}, E)$ defines a set of precedence constraints: for each arc $(i, j) \in E$, the associated constraint is $s(i) + p_i \le s(j)$. The problem is to find, if possible, a feasible schedule. This problem is denoted by $P|prec, r_j, d_j|\star$ using the Graham notation [10]. This problem is difficult to be solved exactly; indeed the $P|prec, p_j = 1|C_{\max}$ problem was proved to be NP-hard by Ullman [18].

The development of fixed-parameter tractable algorithms (FPT algorithms in short) makes it possible to push a little further the study of the existence of an efficient algorithm for some instances of a difficult problem [6,9]. A fixed-parameter tractable algorithm solves any instance of size $n$ of the problem with parameter $k$ in a time $\mathcal{O}(f(k) \times \text{poly}(n))$, where $f$ is allowed to be a computable superpolynomial function and $\text{poly}(n)$ a polynome of $n$.

The article of Mnich and van Bevern [14] surveys the existence of a FPT algorithm for classical scheduling problems and identifies 15 difficult questions in this context. Most of the results obtained so far conclude the non-existence of FPT algorithms for the considered parameters.

Among the key parameters with precedence constraints, several authors considered the parameter $w(G)$, the width of the precedence graph, since it seems to capture the parallelism of the instance. However, this parameter led mainly to negative results. For example, even for unit processing times, Bodlaender and Fellows [2] proved that the problem $P|prec, p_i = 1|C_{\max}$ is W[2]-hard parameterized by $w(G)$ and the number of machines. This discards $w(G)$ and the tuple of parameters $(w(G), p_{\max})$ to be good parameters of an FPT algorithm for our problem. The only known positive result is a FPT by van Bevern et al. [1] for the resource constrained scheduling problem with the tuple of parameter $(w(G), \lambda)$ where $\lambda$ as the maximal allowed lag of a task computed from the earliest schedule defined by precedence constraints defined.

Besides, Munier Kordon [15] developed recently a FPT algorithm based on dynamic programming for the decision problem $P|prec, r_j, d_j, p_j = 1|\star$. The parameter considered is the pathwidth $\mu = \max_{t \ge 0} |\{i \in \mathcal{T} \text{ s.t. } r_i \le t < d_i\}|$ which corresponds to the maximal number of overlapping jobs time windows at a single time $t$. This parameter hence seems then to be more powerful than the width of the precedence graph to obtain positive results. This approach was extended by Hanen and Munier Kordon in [11] to handle different processing times, but with the couple of parameters $(\mu, p_{\max})$ where $p_{\max} = \max_{i \in \mathcal{T}} p_i$; the time complexity of this algorithm belongs to $\mathcal{O}(f(\mu, p_{\max}) \times n^4)$. They also proved that the scheduling problem $P2|r_i, d_i|\star$ parameterized by the pathwidth is para-NP-complete as well as $P|prec, r_i, d_i|\star$ parameterized by $p_{\max}$; it follows that unless $\mathcal{P} = \mathcal{NP}$, there is no FPT algorithm for $P|prec, r_i, d_i|\star$ parameterized by only one of these parameters.

Branch-and-Bound methods are usually considered to develop efficient algorithms for NP-complete scheduling problems. In the nineties, several authors developed Branch-and-Bound methods to handle the resource-constrained project scheduling denoted by $PS|prec|C_{\max}$; see Brucker et al. [4] for the notation and a survey on these methods. The Demeulemeester and Herroelen algorithm (denoted by the DH algorithm from now) [7] is one of the most efficient Branch-and-Bound methods to solve efficiently this class of problems [8]. To our knowledge, there is no worst-case complexity analysis of this algorithm.

We first proved that the tree-based exploration scheme of the DH algorithm [7] can be transformed into the construction of a state graph $\mathcal{G}$. The nodes of the state graph $\mathcal{G}$ correspond to those of the exploration tree and its path to feasible schedules. We also extended the initial DH definition of branching to handle release times and deadlines. Bounding techniques are not taken into account.

Several new original dominance properties based on the time windows structure follow and constitute another important contribution of this paper. They allowed us to prove that the number of states of the state graph is linear in the number of jobs for fixed values of the parameters $\mu$ and $p_{\max}$. Moreover, it can be built by a fixed parameter tractable algorithm in $\mathcal{O}(h(\mu, p_{\max}) \times n^3)$. This indicates the potential of the proposed algorithm for scheduling problems with tight time windows in which both parameters $\mu$ and $p_{\max}$ are not significantly high. We observed that the complexity obtained here is better than the Hanen and Munier Kordon algorithm [11].

Our approach also illustrates that FPT algorithms can be built from Branch-and-Bound schemes that have been proven to be very efficient in practice only with a small overhead. This is an original approach that could be further applied to other problems.

The practical efficiency of the DH algorithm has already been measured [8] and the purpose of this paper is not to pretend that the approach developed here outperforms the existent ones. Instead, we aim to compare the performance of our algorithm on randomly generated instances with small values of the parameters with the theoretical upper bound of complexity. Our experiments show that the practical time complexity of the state graph generation also strongly depends on the pathwidth $\mu$. We also observed that the state graph can be completely generated for small values of the parameters even without bounding techniques.

The remainder of this paper is organized as follows. Section 2 is devoted to the definition of the state graph $\mathcal{G}$ inspired by the DH approach [7]. We specifically explain, in this section, the definition of states, how to generate successor states from a given state and characteristics of the longest paths of the state graph. Section 3 presents the new dominance rules that allow to restrict the definition of the considered states; our general dynamic programming (DP in short) algorithm to build the state graph $\mathcal{G}$ is also described. In the proposed dominance rules, we identify two sets of jobs such that the first set includes the jobs that have to be included in a partial feasible schedule with a given number of jobs whereas the second set includes the jobs that cannot be included in this partial feasible schedule. An upper bound on the number of states is established in Sect. 4 followed by the proof that the DP algorithm is FPT. Computational experiments for the DP algorithm are shared in Sect. 5. We conclude with final remarks in Sect. 6.

## 2 Definition of the State Graph $\mathcal{G}$

We prove in this section that the set of feasible active schedules associated to an instance of the considered scheduling problem can be represented by the maximum paths of an acyclic state graph $\mathcal{G}$. The definition of the nodes of this graph, called the states, comes from the nodes of the Branch-and-Bound DH algorithm [7] and is described in Subsect. 2.1. Each state $v$ is associated with a non-empty subset of partial schedules. Subsection 2.2 describes the definition of the eligible jobs among which successor states of a given state $v$ are built. Subsection 2.3 defines the successors of a state $v$. The two main differences with the DH algorithm are that release times and deadlines are considered and that, as we tackle a decision problem, we do not consider bounding techniques to prune states. Lastly, Subsect. 2.4 enhances the relation between the longest paths of the state graph $\mathcal{G}$ and active feasible schedules.

In Fig. 1, we present an example for 11 jobs and 3 machines with the job attributes and the precedence graph $G = (\mathcal{T}, E)$. This example will be used to illustrate the components of the DP algorithm throughout the paper.

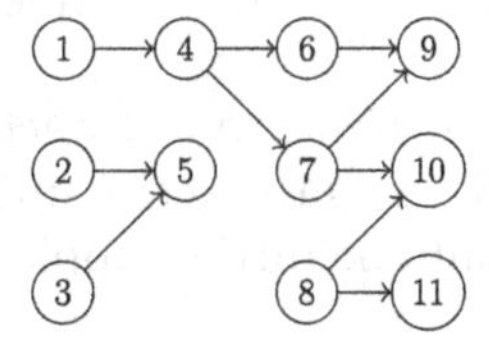


| *jobs* | 1 | 2 | 3 | 4 | 5 | 6 | 7 | 8 | 9 | 10 | 11 |
|---|---|---|---|---|---|---|---|---|---|---|---|
| $r_i$ | 0 | 0 | 1 | 2 | 5 | 7 | 7 | 9 | 11 | 12 | 13 |
| $d_i$ | 5 | 6 | 6 | 9 | 11 | 12 | 13 | 17 | 17 | 19 | 18 |
| $p_i$ | 2 | 4 | 2 | 4 | 5 | 3 | 4 | 2 | 3 | 2 | 1 |

**Fig. 1.** An instance of a scheduling problem $P|prec, r_i, d_i|\star$ for $n = 11$ jobs and $m = 3$ parallel machines.

### 2.1 Basic Definitions and States

**Definition 1 (Active and Semi-active schedule [16]).** *A feasible schedule is called* **semi-active** *(resp.* **active***) if no job can be left shifted by one time unit (resp. scheduled earlier) without changing the starting time of another job.*

**Definition 2 (Partial feasible schedule).** *Let $V \subseteq \mathcal{T}$ and $G_V = (V, E)$ be the precedence sub-graph of $G$ restrained to the set of jobs $V$. A* **partial feasible schedule** *is a feasible schedule of a subset of jobs $V$ following the precedence graph $G_V = (V, E)$ and all the constraints on jobs following the initial problem (release times, deadlines and machine limitations).*

**Definition 3 (States[7]).** *A* **state** *$v$ is a quadruplet $v = (V, t, P, M)$ where $V \subseteq \mathcal{T}$ is a set of jobs, $t \in \mathbb{N}$ is a date, $P \subseteq V$, and $M \in \mathbb{N}^{|P|}$ is a vector indexed following $P$. Moreover, there exists a partial feasible schedule $s$ of jobs $V$ such that:*

1. *Every job $i \in V \backslash P$ is completed before $t$, i.e. $s(i) + p_i < t$;*
2. *Every job $i \in P$ starts before $t$ and is completed at time $M_i \geq t$, i.e. $s(i) = M_i - p_i < t \leq M_i$.*

*Hereafter, we use $V(v)$, $t(v)$, $P(v)$, and $M(v)$ to refer to set $V$, time moment $t$, set $P$ and function $M$ of state $v$. The* **level** *of a state $v$ is the number of jobs in $V(v)$.*

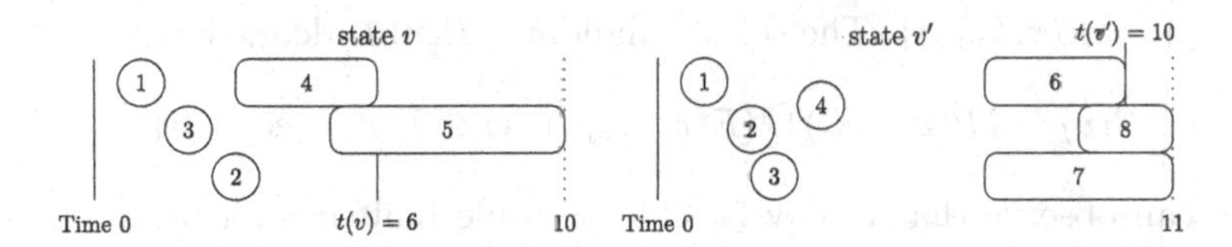


**Fig. 2.** On the left, the state $v$ with $V(v) = \{1, 2, 3, 4, 5\}$, $t(v) = 6$, $P(v) = \{4, 5\}$, $M_4(v) = 6$ and $M_5(v) = 10$. On the right, the state $v'$ with $V(v') = \{1, 2, 3, 4, 6, 7, 8\}$, $t(v') = 10$, $P(v') = \{6, 7, 8\}$, $M_6(v') = 10$, and $M_7(v') = M_8(v') = 11$.

Figure 2 presents two states $v$ and $v'$. The exact completion times of the jobs in set $P(v)$ and $P(v')$ are respectively stored in $M(v)$ and $M(v')$. Jobs in $V(v) \backslash P(v) = \{1, 2, 3\}$ are completed in time period $[0, 5]$ yet their completion times are not recorded in the state. Similarly, jobs in $V(v') \backslash P(v') = \{1, 2, 3, 4\}$ are completed in time period $[0, 9]$.

### 2.2 Set $R(v)$ of Candidate Jobs and $t_{\min}$

This section aims at computing first the set $R(v)$ of candidate jobs among which maximal subsets of at most $m$ jobs are selected to be scheduled in a new partial schedule that defines a new candidate state.

Let us consider a state $v$ and a time instant $t \geq t(v)$. For any job $i$ we denote by $\Gamma^{-\star}(i)$ the set of all ancestors of $i$ in the precedence graph $G$. We then define the following three subsets of jobs:

- $IP(v, t) = \{i \in P(v), M_i(v) > t\}$ is the set of jobs of $P(v)$ that are in progress at time $t$;
- $E(v, t) = \{i \in \mathcal{T} \backslash V(v), \Gamma^{-\star}(i) \subseteq V(v) \backslash IP(v, t)\}$ is the set of eligible jobs at time $t$ following $v$, i.e. these jobs are not in $V(v)$ and all of their ancestors are in $V(v)$ and completed by time $t$;
- $D(v, t) = E(v, t) \cap \{i \in \mathcal{T}, r_i \leq t\}$, the set of tasks schedulable at time $t$ following precedence relations and release times.

Two particular dates are considered: the first one is defined by $t_{\min} = \min\{t, t \geq t(v) \text{ and } D(v, t) \neq \emptyset\}$ as the earliest time for which a new job $j$ of $\mathcal{T} \backslash V(v)$ can start in any partial feasible schedule associated with state $v$.

Now, jobs from $E(v, t_{\min}) \backslash D(v, t_{\min})$ may be slightly delayed because of their release time if $r_i > t_{\min}$. In order to consider all jobs from $E(v, t_{\min})$ that can be scheduled before the completion of a job $i \in IP(v, t_{\min}) \cup (\mathcal{T} \backslash V(v))$, we define the earliest completion time of $i$ by

$$ect(v, i) = \begin{cases} M_i(v) & \text{if } i \in IP(v, t_{\min}) \\ \max\{t_{\min}, r_i\} + p_i & \text{if } i \in \mathcal{T} \backslash V(v). \end{cases}$$

If $ect(v, i) > d_i$ for some job $i \in IP(v, t_{\min}) \cup (\mathcal{T} \backslash V(v))$ then the state $v$ can be pruned. Otherwise, the earliest completion time of any eligible job in progress at $t_{\min}$ or starting not earlier than $t_{\min}$ is defined as $ect^{\star}(v) = \min\{ect(v, i), i \in E(v, t_{\min}) \cup IP(v, t_{\min})\}$. The set of candidates $R(v)$ is defined as:

$$R(v) = IP(v, t_{\min}) \cup (E(v, t_{\min}) \cap \{i \in \mathcal{T}, r_i < ect^{\star}(v)\}).$$

One can observe that in any feasible schedule built from a partial schedule associated with state $v$, jobs in $\mathcal{T} \backslash (V(v) \cup R(v))$ cannot start their execution in the interval $[t_{\min}, ect^{\star}(v))$. Moreover, no job of $R(v)$ will complete earlier than $ect^{\star}(v)$. Thus, no additional job $\mathcal{T} \backslash (V(v))$ is to be considered to build the immediate successor states of state $v$.

Considering the example state $v$ in Fig. 2, computation of set $R(v)$ is performed in the following three steps. Firstly we state $t_{\min} = 7$, the earliest possible starting time of a job in $\mathcal{T} \backslash V(v)$. Jobs 6 and 7 can be scheduled at time 7, i.e. $D(v, t_{\min}) = \{6, 7\}$. In the second step, we calculate $ect^{\star}(v)$ which is the earliest completion time among the jobs 6, 7 and job 5 (the in-progress job at time $t_{\min}$). Here $ect^{\star}(v) = 10$ as the earliest completion time of jobs 5, 6 and 7 are 10, 10 and 11, respectively. In the third step, we check if there exists eligible jobs that are released in $(t_{\min}, ect^{\star}(v))$. In our example, job 8 is eligible to be started at time $9 \in (7, 10)$. Eventually, set $R(v) = \{5, 6, 7, 8\}$.

### 2.3 Successors of a State $v$

Now, for each subset $C \subseteq R(v)$ of $|C| = \min(m, |R(v)|)$ jobs, we derive if possible a new state $u$ successor of $v$ as follows:

- Jobs from $IP(v, t_{\min})$ are discarded if not included in $C$, and thus $V(u) = (V(v) \backslash IP(v, t_{\min})) \cup C$;
- $P(u) = C$ and for every job $j \in C$, $M_j(u) = ect(v, j)$;
- The time instant $t(u) = \min_{j \in C} M_j(u)$.

An additional test is done to ensure that no job in a partial schedule associated with $u$ derived from $v$ can be locally left shifted. Let us first consider the set $Q = \{i \in P(v), M_i(v) < t_{\min}\}$, that is the set of jobs in $P(v)$ that complete before time $t_{\min}$. We also consider the set $IP(v, t_{\min}) \backslash C$ of jobs removed from $P(v)$ to build $V(u)$. We observe that, if $Q \cup (IP(v, t_{\min}) \backslash C) \neq \emptyset$ then at least one machine is empty in the interval $[t_{\min} - 1, t_{\min})$. So, if a job $i \in C \backslash P(v)$ is schedulable strictly before the instant $t_{\min}$, then the state $u$ can be discarded as the associated schedule is not semi-active.

Consider state $v$ in Fig. 2. As $R(v) = \{5, 6, 7, 8\}$ and $m = 3$, for each subset of $R(v)$ with 3 jobs, a successor state will be derived from state $v$. State $v'$ in Fig. 2 is generated by considering subset $C = \{6, 7, 8\}$. While job 5 is included in set $V(v)$, it is not a part of $V(v')$ since it is not in subset $C$ generating state $v'$. Thus, $V(v')$ is equal to $(V(v)\backslash\{5\}) \cup \{6, 7, 8\}$. Set $P(v')$ is equal to subset $C$ of which job completion times are 10, 11 and 11 (as stored in $M(v')$). Accordingly, $t(v')$ is set to the minimum of the completion times in $M(v')$ which is 10. While computing set $R(v)$, we only consider the jobs that can be scheduled between $t(v) = 6$ and $ect^{\star}(v) = 10$. Other jobs that can start at time 10 or later will be handled in the successor states of state $v'$.

### 2.4 Longest Path of the State Graph

For any value $\alpha \in \{1, \ldots, n\}$, $\mathcal{V}_\alpha$ denotes the set of states of level $\alpha$. We set then $\mathcal{V}_0 = \{u_0 = (\emptyset, 0, \emptyset, \bullet)\}$. Here, $\bullet$ represents an empty vector $M$.

By definition of states, each path from the state $u_0$ to a state $u_n$ of $\mathcal{V}_n$ is associated to a feasible schedule of makespan $\max_{i \in P(u_n)} M_i(u_n)$. We proved in [17] that conversely, every active schedule corresponds to a path from $u_0$ to a state of $\mathcal{V}_n$.

We conclude that any state $u \in \cup_{\alpha=0}^{n-1} \mathcal{V}_\alpha$ which does not belong to such a path can be discarded, if possible.

**Definition 4 (Perfect state and schedule associated with a perfect state).** *A state $u$ is a* **perfect state** *if there exists a path from $u_0$ to $u$ and from $u$ to a state of $\mathcal{V}_n$. If $u$ is a perfect state, a* **schedule $s$ is said to be associated with** *$u$, if it satisfies the following properties:*

1. *Every job $i \in V(u)\backslash P(u)$ is completed before $t(u)$, i.e. $s(i) + p_i < t(u)$;*
2. *Every job $i \in \mathcal{T}\backslash V(u)$ starts after time $t$, i.e. $s(i) \geq t(u)$;*
3. *Every job $i \in P(u)$ such that $M_i = t(u)$ starts at time $s(i) = M_i - p_i$. Every job $i \in P(u)$ with $M_i > t(u)$ starts either at time $M_i - p_i$ or at time $s(i) \geq t(u)$.*

In the next section we define dominance properties satisfied by perfect states.

## 3 Implementation of the DP Algorithm

This section aims at developing an algorithm building the state graph $\mathcal{G}$ described previously. In order to limit the number of states, two original properties on the perfect states structure are proved in Subsect. 3.1. Subsection 3.2 recalls a dominance property considered by the DH [7]. Our DP algorithm is briefly presented in Subsect. 3.3.

### 3.1 Dominance on States Structure

For each value $\alpha \in \{0, \ldots, n\}$, we define $Z_\alpha$ as the first $\max\{0, \alpha - \mu\}$ jobs (to recall, $\mu = \max_{t \geq 0} |\{i \in \mathcal{T} \text{ s.t. } r_i \leq t < d_i\}|$), when jobs are sorted in increasing order of their deadlines, i.e. $d_1 \leq d_2 \leq ... \leq d_n$. We note that if the job deadlines are not all different, we break ties with job indexes. Thus, the size of set $Z_\alpha$ is always $\max\{0, \alpha - \mu\}$.

Similarly, for each value $\alpha \in \{0, \dots, n\}$, let $Z'_\alpha$ be the set of the first $\min\{n - \max\{0, \alpha - \mu\}, 2\mu\}$ jobs that are not included in $Z_\alpha$ when jobs are sorted in increasing order of their release times such that $r_1 \leq r_2 \leq ... \leq r_n$. Again, we break ties considering the job indexes if necessary.

For convenience, we provide the cardinality of sets $Z_\alpha$ and $Z'_\alpha$ for different $n$ and $\alpha$ values in Table 1.

**Table 1.** Values $|Z_\alpha| = max\{0, \alpha - \mu\}$, $|Z'_\alpha| = \min\{n - max\{0, \alpha - \mu\}, 2\mu\}$ and $|Z_\alpha| + |Z'_\alpha|$ following $n$, $\alpha$ and $\mu$.

| Case | Subcase | $\|Z_\alpha\|$ | $\|Z'_\alpha\|$ | $\|Z_\alpha\| + \|Z'_\alpha\|$ |
|---|---|---|---|---|
| $n < 2\mu$ | $\alpha \leq \mu$ | 0 | $n$ | $n$ |
| | $\alpha > \mu$ | $\alpha - \mu$ | $n - (\alpha - \mu)$ | $n$ |
| $n \geq 2\mu$ | $\alpha \leq \mu$ | 0 | $2\mu$ | $2\mu$ |
| | $\mu < \alpha < n - \mu$ | $\alpha - \mu$ | $2\mu$ | $\alpha + \mu$ |
| | $\alpha \geq n - \mu$ | $\alpha - \mu$ | $n - (\alpha - \mu)$ | $n$ |

**Lemma 1.** *For any value $\alpha \in \{1, \dots, n\}$ and any perfect state $u \in \mathcal{V}_\alpha$, $Z_\alpha \subseteq V(u)$.*

*Proof.* For $\alpha \leq \mu$ we have $Z_\alpha = \emptyset$. Therefore, we consider a state $u \in \mathcal{V}_\alpha$ with $\alpha > \mu$. Let also $S$ be any feasible schedule associated with $u$. Let $t$ be the starting time of the job of $V(u)$ starting the latest in $S$, i.e. $t = \max_{j \in V(u)} s(j)$. Thus, for each job $j \in V(s)$, $r_j \leq s(j) \leq t$. Moreover, by definition of $S$ and $V(u)$, jobs in $\mathcal{T} \backslash V(u)$ can start at time $t(u)$ at the earliest, i.e. $t < t(u) \leq s(j)$ for every $j \in \mathcal{T} \backslash V(u)$.

By contradiction, assume that there exists a job $i \in Z_\alpha$ with $i \in \mathcal{T} \backslash V(u)$. Then, $s(i) > t$ and thus $d_i > t$. Now, by definition of $Z_\alpha$, all jobs in $V(u) \backslash Z_\alpha$ have a deadline greater than or equal to $d_i$ i.e. $d_j \geq d_i > t, \forall j \in V(u) \backslash Z_\alpha$. Two cases must be considered:

- If $r_i > t$, then $\forall j \in V(u) \backslash Z_\alpha$, $r_j \leq t < r_i < d_i \leq d_j$. Since $|V(u) \backslash Z_\alpha| \geq \mu$, there will be at least $\mu$ jobs overlapping with the time window of job $i$ which contradicts the definition of $\mu$.
- Similarly, if $r_i \leq t$, then $\forall j \in (V(u) \backslash Z_\alpha) \cup \{i\}, r_j \leq t < d_i \leq d_j$. All these at least $\mu + 1$ jobs overlap at time $t$, which contradicts the definition of $\mu$. □

**Lemma 2.** *For any value $\alpha \in \{1, \dots, n\}$ and any perfect state $u \in \mathcal{V}_\alpha$, $V(u) \subseteq Z_\alpha \cup Z'_\alpha$.*

*Proof.* If $n < 2\mu$ or if $\alpha \geq n - \mu$, $|Z_\alpha \cup Z'_\alpha| = |Z_\alpha| + |Z'_\alpha| = n$, and $Z_\alpha \cup Z_{\alpha'} = \mathcal{T}$ as shown in Table 1 and the proposition holds for these cases. Therefore, let us consider $n \geq 2\mu$ and a state $u \in \mathcal{V}_\alpha$ with $\alpha < n - \mu$; in this case $|Z'_\alpha| = 2\mu$.

By contradiction, let us suppose the existence of a job $i \in V(u) \backslash (Z_\alpha \cup Z'_\alpha)$. We first prove that $|Z'_\alpha \backslash V(u)| \geq \mu + 1$. Indeed, by Lemma 1, $Z_\alpha \subseteq V(u)$. Thus, $V(u)$ can be partitioned into the 3 sets: $Z_\alpha$, $\{i\}$ and the remaining jobs set $R$. Here, $|R| = |V(u) \backslash (Z_\alpha \cup \{i\})| = |V(u)| - |Z_\alpha| - 1 \leq \alpha - (\alpha - \mu) - 1 = \mu - 1$. Now, since $(Z_\alpha \cup \{i\}) \cap Z'_\alpha = \emptyset$ and $Z'_\alpha \cap V(u) \subseteq R$, thus $|Z'_\alpha \backslash V(u)| \geq |Z'_\alpha| - |R|$. Now, since $|Z'_\alpha| = 2\mu$ and $|R| \leq \mu - 1$, we get $|Z'_\alpha \backslash V(u)| \geq \mu + 1$.

Let $S$ be a semi-active schedule associated with $u$. Let us denote now by $t = \max_{j \in V(u)} s(j)$ the starting time of the job of $V(u)$ starting the latest in $S$. We prove that, for each $j \in Z'_\alpha \backslash V(u)$, $r_j \leq t < d_j$. Indeed, each job $j \in Z'_\alpha \backslash V(u)$ verifies $s(j) \geq t(u) > t$, thus $d_j > t$. Now, since job $i$ is scheduled before or at time $t$, $r_i \leq s(i) \leq t$. As $i \notin Z_\alpha \cup Z'_\alpha$ and $r_i \geq r_j$ for every job $j \in Z'_\alpha \backslash V(u)$, we get $r_j \leq r_i \leq t$.

Thus all the time windows of jobs in $Z'_\alpha \backslash V(u)$ overlap during interval $(t, t+1)$. Since $|Z'_\alpha \backslash S_\alpha| \geq \mu + 1$, this contradicts the definition of parameter $\mu$. □

**Theorem 1.** *For any value $\alpha \in \{0, \ldots, n\}$ and any perfect state $u \in \mathcal{V}_\alpha$, $P(u) \cap Z_\alpha = \emptyset$, and thus $Z_\alpha \subseteq V(u) \backslash P(u)$ and $P(u) \subseteq Z'_\alpha$.*

*Proof.* Since $Z_\alpha = \emptyset$ for $\alpha \leq \mu$, we only consider $\alpha > \mu$. In this case, by Lemma 1, $|V(u) \backslash Z_\alpha| = \mu$.

By contradiction, let us consider a job $i \in P(u) \cap Z_\alpha$. Since $i \in P(u)$, in the partial semi-active schedule associated with $u$, $i$ is either in-progress or completed at time $t(u)$ and therefore $d_i \geq t(u) > r_i$. Now, as $i \in Z_\alpha$, every job $j \in V(u) \backslash Z_\alpha$ verifies $d_j \geq d_i \geq t(u)$. Moreover $r_j \leq s(j) < t(u)$.

Thus, every job $j \in \{i\} \cup (V(u) \backslash Z_\alpha)$ verifies $r_j < t(u) \leq d_j$; we deduce that there are at least $\mu + 1$ jobs $j$ for which $(t(u) - 1, t(u)) \subset (r_j, d_j]$ which contradicts the definition of $\mu$.

Lastly, by Lemma 1, $Z_\alpha \subseteq V(u)$, and thus $Z_\alpha \subseteq V(u) \backslash P(u)$. By Lemma 2 this implies that $P(u) \subset Z'_\alpha$, which achieves the proof. □

If a state $u$ does not verify one of the inclusion properties expressed by Theorem 1, then $u$ is not a perfect state and will be discarded.

For our example, the level of state $v$ in Fig. 2 is 5, i.e. $v \in \mathcal{V}_5$, while $Z_5 = \{1\}$ and $Z'_5 = \{2, 3, 4, 5, 6, 7, 8, 9\}$. Both Lemmas 1 and 2 and Theorem 1 hold for states $v$ and $v'$.

### 3.2 Dominance of Demeulemeester and Herroelen

The following dominance property proved by Demeulemeester and Herroelen [7] is still valid in the presence of release times and deadlines:

**Proposition 1.** *[7] Consider two states $v$ and $v'$ with $V(v) = V(v')$, and such that $t(v') \geq \max_{i \in P(v) \backslash P(v')} M_i(v)$ and $\forall i \in P(v) \cap P(v'), M_i(v) \leq M_i(v')$. Then if $v'$ is perfect then $v$ is perfect, so $v'$ can be discarded.*

### 3.3 Steps of the Dynamic Programming Algorithm

The main steps of the DP algorithm are presented by Algorithm 1. Line 4 computes $R(v)$ and $t_{\min}$ as described in Sect. 2.2. The function *NewState* called at line 6 builds a new state $u$ following Subsect. 2.3. The conditions of Theorem 1 are also checked and it returns false if the state is discarded. Function *AddDiscardOrReplace* decides to add $u$ or not to $\mathcal{V}_\alpha$ and maintains $\mathcal{V}_\alpha$ as a list of undominated states according to Proposition 1.

**Algorithm 1.** DP algorithm for building the state graph $\mathcal{G}$

1: $\mathcal{V}_0 = \{(\emptyset, 0, \emptyset, \emptyset)\}$, $\mathcal{V}_\alpha = \emptyset$ for $\alpha \in \{1, \ldots, n\}$, $\mathcal{A} = \emptyset$, $\mathcal{S} = \mathcal{V}_0$
2: **while** $\mathcal{S} \neq \emptyset$ **do**
3: Pick a state $v \in \mathcal{S}$ and remove it from $\mathcal{S}$
4: Compute $R(v), t_{\min}$
5: **for** each subset $C \neq \emptyset$ of $R(v)$ s.t. $|C| = \min(m, |R(v)|)$ **do**
6: $u \leftarrow NewState(v, t_{\min}, C)$
7: **if** $u \neq false$ **then**
8: $u \leftarrow AddDiscardOrReplace(u, \mathcal{V}_{\alpha'})$ where $\alpha' = |V(u)|$
9: **if** $u \neq false$ **then**
10: $\mathcal{S} = \mathcal{S} \cup \{u\}$, $\mathcal{A} \leftarrow \mathcal{A} \cup \{(v, u)\}$
11: **end if**
12: **end if**
13: **end for**
14: **end while**
15: **return** $\mathcal{G}(\mathcal{V}, \mathcal{A})$ where $\mathcal{V} = \bigcup_{\alpha=0}^{n} \mathcal{V}_\alpha$

Any search strategy (breadth-first, depth-first, other) can be used to build the state graph $\mathcal{G}$. To solve the decision problem, we just have to stop whenever a state $v$ such that $V(v) = \mathcal{T}$ is reached (i.e. belongs to $\mathcal{G}$). If an optimization function is considered for which active schedules are dominant, the DH dominance can be modified and discarding states based on bounds can be easily added to this framework.

## 4 Complexity Analysis of the DP Algorithm

This section establishes that when the breadth-first search is used, the DP algorithm is fixed-parameter tractable for parameters $(\mu, p_{\max})$. The following lemma uses dominance properties to bound the whole number of states.

**Lemma 3.** *For any perfect state $v$, the number of perfect states $u$ such that $V(u) = V(v)$ is bounded by $(2 \times p_{\max})^\mu$.*

*Proof.* Consider a perfect state $v$ of level $\alpha$, i.e. $|V(v)| = \alpha$.

- By Theorem 1, $Z_\alpha \subseteq V(v)\backslash P(v) \subseteq V(v)$, thus $|V(v)\backslash Z_\alpha| = |V(v)| - |Z_\alpha| = \alpha - \max\{0, \alpha - \mu\} \leq \mu$. Now, by Theorem 1, we also get $P(v) \subseteq V(v)\backslash Z_\alpha$; since $|V(v)\backslash Z_\alpha| \leq \mu$, the total number of possibilities for $P(v)$ when $V(v)$ is fixed is then bounded by $2^\mu$;
- Let us suppose now that $V(v)$ and $P(v)$ are fixed. Then, if $t(v)$ is fixed, each job $i \in P(v)$ must have its completion time $M_i(v)$ in $\{t(v), \ldots, t(v) + p_i - 1\}$. Thus, $(p_{\max})^{|P(v)|}$ is an upper bound of the total number of possible $M(v)$ vectors. Moreover, by Proposition 1, for any fixed $M(v)$ vector, only the smallest possible value of $t(v)$ needs to be considered.

So, for a given subset $V(v)$, the number of states is bounded by $(2 \times p_{\max})^\mu$, and the lemma is proved. □

**Lemma 4.** *The total number of states of level $\alpha$ is bounded by $f(\mu, p_{\max})$ with $f(\mu, p_{\max}) = \binom{2\mu}{\mu} \times (2 \times p_{\max})^\mu$.*

*Proof.* Consider a perfect state $v$ of level $\alpha$, i.e. $|V(v)| = \alpha$. As seen above, by Theorem 1 we get $|V(v)\backslash Z_\alpha| \leq \mu$. Moreover, by Lemma 2 $V(v) \subseteq Z_\alpha \cup Z'_\alpha$ and by definition $|Z'_\alpha| \leq 2\mu$. Thus, $V(v)$ contains $Z_\alpha$ and at most $\mu$ elements of $Z'_\alpha$; the number of possibilities for $V(v)$ is thus bounded by $\binom{2\mu}{\mu}$.

Now, by Lemma 3, the total number of perfect states associated to a set $V(v)$ is bounded by $(2 \times p_{\max})^\mu$. Thus, the total number of states of level $\alpha$ is bounded by $\binom{2\mu}{\mu} \times (2 \times p_{\max})^\mu$, which achieves the proof. □

We can now state our main result.

**Theorem 2.** *Algorithm 1 using breadth-first search is a FPT algorithm of time complexity*

$$\mathcal{O}\left(2^{4\mu} \times p_{\max}^{2\mu} \times \sqrt{\mu} \times n^3\right).$$

*Proof.* The complete proof is given in [17]. We just outline the main arguments.

1. According to Lemma 4, there are at most $f(\mu, p_{\max}) = \binom{2\mu}{\mu} \times p_{\max}^\mu \times 2^\mu$ states of level $\alpha$ for $\alpha \in \{0, \ldots, n\}$. Thus, the whole number of states is $\mathcal{O}(f(\mu, p_{\max}) \times n)$;
2. For each state $v$ of level $\alpha$, we proved in [17] that $|R(v)| \leq \mu$, and that the computation of $R(v)$ and $t_{\min}$ is in time $\mathcal{O}(n^2\mu)$ (line 4 of Algorithm 1);
3. The number of subsets $C$ in line 5 is bounded by $\binom{\mu}{\lceil \mu/2 \rceil}$. A single call to *NewState*$(v, t_{\min}, C)$ is in $\mathcal{O}(n)$, so that the complexity of lines 5:6 for a state $v$ is $\mathcal{O}(\binom{\mu}{\lceil \mu/2 \rceil} \times n)$;
4. Lastly, once a new state $u$ is built, if the level of $u$ is $\alpha$, *AddDiscardOrReplace* first recognizes if a state $u'$ with $V(u') = V(u)$ has already been stored in $\mathcal{V}_\alpha$. As $u$ fulfills Theorem 1, $V(u')$ and $V(u)$ would only differ by how they intersect $Z'_\alpha$. So, the set $V(u)$ can be encoded with respect to set $Z'_\alpha$ i.e. using $2\mu$ bits. Using an appropriate data structure, $V(u)$ can thus be searched in $\mathcal{O}(\mu^2 \ln(\mu))$. Then, by Lemma 3, at most $(2 \times p_{\max})^\mu$ states are compared to $u$, each in $\mathcal{O}(\mu)$. So $g(\mu, p_{\max}) = \mu(\mu \ln(\mu) + (2 \times p_{\max})^\mu)$ steps are needed for each new state $u$ in line 8.

So, we get the overall time complexity

$$\mathcal{O}\left(f(\mu, p_{\max})\left(n^3 \times \mu + n^2 \times \binom{\mu}{\lceil \mu/2 \rceil} + n \times g(\mu, p_{\max})\binom{\mu}{\lceil \mu/2 \rceil}\right)\right)$$

We can then use Stirling's formula (i.e. $n! \sim \sqrt{2\pi n}\left(\frac{n}{e}\right)^n$) to show that $\binom{2\mu}{\mu} \leq \frac{2^{2\mu}}{\sqrt{\mu}}$) and to approximate $\binom{2\mu}{\mu}$ and $\binom{\mu}{\lceil \mu/2 \rceil}$, which achieves the proof. □

# 5 Computational Experiments

We conduct preliminary experiments in order to analyse the practical limit of the complete state graph generation. We also measure the execution time when the state graph generation is stopped as soon as a feasible schedule is found.

## 5.1 Data Generation

We develop a problem instance generator that takes values of $n, m, \mu$ and $p_{\max}$ as inputs and returns an instance with the corresponding parameters. The details of the data generation are presented in the companion paper [17].

We consider for our experiments $\mu \in \{5, 10, 15, 20, 25\}$, $n \in \{50, 100, 250, 500\}$ and $m \in \{2, 5, 10\}$. We first use small values of processing times by setting $p_{\max} = \mu$. Then we consider the case $p_{\max} = n$ that may lead to a high worst case complexity. We generate instances for all cross-combinations of the possible parameter values except the cases where $\mu < m$. For each distinct tuple $(n, \mu, m, p_{\max})$, we generate 15 instances. Instances with 50 and 100 jobs are referred to moderate-size instances as the instances with 250 and 500 jobs are referred to as large-size instances. Similarly, when $p_{\max}$ is equal to $\mu$ and $n$, it is referred to as small and high, respectively.

## 5.2 Computational Results

In our computational experiments, we apply the depth-first search in accordance with the objective of finding a feasible solution. The enumeration of subsets $C$ on line 5 of Algorithm 1 uses sorted earliest starting times of the jobs in $R(v)$ where ties are broken considering the ascending order of deadlines. Thus, the first chosen new state schedules the jobs with the earliest starting times (and earliest deadlines in case of ties) in set $R(v)$ and thereby follows the Jackson's rule [12]. We use one hour time limit for each instance such that the DP algorithm is terminated after one hour if the state graph cannot be completely generated yet.

In Table 2, we provide the percentage of the instances for which the state graph can be generated completely. In our results, the impact of the instance size on the complete state graph generation percentages is less significant according to the impacts of other parameters, especially $\mu$. This is consistent with the complexity of the proposed FPT so that its complexity is polynomial in the number of jobs $n$.

**Table 2.** Complete state graph generation percentages for different tuples $(n, p_{\max}, m, \mu)$.

| $n$ | $p_{\max}$ | $m$ | $\mu$ | | | | |
|---|---|---|---|---|---|---|---|
| | | | 5 | 10 | 15 | 20 | 25 |
| moderate | small | 2 | – | 100.0 | 100.0 | 66.7 | 0.0 |
| | | 5 | – | 100.0 | 80.0 | 0 | 0.0 |
| | | 10 | – | – | 100.0 | 86.7 | 10.0 |
| | high | 2 | 100.0 | 100.0 | 100.0 | 66.7 | 0.0 |
| | | 5 | – | 100.0 | 66.7 | 0.0 | 0.0 |
| | | 10 | – | – | 100.0 | 73.3 | 13.3 |
| large | small | 2 | 100.0 | 100.0 | 100.0 | 50.0 | 0.0 |
| | | 5 | – | 100.0 | 33.3 | 3.3 | 0.0 |
| | | 10 | – | – | 100.0 | 70.0 | 16.7 |
| | high | 2 | 100.0 | 100.0 | 83.3 | 10.0 | 0.0 |
| | | 5 | – | 100.0 | 13.3 | 0.0 | 0.0 |
| | | 10 | – | – | 100.0 | 70.0 | 13.3 |

- We first note that $\mu$ seems to be a key parameter in practice, since the percentages are clearly decreasing with $\mu$ in every cases. For $\mu = 10$ the whole state graph can be generated, for $\mu = 25$ it is hopeless;
- The value of $m$ has an impact. We can observe that for $m = 2$ or $m = 10$ the percentages are often similar, whereas when $m = 5$ the percentage dramatically decreases. This could be partially explained since the number of enumerated sets $C$ is bounded by $\binom{\mu}{m}$ which is lower for low or high values of $m$;
- The impact of $n$ is quite limited with respect to $\mu$ when $m$ is either 2 or 10, even for $p_{\max} = n$.

Besides, we observed that higher number of states can be pruned by the dominance criterion as the number of machines gets smaller. Specifically, the overall percentages of the dominated states over the total number of states generated are 63.5%, 45.5% and 28.7% when the number of machines is 2, 5 and 10, respectively.

In all our experiments, when the state graph was completely generated, instance required less than 1812.7 s on average. Most of the instances required much less time.

We also analyzed when the first feasible solutions are found in the feasible instances. For most of them, we can find a feasible solution in less than 0.01 s. For only 18 of all feasible instances, the first feasible solution finding time is greater then 0.10 s and only for 5 of them, it is greater than 5 s.

## 6 Conclusion

In this paper we developed a new dynamic programming approach to solve the decision problem $P|prec, r_i, d_i|\star$ starting from the Demeulemeester and Herroelen Branch-and-Bound algorithm [7]. We proved that the tree built by this algorithm can be transformed into a state graph. New dominance rules based on the release times and deadlines were provided allowing to bound the number of states and proving that our algorithm is FPT with respect to parameters $(\mu, p_{\max})$ when the breadth-first search is used. Preliminary experiments highlighted that the practical efficiency of our algorithm depends mainly on parameter $\mu$.

Branch-and-Bound methods are widely used and often efficient to solve practically scheduling problems; however, their worst case complexity is rarely studied. Parameterized complexity offers a new angle of approach to measure the parameters that explain an efficiency or inefficiency for some instances. Thus, as a perspective of this work, the study of other Branch-and-Bound-based methods for more general scheduling problems and their adaptation in FPT, depending on the parameters, seems promising.

**Acknowledgments.** This work was supported by the EASI project funded by Sorbonne Universités.

## References

1. van Bevern, R., Bredereck, R., Bulteau, L., Komusiewicz, C., Talmon, N., Woeginger, G.J.: Precedence-constrained scheduling problems parameterized by partial order width. In: Kochetov, Y., Khachay, M., Beresnev, V., Nurminski, E., Pardalos, P. (eds.) DOOR 2016. Lecture Notes in Computer Science, pp. 105–120. Springer International Publishing, Cham (2016). https://doi.org/10.1007/978-3-319-44914-2_9
2. Bodlaender, H.L., Fellows, M.R.: W[2]-hardness of precedence constrained k-processor scheduling. Oper. Res. Lett. **18**(2), 93–97 (1995). Sep
3. Brucker, P.: Scheduling Algorithms, 4th edn. Springer, Cham (2004)
4. Brucker, P., Drexl, A., Möhring, R., Neumann, K., Pesch, E.: Resource-constrained project scheduling: notation, classification, models, and methods. Eur. J. Oper. Res. **112**(1), 3–41 (1999)
5. Chen, B., Potts, C.N., Woeginger, G.J.: A review of machine scheduling: complexity, algorithms and approximability. In: Du, D.Z., Pardalos, P.M. (eds.) Handbook of Combinatorial Optimization, pp. 1493–1641. Springer, US, Boston, MA (1998). https://doi.org/10.1007/978-1-4613-0303-9_25
6. Cygan, M., et al.: Parameterized Algorithms, 1st edn. Springer Publishing Company, Cham (2015). https://doi.org/10.1007/978-3-319-21275-3
7. Demeulemeester, E., Herroelen, W.: A branch-and-bound procedure for the multiple resource-constrained project scheduling problem. Manage. Sci. **38**(12), 1803–1818 (1992)
8. Demeulemeester, E.L., Herroelen, W.S.: New benchmark results for the resource-constrained project scheduling problem. Manage. Sci. **43**(11), 1485–1492 (1997)
9. Downey, R.G., Fellows, M.R.: Fundamentals of Parameterized Complexity, 1st edn. Springer-Verlag, London (2013). https://doi.org/10.1007/978-1-4471-5559-1

10. Graham, R., Lawler, E., Lenstra, J., Kan, A.: Optimization and approximation in deterministic sequencing and scheduling: a survey. In: Hammer, P., Johnson, E., Korte, B. (eds.) Discrete Optimization II, Annals of Discrete Mathematics, vol. 5, pp. 287–326. Elsevier (1979)
11. Hanen, C., Munier Kordon, A.: Fixed-parameter tractability of scheduling dependent typed tasks subject to release times and deadlines. J. Schedul. (2023). https://doi.org/10.1007/s10951-023-00788-4
12. Jackson, J.R.: Scheduling a production line to minimize maximum tardiness. University of California, Technical report (1955)
13. Leung, J.Y.T.: Handbook of Scheduling: Algorithms, Models, and Performance Analysis, 1st edn. Chapman & Hall/CRC, Boca Raton (2004)
14. Mnich, M., van Bevern, R.: Parameterized complexity of machine scheduling: 15 open problems. Comput. Oper. Res. **100**, 254–261 (2018)
15. Munier Kordon, A.: A fixed-parameter algorithm for scheduling unit dependent tasks on parallel machines with time windows. Discret. Appl. Math. **290**, 1–6 (2021)
16. Sprecher, A., Kolisch, R., Drexl, A.: Semi-active, active, and non-delay schedules for the resource-constrained project scheduling problem. Eur. J. Oper. Res. **80**(1), 94–102 (1995)
17. Tarhan, I., Carlier, J., Hanen, C., Jouglet, A., Munier Kordon, A.: Parametrized analysis of an enumerative algorithm for a parallel machine scheduling problem (2022). (hal-03840284)
18. Ullman, J.D.: Np-complete scheduling problems. J. Comput. Syst. Sci. **10**(3), 384–393 (1975)

# SparkEdgeEmu: An Emulation Framework for Edge-Enabled Apache Spark Deployments

Moysis Symeonides[1(✉)], Demetris Trihinas[2], George Pallis[1], and Marios D. Dikaiakos[1]

[1] Department of Computer Science, University of Cyprus, Nicosia, Cyprus
{msymeo03,pallis,mdd}@ucy.ac.cy
[2] Department of Computer Science, University of Nicosia, Nicosia, Cyprus
trihinas.d@unic.ac.cy

**Abstract.** Edge Computing emerges as a stable and efficient solution for IoT data processing and analytics. With big data distributed engines to be deployed on edge infrastructures, users seek solutions to evaluate the performance of their analytics queries. In this paper, we introduce SparkEdgeEmu, an interactive framework designed for researchers and practitioners who need to inspect the performance of Spark analytic jobs without the edge topology setup burden. SparkEdgeEmu provides: (i) parameterizable template-based use cases for edge infrastructures, (ii) real-time emulated environments serving ready-to-use Spark clusters, (iii) a unified and interactive programming interface for the framework's execution and query submission, and (vi) utilization metrics from the underlying emulated topology as well as performance and quantitative metrics from the deployed queries. We evaluate the usability of our framework in a smart city use case and extract useful performance hints for the Apache Spark code execution.

**Keywords:** Edge Computing · Internet of Things · Big Data

## 1 Introduction

The proliferation of the Internet of Things (IoT) has led to an explosion in installations of IoT devices and in the amount of IoT-generated data. Recent reports estimate that by 2025 IoT will comprise around 41 billion devices in operation worldwide, producing on a daily basis about 80ZB of data [9]. However, typical IoT devices do not have adequate storage capacity and processing power to perform analytics tasks. Thus, application designers and operators recognized the need to offload IoT data into more powerful computing platforms placed at the proximity of IoT data sources, to cope with processing, storage, and latency requirements of "earthbound" applications. This has led to the emergence of the Edge Computing paradigm, which offers in-place processing, data transfer


J. Cano et al. (Eds.): Euro-Par 2023, LNCS 14100, pp. 154–168, 2023.
https://doi.org/10.1007/978-3-031-39698-4_11

minimization, and on-time result calculation by deploying analytic tasks on edge-driven compute nodes. A typical edge node, however, does not have the capacity to host and run demanding analytics jobs that arise in many application use cases. Therefore, big data engines, like Apache Spark, provide implementations, which distribute computation and data to multiple edge nodes, and take advantage of their aggregate capacity. These implementations hide the complexity arising from machine communication, task scheduling, fault tolerant operation, etc., behind higher-level abstractions for performing queries on IoT data [20]. However, predicting the resource needs and the performance behavior of analytic queries running on edge nodes that are deployed on a wide geographic area, exposed to possibly sub-optimal environmental conditions with limited computing resources and often unstable network connectivity, is a challenging endeavor [17,19]. It is expensive and time-consuming to develop, configure, test, and reproduce the conditions of large-scale, physical testbeds; consequently, testing and performance evaluation become major barriers for edge processing.

To alleviate the difficulties of a physical testbed, users attempt to evaluate the performance of their tasks via emulation frameworks [3,11], which mimic the conditions and effects of a physical deployment on the deployed services. Even if emulators achieve near-to-real conditions for the deployed services, users have to describe, containerize, and configure these services. Furthermore, emulation frameworks usually provide modeling toolkits that users require to define every emulated node and its properties manually, including processing capabilities, network configurations, deployed services, etc. Then, users need to evaluate the performance of the submitted exploratory queries on scattered datasets by extracting quantitative and utilization metrics from the deployed big data distributed engine and the underlying infrastructure [13]. Considering that the majority of analytic platform users are data scientists, they are not aware of distributed engine deployment, configuration, and monitoring.

To address these challenges, we introduce SparkEdgeEmu, a framework for interactive performance and bottleneck analysis of Apache Spark jobs deployed over emulated edge testbeds. Users only need to fulfill use case templates, leaving the framework to bootstrap the emulated testbed, deploy Spark services, inject the respective datasets , and capture monitoring metrics for post-execution performance analysis. The main contributions of this work are: (i) the *Modeling Abstractions* for parameterizable templates of scalable edge topologies, through which users select the respective use case and its parameters, as well as the topology's compute and network resources, (ii) an *Open-source Implementation*[1] of the SparkEdgeEmu that translates the use case model to a large-scale emulated Apache Spark testbed, providing multi-host scalability, inherited from its underlying emulator [19], query- and topology-level metrics for post-experiment performance evaluation and bottleneck identification analysis, which consequently helps in the query optimization process, and (iii) an *Experimental Study* of analytic queries executed on a city-scale testbed that uncovers hidden insights of the queries performance and the Apache Spark footprint.

[1] https://www.github.com/UCY-LINC-LAB/SparkEdgeEmu.

The rest of the paper is structured as follows: Sect. 2 describes the related work. Sections 3 and 4 show the framework and its implementation details, respectively. Section 5 presents the experiments and Sect. 6 concludes the paper.

## 2 Related Work

To evaluate the performance of a system, users typically embrace benchmarking suites that provide both workloads and monitoring capabilities. There is a plethora of benchmarking tools related to big data analytics. For instance, Yahoo YCSB [7] provides a range of diverse tools for DBMS benchmarking. Moreover, SparkBench [15] introduces ML, graph computation, SQL queries, and streaming workloads for Apache Spark. A study of latency and throughput between big data streaming engines is presented in [6], while Karimov et al. [13] provide a novel definition for the latency of stateful operators, a method to measure it and decouple the underlying systems from the driver that controls the experimentation to have fair results. An edge-oriented and automated approach is proposed in [10]. The authors introduce BenchPilot, a framework that is capable of performing repeatable and reproducible experiments on Edge micro-DCs. Even if the benchmarking studies alleviate the difficulties of analytic workload creation and experimentation, *they consider an already deployed edge infrastructure, which is sometimes unrealistic during the design phase.*

To create realistic testing conditions without facing the cost and the configuration effort of a real edge cluster, users turn to emulation frameworks. Frameworks like FogBed [8] and EmuEdge [22] notably expand network emulators (e.g., MiniNet [14]) to provide fog/edge resource and network heterogeneity. Interestingly, Beilharz et al. introduce Marvis [3], a hybrid testbed that combines simulated events with emulated infrastructure for evaluating distributed IoT applications. The system integrates the ns-3 network simulator with virtualization technologies and domain-specific simulators (e.g., traffic simulators). However, these solutions inherit the restrictions of the network emulators like strict modeling (i.e., the configuration of routers, gateways, IP masks) and limited scalability. To tackle these issues, a series of emulation frameworks introduce distributed cloud technologies via multi-host overlay networks and virtualization technologies. For example, MockFog [11] is a fog emulator that is deployable on AWS and OpenStack clusters, provides the required heterogeneity, and enables users to inject network faults at run-time. Moreover, other container-based Fog and 5G emulation frameworks [16,19,21] offer multi-host scalability, realistic emulation via ad-hoc topology updates, automated service deployment, and emulation monitoring. However, *none of the above solutions are focused on Spark analytic queries, leaving users to handle the barrier of containerization, configuration, deployment, and monitoring of the distributed processing engines.*

## 3 System Overview

The time-consuming infrastructure setup required for studying analytic queries' performance on the edge increases product time-to-market and turns analysts'

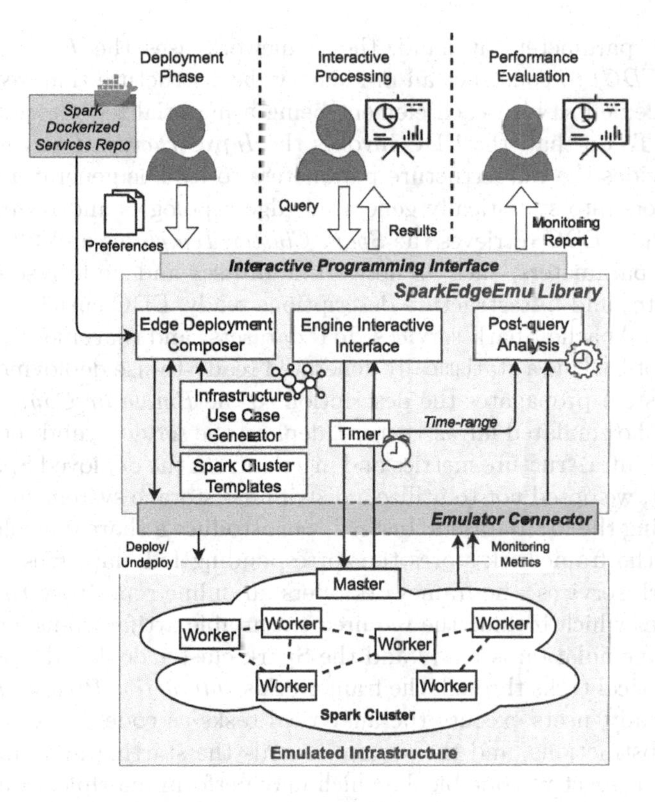


Fig. 1. System Overview

attention away from the actual purpose of query performance evaluation. To ease understanding, let us consider a use case where a data scientist wants to evaluate the performance of his/her analytic queries on a realistic smart city edge deployment. In particular, the data scientist needs an installed city-scale edge infrastructure along with a deployed big data engine to submit his/her queries and monitor their performance. However, operators are almost impossible to provide a ready-to-use infrastructure from the beginning of a project. Thus, users can only evaluate the performance of the analytic queries in a local virtualized environment or a rented Cloud cluster. This results in an error-prone performance that may over- or under-estimate the edge capabilities.

Contrary to this approach, users can embrace the SparkEdgeEmu Framework. The high-level overview of the framework is depicted in Fig. 1. The onboarding starts with the selection of a predefined use case via the framework's *modeling abstractions*, along with the definition of parameters like the number and the density of edge nodes, processing, and network QoS, which are based on statistical distributions extracted from real-world deployments [1,4,5,18]. For instance, for a smart city use case, users select the number of neighborhoods, the number of compute devices per neighborhood, cloud servers, and their capabilities and connectivity characteristics. Then, users submit the parameterized model to the platform via the *Interactive Programming Interface*.

With the parameters at hand, the framework uses the *Edge Deployment Composer (EDC)* to construct an in-memory data structure that keeps a set of deployable elements, with each element being a materialized view of the user's preferences. To do that, the EDC invokes the *Infrastructure Use Case Generator* and provides the infrastructure parameters to it. The generator transforms the parameters into statistically generated edge topologies and returns them to the EDC. Then, EDC retrieves the *Spark Cluster Templates* and fills them with service-level parameters, such as network addresses and node resources. With both templates and infrastructure descriptions ready, EDC enriches the topologies with the Apache Spark services, IoT datasets, and placement preferences. The output of EDC is a statistically generated ready-to-use deployment description. The system propagates the description to the *Emulator Connector*, which instantiates the emulated infrastructure, deploys the services, and retrieves both the emulated infrastructure metrics and metrics from the deployed Spark cluster. In this paper, we opted not to utilize a distributed storage system such as HDFS for distributing the IoT datasets. Instead, we introduce a shareable folder on each node where the framework stores the corresponding IoT data files[2]. Regarding Apache Spark services, the framework offers an online repository that contains docker images which include the required executable artifacts and binaries.

When the emulation is ready and the Spark cluster deployed, the users can submit analytical tasks through the framework's *Interactive Programming Interface*. Specifically, users execute the analytical tasks as code blocks via the programming abstractions, and the system records the starting and ending timestamps of the respective code block, which may perform multiple sequential analytic queries. When they are finished, users are aware of the duration of the queries and retrieve the captured metrics via the Post-query Analysis module.

The *Post-query Analysis* module requests the underlying infrastructure utilization metrics and big data engine statistics from the Emulator Connector, filtered by the code block's starting and ending timestamps. Finally, users may perform high-level analysis on the retrieved metrics generating a more clear overview of the submitted queries' performance.

## 4 Implementation Aspects

This section presents the framework's implementation aspects for SparkEdgeEmu key components.

**Modeling Abstractions.** There are several emulators that provide high-level modeling abstractions [16,19]. However, their users need to describe every single compute node and its network connections, which makes the design of a large-scale deployment challenging. To bridge the gap between scalability and expressivity, we introduce high-level template-based infrastructure and use case modeling abstractions. Model 1.1 depicts an example of system's modeling. Specifically, the users introduce the types of the devices (`devices_types`) and

[2] Possible issues regarding storage, like security concerns, are out of our scope. However, we plan to introduce an emulated distributed storage as a future extension.

connections (`connection_types`). For the devices, users have to specify the `name` of the device, the `processor`'s capabilities (including `cores` and `clock_speed`), the device's `memory`, and the `disk` capabilities (e.g., `technology`, `size`, `read` & `write` throughput, etc.). Moreover, a connection type has an identifier (`name`), and `uplink` & `downlink` QoS that include `data_rate`, `latency`, and `error_rate`.

We note that SparkEdgeEmu provides out-of-the-box profiles for popular edge devices, e.g., raspberries (`rpi3b`), and connections, e.g., `4G`, `5G`, and `wifi` standards, which users use without having to define them again. Finally, the `usecase` primitive materializes a randomized edge deployment. Specifically, use case includes a `usecase_type` that defines the selected template and a set of parameters, through which users configure the template. For instance, in Model 1.1, the use case refers to a `smart_city` template and users set its parameters, such as number of regions, devices per region and their types, the network type, etc.

```
1   infrastructure:
2       devices_types:
3       - name: small-vm
4         processor:
5           cores: 4
6           clock_speed: 1.5GHz
7         memory: 4GB
8         disk:
9           technology: SSD
10          size: 32GB
11          read: 95MB/s
12          write: 90MB/s
13        ....
14      connection_types:
15      - name: 5G
16        downlink:
17          data_rate: 90MBps
18          latency: 2ms
19          error_rate: 0.1%
20        uplink: ....
21  usecase:
22      usecase_type: smart_city
23      parameters:
24          num_of_regions: 3
25          num_of_devices_per_region: 7
26          edge_devices: [rpi3b , nuc]
27          edge_connection: 5G
28          cloudlets: [small-vm]
```

**Model 1.1.** Infrastructure & Use Case Parameters

**Interactive Programming Interface.** Next, SparkEdgeEmu users start the experimentation utilizing a Python-based programming interface (e.g., Code 1.1). The users execute the SparkEdgeEmu functions locally, while the framework handles communication with the underlying emulator and the emulated Apache Spark cluster. For the emulation, users submit the described use case creating a connector object (lines 1–4), and deploy the use case to the underlying emulation framework (line 5). In addition, our choice of Python enables us to leverage PySpark, a Python library that facilitates connectivity to an Apache Spark cluster. By instantiating an Apache Spark session object, users can submit their Spark code to the cluster simply by specifying the IP address of the master. Within the SparkEdgeEmu programming interface, we have implemented the "*create_spark_session*" function, which generates a session object with a pre-configured emulated Spark Master IP (lines 7–9). Through this function, users identify the Spark connection's configurations (e.g., executors' processing capabilities) and get an Apache Spark session object, which interactively communicates with the underlying emulated Apache Spark cluster. When users execute queries in code-blocks under the "*with connector.timer()*" statement (line 10), the system captures the duration of their execution. In this way, the system keeps the starting and ending point of the code block (lines 10–14) and can retrieve metrics from this period (line 15). The metrics include statistics from the deployed Apache Spark queries, e.g., the number of tasks (line 16) and metrics from the emulated infrastructure, e.g., CPU utilization (line 17).

```
1  connector = EmulatorConnector(
2                  controller_ip = '...',
3                  usecase = 'usecase.yaml'
4              )
5  connector.deploy()
6
7  spark_session = connector.create_spark_session(
8          app_name = 'app-1', configs = { ... } )
9
10 with connector.timer():
11     df = spark_session.read.csv('data.csv')
12     df.groupBy('DOLocationID') \
13       .agg({'driver_pay':'avg'}).collect()
14     ....
15 monitoring_data = connector.get_metrics()
16 monitoring_data['rpi3_b_0'].tasks.plot()
17 monitoring_data['rpi3_b_0'].cpu_util.plot()
```

**Code 1.1.** Programming Interaction Primitives

**Infrastructure Use Case Generator.** To materialize the infrastructure generator, we adopt and extend Ether [18], which is a framework for synthesizing plausible edge infrastructure configurations from a set of reference use cases, which are grounded on empirical data, including smart cities [4], Industrial IoT deployment [5], mobile edge clouds and vehicular networks [1]. Developers can utilize Ether's programming primitives and building blocks to create reusable edge infrastructure configurations and topologies. In our case, the Infrastructure Generator translates the use case modeling abstractions into Ether's programming primitives, and Ether creates an in-memory graph keeping all required information for both networks and compute nodes. However, Ether does not have all network or compute properties that our system needs. For example, Ether defines processing power as CPU cycles without considering the number of cores. For the latter, we extend Ether's node abstraction to encapsulate also CPU's number of cores and clock frequency. Moreover, an Ether-enabled use

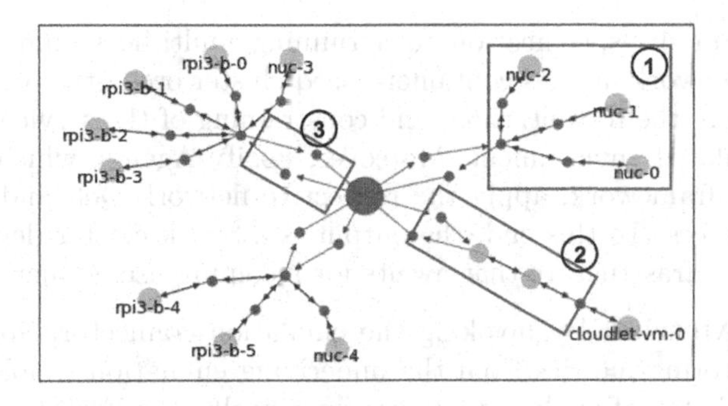


**Fig. 2.** Ether's Visualization for Smart City Use Case

case is framed in a geospatial context through which users evaluate the effects of geographically distributed edge systems. In such a setup, the nodes are distributed across a region by following a specific distribution, e.g., uniform or lognormal. Ether generates the respective connectivity for the nodes and produces the underlying network fabric. We upgrade the latter functionality by introducing realistic wireless signal quality models for 5G MIMO channels [21]. Figure 2 shows a representation of an auto-generated smart city use case with three neighborhoods and one cloudlet. The placement of nodes in a neighborhood follows lognormal distribution, as is highlighted in [2, 18], thus, each neighborhood has a different number of nodes. For instance, rectangle ① depicts a neighborhood with three Intel's Next Unit of Computing (NUC) nodes [12], while others have more nodes or include RPi3s. The yellow ② and green circles ③ depict network components, like switches, and uplink/downlink connections, respectively.

**Emulation & Deployment.** With the edge topology created, the *Edge Topology Composer* is responsible for the creation of the underlying emulation framework model. Specifically, the system fills the Spark templates with proper parameters to generate the Spark services and place them on the auto-generated topology. There are two types of templates for a Spark Cluster, one for the master node and one for the workers' nodes. In these templates, the Edge Topology Composer provides properties, like topology nodes' network addresses, hostnames, other Spark parameters, etc. When the templates are ready, Edge Topology Composer explores the in-memory graph of the infrastructure generator, utilizing Ether's exploration methods for graph and node-to-node analytics like, node's properties identification, uplink and downlink network QoS, link capacity, etc. Thus, the composer keeps the compute nodes' capabilities, identifies the network QoS links among the edge nodes, and forms the underlying emulation model by utilizing the Emulator Connector.

In our prototype, we create a connector for the Fogify emulation framework [19]. Fogify provides a programmable way to produce its model, multi-host scalability, and a less than 10% performance difference between emulation and physical infrastructure. Fogify's connector creates the emulation model and submits it through Fogify's API. Fogify validates the submitted description and translates the model specification to a running multi-host emulated environment. The framework utilizes container-based cluster orchestrators (e.g., docker swarm) to ensure the instantiation, and constraining of the services on the containerized emulated environment. Moreover, Fogify Agents, which are internal services of the framework, apply the respective network QoS and monitor the emulated instances. To this end, the output is a Spark cluster deployed on the emulated edge infrastructure that awaits for incoming user's queries.

**Monitoring Metrics.** By invoking the emulation connector, SparkEdgeEmu retrieves monitoring metrics from the underlying emulation topology after the execution of a batch of analytics queries. Specifically, the Fogify emulator offers a wide range of infrastructure utilization metrics, including CPU utilization, memory usage, network traffic, disk I/Os, etc. However, users do not only require metrics from the underlying infrastructure but also metrics and statistics from the running big data engine, e.g., the average execution time per task or the number of assigned tasks for a specific cluster node. Moreover, holistic metrics, like the overall execution latency or the overall consumed resources, are also important for the performance evaluation of analytics queries. For that reason, we extended Fogify's monitoring system to store metrics from a running deployed Apache Spark cluster. Specifically, Fogify's monitoring subsystem periodically polls the internal monitoring API of the deployed Apache Spark cluster and saves the retrieved measurements. The spark-related metrics refer to each worker and include (i) assigned, completed, and failed tasks, (ii) JVM memory, (iii) cached data size, (vi) CPU time, (v) per-task duration, and so on. Finally, SparkEdgeEmu offers methods for exposing these metrics in a unified manner through which users can combine, process, and analyze them.

## 5 Experimental Study

Next, we examine the use case of smart city deployment on Edge computing topology and analytic queries.

**Topology, Workload and IoT Data.** For the topology generation, we utilize the model of the smart city use case as introduced at Model 1.1 and the exemplary code snippet of Code 1.1. For the parameters of the use case, we set the number of neighborhoods equals to 3, the average number of edge devices in each neighborhood to 7, including Pi4 (4 GB), Pi3b+ raspberries, and NVIDIA Jetson Nanos. Except for the edge devices, we also introduce a cloudlet server with 8 CPUs@2.4 GHz and 8 GB memory. The generated topology includes 22 edge nodes and one cloudlet, with the first neighborhood having 4xRPi4, 2xRPi3b, and 1xJetson-Nano, the second neighborhood having 1xRPi4, 4xRPi3b, and 3xJetson-Nano, and, finally, the third neighborhood including 1xRPi4, 2xRPi3b, and 4xJetson-Nano. As a representative dataset, we utilize a publically available and real-world dataset comprised of For-Hire Vehicle ("FHV") trip routes in the first half of 2022 from New York city[3]. Each vehicle is equipped with an IoT

[3] https://goo.gl/X9rCpq.

**Table 1.** Submitted Queries

| Query | Description |
|---|---|
| Q1 | The average of payment grouped by the drop-off location |
| Q2 | The number of trips (count) per company |
| Q3 | The overall amount of tips that passengers provided |

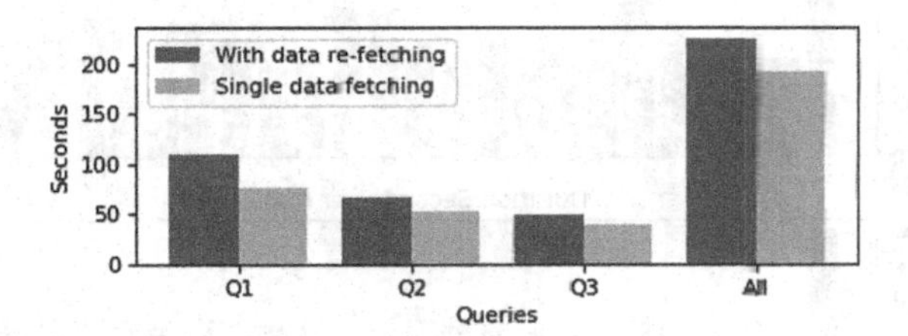


**Fig. 3.** Queries Execution Duration

tracking device to record 24 metrics for each route, including charged amount, tip amount, pickup/dropoff location, etc. We set the dataset to be stored and distributed over the edge nodes, and we submit three analytic queries on it with their descriptions to be on Table 1. All queries include multiple stages with the first stage digesting the input IoT data parquet[4] files. Each trial is repeated 10 times with final results depicting the overall measurements of all runs. All experiments are conducted with SparkEdgeEmu to be run on a server with 48cores@2.450 GHz and 176 GB memory.

### 5.1 Experiments and Results

**Code-Block Performance Evaluation Differences.** Firstly, we evaluated the performance of the queries (Table 1) deployed on the emulated topology. We examine each separate query but also all queries together as a code-block. Furthermore, we examine also how the data fetching influences the performance of the deployed queries. To evaluate the latter, we re-fetch the data at the beginning of each code-block execution, while to avoid the re-fetching, we retrieve the data once and keep them in memory. Figure 3 illustrates the average execution time of ten runs of each configuration. We observe that the execution time follows the same order (Q1>Q2>Q3) independently of the data-fetching approach. If we evaluate the semantics of the queries, we easily recognize that the Q1 is a group-by query that performs average, while Q2 is again a group-by query but only counts the data points. Intuitively, the averaging of a batch of data is heavier than a simple count. Furthermore, the group-by is performed in a different field, with the cardinality of drop-off locations being much higher than the number of car-sharing companies. For similar reasons, it is reasonable Q3 to be the most light-weight query in execution. According to the data fetching, it influences

[4] https://parquet.apache.org/.

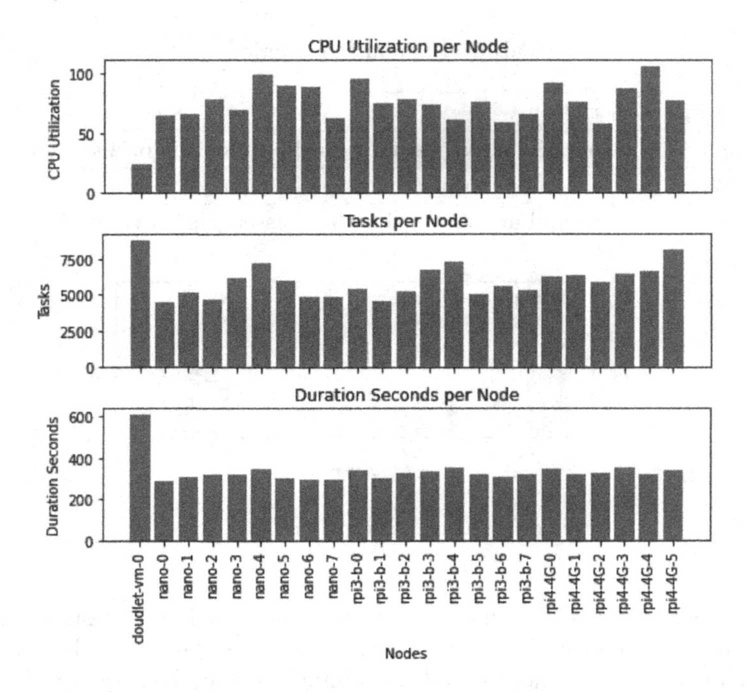


**Fig. 4.** CPU-related Metrics of the Experiment

the execution time in all experiments with an average overhead of about 25%. The latter indicates that Apache Spark does not identify possible optimizations in data-fetching during the repeatable executions and users should be aware of that. In conclusion, *SparkEdgeEmu Framework helps in performance analysis and performance bottleneck identification. During the experimentation, we highlight that the performance of group-by queries is characterized by the number of key elements and aggregation function, while Apache Spark seems to be unaware of data re-fetching and re-computations.*

For the rest of the experiments, we use metrics captured from the execution of all queries without data re-fetching.

**CPU & Analytic Tasks.** SparkEdgeEmu helps users to identify also the workload placement and nodes' utilization of the underlying cluster through its wide range of monitoring metrics. For instance, Fig. 4 depicts three bar charts from workload-related metrics, namely, the emulated node CPU utilization, the assigning tasks of Apache spark, and the cumulative duration in seconds that Apache Spark considers. Interestingly, we observe that the cloudlet VM was underutilized during the experimentation even if Apache Spark was assigned to it for most of the tasks. Moreover, Spark measured that cloudlet workers spent much more CPU time (Duration Seconds) than edge devices. As benchmarking efforts have already identified [10], *distributed processing big data engines tend to assign more tasks to more powerful nodes, while these nodes usually are underutilized in Edge topologies.*

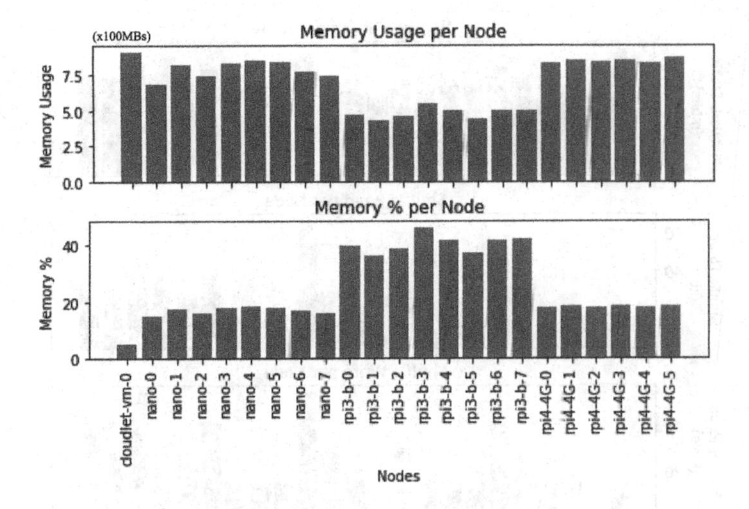


**Fig. 5.** Memory-related metrics of the Experiment

**Memory Consumption.** Another metric that influences the performance of the Apache Spark cluster is the consumed memory of the cluster's nodes. Figure 5 illustrates the consumed memory in bytes (x$10^8$) and the utilization percentage for every emulated node. We have to note here that we keep the default Apache Spark parameters in all experiments, so the default memory that an engine's worker can utilize is 1 GB. One can clearly identify that all nodes have about 700-750 MB occupied memory except for raspberries 3b which have about 400-500 MB. Since RPi3b has only 1 GB of memory, the average percentage of occupied memory is 40% for this device. In summary, *Apache Spark occupied less memory on edge memory-constrained devices, even if it assigns to them a similar number of tasks as the other Edge nodes (Fig.* 4).

**Network Traffic & Shuffling Data.** Figure 6 depicts network-related data extracted from both emulated infrastructure and Apache Spark cluster. Specifically, the first plot highlights the network traffic (both incoming and outgoing) in bytes (x$10^7$), while the second and the third plot illustrate the bytes generated from Spark's Shuffling Read and Write, respectively. Apache Spark generates shuffling data among different stages (usually when join or group operator is performed). So, the *Shuffle Write* metric illustrates how many bytes are generated from a local stage and should be transferred to another operator, while *Shuffle Read* metric is how many bytes are consumed by the current worker. An interesting observation is that the size of the network traffic captured by the emulator is higher than the traffic between the stages captured by the Apache Spark engine. The extra traffic among the cluster nodes could be health-check and the task-assigning messages that the engine uses to keep the cluster and processing alive. To this end, *the health-check and the task-assigning messages contribute a non-negligible extra overhead in network traffic.*

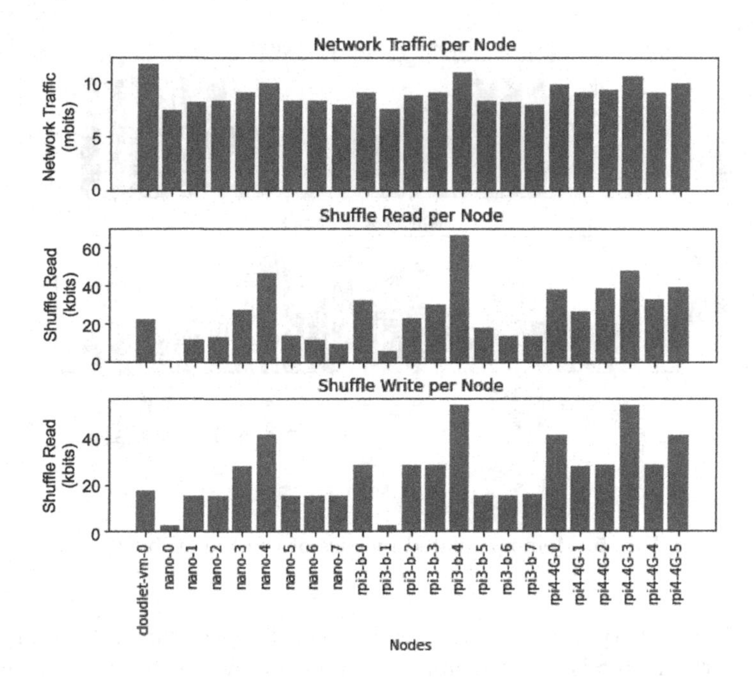


**Fig. 6.** Network-related metrics of the Experiment

# 6 Conclusion and Future Work

In this paper, we introduce SparkEdgeEmu, an interactive framework that facilitates in performance evaluation and assessment of analytic processing on Edge-enabled Apache Spark clusters. It provides a unified interface through which data analysts can: (i) create auto-generated scenario-based Edge topologies, (ii) materialize the topologies into a real-time emulation with a deployed Apache Spark cluster, (iii) submit analytic tasks and observe its results, (iv) inspect and monitor the execution of the map-reduce tasks, and (v) perform post-experimentation analysis on the captured measurements. Furthermore, we provided implementation details about the framework's programming abstractions, infrastructure generation, underlying emulation, and monitoring metrics extraction. Finally, we evaluated the useability of our approach via a representative city-scale use case and performed a wide analysis of IoT data and deployment performance.

**Future Work.** We plan to add more underlying emulators and test their accuracy by comparing them to real-world deployments. To evaluate them properly, we'll deploy edge devices in different locations, install Apache Spark on them, and collect utilization and performance metrics. Next, we will use the same parameters in our system and compare the metrics we collected with the emulated results. Moreover, to enhance the realism of our deployment, we plan to replace the data shareable folder with a distributed storage emulation, such as HDFS.

## References


1. 5G Automotive Association: C-ITS vehicle to infrastructure services: How C-V2X technology completely changes the cost equation for road operators. White paper (2019)
2. Austria, S.: Federal ministry for climate action, environment, energy, mobility, innovation and technology. https://www.senderkataster.at/
3. Beilharz, J., et al.: Towards a staging environment for the internet of things. In: 2021 IEEE International Conference on Pervasive Computing and Communications Workshops (PerCom Workshops), pp. 312–315 (2021)
4. Catlett, C.E., Beckman, P.H., Sankaran, R., Galvin, K.K.: Array of things: a scientific research instrument in the public way: platform design and early lessons learned. In: Proceedings of the 2nd International Workshop on Science of Smart City Operations and Platforms Engineering, pp. 26–33. ACM (2017)
5. Chen, B., Wan, J., Celesti, A., Li, D., Abbas, H., Zhang, Q.: Edge computing in IoT-based manufacturing. IEEE Commun. Mag. **56**(9), 103–109 (2018)
6. Chintapalli, S., et al.: Benchmarking streaming computation engines: storm, flink and spark streaming. In: IEEE IPDPSW (2016)
7. Cooper, B.F., Silberstein, A., Tam, E., Ramakrishnan, R., Sears, R.: Benchmarking cloud serving systems with YCSB. In: SoCC. ACM (2010)
8. Coutinho, A., Greve, F., Prazeres, C., Cardoso, J.: Fogbed: a rapid-prototyping emulation environment for fog computing. In: IEEE ICC (2018)
9. Dignan., L.: IoT devices to generate 79.4 ZB of data in 2025, says IDC (2019). https://bit.ly/3MVTY15
10. Georgiou, J., Symeonides, M., Kasioulis, M., Trihinas, D., Pallis, G., Dikaiakos, M.D.: BenchPilot: repeatable & reproducible benchmarking for edge micro-DCs. In: Proceedings of the 27th IEEE ISCC (2022)
11. Hasenburg, J., Grambow, M., Bermbach, D.: MockFog 2.0: automated execution of fog application experiments in the cloud. IEEE TCC **11**(01), 1 (2021)
12. Intel: Intel NUC for edge compute. https://www.intel.com/content/www/us/en/products/docs/boards-kits/nuc/edge-compute.html
13. Karimov, J., Rabl, T., Katsifodimos, A., Samarev, R., Heiskanen, H., Markl, V.: Benchmarking distributed stream data processing systems. In: IEEE ICDE (2018)
14. Lantz, B., Heller, B., Mckeown, N.: A network in a laptop: rapid prototyping for software-defined networks. In: ACM SIGCOMM HotNets Workshop (2010)
15. Li, M., Tan, J., Wang, Y., Zhang, L., Salapura, V.: Sparkbench: a comprehensive benchmarking suite for in memory data analytic platform spark. In: ACM International Conference on Computing Frontiers (2015)
16. Nikolaidis, F., Chazapis, A., Marazakis, M., Bilas, A.: Frisbee: a suite for benchmarking systems recovery. In: Proceedings of the 1st Workshop on High Availability and Observability of Cloud Systems. HAOC (2021)
17. Rathijit, S., Abhishek, R., Alekh, J.: Predictive price-performance optimization for serverless query processing. In: International Conference on Extending Database Technology, EDBT (2023)
18. Rausch, T., Lachner, C., Frangoudis, P.A., Raith, P., Dustdar, S.: Synthesizing plausible infrastructure configurations for evaluating edge computing systems. In: 3rd USENIX Workshop on Hot Topics in Edge Computing (HotEdge 20). USENIX Association (2020)
19. Symeonides, M., Georgiou, Z., Trihinas, D., Pallis, G., Dikaiakos, M.D.: Fogify: a fog computing emulation framework. In: IEEE/ACM SEC (2020)

20. Symeonides, M., Trihinas, D., Georgiou, Z., Pallis, G., Dikaiakos, M.: Query-driven descriptive analytics for IoT and edge computing. In: Proceedings of IEEE International Conference on Cloud Engineering (IC2E 2019) (2019)
21. Symeonides, M., Trihinas, D., Pallis, G., Dikaiakos, M.D., Psomas, C., Krikidis, I.: 5G-slicer: an emulator for mobile IoT applications deployed over 5G network slices. In: IEEE/ACM IoTDI (2022)
22. Zeng, Y., Chao, M., Stoleru, R.: EmuEdge: a hybrid emulator for reproducible and realistic edge computing experiments. In: IEEE ICFC (2019)

# ODIN: Overcoming Dynamic Interference in iNference Pipelines

Pirah Noor Soomro(✉), Nikela Papadopoulou, and Miquel Pericàs

Chalmers University of Technology, Gothenburg, Sweden
{pirah,nikela,miquelp}@chalmers.se

**Abstract.** As an increasing number of businesses becomes powered by machine-learning, inference becomes a core operation, with a growing trend to be offered as a service. In this context, the inference task must meet certain service-level objectives (SLOs), such as high throughput and low latency. However, these targets can be compromised by interference caused by long- or short-lived co-located tasks. Prior works focus on the generic problem of co-scheduling to mitigate the effect of interference on the performance-critical task. In this work, we focus on inference pipelines and propose ODIN, a technique to mitigate the effect of interference on the performance of the inference task, based on the online scheduling of the pipeline stages. Our technique detects interference online and automatically re-balances the pipeline stages to mitigate the performance degradation of the inference task. We demonstrate that ODIN successfully mitigates the effect of interference, sustaining the latency and throughput of CNN inference, and outperforms the least-loaded scheduling (LLS), a common technique for interference mitigation. Additionally, it is effective in maintaining service-level objectives for inference, and it is scalable to large network models executing on multiple processing elements.

**Keywords:** CNN parallel pipelines · Online tuning · Design space exploration · Interference mitigation · Inference serving

## 1 Introduction

As machine learning becomes the backbone of the digital world, there is an increasing demand for predictions as a service. This has led to the advent of inference-serving systems [7,19,21,24,25]. These systems deploy pre-trained model pipelines, i.e. inference pipelines, on the cloud, serving inference queries to users and applications, often under strict quality-of-service (QoS) requirements for the response times and throughput of the queries [32], expressed as service level objectives (SLOs). However, due to the limited availability of resources of cloud systems, in combination with high demand, inference pipelines are often co-located with other workloads, either as part of the inference-serving system, which may opt to co-locate multiple inference pipelines [22,31], or as part of


J. Cano et al. (Eds.): Euro-Par 2023, LNCS 14100, pp. 169–183, 2023.
https://doi.org/10.1007/978-3-031-39698-4_12

common multi-tenancy practices of cloud providers [9,10] to increase utilization. The resulting interference from the co-located workload can have devastating effects on inference performance, leading to violation of the SLOs.

The mitigation of the effect of interference from co-located workloads on the performance of a critical application has been studied extensively. Several scheduling techniques focus on the generic problem of workload colocation, trying to retain or guarantee the performance of one critical or high-priority workload under interference [4,5,9,10], while more recent works focus on the problem of colocating inference pipelines specifically [17,22,25]. Most of these techniques perform extensive offline profiling and/or characterization of workloads and workload colocations, and build pre-trained machine-learning models or analytical models for each system, while a brief profiling phase may also be required to characterize a workload [9,10]. These techniques proactively partition resources to the workloads to mitigate the effect of interference, but may reactively repartition resources or evict colocated workloads in response to changes in the observed performance or interference. Finally, some techniques only focus on interference effects affecting specific resources, such as GPU accelerators [4,5].

One way to achieve high throughput and low latency for inference pipelines is pipeline parallelism. Pipeline parallelism in the form of layer pipelining has been used extensively in training [12,14,20,23], and in inference [16,30], in combination with operator parallelism, as it is able to reduce data movement costs. To exploit pipelined parallelism, several techniques focus on finding near-optimal pipeline schedules online, using heuristics to tackle the large search space [3,15,28,29]. The ability to rebalance pipeline stages online leaves ample room for the optimization of the execution of a pipeline under the presence of interference, where such a reactive technique can detect and mitigate performance degradation, by making better utilization of the existing resources.

In this work, we propose ODIN, an online solution that dynamically detects interference and adapts the execution of inference pipelines on a given set of processing elements. Thus, inference-serving systems can exploit them to reduce SLO violations in the presence of interference without eviction or resource repartitioning. ODIN does not require offline resource utilization profiles for the inference, and relies only on runtime observed execution times of pipeline stages, therefore being easily applicable to any system. Additionally, ODIN avoids the costly process of building system-specific or pipeline-specific models to characterize interference. Instead, it dynamically reacts and adapts to the presence of interference while executing the inference pipeline. ODIN by itself does not have a notion of SLOs. It is a best-effort solution to quickly achieve near-optimal throughput and latency in the presence of interference, which thereby results in improved SLO conformance compared to a baseline least-loaded scheduler (LLS).

ODIN employs a heuristic pipeline scheduling algorithm, which uses the execution times of pipeline stages, compares them against interference-free performance values, and then moves network layers between pipeline stages, with the goal to reduce the work on the execution unit affected by interference, while maximizing the overall throughput of the pipeline. To minimize the duration of the mitigation phase and quickly react to performance changes due to interference, the heuristic takes into account the extent of the performance degradation. We extensively test ODIN with 12 different scenarios of interference in 9 different frequency-duration settings and compare against the baseline least-loaded scheduler (LLS), which selects the least-loaded execution unit to assign work to. Our experiments show that ODIN sustains high throughput and low latency, including tail latency, under the different interference scenarios, and reacts quickly with a short mitigation phase, which takes 5–15 timesteps, outperforming LLS by 15% in latency and 20% in throughput on average. Additionally, with an SLO set at 80% of the original throughput, our solution is able to avoid 80% of SLO violations under interference, in contrast to LLS, which only delivers 50% SLO conformance. We also test the scalability of ODIN with a deep neural network model on highly parallel platforms, showing that the quality of the solution is independent of the number of execution units and depth of neural network.

## 2 Background and Motivation

Parallel inference pipelines provide a way to maximize the throughput of inference applications, as layer-wise parallelism offers reduced communication and minimizes the need to copy weights between execution units [2]. The parallelism exposed in parallel inference pipelines is across layers, with each layer being assigned to a pipeline stage, as well as within layers, where operators are parallelized for faster execution. A common way to execute pipelines is the "bind-to-stage" approach [18], where each stage of the pipeline is assigned to a unique set of compute units, i.e. an execution place, without sharing resources with other stages. In our work, we also assume that execution places do not share resources, therefore a pipeline stage will not experience interference from pipeline stages running on other execution places. To achieve high throughput, the pipeline stages need to be balanced, otherwise, throughput becomes limited by pipeline stalls, as the pipeline stages have a linear dependence.

Figure 1 shows a motivating example of an inference pipeline for VGG16, a CNN model. The pipeline consists of 4 stages, each consisting of 3 to 5 layers of the network model (Fig. 1a), in a configuration where the pipeline stages are balanced in terms of execution time. Assuming a workload is colocated on the execution place which executes the fourth stage of the pipeline, the execution time of this stage increases due to interference, causing the throughput to decrease by 46% (Fig. 1b). A static solution would dedicate the resources to the colocated workload, and would use only 3 execution places. To maintain high throughput, the pipeline stages would also be reduced to 3, leading to a sub-optimal solution (Fig. 1c). A dynamic solution would attempt to rebalance the initial four pipeline stages, to mitigate the effect of interference on the execution time of the fourth stage. An exhaustive search for an optimal new configuration is able to restore the initial throughput loss (Fig. 1d), however this exhaustive search required 42.5 min to complete.

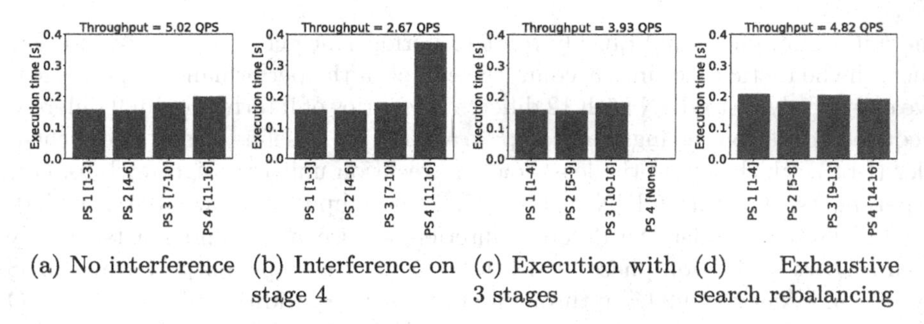


(a) No interference (b) Interference on stage 4 (c) Execution with 3 stages (d) Exhaustive search rebalancing

**Fig. 1.** Throughput and execution time of a 4-stage pipeline for VGG-16.

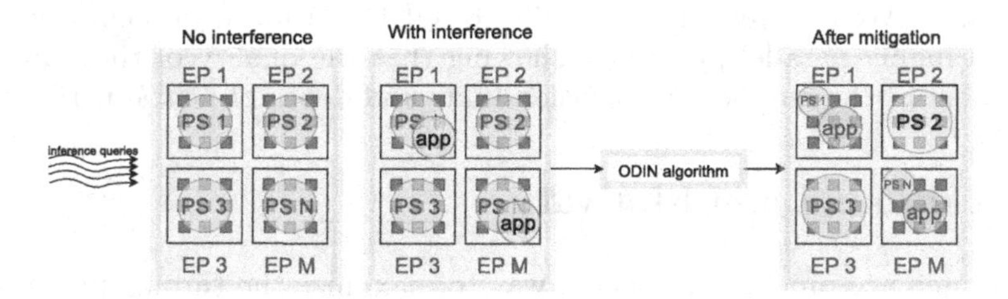


**Fig. 2.** System overview

This experiment allows us to make the following observations: First, the effect of interference on a parallel inference pipeline can be mitigated by rebalancing the pipeline stages. Second, partitioning the resources between the colocated workload and the inference pipeline leads to a shorted pipeline and a suboptimal throughput. Third, dynamic reaction to interference is able to largely restore throughput loss on the inference pipeline. Fourth, an exhaustive search for an optimal configuration is infeasible in a reactive, dynamic solution. The above observations motivate our work, which proposes an online scheduling technique for the pipeline stages of inference pipelines.

## 3 ODIN: A Dynamic Solution to Overcome Interference on Inference Pipelines

### 3.1 Methodology

In this work, we consider a system with a set of resources named execution places (EPs). Each execution place may consist of multiple cores, but execution places do not share performance-critical resources between them, e.g. caches, memory controllers/links. Inference pipelines are linear and are implemented with a bind-to-stage approach, where a single pipeline stage (PS) is assigned to a single EP, i.e. a unique set of resources of the system, and pipeline stages do not share resources. Pipeline stages can exploit the multiple resources within an EP by other means of parallelism, e.g. operator parallelism. A pipeline configuration defines the mapping of pipeline stages to execution places and the assignment of layers of a neural network model to PSs. We additionally assume that, in an interference-free system where the inference pipeline utilizes all the available execution places, the stages are already effectively balanced across the execution places. If a workload is colocated with a pipeline stage on one of the EPs, causing interference and increase of the execution time of this stage, the heuristics which form the backbone of our solution attempts to reduce the total work on the affected pipeline stage, moving network layers to non-affected pipeline stages. A high-level overview of our approach, ODIN, is presented in Fig. 2. Our approach operates online and is agnostic to any other colocated application. At runtime, we monitor the execution time of pipeline stages, and scan for changes in the performance of the slowest pipeline stage. If its execution time has increased, we consider it as affected by an interfering application and trigger the online rebalancing of pipeline stages, to find a new configuration, using our heuristic algorithm. If its execution time has decreased, we consider that any effect of interference is no longer present, and once again trigger online rebalancing to find a new configuration that reclaims resources from the colocated, interfering workload.

### 3.2 ODIN: A Heuristic-Based Approach for Pipeline Stage Re-balancing Under Interference

We describe our approach, ODIN, to mitigate the effect of interference on parallel inference pipelines, and the heuristics it uses to find new configurations for the pipeline stages at runtime. The complete steps of our approach are presented in Algorithm 1. The algorithm takes as input the current configuration $C$, which tracks the number of network layers belonging to each pipeline stage, and a tuning parameter $\alpha$. As the algorithm starts operating without interference, the current configuration is considered to be optimal, and the pipeline throughput is the one given by the current configuration. During execution, the execution time of PSs is monitored. Interference is detected when the execution time $t$ of one of the pipeline stages increases. We identify the affected PS ($PS_{affected}$) as the slowest stage in the current configuration, and this determines the throughput of the pipeline. The goal of the algorithm is then to rebalance the pipeline stages by removing layers from the affected PS, to reduce its work. We note that, removing layers from the affected PS may reduce the length of the pipeline by 1. We apply two heuristics to find a new configuration:

1) **Set the direction for moving work:** To remove layers from the affected PS, we first determine the direction of moving the layers. As the layers of an inference pipeline execute one after the other (forward pass), we can only remove layers from the head or tail of the $PS_{affected}$. At the first attempt, the algorithm does not know which layers of the $PS_{affected}$ have experienced performance degradation due to interference, so we initially remove layers from both ends, as shown in Lines 6–10, and move them to the preceding and subsequent pipeline stages respectively. Next, we calculate the sum of the execution time of PSs on both sides of the $PS_{affected}$ and set the direction to move layers. We then find the PS with the lowest execution time $PS_{lightest}$ in that direction, starting from $PS_{affected}$, and move one layer to $PS_{lightest}$, as shown in Lines 18–20.

**Algorithm 1.** ODIN Algorithm

```
Require: C, α                                          ▷ C = pipeline configuration
 1: T ← THROUGHPUT(C)                                  ▷ T = throughput of the pipeline
 2: C_opt ← C                                          ▷ Optimal pipeline configuration
 3: γ ← 0                                              ▷ counter variable
 4: while γ < α do
 5:     PS_affected ← GET_INDEX(max(t(C)))
 6:     if γ = 0 then
 7:         C[PS_affected + 1] += 1
 8:         C[PS_affected − 1] += 1
 9:         C[PS_affected] −= 2
10:     end if
11:     S_left ← SUM(t(C[0], C[PS_affected]))
12:     S_right ← SUM(t(C[PS_affected + 1], C[N]))
13:     if S_left < S_right then
14:         direction ← left
15:     else
16:         direction ← right
17:     end if
18:     PS_lightest ← GET_INDEX(t(C, PS_affected, direction))
19:     C[PS_affected] −= 1
20:     C[PS_lightest] += 1
21:     T_new ← THROUGHPUT(C)
22:     if T_new < T then
23:         γ += 1
24:     else if T_new = T then
25:         C[PS_affected] −= 1
26:         C[PS_lightest] += 1
27:         γ += 1
28:     else
29:         γ ← 0
30:         T ← T_new
31:         C_opt ← C
32:     end if
33: end while
34: return C_opt
```

2) **Avoiding Local optimum:** Our first heuristic may result in a local, rather than a global optimum. A possible solution for this is to randomly choose a completely new starting configuration, and rebalance again. However, this can lead to loss of information. Since our initial configuration is optimal for the execution of the pipeline in an interference-free case, in the case of a local optimum, we deliberately move more layers from the $PS_{affected}$ to the $PS_{lightest}$, to create a different configuration and continue the exploration.

The extent of exploration is controlled by variable $\alpha$ which is provided as an input to the algorithm. As the algorithm is applied online, while the inference pipeline is running, the value of $\alpha$ can be tuned to reduce the number of trials for

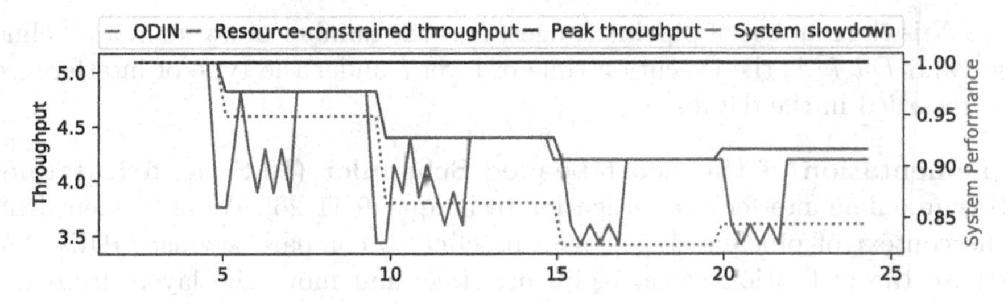


**Fig. 3.** A timeline of a VGG16 inference pipeline, running with ODIN, which reacts to mitigate interference at time steps 5, 10, 15, and 20.

faster exploration. Figure 3 shows a timeline of an inference pipeline for VGG16, executing on four EPs with pipeline stages, where ODIN runs to mitigate the effects of interference. Initially, there is no interference, the inference pipeline is balanced with an optimal configuration and achieves its peak throughput. At time steps 5, 10, and 15, a new workload is co-located on a different execution place, slowing down the system for the inference pipeline, reducing what we define as the resource-constrained throughput, i.e. the throughput the inference pipeline can attain in the presence of interference. At each of these time steps, ODIN automatically detects the throughput degradation and rebalances the pipeline until it finds a successful solution. At time step 20, one of the interfering workloads is removed, and ODIN executes again, to restore the pipeline throughput by claiming back the resources previously used by the colocated workload.

### 3.3 Implementation Details

**Database Creation:** In our evaluation, we use simulation to be able to apply ODIN on any type and size of the underlying system. We, therefore, replace online monitoring with an offline database. We first collect the execution time of the $m$ individual network layers of the inference pipelines under consideration, when executing alone (without any interference), on a real platform. On the same platform, we collect the execution time of the individual network layers when executing alongside co-located applications, producing $n$ different interference scenarios. We then store these collected $m \times (n+1)$ measurements in a database, and use them in simulation. We consider the real platform to be a single execution place for ODIN, and simulate multiple execution places of the same type. To emulate interference, during simulation, we randomly select an interference scenario for an execution place and look up the corresponding execution time in the database.

**Throughput Calculation:** We use the measurements in our database $D$ of size $m \times n$ to calculate the throughput of a pipeline, as follows:

$$T = \frac{1}{max_{i=0}^{N} \sum_{l=0}^{P} D[l,k]}$$

where $N$ is the number of pipeline stages, $P$ is the number of layers in a pipeline stage, and $D[l, k]$ is the execution time of layer $l$ under the type of interference $k$, as recorded in the database $D$.

**Implementation of the Least-Loaded Scheduler (LLS) as a Baseline:** LLS is an online interference mitigation technique [9,11,26]. We implement LLS in the context of pipeline stages, as a baseline to compare against ODIN. We calculate the utilization of each pipeline stage and move the layers from the most utilized to the least utilized stage recursively until the throughput starts decreasing. The utilization of a stage $\upsilon_i$ is calculated as:

$$\upsilon_i = \left(1 - \frac{w_i}{w_i + t_i}\right)$$

where $t_i$ is the execution time of a pipeline stage, and $w_i$ is the waiting time of the stage, calculated as $w_i = w_{i-1} + ti - 1 - t_i$, with $w_0 = 0$.

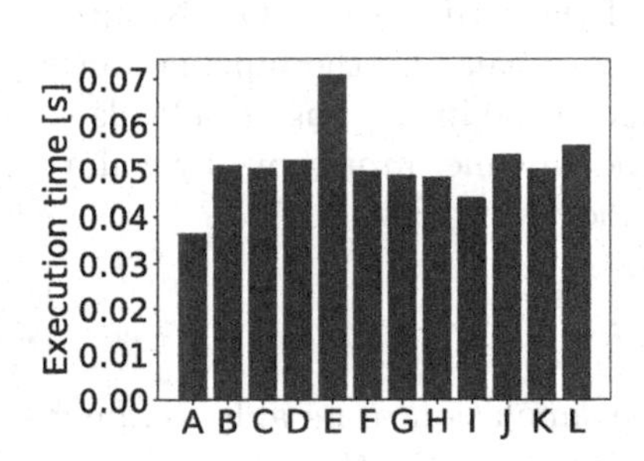


**Fig. 4.** Performance impact

**Table 1.** Interference scenarios

| Mode of execution | Core assignment on Alder Lake |
|---|---|
| A | CNN:[0–7] |
| B | CNN: [0–7], IBench-MemBW: [0] |
| C | CNN: [0–7], IBench-MemBW: [0–1] |
| D | CNN: [0–7], IBench-MemBW: [0–3] |
| E | CNN: [0–7], IBench-MemBW: [0–7] |
| F | CNN: [0–7], IBench-CPU: [0] |
| G | CNN: [0–7], IBench-CPU: [0–1] |
| H | CNN: [0–7], IBench-CPU: [0–3] |
| I | CNN: [0–7], IBench-CPU: [0–7] |
| J | CNN: [0–3], IBench-MemBW: [4–7] |
| K | CNN: [0–3], IBench-CPU: [4–7] |
| L | CNN: [0–3], IBench-CPU: [4–7], IBench-MemBW[4–7] |

# 4 Evaluation

## 4.1 Experimental Setup

We execute ODIN in a simulated system for inference serving, which consists of multiple execution places, and each execution place consists of a fixed number of 8 cores. To generate our database, we use an Intel i9-12900K (AlderLake) server, which consists of 8 2xP-cores (Performance) and 8 2xE-cores (Efficient). We consider the set of 8 P-cores as a single execution place in our system.

For the neural network models we examine as inference pipelines, our database consists of measurements for each layer without interference, as well as measurements for each layer with 12 different co-located workloads, in different settings. To create the co-located workloads, we use two interference benchmarks from the `iBench` suite [8], the `CPU` benchmark that stresses the CPU and the `memBW` benchmark that stresses the memory bandwidth. We then create our 12 scenarios of colocation by assigning the network layers and interference benchmarks different numbers of threads, and pinning them to different cores. Table 1 showcases the colocation scenarios considered in our database, and Fig. 4 demonstrates the performance impact of interference for all these colocation scenarios on a single layer of the VGG16 network model.

For our evaluation, we consider the inference pipelines of three popular CNN models: VGG16 [27], ResNet-50 and ResNet-152 [13], with 16, 50, and 152 layers respectively, implemented with the Keras [6] framework.

### 4.2 Interference Mitigation with ODIN

To evaluate the effectiveness of ODIN, we compare its latency and throughput for different values of $\alpha$, which sets the extent of exploration, against LLS, in several interference scenarios. In particular, we consider a system of 4 executions places of 8 cores each, which serves inference queries with two network models, VGG16, and ResNet-50. We assume a fixed number of 4000 queries, and induce random interference on different execution places, based on the colocation scenarios described in Table 1. We consider different values for the frequency (frequency periods of 2, 10, and 100 queries) and duration (2, 10, and 100 queries) of interference, and evaluate the end-to-end latency and throughput distribution of each inference pipeline.

**Latency:** Figure 5 shows the latency distribution of the two inference pipelines under interference. We observe that ODIN outperforms LLS in all scenarios, delivering lower latency. We highlight the effect of the $\alpha$ parameter of ODIN on latency. A higher value of $\alpha$ yields lower latency, because the longer exploration phase allows ODIN to find an optimal configuration. On the other hand, if the frequency of interference is high, a low value of $\alpha$ is able, in most cases, to produce an equally good solution with lower exploration time. ODIN $\alpha = 10$ yields better latency than ODIN $\alpha = 2$ this is because the former takes more trials to find a schedule, however if the frequency of interference is high then it may take longer to find a solution or end up with sub-optimal solution. We additionally note that both ODIN and LLS are more effective in cases where interference appears with lower frequency and for longer periods. This is particularly evident in Fig. 5. For the pair of [frequency period = 2, duration = 2], the distribution of latency shows many outliers, as an optimal configuration found by the algorithm for one period of interference may be applied to the next period, where the pattern of interference has changed. Overall, however, ODIN outperforms LLS in all scenarios, offering 15.8% better latency on average with $\alpha = 10$ and 14.1% with $\alpha = 2$.

**Throughput:** We then compare the throughput of the inference pipelines under interference, for ResNet50 and VGG16, with ODIN and LLS, for the same interference scenarios, in Fig. 6. Again, ODIN offers higher throughput than LLS in most cases. The case of VGG16 highlights our observation about the lower performance in the case of high frequency, where all three techniques show outliers of low throughput, however, ODIN is more able to adapt to interference of longer duration compared to LLS. We observe additionally that for the case of the highest frequency period-duration pair [100, 100], LLS and ODIN have comparable performance, as the near-optimal solutions were obtained with minimal changes of the pipeline configurations. Overall, on average, ODIN achieves 19% higher throughput than LLS with any choice of $\alpha$.

**Tail Latency:** Besides the latency distribution, we separately examine the tail latency (99th percentile), as it can be a critical metric in inference-serving systems, and it is also indicative of the quality of the solutions found by ODIN. Figure 7 shows the distribution of the tail latency across all the queries considered in the interference scenarios examined in this Section. For both ResNet50 and VGG16, ODIN results in significantly lower tail latencies than LLS. For the case of VGG16, we additionally observe that a higher value of $\alpha$ for ODIN can produce better solutions, resulting in lower tail latencies. On average, ODIN results in 14% lower tail latencies than LLS.

**Exploration Overhead:** Upon detection of interference, both ODIN and LLS begin the rebalancing phase, during which queries as processed serially, until a new configuration of the pipeline stages is found. On average, the number of queries that will be processed serially during a rebalancing phase is 1 for LLS, and 4 and 12 for ODIN with $\alpha = 2$ and $\alpha = 10$ respectively. Figure 8 shows the percentage of time required to rebalance the pipeline stages, for the window of 4000 queries. It is evident that, if the type of interference changes frequently and is short-lived, the overhead of ODIN is higher, as the system is almost continuously in a rebalancing phase. However, when the duration of interference is longer, as the effect of interference on the inference pipeline may be the same, rebalancing may not be triggered, as the selected configuration is already optimal, therefore the rebalancing overhead decreases. Longer frequencies and durations of interference are favored by both ODIN and LLS.

### 4.3 Maintaining QoS with ODIN

To evaluate the ability of ODIN to mitigate interference on an inference pipeline, we consider its quality-of-service (QoS) in terms of SLO violations [1,25]. We use throughput as the target QoS metric, and consider the SLO level as the percentage of the peak throughput, i.e. the throughput of the inference pipeline when executing alone. We then profile the number of queries which violate this SLO using ODIN and LLS. We additionally compare the SLO violations with respect to the resource-constrained throughput, i.e. the throughput achieved when a colocated workload causes interference, and an optimal configuration of the pipeline is found through exhaustive search. We present the results in Fig. 9. Although neither ODIN or LLS are able to offer any performance guarantees, resulting in many violations when the SLO level is strict, ODIN results in less than 20% of SLO violations for SLO levels lower than 85%, and can sustain 70% of the original throughput for any interference scenario, in contrast to LLS, which, in the extreme case of VGG16, violates even an SLO of 35% of the original throughput. Additionally, the comparison of SLO violations for the SLO set w.r.t. the resource-constrained throughput shows that ODIN is able to find near-optimal configurations in most cases, which are close to those found by the exhaustive search. Our conclusion is that, while ODIN cannot provide any strict guarantee for a set SLO, it can sustain high throughput under looser SLOs and therefore can be an effective solution for overprovisioned systems. For example, an inference-serving system that can tolerate 10% of SLO violations would require to overprovision resources by 42% with ODIN, compared to 150% for LLS.

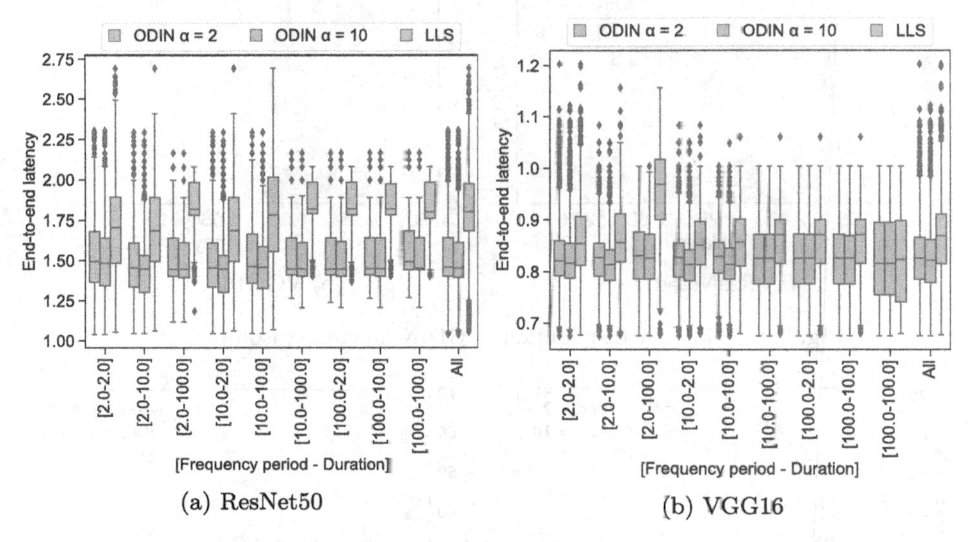


(a) ResNet50

(b) VGG16

**Fig. 5.** Inference pipeline latency (lower is better) with ODIN, in comparison to LLS, over a window of 4000 queries, for interference of different frequency period and duration.

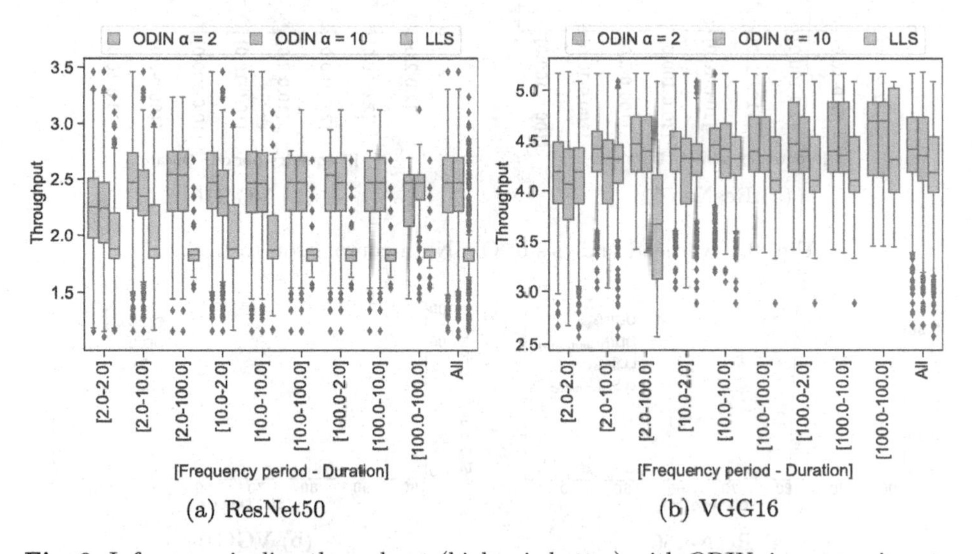


(a) ResNet50

(b) VGG16

**Fig. 6.** Inference pipeline throughput (higher is better) with ODIN, in comparison to LLS, over a window of 4000 queries, for interference of different frequency period and duration.

### 4.4 Scalability Analysis of ODIN

We finally analyze the scalability of ODIN on high numbers of execution places, with deep network models that can run with multiple pipeline stages. For this, we use ResNet152, which consists of 152 layers. We consider, however, residual

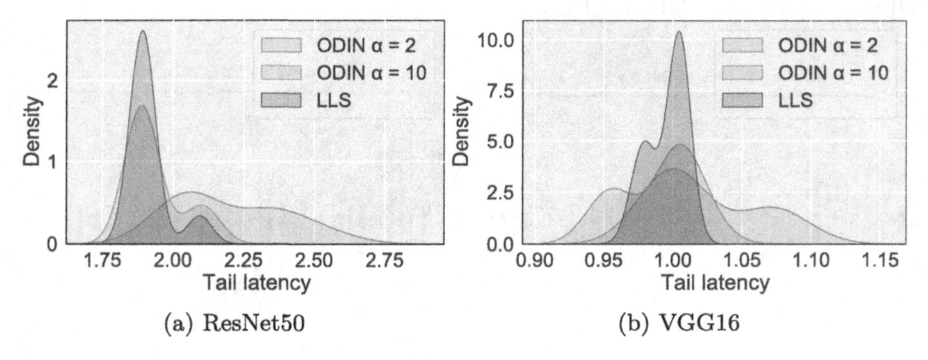


(a) ResNet50 (b) VGG16

**Fig. 7.** Tail latency distribution of ODIN, in comparison to LLS.

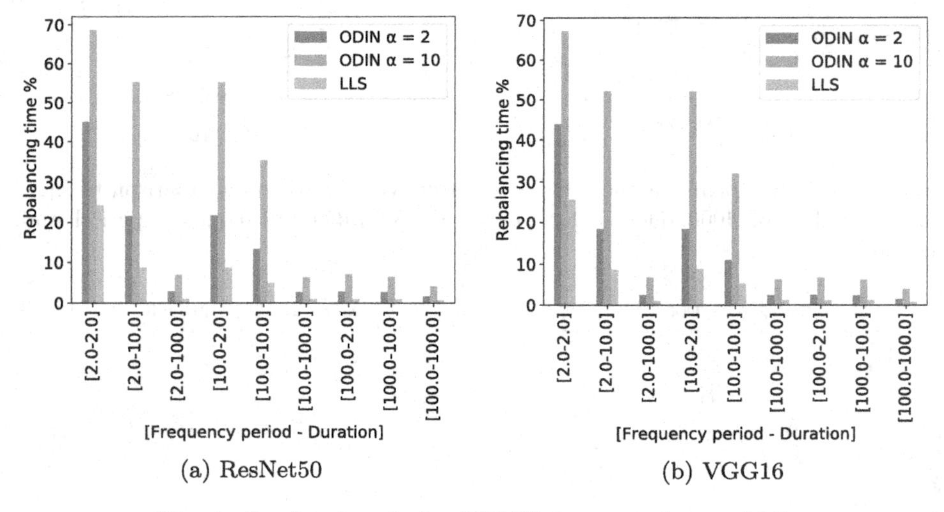


(a) ResNet50 (b) VGG16

**Fig. 8.** Overhead analysis of ODIN, in comparison to LLS.

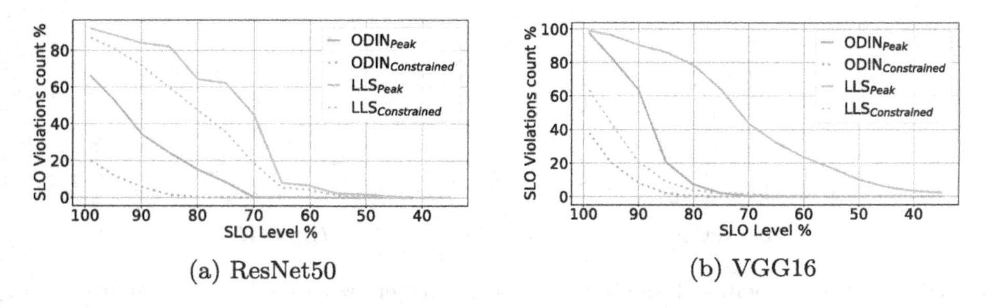


(a) ResNet50 (b) VGG16

**Fig. 9.** Quality-of-service of ODIN, in comparison to LLS, for different SLO levels.

blocks as a single unit, so the maximum number of pipeline stages ResNet152 could run with is 52. We scale the number of execution places from 4 up to 52, and consider a window of 4000 queries, with interference of a frequency period of 10 and duration of 10 queries. Figure 10 shows the latency and throughput of ODIN for the different numbers of EPs. The latency is not affected as the number of EPs increases, therefore ODIN is effective at finding optimal pipeline configurations on multiple execution places. Equivalently, throughput increases with the number of EPs, suggesting high parallelism of the pipeline, and for 52 EPs, the achieved throughput is comparable to the peak throughput of the inference pipeline, under no interference.

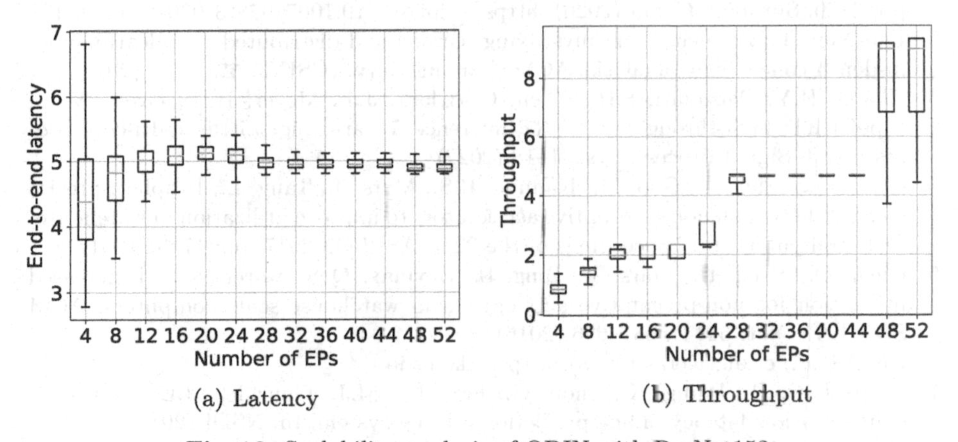


(a) Latency (b) Throughput

**Fig. 10.** Scalability analysis of ODIN with ResNet152.

## 5 Conclusion

In this work, we have proposed ODIN, an online pipeline rebalancing technique that mitigates the effect of interference on inference pipelines. ODIN utilizes the execution times of the pipeline stages to readjust the assignment of layers to pipeline stages, according to the available resources, rebalancing the pipeline. We show that ODIN outperforms the baseline LLS in latency and throughput under different interference scenarios. Additionally, ODIN maintains more than 70% of the peak throughput of the pipeline under interference, and achieves very low SLO violations compared to LLS. Finally, ODIN scales well with deeper networks and large platforms. ODIN is online and dynamic, and requires minimal information from the inference pipeline, therefore applies to any type of inference pipeline and interference scenario. The abstraction of the hardware into execution places allows ODIN to be applied to different types of hardware platforms. As future work, we plan to parallelize the pipeline during rebalancing, and validate the utility of ODIN on heterogeneous platforms.

**Acknowledgement.** This work has received funding from the project PRIDE from the Swedish Foundation for Strategic Research with reference number CHI19-0048. The computations were enabled by resources provided by the Swedish National Infrastructure for Computing (SNIC) at NSC, partially funded by the Swedish Research Council through grant agreement no. 2018-05973.

## References

1. Alves, M.M., Teylo, L., Frota, Y., Drummond, L.M.A.: An interference-aware strategy for co-locating high performance computing applications in clouds. In: Bianchini, C., Osthoff, C., Souza, P., Ferreira, R. (eds.) WSCAD 2018. CCIS, vol. 1171, pp. 3–20. Springer, Cham (2020). https://doi.org/10.1007/978-3-030-41050-6_1
2. Ben-Nun, T., Hoefler, T.: Demystifying parallel and distributed deep learning: an in-depth concurrency analysis. ACM Comput. Surv. (CSUR) **52**, 1–43 (2019)
3. Chang, H.Y., Mozafari, S.H., Chen, C., Clark, J.J., Meyer, B.H., Gross, W.J.: PipeBERT: high-throughput BERT inference for arm big. Little multi-core processors. J. Signal Process. Syst. 1–18 (2022)
4. Chen, Q., Yang, H., Guo, M., Kannan, R.S., Mars, J., Tang, L.: Prophet: precise QoS prediction on non-preemptive accelerators to improve utilization in warehouse-scale computers. In: Proceedings of the 22nd ASPLOS 2017, pp. 17–32 (2017)
5. Chen, Q., Yang, H., Mars, J., Tang, L.: Baymax: QoS awareness and increased utilization for non-preemptive accelerators in warehouse scale computers. ACM SIGPLAN Not. **51**(4), 681–696 (2016)
6. Chollet, F., et al.: Keras (2015). https://keras.io
7. Crankshaw, D., Wang, X., Zhou, G., Franklin, M.J., Gonzalez, J.E., Stoica, I.: Clipper: a low-latency online prediction serving system. In: NSDI (2017)
8. Delimitrou, C., Kozyrakis, C.: iBench: quantifying interference for datacenter applications. In: IISWC, pp. 23–33. IEEE (2013)
9. Delimitrou, C., Kozyrakis, C.: Paragon: QoS-aware scheduling for heterogeneous datacenters. ACM SIGPLAN Not. **48**(4), 77–88 (2013)
10. Delimitrou, C., Kozyrakis, C.: Quasar: resource-efficient and QoS-aware cluster management. ACM SIGPLAN Not. **49**(4), 127–144 (2014)
11. Devi, D.C., Uthariaraj, V.R.: Load balancing in cloud computing environment using improved weighted round robin algorithm for nonpreemptive dependent tasks. Sci. World J. **2016** (2016)
12. Fan, S., et al.: DAPPLE: a pipelined data parallel approach for training large models. In: Proceedings of the 26th ACM SIGPLAN Symposium on Principles and Practice of Parallel Programming, pp. 431–445 (2021)
13. He, K., Zhang, X., Ren, S., Sun, J.: Deep residual learning for image recognition. In: Proceedings of the IEEE Conference on Computer Vision and Pattern Recognition, pp. 770–778 (2016)
14. Huang, et al.: GPipe: efficient training of giant neural networks using pipeline parallelism. In: Advances in Neural Information Processing Systems, vol. 32 (2019)
15. Jeong, E., Kim, J., Tan, S., Lee, J., Ha, S.: Deep learning inference parallelization on heterogeneous processors with TensorRT. IEEE Embed. Syst. Lett. **14**(1), 15–18 (2021)
16. Kang, D., Oh, J., Choi, J., Yi, Y., Ha, S.: Scheduling of deep learning applications onto heterogeneous processors in an embedded device. IEEE Access **8**, 43980–43991 (2020)

17. Ke, L., Gupta, U., Hempsteadis, M., Wu, C.J., Lee, H.H.S., Zhang, X.: Hercules: heterogeneity-aware inference serving for at-scale personalized recommendation. In: HPCA, pp. 141–144. IEEE (2022)
18. Lee, I.T.A., Leiserson, C.E., Schardl, T.B., Zhang, Z., Sukha, J.: On-the-fly pipeline parallelism. ACM Trans. Parallel Comput. (TOPC) **2**(3), 1–42 (2015)
19. Lee, Y., Scolari, A., Chun, B.G., Santambrogio, M.D., Weimer, M., Interlandi, M.: PRETZEL: opening the black box of machine learning prediction serving systems. In: OSDI, vol. 18, pp. 611–626 (2018)
20. Li, S., Hoefler, T.: Chimera: efficiently training large-scale neural networks with bidirectional pipelines. In: Proceedings of the International Conference for High Performance Computing, Networking, Storage and Analysis, pp. 1–14 (2021)
21. Liberty, E., et al.: Elastic machine learning algorithms in Amazon SageMaker. In: SIGMOD, pp. 731–737 (2020)
22. Mendoza, D., Romero, F., Li, Q., Yadwadkar, N.J., Kozyrakis, C.: Interference-aware scheduling for inference serving. In: Proceedings of the 1st Workshop on Machine Learning and Systems, pp. 80–88 (2021)
23. Narayanan, et al.: PipeDream: generalized pipeline parallelism for DNN training. In: Proceedings of the 27th ACM Symposium on Operating Systems Principles, pp. 1–15 (2019)
24. Olston, C., et al.: TensorFlow-serving: flexible, high-performance ML serving. arXiv preprint arXiv:1712.06139 (2017)
25. Romero, F., Li, Q., Yadwadkar, N.J., Kozyrakis, C.: INFaaS: automated model-less inference serving. In: USENIX Annual Technical Conference, pp. 397–411 (2021)
26. Shaw, S.B., Singh, A.: A survey on scheduling and load balancing techniques in cloud computing environment. In: ICCCT, pp. 87–95. IEEE (2014)
27. Simonyan, K., Zisserman, A.: Very deep convolutional networks for large-scale image recognition. arXiv preprint arXiv:1409.1556 (2014)
28. Soomro, P.N., Abduljabbar, M., Castrillon, J., Pericàs, M.: An online guided tuning approach to run CNN pipelines on edge devices. In: CF 2021 (2021)
29. Soomro, P.N., Abduljabbar, M., Castrillon, J., Pericàs, M.: Shisha: online scheduling of CNN pipelines on heterogeneous architectures. In: Wyrzykowski, R., Dongarra, J., Deelman, E., Karczewski, K. (eds.) PPAM 2022. LNCS, vol. 13826, pp. 249–262. Springer, Cham (2022). https://doi.org/10.1007/978-3-031-30442-2_19
30. Wang, S., et al.: High-throughput CNN inference on embedded arm big. Little multicore processors. IEEE Trans. Comput.-Aided Design Integr. Circuits Syst. **39**(10), 2254–2267 (2019)
31. Yeung, G., Borowiec, D., Yang, R., Friday, A., Harper, R., Garraghan, P.: Horus: an interference-aware resource manager for deep learning systems. In: Qiu, M. (ed.) ICA3PP 2020. LNCS, vol. 12453, pp. 492–508. Springer, Cham (2020). https://doi.org/10.1007/978-3-030-60239-0_33
32. Zhang, C., Yu, M., Wang, W., Yan, F.: MArk: exploiting cloud services for cost-effective, SLO-aware machine learning inference serving. In: USENIX Annual Technical Conference, pp. 1049–1062 (2019)

# DAG-Based Efficient Parallel Scheduler for Blockchains: Hyperledger Sawtooth as a Case Study

Manaswini Piduguralla(✉), Saheli Chakraborty, Parwat Singh Anjana, and Sathya Peri

Indian Institute of Technology Hyderabad, Kandi 502284, Telangana, India
{cs20resch11007,ai20mtech12002, cs17resch11004}@iith.ac.com, sathya_p@cse.iith.ac.in

**Abstract.** Blockchain technology is a distributed, decentralized, and immutable ledger system. It is the platform of choice for managing smart contract transactions (SCTs). Smart contracts are pieces of code that capture business agreements between interested parties and are commonly implemented using blockchains. A block in a blockchain contains a set of transactions representing changes to the system and a hash of the previous block. The SCTs are executed multiple times during the block production and validation phases across the network. In most of the existing blockchains, transactions are executed sequentially.

In this work, we propose a parallel direct acyclic graph (DAG) based scheduler module for concurrent execution of SCTs. This module can be seamlessly integrated into the blockchain framework, and the SCTs in a block can be executed efficiently, resulting in higher throughput. The dependencies among the SCTs of a block are represented as a DAG data structure which enables parallel execution of the SCTs. Furthermore, the DAG data structure is shared with block validators, allowing resource conservation for DAG creation across the network. To ensure secure parallel execution, we design a secure validator capable of validating and identifying incorrect DAGs shared by malicious block producers. For evaluation, our framework is implemented in Hyperledger Sawtooth V1.2.6. The performance across multiple smart contract applications is measured for the various schedulers. We observed that our proposed executor exhibits a 1.58 times performance improvement on average over serial execution.

**Keywords:** Smart Contract Executions · Blockchains · Hyperledger Sawtooth · Parallel Scheduler

---

Funded by Meity India: No.4(4)/2021-ITEA & 4(20)/2019-ITEA. This is part of the National (Indian) Blockchain Framework Project.


J. Cano et al. (Eds.): Euro-Par 2023, LNCS 14100, pp. 184–198, 2023.
https://doi.org/10.1007/978-3-031-39698-4_13

## 1 Introduction

Blockchain platforms help establish and maintain a decentralized and distributed ledger system between untrusting parties [14]. The blockchain is a collection of immutable blocks, typically in the form of a chain. Each block points to its previous block by storing its hash. A block in the blockchain consists of several *smart contract transactions (SCTs)*, which are self-executing contracts of agreement between two or more parties that are written in the form of computer code. These help in the execution of agreements among untrusted parties without the necessity for a common trusted authority to oversee the execution. The development and deployment of smart contracts on blockchain platforms are growing rapidly.

A blockchain network usually consists of several nodes (ranging from thousands to millions depending on the blockchain), each of which stores the entire contents of the blockchain. Any node in the blockchain can act as a *block producer.* A producer node selects transactions from a pool of available transactions and packages them into a block. The proposed block is then broadcast to other nodes in the network. A node receiving the block acts as a *validator.* It validates the transactions in the block by executing them one after another. Thus a node can act as a producer while producing the block and as a validator for blocks produced by other nodes in the network.

Agreement on the proposed block by the nodes of the blockchain is performed through various consensus mechanisms, like proof of work (PoW) [14], proof of stake (PoS) [18], proof of elapsed time (PoET) [13], etc. For a block to be added to the blockchain, the transactions of the block are processed in two contexts: (a) first time by the block producer when the block is produced; (b) then by all the block validators as a part of the block validation. Thus the SCT code is executed multiple times by the producer and the validators.

The majority of blockchain technologies execute the SCTs in a block serially during the block creation and validation phases. This is one of the bottlenecks for higher throughput and scalability of blockchain models [10]. The throughput of the blockchain can be improved by concurrent execution of transactions. In order to enable concurrent transaction processing, it is crucial to ensure the avoidance of running interdependent transactions simultaneously. Moreover, when executing transactions concurrently at each validator, they must yield an identical end state in the database.

This work proposes a framework for executing transactions concurrently on producers and validators. We have implemented our framework in Hyperledger Sawtooth 1.2.6. [2]. We have chosen Sawtooth (explained in Sect. 2) as our platform of choice due to its existing support for parallel execution of SCTs, which provides us with an ideal environment to compare and test against both serial and parallel schedulers. This approach could be implemented in any blockchain with an order-execute blockchain model [4]. The major contributions of the paper are as follows:

- We introduced two important modules: a parallel scheduler and a secure validator are introduced in this work. The parallel scheduler module is respon-

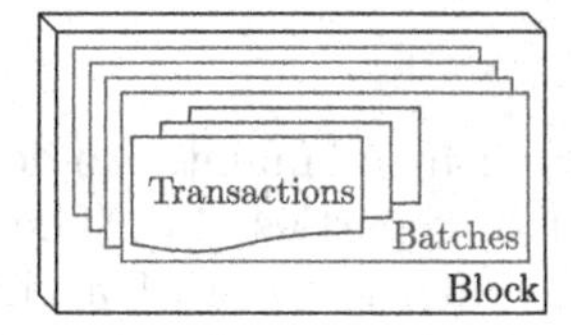


**Fig. 1.** Structure of a Hyperledger Sawtooth block.

sible for identifying transaction dependencies within a block and scheduling them for conflict-free execution using a directed acyclic graph (DAG). The DAG is shared along with the block and validated by the secure validator module, which helps detect any malicious block producers. Section 3 provides a comprehensive explanation of the framework.
- We observed that our proposed executor achieves average speedups of 1.58 times and 1.29 times over Sawtooth's default serial executor and built-in parallel executor, respectively. The implementation details, experiment design, and results are discussed in Sect. 4.

The overview of the related work aligned with the proposed approach is discussed in Sect. 5, while the conclusion and future steps are discussed in Sect. 6.

## 2 Background on Hyperledger Sawtooth

The Hyperledger Foundation is an open-source collaboration project by the Linux Foundation to establish and encourage cross-industry blockchain technologies. Sawtooth is one of the most popular blockchain technologies being developed for permission and permissionless networks. It is designed such that transaction rules, permissions, and consensus algorithms can be customized according to the particular area of application. Some of the distinctive features of Sawtooth are modularity, multi-language support, parallel transaction execution, and pluggable consensus. The modular structure of Sawtooth helps in modifying particular operations without needing to make changes throughout the architecture.

In Sawtooth, smart contracts are referred to as *transaction families*, and the logic for the contract is present in the respective families' transaction processors. Modifications to the state are performed through transactions, and they are always wrapped inside a batch. A batch is the atomic unit of change in the system, and multiple batches are combined to form a block (Fig. 1). The node architecture of Sawtooth includes five modules that play crucial roles in blockchain development: global state, journal, transaction scheduler, transaction executor, and transaction processor. The global state containing the data of transaction families of Sawtooth is stored using a Merkle-Radix tree data structure. The Journal module contains a block completer, block validator, and block publishers that deal with creating, verifying, and publishing blocks. It is the responsibility of the Transaction Scheduler module to identify the dependencies between transactions and schedule transactions that result in conflict-free execution. In order to execute a transaction, the transaction executor collects the context of the transaction.[1]

Hyperledger Sawtooth architecture includes a parallel transaction scheduler (tree-scheduler) that uses a Merkle-Radix tree with nodes that are addressable by state addresses. This tree is called the predecessor tree. Each node in the tree represents one address in the Sawtooth state, and a read list and write list are maintained at each node. Whenever an executor thread requests the next transaction, the scheduler inspects the list of unscheduled transactions and the status of their predecessors. The drawbacks of the tree scheduler are that the status of predecessor transactions needs to be checked before a transaction can be scheduled. The construction of the tree data structure is serial. The number of addresses accessed in a block is generally higher than the total number of transactions. A data structure based on addresses typically requires more memory space compared to a transaction-based data structure. The block producers and validators both construct the tree at their end instead of the block producer sharing the tree with the validators.

The proposed framework for transaction execution on the blockchain would improve the throughput of SCTs by making the block creation and validation process concurrent. SCTs that are independent of each other are executed in parallel in the framework. The dependencies are represented as a DAG based on transaction inputs and outputs. DAG sharing and secure validator module designs are also included in the framework to further optimize block validation.

## 3 Proposed Framework

In this section, the proposed framework for parallel transaction execution in blockchains through static analysis of the block is detailed. This framework introduces *parallel scheduler* and *secure validator* modules into the blockchain node architecture, as shown in Fig. 2. The parallel scheduler (SubSect. 3.1) is responsible for identifying the dependencies among the transactions in the block and scheduling them for conflict-free execution. This is done by determining the dependencies among the transactions. The identified dependencies are represented by a DAG that is shared along with the block to minimize the validation time of the blockchain, the idea explored in [6,7,10]. DAG shared along with the blocks are received and validated by the *secure validator* (SubSection 3.2). Through the validation process, the secure validator determines if any malicious block producer has shared a graph with some crucial edge (dependency) missing. This section presents pseudo-codes for the modules as well as a detailed framework.

### 3.1 Parallel Scheduler

The parallel scheduler module is part of the block producer in the proposed framework. It performs the operations of DAG creation and conflict-free transaction execution. Both processes are multi-threaded for higher throughput.

[1] The detailed architecture is explained in Appendix A of [15].

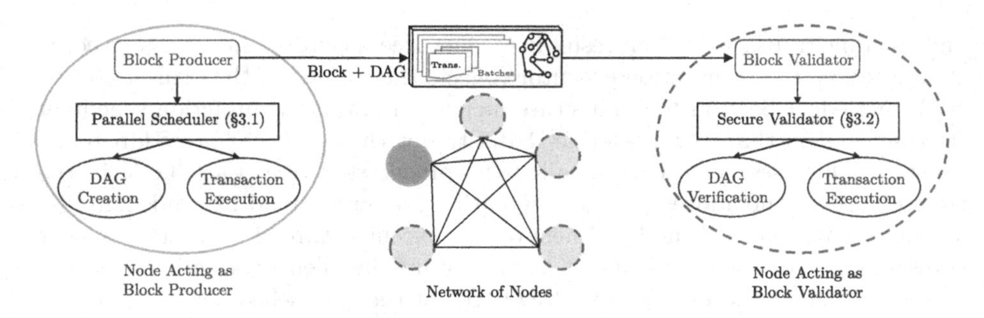


**Fig. 2.** Proposed framework in the blockchain

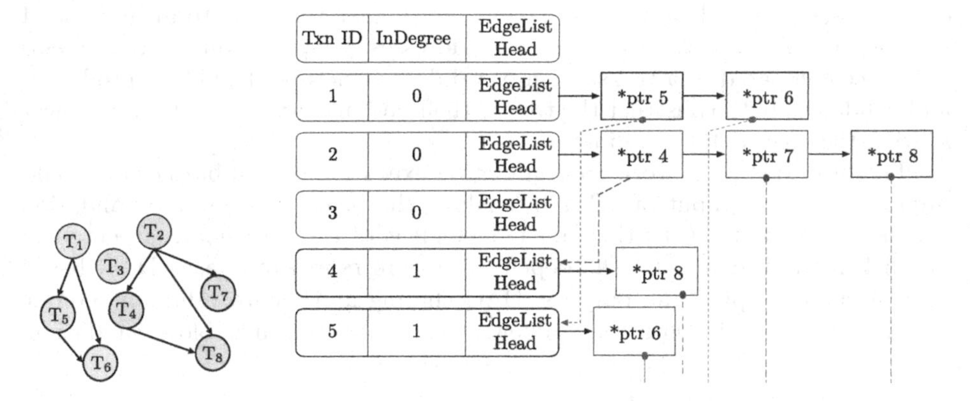


**Fig. 3.** DAG representation of dependencies in the block.

**Fig. 4.** Linked list representation of the DAG.

**DAG Creation:** The DAG creation is initiated when the block producer creates the next block in the blockchain. In blockchains like Sawtooth, the addresses that the transactions read from, and write to, are present in the transaction header. Using this information, we can derive the addresses based on the transaction details without having to execute the transaction. By examining the *input* (read) and *output* (write), the parallel scheduler calculates the dependencies among transactions, as described in the following explanation.

On receiving a block (from the block publisher module), the producer deploys multiple threads to generate the DAG. Firstly, a unique id is assigned to the transactions based on their order in the block ($T_1, T_2, T_3...$) using a global atomic counter as shown in the Algorithm 1, Line 3. The input addresses of the transaction ($T_a$) are compared with all the output addresses of transactions (e.g., $T_b$) with a higher ID. Correspondingly, the output addresses of $T_a$ are compared with the input and output addresses of $T_b$ as shown in Algorithm 1 from Line 10 to Line 24. If there are any common addresses identified in the above checks, an edge is added from $T_a$ to $T_b$ in the DAG. An adjacency matrix data structure is implemented for representing the graph, and an atomic array is used to maintain the indegree count of the vertices. We have also implemented a module with a concurrent linked list structure, as shown in Fig. 4. The pseudo-code is detailed in Algorithm 1, and one can refer to appendix C in [15] for an in-depth explanation. We have also proved the safety of our proposed framework for concurrent execution, available in Appendix B in [15].

**Algorithm 1.** Multi-threaded createDAG(): $m$ threads concurrently create DAG

```
1: procedure CREATEDAG(block)        ▷ The block to be produced or validated is the input
2:    while true do
3:       T_i ← txnCounter.get&inc()           ▷ Claim the next transaction available
4:       if T_i > txn_count then
5:          txnCounter.dec()
6:          return                     ▷ Return if all the transactions are processed
7:       end if
8:       Graph_Node *txn = new Graph_Node
9:       DAG→add_node(T_i, txn)                     ▷ adding the node to the graph
10:      for T_j = T_i + 1 to txn_count do        ▷ finding dependent transactions
11:         flagEdge=false
12:         if T_i.readList ∩ T_j.writeList then    ▷ Checking for RW and WW conflicts
13:            flagEdge=True
14:         end if
15:         if T_i.writeList ∩ T_j.readList then
16:            flagEdge=True
17:         end if
18:         if T_i.writeList ∩ T_j.writeList then
19:            flagEdge=True
20:         end if
21:         if flagEdge then
22:            DAG→add_edge(T_i, T_j)
23:         end if
24:      end for
25:   end while
26: end procedure                     ▷ Threads join when the DAG is complete
```

**Algorithm 2.** Multi-threaded selectTxn(): threads concurrently search DAG for the next transaction to execute

```
27: procedure SELECTTXN(DAG)
28:    for T_i = pos To txn_count do   ▷ iterate over until all transactions to find transaction for
   execution
29:       if T_i.indeg == 0 then                 ▷ Checking for txn with zero indegree
30:          if T_i.indeg.CAS(0, −1) then
31:             pos ← T_i                   ▷ store the last position for fast parsing
32:             return T_i
33:          end if
34:       end if
35:    end for
36:    for T_i = 0 To pos do  ▷ iterate over until all transactions to find transaction for execution
37:       if T_i.indeg == 0 then                 ▷ Checking for txn with zero indegree
38:          if T_i.indeg.CAS(0, −1) then
39:             pos ← T_i                   ▷ store the last position for fast parsing
40:             return T_i
41:          end if
42:       end if
43:    end for
44:    return −1 ▷ Threads returns when a transaction is selected or all transactions are executed.
45: end procedure
```

**Transaction Execution:** Once the dependency DAG is constructed, the block producer proceeds to execute the transactions within the block in parallel. It ini-

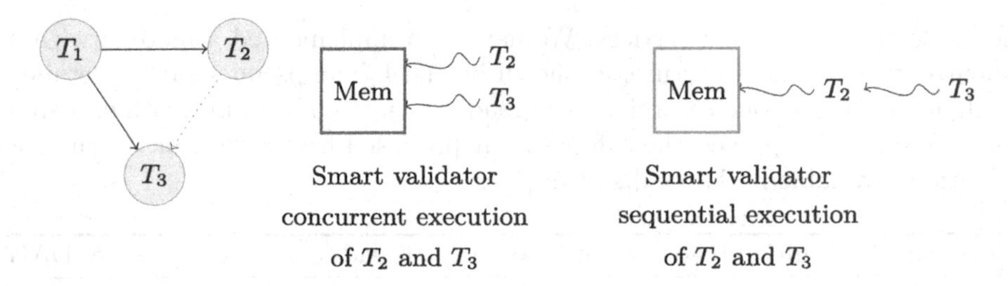


**Fig. 5.** Example scenario of smart validator proposed by Anjana et al. in [6]

tiates multiple threads to process the transactions. Each thread selects a transaction for execution using the indegree array like in Line 30 of Algorithm 2. If the indegree of a transaction is zero, it indicates that the transaction does not have any predecessor-dependent transactions and can be executed ($T_1, T_3$, and $T_2$ in Fig. 3). If no such transactions are available, the threads wait until one is available or end execution if all the transactions have completed execution. Upon selecting a transaction, it is executed, and the indegrees of all the outgoing edge transactions ($T_5$ and $T_6$ for $T_1$) are decremented by 1. Then, the next transaction with zero indegree is searched for. This search can be optimized by initiating the search from the last transaction ID selected. The last transaction ID selected is stored in the variable *pos* in the Algorithm 2 and is used in Line 28 and Line 36. This further reduces the time it takes to find the next transaction as the search starts from *pos* as shown in the Algorithm 2 Line 28. The pseudo-code for the execution of each thread while selecting a transaction is present in Algorithm 2.

### 3.2 Secure Validator

DAG sharing and smart multi-threaded validation have been explored in [6] by Anjana et al. Two important computation errors discussed in [6] are *False Block Rejection* (FBR), where a valid block is incorrectly rejected by a validator, and *Edge Missing BG* (EMB), where an edge is removed from DAG before sharing by a malicious block producer. The solution proposed for the issue of EMB by Anjana et al. in [6] focuses on identifying missing edges between transactions only when they are executed concurrently. However, when a validator executes transactions sequentially, the block may still be accepted. Consequently, a parallel validator would reject the block, while a serial validator would accept it as depicted in the Fig. 5. This discrepancy can potentially result in inconsistencies in the final states of the blockchain across different nodes, which is undesirable. To address this issue without sacrificing concurrent block execution, we propose a solution.

A malicious block producer can add extra edges to slow the validator by forcing it to serially execute the block transaction. This case of malicious behaviour is not considered by Anjana et al. [6]. We have denoted the condition as *Extra edge BG* (EEB). In this work, we propose a solution overcoming the drawbacks of the previous solution in resolving FBR and EMB while addressing EEB error.

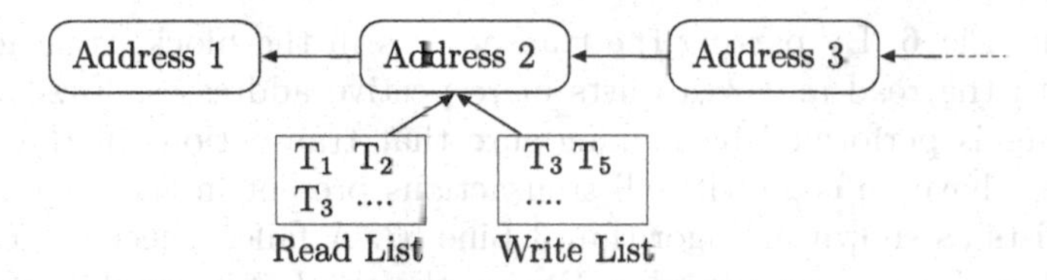


**Fig. 6.** Linked list address data for secure validator.

**Algorithm 3.** Multi-threaded secureValidator(): $m$ threads concurrently verify the DAG shared

```
46: procedure SECUREVALIDATOR(DAG)
47:     while !mBlockProducer do
48:         Adds ← addsCounter.get&inc()              ▷ Claim the next address for analyzing
49:         if Adds > adds_count then
50:             addsCounter.dec()
51:             return                                 ▷ Return if all the address are processed
52:         end if
53:         for i = 0 To lenght(Adds.readList) do      ▷ procedure for checking for missing edges
54:             T_i ← Adds.readList[i]
55:             for j = 0 To lenght(Adds.writeList) do         ▷ read-write dependencies
56:                 T_j ← Adds.writeList[j]
57:                 if !checkEdge(T_i, T_j) then
58:                     mBlockProducer ← True
59:                     return
60:                 end if
61:                 incDeg(T_i, T_j)      ▷ Increment the indegree of lower txn and mark the edge
62:             end for
63:         end for
64:         for i = 0 To lenght(Adds.writeList) do
65:             T_i ← Adds.writeList[i]
66:             for j = 0 To lenght(Adds.writeList) do         ▷ write-write dependencies
67:                 T_j ← Adds.writeList[j]
68:                 if !checkEdge(T_i, T_j) then
69:                     mBlockProducer ← True
70:                     return
71:                 end if
72:                 incDeg(T_i, T_j)      ▷ Increment the indegree of lower txn and mark the edge
73:             end for
74:         end for
75:         for i = 0 to txn_count do                  ▷ procedure for checking for extra edges
76:             if T_i.inDeg ≠ T_i.calDeg then  ▷ if shared indegree is equal to calculated indegree
77:                 mBlockProducer ← True
78:                 return
79:             end if
80:         end for
81:     end while
82: end procedure
```

**DAG Validation:** The DAG created by the block producer in the blockchain network is shared with the validators in the network. This helps validators save on the time taken for DAG creation. In order to address the issues caused by FBR, EMB, and EEB errors due to DAG sharing, we have proposed *secure validator* for verifying DAGs which is described in Algorithm 3. The secure validator checks for missing edges and extra edges present in the DAG shared. This is performed by multiple threads for swift graph verification. For all the addresses accessed in the block, a read list and a write list are maintained as shown in the Fig. 6. By parsing the transactions in the block, transaction IDs are added to the read and write lists of respective addresses. First, check for missing edges is performed by making sure that transactions in the write list of an address have an edge with all transactions present in the respective read and write lists as shown in Algorithm 3 Line 57. A failed check indicates that the DAG shared has a missing edge. During the check, the number of outgoing edges is calculated for each transaction as in Line 72 Algorithm 3.

From Line 75 to Line 80, we compare the sum of the outgoing edges obtained in the above operation with the in-degree array shared along the block. This function identifies if any extra edges are present in the DAG. As a result, the secure validator verifies the DAG and recognizes malicious block producers (if any). The procedure to handle such nodes depends on the type and functionalities of blockchain technology. This way, we eliminate the FBR, EMB, and EEB errors and validate the DAG shared. Detailed algorithms with extensive explanations can be obtained by referring to appendix C in [15].

## 4 Experiments Analysis

### 4.1 Implementation Details

We have chosen Hyperledger Sawtooth as our testing platform since it has good support for parallelism and already has an inbuilt parallel scheduler. To incorporate the DAG framework into the Sawtooth architecture, we have to modify the current parallel scheduler module. Due to the modular nature of Sawtooth, any modifications made to a module can be restricted within the module itself without impacting the remaining modules of the architecture. Ensuring this however requires that the modifications to modules are performed with great care.

We have now implemented the DAG sharing and secure validator modules in Sawtooth 1.2.6. Our modules are in CPP language while the Sawtooth core was developed in both Rust and Python. We have chosen CPP for its efficient support for concurrent programming. For DAG sharing, we have modified the block after the block producer has verified that all the transactions in the block are valid. In Sawtooth 1.2.6 we used the input and output addresses present in the transaction structure. Every transaction in the DAG is represented by a graph node and the outgoing edges indicate dependent transactions. In order to ensure efficient validation, the DAG is also stored in the block [5,6,10] and shared across the blockchain network. We have used the dependencies list component of the transaction structure (in Sawtooth) to incorporate DAG into the block.

Initially, we implemented the DAG using a linked list data structure. This is ideal when the size of the graph is unknown and the graph needs to be dynamic. Given that the number of transactions in a block does not change and the limit to the number of transactions a block can contain, we have designed an adjacency matrix implementation for DAG. The results have shown further improvement over the linked list implementation. This is because the adjacency matrix is direct access whereas the linked list implementation would require traversal across the list to reach the desired node.

In Sawtooth 1.2.6 block validators, the secure validator is implemented. The DAG is recreated using the dependencies list provided in the transaction by the block producer. This saves the time taken to create the DAG for concurrent execution again in the validators. The secure validator performs various checks for missing edges that should have been present in the DAG shared by the block producer as explained in Subsect. 3.2.

**Transaction Families:** We implemented four transaction families to test the performance of our approach: (a) SimpleWallet, (b) Intkey, (c) Voting and (d) Insurance. In SimpleWallet one can create accounts, deposit, withdraw and transfer money. In Intkey clients can increment and decrement values stored in different variables. In Voting, the operations are 'create parties', 'add voters' and the voters can 'vote' one of the parties. The insurance family is a data storage transaction family where user details like ID, name, and address details are stored and manipulated.[2] To control the percentage of conflicts between transactions, one must have control over the keys created. We have modified the batch creation technique in these transaction families to allow the user to submit multiple transactions in a batch. This way we can not only just control the number of transactions in a batch but also the conflicts among the transactions in a batch. We individually observed each transaction family behaviour under various experiments and a mix of all four types of transactions in a block.

### 4.2 Experiments

We have conducted several experiments to extensively test our proposed framework. In order to assess the framework's performance across different scenarios, we have devised three conflict parameters (CP) that indicate the level of dependency among the transaction. The conflict parameters, CP1, CP2, and CP3, are metrics used to assess different aspects of a DAG representing transactions. CP1 measures the proportion of transactions in the DAG that have at least one dependency. It indicates how interconnected the transactions are, with higher values suggesting a greater level of dependencies. CP2 represents the ratio of dependencies to the total number of transactions in the DAG. It provides insights into the density of dependencies within the graph. A higher CP2 value indicates a higher density of dependencies among transactions. CP3 quantifies the degree of parallelism in the DAG by calculating the number of disjoint components, which are subgraphs without interconnections. A lower CP3 value suggests a higher level of parallelism, indicating that transactions can be executed independently in separate components. By evaluating these conflict ratios, one can gain a deeper understanding of the interdependencies and parallelizability of transactions within the DAG.

We have designed four experiments, each varying one parameter while the rest of the parameters are constant. The four parameters are (1) the number of blocks, (2) the number of transactions in the block, (3) the degree of dependency, and (4)

[2] The transaction family code can be accessed here: https://github.com/PDCRL/ConcSawtooth.

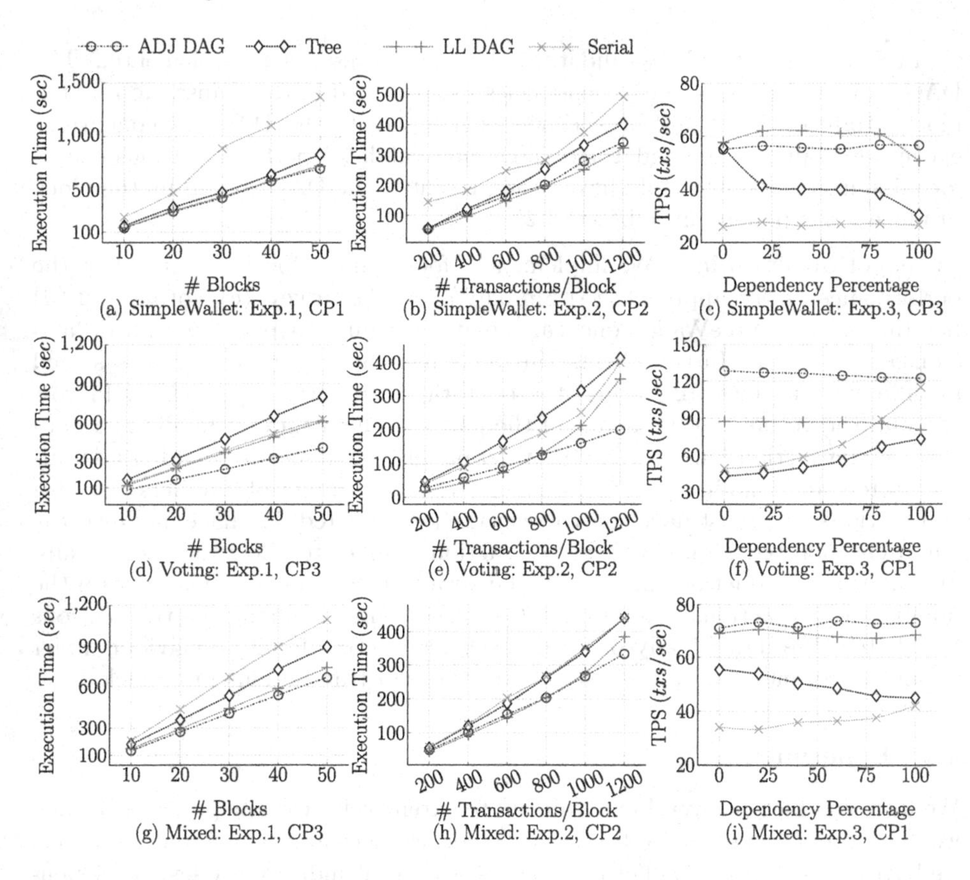


**Fig. 7.** Detailed analysis of our proposed framework performance with both adjacency matrix and linked list implementations in Sawtooth 1.2.6.

the number of threads. The experimental setup is named one to four, respectively. We have named the adjacency matrix implementation of our proposed framework as *Adj_DAG* and linked list implementation as *LL_DAG*. The Sawtooth inbuilt parallel scheduler uses a tree data structure; accordingly, we have named it as *Tree* and serial execution output as *Serial* in our results. We have observed that due to the presence of global lock in Python, the change in the number of threads has not impacted the performance significantly. Due to this, we have not presented the results of the experiment (4) in this work.

It can be observed from Fig. 7 that the adjacency matrix and linked list implementation of our proposed framework perform significantly better than the tree-based parallel scheduling and serial execution. We have illustrated here some of the experiments we have conducted, and the rest can be found in the associated technical report [15] (Appendix D). Figure 7(a), (d), and (g) illustrate the impact of change in the number of blocks on various schedulers. On average the speedup of *Adj_DAG* over *Serial* is 1.58 times and *LL_DAG* is 1.43 times, while *Tree* is 1.22 times. The average speedup of *Adj_DAG* over *Tree* is 1.29 and *LL_DAG* is 1.17 times.

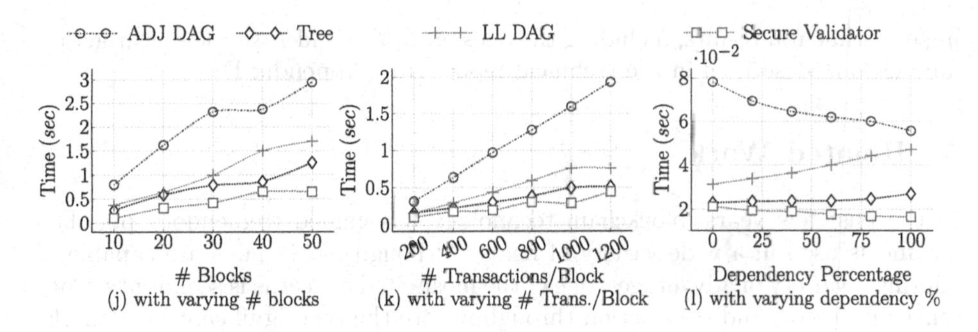


**Fig. 8.** Comparison of data structure creation time for all the parallel schedulers

Experiment (2) results are depicted in Fig. 7(b), (e), and (h). We can observe that the gap between serial and parallel schedulers increases with an increase in the number of transactions in the block. We observe that the higher the number of transactions greater the scope for concurrency. For Experiment (3), we have varied the degree of dependency between the transactions and measured its impact on the transactions per second (TPS). The dependency among the transactions is increased by making multiple transactions access the same accounts/addresses. Ideally, varying the conflict percentage without changing the number of transactions should not impact serial execution throughput. However, a decrease in the number of different memory accesses due to caching improves the execution time. We can observe this phenomenon in serial execution time in Fig. 7(c), (f), and (i). Interestingly these opposing effects, temporal locality, and increase in conflicts balance each other, and a steady TPS is maintained for *ADJ_DAG* and *LL_DAG* algorithms. But, in *Tree* scheduler, the performance further decreases with increased conflicts as it dominates over the temporal locality.

Figure 7(d), (e), and (f) show the Voting transaction family behavior under experiments (1), (2), and (3). Unlike the other transaction families, *Serial* execution is faster than *Tree* scheduler with this family. We discovered that the reason for this is that the entire list of voters list and parties are accessed for any transaction (operation) in this family instead of the one particular voter and party address. This causes higher overheads which leads to the observation that the design of the transaction family (smart contract) plays a crucial role in performance optimization. One can observe that the *ADJ_DAG* and *LL_DAG* still perform better as they use transactions to represent the dependency data structure, unlike *Tree* scheduler that uses addresses.

The *secure validator* framework efficiently verifies the DAG shared by the block producer and eliminates the need to reconstruct the DAG at every block validator. The execution time of the secure validator and adjacency DAG scheduler will only vary in the dependency graph creation aspect. To highlight the savings achieved through secure validator, we analyzed the dependency data structure creation and verification time for various schedulers in Fig. 7. One can observe that the *secure validator* takes the least execution time, as seen in the Fig. 8(j), (k), and (l). Figure 8(l) shows that *secure validator* is stable against the variations in the dependency in the graph. Due to lack of space, the remaining experimental results, including the ones on *Intkey* and *Insurance* transaction families, are described in the technical report [15] (Appendix D).

## 5 Related Work

In the past few years, blockchain technology has gained tremendous popularity and is used in a wide variety of fields. Although blockchains are capable of offering a variety of advantages, one of the most cited concerns is scalability. Consensus protocols and transaction throughput are the two significant bottlenecks of blockchain performance. In contrast to PoW, alternative consensus protocols like PoS and PoET are introduced to minimize consensus time. However, transaction throughput continues to be a hindrance to scalability. Exercising parallel execution of transactions in a block is one of the solutions to optimize blockchains.

Dickerson et al. [10] introduced the concept of parallel execution of Ethereum [1] transactions using Software Transactional Memory (STM). The block producer executes transactions in the block using STM, and the serializable concurrent state is discovered. This is then shared with the validators to achieve deterministic execution. Following this, there have been multiple STM-based concurrent transaction execution frameworks for blockchains [3,7,11]. Besides the significant overhead associated with executing transactions through STMs, transactions sometimes fail due to dependencies and must be re-executed. Another drawback is that they cannot have operations that cannot be undone, which is a significant obstacle to smart contract design. During concurrent execution, STM-based approaches identify conflicts among transactions dynamically, i.e., during execution. This results in various transactions failing or rolling back to resolve the conflict. This has a significant impact on throughput and is not optimal for blocks with high interdependencies. In general, a dynamic approach is ideal, but it is not necessary for blockchains whose addresses are either included in the transactions or are easily inferred. For such systems, we propose a parallel execution framework for transactions in a block.

Sharding is another popular technique to address scaling issues in blockchains. In this, the nodes present in the network are categorized into small groups. Each group processes transactions parallelly with the other groups. Sharding is being explored earnestly as a solution to scalability issues [8,9,12,17,19,20]. The criteria for sharding are different in each approach. Few are specifically designed for monetary transactions in blockchains [12,19]. This leads to smart contract transactions being processed on a single shard leading to an inefficient distribution of computational work. The implementation of transactions that span across smart contracts becomes intricate with sharding. Protocols have to be designed specifically for inter-shard communication, further increasing the complexity of the design [9].

The Aeolus blockchain [20], is specifically tailored for Internet of Things (IoT) devices that face limitations in executing multiple transactions rapidly. Aeolus addresses this challenge by harnessing the computing resources available in a cluster of nodes to reduce the time required for transaction execution, thereby enhancing the overall performance of the blockchain. The sharding technique limits the degree of parallelization to the number of shards irrespective of actual capacity. If the shards are dynamic, in the worst case, the number of shards is equal to the number of transactions. Sharding is considered unsuitable for transactions with high inter-dependencies. In contrast, we designed an efficient parallel scheduler for blockchain nodes to execute block transactions concurrently. Our proposed approach can be implemented on top of the sharding approach to improve the efficiency of individual nodes within each shard, where transactions in a block can be executed in parallel.

## 6 Conclusion and Future Work

In this paper, we proposed a concurrent transaction execution framework for blockchains. We proposed a parallel scheduler and a secure validator module for the blockchain node architecture. The parallel scheduler is responsible for identifying the dependencies among the transactions in the block and scheduling them for conflict-free execution. The dependencies are represented by a DAG and are shared along with the block to minimize the validation time of validating nodes. DAGs are validated using the secure validator, which determines if a malicious block producer has shared inaccurate graphs. The proposed approach has been thoroughly tested in Hyperledger Sawtooth 1.2.6 [2] and is flexible enough to be implemented in any blockchain that follows the order-execute paradigm [4]. One possible future step would be to extend the implementation of the proposed approach to different blockchain platforms and compare their performance. Further, fault tolerance and scalability for each blockchain node on its own (i.e., horizontal scaling of each validator node) can be explored.

**Acknowledgements and Data Availability.** We would like to express our sincere gratitude to the paper and artifact reviewers who dedicated their time and expertise to evaluate our work. We would also like to extend our gratitude to the members of the MeitY and NBF (National Blockchain Framework) project for their support throughout the research. The modified Sawtooth node developed in this work with both implementations discussed is available at the Figshare repository: https://doi.org/10.6084/m9.figshare.23544960 [16].

## References

1. Ethereum: A Next-Generation Smart Contract and Decentralized Application Platform. https://ethereum.org/
2. Hyperledger Sawtooth. https://sawtooth.hyperledger.org/
3. Amiri, M.J., Agrawal, D., El Abbadi, A.: ParBlockchain: leveraging transaction parallelism in permissioned blockchain systems. In: 2019 IEEE 39th International Conference on Distributed Computing Systems (ICDCS), pp. 1337–1347 (2019)
4. Androulaki, E., et al.: Hyperledger fabric: a distributed operating system for permissioned blockchains. In: EuroSys (2018)

5. Anjana, P.S., Kumari, S., Peri, S., Rathor, S., Somani, A.: An efficient framework for optimistic concurrent execution of smart contracts. In: PDP, pp. 83–92 (2019)
6. Anjana, P.S., Attiya, H., Kumari, S., Peri, S., Somani, A.: Efficient concurrent execution of smart contracts in blockchains using object-based transactional memory. In: Georgiou, C., Majumdar, R. (eds.) NETYS 2020. LNCS, vol. 12129, pp. 77–93. Springer, Cham (2021). https://doi.org/10.1007/978-3-030-67087-0_6
7. Anjana, P.S., Kumari, S., Peri, S., Rathor, S., Somani, A.: OptSmart: a space efficient Optimistic concurrent execution of Smart contracts. Distrib. Parallel Databases (2022)
8. Baheti, S., Anjana, P.S., Peri, S., Simmhan, Y.: DiPETrans: a framework for distributed parallel execution of transactions of blocks in blockchains. Concurr. Comput.: Pract. Exp. **34**(10), e6804 (2022)
9. Dang, H., Dinh, T.T.A., Loghin, D., Chang, E.C., Lin, Q., Ooi, B.C.: Towards scaling blockchain systems via sharding. In: Proceedings of the 2019 International Conference on Management of Data, SIGMOD 2019, pp. 123–140. Association for Computing Machinery, New York (2019)
10. Dickerson, T., Gazzillo, P., Herlihy, M., Koskinen, E.: Adding concurrency to smart contracts. In: PODC 2017, pp. 303–312. Association for Computing Machinery, New York, NY, USA (2017)
11. Gelashvili, R., et al.: Block-STM: scaling blockchain execution by turning ordering curse to a performance blessing (2022)
12. Kokoris-Kogias, E., Jovanovic, P., Gasser, L., Gailly, N., Syta, E., Ford, B.: OmniLedger: a secure, scale-out, decentralized ledger via sharding. In: 2018 IEEE Symposium on Security and Privacy (SP), pp. 583–598 (2018)
13. Kunz, T., Black, J.P., Taylor, D.J., Basten, T.: POET: target-system independent visualizations of complex distributed-applications executions. Comput. J. **40**(8), 499–512 (1997)
14. Nakamoto, S.: Bitcoin: a peer-to-peer electronic cash system (2008). https://bitcoin.org/bitcoin.pdf
15. Piduguralla, M., Chakraborty, S., Anjana, P.S., Peri, S.: An efficient framework for execution of smart contracts in hyperledger sawtooth (2023). https://doi.org/10.48550/arXiv.2302.08452
16. Piduguralla, M., Saheli, C., Anjana, P.S., Peri, S.: Artifact and instructions to generate experimental results for Euro-Par conference proceeding 2023 paper: DAG-based Efficient Parallel Scheduler for Blockchains: Hyperledger Sawtooth as a Case Study (2023). https://doi.org/10.6084/m9.figshare.23544960
17. Valtchanov, A., Helbling, L., Mekiker, B., Wittie, M.P.: Parallel block execution in SoCC blockchains through optimistic concurrency control. In: 2021 IEEE Globecom Workshops (GC Wkshps), pp. 1–6 (2021)
18. Vasin, P.: Blackcoin's proof-of-stake protocol v2, p. 71 (2014). https://blackcoin.co/blackcoin-pos-protocol-v2-whitepaper.pdf
19. Zamani, M., Movahedi, M., Raykova, M.: RapidChain: scaling blockchain via full sharding. In: Proceedings of the 2018 ACM SIGSAC Conference on Computer and Communications Security, CCS 2018, pp. 931–948. Association for Computing Machinery, New York (2018)
20. Zheng, P., et al.: Aeolus: distributed execution of permissioned blockchain transactions via state sharding. IEEE Trans. Industr. Inf. **18**(12), 9227–9238 (2022)

# INSTANT: A Runtime Framework to Orchestrate In-Situ Workflows

Feng Li[1] and Fengguang Song[2](✉)

[1] Purdue University, Indianapolis, IN 46202, USA
li2251@purdue.edu

[2] Indiana University Purdue University, Indianapolis, IN 46202, USA
fgsong@iupui.edu

**Abstract.** In-situ workflow is a type of workflow where multiple components execute concurrently with data flowing continuously. The adoption of in-situ workflows not only accelerates mission-critical scientific discoveries but also enables responsive disaster predictions. Although there are recent studies on the performance and efficiency aspects of in-situ workflows, the support for portability and distributed computing environments is limited. We present INSTANT, a runtime framework to configure, plan, launch, and monitor in-situ workflows for distributed computing environments. INSTANT provides intuitive interfaces to compose abstract in-situ workflows, manages in-site and cross-site data transfers with ADIOS2, and supports resource planning using profiled performance data. We use two real-world workflows as use cases: a coupled wildfire spreading workflow and a computational fluid dynamics (CFD) workflow coupled with machine learning and visualization. Experiments with the two real-world use cases show that INSTANT effectively streamlines the orchestration of complex in-situ workflows, and its resource planning capability allows INSTANT to plan and carry out efficient in-situ workflow executions under various computing resource availability.

**Keywords:** in-situ workflow · scientific computing · high-performance computing · urgent computing

## 1 Introduction

Workflows have been widely used to enable scientific discoveries in different domains. A workflow describes the sequence of operations and the data/control dependencies among the operations. Traditionally, data dependencies of workflows are facilitated with offline file transfers, however with the increasing amount of data in different scientific domains, there is a trend to pursue in-situ workflows, where multiple components execute concurrently, with data flowing continuously across the workflow's lifespan. Although some researchers may use "in-situ" to describe the situation where different components co-locate in the same computing environment to reduce data transfer overhead [1,2], "in-situ" in this paper refers to "processing data as it is generated" as discussed in [3].


J. Cano et al. (Eds.): Euro-Par 2023, LNCS 14100, pp. 199–213, 2023.
https://doi.org/10.1007/978-3-031-39698-4_14

There are continuous community efforts to support in-situ analysis for different application domains, one of which is the ADIOS2 project. ADIOS2 (the second generation of the Adaptable Input Output System [4]) provides applications with a generic interface to switch among multiple file-based or streaming-based data transport methods. Parallel applications can use ADIOS2 APIs to read or write multi-dimensional data, and their choices of underlying I/O engines (transport methods) can be delayed to the runtime, by providing an external XML configuration file. This adaptive design makes it easier to conduct in-situ analysis for traditional HPC applications. ADIOS2 allows a group of $m$ MPI processes each writing to a portion of multi-dimensional domain space, and another group of $n$ MPI processes reading concurrently with data layouts different from the writer processes. There are also an increasing number of domain applications that have recently adopted ADIOS2, such as OpenFOAM [5] (computational fluid dynamics) and LAMMPS [6] (molecular dynamics).

Although the ADIOS2 library itself provides a universal interface to pairwisely connect various applications such as simulation, analysis, and visualization, it lacks the ability to compose and manage complex in-situ workflows. The loosely-couple model of ADIOS2 allows domain scientists to focus on each individual component's performance and usability, however, there is no high-level control or view of a workflow as a whole. As a result, the performance of in-situ workflows cannot be properly captured, and the in-situ workflows have limited portability and reproducibility due to the hardcoded and low-level ADIOS2 configurations.

Cheetah is a software framework to create "campaigns" for coupled simulation-analysis-reduction (SAR) computations [7]. Although Cheetah utilizes ADIOS2 to couple multiple component applications, it focuses on searching for good runtime parameter combinations in a single site through parameter sweeping, and it lacks the ability to compose workflows with a general DAG-like layout. Traditional workflow systems use the high-level DAG (Directed Acyclic Graph) abstraction to describe a workflow and allow the components of a workflow to be executed orderly following the precedence specified in the DAG. However, unlike traditional workflow, in-situ workflows feature in-situ data dependencies, which require special handling from workflow systems [8]. The integration of in-situ workflow and traditional task-based workflow has recently been explored in PyCOMMPs and Pegasus workflow management systems [9,10]. However, these two integrations both rely on the Decaf library [11] for in-situ data transports, such that the in-situ transfer is limited to a single HPC site.

In order to provide high-level composition and orchestration support for complex in-situ workflows in distributed computing environments, we design and implement a runtime framework called INSTANT. INSTANT takes in an abstract workflow that consists of ADIOS2-enabled components, and generates executable workflows for running on distributed computing resources. The resource planning capability of INSTANT allows an abstract in-situ workflow to be mapped efficiently on different platforms, or across multiple platforms, based on workflow characteristics gathered through performance monitoring. The execution engine of INSTANT then launches the components of the workflow to the mapped computing environments and configures dataflow correspondingly. The flexible configuration interface of INSTANT not only makes the in-situ workflows portable and easily reproducible, but also enables instant deployment of critical pipelines.

In our experiments, we use two high-impact real-world workflow applications as use cases: a wildfire spreading workflow, and a CFD workflow coupled with real-time machine learning and visualization. Experiment results show that INSTANT realizes flexible configurations of in-situ workflows and allows efficient executions of in-situ workflows under different resource availabilities.

To the best of our knowledge, this work makes the following contributions:

1. A runtime framework to compose, plan, launch, and monitor complex in-situ workflows across multiple distributed environments.
2. An customized *DataX* I/O engine that supports flexible data interactions for wide-area networks.
3. Use case studies and performance analysis of real-world in-situ workflows, including a wildfire spreading workflow and a real-time "CFD + machine learning/visualization" workflow.

In the rest of this paper, we introduce the general design of the INSTANT runtime system in Sect. 2. We show the experiments with two real-world use cases in Sect. 3 and discuss the related work in Sect. 4. We assess the limitations and practical design decisions in Sect. 5, and then conclude the paper in Sect. 6.

## 2 Methodology

INSTANT mainly includes two main components, a "mapper" and an "execution engine", as shown in colored boxes in the Fig. 1. The mapper takes in an abstract workflow as input and decides how to map the components of the workflow to a diverse set of sites. Such decisions are then instantiated as the "executable workflow" in the figure. The executable workflow is launched by the "execution engine" to the selected computing resources, which can be a grid, a computer cluster, or the local execution environment. Besides orchestrating remote jobs, the execution engine also sets up dataflows between workflow components (either same-site or cross-site using ADIOS2), and collects performance data which are used in turn for resource planning.

The separation of resource planning and execution engine are also seen in traditional workflow systems. However components execute one-after-another in a traditional task-based workflow system, and the data dependency is typically realized as offline file transfers. In comparison, INSTANT targets in-situ workflows, where components execute concurrently and the data transfer is continuous data flow instead of one-time file transfers. INSTANT allows a workflow

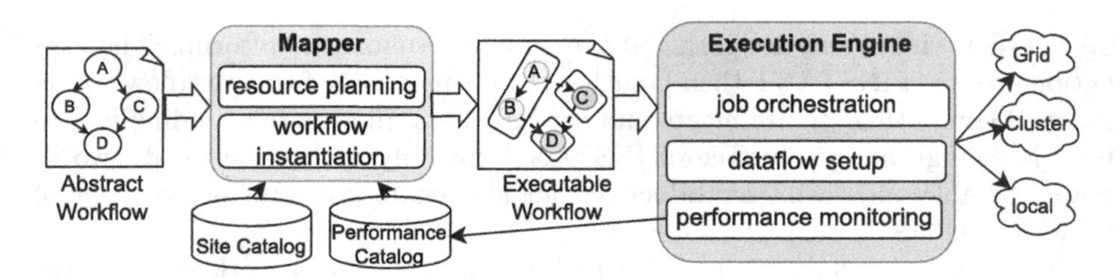


**Fig. 1.** Overview of the INSTANT runtime framework.

described similarly to traditional workflows as DAG, and it intelligently decides the placements of workflow components and sets up the ADIOS2-based dataflow.

### 2.1 Mapper

The mapper takes in the abstraction of a workflow, site catalog and performance catalog as input information and generates an "executable workflow" as the intermediate result.

**Workflow Abstraction.** A workflow abstraction defines how each component is invoked for execution, and how data flows between components. The abstraction is resource independent, meaning that the same workflow can be executed on a local computer, a remote cluster, or a grid consisting of several clusters. The abstraction is designed in a way that a workflow user only needs to interact with the locally-install toolkit interfaces provided by INSTANT, without the need for preparing individual job scripts for remote submissions.

Listing 1 shows an abstract workflow description of a simple HeatTransfer workflow, which solves a 2D passion equation for temperature in homogeneous media using finite differences [12]. The HeatTransfer workflow contains two components, and the data writer runs iteratively and sends data to the reader continuously. In the abstraction file, the "name" field is the unique identifier of each component, and "exe" and the "args" fields describe the relative path of the component executable files and the runtime arguments, respectively. In the "dataflows" section, each entry describes a data flow between a pair of components. In this simple example, there is only a single data flow, which is from the "producer" component to the "consumer" component. The "IOFrom" and "IOTo" fields are the names of ADIOS2 IOs, and these IO names allow each component to initialize its IO engines based on the configuration of ADIOS2 XML configuration files provided later during runtime. As shown in Fig. 2, the two IOs only allocate a "virtual" communication channel of two components. The corresponding engine choices for these IOs depend on the actual resource planning, which we introduce below.

```
{
    "components": [
        {
            "name": "producer",
            "exe":"heatTransfer_write_adios2",
            "args": ["adios2.xml", heat.bp, ...],
            "deployment": "$INSTANT_PATH/"
        },
        {
            "name": "consumer",
            "exe": "heatTransfer_read",
            "args": ["adios2.xml", heat.bp, ...],
            "deployment": "$INSTANT_PATH/"
        }],
    "dataflows": [
        {
            "componentFrom": "producer",
            "componentTo":"consumer",
            "IOFrom": "writer",
            "IOTo": "reader",
            "type": "Insitu"
        }]
}
```

**Listing 1.** The abstract workflow file for an example Heat-Transfer workflow.

**Fig. 2.** The abstract workflow represented in Listing 1.

**Resource Planning.** The resource planning utility decides where (which sites) and how (the number of processing units) to launch each component.

In an in-situ workflow, data continuously flows between components during the workflow lifetime in a pipeline fashion, and the overall speed of the workflow depends on the slowest segment [9,13]. INSTANT utilizes existing site catalog, collected performance data and resource planning to help an in-situ workflow to achieve better efficiency. The site catalog contains two parts:

- Compute-capability information: number of processing units (e.g. CPU cores) available at each site, and performance of each processing unit[1].
- Connectivity information: latency and bandwidth matrices between available sites.

The collected performance metrics mainly include the compute cost of each component and transfer sizes between components.

Currently, we utilize CPLEX as our default resource planning method. CPLEX together with its Optimization Programming Language (OPL) [14,15] allows us to define and solve the in-situ workflow optimization problem using a syntax similar to formal mathematical representations. The built-in optimization model optimizes the "throughput", which is the number of steps the whole workflow can advance in a second. We first create the mathematical optimization model using OPL, respecting the actual resource limits and the pipelined execution constraints. Then CPLEX can build up a search space with reasonable

[1] The per-processing-unit performance is currently recorded in the form of giga-floating-point operations per second (GFLOP/S).

combinations of different decision variables and search for the best solution. We have also developed a more efficient heuristic-based algorithm for the same optimization goal of maximizing workflow throughput, however we mainly discuss the CPLEX resource planning method in this paper for its simplicity.

The resulting resource plan is the decision on where to place each component, and how much computing resource to allocate for each component. Listing 2 then shows a possible launching plan of the previous HeatTransfer workflow. In the example workflow, the two components are assigned to two separate computing environments (PSC Bridges2 and IU Bigred 200) with different numbers of processing units respectively.

```
1  {
2    "plans":[
3      {
4        "name": "producer",
5        "site": "bridges2",
6        "nprocs": 4
7      },
8      {
9        "name": "consumer",
10       "site": "bigred200",
11       "nprocs": 2
12     }
13   ]
14 }
```

**Listing 2.** An example workflow plan file (cross-site plan).

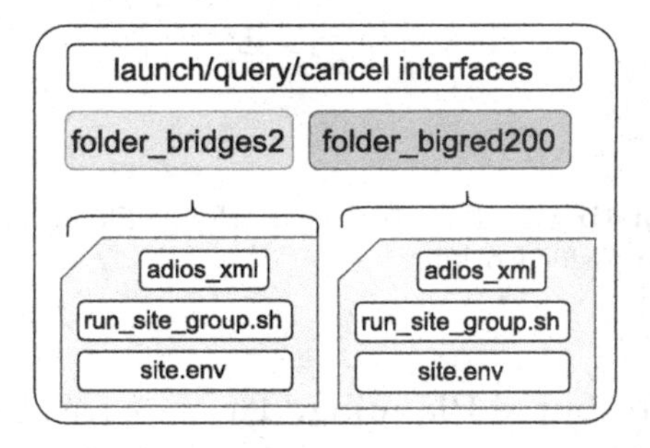


**Fig. 3.** Folder structure of an example executable workflow.

**Instantiation.** Once the planning utility decides how to map each component, it can generate the "executable workflow". The executable workflow is an instantiation of the workflow plan and contains the required recipes to launch the workflow. The executable workflow is generated by first grouping components based on their site choices and then creating submission folders for each site group. Listing 3 shows the user interfaces of instantiating the executable workflow, where the "heat-transfer-dag.json" is the abstract workflow file, and "chosen-plan.json" is the plan file (either manually configured or generated by INSTANT resource planning utility). The output folder "testbed_folder" stores all generated contents of the executable workflow.

```
1 python3 scripts/instant_instantiate.py -c heat-transfer-dag.json -p chosen-
      plan.json -o testbed_folder
```

**Listing 3.** User interface to create a excutable executable workflow.

Figure 3 shows the contents of the output folder, where users can use the launch/query/cancel interfaces to orchestrate the remote executions of the in-situ workflow. Two submission sub-folders are created for the two sites planned for workflow execution. Specifically, each site submission sub-folder includes a job script to invoke individual components assigned to the site (run_site_group.sh), an ADIOS2 configuration file to specify the choices of I/O engines (adios_xml), and an environment setup script (site.env).

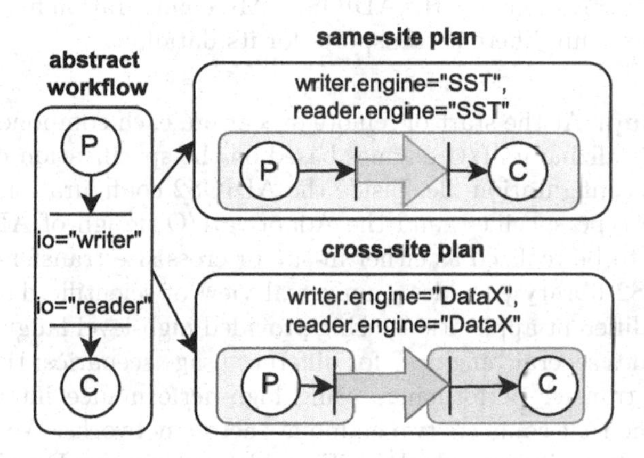


**Fig. 4.** INSTANT sets up either same-site or cross-site dataflow based on the plan.

The generated ADIOS2 XML configuration file allows the dataflow correctly configured in the later execution stage. Figure 4 shows how the generated ADIOS2 XML configuration file is used to prepare the workflows for same-site and cross-site launching. The original abstract workflow only defines the name of the ADIOS2 IOs, however, the actual transport method (the choice of ADIOS2 engine) is not determined until the planning is finished. In Fig. 4, the "same-site" plan sets the engine type of both ends to "SST", which is the high-performance in-cluster transport provided by ADIOS2. In contrast, for a cross-site plan, the engine type is then configured as "DataX". The "DataX" is our customized ADIOS2 engine type to enable flexible data coupling across clusters, which we introduce later in this paper in Sect. 2.2.

### 2.2 Execution Engine

When the executable workflow is ready, the "execution engine" can launch the components to the target sites. The execution engine has three main goals:

- Job orchestration: launch, monitor and control the execution of remote jobs.
- Dataflow setup: set up and maintain the data communication channel for both in-site and cross-site dataflows.
- Performance monitoring: collect performance data which can then be used for resource planning to further improve the workflow execution efficiency.

**Job Orchestration.** As previously shown in Fig. 3, the executable workflow exposes interfaces to launch, cancel and query the status of the workflow. The "launch" interface first copies the site-specific submission folders to the target sites, and then submits the site-specific job scripts (run_site_group.sh) to the HPC batch system. The query and cancel interfaces work similarly by issuing corresponding batch system job control commands. The submission folder copied to the target sites also contains the ADIOS2 XML configuration file, which allows components to set up different transports for its dataflow.

**Dataflow Setup.** At the start of remote execution, each component sets up its dataflow by initializing its I/O engines based on the specification defined in the ADIOS2 XML configuration file. Inside the ADIOS2 configuration file, each IO has the engine type specified, and the Adaptive I/O design of ADIOS2 allows the transports to be realized as either in-site or cross-site transfers.

The ADIOS2 library provides a universal view of scientific data and allows easy gluing of different applications using provided high-level language bindings. ADIOS2 provides several "engines" for different usage scenarios: the SST engine that max out transfer performance using high-performance interconnect; the DataMan engine that connects two endpoints across networks. We designed and developed a new engine called "DataX", which reuses the DataMan engine's ZeroMQ communication patterns, with the following features added:

1. Support arbitrary m-to-n process mapping.
2. Support scenarios that both sites are behind the firewall.

For feature #1, the current DataMan engine[2] only supports 1-to-1 process mapping (i.e., both DataMan producer and consumer have to use a single process), and DataMan is mainly used for cross-site communication between data transfer nodes of two clusters. In comparison, the more general ADIOS2 interface supports m-to-n process mapping: producer and consumer components can each be a group of MPI processes and have different access patterns of the global space. To provide such universal m-to-n process mapping for cross-site communication, our "DataX" engine adds additional support for data aggregation and redistribution for MPI ranks on both sides of the communication. This feature enables the support of the same flexible m-to-n process mapping even across wide-area networks, which allows a dataflow easily configured as same-site or cross-site.

For feature #2, the current implementation of DataMan requires the IP address and port of the reader to be accessible to the data writers, in order to establish the ZeroMQ data communication channel. However, it is common that HPC compute nodes are behind firewalls and not exposed to the outside of the institution, which makes it difficult to enable cross-site communication for in-situ workflows. For this reason, the INSTANT framework also includes a "relay" service, which creates endpoints in an accessible place that both ends can connect to. The relay service is implemented as an array of ZeroMQ "queue" devices[3] allocated in cloud virtual machines, which allows both sender and receiver to get connected even if they are both behind firewalls.

[2] As of March 2023 when we submitted this work.

[3] ZeroMQ queue device: http://api.zeromq.org/2-1:zmq-device.

**Performance Monitoring.** Here we explain what information is needed for INSTANT to support resource planning, and how the required performance data is collected.

The resource planning utility mentioned in Sect. 2.1 requires several types of performance data to conduct resource planning: the per-step compute work of each component, the per-step transfer size of each data communication pair, and environment-related information such as latency/bandwidth between sites. We have added customized hooks for the *BeginStep* and *EndStep* ADIOS2 APIs, so that the ADIOS2 library automatically records the start and end time of each ADIOS2 step. For each component, the actual time spent on computing can be inferred from the elapsed time between the EndStep for reader operations and the BeginStep of the next write operations. The inferred compute time $T_{compute}$ and the documented performance data of the environments can then be used to calculate the actual computation work size $work = core\_speed \times num\_cores \times T_{compute}$. In the customized hooks, we also record the number of bytes written for each variable in each step. For component pairs that transfer multiple variables, the recorded transfer sizes are added together to obtain the per-step transfer size between the two components. The addition of customized hooks is transparent to workflow composers because the same set of ADIOS2 APIs are used. The bandwidth and latency information between HPC sites are obtained using iperftools and Linux ping command.

Our experiments in Sect. 3.2 demonstrate that through performance data collected from a previously-executed in-situ workflow, INSTANT can produce efficient resource plans for same-environment and cross-environment executions.

## 3 Use Cases

In this section, we show two real-world use cases of INSTANT. In the first use case we WRF-SFIRE, a coupled atmosphere-fire model, and demonstrates how INSTANT can help accelerate the model coupling, and at the same time provide users with extensive flexibility/functionality. In the second use case, we use a real-time “CFD + machine learning/visualization” workflow, and show the advantage of INSTANT's resource planning and launching capability especially when computing resources are limited.

### 3.1 WRF-SFIRE

The first experiment uses WRF-SFIRE, which is a coupled atmosphere-fire model that is used for urgent simulations and forecasting of wildfire propagation [16]. WRF-SFIRE combines the state-of-the-art Weather Research and Forecasting model (WRF) and a surface fire spreading model (SFIRE). The atmosphere properties from WRF (e.g. surface air temperate, humidity, and wind) drive the SFIRE model, which then calculates the spreading of the fire line. The default/baseline WRF-SFIRE is a tightly-coupled model: the SFIRE model is implemented as one of the physics plugins of WRF, and WRF and SFIRE are built into the same binary executable. During runtime, the executable alternates between WRF and SFIRE models, which share the same memory space and CPU resources (i.e., time-division).

We compare the baseline tightly-coupled WRF-SFIRE method with the other two methods enabled by INSTANT, as shown in Fig. 5a. Unlike the baseline method where WRF and SFIRE are tightly coupled, the INSTANT-enabled methods create decoupled in-situ workflows using ADIOS2. The "INSTANT w/ 1fire" method has two executable binaries: a WRF model without SFIRE component, and a standalone SFIRE executable. We developed the decoupled method based on the recent ADIOS2 IO backend for WRF [17][4]. Instead of utilizing the NetCDF for periodical variable output, the output data from WRF are sent out through ADIOS2 format for data streaming. For the data receiver side, we added ADIOS2 support for the standalone SFIRE by changing the default NetCDF I/O routines to corresponding ADIOS2 I/O routines. The "INSTANT w/ 2fires" method uses the same two executable binaries, but the WRF model sends data streams to two separate SFIRE simulations. This allows the workflow to use the same WRF output data to predict fire lines under different ignition conditions.

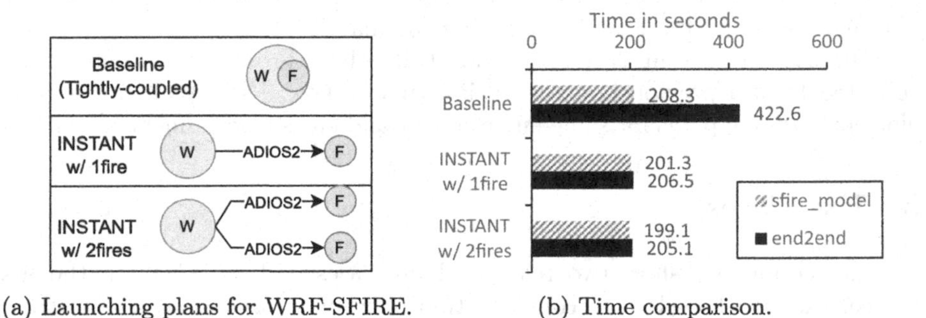


(a) Launching plans for WRF-SFIRE. (b) Time comparison.

**Fig. 5.** Time comparison of the WRF-SFIRE workflow w/ and w/o INSTANT support.

For all three methods, we use the "hill" example included in the WRF-SFIRE repository, which simulates 5 min of the fire propagation in a 60 m × 60 m hill area. Figure 5b shows the time comparison with different execution methods. For each method, we plot the total end-to-end time (from the first step of the WRF model to the last step of the SFIRE model), and also the sfire_model time (elapsed time used for the SFIRE model execution). From Fig. 5b, we can see that the default tightly-coupled method has the longest end-to-end time of 422.6 seconds. This lengthy time is caused by the time-division pattern of tightly-coupled execution: the same processors need to be time-sliced to alternate through WRF and SFIRE executions.

[4] The integration of ADIOS2 into the WRF is being added for future WRF releases https://github.com/wrf-model/WRF/pull/1787.

In comparison, the decoupled executions enabled by INSTANT deploy the WRF and SFIRE models in separate computing resources, and allow the data transfer to happen asynchronously without blocking the WRF atmosphere execution. For "INSTANT w/ 1fire" and "INSTANT w/ 2fires" methods, the total time is greatly reduced to 206.5 and 205.1 s, respectively, both resulting in more than 2 times speedup. In both cases, the end-to-end time is close to the time spent on the sfire_model. Moreover, compared with the base 1fire method, the 2fire method does more with similar time: two separate SFIRE models are concurrently executed, which gives more insights for disaster monitoring/prevention, without running the WRF atmosphere model multiple times. Overall, INSTANT enables flexible composition of in-situ workflows by allowing simulation connected with interchangeable analytics components.

### 3.2 Computational Fluid Dynamics with Real-Time Machine Learning/Visualization

In the second use case, we use a real-time "CFD + machine learning and visualization" in-situ workflow application [18] to demonstrate how INSTANT can process execution patterns through collected performance data, generate efficient execution plans, and launch the proposed workflow to accelerate applications.

Figure 6a shows the workflow layout of the CFD-based workflow. The first *CFD* component application is a parallel icoFoam CFD simulation implemented with the OpenFOAM package to simulate a 2-D lid-driven cavity flow problem. Then the simulation output is partitioned into a number of 2D regions based on the geometric information, and the task is to cluster the regions into different categories based on the flow pattern. The *DivCal* component, to calculate the L2 divergences between a group of sampled regions. Then, the *K-MedoidsClustering* component groups all the sampled regions using k-medoid with the calculated divergence information. After that, the *AssignClusterIDs* component assigns a label for each region, based on its divergence from the medoid regions. Finally the *CatalystVis* component visualizes the clustering results using the ParaView Catalyst in-situ visualization toolkit [19].

We configure a grid size of $1024 \times 1024$ for the CFD simulation and a region size of $16 \times 16$, which results in a total number of 4096 regions. We compare the following three cases: *baseline*, *INSTANT-1site*, and *INSTANT-distrib*. The *baseline* case is a reference execution plan, which uses small-size allocation just to gather performance data for resource planning[5]. The two other methods use the collected performance data from the baseline execution and generate plans for two different resource availability scenarios. The *INSTANT-1site* method assumes there is a total of 32 cores available on a single HPC site (IU Quartz HPC); while the *INSTANT-distrib* method assumes there are 32 cores available in a distributed environment (two HPC systems: IU Quartz and Bridges2, each with 16 cores).

[5] We have used 4,2,1,2,1 processes for the 5 components, respectively.

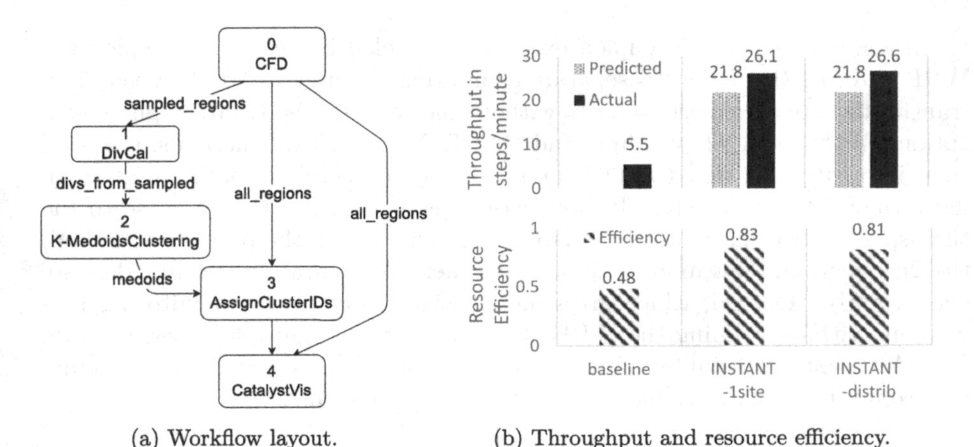


(a) Workflow layout. (b) Throughput and resource efficiency.

**Fig. 6.** A CFD simulation + machine learning/visualization in-situ workflow. INSTANT achieves better throughput and resource efficiency through resource planning.

We use throughput and resource efficiency as the metrics to compare the above three methods. Throughput is measured in "steps per minute", which corresponds to the speed the workflow can advance in a pipelined fashion. The resource efficiency, on the other hand, is calculated by:

$$E_{\text{resource}} = \frac{\sum_{c_i \in C} n_{c_i} p_{c_i} T_{\text{compute}}(c_i)}{(\sum_{c_i \in C} n_{c_i} p_{c_i}) T_{\text{step}}}$$

Here $C$ is the set of all components of the workflow, $n_{c_i}$ is the number of processing units allocated to component $c_i$, and $p_{c_i}$ denotes the performance of each assigned processing unit. The $T_{\text{step}}$ is the workflow step time, which indicates the time required for the whole workflow to advance a step in the pipelined fashion. The $T_{\text{compute}}(c_i)$ is the time a component $c_i$ uses for compute work instead of idling caused by pipeline stall. Overall, a higher resource efficiency indicates that components are assigned with the proper amount of computing resources, and the whole workflow experiences less idling.

Figure 6b shows the throughput and resource efficiency of the CFD workflow of the three methods. The upper part of the figure shows the throughput of the three methods, where the base case has a relatively low throughput of 5.5 steps per minute. With the performance gathered from the base case, the INSTANT creates plans for the *INSTANT-1site* and *INSTANT-distrib* methods. For those two methods, INSTANT can first give rough predictions of the throughput even before the execution, based on the results of resource planning. After the actual launching, INSTANT achieves 4.75 and 4.83 times better throughput for the 1-site and distributed setups, respectively, compared with the baseline. SNL-based methods also achieve better resource efficiency than the baseline, as shown in the bottom part of Fig. 6b. Overall, INSTANT can help workflow users conveniently gather performance data from historical runs, and generate adequate resource plans for efficient executions at different resource availabilities.

# 4 Related Work

Traditional workflow management systems such as Pegasus [20] and Kepler [21] provide interfaces for workflow users to compose, launch and collect results for task-based workflows. In these works, the data dependencies are carried out through file transfers, and each task can only start only after all its predecessors finish. Resource planning methods have also largely been developed following such assumptions of execution precedence. Our INSTANT framework, however, assumes a different pipelined execution pattern, and allows for special resource planning methods to target the emerging in-situ workflows.

The Cheetah/Savanna workflow environment [7] is a toolset to automate performance studies of coupled simulation-analysis-reduction HPC computations. Cheetah is used to compose a campaign of workflows, considering large configuration space such as process placement and I/O choices, and Savanna is a runtime engine that orchestrates individual workflows on target platforms. Although Cheetah/Savanna workflow environment supports different HPC platforms, it focuses on the fine-grained performance study on each individual platform, and the effect of collaboration of multiple platforms is largely unexplored.

BeeFlow [8] is a workflow management system that supports traditional workflows and also workflows with in-situ data dependencies. It utilizes event-synchronization primitives to enforce in-situ workflow logic. BeeFlow replies on Docker containers for application deployment, and the execution is constrained to one site for a single run. In comparison, INSTANT allows native parallel component applications, and the applications can be planned and deployed across multiple sites for efficient executions.

# 5 Discussion

## 5.1 Co-allocation of Computation Resources and Queue Time Waste

Currently, different site groups of a workflow are submitted subsequently to the planned sites, and we assume the components can start execution at around the same time. In the case when an HPC site experiences long job queue waiting time, the job submitted to the other sites will wait during the ADIOS2 environment initialization until the delayed job starts. For mission-critical applications, allocation reservation or increasing job queue priority can also better ensure that applications be launched and started around the same time.

## 5.2 Application Deployment in Distributed Computing Environments

One challenge in supporting the flexible execution of in-situ workflows on various platforms is the software deployment of component applications on different computing environments. To let components have the flexibility to be placed on either of the available sites, executables of the components should also be either available or deployable on those sites. Workflow systems such as Pegasus maintain a "transformation catalog", to locate the executables for workflow components. Other systems use container technologies to deploy applications before execution. In our current implementation, we deploy component applications on the target sites using Spack environment [22]. INSTANT specifies a list of required software packages (e.g., OpenFOAM and ParaView) as a Spack environment file, which allows the same set of software environments to be easily installed/reproduced on various platforms.

## 6 Conclusion

We design and implement a runtime framework called INSTANT, which allows for easy configuration, planning, and deployment of in-situ workflows across multiple execution environments. The INSTANT framework contains a mapper component and an execution engine. The mapper can generate efficient execution plans based on available computing environments and workflow characteristics, and the execution engine allows the execution workflow to be deployed either on one site or across multiple sites. We conduct our experiments with a wildfire-spreading workflow and a real-time "CFD with machine learning and visualization" workflow. Experiment results show that INSTANT allows easier composition of in-situ workflows and built-in resource planning functionality improves the workflow throughput and resource efficiency. Future work includes supporting more applications from various domains. This will also allow for a more thorough performance study for a broad set of applications and workflows.

**Acknowledgements.** This work is supported by the National Science Foundation Award #1835817. We want to thank Greg Eisenhauer who provided useful suggestions and clarifications on ADIOS2 cross-site in-situ data transport, and also Michael Laufer who offered generous help and guidance on the WRF-ADIOS2 integration.

## References

1. Bennett, J.C., Abbasi, H., Bremer, P.-T., et al.: Combining in-situ and in-transit processing to enable extreme-scale scientific analysis. In: Proceedings of the International Conference on High Performance Computing, Networking, Storage and Analysis, SC 2012, pp. 1–9. IEEE (2012)
2. Sewell, C., Heitmann, K., Finkel, H., et al.: Large-scale compute-intensive analysis via a combined in-situ and co-scheduling workflow approach. In: Proceedings of the International Conference for High Performance Computing, Networking, Storage and Analysis, pp. 1–11 (2015)
3. Childs, H., Ahern, S.D., Ahrens, J., et al.: A terminology for in situ visualization and analysis systems. Int. J. High Perform. Comput. Appl. **34**(6), 576–691 (2020)
4. Godoy, W.F., Podhorszki, N., Wang, R., et al.: ADIOS 2: the adaptable input output system. A framework for high-performance data management. SoftwareX **12**, 100561 (2020)

5. Jasak, H., Jemcov, A., Tukovic, Ž.: OpenFOAM: a C++ library for complex physics simulations. In: International Workshop on Coupled Methods in Numerical Dynamics, Dubrovnik, Croatia, p. 20. IUC (2007)
6. Plimpton, S.: Fast parallel algorithms for short-range molecular dynamics. J. Comput. Phys. **117**(1), 1–19 (1995)
7. Mehta, K., Allen, B., Wolf, M., et al.: A codesign framework for online data analysis and reduction. Concurr. Comput.: Pract. Experience **34**(14), e6519 (2021)
8. Chen, J., Guan, Q., Zhang, Z., et al.: BeeFlow: a workflow management system for in situ processing across HPC and cloud systems. In: 2018 IEEE 38th International Conference on Distributed Computing Systems (ICDCS), pp. 1029–1038. IEEE (2018)
9. Do, T.M.A., et al.: Accelerating scientific workflows on HPC platforms with in situ processing. In: 2022 22nd IEEE International Symposium on Cluster, Cloud and Internet Computing (CCGrid), pp. 1–10 (2022)
10. Yildiz, O., Ejarque, J., Chan, H., Sankaranarayanan, S., Badia, R.M., Peterka, T.: Heterogeneous hierarchical workflow composition. Comput. Sci. Eng. **21**(4), 76–86 (2019)
11. Dreher, M., Peterka, T.: Decaf: decoupled dataflows for in situ high-performance workflows. (ANL/MCS-TM-371) (2017)
12. ORNL. ADIOS2 HeatTransfer workflow. http://github.com/ornladios/ADIOS2/blob/release_28/examples/heatTransfer/ReadMe.md
13. Fu, Y., Li, F., Song, F., Chen, Z.: Performance analysis and optimization of in-situ integration of simulation with data analysis: zipping applications up. In: Proceedings of the 27th International Symposium on High-Performance Parallel and Distributed Computing, HPDC 2018, pp. 192–205. ACM (2018)
14. IBM. IBM ILOG CPLEX Optimization Studio OPL Language User's Manual. Technical Report Version 12 Release 8 (2017)
15. Laborie, P., Rogerie, J., Shaw, P., Vilím, P.: IBM ILOG CP optimizer for scheduling. Constraints **23**(2), 210–250 (2018)
16. Mandel, J., Beezley, J.D., Kochanski, A.K.: Coupled atmosphere-wildland fire modeling with WRF 3.3 and SFIRE 2011. Geosci. Model Dev. **4**(3), 591–610 (2011)
17. Laufer, M., Fredj, E.: High performance parallel I/O and in-situ analysis in the WRF model with ADIOS2. arXiv preprint arXiv:2201.08228 (2022)
18. Li, F., Song, F.: Building a scientific workflow framework to enable real-time machine learning and visualization. Concurr. Comput.: Pract. Experience **31**(16), e4703 (2019)
19. Fabian, N., Moreland, K., et al.: The ParaView coprocessing library: a scalable, general purpose in situ visualization library. In: 2011 IEEE Symposium on Large Data Analysis and Visualization, pp. 89–96 (2011)
20. Deelman, E., Vahi, K., et al.: Pegasus, a workflow management system for science automation. Futur. Gener. Comput. Syst. **46**, 17–35 (2015)
21. Ludäscher, B., Altintas, I., Berkley, C., et al.: Scientific workflow management and the Kepler system. Concurr. Comput.: Pract. Experience **18**(11), 1039–1065 (2006)
22. Gamblin, T., LeGendre, M., Collette, M.R., et al.: The Spack package manager: bringing order to HPC software chaos. In: Proceedings of the International Conference for High Performance Computing, Networking, Storage and Analysis, pp. 1–12 (2015)

# How Do OS and Application Schedulers Interact? An Investigation with Multithreaded Applications

Jonas H. Müller Korndörfer[1], Ahmed Eleliemy[1], Osman Seckin Simsek[1], Thomas Ilsche[2], Robert Schöne[2], and Florina M. Ciorba[1](✉)

[1] University of Basel, Basel, Switzerland
{jonas.korndorfer,ahmed.eleliemy,osman.simsek,florina.ciorba}@unibas.ch
[2] Technische Universität Dresden, Dresden, Germany
{thomas.ilsche,robert.schoene}@tu-dresden.de

**Abstract.** Scheduling is critical for achieving high performance for parallel applications executing on high performance computing (HPC) systems. Scheduling decisions can be taken at batch system, application, and operating system (OS) levels. In this work, we investigate the interaction between the Linux scheduler and various OpenMP scheduling options during the execution of three multithreaded codes on two types of computing nodes. When threads are unpinned, we found that OS scheduling events significantly interfere with the performance of compute-bound applications, aggravating their inherent load imbalance or overhead (by additional context switches). While the Linux scheduler balances system load in the absence of application-level load balancing, we also found it decreases performance via additional context switches and thread migrations. We observed that performing load balancing operations both at the OS and application levels is advantageous for the performance of concurrently executing applications. These results show the importance of considering the role of OS scheduling in the design of application scheduling techniques and vice versa. This work motivates further research into coordination of scheduling within multithreaded applications and the OS.

**Keywords:** OS scheduling · Application thread-level scheduling · Linux · CFS · LB4OMP · lo2s · OpenMP

## 1 Introduction

The even distribution of work in a parallel system is a principal challenge for achieving optimal efficiency, as uneven distribution (*load imbalance*) leads to underutilized hardware. On the one hand, the application or its runtime needs to distribute work evenly across threads (or processes), e.g., by OpenMP loop scheduling. The operating system (OS) scheduler can amplify or mitigate load imbalances by scheduling application threads among cores/hardware threads. OS scheduling decisions are most impactful if there are more execution threads—including application threads and background tasks—than processor cores.


J. Cano et al. (Eds.): Euro-Par 2023, LNCS 14100, pp. 214–228, 2023.
https://doi.org/10.1007/978-3-031-39698-4_15

All supercomputers on the TOP500 list use Linux[1] and therefore its Completely Fair Scheduler (CFS) [13]. OS-level load balancing operations such as *context switches* and *thread migrations* can be costly and influence application performance. Moreover, application characteristics can also influence the OS scheduler actions regarding load balancing. The relation between OS-level and application thread-level scheduling and load balancing is **key** to increasing performance and utilization of today's complex and extremely large supercomputers but has not yet been explored. In this work, we investigate this interaction and pursue answers to three specific research questions presented in Sect. 4.

We selected applications with different load imbalance characteristics to create distinct scenarios for the OS scheduler. The applications contain loops parallelized and scheduled with OpenMP. We modified the loop `schedule` clauses to use LB4OMP [12], a load balancing library that provides dynamic and adaptive loop self-scheduling techniques in addition to the standard options. To measure the Linux OS scheduler events during the execution of parallel applications we use lo2s [11], a lightweight node-level tool that monitors applications and the OS.

This work makes the following **contributions:** 1) An in-depth investigation of the *interaction between OS- and application-level scheduling and load balancing* and its influence on system and application performance. 2) *Exposes opportunities for performance improvement* by bridging OS- and application-level schedulers. Overall, the presented results pave the way for cooperation between these levels of scheduling.

This work is organized as follows. Section 2 reviews the related literature while Sect. 3 contextualizes the scheduling considerations relevant to this work. The approach proposed to study the interaction between scheduling levels is described in Sect. 4. The experimental design and performance analysis are discussed Sect. 5. The conclusions and outline directions for future work are presented in Sect. 6.

## 2 Related Work

Earlier work has exclusively studied the performance of different application thread-/process-level scheduling techniques [7,12] or the relation between application thread-level and application process-level scheduling [8,15,16].

The OS noise was investigated in different scenarios and experimentation strategies [1,19,20]. The OS noise was evaluated as a single "composed component" that consists of scheduling, kernel events, OS services, and maintenance tasks. In this work, we break this noise into its constituents and assess the influence of Linux OS scheduler on the performance of multithreaded applications.

Wong et al. showed that local scheduling decisions in Linux with CFS are efficient [21]. Bouron et al. showed that the FreeBSD ULE scheduler achieves comparable performance to Linux CFS [6]. While CFS is in general efficient, Lozi et al. [14] show that its implementation is still updated when bugs are found.

In contrast to the above-cited literature, this work investigates the influence of the Linux CFS on the performance of several multithreaded applications

[1] https://www.top500.org/statistics/details/osfam/1/.

and quantifies this interaction. Through selected specific kernels, benchmarks, and mini-apps that exhibit varied load imbalance characteristics (which we also modify by employing various OpenMP scheduling techniques) we observe their effects on the OS scheduler's behavior.

# 3 Scheduling in Context

## 3.1 Linux OS Scheduling

To rebalance work between different CPUs[2], the Linux kernel uses *scheduler domains*, which *"mimic[...] the physical hardware"* [5]. Figure 1 shows the scheduler domains of the dual socket system used in the experiments. The domains include SMT (Symmetric Multi-Threading), MC (Multi-Core), NODE, and NUMA (twice). While SMT includes all logical CPUs of a single processor core, MC includes all cores with a common LLC (Last Level Cache), i.e., one core complex [2, Sect. 1.8.1]. NODE refers to all CPUs of a NUMA node. NUMA refers to properties of NUMA systems that are not matched by previous domains – in our example, the two NUMA domains represent CPUs of one processor and all CPUs, respectively. Each domain also serves as a scheduling group in the higher level domain, e.g., the four SMT domains are scheduling groups in the MC domain.

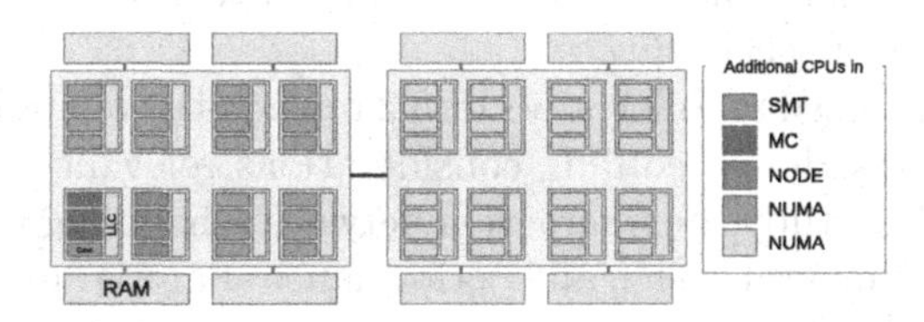


**Fig. 1.** Scheduler domains of a dual socket AMD Epyc 7502 system. Four cores are a core complex, two core complexes define a NUMA node.

Bligh et al. [5] also state that work rebalancing is triggered at regular intervals. This is done by *stopper threads*, which exist per CPU[3]. The threads visit their scheduler domains and try to find more loaded scheduling groups from which they steal work and enqueue it in their local group. The rebalancing interval is typically between one and hundreds of milliseconds, depending on the scheduler domain, and typically grows with the number of CPUs being included in the domain. The exact values for each domain are listed as `min_interval` and `max_interval` in the domains entries in Linux' debugfs. Linux can also reschedule tasks (in our case OpenMP application threads) when they change state, e.g., when they switch between active (`TASK_RUNNING`) and idle (`TASK_SUSPENDED`). To save energy, stopper threads can be turned off during idle periods on tickless kernels. Here, a *"NOHZ balancer core is responsible [...] to run the periodic load balancing routine for itself and on behalf of [...] idle cores.*" [14, Sect. 2.2.2].

[2] In Linux systems, a CPU refers to a hardware thread managed by the OS.

[3] https://github.com/torvalds/linux/blob/master/kernel/stop_machine.c.

### 3.2 Application Thread-Level Scheduling

Application thread-level scheduling is used to improve the execution of a given application. E.g., load-imbalanced loops with *static* scheduling leads to idle application threads and therefore possibly underutilized CPUs while *dynamic* scheduling leads to fewer idle application threads.

The applications considered in this work exhibit various load imbalance characteristics and we modify their parallel loops to use techniques from the LB4OMP library [12]. We select six scheduling techniques representing distinct classes: static (`static`), work-stealing (`static_steal`), dynamic self-scheduling (`SS`, `FAC2`, `GSS`), and adaptive self-scheduling (`AF`). 1) `static`: straightforward compile-time parallelization as per OpenMP standard, smallest to no scheduling overhead and high data locality, no load rebalancing during execution. 2) `static_steal`: LLVM's implementation of static scheduling with work stealing; Steal operations are costly with loss of data locality. 3) **dynamic,1** (`SS`) [17]: OpenMP standard-compliant. Each work request is assigned one loop iteration; Best load balance at the cost of considerable scheduling overhead and severe loss of data locality. 4) **guided** (`GSS`) [18] and (5) `FAC2` [10] are *dynamic & non-adaptive* scheduling techniques. Both assign large chunks of iterations early in the loop execution and later gradually smaller chunks, achieving load balancing at low scheduling overhead. 6) **adaptive factoring** (`AF`) [4] is a *dynamic & adaptive* scheduling technique. `AF` collects information about currently executing loop iterations to adapt the next chunk size accordingly and achieve load balancing at a possibly considerable scheduling overhead and loss of data locality.

## 4 Interaction Between OS and Application Scheduler

The next two subsections present our proposed methodology to answer the following research questions.

**RQ.1** What is the influence of OS scheduling events on the performance of applications with various load imbalance characteristics?
**RQ.2** How does simultaneous load balancing at OS- and application thread-level impact overall application performance and system cores load balance?
**RQ.3** Does the OS exploit system idleness caused by application thread-level load imbalance?

### 4.1 Quantifying OS Scheduler Influence on Application Performance

Quantifying the OS influence on application performance and core utilization is challenging. For instance, an application may issue system calls to read a file from the disk; the OS will do a context switch and may schedule other tasks while the data is being read from the disk. In this case the application is not delayed while it waits for the I/O. In other cases, the OS scheduler may decide to migrate an application thread to another core. The OS scheduler often makes

**Table 1.** Symbol definitions

| | |
|---|---|
| $P$ | Total amount of processing elements (logical cores) assigned to an application |
| $i$ | CPU ID, $0 \leq i < P$ |
| $T_{par}$ | Parallel execution time of an application (maximum of execution times of each processing element) |
| $T_c$ | Parallel cost of executing an application on $P$ processing elements, $T_c = P \times T_{par}$ |
| $x$ | Event type: $A$ (application), $C$ (context switch), $D$ (idle), and $O$ (other) |
| $X_i$ | Set of events of type $x$ occurring on the $i^{th}$ CPU |
| $X$ | Set of all events of type $x$, $X = \bigcup_{i=0}^{P-1} X_i$ |
| $t(X_i)$ | Duration of all events of type $x$ on the $i^{th}$ CPU |
| $f(X)$ | Percentile influence of all events of type $x$ on the application's parallel cost $T_c$, $f(X) = \frac{\sum_{i=0}^{P-1} t(X_i)}{T_c}\%$ |
| $r(X)$ | Average rate of events of type $X$, $r(X) = \frac{\lvert X_i \rvert}{T_{par}}$ |
| $c.o.v$ | Load imbalance based on σ (standard deviation) and μ (mean) of cores finishing times |

such decisions to *balance the system cores* either globally via thread migrations or locally via context switches. However, these scheduling decisions may ultimately *lead to load imbalance at the application level*, i.e., context switches and thread migrations cause performance variability between application threads.

To quantify the OS scheduler's influence on a specific application, we monitor and capture all events that occur while the OS schedules the application. The captured events are classified into: application events **A**, context switches **C**, idle events **D**, or other **O**. This classification allows to quantify and compare the influence of individual event types in various scenarios (see Sect. 5).

Table 1 summarizes the notation and metrics employed in this work. In particular, $f(X)$ represents the influence of a specific type of event as the percentage of the aggregated duration of all events of that specific type on all cores to the parallel cost of the application. Events also have an indirect influence that is observable but not explicitly measurable. For instance, frequent context switches create locality loss and delay certain application threads. Thus, the influence of these context switches goes beyond their duration. To infer such indirect influence, we measure the rate of a specific type of event. For instance, abnormally high context switch rates may explain performance degradation (see Sect. 5.3).

### 4.2 Recording Linux OS Scheduling Events

We record Linux OS scheduling events with the **lo2s** performance measurement tool [11]. lo2s leverages the Linux kernel to collect occurrences of hardware and software events including two special context switch records: one for switching away from a process and one for switching into the new current process. These records are generated at the beginning and end of the scheduler `context_switch` implementation in `kernel/sched/core.c`. lo2s reads the buffers when reaching a watermark or at the end of monitoring and writes them to OTF2 [9] files.

In this work, we use one buffer for each of the systems CPUs and register the tracepoint event `sched:sched_migrate_task`, which is generated by the Linux scheduler implementation of `set_task_cpu` in `kernel/sched/core.c`. This event is caused by different sources, e.g., when a program calls specific syscalls, or when a stopper thread or the swapper re-balance work. Each occurrence of this tracepoint translates to an OTF2 metric event that includes numeric values of the involved process and CPU ids as well as priority. The OTF2 representation of the context switch events gives complete information about when which thread was (de)scheduled on any CPU. The information is recorded as calling-context enter and leave events where each calling-context represents the process that was (de)scheduled. This includes a calling-context for `idle` with a `pid` of `0`. The full lo2s command used in this work is `lo2s -a -t sched:sched_migrate_task`.

From the recorded data, we extract information on *how often* a context switch was performed and how much time the `context_switch` implementation took in total in between the monitoring records. We specifically filter the (de)scheduling of application threads to collect how often and for how long they were scheduled. The same is true for the time spent idle (idle OS threads).

## 5 Performance Results and Discussion

We test the proposed methodology (see Sect. 4) through a performance analysis campaign and offer quantitative answers to the three research questions. For the experiments, we use an application, a benchmark, and a kernel, which we execute on two types of compute nodes (Table 2 and Sect. 5.1), operated by distinct Linux kernel versions. All codes are compiled with Intel compiler version 2021.6.0. We employ 6 different application thread-level scheduling techniques from the LB4OMP library (Sect. 3.2). The LB4OMP library requires OpenMP and we use the LLVM OpenMP runtime library version 8.0. For all measurements regarding OS and application events, we use lo2s version v1.6.0 (Sect. 4.2). Each experiment configuration was repeated 5 times. The average *c.o.v.* of all measurements considering parallel execution time was 0.0133. The highest *c.o.v.* appears for NAS-BT.C executing on `conway`, active wait policy, notPin, and static scheduling technique: 0.0937. The majority of all other measurements are below 0.02 *c.o.v.*

### 5.1 Applications

Depending on their characteristics (memory-, compute-, and/or I/O-bound), applications may drive the OS scheduler to perform more scheduling operations (context switches, thread migration) than others. OS threads executing load-imbalanced applications will naturally idle more often than when executing well-balanced applications. These idle times can be exploited by the OS scheduler. Preemption or migration of threads can also decrease data locality. **To investigate these aspects, we focus mainly on compute-bound applications with different characteristics regarding their load imbalance behavior.**

Calculating the **Mandelbrot** set is a highly compute-bound kernel. We implement this kernel in a time-stepping fashion. The code comprises an outer loop enclosing three other loops that, when scheduled with `static`, present:

constant, increasing, and decreasing load imbalance characteristics across time steps. **NAS-BT.C** is a block tridiagonal solver for synthetic systems of nonlinear partial differential equations, part of the NAS OpenMP parallel benchmarks version 3.4.2 [3]. When NAS-BT.C is scheduled with `static`, it shows low load imbalance. **SPH-EXA**[4] is a Smoothed Particle Hydrodynamics (SPH) simulation framework. In this work, SPH-EXA simulates a Sedov blast wave explosion. This application exhibits both memory- and compute-bound characteristics and when executed with `static` results in mild load imbalance.

These applications comprise loops and employ OpenMP loop parallelization and scheduling to exploit hardware parallelism on shared memory systems. We modified their most time-consuming loops to use the OpenMP `schedule (runtime)` clause to call different scheduling techniques from LB4OMP [12]. Specifically, all OpenMP loops in Mandelbrot were changed from no `schedule` clause (which defaults to `static`) to `schedule(runtime)`. In NAS-BT.C, 12 out of 28 loops use the `NOWAIT` loop clause. The scheduling of these loops cannot be changed from the current `static` scheduling as the correctness in NAS-BT.C depends on those loops' iterations executing in the predefined order. Therefore, we only modified the 3 most time-consuming loops: x_solve, y_solve, z_solve. For SPH-EXA, the 4 most time-consuming loops: `IAD`, `findPeersMac`, `momentumAndEnergy`, and `updateSmoothingLength` were modified, out of 16 OpenMP loops.

### 5.2 Design of Experiments

The experimental evaluation of the proposed methodology requires designing and performing experiments with several factors, each with multiple values. This yields a set of 2'520 factorial experiments, summarized in Table 2. **N** denotes the number of iterations of an applications' loop that we will schedule, **S** – the number of time-steps, and **P** – the number of system cores. In the following sections, we explore the interaction between OS-level and application thread-level scheduling using the metrics described in Sect. 4.1 and Table 2.

### 5.3 Influence of OS Scheduling Events on Application Performance

Here, we decouple OS- from application-related events to answer **RQ.1**. This allows us to investigate the direct impact of different OS scheduler-related operations on the parallel cost. Figure 2 shows several heat maps which represent the influence of OS scheduler-related events on the parallel cost of the different applications/configurations executing on the two systems. That is, the color of the cells represents $1 - f(A)$.

**Cells with a dark shade of** red **show a larger influence of non-application events on parallel cost than cells with a** blue **shade.** Information about the cells' annotations and $x$ and $y$ axis can be found in the caption of Fig. 2. The title of each heat map identifies the application and system, and

[4] https://github.com/unibas-dmi-hpc/SPH-EXA/tree/ccef6cc.

**Table 2.** Design of factorial experiments (960 experiments in total)

| Factors | Values | Properties |
|---|---|---|
| Program | Mandelbrot set | N = 262,144 S = 60 Total loops = 3 Mod. loops = 3 |
| | NAS-BT.C | N = 164,836 S = 200 Total loops = 28 Mod. loops = 3 |
| | SPH-EXA Sedov | N = 15,625 S = 60 Total loops = 16 Mod. loops = 4 |
| OpenMP loop scheduling | `static` | Standard, straightforward parallelization |
| | `dynamic,1 (SS)` | Standard, dynamic and non-adaptive |
| | `guided (GSS)` | Standard, dynamic and non-adaptive |
| | `static_steal` | LB4OMP, dynamic and non-adaptive |
| | `FAC2` | LB4OMP, dynamic and non-adaptive |
| | `AF` | LB4OMP, dynamic and adaptive |
| OpenMP placement | pinned | `OMP_PROC_BIND=close, OMP_PLACES=cores` |
| | unpinned | `OMP_PROC_BIND=false, OMP_PLACES={0:P}:1` |
| OpenMP wait policy | passive | `OMP_WAIT_POLICY=passive` (LLVM default) |
| | active | `OMP_WAIT_POLICY=active` |
| Systems | `ariel` | Intel Xeon Gold Skylake 6154 (2 sockets, 18 cores each) |
| | | $P = 36$ cores, hyperthreading disabled |
| | | Ubuntu 22.04, Linux kernel 5.15.0-52 x86_64, CFS |
| | `conway` | AMD Epyc 7502 (2 sockets, 32 cores each)) |
| | | $P = 64$ cores, no hardware multithreading |
| | | Ubuntu 22.04, Linux kernel 6.0.3 x86_64, CFS |

reminds the key characteristics of the application. The application thread-level scheduling techniques are ordered along the $x$ axis according to their scheduling overhead [12], from lowest (`static`), to the highest (`SS`).

In Fig. 2, one can observe that the largest OS influence is due to the time spent idle during the execution (**5th** row of annotations on the cells of the heat maps). Only results for experiments configured with the **passive** wait policy are shown in Fig. 2. The results for **active** wait policy were subtracted, as they show the same behavior for all applications and systems with the influence of non-application events on the parallel cost close to 0%. This is due to application threads never being allowed to become idle (they persist in *busy wait* at the end of the OpenMP loops), which prevents the OS from freeing cores. This phenomenon makes the idle times practically disappear and other events, such as context switches, are significantly reduced.

The pinning strategies reveal a more general behavior. **Unpinned** executions increase the amount of time spent idle during the execution of the applications, indicating that the OS level load balancing attempts (via thread migrations) end up increasing system idleness. One can observe that for the `ariel` system, the performance impact of not pinning application threads is lower than on `conway`. Since `conway` has almost twice the amount of cores than `ariel`, it increases the likelihood that the OS load balancing operations (performed to preserve OS-level load balance) will create short delays on application threads which can induce or increase application-level load imbalance. Thereby, increasing the amount of time spent idle during the applications' execution. We discuss this phenomenon further in Sect. 5.4.

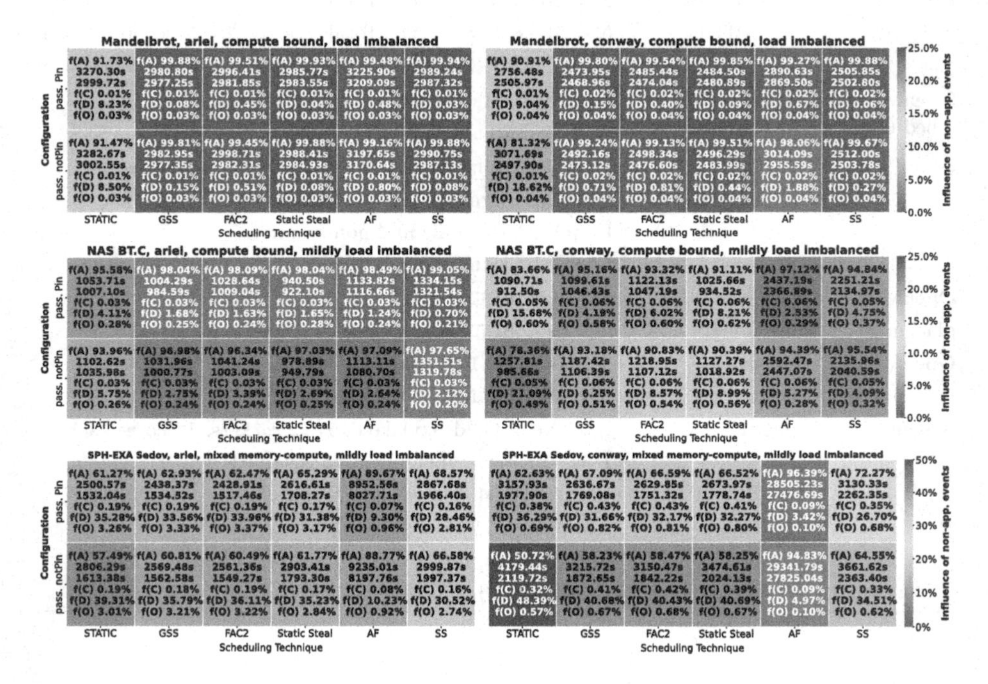


**Fig. 2.** Influence of OS scheduler-related events on the parallel cost of different applications/configurations executing on the two systems. The $x$ axis shows the application thread-level scheduling techniques, while the $y$ axis identifies the different configurations. The heat bar presents $1-f(A)$, which determines the heat map cells' colors. The annotations of each cell show: **1st line**, the relative time spent in application events $f(A)$; **2nd line**, the parallel cost $T_c$; **3rd line**, the application related events time $t(A_i)$; **4th line**, the relative time spent in context switch operations $f(C)$; **5th line**, the relative time spent in idle events $f(D)$; **6th line**, the relative time spent in other events $f(O)$.

From Fig. 2, Mandelbrot executions with `static` scheduling show a large percentage of time spent idle during the executions (`ariel` **Pin** 8.23%, **notPin** 8.50% | `conway` **Pin** 9.04%, **notPin** 18.62%). This happens as the kernel itself is highly load imbalanced which creates several opportunities for the OS to schedule other tasks or, in this case, turn the cores idle. The load imbalance in Mandelbrot greatly affects the performance of the kernel. This can be noticed as all application thread-level scheduling techniques outperform `static` by improving application-level load balancing and also indirectly improving OS-level load balancing by reducing the time spent idle on the cores.

NAS-BT.C (see Fig. 2) makes for an interesting case as it starts with 19 short loops interconnected by the `NOWAIT` loop clause. These loops become slightly desynchronized during execution, which accumulates until the end of the loop barrier in every time step. This causes a significant amount of idle time. Although this desynchronization can create a considerable amount of time spent idle when the application is executed with `static` on all loops (**`ariel` Pin** 4.11%, **notPin** 5.75% | **`conway` Pin** 15.68%, **notPin** 21.09%), it does not translate into considerable application performance loss.

For SPH-EXA, one can observe that the direct influence on parallel cost from context switches $f(C)$ and other events $f(O)$ is very low (smaller than 1%) for all experiments. SPH-EXA (see Fig. 2) loops are executed numerous times within each time step. This makes the application threads encounter the OpenMP end loop barriers also numerous times for each time step, creating very frequent and short idle periods.

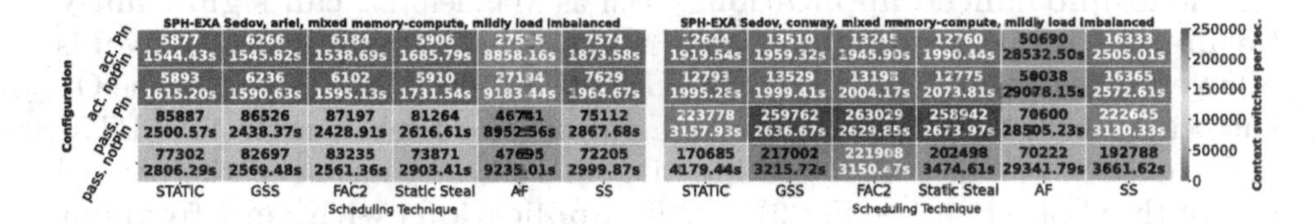


**Fig. 3.** Context switches per second, $r(C)$, for SPH-EXA executing on both systems `ariel` and `conway`. The $x$ axis shows the different scheduling techniques and the $y$ axis identifies the different configurations. The heat bar shows the context switch rate, blue cells show a lower rate while red cells show a higher rate. The annotations in each cell show: **1st line**, the actual context switches per second, $r(C)$, represented by the cells' color; **2nd line**, the parallel cost $T_c$. (Color figure online)

We experiment with SPH-EXA to demonstrate the indirect influence that excessive context switches can have on the performance of applications. Figure 3 shows the number of context switches per second, $r(C)$, when SPH-EXA executed on both systems `ariel` and `conway`. Figure 3 includes the results for wait policy **active** to highlight the excessive context switches that were performed when SPH-EXA was executed with **passive** wait policy.

Using the frequency of context switches, one can infer their indirect influence on the performance of SPH-EXA. In Fig. 3, the executions configured with **wait policy passive**, on both systems, show more than 10× context switches per second than with **wait policy active**. This indirectly affects the performance of SPH-EXA as not only the direct cost of context switches is increased, but also thread wake-up times and loss of data locality. One can notice that by forcing the application threads to stay in a busy wait state at the end of the OpenMP loops (wait policy active), the OS does not preempt the threads so frequently, which lowers the context switches per second (Fig. 3) and the amount of time spent idle (Fig. 2).

Without wait policy active, the OS scheduler does not know the characteristics of the application being executed and keeps trying to free the cores that contain idle application threads even if the idle time is extremely short and rather frequent. Although wait policy active works as a solution for this case, it will prevent the OS from exploiting idle times, which is not ideal for collocation. A solution to this problem can be **coordination and information exchange** between application thread-level and OS-level scheduling where the application scheduler signals the OS scheduler that a few threads are in a busy wait state. Also, the OS can be notified that the application is executing exclusively. This would allow the OS to make more informed decisions. A common case for HPC systems is exclusive execution where, instead of making the cores idle, the OS could keep the application threads scheduled and only preempt them when there is something that is actually ready to execute.

**The results in Fig. 2 and Fig. 3 allow an answer to RQ.1**. The influence of OS scheduling events on the performance of applications manifests in different ways, depending on the application characteristics. Extremely **compute-bound and load-imbalanced applications**, such as Mandelbrot, **can significantly be affected by OS scheduling events when load balancing at OS-level is allowed** (not pinned threads). Results with unpinned threads show that the OS balancing the load across cores ends up aggravating load imbalance in NAS-BT.C and Mandelbrot, which increased idle time and directly increased the parallel cost of the application (see Fig. 2). Finally, **applications with very frequent and short loops**, such as SPH-EXA, can **end up triggering the OS to perform too frequent context switches** to keep the system state updated with idle cores, **which creates a significant overhead on the application execution.**

### 5.4 Interaction Between OS- And Application-Level Scheduling

In this section, we first compare **system level load imbalance** and application performance for Mandelbrot to answer **RQ.2** (Fig. 4).

To calculate the *c.o.v.* shown in Fig. 4, we consider each system core individually and measure the time spent in application-related events on each core, $t(A_i)$. This time is then used to calculate the *c.o.v.* of the system cores considering only application-related events (see *c.o.v.* in Table 2). The active wait policy results were subtracted from the figure as they always show *c.o.v.* close to zero due to threads practically never becoming idle.

For **Mandelbrot with pinned threads (Pin)** in Fig. 4, executed with `static`, the application load imbalance directly translates to load imbalance across the system cores as the OS is not allowed to migrate application threads. Furthermore, all dynamic application thread-level scheduling techniques achieved similar performance and balanced the execution of Mandelbrot achieving *c.o.v.* close to zero. This means that **balancing the execution of pinned threads, the system cores load is directly balanced too.**

**The results for Mandelbrot with unpinned threads (notPin), in Fig. 4 allow an answer to RQ.2**. During execution of Mandelbrot with `static`, the **OS reduced system cores load imbalance** by migrating overloaded threads to idle cores. However, the additional context switches and thread migration operations lowered Mandelbrot's performance in comparison to executions with pinned threads. For example, the *c.o.v.* of the conway system with pinned threads (**Pin**) was 0.0824 and the parallel cost was 2756.48 s while the *c.o.v.* with unpinned threads (**notPin**) was 0.0468 and the parallel cost was 3071.69 s. In Sec. 5.3, fourth row of the heat maps at the top of Fig. 2, one can observe that **the additional operations required to improve the system cores load balance end up increasing the amount of time spent idle during the execution.**

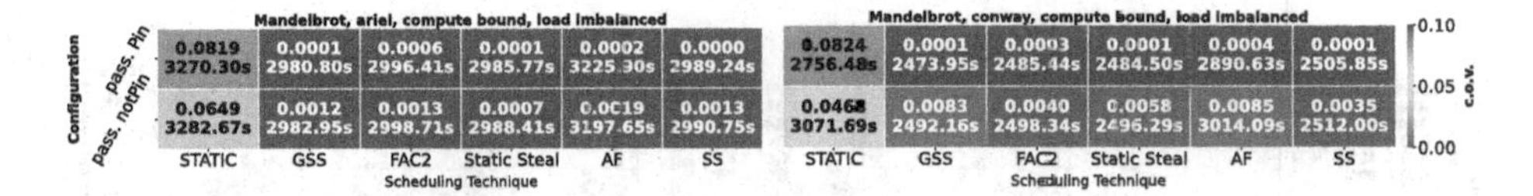


**Fig. 4.** System cores load imbalance using *c.o.v.* metric. The $x$ axis shows the different scheduling techniques at application thread-level while the $y$ axis identifies the configurations. The heat bar shows the *c.o.v.* for the heat maps. Cells with a red shade show higher *c.o.v.* than cells with a blue shade. Higher *c.o.v.* indicates a higher system level load imbalance. The annotations show: **1st line**, the actual *c.o.v.* shown by the cell color; **2nd line**, the parallel cost ($T_c$). (Color figure online)

One can observe in Fig. 4 that when the OS performs load balancing across cores (**notPin**) and the application (Mandelbrot) also performs load balancing with dynamic scheduling techniques, the resulting *c.o.v.* is higher than when the OS does not interfere (**Pin**). This indicates that **simultaneous load balancing operations both in the application thread-level and the OS-level schedulers result in application performance loss and a higher system cores load imbalance** (higher *c.o.v.*).

This phenomenon is explained by the fact that the OS scheduler is designed to achieve fairness for multiple applications which compete for resources. In contrast, application thread-level scheduling is a cooperative approach for all threads executing on resources with the common objective to keep the execution flow balanced and complete the work as fast as possible. The key issue here is that **on most HPC systems, nodes are allocated exclusively**, with only one application executing at any time on each node. **This decreases the fairness requirement, making OS-level scheduling less competitive and increasing the need for it to be more cooperative. One must consider modifications to the Linux OS scheduler, for HPC systems to allow the OS scheduler to receive information from other levels of scheduling that would help avoid focusing on fairness when it is not needed.**

**To answer RQ.3, we evaluate whether the OS exploits system idleness to collocate Mandelbrot and NAS-BT.C on the nodes.** We selected these applications as they show both the highest (Mandelbrot) and lowest (NAS-BT.C) *c.o.v.* among all applications, respectively.

Figure 5 presents the influence of OS scheduler-related events on the parallel cost of Mandelbrot and NAS-BT.C when they execute concurrently. It shows that for both systems and **Pin/notPin** strategies, when the applications were executed concurrently and scheduled with `static`, the amount of idle time in the system decreased compared to the same configurations when the applications were executed exclusively (as shown in Fig. 2 results for Mandelbrot and NAS-BT.C, with `static`). This shows that the OS benefited from at least a portion of the idleness generated by Mandelbrot to schedule NAS-BT.C and vice versa (**RQ.3**).

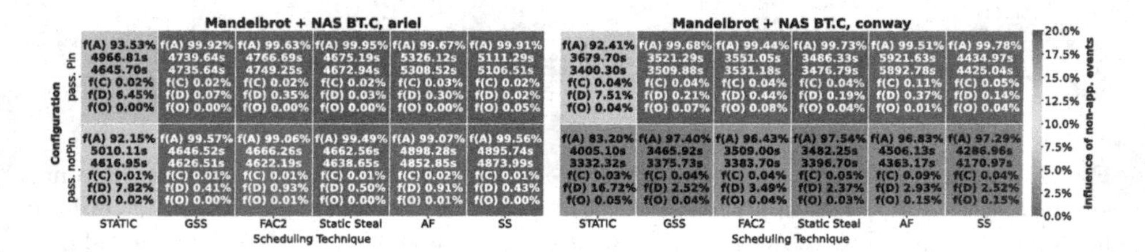


**Fig. 5.** Influence of OS scheduler-related events on the parallel cost of Mandelbrot and NAS-BT.C when executing concurrently on the two systems. For these experiments, we consider application events as any event that is related to any of the two applications. The axes and annotations to the cells of the heat maps follow the same pattern as Fig. 2.

To confirm that the OS efficiently exploits system idleness (**RQ.3**), we analyze the executions with unpinned application threads (**notPin**) as the OS performs balancing such threads across cores. As the OS can move threads, it should migrate NAS-BT.C threads to cores where the threads from Mandelbrot are underloaded. This is confirmed by the results in Fig. 5, which show that with the exception of `static`, the executions with unpinned threads outperform executions with pinned threads on both systems. For example, the parallel cost of the applications executed on `ariel` with `GSS` scheduling technique and pinned (**Pin**) threads was 4739.64 s, while for free threads (**notPin**), it was 4646.52 s. **This confirms that the OS exploits system idleness (RQ.3) and shows that when there is competition in the system, performing load balancing at both OS- and application thread-level is advantageous (RQ.2).**

## 6 Conclusion

This work investigates the interaction between OS-level and application thread-level scheduling to explain and quantify their precise roles in application and system performance. We distinguish OS-related events from application-related events and proposed metrics to quantify the interaction between OS-level and application thread-level scheduling strategies and decisions. Through an extensive performance analysis campaign, we show that the interaction between OS and application scheduling significantly influences system load balance and application performance. We also expose collaboration points between OS- and application thread-level scheduling that can be leveraged to improve performance and load balancing decisions at the OS-level scheduling.

Future work will consider memory-bound applications and tuning of the Linux kernel parameters. Modifying the kernel to receive information about application scheduling decisions will also help coordinate scheduling and load balancing decisions at the OS level.

**Acknowledgment.** The work is jointly supported by the European Union's Horizon 2020 research and innovation programme (grant agreement No. 957407, DAPHNE) and the Swiss Platform for Advanced Scientific Computing (PASC) project SPH-EXA2.

## References


1. Akkan, H., Lang, M., Liebrock, L.: Understanding and isolating the noise in the Linux kernel. Int. J. High Perform. Comput. Appl. **27**(2), 136–146 (2013)
2. AMD: Preliminary Processor Programming Reference (PPR) for AMD Family 17h Model 31h, Revision B0 Processors (2020)
3. Bailey, D., Harris, T., Saphir, W., Van Der Wijngaart, R., Woo, A., Yarrow, M.: The NAS Parallel Benchmarks 2.0. Technical report (1995)
4. Banicescu, I., Liu, Z.: Adaptive factoring: a dynamic scheduling method tuned to the rate of weight changes. In: Proceedings of the High Performance Computing Symposium, pp. 122–129 (2000)
5. Bligh, M.J., Dobson, M., Hart, D., Huizenga, D.: Linux on NUMA systems. In: Proceedings of the Linux Symposium, pp. 89–102 (2004)
6. Bouron, J., et al.: The battle of the schedulers: FreeBSD ULE vs. Linux CFS. In: USENIX ATC, pp. 85–96 (2018)
7. Ciorba, F.M., Iwainsky, C., Buder, P.: OpenMP loop scheduling revisited: making a case for more schedules. In: de Supinski, B.R., Valero-Lara, P., Martorell, X., Mateo Bellido, S., Labarta, J. (eds.) IWOMP 2018. LNCS, vol. 11128, pp. 21–36. Springer, Cham (2018). https://doi.org/10.1007/978-3-319-98521-3_2
8. Eleliemy, A., Mohammed, A., Ciorba, F.M.: Exploring the relation between two levels of scheduling using a novel simulation approach. In: ISDPC, p. 8 (2017)
9. Eschweiler, D., Wagner, M., Geimer, M., Knüpfer, A., Nagel, W.E., Wolf, F.: Open trace format 2: the next generation of scalable trace formats and support libraries. In: Applications, Tools, and Techniques on the Road to Exascale Computing, pp. 481–490 (2012)
10. Flynn Hummel, S., Schonberg, E., Flynn, L.E.: Factoring: a method for scheduling parallel loops. J. Commun. **35**, 90–101 (1992)
11. Ilsche, T., Schöne, R., Bielert, M., Gocht, A., Hackenberg, D.: lo2s - multi-core system and application performance analysis for Linux. In: Proceedings of the IEEE CLUSTER, pp. 801–804 (2017)
12. Korndörfer, J.H.M., Eleliemy, A., Mohammed, A., Ciorba, F.M.: LB4OMP: a dynamic load balancing library for multithreaded applications. IEEE TPDS **33**(4), 830–841 (2022)
13. Linux Kernel Documentation: CFS Scheduler. https://www.kernel.org/doc/html/latest/scheduler/sched-design-CFS.html. Accessed 07 June 2022

14. Lozi, J.P., Lepers, B., Funston, J., Gaud, F., Quéma, V., Fedorova, A.: The Linux scheduler: a decade of wasted cores. In: Proceedings of the EuroSys (2016)
15. Mohammed, A., Cavelan, A., Ciorba, F.M., Cabezón, R.M., Banicescu, I.: Two-level dynamic load balancing for high performance scientific applications. In: Proceedings of the SIAM Conference on Parallel Processing for Scientific Computing, pp. 69–80 (2020)
16. Mohammed, A., Korndörfer, J.H.M., Eleliemy, A., Ciorba, F.M.: Automated scheduling algorithm selection and chunk parameter calculation in OpenMP. IEEE TPDS **33**(12), 4383–4394 (2022)
17. Peiyi, T., Pen-Chung, Y.: Processor self-scheduling for multiple-nested parallel loops. In: Proceedings of the International Conference on Parallel Processing, pp. 528–535 (1986)
18. Polychronopoulos, C.D., Kuck, D.J.: Guided self-scheduling: a practical scheduling scheme for parallel supercomputers. J. Trans. Comput. **100**, 1425–1439 (1987)
19. Wächtler, S., Sojka, M.: OS noise: Linux vs. Microkernel. In: Proceedings of the OSADL (2012)
20. Wang, L., Zhao, Y., Wang, Z.: Measurement and control of Linux operating system noise on the godson-3A shared-memory multicore platform. In: Proceedings of the IEEE HPCC & EUC, pp. 474–481 (2013)
21. Wong, C., Tan, I., Kumari, R., Lam, J., Fun, W.: Fairness and interactive performance of O(1) and CFS Linux kernel schedulers. In: Proceedings of the ITSim, pp. 1–8 (2008)

# Assessing Power Needs to Run a Workload with Quality of Service on Green Datacenters

Louis-Claude Canon[1], Damien Landré[1,2](✉), Laurent Philippe[1], Jean-Marc Pierson[2], and Paul Renaud-Goud[2]

[1] Université de Franche-Comté, CNRS, institut FEMTO-ST, 25000 Besançon, France
{lccanon,damien.landre,lphilipp}@femto-st.fr

[2] IRIT, Université de Toulouse, CNRS, Toulouse INP, UT3, Toulouse, France
{Damien.Landre,jean-marc.pierson,paul.renaud.goud}@irit.fr

**Abstract.** Datacenters are an essential part of the internet, but their continuous development requires finding sustainable solutions to limit their impact on climate change. The DATAZERO2 project aims to design datacenters running solely on local renewable energy. In this paper, we tackle the problem of computing the minimum power demand to process a workload under quality of service constraint in a green datacenter. To solve this problem, we propose a binary search algorithm that requires the computation of machine configurations with maximum computing power. When machines are heterogeneous, we face the problem of choosing the machines and their DVFS state. A MILP (Mixed-Integer Linear Programming), to find the optimal solution, and four heuristics that give satisfactory results in a reasonable time are proposed. The bests reach an average deviation from the optimal solution of 0.03% to 0.65%.

**Keywords:** Green datacenter · Power consumption · Optimization

## 1 Introduction

Since a decade datacenters have become an essential part of the internet, either being at the edge or at the center, and their number and size are continuously increasing, as their global energy consumption. These datacenters represented in 2018 1% of the global energy consumption, that is to say 6% more than in 2010 [14]. It is estimated [4] that, by 2025, energy consumption will have multiplied by 2.9 and greenhouse gas emissions by 3.1. To reduce the datacenter impact on climate change several research works propose solutions to optimize their energy consumption [6,18]. These solutions are essential on the way to efficiency, but cannot achieve a drastic reduction of the carbon footprint. Other projects and research works claim to reduce their brown energy consumption [2,10]. The objective of the DATAZERO project [21] (2015–2019) and DATAZERO2 (2020–2024) is to investigate the solutions to design and operate a datacenter only fueled by renewable energies. By design, this project builds


J. Cano et al. (Eds.): Euro-Par 2023, LNCS 14100, pp. 229–242, 2023.
https://doi.org/10.1007/978-3-031-39698-4_16

on a negotiation [24] between the electrical management (power production and storage) and the IT management (workload processing) to choose a power command that will be applied in the next time window, typically the coming 72 h. A power command refers to the control commands that are asked to the electrical side, so that the needed power is provided along the time window.

The negotiation is developed as a process based on game theory that loops on asking for IT consumption and power production predictions over the time window to converge after several iterations on an acceptable solution for both the IT and electrical management. The result of the negotiation is a power command for the time window, represented as a time series of power values for each time interval, called a power profile. This power command is then applied on the infrastructure. The negotiation therefore needs predictions of the power needs during the time window. In this article, we tackle the problem of computing the minimum power profile required to process a workload forecast. We do not address the problem of workload forecast that has been widely studied already [15]. Rather, we investigate the problem of transforming a workload prediction to an optimized usage of a given infrastructure, called a plan, that minimizes the electrical power needs. This plan is made for how the machine will be switched-on and off based on the negotiated power profile. It is sent to an online module, which applies it and adapts it to events, due to the uncertainty of the plan. [8]. Since the negotiation process is interactive, this computation must last a reasonable time [24]. It must be noted already that we consider a consolidated workload, and not individual jobs. Therefore, a workload represents the total amount of work units that have to be processed along time. A workload possibly aggregates the work units of several jobs that may concurrently use the infrastructure and share each of the machines of the infrastructure.

This paper contributes with multiple variants of an algorithm that computes a minimized power profile. The algorithm realizes this computation in steps. The main step iterates on each time interval of the time window. For each time interval, a binary search algorithm is used to find a minimized power value. Last, for each power value, the algorithm computes the maximum processing capacity that can be reached using the datacenter machines and tries to schedule the workload under quality of service (QoS) constraints, using the processing capacity. We propose several solutions, a MILP and different heuristics, to compute the maximum computing capacity for a power value.

In the following, related work is detailed in Sect. 2. Section 3 formally defines the problem of computing a capping value from a workload forecast and maximizing a processing capacity within a given power value. Section 4 and Sect. 5 respectively present the binary search algorithm and the heuristics proposed to solve the problem. Section 6 presents experiments and results. Finally, Sect. 7 summarizes the paper, highlighting the main conclusion.

## 2 Related Work

In order to minimize energy or power consumption while possibly meeting another criteria, different online approaches are considered in the literature.

In [27], an online method manages energy consumption and workload scheduling for hybrid geo-distributed datacenters. Several variables are taken into account such as the variation of the electricity price, the power consumption of the cooling, machines, or constraints on renewable energy. In a similar way, in [20] a genetic based online algorithm optimizes energy consumption, performance degradation as well as power grid cost for multiple hybrid datacenters. Zhang et al. [26] propose PoDD, an online power-capping algorithm to maximize performances of homogeneous servers for dependent application workloads. The applications are composed of a front-end and a back-end, and the front-end produces the data consumed by the back-end. A similar method is also proposed for heterogeneous nodes of a datacenter [7]. In [25], different online algorithms are introduced to minimize the performance degradation and the total energy consumed: LmsReg, based on regression, which detects overloaded servers and migrates virtual machines, and MuP, which addresses the trade-off between power consumption, number of migrations, server performance and the total number of servers that have been switched-off in the selection of virtual machines. These algorithms migrate virtual machines from over-loaded servers to under-loaded servers. Other methods using virtual machine allocation and migration are proposed [12,16,17]. In [13], an online holistic approach schedules virtual machines to minimize the total energy consumption of the datacenter by considering the datacenter as a whole and not trying to divide it into several parts to be treated separately from each other. But these works focus only on the objective of reducing online energy consumption by allocating and migrating virtual machines. In our case, we seek to minimize a forecast of power demand.

In [17], an online multi-objective algorithm optimizes energy consumption, by taking into account QoS, energy, number of active servers and number of virtual machine migrations on servers. A similar method in [9] is used by considering DVFS (Dynamic Voltage and Frequency Scaling), temperature-dependent task scheduling, dynamic resource provisioning, and cooling management. But the optimization is also done online, with a non-clairvoyant approach.

In [11], in the context of cloud datacenters, an online clairvoyant method for predicting the total energy consumption of the datacenter is proposed to improve the datacenter energy management that controls and coordinates all the equipment. This method evaluates the importance of the variables of the equipment to make the prediction. Then a neural network computes the prediction on the total energy consumption, a single value for the coming 20 min. Finally, an online module is in charge of updating the model based on the forecast errors.

In [8], the authors develop a complementary approach to ours. An online module is based on offline decisions, adapting them to real-time events via different compensation policies, to stay as close to the offline plan. The module is responsible for compensating energy utilization, scheduling and servers in a green datacenter. Different compensation policies are evaluated according to five metrics. The results indicate that compensation are necessary and simply following the plan is not enough, due to the uncertainty of the plan.

Finally, all these studies address the online problem and, to the best of our knowledge, there is no work addressing the offline minimization of power consumption in the case of homogeneous or heterogeneous machines with different amount of work to process, under the constraint of deadline violations.

# 3 Problem Definition, Model and Objective

The power management system, running solely on renewable energy, needs to plan its power sources and storage usage to correctly fuel the machines. Due to technical constraints [21], the power command delivered to the machines must be constant over a minimum time duration, a time interval, that ranges from 15 min to one hour. To give the power usage over a time window, we thus need to define a power profile that gives, for each time interval, a constant power need value. Since the power supply only relies on intermittent renewable energies, saving as much energy as possible, and storing it, is essential to operate the datacenter during periods of underproduction. The problem we face is hence to compute the minimum power profile needed to process a given workload.

On the other hand, the time intervals are independent. For this reason, in the following we concentrate on finding the minimal value $P$ for one interval, then the same method is applied to each time interval of the time window. Note that the problem is tackled as an offline problem, but it is also constrained by the interactivity of the negotiation, which requires several exchanges before converging to a solution. The problem must hence be resolved in a reasonable time. In the following, we first define the problem and its associated model, then we define the objectives.

In the context of this paper, the workload forecast is an input of the problem and the solution must be able to handle any workload, whatever its characteristics. Since the temporalities are different between the power and the load variations, a time interval is subdivided into multiple time steps and the workload gives the variation of the load on time steps, which duration typically ranges from 1 s to one minute. Formally, we denote by $T$ the number of time steps, and we normalize the time axis such that the $t^{\text{th}}$ time step begins at time $t-1$, for $t \in \mathcal{T} = \{1, \ldots, T\}$. We define $\Delta t$ as the duration of a time step in seconds.

The workload is composed of several load parts, each arriving at a given time step. We define the total workload as a set of $W$ load parts, $l_k$ for $k \in \mathcal{W} = \{1, \ldots, W\}$. A load part $l_k$ is defined by its release time $r_k$ (*i.e.* the time step when $l_k$ arrives), its amount of operations to be processed $p_k$ and a deadline $d_k$ such that, if the load part cannot be processed before $d_k$, it is killed. For instance, on the first time step of Fig. 1, the workload is composed of two load parts, $l_1$ and $l_2$. $p_1$, the amount of operations of $l_1$, is two times larger than $p_2$. The deadline $d_k$ is defined as a duration. It enforces that load parts arriving in the same time step may have different QoS constraints. A load part $l_k$, which arrives at the time step $t = r_k$ with a deadline $d_k$ must be finished no later

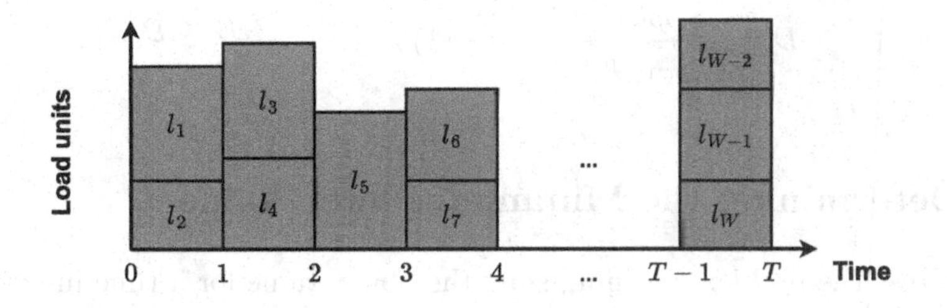


**Fig. 1.** Load parts and amount of operations of a workload forecast.

than $r_k + d_k$. All the operations of a load part $l_k$ have the same deadline $d_k$. For instance, in Fig. 1 if load part $l_1$ has a deadline $d_1 = 2$ steps, then it can be processed partially or completely during time steps 1 and/or 2.

The datacenter is composed of $M$ machines which are noted machine $i$ with $i \in \mathcal{M} = \{1, \ldots, M\}$. Considering the power consumption, machine $i$ dissipates a power $static_i$ when it is idle. Each machine $i$ can be set in $S_i$ different DVFS states [9]. The DVFS state of a machine is noted $j \in \mathcal{S}^{(i)} = \{0, \ldots, S_i\}$. The set of machines with their DVFS states defines the configuration of the datacenter. We note $\mathcal{S}$ the set of DVFS states of all machines, $\mathcal{S} = \{\mathcal{S}^{(1)}, \ldots, \mathcal{S}^{(M)}\}$. A DVFS state $j$ defines $g^{(i)}_{\max_j}$, the maximum amount of operations per second that machine $i$ can process, and $power^{(i)}_j$, the consumed power per operation per second. For the sake of simplicity, we consider an average value for this consumed power. The model could be extended to consider different power consumption for different operations, since consumption can vary depending whether the workload is CPU, I/O, memory or network intensive. If machine $i$ is switched-on, it computes $g^{(i)}$ operations per second with $0 \le g^{(i)} \le g^{(i)}_{\max_j}$ while dissipating $power^{(i)}_j$ power per operation per second. Therefore, if a machine $i$ computes several load parts $l_k$ in state $j$ during a time $\Delta t$ with an amount of operations to be processed $g^{(i)}\Delta t = \sum_{k \in \mathcal{W}} p_k \le g^{(i)}_{\max_j}\Delta t$, it consumes a power of $P_i = static_i + g^{(i)} \times power^{(i)}_j$. We assume that, when a machine is off, its DVFS state is $j = 0$ and it does not consume any power, nor does it process any operation. Last, the power consumption $P$ of a configuration is $P = \sum_{i \in \mathcal{M}} P_i$ and its maximum available computing power $w^{(p)}$ is $w^{(p)} = \sum_{i \in \mathcal{M}} g^{(i)}\Delta t$.

The objective of this optimization problem is thus to find a machine configuration (off, on and other DVFS states) that delivers enough computing power to process the workload while consuming the lowest power $P$. In addition, to give the users a flowtime guarantee, we define *opk* as the total amount of operations missing their deadline and the ratio $D$ as the amount of operations killed over the amount of operations to be processed during the time interval (1). This ratio must not exceed a fixed threshold $D_{\max}$ (2) to meet the flowtime guarantee.

$$D = \frac{opk}{\sum_{k \in \mathcal{W}} p_k} \quad (1) \qquad\qquad D \leq D_{\max} \quad (2)$$

## 4 Determining the Minimum Power Value

To address the problem of minimizing the power value for a time interval under the deadline violation constraint we propose a binary search algorithm (Algorithm 1). For a given power value $P$, the algorithm first computes a machine configuration that maximises the computing power and then schedules the workload to determine the deadline violation ratio $D$ of the time interval.

**Algorithm 1:** Binary search algorithm to minimize the power need to run a workload on a configuration violation ratio

**Data**: $\mathcal{M}, \mathcal{S}, \mathcal{W}, \mathcal{T}, \epsilon, D_{\max}, \Delta t$
**Result**: minimize $P$
1 **begin**
2 $\quad P_{\min} \leftarrow 0$; $P_{\max} \leftarrow \sum_{i \in \mathcal{M}} (static_i + power^{(i)}_{S_i} \times g^{(i)}_{\max S_i})$
3 $\quad$ **while** $P_{\max} - P_{\min} \geq \epsilon$ **do**
4 $\quad\quad P \leftarrow (P_{\min} + P_{\max})/2$
5 $\quad\quad w^{(p)} \leftarrow config(\mathcal{M}, \mathcal{S}, P, \Delta t)$
6 $\quad\quad opk \leftarrow 0$; $\bar{\mathcal{W}} \leftarrow \mathcal{W}$
7 $\quad\quad$ **for** $t \in \mathcal{T}$ **do**
8 $\quad\quad\quad \bar{w}^{(p)} \leftarrow w^{(p)}$
9 $\quad\quad\quad \bar{\mathcal{W}}, opk \leftarrow schedule(\bar{\mathcal{W}}, opk, \bar{w}^{(p)}, t)$
10 $\quad\quad D \leftarrow opk / \sum_{k \in \mathcal{W}} p_k$
11 $\quad\quad$ **if** $D \leq D_{\max}$ **then** $P_{\max} \leftarrow P$ **else** $P_{\min} \leftarrow P$

The dichotomy is initiated (line 1) by setting the maximum power $P_{\max}$ to the case where all the machines are used to their maximum capacity and the minimum power $P_{\min}$ to 0. Then the algorithm iterates until the difference between the two power values is lower than $\epsilon$, the stopping criterion of the algorithm. At each iteration the algorithm computes, with the *config* function [22] (line 5), the machine configuration with the largest possible computing power $w^{(p)}$ for the power value $P$ of the current iteration. The *schedule* function is then used for each time step $t$ of the time interval $\mathcal{T}$ (lines 7 to 9) to determine the schedule and the *opk* value, the number of killed operations. The *schedule* function simply uses EDF (Earliest Deadline First) algorithm to schedule the load parts on the time steps. Then, if the ratio of violated deadlines $D$ does not exceed the threshold $D_{\max}$ (line 11), it means that the computing power is sufficient and the power value $P_{\max}$ can be decreased to $P$. Otherwise, $D$ exceeds $D_{\max}$ and the power $P_{\min}$ must be increased to $P$.

Several propositions of the *config* function are given in the following section.

## 5 Maximizing the Computing Power

The *config* function computes the most powerful machine configuration that can be fueled with the power $P$, fixed by the binary search algorithm. This computation obviously depends on the machine characteristics. The simplest case is when machines are homogeneous with only two DVFS states (switch-on or -off) since machines are undifferentiated and it is sufficient to calculate how many machines can be powered with $P$ to provide the most powerful configuration. If homogeneous machines have several DVFS states there is already a decision to take between switching-on a new machine or setting an already started machine in a higher DVFS state. In the heterogeneous case, several configurations are possible for a given power value, but all of them do not provide the same computing power. It is therefore important to improve the power efficiently by determining an optimal machine configuration. The difficulty lies in the choice of the machines to be switched-on and their DVFS state. In the following, we concentrate on the case of heterogeneous machines with multiple DVFS states, which includes the homogeneous case.

From the complexity view point, the problem of computing the maximum computing power $w^{(p)}$ with heterogeneous machines is at least as difficult as the partition problem and is thus NP-Hard. The corresponding decision problem is trivially in NP as we can verify a solution from the decision variables $g^{(i)}$ in polynomial time. Besides, any instance of the partition problem can be directly reduced to our problem: for each integer $z_i$, we consider a machine such that $static_i = 0$ and $g^{(i)}$ has only two possible values, *i.e.* 0 or $g^{(i)}_{\max_j} = z_i$. Note that, in the general case, the $g^{(i)}$ are coded in a discrete variable that ranges from 0 to $g^{(i)}_{\max_j}$. In this particular case, we just give the lowest possible value to $g^{(i)}_{\max_j}$. In that case, the power consumed by a computing machine becomes constant, $P_i = static_i + g^{(i)}_{\max_j} = z_i$. Furthermore, we set the total power available $P = \frac{1}{2}\sum_i z_i$. There is a schedule with maximum computing power $w^{(p)} = P$ if and only if the partition problem has a valid solution. Since this problem is NP-Hard, we first designed a MILP (Mixed-Integer Linear Programming).

**Mixed Integer Linear Programming:** We define the decision variable $x_{i,j}$ to determine the machines to be switched-on or -off and their DVFS state. For each machine $i$ and for each DVFS state $j$, $x_{i,j} = 1$ if the DVFS state $j$ of machine $i$ is selected, otherwise $x_{i,j} = 0$. These variables hence define the machine configuration. For a machine, we consider that only one DVFS state can be selected and remains the same for the entire duration of the time interval.

The MILP is described in (3). The objective function is to maximize the computing power of the machines. Using the binary decision variable $x_{i,j}$, the first constraint states that a machine $i$, for all $i \in \mathcal{M}$, must have a single DVFS state $j$ among all possible DVFS states of the machine, from 0 to $S_i$ (including the switched-off state $j = 0$). Depending on the selected DVFS state we express, for all $i \in \mathcal{M}$, that the computing power must not exceed the maximum computing capacity of the machine, with the second constraint. Then, knowing the DVFS state and the computing power of the machine, the third constraint bounds the power consumption of the machine, for all $i \in \mathcal{M}$. Finally, the fourth constraint imposes that the total power consumption of the machines must not exceed the power $P$ value given by the binary search algorithm.

$$\begin{cases} \text{maximize } \sum_{i=1}^{M} g^{(i)}, s.t.: \\ \sum_{j=0}^{S_i} x_{i,j} = 1 \\ g^{(i)} \leq \sum_{j=0}^{S_i} (x_{i,j} \times g_{\max_j}^{(i)}) \\ P_i = \sum_{j=1}^{S_i} x_{i,j}(static_i + g^{(i)} power_j^{(i)}) \\ \sum_{i=1}^{M} P_i \leq P \end{cases} \tag{3}$$

Under the following constraints.

$$\begin{cases} \forall i \in \mathcal{M}, \forall j \in \mathcal{S}^{(i)} & x_{i,j} \in \{0,1\} \\ \forall i \in \mathcal{M} & g^{(i)} \geq 0 \\ \forall i \in \mathcal{M} & P_i \geq 0 \end{cases}$$

As shown by the experiments in Sect. 6, the MILP calculation takes 2.83 s in average and up to 50 s in complex cases. This calculation has to be repeated for each iteration, usually more than 15, of the binary search algorithm. Its runtime, including the configuration computation and the scheduling, then varies from 42 s to more than 100 s, depending on the stopping criterion $\epsilon$. Hence, the total runtime ranges from 50 minutes to more than 2 hours to determine a power profile. As previously explained the power profile is used in the negotiation process to anticipate the power which makes several iterations before taking a decision. Although based on offline calculations, the MILP is therefore used in an interactive process for which waiting one hour for a proposition does not make sense. For this reason, we propose in the following heuristics providing solutions in a shorter time.

**Random Choice Heuristic:** A first trivial heuristic proposal is to randomly choose the type of machine to switch-on. When a machine is switched-on, it is allocated the power needed to provide the maximum computing power. The DVFS state chosen is the one maximizing the computing power, according to the remaining power. This step is repeated until the power is insufficient and/or there are no more machines to switch-on. The advantage of this heuristic is its fast execution time, but it provides unsatisfactory results compared to the other presented in the following in the heterogeneous case.

**Balance Power-Performance (BPP) Heuristic:** The BPP heuristic evaluates the most suitable machines and its DVFS states to switch-on according to two metrics: (i) computing power and (ii) performance ratio. The computing power criteria is chosen since the objective is to maximize the total computing power of the machines $w^{(p)}$. The performance ratio criteria is chosen to minimize the power consumed per unit of computing power.

These two metrics are used to compute a normalized score depending on a given power and an $\alpha$ parameter. The $\alpha$ parameter (with $0 \leq \alpha \leq 1$), given as input, controls the trade-off between computing power and performance ratio. The nearer alpha is to 0, the more weight is given to the computing power in the choice of the machine to be switched-on, and inversely. Depending on the alpha parameter value, the configurations proposed by BPP can be different. For this reason, several alpha values are assessed in order to produce different machine configurations and the algorithm returns the one maximizing the total computing power. BPP switches-on the machine with the highest score.

This heuristic is very efficient in the homogeneous and heterogeneous case with a very satisfactory execution time.

**Best State Redistribute Without Static (BSRWS) Heuristic:** The BSRWS heuristic focuses on the performance ratio of the machines. This heuristic switches-on as many machines with the best performance ratio as it is possible without exceeding the given power. If no more machine can be switched-on and there is power left, either because all the machines are on or because there is not enough power to switch-on more machines, the remaining power is redistributed to the switched-on machines. This redistribution increases the DVFS state of the switched-on machines and thus their computing power.

The advantage of this heuristic is its accuracy with a satisfactory execution time, which however increases with power. In the heterogeneous case, some solutions deviate from the optimal because it switches-on too many machines.

**Best State Redistribute Without Static and Removing (BSRWS-AR) Heuristic:** The BSRWS-AR heuristic focuses on the performance ratios of the machines and explore more machine configurations. This heuristic is an improvement of the BSRWS heuristic. The latter is run several times and, at each iteration, it removes a machine of the configuration in order to test configurations with fewer switched-on machines. More power can be redistributed to increase the DVFS state and the computing power of the remaining machines.

The advantage of this heuristic is its accuracy compared to BSRWS in the homogeneous and heterogeneous case. However, its execution time is much higher and increases strongly with power.

## 6 Experiment and Results

We present here an experiment that considers the example of a medium-sized datacenter of 267 kW [21] and 10 machine types. Note that, due to the paper length constraint, we only present this example but different size of datacenter are experimented and given in the research report [22] to completely assess our heuristics. The machine types are taken from the GRID5000 platform [3]. We have implemented the MILP and the heuristics in Python[1,2]. We remind the

[1] The source code in zip file is available here.

[2] Experiments have been run on Ubuntu 22.04.1 LTS, Intel Core i7-11850H processor, 32.0 Go of memory, Python 3.10 and PulP 2.6.0 with Gurobi 9.5.1 solver.

reader that on this part there is no related work in the literature to compare to. Input data includes 1241 machines divided into the 10 types. Note that no workload is used for the experiment, as we only assess the quality of the solutions of the heuristics compared to the MILP in the determination of the computing power. Data on the characteristics of the machines are known in advance [19,23]. For each type of machine, we know all the data described in Sect. 3. All data are average values coming from experiments on Grid5000 performed in the context of the ANR ENERGUMEN [1] project.

To illustrate the characteristics of the set of machines, Fig. 2 shows the best performance ratio of the 10 machine types in W/GFlop depending on power, taking into account static power of the machines (the leftmost of each curve) and their DVFS states. It is worth noticing the continuity of the performance ratio curves, even when changing the DVFS state, for almost all machines. The Gemini machines, having the highest static power, are shown on the right figure. The other machines are grouped on the left. The lower the static power of a machine and the better the performance ratio, the more advantageous it is to switch-on this machine, depending on power. For instance, on a simple case, if the available power is 1000 W, the best is to use 9 Gros machines than any other combination (visually and confirmed by the MILP solution), if we have these 9 Gros machines at hand. Otherwise, with less Gros machines, a different combination has to be used involving Gros and other types of machines. Also note that some performance ratios of machine types cross others.

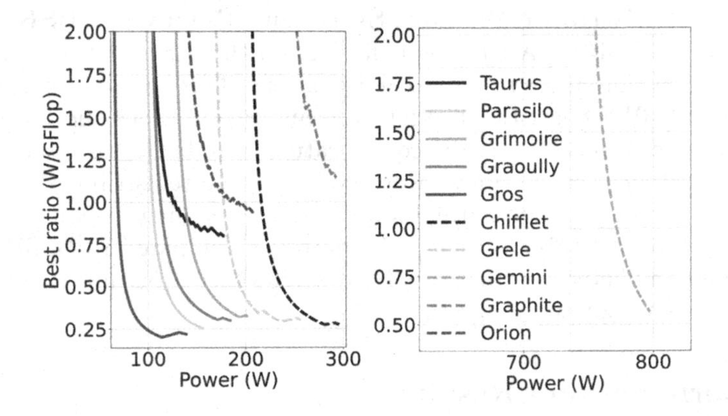


**Fig. 2.** Best performance ratio in W/GFlop depending on power.

Figure 3 shows the maximum computing power given by the MILP and the heuristics for different power values, from 63 W (the minimum power required to switch-on a machine) to 267 kW (the maximum power that can be required by all machines when running at maximum frequencies) by steps of 100 W.

The RC (Random Choice) heuristic is run 100 times to show the dispersion of the solutions and the average computing power for each power value. The minimum and maximum computing power are shown in red.

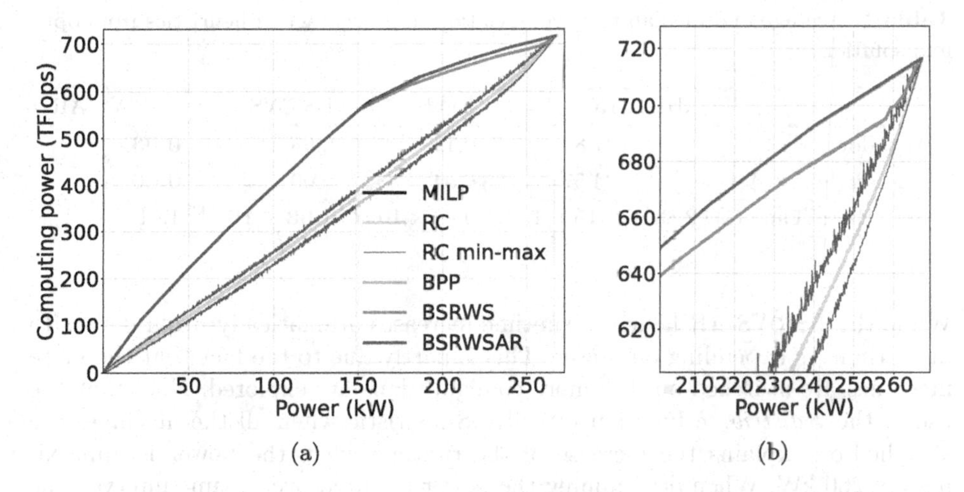


**Fig. 3.** (a): Comparison of the maximum computing power computed by the MILP and heuristics depending on power value from 63 W to 267 kW by steps of 100 W. (b): Zoom on 200 kW to 267 kW by steps of 100 W. (Color figure online)

The RC heuristic significantly deviates from the optimal solution with an average deviation of 31.84% (Table 1). This is not surprising. Since the choice of the machine type is random, the RC heuristic may switch-on the least efficient machines. This occurs mostly in the heterogeneous case, according to our experiences. The BPP (Balance Power-Performance) heuristic with alpha from 0 to 1 by steps of 0.05 for each power value and BSRWS-AR heuristic (Best State Redistribute Without Static And Removing) are the closest to the optimal solution. Their average deviation from the optimal is 0.12% and 0.03% respectively (Table 1). Note that the BSRWS-AR heuristic performs better than the BSRWS (Best State Redistribute Without Static) heuristic, since it explores more configurations. Also, BPP outperforms BSRWS and BSRWS-AR in other cases of heterogeneity. From 150 kW to 260 kW, the deviation from the optimal is more significant for BSRWS (Fig. 3). But our different experiences show that this is not always the case. The BSRWS heuristic has an average deviation of 0.65%. Note that from 260 kW, the BSRWS heuristic reduces its deviation from the optimal because there is enough power to switch-on all the machines and redistribute the remaining power to increase their DVFS state. In terms of accuracy, BPP and BSRWS-AR are the most satisfying heuristics, but BPP is significantly faster than BSRWS-AR. This is mostly the case in our experiments.

Figure 4 gives the runtimes of the MILP and the heuristics depending on power. Note that the y-axis is plotted on a logarithmic scale. There is a general trend for all the runtimes to increase with power. This is intuitive since the more power, the more machines the heuristics have to consider. Compared to the MILP that has an average runtime of 2.83 s per power value, the heuristics are more time efficient to find a configuration. The runtime of the BPP heuristic is of the order of milliseconds and increases slightly depending on power.

**Table 1.** Average and median relative deviation in percentage of heuristics from optimal solution.

| | MILP | RC | BPP | BSRWS | BSRWS-AR |
|---|---|---|---|---|---|
| Avg. dev. (%) | – | 31.84 | 0.12 | 0.65 | **0.03** |
| Median dev. (%) | – | 34.57 | 0.04 | 0.09 | **0.00** |
| Avg. Exec. Time (s) | 2.83 | $1.15 \times 10^{-3}$ | $9.07 \times 10^{-3}$ | $\mathbf{1.03 \times 10^{-3}}$ | 1.61 |

While the BSRWS-AR heuristic runtime increases dramatically: from 0.4 ms to more than 4 s depending on power. This is partly due to the fact that the more machines are switched-on, the more configurations are explored. Note that the use of the *redistribute* function in BSRWS heuristic when all the machines are switched-on explains the increase of the runtime when the power is approximately 260 kW. When determining the power required over a time interval, the runtime of the binary search algorithm varies from 0.11 s to 2.75 s, using the BPP heuristic and depending on the stopping criterion $\epsilon$.

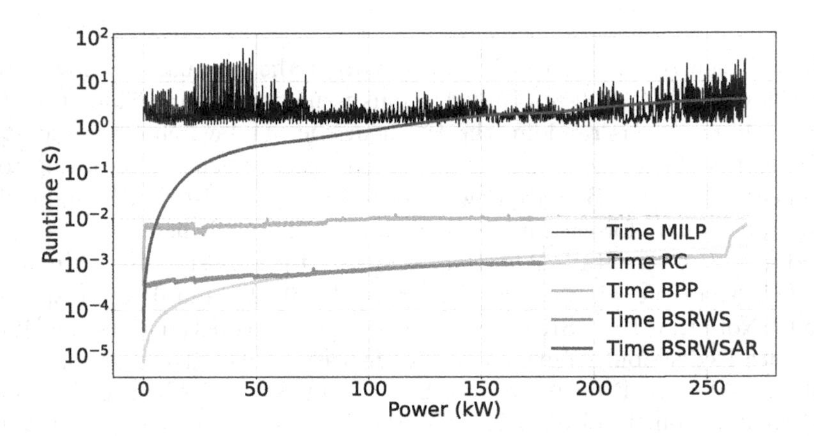


**Fig. 4.** Runtime of the MILP and the heuristics depending on power

## 7 Conclusion

In this paper, we tackle the problem of minimizing a power value to switch-on just enough machines to process a workload over a time interval while respecting quality of service constraints. We propose a binary search algorithm to solve this problem with multiple variants. This algorithm uses two functions, one that computes the maximum computing power that is obtained knowing a given power, and another that schedules the workload on the switched-on machines. Since computing the maximum processing power is NP-Hard in the heterogeneous case, we propose a MILP and 3 non-trivial heuristics and compare their performance and runtime. Heuristics give satisfactory results in a reasonable time, with an average relative deviation from optimal solution of 0.12%, 0.65% and 0.03%. Looking at the results and runtime, the BPP (Balance Power-Performance) heuristic seems the most suitable to solve this problem in a reasonable time.

These different approaches show that using DVFS states in a heterogeneous environment allows approaching the optimal configuration of the machines and thus efficiently using energy. In future work, we plan to compare the BS approach to an integrated solution, then we will take the switching-on and switching-off and their consumption into consideration to integrate the cost of changing a configuration between two time intervals. Last, we plan to introduce uncertainty in the machine choice to better anticipate the workload variations.

**Acknowledgments and Data Availability Statement.** This work was supported by the DATAZERO2 project ("ANR-19-CE25-0016") and by the EIPHI Graduate school ("ANR-17-EURE-0002"). We would like to thank the ENERGUMEN project ("ANR-18-CE25-0008") and Grid5000 for providing some of the data used in this article. The scripts and instructions necessary to reproduce and analyze our result are available in a Figshare repository [5].

## References

1. Energy saving in large scale distributed platforms - Energumen (2018). https://anr.fr/Project-ANR-18-CE25-0008. Accessed 20 Nov 2022
2. Apple: Environmental Progress Report (2022). https://www.apple.com/environment/. Accessed 20 May 2022
3. Clusters Grid5000 (2022). https://www.grid5000.fr/. Accessed 21 Oct 2022
4. Bordage, F.: The environmental footprint of the digital world. GreenIT (2019)
5. Canon, L.-C., Landré, D., Philippe, L., Pierson, J.-M., Renaud-Goud, P.: Artifact and instructions to generate experimental results for euro-par'2023 paper: assessing power needs to run a workload with quality of service on green datacenters (2023). https://doi.org/10.6084/m9.figshare.23544939
6. Chaithra, P.: Eco friendly green cloud computing. J. Res. Proc. **1**(2), 41–52 (2021)
7. Ciesielczyk, T., et al.: An approach to reduce energy consumption and performance losses on heterogeneous servers using power capping. J. Sched. **24**, 489–505 (2021)
8. Fontana de Nardin, I., Stolf, P., Caux, S.: Mixing offline and online electrical decisions in data centers powered by renewable sources. In: IECON-48th Annual Conference of the IEEE Industrial Electronics Society, pp. 1–6. IEEE (2022)
9. Fang, Q., Wang, J., Gong, Q., Song, M.: Thermal-aware energy management of an HPC data center via two-time-scale control. IEEE Trans. Industr. Inf. **13**(5), 2260–2269 (2017)
10. Greendatanet research project (2013–2016). https://www.greendatanet-project.eu/. Accessed 28 May 2021
11. Hsu, Y.F., Matsuda, K., Matsuoka, M.: Self-aware workload forecasting in data center power prediction. In: 2018 18th IEEE/ACM International Symposium on Cluster, Cloud and Grid Computing (CCGrid), pp. 321–330. IEEE (2018)
12. Kurdi, H.A., Alismail, S.M., Hassan, M.M.: LACE: a locust-inspired scheduling algorithm to reduce energy consumption in cloud datacenters. IEEE Access **6**, 35435–35448 (2018)

13. Li, X., Garraghan, P., Jiang, X., Wu, Z., Xu, J.: Holistic virtual machine scheduling in cloud datacenters towards minimizing total energy. IEEE Trans. Parallel Distrib. Syst. **29**(6), 1317–1331 (2017)
14. Masanet, E., Shehabi, A., Lei, N., Smith, S., Koomey, J.: Recalibrating global data center energy-use estimates. Science **367**(6481), 984–986 (2020)
15. Masdari, M., Khoshnevis, A.: A survey and classification of the workload forecasting methods in cloud computing. Clust. Comput. **23**(4), 2399–2424 (2020)
16. Mazumdar, S., Pranzo, M.: Power efficient server consolidation for cloud data center. Futur. Gener. Comput. Syst. **70**, 4–16 (2017)
17. Nikzad, B., Barzegar, B., Motameni, H.: Sla-aware and energy-efficient virtual machine placement and consolidation in heterogeneous DVFS enabled cloud datacenter. IEEE Access **10**, 81787–81804 (2022)
18. Pahlevan, A., Rossi, M., del Valle, P.G., Brunelli, D., Atienza Alonso, D.: Joint computing and electric systems optimization for green datacenters. Technical report, Springer (2017)
19. Pedretti, K., et al.: A comparison of power management mechanisms: P-states vs. node-level power cap control. In: International Parallel and Distributed Processing Symposium Workshops. IEEE (2018)
20. Peng, Y., Kang, D.K., Al-Hazemi, F., Youn, C.H.: Energy and QoS aware resource allocation for heterogeneous sustainable cloud datacenters. Opt. Switch. Netw. **23**, 225–240 (2017)
21. Pierson, J.M., et al.: DATAZERO: datacenter with zero emission and robust management using renewable energy. IEEE Access **7**, 103209–103230 (2019)
22. Research report: Assessing power needs to run a workload with quality of service constraint on green datacenters (2023). https://members.femto-st.fr/Laurent-Philippe/sites/femto-st.fr.Laurent-Philippe/files/content/articles/rr-1-2023.pdf
23. Standard performance evaluation corporation. https://spec.org/. Accessed 28 Feb 2023
24. Thi, M.T., et al.: Negotiation game for joint IT and energy management in green datacenters. Futur. Gener. Comput. Syst. **110**, 1116–1138 (2020)
25. Yadav, R., Zhang, W., Li, K., Liu, C., Shafiq, M., Karn, N.K.: An adaptive heuristic for managing energy consumption and overloaded hosts in a cloud data center. Wireless Netw. **26**, 1905–1919 (2020)
26. Zhang, H., Hoffmann, H.: PoDD: power-capping dependent distributed applications. In: Proceedings of the International Conference for High Performance Computing, Networking, Storage and Analysis, pp. 1–23 (2019)
27. Zhao, M., Wang, X., Mo, J.: Workload and energy management of geo-distributed datacenters considering demand response programs. Sustain. Energy Technol. Assess. **55**, 102851 (2023)

# Architectures and Accelerators

# Improving Utilization of Dataflow Architectures Through Software and Hardware Co-Design

Zhihua Fan[1,2], Wenming Li[1,2(✉)], Shengzhong Tang[1,2], Xuejun An[1,2], Xiaochun Ye[1,2], and Dongrui Fan[1,2]

[1] SKLP, Institute of Computing Technology, Chinese Academy of Sciences, Beijing, China
{fanzhihua,tangshengzhong20s,axj,yexiaochun,fandr}@ict.ac.cn
[2] University of Chinese Academy of Sciences, Beijing, China
liwenming@ict.ac.cn

**Abstract.** Dataflow architectures can achieve much better performance and higher efficiency than general-purpose core, approaching the performance of a specialized design while retaining programmability. However, dataflow architectures often face challenges of low utilization of computational resources if the application algorithms are irregular. In this paper, we propose a software and hardware co-design technique that makes both regular and irregular applications efficient on dataflow architectures. First, we dispatch instructions between dataflow graph (DFG) nodes to ensure load balance. Second, we decouple threads within the DFG nodes into consecutive pipeline stages and provide architectural support. By time-multiplexing these stages on each PE, dataflow hardware can achieve much higher utilization and performance. We show that our method improves performance by gmean 2.55× (and up to 3.71×) over a conventional dataflow architecture (and by gmean 1.80× over Plasticine) on a variety of challenging applications.

**Keywords:** Dataflow Architecture · Decoupled Architecture

## 1 Introduction

Dataflow architecture is an emerging class of reconfigurable arrays designed for modern analytical workloads. The program offloaded to dataflow fabrics will be converted to a dataflow graph (DFG) by dataflow compiler. A DFG consists of a set of nodes and directed edges that connect the nodes. The nodes represent the computing, while the edges represent data dependencies between nodes. Figure 1 illustrates a typical dataflow architecture, which consists of a PE (Processing Element) array, a configuration buffer and a data buffer. The PE array is formed by multiple PEs that are connected by the network-on-chip. Each PE is composed of a router, a local buffer, a register file, and several function units.


J. Cano et al. (Eds.): Euro-Par 2023, LNCS 14100, pp. 245–259, 2023.
https://doi.org/10.1007/978-3-031-39698-4_17

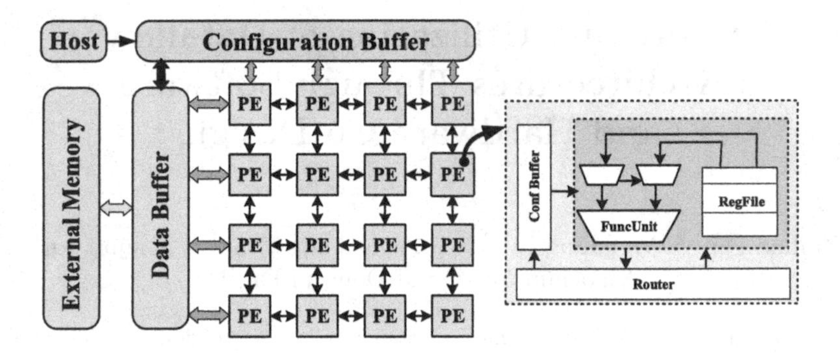


**Fig. 1.** A typical dataflow architecture.

Most dataflow architectures are restricted to regular applications, i.e., those with structured access patterns and data reuse, like neural networks [1] and dense linear algebra [2]. These characteristics are necessary to produce a high-performance pipeline that can be spatially and statically mapped to a dataflow fabric. However, dataflow architectures struggle with irregular applications, i.e., those with complex control flow and memory access patterns, lack data sharing characteristics and data reuse. These applications arise in many important domains, like graph analytic, sparse linear algebra and signal processing. Dataflow architectures are ill-equipped to handle these operations.

Abundant prior works have been proposed to accelerate irregular applications on dataflow architectures (in Sect. 2): pipeline parallelism [3–5], decoupled access-execute architectures [6–9] and dedicated interfaces between cores or threads [10,11]. Nevertheless, these solutions can be further improved because they (in Sect. 3): (i) suffer from load imbalance, as they rarely take into account the imbalance between DFG nodes, but we found the imbalance impacts the software pipeline execution significantly. (ii) lack of fine-grained pipelining scheduling. The schedule of each DFG node is coarse-grained and non-preemptive, which miss opportunities to exploit more parallelism within DFG nodes to boost utilization. To this end, we introduce a software and hardware co-design method to improve the hardware utilization of dataflow architectures. In summary, we make the following contributions:

- We present a method to solve the load imbalance between DFG nodes. This approach dispatches instructions between DFG nodes to ensure load balance.
- We introduce *decoupled execution model*. It decouples the thread within DFG node into four consecutive pipeline stages. Each stage is an atomic schedule and execution unit. In this way, a PE can be shared by at most four different DFG nodes at the same time and the memory access and data transfer latency can be overlapped as much as possible.
- We provide architectural support for the decoupled execution model. By decoupling the datapath of different stages and equipping with a dedicated scheduler within each PE, the DFG nodes of different iterations can be pipelined more efficiently.

- We evaluate our methods on a wide range of applications, demonstrating their applicability. Experiments show our methods improve performance by gmean 2.55× (and up to 3.71×) over a conventional dataflow architecture (and by gmean 1.80× over Plasticine [4]).

## 2 Background and Related Works

In this section, we briefly introduce the background and works related to improving the utilization of dataflow architectures.

*Pipeline Parallelism:* Dataflow architectures are amenable to creating static spatial pipelines, in which an application is split into DFG nodes and mapped to functional units across the fabric [1–4,12]. To perform a particular computation, operands are passed from one functional unit to the next in this fixed pipeline. Pipette [5] structures irregular applications as a pipeline of DFG nodes connected by queues. The queues hide latency when they allow producer nodes to run far ahead of consumers. Zhongyuan et al. [13] design a global synchronization mechanism, which help reducing the nodes and edges in modified DFG. and propose a complete and systematic DFG modification flow which saves more resources. These efforts may be inefficient for irregular workloads because they rarely take into account the load imbalance between DFG nodes.

*Decoupled Architectures:* Fifer [6] decouples memory access datapath from computing pipeline. Each DFG node is divided into two stages: access and execution. Equipped with a dedicated scheduler, at most two DFG nodes can be executed on the same PE at the same time. In this way, memory access latency can be overlapped and the utilization can be further improved. DESC [7] proposes a framework that has been inspired by decoupled access and execution, and updates and expands for modern, heterogeneous processors. REVEL [8] extends the traditional dataflow model with primitives for inductive data dependences and memory access patterns, and develops a hybrid spatial architecture combining systolic and dataflow execution. RAW [9] introduces hardware support for decoupled communication between cores, which can stream values over the network. Käsgen et al. [14] present a new mechanism that resolves data and structural hazards in processing elements that feature in-order issue, but out-of-order completion of operations. Different from these partial design, our methods is fully decoupled PE.

*Custom Interface:* Chen et al. [11] propose subgraph decoupling and rescheduling to accelerate irregular applications, which decouples the inconsistent regions into control-independent subgraphs. Each subgraph can be rescheduled with zero-cost context switching and parallelized to fully utilize the PE resources. TaskStream [10] introduces a task execution model which annotates task dependences with information sufficient to recover inter-task structure. It enables work-aware load balancing, recovery of pipelined inter-task dependences, and recovery of inter-task read sharing through multicasting. MANIC [15] introduces vector-dataflow execution, allowing it to exploit the dataflow in a sequence of vector instructions and amortize instruction fetch and decode over a whole vector of operations. By forwarding values from producers to consumers, MANIC avoids costly vector register file accesses. However, the schedule mechanism of DFG nodes within each PE is coarse-grained and non-preemptive. The PE can switch to the next iteration or other nodes only after finishing all instructions of the current DFG node.

## 3 Motivation

Irregular applications are common in real-life workloads and benchmark suites, such as graph analytics, sparse linear algebra and databases. As reported in Fig. 2 (a), the average percentage of unstructured access, complex control flow and imperfect loops can be over 50% in three widely-used benchmarks. Figure 2 (b) reports the utilization of the dataflow fabrics using the methods we discussed earlier (Sect. 2). Obviously, the hardware utilization is pretty low and at least half of the PEs are under-utilized during execution. We obtain these results from experiments with a dataflow simulator, using the methods introduced in [4] and [6], respectively.

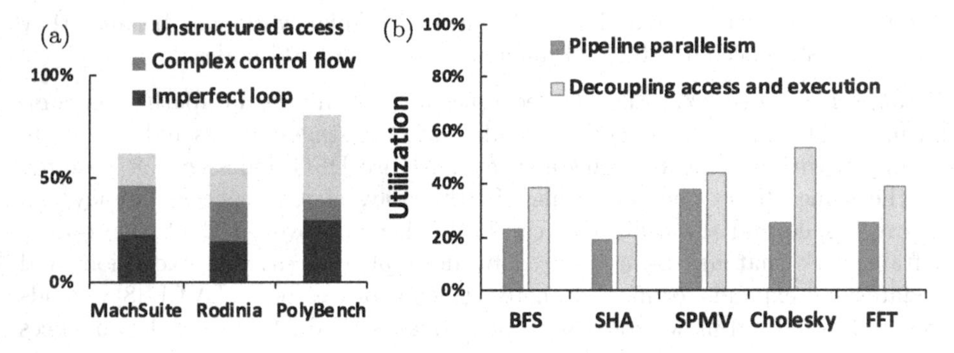


**Fig. 2.** (a) Percentage of irregular applications in several typical benchmark suites [11]. (b) Utilization of the fabrics using previous methods.

For a concrete example, we use BFS (Breadth First Search), a common graph algorithm that searches the distance from a source vertex *src* to all vertices reachable from it. BFS is a challenging irregular workload due to its multiple levels of indirection: it uses elements from cur_fringe to access offsets, which is then used to access neighbors, which in turn is used to access distances. It is a typical irregular application consisting of imperfect loop, complex control flow and unstructured memory access. Figure 3 shows the pseudo-code for BFS and illustrate its implementation on dataflow fabric using pipeline parallelism and decoupling access-execution [6].

*Challenge 1: Load Imbalance.* In Fig. 3 , the process current fringe node reads vertices from cur_fringe, whose neighbors are identified in the enumerate neighbors node. For each of these neighbors, the fetch distances node loads the distance

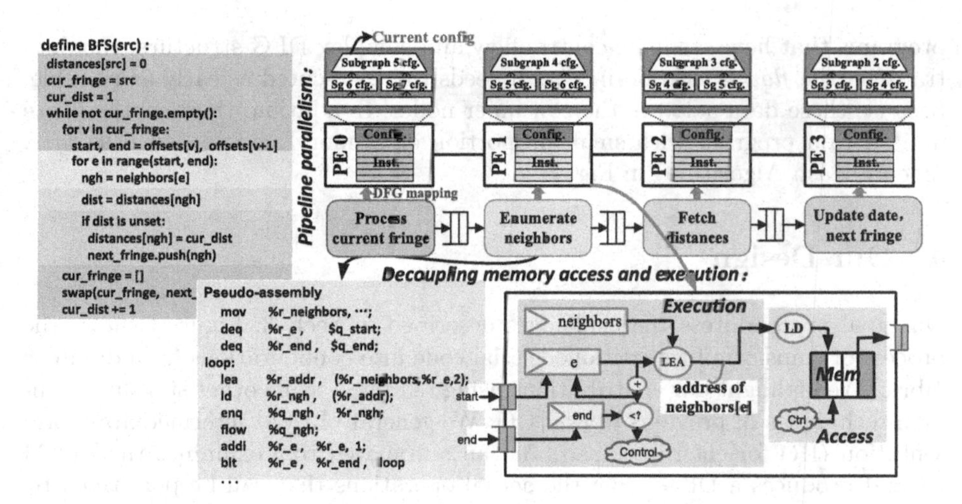


**Fig. 3.** Illustration of breadth-first search (BFS) using pipeline parallelism and decoupling memory access and execution.

of this neighbor, which is checked against the current distance from the source by the update data node. By decomposing a large graph into multiple subgraphs, the BFS algorithm can be executed in a pipelined manner among these four PEs, as shown at the top of Fig. 3. After instruction assembly, the number and type of instructions are different between DFG nodes, and even the number of iterations is different. The enumerate neighbor node contains loop, address calculation. The updating node deals with branch, while the getting distance nodes only requires getting distance. The node with the longest delay among the four nodes will block the pipelined execution.

*Challenge 2: Lack of Fine-Grained Pipelining Scheduling.* The conventional, coupled load interface is a simple connection to the memory hierarchy and stalls the PE on cache misses. Simple memory access patterns, like streaming linearly through memory, do not need to be decoupled, and would be suitable for this interface, while some accesses are known to miss frequently, causing lengthy stalls. Decoupled architecture allows these accesses to be further from DFG execution, which is equipped with a small finite state machine within the PE, as shown in Fig. 3 (bottom). The access datapath now performs the memory access, which will obtain the neighbor id *ngh* as a result. Once this value is available, *ngh* is placed in the output queue to be sent to the consumer node. Even if a memory access to the neighbor array results in a cache miss, the enumeration neighbor node can still perform computations on other subgraphs at the same time, causing the DFG pipeline to stall only when the input queue of the computation is empty or the access queue is full.

However, for irregular applications, it is not enough to only decouple computation and memory access in a coarse-grained manner. In the dataflow-driven model, a DFG node can be fired only if its source operands are ready. Thus, for programs that have complex control flow and complex DFG structure, the data transfer (the *flow* operation in Fig. 3) needs to be executed as early as possible, because these data activate the consumer nodes. In addtion, these methods are limited to a program with small proportion of memory accesses, such as SHA (Secure Hash Algorithm) in Fig. 2.

# 4 Our Design

Our goal is to address the challenges described in Sect. 3. Figure 4 shows the process of transforming partitioned serial code into configurations for a dataflow fabric. We highlight our contributions using red lines, while other steps are common techniques in previous works [1,6]. We generate LLVM intermediate representation (IR) for each workload, and an automated tool examines the LLVM IR and produces a DFG using the actual operations that can be performed by PE's functional units.

In order to solve the load imbalance among DFG nodes, *DFG balancing* is introduced, which is a heuristic algorithm that achieves load balancing through instruction scheduling among DFG nodes. To exploit more parallelism and accelerate irregular applications, we propose *decoupled execution model*, a novel execution and schedule mechanism for DFG threads. Moreover, a *decoupled PE architecture* is provided to support the decoupled execution model efficiently.

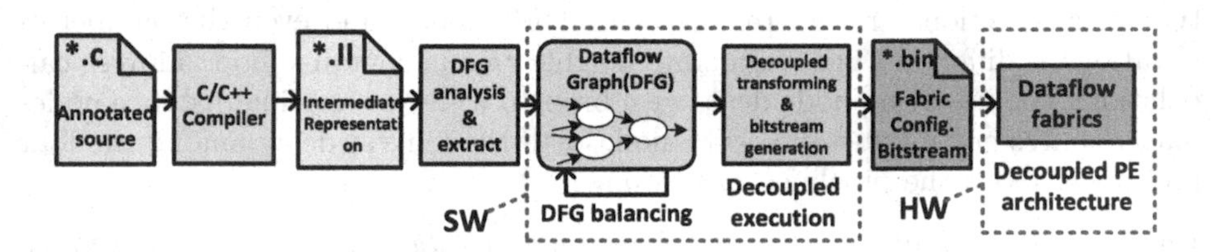


**Fig. 4.** Workflow of our methods.

## 4.1 Load Balancing

DFG balancing is a heuristic algorithm and it intends to dispatch instructions from high-load nodes to low-load nodes. Note that it is hard to generate an absolutely balanced DFG because: 1) the delay of each nodes is unpredictable during execution, like stalls caused by hazard or memory access. 2) allocating the same number of instructions to each DFG node is expensive and is limited by the applications itself, which often leads to non-convergence. Thus, we aim to generate a relatively balanced DFG based on the number and type of instructions.

The algorithm of DFG balancing is described in Algorithm 1. A DFG $G = (V, E)$ generated by the earlier stages in the toolchain (Fig. 4) and a threshold $\theta$ are the inputs. The first step is to sort the DFG nodes in depth-first order and estimate their latency (Line 1–4). When estimating the latency of each

**Algorithm 1.** Instruction Reschedule Algorithm

**Input:** a dataflow graph $G = (V, E)$, and a threshold $\theta \in \mathbb{Z}^+$
**Output:** a more balanced dataflow graph $G' = (V', E')$
1: Init set $CP \leftarrow$ sortbyDFS($G$) ▷ Step ①
2: Init $C_{num} \leftarrow$ getNumofNodes($CP$)
3: Init $List[] \leftarrow$ getLatencyofEachNode($CP$,$inst\_latency$)
4: Set $\chi \leftarrow \sum_{n=1}^{C_{num}}$ List[] / $C_{num}$
5: **for** each node $n_i$ in $CP$ **do** ▷ Step ②
6: Set $load \leftarrow$ List($n_i$)
7: **if** $load \geqslant \chi + \theta$ **then**
8: dispInst2Downstream($selInst$,$n_i$,$n_{i+1}$)
9: **end if**
10: **if** $load \leqslant \chi$ - $\theta$ **then**
11: dispInsfromDownstream($selInst$,$n_i$,$n_{i+1}$)
12: **end if**
13: **end for**
14: **return** generate $G' \leftarrow$ refresh($G$, $CP$) ▷ Step ③

node (Line 3), we need to refer to the instruction type ($inst\_latency$), because the execution time of different instructions may be different, which is related to the instruction set architecture (ISA). For simplicity, this evaluation only considers the number of instructions and their latency, and the PE only support partial RISC-V ISA (RV64I) and some dedicated dataflow instructions (*flow*). A comparison factor $\chi$ is used in Algorithm 1, which is calculated in Line 4, where the $List[\,]$ array maintains the latency of each node on the critical path. It will be used as a reference in Step 2.

The principle of Step 2 is to find the imbalance DFG nodes and perform instruction redispatch (Line 5–13). The threshold $\theta$ and the comparison factor $\chi$ are used to obtain an interval ( $\chi$ - $\theta$, $\chi + \theta$). If a node's latency is in this interval, it is a suitable node. If a node's latency is greater (or less) than this interval's upper (or lower) bound, it can be seen a heavy (or light) node, respectively. For a heavy/light node, the algorithm will dispatch computing instructions to/from its downstream node. If a heavy node has no downstream nodes, the node will be split into two nodes. We found it difficult to find a threshold $\theta$ that fits all applications. The smaller the $\theta$ is, the more balanced DFG is generated, but Algorithm 1 becomes more complex and harder to converge. When the $\theta$ is larger, the overhead of Algorithm 1 will decrease, but the performance of the application will also decrease. We found that a good trade-off between performance and cost can be achieved when the $\theta$ is set in a range of [3,5]. The final step of Algorithm 1 is to update the DFG according to the adjusted $CP$ and to generate the final DFG $G'$.

### 4.2 Decoupled Model

The decoupled execution model defines a novel scheme to schedule and trigger DFG nodes and exploit instruction block level parallelism. The code of each node consists of up to four consecutive stages: *Load stage, Calculating stage, Flow stage* and *Store stage*, which we describe below:

- Ld (Load) Stage: This stage loads data from the memory hierarchy to the in-PE local memory.
- Cal (Calculating) Stage: This stage completes calculations. A node can enter the Cal stage only when the following two conditions are met: first, its Ld stage (if it exists) has already finished; second, it has received all the necessary data from its predecessor nodes.
- Flow Stage: This stage transfers data from the current node to its successors.
- ST (Store) Stage: This stage transfers data from the in-PE operand memory to the memory hierarchy.

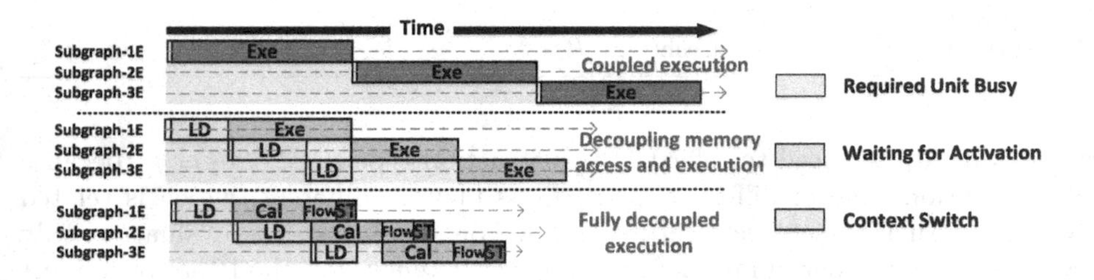


**Fig. 5.** Comparison of three different execution models.

Correspondingly, instructions in a DFG node will be rearranged according to their types and divided into four different blocks. The block is a basic schedule and trigger unit. Different from traditional out-of-order execution, the decoupled execution model exploits more instruction-block level parallelism without complex control logic, such as reorder buffer. Figure 5 takes the process of enumerating neighbor nodes of BFS (in Fig. 3) as an example to show the comparison between the decoupled execution model and the previous two execution models. In the coupled model (top), the execution of DFG nodes adopts a non-preemptive mechanism. The subgraph-1 will not release the PE resources until the end of execution. After decoupling the memory access in DFG node (middle), the subgraph-2 can perform the memory access operation after the LD stage of the subgraph-1 is finished. In this way, the PE can process up to two subgraphs at the same time. But the execution of subgraph-3 requires a long waiting delay. This is because the subgraph-2 occupies PE resources due to the coarse-grained (partial) decoupling. Fortunately, this problem can be addressed in the fully decoupled execution model (bottom). Through a more fine-grained scheduling mechanism, PE can process more subgraphs at the same time, and can overlap more delays, such as memory access and data flow.

### 4.3 Decoupled Architecture

Figure 6 illustrates the top-level diagram of our dataflow architecture, which is comprised of a set of identical decoupled processing elements (dPE). To support the decoupled execution model, separated four-stage components are designed within each PE to correspond to the four different states of the nodes. The function of the controller is to maintain and schedule the execution of different node states. And to ensure the correctness of the execution, separate operand RAM space is provided for different iterations. And a shared operand RAM space is set up to store the data that has dependencies between iterations, which are marked by special registers in the instructions.

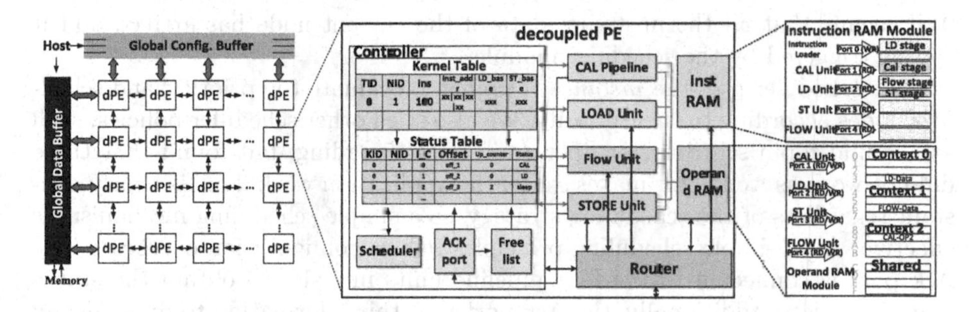


Fig. 6. The decoupled PE architecture.

The dPE consists of a calculation pipeline, a load unit, a store unit, a flow unit, an instruction RAM module, an operand RAM module, a controller and a router (in the middle of Fig. 6). These four separate functional components (CAL, LOAD, FLOW, STORE) and the controller are designed for the decoupled model, which are different from previous structures. The calculation pipeline is a data path for arithmetic operations and logical operations. It fetches instructions from the instruction RAM module and performs computations on source data. The load/store unit transfers data from/to on-chip data memory to/from operand RAM module, respectively. And the flow unit dispatches data to downstream dPEs. Each execution unit has a corresponding state, as described in Fig. 5, and such a decoupling method is the key to improving the utilization.

The controller plays a non-negligible role in the state transition and DFG nodes triggering. It consists of a kernel table, a status table, a free list, a dedicated acknowledgment buffer (Ack port), and a scheduler module. The kernel table stores the configurations of the nodes mapped to the dPE, which contain the task ID (*TID*), node ID (*NID*), instance number (*instance*), instruction address list (*inst_addr*) and data address (*LD_base&ST_base*). The *TID* and *NID* are used to identify task and DFG node, because the PE array can be mapped to multiple tasks at the same time, and a PE can be mapped to multiple nodes. The *instance* is a value related to the pipeline parallelism, which indicates how many times the DFG node needs to be executed. Taking BFS as an example, for a large graph, it may need to be decomposed into many subgraphs, such as 100, then each DFG node needs to be executed 100 times. The *inst_ addr* records the location of the four-stage instruction of the DFG node in the instruction RAM. The *LD_ base&ST_ base* are the base addresses for the source and destination, which can work with the *offset* in the status table to access the data in the operand RAM.

The status table maintains the runtime information for different instances. It uses the *instance_ counter* to record different instances of DFG nodes. Although different instances share the same instructions, they handle different data. Therefore, the offsets (*offset*) of different instances are different. In addtion, the status table records the activations (*Up_ counter*) and status informations. The value of *Up_ counter* decreases with the arrival of activation data. When this value is 0, it means that all the upstream data of the current node has arrived and it can be triggered by the scheduler module.

The scheduler uses the *instance_ counter* to evaluate the priority, and schedules nodes according to their priority. We also tried other scheduler policies, such as a round-robin scheduler or finer-grain multithreading, but found that these did not work as well. This makes sense: the application work done is nearly constant regardless of the scheduling strategy, so a simple scheduling mechanism is effective. Also, simple scheduling principles reduce configuration overhead. The Ack port is connected to the four pipeline units in order to obtain the status of each section. Additionally, the Ack port uses this information to dynamically modify the contents of the state table for scheduling by the scheduler. And the free list queue maintains free entries in this buffer.

The instruction RAM module consists of multiple single-port SRAM banks. Each bank can be occupied by a single functional unit at any time. The operand RAM module consists of multiple 1-write-1-read SRAM banks. To ensure the pipeline execution between instances, a separate context is allocated for each iteration. Considering that there may be dependent data between instances, a shared context is established in the operand RAM. Shared data are marked by special registers in the instructions.

## 5 Methodology

**Setup.** We develop a cycle-accurate micro-architecture simulator for hardware utilization and performance evaluation. The simulator is developed in C language based on SimICT framework [16] and can simulate behaviors such as memory access, data transfer, scheduling, etc. We calibrate the error to within ±7% using RTL environment. We also implement our architecture using Verilog. We use Synopsys Design Compiler and a TSMC 28nm GP standard VT library to synthesize it and obtain area, delay and energy consumption, which meets timing at 1 GHz. Table 1 shows the hardware parameters.

Table 1. Hardware Parameters.

| Component | | Parameter | Area ($mm^2$) | Power (mW) |
|---|---|---|---|---|
| dPE | Func. Units | INT&FP32 | 0.046(26.90%) | 7.92(29.61%) |
| | Controller | – | 0.012(7.27%) | 1.20(4.97%) |
| | Inst. RAM | 4KB | 0.003(1.81%) | 0.38(1.56%) |
| | Oper. RAM | 64KB | 0.812(47.27%) | 9.93(41.18%) |
| | Routers | – | 0.028(16.72%) | 4.67(19.41%) |
| | *Total* | | *0.1719* | *24.1019* |
| PE Array | | 8 × 8 | 11(79.38%) | 1542(84.45%) |
| NoC | | 2D mesh | 0.65(4.72%) | 70.65(3.86%) |
| Glo. Data Buf. | | 1MB(SPM) | 1.67(12.06%) | 150.57(8.79%) |
| Glo. Conf. Buf. | | 0.2MB(SPM) | 0.35(2.50%) | 38.11(2.08%) |
| DMA | | 2 channels | 0.19(1.37%) | 14.65(0.8%) |
| ***Total*** | | | ***13.8647*** | ***1826*** |

**Benchmarks.** To evaluate our methods, we use the benchmarks from Fifer [6] and literature [11]. These irregular workloads contain imperfect loops, complex control flow and unstructured access. And we used the same input data as those in the literatures [6,11]. Table 2 lists the selected workloads.

Table 2. Workloads for Evaluation.

| Workload | Characteristic | Benchmark suite |
|---|---|---|
| GEMM, Viterbi(VIT)<br>Sort, FFT | Imperfect loop<br>Complex control flow | MachSuite<br>adopt from [11] |
| CFD<br>HotSpot(HS)<br>LUD, GE | Imperfect loop<br>Complex control flow<br>Loop dependency | Rodinia<br>adopt from [11] |
| Gesummv(GES)<br>Cholesky | Imperfect loop<br>Complex control flow | PolyBench<br>adopt from [11] |
| BFS,PageRank<br>CC, Radii | Unstructured access<br>Imperfect loop | Fifer [6] |

# 6 Evaluation

## 6.1 Results and Analysis

To evaluate the effectiveness of the methods we proposed, we implement the following four different experiments.

- **Baseline (Base).** It is our baseline, using only pipeline parallelism to accelerate irregular applications.

- **Baseline + DFG Reorganization (D1).** It combines the pipeline parallelism with DFG balancing technique.
- **Baseline + Decoupled Model & Architecture (D2).** It combines the pipeline parallelism with decoupled model and hardware.
- **Baseline + DFG Reorganization + Decoupled Model & Architecture (D3).** It combines the pipeline parallelism with our three methods.

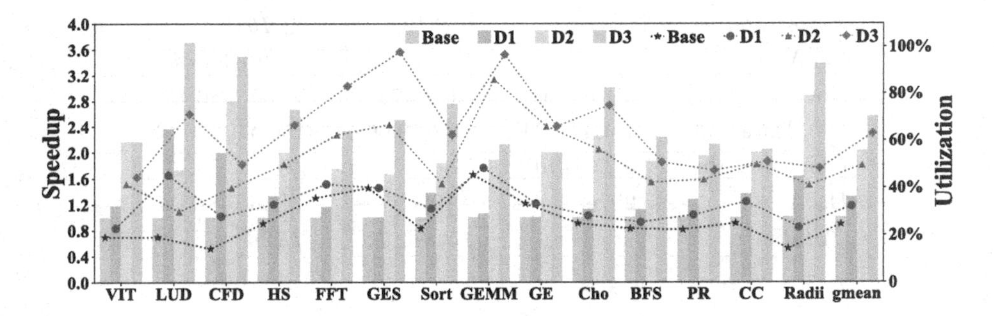


**Fig. 7.** Utilization (in marker) and speedup (in bar) over the baseline.

Figure 7 demonstrates the effectiveness of our proposed methods in terms of performance and utilization improvements. DFG balancing (D1) achieves an average performance improvement of 1.31×. Decoupled execution technique (D2) improves performance by gmean 2.03× over the baseline. By combining these approaches (D3), the performance of the dataflow fabric can be improved by 2.55×, and the average computing resource utilization has also reached 65.12%. In most cases, decoupled execution achieves better performance and utilization improvements compared to DFG balancing.

For imperfect loop like GEMM, Gesummv and GE, the inner and outer loops are almost equal in size and the load of each DFG node is more balanced. Thus the effect of DFG balancing is not very obvious while the improvement of the decoupled execution is obvious. Because decoupled execution can overlap the delays caused by memory access and data transfer and improve the utilization up to 96.8%. For dependency loop like LUD, data dependence reduces the utilization by limiting inter sibling loops parallelism and explicit data barrier also exacerbates the problem, which limit the effectiveness of decoupled model. For kernels with branches such as Sort, FFT and HotSpot, the utilization is significantly degraded in baseline, especially in Sort (only 22.7%), which has plenty of elseif statements. Our design decouples the data transfer stage so that activations can be delivered to downstream nodes as early as possible. Even though we didn't use prediction techniques, it still achieves a speedup of 2.75×.

*Cost.* The hardware overhead of decoupled execution is shown in Table 1. The area and power consumption of the controller used for scheduling in dPE only account for 7.27% and 4.97%, respectively. We evaluate Algorithm 1 on Intel(R)

Core(TM) i7-7700 CPU@2.80GHz. This time is 5.1% of the execution time on average, so it has negligible effect when performed at runtime.

### 6.2 Comparison with Other Dataflow Architectures

For comparison, we use three typical dataflow architectures, i.e. Plasticine [4], Fifer [6] and Yin et al. [11]. Plasticine features pipeline parallelism. Fifer features decoupling access and execution. Yin et al. [11] features subgraph rescheduling (detailed in Sect. 2). The hardware parameters of the three architectures are shown in Table 3, where we align them with similar peak performance. To model their performance and utilization, we leverage the open source implementations for Plasticine [4] and Fifer [6]. For work [11], we obtained data from the paper.

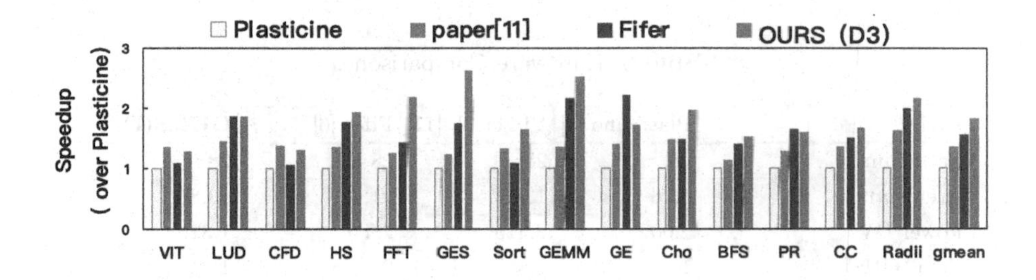


**Fig. 8.** Performance comparisons normalized to Plasticine.

*Performance.* Figure 8 illustrates the speedup comparisons normalized to Plasticine. Our design (D3) outperforms the Plasticine by gmean 1.81× and by up to 2.53×. This speedup comes from D3's ability to further shorten the interval between different iterations of the DFG pipeline execution. Compared with work [11], D3 achieves average 1.34× performance improvement. The reason for limiting the performance of paper [11] is that the execution of DFG nodes still adopts a coarse-grained mechanism, resulting in an average utilization of only 39.04%. Fifer achieves an average 1.54× performance improvement. These performance

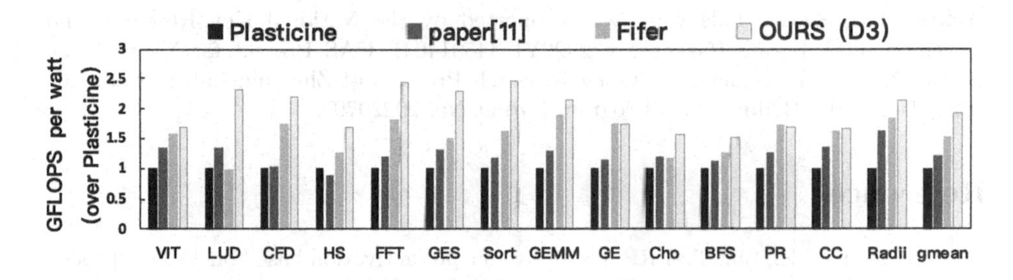


**Fig. 9.** Energy efficiency comparisons normalized to Plasticine.

gains come from decoupling memory access. However, for computationally intensive applications like VIT (1.09×) and CFD (1.05×), the improvement is not obvious.

*Energy Efficiency.* Figure 9 shows the energy efficiency (***performance-per-watt***) comparisons normalized to Plasticine. On average, Our design (D3) achieves 1.94× efficiency improvement over Plasticine, 1.58× over work [11] and 1.26× over Fifer. The coarse-grained scheduling mechanism employed in Plasticine results in lower utilization, resulting in poor energy efficiency performance. Work [11] achieves a relatively high energy efficiency in most cases by rescheduling at software level. But for HotSpot and CFD, it consumes more energy on buffer accesses due to the frequently subgraph switching. In Fifer, a large number of buffers are added between PEs to reduce the impact of load imbalance. But the energy overhead of these buffers is very large.

**Table 3.** Hardware Comparisons.

| Arch | Plasticine [4] | Yin et al. [11] | Fifer [6] | **OURS(D3)** |
|---|---|---|---|---|
| Tech (nm) | 28 | 28 | 28 | 28 |
| Area ($mm^2$) | 12.6 | 13.95 | 21.44 | 13.86 |
| Power (W) | 2.002 | 2.415 | 2.476 | 1.826 |
| Freq (GHz) | 1 | 0.8 | 2 | 1 |
| PeakPerf (GFLOPS) | 523 | 576 | 640 | 512 |
| Efficiency (GFLOPS/W) | 58.25∼99.79 | 27.85∼137.29 | 113.88∼218.17 | 116.64∼280.39 |

## 7 Conclusion

This paper presents a software and hardware co-design technique that makes both regular and irregular applications efficient on dataflow architectures. We propose an instruction schedule method to solve load imbalances and a more fine-grained scheduling and trigger mechanism. Experiments exhibited by our methods achieve significant utilization and performance improvement on key application domains with small modifications.

**Acknowledgment.** This work was supported by the National Key Research and Development Program (Grant No. 2022YFB4501404), CAS Project for Youth Innovation Promotion Association, Open Research Projects of Zhejiang Lab (Grant NO. 2022PB0AB01), Beijing Nova Program (Grant No. 2022079).

## References

1. Wu, X., Fan, Z., Liu, T.: LRP: predictive output activation based on SVD approach for CNN s acceleration. In: DATE, pp. 831–836 (2022)

2. Ye, X., Tan, X., Wu, M., et al.: An efficient dataflow accelerator for scientific applications. Future Gener. Comput. Syst. **112**, 580–588 (2020)
3. Zhang, Y., Zhang, N., Zhao, T.: Sara: scaling a reconfigurable dataflow accelerator. In: ISCA, pp. 1041–1054 (2021)
4. Prabhakar, R., Zhang, Y.: Plasticine: a reconfigurable architecture for parallel patterns. In: ISCA, pp. 389–402 (2017)
5. Nguyen, Q.M., Sanchez, D.: Pipette: improving core utilization on irregular applications through intra-core pipeline parallelism. In: MICRO, pp. 596–608 (2020)
6. Nguyen, Q.M., Sanchez, D.: Fifer: practical acceleration of irregular applications on reconfigurable architectures. In: MICRO, pp. 1064–1077 (2021)
7. Ham, T.J., Aragón, J.L., Martonosi, M.: DeSC: decoupled supply-compute communication management for heterogeneous architectures. In: MICRO, pp. 191–203 (2015)
8. Weng, J., Liu, S., et al.: A hybrid systolic-dataflow architecture for inductive matrix algorithms. In: HPCA, pp. 703–716 (2020)
9. Taylor, M.B., Kim, J., et al.: The raw microprocessor: a computational fabric for software circuits and general-purpose programs. IEEE Micro **22**(2), 25–35 (2002)
10. Dadu, V., Nowatzki, T.: Taskstream: accelerating task-parallel workloads by recovering program structure. In: ASPLOS, pp. 1–13 (2022)
11. Yin, C., Wang, Q.: Subgraph decoupling and rescheduling for increased utilization in CGRA architecture. In: DATE, pp. 1394–1399 (2021)
12. Capalija, D., Abdelrahman, T.S.: A high-performance overlay architecture for pipelined execution of data flow graphs. In: 2013 23rd International Conference on Field programmable Logic and Applications, pp. 1–8 (2013)
13. Zhao, Z., Sheng, W., Jing, N., He, W., et al.: Resource-saving compile flow for coarse-grained reconfigurable architectures. In: ReConFig, pp. 1–8 (2015)
14. Kasgen, P.S., Weinhardt, M., Hochberger, C.: Dynamic scheduling of pipelined functional units in coarse-grained reconfigurable array elements. In: Schoeberl, M., Hochberger, C., Uhrig, S., Brehm, J., Pionteck, T. (eds.) ARCS 2019. Lecture Notes in Computer Science, vol. 11479, pp. 156–167. Springer, Cham (2019). https://doi.org/10.1007/978-3-030-18656-2_12
15. Gobieski, G.: Manic: a vector-dataflow architecture for ultra-low-power embedded systems. In: MICRO (2019)
16. Ye, X., Fan, D., Sun, N., Tang, S., Zhang, M., Zhang, H.: SimICT: a fast and flexible framework for performance and power evaluation of large-scale architecture. In: ISLPED, pp. 273–278 (2013)

# A Multi-level Parallel Integer/Floating-Point Arithmetic Architecture for Deep Learning Instructions

Hongbing Tan, Jing Zhang, Libo Huang(✉), Xiaowei He, Dezun Dong, Yongwen Wang, and Liquan Xiao

National University of Defense Technology, Changsha 410073, China
{tanhongbing,libohuang}@nudt.edu.cn

**Abstract.** The extensive instruction-set for deep learning (DL) significantly enhances the performance of general-purpose architectures by exploiting data-level parallelism. However, it is challenging to design arithmetic units capable of performing parallel operations on a wide range of formats to perform DL instructions (DLIs) efficiently. This paper presents a multi-level parallel arithmetic architecture capable of supporting intra- and inter-operation parallelism for integer and a wide range of FP formats. For intra-operation parallelism, the proposed architecture supports multi-term dot-product for integer, half-precision, and BrainFloat16 formats using mixed-precision methods. For inter-operation parallelism, a dual-path execution is enabled to perform integer dot-product and single-precision (SP) addition in parallel. Moreover, the architecture supports the commonly used fused multiply-add (FMA) operations in general-purpose architectures. The proposed architecture strictly adheres to the computing requirements of DLIs and can efficiently implement them. When using benchmarked DNN inference applications where both integer and FP formats are needed, the proposed architecture can significantly improve performance by up to 15.7% compared to a single-path implementation. Furthermore, compared with state-of-the-art designs, the proposed architecture achieves higher energy efficiency and works more efficiently in implementing DLIs.

**Keywords:** Deep Learning instruction · data-level parallelism · Arithmetic Architecture · Dot-Product · Mixed-Precision · Inter- and Intra-operation Parallelism

## 1 Introduction

Recently, deep learning has enabled significant advances in a variety of applications, with performance that is comparable to or even surpassing that of humans in certain scenarios. However, the rapidly increasing computing requirements of advanced deep learning models have resulted in a performance bottleneck


J. Cano et al. (Eds.): Euro-Par 2023, LNCS 14100, pp. 260–274, 2023.
https://doi.org/10.1007/978-3-031-39698-4_18

in hardware platforms [16]. Consequently, numerous research efforts have been devoted to the efficient implementation of deep learning algorithms on hardware. An interesting trend that has emerged is the exploitation of specific instructions by many general-purpose architectures to facilitate the efficient implementation of deep learning algorithms [2,3].

In most general-purpose architectures, deep neural networks (DNN) training and inference employ fused multiply-add (FMA) instructions using 32-bit single-precision (SP) floating-point. However, the complex datapath of SP FMA architecture is costly and results in large latency during hardware implementation, leading to high energy consumption during deep learning algorithm execution. To address this issue, some general-purpose architectures have extended their instruction set to support low-precision operations to reduce hardware costs and improve DNN performance. For example, mainstream instruction-set architectures such as AVX-512, Arm v8-SVE, and Arm v9-SME have introduced 16-bit half-precision (HP) and BrainFloat16 (BF16) formats. Due to the narrower bitwidth, 16-bit numbers can not only save memory resources but can also exploit more data-level parallelism than SP formats. However, the potential of using HP or BF16 throughout the entire training process is not fully exploited by any proposal. Numerical issues arise due to the reduced mantissa bits budget of BF16 [9] and the limited dynamic range of HP [13]. To overcome these issues, mixed-precision methods are utilized by performing low-precision multiplication to improve performance while accumulating the products in higher precision to maintain high accuracy. In comparison to DNN training, inference is more robust to computation errors. Therefore, 8-bit integer operations are commonly used to efficiently perform DNNs with higher energy efficiency [19].

In DNN tasks, low precision operations are primarily utilized in computation-intensive layers, such as the general matrix multiplication (GEMM) layer. On the other hand, precision-intensive layers, like BatchNorm and SoftMax, require SP operations to prevent accuracy loss. In particular, BatchNorm layers necessitate a larger number of SP additions during both DNN training and inference. Therefore, in this paper, we propose a multi-level parallel integer/floating-point arithmetic architecture to address the precision and parallelism requirements of DLIs. The primary contribution of our research is summarized below.

- The proposed arithmetic architecture supports both inter- and intra-operation parallelism, making it highly efficient at exploiting data-level and instruction-level parallelism for deep learning instructions.
- The architecture supports both integer and FP formats on single-path or dual-path execution, providing different latencies for integer and FP operations. This enhances the performance of DNN training and inference.
- The architecture also supports mixed-precision dot-product, wherein multiple products in low precision are accumulated into higher precision formats to improve throughput and maintain accuracy. Specifically, 4-term operations for HP or BF16 formats and 8-term operations for INT8 are performed at each cycle.

- The flexible dataflow of the proposed architecture allows for circuit reuse, reducing area requirements and power consumption. As a result, it achieves higher energy efficiency and operates more efficiently in implementing DLIs than other designs.

The remainder of this paper is organized as follows. Section 2 introduces the supported formats the functions of DLIs. Section 3 introduces the related works. In Sect. 4, the multi-level parallel integer/floating-point arithmetic architecture is presented. Section 5 covers the circuit implementation. Then the synthesis results, the analysis and the comparison with the previous designs are presented in Sect. 6. Finally, Sect. 7 gives the conclusion of the whole work.

## 2 Background

### 2.1 Integer and Floating-Point Formats

Standard floating-point formats are defined in IEEE754-2008 standard [6] which consists of three components: the 1-bit sign ($S$), the $e$-bit biased exponent ($E$), the $m$-bit mantissa ($M$). The sign bit determines whether the number is a positive or negative number. The mantissa determines the numerical accuracy while the exponent determines the dynamic range. Although the BF16 format is not included in IEEE 754-2008, it has the same components and also follows the IEEE 754 rule. The integer representation is less complicated than floating-point numbers, which only consists of two components, 1-bit sign and ($N-1$)-bit mantissa. The numerical formats of each operand supported by the proposed arithmetic architecture are shown in Fig. 1.

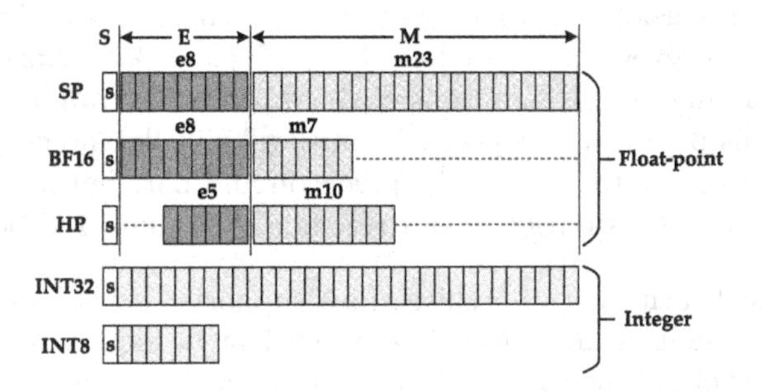


**Fig. 1.** Supported numerical formats of the proposed arithmetic architecture.

### 2.2 The Computing Requirement of DLIs

General-purpose architectures have been leveraged for accelerating deep learning algorithms by exploiting DLIs. Unlike conventional SP instructions, DLIs focus on data-level parallelism and low-precision computing to improve performance and reduce energy consumption. For example, dot-product instructions can significantly enhance performance by combining multiple instructions into one, thereby maximizing the use of computing resources and avoiding potential bandwidth bottlenecks when performing GEMM. Various DLIs have been proposed for integer and FP formats on general-purpose architectures such as Intel's AVX-512, Arm's v8-SVE and v9-SME, as shown in Table 1. The Vector Neural Network Instructions (VNNI) support 512-bit vector operations that can be configured to perform 16 parallel dot-product operations for integer and floating-point numbers [2]. SVE and SME have designed different DLIs for vector or matrix operations of varying formats, which can offer higher throughput and enable efficient implementation of DNN algorithms.

**Table 1.** Computing requirement of the instructions in DLIs

| Instruction | ISA | Bitwidth | Function | Format |
|---|---|---|---|---|
| VNNI | AVX-512 | 512-bit | 16 × [1, 2] × [2, 1] | BF16 & HP & INT16 |
| | | | 16 × [1, 4] × [4, 1] | INT8 |
| BFDOT | Arm v8 SVE | 32-bit | [1, 2] × [2, 1] | BF16 |
| SDOT & UDOT | Arm v8 SVE | 64-bit | [1, 8] × [8, 1] | INT8 |
| SMMLA | Arm v8 SVE | 128-bit | [2, 8] × [8, 2] | INT8 |
| BFMMLA | Arm v8 SVE | 128-bit | [2, 4] × [4, 2] | BF16 |
| Arm v9 SVE2 & SME [3]: wider vector operations and matrix multiplications | | | | |

## 3 Related Work

Previous works have proposed various arithmetic architectures that support multiple precision and parallel operations for deep learning algorithms. The FMA units proposed by [20] and [12] support a wide range of FP formats for flexible use in different applications. While their supported FP formats can be efficiently used in DNN training, they have higher costs in performing DNN inference than integer operations. Sohn et al. [17] proposed a 4-term dot-product unit that achieves better performance and accuracy compared to a network of traditional FP units. However, it only supports SP format, which incurs more overhead than reducing precision in performing DNN tasks. Zhang et al. [21] proposed an integer and FP multiply-accumulate (MAC) unit for DNN algorithms. This MAC unit supports scalar operations for HP format and dot-product for INT8 numbers. Although their integer dot-product offers high performance for DNN inference, the scalar HP operations cause large latency in implementing DLIs that require vector or matrix operations. Mach et al. [11] proposed an FMA unit that exploits 8-bit FP format (FP8), which offers higher throughput than 16-bit FP formats with less overhead. However, the FP8 format can only be used in limited scenarios of DNN training, and it costs more energy than INT8 in performing DNN inference. In general, it is significant to design arithmetic architectures that support parallel operations for both integer and FP formats, offering an efficient implementation for DLIs.

# 4 The Configurable Integer/Floating-Point Arithmetic Architecture

## 4.1 The Flexible Dataflow of the Dual-Path Architecture

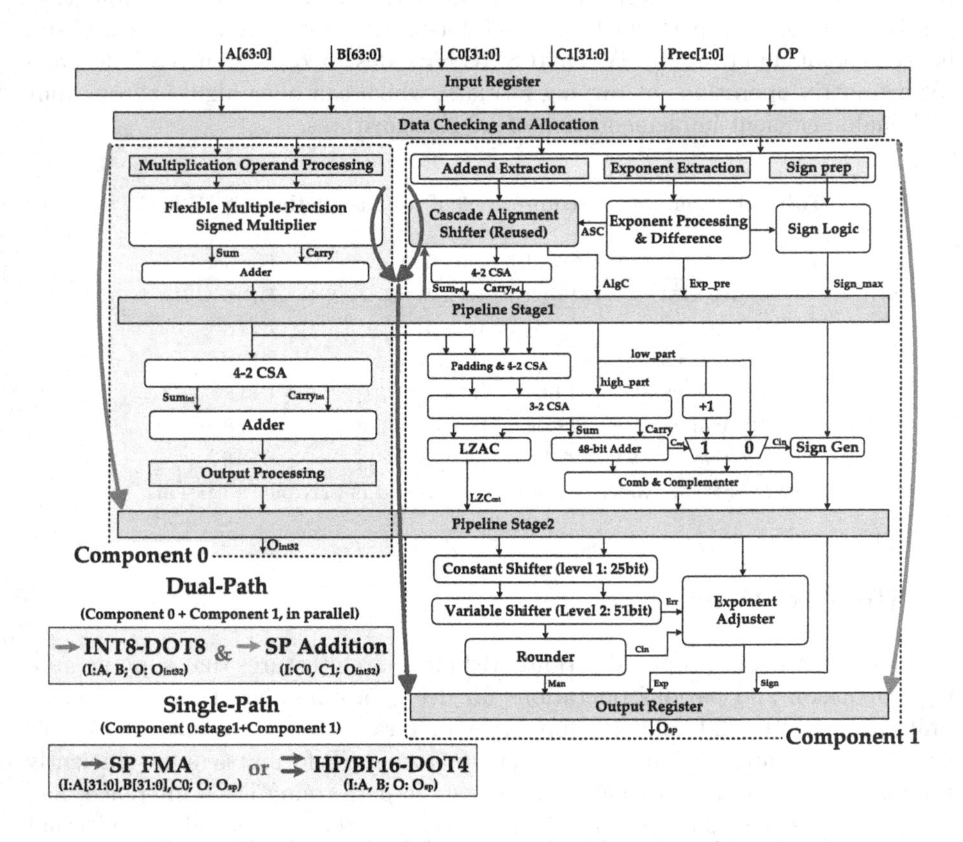


**Fig. 2.** The datapath of the proposed arithmetic architecture.

To achieve both data-level and instruction-level parallelism for DLIs, we propose an arithmetic architecture that supports dual-path and single-path execution for a variety of operations. The configurable architecture, shown in Fig. 2, is divided into two components to support dual-path operations, and the dataflow and latency are optimized based on the datapath of the supported operations. Input data is checked and then allocated to the corresponding component based on the operation being performed. In deep learning tasks, subnormal data is often flushed to zero to save hardware costs due to the high robustness of such tasks. Exceptional data, such as NaN, will trigger an error and be logged without processing. We re-use circuits to reduce hardware costs by rearranging the dataflow of the proposed architecture. Specifically, a four-segment alignment shifter is utilized to align the four products of HP/BF16-DOT operations by rotating the dataflow (red arrow). It can also be utilized to align the SP addends when combined. These two components are controlled by a 1-bit signal, $OP$, which determines whether single-path or dual-path execution is used. The 2-bit signal, $Prec$, is used to determine the data format. For dual-path execution, the integer dot-product and SP addition operations run independently in parallel using the two components, which not only improves throughput but also provides instruction-level parallelism for DLIs. In single-path execution, the entire architecture is utilized and fully pipelined to perform SP FMA or 4-term dot-product for BF16 and HP formats: BF16-DOT4 and HP-DOT4.

To save energy consumption, we use a coarse-grained low-power technology in the proposed design, allowing unused logic to be gated in specific operations. For example, when performing INT8-DOT8, the entire logic of component 1 can be gated.

### 4.2 The Bit-Partitioning Method for Multiplier Design

To incorporate SP and reduced precision operations into the proposed architecture, we adopt a bit-partitioning approach to partition the bitwidth $W_p$ of SP operands into several segments. The bit-partitioning method must comply with the requirement of DLIs that the number of parallel operations of vector and matrix instructions are powers of two. Therefore, we need to comprehensively analyze the bitwidth of the multiplier unit to maximize hardware usage. We determine the number of segments $N$ using bit-partitioning methods with various bitwidths $W_m$ of the supported formats.

$$N = 2^{\left\lceil log2(\frac{W_p}{W_m})\right\rceil} \tag{1}$$

During partition processing, redundant bits are generated which can be used to evaluate the utilization of the multiplier unit. The number of these redundant bits, denoted as $n_r$, can be calculated by subtracting the bit width of the partition ($W_p$) from the total bit width of the multipliers.

$$n_r = W_m \times N - W_p \tag{2}$$

The number of redundant bits per segment, denoted as $n_{rps}$, represents the redundancy performance that is averaged over each segment. When calculating $n_{rps}$, both the horizontal and vertical redundant bits should be taken into account. This can be summarized as follows:

$$n_{rps} = \frac{n_{rh}}{N_h} + \frac{n_{rv}}{N_v} \tag{3}$$

where the $N_h$ and $N_v$ mean the segments in the horizontal and vertical partition. Based on the supported formats, the minimum value of $W_m$ for INT8 is restricted to 7. To analyze the redundancy performance and parallel operations per cycle, we have compiled a list of multiplier sizes ranging from 7 to 12. As shown in Table 2, the parameter vector $(N_{INT8}, N_{hp}, N_{sp}, n_{rps})$ are listed, where the $N_{INT8}, N_{hp}, N_{sp}$ denote the parallel multiplications for INT8, HP, SP operations, respectively. When the $W_m$ between 7 to 11, more parallel operations are supported for INT8 numbers, but it will cause a low redundancy performance. The $12 \times 12$ multiplier will cause low redundancy performance and fewer parallel operations for INT8 precision. So, the $12 \times 7$ multiplier is selected as the basic unit to construct the multiplier array of the proposed design.

**Table 2.** Analysis of bitwidth for the configurable multiplier

| Bitwidth | (7-11)-bit | 12-bit |
|---|---|---|
| (7-11)-bit | (16, 4, 1, >10) | (8, 4, 1, 5) |
| 12-bit | ( 8, 4, 1, 5) | (4, 4, 1, 12) |

## 5 Circuit Implementation

### 5.1 Configurable Multiple-Precision Multiplier Array

We implement a configurable multiplier array using low-precision-combination (LPC) techniques, which utilizes eight $12 \times 7$ multiplier units. For the multiplier unit design, we employ the radix-4 modified Booth algorithm [4] to reduce hardware costs. The sub-array organization, comprising two multiplier units, is illustrated in Fig. 3, which includes the multiplicand, multiplier, and generated partial product (PP) array. Before inputting the multiplicand and multiplier into the sub-array, they must first be processed into a unified format, as depicted at the top of Fig. 3. The sub-arrays can be configured to operate with different numeric formats, including INT8, HP/BF16, and SP.

When performing INT8-DOT8 mode, the two products generated by two multipliers are first right-aligned and then added by a 4-to-2 carry save adder (CSA). However, in HP/BF16-DOT4 mode, the two multipliers are combined to realize the 11-bit multiplication. As for SP mode, the sub-array generates a $12 \times 12$ result, and the entire multiplier array consists of four sub-array cells to generate the complete SP result. Our proposed design constructs the complete multiplier array by replicating four sub-arrays and summing up their results through a 4-to-2 adder. This multiplier array is capable of performing eight INT8 operations, four HP/BF16 operations, or one SP operation.

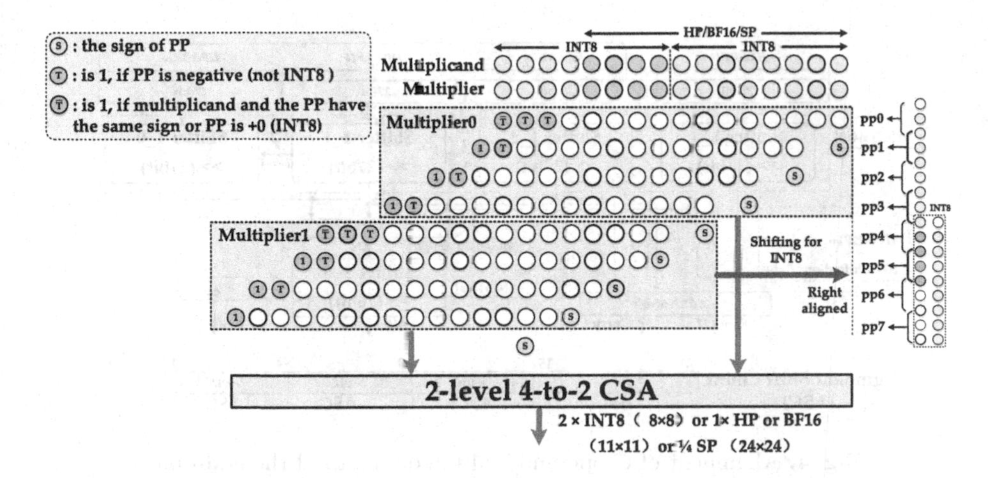


**Fig. 3.** Partial product generation and partial product array of the sub-array.

### 5.2 Cascade Alignment Shifter and Product Processing

The proposed design saves costs by reusing the alignment shifter in both the SP operations and HP/BF16-DOT4. The alignment shifting methods used are similar to those in a previous FMA design [8]. To perform the alignment of SP operations, a 76-bit shifter is required, while a 27-bit shifter is needed for HP/BF16-DOT4. To implement the alignment of the supported operations, the alignment shifter is split into four segments using LPC methods, as shown in Fig. 4. Four 27-bit 5-level shifters and a 76-bit 2-level shifter are designed to construct the entire 7-level alignment shifter in cascade methods. During HP-DOT4 and BF16-DOT4, the four 27-bit shifters run independently to perform the alignment of products. The aligned products are then added together using a 4-to-2 CSA to reduce latency. In SP operations, the lower three 27-bit shifters are combined to perform the head 5-level alignment of addend C. The final shifting is completed using a 76-bit shifter in the later 2-levels, which runs in cascade.

### 5.3 Adder, Leading Zero Anticipator, Normalization and Rounding

In the proposed design, a total of 76-bit vectors need to be added. For the most significant 26 bits, an incrementer is used since only one of the two vectors contains useful data. For the less significant 48 bits, a carry propagate adder (CPA) is used for the addition. In SP operations, the whole 76-bit adder is used, while only the 48-bit CPA is used in dot-product operations. To reduce latency, a leading zero anticipator (LZA) [15] is used to anticipate both leading zeros and leading ones, working in parallel with the addition. The leading zero numbers are then used in both normalization and exponent adjustment, removing the heading zeros of the addition results, and generating the exponent. The roundTiesToEven

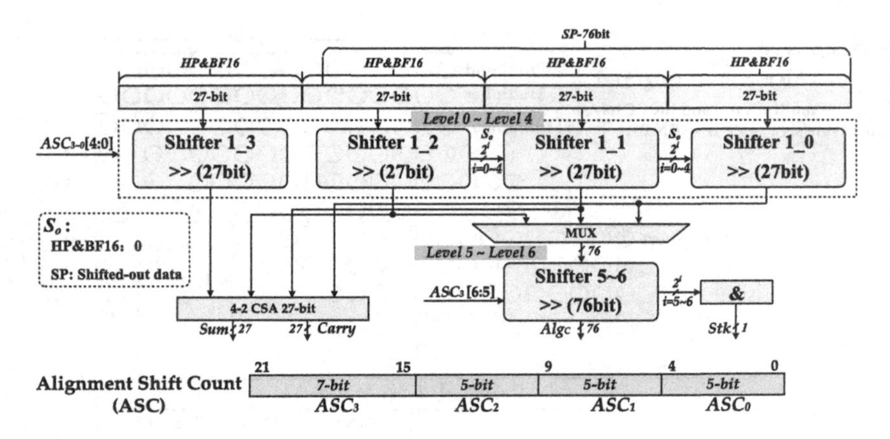


**Fig. 4.** Alignment of $C$ operand and the datapath of the addition.

mode [1] is applied to the rounding of the normalized mantissa. Finally, the result is generated by combining the processed sign, adjusted exponent, and rounded mantissa.

## 6 Synthesis and Evaluation

The proposed design was implemented using Verilog HDL, and its correctness was verified through extensive testing using vectors generated by testfloat [7]. In addition to the proposed architecture, we also implemented baseline FMA designs for SP, BF16, HP, and INT8 formats to compare them with the proposed arithmetic architecture. All of these designs were synthesized in the typical corner of 28 nm CMOS technology using synthesis tools. Subsequently, we generated timing and area metrics to evaluate the designs. We used the synthesized netlist and the activity file generated from post-synthesis simulations, aided by Static Timing Analysis (STA) tools, to estimate power consumption.

All designs were synthesized with a time constraint of 0.45 ns, and the synthesis results are presented in Fig. 5. Due to its complex architecture and wider datapath, the proposed architecture consumes more power and area than the baseline designs. However, the proposed design can perform a broader range of operations with higher performance, including INT8-DOT8, BF16-DOT4, HP-DOT4, and standard SP FMA operations, as discussed in previous sections. This is mainly due to two factors: firstly, the architecture of the baseline designs is simple with a narrower datapath, and they are synthesized under a loose time constraint. Secondly, the proposed design requires more logic to support a wide range of formats and various operations. To achieve the same functionality as the proposed arithmetic unit, we would require 4 HP MIX-FMAs, 4 BF MIX-FMAs, 1 SP FMA, and 8 INT8 FMAs. However, the proposed arithmetic unit is 67.2% more area-efficient than the combination (Comb) of these FMAs.

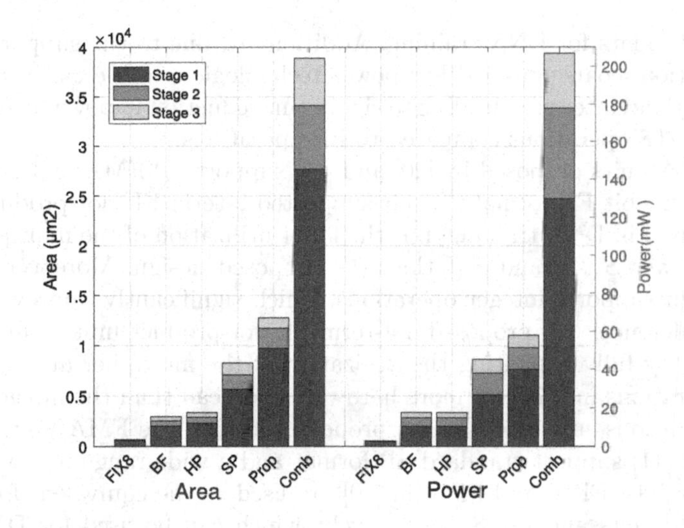


**Fig. 5.** Synthesis results of the proposed design and baseline designs.

## 6.1 Comparisons with Related Works

Table 3 presents a comparison of the latency, performance, power consumption, and energy efficiency of our proposed arithmetic architecture with those of previous works. As the previous works were synthesized under different processes, we scaled their areas to the same process feature size to ensure a fair comparison. The total area of a design is directly proportional to the area of a unit transistor; therefore, we generated a normalized area ($NArea$) by dividing the total area by the square of the process feature size ($F^2$). Furthermore, the performance of an arithmetic unit in hardware implementation is strictly constrained by the silicon area. Hence, we calculated the scaled throughput ($S\_TP$) based on the normalized area for performance comparison.

$$S\_TP = Freq \times \frac{1}{NArea} \times OPs \tag{4}$$

where $OPs$ represents the parallel operations per cycle, ($1\ MAC = 2\ OPs$), and $Freq$ refers to the frequency of the designs. In contemporary DL systems, 16-bit FP and 8-bit integer formats are commonly used in DNN training and inference, respectively. While SP formats offer a larger dynamic range and higher precision than 16-bit FP numbers, their impact on the accuracy of DL models during training is often negligible. This is due to the use of mixed-precision methods that accumulate the HP numbers to the SP format, effectively reducing the accuracy gap between the two formats. Therefore, equivalent formats are utilized for the evaluation of $S\_TP$ and energy efficiency ($EE$) in DNN training and inference due to the limited support of formats in some works. For example, during mixed-precision methods, 16-bit FP operation products are accumulated into SP formats, enabling 32-bit SP formats and 16-bit FP formats to be considered equivalent formats for DNN training. Additionally, due to the support of dual-path execution, coarse-grained low-power technologies can be easily utilized in the dual-path architecture, leading to significant reduction in power consumption in INT8-DOT8 operations compared to FP operations.

The FMA units proposed by [20] and [18] support SP FMA and 2-term dot-product for 16-bit FP formats. Their supported 2-term FP dot-product can be efficiently used in DNN training, but the lower utilization of the multiplier array results in lower $S\_TP$ and $EE$ than the proposed design. Moreover, the proposed design supports integer operations, which significantly improves the $EE$ for DNN inference. [17] proposed a 4-term SP dot-product unit to improve the throughput by fully exploiting the utilization of the multiplier array. However, the SP operations in [17] cost more hardware overhead than the integer and 16-bit FP operations supported by the proposed design. The FMA units designed by [10] and [11] support standard SP format and a wide range of low precision FP formats. The FP20 and FP14 in [10] are used as the equivalent formats for 16-bit FP formats and INT8, respectively, which can be used for DNN training and inference. Also, the FP8 in [11] and INT8 are equivalent formats for DNN inference. Due to coarse-grained lower techniques, the proposed design has higher $EE$ in DNN training and inference than [10] and [11]. The mixed-precision operations for HP numbers are supported by [21] and [5], which are useful in DNN training. However, the scalar operations for HP numbers result in lower $S_TP$ and higher $EE$ than the proposed design. The FMA unit in [21] supports INT8-DOT2 for DNN inference, but the proposed design exploits more parallel operations to significantly enhance the throughput. In general, compared with other works, the proposed design exploits more types of operations dedicated to DNN training and inference, such as INT8-DOT8, HP-DOT4, and BF16-DOT4, to achieve higher throughput and energy efficiency. The supported parallel operations can be efficiently used for the data-level parallelism of DLIs and accelerate the implementation of DNN training and inference.

**Table 3.** Comparison of the proposed arithmetic architecture with previous works

| Design | Functions for DNN algorithms | Cycle | Delay | Freq | Area | NArea | Power | $S\_TP$ | | EE(GOPS/W) | |
|---|---|---|---|---|---|---|---|---|---|---|---|
| | | | ns | GHz | $\mu m^2$ | $\mu m^2/F^2$ | (mW) | If | Tr | If | Tr |
| [20]-90 nm | 1 SP, 2 HP DOT2 | 4 | 1.5 | 0.67 | 17,2014 | 21.2 | 26.2 | 0.13 | 0.13 | 102.3 | 102.3 |
| [10]-32 nm | 1 SP, 2 FP20‡, 4 FP14‡ FMA | 3 | 0.69 | 1.45 | 45,000 | 43.9 | 60.0 | 0.13 | 14.1 | 96.7 | 193.3 |
| [17]-45 nm | 1 SP DOT4 | 4 | 0.64 | 1.56 | 63,200 | 31.2 | 32.7 | 0.4 | 0.4 | 381.7 | 381.7 |
| [11]-22 nm | 2 SP, 4 HP, 4 BF16, 8 FP8$^{\alpha}$ FMA | 3,2$^{\alpha}$ | 1.08 | 0.92 | 49,000 | 101.2 | 57.4 | 0.15 | 0.08 | 128.9 | 257.8 |
| [21]-90 nm | 1 HP FMA, 1 INT8$^{\beta}$-DOT2 | 3,2$^{\beta}$ | 0.8 | 1.25 | 42,711 | 5.3 | 14.1 | 0.47 | 0.24 | 354.6 | 177.3 |
| [5]-28 nm | 1 HP MIX-FMA | 6 | 2.0 | 0.5 | 2,690 | 3.4 | – | 0.29 | 0.29 | – | – |
| [18]-28 nm | 1 SP/2 HP FMA, 1 HP/BF16 DOT2 | 4 | 0.45 | 2.22 | 13,032 | 16.6 | 73.1 | 0.53 | 0.53 | 121.5 | 121.5 |
| Prop-28 nm | 1 INT8-DOT8 & 1 SP ADD$^{\gamma}$ | 2,3$^{\gamma}$ | 0.45 | 2.22 | 12,765 | 16.3 | 20.5† | 2.18 | – | 1,734.4 | – |
| | 1 SP FMA$^{\gamma}$, 1 HP/BF16 DOT4 | 3$^{\gamma}$,4 | 0.45 | 2.22 | 12,765 | 16.3 | 57.9 | – | 1.09 | – | 307.0 |

‡ FP20 = SP using only 12 bit of precision, FP14 = SP using only 6 bit of precision
† power for INT8-DOT8; $If$: Inference; $Tr$: Training

### 6.2 Evaluation of the DLIs Implementation

The Arm v8-SVE instruction-set architecture has been expanded to support DLIs for DNN algorithms, including BFDOT, UDOT, SDOT, SMMLA, and BFMMLA. The proposed arithmetic architecture supports dot-product computations for BF16, HP, and INT8 numbers, allowing for data-level parallelism to efficiently execute DLIs. To implement these instructions, multiple arithmetic units must be organized into vector or matrix formats, with $1 \times 1$ or $2 \times 2$ arithmetic units required for these DLIs, as indicated in Table 4. Previous arithmetic units support fewer formats and are unable to implement DLIs directly, so equivalent formats are used to achieve the same function as the DLIs in performing DNN tasks. By considering the throughput of DLIs and the number of parallel operations for specific formats in prior research, the number of arithmetic units ($Num.U$) is determined. Previous studies have focused on supporting FP formats or short vector operations for integer formats, requiring additional units to implement DLIs. As indicated in Table 4, the proposed arithmetic architecture reduces energy costs by more than 90% for integer instructions U/SDOT and SMMLA, compared to prior research. For the implementation of FP instructions BFDOT and BFMMLA, the proposed arithmetic architecture can achieve a maximum energy cost reduction of 44%.

**Table 4.** Comparison of energy consumption for achieving the same functions of DLIs

| Design | BFDOT | | U/SDOT | | SMMLA | | BFMMLA | |
|---|---|---|---|---|---|---|---|---|
| | Num.U | Energy(pJ) | Num.U | Energy(pJ) | Num.U | Energy(pJ) | Num.U | Energy(pJ) |
| [10] | $1 \times 1$ | 124.2 | $2 \times 1$ | 248.4 | $8 \times 1$ | 993.6 | $8 \times 1$ | 993.6 |
| [20] | $1 \times 1$ | 157.2 | $4 \times 1$ | 628.8 | $16 \times 1$ | 2,515.2 | $16 \times 1$ | 2515.2 |
| [11] | $1 \times 1$ | 185.98 | $1 \times 1$ | 123.98 | $4 \times 1$ | 495.92 | $4 \times 1$ | 743.92 |
| [21] | – | – | $4 \times 1$ | 90.24 | $16 \times 1$ | 360.96 | – | – |
| [18] | $1 \times 1$ | 131.58 | $4 \times 1$ | 526.32 | $16 \times 1$ | 2,105.28 | $4 \times 1$ | 526.32 |
| Prop | $1 \times 1$ | 104.22 | $1 \times 1$ | 18.45 | $2 \times 2$ | 73.8 | $2 \times 2$ | 416.88 |

$Energy = Delay \times Cycles \times Power \times Num.U$.

### 6.3 Evaluation of the Inter-operation Parallelism

The proposed arithmetic architecture supports inter-operation parallelism on dual-path execution, enabling instruction-level parallelism for DLIs. This architecture enables instruction-level parallelism and can be evaluated against a single-path implementation that supports the same functionalities but implements them serially. In DNN inference, both integer and FP formats are necessary in different layers. INT8 operations are used for the GEMM layer, while non-GEMM layers such as BatchNorm, SoftMax, ResNet-add, and All-Reduce require a large number of SP operations. Although DNN models are structurally serial, dataflow parallelism can be exploited in certain layers to improve performance. Therefore, practical DNN models require parallel INT8 and SP instructions to accelerate inference. The runtime of DNN models is determined by the ratio of INT8 and SP operations. INT8 operations in GEMM layers account for the majority of DNN inference computation, with a ratio of $R_{int}$. The ratio of SP operations is $R_{sp}$ ($R_{int} + R_{sp} = 1$), and only a portion of the SP operations, $Rp_{sp}$, can run in parallel with the integer operations, while the remainder runs in serial in a ratio of $Rs_{sp}$ ($Rp_{sp} + Rs_{sp} = 1$). The scaled runtimes for single-path and dual-path implementation can be calculated as follows:

$$T_{single-path} = \frac{R_{int}}{OP_{int}} + \frac{R_{sp}}{OP_{sp}} \tag{5}$$

$$T_{dual-path} = max(\frac{R_{int}}{OP_{int}}, \frac{Rp_{sp}}{OP_{sp}}) + \frac{Rs_{sp}}{OP_{sp}} \tag{6}$$

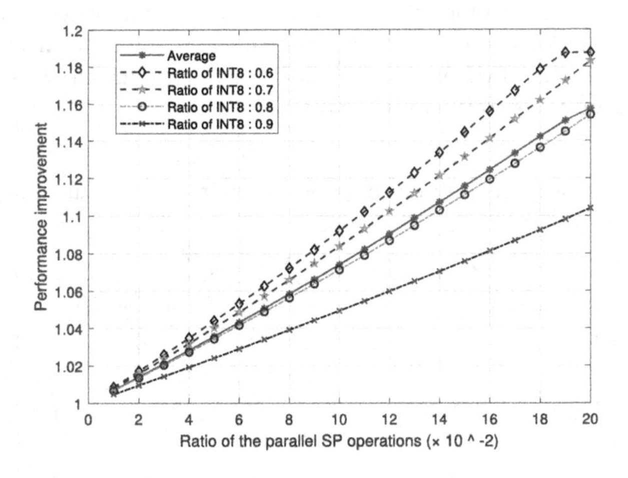


**Fig. 6.** The performance improvement than a single-path implementation.

In practical DNN inference tasks, the proportion of integer operations is typically over 0.6, while the proportion of parallel SP operations is often less than 0.2 [14]. Figure 6 shows a line chart comparing the performance of different ratios of INT8 and FP operations. Due to the inter-parallelism on the dual-path execution, the average performance improvement is up to 15.7% compared to the single-path implementation.

## 7 Conclusion

In this paper, we present a multi-level parallel arithmetic architecture that supports integers and a wide range of FP formats. Our proposed architecture supports multi-term dot-product for integer, HP, and BF16 formats, which enables the exploitation of data-level parallelism in DLIs. The dot-product operation is implemented using mixed-precision methods that use lower precision to improve performance while accumulating to higher precision to avoid accuracy loss. Furthermore, our proposed architecture supports dual-path execution, where the INT8-DOT8 and SP addition can be performed in parallel. The inter-operation parallelism in dual-path execution can be efficiently utilized in performing DNN inference, resulting in a 15.7% improvement in performance compared to a single-path implementation. Our proposed architecture exhibits higher energy efficiency compared to state-of-the-art designs for implementing DLIs, making it more efficient for DNN applications.

**Acknowledgment.** This work is supported in part by NSFC (No. 62272475, 62090023) and NSFHN (No. 2022JJ10064).

## References

1. IEEE standard for floating-point arithmetic. IEEE Std 754-2019 (Revision of IEEE 754-2008), pp. 1–84 (2019). https://doi.org/10.1109/IEEESTD.2019.8766229
2. Arafa, M., et al.: Cascade lake: next generation Intel Xeon scalable processor. IEEE Micro **39**(2), 29–36 (2019)
3. Arm: Arm A64 instruction set architecture - Armv9, for Armv9-a architecture profile (2021). https://developer.arm.com/documentation/ddi0602/2021-12
4. Booth, A.D.: A signed binary multiplication technique. Q. J. Mech. Appl. Math. **4**(2), 236–240 (1951)
5. Brunie, N.: Modified fused multiply and add for exact low precision product accumulation. In: 2017 IEEE 24th Symposium on Computer Arithmetic (ARITH), pp. 106–113. IEEE (2017)
6. Dan, Z., et al.: IEEE standard for floating-point arithmetic. IEEE Std 754-2008, pp. 1–70 (2008)
7. Hauser, J.: Berkeley testfloat (2018). https://www.jhauser.us/arithmetic/testfloat.html
8. Huang, L., Ma, S., Shen, L., Wang, Z., Xiao, N.: Low-cost binary128 floating-point FMA unit design with SIMD support. IEEE Trans. Comput. **61**(5), 745–751 (2011)
9. Kalamkar, D., et al.: A study of BFLOAT16 for deep learning training. arXiv preprint arXiv:1905.12322 (2019)
10. Kaul, H., et al.: A 1.45 GHz 52-to-162GFLOPS/W variable-precision floating-point fused multiply-add unit with certainty tracking in 32 nm CMOS. In: 2012 IEEE International Solid-State Circuits Conference, pp. 182–184. IEEE (2012)
11. Mach, S., Schuiki, F., Zaruba, F., Benini, L.: FPnew: an open-source multiformat floating-point unit architecture for energy-proportional transprecision computing. IEEE Trans. Very Large Scale Integr. (VLSI) Syst. **29**(4), 774–787 (2020)
12. Mao, W., et al.: A configurable floating-point multiple-precision processing element for HPC and AI converged computing. IEEE Trans. Very Large Scale Integr. (VLSI) Syst. **30**(2), 213–226 (2021)
13. Micikevicius, P., et al.: Mixed precision training. arXiv preprint arXiv:1710.03740 (2017)
14. Murshed, M.S., Murphy, C., Hou, D., Khan, N., Ananthanarayanan, G., Hussain, F.: Machine learning at the network edge: a survey. ACM Comput. Surv. (CSUR) **54**(8), 1–37 (2021)

15. Schmookler, M.S., Nowka, K.J.: Leading zero anticipation and detection-a comparison of methods. In: Proceedings 15th IEEE Symposium on Computer Arithmetic, ARITH-15 2001, pp. 7–12. IEEE (2001)
16. Sevilla, J., Heim, L., Ho, A., Besiroglu, T., Hobbhahn, M., Villalobos, P.: Compute trends across three eras of machine learning. In: 2022 International Joint Conference on Neural Networks (IJCNN), pp. 1–8. IEEE (2022)
17. Sohn, J., Swartzlander, E.E.: A fused floating-point four-term dot product unit. IEEE Trans. Circuits Syst. I Regul. Pap. **63**(3), 370–378 (2016)
18. Tan, H., Tong, G., Huang, L., Xiao, L., Xiao, N.: Multiple-mode-supporting floating-point FMA unit for deep learning processors. IEEE Trans. Very Large Scale Integr. (VLSI) Syst. **31**(02), 253–266 (2023)
19. Vanholder, H.: Efficient inference with tensorrt. In: GPU Technology Conference, vol. 1, p. 2 (2016)
20. Zhang, H., Chen, D., Ko, S.B.: Efficient multiple-precision floating-point fused multiply-add with mixed-precision support. IEEE Trans. Comput. **68**(7), 1035–1048 (2019)
21. Zhang, H., Lee, H.J., Ko, S.B.: Efficient fixed/floating-point merged mixed-precision multiply-accumulate unit for deep learning processors. In: 2018 IEEE International Symposium on Circuits and Systems (ISCAS), pp. 1–5. IEEE (2018)

# Lock-Free Bucketized Cuckoo Hashing

Wenhai Li, Zhiling Cheng(✉), Yuan Chen, Ao Li, and Lingfeng Deng

Wuhan University, Wuhan, China
chengzl@whu.edu.cn

**Abstract.** Concurrent hash tables are one of the fundamental building blocks for cloud computing. In this paper, we introduce lock-free modifications to in-memory bucketized cuckoo hashing. We present a novel concurrent strategy in designing a lock-free hash table, called LFBCH, that paves the way towards scalability and high space efficiency. To the best of our knowledge, this is the first attempt to incorporate lock-free technology into in-memory bucketized cuckoo hashing, while still providing worst-case constant-scale lookup time and extremely high load factor. All of the operations over LFBCH, such as get, put, "kick out" and rehash, are guaranteed to be lock-free, without introducing notorious problems like false miss and duplicated key. The experimental results indicate that under mixed workloads with up to 64 threads, the throughput of LFBCH is 14%–360% higher than other popular concurrent hash tables.

**Keywords:** buckized cuckoo hashing · lock-free · data structure · multicore · parallel computing

## 1 Introduction

With the rapid growth of data volume in the Big Data era, the massive amount of data puts increasing pressure on cloud computing systems [1,18]. As a key component of these systems [3,7–9,15], a high-performance hash table is very important for application usability. In step with Moore's law, the improvement in CPU performance has relied on the increase in the number of cores, leading to higher demands for the scalability of hash tables [16]. Consequently, improving the concurrent performance of hash tables on multicore architectures has become a crucial step in designing data-intensive platforms. In practice, the open-addressing hash table is widely used due to its ability to limit the memory usage of the hash table. However, with the increase in application scale, it is challenging to drive concurrent operations on a dense open-addressing hash table.

As an open-addressing hash table, cuckoo hashing was first proposed in 2004 [14]. It utilizes two hash functions to guarantee a constant-time worst-case complexity for the search operation. It introduces a critical step called "kick out", which will be invoked when other keys have occupied both of the positions corresponding to an insertion. The action involves kicking one of the occupying


J. Cano et al. (Eds.): Euro-Par 2023, LNCS 14100, pp. 275–288, 2023.
https://doi.org/10.1007/978-3-031-39698-4_19

keys to its alternative position, creating space for the incoming insertion. This process is similar to that of a cuckoo bird, which always kicks out the eggs of other birds and places its eggs in the nest, hence the name cuckoo hash. If the alternative location of the kicked key is also occupied, a cascade kick is triggered. As the cascade kick could easily form a loop, in general, the load factor of the primitive design cannot exceed 50%. The bucketized cuckoo-hashing scheme introduces multiple slots per bucket for alleviating the kicking loops. This makes the process applicable for use cases with a load factor exceeding 95% [10].

Another essential problem is concurrency. In cuckoo hashing, it could be very difficult to efficiently prevent the kicking process from affecting readers and writers. As a widespread implementation of bucketized cuckoo hashing, libcuckoo [13] conducts a fine-grained locking approach to reduce the blocking overhead of concurrent threads. It can be shown that the throughput of libcuckoo significantly degrades as long as the number of worker threads continuously increases, e.g., with more than 16 worker threads. Lock-free technique [2] has also been applied to cuckoo hashing. Lfcuckoo [13] accelerates the primitive cuckoo hashing using atomic primitives, such as LOAD, STORE, and Compare-and-Swap (CAS). Two correctness issues, i.e., *false miss* and *duplicated key*, have been addressed in the presence of lock-freedom by lfcuckoo. However, the solution can hardly be applied to the bucketized use case, making it impractical.

To implement a concurrent hash table that can efficiently exploit the increasing number of cores, we introduce lock-free techniques to in-memory bucketized cuckoo hashing. We use single-word atomic primitives to optimize concurrent operations over the bucketized data structure, with thorough consideration of the kicking process for cuckoo hashing. We revise lfcuckoo's helper mechanism for the use case with bucketized data structure. For the false miss problem, inspired by hazard pointers [12], we present a mechanism based on hazard hash value that detects the conflicting hash values when performing "kick out". If a search operation gets a miss and detects the hash value derived from its required key conflict with a key being kicked out, it will retry to ensure that it does not return a false miss when the key is present in the hash table. As for the problem of duplicated keys, we generate a snapshot of the target bucket and delete any duplicated keys within it when necessary. In addition to addressing the two issues that affect correctness, we have also presented lock-free lazy rehash which has never been addressed in the previous studies. To address the issue of data hotspots [4], we have also implemented the hotspot detection and adjustment mechanism, improving the performance of the hash table under a highly skewed workload. Ultimately, we implemented lock-free bucketized cuckoo hashing, which is functionally correct, space-efficient, and scalable.

The rest of this paper is organized as follows. Section 2 gives the basic concepts of libcuckoo and lfcuckoo. Section 3 presents the data structure of LFBCH followed by its basic operations. Section 4 shows the implementation details of the lock-free hash table. Section 5 evaluates the hash table based on benchmark workloads. The related works and the conclusion of this paper are given in Sect. 6 and Sect. 7, respectively.

# 2 Preliminaries

In this section, we present the basic concepts of bucketized cuckoo hashing and the lock-free revision for primitive cuckoo hashing. Problems when driving lock-free operations over a bucketized hash table are discussed.

## 2.1 Bucketized Cuckoo Hashing

Libcuckoo is a popular implementation of cuckoo hashing that supports lock-based operations using a bucketized hash table. We will use it as an example to illustrate the critical components of a bucketized hash table in the context of cuckoo hashing.

**Data Structure.** Figure 1 demonstrates the basic structure of libcuckoo by a typical configuration with two cuckoo-hashing functions and a four-way set-associative bucket. A key calculated by two hash functions is mapped to two buckets, each consisting of four set-associative slots. For concurrency, libcuckoo employs a lock strip technique. Each request first acquires locks corresponding to both target buckets before accessing them. Libcuckoo exhibits good scalability when the user requests follow a uniform distribution in their request keys. However, due to the overhead incurred by lock contention, the system performance sharply degrades when the number of worker threads increases on skewed workloads, even in read-only applications.

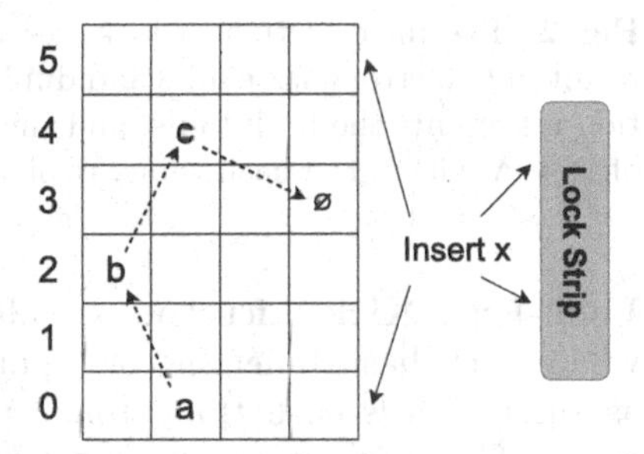


**Fig. 1.** Demonstration of the kicking process of libcuckoo, where a kick path $a \rightarrow b \rightarrow c \rightarrow \emptyset$ is found to make free slot for a new insertion key "x". $\emptyset$ denotes an empty slot. The three keys, i.e., $c, b, a$, will be moved to their alternative slots following the directions of the arrows.

**Kick Process.** The kick process is divided into two stages, i.e., path search and item movement along the kick path. The goal of the path search stage is to find a path for cascade kicking out. For example, Fig. 1 shows how to kick item "a" to make space for a new insertion "x". Libcuckoo finds the kick path by evaluating a BFS search, which guarantees the shortest path [10]. In the second stage, it moves the keys reversely along the kick path. This will leave an empty slot in the head of the kick path, which can be used to accommodate the new insertion key. Rather than locking the entire kicking path, libcuckoo utilizes fine-grained locks to ensure the correctness of the kicking process.

## 2.2 Difficulties when Supporting Lock-Free Operations

Next, we analyze the critical idea of introducing a lock-free technique into cuckoo hashing. Based on a primitive revision, i.e., lfcuckoo, we highlight the difficulties when considering lock freedom over bucketized cuckoo hashing.

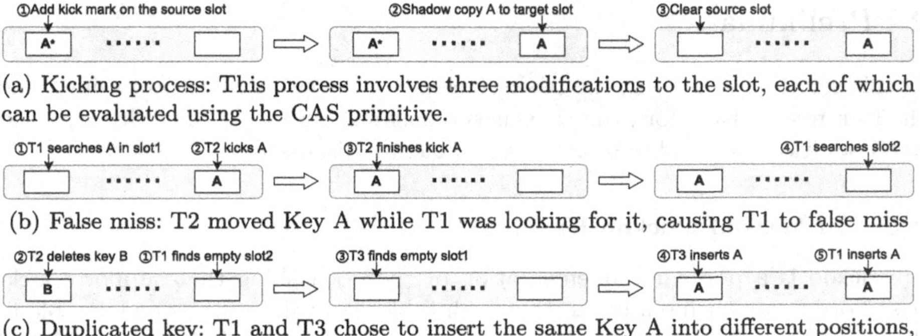


(a) Kicking process: This process involves three modifications to the slot, each of which can be evaluated using the CAS primitive.

(b) False miss: T2 moved Key A while T1 was looking for it, causing T1 to false miss

(c) Duplicated key: T1 and T3 chose to insert the same Key A into different positions, resulting in duplicated key

**Fig. 2.** The introduction of lock-free techniques into cuckoo hashing can potentially result in two errors: false miss and duplicated key. The gray rounded box in the illustration represents the hash table, and the white boxes indicate the two possible positions of Key A within the hash table. (Color figure online)

**Lock-Free Kick.** Lfcuckoo is built on a single-slot cuckoo hashing structure, where each hash function corresponds to a single slot. The slots are designed as single words such that atomic primitives can be applied for lock-free purposes. The single item movement in the kicking process is shown in Fig. 2(a). Lfcuckoo marks the least significant bit (LSB) of the source slot pointer at the first step of the kick process. Marking the LSB on the source slot helps to prevent the kick operation from blocking write operations. Other write operations call a helper function to help the "kick out" thread when they detect the kick mark. The helper function encapsulates the processes of slot copy and source clearance, making the kicking process lock-free. While this mechanism makes sense in single-slot cuckoo hashing, it cannot be directly applied to bucketized cuckoo hashing. As multiple target slots in each bucket can be selected as evictee by each movement, a helper thread cannot determine to which slot the marked key should be kicked to.

**False Miss.** As shown in Fig. 2(b), a false miss refers to the scenario that a key is present in the hash table but a search operation fails to find it. Lfcuckoo resolves false misses by detecting the interleaving kicks based on a kicking counter in the highest 16 bits of the slot. The search operation must be evaluated twice to detect the modifications to the counter on each slot. A false miss might occur if the counter changes within any of the two rounds. It then restarts the search process to make sure whether the key exists. However, using a counter is not entirely safe as there is a risk of fatal errors resulting from short, recycling counters conflicting with each other. Additionally, the presence of version numbers occupies the space available for tags, which is an essential part of reducing memory access and speeding up searches. On the other hand, version numbers are also inapplicable to bucketized cuckoo hashing due to the expansion of slot numbers.

**Duplicated Key.** Figure 2(c) shows an example of the duplicated key caused by three interleaved modifications. To address this issue, at any time a duplicated key is found by a search process, lfcuckoo always removes the key in the later slot of the search sequence. The solution of lfcuckoo makes sense since each key has only two possible locations, both cannot be selected as evictees due to the duplicate key in their alternative slot. However, in the bucketized cuckoo hashing, a kicking process may be interleaved with the duplicated key check process. It thus might cause the duplicated key check process to miss duplicated keys or to get an intermediate state of the kicking out process.

## 3 Overview of LFBCH

In this section, we provide an overview of our bucketized cuckoo hashing, including its data structure and fundamental operations.

### 3.1 Data Structure

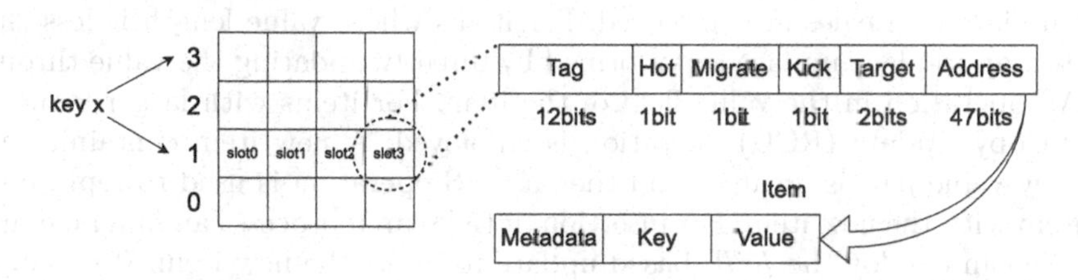


**Fig. 3.** Data structure of LFBCH with the fine-grained division of its 64-bit slot especially for supporting lock-free operations.

The basic structure of LFBCH is an array-typed bucketized hash table with two hash functions and four slots per bucket. Each slot is 64 bits wide and can be manipulated by atomic primitives. The atomic LOAD result of the slot is referred to as an entry.

As shown in Fig. 3, the entry can be divided into the following fields:

- *Address.* A 47-bit address is generally sufficient to locate a key-value pair for purposes of alignment.
- *Target.* Used to identify the target slot index of an in-flight entry.
- *Kick/Migrate.* Mark that the entry is being kicked/rehash migrated.
- *Hot.* Identify whether an item is frequently accessed.
- *Tag.* A signature of the hash value for each key. Enhances query efficiency by filtering out memory accesses to keys with different signatures.

The compact bucket structure of LFBCH is similar to that of libcuckoo, enabling it to support a load factor of up to 95%. Additionally, with the introduction of lock-free techniques, LFBCH offers significantly better scalability than libcuckoo, which employs a lock strip for synchronization. Next, we show how to drive lock-free operations based on the data structures.

### 3.2 Basic Operations

In this section, we consider three basic operations, i.e., Get, Put, and Delete. We focus on the use cases without the kicking and rehash processes and leave more details of the two processes in Sect. 4.

**Get.** Given two distinct hash functions, we can determine two target buckets based on the two hash values of a Get key. We refer to the two hash functions as the primary hash function and the secondary hash function, and the buckets they map to as the primary bucket and the secondary bucket, respectively. Searches always start from the primary bucket and traverse all eight slots across both buckets. It in turn considers each slot by triggering an atomic LOAD to obtain the entry thereon. If all of the eight comparisons have failed, a result of a miss will return. It is worth noting that an interleaving kicking process may issue false misses, as demonstrated in Fig. 2(b). We will detail the resolution in Algorithm 1.

**Put.** The semantic of the put operation is inserting when the key is missing and updating when the key is hit. We will discuss the two cases separately. For an update operation, only one slot returned from the search process is considered. Two update strategies are employed. For items whose value length is less than 8 bytes, an in-place update is performed by directly updating the value through a CAS operation in the value field of the item. For items with larger values, a Read-Copy-Update (RCU) operation is employed. A new item containing the new key-value pair is created, and then a CAS operation is used to replace the old item with the new item. For insertion, if the search process can find an empty slot, we can employ the *RCU*-based update to insert the new item. If no empty slot is found, the kick-out algorithm kicks out a key within the target buckets to make room for the insertion. After the kick-out algorithm finishes, an empty slot will appear within the target bucket, and we can perform insertion on the empty slot. After the insertion, the action to check and resolve the duplicated key starts. The details are described in Sect. 4.2. Note that if we find a kick mark on the entry of the target key during the search process. We need to call the helper function to help kick out and re-execute the PUT operation from the beginning. The details are covered in Sect. 4.1.

**Delete.** The Delete operation has similar logic to the Put. If the key is not found, a failure will be returned. Otherwise, we perform a CAS operation to replace the target slot with an empty entry atomically.

## 4 Detailed Algorithm Description

This section will detail the critical designs in lock-free bucketized cuckoo hashing, including lock-free kicking, preventing duplicated key, lock-free rehashing, and hotspot perception.

### 4.1 Lock-Free Kick on Bucketized Cuckoo Hashing

Our lock-free kicking algorithm has two primary components: path search and item movement along the kick path.

**Path Search.** Regarding path search, we have adopted the BFS algorithm employed by libcuckoo without locking. However, since other threads may modify the state of the hash table during the search process, the state of the hash table may be modified by other threads during the path search process. For example, the empty slot at the tail may be filled with a key after the search path is formed. Any inconsistencies between the actual state and the kick path are checked for in the following item movement along the kick path phase. If any discrepancies are found, the kicking-out process is restarted from the beginning to ensure correctness.

**Item Movement Along Kick Path.** Once a kick path is found, the items need to be moved along the kick path. Proceeding from the tail towards the head, the process moves one item at a time. The fundamental operations of the single-item movement process are similar to those performed by lfcuckoo and can be referred to in Fig. 2(a). We have added our method to prevent false misses and improve the handling of bucketized environments. The specific method is shown in Algorithm 1.

Meanings of the key variables adopted by the algorithm are as follows: The *table* represents the entire hash table. The *source_bucket* and *source_slot* represent the bucket and source slot indexes. We abbreviate the two variables as *sb* and *ss*. Similarly, *target_bucket* and *target_slot* are respectively abbreviated as *tb* and *ts*. The *source_entry* represents the value of the uint64_t variable maintained on the source slot. The *kick_marked_entry* is the kick-marked result of source_entry.

Two global arrays are defined (lines 1–2) with lengths equal to the number of global threads. Each thread is mapped to a specific position in the array according to its thread id. Padding is used to avoid false sharing issues. The functions of these global arrays are: *hash_record*. The working thread stores the hazard hash value of the key calculated by the primary hash function in the corresponding position of the hash record array at the beginning of every operation, for conflict detection performed by the kicking threads; *retry_flags*. Once the hazard hash value of another worker thread is found to conflict with the moving item, the retry_flag at the corresponding position of the reader will be set, indicating this worker thread might be affected by movement.

The item_move function (line 4) begins with two initial checks. The first "if" statement (line 6) checks if the source slot is empty. If it is empty, the item_move function can return success directly. The second "if" statement (line 8) checks if the source slot has been marked with a "kick mark" by other threads, indicating that another thread is concurrently accessing it for an item move operation. A helper function is then invoked to help the moving process and prevent blocking. The target slot information has been added to the kick_marked_entry (line 11) for a potential helper to obtain (line 18). Otherwise, other threads cannot determine which slot they should help kick into. The helper will get the target bucket information by calculating the two possible bucket locations of the intended key based on the item associated with the kick_marked_entry. The bucket that differs from the source bucket is identified as the target bucket.

**Algorithm 1.** Lock Free Single Item Movement

```
1: atomic < bool > retry_flags[thread_num]
2: atomic < uint64_t > hash_record[thread_num]
3:
4: function single_item_move(sb, ss, tb, ts)
5:     source_entry ← table[sb][ss].LOAD()
6:     if source_entry == empty_entry then
7:         return true
8:     if is_kick_marked(source_entry) then
9:         helper(sb, ss, source_entry)              ▷ source entry here is kick marked
10:        return false
11:    kick_marked_entry ← source_entry, ts
12:    if !table[sb][ss].CAS(source_entry, kick_marked_entry) then
13:        return false
14:    return copy(sb, ss, tb, ts, kick_marked_entry)
15:
16: function helper(sb, ss, kick_marked_entry)
17:    key, hash ← kick_marked_entry
18:    tb ← hash, sb; ts ← kick_marked_entry
19:    copy(sb, ss, tb, ts, kick_marked_entry)
20:
21: function copy(sb, ss, tb, ts, kick_marked_entry)
22:    if table[tb][ts].CAS(empty_entry, source_entry) then
23:        hash ← source_entry
24:        set_retry_if_hazard(hash)
25:        if table[sb][ss].CAS(kick_marked_entry, empty_entry) then
26:            return true
27:    if key_in(ss, sb) == key_in(ts, tb) then
28:        hash ← source_entry
29:        set_retry_if_hazard(hash)
30:        table[sb][ss].CAS(kick_marked_entry, empty_entry)
31:        return false
32:    table[sb][ss].CAS(kick_marked_entry, source_entry)
33:    return false
34:
35: function set_retry_if_hazard(hash)
36:    for i = 0 → thread_num − 1 do
37:        if hash_record[i].LOAD() == hash then     ▷ Check hazard value
38:            retry_flags[i].STORE(true)
39:
40: function search(key)
41:    hash_record[thread_id].STORE(hash)            ▷ Store hazard value
42:    while true do
43:        bool hit ← search_two_buckets(key)
44:        if hit then
45:            return key_hit
46:        else if retry_flags[thread_id].LOAD() then
47:            retry_flags[thread_id].STORE(false)
48:            continue
49:        else
50:            return key_miss
51:
```

In the copy function (line 21), a CAS operation is first used to update the target slot with the source entry (line 22). If the CAS operation succeeds, a CAS operation is then used to clear the source slot (line 25). If this clearing operation succeeds, the copy operation is considered successful and the function returns true.

Before clearing the source slot (line 25), the function set_retry_if_hazard is invoked to prevent other threads from returning false misses that may have been affected by the item movement process. This function (line 35) traverses the hash_record array to determine if the hash value of the key being moved conflicts with the hazard hash value of a key being operated on by another thread. If it is, the retry_flag of the corresponding thread is set, informing other threads that the search may have been affected by the item movement process and a false miss may have occurred. To avoid false misses, the search algorithm (line 40) begins by storing the hash value of the target key in the corresponding position of the hash_record array. If it gets a miss and the corresponding retry_flag is set, it indicates that the miss may be a false miss. In this case, the retry flag is cleared, and the search operation is performed again.

If either of the two CAS operations (line 22, line 25) fails, it indicates that the state of the hash table has been modified by another thread, and failure handling is required. Firstly, it is necessary to check whether the keys in the target and source positions are the same. If they are the same, it means that another thread has already completed the entry copying operation. In this case, the source slot needs to be cleared (lines 28–30), and the function returns false. If the keys are not the same, it means that either the target slot or the source slot has already been modified by another thread. In either case, the copy operation cannot succeed. At this point, a CAS operation is used to attempt to clear the kick-out mark in the source slot (line 32) and restore it to its state before the mark was set. The function then returns false.

### 4.2 Prevent Duplicated Key

Unlike the temporary duplicated keys that may arise during item movement, the presence of duplicated keys resulting from distinct threads inserting the same key into different empty slots can cause errors in the hash table. We conduct a post-checking step after each insertion to solve this problem.

The specific methodology is shown in Algorithm 2. The *check_duplicate_key* function is called after each successful insertion. The duplicated key check will pass only when the number of target keys in the obtained snapshot equals 1. Since in the vast majority of cases, post-checking only scans buckets that have already been scanned during the search phase and passes the check without introducing additional overhead, our post-checking mechanism is efficient.

### 4.3 Lock Free Rehash

When the load factor of the hash table is excessively high, rehash is necessary. Similar to that of libcuckoo, our rehash mechanism employs a lazy rehash strategy, whereby items are shallow-copied gradually from the old table to the newly created table. However, unlike libcuckoo, we use a global atomic bitmap to identify whether each bucket has been migrated. Moreover, for each item migration from the old table, we use a mechanism similar to the single item movement within a table, but with migrate marks instead of kick marks. Therefore, the guarantee of lock-free rehashing is ensured.

**Algorithm 2.** Post-checking Process for Duplicated Key

```
1: //b : bucket_index, s : slot_index
2:
3: function check_duplicate_key(key)
4:     Start :
5:     Initialize snapshot
6:     for each slot in two buckets do
7:         snapshot.append(⟨b, s, slot.LOAD()⟩)              ▷ 8 slots in total
8:     if retry_flag[thread_id].LOAD() then
9:         retry_flag[thread_id].STORE(false)
10:        goto Start
11:    count = 0
12:    for ⟨b, s, entry⟩ in snapshot do
13:        if is_kick_marked(entry) then
14:            helper(b, s, entry)
15:            goto Start
16:        key_extract ← entry
17:        if key equals key_extract then
18:            task ← b, s, entry
19:            count++
20:    if count ≤ 1 then
21:        return
22:    else
23:        table[task.b][task.s].CAS(entry, empty_entry)
24:        goto Start
```

### 4.4 Hot Key Perception and Adjustment

Although bucketized cuckoo hashing minimizes memory access and cache misses due to its compact slot layout, queries on keys in the secondary bucket result in one additional cache miss compared to the primary bucket. Additionally, due to skewed key distribution in practice, when a hotspot key is placed in the secondary bucket, accessing it incurs additional overhead. Therefore, we have optimized our implementation by placing hotspot keys as far forward as possible in the primary bucket to reduce the number of comparisons required for access.

The specific method of adjusting hotspots is to displace the first non-hotspot key located before the hotspot key in the search sequence and subsequently place itself in the vacated position. The process of displacing a key is the same as the kicking process, except that there is no cascading displacement. If the secondary bucket of a non-hotspot key is full, it is skipped. Hotspot keys are determined based on whether the slot has a "hot" mark, which is applied the first time the key is updated. Considering the scenarios with their hotspots frequently evolving, the "hot" marks on all the slots in the bucket will be cleared after each successful adjustment of a hotspot key. If all the keys before the search sequence of a hotspot key are hotspot keys, no adjustment is performed.

## 5 Experiments

In this section, we evaluate the performance of LFBCH using YCSB benchmarks. We compare the throughput and scalability of LFBCH with that of libcuckoo and the hash table faster [3] use. We also provide the results with the hotspot optimization.

**Environment.** We conducted experiments on a machine comprising two AMD EPYC 7742 64-Core Processors with 1.50 GHz processors. Each processor has two sockets, each with 64 cores. The RAM capacity is 1024 GB. It runs Ubuntu 16.04.7 LTS OS with Linux 4.4 kernel. Only 64 cores in one socket were utilized, and each thread was bound to a specific core. Jemalloc library is used to allocate memory. All code is compiled using gcc/g++−7.5.0 with parameter −O2. Memory reclamation is not carried out to eliminate the influence of different memory reclamation algorithms on the hash table throughput.

**Table 1.** Load factor within different slot number

| Slot Per Bucket | 1 | 2 | 4 | 8 |
|---|---|---|---|---|
| Load Factor | 50% | 87% | 95% | 95% |

**BaseLine and Workloads.** We employed libcuckoo and the hash table faster uses in contrast to LFBCH. As shown in Table 1, since each bucket in lfcuckoo

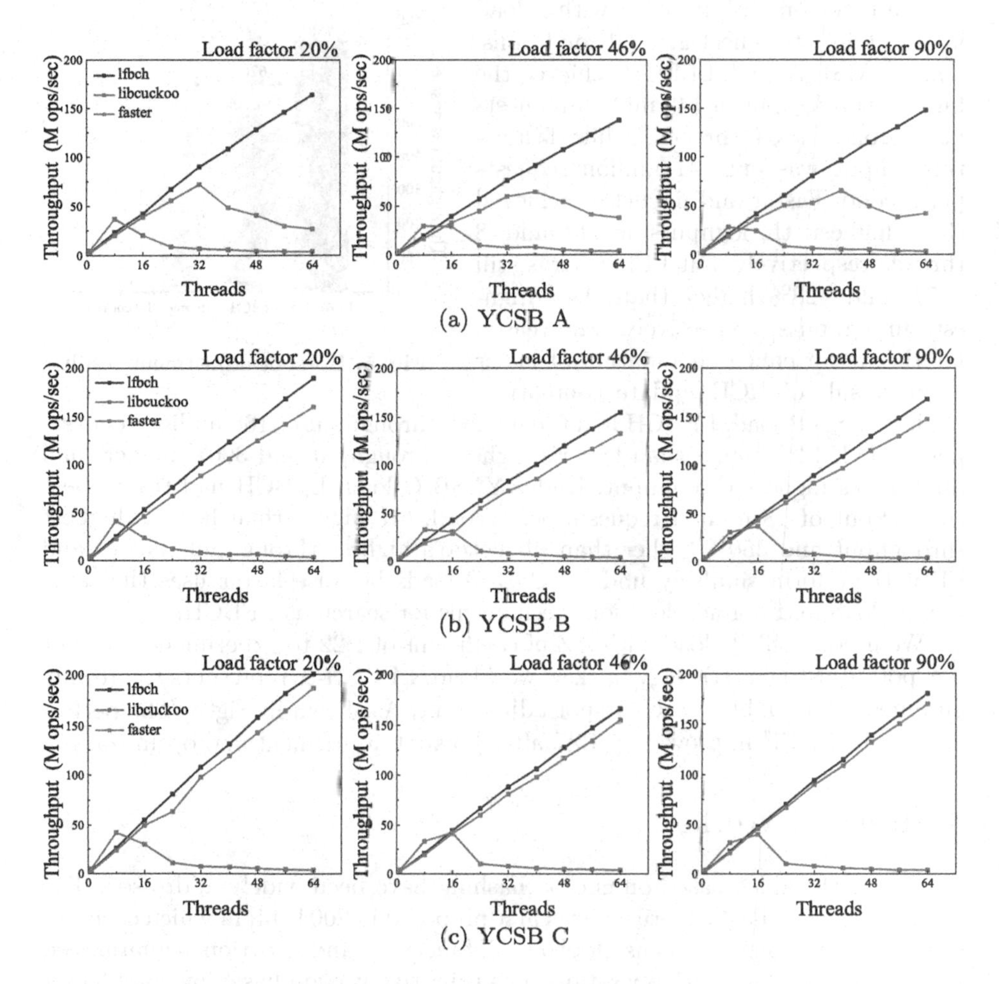


**Fig. 4.** The throughput under different load factors and different YCSB loads varies with the worker threads.

only has a single slot, the load factor cannot exceed 50%, making it impractical and thus not included in the comparison experiments. In each test, the number of buckets for Libcuckoo and LFBCH was set at $2^{27}$. Because of the batch chain structure of the faster hash table, it has half as many buckets. We conduct experiments using the YCSB core workloads A, B, and C [6]. The Zipfian distribution parameter in YCSB is set to 0.99. For each item, we set both the key size and the value size to be 8 bytes.

**Results.** The throughput test result is shown in Fig. 4. We observed that the throughput of libcuckoo decreases when the number of threads exceeds 16 in all cases. At 64 threads, the throughput is less than five million requests per second. In contrast, the throughput of LFBCH increases linearly for all thread counts. When the load type is the same, the performance of each hash table is better when the load factor is low, compared to when the load factor is high.

We focus on the situation with a load factor of 46% to reflect general conditions. Under YCSB A load, LFBCH achieved the highest throughput of 148 million requests per second at 64 threads, while faster's throughput was only 41 million requests per second. Faster and libcuckoo achieved their highest throughputs at 40 and 8 threads respectively, but LFBCH was still 127% and 428% higher than their highest throughputs, respectively. The reason for the performance degradation of faster is the result of RCU update contention.

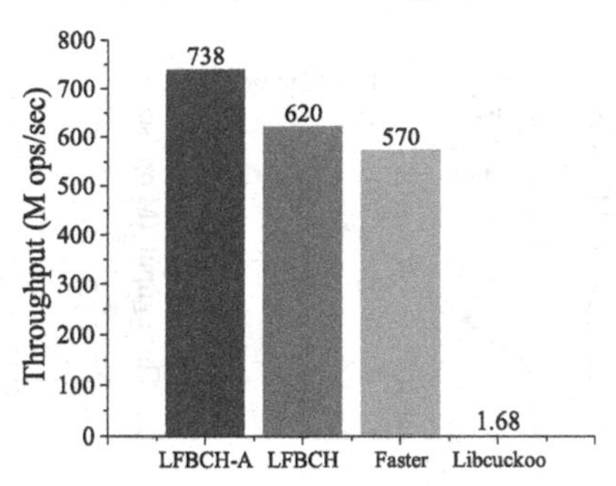


**Fig. 5.** Hotspot adjustment result

Under YCSB B load, LFBCH had the highest throughput of 168 million requests per second, 14% higher than faster's highest throughput and 360% higher than libcuckoo's highest throughput. Under YCSB C load, LFBCH had the highest throughput of 18 million requests per second, 6% higher than faster's highest throughput and 350% higher than libcuckoo's highest throughput. Faster and LFBCH perform similarly under YCSB C loads because faster uses the same atomic load and tag acceleration mechanisms for search as LFBCH.

We used YCSB C load with a Zipf coefficient of 1.22 to experiment with our hotspot adjustment strategy in skew workload. LFBCH-A represents the results obtained after enabling the hotspot adjustment. As shown in Fig. 5, The performance of LFBCH improved by 19% after hotspot adjustment and optimization.

## 6 Related Works

Various hash tables based on cuckoo hashing have been widely addressed. The primitive cuckoo hash algorithm was first proposed in 2004 [14] in which each key is mapped to two positions using two hash functions, and insertion is guaranteed by the use of a "kick out" operation. The primitive version has a low load factor and no concurrency scheme.

Memc3 [8] allows multiple readers and a single writer concurrently access the bucketized cuckoo hashing. Xiaozhou Li's work [10] introduced HTM into bucketized cuckoo hashing. It has inherent limitations of HTM, which can lead to significant performance degradation when transactions fail frequently. As a widely used cuckoo-based hash table, libcuckoo [11] employs a bucketized structure and utilizes fine-grained locks to control concurrent access. However, the performance degradation caused by the competition when the number of threads increases cannot be avoided. Lfcuckoo [13] made a Lock-free improvement to the primitive cuckoo hashing, but it has not been extended to bucketized cuckoo hashing, leading to low space utilization efficiency. Level hash [5] has also employed a lock-free technique in bucketized cuckoo hashing, but it is designed for the scenario of persistent memory.

The work of hotspot adjustment for our hash table is inspired by hotring [4]. It speeds up the performance of the chained hash table in the case of data skew by pointing the linked list header pointer to the hotspot key.

## 7 Conclusion

We introduced lock-free techniques into bucketized cuckoo hashing and proposed LFBCH, which paves the way toward scalability and high space efficiency. All of the operations over LFBCH are guaranteed to be lock-free, without introducing notorious problems like false miss and duplicated key. Lock-free rehash and hotspot adjustment are also implemented in LFBCH. The throughput of LFBCH is 14%–360% higher than other popular concurrent hash tables.

Accessing the same shared data structure introduces additional latency when the working threads are distributed across CPU sockets. In the future, optimizations can be made to improve the performance of LFBCH in scenarios where it is distributed across CPU sockets.

**Acknowledgment and Data Availability Statement.** This work was sponsored by the National Science Foundation, grant 61572373. Besides the reviewers, we would like to thank High Performance Computing Center at the Computer School of Wuhan University. The Code is available in the Figshare repository: https://doi.org/10.6084/m9.figshare.23550111 [17]

## References

1. Armbrust, M., et al.: A view of cloud computing. Commun. ACM **53**(4), 50–58 (2010)
2. Barnes, G.: A method for implementing lock-free shared-data structures. In: Proceedings of the Fifth Annual ACM Symposium on Parallel Algorithms and Architectures, pp. 261–270 (1993)
3. Chandramouli, B., Prasaad, G., Kossmann, D., Levandoski, J., Hunter, J., Barnett, M.: Faster: a concurrent key-value store with in-place updates. In: Proceedings of the 2018 International Conference on Management of Data, pp. 275–290 (2018)

4. Chen, J., et al.: Hotring: a hotspot-aware in-memory key-value store. In: FAST, pp. 239–252 (2020)
5. Chen, Z., Hua, Y., Ding, B., Zuo, P.: Lock-free concurrent level hashing for persistent memory. In: Proceedings of the 2020 USENIX Conference on USENIX Annual Technical Conference, pp. 799–812 (2020)
6. Cooper, B.F., Silberstein, A., Tam, E., Ramakrishnan, R., Sears, R.: Benchmarking cloud serving systems with YCSB. In: Proceedings of the 1st ACM Symposium on Cloud Computing, pp. 143–154 (2010)
7. DeWitt, D.J., Katz, R.H., Olken, F., Shapiro, L.D., Stonebraker, M.R., Wood, D.A.: Implementation techniques for main memory database systems. In: Proceedings of the 1984 ACM SIGMOD International Conference on Management of Data, pp. 1–8 (1984)
8. Fan, B., Andersen, D.G., Kaminsky, M.: MemC3: compact and concurrent MemCache with dumber caching and smarter hashing. In: Presented as part of the 10th {USENIX} Symposium on Networked Systems Design and Implementation ({NSDI} 13), pp. 371–384 (2013)
9. Garcia-Molina, H., Salem, K.: Main memory database systems: an overview. IEEE Trans. Knowl. Data Eng. **4**(6), 509–516 (1992)
10. Li, X., Andersen, D.G., Kaminsky, M., Freedman, M.J.: Algorithmic improvements for fast concurrent cuckoo hashing. In: Proceedings of the Ninth European Conference on Computer Systems, pp. 1–14 (2014)
11. M, K.: libcuckoo. https://github.com/efficient/libcuckoo
12. Michael, M.M.: Hazard pointers: safe memory reclamation for lock-free objects. IEEE Trans. Parallel Distrib. Syst. **15**(6), 491–504 (2004)
13. Nguyen, N., Tsigas, P.: Lock-free cuckoo hashing. In: 2014 IEEE 34th International Conference on Distributed Computing Systems, pp. 627–636. IEEE (2014)
14. Pagh, R., Rodler, F.F.: Cuckoo hashing. J. Algorithms **51**(2), 122–144 (2004)
15. Ghemawat, S., Dean, D.: levelDB. https://github.com/google/leveldb
16. Shalf, J.: The future of computing beyond Moore's law. Phil. Trans. R. Soc. A **378**(2166), 20190061 (2020)
17. Li, W., Cheng, Z., Chen, Y., Li, A., Deng, L.: Artifact and instructions to generate experimental results for euro-par 23 paper: Lock-free bucketized cuckoo hashing (2023). https://doi.org/10.6084/m9.figshare.23550111
18. Wu, S., Li, F., Mehrotra, S., Ooi, B.C.: Query optimization for massively parallel data processing. In: Proceedings of the 2nd ACM Symposium on Cloud Computing, pp. 1–13 (2011)

# BitHist: A Precision-Scalable Sparse-Awareness DNN Accelerator Based on Bit Slices Products Histogram

Zhaoteng Meng[1,2], Long Xiao[1,2], Xiaoyao Gao[1,2], Zhan Li[1,2], Lin Shu[1,3], and Jie Hao[1,3](✉)

[1] Institute of Automation, Chinese Academy of Sciences, Beijing, China
mengzhaoteng2019@ia.ac.cn
[2] School of Artificial Intelligence, University of Chinese Academy of Sciences, Beijing, China
[3] Guangdong Institute of Artificial Intelligence and Advanced Computing, Guangzhou, China
jie.hao@ia.ac.cn

**Abstract.** Memory and power-sensitive edge devices benefit from quantized models based on precision-scalable CNN accelerators. These accelerators can process CNN models that with different data precisions, which rely on the precision scalable multiply-accumulate (MAC) unit. Among all types of MAC units, the spatial precision scalable MAC (SPM) unit is an attractive one as it is flexible and can convert the decrease in data width into an increase in throughput. However, it becomes energy-inefficient due to the need for more shifters and high-width adders as the bit width of the operand increases. Taking advantage of the limited number of unique products of 2-bit unsigned multiplication in the existing SPM, this paper proposes a new MAC method based on the unique product histogram, which is orthogonal to the existing methods. Based on the proposed MAC method, this paper also proposes the *BitHist*, an efficient DNN accelerator that exploits both bit-level and data-level sparsity. The evaluation results illustrate that BitHist saves 57% of the area compared to the BitFusion and provides up to 4.60× throughput per area and 17.4× energy efficiency. Additionally, BitHist can achieve a 2.28× performance gain from sparsity exploitation.

**Keywords:** CNN accelerator · precision-scalable · multiply-accumulation · sparse exploration

## 1 Introduction

Convolutional Neural Network (CNN) based models have achieved gratifying performance in computer vision [23], autonomous decision making [15], and nat-

Supported by the National Science and Technology Major Project from Minister of Science and Technology, China (Grant No. 2018AAA0103100), National Natural Science Foundation of China under Grant 62236007, and Guangzhou Basic Research Program under Grant 202201011389.


J. Cano et al. (Eds.): Euro-Par 2023, LNCS 14100, pp. 289–303, 2023.
https://doi.org/10.1007/978-3-031-39698-4_20

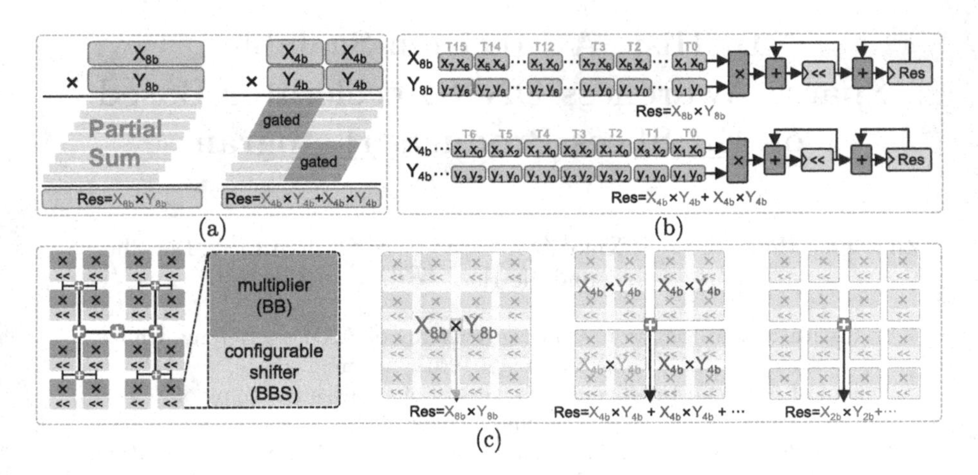


**Fig. 1.** Three types of precision-scalable MAC. (a) Traditional method. (b) TPM method. (c) SPM method.

ural language processing [7]. However, due to the vast parameters and intensive computing, the deployment of these models on edge devices is permanently restricted by limited storage capacity and computing resources. Common compression techniques, including low-rank compression [8], knowledge distillation [5], pruning, and quantization [6] are employed to reduce the computational and storage load on edge devices.

Quantization can reduce off-chip data access and power consumption by reducing the weight or activation to 16bit or even 1bit without significantly reducing the accuracy of the model [3,14,16,20,25]. There have been already many CNN accelerators that can support quantized network deployment [1,2, 11,24]. Still, they generally only support one quantized data precision, which cannot fully benefit from quantized models. Other work aims to fully exploit the potential of quantization techniques to improve performance since the data bit width of CNNs is variable among layers [17] or groups [4]. These multi-precision accelerators [9,13,18] are compatible with the computation of multiple data bit widths in CNN models.

The primary calculation mode of CNN is multiply-accumulate (MAC) calculation, so the accelerator's ability to calculate the mixed-precision model comes from the precision-scalable MAC unit. Figure 1 shows three designs of precision-scalable MAC units. One traditional precision-scalable MAC [19] is designed to compute multiplications of low-bit-width data by gating the computational unit. But it is wasteful regarding throughput per area since it leaves many idle gates. Another type is temporal precision-scalable MACs (TPM) such as Bit-Serial [12]. It produces and temporally accumulates several partial products for a multiplier. However, the processing time of TPM increases quadratically with bit width in the case of symmetric precision.

Some other types of attractive design are spatial precision-scalable MACs (SPM) such as BitFusion [22]. The subunits array in a high-bit-width MAC can be recombined as several multipliers with reduced precision. SPM can translate reductions in data precision into improvements in throughput and energy efficiency while maintaining high hardware utilization. Even with the above exciting benefits of SPM, the additional adder and shift logic will incur significant area overhead as scale increases to support the parallel additions of partial products into a single final product.

To overcome the shortcomings of the above MAC architectures, this paper proposed a new precision-scalable MAC method orthogonal to existing work. Based on the new MAC method, we propose an energy-efficient precision-scalable DNN accelerator called *BitHist*. We highlight our contributions as follows:

- This paper proposes a method for bit-width scalable MAC based on histogram by taking advantage of the finite unique products (UPs) of the 2-bit unsigned multiplication in the SPM method. It avoids many redundant 2-bit multiplications in the SPM method and saves half of the area.
- The proposed method simultaneously exploits bit-level and data-level sparsity. The encoding we adopt avoids potential slice products with value 0. We employ flag distillation to address the flag sparsity introduced in the proposed method, which further improves the throughput per area of the MAC unit and makes it sensitive to data-level sparsity.
- Based on the above method, we construct *BitHist*, an area-efficient precision-scalable DNN accelerator. The evaluation results show that it is 4.60× area and 17.4× energy efficient than the existing work without exploiting sparsity. With exploiting sparsity, BitHist can achieve a 2.28× performance gain.

The rest of this paper is organized as follows. Section 2 reviews BitFusion and its redundant computations. Section 3 describes our method based on the histogram of UPs. Section 4 explains the architecture based on the method mentioned in Sect. 3. Section 5 illustrates the performance of our architecture. Finally, Sect. 6 gives the conclusion.

## 2 Motivation

### 2.1 Bit-Level Fusion and Decomposition

As a typical architecture of the SPM method, BitFusion can provide precision flexibility by splitting the operands into bit slices. More specifically, when a MAC operation involving $L$ pair multiplications is performed spatially, the p-bit $x$ and q-bit $y$ are split into 2-bit slices as shown in Fig. 2(a). M × N signed multiplications of slice pairs are calculated. The partial sums of the result are obtained by multiplying the product of signed multiplication with a shift factor $\alpha_{m,n}$. The computing paradigm of 2-bit-based SPM can be described by (1) and (2), where $slc.x_{[m]}$ is the (m+1)th 2-bit segment of $x$.

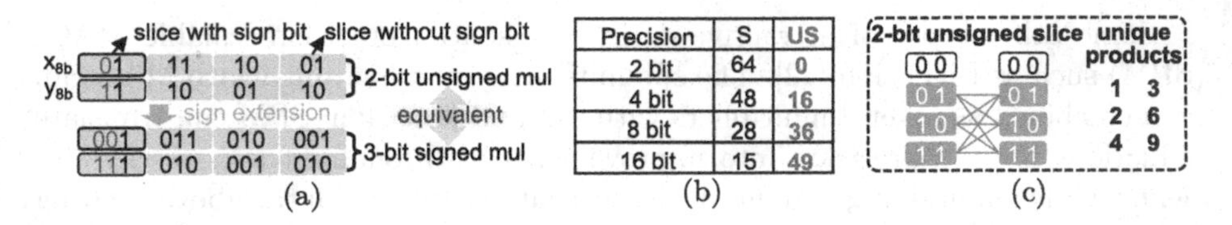


| Precision | S | US |
|---|---|---|
| 2 bit | 64 | 0 |
| 4 bit | 48 | 16 |
| 8 bit | 28 | 36 |
| 16 bit | 15 | 49 |

**Fig. 2.** The redundant computations in slice-level multiplications. (a) The operands segmentation and sign extension in BitFusion. (b) The number of operations that can be reduced to unsigned multiplication at different data precisions, S means signed multiplication, and US means unsigned multiplication. (c) All combinations of 2-bit unsigned multiplication.

$$\mathrm{SUM} = \sum_{l=0}^{L-1} x_{pb,l} \cdot y_{qb,l} = \sum_{l=0}^{L-1} \sum_{m=0}^{M-1} \sum_{n=0}^{N-1} slc.x_{[m]} \cdot slc.y_{[n]} \cdot \alpha_{m,n,l} \tag{1}$$

with

$$M = p/2, \quad N = q/2, \quad \alpha_{m,n} = 2^{2(m+n)} \tag{2}$$

### 2.2 The Redundant Computation in Bit-Level Computation

The multiplications between slice pairs are performed in the array shown in Fig. 1(c). The basic unit consists of a multiplier called BitBrick (BB) and a configurable shifter named BitBrick Shifter (BBS). All slices are extended to a 3-bit signed number according to their positions and source operands signs. The slices without sign bit will be extended with sign bit 0, and the slices with sign bit will be extended with the sign bit of the source operand. A basic observation is that multiplications between 3-bit signed numbers whose sign bit is 0 are equivalent to multiplications between 2-bit unsigned numbers. Figure 2(b) lists the number of equivalent 2-bit unsigned multiplications when performing different precision MAC operations in an array with 64 basic units. The number of equivalent unsigned operations increases as the bit width of the operand becomes larger. Figure 2(c) shows the combinations of 2-bit number multiplications. There are only nine valid combinations and six UPs of 2-bit unsigned multiplication, which means that many calculations in the BBs are repeated. Such redundancy increases with the improvement of data precision. The case is further exacerbated when the sign of the operand is 0. This inspires us to reduce the area overhead of the SPM method and to improve energy efficiency by exploiting the redundancy.

## 3 MAC Based on Bit-Slices Products Histogram

This section describes the proposed histogram-based MAC method. It has been mentioned that if the operands of a signed multiplication are positive, all of the slice multiplications are equivalent to 2-bit unsigned multiplications. This is still

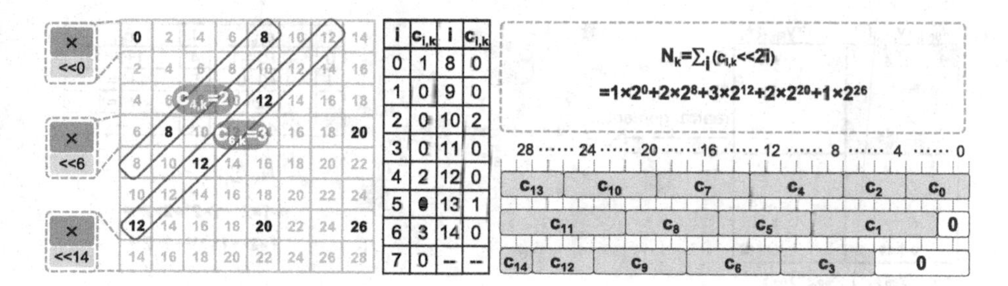


**Fig. 3.** Calculation of $N_k$.

the case when both operands are negative. However, in a general MAC, not every product is positive, which determines that the multiplication between bit slices in Eq. (1) must be a signed operation. To unify all multiplications of bit slices into unsigned multiplications, we use Eq. (3) to calculate the MAC of the absolute values of the original operands and absorb the signs of the $slc.x_{[m]} \cdot slc.y_{[n]}$ into the shift coefficients $\alpha_{m,n,l}$.

$$\text{SUM} = \sum_{l=0}^{L-1} |x|_{pb,l} \cdot |y|_{qb,l} = \sum_{l=0}^{L-1} \sum_{m=0}^{M-1} \sum_{n=0}^{N-1} slc.|x|_{[m]} \cdot slc.|y|_{[n]} \cdot \alpha'_{m,n,l} \tag{3}$$

with

$$\alpha'_{m,n,l} = \begin{cases} \alpha_{m,n,l} & , x_l \cdot y_l > 0 \\ -\alpha_{m,n,l} & , x_l \cdot y_l < 0 \end{cases} \tag{4}$$

As $|x|$ and $|y|$ are positive, $\text{slc.}|\text{x}|_{[\text{m}]} \cdot \text{slc.}|\text{y}|_{\text{m}}$ can be calculated as an unsigned multiplication. As Fig. 1(c) shows, there are six UPs in the multiplication of 2-bit unsigned segments, so we can further express (3) as

$$\text{SUM} = \sum_{k=1,2,3,4,6,9} \sum_{\alpha' \in A} \alpha'_{m,n,l} \cdot k = \sum_{k=1,2,3,4,6,9} N_k \cdot k \tag{5}$$

Equation (5) provides a new method of MAC unit design. It shows that we can convert the calculation of MAC result into solving the coefficients of UPs, that is, building a histogram for UPs. We present an example in Fig. 3 to illustrate how to calculate the coefficient $N_k$ of the unique product $k$ in a 16-bit fixed-point multiplication. The left side of Fig. 3 is a simplified BitFusion array that performs $x_{16b} \times y_{16b}$. The black number indicates that the unique product $k$ appears at this position. We use $c_{i,k}$ to represent the total number of occurrences of $k$ in the area that needs to be shifted left by 2i bits. If $x_{16b} \times y_{16b}$ is a positive number, one occurrence is recorded as +1; otherwise, it is recorded as −1. Then $N_k$ can be obtained by $N_k = \sum_{i=0}^{14}(c_{i,k} \times 2^{2i})$. It is worth mentioning that $N_k$ can be obtained by shifting and splicing $c_{i,k}$ without multiplication and too many additions.

The compatibility to 8-bit MAC is shown in Fig. 4. It shows the calculation of $N_k$ when $\sum_{l=0}^{3} x_{8b,l} \times y_{8b,l}$ is performed. With 8-bit precision, the bit slice product will be shifted to the left by fewer bits, but more products will be shifted

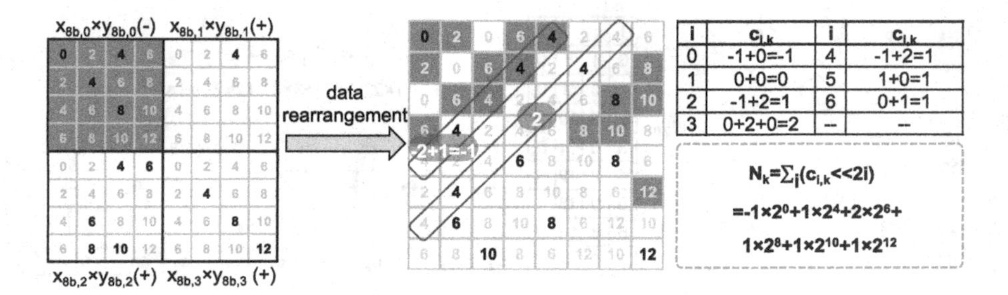


**Fig. 4.** Precision compatible method. The architecture corresponding to the calculation process shown in Fig. 3 is reused through data rearrangement. The gray background in the figure indicates that the product of the operands is negative.

by the same number of bits. For instance, there are three bit slice products that will be shifted by 4 bits in the 16-bit case, but there are twelve products in the 8-bit case that will be shifted by 4 bits. As a result, the architecture used to compute $c_{2,k,16b}$ cannot be used directly to compute $c_{2,k,8b}$. This problem can be solved by rearranging the bit slice pairs. In this way, the calculation of $c_{2,k,8b}$ is divided into two parts, which uses the calculation architecture of $c_{4,k,16b}$ and $c_{6,k,16b}$. The MACs of other precisions are processed in the same way, including the calculation of asymmetric quantized data.

It is worth mentioning that the precision-scalable MAC method we proposed is transparent to software stacks and programmers. It can be easily compatible with the existing precision-scalable accelerators.

## 4 BitHist Accelerator

Based on the above MAC method, we proposed a precision-scalable sparse-awareness DNN accelerator called BitHist. A single MAC's architecture and data flow is described in Sect. 4.1. Then Sect. 4.2 introduces the design of BitHist, including data tiling, overall architecture, and sparsity exploration.

### 4.1 MAC Unit Based on Bitslices Products Histogram

The architecture of a single MAC that can calculate $x_{16b} \times y_{16b}$, $\sum_{l=0}^{3} x_{8b,l} \times y_{8b,l}$, $\sum_{l=0}^{15} x_{4b,l} \times y_{4b,l}$, and $\sum_{l=0}^{127} x_{2b,l} \times y_{2b,l}$ is shown in Fig. 5(a). The Preprocess and Reshape Unit (PRU) converts all operands to positive numbers and splits the positive numbers into 2-bit slices. In Unique Product Encoder (UPE), the 64 pairs of reshaped bit slices from PRU are encoded as six 64-bit vectors, each giving the distribution of six unique products among these segment pairs. Each vector is processed in a branch to generate the partial sum $N_k \cdot k$. The branch consists of two units, Histogram Generator (HG) and PSUM Generator (PG). HG calculates the coefficients $c_{i,k}$ according to the vectors and generates $N_k$ by concatenating the coefficients $c_{i,k}$. Next, the PSUMs of each unique product

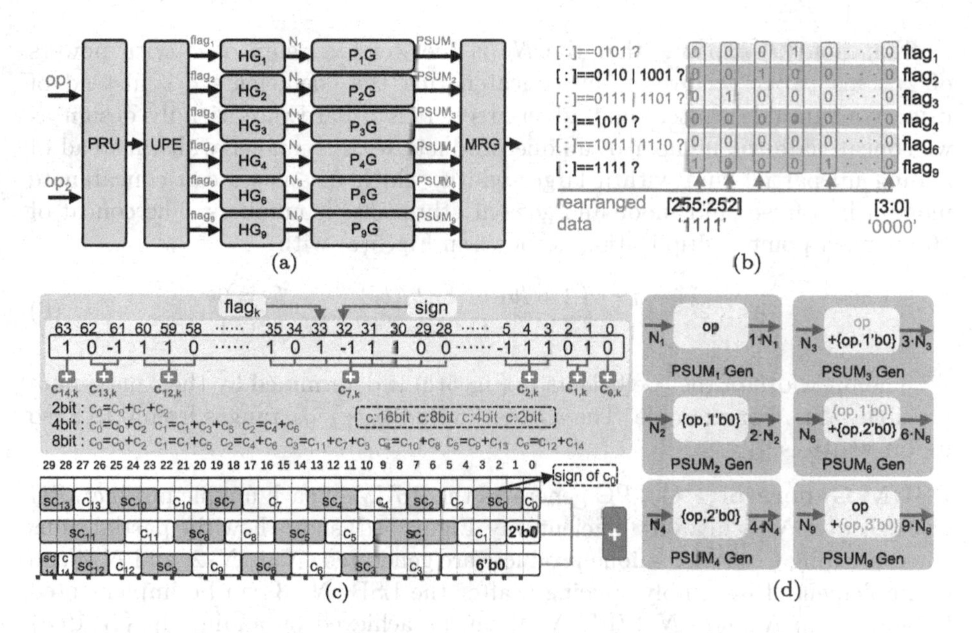


**Fig. 5.** (a) The overall architecture of BitHist. (b) Unique Product Encoder(UPE). (c) Histogram Generator(HG). (d) PSUM Generator(PSUM Gen).

can be computed in PG in a hardware-friendly way. The MAC Result Generator(MRG) is a six-input binary tree adder that produces the final results.

**Preprocess and Reshape Unit(PRU).** The absolute values of operands are split into 2-bit slices, and the slice pairs are rearranged in a pre-defined order in the PRU. A sign bit of each multiplication result in a MAC is obtained from original operands with XOR gates. The sign bits are reordered the same way as the slice pairs are.

**Unique Product Encoder(UPE).** UPE generates a 6-bit one-hot vector for each 4-bit slice pair to indicate which of the six unique products the product of this slice pair is. As Fig. 5(b) shows, sixty-four 6-bit one-hot vectors generate six 64-bit flags for each unique product, each of which gives the positions where the unique product appears. Based on the flags, we can get the number of occurrences of each unique product. It is worth mentioning that each one-hot code generation only uses a few gates instead of a 2-bit unsigned multiplier, and the overhead of this unit can be amortized due to the data reuse in DNN.

**Histogram Generator(HG).** As Fig. 5(c) shows, HG receives the $flag_k$ from UPE and signs from PRU to generate coefficients $c_{i,k}$. Due to the rearrangement of all pairs, we can get $c_{i,k}$ by adding the bits in a certain segment of $flag_k$. For example, $c_{1,k,16b}$ can be calculated by adding up the bit of $flag_k[2:1]$ , and $c_{13,k,16b}$ can be computed from $flag_k[60:58]$. The bits in the flag are signed ($+1$ or $-1$), and the sign depends on the original operands' product at that position.

Equation (9) explains that the $N_k$ is the weighted sum of $c_i$ with powers of 2. This paper achieves it by concatenating the coefficients $c_{i,k}$ instead of using configurable shifters and adder trees. It is a hardware-friendly design as we concatenate the number of unique products with a smaller width instead of adding up partial sum with a larger width, which means we can concatenate more $c_i$ in a fixed shift mode and get only three 30-bit numbers. The concat of 16-bit fixed-point multiplication is shown in Fig. 5(c) with

$$A^6 \times 2^5 + B^6 = \begin{cases} \{A^6, b_4, b_3, b_2, b_1, b_0\} & , b_5 = 0 \\ \{(A^6 - 1), b_4, b_3, b_2, b_1, b_0\}, & b_5 = 1 \end{cases} \tag{6}$$

The bit width of the coefficients in Fig. 5(c) is determined by their maximum possible value. For example, The absolute value of $c_{7,k,16b}$ ranges from 0 to 8, so its bit width is 4.

**PSUM Generator(PG).** PG generates the PSUM of each unique product. PG also executes $N_k \cdot k$ in a very efficient way. Figure 5(d) shows how the partial sums corresponding to the six unique products are generated. $N \cdot 1$, $N \cdot 2$, and $N \cdot 4$ can be implemented by simply splicing 0 after the LSB. $N \cdot 3$ can be implemented by adding up $N$ and $\{N, 1'b0\}$, $N \cdot 6$ can be achieved by adding up $\{N, 1'b0\}$ and $\{N, 2'b0\}$, and $N \cdot 9$ can be achieved by adding up $N$ and $\{N, 3'b0\}$.

The architecture is able to achieve the high throughput of 2-bit precision MAC. The value range of a 2-bit signed number is -2, -1, 0, and 1. It only has three unique products (i.e., 1, 2, and 4) when the precision of operands is 2bit. $N \cdot 3$, $N \cdot 6$ and $N \cdot 9$ can be reconfigured as $\{N, 1'b0\}$, $\{N, 2'b0\}$, and $N$, so the six branches can calculate two MACs in 2-bit case.

**Vector Implementation.** As shown in Fig. 5(c), the sign bit in the splicing mode is greater than 1 bit when calculating the multiplication of 16-bit fixed-point numbers. It means that the value of coefficient $c_i$ can be further expanded, and the splicing result is still correct. We can increase the bit width of $flag_k$ up to 256bit to calculate $\sum_{l=0}^{3} x_{16b,l} \times y_{16b,l}$, $\sum_{l=0}^{15} x_{8b,l} \times y_{8b,l}$, $\sum_{l=0}^{63} x_{4b,l} \times y_{4b,l}$, and $\sum_{l=0}^{511} x_{2b,l} \times y_{2b,l}$.

### 4.2 Dataflow and Architecture of BitHist

**Mapping to Matrix Multiplication for Convolution Layers.** BitHist adopts NVDLA-like [10] dataflow. The input activation and kernels are divided into several data cubes, and the channel of each data cube is $c$ byte. BitHist calculates the channels of the output activation in parallel. As what Fig. 6(b) shows, matrix multiplication between data cubes $W_0^i (i = 1, 2, ..., k)$ and $A_0$ are performed in parallel. Then, $W_0^i$ will be reused until all matrix multiplications related to $W_0^i$ during convolution have been performed ($A_0, A_1, ..., A_s$ in block0, see Fig. 6(a)). After that, $W_1^i (i = 1, 2..., k)$ is loaded, and $A_1, A_2, ..., A_p$ in block1 will be calculated with them in serial. The activation data cube is updated in the order of 1,2,3 in the circle which is shown in Fig. 6(a). The activation data cube is reused in different blocks, and the weight data cube is reused within a block.

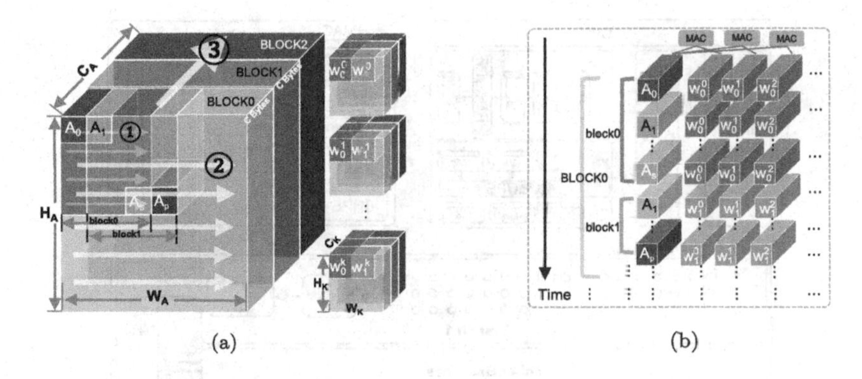


**Fig. 6.** Mapping to matrix multiplication for convolution layer.

**Architecture of BitHist.** The overall architecture of BitHist is shown in Fig. 7. Activation and weight data are loaded from off-chip DRAM via DMA and sent to the activation buffer (blue) and weight buffer (green). PRU and UPE serially process the data in each buffer and generate the flags of rearranged bit slices.

The PE groups in BitHist calculate 16 output activation channels in parallel, and each PE group computes activations in an output channel plane. There are four sparsity-sensitive BHPEs in a PE group, and each BHPE consists of three MAC units.

The unique product flags are generated in two steps. In step 1, the rearranged bit slices' flags of activation and weight are generated separately. In step 2, the unique product flags are generated in the PE groups by bitwise AND of the operands' flags. For example, the rearranged flag of activation slices is $flag_{at01} =$ 0011, and the rearranged flag of weight slices is $flag_{wt11} = 1010$. We can get the flag of unique product 3 which is 0010 by $flag_{UP0011} = flag_{at01} \& flag_{wt11}$, which indicates that the product of the second slice pair among the rearranged pairs is 3.

**Sparsity Exploitation in BHPE.** As shown in Fig. 5(b), the flag vector obtained by UPE is sparse. Two factors cause this sparseness. First, when UPE encodes the reordered slices, the combination with a product of 0 is naturally encoded as 0. Second, the encoding vector generated by UPE for each pair is one-hot, which makes it impossible for two 1 to appear in the same position of the six flag vectors. This inherent property of the flag vector allows us to explore sparsity to improve performance further. We take the distillation operation to process the same flag vector (such as $flag_1$) of different MAC units. As Fig. 7 shows, there are three $flag_1$ vectors ($flag_1^1$, $flag_1^2$, and $flag_1^3$) from three MAC units in a BHPE, which represents the occurrence of the unique product 1 in each MAC. It will take three cycles to generate coefficients for these vectors sequentially without additional processing. Now, if we perform the distillation operation on the vectors, that is, distilling all flag bit 1 into the upper position, there will be a chance to shorten the execution time to two cycles or one cycle. This mechanism effectively reduces the invalid calculation caused by sparse flags.

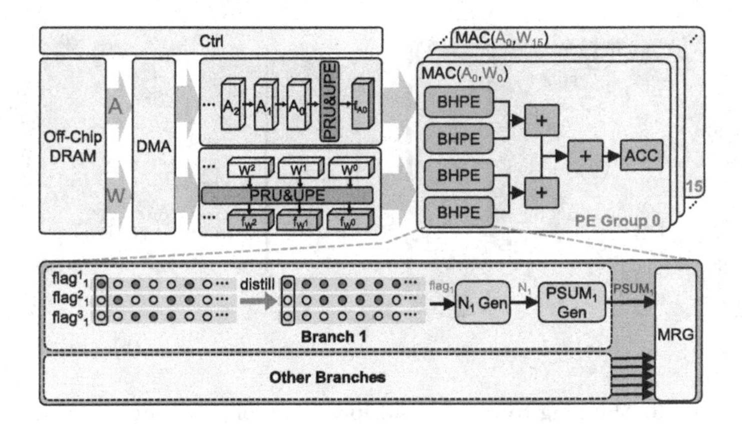


**Fig. 7.** The overall architecture of BitHist.

It can also take advantage of data-level sparsity as the flags encoded from value zero have only bit 0. When the flag bits in the six branches of the three mac are all calculated, BHPE requests new data from the operands buffer.

# 5 Evaluation

## 5.1 Experiment Methodology

We implement the BitFusion [22] with 64 basic units as our baseline, and we also implement two state-of-the-art precision-scalable CNN accelerators, Subword Parallel [19]and Loom [21], which are shown in Fig. 1(a) and Fig. 1(b). All the above architectures are designed to support up to 16-bit precision data calculation. We implement them using Verilog RTL. We use Synopsys Design Compiler for synthesis and PrimeTime PX for the power evaluation. The technology node is SMIC 28 nm, and the frequency is 200 MHz. Furthermore, we perform inference on LeNet, ResNet18, and VGG16 using a custom cycle-accurate simulators with the MNIST dataset. The proposed method and architecture do not affect the accuracy of calculation, so the choice of models and datasets does not affect the metrics at the architecture level. The metrics are obtained by averaging the metrics of the three networks.

We first report the metrics of a single BitHist MAC unit and compare it with BitFusion to demonstrate the effectiveness of our method in removing the redundant 2-bit multiplications. Then we tested the throughput and energy efficiency of the four architectures on the selected benchmark. In each precision case, the activation and weight are quantized to 2bit, 4bit, 8bit, and 16bit, respectively. Since none of the three comparison works has exploitation of sparsity, we use the non-sparse version of BitHist (BH-NS) for the above comparison. Finally, we show the performance gain of BitHist with the sparsity exploitation.

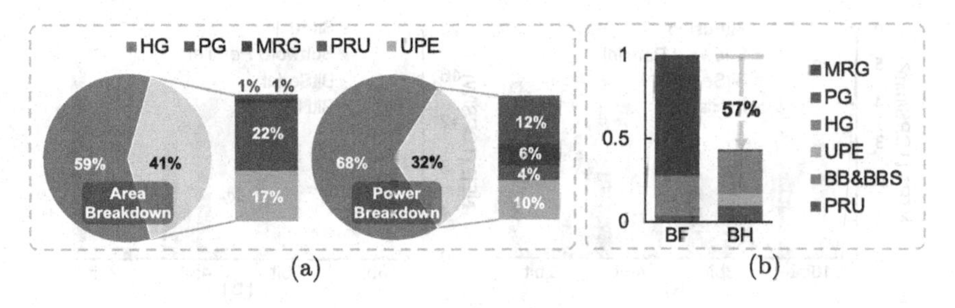


**Fig. 8.** Area and power of BH-NS. (a) Area and power breakdown. (b) Area overhead compared with BitFusion. All values in the figure are matrics of a single MAC rather than vector MACs.

## 5.2 Area and Power at MAC Unit Level

Figure8(a) shows the area and power breakdown of a BitHist MAC unit. It can be seen that HG generates the main area and power overhead. It is because HG needs more adders to get the number of unique products. Besides, to achieve precision compatibility shown in Fig. 5(c), an adder tree is implemented in HG.

Figure8(b) shows the area overhead comparison between a BitHist MAC unit and a BitFusion MAC unit. We implement BitFusion in the same data reuse way as BitHist to distribute the area overhead of its PRU. At a single MAC unit level, BitHist MAC still saves 57% area overhead to BitFusion. It is mainly due to the hardware-friendly design of the architecture. The bit width of the adder's input in HG is low, and $N_k \cdot k$ can be calculated with low hardware cost. Evaluation results show that calculation of $\text{PSUM}_{0001}$, $\text{PSUM}_{0010}$, and $\text{PSUM}_{0100}$ does not incur any area and power overhead. Another key area-saving design is that BitHist uses concat operations instead of expensive shift logic and binary adder trees. Six branches yield 18 partial sums in total, which greatly reduces the overhead of the final adder tree compared to BitFusion's 64 partial sums (the red part in Fig. 8(b)). Besides, the area overhead of the concat and adder tree of HG can be amortized due to the vector MAC design. In addition, data reuse will further amortize the area overhead of UPE in BH-NS at the accelerator level, which increases the throughput per unit area of BH-NS to nearly 2.33 $\times$ that of BitFusion.

## 5.3 Performance Comparison

**Latency.** Both BitHist, BitFusion and Subword Parallel can be pipelined and they can produce a valid result per cycle after several cycles latency. But the Loom cannot be effectively pipelined as it divides a complete calculation into several slices productions in the time dimension, and there is a considerable delay before each valid result is produced.

**Area and Power Efficiency.** Figure 9(a) shows the normalized throughput per area (NTPA) comparison, and Fig. 9(b) shows the normalized energy efficiency (NEE) comparison. Metrics in the different precision cases are normalized

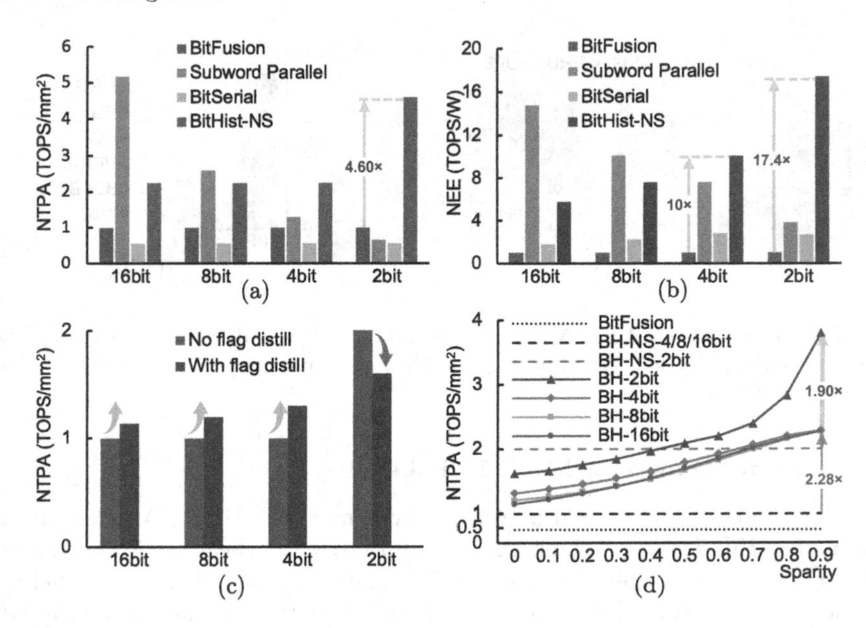


**Fig. 9.** Evaluation results. (a) Comparison of normalized throughput per area (NTPA). (b) Comparison of normalized energy efficiency (NEE). All accelerators are implemented as symmetric precision scaling. (c) Comparison of TPA between BH-NS and BH when executing the unpruned models. It shows the performance boost of BitHist with bit-level sparsity exploitation. (d) Sparsity sensitivity of BitHist, and it shows the performance boost with data-level sparsity exploitation.

to BitFusion's performance ratio. Subword Parallel has more advantages when computing high-precision data. But the TPA and EE decrease rapidly as the data bit width decreases, mainly due to the waste of a large number of computing resources caused by gating. The bit-serial approach suffers from low TPA and EE due to the register area and energy overhead. On the contrary, the TPA and EE of BitFusion and BitHist can show quadratic growth with the reduction of data bit width.

Furthermore, thanks to avoiding redundant bit slice multiplications and adopting a hardware-friendly design, BitHist is superior to BitFusion in terms of TPA and EE. In the 2-bit case, the TPA of BitHsit is 4.60× that of BitFusion, and it is 2.30× that of BitFusion in other cases. In each precision case, the energy efficiency of BitHist is 5.74×, 7.62×, 10.05×, and 17.40× that of the baseline. It is worth mentioning that our work has extremely advantageous TPA and EE in the 2-bit case. The branches of unique products 3, 6, and 9 can be reconfigured to compute unique products 1, 2, and 4. Therefore, in the case of 2bit, the throughput of BitHist is doubled, with a few additional bandwidth costs paid.

### 5.4 Performance Boost with Sparse Exploitation

The distillation of the flags makes BH exploit the bit-level sparsity. It further amortizes the hardware overhead of HG since it enables the generation logic of coefficients $c_i$ in HG to handle more than one flag vector in a cycle. At the same time, reducing the number of 0 in the flag vector also improves the efficiency of HG. Yet, it must be pointed out that the distillation operation itself introduces overhead. This is a design trade-off, and the overhead of distilling four or more flags simultaneously is unacceptable. We implement three-flag distillation in BitHist. Figure 9(c) shows the boost of NTPA with flag distillation. Compared with BH-NS, BH has achieved NTPA gain except for the 2-bit case. This is because the unique product of 2-bit unsigned multiplication is less, and the flag is denser. The distillation of the flags also makes BHPE benefit from data-level sparsity. We manually pruned the models and evaluated the sparsity sensitivity of BitHist. Figure 9(d) shows the performance improvement of BH at different levels of model sparsity. The results show that BitHist can achieve a performance gain of up to 2.28× from sparsity exploitation.

## 6 Conclusion

This paper proposes a multiply-accumulation method based on the histogram of the unique products of unsigned 2-bit multiplication. It effectively alleviates the high hardware overhead caused by the configurable logic of the spatial precision-scalable MACs. This paper also introduces an accelerator based on the proposed MAC method. The results demonstrate that the accelerator without sparsity exploitation can provide at most 17.40× higher energy efficiency and 4.60× higher throughput per area than baseline in various precision cases. Benefiting from the bit-level and data-level sparsity, the accelerator's performance is further improved.

## References

1. Agrawal, A., et al.: 9.1 A 7nm 4-core AI chip with 25.6TFLOPS hybrid fp8 training, 102.4TOPS INT4 inference and workload-aware throttling. In: 2021 IEEE International Solid- State Circuits Conference (ISSCC), vol. 64, pp. 144–146 (2021). https://doi.org/10.1109/ISSCC42613.2021.9365791
2. Chen, Y.H., et al.: Eyeriss: a spatial architecture for energy-efficient dataflow for convolutional neural networks. ACM SIGARCH Comput. Archit. news **44**(3), 367–379 (2016). https://doi.org/10.1145/3007787.3001177
3. Courbariaux, M., et al.: Binaryconnect: training deep neural networks with binary weights during propagations. In: Cortes, C., Lawrence, N., Lee, D., Sugiyama, M., Garnett, R. (eds.) Advances in Neural Information Processing Systems, vol. 28. Curran Associates, Inc. (2015). https://proceedings.neurips.cc/paper/2015/file/3e15cc11f979ed25912dff5b0669f2cd-Paper.pdf
4. Delmas, A., Sharify, S., Judd, P., Nikolic, M., Moshovos, A.: Dpred: Making typical activation values matter in deep learning computing. CoRR, vol. abs/1804.06732 (2018). https://doi.org/10.48550/arXiv.1804.06732

5. Gou, J., et al.: Knowledge distillation: a survey. Int. J. Comput. Vis. **129**, 1789–1819 (2021). https://doi.org/10.1007/s11263-021-01453-z
6. Han, S., et al.: Deep compression: compressing deep neural networks with pruning, trained quantization and huffman coding. arXiv preprint arXiv:1510.00149 (2015). https://doi.org/10.48550/arXiv.1510.00149
7. Hu, D.: An introductory survey on attention mechanisms in NLP problems. In: Bi, Y., Bhatia, R., Kapoor, S. (eds.) IntelliSys 2019. AISC, vol. 1038, pp. 432–448. Springer, Cham (2020). https://doi.org/10.1007/978-3-030-29513-4_31
8. Idelbayev, Y., et al.: Low-rank compression of neural nets: learning the rank of each layer. In: Proceedings of the IEEE/CVF Conference on Computer Vision and Pattern Recognition (CVPR) (2020). https://doi.org/10.1109/CVPR42600.2020.00807
9. Im, D., et al.: DSPU: a 281.6 mw real-time depth signal processing unit for deep learning-based dense RGB-D data acquisition with depth fusion and 3d bounding box extraction in mobile platforms. In: 2022 IEEE International Solid-State Circuits Conference (ISSCC), vol. 65, pp. 510–512. IEEE (2022). https://doi.org/10.1109/ISSCC42614.2022.9731699
10. Internet: NVDLA open source project. [EB/OL]. https://nvdla.org
11. Jiao, Y., et al.: 7.2 a 12nm programmable convolution-efficient neural-processing-unit chip achieving 825TOPS. In: 2020 IEEE International Solid- State Circuits Conference - (ISSCC), pp. 136–140 (2020). https://doi.org/10.1109/ISSCC19947.2020.9062984
12. Judd, P., et al.: Stripes: bit-serial deep neural network computing. IEEE Comput. Archit. Lett. **16**(1), 80–83 (2017). https://doi.org/10.1109/LCA.2016.2597140
13. Kang, S., et al.: 7.4 GANPU: a 135TFLOPS/W multi-DNN training processor for GANs with speculative dual-sparsity exploitation. In: 2020 IEEE International Solid- State Circuits Conference - (ISSCC), pp. 140–142 (2020). https://doi.org/10.1109/ISSCC19947.2020.9062989
14. Kapur, S., et al.: Low precision RNNs: quantizing RNNs without losing accuracy. arXiv preprint arXiv:1710.07706 (2017). 10.48550/arXiv. 1710.07706
15. Kim, M., Ham, Y., Koo, C., Kim, T.W.: Simulating travel paths of construction site workers via deep reinforcement learning considering their spatial cognition and wayfinding behavior. Autom. Constr. **147**, 104715 (2023)
16. Li, F., et al.: Ternary weight networks. arXiv preprint arXiv:1605.04711 (2016). 10.48550/arXiv. 1605.04711
17. Lin, D.D., Talathi, S.S., Annapureddy, V.S.: Fixed point quantization of deep convolutional networks. In: Computer ENCE (2016). https://doi.org/10.48550/arXiv.1511.06393
18. Lu, H., et al.: Distilling bit-level sparsity parallelism for general purpose deep learning acceleration. In: MICRO-54: 54th Annual IEEE/ACM International Symposium on Microarchitecture, pp. 963–976 (2021). https://doi.org/10.1145/3466752.3480123
19. Mei, L., et al.: Sub-word parallel precision-scalable mac engines for efficient embedded DNN inference. In: 2019 IEEE International Conference on Artificial Intelligence Circuits and Systems (AICAS), pp. 6–10 (2019). https://doi.org/10.1109/AICAS.2019.8771481
20. Nagel, M., et al.: A white paper on neural network quantization. arXiv preprint arXiv:2106.08295 (2021). https://doi.org/10.48550/arXiv.2106.08295
21. Sharify, S., Lascorz, A.D., Siu, K., Judd, P., Moshovos, A.: Loom: exploiting weight and activation precisions to accelerate convolutional neural networks. In: 2018

55th ACM/ESDA/IEEE Design Automation Conference (DAC), pp. 1–6 (2018). https://doi.org/10.1109/DAC.2018.8465915
22. Sharma, H., et al.: Bit fusion: bit-level dynamically composable architecture for accelerating deep neural network. In: 2018 ACM/IEEE 45th Annual International Symposium on Computer Architecture (ISCA), pp. 764–775 (2018). https://doi.org/10.1109/ISCA.2018.00069
23. Tropea, M., et al.: Classifiers comparison for convolutional neural networks (CNNs) in image classification. In: 2019 IEEE/ACM 23rd International Symposium on Distributed Simulation and Real Time Applications (DS-RT), pp. 1–4 (2019). https://doi.org/10.1109/DS-RT47707.2019.8958662
24. Yuan, Z., et al.: A sparse-adaptive CNN processor with area/performance balanced n-way set-associate PE arrays assisted by a collision-aware scheduler. In: 2019 IEEE Asian Solid-State Circuits Conference (A-SSCC), pp. 61–64 (2019). https://doi.org/10.1109/A-SSCC47793.2019.9056918
25. Zhu, C., et al.: Trained ternary quantization. arXiv preprint arXiv:1612.01064 (2016). https://doi.org/10.48550/arXiv.1612.01064

# Computational Storage for an Energy-Efficient Deep Neural Network Training System

Shiju Li[1], Kevin Tang[1], Jin Lim[1], Chul-Ho Lee[2], and Jongryool Kim[1(✉)]

[1] Memory Forest x&D Solution Laboratory, SK Hynix, San Jose, CA, USA
{shiju.li,kevin.tang,jin.lim,jongryool.kim}@us.skynix.com
[2] Department of Computer Science, Texas State University, San Marcos, TX, USA
chulho.lee@txstate.edu

**Abstract.** Near-storage data processing and computational storage have recently received considerable attention from the industry as energy- and cost-efficient ways to improve system performance. This paper introduces a computational-storage solution to enhance the performance and energy efficiency of an AI training system, especially for training a deep learning model with large datasets or high-dimensional data. Our system leverages dimensionality reduction effectively by offloading its operations to computational storage in a systematic manner. Our experiment results show that it can reduce the training time of a deep learning model by over 40.3%, while lowering energy consumption by 38.2%.

**Keywords:** Deep Neural Networks · Computational Storage · Near-Storage Data Preprocessing · Model Training · Energy Efficiency

## 1 Introduction

Deep neural networks (DNNs) have played a pivotal role in numerous domains such as computer vision, natural language processing, biomedical analysis, and robotics. However, their development and deployment present challenges. When training a DNN model on a large dataset or high-dimensional data, storing all the training data in GPUs can quickly become impractical due to the limited memory capacity of GPUs, leading to out-of-memory errors and thus preventing further training. To overcome this problem, one can access the data in smaller, buffered chunks by partitioning the data. Nonetheless, even with data partitioning, there are still limitations due to the relatively slower growth of memory performance.

The speed at which data can be read from memory is slower than the speed at which data can be processed in GPUs, which makes accessing data from memory become a bottleneck. This can slow down the training process and potentially cause issues with model convergence. The problem is further compounded when multiple epochs of training are required or when hyperparameter tuning is necessary. In such cases, the same data must be repeatedly accessed, leading to


J. Cano et al. (Eds.): Euro-Par 2023, LNCS 14100, pp. 304–319, 2023.
https://doi.org/10.1007/978-3-031-39698-4_21

even slower storage access and exacerbating the performance bottleneck. This is known as the "GPU memory capacity wall" [17]. As the size of the dataset and the complexity of the model increase rapidly, the amount of memory required to store the data also goes up dramatically.

To cope with the memory problem associated with training a DNN model, one common approach is to distribute the training of each model across multiple GPUs [12]. This approach involves splitting the dataset or model variables across the GPUs, resulting in faster training time and improved performance. However, it can lead to a linear increase in GPU and energy costs. Another recent approach is to take advantage of the host CPU memory as a buffer to offload some of the impending tensors during training [9]. However, this approach can result in low training throughput and significant CPU memory interference in practice, which motivates the need to relieve the burden of utilizing the CPU during training. Instead of addressing the memory problem at a hardware level, an orthogonal approach is to preprocess the training data in a way that accelerates model training while mitigating the memory problem.

Dimensionality reduction (DR) is one such approach that can be leveraged, especially for high-dimensional data that often contain a lot of redundant features and thus increase space and computational time complexity while being prone to overfitting. In particular, random projection (RP) [2] can effectively reduce the computation and storage burden of deep learning without significant information loss. One of its key advantages is its tangible benefits to counteract the burdensome computational requirements and its versatile ability to meet the needs of real-time processing [8]. Besides, unlike other techniques such as principal component analysis (PCA) and independent component analysis (ICA), RP's inherent simplicity and parallelism enable its efficient implementation in field programmable gate arrays (FPGAs) [4,21], which is particularly useful for developing high-performance computing systems.

In this work, we propose a computational-storage solution that provides accelerated data preprocessing for DNN training by performing data preprocessing steps, such as RP near the SSD to minimize overall data movement. Computational storage (CS) enables us to achieve low end-to-end latency and high energy efficiency. The system can greatly reduce the training time and improve the accuracy of the model. This not only solves the memory problem during DNN training but also ensures lower energy consumption.

Our contributions in this paper can be summarized as follows:

- We propose a CS solution that accelerates data preprocessing for AI training by integrating dimensionality reduction into a compute component inside CS.
- The proposed CS solution can significantly reduce training time and energy consumption of lightweight DNN models such as multilayer perceptron (MLP). Experiment results on real-world datasets show a clear difference in training time between systems with and without a CS. In particular, we demonstrate that the computation offloading of RP as data processing to CS can dramatically reduce energy consumption and even improve model accuracy for datasets with a large number of features.

- To amplify the benefits of near-storage data preprocessing in CS compared with other accelerators, we propose a system that supports large dataset DNN training, which can improve the performance of the convolutional recurrent neural network (CRNN) model in text recognition. Experiment results on large datasets show distinct benefits with RP compared to the one without RP. Performing RP using CS can achieve similar accuracy to the CRNN model while ensuring low end-to-end latency and high-energy efficiency.

## 2 Background and Related Work

**Computational Storage on DNN.** Computational storage, also known as in-situ storage, is a technique that allows data to be processed in or near a storage device, rather than the main CPU of a host. The idea of integrating in-memory computing with DNNs has gained significant attention recently, enabling data processing to be performed directly in memory and significantly reducing the latency and energy consumption of DNN operations. Specifically, it has emerged as a promising solution for accelerating both convolutional neural networks (CNNs) and recurrent neural networks (RNNs).

By using custom hardware designs, quantization methods, pruning techniques, and memory access patterns, it is possible to significantly improve the performance of CNN inference on CS devices like FPGAs, enabling the deployment of CNNs on resource-constrained devices and accelerating their use in large-scale applications [1]. By leveraging the high parallelism and energy efficiency of FPGAs, researchers have been able to dramatically speed up the training process of CNNs. Qiu et al. [23] present a novel architecture optimized for the specific characteristics of CNNs, including weight sharing, sparse connectivity, and convolutional operations. Guo et al. [6] present a design flow for mapping CNNs onto an embedded FPGA. Ma et al. [20] optimize the convolution operation to accelerate deep neural networks on FPGA.

CS has also been explored as a potential solution to overcome the computational limitations of traditional CPU and GPU implementations in RNNs. Nurvitadhio et al. [22] evaluate the performance of various hardware accelerators for RNNs and find that FPGA-based implementations outperform other baselines by several orders of magnitude while providing better energy efficiency. Guan et al. [5] propose an FPGA-based accelerator for long short-term memory RNNs, which leverages a custom pipelined architecture with optimized memory access patterns and quantization methods. Li et al. [19] present a hardware implementation of RNNs on an FPGA using a hybrid approach that combines fixed-point and floating-point arithmetic to balance performance and energy consumption. These studies demonstrate the potential of CS, specifically FPGAs, to enable high-performance, low-power, and real-time processing of deep neural networks.

**Random Projection.** The Johnson-Lindenstrauss Lemma, which serves as the theoretical underpinning of Random Projection (RP) [14], states that a set of points in a high-dimensional space can be embedded into a space of much lower dimension in a way that nearly preserves distances between the points. The level

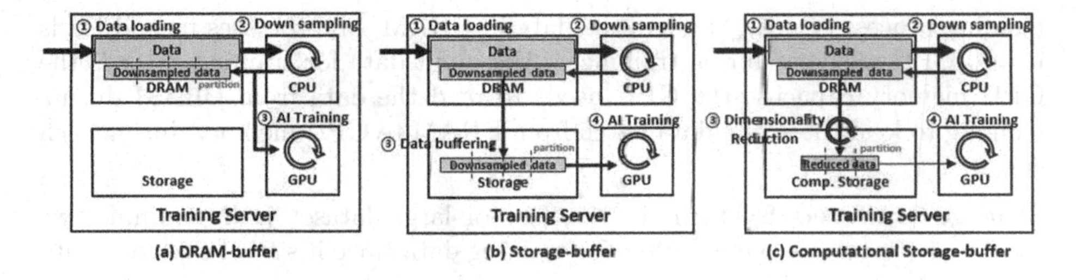


**Fig. 1.** Comparison of DNN training systems with data preprocessing

of distortion created by an RP $p$ is validated by the capacity of $p$ to determine an $\epsilon$-embedding with a reasonable probability. The definition is as follows: $(1 - \epsilon)||\boldsymbol{u} - \boldsymbol{v}||^2 \leq ||p(\boldsymbol{u}) - p(\boldsymbol{v})||^2 \leq (1+\epsilon)||\boldsymbol{u} - \boldsymbol{v}||^2$, where $\boldsymbol{u}$ and $\boldsymbol{v}$ are arbitrary rows taken from a dataset matrix $\mathbb{A}$ with shape $(n, d)$.

From an algorithmic perspective, $p$ is implemented by multiplying the dataset matrix $\mathbb{A}$ with a random matrix $\mathbb{B}$, where $\mathbb{B}$ has dimensions $d \times k$. The elements of $\mathbb{B}$ are independent random variables, with numerous potential constructions such as standard Gaussian or sub-Gaussian distributions. The latter is more commonly used for sparse data. Of significance is the fact that the development of $\mathbb{B}$ is independent of $\mathbb{A}$, indicating that RP is data-insensitive and compatible with partitioned or parallel computation for large datasets. The quantity of $k$ is calculated mathematically to attain a specific accuracy, which is indicated by the value of $\epsilon$. A desirable property is that $k$ is dependent only on the logarithmic size of the data, i.e., $k = O(\ln n)$. Considering that the complexity of many algorithms increases exponentially with respect to $d$, the dimension reduction from $d$ to $k$ is significantly beneficial. The storage requirement for $n$ column vectors is cut down from $dn$ to $kn = O(n \log n)$.

RP has proven to be a powerful and versatile technique for feature extraction in DNN. Piotr et al. [26] incorporate an RP layer into the DNN architecture to deal with extremely high-dimensional data. Jiang et al. [11] present a lightweight privacy-preserving collaborative learning approach for Internet of Things (IoT) devices using Independent Random Projection (IRP) since it can preserve the important features of the data while removing the sensitive information for individuals. Hashemifar et al. [7] efficiently combine deep Siamese-like convolutional neural networks and RP to construct a DPPI model for predicting PPIs by associating with protein evolutionary information. Jindal et al. [13] propose a method for securing biometric data and preserving user privacy in face recognition systems, using a combination of deep CNN and RP.

## 3 Computational Storage for DNN Prepossessing

**DRAM Buffered System.** The traditional DRAM-buffered DNN training system consists of three steps: data loading, preprocessing, and training. As shown in Fig. 1a, assuming we have a data source outside the host, the lightweight DNN training process typically buffers the data in DRAM, preprocesses it, and loads it into GPU memory during training. If the input data for training exceeds the GPU memory capacity, the GPU needs to read the data from DRAM during training to load the entire data batch from DRAM to GPU memory during each epoch.

**Storage Buffered System.** In the case of large-dataset DNN training, we need to use local storage to buffer the training data since it's too large to fit into DRAM. As depicted in Fig. 1b, the original data is first transmitted from the objective storage to the local storage. Then, it is partitioned and preprocessed in the CPU. After that, the data is buffered back into the local storage once again. During training, these data are read as multiple training batches into DRAM by the training batch generator and are finally fed into the GPU for training. Since the process of reading the training batches is repeated for every epoch, the IO time cost is non-negligible.

**Computational Storage Buffered System.** We propose a system that offloads RP as data processing to the CS, as illustrated in Fig. 1c. This system can minimize data movement in machine learning workloads by performing preprocessing steps near the SSD. In most cases, reading data from the storage is relatively slow. Therefore, instead of performing all the preprocessing on CPU and buffering the preprocessed data on DRAM before training, we can apply DR as an inline operation beside downsampling, and the reduced data can be stored in the CS. To apply DR, the system first loads the downsampled data from the host memory to the working memory on the CS. The compute unit on the CS performs a DR and stores the reduced data in its storage. Then, the reduced data is transferred to the GPU for training through peer-to-peer direct memory access (P2P-DMA). By applying DR to the data writing process for buffering, additional data movement and CPU usage for performing DR are eliminated, and memory space on DRAM can be saved. Furthermore, the reduced data is transmitted to the GPU, which can decrease both the data transfer time from the storage to the GPU and the training time in the GPU as it will reduce the training model size.

Our system will be more effective when dealing with large-dataset DNN training. Instead of relying heavily on CPU memory bandwidth, we use the CS to perform the DR and store the reduced-size data for GPU training. On one hand, the CS is utilized by the training batch generator to produce training batches locally, avoiding consumption of host CPU cycles or DRAM bandwidth. On the other hand, P2P-DMA enables direct memory access between a GPU and CS without using the host DRAM buffer, minimizing host intervention during SSD read/write. Thus, we fully utilize the benefits of CS and greatly relieve the burden on the CPU.

## 4 System Implementation Details

We perform RP using a single precision general matrix multiply (SGEMM) kernel with a U200 FPGA. The kernel is implemented using Xilinx OpenCL HLS.

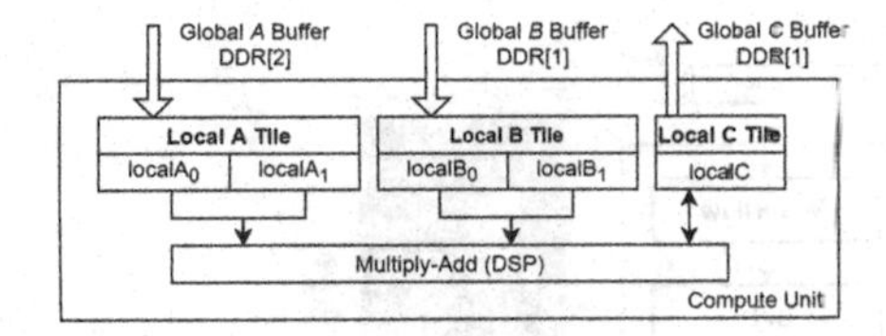


**Fig. 2.** Matrix-multiply CU layout: local A and B tiles are double-buffered to enable simultaneous writes from global memory and computation of C tile

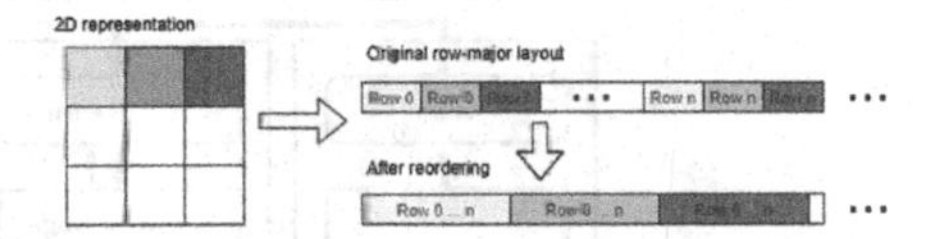


**Fig. 3.** Comparison of the layout of tiles in memory between row-major data layout and after data reordering

Under the HLS development flow, the FPGA is managed by the Xilinx Runtime (XRT), which provides the APIs and drivers to reprogram and communicate with the FPGA from the host. We use Xilinx Vitis 2021.2 and XRT 2.12.427 to develop and evaluate the kernels, targeting the *xilinx_u200_gen3x16_xdma_base_2* platform. The SGEMM accelerator consists of a portion running on the U200 FPGA, and management code using OpenCL running on the host.

**SGEMM Kernel Using Xilinx OpenCL HLS.** We implement a tiled SGEMM accelerator function via multiple compute units (CUs) to compute tiles of the output matrix in parallel. The SGEMM kernel is used to perform RP and obtain the result matrix $\mathbb{C} = \mathbb{A}\mathbb{B}$.

The design of the CU is shown in Fig. 2, and consists of DSP units to perform multiply-add and BRAM blocks for storing the input/output tiles. As FPGA on-chip memory resources are limited compared to external memory, full matrices are first transferred to FPGA's external DRAM, and tiles are loaded to BRAMs on the CU as needed to perform the matrix multiplication. The input matrices are double-buffered to overlap the write from external DRAM and the read for computation of the output tile.

However, there is a tradeoff in employing double-buffering, as it comes at the cost of doubling the BRAM requirement of the kernel. As FPGA on-chip memory is limited, the tile size must be reduced to compensate, resulting in a higher memory bandwidth requirement. For this reason, we buffer the input $\mathbb{A}/\mathbb{B}$ tiles, but do not double-buffer the output $\mathbb{C}$ tile. The number of $\mathbb{A}/\mathbb{B}$ tile accesses scales per-tile with the matrix size, while the number of $\mathbb{C}$ accesses does not. For large matrices, the performance gain from double-buffering $\mathbb{C}$ is minimal compared to the associated penalty for reducing tile size.

To take full advantage of the FPGA's DRAM memory bandwidth, the data access pattern must be sequential. Xilinx HLS provides two main optimizations for memory accesses, burst transfers and read/write widening, which require a sequential, regular access pattern. Under a standard row- or column-major matrix layout, tiles are located in a non-contiguous region of memory, disabling possible optimizations. To resolve this issue, the host performs a reordering of input matrices to a tiled data format before transferring to the SGEMM kernel as shown in Fig. 3. Applying a data reordering incurs a host memory bandwidth overhead, but this cost reduces the overall execution time by setting up the FPGA to burst read/write these tiles from a contiguous region of memory.

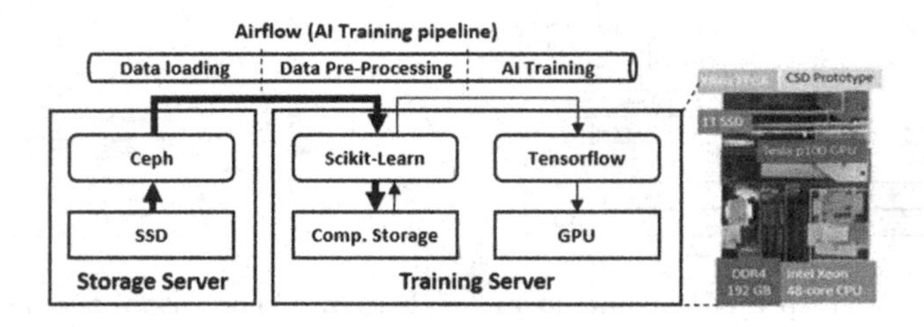


**Fig. 4.** Computational storage prototype and training system testbed

**OpenCL Host Application.** The host application provides an API (C++, scikit-learn) for the user to perform matrix-multiplications using the U200 FPGA. Internally, it uses OpenCL queues to schedule the I/O and kernel execution. Tiles of the output matrix are grouped into OpenCL work-items and divided to CUs to compute the result in parallel.

Because the matrix data originally resides outside the FPGA DRAM (either in host DRAM or in SSD), in practice there is an additional cost of loading data to the FPGA. When considering the latency of a single matrix-multiply operation, this depends on both the PCIe transfer and kernel computation latencies. To hide this latency, we implement an asynchronous API and pipeline the host-FPGA I/O and kernel computation.

**P2P-DMA.** On a BIOS with support for large memory-mapped IO, the U200 FPGA can map its 64 GB of DDR to the host memory space, allowing for peer-to-peer (P2P) DMA transfer. If data is intended to be read or written to SSD, PCIe bandwidth can be saved by enabling P2P DMA and transferring data directly between FPGA and SSD, bypassing the buffer in host memory. We use this feature in the output phase to directly write the reduced matrix to the SSD.

**DNN Training System with Computational Storage.** Figure 4 depicts the basic setup of the testbed for our proposed CS-enabled training system. This testbed consists of an object storage server and a training server that uses GPUs and a CS prototype that employs the Xilinx Alveo™ U200 FPGA with a 3.84 TB PE8010 SK hynix NVMe SSD. The prototype supports two types of APIs: (1) C++ API and (2) scikit-learn API to apply DR in the CS and output the result either to host DRAM or to the SSD via P2P-DMA.

The overall training tasks are managed and orchestrated by Apache AirFlow [3]. The data are originally stored in Ceph [25] and transferred to CS for buffering, then copied to the GPU for training. To enable DNN services, we use TensorFlow 2.9.1, which uses CUDA 11.4 and cuDNN 8.2 for GPU acceleration, along with an NVIDIA®Tesla®P100 GPU with 16 GB memory. The testbed uses a 3.0 GHz 48-core Intel®Xeon®Gold 6136 CPU with DDR4-2666 192 GB DRAM, along with the P100 GPU and CS prototype.

For DNN training system using CS, the original data (training, validation and test dataset) are initially stored in different containers of Ceph in the storage server. They are first transferred to DRAM of the local server for buffering, then downsampled by CPU, sent to CS for RP, and finally saved in CS. The down-sampling typically includes data cleaning, data integration, data transformation and data augmentation. Thus, downsampling as a necessary part of preprocessing may increase the data size. For large scale training tasks, the training data is too large to fit entirely into DRAM, so it must be first partitioned according to the DRAM size and training batch size. The partitioned data are then down-sampled in the CPU, processed, and stored in the CS. This process is repeated to preprocess the entire training data.

## 5 Case Studies and Experiment Results

In this section, we present three case studies and extensive experiment results to demonstrate the efficacy of our AI training system with CS compared to other baselines, including deep learning models with large datasets or high dimensional data. We evaluate the performance of different systems based on three standards: AI task runtime, training accuracy, and energy cost.

**Table 1.** Dataset summary

| Task # | Dataset | Size | # of Samples | # of Classes |
|---|---|---|---|---|
| 1 | Chest X-Ray Images | 1.15 GB | 5863 | Pneumonia (P) and Normal (N) |
| 2 | Single-Cell RNA-Seq | 71.9 MB | 638 | Non-Diabetic (ND) and Type 2 Diabetic (T2D) |
| 3 | MJSynth | 32 GB | 8919273 | 62 classes (0–9, a–z, A–Z) |
| 3 | ICDAR 2003 (Test) | 33 MB | 860 | 62 classes (0–9, a–z, A–Z) |
| 3 | ICDAR 2013 (Test) | 65 MB | 857 | 62 classes (0–9, a–z, A–Z) |

**Case Studies.** In this work, we applied our lightweight DNN training system to two real-world binary classification tasks using MLP: pediatric pneumonia chest X-ray classification and RNA-seq cell types classification. For the first task, the goal was to differentiate pneumonia and normal chests from chest radiograph images [16]. For the second task, we used a real transcriptomics dataset from single-cell RNA-seq studies [18]. We need to perform binary classification of ND and T2D cell types for each RNA-seq sample. To demonstrate the performance of our large-dataset DNN training system, we focus on an unconstrained scene text recognition task. We use MJSynth [10], a synthetically generated word image dataset containing 9 million samples, for training and validation. Note that there is no lexicon as a reference to improve the training accuracy. ICDAR 2003 and ICDAR 2013 [15] are two test datasets. All datasets are summarized in Table 1.

The MLP model in the first two tasks has four neural layers, including three fully connected layers with Relu activation and dropout rate of 0.2, and a final layer with 1 neuron and sigmoid activation. Binary cross-entropy is set as the loss function. In the beginning of task 1, we have five groups of square images with different pixels. The entire sample sets are split into training and validation at a ratio of 4:1 for each group. We flattened the image data and applied RP to these image samples in CS to reduce the dimension. The number of neurons for

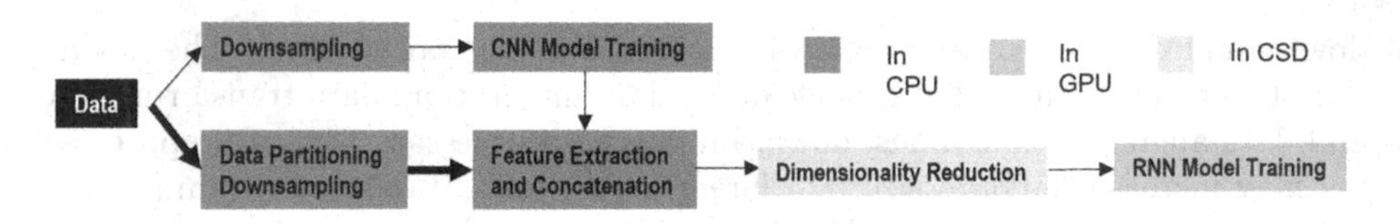


**Fig. 5.** Entire workflow for unconstrained scene text recognition

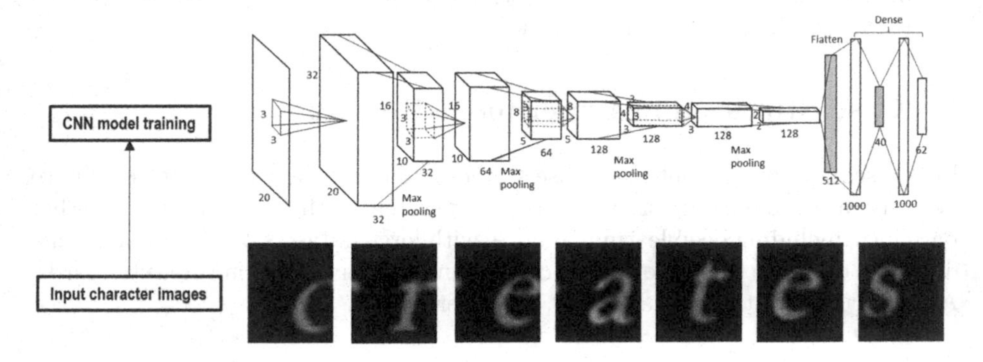


**Fig. 6.** CNN model training in CDRNN

each FC layer was set to be the same and equal to the number of pixels. In task 2, the dimension of the input data was 638 × 26616. In the preprocessing, we split the data into training and test samples, with 95% and 5% respectively. The training samples were further split into training and validation samples at a ratio of 3:1. After RP, feature size in all samples was reduced to 1000. We changed the batch size to show the performance robustness of our training system.

For task 3, we propose a large-dataset CS-based DNN training system using CDRNN [27], whose main workflow is summarized in Fig. 5. To extract robust features for text recognition, we first train a case-sensitive character classifier using 0.1 million images samples (see Fig. 6). These word images are evenly chopped into multiple character images based on the length of the label of each word, in which each character image is given the corresponding label. There are 0.65 million input samples for CNN training. Second, for each resized word image sample with a height of 32, we use a sliding window of size equal to 32 to shift it, and convert the captured image patch to a multi-layer CNN feature sequence by passing them through pre-trained CNN model in CPU. Specifically, we extract the output of the flatten layer and the smallest fully connected layer, and concatenate them into a feature sequence with 552 dimensions. Third, we use RP to embed the original 552-dimension features into 80-dimension random subspace in the CS. After such an 85% dimensionality reduction, we train a RNN model, which recognizes reduced feature sequence sample, in the GPU. The RNN model contains two bidirectional LSTM layers with each of 256 nodes. Finally, we use connectionist temporal classification (CTC) to remove the repeated labels

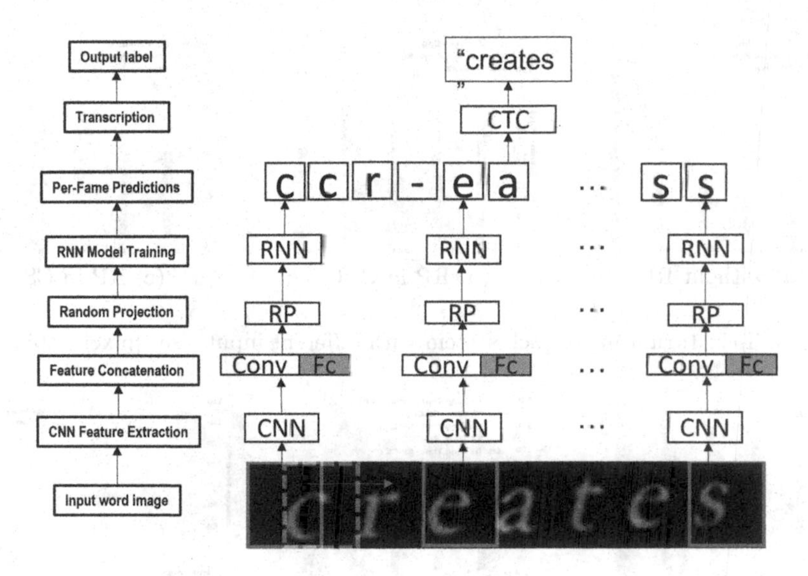


**Fig. 7.** CDRNN workflow

and non-character labels in its last output. The Adam optimizer is utilized with a defaulted learning rate. We present the entire workflow in Fig. 7.

We use a customized training batch generator to generate the batch during the training for each system. Note that we partition the original data based on the determined batch size and ensure that each partition of data covers one exact batch. During the data partition period, we write each batch from the DRAM into local storage. We also include the well-known CRNN model [24] as a baseline that uses a storage-buffered DNN training system for performance comparison. The structure of the model is the same as the one in [24]. We make the batch size used in CRNN the same as the size of input in our proposed system. Comparing CDRNN with CRNN, the total model size has reduced from 8.7 million parameters to 3.2 million parameters, where the latter is obtained by adding the number of model parameters in CNN and RNN.

All systems are tested with three different workloads (0.1M, 1M and 9M images) under a large DNN training environment, indicating that all training data are either buffered in local storage or CS before training, instead of stored in DRAM. For each workload, we split the training data into training and validation at a ratio of 4:1. Note that though the raw size of 9M images dataset in memory is 32 GB, processed data size in memory will increase to 734.4 GB after downsampling, which is far larger than the DRAM size.

**Experiment Results.** We first evaluated the performance of different systems on Task 1. We show the runtime of each baseline with different input image sizes in Fig. 8. It is evident that the loading time of all systems is almost the same with a fixed input image size. With the increase of image size, the runtime of the baseline that has no RP preprocess increases linearly with the square of pixels,

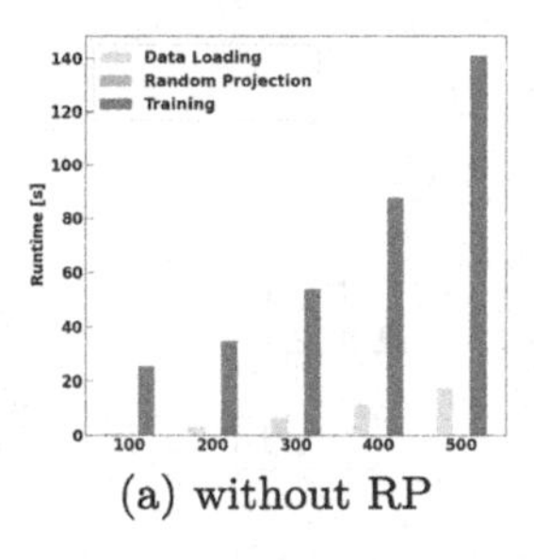


(a) without RP

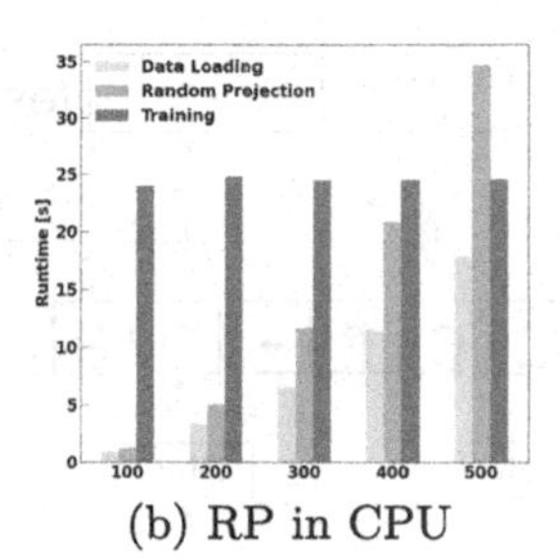


(b) RP in CPU

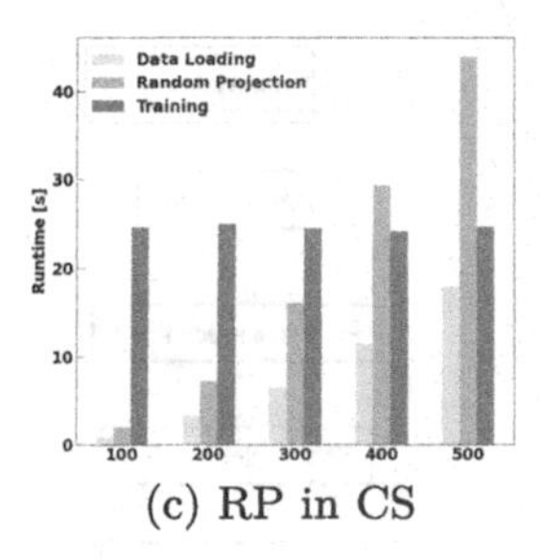


(c) RP in CS

**Fig. 8.** Task 1: runtime in each system with different input sizes [pixel × pixel]

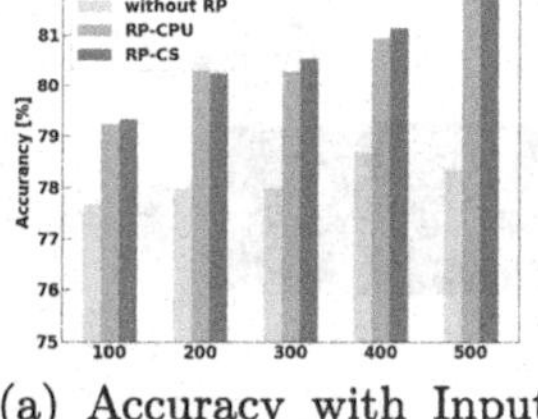


(a) Accuracy with Input Size (Pixel×Pixel)

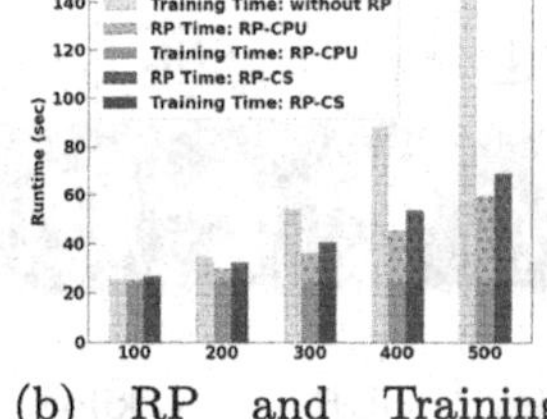


(b) RP and Training Time with Input Size (Pixel×Pixel)

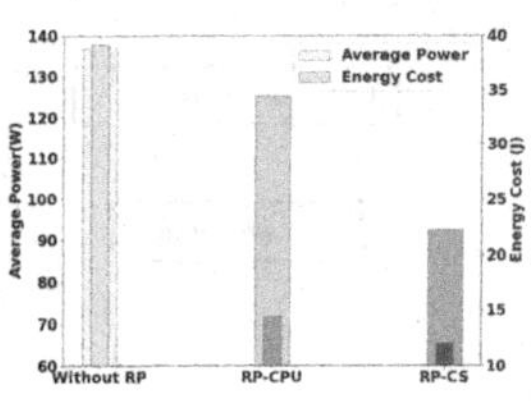


(c) Average Power and Energy Consumption with Systems

**Fig. 9.** Task 1: AI system performance comparison

but the training times of the two RP-involved systems are almost the same since the reduced feature sizes are similar across different input sizes.

We next present the performance differences among the three systems. As shown in Fig. 9a, the accuracy of the model is relatively higher with a larger input size, as it will keep more features. The systems with RP have an apparent edge over the non-RP ones. According to Fig. 9b, it is noticeable that the RP process can reduce the training time by more than 50%. It can be seen that the increase of training time for non-RP with increasing input size is much larger than the increase of RP time in the RP-involved system. We present the average power and total energy consumption collected under input size 500 × 500 based on the results in Fig. 9c. Average power and energy consumption measurements exclude the idle power consumed in the background system. We find that, when compared to the system without RP and the one using RP in CPU, our system can save about 33% and 26% of average power, and further reduce 70% and 16% of total energy consumption, respectively.

We then report the results from Task 2. As shown in Fig. 10a, the training accuracy decreases significantly with increasing batch size for the system without RP, but remains almost unchanged for the systems with RP, even with varying batch sizes. As depicted in Fig. 10b, the training time for all systems decreases with increasing batch size. RP-based systems have a greater advantage over the non-RP system with smaller batch sizes in terms of training time and end-to-end

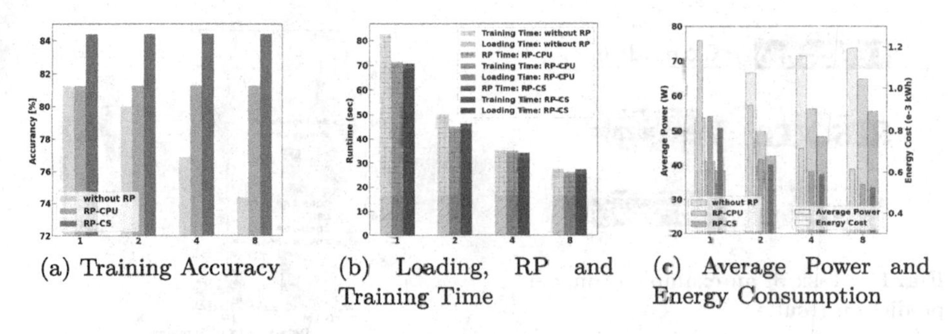


(a) Training Accuracy (b) Loading, RP and Training Time (c) Average Power and Energy Consumption

**Fig. 10.** Task 2: AI system performance comparison under different batch sizes

runtime. The runtime performance between RP-CPU and RP-CS is very similar. We can also observe that data loading time occupies more than half of the total end-to-end runtime when the batch size is over 8. The average power and total energy consumption are collected in Fig. 10c. Regarding the overall trend, the average power for all systems increases with increasing batch size. However, the energy consumption decreases with increase of batch size. It is worth noting that when compared to the system without RP and the one using RP in CPU, by taking the average power and energy values of four different batch sizes, our system can save about 30% and 12% of average power, and further reduce 24% and 4% of total energy consumption, respectively.

**Table 2.** Task 3: accuracy of model with different training data sizes and systems

| Workload Size | Accuracy | | | Systems |
|---|---|---|---|---|
| Dataset Type | Test dataset | Test dataset | validation dataset | |
| Dataset Name | ic03 | ic13 | MySynth | |
| 0.1M images | 68.14 | 68.61 | 71.3 | CRNN |
| | 67.33 | 68.26 | 74.6 | CDRNN without RP |
| | 61.28 | 64.29 | 69 | CDRNN RP in CPU |
| | 63.14 | 66.04 | 70 | CDRNN RP in CS |
| 1M images | 77.67 | 77.36 | 83.23 | CRNN |
| | 76.74 | 75.61 | 85.60 | CDRNN without RP |
| | 73.72 | 73.16 | 80.40 | CDRNN RP in CPU |
| | 72.84 | 72.23 | 79.80 | CDRNN RP in CS |
| 9M images | 84.53 | 83.78 | 90.66 | CRNN |
| | 83.72 | 82.15 | 88.27 | CDRNN without RP |
| | 81.86 | 80.05 | 86.83 | CDRNN RP in CPU |
| | 81.98 | 79.93 | 86.21 | CDRNN RP in CS |

We finally investigate the performance of each system in Task 3. We first present a few examples of the test results for our system in Fig. 11, where the

**Fig. 11.** Task 3: an example of model prediction results

| | RP in CPU | RP in CS |
|---|---|---|
| Random Projection time (sec) | 658.4635 | 1169.6614 |
| Random Projection CPU time (sec) | 18190.0139 | 794.9510 |
| Average CPU usage | 2762.49% | 67.96% |
| Data Partition time (sec) | 817.5243 | 750.0470 |
| Average Power (W) | 270.1518 | 129.2372 |
| Energy Cost (kWh) | 0.1105 | 0.0698 |

**Fig. 12.** Task 3: RP Phase Comparison

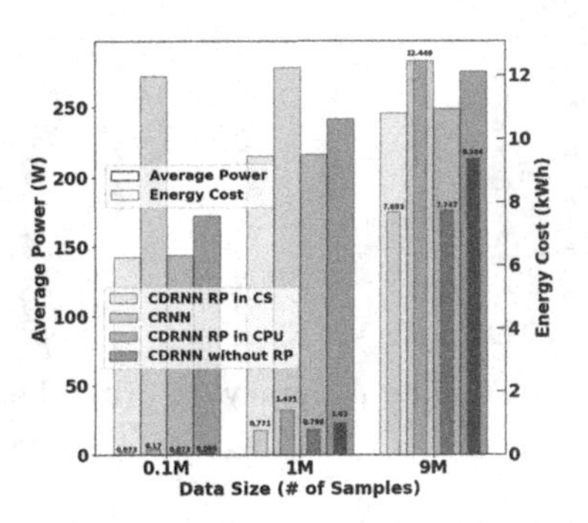


**Fig. 13.** Task 3: comparison of average power and energy consumption for different number of training sample with each system

predicted results are shown on the left caption above each word image, and the ground truths are on its right. We compare the performance of different systems in Table 2, which reports the accuracy under four different systems, including our CDRNN system when the RP preprocessing is done in CS and CPU. The only difference between the systems is where RP is conducted. We also consider the case where RP is excluded and the original CNN feature is directly fed into the RNN. We observe that the CRNN system is the best in terms of accuracy. However, its advantage decreases with increasing dataset size. The accuracy of CDRNN without RP is around 2% higher than the CDRNN with RP due to a certain amount of distortion and information loss in RP. However, we notice that the gap narrows greatly with the increase in workload size. The accuracy difference between RP-CPU and RP-CS is negligible and purely due to the randomness of the transformation matrix. We also observe that when the dataset is small, for all systems, the accuracy on ic13 is higher than that on ic03. However, the conclusion reverses for the large dataset.

Next, we examine the runtime of each system, which consists of four main phases, including data loading, downsampling and data partitioning, RP, and training. The end-to-end latency is the sum of the runtimes of all phases. Notice that we include the feature extraction step into the downsampling step, which consumes a certain amount of time for CDRNN-related systems. As shown in Table 3, CDRNN with RP significantly outperforms CRNN and is remarkably better than CDRNN without RP across different datasets. We find that, when compared to the systems of CRNN and CDRNN without RP on the 9M dataset, our system has a 40.3% and 10% percent training time reduction, respectively, and a 29.3% and 8.2% percent end-to-end latency reduction, respectively.

Finally, we measured the average power and total energy consumption collected under the systems, as shown in Fig. 13. Overall, both the average power

**Table 3.** Task 3: runtime of systems with different training data sizes (hour)

| Data Size | Systems | Data Loading | Downsampling-Partition | Random Projection | Training | End to End |
|---|---|---|---|---|---|---|
| 0.1M images | CRNN | 0.0151 | 0.0035 | 0.0000 | 0.6050 | 0.6236 |
| | CDRNN without RP | 0.0150 | 0.0313 | 0.0000 | 0.5058 | 0.5521 |
| | CDRNN RP in CPU | 0.0152 | 0.0333 | 0.0021 | 0.4595 | 0.5101 |
| | CDRNN RP in CS | 0.0151 | 0.0335 | 0.0032 | 0.4593 | 0.5111 |
| 1M images | CRNN | 0.1509 | 0.0355 | 0.0000 | 4.9887 | 5.1396 |
| | CDRNN without RP | 0.1508 | 0.3307 | 0.0000 | 3.7417 | 4.2232 |
| | CDRNN RP in CPU | 0.1508 | 0.3537 | 0.0201 | 3.1543 | 3.6790 |
| | CDRNN RP in CS | 0.1507 | 0.3464 | 0.0324 | 3.0478 | 3.5773 |
| 9M images | CRNN | 1.3512 | 0.3172 | 0.0000 | 43.9855 | 44.3024 |
| | CDRNN without RP | 1.3515 | 3.5569 | 0.0000 | 29.1916 | 34.1000 |
| | CDRNN RP in CPU | 1.3514 | 3.5096 | 0.1477 | 26.1004 | 31.1486 |
| | CDRNN RP in CS | 1.3517 | 3.3485 | 0.3251 | 26.2821 | 31.3074 |

and energy consumption for all systems increase with increasing dataset size. The results demonstrate the superiority of our CS-based CDRNN system over all other systems. Compared to the CRNN and CDRNN without RP systems, by taking the average power and energy cost on the largest tested dataset, our system can save about 13.2% and 10.7% of average power, and further reduce 38.2% and 18% of total energy consumption, respectively. Specifically, our system can save up to 47.7% and 23.5% of average power, and further reduce 57.1% and 17.4% of total energy consumption, respectively. To show the benefit of our system over RP in the CPU system, we directly compare the energy consumption and CPU time in RP Phase for 9M dataset in Fig. 12. The CPU usage of RP-in-CPU is 40.6 times larger than RP-in-CS, and the energy cost of RP-in-CPU is 58.3% larger than RP-in-CS.

## 6 Conclusion and Future Work

This paper has presented a computational storage prototype and its use case for an AI training system. Our performance evaluation has shown that computational storage can be used to improve both training time and model performance and reduce its overall power consumption. While we have demonstrated the effectiveness of leveraging computational storage for an AI training system, there are several interesting directions as future work. We plan to extend our implementation to enable general sparse matrix-matrix multiplication (SpGEMM) in FPGA so that our system can deal with much higher dimensional data. Our system can also be extended to accelerating in-storage AI inference by using dimensionality reduction for feature extraction.

## References


1. Abdelouahab, K., Pelcat, M., Serot, J., Berry, F.: Accelerating CNN inference on FPGAs: a survey. arXiv preprint arXiv:1806.01683 (2018)
2. Achlioptas, D.: Database-friendly random projections. In: Proceedings of the Twentieth ACM SIGMOD-SIGACT-SIGART Symposium on Principles of Database Systems, pp. 274–281 (2001)
3. Apache Airflow (2020). https://airflow.apache.org
4. Fox, S., Tridgell, S., Jin, C., Leong, P.H.W.: Random projections for scaling machine learning on FPGAs. In: 2016 International Conference on Field-Programmable Technology (FPT). IEEE (2016)
5. Guan, Y., Yuan, Z., Sun, G., Cong, J.: FPGA-based accelerator for long short-term memory recurrent neural networks. In: ASP-DAC. IEEE (2017)
6. Guo, K., et al.: Angel-eye: a complete design flow for mapping CNN onto embedded FPGA. IEEE Trans. Comput.-Aded Des. Integr. Circuits Syst. **37**, 35–47 (2017)
7. Hashemifar, S., Neyshabur, B., Khan, A.A., Xu, J.: Predicting protein-protein interactions through sequence-based deep learning. Bioinformatics **34**, i802–i810 (2018)
8. Ibrahim, H., Loo, C.K., Alnajjar, F.: Speech emotion recognition by late fusion for bidirectional reservoir computing with random projection. IEEE Access **9**, 122855–122871 (2021)
9. Ito, Y., Matsumiya, R., Endo, T.: ooc_cuDNN: accommodating convolutional neural networks over GPU memory capacity. In: 2017 IEEE International Conference on Big Data (Big Data). IEEE (2017)
10. Jaderberg, M., Simonyan, K., Vedaldi, A., Zisserman, A.: Synthetic data and artificial neural networks for natural scene text recognition. arXiv preprint arXiv:1406.2227 (2014)
11. Jiang, L., Tan, R., Lou, X., Lin, G.: On lightweight privacy-preserving collaborative learning for internet of things by independent random projections. ACM Trans. Internet Things **2**, 1–32 (2021)
12. Jiang, Y., Zhu, Y., Lan, C., Yi, B., Cui, Y., Guo, C.: A unified architecture for accelerating distributed DNN training in heterogeneous GPU/CPU clusters. In: Proceedings of the 14th USENIX Conference on Operating Systems Design and Implementation (2020)
13. Jindal, A.K., Chalamala, S.R., Jami, S.K.: Securing face templates using deep convolutional neural network and random projection. In: ICCE. IEEE (2019)
14. Johnson, W.B.: Extensions of Lipschitz mappings into a Hilbert space. Contemp. Math. **26**(1984), 189–206 (1984)
15. Karatzas, D., et al.: ICDAR 2013 robust reading competition. In: ICDAR. IEEE (2013)
16. Kermany, D.S., et al.: Identifying medical diagnoses and treatable diseases by image-based deep learning. Cell **172**, 1122–1131 (2018)
17. Kwon, Y., Rhu, M.: Beyond the memory wall: a case for memory-centric HPC system for deep learning. In: MICRO. IEEE (2018)
18. Lawlor, N., et al.: Single-cell transcriptomes identify human islet cell signatures and reveal cell-type-specific expression changes in type 2 diabetes. Genome Res. **27**, 208–222 (2017)
19. Li, S., Wu, C., Li, H., Li, B., Wang, Y., Qiu, Q.: FPGA acceleration of recurrent neural network based language model. In: 2015 IEEE 23rd Annual International Symposium on Field-Programmable Custom Computing Machines. IEEE (2015)

20. Ma, Y., Cao, Y., Vrudhula, S., Seo, J.: Optimizing the convolution operation to accelerate deep neural networks on FPGA. VLSI **26**, 1354–1367 (2018)
21. Nazemi, M.: Eshratifar, A.E., Pedram, M.: A hardware-friendly algorithm for scalable training and deployment of dimensionality reduction models on FPGA. In: ISQED. IEEE (2018)
22. Nurvitadhi, E., Sim, J., Sheffield, D., Mishra, A., Krishnan, S., Marr, D.: Accelerating recurrent neural networks in analytics servers: comparison of FPGA, CPU, GPU, and ASIC. In: FPL. IEEE (2016)
23. Qiu, J., et al.: Going deeper with embedded FPGA platform for convolutional neural network. In: International Symposium on FPGA (2016)
24. Shi, B., Bai, X., Yao, C.: An end-to-end trainable neural network for image-based sequence recognition and its application to scene text recognition. PAMI **39**, 2298–2304 (2016)
25. Weil, S.A., Brandt, S.A., Miller, E.L., Long, D.D.E., Maltzahn, C.: Ceph: a scalable, high-performance distributed file system. In: Proceedings of the 7th Symposium on Operating Systems Design and Implementation, pp. 307–320 (2006)
26. Wójcik, P.I.: Random projection in deep neural networks. arXiv preprint arXiv:1812.09489 (2018)
27. Wu, R., Yang, S., Leng, D., Luo, Z., Wang, Y.: Random projected convolutional feature for scene text recognition. In: 2016 15th International Conference on Frontiers in Handwriting Recognition (ICFHR), 132–137. IEEE (2016)

# Data Analytics, AI, and Computational Science

# Optimizing Data Movement for GPU-Based In-Situ Workflow Using GPUDirect RDMA

Bo Zhang[1](✉), Philip E. Davis[1], Nicolas Morales[2], Zhao Zhang[3], Keita Teranishi[4], and Manish Parashar[1]

[1] Scientific Computing and Imaging Institute, University of Utah, Salt Lake City, UT 84112, USA
{bozhang,philip.davis,parashar}@sci.utah.edu

[2] Sandia National Laboratories, Livermore, CA 94551, USA
nmmoral@sandia.gov

[3] Texas Advanced Computing Center, Austin, TX 78758, USA
zzhang@tacc.utexas.edu

[4] Oak Ridge National Laboratory, Oak Ridge, TN 37830, USA
teranishik@ornl.gov

**Abstract.** The extreme-scale computing landscape is increasingly dominated by GPU-accelerated systems. At the same time, in-situ workflows that employ memory-to-memory inter-application data exchanges have emerged as an effective approach for leveraging these extreme-scale systems. In the case of GPUs, GPUDirect RDMA enables third-party devices, such as network interface cards, to access GPU memory directly and has been adopted for intra-application communications across GPUs. In this paper, we present an interoperable framework for GPU-based in-situ workflows that optimizes data movement using GPUDirect RDMA. Specifically, we analyze the characteristics of the possible data movement pathways between GPUs from an in-situ workflow perspective, and design a strategy that maximizes throughput. Furthermore, we implement this approach as an extension of the DataSpaces data staging service, and experimentally evaluate its performance and scalability on a current leadership GPU cluster. The performance results show that the proposed design reduces data-movement time by up to 53% and 40% for the sender and receiver, respectively, and maintains excellent scalability for up to 256 GPUs.

**Keywords:** In-Situ · Workflow · GPU · GPUDirect RDMA · Extreme-Scale Data Management

## 1 Introduction

Emerging HPC systems have widely adopted Graphic Processing Units (GPUs) for their massive computing capability and high power efficiency. As of November 2022, seven of the top ten systems on the TOP500 list [23] have GPUs. Scientific simulations and analyses benefit from both the parallelism and energy


J. Cano et al. (Eds.): Euro-Par 2023, LNCS 14100, pp. 323–338, 2023.
https://doi.org/10.1007/978-3-031-39698-4_22

efficiency of GPUs' architecture [12]. A variety of applications and tools, such as LAMMPS [9] and ZFP [16], have released GPU-optimized versions.

However, a vast I/O gap still remains for the loosely-coupled in-situ workflow [15], which typically consists of several scientific applications as its components. Within in-situ workflows, the component applications run on GPUs/CPUs and exchange data through a high-speed network. Although individual applications can leverage GPUs, the inter-GPU and GPU-CPU I/O cross codes are implemented in an ad hoc manner, which is prone to suboptimal performance. On the other hand, the latest hardware-specific technique, i.e., GPUDirect RDMA (GDR) [3], is available on many modern HPC systems and offers a performance improvement opportunity, while requiring deep hardware knowledge and low-level programming skills from domain scientists.

Existing solutions to the I/O across components in the workflows view the devices (GPU) and hosts (CPU) as individual entities and employ a sequential $device \rightleftharpoons host \rightleftharpoons network$ pathway. As can be seen, the involvement of the hosts is nonessential, and it slows down the I/O performance due to unnecessary data movement to/from the hosts. This slowdown will be exacerbated at larger scales. In addition, involving hosts during I/O across components requires the developers transfer data between hosts and devices with low-level GPU programming APIs, such as CUDA, HIP, etc. It is nontrivial for domain scientists to program with these low-level APIs, and such a programming approach often results in ad hoc solutions that are limited in both interoperability and portability, especially in cases of massive variables or complex I/O patterns.

Porting existing in-situ workflow to GPUs is an ongoing effort in many scientific computing communities. Figure 1 illustrates the challenges of this workflow porting problem: Some of the components have already been ready to run on GPUs, whereas others are in the porting process or still left as legacies. This heterogeneity complicates the I/O management between components in different porting stages and thus makes the plug-n-play almost impossible. Complex data communication patterns and a great number of variables make the situation even worse. For example, the I/O engine of MURaM workflow [19] contains seven separate procedures with 50 1-D variables, 63 2-D variables, and 34 3-D variables in total. We realized that although moving data between GPU and

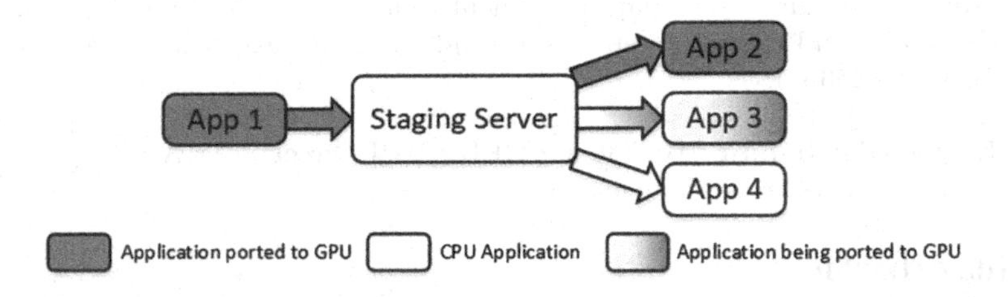


**Fig. 1.** A typical ongoing GPU-based in-situ workflow porting process. The main simulation has already been ported to GPU. Other components are ported, being ported, or still remain the CPU version. The I/O between components also has to change according to the data source/destination.

the host plus conventional communications between host buffers and the network remains a solution, it requires greatly repetitive code refactoring efforts during the porting process but still gains no flexibility of being ported to other GPU ecosystems. In addition, we observed that the I/O performance degraded severely due to consecutive staging at the host buffer, which can be bypassed to reduce the I/O overhead for most cases.

Based on these insights, we investigate several designs for inter-application bulk communications from/to GPUs and introduce a GDR design that circumvent unnecessary data movement path through the host. We therefore propose the first interoperable I/O abstraction for GPU-based in-situ workflow and implement it as an extension of the DataSpaces [10] data staging service. We make the following key contributions in this paper:

- We investigate several designs for bulk data exchanges between GPU applications with respect to the features of in-situ workflow, and then propose a GDR design that reduces I/O overhead by circumventing the host.
- We propose the first interoperable I/O abstraction for GPU-based in-situ workflow, implemented as the extension of the DataSpaces data staging service, which reduces the software refactoring cost and enables plug-n-play in the workflow porting process.
- We evaluate the proposed designs on current leadership GPU clusters using both synthetic and real workflows running on up to 256 GPUs and demonstrate that they can reduce up to 53% and 40% of the I/O time for sender and receiver, respectively, in comparison to the baseline.

# 2 Background

## 2.1 In-Situ Workflow

The traditional scientific workflow model first writes the simulation data to persistent storage, and then reads it back into memory for the analysis or visualization later, which is defined as a *post-hoc* method since it reflects that the visualization or analysis is performed "after the fact" [8]. We have witnessed a significant performance slowdown for this method as the computational throughput scaled up [5,6,17]. An alternative approach, which is named by the umbrella term *in-situ*, saves the huge I/O cost by removing the nonessential involvement of

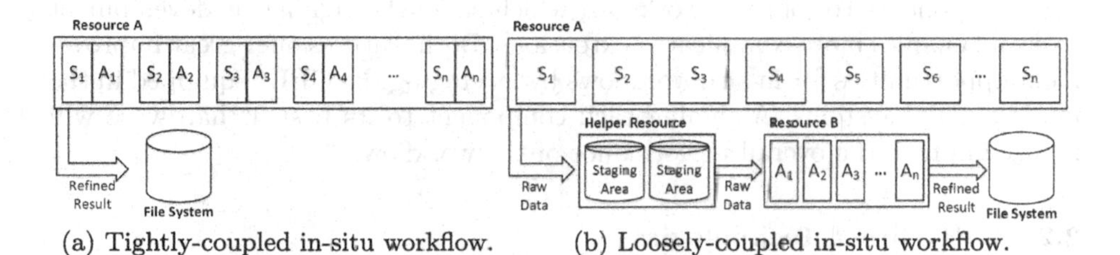


(a) Tightly-coupled in-situ workflow. (b) Loosely-coupled in-situ workflow.

**Fig. 2.** A schematic illustration of in-situ workflow paradigms.

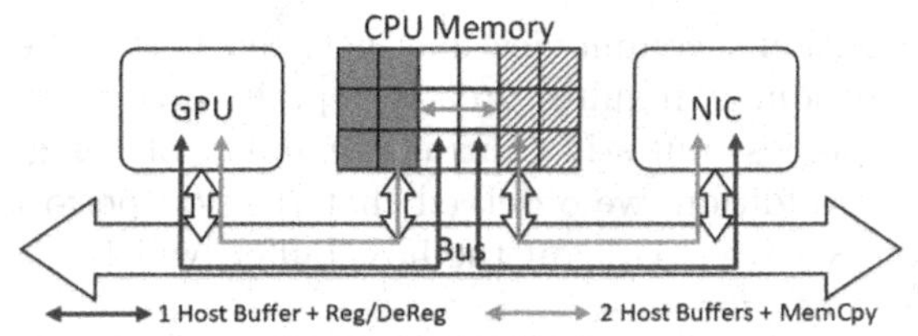


**(a) Vanilla data flow between GPU and NIC. The red path requires the data to be staged in only one host buffer but needs a sequential DMA deregistration and registration by GPU/NIC or NIC/GPU, respectively. The blue path allows GPU and NIC to register at two host buffers, but an extra memory copy is needed.**

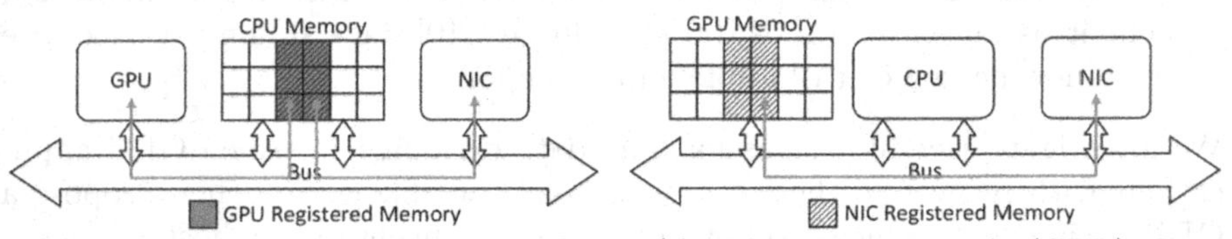


**(b) GPUDirect data flow between GPU and NIC. GPU and NIC and register at the same host buffer at the same time.**

**(c) GPUDirect RDMA (GDR) data flow between GPU and NIC. CPU data staging is avoided.**

**Fig. 3.** Data flow paths between GPU and network interface card (NIC).

persistent storage. Two paradigms have emerged from the in-situ model: *tightly-coupled* method and *loosely-coupled* method [15]. The tightly-coupled paradigm is illustrated in Fig. 2a. Simulation and analysis run in the same process using the same set of computing resources. They alternate in each iteration, sharing the data stored in the memory, and finally output the refined result to the file system. As for the loosely-coupled paradigm, simulation and analysis run asynchronously in the separate process groups on their dedicated resources, as shown in Fig. 2b. They exchange the shared data over the high-speed network with the help of a staging server, which takes extra resources to manage the data forwarding.

The loosely-coupled in-situ workflow maintains its flexibility and modularity by isolating the computational tasks at an appropriate granularity. We define each isolated computational task that runs separately as an individual *component* in the context of loosely-coupled in-situ workflow. Then, the flexibility means that the running scale of each component can be configured individually according to its characteristics, avoiding the inefficiency under the holistic resources allocation. Besides, the modularity supports easy plugin-and-play for new components to join the workflow, which saves the significant development cost and enables more complicated extensions. Both features offer great improvement opportunities for in-situ workflows by leveraging the GPUs equipped in the modern HPC systems. Assigning each component to its best-fit hardware will finally improve the overall performance of the workflow.

### 2.2 GPUDirect Technologies

Direct Memory Access (DMA) requires memory registration before data access. The DMA engine of GPU has to register a CPU memory region to enable asynchronous data movement, and the network interface card (NIC) also requires this registration to transfer data over the network. Therefore, as shown in Fig. 3a, either GPU and NIC registering the same host buffer sequentially or registering two separate host buffers at the same time but introducing an extra data copy is required for GPU data communication. Both the de-register/register process and the extra memory copy can be summarized as the DMA overhead that increases I/O latency. NVIDIA GPUDirect technologies eliminate unnecessary memory copies between GPUs and other devices, decrease CPU overheads, and reduce latency [3], thereby significantly enhancing data movement and access for GPUs. Released with CUDA 4.0, the initial GPUDirect enabled both GPU and NIC to register the same memory region on the CPU, avoiding the DMA overhead at the host as shown in Fig. 3b. From CUDA 5.0, GPUDirect RDMA (GDR) is released as the extension of GPUDirect, which supports GPU memory registration by any third-party standard PCIe device. Figure 3c illustrates the direct data exchange path between GPU and NIC.

AMD GPUs also support this peer-direct technique in their ROCm ecosystem, namely ROCmRDMA [2]. In this work, however, we use the umbrella term *GPUDirect RDMA (GDR)* to refer to all direct data exchange solutions between GPU and NIC. We focus on NVIDIA GPUs with the CUDA programming ecosystem and the RDMA-enabled network in the rest of the paper.

## 3 Related Work

Over last ten years, a fair amount of contributions from HPC community have been made to accelerate GPU-related I/O in widely used programming models and network substrates by GPUDirect technologies. Wang et al. proposed MVAPICH2-GPU [26], which is the first GPU-aware MPI implementation with the GPUDirect optimization for CUDA-based GPUs. Potluri et al. upgraded the GPU-aware MPI libraries using GPUDirect RDMA (GDR) and proposed a hybrid solution that benefits from the best of both GDR and host-assisted GPU communication [18]. Shi et al. designed GDRCopy [22], a low-latency copy mechanism between GPU and host memory based on GDR, which improved the efficiency of small message transfer. NVIDIA NCCL [13], as a popular backend for leading deep learning frameworks, also supported GDR in its communication routine set. In addition, programming frameworks that simplify the GPU application porting process have been explored as well. Kokkos [24], RAJA [7] and SYCL [20] support compile-time platform specification for applications written in their abstractions. However, research work in either data movement optimization or I/O abstraction from a workflow perspective is extremely limited. ADIOS2 [11], a high-performance I/O framework that often plays as a data coupler between components in a workflow, is extended to support GPU-aware I/O [1]. However, its GPU I/O support works only for binary-pack version 4 (BP4) and BP5 file engines, which are still solutions based on persistent storage. Zhang et al. explored the data layout mismatch in the CPU-GPU hybrid loosely-coupled in-situ workflow and proposed a solution to minimize the data reorganization overhead [27]. However, they did not optimize the data movement pathway for GPU components. Wang et al. presented a conceptual overview of the GPU-aware data exchange in an in-situ workflow [25], but they proposed only a preliminary idea with neither implementation details nor quantitative evaluation at scale. Our work is distinguished from related efforts in being the first interoperable GPU-aware I/O abstraction for the inter-component data exchange in loosely-coupled in-situ workflows. We provide a systematically comprehensive evaluation of the GDR design at the largest scales we were able to reach on a state-of-the-art production HPC system equipped with GPUs.

# 4 Design

In this section, we discuss the baseline and optimized designs for the inter-application bulk data movement from/to GPUs. As shown in Fig. 1, components in the workflow can be generally classified in three categories as staging server, sender, and receiver. The staging server typically works as a memory-bounded component that is responsible for storing the intermediate shared data and processing the asynchronous I/O requests made by all other applications. Therefore, even if the staging server may also run on nodes equipped with GPUs, CPU main memory is still chosen as the primary storage media for its consideration of capacity and cost. The sender is typically a simulation that produces multidimensional data on GPUs and sends it out to the staging server. The receiver is usually an analysis or a visualization that fetches the data from the staging server and consumes it. A loosely-coupled in-situ workflow has only one staging server component and at least one sender and one receiver. In the following subsections, we discuss these two parts, respectively. We also present the implementation overview of the proposed I/O framework and demonstrate its interoperability through a code snippet.

## 4.1 Sender Side

**Baseline Design.** To send the GPU data out to the staging server, the baseline design simply uses CUDA memory copy from device to host and then sets up a conventional CPU-CPU bulk data transfer between the sender and staging server. This straightforward approach takes the bulk I/O as an ensemble by concatenating the GPU to CPU and CPU to the staging server data transfer together, which runs sequentially after the meta-data preparation phase on the CPU. The DMA control sequence introduced in Sect. 2.2 must be gone through between the two concatenated I/O procedures, which increases the overall latency. Although this design is intuitive and simple to implement, its weakness becomes apparent when frequent and consecutive `put` requests are made because the fixed overhead is incurred for every request.

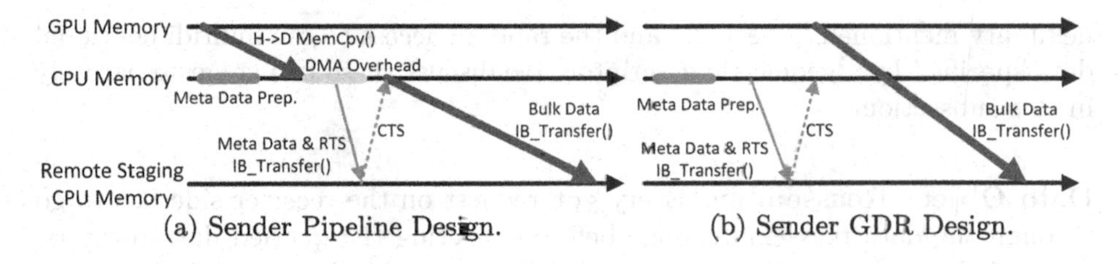


(a) Sender Pipeline Design. (b) Sender GDR Design.

**Fig. 4.** A schematic illustration of sender side designs.

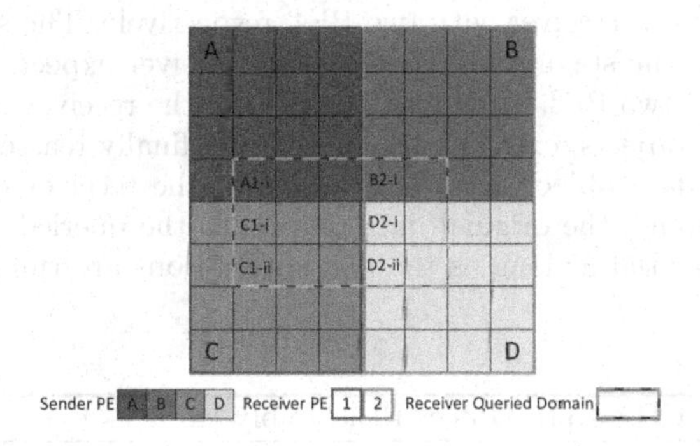


**Fig. 5.** Data Object Reassembly on the receiver side. 4 PEs of the sender put local $4 \times 4$ 2D arrays into a global $8 \times 8$ domain. 2 PEs of the receiver expect to get a subset of the $8 \times 8$ shared domain, a $3 \times 3$ array and a $3 \times 2$ array, respectively. Receiver PE1 has to find the data object A, copy the memory line once, and find data object C, copy the memory line twice. Receiver PE2 has to find the data objects B, D and copy the memory line accordingly.

**Pipeline Design.** We are able to optimize the baseline design by overlapping independent tasks after splitting the entire send procedure into several stages and analyzing their dependencies carefully. Figure 4a illustrates the pipeline design that requires no additional prerequisites. The meta-data are prepared on the host when the bulk data is copied from GPU to the host. Also, the DMA operations partially overlap with the connection setup between the sender and the staging server. This design exploits the potential overlaps between different stages of the send procedure by leveraging the asynchrony on both the GPU and CPU.

**GDR Design.** As long as the GPU data are transferred to the staging server, the less intermediate stages result in better performance. We fully circumvent the host involvement by employing GDR in the bulk data transfer. Figure 4b presents the neat GDR design. After the essential meta-data preparation and connection setup phase, data are directly sent from GPU memory to the staging server. No memory allocations and DMA overhead are incurred in this design.

### 4.2 Receiver Side

Due to the simplicity of the sender design, on the receiver side, a data object reassembly stage is introduced in addition to the bulk data I/O for the scale flexibility mentioned in Sect. 2.1 and the random access to the multidimensional data specified by a geometric descriptor. We discuss these two stages separately in this subsection.

**Data Object Reassembly.** Every `get` request on the receiver side has to go through the data reassembly stage before delivering the queried data to users. Figure 5 demonstrates the necessity of data reassembly by an example. A 2-D data domain is shared by two applications served as a sender with four processing elements(PEs) and a receiver with two PEs, respectively. The sender puts four data objects into the staging server, while the receiver expects to get a subset of data in each of two PEs. Therefore, each PE in the receiver has to figure out the original data objects, extract each subset, and finally reassemble the subset to a contiguous data object accordingly. Even if the receiver query the entire domain, reassembling the original data objects to the queried contiguous data object is still essential as long as the two applications are running at different scales.

**Algorithm 1.** CUDA Data Object Reassembly Kernel

**Input:** $src\_obj$, $dst\_obj.bbox$ {bounding box descriptor}
**Output:** $dst\_obj.data$

$its\_bbox \leftarrow$ Intersection($src\_obj.bbox$, $dst\_obj.bbox$)
$src\_nx, src\_ny, src\_nz \leftarrow$ Distance($src\_obj.bbox$)
$dst\_nx, dst\_ny, dst\_nz \leftarrow$ Distance($dst\_obj.bbox$)
$sub\_nx, sub\_ny, sub\_nz \leftarrow$ Distance($its\_bbox$)
$i \leftarrow blockIdx.x * blockDim.x + threadIdx.x$
$j \leftarrow blockIdx.y * blockDim.y + threadIdx.y$
$k \leftarrow blockIdx.z * blockDim.z + threadIdx.z$
**if** $i < sub\_nx$ **and** $j < sub\_ny$ **and** $k < sub\_nz$ **then**
  $dst\_idx \leftarrow i + j * dst\_nx + k * dst\_nx * dst\_ny$
  $src\_idx \leftarrow i + j * src\_nx + k * src\_nx * src\_ny$
  $dst\_obj.data[dst\_idx] \leftarrow src\_obj.data[src\_idx]$
**end if**

The existing solution for data object reassembly is based purely on CPU. It iteratively calls `Memcpy()`, which moves a data line along the lowest dimension at once, for the multidimensional data. Since the data destination is ported to GPU memory in the GPU applications, we design a CUDA kernel to accelerate this data object reassembly task by utilizing the intrinsic parallelism of GPU architecture. Algorithm 1 describes the details of the kernel. Although an individual kernel supports only up to 3-D data object reassembly, it can be iteratively launched several times for data in more dimensions. Asynchronous kernel launch is utilized for concurrency depending on the capability of the target CUDA device.

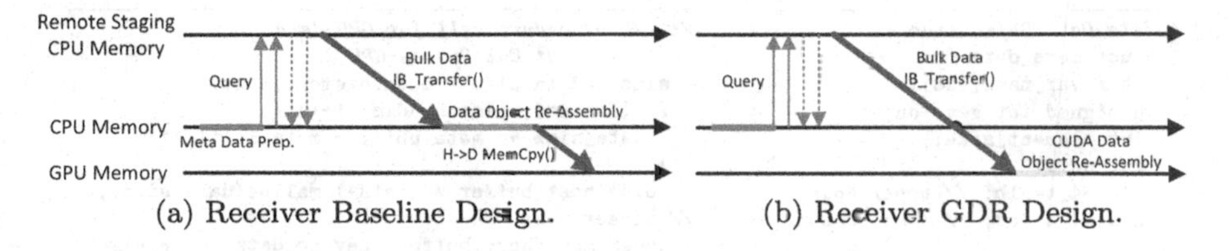


**Fig. 6.** A schematic illustration of receiver side designs.

**Bulk Data Transfer.** The bulk data I/O path on the receiver side keeps the same options as the sender side: CPU-CPU transfer plus CUDA memory copy from host to device or GDR. Therefore, we propose three receiver designs as the combination of bulk data transfer and data object reassembly options. Figure 6a illustrates the baseline design that reassembles the received data objects on the host to a new CPU buffer, and then transfers it to the GPU destination. Because two buffers are used on the host and the data object reassembly intrinsically finishes the memory copy between them, no DMA overhead is incurred in this design. The hybrid design takes the conventional I/O path but uses the CUDA kernel for data object reassembly. It holds only one buffer for both receiving data from the staging server and transferring to the GPU, but its DMA overhead partially overlaps with the CUDA kernel computation since multiple data objects are received typically and the following work is done asynchronously. The GDR design keeps clear as shown in Fig. 6b. There is no CPU involvement, and the data object reassembly is done by CUDA kernels.

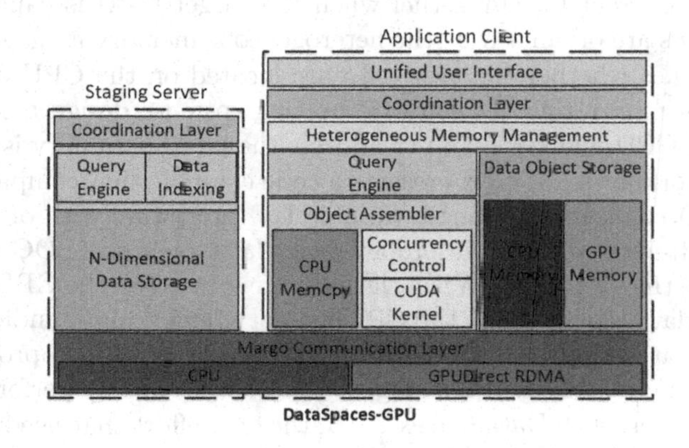


**Fig. 7.** Architecture of DataSpace-GPU. Existing modules are extended to support both GPU computation and storage under the heterogeneous memory management layer.

### 4.3 Implementation and Interoperability

Our designs are implemented in the existing DataSpaces staging framework as an extension to support the data exchanges from/to GPU components inside an in-situ workflow. Figure 7 presents a schematic overview of the DataSpaces-GPU.

```
/* Meta Data Defination */
  struct meta_data {
    char var_name[128];
    unsigned int version;
    int element_size;
    int ndim;
    uint64_t* lb; // upper bound
    uint64_t* ub; // lower bound
  };

  struct meta_data meta;
  void* host_data, device_data;

/* Meta Data Preparation */
  prepare(meta);
```

```
/* I/O procedure call for GPU data
     without DataSpaces-GPU */
  size_t data_size = meta.element_size;
  for(int i=0; i<meta.ndim; i++) {
    data_size *= meta.ub[i] - meta.lb[i] +1;
  }
  void* host_buffer = (void*) malloc(data_size);
// Sender Side
  cudaMemcpy(host_buffer, device_data, data_size,
          cudaMemcpyDeviceToHost);
  dspaces_put(meta, host_buffer);
// Receiver Side
  dspaces_get(meta, host_buffer);
  cudaMemcpy(device_data, host_buffer, data_size,
          cudaMemcpyHostToDevice);
  free(host_buffer);
```

```
/* I/O procedure call for
    CPU data */
// Sender Side
  dspaces_put(meta, host_data);
// Receiver Side
  dspaces_get(meta, host_data);
```

```
/* I/O procedure call for GPU data
     with DataSpaces-GPU */
// Sender Side
  dspaces_put(meta, device_data);
// Receiver Side
  dspaces_get(meta, device_data);
```

**Fig. 8.** Code example of porting a single variable I/O procedure to GPU with or without DataSpaces-GPU.

It leverages the existing components by reusing its data transport, indexing, and querying capabilities. The GDR capability of the Margo [21] communication layer is employed by the GPU memory extension of the data object storage module at the application client. The object assembler module adds support to launch the concurrent CUDA kernel when the target GPU is capable. All the GPU extensions are organized by the heterogeneous memory management layer, which determines whether the user data are located on the CPU or GPU. For the purpose of minimizing the software porting cost, we design a set of unified APIs for both CPU and GPU I/O to address the interoperability issue with the legacy CPU workflows. Figure 8 presents a code example that compares the lines of code (LOC) changes for a single variable I/O procedure with or without our framework. After setting up the proper meta-data, only one LOC is needed to send or receive the CPU data. When the data are located on the GPU, we need to calculate the data size, manage the CPU memory buffer, and handle the CUDA memory copy at the sender and receiver side, respectively. Approximately 10 LOC are added on each side for a single variable without any performance optimization. However, with DataSpaces-GPU, the only effort that needs to be made is changing the CPU pointer to the GPU pointer and no extra code is required, which saves great software porting costs, especially when many variables are communicated or the communication pattern is complex. DataSpaces-GPU thus enables procedure-wise I/O plug-n-play in the entire workflow porting process.

## 5 Evaluation

In this section, we present an evaluation of the proposed GDR design compared to the conventional host-based designs in terms of both time-to-solution and scalability. The end-to-end benchmark is tested using a synthetic workflow emulator, and the weak scaling experiment is performed on a real scientific workflow that consists of LULESH-CUDA [14] and ZFP-CUDA.

Our synthetic workflow emulator uses two application codes, namely writers and readers, to simulate the inter-application data movement behaviors in real loosely-coupled in-situ workflows. Writers produce simulation data and send it to the staging servers, whereas readers fetch the data from staging servers and then perform some analysis. In our real workflow experiment, LULESH is the simulation that writes the data out and ZFP is the reader. The data are organized in a 3-D Cartesian grid format with $X \times Y \times Z$ scale in both workflows.

All the experiments were performed on the Phase 2 GPU nodes of the Perlmutter supercomputer at National Energy Research Scientific Computing (NERSC). Phase 2 GPU nodes have a single socket of an AMD EPYC 7763 (Milan) 64-core processor with 160GB of DDR4 RAM. Each node equips four NVIDIA Ampere A100 GPUs with four Slingshot-11 Cassini NICs. All the nodes run libfabric-1.15.0 with Cray Slingshot-11 `cxi` support. All four NICs are leveraged and evenly mapped to the PEs on each node. Concurrent CUDA kernel launch is enabled, and the maximum number of concurrent kernel launch is set to 32 as the default. In subsequent sections, all measured times refer to the wall time of the blocking I/O routine that guarantees the message is sent to the destination. All the test runs have been executed three times, and the average result is reported.

**Table 1.** Experimental setup configurations for end-to-end benchmark

| | |
|---|---|
| No. of Parallel Writer Cores/GPUs/Nodes | 128 / 64 / 16 |
| No. of Parallel Reader Cores /GPUs/Nodes | 128/64/16 |
| No. of Staging Cores/Nodes | 32/8 |
| Total I/O Iterations | 10 |
| I/O Iteration Frequency | Every 2 s |

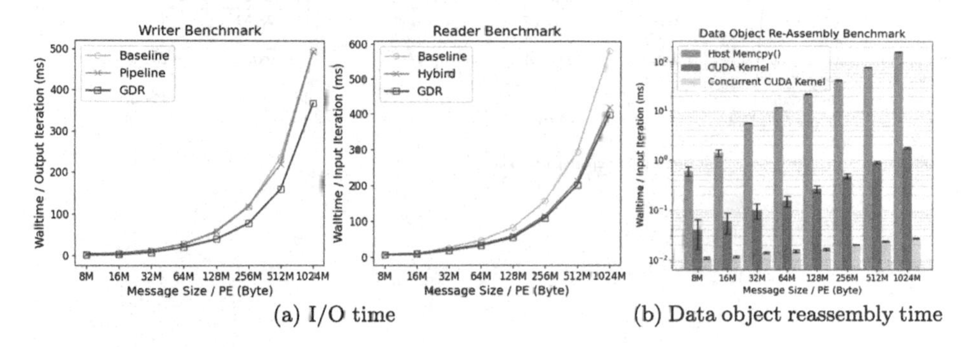


(a) I/O time (b) Data object reassembly time

**Fig. 9.** Performance comparison per I/O iteration among proposed designs with increasing message size.

### 5.1 End-to-End Benchmark

This experiment compares the I/O performance between applications and staging servers for various message sizes using different designs introduced in Sect. 4. Table 1 details the setup for all test cases in this experiment. In order to alleviate the iterative interference, we set the I/O frequency to 2 s. The message size we choose to evaluate starts from 8 MB, which is the smallest data size for a single variable in each parallel PEs in a typical fine-grained domain decomposition.

Figure 9a presents the benchmark result for writers and readers, respectively. In general, although GDR is designed to optimize small and frequent communication to/from GPUs, it achieves better performance in bulk data transfer than other host-involved designs as well. On the writer side, the baseline method and pipeline method show almost the same trend, which means the overhead of sending metadata is negligible in the bulk data movement. Compared to the baseline and pipeline methods, the GDR method reduces 53% of the put time for the 8 MB bulk transfer while still maintaining a 34% of reduction when sending 1024 MB messages.

On the reader side, the hybrid and GDR methods achieve up to 28% and 33% reduction of the get time compared to the baseline. The GDR method always performs slightly better than the hybrid method since it avoids the DMA overhead introduced in Sect. 2.2. Both methods use the CUDA kernel for the data object reassembly instead of the host `Memcpy()` function, which contributes mainly to the performance improvement. Figure 9b extracts and compares the data object reassembly performance from the overall I/O time. The CUDA kernel accelerates the data object reassembly task by up to 90x as the message size increases. By utilizing the asynchronous kernel execution feature of CUDA devices, launching the kernels concurrently with a barrier that waits all kernels to complete can even achieve an acceleration up to 6000x.

**Table 2.** Experimental setup configurations of data domain, core-allocations and size of the staged data for shock hydrodynamics workflow

| Data Domain | 512 × 512 × 512 | 768 × 768 × 768 | 1024 × 1024 × 1024 | 1280 × 1280 × 1280 | 1536 × 1536 × 1536 |
|---|---|---|---|---|---|
| No. of LULESH-CUDA Cores/GPUs/Nodes | 8/8/2 | 27/27/7 | 64/64/16 | 128/128/32 | 256/256/64 |
| No. of ZFP-CUDA Cores/GPUs/Nodes | 8/8/2 | 27/27/7 | 64/64/16 | 128/128/32 | 256/256/64 |
| No. of Staging Cores/Nodes | 4/1 | 16/4 | 32/8 | 64/16 | 128/32 |
| Total Staged Data Size (3 variables, 10 I/O Iterations) | 30 GB | 60 GB | 120 GB | 240 GB | 480 GB |
| I/O Iteration Frequency | Every 100 computing iteration | | | | |

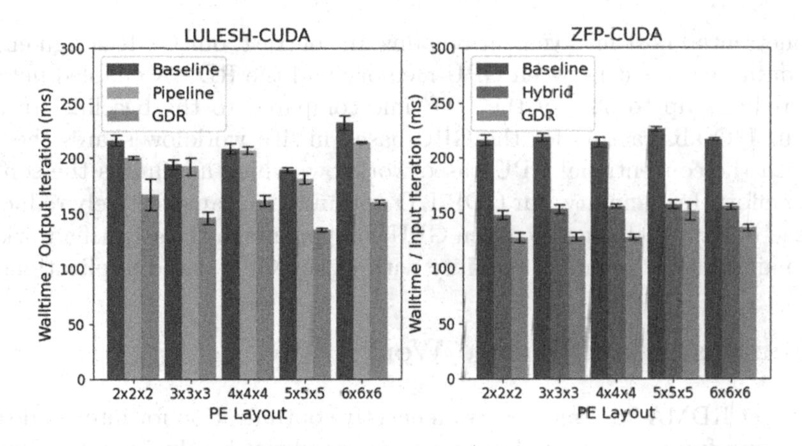


**Fig. 10.** Weak scaling comparison of I/O time per I/O iteration among proposed designs in the LULESH workflow.

### 5.2 Real Scientific Workflow

In addition to evaluations based on the synthetic workflow emulator, we also apply our proposed designs to a CUDA-based shock hydrodynamics simulation workflow. We use the LULESH-CUDA component for the simulation purpose, which generates 3-D data and sends them to the staging servers. For the analysis, the ZFP-CUDA component gets the data from the staging servers, compresses and writes it to the persistent storage. We select three scalar data fields (energy, pressure, mass) from 13 variables to perform the inter-application data exchange. The experimental configurations of our hydrodynamics workflow tests are listed in Table 2. Since LULESH supports only cubic PEs increment, our evaluation was performed with 8, 27, 64 cores, with a $1:1$ mapping to GPUs and a $\sim$4:1 mapping to nodes. The grid domain sizes were chosen such that each core was assigned a spatial local domain of size $256 \times 256 \times 256$. We keep this same data volume per LULESH/ZFP core to perform a weak scaling test in this evaluation.

Figure 10 compares the proposed designs in the weak scaling workflow with a fixed ratio of LULESH/ZFP resources to the staging server. The GDR design still takes $\sim$24% less time to consecutively send the data fields out compared to others, while performing $\sim$40% and $\sim$17% better in fetching the data fields than the baseline and hybrid design, respectively. The I/O time remains relatively constant for all designs as the overall problem size and total resources increase. Little overhead is introduced as the amount of resources increases, which indicates that all proposed designs maintain great scalability to solve the problem in a larger scale.

From our synthetic and real scientific workflow evaluations, we can infer that the straightforward baseline design of data movement between GPU applications performs poorly at any scale due to the sequential *device* $\rightleftharpoons$ *host* $\rightleftharpoons$ *network* pathway. Pipelining I/O design on the sender side and applying CUDA kernels for data object reassembly on the receiver side improves the performance, but nonessential host involvement remains. In contrast, our GDR design enables direct data movement between GPU memory and the RDMA-enabled network, which reduces up to 53% of the I/O time compared to the baseline. In addition, our I/O abstraction for the GPU-based in-situ workflow shares the same API with the conventional CPU-based workflow, which minimizes the software porting effort. In summary, our GDR I/O optimization can effectively reduce the overhead of data exchanges between GPU components in the scientific workflow, while maintaining the interoperability with legacy CPU-based applications.

## 6 Conclusion and Future Work

GPUDirect RDMA has emerged as an effective optimization for inter-node communications from/to GPUs, but it has been adopted only by I/O substrate designed for individual applications. In this paper, we present a novel design that applies GPUDirect RDMA to the bulk data movement between GPU applications within a workflow. Also, we propose the first interoperable I/O abstraction for GPU-based in-situ workflows, which simplifies the GPU workflow porting process and enables procedure-wise plug-n-play through the unified interface. We implemented the proposed solution based on the DataSpaces framework and evaluated it on the NERSC Perlmutter system. Our experimental results, using both synthetic and real GPU workflows, demonstrate that the proposed solution yields an I/O improvement of up to 53% and 40% for sender and receiver, respectively, while maintaining great scalability for up to 256 processing elements on 256 GPUs. As future work, we plan to investigate the performance portability of our design on other network hardware, such as Mellanox EDR and HDR interconnect. We also plan to provide comprehensive support to AMD GPUs in our workflow I/O abstraction.

**Acknowledgements and Data Availability.** This research used resources of the National Energy Research Scientific Computing Center, which is supported by the Office of Science of the U.S. Department of Energy under Contract No. DE-AC02-05CH11231. Sandia National Laboratories is a multimission laboratory managed and operated by National Technology & Engineering Solutions of Sandia, LLC, a wholly owned subsidiary of Honeywell International Inc., for the U.S. Department of Energy's National Nuclear Security Administration (NNSA) under contract DE- NA0003525. This work was funded by NNSA's Advanced Simulation and Computing (ASC) Program. This manuscript has been authored by UT-Battelle LLC under contract DE-AC05-00OR22725 with the US Department of Energy (DOE). This work is also based upon work by the RAPIDS2 Institute supported by the U.S. Department of Energy, Office of Science, Office of Advanced Scientific Computing Research through the Advanced Computing (SciDAC) program under Award Number DE-SC0023130. The datasets and code generated during and/or analysed during the current study are available in the Figshare repository: https://doi.org/10.6084/m9.figshare.23535855 [4]. This paper describes objective technical results and analysis. Any subjective views or opinions that might be expressed in the paper do not necessarily represent the views of the U.S. Department of Energy or the United States Government.

## References


1. ADIOS 2 Documentation (2022). https://adios2.readthedocs.io/en/latest/advanced/gpu_aware.html
2. AMD ROCm Information Portal - v4.5 (2022). https://rocmdocs.amd.com/en/latest/Remote_Device_Programming/Remote-Device-Programming.html
3. NVIDIA GPUDirect RDMA Documentation (2022). https://docs.nvidia.com/cuda/gpudirect-rdma/index.html
4. Zhang, B., Davis, P.E., Morales, N., Zhang, Z., Teranishi, K., Parashar, M. Artifact and instructions to generate experimental results for Euro-Par 2023 paper: SymED: Adaptive and Online Symbolic Representation of Data on the Edge, 2023. https://doi.org/10.6084/m9.figshare.23535855
5. Ahrens, J., Rhyne, T.M.: Increasing scientific data insights about exascale class simulations under power and storage constraints. IEEE Comput. Graph. Appl. **35**(2), 8–11 (2015)
6. Asch, M., et al.: Big data and extreme-scale computing: pathways to convergence-toward a shaping strategy for a future software and data ecosystem for scientific inquiry. Int. J. High Perform. Comput. Appl. **32**(4), 435–479 (2018)
7. Beckingsale, D.A., et al.: RAJA: portable performance for large-scale scientific applications. In: 2019 IEEE/ACM International Workshop on Performance, Portability and Productivity in HPC (P3HPC), pp. 71–81. IEEE (2019)
8. Bethel, E., et al.: In Situ Methods, Infrastructures, and Applications on High Performance Computing Platforms, a State-of-the-art (STAR) Report (2021)
9. Brown, W.M.: GPU acceleration in LAMMPS. In: LAMMPS User's Workshop and Symposium (2011)
10. Docan, C., Parashar, M., Klasky, S.: Dataspaces: an interaction and coordination framework for coupled simulation workflows. In: Proceedings of the 19th ACM International Symposium on High Performance Distributed Computing, pp. 25–36 (2010)
11. Godoy, W.F., et al.: Adios 2: the adaptable input output system. a framework for high-performance data management. SoftwareX **12**, 100561 (2020)
12. Goswami, A., et al.: Landrush: rethinking in-situ analysis for GPGPU workflows. In: 2016 16th IEEE/ACM International Symposium on Cluster, Cloud and Grid Computing (CCGrid), pp. 32–41. IEEE (2016)
13. Jeaugey, S.: Nccl 2.0. In: GPU Technology Conference (GTC), vol. 2 (2017)
14. Karlin, I., Keasler, J., Neely, R.: Lulesh 2.0 updates and changes. Technical report LLNL-TR-641973, August 2013
15. Kress, J., Klasky, S., Podhorszki, N., Choi, J., Childs, H., Pugmire, D.: Loosely coupled in situ visualization: a perspective on why it's here to stay. In: Proceedings of the First Workshop on In Situ Infrastructures for Enabling Extreme-Scale Analysis and Visualization, pp. 1–6 (2015)
16. Lindstrom, P.: Fixed-rate compressed floating-point arrays. IEEE Trans. Vis. Comput. Graph. **20**(12), 2674–2683 (2014)
17. Moreland, K.: The tensions of in situ visualization. IEEE Comput. Graph. Appl. **36**(2), 5–9 (2016)
18. Potluri, S., Hamidouche, K., Venkatesh, A., Bureddy, D., Panda, D.K.: Efficient inter-node MPI communication using GPUDirect RDMA for InfiniBand clusters with NVIDIA GPUs. In: 2013 42nd International Conference on Parallel Processing, pp. 80–89. IEEE (2013)

19. Pulatov, D., Zhang, B., Suresh, S., Miller, C.: Porting IDL programs into Python for GPU-Accelerated In-situ Analysis (2021)
20. Reyes, R., Brown, G., Burns, R., Wong, M.: SYCL 2020: more than meets the eye. In: Proceedings of the International Workshop on OpenCL, p. 1 (2020)
21. Ross, R.B., et al.: Mochi: composing data services for high-performance computing environments. J. Comput. Sci. Technol. **35**(1), 121–144 (2020)
22. Shi, R., et al.: Designing efficient small message transfer mechanism for inter-node MPI communication on InfiniBand GPU clusters. In: 2014 21st International Conference on High Performance Computing (HiPC), pp. 1–10. IEEE (2014)
23. Strohmaier, E., Dongarra, J., Simon, H., Meuer, M.: TOP500 List, November 2022. https://www.top500.org/lists/top500/2022/11/
24. Trott, C.R., et al.: Kokkos 3: programming model extensions for the exascale era. IEEE Trans. Parallel Distrib. Syst. **33**(4), 805–817 (2021)
25. Wang, D., Foran, D.J., Qi, X., Parashar, M.: Enabling asynchronous coupled data intensive analysis workflows on GPU-accelerated platforms via data staging
26. Wang, H., Potluri, S., Luo, M., Singh, A.K., Sur, S., Panda, D.K.: MVAPICH2-GPU: optimized GPU to GPU communication for InfiniBand clusters. Comput. Sci.-Res. Dev. **26**(3), 257–266 (2011)
27. Zhang, B., Subedi, P., Davis, P.E., Rizzi, F., Teranishi, K., Parashar, M.: Assembling portable in-situ workflow from heterogeneous components using data reorganization. In: 2022 22nd IEEE International Symposium on Cluster, Cloud and Internet Computing (CCGrid), pp. 41–50. IEEE (2022)

# FedGM: Heterogeneous Federated Learning via Generative Learning and Mutual Distillation

Chao Peng, Yiming Guo(✉), Yao Chen, Qilin Rui, Zhengfeng Yang, and Chenyang Xu

Shanghai Key Laboratory of Trustworthy Computing, Software Engineering Institute, East China Normal University, Shanghai, China
{cpeng,zfyang,cyxu}@sei.ecnu.edu.cn,
{yiming.guo,51205902080,51205902132}@stu.ecnu.edu.cn

**Abstract.** Federated learning is a distributed machine learning that enables models to aggregate on the server after local training to protect privacy. However, user heterogeneity presents a challenge in federated learning. To address this issue, some recent work has proposed using knowledge distillation. But the application of knowledge distillation in federated learning is dependent on the proxy dataset, which can be difficult to obtain in practice. Additionally, the simple average aggregation method of model parameters may fail to achieve a global model with good generalization performance, and may also lead to potential privacy breaches. To tackle these issues, we propose FedGM, a data-free federated knowledge distillation method that combines generative learning with mutual distillation. FedGM addresses user heterogeneity while also protecting user privacy. We use a conditional generator to extract global knowledge to guide local model training and build a proxy dataset on the server-side to perform mutual distillation. Extensive experiments on benchmark datasets show that FedGM outperforms state-of-the-art approaches in terms of generalization performance and privacy protection.

**Keywords:** Federated Learning · User heterogeneity · Knowledge Distillation · Generative Learning

## 1 Introduction

With the advent of edge computing, edge devices such as mobile phones, vehicles, and facilities are generating more data than ever before. However, integrating this data directly can be challenging due to privacy restrictions and industry competition. Federated Learning (FL) is a novel machine learning approach that decentralizes computing power and data resources. It enables clients to leverage their local data for most of the computation by generating a local model, while the global server only aggregates and updates the model parameters based on the information received from clients, thus can ensure a basic level of privacy while also allowing for the use of decentralized data resources.


J. Cano et al. (Eds.): Euro-Par 2023, LNCS 14100, pp. 339–351, 2023.
https://doi.org/10.1007/978-3-031-39698-4_23

Classic aggregation algorithms for FL, represented by FedAvg [1], typically average model parameters trained by each client element-wise. However, FL faces a practical challenge from user heterogeneity, that is, in a scenario with $K$ clients, the datasets $\{(\mathcal{X}_1, \mathcal{Y}_1), \cdots, (\mathcal{X}_k, \mathcal{Y}_k)\}$ that belong to different clients $i, j \in \{1, 2, \ldots, K\}$ may follow different data distributions $(x, y) \sim \mathcal{P}_i(x, y) \neq \mathcal{P}_j$. This user heterogeneity can result in a significant reduction in accuracy for FedAvg compared to Independent and Identically Distributed (IID) data.

To deal with user **heterogeneity** in Federated Learning, many approaches have been suggested, primarily from two complementary perspectives: one is to regulate the local model's deviation from the global model in the parameter space to stabilize local training, such as FedProx [2], while the other tries to enhance the effectiveness of the model aggregation method, with knowledge distillation emerging as an effective solution, such as FedDF [3]. By using a proxy dataset to transfer ensemble knowledge from local models to the global model, knowledge distillation can mitigate the model drift problem caused by user data heterogeneity more effectively than simple parameter-averaging. However, a proxy dataset saved on the server-side is required for using knowledge distillation, which usually consists of partial data provided by users or collected unlabeled data. This is not feasible in many application fields due to two reasons: 1) the risk of user privacy leakage, and 2) the low quality of wild data.

Based on our observation of user heterogeneity and shortcomings of existing methods, in this work, we introduce a novel approach for federated learning, namely Heterogeneous Federated Learning via Generative Learning and Mutual Distillation (FedGM), in response to the problem of user heterogeneity. Inspired by FedGen [4] and Deep Mutual Learning (DML) [5], our FedGM combines the strengths of generative learning to transfer global knowledge to clients with mutual distillation to improve the performance of the global model and communication effectiveness. FedGM learns the global data distribution from user models' prediction rules using a conditional generator, which can produce feature representations that match user predictions for given target labels. As a result, the purpose of transferring global knowledge is achieved by broadcasting the generator to clients and generating augmented samples to guide the training of local models. In addition, a proxy dataset is constructed with the learned generator to perform mutual distillation on the server-side, facilitating the ensemble of a more robust and generalizable global model by learning secondary information from the prediction of peer models.

Concretely, our main contributions are as follows:

- We propose a data-free approach to knowledge transfer in federated learning using a generative model to learn the global data distribution and constructing a proxy dataset on the server-side.
- Our proposed approach, FedGM, combines generative learning with mutual distillation to overcome the challenges of user heterogeneity. The global generator is broadcasted to clients to adjust the update of their local models, while mutual distillation is performed on the server-side to assemble a more robust global model.

- We evaluate FedGM on three benchmark datasets, and the results show that our proposed approach outperforms the state-of-the-art in terms of generalization performance and communication rounds.

## 2 Related Work

**Federated Learning.** Federated learning involves training machine learning models on remote devices or isolated data centers while keeping the data decentralized [1]. Recent research in this area has focused on addressing various challenges associated with FL, such as communication efficiency, privacy, and data heterogeneity [6]. A variety of approaches have been proposed to address heterogeneity, including personalized models that learn separate but related models for each device [7], regularization techniques that impose a proximal term on local training [2], and methods for sharing local or proxy data on the server-side [8,9]. However, these approaches may not be practical and can impose a heavy burden on network bandwidth. Furthermore, sending client's local data to the server violates the fundamental privacy principle of federated learning.

**Knowledge Distillation.** Knowledge distillation (KD) for neural networks is first introduced in [10], using a pre-trained teacher neural network (generally larger in size) on the dataset to guide and supervise the training of a student neural network (generally much smaller than the teacher network). The main problem solved by knowledge distillation is how to transfer the knowledge learned by the teacher network to the student network [11]. In particular, DML [5] has been proposed to weaken the fixed teacher-student relationship, where a group of student networks learn collaboratively and transfer knowledge to each other during the training process. Additionally, some data-free KD methods have been developed to address the issue of unavailable data. In particular, in [12–14], the transferred data is generated by GAN. Data-free distillation shows great potential when data is not available, and we aim to combine state-of-the-art knowledge distillation techniques with federated learning to enhance the generalizability and communication efficiency of models in heterogeneous federated learning.

**KD in Federated Learning.** To address user heterogeneity in federated learning, knowledge distillation has materialized as an effective method. Several approaches have been proposed, such as FD [8], which synchronizes the logits of each label accumulated during local training, and then uses the average logits of each label as the distillation regularizer for the next round of local training. FedMD [15] and Cronus [16] consider learning by mean logits per sample on public datasets. FedDistill [17] obtains the metrics of the logit vector output from user models and shares this metadata with users for knowledge distillation. FedMix [18] uses a data augmentation approach, where local training is enhanced with the help of batch average data shared by users. However, most of these approaches perform data-dependent distillation, which poses privacy risks. In contrast, our FedGM extracts global knowledge from user models via generative learning in a data-free way, reducing these risks. Moreover, FedGM performs mutual distillation on the server-side to ensemble a global model, rather than simple parameter averaging.

# 3 Preliminaries

## 3.1 Typical Federated Learning Setup

The goal of conventional federated learning (FedAvg) is to learn a shared model over decentralized data, by optimizing the global objective function in a distributed manner, where the global view of the entire dataset is obtained by taking the union of all the decentralized datasets. We consider an instance space $\mathcal{X} \subset \mathbb{R}^p$, a latent feature space $z \subset \mathbb{R}^d$ with $d < p$, and an output space $\mathcal{Y} \subset \mathbb{R}$. We consider private data, denoted as $(\mathcal{X}_k, \mathcal{Y}_k)$ drawn from distinct distribution $\mathcal{P}_k(x, y)$ from $K$ clients, federated learning on each client begins with downloading the global weight vector $w^g \in \mathbb{R}^d$ from the server. To optimize the local objective function, each client applies the gradient descent algorithm for a number of epochs on its local data and updates its local model parameters:

$$F_k(w^k) := \mathbb{E}_{x \sim \mathcal{P}_k} \left[ l \left( f(w^k), c^*(x) \right) \right], \tag{1}$$

$$w^k \leftarrow w^k - \eta \nabla F_k(w^k) \tag{2}$$

where $F_k(w^k)$ is the risk of the $k$-th client local model, $f$ is the forward method, $l$ is the loss function, $c^*$ is a ground-truth labeling function, $\eta$ is the learning rate, and $\nabla F_k \left( w^k \right) \in \mathbb{R}^d$ is the gradient of $F_k(w^k)$. After a period of local updates, clients upload their local model weights $w^k$ to the server, and then the server aggregates these weights by weighted averaging:

$$w^g \leftarrow \sum_{k=1}^{K} \frac{n_k}{n} w^k \tag{3}$$

where $w^g$ is the weights of the global model, $n_k$ is the number of local private samples of the $k$-th client, and $n$ is the number of samples overall clients. The training process continues until the global model reaches convergence. The advantage of this approach is that it enables collaborative learning without exposing the private local data of each client. However, a potential challenge is that the local data distributions $\mathcal{P}_k$ may differ from the joint data distribution $\mathcal{P}_{\text{joint}}$ , which violates the assumption that $\mathbb{E}_{\mathcal{P}_k}[F_k(w^k)] = f(w^g)$ under non-IID settings. In practical application scenarios, user data is often non-IID, so FL faces the challenge of user heterogeneity. Thus, applying model averaging directly for aggregation may not result in an optimal global model.

### 3.2 Knowledge Distillation

Knowledge distillation can transfer dark knowledge from the large teacher model with superior capability to the student model with fewer parameters while maintaining performance. We can simplify the loss function of the student model as follows:

$$L_{\text{student}} = L_{\text{CE}} + D_{\text{KL}}\left(p_{\text{teacher}} \| p_{\text{student}}\right), \tag{4}$$

$$p_{\text{teacher}} = \frac{\exp(z/T)}{\sum_i \exp\left(z_i/T\right)} \tag{5}$$

where $L_{\text{CE}}$ is Cross-Entropy Loss and $D_{\text{KL}}$ is Kullback Leibler (KL) Divergence, $p_{\text{teacher}}$ and $p_{\text{student}}$ are the predictions of the teacher and student models, respectively. Let $T$ be a hyper-parameter that represents the temperature, $z_i$ be the logits of the $i$-th student model, and $z$ be the logits of the teacher model. Previous studies have shown that the prediction of the teacher model can provide more informative guidance (soft targets) than a one-hot label (hard targets) for knowledge distillation, which can significantly enhance the performance of the student model.

## 4 Methodology

In this section, we clarify our proposed approach in detail. Algorithm 1 shows a summary, and Fig. 1 visualizes the overview of its learning procedure.

### 4.1 Global Knowledge Extraction

Inspired by FedGen [4], we try to get a global view of the data distribution without acquiring private data, which we call global knowledge. In the training process, we try to use distilled global knowledge to guide the learning of local models. In order to make the global knowledge as consistent as possible with the ground-truth data distribution, we consider a conditional distribution to represent the global knowledge:

$$\mathcal{P}^*_{\text{joint}} = \underset{\mathcal{P}_{\text{joint}}:\mathcal{Y}\to\mathcal{X}}{\arg\max}\ \mathbb{E}_{y\sim p(y)}\mathbb{E}_{x\sim\mathcal{P}_{\text{joint}}(x|y)}[\log p(y \mid x)]. \tag{6}$$

In above equation, $p(y)$ and $p(y \mid x)$ are both unknown, where the former is the ground-truth prior and the latter is the posterior distributions of the target labels. To make Eq. (6) optimizable w.r.t $\mathcal{P}_{\text{joint}}$, we use the empirical approximations to estimate $p(y)$ and $p(x \mid y)$. When applied in practice, we can obtain $\hat{p}(y)$ by asking users to provide the training label count while they upload models. Then we use the ensemble knowledge from user models to approximate $p(y \mid x)$:

$$\log \hat{p}(y \mid x) \propto \frac{1}{K}\sum_{k=1}^{K} \log p\left(y \mid x; w^k\right). \tag{7}$$

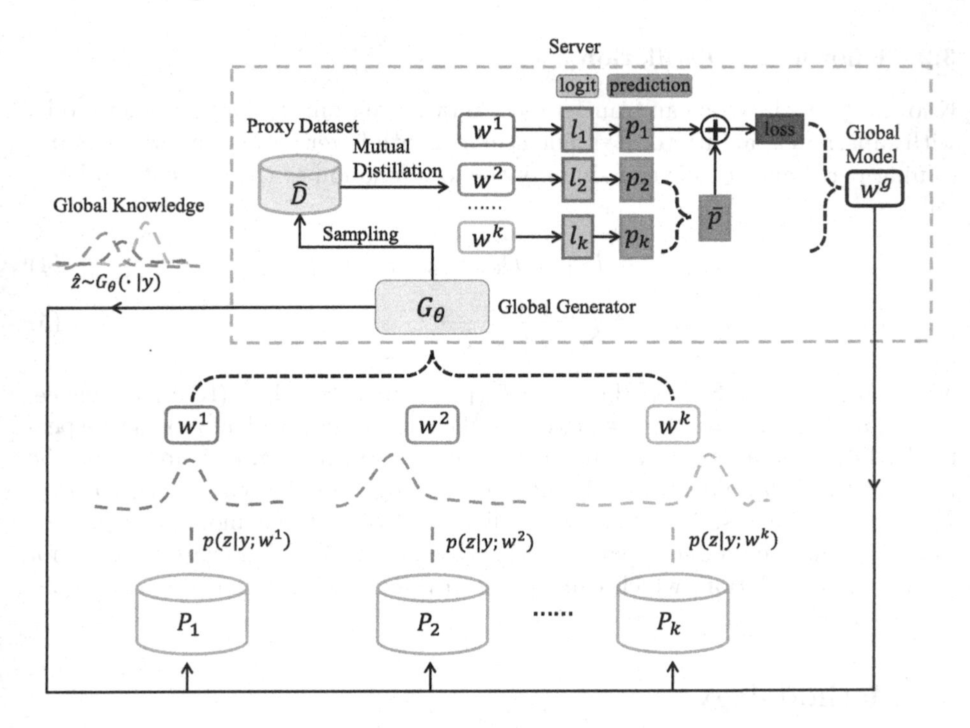


**Fig. 1.** Overview of FedGM

Even though we can estimate the approximation by using the above method, it is also challenging to optimize Eq. (6) by direct computation on the input space $\mathcal{X}$, due to two reasons: the computational overload brought by the high-dimensional space and the leakage of user information. Therefore, we try to recover a latent space with an induced distribution $G^* : \mathcal{Y} \rightarrow \mathcal{Z}$ that is more compact than the original space while avoiding user information leakage:

$$G^* = \underset{G:\mathcal{Y}\rightarrow\mathcal{Z}}{\arg\max} E_{y\sim\hat{p}(y)} E_{z\sim G(z|y)} \left[ \sum_{k=1}^{K} \log p\left(y \mid z; w^k\right) \right]. \tag{8}$$

Next, our goal is to learn a conditional generator $G$ to perform knowledge extraction. We set the parameter of $G$ as $\theta$, and optimize the following objective:

$$\min_{\theta} J(\theta) := \mathbb{E}_{y\sim\hat{p}(y)} \mathbb{E}_{z\sim G_\theta(z|y)} \left[ l\left( \sigma\left( \frac{1}{K} \sum_{k=1}^{K} g\left(z; w^k\right) \right), y \right) \right] \tag{9}$$

where $\sigma$ is the activation function and $g$ is the logit-output. Specifically, to diversify the outputs of $G(\cdot \mid y)$, we add the noise vector $\epsilon \sim \mathcal{N}(0, I)$ to the generator. Therefore, $z \sim G_\theta(\cdot \mid y) \equiv G_\theta(y, \epsilon \mid \epsilon \sim \mathcal{N}(0, I))$. Given an arbitrary target label, the generator is to be optimized so that the feature representation produced by the generator can be ideally predicted in the user model, in other words, the generator simulates the consensus of local users, resulting in a global view of the user data.

After learning the generator $G_\theta$, we broadcast it to local users so that each user model can use $G_\theta$ to generate new augmented samples $z \sim G_\theta(\cdot \mid y)$, and add it to the training process to train along with the local data. Therefore, in order to enable the local model $w^k$ to generate more accurate predictions for augmented samples, we need to add another part of the objective function to maximize the ideal predictions probability:

$$\min_{w^k} J\left(w^k\right) := F_k(w^k) + \hat{\mathbb{E}}_{y \sim \hat{p}(y), z \sim G_\theta(z|y)}\left[l\left(f\left(z; w^k\right); y\right)\right] \tag{10}$$

where $F_k(w^k) := \frac{1}{n_k}\sum_{x_i \in \mathcal{P}_k}\left[l\left(f(x_i, w^k), c^*(x_i)\right)\right]$is the empirical risk given local data $\mathcal{P}_k$.

## 4.2 Mutual Distillation

We use the learned generator to create pseudo-samples that reflect the global consensus and form a proxy dataset. Then, we apply knowledge distillation to optimize the original aggregation method on the server. However, we do not have a well-trained teacher model in the training process before convergence. Therefore, we adopt deep mutual learning (DML) [5] as our server aggregation strategy, which is based on knowledge distillation. In contrast to the conventional one-way knowledge transfer from a pre-trained teacher model to an untrained student model, DML enables bidirectional learning between two models during the training process. The loss functions of the two models are given by:

$$L_{w^1} = L_{C_1} + D_{KL}\left(p_2 \| p_1\right), \tag{11}$$

$$L_{w^2} = L_{C_2} + D_{KL}\left(p_1 \| p_2\right) \tag{12}$$

where $p_1$ and $p_2$ denote the predictions of the two networks. The objective of the two models is to learn from the proxy datasets while minimizing the discrepancy between their predictions. The proposed DML approach can also be naturally extended to multiple networks.

Therefore, when users upload their local models $w^1, w^2, ..., w^k$ to the server, the local models are trained to learn from secondary information on the proxy dataset. And the global model $w^g$ is obtained by aggregating the local models after mutual distillation. The objective function for optimizing $w^k, (1 \leq k \leq K)$ becomes

$$L_{w^k} = L_{C_k} + \frac{1}{K-1}\sum_{l=1, l \neq k}^{K} D_{KL}\left(\boldsymbol{p}_l \| \boldsymbol{p}_k\right). \tag{13}$$

For model fusion, the local models are evaluated on mini-batches $(\mathbf{d})$ of the proxy dataset and their logit outputs are used to integrate the global model. Thus, the local models are ensembled into a global model $w^g$ that users can download,

$$w_j^g := w_{j-1}^g - \eta \frac{\partial \mathrm{KL}\left(\sigma\left(\frac{1}{|\mathcal{S}_t|}\sum_{k \in \mathcal{S}_t} f\left(w^k, \mathbf{d}\right)\right), \sigma\left(f\left(w_{j-1}^g, \mathbf{d}\right)\right)\right)}{\partial w_{j-1}^g} \tag{14}$$

where $S_t$ is the random subset of the $K$ clients.

Through all the steps above, our proposed method can now extract the global knowledge and realize the mutual distillation among the models. During the implementation, we used interactive learning to produce a lightweight generator that relied on local model prediction rules, and further used this generator to enable local users to learn from consensus knowledge. We also use it to build a proxy dataset stored on the central server for mutual distillation, which allowed local models to learn from each other and ensemble into a better performing global model.

**Algorithm 1.** FedGM: Heterogeneous Federated Learning via Generative Model and Mutual Distillation

**Require:** global model parameters $w^g$, local model parameters $\{w^k\}_{k=1}^K$, generator parameters $\theta$, $\hat{p}(y)$ uniformly initialized, local steps $T$, learning rate $\alpha, \beta$, batchsize $B$, local label counter $c_k$, global mutual distillation epochs $N$.

1: **repeat**
2: $S_t \rightarrow$ random subset ($C$ fraction) of the $K$ clients
3: server broadcast $w^g, \theta, \hat{p}(y)$ to $S_t$
4: **for** each client $k \in S_t$ in parallel **do**
5: $w^k \leftarrow w^g$
6: **for** $t = 1...T$ **do**
7: $\{x_i, y_i\}_{i=1}^B \sim \mathcal{P}_k, \{\hat{z}_i \sim G_\theta(\cdot \mid \hat{y}_i), \hat{y}_i \sim \hat{p}(y)\}_{i=1}^B$
8: update label counter $c_k$.
9: **end for**
10: user upload $w^k, c_k$ to server
11: **end for**
12: server updates $\hat{p}(y)$ based on $\{c_k\}_{k \in S_t}$
13: $\theta \leftarrow \theta - \alpha \nabla_\theta J(\theta)$
14: build proxy dataset $\{\hat{z}_i \sim G_\theta(\cdot \mid \hat{y}_i), \hat{y}_i \sim \hat{p}(y)\} \rightarrow \hat{\mathcal{D}}$
15: **for** $j = 1...N$ **do**
16: sample a mini-batch of samples $\mathbf{d} \in \hat{\mathcal{D}}$
17: local models $\{w^k\}_{k=1}^K$ perform mutual distillation
18: $L_{w^k} = L_{C_k} + \frac{1}{K-1} \sum_{l=1, l \neq k}^K D_{\mathrm{KL}}(\boldsymbol{p}_l \| \boldsymbol{p}_k)$
19: ensemble global model
20: $w_j^g := w_{j-1}^g - \eta \frac{\partial \, \mathrm{KL}\left(\sigma\left(\frac{1}{|S_t|} \sum_{k \in S_t} f(w^k, \mathbf{d})\right), \sigma\left(f(w_{j-1}^g, \mathbf{d})\right)\right)}{\partial w_{j-1}^g}$
21: **end for**
22: **until** training stop

# 5 Experiments

In this section, we validate the performance of FedGM and compare the performance of our approach with other key related work.

## 5.1 Datasets

To verify the effectiveness of our proposed FedGM, we conduct a series of experiments on three benchmark datasets.

- **MNIST** [19] is a 10-classification handwriting digit dataset, with the number of 0 to 9. The dataset consists of 60000 training images and 10000 testing images, with 6000 and 1,000 images ($28 \times 28$ pixels) per digit, respectively.
- **EMNIST** [20] is an extension of MNIST to handwritten letters. The dataset consists of 4800 training images and 800 testing images($28 \times 28$ pixels) per letter respectively in 26 classes.
- **CIFAR-10** [21] consists of 50000 training images and 10000 test images in 10 classes, with 5000 and 1000 images per class.

## 5.2 Baseline

To validate the performance of our approach, we select the following work as the baseline.

- **FedAvg** [1] is one of typical FL methods, which directly manipulate received model parameters.
- **FedProx** [2] limits the local model updates with a proximal term for better local training under heterogeneous systems.
- **FedDF** [3] performs ensemble distillation with unlabeled data on the server for effective model fusion.
- **FedGen** [4] is a data-free federated distillation method with flexible parameter sharing.

## 5.3 Implementation Details

We use the following settings for our experiments if not specified otherwise: 200 rounds of global communication, 20 user models with an active-user ratio $C = 50\%$, a local update step size $T = 20$ with a mini-batch size $B = 32$ for each step. We simulate the typical federated learning setting by using at most 50% of the total training dataset distributed to user models, and the whole testing dataset for performance evaluation. We adopt the network architecture of [1] for the classifier. We set the mutual distillation iterations $N = 50$ and the distillation mini-batch $\mathbf{d} = 32$ with the same size as $B$.

To simulate the non-iid federated setting, we follow prior work and use the Dirichlet distribution $Dir(\alpha)$ to model non-iid data distributions. A higher $\alpha$ value means lower data heterogeneity. Figure 2 shows the effects of different $\alpha$ values on the heterogeneity for the MNIST dataset.

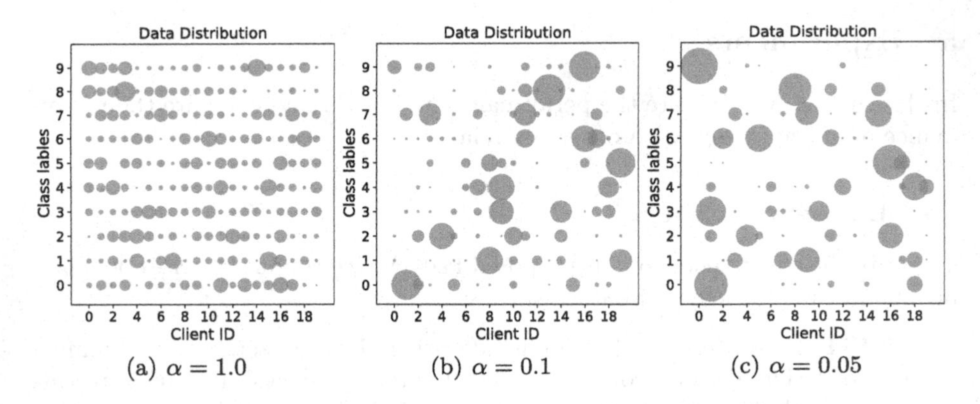


(a) $\alpha = 1.0$ (b) $\alpha = 0.1$ (c) $\alpha = 0.05$

**Fig. 2.** Visualization of different user heterogeneity on MNIST dataset

## 5.4 Overall Performance

**Impacts of Data Heterogeneity:** Table 1 records the top-1 average test accuracy of all methods involved in comparison on MNIST and EMNIST, and Table 2 records the top-3 average test accuracy on CIFAR10. As we can see from the table, our proposed FedGM achieves better and more robust results at different levels of user heterogeneity, and the greater the heterogeneity of data distribution (the smaller the value of $\alpha$), the greater the increase of FedGM.

**Table 1.** Performance overview given different data settings on MNIST and EMNIST. A higher $\alpha$ value means lower data heterogeneity. $T$ denotes the local training steps (communication delay).

| Top-1 Test Accuracy | | | | | | |
|---|---|---|---|---|---|---|
| Dataset | Setting | FedAvg | FedProx | FedDF | FedGen | FedGM |
| MNIST ($T$=20) | $\alpha$=0.05 | 87.70±2.07 | 87.49±2.05 | 90.02±0.96 | 91.30±0.74 | **93.06±0.78** |
| | $\alpha$=0.1 | 90.16±0.59 | 90.10±0.39 | 91.11±0.43 | 93.03±0.32 | **94.31±0.45** |
| | $\alpha$=1.0 | 93.84±0.25 | 93.83±0.29 | 93.37±0.40 | 95.52±0.07 | **95.82±0.10** |
| EMNIST ($T$=20) | $\alpha$=0.05 | 62.25±2.82 | 61.93±2.31 | **70.40±0.79** | 68.53±1.17 | 69.72±0.64 |
| | $\alpha$=0.1 | 66.21±2.43 | 65.29±2.94 | 70.94±0.76 | 72.15±0.21 | **73.50±0.40** |
| | $\alpha$=10.0 | 74.83±0.69 | 74.24±0.81 | 74.36±0.40 | 78.43±0.74 | **79.02±0.14** |
| EMNIST ($\alpha$=1.0) | $T$=20 | 74.83±0.99 | 74.12±0.88 | 75.43±0.37 | 78.48±1.04 | **80.03±0.21** |
| | $T$=40 | 77.02±1.09 | 75.93±0.95 | 77.58±0.37 | 78.92±0.73 | **80.31±0.19** |

**Table 2.** Performance overview given different data settings on CIFAR10. A higher $\alpha$ value means lower data heterogeneity.

| Top-3 Test Accuracy | | | | | | |
|---|---|---|---|---|---|---|
| Dataset | Setting | FedAvg | FedProx | FedDF | FedGen | FedGM |
| CIFAR10 ($T$=20) | $\alpha$=0.05 | 67.55±1.25 | 66.83±1.0 | 62.94±1.21 | 72.41±1.25 | **74.01±1.07** |
| | $\alpha$=0.1 | 73.16±0.86 | 72.50±0.92 | 71.87±1.02 | 72.84±0.31 | **74.45±0.77** |
| | $\alpha$=10.0 | 82.78±0.1 | 82.48±0.06 | 85.84±0.18 | 84.19±0.26 | **85.91±0.12** |

This result confirms our motivation: FedProx and FedDF are optimized based on the average of local model parameters by FedAvg, FedDF is extracted from the global model obtained by FedAvg, so as the degree of non-iid increases, there will be a certain effect, but the improvement is limited. Unlike FedDF, our method achieves a significant performance gain compared to FedAvg. Among the baselines, FedGen is one of the most competitive ones and achieves good results in most cases. However, it does not fully exploit knowledge distillation. We attribute our method's better performance to the improved generalization performance of both local and global models obtained by mutual distillation. With the help of conditional generator, we distill local users' knowledge into global knowledge. Users supplement their local data by sampling from the generator which represents global knowledge so that the local objective function does not deviate excessively from the global one and mitigates potential distribution differences among users. Proxy dataset is constructed on the server-side with pseudo-samples generated by the generator, allowing user models to perform mutual distillation on the server to obtain a global model with better generalization performance, further alleviating the heterogeneity of data distribution. Baselines such as FedAvg and FedProx do not address global knowledge transfer or use a proxy dataset representing global data distribution for distillation.

**Learning Efficiency:** As shown in Fig. 3, FedGM achieves faster and more stable convergence, and outperforms other baselines on MNIST under $\alpha = 0.1, r = 50\%$. Although FedGen exhibits higher learning efficiency than other baselines, with the help of the proxy dataset on sever side and mutual distillation, our approach has less fluctuation in accuracy during the training process and results in a better accuracy.

### 5.5 Sensitivity Analysis

**Effects of Communication Frequency:** We conduct a comparative analysis of the impact of different local update steps $T$ on the performance of FedGM on EMNIST. A higher value of $T$ will lead to longer communication delays between global communications. Therefore, an appropriate local update step can effectively improve global communication efficiency. As shown in Table 1, our method maintains its performance under various communication delay scenarios. In other words, our method has better communication efficiency.

**Effects of Mutual Distillation Epochs:** Figure 4 shows the performance of our proposed method on EMNIST under different mutual distillation epochs. The results show that the performance first improves significantly as the epoch increases, but then decreases gradually. The reason is that when the epoch is small, user models can not fully learn the secondary information from each other. When the epoch becomes larger, user models have learned to overfit the proxy dataset, resulting in the global model producing negative guidance for local training. After comprehensive consideration, choosing $epoch = 50$ is more appropriate.

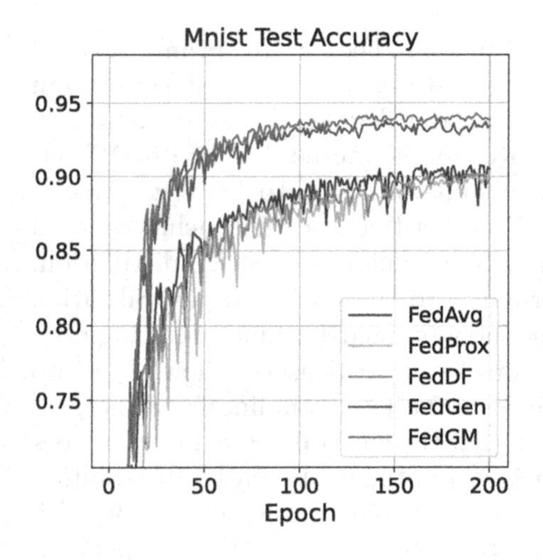


**Fig. 3.** Performance on MNIST under $\alpha = 0.1, r = 50\%$.

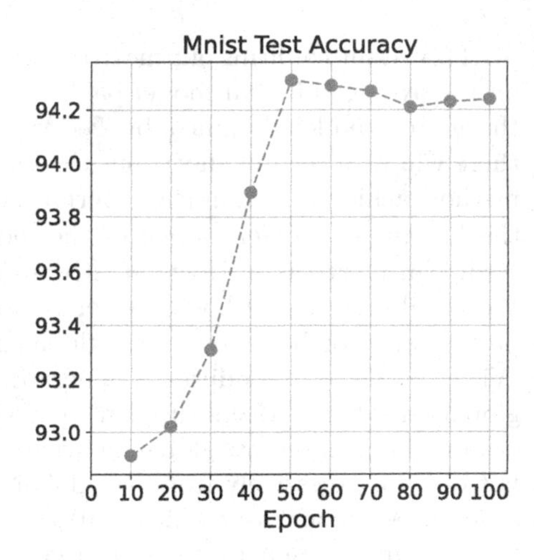


**Fig. 4.** The influence of global mutual distillation epoch on MNIST

## 6 Conclusion

This paper presents FedGM, a solution to the challenging problem of user heterogeneity in federated learning. FedGM combines generative learning with mutual distillation to improve generalization performance in a data-free manner. Empirical experiments demonstrate that our proposed approach achieves significantly better performance, with greater stability and fewer communication rounds than previous methods.

**Acknowledgements.** This work is partially supported by the Scientific and Technological Innovation 2030 Major Projects under Grant 2018AAA0100902 and the Shanghai Science and Technology Commission under Grant No. 20511100200.

## References

1. McMahan, B., Moore, E., Ramage, D., Hampson, S., y Arcas, B.A.: Communication-efficient learning of deep networks from decentralized data. In: Artificial intelligence and statistics, pp. 1273–1282. PMLR (2017)
2. Li, T., Sahu, A.K., Zaheer, M., Sanjabi, M., Talwalkar, A., Smith, V.: Federated optimization in heterogeneous networks. In: Proceedings of Machine Learning and Systems, vol. 2, pp. 429–450 (2020)
3. Lin, T., Kong, L., Stich, S.U., Jaggi, M.: Ensemble distillation for robust model fusion in federated learning. In: Advances in Neural Information Processing Systems, vol. 33, pp. 2351–2363 (2020)
4. Zhu, Z., Hong, J., Zhou, J.: Data-free knowledge distillation for heterogeneous federated learning. In: International Conference on Machine Learning, pp. 12878–12889. PMLR (2021)

5. Zhang, Y., Xiang, T., Hospedales, T.M., Lu, H.: Deep mutual learning. In: Proceedings of the IEEE Conference on Computer Vision and Pattern Recognition, pp. 4320–4328 (2018)
6. Li, T., Sahu, A.K., Talwalkar, A., Smith, V.: Federated learning: challenges, methods, and future directions. IEEE Sig. Process. Mag. **37**(3), 50–60 (2020)
7. Fallah, A., Mokhtari, A., Ozdaglar, A.: Personalized federated learning with theoretical guarantees: a model-agnostic meta-learning approach. In: Advances in Neural Information Processing Systems, vol. 33, pp. 3557–3568 (2020)
8. Jeong, E., Oh, S., Kim, H., Park, J., Bennis, M., Kim, S.-L.: Communication-efficient on-device machine learning: Federated distillation and augmentation under non-IID private data. arXiv preprint arXiv:1811.11479 (2018)
9. Zhao, Y., Li, M., Lai, L., Suda, N., Civin, D., Chandra, V.: Federated learning with non-IID data. arXiv preprint arXiv:1806.00582 (2018)
10. Hinton, G., Vinyals, O., Dean, J., et al.: Distilling the knowledge in a neural network. arXiv preprint arXiv:1503.02531 (2015)
11. Gou, J., Yu, B., Maybank, S.J., Tao, D.: Knowledge distillation: a survey. Int. J. Comput. Vis. **129**(6), 1789–1819 (2021)
12. Chen, H., et al.: Data-free learning of student networks. In: Proceedings of the IEEE/CVF International Conference on Computer Vision, pp. 3514–3522 (2019)
13. Ye, J., Ji, Y., Wang, X., Gao, X., Song, M.: Data-free knowledge amalgamation via group-stack dual-GAN. In: Proceedings of the IEEE/CVF Conference on Computer Vision and Pattern Recognition, pp. 12516–12525 (2020)
14. Yoo, J., Cho, M., Kim, T., Kang, U.: Knowledge extraction with no observable data. In: Advances in Neural Information Processing Systems vol. 32 (2019)
15. Li, D., Wang, J.: FedMD: heterogenous federated learning via model distillation. arXiv preprint arXiv:1910.03581 (2019)
16. Chang, H., Shejwalkar, V., Shokri, R., Houmansadr, A.: Cronus: robust and heterogeneous collaborative learning with black-box knowledge transfer. arXiv preprint arXiv:1912.11279 (2019)
17. Seo, H., Park, J., Oh, S., Bennis, M., Kim, S.-L.. Federated knowledge distillation. arXiv preprint arXiv:2011.02367 (2020)
18. Yoon, T., Shin, S., Hwang, S.J., Yang, E.: FedMix: approximation of mixup under mean augmented federated learning. arXiv preprint arXiv:2107.00233 (2021)
19. LeCun, Y., et al.: Handwritten digit recognition with a back-propagation network. In: Advances in Neural Information Processing Systems, vol. 2 (1989)
20. Cohen, G., Afshar, S., Tapson, J., Van Schaik, A.: EMNIST: extending MNIST to handwritten letters. In: 2017 International Joint Conference on Neural Networks (IJCNN), pp. 2921–2926. IEEE (2017)
21. Krizhevsky, A., Hinton, G., et al.: Learning multiple layers of features from tiny images (2009)

# DeTAR: A Decision Tree-Based Adaptive Routing in Networks-on-Chip

Xiaoyun Zhang, Yaohua Wang, Dezun Dong(✉), Cunlu Li, Shaocong Wang, and Liquan Xiao

National University of Defense Technology, Changsha, Hunan, China
{zhangxiaoyun,yhwang,dong,cunluli,wangshaocong,xiaoliquan}@nudt.edu.cn

**Abstract.** The deployment of heuristic algorithms is extensively utilized in the routing policy of Networks-on-Chip (NoCs). However, the escalating complexity and heterogeneity of multi-core architectures present a formidable task for human-designed efficient heuristic routing policies. Although recent works have exhibited that machine learning (ML) can learn efficacious routing policies that surpass human-designed heuristics in simulation, the intricate design and costly hardware overhead of ML-based routing algorithms preclude their practical application in NoCs. In this paper, we propose a Decision Tree-based Adaptive Routing algorithm, DeTAR, which is effective yet simple. The key insight of DeTAR is that routing decisions can be treated as selecting and prioritizing the key features among various NoCs' metrics like free Virtual Channels (VCs), the buffer length, etc., that better affect the routing decision. This reveals a natural match between the adaptive routing algorithm and the Decision Tree (DT) model. We trained DeTAR from network behavior datasets and evaluated the DeTAR routing algorithm against existing routing algorithms. Our simulation results show that the average saturation throughput can be improved by up to 17.59% compared with existing heuristic routing algorithms. Compared with the previous ML-based adaptive routing algorithm, the area of our routing logic is reduced by 88.95% without significant performance degradation.

**Keywords:** Networks-on-Chip · Machine Learning · Decision Tree Model · Adaptive Routing Algorithm

## 1 Introduction

Routing algorithm plays a key role in the overall performance of Networks-on-chip (NoCs), which select an output port by specific rules to determine packet transmission paths [15]. Dimension Order Routing (DOR) [6] is a classical deterministic routing algorithm and has low hardware cost. However, it suffers from poor load balance across different routes in NoCs. Heuristic adaptive routing algorithms (such as Dynamic XY (DyXY) [14], Regional Congestion Awareness (RCA) [11], Destination-Based Adaptive Routing (DBAR) [15], Footprint [10],


J. Cano et al. (Eds.): Euro-Par 2023, LNCS 14100, pp. 352–366, 2023.
https://doi.org/10.1007/978-3-031-39698-4_24

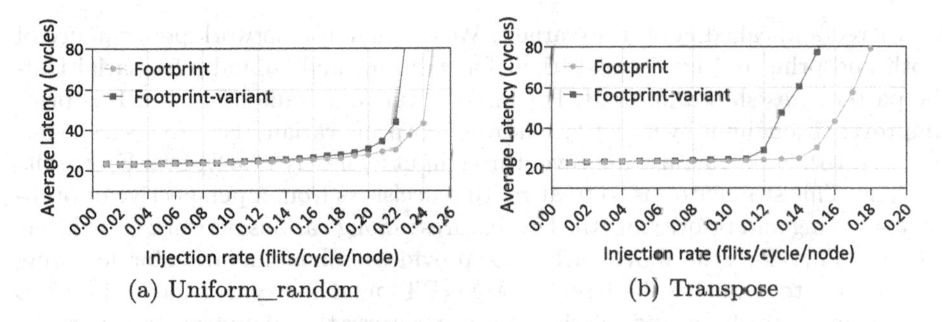


(a) Uniform_random (b) Transpose

**Fig. 1.** Latency-throughput comparison of Footprint [10] and Footprint-variant with $4 \times 4$ 2D mesh for uniform_random and adversarial (such as transpose) traffic patterns, where Footprint-variant changes the priority of Footprint's decision metrics.

etc.) improve this problem by selecting routing ports based on the network state information, including the number of free Virtual Channels (VCs), the buffer length, etc. Designing an effective routing algorithm requires carefully deliberating complex trade-offs between network performance and hardware cost, which is progressively more arduous for human designers. Therefore, experts have initiated exploring machine learning (ML) techniques to design routing policies.

Recent works have shown that ML techniques can learn effective routing policies. However, these works usually adopt reinforcement learning (RL) techniques of ML and outperform human-designed heuristics in simulation. Boyan et al. [4] first proposed the routing algorithm based on Q-learning, Q-Routing, which employs a large Q-table (2KB overhead in $8 \times 8$ 2D Mesh) to store the Q-value for each state-action pair. Dual Reinforcement Q-Routing (DRQ-Routing [13]) uses backward exploration in addition to forwarding exploration (as that of Q-Routing), which increases the cost of storing the Q-table. Reinforcement learning framework for adaptive routing (RELAR) [20] introduces a complex neural network unit to approximate the state-action pair. This neural network still requires tuning some model parameters for training and learning. However, RL-based routing policies are hindered by two impediments. First, the RL model must undergo the tuning and evaluation of numerous parameters to ensure efficient performance [4]. Second, the RL-based routing policies face the substantial hardware cost incurred during model deployment, which comprises complex computation resources and large parameter memory space.

To solve the above problems, the key insight of this paper is that routing decisions can be treated as selecting and prioritizing the key features among various network state information like free VCs, the buffer length, etc., which significantly impact the routing decision. We present an example to illustrate the impact of changing the priority of decision metrics in Footprint [10]. We select the Footprint since it is a state-of-the-art heuristic adaptive routing algorithm. Footprint uses free VCs and footprint VCs (VCs with the same destination as the current packet) as decision metrics. By reordering the priority of these metrics, we can observe how the network performance is affected. Footprint's decision-making metrics are reordered and called Footprint-variant. We evaluate the network performance of both Footprint and Footprint-variant for uniform_random and adversarial traffic patterns, as shown in Fig. 1. For uniform_random traffic (Fig. 1a), Footprint improves throughput by nearly 8.33% over Footprint-variant. For adversarial traffic (Fig. 1b), Footprint also improves throughput by nearly 17.64% over Footprint-variant. This stimulates us to treat routing decisions from a perspective of properly selecting and prioritizing the key features among various network state information. Therefore, the above verification provides a solid foundation for designing routing strategies using the Decision Tree (DT) model, a typical supervised ML model aiming to obtain and prioritize the key features that significantly impact the target decision from a set of data features [17]. To this end, we propose a Decision Tree-based Adaptive Routing (DeTAR) algorithm on 2D mesh network topology.

To the best of our knowledge, we are the first to employ the DT model in the NoCs routing algorithm design, and we build the dataset for the DT model. We set a relatively comprehensive collection of commonly used network state information at the beginning, including packet size, free VCs [11], free buffer size [14], footprint VCs, remaining hops, and crossbar demand (the number of active requesters for a given output port). We then label routing decisions by comparing the real latency with theoretical latency and achieve a balanced amount of positive and negative routing decisions via empirical parameter settings of the theoretical latency model. Next, we exploit the dataset to train the DT model and assist in the design of DeTAR. DeTAR prioritizes the network state information in an order as follows: packet size and free buffer size. Finally, we implement the DeTAR with three comparators and three multiplexers in a router. The comparators help check the routing state information and control the selection of multiplexers in a prioritized manner, which enables us to achieve low hardware costs.

The major contributions of this paper are as follows:

(1) We are the first to employ the DT model for routing policy designs. We construct the dataset for the DT model by extracting a comprehensive collection of network states from simulation trajectories and label routing decisions.
(2) We propose a Decision Tree-based Adaptive Routing (DeTAR) algorithm and implement DeTAR with a few comparators and multiplexers while achieving low hardware cost.
(3) We evaluate the proposed DeTAR routing, and the simulation results show that the average saturation throughput can be improved by up to 17.59% compared with existing routing algorithms. Compared with Q-Routing, the area of DeTAR is reduced by 88.95%.

## 2 Background and Related Work

### 2.1 Machine Learning in Adaptive Routing Design

ML techniques can effectively solve many critical problems in NoCs, such as low power [9], arbitration policy [21], routing algorithm [4], and network congestion determination [12]. One of the widely recognized applications of ML in NoCs is adaptive routing. The Q-Routing algorithm [4], founded on the Q-learning model of RL, is a classical work. This algorithm involves the construction of a Q-table for each router to store the Q-value. This value estimates the time it takes to send a packet to its destination through neighboring routers. After the router selects the next-hop router, it needs to return the new Q-value and update the Q-value of the router. DRQ-Routing [13] incorporates a double-strengthening mechanism that involves both forward and backward exploration techniques to update the Q-value. Predictive Q-Routing (PQ-Routing [5]) uses memory to store experience by predicting traffic trends to increase the learning rate. Hierarchical cluster-based adaptive routing (C-Routing [18]) divides the network into several clusters; each cluster maintains a Q-table instead of each node and can reduce the size of the Q-table by four times. A highly adaptive routing algorithm based on Q-learning is proposed, HARAQ [8], which adopts a scalable Q-table and minimizes storage overhead. However, researchers have employed deep reinforcement learning (DRL) to optimize routing algorithm design to mitigate the storage overhead attributed to Q-table. Wang et al. [20] proposed an adaptive routing framework based on DRL, RELAR, where the framework utilizes a neural network to approximate the Q-table. Initially, it is important to note that the previous works utilizing RL for designing routing algorithms are primarily focused on enhancing the precision of the Q-learning approach and minimizing the Q-table size. Secondly, these methods require adjusting multiple parameters and conducting online training, leading to increased hardware costs and the complexity of actual deployment. Hence, this paper aims to develop a minimal adaptive routing algorithm that reduces hardware costs, thereby facilitating deployment.

To address these issues, we propose a Decision Tree-based Adaptive Routing (DeTAR) algorithm, which leverages the DT model to identify the key metrics that affect network performance and prioritize them accordingly. Another factor is that the DT model's simple architecture makes it easy to deploy.

### 2.2 Decision Tree Models

Tree-based model is a supervised learning model widely used for decision-making problems, which aims to identify crucial features significantly impacting the target decision [17]. Common tree-based models include decision trees, random forests, and gradient-boosted trees [22]. In contrast, the random forests and gradient-boosted trees are complex and have more parameters, which could increase the difficulty of training and implementation [17]. In this paper, we exploit the DT model because this model can be efficiently implemented in hardware.

A decision tree comprises a root node and several internal and leaf nodes. During training, this model first analyzes datasets and calculates the information gain of all features. It selects the feature with the largest information gain value as the root node and divides the dataset based on the feature value of the root node. This procedure repeats until reaching the termination conditions. Thus, the leaf nodes represent the decision result. The first selected feature is the root node, which carries the most weight in the decision-making process, followed by

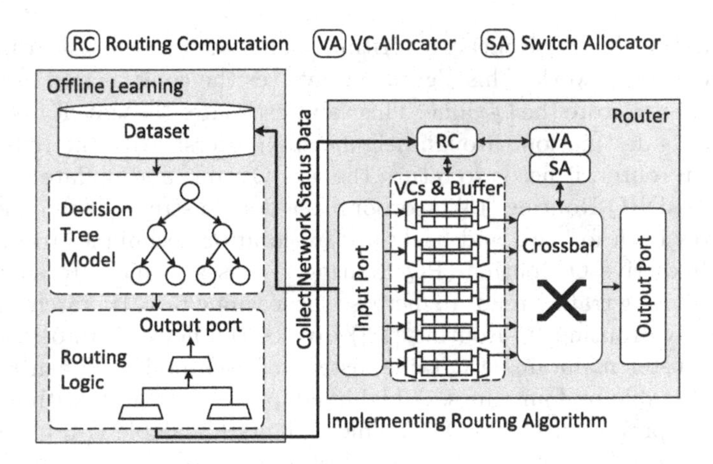


**Fig. 2.** The overall framework of the DeTAR routing design scheme.

the second feature. Overall, decision tree generation is selecting and prioritizing data features. This paper provides a key insight that treats routing decisions from a perspective of properly selecting and prioritizing the key features among various network state information. Therefore, the DT model reveals a natural match to the design of the adaptive routing algorithm.

# 3 Design of DeTAR Routing

This section presents the design details of the DeTAR algorithm. The overall framework of the DeTAR routing design scheme has been shown in Fig. 2. During the simulation of NoCs, we collect network state information as features and determine labels to create a training dataset. Then, we inject this dataset into the DT model for training to generate a decision tree and convert it into an achievable routing policy. Finally, we deploy the routing logic to the routing computation unit to implement the DeTAR adaptive routing algorithm.

## 3.1 Construction of Dataset

DT model is a supervised learning approach that relies on constructing a dataset by collecting network state information as features and assigning labels. Collect network state information from simulation traces generated during NoCs routing computation. We collect this information relevant to the output port for each routing computation and form a feature vector. A feature vector consists of a list of features from all messages via the same output port. We then use message transfer times to evaluate how routing policies affect network latency, providing a basis for data labeling. We explain the detailed design below.

**(1) Determine data features.** For routing design, we consider the complete set of features, which include **Packet Size**, i.e., the size of the packet;

**Remaining hops**, i.e., the number of hops from the packet's current to destination router; **Free VCs**, i.e., the number of free VCs; **Free Buffer Size**, i.e., the number of the free buffer of input port; **Footprint VCs**, i.e., the number of footprint VCs with the same destination as the current packet; **Crossbar Demand**, i.e., the number of active requesters for a given output port. These features (e.g., packet size) should significantly impact routing decisions. Packet Size and Remaining hops are related to network latency. Free VCs and Free Buffer Size may correlate to network states and decision behaviors. Footprint VCs and Crossbar Demand are related to traffic patterns. Note that each message needs six integers (one each for the six features).

**(2) Determine data labels.** Network latency is typically employed to evaluate the network performance, laying the foundation for the data labels. At low loads, the theoretical latency ($T$) can be roughly estimated as the sum of header latency ($T_h$) and serialization latency ($T_s$). The header latency equals the packet's hop count ($H$) multiplied by per-hop router latency ($t_r$). The per-hop router latency equals the number of pipeline stages ($P$) multiplied by the cycle time ($t_c$). The resulting additional serialization latency ($L/b$) is the latency for the body to travel across the channel. $L$ is the length of a packet, and $b$ is the bandwidth of the channels. We estimate the $T$ using the following equation.

$$T = T_h + T_s = H \times t_r + L/b = H \times P \times t_c + L/b \tag{1}$$

However, this $T$ calculation ignores the time of multiple packets competing for the same output ports, which varies based on the actual transmission and is known as contention time ($T_c$). Therefore, we take the sum of $L/b$, $T_c$ collectively called **tolerance**, can set the constants $P$ and $t_c$ based on experimental simulations, and their product can be replaced by a single constant $a$. We estimate the actual latency (*Actual_T*) using the following equation

$$Actual\_T = H \times P \times t_c + L/b + T_c = H \times a + tolerance. \tag{2}$$

Similar to the principle of error analysis, we compare the difference value between the *Actual_T* and the $T$. If this value exceeds 0, the label is 0, representing the negative samples; otherwise, the label is 1, meaning the positive samples. Therefore, in this paper, we mitigate the issue of data imbalance by regulating the dataset's sample size with the same labels by adjusting the tolerance value. For example, through extensive experimental analysis for uniform_random traffic pattern, we found that setting the tolerance value to 17 determines the label and solves the data imbalance problem. Still, we also evaluated other traffic patterns and verified the generalization ability. In addition to marking the dataset, this tolerance value can also control the number of dataset samples in different categories. As mentioned, selecting features and determining labels to construct datasets require human involvement.

### 3.2 Learning a Routing Policy

As introduced in the previous subsection, we have completed the construction of the training dataset. This paper selects the minimal adaptive routing algorithm

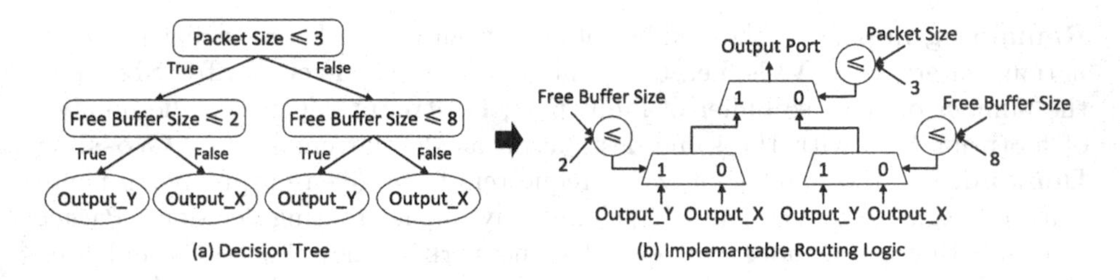


**Fig. 3.** Convert decision tree to implementable routing logic.

as the learning object since it can be transformed into a binary classification problem. Then, the subsection mainly describes the training of the DT model to obtain a decision tree, which is employed in designing the routing policy.

We utilize an online training-based method combined with obtaining global state information that can be intuitively employed to achieve optimal performance. Unfortunately, the following hinder the implementation of this method. (1) It is expensive to store network state information; (2) Collecting network state information and online training ML model increase latency. Therefore, we adopt the offline training method to learn the routing policy. The advantage of this method is that the DT model can be fully trained through a large number of datasets to obtain a more accurate DT model and improve the decision-making ability of the DeTAR algorithm. In addition, offline training can also avoid problems such as latency and resource occupation during online training.

This paper employs the ID3 (Iterative Dichotomiser) algorithm since its simple structure can be easily converted to a logic circuit with acceptable deployment overhead after offline training. The ID3 algorithm computes the information gain of each feature, selects the optimal feature to divide the current dataset, and generates child nodes. Then, the identical process is iteratively applied to each child node until all data is correctly classified or no further divisions can be made. The offline training process of the ID3 model uses information gain to select the optimal features as nodes and build a decision tree. The result of the ID3 model is a decision tree, as shown in Fig. 3(a). Figure 3(a) is a 2-depth decision tree. Each non-leaf node in the decision tree represents a feature (packet size or free buffer size). The leaf node represents the output port outcomes (*Outport_X* and *Outport_Y*). In this decision tree, any path from the root node to the leaf node is a decision rule, a simple IF-THEN statement consisting of conditions and predictions. Therefore, we can map each decision rule to a piece of pseudocode. An essential parameter of the ID3 algorithm is the max-depth, which can also be used as a termination condition. More details about the max-depth parameter will be detailed in the evaluation section.

Figure 3(a) suggests that this decision tree tends to utilize the packet size and free buffer size, where the root node is the feature of packet size with the highest decision priority, followed by free buffer size. However, it is apparent that the packet size is a significant feature since a larger packet tends to wait longer at a router, which increases the likelihood of blocking other packets or holding

**Algorithm 1. DeTAR** Routing Algorithm Description.

**Input:** $Packet_{size}$, $FreeBuffer_x$.
**Output:** The output direction, $OutDir$.
1: **if** $Packet_{size} \leq 3$ **then**
2: **if** $FreeBuffer_x \leq 2$ **then** $OutDir = P_y$; **else** $OutDir = P_x$;
3: **else**
4: **if** $FreeBuffer_x \leq 8$ **then** $OutDir = P_y$; **else** $OutDir = P_x$;
5: **end if**

onto critical resources. Free buffer size also makes sense since a router with a larger free buffer size is less likely to be congested. It is worth noting that this analysis guides on selecting key features. However, converting these analyses into practical routing policies still lies on human designers.

### 3.3 Analysis of the DeTAR Routing Algorithm

Algorithm 1 is the DeTAR routing algorithm learned by the decision tree with a max-depth of 2. The routing policy utilizes packet size as a key feature, where each packet is handled differently based on its size. This routing policy dictates that larger packets should reserve more free buffers while smaller packets should reserve fewer free buffers. This routing policy generated by our approach resembles the dynamic buffer allocation concept, where buffer sizes are adjusted based on packet size to mitigate network congestion.

DeTAR employs 2D mesh and has at most two possible output ports, one in each dimension ($P_x$ or $P_y$). DeTAR needs to count the packet size ($Packet_{size}$) and free buffer size ($FreeBuffer_x$) of one output port (X or Y dimension, but this paper selects X dimension) as input. These candidate ports only have X and Y dimensions in the minimum adaptive routing algorithm. When selecting an output port, DeTAR first determines which dimension is likely to be congested based on the current network status and then avoids selecting the port on this dimension. The metric values of packets are compared against the decision values to determine the output port based on the packet size and free buffer size. By the way, DeTAR is deadlock-free since it is based on Duato's theory [7]. In this theory, packets can be routed fully adaptive but should wait on escape channels to avoid routing deadlock. The escape VC is added to handle the deadlock, and the first VC in each port is used as an escape VC in our design. Once a deadlock occurs, the corresponding packets are injected into the escape VC. Packets in the escape VC are transmitted using the DOR algorithm while ensuring no deadlocks occur.

### 3.4 Generating Implementable Routing Logic

According to the above steps, we have successfully constructed the dataset, trained the DT model to generate a decision tree, and designed a routing algorithm based on this decision tree. This subsection mainly describes transforming the decision tree into achievable routing logic.

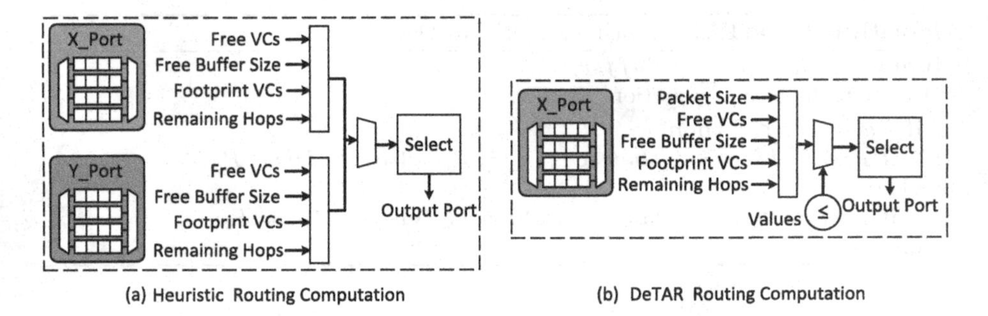


**Fig. 4.** Analysis and comparison of two routing computation units in router architecture: the heuristic adaptive routing algorithm and the DeTAR.

Figure 3 shows how the decision tree is converted into an implementable routing logic. Figure 3(a) is a 2-depth decision tree. Figure 3(b) is the implementable routing logic converted according to the decision tree. Each non-leaf node is implemented using a two-input multiplexer and a comparator. This routing logic needs three comparators and three multiplexers, where the comparators check whether the routing state information meets a certain threshold and control the selection of multiplexers accordingly in a prioritized manner. In the last step, we need to deploy the routing logic into the routing computation unit. We compare and analyze two routing computation units in router architecture: the heuristic adaptive routing algorithm and the DeTAR algorithm, as shown in Fig. 4. In the minimum routing algorithm, the heuristic adaptive routing algorithm typically involves considering two potential ports in the X and Y dimensions. This algorithm relies on the network state information in two dimensions to determine the output port. DeTAR only counts the metric value for the output port in the X dimension of the router and compares it with the decision values to determine the output port. It is worth noting that the decision values of the trained decision tree model are shared with each router. Therefore, DeTAR is a hardware-efficient design compared with the heuristic adaptive routing algorithms.

## 4 Evaluation

This paper employs the Garnet2.0 [1] network model in full-system simulator Gem5 [3]. We have modified this platform for data collection as well as evaluating the performance of the DeTAR. The offline training of the DT model is implemented in Python, leveraging scikit-learn [16] tools. To evaluate the area, we synthesize the generated routing logic modules using Synopsys Design Compiler, targeting a TSMC 90 nm technology library and 2 GHz clock frequency.

As DeTAR does not impose specific restrictions on router architecture, we select an input-queued VC-based router architecture as our baseline router architecture. This router has 4 VCs per virtual network and 4-flit depth per VC and variable packet size ({1,5}uniformly distributed). To obtain a wide range of

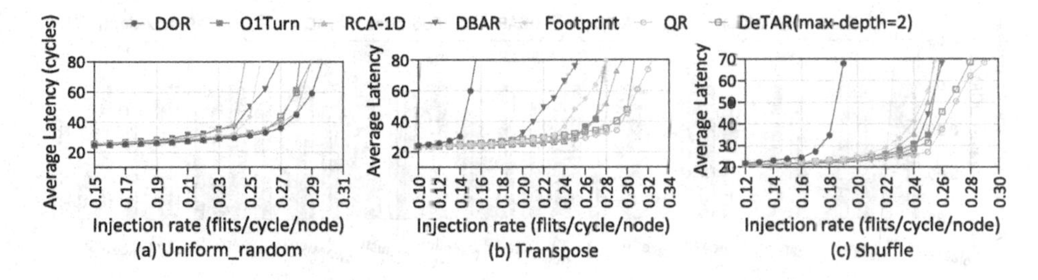


**Fig. 5.** Latency-throughput comparison of alternative routing algorithms with 4 × 4 mesh network topology and variable packet size for different synthetic traffic patterns.

feature values, we use 4×4 2D mesh and DOR with an injection rate of 0.31 packets/node/cycle under uniform_random traffic. We select this particular injection rate since it is the network saturation point (the average packet latency increases dramatically after this point) and can collect different network status data. We collect network status information for the output ports in the X dimension of a router since this paper focuses on the minimum adaptive routing algorithm. Then, this router is located in the middle area of the network topology since a transmission path involves multiple routing decisions that overlap and intersect. However, collecting data this way aims to ensure the dataset's quality. In addition to evaluating performance under uniform_random traffic patterns, we also assess the routing algorithms using other synthetic traffic patterns (such as transpose and shuffle) and PARSEC workloads [2] to check if the DeTAR is scalability in real workloads. We compare DeTAR with other routing algorithms, and the corresponding routing algorithms are as follows. (1) DOR, a dimension-ordered deterministic routing algorithm [6]; (2) O1Turn, an oblivious routing algorithm [19]; (3) RCA-1D, a regional congestion awareness adaptive routing algorithm [11]; (4) DBAR, a destination-based adaptive routing algorithm [15]; (5) Footprint, a state-of-the-art adaptive routing algorithm [10]; (6) Q-Routing (QR), an adaptive routing algorithm based on Q-Learning [4]. DeTAR uses the decision tree with a max-depth of 2 to generate routing decisions.

During model training, we conducted simulations for a total of 50,000 cycles, with 20,000 cycles dedicated to warming up the network, 20,000 cycles for DT model training, and the remaining cycles for testing the DT model. In decision tree generation, each node is evaluated before division. If the division of the current node cannot improve the generalization ability of the decision tree, the division is stopped, and the current node is marked as a leaf node.

### 4.1 Scalable to Different Injection Rates

Figure 5(a) shows the performance comparison between baseline routing algorithms and DeTAR across different injection rates on the uniform_random traffic pattern. This figure only shows the region around the network saturation point, as routing algorithms have little effect on NoCs performance under low injection rates. Regarding network throughput, DeTAR performs superior to RCA-1D,

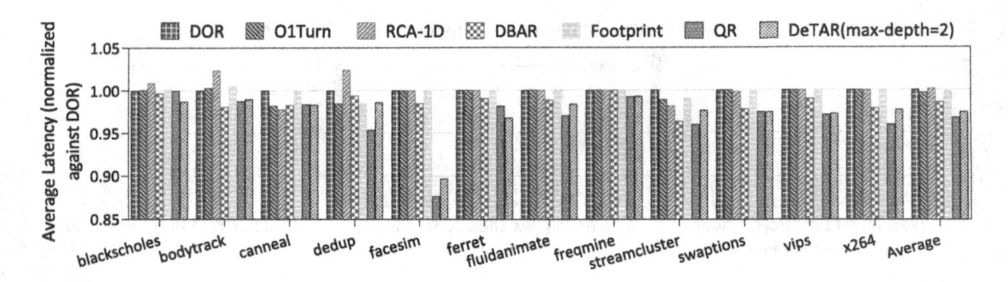


**Fig. 6.** Comparison of DeTAR and alternative routing algorithms using PARSEC workloads. The average latency of adaptive routing algorithms is normalized to that of DOR.

DBAR, and Footprint while being close to DOR and O1Turn. The performance of the DeTAR is slightly better than heuristic adaptive routing algorithms but is slightly lower than the QR. This is because QR uses online training to make routing decisions, and this method can better monitor network status. However, QR also increases hardware overhead, making it challenging to adopt in NoCs. Under the same traffic pattern, DeTAR can generalize in situations of different injection rates and outperforms heuristic adaptive routing algorithms. Mainly, DeTAR improves saturation throughput by 11.5% compared with Footprint.

### 4.2 Generalization to Different Traffic Patterns

Figure 5(b, c) shows the performance comparison between different routing algorithms under non-uniform traffic patterns, such as transpose and shuffle traffic patterns. Similarly, DeTAR outperforms the heuristic routing algorithm in average packet latency. While the DeTAR is trained using uniform_random traffic, its high generalization makes it outperform other routing algorithms under other traffic patterns as well. However, DeTAR does have a little performance gap with the QR [4], which is based on RL and relies on network environment exploration to enable a more feasible global adaptive routing. Unlike QR, DeTAR adopts a decision tree model to explore the priority of network state features, which is an approximate local optimum. DeTAR exhibits poorer performance than QR, which is dynamically updated based on the global network state environment, and serves as an approximate global optimum. However, compared with heuristic routing algorithms, DeTAR improves the saturation throughput by 23.69%.

### 4.3 Real Workloads

We demonstrate the scalability of DeTAR under PARSEC workloads in this section. Figure 6 shows the average packet latency (normalized to DOR's latency) across PARSEC workloads, where the bars at the end show the average result across all workloads. DeTAR achieves better results for all cases, where the average packet latency of DeTAR outperforms DOR by up to 2.61%. For blackscholes, the DeTAR routing algorithm improves minimally over DOR. For facesim,

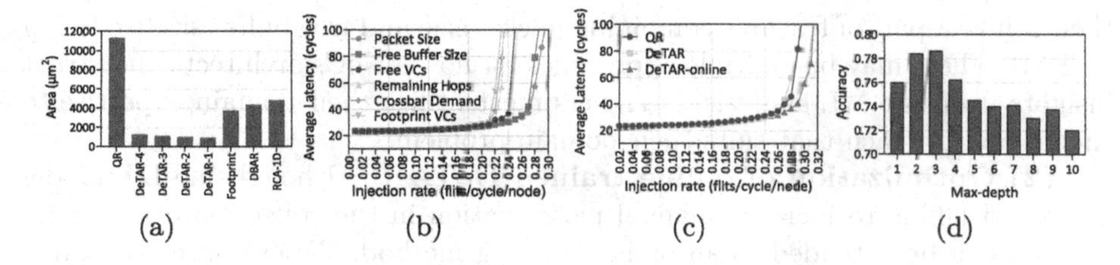


**Fig. 7.** (a) Area comparison of different routing algorithms. (b) Throughput comparison of different network features for uniform_random traffic pattern. (c) Throughput comparison of online trained DeTAR-online optimization with DeTAR and QR routing algorithms under uniform_random traffic pattern. (d) Impact of max-depth parameters on the classification accuracy.

the average packet latency of DeTAR outperforms DOR by up to 10.3%. The working set of facesim is larger than that of blackscholes, as blackscholes has the smallest working set among all the PARSEC workloads [2]. However, in the above experiment, we evaluate performance under uniform_random traffic patterns, other synthetic traffic patterns (transpose and shuffle), and PARSEC workloads. These can all prove that DeTAR is scalability.

### 4.4 Area of the DeTAR Routing Logic

Figure 7(a) shows the area comparison of different adaptive routing algorithms. The implementation overhead of DeTAR adds information about the free buffer size. The count of the free buffer size does not need to add additional registers but only uses the credit link in the router architecture. The QR shows the area of this implementation where the Q-table should use memory to implement. Compared with QR implementation, DeTAR can reduce the area overhead by 88.95% with slight performance degradation. Compared with Footprint, DeTAR can reduce the area overhead by 66.32% without significant performance degradation. As the max-depth used in the decision tree model increases, the area of DeTAR also increases. This is because the number of comparators and multiplexers used by DeTAR also increases.

### 4.5 Discussion

In this subsection, we present an analysis of observations and parameters based on our ML experience for NoCs adaptive routing.

**(1) Verify the validity of DeTAR.** The learning process of the DT model relies on features and domain knowledge, which select decision metrics critical for the overall network performance and set the priority of these metrics accordingly. Figure 7(b) compares the impact of different features on network performance when they are separately used in routing strategies. Not surprisingly, packet size was the feature that performed best, which can be verified to be consistent with the feature priority obtained from the result of the DT model learning. We then utilize a pair of features combining packet size and free buffer size to design DeTAR. There may be multiple approaches for how a NoCs architect can extract insights from the ML analysis. Designers must utilize their domain expertise to choose an approach that suits their domain problem.

**(2) Optimization of online trained DeTAR.** Although the DT model is trained offline to increase manual participation in the collection of datasets, DeTAR can be extended to an online training method. We evaluate the online version of DeTAR (DeTAR-online) and compare it with QR and DeTAR under uniform_random traffic pattern, as shown in Fig. 7(c). DeTAR-online outperforms QR and DeTAR with a 6.9% increase in throughput. This experiment verifies that the design scheme of the DeTAR can be scalability in an online training mode, reducing manual participation.

**(3) Different max-depth of the DT model.** To explore the impact of the max-depth parameter of the DT model on performance, we discuss different max-depth values. Figure 7(d) shows the effect of max-depth values on classification accuracy from 1 to 10. The larger the max-depth value, the lower the classification accuracy. As suggested in previous studies, the max-depth is a critical parameter, and ensure it is not too large to avoid overfitting. To make a trade-off between hardware overhead and network performance, although the accuracy when the max-depth value is 3 is greater than that when the max-depth value is 2, the main research object of this paper is the maximum value of 2. Therefore, a larger max-depth value can result in sub-optimal network performance. On the other hand, aggressively lowering the max-depth values also reduces hardware overhead.

## 5 Conclusion

This paper has presented a novel methodology for distilling routing logic, the Decision Tree-based Adaptive Routing algorithm, DeTAR. We design DeTAR from a key insight that routing decisions can be treated as selecting and prioritizing the key features of various network state information. The DT model can select and prioritize critical factors for the target decision. This reveals a natural match between the adaptive routing algorithm and the DT model. We collect network state data from the NoCs simulation process and build the training dataset. This method uses the ID3 algorithm and offline training to obtain a decision tree. Then, this decision tree is transformed into implementable routing logic. Finally, we implement DeTAR with a few comparators and multiplexers, achieving low hardware costs. We demonstrate that DeTAR provides significant improvement in performance across synthetic traffic patterns and real workloads.

**Acknowledgments.** The authors would like to express their sincere gratitude to the anonymous reviewers for their invaluable comments and suggestions. This work is supported by the National Key Research and Development Program of China under Grant No.2021YFB0300101, the Natural Science Foundation of China (NSFC) under Grant No.62002368, and the Excellent Youth Foundation of Hunan Province under Grant

No.2021JJ10050. Dezun Dong is the corresponding author of this paper. Xiaoyun Zhang and Yaohua Wang contributed equally to this research.

## References

1. Agarwal, N., Krishna, T., Peh, L.S., Jha, N.K.: GARNET: a detailed on-chip network model inside a full-system simulator. In: Proceedings of the 2009 IEEE International Symposium on Performance Analysis of Systems and Software (ISPASS), pp. 33–42 (2009)
2. Bienia, C., Kumar, S., Singh, J.P., Li, K.: The PARSEC benchmark suite: characterization and architectural implications. In: Proceedings of the 17th annual International Conference on Parallel Architectures and Compilation Techniques (PACT), pp. 72–81 (2008)
3. Binkert, N., Beckmann, B., Black, G., Reinhardt, S.K., Saidi, A.: The gem5 simulator. ACM SIGARCH Comput. Archit. News. **39**(2), 1–7 (2011)
4. Boyan, J., Littman, M.: Packet routing in dynamically changing networks: a reinforcement learning approach. In: Advances in Neural Information Processing Systems vol. 6, pp. 1–8 (1994)
5. Choi, S., Yeung, D.Y.: Predictive Q-routing: a memory-based reinforcement learning approach to adaptive traffic control. In: Advances in Neural Information Processing Systems, vol. 8, pp. 1–7 (1999)
6. Dally, W.J., Towles, B.P.: Principles and Practices of Interconnection Networks. Morgan Kaufmann, Burlington (2004)
7. Duato, J.: A new theory of deadlock-free adaptive routing in wormhole networks. IEEE Trans. Parallel Distrib. Syst. (TPDS). **4**(12), 1320–1331 (1993)
8. Ebrahimi, M., et al.: HARAQ: congestion-aware learning model for highly adaptive routing algorithm in on-chip networks. In: Proceedings of the Sixth Annual International Symposium on Networks-on-Chip (NoCs), pp. 19–26 (2012)
9. Fettes, Q., Clark, M., Bunescu, R., Karanth, A., Louri, A.: Dynamic voltage and frequency scaling in NoCs with supervised and reinforcement learning techniques. IEEE Trans. Comput. (TC). **68**(3), 375–389 (2019)
10. Fu, B., Kim, J.: Footprint: regulating routing adaptiveness in networks-on-chip. In: Proceedings of the 44th Annual International Symposium on Computer Architecture (ISCA), pp. 691–702 (2017)
11. Gratz, P., Grot, B., Keckler, S.W.: Regional congestion awareness for load balance in networks-on-chip. In: Proceedings of the 14th annual International Symposium on High Performance Computer Architecture (HPCA), pp. 203–214 (2008)
12. Kakoulli, E., Soteriou, V., Theocharides, T.: HPRA: a pro-active hotspot-preventive high-performance routing algorithm for networks-on-chips. In: IEEE 30th International Conference on Computer Design (ICCD), pp. 249–255 (2012)
13. Kumar, S., Miikkulainen, R.: Dual reinforcement Q-routing: an on-line adaptive routing algorithm. In: Proceedings of the Artificial Neural Networks in Engineering Conference, pp. 231–238 (1997)
14. Li, M., Zeng, Q.A., Jone, W.B.: DyXY: a proximity congestion-aware deadlock-free dynamic routing method for network on chip. In: Proceedings of the 43rd Annual Design Automation Conference (DAC), pp. 849–852 (2006)
15. Ma, S., Enright Jerger, N., Wang, Z.: DBAR: an efficient routing algorithm to support multiple concurrent applications in networks-on-chip. In: Proceedings of the 38th Annual International Symposium on Computer Architecture (ISCA), pp. 413–424 (2011)

16. Pedregosa, F., et al.: Scikit-learn: machine learning in python. J. Mach. Learn. Res. **12**, 2825–2830 (2012)
17. Penney, D.D., Chen, L.: A survey of machine learning applied to computer architecture design (2019). http://arxiv.org/abs/1909.12373
18. Puthal, M.K., Singh, V., Gaur, M., Laxmi, V.: C-routing: an adaptive hierarchical NoC routing methodology. In: Proceedings of the Annual 19th International Conference on VLSI and System-on-Chip (VLSI-SoC), pp. 392–397 (2011)
19. Seo, D., Ali, A., Lim, W.T., Rafique, N.: Near-optimal worst-case throughput routing for two-dimensional mesh networks. In: Proceedings of the 32nd Annual International Symposium on Computer Architecture (ISCA), pp. 432–443 (2005)
20. Wang, C., Dong, D., Wang, Z., Zhang, X., Zhao, Z.: RELAR: a reinforcement learning framework for adaptive routing in network-on-chips. In: Proceedings of the 2021 IEEE International Conference on Cluster Computing (CLUSTER), pp. 813–814 (2021)
21. Yin, J., et al.: Experiences with ML-driven design: a NoC case study. In: Proceedings of the 26th Annual International Symposium on High Performance Computer Architecture (HPCA), pp. 637–648 (2020)
22. Zhou, Z.-H.: Machine Learning. Springer, Singapore (2021). https://doi.org/10.1007/978-981-15-1967-3

# Auto-Divide GNN: Accelerating GNN Training with Subgraph Division

Hongyu Chen, Zhejiang Ran, Keshi Ge, Zhiquan Lai, Jingfei Jiang, and Dongsheng Li(✉)

National Laboratory for Parallel and Distributed Processing (PDL), Computer College, National University of Defense Technology, Changsha, China
dsli@nudt.edu.cn

**Abstract.** Graph Neural Networks (GNNs) have gained considerable attention in recent years for their exceptional performance on graph-structured data. Sampling-based GNN training is the most common method used for training GNNs on large-scale graphs, and it is often accelerated by caching feature data on the GPU. However, the emergence of more complex models and datasets with higher feature dimension requires more GPU memory for training, which limits the acceleration performance of GPU caching and can even result in out-of-memory errors. To release more GPU memory for the cache in a transparent way, we propose a *subgraph division* method, which trains several smaller micrographs instead of an entire subgraph at each training iteration. However, it is non-trivial to combine subgraph division with GPU caching due to the redundancy between micrographs. To tackle this challenge, we introduce an *auto-profile* method that searches for the best-performing subgraph division scheme based on training perception and probability analysis. Additionally, we develop an *estimation-based caching strategy* to lift the caching hitting rate against the diverse graph structures. These ideas are integrated to *Auto-Divide GNN*, a framework for accelerating sampling-based GNN training. The multi-GPU evaluations on three representative GNN models and five large graphs demonstrate that Auto-Divide GNN achieves significant speedups of up to 5.61× and 3.13× over two state-of-the-art GNN frameworks, DGL and PaGraph, respectively.

**Keywords:** Graph Neural Networks · Accelerate Training · Subgraph Division · GPU Caching

## 1 Introduction

Recently, Graph Neural Networks [5,9,13] the application of deep learning methods to graph-structured data, have achieved remarkable success, particularly in node classification [9], link prediction [17], and graph classification [15] tasks.

H. Chen and Z. Ran—These authors contribute equally to this work and should be considered as co-first authors.


J. Cano et al. (Eds.): Euro-Par 2023, LNCS 14100, pp. 367–382, 2023.
https://doi.org/10.1007/978-3-031-39698-4_25

Real-world graphs are often large-scale and associated with rich feature data. When dealing with such graphs, it is highly challenging to process the entire graph as one batch for limited memory in GNN training. Consequently, recent works [4,7] have turned to sampling-based GNN training, which repeatedly samples subgraphs from the original graph and collects feature data to form minibatch data for training. However, sampling-based GNN training suffers from inefficiencies due to the data loading problem, which involves the heavy and frequent transmission of data from host memory to GPU memory. To address this challenge, PaGraph [11] introduced GPU caching that leverages free GPU memory to cache the feature data to reduce data transmission. And PaGraph proposes a caching strategy based on the out-degree of nodes. Further, GNNLab [16] adopts a more general caching strategy based on pre-sampling. BGL [12] employs a dynamic cache engine to minimize feature retrieving traffic.

Unfortunately, the effectiveness of GPU caching is constrained by the two main bottlenecks. Firstly, the limited GPU memory. On the one hand, the GPU caching solutions listed above require a significant volume of GPU memory to cache node features. On the other hand, GNN training also requires a large memory footprint. Thus, the caching solution has to compete for GPU memory with the GNN training. As the trend of deploying more model layers, wider layer hidden sizes, and advanced aggregators (e.g. LSTM), this memory competition becomes severe. In extreme cases, such as mobile devices or desktop GPUs, this can even lead to out-of-memory errors. The default solution to release GPU memory for caching involves manually changing the model training algorithm or tuning hyperparameters (e.g., minibatch size). However, this manual tuning method increases the users' workload. What's worse, the hyperparameters changing may interfere with the model update information, such as gradients, and thus deteriorate the model's accuracy and training convergence [8].

Secondly, the efficacy of GPU caching is also determined by the caching strategy. However, current strategies often overlook the diversity of graph structure. For instance, the caching strategy of PaGraph [11] is only efficient when the graph has a power-law degree distribution, otherwise, its performance is poor.

In such circumstances, we propose Auto-Divide GNN, a sampling-based multi-GPU GNN training framework targeting large graphs. Auto-Divide GNN focuses on unleashing the power of GPU caching to accelerate GNN training by solving the GPU memory competition in a transparent way. Our key idea of this framework is *subgraph division*, which trains several smaller micrographs instead of an entire subgraph at each training iteration. This design can release GPU memory for caching since training on micrographs consumes much less GPU memory in model computation. To provide a transparent view for users and guarantee the model accuracy and training convergence, we accumulate the gradients yielding from each micrograph and defer updating the model parameters, until the end of an iteration. In this way, model training with subgraph division is equivalent to using the user-defined minibatch size.

However, combining subgraph division directly with GPU caching is challenging because there is a large number of redundant nodes between micrographs, i.e., a node could simultaneously be an input node to multiple micrographs.

Such duplication will further cause extra massive computation and transmission. This conflicts with the training speedup brought by subgraph division. A reasonable subgraph division scheme can maximize the available GPU caching space while reducing redundancy to achieve the best acceleration performance. The manual search for such an optimal subgraph division scheme is burdensome for the researchers. To tackle this challenge, we propose an *auto-profile* method to search for the optimal division scheme. We first identify the pattern of the optimal subgraph division scheme. Then we estimate the end-to-end time of all alternative schemes under this pattern by training perception and probability analysis. Finally, we select the scheme that promises to be the best performance.

Besides the subgraph division scheme, to lift the cache hitting rate against diverse graph structures, we propose estimation-based caching, a caching strategy based on the auto-profile method. Specifically, it will cache the nodes estimated to be sampled most frequently, thus, it can achieve robustness and efficiency.

We evaluate the performance of Auto-Divide GNN by executing three typical GNN models (i.e., GraphSAGE [4], GCN [9], and GAT [13]) over five representative datasets, and compare it with the state-of-the-art GNN system DGL [14] and PaGraph [11]. Experimental results show that Auto-Divide GNN outperforms DGL and PaGraph by up to 5.61× and 3.13×, and reduces average 95.05% and 82.17% data loading time, respectively.

**Contributions.** We make the following contributions in this paper.

1. An analysis of the bottlenecks of GPU caching technology (Sect. 2.3).
2. A novel subgraph division design for sampling-based GNN training that reduces GPU memory consumption without adjusting the training strategy and hyperparameters (Sect. 3.1).
3. An auto-profile method searches for the optimal subgraph division scheme to combine with GPU caching, as well as a derived caching strategy with near-ideal performance (Sect. 3.2).
4. An extensive evaluation with three models and five GNN datasets to show the efficacy of Auto-Divide GNN (Sect. 4).

## 2 Background and Motivation

### 2.1 Sampling-Based GNN Training

The basic idea behind Graph neural networks (GNNs) is that each node aggregates features from its neighboring nodes and performs neural network-based transformations. Minibatch training, i.e., sampling-based GNN training, is the most widely used approach. This method is typically executed in a CPU-GPU hybrid architecture, where the graph structure data and node feature data are stored in the server host memory, while the model training is performed on the GPU. The training process is shown in Algorithm 1. The training nodes are first divided into multiple minibatches, which are then processed one by one. In each iteration, three steps of subgraph sampling, feature loading and model

**Algorithm 1:** Minibatch training procedure.

**Input** : graph $G = (V, E)$, training nodes set $V_t$, node feature data $H$, GNN model *model*, minibatch size *bs*

```
1 {V_1, V_2, ..., V_B} ← Split(V_t, bs) // minibatches of training nodes
2 for b ← 1 to B do
3 |  G_b ← Sample(G, V_b)
4 |  H_input ← LoadFeature(H, G_b)
5 |  loss ← L(model(G_b, H_input), label_{V_b})
6 |  loss.backward()
7 |  UpdateParameters(model.parameters())
```

computation will be performed. The training nodes in each minibatch are also the output nodes. This is because the predicted values for these nodes will be used to compare with their labels for the subsequent calculation of loss.

### 2.2 Acceleration Based on GPU Caching

A significant challenge faced by sampling-based GNN training is the heavy burden of data transfer from host memory to GPU memory in feature loading. This problem is caused by the exponential growth of the number of input nodes and their corresponding feature data, as well as the limited PCIe bandwidth.

To address this challenge, PaGraph [11] first proposed to selectively cache the features associated with specific nodes in GPU memory. During the model training, the input features of the minibatch will be retrieved from the host memory and GPU cache respectively. Those nodes that are sampled more frequently will be cached. Thus GPU caching reduces the data movement from CPU to GPU to a certain extent.

### 2.3 Bottlenecks of GPU Caching

There are two main bottlenecks in training with GPU caching.

*Firstly*, more model layers, wider layer hidden sizes, and advanced aggregators (e.g. LSTM) improve the performance of GNN models, but also significantly increase the memory usage of GPU during model training. With limited GPU memory capacity, this leaves very little memory for GPU caching, resulting in poor acceleration as well. Table 1 presents the peak training memory footprint for each Model-Dataset pair under the setting of Table 2 and Table 3. This shows that in many cases, the peak memory usage is already approaching the upper limit of desktop GPUs. Therefore, the effectiveness of GPU caching is greatly diminished. While hyperparameter tuning and training strategy modification can reduce excessive memory consumption, they often come at the cost of worse model performance and convergence.

*Secondly*, the design of caching strategy is also influential. PaGraph adopts a static caching strategy that chooses the nodes with a high out-degree to cache.

**Table 1.** Peak training memory footprint. (GB)

| Models | Ogbn-Products | Wikipedia | Live-Journal | Live-Journal-2008 | Enwiki |
|---|---|---|---|---|---|
| GraphSAGE | 9.92 | 6.45 | 9.04 | 8.95 | 8.67 |
| GCN | 6.90 | 8.82 | 11.64 | 11.60 | 10.69 |
| GAT | 12.62 | 7.34 | 10.44 | 10.48 | 10.18 |

But this strategy is based on the assumption that the graph has a highly skewed power-low degree distribution, which is not always met. GNNLab [16] employs a caching policy based on pre-sampling which requires pre-processing of multiple epochs. BGL [12] design a dynamic cache engine to acquire a higher cache hitting rate. The cost, however, is the decrease in model accuracy due to the need for using the specified partition and sampling algorithm.

Therefore, it is urgent to develop a user-transparent approach to reduce the training memory overhead and a more general caching strategy.

## 3 Design

Auto-Divide GNN reduces the memory consumption during model training by subgraph division, which processes multiple smaller micrographs instead of one subgraph in an iteration. The gradients of these micrographs are accumulated to update the model parameters at the end of the iteration, ensuring that the effective minibatch size for updating model parameters is equal to the user-defined minibatch size. Subgraph division, therefore, reduces memory usage during model training without the need to adjust hyperparameters or model algorithms. More details about subgraph division are presented in Sect. 3.1.

Subgraph division reserves more available memory for GPU caching. However, combining subgraph division with GPU caching is challenging because it introduces redundant nodes across micrographs, leading to an increase in computation and transmission. This makes selecting the optimal subgraph division scheme crucial for users. In Sect. 3.2, we introduce an auto-profile method that selects the optimal subgraph division scheme based on an accurate estimation of the end-to-end time of micrographs. This approach enables Auto-Divide GNN to achieve significant acceleration performance when subgraph division is coupled with GPU caching. Additionally, based on the auto-profile method, we have derived a more general and effective caching strategy compared to others.

Figure 1 presents the training pipeline of the Auto-Divide GNN. After initializing the Auto-Divide GNN framework, we execute several epochs to obtain the necessary information about the performance of the machine, and then calculate the best subgraph division scheme based on our auto-profile method. Then we start model training with subgraph division until the model convergences.

### 3.1 Subgraph Division

We propose subgraph division, and introduce it into sampling-based GNN training. Algorithm 2 describes the training pipeline. At the start of training, *mbs*, the

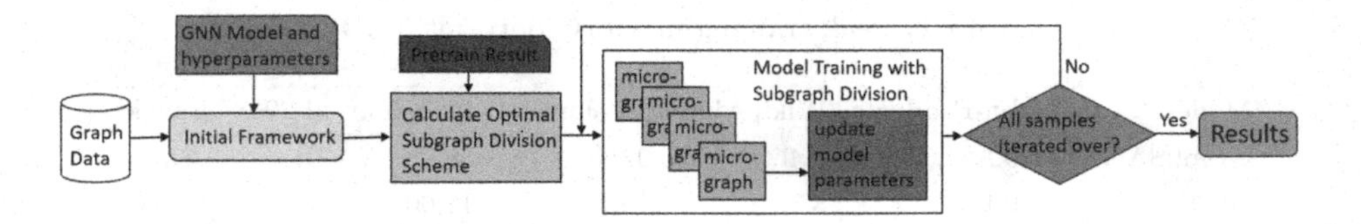


**Fig. 1.** Training pipeline of Auto-Divide GNN.

---

**Algorithm 2:** Training with subgraph division.

---

**Input** : graph $G = (V, E)$, training nodes set $V_t$, node feature data $H$, GNN model *model*, minibatch size *bs*

1 $mbs, t \leftarrow$ `AutoProfile(`$model, bs$`)`
2 $\{V_1, V_2, ..., V_B\} \leftarrow$ `Split(`$V_t$`, `$mbs$`) // microbatches of training nodes`
3 **for** $b \leftarrow 1$ **to** $B$ **do**
4 $\quad G_b \leftarrow$ `Sample(`$G$`, `$V_b$`) // sample micrograph`
5 $\quad H_{input} \leftarrow$ `LoadFeature(`$H$`, `$G_b$`)`
6 $\quad loss \leftarrow \mathscr{L}(model(G_b, H_{input}), label_{V_b})$
7 $\quad loss.backward()$
8 $\quad$ **if** $b \ mod \ t == 0$ **then** `// Every t micorbatches`
9 $\quad\quad$ `UpdateParameters(`$model.parameters()$`)`

---

microbatch size and $t$, the number of microbatches in one iteration, are obtained by pre-processing or manual setting in Line 1. Then training nodes are splitted into microbatches based on *mbs* in Line 2. After that, the subgraph sampling, feature loading and model computation in Line 4–7 are the same as the steps in Algorithm 1. The difference, however, is that training with subgraph division only updates the model parameters after $t$ microbatches, as shown in Line 8–9. And we refer to $t$ microbatches and one parameter updating as one iteration. While in minibatch training procedure, the model parameters are updated after each minibatch has been processed.

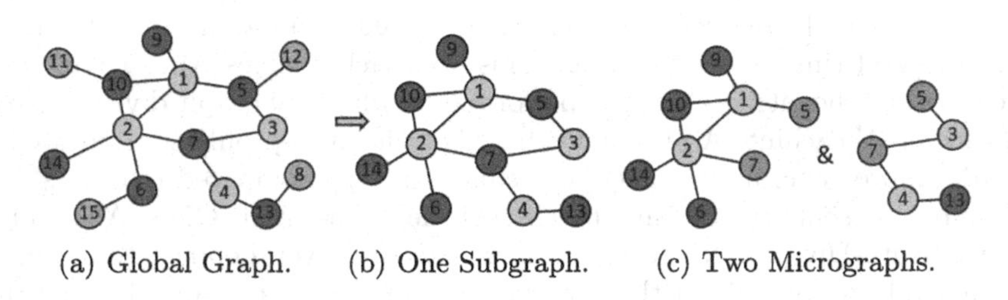

(a) Global Graph. (b) One Subgraph. (c) Two Micrographs.

**Fig. 2.** Schematic of subgraph division.

Figure 2 provides an example of subgraph division. Nodes 1, 2, 3, and 4 are training nodes, while the other nodes are ordinary ones. With a user-defined *minibatch size* of 4, Fig. 2(b) shows a subgraph sampled from the 4 training nodes, which are also the output nodes of the subgraph. As the training nodes will sample their *1-hop* neighbors to form a subgraph, neighboring nodes beyond *1-hop* will not be sampled (e.g., nodes 8, 11, 12, and 15). As a comparison, Fig. 2(c) illustrates the two micrographs used to replace the subgraph in Fig. 2(b). One micrograph is sampled from training nodes 1 and 2, while another is from nodes 3 and 4. The sum of output nodes of the micrographs in one iteration is equal to the *minibatch size*. Clearly, the micrograph is smaller than the subgraph, resulting in lower peak memory overhead for training. However, the computations and transfers of redundant nodes are also inevitable, such as the nodes 5 and 7 in Fig. 2(c).

While in training with subgraph division, the GNN model computes multiple microbatches one by one in a single iteration. The gradients calculated from each microbatch are not immediately used to update the model parameters after the backward propagation; instead, they are accumulated and used to update the model parameters together at the end of the iteration. This means that the model parameters remain the same throughout this iteration until the final update.

So when the sum of the output nodes of the microbatches in a single iteration is equivalent to *minibatch size*, the gradients for one update are calculated from *minibatch size* samples, which means the effective minibatch size is equal to the user-defined minibatch size. This demonstrates that subgraph division does not affect model performance and convergence, and reduces peak training memory overhead in a way that is transparent to the users.

### 3.2 Automatic Profiling

**Pattern of Optimal Subgraph Division Scheme.** Based on the analysis, we propose three principles for the selection of the subgraph division scheme:

1. Reduce the size of micrographs to maximize available GPU memory for caching feature data.
2. Minimize the number of micrographs in an iteration to reduce redundancy.
3. Ensure that the sum of output nodes of micrographs in an iteration is equal to the user-defined minibatch size.

Under these constraints, we propose a model for the optimal subgraph division scheme: in a single iteration, there will be $k$ **main micrographs** (sampled from *main microbatch size* training nodes) and 1 **append micrograph** (sampled from *append microbatch size* training nodes) if the *minibatch size* is not evenly divisible by *main microbatch size*. The following formula is more clear:

$$\begin{cases} minibatch\ size = k \times main\ microbatch\ size + append\ microbatch\ size \\ append\ microbatch\ size = minibatch\ size\ \%\ main\ microbatch\ size \end{cases} \quad (1)$$

**Searching Algorithm.** We consider the search space to be all possible subgraph division schemes under Eq. 1, and we traverse this space to find the scheme with the best performance by estimating the end-to-end time of each subgraph division scheme, which can be easily achieved by estimating the end-to-end time of a single micrograph.

We begin by modeling the end-to-end time of a micrograph, which is illustrated in Fig. 3 along with its various components and their relationships. This

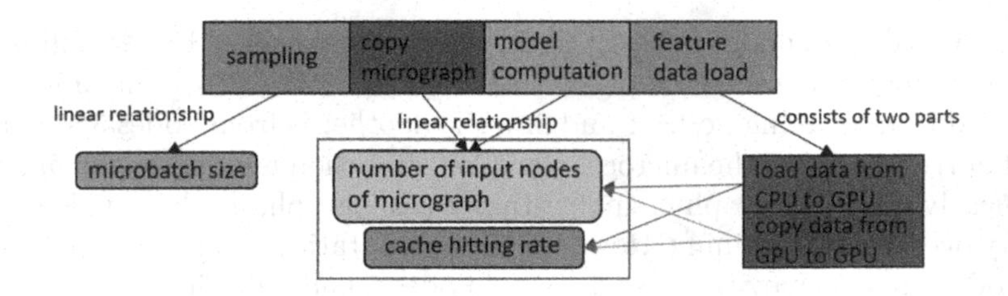


**Fig. 3.** The model for end-to-end processing time of single micrograph.

time can be divided into four parts: sampling time, micrograph copy time, model computation time, and feature data load time. Our observations show that the sampling time is directly proportional to the *microbatch size*, while the micrograph copy time, the model computation time, and the peak GPU memory overhead during training are directly proportional to the number of input nodes in the micrograph. The feature data load time is dependent on two parts: the data loaded from the CPU to the GPU and the data copied from the GPU to the GPU, which can also be estimated from the number of input nodes and the cache hitting rate. Therefore, the key to estimating the end-to-end time of a micrograph lies in the estimation of the number of input nodes and the cache hitting rate, which can be calculated by computing $\boldsymbol{E_u}$, the estimated number of times that each node $u$ will be sampled.

Algorithm 3 presents the complete process of estimating the end-to-end time of a single micrograph. The algorithm first calculates the number of times each node is sampled in Line 2–9. Line 10 computes the number of input nodes of the micrograph. Finally, Line 11–14 estimate the end-to-end time of the micrograph based on previous calculations.

In the algorithm, probability map $PM$ is a hash map with node numbers as keys and lists $\{p_1, p_2, ..., p_n\}$ as values. Here, $p_i$ represents the probability that the $i$-th *L-hop* neighborhood training node of node $u$ samples node $u$. We obtain $PM$ through pre-sampling. The function FuncPeakMem, FuncTimeSample, FuncTimeCopyMicrograph, and FuncTimeModelComputation are all univariate linear functions, as we described before. The other three functions GroupProbability, GetHittingRate, and FuncTimeDataLoad, are calculated using the following equations:

$$\begin{cases} GroupProbability(\{p_1, p_2, ..., p_n\}) = 1 - \prod_{i=1}^{n}(1 - p_i) \\ GetHittingRate(m) = \frac{\sum_{u \in Top_m} E_u}{\sum_{u \in N} E_u} \\ FuncTimeDataLoad(n, hitting\_rate) = \frac{n \times hitting\_rate}{v_{g2g}} + \frac{n \times (1 - hitting\_rate)}{v_{c2g}} \end{cases} \quad (2)$$

where $Top_m$ is the set of the top $m$ nodes with the highest frequencies of being sampled, and the $v_{g2g}$ and $v_{c2g}$ are the transfer speed from GPU to GPU and CPU to GPU respectively.

**Algorithm 3:** Estimate the end-to-end time of one micrograph.

**Input** : graph $G$, microbatch size $mbs$, node set $N$, total GPU memory size $GPU\_size$, node feature size $feature\_size$, probability map $PM$
**Output**: an estimated end-to-end time of a single micrograph

```
1  Total_E_u ⟵ 0 ;                                // total sampled times of all nodes
2  foreach node u ∈ N do
3      {p_1, p_2, ..., p_n} ⟵ RandomShuffle(PM[u])
4      E_u ⟵ 0 ;                                   // sampled times of node u
5      k ⟵ n / (|N|/mbs) ;                         // split training neighbors into k group
6      for i ← 0 to |N|/mbs − 1 do
7          start ⟵ i × k + 1, end ⟵ min((i + 1) × k, n)
8          E_u ⟵ E_u + GroupProbability({p_start, p_start+1, ..., p_end})
9      Total_E_u ⟵ Total_E_u + E_u
10 num_input_nodes ⟵ Total_E_u / (|N|/mbs) ;      // number of input nodes
11 free_memory ⟵ GPU_size - FuncPeakMem(num_input_nodes)
12 num_cache_nodes ⟵ free_memory / feature_size
13 cache_hitting_rate ⟵ GetHittingRate(num_cache_nodes)
14 end2end_time ⟵ FuncTimeSample(mbs) +
   FuncTimeCopyMicrograph(num_input_nodes) +
   FuncTimeModelComputation(num_input_nodes) +
   FuncTimeDataLoad(num_input_nodes, cache_hitting_rate)
15 return end2end_time
```

**Estimation-Based Caching Strategy.** Drawing on our previous analysis and calculations, we propose an estimation-based caching strategy that prioritizes caching the nodes with the highest estimated frequency of being sampled. This caching strategy has demonstrated near-ideal results in practice and is also adaptable to a wider range of graph structures and sampling algorithms.

# 4 Evaluation

## 4.1 Experimental Setup

**Environments.** We use the server with 4 NVIDIA 3090 GPUs (24 GB memory), two 24-core Intel Xeon CPUs (2.40 GHz), and 512 GB DDR4 host memory. The machine is installed with Ubuntu 18.04, CUDA library v11.3. Our experiments are carried out on PyTorch of version 1.13 and DGL [14] of version 0.9.2.

**Datasets.** We conduct the experiments on the following five representative datasets, Ogbn-Products [6], Wikipedia-20070206 (for short, Wikipedia) [3], Live-Journal [1], Live-Journal-2008 [3], Wikipedia-links-English (for short, Enwiki) [10]. Table 2 shows the details of the datasets. As the four datasets other than Ogbn-Products only provide graph structures, we generate random feature data and labels for them based on specific dimensions, following the setting of PaGraph [11].

**Models.** We use three typical GNN models, GraphSAGE (for short, GSAGE) [4], GCN [9], and GAT [13]. Specifically, we train GCN with neighborhood sampling due to limited GPU memory, and GraphSAGE with mean aggregator. Detailed parameter settings of GNN models and datasets are shown in Table 3.

**Baselines.** We evaluate our approach against two baselines: DGL [14], the most widely-used industrial GNN framework, which performs sampling-based GNN training without GPU caching, and PaGraph [11], a state-of-the-art GNN framework that utilizes GPU caching with a node-degree based caching strategy. To ensure fairness in the experiments, we reconstructed PaGraph in our software environment. Unless stated otherwise, all the performance numbers are the average of results from 12 epochs.

**Table 2.** Statistics of datasets. (M: million)

| Datasets | Ogbn-Products | Wikipedia | Live-Journal | Live-Journal-2008 | Enwiki |
|---|---|---|---|---|---|
| vertex# | 2.44M | 3.57M | 4.85M | 5.36M | 13.6M |
| edge# | 123.7M | 45.0M | 68.99M | 79.02M | 437.2M |
| feature dimension | 100 | 1000 | 600 | 600 | 600 |

**Table 3.** Parameter settings of GNN models.

| Model | layers | Hidden size | sampling | minibatch size | attention heads |
|---|---|---|---|---|---|
| GSAGE | 3 | 512 | (10, 15, 25) | 4096 | × |
| GCN | 3 | 512 | (10, 15, 25) | 4096 | × |
| GAT | 3 | 128 | (10, 15, 25) | 2048 | 3 |

### 4.2 Overall Performance

We conduct the experiment of training three GNN models over five datasets with four GPUs and present the end-to-end training performance of the three frameworks in Fig. 4, 5, 6. Considering the impact of GPU memory on the experiment and the specifications of common desktop GPUs, we manually set the available total GPU memory to 10, 12, and 14 GB respectively.

**Different Frameworks.** DGL does not cache feature data on GPU, which results in significant time consumption during data loading. As a result, Auto-Divide GNN outperforms DGL by up to 5.61× (GAT + Wikipedia + 14 GB), with an average speedup of 3.17×. PaGraph's performance is better than DGL because of GPU caching. Nevertheless, Auto-Divide GNN still achieves up to 3.13× speedup (GCN + Live-Journal-2008 + 12 GB), with an average speedup of 1.71×. This is because of Auto-Divide GNN's superior allocation of limited GPU memory compared to PaGraph. With an equivalent GPU memory capacity, Auto-Divide GNN has a larger cache space and can effectively reduce data loading time. In addition, Auto-Divide GNN prevents the extreme case of out-of-memory errors, which cannot be avoided by other baselines.

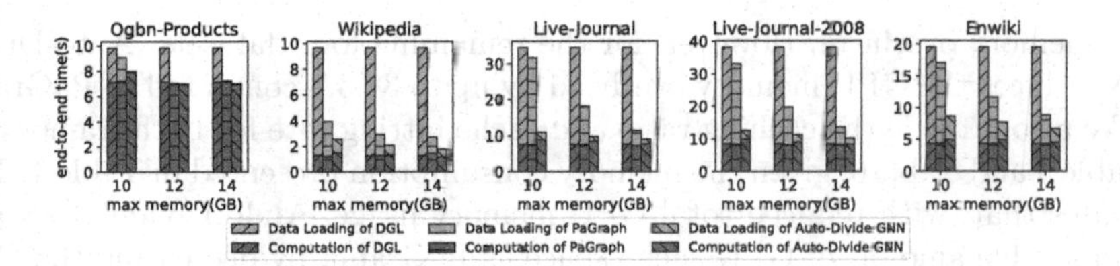


**Fig. 4.** Training GraphSAGE model over 5 datasets.

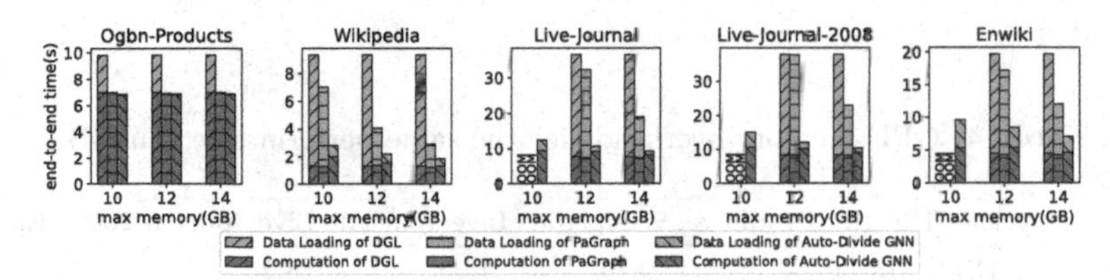


**Fig. 5.** Training GCN model over 5 datasets.

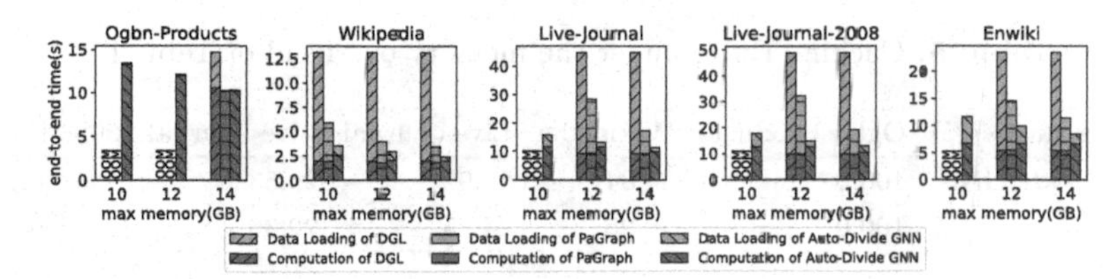


**Fig. 6.** Training GAT model over 5 datasets.

**Time Breakdown.** We divided the end-to-end time into two parts, computation, and data loading. Computation time includes sampling time, micrograph copy time, and model computation time, while data loading time refers to the feature data load time. Compared to DGL and PaGraph, the average reduction of data loading time by Auto-Divide GNN is 95.05% and 82.17%, respectively. Furthermore, the average increase in computation time for Auto-Divide GNN is only 9.08% and 11.07%, respectively. Given that data loading time dominates the end-to-end time, the small increase in computation time is negligible.

### 4.3 Decrease of GPU Memory Overhead

To demonstrate the effectiveness of Auto-Divide GNN in reducing GPU memory consumption, we compared the GPU memory consumption of Auto-Divide GNN and PaGraph in training the GraphSAGE model over five datasets while achieving the same acceleration performance.

Table 4 compares the GPU memory overhead of Auto-Divide GNN and PaGraph, with both frameworks achieving the same end-to-end training time. Since the feature data of the Ogbn-Products dataset can be fully cached on a 12 GB GPU, subgraph division is unnecessary and both frameworks have the same

GPU memory overhead. However, for the remaining four datasets, Auto-Divide GNN reduces the GPU memory overhead by up to 38.3% compared to PaGraph.

We also provide the caching ratio and cache hitting rate for both frameworks in Table 5 and Table 6, given the memory consumption presented in Table 4. This indicates that, with reduced total GPU memory usage, Audo-Divide GNN gets a comparable amount of GPU cache space as PaGraph, by decreasing the GPU memory overhead during training. As a result, Auto-Divide GNN achieves a similar or higher caching ratio, leading to a higher cache hitting rate and similar speedup.

**Table 4.** GPU memory overheads for the same performance. (in GB)

| Memory Overhead | Ogbn-Products | Wikipedia | Live-Journal | Live-Journal-2008 | Enwiki |
|---|---|---|---|---|---|
| Auto-Divide GNN | 10.71 | 9.70 | 7.99 | 8.20 | 7.40 |
| PaGraph | 10.70 | 12.00 | 12.00 | 11.99 | 12.00 |

**Table 5.** Caching Ratio under the memory overhead of Table 4.

| Caching Ratio (%) | Ogbn-Products | Wikipedia | Live-Journal | Live-Journal-2008 | Enwiki |
|---|---|---|---|---|---|
| Auto-Divide GNN | 100.0 | 34.84 | 28.92 | 26.53 | 12.96 |
| PaGraph | 100.0 | 40.25 | 24.25 | 22.36 | 10.40 |

**Table 6.** Hitting Rate under the memory overhead of Table 4.

| Hitting Rate (%) | Ogbn-Products | Wikipedia | Live-Journal | Live-Journal-2008 | Enwiki |
|---|---|---|---|---|---|
| Auto-Divide GNN | 100.0 | 85.43 | 80.64 | 79.52 | 75.71 |
| PaGraph | 100.0 | 79.15 | 63.47 | 62.39 | 55.21 |

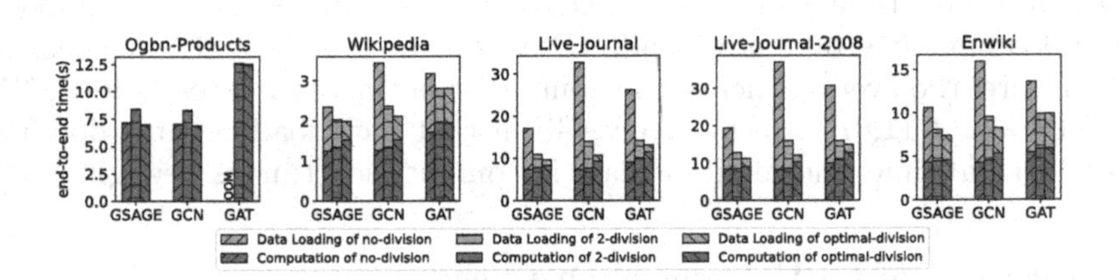


**Fig. 7.** The end-to-end time using different dividing methods.

## 4.4 Benefit of Auto-profile Method

To demonstrate the impact of subgraph division scheme selection, we evaluate three different dividing methods: no-division (using the original minibatch size), 2-division (using minibatch size/2 as the main microbatch size), and optimal-division (using the microbatch sizes calculated by Auto-Divide GNN).

The evaluation results (using GPU memory of 12 GB) in Fig. 7 show that optimal-division achieves an average speedup of 1.12× (up to 1.31×) and 1.74× (up to 3.06×) over 2-division and no-division, respectively. This result illustrates the necessity of the auto-profile method for searching the optimal subgraph division scheme.

Notably, in the following two scenarios, GAT on Wikipedia and GAT on Enwiki, the optimal subgraph division is 2-division. Therefore, optimal-division and 2-division have the same acceleration performance in these cases.

### 4.5 Ablation Experiments

We conducted an experiment to demonstrate the impact of our two acceleration components, namely subgraph division and caching strategy. We introduced a new baseline, cache_estimation, which combines PaGraph with our estimation-based caching strategy.

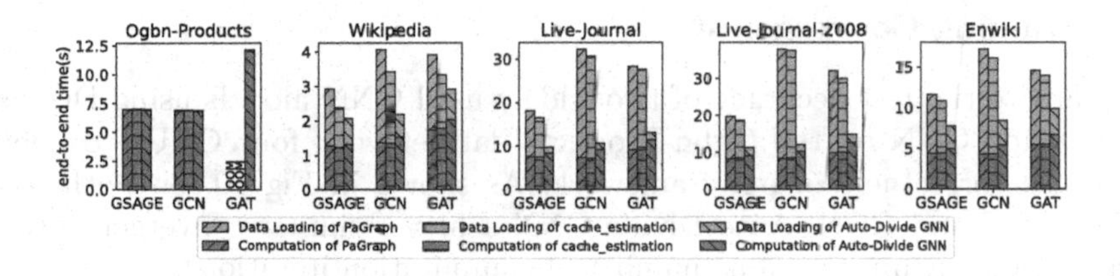


**Fig. 8.** The end-to-end time for 3 baselines including cache_estimation.

Figure 8 presents the end-to-end time of the three baselines (using GPU memory of 12 GB). Compared with PaGraph, cache_estimation achieves an average speedup of 1.14× (up to 1.44×) in data loading, indicating the superiority of our estimation-based caching strategy over PaGraph's node-degree based strategy.

While the comparison between Auto-Divide GNN and cache_estimation confirms the effectiveness of subgraph division: with a significant reduction in data loading time and a slight increase in computation time, Auto-Divide GNN achieves an average speedup of 1.72× (up to 3.10×) over cache_estimation.

### 4.6 Scalability

We conduct the scalability evaluation of our framework. Figure 9 shows the throughputs of training GraphSAGE, GCN, and GAT on two representative real-world datasets (Live-Journal and Enwiki) with different numbers of GPUs. Overall, Auto-Divide GNN outperforms PaGraph and DGL and achieves near-linear scalability. For example, throughput on 4-GPU is 3.83× of which on the one of a single GPU when training the GAT model on the Live-Journal dataset, while PaGraph can only achieve a speedup of 2.97× in the same situation.

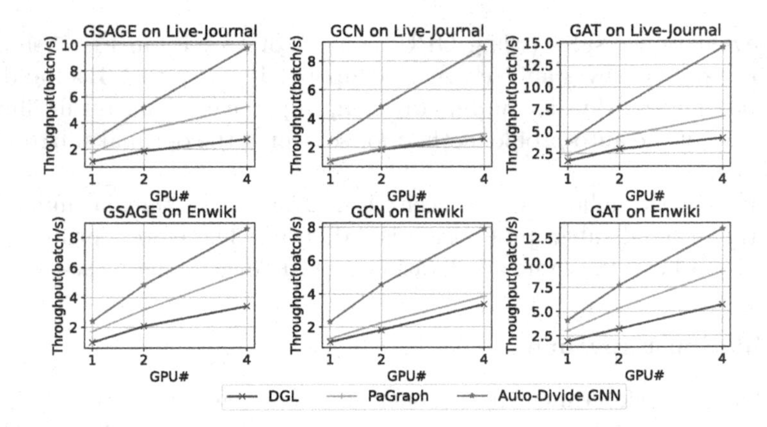


**Fig. 9.** Scalability of DGL, PaGraph, and Auto-Divide GNN in training 3 GNN models over 2 datasets.

### 4.7 Training Convergence

We evaluate the test accuracy of two widely used GNN models using DGL and Auto-Divide GNN on the Ogbn-Products dataset with four GPUs to demonstrate the correctness of our framework. As shown in Fig. 10, on both model GraphSAGE and GCN, Auto-Divide GNN achieves similar convergence to the original DGL within the same number of computation iterations.

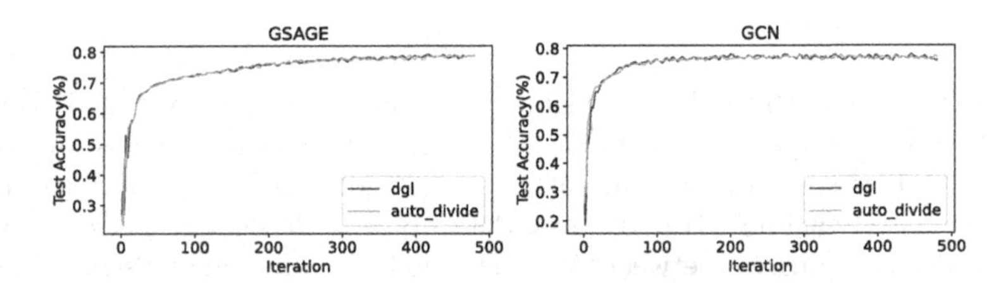


**Fig. 10.** Test accuracy of DGL and Auto-Divide GNN during 4-GPU training. (Dataset: Ogbn-Products dataset)

## 5 Related Works

**Frameworks.** We will discuss several sampling-based GNN training frameworks that also rely on GPU caching. PaGraph [11] introduces a partitioning algorithm to assign different cache contents to different GPUs in addition to GPU caching. The core idea of GNNLab [16] is a factored design for multiple GPUs, where each GPU focuses on either the sampling or training task. BGL [12] also isolates resources between different data preprocessing stages to reduce contention.

Auto-Divide GNN does not conflict with these developments and can benefit from these novel designs. In addition, the subgraph division approach and auto-profile method of Auto-Divide GNN have addressed the inefficiency challenge in GPU caching that other frameworks are powerless to tackle.

## 6 Conclusion

In this paper, we introduce Auto-Divide GNN, a novel system designed for efficient sampling-based GNN training over GPUs. Auto-Divide GNN employs subgraph division to reduce GPU memory consumption and adopts an auto-profile method to combine subgraph division with GPU caching. Our experimental results demonstrate that Auto-Divide GNN achieves up to 5.61× and 3.13× speedup and reduces average 95.05% and 82.17% data loading time compared to two state-of-the-art baselines, DGL and PaGraph, respectively.

**Acknowledgments and Data Availability.** This work was supported by the National Nature Science Foundation of China under Grant No. 62025208. The datasets and code generated during and analysed during the current study are available in the figshare repository: https://doi.org/10.6084/m9.figshare.23544639 [2].

## References

1. Backstrom, L., Huttenlocher, D., Kleinberg, J., Lan, X.: Group formation in large social networks: membership, growth, and evolution. In: Proceedings of the 12th ACM SIGKDD International Conference on Knowledge Discovery and Data Mining, pp. 44–54 (2006)
2. Chen, H., Ran, Z., Ge, K., Lai, Z., Jiang, J., Li, D.: Auto-divide GNN: accelerating GNN training with subgraph division. Presented in Euro-Par 2023 paper (2023). https://doi.org/10.6084/m9.figshare.23544639
3. Davis, T.A., Hu, Y.: The University of Florida sparse matrix collection. ACM Trans. Math. Softw. **38**(1), 1–25 (2011). https://doi.org/10.1145/2049662.2049663
4. Hamilton, W., Ying, Z., Leskovec, J.: Inductive representation learning on large graphs. In: Advances in Neural Information Processing Systems, vol. 30 (2017)
5. Hamilton, W.L., Ying, R., Leskovec, J.: Representation learning on graphs: methods and applications. IEEE Data Eng. Bull. **40**(3), 52–74 (2017). https://sites.computer.org/debull/A17sept/p52.pdf
6. Hu, W., et al.: Open graph benchmark: datasets for machine learning on graphs. In: Advances in Neural Information Processing Systems, vol. 33, pp. 22118–22133 (2020)
7. Huang, W., Zhang, T., Rong, Y., Huang, J.: Adaptive sampling towards fast graph representation learning. In: Advances in Neural Information Processing Systems, vol. 31 (2018)
8. Keskar, N.S., Mudigere, D., Nocedal, J., Smelyanskiy, M., Tang, P.T.P.: On large-batch training for deep learning: generalization gap and sharp minima. In: 5th International Conference on Learning Representations, ICLR 2017, Toulon, France, 24–26 April 2017, Conference Track Proceedings. OpenReview.net (2017). https://openreview.net/forum?id=H1oyRlYgg

9. Kipf, T.N., Welling, M.: Semi-supervised classification with graph convolutional networks. In: 5th International Conference on Learning Representations, ICLR 2017, Toulon, France, 24–26 April 2017, Conference Track Proceedings. OpenReview.net (2017). https://openreview.net/forum?id=SJU4ayYgl
10. KONECT: Wikipedia links, English network dataset - KONECT (2022). https://konect.uni-koblenz.de/networks/wikipedia_link_en
11. Lin, Z., Li, C., Miao, Y., Liu, Y., Xu, Y.: PaGraph: scaling GNN training on large graphs via computation-aware caching. In: Proceedings of the 11th ACM Symposium on Cloud Computing, pp. 401–415 (2020)
12. Liu, T., et al.: BGL: GPU-efficient GNN training by optimizing graph data I/O and preprocessing. In: The 20th USENIX Symposium on Networked Systems Design and Implementation (NSDI) (2023)
13. Veličković, P., Cucurull, G., Casanova, A., Romero, A., Liò, P., Bengio, Y.: Graph attention networks. In: International Conference on Learning Representations (2017)
14. Wang, M.Y.: Deep graph library: towards efficient and scalable deep learning on graphs. In: ICLR Workshop on Representation Learning on Graphs and Manifolds (2019)
15. Yan, S., Xiong, Y., Lin, D.: Spatial temporal graph convolutional networks for skeleton-based action recognition. In: Thirty-Second AAAI Conference on Artificial Intelligence (2018)
16. Yang, J., et al.: GNNLab: a factored system for sample-based GNN training over GPUs. In: Proceedings of the Seventeenth European Conference on Computer Systems, pp. 417–434 (2022)
17. Zhang, M., Chen, Y.: Link prediction based on graph neural networks. In: Advances in Neural Information Processing Systems, vol. 31 (2018)

# Model-Agnostic Federated Learning

Gianluca Mittone[1(✉)], Walter Riviera[2], Iacopo Colonnelli[1], Robert Birke[1], and Marco Aldinucci[1]

[1] University of Turin, Turin, Italy
{gianluca.mittone,iacopo.colonnelli,robert.birke, marco.aldinucci}@unito.it
[2] University of Verona, Verona, Italy
walter.riviera@univr.it

**Abstract.** Since its debut in 2016, Federated Learning (FL) has been tied to the inner workings of Deep Neural Networks (DNNs); this allowed its development as DNNs proliferated but neglected those scenarios in which using DNNs is not possible or advantageous. The fact that most current FL frameworks only support DNNs reinforces this problem. To address the lack of non-DNN-based FL solutions, we propose MAFL (Model-Agnostic Federated Learning). MAFL merges a model-agnostic FL algorithm, AdaBoost.F, with an open industry-grade FL framework: Intel® OpenFL. MAFL is the first FL system not tied to any machine learning model, allowing exploration of FL beyond DNNs. We test MAFL from multiple points of view, assessing its correctness, flexibility, and scaling properties up to 64 nodes of an HPC cluster. We also show how we optimised OpenFL achieving a 5.5× speedup over a standard FL scenario. MAFL is compatible with x86-64, ARM-v8, Power and RISC-V.

**Keywords:** Machine Learning · Federated Learning · Federated AdaBoost · Software Engineering

## 1 Introduction

Federated Learning (FL) is a Machine Learning (ML) technique that has gained tremendous popularity in the last years [9]: a shared ML model is trained without ever exchanging the data owned by each party or requiring it to be gathered in one common computational infrastructure. The popularity of FL caused the development of a plethora of FL frameworks, e.g., Flower [4], FedML [7], and HPE Swarm Learning [23] to cite a few. These frameworks only support one ML model type: Deep Neural Networks (DNNs). While DNNs have shown unprecedented results across a wide range of applications, from image recognition [11] to natural language processing [22], from drug discovery [24] to fraud detection [10], they are not the best model for every use case. DNNs require massive amounts of data, which collecting and eventually labelling is often prohibitive; furthermore, DNNs are not well-suited for all types of data. For example, traditional ML models can offer a better performance-to-complexity ratio on tabular data


J. Cano et al. (Eds.): Euro-Par 2023, LNCS 14100, pp. 383–396, 2023.
https://doi.org/10.1007/978-3-031-39698-4_26

than DNNs [17]. DNNs also behave as black-box, making them undesirable when the model's output has to be explained [8]. Lastly, DNNs require high computational resources, and modern security-preserving approaches, e.g. [16,21], only exacerbate this issues [14].

We propose the open-source **MAFL**[1] (*Model-Agnostic Federated Learning*) framework to alleviate these problems. MAFL leverages *Ensemble Learning* to support and aggregate ML models independently from their type. Ensemble Learning exploits the combination of multiple *weak learners* to obtain a single *strong learner*. A weak learner is a learning algorithm that only guarantees performance better than a random guessing model; in contrast, a strong learner provides a very high learning performance (at least on the training set). Since weak learners are not bound to be a specific ML model, Ensemble Learning techniques can be considered *model-agnostic*. We adopt the AdaBoost.F algorithm [18], which leverages the AdaBoost algorithm [6] and adapts it to the FL setting, and we marry it with an open-source industry-grade FL platform, i.e., Intel® OpenFL [5]. To our knowledge, MAFL is the first and only model-agnostic FL framework available to researchers and industry at publication.

The rest of the paper introduces the basic concepts behind MAFL. We provide implementation details underlying its development, highlight the challenges we overcame, and empirically assess our approach from the computational performances and learning metrics points of view. To summarise, the contributions of this paper are the following:

- we introduce MAFL, the first FL software able to work with any supervised ML model, from heavy DNNs to lightweight trees;
- we describe the architectural challenges posed by a model-agnostic FL framework in detail;
- we describe how Intel® OpenFL can be improved to boost computational performances;
- we provide an extensive empirical evaluation of MAFL to showcase its correctness, flexibility, and performance.

## 2 Related Works

*FL* [15] usually refers to a centralised structure in which two types of entities, a single *aggregator* and multiple *collaborators*, work together to solve a common ML problem. A FL framework orchestrate the federation by distributing initial models, collecting the model updates, merging them according to an aggregation strategy, and broadcasting back the updated model. FL requires a *higher-level software infrastructure* than traditional ML flows due to the necessity of exchanging model parameters quickly and securely. Model training is typically delegated to de-facto standard (deep) ML frameworks, e.g., PyTorch and TensorFlow.

Different *FL frameworks* are emerging. Riviera [19] provides a compelling list of 36 open-source tools ranked by community adoption, popularity growth, and

[1] https://github.com/alpha-unito/Model-Agnostic-FL.

feature maturity, and Beltrán [3] reviews 16 FL frameworks, identifying only six as mature. All of the surveyed frameworks support supervised training of DNNs, but only FATE [12], IBM-Federated [13], and NVIDIA FLARE [20] offer support for a few different ML models, mainly implementing federated K-means or Extreme Gradient Boosting (XGBoost): this is due to the problem of defining a model-agnostic aggregation strategy. DNNs' client updates consist of tensors (mainly weights or gradients) that can be easily serialised and mathematically combined (e.g., averaged), as are also the updates provided by federated K-means and XGBoost. This assumption does not hold in a model-agnostic scenario, where the serialisation infrastructure and the aggregation mechanism have to be powerful enough to accommodate different update types. A truly model-agnostic aggregation strategy should be able to aggregate not only tensors, but also complex objects like entire ML model. AdaBoost.F is capable of doing that. Section 3 delves deeper into the state-of-the-art of federated ensemble algorithms.

As a base for developing MAFL, we chose a mature, open-source framework supporting only DNNs: Intel® OpenFL [5]. The reason for this choice is twofold: (i) its structure and community support; and (ii) the possibility of leveraging the existing ecosystem by maintaining the same use and feel. Section 4 delves into the differences between plain OpenFL and its MAFL extension, showing how much DNN-centric a representative modern FL framework can be.

## 3 Model-Agnostic Federated Algorithms

None of the frameworks mentioned in Sect. 2 supports model-agnostic FL algorithms, i.e., they cannot handle different ML models seamlessly. The reason is twofold. On the one hand, modern FL frameworks still try to achieve sufficient technical maturity, rather than adding new functionalities. On the other hand, model-agnostic federated algorithms are still new and little investigated.

Recently, [18] proposed three federated versions of AdaBoost: *DistBoost.F*, *PreWeak.F*, and *AdaBoost.F*. All three algorithms are model-agnostic due to their inherent roots in AdaBoost. Following the terminology commonly used in ensemble learning literature, we call *weak hypothesis* a model learned at each federated round and *strong hypothesis* the final global model produced by the algorithms. The general steps of an AdaBoost-based FL algorithm are the following:

1. The aggregator receives the dataset size $N$ from each collaborator and sends them an initial version of the weak hypothesis.
2. The aggregator receives the weak hypothesis $h_i$ from each collaborator and broadcasts the entire hypothesis space to every collaborator.
3. The errors $\epsilon$ committed by the global weak hypothesis on the local data are calculated by each client and sent to the aggregator.
4. The aggregator exploits the error information to select the best weak hypothesis $c$, adds it to the global strong hypothesis and sends the calculated AdaBoost coefficient $\alpha$ to the collaborators.

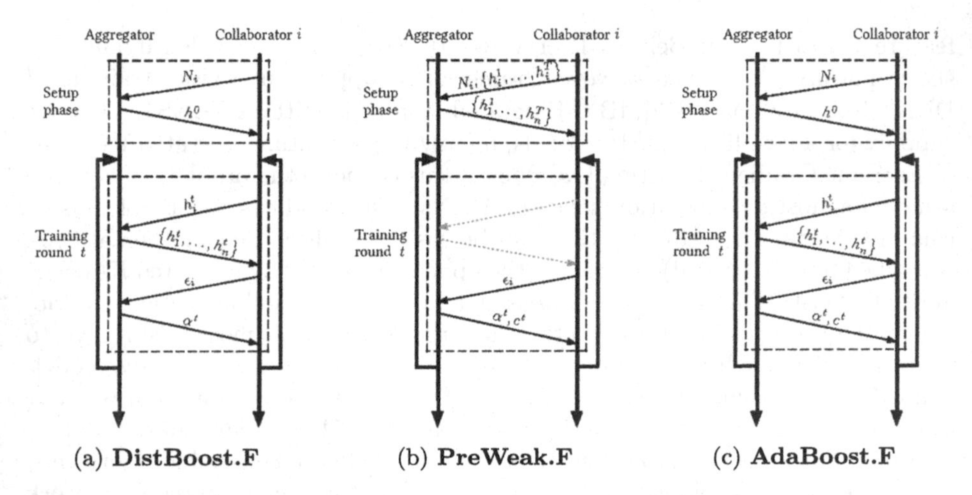


(a) **DistBoost.F** (b) **PreWeak.F** (c) **AdaBoost.F**

**Fig. 1. The three protocols implied by DistBoost.F, PreWeak.F, and AdaBoost.F**. $N$ is the dataset size, $T$ is the number of training rounds, $h$ the weak hypothesis, $\epsilon$ the classification error, $\alpha$ the AdaBoost coefficient. The subscript $i \in [1, n]$ indices the collaborators and the superscript $t$ the training rounds (with 0 standing for an untrained weak hypothesis). $c \in [1, n]$ is the index of the best weak hypothesis in the hypothesis space. The red dotted line in PreWeak.F indicates the absence of communication.

Note that $N$ is needed to adequately weight the errors committed by the global weak hypothesis on the local data, thus allowing to compute $\alpha$ correctly.

Figure 1 depicts the protocol specialisations for the three algorithms described in [18]. They are similar once abstracted from their low-level details. While step 1 is inherently a setup step, steps 2–4 are repeated cyclically by DistBoost.F and AdaBoost.F. PreWeak.F instead fuses steps 1 and 2 at setup time, receiving from each collaborator $T$ instances of already trained weak hypotheses (one for each training round) and broadcasting $n \times T$ models to the federation. Then, each federated round $t$ loops only on steps 3 and 4 due to the different *hypothesis space* the algorithms explore. While DistBoost.F and AdaBoost.F create a weak hypothesis during each federated round, PreWeak.F creates the whole hypothesis space during step 2 and then searches for the best solution in it.

All three algorithms produce the same strong hypothesis and AdaBoost model, but they differ in the selection of the best weak hypothesis at each round:

- DistBoost.F uses a committee of weak hypotheses;
- PreWeak.F uses the weak hypotheses from a fully trained AdaBoost model;
- AdaBoost.F uses the best weak hypothesis trained in the current round.

The generic model-agnostic federated protocol is more complex than the standard FL one. It requires one more communication for each round and the exchange of complex objects across the network (the weak hypotheses), impacting

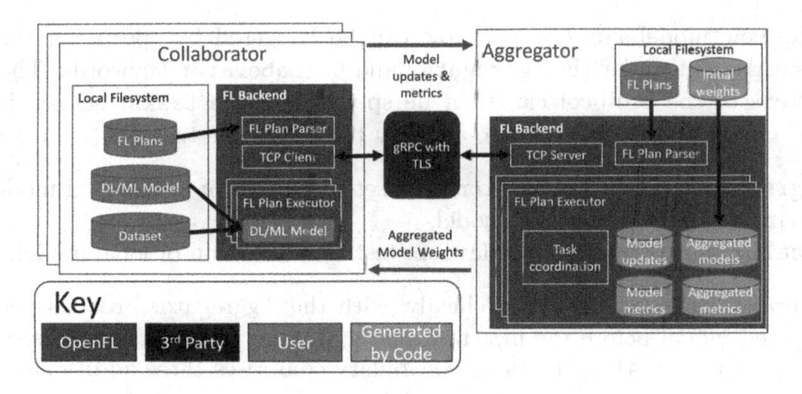


**Fig. 2.** OpenFL architecture from [5]. The proposed extension targets only the inner components (coloured in blue). (Color figure online)

performance. Note that each arrow going from collaborator $i$ to the aggregator in Fig. 1 implies a synchronisation barrier among all the collaborators in the federation. Increasing the number of global synchronisation points reduces concurrency and increases the sensitivity to stragglers. It is worth noting that once an FL framework can handle the common protocol structure, implementing any of the three algorithms requires the same effort. For this study, we implemented AdaBoost.F for two main reasons. First, its protocol covers the whole set of messages (like DistBoost.F), making it computationally more interesting to analyse than PreWeak.F. Besides, AdaBoost.F achieves the best learning results out of the three, also when data is heavily non-IID across the collaborators.

# 4 MAFL Architecture

Redesigning OpenFL comprises two main goals: allowing more flexible protocol management and making the whole infrastructure model agnostic. During this process, we aimed to make the changes the least invasive and respect the original design principles whenever possible (see Fig. 2).

## 4.1 The Plan Generalization

The *Plan* guides the software components' run time. It is a YAML file containing all the directives handling the FL learning task, such as which software components to use, where to save the produced models, how many rounds to train, which tasks compose a federated round, and so on. The original OpenFL Plan is rather primitive in its functions. It is not entirely customisable by the user, and many of its fields are overwritten at run time with the default values. Due to its unused power, the parsing of the plan file has been extended and empowered, making it capable of handling new types of tasks, along with a higher range of arguments (and also making it evaluate *every* parameter in the file).

The new model-agnostic workflow can be triggered by specifying the `nn: False` argument under the `Aggregator` and `Collaborator` keywords. The specific steps of the protocol can then be specified in the `tasks` section. In the Intel® OpenFL framework, there are only three possible tasks:

- `aggregated_model_validation`: test set validation of aggregated model;
- `train`: local training of the model;
- `locally_tuned_model_validation`: test set validation of local model.

The three tasks are executed cyclically, with the Aggregator broadcasting the aggregated model before the first task and gathering the local models after the training step. In MAFL, the tasks vocabulary comprises three additional tasks:

- `weak_learners_validate`: test set validation of the weak learners;
- `adaboost_update`: update of the global parameters of AdaBoost.F on the Collaborators and the ensemble model on the Aggregator;
- `adaboost_validate`: local test set validation of the aggregated AdaBoost.F model.

The `weak_learners_validate` task is similar to `aggregated_model_validation`. However, it returns additional information for AdaBoost.F, such as which samples are correctly predicted/mispredicted and the norm of the samples' weights.

The extended set of tasks allows users to use new FL algorithms, such as AdaBoost.F. Additionally, if the `adaboost_update` task is omitted, it is possible to obtain a simple *Federated Bagging* behaviour. Switching behaviour requires small actions other than changing the Plan; however, both functionalities are documented with tutorials in the code repository.

### 4.2 Expanded Communication Protocol

New messages have been implemented into the original *communication protocol*, allowing the exchange of values other than ML models and performance metrics since AdaBoost.F relies on exchanging locally calculated parameters. Furthermore, Intel® OpenFL only implements two synchronisation points in its original workflow: one at the end of the federation round and one when the Collaborator asks the Aggregator for the aggregated model. These synchronisation points are hard-coded into the software and cannot be generalised for other uses.

For the AdaBoost.F workflow, a more general synchronisation point is needed: not two consecutive steps can be executed before each Collaborator has concluded the previous one. Thus a new `synch` message has been added to the *gRPC* protocol. The working mechanism of this synchronisation point is straightforward: the collaborators ask for a `synch` at the end of each task, and if not all collaborators have finished the current task, it is put to sleep; otherwise, it is allowed to continue to the next task. This solution, even if not the most efficient, respects the Intel® OpenFL internal synchronisation mechanisms and thus does not require any different structure or new dependency.

### 4.3 Core Classes Extension

The following core classes of the framework have been modified to allow the standard and model-agnostic workflows to coexist (see Fig. 2 for an overview).

The `Collaborator` class can now offer different behaviours according to the ML model used in the computation. Suppose the Plan specifies that the training will not involve DNNs. In that case, the Collaborator will actively keep track of the parameters necessary to the AdaBoost.F algorithm, like the mispredicted examples, the weight associated with each data sample, and the weighted error committed by the models. Additionally, the handling of the internal database used for storage will change behaviour, changing tags and names associated with the entries to make possible finer requests to it.

The `Aggregator` can now generate any ML models (instead of only DNNs weights), handle aggregation functions instantiated dynamically from the plan file, and handle the synchronisation needed at the end of each step. New methods allow the Aggregator to query the internal database more finely, thus allowing it to read and write ML models with the same tags and name as the Collaborator.

`TensorDB`, the internal class used for storage, has been modified to accommodate the new behaviours described above. This class implements a simple *Pandas* data frame responsible for all model storage and retrieving done by the Aggregator and Collaborators. Furthermore, its `clean_up` method has been revised, making it possible to maintain a fixed amount of data in memory. This fix has an important effect on the computational performance since the query time to this object is directly proportional to the amount of data it contains.

Finally, the more high-level and interactive classes, namely `Director` and `Envoy`, and the serialization library have been updated to work correctly with the new underlying code base. These software components are supposed to be long-lived: they should constantly be running on the server and clients' hosts. When a new experiment starts, they will instantiate the necessary `Aggregator` and `Collaborators` objects with the parameters for the specified workflow.

This effort results in a model-agnostic FL framework that supports the standard DNNs-based FL workflow and the new AdaBoost.F algorithm. Using the software in one mode or another does not require any additional programming effort from the user: a few simple configuration instructions are enough. Additionally, the installation procedure has been updated to incorporate all new module dependencies of the software. Finally, a complete set of tutorials has been added to the repository: this way, it should be easy for any developer to get started with this experimental software.

## 5 Evaluation

The complete set of tutorials replicating the experiments from [18] are used to assess MAFL's correctness and efficiency. We run them on a cloud and HPC infrastructure, both x86-64 based, and Monte Cimone, the first RISC-V based HPC system; however, MAFL runs also on ARM-v8 and Power systems.

### 5.1 Performance Optimizations

Using weak learners instead of DNNs drastically reduces the computational load. As an example, [1] reports 18.5 vs 419.3 s to train a 10-leaves decision tree or a DNN model, respectively, on the PRAISE training set (with comparable prediction performance). Moreover, AdaBoost.F requires one additional communication phase per round. This exacerbates the impact of time spent in communication and synchronisation on the overall system performance. To reduce this impact, we propose and evaluate different optimisations to reduce this overhead. Applying all proposed optimisations, we achieve a 5.5× speedup on a representative FL task (see Fig. 3). As a baseline workload, we train a 10-leaves decision tree on the Adult dataset over 100 rounds using 9 nodes (1 aggregator plus 8 collaborators). We use physical machines to obtain stable and reliable computing times, as execution times on bare-metal nodes are more deterministic than cloud infrastructures. Each HPC node is equipped with two 18-core Intel® Xeon E5-2697 v4 @2.30 GHz and 126 GB of RAM. A 100 Gb/s Intel® Omni-Path network interface (in IPoFabric mode) is used as interconnection network. Reported times are average of five runs ± the 95% CI.

We start by measuring the execution time given by the baseline: 484.13 ± 15.80 s. The first optimisation is to adapt the buffer sizes used by gRPC to accommodate larger models and avoid resizing operations. Increasing the buffer from 2 MB to 32 MB using decision trees reduced the execution time to 477.0 ± 17.5 s, an improvement of ∼ 1.5%. While this seems small, the larger the models, the bigger the impact of this optimisation. The second optimisation is the choice of the serialisation framework: by using `Cloudpickle`, we reduce the execution time to 471.4 ± 6.1 s, an improvement of ∼2.6%. Next, we examine `TensorDB`, which grows linearly in the number of federated rounds, thus slowing down access time linearly. We modified the `TensorDB` to store only the essential information of the last two federation rounds: this results in a stable memory occupation and access time. With this change, the execution time drops to 414.8 ± 0.9 s, an improvement of ∼14.4% over the baseline.

Lastly, two `sleep` are present in the MAFL code: one for the end-round synchronisation and another for the `synch` general synchronisation point, fixed respectively at 10 and 1 s. Both have been lowered to 0.01 s since we assessed empirically that this is the lowest waiting time still improving the global execution time. This choice has also been made possible due to the computational infrastructures exploited in this work; it may not be suitable for wide-scale implementations in which servers and clients are geographically distant or compute and energy-constrained. With this sleep calibration, we obtained a global execution time of 250.8 ± 9.6 s, a ∼48.2% less than the baseline. Overall, with all the optimisations applied together, we can achieve a final mean execution time of 88.6± s, i.e. a 5.46× speedup over the baseline.

### 5.2 Correctness

We replicate the experiments from [18] and compare the ML results. These experiments involve ten different datasets: `adult`, `forestcover`, `kr-vs-kp`,

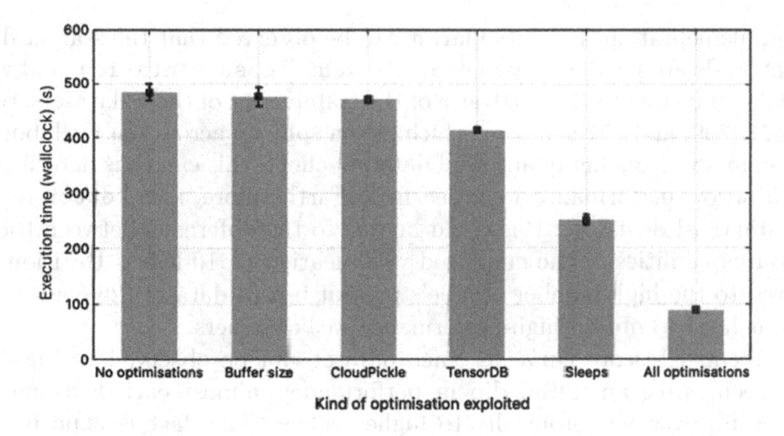


**Fig. 3.** Ablation study of the proposed software optimisations; the 95% CI has been obtained over five executions.

**Table 1.** Mean F1 scores ± standard deviation over 5 runs.

| Dataset | Classes | Reference | MAFL |
|---|---|---|---|
| Adult | 2 | 85.58 ± 0.06 | 85.60 ± 0.05 |
| ForestCover | 2 | 83.67 ± 0.21 | 83.94 ± 0.14 |
| Kr-vs-kp | 2 | 99.38 ± 0.29 | 99.50 ± 0.21 |
| Splice | 3 | 95.61 ± 0.62 | 96.97 ± 0.65 |
| Vehicle | 4 | 72.94 ± 3.40 | 80.04 ± 3.30 |
| Segmentation | 7 | 86.07 ± 2.86 | 85.58 ± 0.06 |
| Sat | 8 | 83.52 ± 0.58 | 84.89 ± 0.57 |
| Pendigits | 10 | 93.21 ± 0.80 | 92.06 ± 0.44 |
| Vowel | 11 | 79.80 ± 1.47 | 79.34 ± 3.31 |
| Letter | 26 | 68.32 ± 1.63 | 71.13 ± 2.02 |

`splice`, `vehicle`, `segmentation`, `sat`, `pendigits`, `vowel`, and `letter`. These are standard ML datasets targeting classification tasks, both binary (`adult`, `forestcover`, `kr-vs-kp`) and multi-class (all the others), with a varying number of features (from the 14 of `adult` up to the 61 of `splice`), and a different number of samples (from the 846 of `vehicle` up to the 495.141 of `forestcover`). Each training set has been split in an IID way across all the Collaborators, while the testing has been done on the entire test set. A simple Decision Tree from SciKit-Learn with ten leaves is used as a weak learner; instead, the AdaBoost class has been created manually. We set the number of federated rounds to 300 and use 10 nodes: 1 aggregator plus 9 collaborators. We note that these optimizations can also benefit the original OpenFL.

Table 1 reports each dataset's reference and calculated F1 scores (mean value ± the standard deviation over five runs). The values reported are fully compatible with the results reported in the original study, thus assessing the correctness of the implementation. In particular, it can be observed that the standard deviation intervals are particularly high for the vehicle, segmentation, and vowel. This fact can be due to the small size of the training set of these datasets, respectively 677, 209, and 792 samples, which, when split up across ten Collaborators, results in an even smaller quantity of data per client: this can thus determine the creation of low-performance weak learners. Furthermore, also letter reported a high standard deviation: this could be due to the difference between the classification capabilities of the employed weak learner (a 10-leaves Decision Tree) compared to the high number of labels present in this dataset (26 classes), thus making it hard to obtain high-performance weak learners.

The mean F1 score curve for each dataset can be observed in Fig. 4a. As can be seen, after an initial dip in performance, almost each learning curve continues to grow monotonically to higher values. This fact is expected since the AdaBoost.F is supposed to improve its classification performance with more weak learners. It has to be observed that, at each federated round, a new weak learner will be added to the aggregated model: the AdaBoost.F grows linearly in size with the number of federated rounds. This characteristic of the algorithm has many consequences, like the increasingly longer time needed for inference and for moving the aggregated model over the network. From Fig. 4a, we can observe that, in the vast majority of cases, a few tens of federated rounds are more than enough to obtain a decent level of F1 scores; this is interesting since it is possible to obtain a small and efficient AdaBoost.F model in little training effort. Instead, for the more complex datasets like letter and vowel, we can observe that it is possible to obtain better performance with longer training efforts. This means that is possible to use AdaBoost.F to produce bigger and heavier models at need, according to the desired performance and inference complexity.

### 5.3 Flexibility

To demonstrate the model-agnostic property of MAFL, we choose the vowel dataset and train different ML model types on it. In particular, one representative ML model has been chosen from each multi-label classifier family available on SciKit-Learn: Extremely Randomized Tree (Trees), Ridge Linear Regression (Linear models), Multi-Layer Perceptron (Neural Networks), K-Nearest Neighbors (Neighbors), Gaussian Naive Bayes (Naive Bayes), and simple 10-leaves Decision Trees as baselines. Figure 4b summarises the F1 curves for the different ML models used as weak learners. Each model has been used out-of-the-box, without hyper-parameter tuning using the default parameters set by SciKit-Learn v1.1.2. All ML models work straightforwardly in the proposed software without needing to code anything manually: it is sufficient to replace the class name in the experiment file. This proves the ease with which data scientists can leverage MAFL to experiment with different model types.

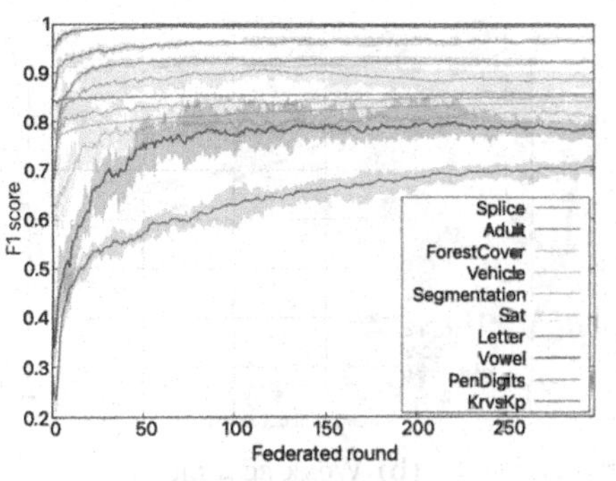


(a) Aggregated AdaBoost.F model F1 score on each test set.

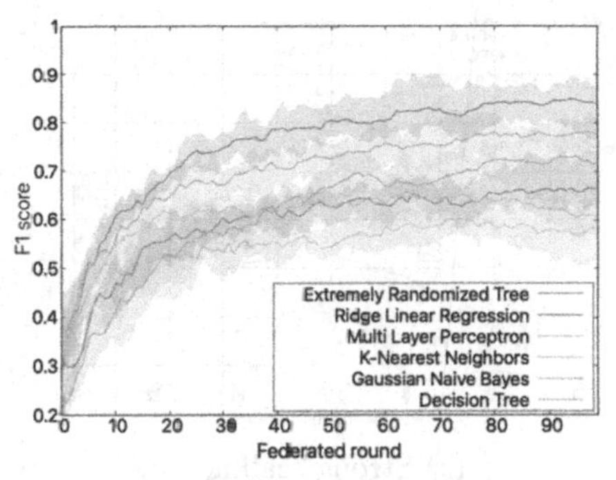


(b) Example of the effect of using different ML models as weak learners.

**Fig. 4.** ML properties of MAFL

### 5.4 Scalability Analysis

We perform this scalability study using the HPC nodes from Sect. 5.1 and Monte Cimone [2], the first available HPC-class cluster based on RISC-V processors. It comprises eight computing nodes equipped with a U740 SoC from SiFive integrating four U74 RV64GCB cores @ 1.2 GHz, 16 GB RAM and a 1 Gb/s interconnection network.

We select the `forestcover` dataset for running these experiments, being the largest dataset used in this study, split into a 485K training samples and 10K testing samples. The weak learner is the same 10-leaves SciKit-Learn Decision Tree from Sect. 5.2. We lowered the number of federated training rounds to 100 since they are enough to provide an acceptable and stable result (10 on the RISC-V system due to the longer computational times required). Different federations have been tested, varying numbers of Collaborators from 2 to 64 by powers of 2. We went no further since OpenFL is designed to suit a cross-silo FL scenario, which means a few tens of clients. We investigated two different scenarios: *strong scaling*, where we increase the collaborators while keeping the same problem size by spitting the dataset samples in uniform chunks across collaborators; and *weak scaling*, where we scale the problem size with the number collaborators by assigning each collaborator the entire dataset. In both cases, the baseline reference time is the time taken by a federation comprising the aggregator and a single collaborator. We report the mean over 5 runs for each experiment.

Figure 5 shows the strong and weak scaling properties of MAFL. The RISC-V plot stops at 7 because we have just 8 nodes in the cluster, and we want to avoid sharing a node between the aggregator and collaborator to maintain the same experiment system setting. In the strong scaling scenario, the software does not scale efficiently beyond 8 HPC nodes, as the execution becomes increasingly communication-bound. The same also affects the weak scaling. Nevertheless, the degradation is sublinear (each point on the x/axis doubles the number of nodes). This is important because the main benefit in the FL scenario is the additional

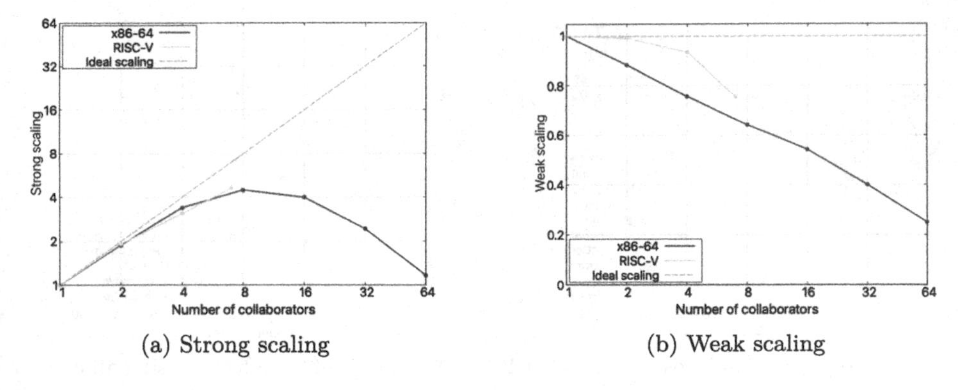


(a) Strong scaling

(b) Weak scaling

**Fig. 5.** Strong and weak scaling properties of MAFL.

training data brought in by each contributor node. The RISC-V cluster exhibits better strong scalability when comparing the two clusters. This is justified by the slower compute speed of the RISC-V cores leading to higher training times, making the execution more compute-bound, especially for a low number of nodes. The weak scalability on the RISC-V cluster suffers from the lower network speed. Since real-world cross-silo federations rarely count more than a dozen participants, it can be assessed that MAFL is suitable for experimenting with such real-world scenarios.

## 6 Discussion

The implementation experience of MAFL and the subsequent experimentation made it evident that current FL frameworks are not designed to be as flexible as the current research environment needs them to be. The fact that the standard workflow of OpenFL was not customisable in any possible way without modifying the code and that the serialisation structure is DNN-specific led the authors to the idea that a new, workflow-based FL framework is needed. Such a framework should not implement a fixed workflow but allow the user to express any number of workflow steps, entities, the relations between them, and the objects that must be exchanged. This property implies the generalisation of the serialisation infrastructure, which cannot be limited to tensors only. Such an approach would lead to a much more straightforward implementation of newer and experimental approaches to FL, both from the architectural and ML perspective.

Furthermore, the use of asynchronous communication can help better manage the concurrent architecture of the federation. These systems are usually slowed down by stragglers that, since the whole system is supposed to wait for them, will slow down the entire computation. In our experience implementing MAFL, a significant part of the scalability issues is determined by the waiting time between the different collaborators taking part in the training. While such an approach would improve the scalability performance of any FL framework, it also underlies the investigation of how to simultaneously handle newer and older updates. This capability would improve the computational performance of gradient and non-gradient-based systems: the relative aggregation algorithms must be revised to accommodate this new logic. This matter is not trivial and deserves research interest. Lastly, due to the possibility of exploiting less computationally requiring models, MAFL can easily be used to implement FL on low-power devices, such as systems based on the new RISC-V.

## 7 Conclusions

A model-agnostic modified version of Intel® OpenFL implementing the AdaBoost.F federated boosting algorithm, named MAFL, has been proposed. The proposed software has been proven to implement the AdaBoost.F algorithm correctly and can scale sufficiently to experiment efficiently with small cross-silo federations. MAFL is open-source, freely available online, easily installable, and has a complete set of already implemented examples. To our knowledge, MAFL is the first FL framework to implement a model-agnostic, non-gradient-based algorithm. This effort will allow researchers to experiment with this new conception of FL more freely, pushing the concept of model-agnostic FL even further. Furthermore, this work aims to contribute directly to the RISC-V community, enabling FL research on this innovative platform.

**Acknowledgments.** This work has been supported by the Spoke "FutureHPC & BigData" of the ICSC - Centro Nazionale di Ricerca in "High Performance Computing, Big Data and Quantum Computing", funded by European Union - NextGenerationEU and the EuPilot project funded by EuroHPC JU under G.A. n. 101034126.

## References

1. Arfat, Y., Mittone, G., Colonnelli, I., D'Ascenzo, F., Esposito, R., Aldinucci, M.: Pooling critical datasets with federated learning. In: IEEE PDP (2023)
2. Bartolini, A., Ficarelli, F., Parisi, E., Beneventi, F., Barchi, F., Gregori, D., et al.: Monte cimone: paving the road for the first generation of risc-v high-performance computers. In: IEEE SOCC, pp. 1–6 (2022)
3. Beltrán, E.T.M., Pérez, M.Q., Sánchez, P.M.S., Bernal, S.L., Bovet, G., Pérez, M.G., et al.: Decentralized federated learning: fundamentals, state-of-the-art, frameworks, trends, and challenges. arXiv preprint arXiv:2211.08413 (2022)
4. Beutel, D.J., Topal, T., Mathur, A., Qiu, X., Parcollet, T., de Gusmão, P.P., et al.: Flower: a friendly federated learning research framework. arXiv preprint arXiv:2007.14390 (2020)
5. Foley, P., Sheller, M.J., Edwards, B., Pati, S., Riviera, W., Sharma, M., et al.: OpenFL: the open federated learning library. Phys. Med. Biol. **67**(21), 214001 (2022)
6. Freund, Y., Schapire, R.E.: A decision-theoretic generalization of on-line learning and an application to boosting. J. Comput. Syst. Sci. **55**(1), 119–139 (1997)
7. He, C., Li, S., So, J., Zhang, M., Wang, H., Wang, X., et al.: FedML: a research library and benchmark for federated machine learning. arXiv preprint arXiv:2007.13518 (2020)

8. Holzinger, A., Langs, G., Denk, H., Zatloukal, K., Müller, H.: Causability and explainability of artificial intelligence in medicine. Wiley Interdisc. Rev. Data Min. Knowl. Discov. **9**(4), 1312 (2019)
9. Kairouz, P., et al.: Advances and open problems in federated learning. Found. Trends Mach. Learn. **14**(1–2), 1–210 (2021)
10. Kleanthous, C., Chatzis, S.: Gated mixture variational autoencoders for value added tax audit case selection. Knowl. Based Syst. **188**, 105048 (2020)
11. Krizhevsky, A., Sutskever, I., Hinton, G.E.: Imagenet classification with deep convolutional neural networks. Commun. ACM **60**(6), 84–90 (2017)
12. Liu, Y., Fan, T., Chen, T., Xu, Q., Yang, Q.: Fate: an industrial grade platform for collaborative learning with data protection. J. Mach. Learn. Res. **22**(1), 10320–10325 (2021)
13. Ludwig, H., Baracaldo, N., Thomas, G., Zhou, Y., Anwar, A., Rajamoni, S., et al.: IBM federated learning: an enterprise framework white paper v0. 1. arXiv preprint arXiv:2007.10987 (2020)
14. Lyu, L., Yu, H., Ma, X., Chen, C., Sun, L., Zhao, J., et al.: Privacy and robustness in federated learning: attacks and defenses. IEEE Trans. Neural. Netw. Learn. Syst. 1–21 (2022)
15. McMahan, B., Moore, E., Ramage, D., Hampson, S., Agüera y Arcas, B.: Communication-efficient learning of deep networks from decentralized data. In: Proceedings of the 20th International Conference on Artificial Intelligence and Statistics AISTATS, vol. 54, pp. 1273–1282. PMLR, Fort Lauderdale, FL, USA (2017)
16. Meese, C., Chen, H., Asif, S.A., Li, W., Shen, C.C., Nejad, M.: BFRT: blockchained federated learning for real-time traffic flow prediction. In: IEEE CCGrid, pp. 317–326 (2022)
17. O'Mahony, N., et al.: Deep learning vs. traditional computer vision. In: Arai, K., Kapoor, S. (eds.) CVC 2019. AISC, vol. 943, pp. 128–144. Springer, Cham (2020). https://doi.org/10.1007/978-3-030-17795-9_10
18. Polato, M., Esposito, R., Aldinucci, M.: Boosting the federation: cross-silo federated learning without gradient descent. In: IEEE IJCNN), pp. 1–10 (2022)
19. Riviera, W., Menegaz, G., Boscolo Galazzo, I.: FeLebrities: a user-centric assessment of federated learning frameworks. TechRxiv (2022)
20. Roth, H.R., Cheng, Y., Wen, Y., Yang, I., Xu, Z., Hsieh, Y.T., et al.: Nvidia flare: federated learning from simulation to real-world. arXiv preprint arXiv:2210.13291 (2022)
21. Sotthiwat, E., Zhen, L., Li, Z., Zhang, C.: Partially encrypted multi-party computation for federated learning. In: IEEE CCGrid, pp. 828–835 (2021)
22. Sutskever, I., Vinyals, O., Le, Q.V.: Sequence to sequence learning with neural networks. In: NeurIPS, pp. 3104–3112 (2014)
23. Warnat-Herresthal, S., Schultze, H., Shastry, K.L., Manamohan, S., Mukherjee, S., Garg, V., et al.: Swarm learning for decentralized and confidential clinical machine learning. Nature **594**(7862), 265–270 (2021)
24. Zhavoronkov, A., Ivanenkov, Y.A., Aliper, A., Veselov, M.S., Aladinskiy, V.A., Aladinskaya, A.V., et al.: Deep learning enables rapid identification of potent DDR1 kinase inhibitors. Nat. Biotechnol. **37**(9), 1038–1040 (2019)

# Scalable Random Forest with Data-Parallel Computing

Fernando Vázquez-Novoa([✉]), Javier Conejero, Cristian Tatu, and Rosa M. Badia

Barcelona Supercomputing Center (BSC-CNS), Barcelona, Spain
{fernando.vazquez,javier.conejero,cristian.tatu,rosa.m.badia}@bsc.es

**Abstract.** In the last years, there has been a significant increment in the quantity of data available and computational resources. This leads scientific and industry communities to pursue more accurate and efficient Machine Learning (ML) models. Random Forest is a well-known algorithm in the ML field due to the good results obtained in a wide range of problems. Our objective is to create a parallel version of the algorithm that can generate a model using data distributed across different processors that computationally scales on available resources. This paper presents two novel proposals for this algorithm with a data-parallel approach. The first version is implemented using the PyCOMPSs framework and its failure management mechanism, while the second variant uses the new PyCOMPSs nesting paradigm where the parallel tasks can generate other tasks within them. Both approaches are compared between them and against MLlib Apache Spark Random Forest with strong and weak scaling tests. Our findings indicate that while the MLlib implementation is faster when executed in a small number of nodes, the scalability of both new variants is superior. We conclude that the proposed data-parallel approaches to the Random Forest algorithm can effectively generate accurate and efficient models in a distributed computing environment and offer improved scalability over existing methods.

**Keywords:** Random Forest · PyCOMPSs · COMPSs · Parallelism · Distributed Computing · Dislib · Machine Learning · HPC

## 1 Introduction

Machine Learning (ML) has gained importance recently and is becoming a widespread tool. It allows the computer to analyze data, extract meaningful information, make valuable predictions, or help the user make critical decisions.

Due to the large amount of data generated in the last years, it is becoming very relevant and valuable. The improvement in computational capacity has led ML to create very accurate models in less time.

Despite the improvements achieved during the previous years on the techniques analysed, there is still a lot of work to be done. The amount of data is growing much faster than the computational and storage systems' capacity.


J. Cano et al. (Eds.): Euro-Par 2023, LNCS 14100, pp. 397–410, 2023.
https://doi.org/10.1007/978-3-031-39698-4_27

From this uneven growth arises the need for parallel computing. This technique aims to use multiple processors (or other resources) simultaneously, distributing the computation among them and reducing the time required. It can also be used to solve large data problems when the data does not fit into the memory of a single computing node by distributing data between several devices, and each one processes the part of the data it has received.

The *distributed computing library* (dislib) [6] was born to solve the previously explained problems. This library built on top of PyCOMPSs [16] focuses on implementing parallel and distributed ML algorithms, giving the user a completely agnostic interface and facilitating its use on distributed computing environments like clusters or supercomputers.

Random Forest is a very widespread ML algorithm that reaches very good results in many problems. This article is about its parallelization using the PyCOMPSs framework in order to include it on dislib, the challenges that arisen and the results obtained. The main contributions of the paper are:

- A new parallel version of Random Forest algorithm.
- An implementation of Random Forest with PyCOMPSs using its failure management mechanism.
- An implementation of Random Forest with PyCOMPSs using nested tasks.

The rest of the article is structured as follows: Sect. 2 presents an overview of the current state of the art of the Random Forest algorithm. The sequential algorithm is presented in Sect. 3. Next, Sect. 4 describes the parallelization performed, based on the parallel framework PyCOMPSs and the dislib (Subsect. 4.1), the parallelization of the algorithm (Subsect. 4.2) and adaptation to the nesting paradigm (Subsect. 4.3). Section 5 provides performance evaluation and the behaviour analysis. Finally, Sect. 6 summarizes the conclusions and future work.

## 2 Related Work

Random Forest [8] is a well known algorithm and it has been implemented in popular ML libraries like scikit-learn [12] or Apache Spark MLlib [11]. Scikit-learn offers a very efficient sequential implementation and also a parallel version. The parallel versions of scikit-learn are limited to its execution on a single computing node, except when using Joblib to control the parallelism. Joblib supports the use of Dask [14] as backend, which allows the use of multiple nodes.

The approach used on MLlib to parallelize the random forest algorithm is based on a data-parallel optimization. The construction of the decision trees on this algorithm relies on the use of histograms [3] for discretizing the continuous variables. This reduces the costs in computation and communication between processes, but it also reduces the accuracy reached by the model. Our implementation maintains the same predictive performance as the original algorithm, which has already shown very good results, without using histograms for discretizing continuous data.

In [1], a simple parallelization approach for random forest building each tree in parallel is presented, but its scalability is limited by the number of trees and not the data. Our work improves scalability using distributed arrays, where the number of tasks depend on the number of blocks and their duration depends on the block size, without relying on arbitrary parameters.

In [5], a random forest algorithm is parallelized with Apache Spark [18], performing feature selection and using vertical data partitioning to allocate subsets to different workers. Two types of tasks are presented: gain-ratio computing tasks and node-splitting tasks. While promising for classification, this approach is not evaluated for regression. In this paper, we aim to develop a general parallel random forest algorithm that works for both classification and regression problems.

## 3 Random Forest Algorithm

The random forest algorithm is an ensemble method that contains multiple decision tree models. To train each tree, a new subspace of the dataset is generated via bootstrap sampling.

There are different approaches for this algorithm, all of them based on creating a model which consists on a set of simple rules inferred from the training data. The nodes of the decision trees can be one of these three different types:

- **Root node:** Represents the entire dataset and is split into at least two subsets assigned to two child sub-nodes.
- **Decision node:** Node that splits into another two sub-nodes.
- **Leaf or Terminal node:** Does not split further and is used to assign predicted classes or values to the samples.

As each decision tree is trained, a set of random attributes is selected for each node splitting. Among these attributes, the most suitable one and its corresponding value (according to a specified criteria) are used to perform the split.

To make predictions with the decision tree, a sample is assigned to the root node and follows the corresponding path down the tree based on its attributes and their values. Once the sample reaches a leaf node, the value of that node is used as the prediction value for the sample.

The prediction in the random forest is done by gathering the predictions from all of the trees and making a voting for classification or an average between the predictions for regression problems.

Using different subspaces for each tree and randomly selecting the features evaluated for each split prevents the random forest from overfitting.

There are several decision tree algorithms that vary the splitting process of the nodes. The most popular ones are ID3 [13], C4.5 [15] which is an improved version of the previous approach and CART [4]. Of the algorithms mentioned, only CART is capable of constructing both classification and regression trees.

The algorithm selected for this work is CART. It selects the best attribute and value for each splitting using the Gini impurity (Eq. 1) for classification trees. When building a regression tree this algorithm uses the Sum of Squares Error (Eq. 2) to select the best attribute and value for the splitting.

$$GiniImpurity = 1 - \sum_{i=1}^{classes} (p_i)^2 \tag{1}$$

$$SSE = \sum_{i=1}^{n} (Y_i - \hat{Y_i})^2 \tag{2}$$

# 4 Parallelization

## 4.1 PyCOMPSs and dislib

COMPS superscalar [9] is a task-based programming model designed to simplify the development of distributed applications. Its interface allows for easy development and its runtime system can efficiently leverage parallelism during execution. The use of PyCOMPSs has many benefits, including infrastructure agnosticism, abstraction of memory and file system, and support for standard programming languages such as Java, Python, and C/C++.

PyCOMPSs [16] provides support for Python. A regular Python script can be easily transformed into a PyCOMPSs application by annotating functions to be run in parallel with a decorator. The runtime system is then able to automatically detect task dependencies and exploit parallelism for improved performance. The runtime detects the tasks' dependencies based on their input and output arguments. A task that has at least one input argument that is the output of another task has a dependency with that previous task.

The dislib library is parallelized using PyCOMPSs. The main concept of the dislib is the distributed array. It works as a regular Python [17] object from the user's perspective but it stores the data in a distributed way. The distributed array (or ds-array for short) is the input to the algorithms of the dislib library. The ds-array is comprised of blocks arranged in a two-dimensional format, with parallelism being achieved through the concurrent execution of algorithmic operations on these blocks.

Because the method presented on this paper is an extension of the dislib library, the input data will be stored in a ds-array structure. This means that the user will be able to control the parallelism by adjusting the number of blocks in the distributed array: with more blocks there will be more tasks in parallel and with less blocks less parallelism and less communications. We will address memory issues by ensuring that each block fits in memory. Our proposed approach will achieve the same result quality as the sequential algorithm, and we will leverage several PyCOMPSs mechanisms (detailed in Sect. 4) to optimize memory usage and reduce synchronization requirements.

### 4.2 Parallelization of the Algorithm

The input dataset for the algorithm is loaded as a ds-array. This means that the data is divided into blocks stored separately in memory. The first step of the Random Forest algorithm consists of generating the bootstraps (random sampling of the dataset) of the dataset that are going to be used on each decision tree. Then, the first level of each decision tree makes only one split, dividing the dataset assigned to it into two (or more) smaller datasets. The sequential algorithm computes the split for the first decision tree, then it computes the next split, and so on until it ends with the first decision tree and starts with the second one. The parallel version of the algorithm aims to make possible to compute all the decision trees concurrently. The first change with respect to the sequential algorithm is the order in which the splits of the decision trees are computed. The parallel version tries to execute concurrently the splits at the same depth for all the decision trees as it is described on Algorithm 1.

Reordering the algorithm's task creation provides greater parallelism. When all tasks at a given level are scheduled together rather than by trees, the later levels of the tree have more parallel tasks to execute, resulting in increased efficiency. By contrast, scheduling by trees leads to a reduction in parallel tasks available as the first trees scheduled finish before the last ones, thereby limiting parallelism.

**Algorithm 1.** Random Forest

```
1: procedure RANDOM_FOREST (X TRAINING DATA, Y LABELS DATA, NT NUMBER OF TREES, F NUMBER
   FEATURES USED)
2:     for j=0 to NT do
3:         Branches[j] ← X, Y, NewNode()
4:     for i = 0 to DistrDepth do
5:         for j=0 to NT do
6:             for branch ∈ Branches[j] do
7:                 x, y, ActualNode ← branch
8:                 Node, Left, Right ← ComputeSplit(x, y)
9:                 ActualNode.Content ← Node
10:                ActualNode.Left ← NewNode()
11:                ActualNode.Right ← NewNode()
12:                NewBranch ← Left, ActualNode.Left
13:                NewBranch ← Right, ActualNode.Right
14:            Branches[j] ← NewBranch
15:    for j=0 to NT do
16:        for branch ∈ Branches[j] do
17:            x, y, ActualNode ← branch
18:            ActualNode ← ConstructSbutree(x, y)
19:    return
```

The pseudocode of the parallel version is present on Algorithm 2. The functions that will run in parallel are annotated with a task decorator and will be: `GetSplitPoints`, `DataPerSplit`, `Gini`, `MSE`, `GetOptimalSplitPoint`, `ApplySplitPoint`, `GenerateNode` and `EvaluateStop`.

Following the pseudocode on Algorithm 2 the first step is to randomly select a set of attributes that are evaluated to determine the optimal split point. Next, the values of these attributes are sorted using the TeraSort algorithm (line 3). This algorithm works also parallelized with PyCOMPSs to sort all features concurrently. Otherwise, a sequential sorting operation will be performed for each attribute.

After sorting the values, the algorithm generates the split points. A modification introduced in the new approach is the use of a single subset of the possible split points. This change does not affect the final accuracy of the model, and it remarkably reduces the computation required on the first splits. For each split point we obtain the necessary information for determining the optimal split point from each block. This step is parallelized by invoking one task per block. To compute the Gini Impurity, we need only the classes present and their number of occurrences in each block partition.

For regression problems, we modified the formula to compute the error. From each block partition, we obtain the mean, the sum of all $Y$ values, and the number of occurrences. With the mean of each partition block (represented in the Equation as $MEAN_i$) and the number of instances it is possible to compute the mean $Y$ for the partition (represented as $\hat{Y}$). The new formula of the error is Eq. 3 ($S_1$ represents the first partition and $S_2$ the second one).

$$Error = \sum_{i \in S_1}^{blocks} (MEAN_i - \hat{Y_1})^2 + \sum_{i=1 \in S_2}^{blocks} (MEAN_i - \hat{Y_2})^2 \quad (3)$$

The split that returns the lowest Gini Impurity or error is selected and it is applied to all the blocks concurrently. This will divide the dataset into two subsets that will be sent to the next `Compute Split` function.

Finally, there is a task called `EvaluateStop` which aims to avoid a synchronization point. When PyCOMPSs tasks are submitted to the runtime, they generate future objects as their result, which can be used as input to other tasks and the runtime will recognize their dependencies and make all the required data transfers. However, future objects cannot be accessed outside the tasks without synchronization. If a synchronization is triggered, the generation of new tasks is stopped, causing the runtime to only launch tasks for a specific split at a time and hurting performance drastically. To avoid the need for synchronization points, PyCOMPSs offers several mechanisms.

The algorithm developed uses the PyCOMPSs failure management mechanism originally designed to enable the runtime to respond to task failures [7]. The way the algorithm is designed will create a large number of tasks, each with finer granularity and therefore more overheads. To improve the situation, we use the failure management mechanism to prune some tasks when we decide a node is a leaf. A node is considered a leaf when it has four or less instances assigned, or all of them are of the same class. When a task finds a leaf node, the task fails. In addition, all tasks dependent on the output of the failed task are canceled and will not be executed. This behavior is illustrated in Fig. 1.

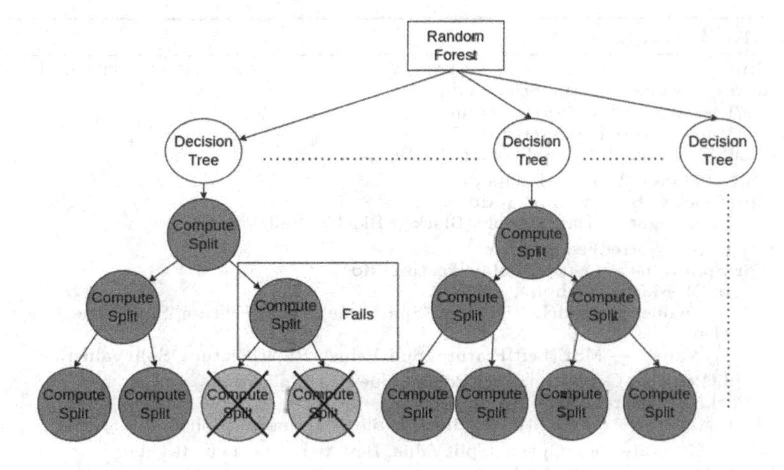


**Fig. 1.** Failure management behaviour. For the sake of simplicity each compute split represents the tasks inside it.

The algorithm would also work fine without this cancellation mechanism. However, it would launch and execute unnecessary tasks as it would have no way to know when a leaf node is created and stop the generation of tasks.

The number of tasks in this algorithm grows exponentially with each level of depth. In addition the granularity of the tasks in each deeper level will be finer. In order to solve this problem, we introduced a parameter that limits the maximum depth at which splits are computed using block level parallelism. Beyond this depth, the task `ConstructSubtree` is called to complete for each non-leaf node the construction of all branches in parallel using the Scikit-learn Decision Tree [12] algorithm. Since these tasks can be successors of the eventually failing tasks, the failure management may also cancel them executing only the necessary `ConstructSubtree` tasks.

### 4.3 Nested Task Solution

On execution, a PyCOMPSs application is deployed following the master-worker paradigm. The PyCOMPSs runtime runs on a master node. It is in charge of analyzing the code, identifying the tasks and their dependencies, orchestrating the data transfers and scheduling them for their execution. The computing nodes that perform the tasks' execution, making the actual computations, are called worker nodes.

PyCOMPSs has recently introduced a new nested task approach [10], which allows tasks to be called from other tasks. Under this paradigm each of the worker nodes is in charge of scheduling their own tasks. A visual representation is given on Fig. 2. On the figure we can see several levels of tasks. The nested tasks are scheduled by the worker node that is executing the outer task. This approach enables partial synchronizations without halting the entire execution. For example, the synchronization only affects the corresponding `Compute Split`

**Algorithm 2.** Compute Split

```
    procedure COMPUTE SPLIT (X TRAINING DATA, Y LABELS DATA, F NUMBER FEATURES EVALUATED)( )
        Features ← randomFeatureSelection(x, f)
 3:     SortedFeatures ← TeraSort(x, Features)
        for Feature ∈ SortedFeatures do
            ListSplitPoints ← GetSplitPoints(Feature)
 6:     for SplitValues ∈ ListSplitPoints do
            for BlockX, BlockY in X, Y do
                Left, Right ← DataPerSplit(BlockX, BlockY, SplitValues)
 9:     for Feature ∈ SortedFeatures do
            for SplitValue ∈ ListSplitPoints[Feature] do
                if Classification then
12:                 Values ← Gini(Left[Feature, SplitValue], Right[Feature, SplitValue])
                else
                    Values ← MSE(Left[Feature, SplitValue], Right[Feature, SplitValue])
15:     OptSplitPoint ← GetOptimalSplitPoint(Values, ListSplitPoints)
        for BlockX, BlockY in X, Y do
            Left, Right ← ApplySplitPoint(BlockX, BlockY, OptSplitPoint)
18:     Node ← GenerateNode(OptimalSplitValue, BestAttribute, Left, Right)
        EvaluateStop(Node, Left, Right)
        return Node, Left, Right
```

task where it is launched, stopping the generation and scheduling of tasks inside that specific `Compute Split` task without affecting the rest of the tasks.

A version of the Random Forest algorithm has also been implemented with this new technique. The nested version has several differences with respect to the previous one. The first difference is that the `fit` function of each decision tree becomes a task. The `ComputeSplit` function is also defined as a task allowing the runtime to schedule tasks within it and synchronize results without stopping the global execution of the algorithm. This eliminates the need for the failure management mechanism. The `ComputeSplit` functions will be executed in parallel. However, some functions inside `ComputeSplit` are no longer defined as tasks due to their fine granularity. Finally, the task generation order and the task scheduling has changed. In the previous section it was mentioned that the trees were generated following a width-depth approach. Now each decision tree's `fit` function is responsible for scheduling its inner tasks so the main program only schedules these first functions and waits for their results. Algorithm 3 provides a pseudocode representation of these changes. This way, in each decision tree, the `ComputeSplit` tasks are scheduled by depth.

**Algorithm 3.** Random Forest

```
1: procedure RANDOM_FOREST (X TRAINING DATA, Y LABELS DATA, NT NUMBER OF TREES, F NUMBER
   FEATURES USED)
2:     for j to NT do
3:         Trees[j] ← X, Y, NewDT()
4:     for j to NT do
5:         x, y, ActualTree ← Trees[j]
6:         Trees[j] ← ActualTree.fit(x, y)
7:     Trees ← compss_wait_on(Trees)
8:     return
```

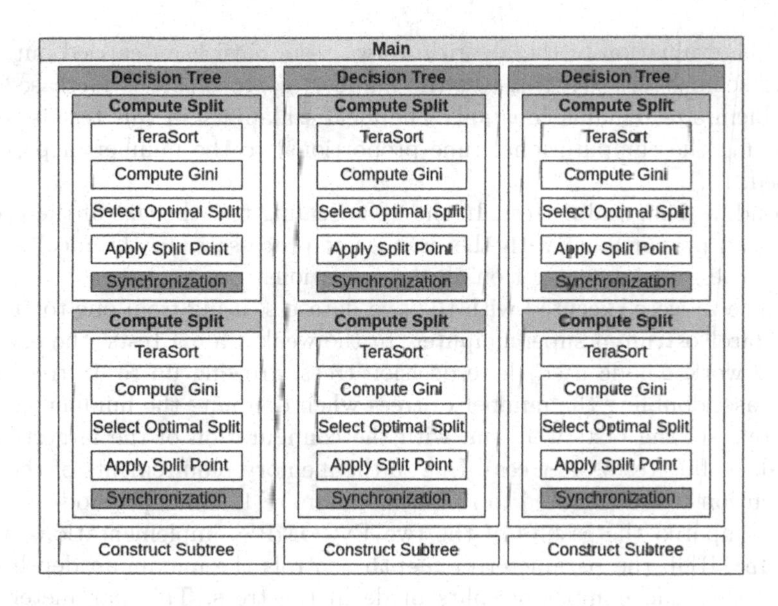


**Fig. 2.** Nested hierarchy tasks: each task schedules the tasks inside it recursively.

## 5 Evaluation

The solutions presented on this paper have been evaluated on a distributed execution environment. More specifically, we evaluated the solution on MareNostrum 4 supercomputer (MN4). It is composed of 3456 nodes, each node has two Intel®Xeon Platinum 8160 (24 cores at 2,1 GHz each), which means 48 cores per node and 96 GB of main memory. 216 of the nodes are high memory nodes with 380 GB of main memory. The peak performance of this supercomputer is 11.15 Petaflops. Its shared storage disks are managed using the Global Parallel File System.

Two different datasets were used to evaluate the solution proposed on this paper, one for classification and another one for regression:

- *HIGGS* [2]: kinematic data from particles, classification dataset with two classes. Class 1 Higgs boson signal, class 0 background. It contains 28 attributes, all with continuous values and 11 million instances, 10.5 million training instances and 500.000 test instances.
- *High Pressure Turbulence (HPT)*: data from fluid particles under high pressure and high temperature conditions. The prediction will be done on the $c\_p$ variable, that measures the heat capacity over the fluid mesh. It contains 5 attributes with continuous values and it is made up of 18.8 million training instances and 4.2 million test instances.

To increase the size of the problem and have longer execution times, the experiments performed with the HIGGS dataset the training data was doubled. This allowed us to better measure the scalability.

For the evaluation of the algorithm, two tests have been carried out. First, a strong scaling test. On this test the number of processors is increased while the problem size remains constant. The ideal scalability in this test is reached by reducing the computational time proportional to the number of processors increased.

Second, a weak scaling test. In the weak scaling test the size of the problem is increased proportional with the number of processors. In the ideal scenario the time will remain constant on all the executions.

Both tests were executed with the two datasets, using from one to 16 nodes of the MareNostrum 4 supercomputer. In the weak scaling tests, the execution with one worker node used three decision trees, growing up to 48 trees in the largest case, doubling the number of trees when doubling the number of nodes. The strong scaling tests were run with the configuration of the largest case of the weak scaling tests (48 trees). Due to the memory requirements of the tasks, the execution was configured to run a maximum of 12 tasks per node.

We compared the results of the two PyCOMPSs implementations against MLlib. In MLlib the parameter `maxDepth` controls the maximum depth of the tree and thus the number of splits made in the trees. This parameter has a direct impact on the execution time, accuracy and error of the predictions of the Random Forest. To make a fair comparison between the execution times of the different approaches, this parameter was adjusted to reach the same accuracy and error with the MLlib Random Forest than the accuracy and errors obtained with both PyCOMPSs approaches. Table 1 shows an example of the results obtained. The results presented here are from a single run, which may have some variability. We found that the results obtained using both PyCOMPSs and Scikit-learn were very similar. Therefore, we concluded that our approach does not alter the results obtained by the traditional method. We also included the results obtained using MLlib to provide a comprehensive overview of all the approaches we evaluated.

**Table 1.** Accuracy and Mean Absolute Error results obtained on the datasets with different approaches.

| | HIGGS accuracy | Mean Absolute Error HPT |
|---|---|---|
| Scikit-learn | 0.753 | 169.605 |
| PyCOMPSs | 0.755 | 171.087 |
| PyCOMPSs Nesting | 0.754 | 170.482 |
| MLlib | 0.722 | 162.233 |

Figure 3 contains the execution times and speedup of the MLlib Random Forest, PyCOMPSs Random Forest (referred as PyCOMPSs from now in advance) and Nested Random Forest for the strong scaling test. Despite the MLlib solution seems to be faster with a smaller number of nodes, its scalability is very limited and with more than 4 compute nodes the execution time increases. This can be

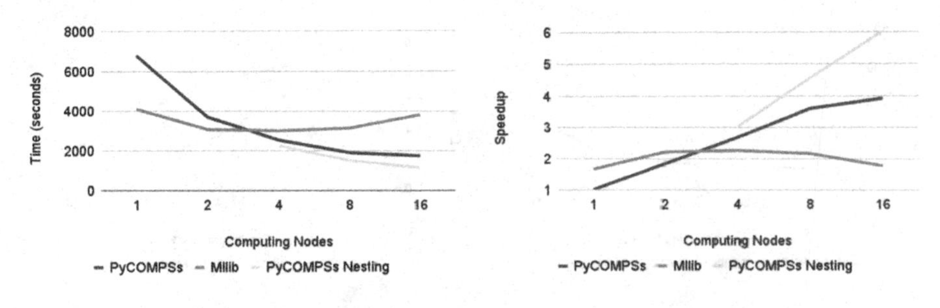


**Fig. 3.** HIGGS dataset execution times and Speedup.

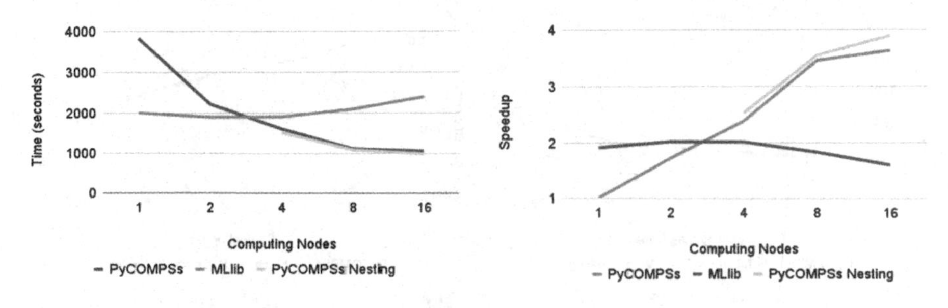


**Fig. 4.** High Pressure Turbulence dataset execution times and Speedup.

caused by an increment in the communication time. The executions with four and more nodes show that both PyCOMPSs implementations scale better than the MLlib solution, especially the Nested version. The execution times with 1 and 16 worker nodes are practically the same when executing with MLlib. With PyCOMPSs, the speedup reached is $\times 4$ and $\times 6$ with the nesting approach. For the executions with the PyCOMPSs non-nested version it is required to use an additional node in all the executions that works as master.

The strong scaling results obtained with the High Pressure Turbulence dataset are shown in Fig. 4. The scalability of all the solutions seem to be worse than with the previous dataset. This can be because a smaller dataset implies less parallelism. The MLlib algorithm shows a worst scalability than in the previous tests, obtaining worst execution times with 8 and 16 nodes than the execution time obtained with one worker node. In this second case, the speed up of both PyCOMPSs executions with 8 and 16 nodes is smaller. As said, the dataset is smaller than the previous one and this causes a reduction in the parallelism that limits the scalability. To compute the speedup, the execution time used as baseline is the time obtained with the first PyCOMPSs solution using one worker node. Both approaches proposed on this paper imply an improvement in scalability over the MLlib solution.

Figure 5 shows the weak scaling results obtained with the HIGGS dataset and Fig. 6 the corresponding ones for the HPT dataset. The execution time used as baseline for computing the efficiency is the time obtained with the first PyCOMPSs solution using one worker node. The MLlib Random Forest is the

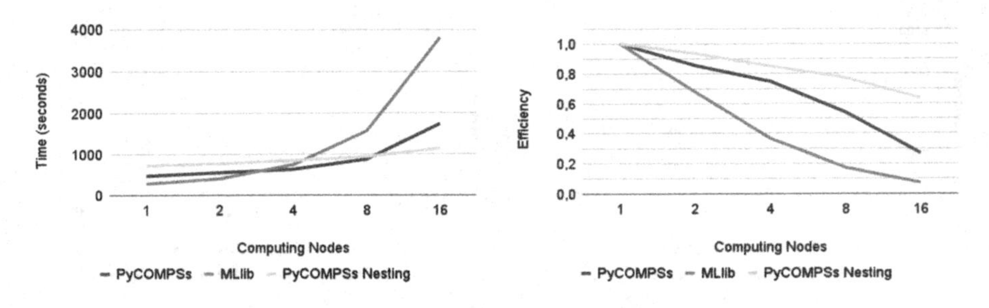


**Fig. 5.** HIGGS dataset execution times and Efficiency.

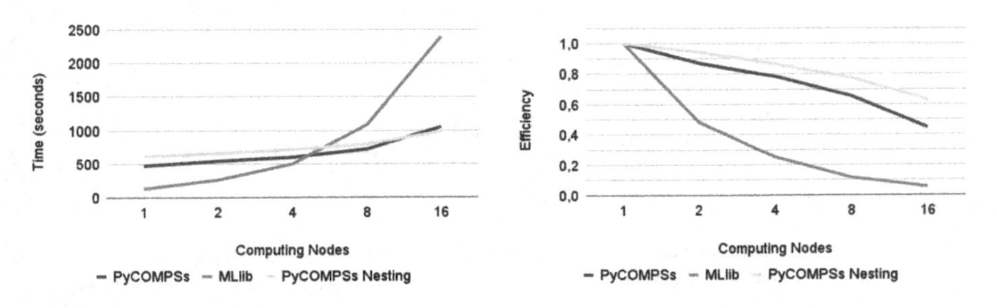


**Fig. 6.** High Pressure Turbulence dataset execution times and Efficiency.

fastest approach on both executions when using one and two nodes. Its bad scalability causes the execution with for nodes to obtain a worst execution time than PyCOMPSs in the classification problem and a very similar result with the regression dataset. From 8 nodes and more, the MLlib approach is clearly worse than both PyCOMPSs and Nesting approaches.

The nesting version starts with the worst execution time. However, its scalability is better and its execution time increases very little, being the approach with shortest execution time when running with 16 nodes on both datasets.

Finally, we experimented with different parameters to enhance MLlib performance, such as the number of executors, number of partitions, etc. The only parameter that had a positive effect on the execution times and scalability was the number of partitions. However, the scalability was still worse than PyCOMPSs scalabilities in all cases. Both PyCOMPSs versions were the optimal choices when using 8 or more nodes.

## 6 Conclusions

Two new data-parallel approaches have been proposed for the Random Forest algorithm. None of the two approaches causes any reduction in accuracy or error obtained with the model. The scalability of both new versions is considerably good, assuming an improvement over the MLlib Random Forest scalability.

The nested approach shows better scalability and efficiency than the regular COMPSs version, demonstrating that nesting is a useful mechanism that efficiently distributes work among multiple nodes.

The challenges faced during the development of the algorithm were the lack of parallelism, which was solved by changing the order of generation of the tasks, scheduling the tasks by depth in the different trees instead scheduling the tasks by tree. The generation of tasks with a very fine granularity was avoided using the COMPSs failure management system. We modified the error function for regression problems to compute the error without synchronizing entire tree nodes. Finally, we developed an approach based on task nesting that solves the initial lack of parallelism and the necessity to use the failure management system and improves the execution time and scalability of the PyCOMPSs algorithm.

Future work may imply exploring machine learning algorithms like Gradient Boosting in order to extend dislib functionalities.

**Acknowledgements.** This work has been supported by the Spanish Government (PID2019-107255GB) and by the MCIN/AEI /10.13039/501100011033 (CEX2021-001148-S), by the Departament de Recerca i Universitats de la Generalitat de Catalunya to the Research Group MPiEDist (2021 SGR 00412), and by the European Commission's Horizon 2020 Framework program and the European High-Performance Computing Joint Undertaking (JU) under grant agreement No 955558 and by MCIN/AEI/10.13039/501100011033 and the European Union NextGenerationEU/PRTR (PCI2021-121957, project eFlows4HPC), and by the European Commission through the Horizon Europe Research and Innovation program under Grant Agreement No. 101016577 (AI-Sprint project).

We thank Núria Masclans and Lluís Jofre from the Department of Fluid Mechanics of the Universitat Politècnica de Catalunya for providing the *High Pressure Turbulence* dataset.

## References

1. Azizah, N., Riza, L.S., Wihardi, Y.: Implementation of random forest algorithm with parallel computing in r. J. Phys: Conf. Ser. **1280**(2), 022028 (2019). https://doi.org/10.1088/1742-6596/1280/2/022028
2. Baldi, P., Sadowski, P., Whiteson, D.: Searching for exotic particles in high-energy physics with deep learning. Nature Commun. **5**(1), 4308 (2014)
3. Ben-Haim, Y., Tom-Tov, E.: A streaming parallel decision tree algorithm. J. Mach. Learn. Res. **11**(2) (2010)
4. Breiman, L., Friedman, J., Olshen, R., Stone, C.: Cart: Classification and Regression Trees (1984). Wadsworth, Belmont, CA (1993)
5. Chen, J., et al.: A parallel random forest algorithm for big data in a spark cloud computing environment. IEEE Trans. Parallel Distrib. Syst. **28**(4), 919–933 (2016)
6. Cid-Fuentes, J.Á., Solà, S., Álvarez, P., Castro-Ginard, A., Badia, R.M.: dislib: Large scale high performance machine learning in python. In: 2019 15th International Conference on eScience (eScience), pp. 96–105. IEEE (2019)
7. Ejarque, J., Bertran, M., Cid-Fuentes, J.Á., Conejero, J., Badia, R.M.: Managing failures in task-based parallel workflows in distributed computing environments. In: Malawski, M., Rzadca, K. (eds.) Euro-Par 2020. LNCS, vol. 12247, pp. 411–425. Springer, Cham (2020). https://doi.org/10.1007/978-3-030-57675-2_26

8. Ho, T.K.: Random decision forests. In: Proceedings of 3rd International Conference on Document Analysis and Recognition, vol. 1, pp. 278–282. IEEE (1995)
9. Lordan, F., et al.: ServiceSs: an interoperable programming framework for the cloud. J. Grid Comput. **12**(1), 67–91 (2013). https://doi.org/10.1007/s10723-013-9272-5
10. Lordan, F., Lezzi, D., Badia, R.M.: Colony: parallel functions as a service on the cloud-edge continuum. In: Sousa, L., Roma, N., Tomás, P. (eds.) Euro-Par 2021. LNCS, vol. 12820, pp. 269–284. Springer, Cham (2021). https://doi.org/10.1007/978-3-030-85665-6_17
11. Meng, X., et al.: Mllib: machine learning in apache spark. J. Mach. Learn. Res. **17**(1), 1235–1241 (2016)
12. Pedregosa, F., et al.: Scikit-learn: machine learning in Python. J. Mach. Learn. Res. **12**, 2825–2830 (2011)
13. Quinlan, J.R.: Induction of decision trees. Mach. Learn. **1**(1), 81–106 (1986)
14. Rocklin, M.: Dask: parallel computation with blocked algorithms and task scheduling. In: Proceedings of the 14th Python in Science Conference, no. 130–136. Citeseer (2015)
15. Salzberg, S.L.: C4. 5: Programs for machine learning by j. ross quinlan. morgan kaufmann publishers, inc., 1993 (1994)
16. Tejedor, E., et al.: Pycompss: parallel computational workflows in python. Int. J. High Perform. Comput. Appl. **31**(1), 66–82 (2017)
17. Van Rossum, G., Drake, F.L.: Python 3 Reference Manual. CreateSpace, Scotts Valley, CA (2009)
18. Zaharia, M., et al.: Apache spark: a unified engine for big data processing. Commun. ACM **59**(11), 56–65 (2016). https://doi.org/10.1145/2934664

# SymED: Adaptive and Online Symbolic Representation of Data on the Edge

Daniel Hofstätter[1(✉)], Shashikant Ilager[1], Ivan Lujic[2], and Ivona Brandic[1]

[1] Vienna University of Technology, Vienna, Austria
{daniel.hofstaetter,shashikant.ilager, ivona.brandic}@tuwien.ac.at
[2] Ericsson Nikola Tesla, Zagreb, Croatia
ivan.lujic@ericsson.com

**Abstract.** The edge computing paradigm helps handle the Internet of Things (IoT) generated data in proximity to its source. Challenges occur in transferring, storing, and processing this rapidly growing amount of data on resource-constrained edge devices. Symbolic Representation (SR) algorithms are promising solutions to reduce the data size by converting actual raw data into symbols. Also, they allow data analytics (e.g., anomaly detection and trend prediction) directly on symbols, benefiting large classes of edge applications. However, existing SR algorithms are centralized in design and work offline with batch data, which is infeasible for real-time cases. We propose SymED - Symbolic Edge Data representation method, i.e., an online, adaptive, and distributed approach for symbolic representation of data on edge. SymED is based on the Adaptive Brownian Bridge-based Aggregation (ABBA), where we assume low-powered IoT devices do initial data compression (senders) and the more robust edge devices do the symbolic conversion (receivers). We evaluate SymED by measuring compression performance, reconstruction accuracy through Dynamic Time Warping (DTW) distance, and computational latency. The results show that SymED is able to (i) reduce the raw data with an average compression rate of 9.5%; (ii) keep a low reconstruction error of 13.25 in the DTW space; (iii) simultaneously provide real-time adaptability for online streaming IoT data at typical latencies of 42 ms per symbol, reducing the overall network traffic.

**Keywords:** Internet of Things · Edge computing · Symbolic data representation · Edge storage and analytics · Data compression · Time series

## 1 Introduction

The Internet of Things (IoT) enables various physical devices to embed with sensors and actuators to exchange data with smart systems over the Internet. Rapid growing IoT data are traditionally transmitted to a centralized cloud to derive insights for smart applications. However, this remote cloud-centric approach does


J. Cano et al. (Eds.): Euro-Par 2023, LNCS 14100, pp. 411–425, 2023.
https://doi.org/10.1007/978-3-031-39698-4_28

not satisfy time-critical IoT application requirements [19,20] and can create network congestion [18]. Consequently, edge computing mitigates these issues by delivering computing, storage, and network resources at the network edge.

Edge nodes are highly distributed resource-limited devices deployed in the proximity of IoT data sources to deliver time-critical processing [19]. Unlike the cloud, edge nodes have limited computation and storage resources. Therefore, it becomes crucial for edge nodes to cope with the velocity and growing volume of data generated and support applications within their resource constraints. Several efforts have been made to reduce network traffic and improve data storage using edge data processing techniques. In [15], authors target edge data reduction focusing on IoT data and adapting a posteriori data reduction techniques to data streams. Nevertheless, this approach does not consider the impact of reduced data on data analytics tasks. Consequently, Symbolic Representation (SR) techniques are promising alternative methods to reduce the data size while maintaining partial semantics of the data [11].

The SR helps reduce the dimension and volume of time series, enabling efficient edge data storage management. The raw data in SR are segmented and represented with symbols that can be reconstructed to their original dimension. Unlike common raw data compression methods, the symbolically converted data in SR can help to directly perform data mining tasks such as pattern matching, substring search, motif discovery, and time series prediction, which are commonly used techniques in IoT applications [5]. However, the state-of-the-art SR algorithms are designed for centralized batch processing systems and perform an offline conversion, where often fixed parameters (e.g., window and alphabet size) are needed, making them infeasible for streaming data in modern IoT systems.

We propose *SymED* (Symbolic Edge Data representation) approach, i.e., an online distributed and adaptive SR method suiting edge data storage management and transmission. SymED is based on the Adaptive Brownian bridge-based symbolic aggregation (ABBA) algorithm, due to its adaptiveness in window and alphabet size. We decompose the algorithm into distributed manner with two main components: sender and receiver. We also incorporate online normalization and clustering for adaptation to streaming data and symbol conversion. Furthermore, SymED allows us to adaptively adjust the reconstruction error and bandwidth usage between sender and receiver depending on hyperparameter configurations. The main contributions include **(i)** a symbolic representation approach for IoT sensor-based time series, investigating the benefits of edge storage and transmission bandwidth scarcity; **(ii)** an online symbolic representation algorithm for real-time symbol generations in edge environments; **(iii)** an empirical evaluation of the proposed solution on real-world data sets, showing different performance profiles and achieving raw data compression of 9.5% on average while minimizing reconstruction error.

## 2 Motivation and Background

**Need for Symbolic Representation on Edge:** SR methods are promising solutions that allow analytic tasks to be performed directly on reduced data and

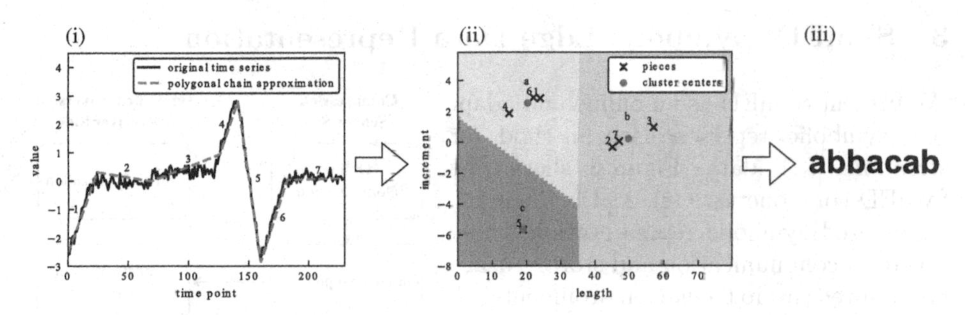


**Fig. 1.** Illustration of ABBA [5]. (i) Creating polygonal chain of linear pieces (left side). (ii) Clustering pieces (middle). (iii) Symbolizing (right side), i.e., *abbacab*.

enable the reconstruction of original data with minimal error. Existing symbolic representation algorithms have limited applicability for edge due to the following design requirements: (1) **Online**: Compression should be continuous and immediate (i.e., stream-based). (2) **Adaptive:** A SR algorithm should be adaptive, allowing flexible compression and reconstruction performance based on application and resource constraints. (3) **Distributed:** A SR should be distributed in edge as IoT sensors themselves do not have enough computational/network capabilities. Existing SR algorithms assume apriori availability of batch data and work offline in a centralized manner.

**Symbolic Representation for Time Series Data:** A SR algorithm transforms time series into a string using finite alphabet size. Let us consider a time series $T = [t_0, t_1, ..., t_N] \in \mathbb{R}^{N+1}$ converted into a symbolic representation $S = [s_1, s_2, ..., s_n] \in \mathbb{A}^n$, with symbols $s_i$ coming from an alphabet of $k$ symbols $\mathbb{A} = \{a_1, a_2, ..., a_k\}$ [5]. The sequence $S$ should be of considerably lower dimension than the original time series $T$, that is $n << N$, and it should only use a small number of meaningful symbols, that is $k << n$. The symbolic representation must also allow a reconstruction, with (i) a minimal and controllable error, and (ii) a shape suitably close to the original time series data.

**Adaptive Brownian Bridge-based Aggregation (ABBA):** Our SymED is based on ABBA symbolic method and adapted for edge environments. Figure 1 shows an example of ABBA symbolic conversion, with the black line on the left side as the original data, and the symbolically represented data on the rightmost side. ABBA adaptively finds linear pieces (7 red dashed lines on the left), where similar pieces are clustered together based on their length and increment values (middle), and each cluster is mapped to a symbol from the alphabet, resulting in a string (right). A tolerance hyperparameter *tol* sets boundaries for the allowed reconstruction error, where a lower value results in a lower reconstruction error, but also a lower compression rate with more symbols. In this example, 230 data points are converted to a word of just 7 symbols (rightmost part of Fig. 1). A similar inverse approach will be applied during the reconstruction of the data. However, many challenges arise when using such algorithms for online and resource-constrained edge environments, which we address in this work.

# 3 SymED: Symbolic Edge Data Representation

We present SymED as an online and adaptive symbolic representation method for streaming IoT data. Figure 2 shows the SymED components. Our goal is to enable distributed symbolic representation where raw data communication and storage usage are limited in IoT-edge environments. A sender (IoT node) normalizes and compresses all incoming data. A receiver (edge node) collects transmitted data to (i) construct linear pieces (line segments), (ii) converts them to symbols in the digitization phase, and (iii) optionally reconstructs pieces or symbols again.

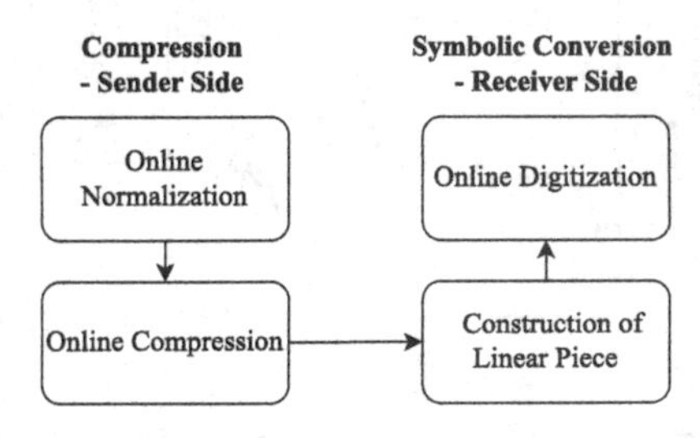


**Fig. 2.** SymED Components.

## 3.1 Sender Side - Compression

The sender compresses data stream $T = [t_0, t_1, ...., t_N]$ for each new data point $t_j \in T$ step-wise. Our compression technique, leverages the existing method [5] to an online setting, with additional online normalization, shown in Algorithm 1. The sender collects and normalizes data stream points $[t_0, t_1, ..., t_m]$ $(m << N)$, and fits them to a linear line. After transmitting only the end point of this line to the receiver, the whole process repeats.

**Online Normalization:** Using normalized data is mandatory for a uniform conversion performance, as data can arrive with arbitrary scaling. A popular normalization technique is the Min-Max-Normalization [1,7]. We use Z-Score-Normalization (standardization) that provides scaling data with zero mean and unit variance. Standardization in an online setting is used for, e.g., improving batch normalization in continual learning [16].

Online normalization also requires a window of data points to consider. There exist multiple windows models [22] for online streaming data. Mainly, (i) *landmark windows*, which span from a landmark of the past to the present, (ii) *sliding windows*, which have a fixed size and data points passing through them in a first-in-first-out fashion, (iii) *damped windows*, which give data points weights decaying exponentially over time. We chose the damped window model due to its simple iterative calculation and the advantage of not requiring extra storage. The standardization parameters are set as exponentially weighted moving average (EWMA) and exponentially weighted moving variance (EWMV) [14], defined as follows:

$$EWMA_j = \alpha t_j + (1 - \alpha)EWMA_{j-1} \tag{1}$$

$$EWMV_j = \alpha(t_j - EWMA_j)^2 + (1 - \alpha)EWMV_{j-1} \tag{2}$$

**Algorithm 1.** SymED - Sender

```
1: function ONLINECOMPRESSION(tol, len_max)
2:     get T_s from memory
3:     err ← 0; bound ← 0; len_ts ← 0
4:     while err <= bound and len_ts <= len_max do
5:         t_j ← GETNEXTDATAPOINT()
6:         append t_j to T_s
7:         UPDATEONLINENORMALIZATIONPARAMS(t_j)
8:         T_sn ← standardize T_s
9:         err ← GETERROR(T_sn)
10:        len_ts ← LENGTH(T_s)
11:        bound ← (len_ts − 2) * tol
12:    T_s ← last 2 elements of T_s
13:    store T_s in memory
14:    return first element of T_s
```

In Eq. 1 and 2, $t_j$ indicates the next data point of the processed stream. The hyperparameter $\alpha$ serves as a weight, which has an exponentially decreasing influence on past data points. Here, EWMA and EWMV have same $\alpha$ value, for simplicity and consistency. Initially, $EWMA_0 = t_0$ and $EWMV_0 = 1.0$ are set. All data kept in memory are standardized newly each iteration with up-to-date EWMA and EWMV. The update process of EWMA and EWMV, using Eqs. 1 and 2, can be found in Algorithm 1 (line 7). Standardization is done through $\frac{t_h - EWMA_j}{\sqrt{EWMV_j}}$, e.g., for each data point $t_h$with $h \leq j$ (line 8).

**Online Compression:** In ABBA compression [5], data is approximated by a polygonal chain of linear pieces, where each piece is bounded by length and squared Euclidean distance error. Linear pieces are defined as $P = [p_1, p_2, ..., p_n]$, where each linear piece $p = (len, inc)$ is a tuple of length and increment value. Our proposed online compression Algorithm 1 only works on one linear piece at a time, instead of converting them all at once, like [5]. After checking the error and maximal length limits in line 4, one of the following cases can happen, (i) no boundaries are reached and the algorithm continues the compression in the next iteration by trying to add another data point $t_{j+1}$ to the time series segment $T_s$, (ii) if $len_{max}$ is surpassed or the error including the current data point $t_j$ is out of bounds (see line 11 for bound value), then the loop terminates. After the loop, $T_s$ is set from $[t_0, ..., t_m]$ back to the points $[t_{m-1}, t_m]$, to initialize the compression of the next segment. Finally, the endpoint of the segment $t_{m-1}$ is returned and sent to the receiver. Originally, the ABBA compression [5] would use $T_s$ to produce a piece $p = (m - 1, t_{m-1} - t_0)$ here, before moving on to compressing the next piece. However, in SymED, we move this step to the receiver. In this way, (i) the size of payload needed to be transmitted is reduced by half, only sending one numeric value ($t_{m-1}$) instead of two ($p$), and (ii) making the receiver more robust to missing sender values. Length and increment of a piece $p_i$ are always relative to its predecessor $p_{i-1}$. One missing piece would break up the polygonal chain of pieces ABBA depends on. SymED avoids this problem by only transmitting data points as absolute values from the sender to the receiver.

**Algorithm 2.** SymED - Receiver

```
1: procedure SymED(tol, scl, k_min, k_max)
2:     S ← []; C ← []; P ← []; t_{i-1} ← 0
3:     while True do
4:         t_i ← getDataPointFromSender()
5:         len ← timeSinceLastUpdate()
6:         inc ← t_i − t_{i-1}
7:         p_i ← (len, inc)
8:         append p_i to P
9:         S, C ← onlineDigitization(P, C, tol, scl, k_min, k_max)
10:        t_{i-1} ← t_i
```

Compressing $m$ data points to one linear piece with length $len = m - 1$ requires $\mathcal{O}(m)$ iterations of the while loop (line 4) and recalculating the error at line 9 in $\mathcal{O}(m)$ time, hence, Algorithm 1 runs in $\mathcal{O}(m^2)$. For the whole data stream of size $N$, assuming each linear piece compresses on average $m$ data points ($m << N$), the complexity is $\mathcal{O}(N)$ [5].

### 3.2 Receiver Side - Symbolic Conversion

The job of the receiver is to listen for data points $t$ coming from sender devices and convert each of two subsequent data points to a linear piece $p$. All pieces $P$ are clustered in an online fashion, to get the converted sequence of symbols $S$, which essentially becomes one symbol longer after each received data point. Optionally, a reconstruction of the data stream can be done on demand. We decided to do the symbolic conversion at the receiver instead of the sender, because (i) the sender is relieved of the computational demands, and (ii) symbolic conversion at the sender would require frequent and costly transmissions of the up-to-date reconstruction centers to the receiver.

**Construction of Linear Pieces:** The receiver Algorithm 2 receives data point $t_i$ in iteration $i$ from a sender. Along with data point $t_{i-1}$ of the previous iteration, the length and increment values $(len, inc)$ of the current linear piece $p_i$ can be constructed. We infer $len$ by taking advantage of the real-time online setting. To do that, the receiver saves timestamp $time_i$ upon the arrival of each $t_i$. Taking the difference in times with $len = time_i - time_{i-1}$ allows us not to have the sender transfer this value. Consequently, $inc = t_i - t_{i-1}$ completes the construction of $p_i$. Afterwards, at line 9, all pieces $P$ found so far get clustered to centers $C$ and converted to a symbolic string $S$ through Online Digitization in Algorithm 3, which also determines the time complexity of Algorithm 2.

**Online Digitization:** The Algorithm 3 uses clustering to group pieces $P = [p_1, p_2, ..., p_n]$ to centers $C = [c_1, c_2, ..., c_k]$. Each center $c$ represents a character of the alphabet $A = [a_1, a_2, ..., a_k]$, mapping $P$ to the symbolic string $S = [s_1, s_2, ..., s_n]$, and the center coordinates are responsible for the reconstruction of length and increment values of $P$. A scaling factor $scl$ is provided to weigh lengths of pieces differently from increments during 2D clustering, for $scl \in (0, \infty)$. The classical approach [5] also considers that $scl \in \{0, \infty\}$, allowing for 1D-clustering either the lengths or increments, while $scl = 0$ is selected to put more emphasis

**Algorithm 3.** SymED - Receiver - Online Digitization

```
1: function ONLINEDIGITIZATION(P, C, tol, scl, k_min, k_max)
2:     if LENGTH(C) < k_min then
3:         L ← [0, 1, ..., LENGTH(P) − 1]
4:         S ← LABELSTOSYMBOLS(L)
5:         C ← P
6:         return S, C
7:     standardize P and C and scale with scl
8:     tol_s ← GETTOLS(tol, P); len_P ← LENGTH(P)
9:     C_init ← C; k_o ← LENGTH(C); k ← k_o − 1; err ← ∞
10:    while k < k_max and k < len_P and err > bound do
11:        k ← k + 1
12:        if k = k_o + 1 then
13:            append last element of P to C_init
14:        else if k > k_o + 1 then
15:            randomly initialize C_init
16:        C, L ← KMEANS(C_init, k)
17:        err ← MAXCLUSTERVARIANCE(P, C, L, k)
18:    de-standardize P, C and de-scale with scl
19:    S ← LABELSTOSYMBOLS(L)
20:    return S, C
```

on the trends of the time series. Our proposed SymED clustering can also be done either in 2D or in 1D, however, we focus mainly on 2D in this work.

For SymED, we use a customized online version of k-means for both 1D and 2D clustering, because k-means is widely studied and provides a suitable streaming-based version [17], feasible for our online implementation. The steps of k-means, calculation of the cluster variances, and checking them against the tolerance boundary $tol_s^2$, follow the standard processes [5].

In the online k-means function within Algorithm 3, instead of the default initialization (randomized seeding), we initialize cluster centers $C_{init}$ with the values from the previous old clusters $C$, to remove the need for restarting a randomly initialized clustering [17]. Consequently, the number of clusters $k$ for the first run of k-means is set to $k_o$, the number of old clusters in $C$, to avoid trying many values of $k$. If an additional cluster is still needed, $k$ is incremented by one, and the clustering is re-run (line 10). We initialize the newly added center with the newest piece, while the rest of the center initialization remains the same, ensuring fast convergence (line 13). Random-based initialization of centers is only chosen in line 15, if the previous attempts of re-using old cluster centers fail. The $k_{min}$ and $k_{max}$ limit the number of clusters, as well as the size of the alphabet. After clustering is done, labels $L = [0, 1, ...]$, are mapped to symbols $[`a', `b', ...]$ and returned as string $S$, along with updated centers $C$.

The runtime of Algorithm 3 is bounded by the complexity of k-means. The average complexity to produce a new symbol is therefore $\mathcal{O}(kn)$ for $k$ clusters and $n$ linear pieces, per k-means iteration. Due to initialized centers and adding pieces one-by-one to the clusters, only very few iterations are needed. To convert a data stream of size $N$ to $n$ symbols, the resulting complexity is $\mathcal{O}(kn^2)$.

**Reconstruction:** Converting a sequence of symbols $S$ back to a time series $\hat{T}$ follows three steps [5]: (i) *Inverse-Digitization*, replacing $S$ with length and increment values $(\widetilde{len}, \widetilde{inc})$ of their corresponding reconstruction centers to reconstruct linear pieces, (ii) *Quantization*, rounding lengths of those linear pieces back to whole numbers, generating $(\widehat{len}, \widehat{inc})$, and (iii) *Inverse-Compression*, interpolating all-time series points for the chain of linear pieces, producing $\hat{T} = [\hat{t_0}, \hat{t_1}, ..., \hat{t_N}]$ This offline reconstruction procedure from symbols works for both ABBA and SymED. Additionally, for SymED, a more accurate online reconstruction for $\hat{T}$ is possible by directly doing the Inverse-Compression step, with the original $(len, inc)$ values of pieces constructed by the receiver.

# 4 Performance Evaluation

## 4.1 Experimental Setup

**Metrics:** To measure the performance of SymED, we consider four main metrics. Namely, (i) *reconstruction error*, (ii) *compression rate*, (iii) *dimension reduction rate*, and (iv) *computational latency*. We measure reconstruction error ($RE$) through the Dynamic Time Warping (DTW) distance [3] between the original time series $T$ and the reconstruction $\hat{T}$, i.e., $RE = dtw(T, \hat{T})$, as in [5]. Additionally, for SymED, we evaluate the reconstruction error not only from symbols $S$, but also from linear pieces $P$, since they are also available for the SymED receiver. The compression rate ($CR$) for ABBA ($CR_{ABBA}$) and SymED ($CR_{SymED}$) is measured as defined in Eq. 3. Here, we measure how many bytes are saved during transmission from the sender to the receiver, instead of just sending an uncompressed raw data stream. We measure the dimension reduction rate ($DRR$), a measure of data size reduction while preserving the original data properties, by comparing lengths of converted symbols $S$ and true time series $T$, i.e., $DRR = \frac{len(S)}{len(T)}$. Here, $len()$ returns the length of the input (count of symbols or data points). Dimension reduction helps to cope with the *curse of dimensionality* when working with high-dimensional data.

$$CR_{ABBA} = \frac{bytes(C) + bytes(S)}{bytes(T)} \qquad CR_{SymED} = \frac{bytes(P)/2}{bytes(T)} \tag{3}$$

In Eq. 3, $bytes()$ returns a total number of bytes for the input. The assumptions of this experimental setting are, a symbol/character is a size of 1 byte, and a numerical/float value has a size of 4 bytes. $S$ is a series of symbols, $T$ is a series of floats, and $C$ is a set of centers, where each center is defined through 2 float valued coordinates. $P$ is a sequence of linear pieces, where a linear piece $p$ is defined over 2 float values. With ABBA, we assume the sender does the symbolic conversion offline in a batch, then sends all symbols $S$ and reconstruction centers $C$ to the receiver. For SymED, we only need to transmit one float value for each $p$, hence $bytes(P)/2$ for $CR_{SymED}$ in Eq. 3. For simplicity, any other bytes regarding a transmission protocol between the sender and receiver are omitted. For all metrics, a lower value means better performance.

The final metric is computational latency, addressing the average amount of computational time needed for each symbol in the online setting. We measure the time required for a SymED sender to perform compression and a receiver to do symbolic conversion and reconstruction on a per-symbol basis. Compared to offline ABBA, we take the total time for all produced symbols, i.e., how long it takes on average to fully convert time series to symbols and reconstruct it again.

**Edge Scenario Setup:** We emulate the sender-receiver setup, where sender is an IoT sensor streaming pre-processed data towards receiver edge node for further processing. The setup is implemented as a multi-thread Python application. SymED is split up as explained in Sect. 3. For ABBA, we assume the sender does offline symbolic conversion of the time series and sends symbols and reconstruction centers to the receiver, where reconstruction happens. Evaluation is done on a Raspberry Pi 4B (4 GB RAM).

**Datasets:** We use UCR Time Series Classification Archive [4] datasets as a representative of IoT data [5]. We filter the *test* split for datasets with a minimal length of 1000 data points, ensuring we have sufficient data for the online normalization to adapt. We sample each dataset by selecting the first time series of each class, e.g., for dataset *ACSF1* with a size of 100 time series and 10 different classes, we take a sample of 10 time series, each with a length of 1460. Table 1 shows 22 selected datasets containing 302 time series with mean length of 1673.

**Baseline and Hyperparameters:** We compare the results of our proposed SymED to the original ABBA, a baseline for reconstruction accuracy. Compared to ABBA, SymED has an additional hyperparameter $\alpha$ for adjusting the weights of online normalization values EWMA and EWMV. Higher $\alpha$ values prefer the most recent data, monitoring short-term variability of EWMA and EWMV, and lower values focus on long-term estimation of mean and variance [14]. We set $0.01 \leq \alpha \leq 0.02$ based on empirical testing, suiting our chosen datasets. Further, we set $k_{min} = 3$ for both ABBA and SymED, meaning that an alphabet of at least three symbols will be used. The only exception is when $|P| < k_{min}$, where too few linear pieces are in $P$ to form $k_{min}$ clusters, resulting $k_{min} = |P|$. We set $k_{max} = 100$, the upper bound for the alphabet size.

For each algorithm and tolerance value, the mean of the results over all datasets (Table 1) is taken. To compensate for the different sizes of datasets, we assign equal weights in the evaluation, i.e., averaging results first for all time series within a dataset, then taking the average once again over all datasets.

**Table 1.** Selected datasets of the UCR Time Series Classification Archive [4].

| Dataset | Type | Size | Length |
|---|---|---|---|
| ACSF1 | Device | 10 | 1460 |
| CinCECGTorso | Sensor | 4 | 1639 |
| EOGHorizontalSignal | EOG | 12 | 1250 |
| EOGVerticalSignal | EOG | 12 | 1250 |
| EthanolLevel | Spectro | 4 | 1751 |
| HandOutlines | Image | 2 | 2709 |
| Haptics | Motion | 5 | 1092 |
| HouseTwenty | Device | 2 | 2000 |
| InlineSkate | Motion | 7 | 1882 |
| Mallat | Simulated | 8 | 1024 |
| MixedShapesRegularTrain | Image | 5 | 1024 |
| MixedShapesSmallTrain | Image | 5 | 1024 |
| PLAID | Device | 11 | 1344 |
| Phoneme | Sensor | 39 | 1024 |
| PigAirwayPressure | Hemodynamics | 52 | 2000 |
| PigArtPressure | Hemodynamics | 52 | 2000 |
| PigCVP | Hemodynamics | 52 | 2000 |
| Rock | Spectrum | 4 | 2844 |
| SemgHandGenderCh2 | Spectrum | 2 | 1500 |
| SemgHandMovementCh2 | Spectrum | 6 | 1500 |
| SemgHandSubjectCh2 | Spectrum | 5 | 1500 |
| StarLightCurves | Sensor | 3 | 1024 |

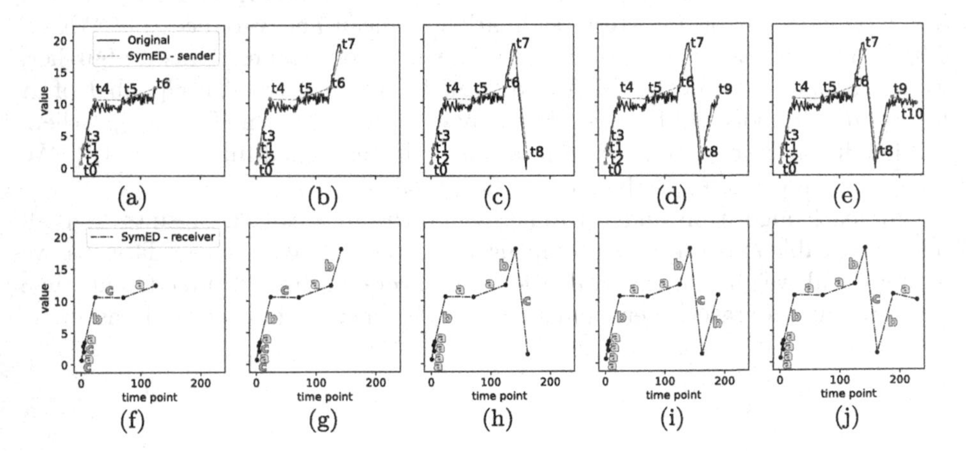


**Fig. 3.** Running example for SymED sender (a-e) and receiver (f-j) algorithms.

## 4.2 Running Example

We provide a running example in Fig. 3, on a time series example of 230 data points, similar to the ABBA [5]. Here, parameters are set as $tol = 0.4$, $\alpha = 0.02$, and $scl = 0$ (1D clustering). In Fig. 3, the sender-side (IoT nodes) steps are depicted in Figs. 3a–3e, the receiver side steps (edge nodes) in Figs. 3f–3j. Each sub-figure shows the generation of one new linear piece and symbol, from left to right. For brevity, we summarized the first seven iterations in Figs. 3a and 3f, then showed the remaining iterations in the remaining figures.

The sender compresses the incoming data stream (solid black line) until a linear piece $p_i$ is formed (red dashed line) and then sends the endpoint $t_i$ of $p_i$ to the receiver. The receiver reconstructs $p_i$ (black dash-dotted line) from $t_i$, and $t_{i-1}$, and does an online clustering to produce the symbol $s_i$ ('a', 'b', or 'c' here). SymED produces 11 symbols in total, namely, *aaaabaabcba*. At the beginning, the first four symbols are produced in very short intervals, due to the online normalization not having adapted to the data yet and also capturing noise. But afterwards, longer linear pieces start to get formed to produce the remaining symbols. Due to the nature of online clustering, older pieces may be assigned to a different cluster after several updates. This can be seen for a linear piece between $t_4$ and $t_5$, which changes from 'c' to 'a' (from Fig. 3g to Fig. 3h).

### 4.3 Results and Analysis

Figures 4a–4c show examples of SymED reconstruction on a few UCR time series, using tolerance $tol = 0.4$. The following metrics in Fig. 5 are evaluated for a range of $tol$ values, going from 0.1 to 2.0 in 0.1 increments. Other common parameters for Figs. 4–5 are $\alpha = 0.01$ and $scl = 1.0$, using 2D clustering.

**Reconstruction Error:** Figure. 5a shows that SymED reconstruction error for symbol generation follows the original ABBA curve, which is a desired behavior. Reconstruction errors from symbols average around 29.25 for SymED and 29.60 for ABBA. In contrast, SymED online reconstruction from linear pieces has less than half the error at 13.25, due to pieces being more true to the original data, before being clustered and converted to symbols.

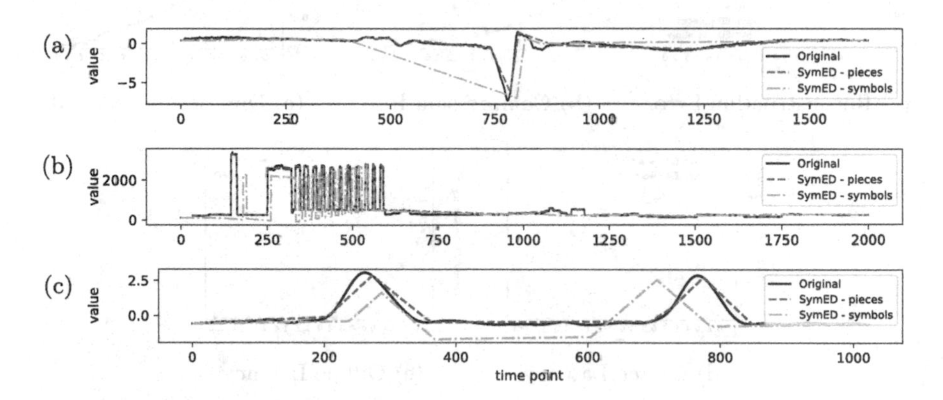


**Fig. 4.** SymED reconstruction example on three representational datasets from the UCR archive: (a) *CinCECGTorso*, (b) *HouseTwenty*, (c) *StarLightCurves*

**Compression Rate:** We compare the results of compression rates in Fig. 5b, measuring the size reduction of transmitted data. As seen in Fig. 5b, ABBA compresses data to 3.1% on average, by taking advantage of transmitting already converted symbols, which are less byte expensive than numerical data points of SymED. SymED's online and distributed nature comes at the cost of having a worse compression rate of 9.5% on average.

**Dimension Reduction Rate:** Figure 5c shows dimension reduction results. Both ABBA and SymED have similar behavior, since their compression phases work in a similar way. Differences occur due to the online normalization of SymED, which takes time to adapt to the data and produces a higher number of linear pieces/symbols early on, also evidenced in Fig. 3. Finally, the SymED has a mean dimension reduction rate of 9.5%, ABBA averages at 7.7%.

**Computational Latency:** Figure 5d compares SymED sender and receiver, how long processing takes per symbol. Lower tolerances produce many short pieces, making clustering at the receiver dominant. In contrast, higher tolerance values produce fewer and longer linear pieces, increasing the compression times for the sender. On average, a SymED sender spends 30 ms on compressing, and a receiver 12 ms on creating and reconstructing a symbol, summing up to 42 ms total per symbol. In Fig. 5e we show the total latencies for processing an entire time series offline. ABBA is overall faster with a mean of 2.0 s, compared to 5.3 s for SmyED, however, SymED is mainly designed for online processing.

To conclude, SymED provides the benefit of lower online reconstruction error and real-time adaptability to streaming data, with a little cost on higher data transmission needs and computational times compared to offline ABBA.

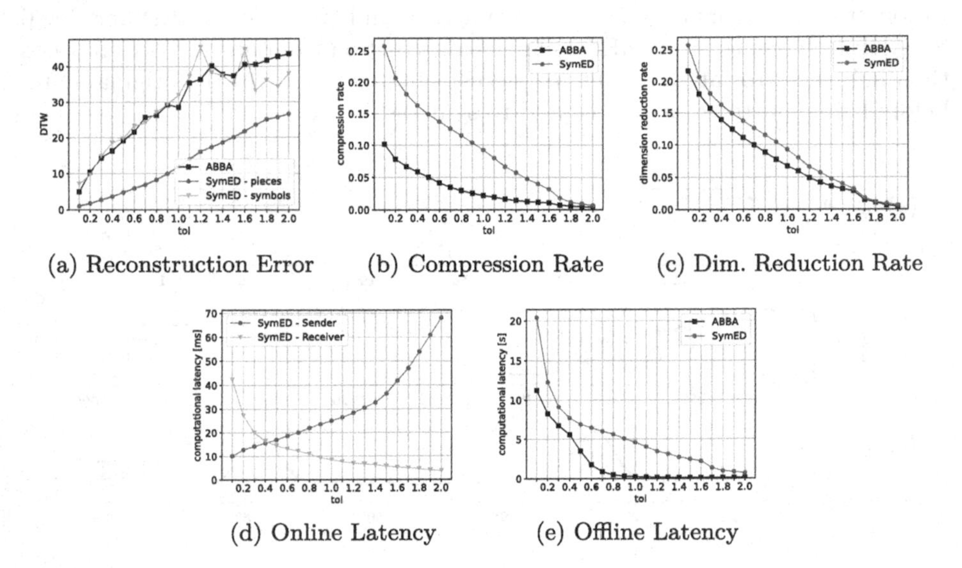

(a) Reconstruction Error (b) Compression Rate (c) Dim. Reduction Rate

(d) Online Latency (e) Offline Latency

**Fig. 5.** Evaluation of ABBA and proposed SymED (averaged over all datasets).

## 5 Related Work

Symbolic representation (SR) algorithms have been used to convert time series data into symbols. The basic algorithm in the symbolic conversion is SAX [11]. Another variant of SAX is proposed in [12], dedicated to online load data compression and reconstruction. The authors split the time series into the event and steady-state segments, while using symbolic conversion only on the latter one. In this version, the alphabet is fixed, while the window length is adaptive, by dividing segments into windows of equal information content. Although they use adaptive window sizes, as in our proposed SymED, they focus on event-based data instead of arbitrary time series. In [9], the author converts sensor data streams to symbols using SAX, followed by classification with a Support Vector Machine (SVM). Works like [10] symbolize sensor data streams using SAX and incorporate data stream annotation in a distributed environment, interacting over a publish/subscribe messaging service. Further, SensorSAX [6], is a SAX variation with dynamic window length, to reduce the energy consumption of IoT sensor streams. While using symbolic conversion to process IoT data, other works lack adaptability by either using a static window size [9,10] or fixed alphabet [6,9,10]. They also sample the data stream and produce symbols in batches, in contrast to producing symbols consecutively in SymED. Adaptive compression of IoT data based on different resource-limited edge conditions is proposed by [13]. However, only the impact on edge-cloud bandwidth and data transfer is considered, without addressing the impact on edge analytics. [17] targets an adaptive streaming-based version of k-means. This solution starts with initial candidate clusters, trying to assign each new data point in the online phase to the nearest cluster, and only does a complete re-clustering if the clusters are not valid anymore. A validity check is done by analyzing the input stream's probability density function, where high deviations signal a concept data drift and require a new cluster initialization. Still, they do not consider the tolerance-dependent variance checks of clusters, as in SymED. Similarly, [20] considers data-sharing edge concepts, while [2] deals with the bandwidth limitation. However, no online concepts are considered with IoT data streams.

Although there exist different techniques for raw data compression in cloud and edge [21], we particularly focus on SR for the edge. SR allows for direct analytics on compressed data, while also enabling reconstruction of the original data. We believe this is a crucial advantage over other raw data compression techniques, reducing both network and storage usage for critical IoT systems.

## 6 Conclusions and Future Work

We proposed SymED, a real-time online symbolic representation method for resource-constrained edge environments. We distribute the symbolic conversion workload between IoT sender and edge receiver devices, and also minimize the number of transmitted bytes between them. Hyperparameters in SymED, such as *tol*, balance reconstruction error and compression performance, while $\alpha$ determines the adaptability to streaming data through online normalization. SymED achieves on average 9.5% on compression rate and dimension reduction rate, with a mean online reconstruction error of 13.25 in the DTW space, while taking a mean time of 42 ms to compute a symbol. Online SymED improves on reconstruction accuracy and adapting to data stream distribution, with a slight overhead in compression and computational efficiency, compared to the offline base algorithm ABBA. Our future plans involve enhancing SymED's performance for time-critical IoT applications by incorporating different clustering mechanisms.

**Acknowledgements and Data Availability.** This work has been partially funded through the Runtime Control in Multi Clouds (RUCON), Austrian Science Fund (FWF): Y904-N31 START-Programm, 2015, Sustainable Watershed Management Through IoT-Driven Artificial Intelligence (SWAIN), CHIST-ERA-19-CES-005, Austrian Science Fund (FWF), 2021, Standalone Project Transprecise Edge Computing (Triton), Austrian Science Fund (FWF): P 36870-N, 2023, Flagship Project High-Performance Integrated Quantum Computing (HPQC) # 897481 Austrian Research Promotion Agency (FFG), 2023. The artifact associated with this paper is available in the *figshare* repository https://doi.org/10.6084/m9.figshare.23536992 [8].

## References

1. Attig, A., Perner, P.: The problem of normalization and a normalized similarity measure by online data. Trans. Case Based Reason. **4**(1), 3–17 (2011)
2. Azar, J., Makhoul, A., Barhamgi, M., Couturier, R.: An energy efficient IoT data compression approach for edge machine learning. Futur. Gener. Comput. Syst. **96**, 168–175 (2019)
3. Berndt, D.J., Clifford, J.: Using dynamic time warping to find patterns in time series. In: Proceedings of the 3rd International Conference on Knowledge Discovery and Data Mining, pp. 359–370 (1994)
4. Dau, H.A., et, a.: The UCR time series classification archive (2019). https://www.cs.ucr.edu/eamonn/time_series_data_2018/ Accessed 03 Apr 2023
5. Elsworth, S., et al.: Abba: Adaptive Brownian bridge-based symbolic aggregation of time series. Data Min. Knowl. Disc. **34**(4), 1175–1200 (2020)
6. Ganz, F., Barnaghi, P., Carrez, F.: Information abstraction for heterogeneous real world internet data. IEEE Sens. J. **13**(10), 3793–3805 (2013)
7. Gupta, V., Hewett, R.: Adaptive normalization in streaming data. In: Proceedings of the 2019 3rd International Conference on Big Data Research, pp. 12–17 (2019)
8. Hofstätter, D., Ilager, S., Lujic, I., Brandic, I.: Artifact and instructions to generate experimental results for Euro-Par 2023 paper: SymED: Adaptive and Online Symbolic Representation of Data on the Edge, 2023. https://doi.org/10.6084/m9.figshare.23536992
9. Khan, M.A., Khan, A., Khan, M.N., Anwar, S.: A novel learning method to classify data streams in the internet of things. In: 2014 National Software Engineering Conference, pp. 61–66. IEEE (2014)
10. Kolozali, S., et al.: A knowledge-based approach for real-time IoT data stream annotation and processing. In: 2014 IEEE International Conference on Internet of Things, and IEEE Green Computing and Communications and IEEE Cyber, Physical and Social Computing (CPSCom), pp. 215–222. IEEE (2014)
11. Lin, J., Keogh, E., Wei, L., Lonardi, S.: Experiencing SAX: a novel symbolic representation of time series. Data Min. Knowl. Disc. **15**, 107–144 (2007)

12. Liu, B., Hou, Y., et al.: Online load data compression and reconstruction based on segmental symbolic aggregate approximation. In: 2021 IEEE 5th Conference on Energy Internet and Energy System Integration (EI2), pp. 466–472. IEEE (2021)
13. Lu, T., Xia, W., Zou, X., Xia, Q.: Adaptively compressing IoT data on the resource-constrained edge. In: 3rd {USENIX} Workshop on Hot Topics in Edge Computing (HotEdge 20) (2020)
14. MacGregor, J., Harris, T.: The exponentially weighted moving variance. J. Qual. Technol. **25**(2), 106–118 (1993)
15. Papageorgiou, A., Cheng, B., Kovacs, E.: Real-time data reduction at the network edge of internet-of-things systems. In: 11th International Conference on Network and Service Management (CNSM), pp. 284–291. IEEE (2015)
16. Pham, Q., Liu, C., Steven, H.: Continual normalization: rethinking batch normalization for online continual learning. In: International Conference on Learning Representations (2022)
17. Puschmann, D., Barnaghi, P., Tafazolli, R.: Adaptive clustering for dynamic IoT data streams. IEEE Internet Things J. **4**(1), 64–74 (2016)
18. Ranjan, R.: Streaming big data processing in datacenter clouds. IEEE Cloud Comput. **1**(1), 78–83 (2014)
19. Satyanarayanan, M.: The emergence of edge computing. Computer **50**(1), 30–39 (2017)
20. Trivedi, A., et al.: Sharing and caring of data at the edge. In: 3rd {USENIX} Workshop on Hot Topics in Edge Computing (2020)
21. Wang, J.B., Zhang, J., Ding, C., Zhang, H., Lin, M., Wang, J.: Joint optimization of transmission bandwidth allocation and data compression for mobile-edge computing systems. IEEE Commun. Lett. **24**(10), 2245–2249 (2020)
22. Zhu, Y., Shasha, D.: Efficient elastic burst detection in data streams. In: Proceedings of the Ninth ACM SIGKDD International Conference on Knowledge Discovery and Data Mining, pp. 336–345 (2003)

# MMExit: Enabling Fast and Efficient Multi-modal DNN Inference with Adaptive Network Exits

Xiaofeng Hou[1], Jiacheng Liu[1], Xuehan Tang[1], Chao Li[1(✉)], Kwang-Ting Cheng[2(✉)], Li Li[1], and Minyi Guo[1]

[1] Department of Computer Science and Engineering, Shanghai Jiao Tong University, Shanghai, China
lichao@cs.sjtu.edu.cn
[2] ACCESS - AI Chip Center for Emerging Smart Systems, InnoHK Centers, The Hong Kong University of Science and Technology, Hong Kong, China
timcheng@ust.hk

**Abstract.** Multi-modal DNNs have been demonstrated to outperform the best uni-modal DNNs by fusing information from different modalities. However, the performance improvement of multi-modal DNNs is always associated with an incredible increase in computational cost (e.g., network parameters, MAC operations, etc.) to handle more modalities, which ultimately makes them impractical for many real-world applications where computing capability is limited.

In this paper, we propose *MMExit*, a multi-modal exit architecture that allows for computing appropriate modalities and layers to predict results for different data samples. To this end, we define a novel metric called *utility of exit (UoE)* to measure the correlations of performance and computational cost for different exits. We then use an *equivalent modality serialization* method to map the two-dimensional exit space into an equivalent linear space and rank the exits according to their UoE to achieve fast and adaptive inference. To train the *MMExit* network, we devise *a joint loss function* which synthesizes the features of different modalities and layers. Our results show that *MMExit* can slash up to 48.72% of MAC operations with the best performance compared to SOTA multi-modal architectures.

**Keywords:** Multi-modal DNNs · Energy-efficient AI · Adaptive Inference

## 1 Introduction

Multi-modal DNNs [11,16,27] have recently attracted lots of attention due to their superior performance. As shown in Fig. 1, a multi-modal DNN typically consists of multiple parallel encoder networks that take different modality data as inputs to obtain the modality features and a subsequent fusion and decision network that fuses the different features as well as outputs the final decision. By fusing the information from different modalities, multi-modal DNNs have been demonstrated to outperform the best uni-modal DNNs in many application domains. For example, in multimedia applications, the multi-modal DNNs have been shown to outperform the best uni-modal DNNs by 5%–30% accuracy through fusing vast amounts of image, video and audio data [2].


J. Cano et al. (Eds.): Euro-Par 2023, LNCS 14100, pp. 426–440, 2023.
https://doi.org/10.1007/978-3-031-39698-4_29

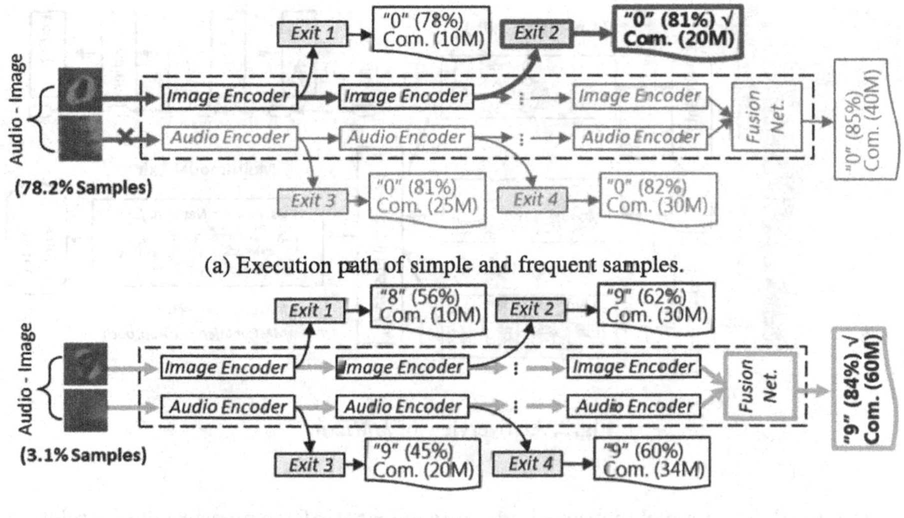


(a) Execution path of simple and frequent samples.



(b) Execution path of difficult but less frequent samples.

**Fig. 1.** The execution paths for different data samples in *avmnist* with *MMExit*.

Despite the performance advantages, multi-modal DNNs often involve more computational costs such as network parameters and Multiply-Accumulate (MAC) operations [23]. It has been shown that multi-modal DNNs can lead to a $0.1\times$–$80\times$ increase in network parameters compared to uni-modal DNNs [16,17]. This would ultimately increase the latency and energy required by inference tasks. For example, experimental results on powerful servers with 17 GPUs and 32 CPUs installed show that the increased parameters of the multi-modal DNNs can lead to a $10\times$ increase in inference latency and power consumption in affective computing applications [16]. This would further make multi-modal DNNs prohibitive in many real-world scenarios such as next-generation mobile robots where computational capability is limited.

In this paper, we propose *MMExit*, an adaptive multi-modal exit architecture that enables the optimal performance and computational cost tradeoffs in multi-modal DNN inference tasks for different data samples. *MMExit* exploits a unique feature of multi-modal DNNs in that different modalities and layers can provide different levels of confidence at different computational costs. For example, it has been shown that text-based features perform better than visual or auditory features in a multi-modal language-emotion analysis task [1]. Therefore, *MMExit* is designed to predict results for most data samples with a minimal computational cost by exiting from appropriate modality and layers as shown in Fig. 1. For very complex data samples, which happen less frequently, *MMExit* would compute more modalities to guarantee better accuracy.

Unlike the previous early-exit architectures for uni-modal DNNs, where exits are explicitly related to the depth of layers, *MMExit* is a **new problem of finding an optimal exit in a 2-dimensional (2D) space composed of modalities and layers**. In this regard, one important challenge is to decide in which modality and layers to exit to reduce the computation cost of the inference task while maintaining high accuracy. To

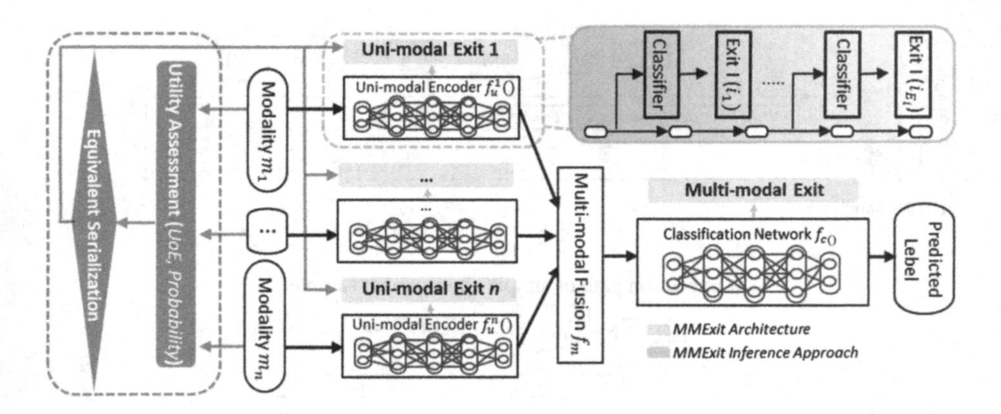


**Fig. 2.** An overview of *MMExit*.

this end, we define a novel metric called *utility of exit (UoE)* to measure the correlations of performance gain and computational effort for different exits. We also use *an equivalent serialization method* to map the 2D exit space into an equivalent linear space which enables us to find the optimal exit fast. Another challenge is how to train the *MMExit* DNNs efficiently. We devise *a joint loss function* which synthesizes the features of different modalities and layers. The experimental results show that *MMExit* can reduce 22.64%–48.72% MACs and 21.44%–45.02% parameters of multi-modal fusion without any performance degradation. To sum up, we make the following contributions:

1. We propose *MMExit*, a multi-modal exit architecture to adaptively reduce the computational cost in multi-modal DNN inference tasks with different data samples.
2. We design a new metric called the utility of exit and the equivalent serialization method to navigate the multi-modal DNN inference tasks to exit adaptively.
3. We define a joint loss function that synthesizes the features of different modalities and layers with a double-stage adaptive re-weighting method to train the *MMExit*.
4. We verify *MMExit* with an extensive number of real-world multi-modal DNN models and datasets based on an open-sourced benchmark.

## 2 *MMExit*: Architecture Design

### 2.1 Problem Setup

**Background.** We first briefly introduce the fundamental multi-modal DNN architecture. Without loss of generality, we consider a classification task that leverages the multi-modal DNN to process and fuse the features from $n$ modalities. We use $m_1, ..., m_n$ to denote these modalities. To train the multi-modal DNN, we construct a dataset that contains $N$ data samples denoted as $\mathcal{D} = \{(x^i_{m_1}, x^i_{m_2}, \cdots, x^i_{m_n}, y_i)\}_{i=1}^N$. The goal is to predict the correct label $y$ with the network and dataset. Figure 2 shows the common structure of the multi-modal DNN. It consists of multiple, parallel modality encoder sub-networks as well as a sequential fusion and classification sub-network, i.e., icons highlighted by black border and white background. These encoder sub-networks are responsible for obtaining the representations of different modalities. Typically, they can be implemented with standard uni-modal DNNs, determined by the characteristics of modality [16]. After that, the fusion and classification sub-network is used to merge the representations of all modalities and produce the final prediction.

**The *MMExit* Architecture.** The key behind *MMExit* is that for most data samples, the feature learned from a fraction of modalities is sufficient to produce the final prediction $y$ with high confidence. For example, it is widely accepted that most data samples can be addressed using simple models [8]. In multi-modal settings, some modalities achieve better performance than others in many cases [16].

Therefore, in the *MMExit* network, we obtain the prediction label $y$ through the exits from the modality encoder sub-networks or the exit after fusion. As shown in Fig. 2, we define two classes of exits. The first is the encoder exit at each encoder sub-network and the second is the fusion exit at the fusion and classification sub-network. Assuming $n$ modalities in the multi-modal DNN application, any inference task has $n + 1$ exits including $n$ encoder exits and one fusion exit. For the $i$-th sub-network, we assume the $j$-th exit point in it is denoted as $e^{(m_i,j)}$. We use a lightweight classification head to transform the features learned at this point into the final predictions.

$$y_e^{(m_i,j)} = f_e^{(m_i,j)}(z_i; \theta_e^{(m_i,j)}) \tag{1}$$

where $y_e^{(m_i,j)}$ is a vector that represents the predicted probability. Then, we calculate the normalized entropy as the confidence of the prediction result from exit $e^{(i,j)}$ as,

$$H(e^{(m_i,j)}) = -\frac{1}{\log(C)} y_e^{(m_i,j)} \log(y_e^{(m_i,j)}) \tag{2}$$

where $C$ is the number of classes in the classification task.

### 2.2 Discussion on *MMExit*

In the DNN inference process, the optimal exit with minimal computational cost is the earliest one to meet the accuracy. In the previous uni-modal early-exit architecture [24], the accuracy and computational cost of an exit is only related to the depth of layers. Thus, it is easy to find the optimal exit fast in the uni-modal network due to the explicit relationship between different exits. However, *in MMExit architecture, there is no fixed relationship between performance and computational cost of the exits on different modality encoder sub-networks*. Thus, we have to determine which modality should be processed in advance in order to provide the expected prediction results with the least amount of computation. In the training process, the uni-modal exit network only needs to set different weights for different exits. However, *when training the MMExit networks, we must determine the weights for different modalities and exits*, which requires a joint training approach to improve the robustness of *MMExit*.

## 3 *MMExit*: Adaptive Inference

### 3.1 Utility Assessment Metric

We define a metric named utility of exit (UoE) to measure the benefit of an exit in terms of its accuracy and computational cost. A larger UoE for an exit indicates the benefit of the performance improvement from the exit outweighs its computational cost. Conversely, a smaller UoE means that the utility of the exit is not good. The mission of the inference process is to find the optimal exit that has the highest UoE, thus avoiding the waste of computation while satisfying the performance.

To compute the UoE of an encoder exit, for the $i$-th modality, we denote its modality encoder sub-network as $f_u^i(\cdot)$. We assume modality $m_i$ has $e_{m_i}$ different exits, forming a set of exit classification network, which denoted by $E_{m_i} = \langle f_e^{(m_i,1)}, f_e^{(m_i,2)}, ..., f_e^{(m_i,e_{m_i})} \rangle$. For the $j$-th exit $f_e^{(m_i,j)} \in E_{m_i}$ of modality encoder sub-network for modality $m_i$, we assume that it can achieve an accuracy of $a_{m_i}^j$ with a computational cost of $c_{m_i}^j$. Then, we can define the utility of the encoder exit as,

$$\mathcal{U}(e_{m_i}^j) = \lambda a_{m_i}^j - (c_{m_i}^j + \sum_{\substack{f:1 \to i-1 \\ g:1 \to e_{m_f}}} c_{m_f}^g + \sum_{\substack{f=i \\ g:1 \to j-1}} c_{m_f}^g) \tag{3}$$

where $\lambda$ represents the preference of different applications for performance and computational cost. Notably, we compute the UoE of the fusion exits in a similar way.

Then, we assume that for a standalone exit network a data sample will exit from $f_e^{(m_i,j)}$ with a probability of $p_{m_i}^j$. Thus, in the *MMExit* network, we formulate the probability of a sample exit from $y$-th exit in $x$-th modality as follows,

$$P_e(x,y) = \prod_{\substack{i:1 \to x-1 \\ j:1 \to e_{m_x}}} (1 - p_{m_i}^j) * \prod_{\substack{i=x \\ j:1 \to y-1}} (1 - p_{m_i}^j) * p_{m_x}^y \tag{4}$$

### 3.2 Equivalent Modality Serialization

In the inference process of *MMExit*, the ultimate goal is to generate an order of exits that can maximize the sum of the utility function for all data samples, which is formulated as,

$$\max \sum_{\substack{i:1 \to n \\ j:1 \to e_{m_i}}} \mathcal{U}(e_{m_i}^j) \tag{5}$$

As shown in Fig. 2, the order of exits in a modality encoder sub-network is fixed and the order between the encoder exits and fusion exit is also fixed. We only need to define the execution order of different modalities. Considering the execution order of the modalities as $O = \{o_1, o_2, ..., o_M\}$, the overall target turns to,

$$\arg\max_{O} \mathcal{U}(O) = \arg\max_{O} \sum_{\substack{i:1 \to M \\ j:1 \to e_{m_i}}} P_e(o_i, j) * \mathcal{U}(e_{o_i}^j) \tag{6}$$

This is a hard problem that cannot be solved with a naive method. To order the modalities, the most explicit way is to traverse all orders and select the order which maximizes the utility sum. However, there is a drawback in that the computational process requires traversing all possible modality orders, which leads to unacceptable computational cost when the number of modalities is large. Therefore, we define an equivalent metric $\phi$, which defines a fast way to select the optimal modality execution order. Assuming $e_{m_i}$ is equal to $e_m$ for all modalities and $p^j_{m_i}$ is approximately close to $p$ for all exits (the experiments show that our method is able to achieve near-optimal performance even when these assumptions are not satisfied.), the $\phi$ is formulated as,

$$\begin{aligned} \phi(i) = (1 - q^{e_m}) * \sum_{j:1 \to e_m} q^{j-1} * p * (\lambda a^j_{m_i} - c^j_{m_i} \\ - \sum_{\substack{f=i \\ g:1 \to j-1}} c^g_{m_f}) - \sum_{j:1 \to e_m} (q^{e_m} * q^{j-1} * p * \sum_{\substack{f=i \\ g:1 \to e_m}} c^g_{m_f}) \end{aligned} \tag{7}$$

The validity of the proposed metric $\phi$ follows the following theorem (the proof is omitted due to the limit of space, but can be easily established using proof by contradiction).

**Theorem 1.** *Given a modality execution ordering* $O = \{o_1, o_2, \cdots, o_n\}$, *if it is satisfied that for any* $i$ *and* $j$ $(i \leq j)$ *we have* $\phi(i) \geq \phi(j)$. *Then we can conclude that* $O$ *is the optimal modality execution ordering.*

### 3.3 *MMExit* Inference Process

In the inference process, the mission of the inference process is to find the optimal exit for a set of data samples. To this end, we can profile the correlation between performance gain and computational cost for each modality by computing the UoE. Then, we rank all the modalities according to their utility functions in an order $O = \{o_1, o_2, \cdots, o_n\}$ with the equivalent serialization method. Notably that the accuracy $a^j_{m_i}$ and the probability $p^j_{m_i}$ can be collected in the training phase. In addition, we leverage a validation set to estimate it and then dynamically change the ordering.

## 4 *MMExit*: Joint Training

### 4.1 Joint Loss Function

To train the proposed *MMExit* classification network, we use the cross-entropy between the predicted and real label as the loss function. We assume the loss function for the $j$-th exit from the $i$-th modality encoder sub-network and the fusion sub-network is respectively represented as $\mathcal{L}^j_i$ and $\mathcal{L}_c$,

$$\mathcal{L}^j_i(y^j_i, \hat{y}) = -\sum \hat{y} \log(y^j_i); \quad \mathcal{L}_c(y_c, \hat{y}) = -\sum \hat{y} \log(y_c) \tag{8}$$

where $\hat{y}$ is the real label and $y^j_i$ and $y_c$ is the predicted label.

Considering that the *MMExit* network has $n$ predicted labels from the $n$ encoder exits and one predicted label from the fusion exit, we formulate the overall loss function using the weighted sum of the losses from all exits.

$$\mathcal{L} = \sum_{i=1}^{M} \sum_{j=1}^{e_{m_i}} w_{ij} \mathcal{L}_i^j(y, \hat{y}) + \mathcal{L}_c(y, \hat{y}) \tag{9}$$

## 4.2 Objective Analysis

The training loss of the *MMExit* network is determined by the features of both the modalities and exit layers. We first analyze the effect of the modalities on training loss. We consider the multi-modal classification network $f_c(z; \theta_c)$ with parameters $\theta_c = \{W \in R^{d_{z_1}+d_{z_2}+\cdots,+d_{z_M}}, b \in R^M\}$ as shown in Sect. 2, the layer of which can be represented as,

$$f_c(x_i) = W\left[f_u^1\left(\theta_u^1, x_1^i\right) \oplus \cdots \oplus f_u^M\left(\theta_u^1, x_M^i\right)\right] + b \tag{10}$$

It's obvious that the weight matrix $W$ can be split into several blocks represented as $W = [W_{m_1}; W_{m_2}; \cdots ; W_{m_M}]$, then we can rewrite the above equation as,

$$f_c(x_i) = W_{m_1} \cdot f_u^1\left(\theta_u^1, x_1^i\right) + \cdots + W_{m_M} f_u^M\left(\theta^v, x_M^i\right) + b. \tag{11}$$

The update of the weight parameter is,

$$W_{m_i}^{t+1} == W_{m_i}^t - \eta \frac{1}{N} \sum_{j=1}^{N} \frac{\partial L}{\partial f_c(x_j)} f_u^i\left(\theta_u^i, x_i^j\right) \tag{12}$$

Then, we can update the overall loss as,

$$\frac{\partial L}{\partial f(x_i)_c} = \frac{e^{(f_c(x_i))_c}}{\sum_{k=1}^{M} e^{(f_c(x_i))_k}} - 1_{c=y_i} \tag{13}$$

where $f(x_i)_c$ is the logits output for class c. It is obvious that the overall gradient will be dominated by the stronger modality (with a smaller gradient), which finally makes the other modalities not converge to the optimal value. To alleviate this, we need to give larger weights to the strong modalities (with lower loss).

Then, we consider the effect of the multi-exit network. We assume training the exits at the sub-network for modality $i$ with loss $\mathcal{L}_i$. Some previous studies have found that training exits sequentially is sub-optimal compared to jointly optimizing all exits [12]. It involves two aspects of the learning objective. On the one hand, the earlier features are not sufficiently predictable and have larger gradients. On the other hand, the earlier part of the network will receive gradient back-propagation from all later exits. The gradient of the s-th block is contributed by the s-th node and the subsequent $(e_{m_i} - s)$ exits denoted as,

$$\nabla_{\theta_u^{i,s}} \mathcal{L}_i = \sum_{j=s}^{e_{m_i}} w_{m_i}^j \nabla_{\theta_u^{i,s}} \mathcal{L}_i^j \tag{14}$$

**Algorithm 1:** *MMExit* Training Algorithm

**Input**: Trained model $\mathcal{M}$, preference $\lambda$, threshold $\epsilon$.
**Output**: Trained *MMExit* model.

```
1  for i = 1, ··· , e do
2      Get the predictions from the model.
3      Calculate the losses and update the running mean according to Eq. (15).
4      if i % 2 = 0 then
5          Calculate {w_i^{m_i}}_{i=1}^M according to Eq. (16).
6          Calculate the loss L_e according to Eq. (17).
7      else
8          Calculate exit weights according to Eq. (16).
9          Calculate the loss L_o according to Eq. (18).
10     Update model parameters with gradient descent.
```

where $\theta_u^{i,s}$ is the features at s-th block. This illustrates that the earlier exits usually have more weight, making them more important in the optimization process and dominating the training process. So, we need to give smaller weights to the earlier exits, which have higher losses in the training process.

Training *MMExit* contains two conflict objectives in terms of the loss value [20]. For the multi-modal part, the training process can be dominated by strong modalities (with less loss), which suppresses the training of weak modalities and is not conducive to better performance of the overall multi-modal model. For the multi-exit part, its exit structure leads to the fact that the early blocks receive the gradient back-propagate from all the later exits, which leads to its possible domination of the whole training process, resulting in poor performance of the whole network. Traditional adaptive methods tend to solve one of these problems by weighting the losses according to the gradient values (or similar metrics) in various ways. They cannot be directly applied to more complex *MMExit* training.

### 4.3 *MMExit* Training Algorithm

Based on previous analysis, we propose a double-stage adaptive re-weighting method to train the *MMExit* network. Firstly, we use the running average of the gradients to weigh the predictive capabilities of different exits. A high gradient always implies a fairly large gap between the predicted label and the true label. For exit $j$ in each modality $i$, we denote the gradient as $g_{(i,j)}$, then we can formulate the average gradient at step $t$ as,

$$\bar{g}_{(i,j)}^{t} = \alpha \bar{g}_{(i,j)}^{t-1} + (1-\alpha) g_{(i,j)} \tag{15}$$

where $\alpha$ is the weight parameters to control the importance of the current value and previous values. Then, we define the weight for different exits as,

$$w_{i,j}^{t} = \frac{\exp(\bar{g}_{(i,j)}^{t}/\tau)}{(m_i - j + 1)\sum_{x \in \mathcal{Q}} \exp(\bar{g}_{x}^{t}/\tau)} \tag{16}$$

**Table 1.** Description of the multi-modal Datasets used.

| Dataset | Data Samples | *Modality* (Encoder sub-network) | Classes |
|---|---|---|---|
| *sarcasm* [5] | 690 | *spoken language* (BERT/GloVe), *visual* (ResNet), *audio* (Librosa) | 2 |
| *mosi* [25] | 2,199 | | 5 |
| *mosei* [25] | 22,777 | | 5 |
| *avmnist* [21] | 70,000 | *image* (Raw), *audio* (Spectogram) | 10 |

where $\mathcal{Q}$ is the set of exits considered in the update step, $\tau$ is the temperature parameter for softmax function. We decrease the temperature parameter during training to help the model focus on some hard parts of the model. With this, we can make better use of the strong modalities and alleviate the effect of the earlier sub-network. Then we can train *MMExit* effectively by balancing different components in the network.

Given the aforementioned discussions, we introduce a novel double-stage cross-training strategy to train the *MMExit* network. The proposed training algorithm is depicted in Algorithm 1. The training process comprises two stages that alternate in consecutive epochs. Specifically, in the even-numbered epochs, the training of the multi-modal part of the network is achieved by using the following model representation,

$$\min \mathcal{L}_e = \sum_{i=1}^{M} \mathcal{L}_i^{m_i} + \mathcal{L}_c \tag{17}$$

In the odd-numbered epochs, the model trains the remaining exits and is denoted as,

$$\min \mathcal{L}_o = \sum_{i=1}^{M} \sum_{j=1}^{m_i-1} \mathcal{L}_i^j \tag{18}$$

# 5 Experiments and Evaluations

## 5.1 Experiment Setup

**Implementation.** We conduct our experiment based on 4 representative multi-modal DNNs and datasets provided by the *Multibench* benchmark [16] from real-world applications (details are shown in Table 1). We construct the *MMExit* networks for each dataset by adding 2 exits per modality to their *late fusion (LF)* networks. LF is the most fundamental method that combines multiple modalities with the concatenation operation. We implement the exits by using one linear layer, which only results in an extra computational cost of less than 0.02% to produce the prediction label. We train and run all these models on a server with one GeForce RTX 2080Ti GPU. We run each experiment 5 times with different random seeds for reliability. Notably that it is easy to apply our *MMExit* method to other state-of-the-art multi-modal networks such as *MIM*, *TF* and *LRTF* to reduce their computational effort. However, for the space limitation, we only apply the *MMExit* to the *Humor Knowledge enriched Transformer (HKT)* [9],

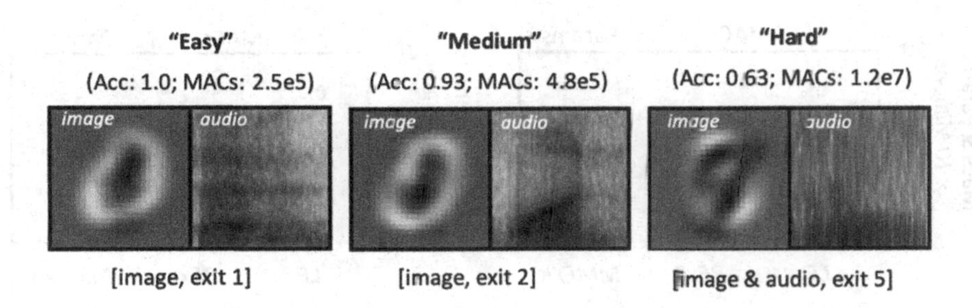


**Fig. 3.** Visualization of *MMExit* under the *avmnist* dataset.

which is one of the latest multi-modal transformer networks and omit the most content of the integration of *MMExit* with other fusion methods.

**Baselines and the State-of-the-Art.** We use the ***late fusion (LF)*** method as our baseline. We also compare *MMExit* with both the uni-modal methods and the most representative multi-modal methods. In each of the ***uni-modal models (Uni1–Uni3)***, we only use the encoder sub-network of one modality and connect it to the classification network to obtain the output predictions. Among these multi-modal methods, ***Tensor fusion network (TF)*** [26] uses tensor outer product to fuse information from different modalities. ***Low rank tensor fusion network (LRTF)*** [18] leverages a modality-specific set of low-rank factors to improve the efficiency of tensor fusion. ***Multiplicative interaction model (MIM)*** [13] further generalizes the tensor products to capture and learn the interactions between different modalities. We also implement another multi-exit method called ***RExit***, which inserts exits without *the equivalent serialization* optimization.

## 5.2 Visualization

We first illustrate that *MMExit* has the ability to adaptively exit from appropriate modalities and network layers for different data samples. In Fig. 3, we plot the results for the *avmnist* dataset which classifies data samples based on two modalities including *image* and *audio*. The data samples of *image* are represented in pixels, and the data samples of *audio* are represented with a $112 \times 112$ spectrogram. First of all, we can see that for a very **"Easy"** sample, *MMExit* is able to perform an accurate recognition at the first exit which significantly saves the computational effort. For more complex sample, *MMExit* extracts more features from the modality of *image* by exiting later at the second exit to obtain the prediction result with high accuracy. For both **"Easy"** and **"Medium"** samples, they can be classified accurately by exiting from different layers of the *image* modality. However, for some **"Hard"** samples, which happens less frequently, it is difficult to obtain its correct label only from the *image* modality. In this case, *MMExit* has to complete both *image* and *audio* modalities to compute the final prediction.

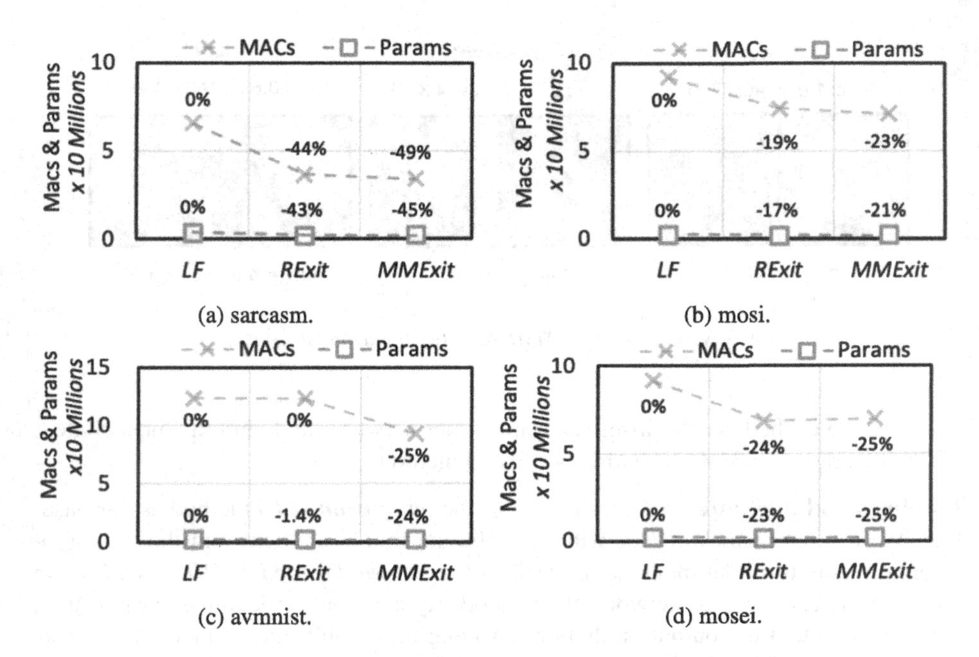


**Fig. 4.** Computational effort under the two exit schemes.

### 5.3 Ablation Study

**Utility Analysis:** To evaluate the equivalent serialization method, we compare both the performance and computation cost including network parameters and MAC operations under *RExit* and *MMExit*. As shown in Fig. 4, both the *RExit* and *MMExit* can reduce the number of MACs and parameters of the *LF* baseline method. For these datasets, *MMExit* can reduce the computation load by 23%–49%. Although *RExit* can reduce 1.4%–44% computational effort as well, *RExit* cannot guarantee the performance (i.e., accuracy and F-scores) with unawareness of the trade-off between the accuracy gain and computational effort as shown in Fig. 5. Overall, the proposed *MMExit* can always find the optimal tradeoffs between computation load and performance.

**Joint Training Algorithm:** To verify the effectiveness of the training algorithm, we compare it with two commonly-used training strategies. In Fig. 6, the *Eloss* represents the ones which treat and train all the exits equally with the same weight [22]. The *Sloss* stands for the ones which group different layers and assign different groups with static weights increasing from previous to latter groups. In the figure, the more overlap of two bars means requiring more computational effort to obtain the performance gains. For example, *Eloss* and *Sloss* explicitly consumes more MACs than *MMExit* . We can see that *MMExit* always intends to guarantee higher accuracy and less computation load compared with other training loss functions under all the datasets.

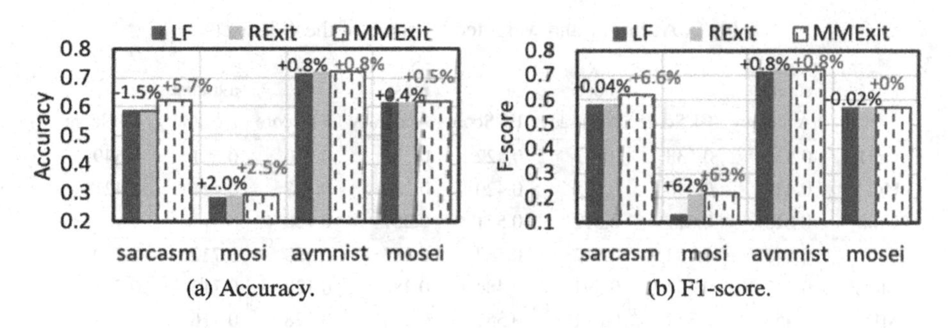


(a) Accuracy. (b) F1-score.

**Fig. 5.** Performance comparison of the two exit schemes.

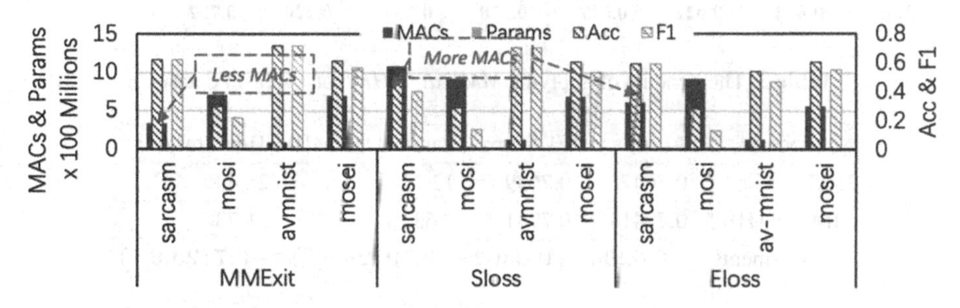


**Fig. 6.** The impact of different training algorithms on the performance gain and computational effort of *MMExit*.

## 5.4 Performance Evaluation

In Table 2, we compare the performance of *MMExit* with both the uni-modal and multi-modal methods under various datasets. It is evident that *MMExit* obtains better output predictions than the uni-modal models by fusing multiple modalities. In addition, *MMExit* can achieve the same or even higher accuracy and F-scores than the *LF* baseline method in all the scenarios. It also achieves the best performance compared to the most state-of-the-art multi-modal methods. It is notable that *MMExit* can be easily applied to more advanced multi-modal networks such as *MIM*, *LRTF* and *HKT* to reduce their computational effort. Table 3 shows that applying the *MMExit* to *HKT* can reduce its parameters, thus significantly reducing the inference latency and improving the performance. Overall, *MMExit* can reduce the computational effort of multi-modal networks without any performance degradation.

## 5.5 Reduction of Computation

An important design objective of *MMExit* is to reduce the computational effort of the existing multi-modal methods. In this part, we compare the MACs and parameters of different methods. As shown in Fig. 7, the *MMExit* reduces 22.64%–48.72% MACs and 21.44%–45.02% parameters of the *LF* method. It even consumes less MACs and parameters that the uni-modal networks. For example, *MMExit* has 13.0% less MACs than the uni-modal network for the *mosi* dataset. Combined with the results in Table 2,

**Table 2.** Accuracy and weighted F1 score of the 4 datasets.

| | sarcasm | | mosei | | mosi | | avmnist | |
|---|---|---|---|---|---|---|---|---|
| | Accuracy | F1 Score | Accuracy | F1 Score | Accuracy | F1 Score | Accuracy | F1 Score |
| Uni1 | 0.536 | 0.538 | 0.573 | 0.422 | 0.286 | 0.130 | 0.651 | 0.649 |
| Uni2 | 0.470 | 0.440 | 0.575 | 0.420 | 0.289 | 0.137 | 0.421 | 0.421 |
| Uni3 | 0.613 | 0.611 | 0.612 | 0.571 | 0.287 | 0.128 | – | – |
| TF | 0.535 | 0.492 | 0.612 | 0.567 | 0.287 | 0.130 | 0.712 | 0.710 |
| LRTF | 0.467 | 0.364 | 0.591 | 0.484 | 0.287 | 0.128 | 0.715 | 0.714 |
| MIM | 0.455 | 0.352 | 0.611 | 0.557 | 0.285 | 0.128 | 0.716 | 0.714 |
| LF | 0.588 | 0.583 | 0.614 | 0.570 | 0.288 | 0.134 | 0.717 | 0.715 |
| *MMExit* | **0.622** | **0.622** | **0.617** | **0.570** | **0.295** | **0.220** | **0.722** | **0.720** |

**Table 3.** The benefits of applying *MMExit* to *HKT* on sarcasm dataset.

| Methods | Accuracy | F1 Score | Parameters (MB) | Time (ms) |
|---|---|---|---|---|
| HKT | 0.7647 | 0.7639 | 12.12 | 28.43 |
| MMExit+HKT | 0.7941 | 0.7941 | 8.63 | 21.73 |
| Improvements | $\mathbf{+0.0294}$ | $\mathbf{+0.0302}$ | $\mathbf{-3.50}$ **(28.9%)** | $\mathbf{-6.7}$ **(23.6%)** |

*MMExit* offers the probability to improve the existing model in terms of performance and efficiency, which is important for real-world deployments. Moreover, the reduction in computation complexity would lead to additional benefits such as speeding up the inference processes as shown in Table 3.

## 6 Related Work

**Multi-modal DNNs:** Multi-modal deep neural networks [27] are designed to merge complementary information from various modalities like text, audio, image, etc. They have been demonstrated to outperform the uni-modal networks in many application fields [16]. The most typical multi-modal architecture consists of multiple heterogeneous encoders to obtain representations of different modalities. These representations are then fused using either early fusion methods [19] or late fusion methods [3]. Recently, multi-modal transformers [14] are proposed, which are powerful but computationally intensive, using only transformers to obtain and fuse multi-modal features. *MMExit is orthogonal to all these methods. It can be used to reduce their computational effort.*

**Early Exit Neural Network:** Early exit which has been extensively studied for uni-modal DNN inference tasks [8], is the most similar to our work. Compared to other state-of-the-art neural network (NN) compression methods such as pruning [6] and quantization [4], early exit [7,8,15,22] aims to reduce the computation of network layers adapted to different inference tasks, thus making DNNs more applicable in some resource-limited application scenarios. For example, some previous work leverages

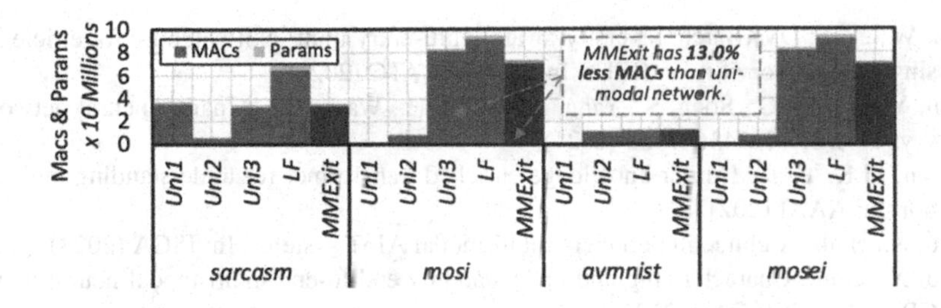


**Fig. 7.** Comparison of computational effort.

early exit [8, 10, 22] to adapt edge DNN tasks to resource-limited AIoT devices. *MMExit is a new adaptive neural architecture for multi-modal DNNs.*

## 7 Conclusion

While multi-modal DNNs have culminated in significant accuracy gain, they also lead to an explosive increase in computational cost, which would hinder their deployment in many real-world applications. To address this, we propose a novel multi-modal exit architecture called *MMExit*. To the best of our knowledge, it is the first multi-modal exit network that provides adaptive inference with minimal computational effort. *MMExit* shows great potential in applying multi-modal networks to the next-generation resource-constrained scenarios such as smart networking devices, mobile robots, etc.

**Acknowledgements.** This work is supported in part by the National Key R&D Program of China under grant No.2021ZD0110104, and the National Natural Science Foundation of China under grant No.62122053. It was also partially supported by ACCESS - AI Chip Center for Emerging Smart Systems, InnoHK funding, Hong Kong SAR. We thank all the anonymous reviewers for their valuable feedback.

## References

1. Akhtar, M.S., Chauhan, D.S., Ghosal, D., Poria, S., Ekbal, A., Bhattacharyya, P.: Multi-task learning for multi-modal emotion recognition and sentiment analysis. In: NAACL-HLT (2019)
2. Arevalo, J., Solorio, T., Montes-y Gómez, M., González, F.A.: Gated multimodal units for information fusion. In: ICLR (2017)
3. Bach, F.R., Lanckriet, G.R., Jordan, M.I.: Multiple kernel learning, conic duality, and the SMO algorithm. In: ICML (2004)
4. Bhattacharjee, A., et al.: MIME: adapting a single neural network for multi-task inference with memory-efficient dynamic pruning. In: DAC (2022)
5. Castro, S., Hazarika, D., Pérez-Rosas, V., Zimmermann, R., Mihalcea, R., Poria, S.: Towards multimodal sarcasm detection (an _obviously_ perfect paper). In: ACL (2019)
6. Choi, K., Yang, H.: A GPU architecture aware fine-grain pruning technique for deep neural networks. In: Sousa, L., Roma, N., Tomás, P. (eds.) Euro-Par 2021. LNCS, vol. 12820, pp. 217–231. Springer, Cham (2021). https://doi.org/10.1007/978-3-030-85665-6_14

7. Cui, W., et al.: DVABatch: diversity-aware multi-entry multi-exit batching for efficient processing of DNN services on GPUs. In: USENIX ATC (2022)
8. Han, Y., Huang, G., Song, S., Yang, L., Wang, H., Wang, Y.: Dynamic neural networks: a survey. TPAMI **44**, 7436–7456 (2021)
9. Hasan, M.K., et al.: Humor knowledge enriched transformer for understanding multimodal humor. In: AAAI (2021)
10. Hou, X., et al.: Architecting efficient multi-modal AIoT systems. In: ISCA (2023)
11. Hou, X., et al.: Characterizing and understanding end-to-end multi-modal neural networks on GPUs. In: IEEE CAL (2022)
12. Huang, G., Chen, D., Li, T., Wu, F., van der Maaten, L., Weinberger, K.Q.: Multi-scale dense networks for resource efficient image classification. In: ICLR (2018)
13. Jayakumar, S.M., et al.: Multiplicative interactions and where to find them. In: ICLR (2020)
14. Kim, W., Son, B., Kim, I.: ViLT: vision-and-language transformer without convolution or region supervision. In: ICML (2021)
15. Laskaridis, S., Kouris, A., Lane, N.D.: Adaptive inference through early-exit networks: design, challenges and directions. In: MobiSys (2021)
16. Liang, P.P., et al.: MultiBench: multiscale benchmarks for multimodal representation learning. In: NeurIPS (2021)
17. Liu, J., Hou, X., Tang, F.: Fine-grained machine teaching with attention modeling. In: AAAI (2020)
18. Liu, Z., Shen, Y., Lakshminarasimhan, V.B., Liang, P.P., Zadeh, A., Morency, L.P.: Efficient low-rank multimodal fusion with modality-specific factors. In: ACL (2018)
19. Neverova, N., Wolf, C., Taylor, G.W., Nebout, F.: Multi-scale deep learning for gesture detection and localization. In: Agapito, L., Bronstein, M.M., Rother, C. (eds.) ECCV 2014. LNCS, vol. 8925, pp. 474–490. Springer, Cham (2015). https://doi.org/10.1007/978-3-319-16178-5_33
20. Peng, X., Wei, Y., Deng, A., Wang, D., Hu, D.: Balanced multimodal learning via on-the-fly gradient modulation. In: CVPR (2022)
21. Pham, H., Liang, P.P., Manzini, T., Morency, L.P., Póczos, B.: Found in translation: learning robust joint representations by cyclic translations between modalities. In: AAAI (2019)
22. Scardapane, S., Scarpiniti, M., Baccarelli, E., Uncini, A.: Why should we add early exits to neural networks? Cogn. Comput. **12**, 954–966 (2020)
23. Sze, V., Chen, Y.H., Yang, T.J., Emer, J.S.: Efficient processing of deep neural networks. In: Synthesis Lectures on Computer Architecture (2020)
24. Teerapittayanon, S., McDanel, B., Kung, H.T.: BranchyNet: fast inference via early exiting from deep neural networks. In: ICPR (2016)
25. Vinyals, O., Toshev, A., Bengio, S., Erhan, D.: Show and tell: lessons learned from the 2015 MSCOCO image captioning challenge. TPAMI **39**, 652–663 (2016)
26. Zadeh, A., Chen, M., Poria, S., Cambria, E., Morency, L.P.: Tensor fusion network for multimodal sentiment analysis. In: EMNLP (2017)
27. Zhang, C., Yang, Z., He, X., Deng, L.: Multimodal intelligence: representation learning, information fusion, and applications. JSTSP **14**, 478–493 (2020)

# Theory and Algorithms

# Distributed Deep Multilevel Graph Partitioning

Peter Sanders and Daniel Seemaier(✉)

Karlsruhe Institute of Technology, Karlsruhe, Germany
{sanders,daniel.seemaier}@kit.edu

**Abstract.** We describe the engineering of the distributed-memory multilevel graph partitioner dKaMinPar. It scales to (at least) 8192 cores while achieving partitioning quality comparable to widely used sequential and shared-memory graph partitioners. In comparison, previous distributed graph partitioners scale only in more restricted scenarios and often induce a considerable quality penalty compared to non-distributed partitioners. When partitioning into a large number of blocks, they even produce infeasible solution that violate the balancing constraint. dKaMinPar achieves its robustness by a scalable distributed implementation of the deep-multilevel scheme for graph partitioning. Crucially, this includes new algorithms for balancing during refinement *and* coarsening.

**Keywords:** algorithms · distributed systems · graph partitioning · multilevel algorithm · balancing

## 1 Introduction

Graphs are a central concept of computer science used whenever we need to model relations between objects. Consequently, handling *large* graphs is very important for parallel processing. This often requires to *partition* these graphs into blocks of approximately equal weight with most edges inside the blocks (balanced graph partitioning). Applications include scientific computing, handling social networks, route planning, and graph databases [3].

In principle, *multilevel graph partitioners* (MGP) achieve high quality partitions for a wide range of input graphs $G$ with a good trade-off between quality and partitioning cost. They are based on first iteratively *coarsening* $G$ by contracting edges or small clusters. The resulting small graph $G'$ is then still a good representation of the overall input and an *initial partition* of $G'$ already induces a good partition of $G$. This is further improved by *uncoarsening* the graph and improving the partition on each level through refinement algorithms.

However, parallelizing multi-level graph partitioning has proved challenging over several decades. While shared-memory graph partitioners have recently matured to achieve high quality and reasonable scalability [1,9,10,14], current distributed-memory partitioners [13,19,25] induce a severe quality deterioration and often are not able to consistently achieve feasible (i.e. balanced) partitions. In particular, high quality partitioners do not scale to the number of processing


J. Cano et al. (Eds.): Euro-Par 2023, LNCS 14100, pp. 443–457, 2023.
https://doi.org/10.1007/978-3-031-39698-4_30

elements (PEs) available in large supercomputers. This situation is exacerbated by the fact that often the number of blocks $k$ should increase linearly in the number of PEs. Previous systems are not able to directly handle large $k$ running into even larger problems with achieving feasibility.

In this paper, we present dKaMinPar which addresses all these issues. Its basis is a distributed-memory adaptation of the deep-multilevel graph partitioning concept [9] that continues the multilevel approach deep into the initial partitioning phase. This makes the large $k$ case much easier and eliminates a parallelization bottleneck due to initial partitioning. Our coarsening and refinement algorithms are based on the label propagation approach previously used in several partitioners [13,19,25]. Label propagation [18,20] greedily moves vertices to other clusters/blocks when this reduces cuts (and does not violate the balance constraint). This is simple, fast, effective and robust even for complex networks. We develop a distributed-memory version with improved scalability, e.g., by using improved sparse-all-to-all primitives. Perhaps the main algorithmic innovation are new scalable distributed techniques allowing to maintain the balance constraint. During coarsening, a maximum cluster weight is approximated by unwinding contractions that lead to overweight clusters. During uncoarsening, block weight constraints are achieved by finding, selecting and applying globally "best" block moves.

The experiments described in Sect. 6 indicate that our implementation has achieved the main goals. It scales to at least 8 192 cores even for complex networks that did not scale on previous distributed solvers. Feasibility is guaranteed, even for large $k$ and quality is typically within a few percent of the shared-memory systems. Section 7 summarizes the results and discusses possible future improvements.

*Contributions*

- Scalable distributed implementation of deep multilevel graph partitioning.
- Simplicity using label propagation for both contraction and refinement.
- New scalable balanced coarsening and uncoarsening algorithm.
- Extensive evaluation on both large real world networks and huge synthetic networks from 3 input families.
- Quality comparable to shared-memory systems.
- Scalability up to (at least) $2^{13}$ machine cores and $2^{39}$ graph edges.
- Works both for complex networks and large number of blocks where previous systems often fail.

## 2 Preliminaries

*Notation and Definitions.* Let $G = (V, E, c, \omega)$ be an undirected graph with vertex weights $c : V \to \mathbb{N}_{>0}$, edge weights $\omega : E \to \mathbb{N}_{>0}$, $n := |V|$, and $m := |E|$. We extend $c$ and $\omega$ to sets, i.e., $c(V') := \sum_{v \in V'} c(v)$ and $\omega(E') := \sum_{e \in E'} \omega(e)$. $N(v) := \{u \mid \{u, v\} \in E\}$ denotes the neighbors of $v$. For some $V' \subseteq V$, $G[V']$ denotes the subgraph of $G$ induced by $V'$. We are looking for *blocks* of nodes

$\Pi := \{V_1, \ldots, V_k\}$ that partition $V$, i.e., $V_1 \cup \cdots \cup V_k = V$ and $V_i \cap V_j = \emptyset$ for $i \neq j$. The *balance constraint* demands that for all $i \in \{1, \ldots, k\}$, $c(V_i) \leq L_{\max} := \max\{(1+\varepsilon)\frac{c(V)}{k}, \frac{c(V)}{k} + \max_v c(v)\}$ for some imbalance parameter $\varepsilon$[1]. The objective is to minimize $\mathrm{cut}(\Pi) := \sum_{i<j} \omega(E_{ij})$ (weight of all cut edges), where $E_{ij} := \{\{u, v\} \in E \mid u \in V_i \text{ and } v \in V_j\}$. We call a vertex $u \in V_i$ that has a neighbor in $V_j$, $i \neq j$, a *boundary vertex*. A *clustering* $\mathcal{C} := \{C_1, \ldots, C_\ell\}$ is also a partition of $V$, where the number of blocks $\ell$ is not given in advance (there is also no balance constraint).

*Machine Model and Input Format.* The distributed memory model used in this work considers $P$ processing elements (PEs) numbered $1..P$, connected by a full-duplex, single ported communication network. The input graph is given with a (usually balanced) 1D vertex partition. Each PE is given a subgraph of the input graph (i.e., a block of the 1D partition) with consecutive vertices. An undirected edge $\{u, v\}$ is represented by two directed edges $(u, v)$, $(v, u)$, which are stored on the PEs owning the respective tail vertices. Vertices adjacent to vertices owned by other PEs are called *interface vertices* and are replicated as *ghost vertices* (i.e., without outgoing edges) on those PEs.

## 3 Related Work

There has been a huge amount of research on graph partitioning so that we refer the reader to overview papers [2–4,24] for most of the general material. Here, we focus on parallel algorithms for high-quality graph partitioning.

*Distributed Graph Partitioning.* Virtually all high-quality partitioners are based on the multilevel paradigm, e.g., ParMETIS [12,13], ParHIP [19,22] and others [5, 27]. These algorithms partition a graph in three phases. First, they build a hierarchy of successively coarse approximations of the input graph, usually by contracting matchings or clusters. Once the graph has only few vertices left (e.g., $n \leq Ck$ for some *contraction limit* $C$), the graph is partitioned into $k$ blocks. Finally, this partition is successively projected onto finer levels of the hierarchy and refined using local search algorithms.

The performance of multilevel algorithms is defined by the algorithmic components used for these phases. Partitioners designed for mesh-partitioning usually contract matchings to coarsen the graph [5,13,27]. However, this technique is not suitable for partitioning complex networks that only admit a small maximum matching. Thus, other partitioners use two-hop matchings [15] or size-constrained label propagation [9,11,19]. Due to its simple yet effective nature, the latter is also commonly used as a local search algorithm during refinement [1,6,9,11,13,19,27].

Label propagation has also been used by non-multilevel graph partitioning algorithms such as XtraPuLP [25], which reports scalability up to $2^{17}$ cores, a

[1] Traditionally, $L_k := (1+\varepsilon)\lceil\frac{c(V)}{k}\rceil$ is used as balance constraint. We relax this constraint since it is otherwise NP-complete to find a feasible partition.

level which has not been reached by multilevel algorithms. However, using label propagation without the multilevel paradigm comes with a pronounced decline in quality; Ref. [9] reports edge cuts for PuLP [26] (non-multilevel) that are on average more than twice as large as those of KaMinPar (multilevel). Across a large and diverse benchmark set, this is considered a lot; most multilevel algorithms achieve average edge cuts within a few percentage points of each other. Another class of highly scalable graph partitioners include geometric partitioners, which work on a geometric embedding of the graph. While these algorithms are orders of magnitude faster than multilevel algorithms [16], they generally compute larger edge cuts and only work on graphs with a meaningful geometric embedding.

*Deep Multilevel Graph Partitioning.* As plain MGP algorithms usually shrink the graph down to $Ck$ vertices, large values for $k$ break the assumption that the coarsest graph is small. This causes their performance to deteriorate [9]. Instead, recursive bipartitioning can be used to compute partitions with large $k$, but this induces an additional $\log k$ factor in running time and makes it more difficult to compute balanced partitions due to the lack of global view. *Deep multilevel graph partitioning* (deep MGP) [9] circumvents these problems by continuing coarsening deep into initial partitioning. More precisely, deep MGP coarsens the graph until only $2C$ vertices are left, independent of $k$. After bipartitioning the coarsest graphs, it maintains the invariant that a (coarse) graph with $n$ vertices is partitioned into $\min\{k, n/C\}$ blocks by using recursive bipartitioning on the current level. By using additional balancing techniques, partitioners based on deep MGP can obtain feasible high-quality partitions with a large number of blocks (e.g., $k \approx 1M$) while often being an order of magnitude faster than partitioners based on plain MGP. Compared to recursive bipartitioning the entire graph, it reduces the additional $\log k$ factor to $\log kC/n$. KaMinPar [9] is a scalable shared-memory implementation of deep MGP which uses size-constrained label propagation during coarsening and refinement.

## 4 Distributed Deep Multilevel Graph Partitioning

In this section, we present dKaMinPar, a distributed graph partitioner that leverages deep MGP. We first describe the distributed deep MGP scheme, which partitions a graph on $P$ PEs into $k$ blocks. For simplicity, we assume that $k$ and $P$ are powers of two. Then, we explain the different algorithmic components for *coarsening*, *initial partitioning*, *refinement* and *balancing* in more detail.

*Distributed Deep Multilevel Partitioning.* Recall that deep MGP [9] follows the traditional multilevel graph partitioning scheme, but coarsens the graph down to a small size independent of $k$. After partitioning the coarsest graph into a small number of blocks, it maintains the invariant that each block of the current partition contains roughly $C$ vertices throughout the uncoarsening phase (until there are $k$ blocks).

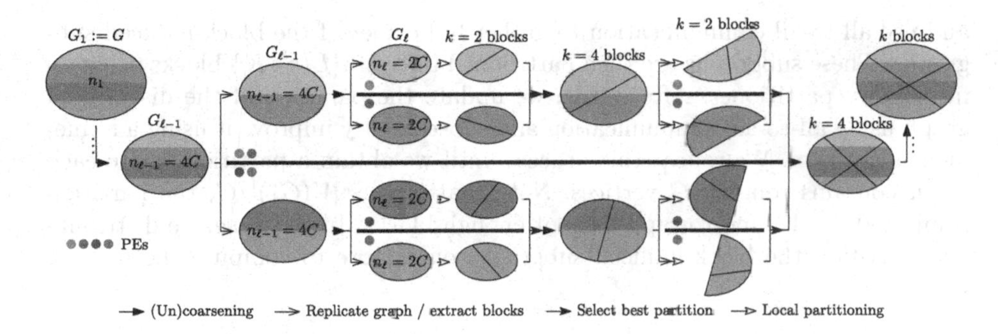


**Fig. 1.** Distributed deep multilevel graph partitioning on $P = 4$ PEs to partition a graph $G$ into $k = 4$ blocks. Unpartitioned graphs are labeled with their number of vertices. During initial partitioning and uncoarsening, blocks are recursively partitioned into $K = 2$ blocks. Bold horizontal lines illustrate PE groups working independently.

To adapt this scheme to the distributed setting, we use distributed algorithms for graph clustering, contraction, and partition refinement (see below). Initial partitioning of the coarsest graph and block-induced subgraphs is done using an in-memory partitioner by gathering full copies of the graphs on individual PEs. Since this process is communication heavy, we generalize the bipartitioning steps of deep MGP to $K$-way partitioning for some tuning parameter $K$. The scheme then works as follows.

We repeatedly coarsen the input graph until only $K \cdot C$ vertices are left, building a hierarchy $G_1 =: G, G_2, \ldots, G_\ell$ of successively coarser graphs. During this process, we exploit parallelism and improve scalablility on coarse levels of the hierarchy by maintaining the invariant that $P$ PEs work on a graph with at least $P \cdot C$ vertices [27]. This leads to more diversification on coarse levels due to the randomized nature of the clustering, initial partitioning and refinement algorithms. More precisely, we check on each level whether the current graph $G_i$ has more than $P \cdot C$ vertices. If so, we split the $P$ PEs into two subgroups $1..\frac{P}{2}$, $\frac{P}{2}+1..P$ and mirror the parts of $G_i$ between PEs $j$ and $\frac{P}{2}+j$, $0 \leq j < \frac{P}{2}$, such that each group obtains an identical copy of $G_i$. The subgroups then continue this procedure recursively. In Fig. 1, we illustrate this process by using bold horizontal lines, duplicating $G_{\ell-1}$ and $G_\ell$. The coarsest graph is then copied to each PE and partitioned into $\min\{k, K\}$ blocks using an in-memory partitioner. The best partition (within each group of PEs) is selected and projected onto $G_{\ell-1}$ by assigning fine vertices to the blocks of their corresponding coarse vertices. From here, we maintain two invariants during uncoarsening:

1. The current partition is feasible, which we ensure using the distributed balancing algorithm described below, and
2. each block contains roughly $C$ vertices (until there are $k$ blocks).

To maintain the latter invariant, assume that the current graph with $|V(G_i)|$ vertices is partitioned into $k' < k$ blocks. Then, assign $k'/P$ blocks to each PE and use all-to-all communication to gather full copies of the block-induced subgraphs. These subgraphs are then partitioned into $\min\{k/k', K\}$ blocks using an in-memory partitioner. Afterwards, we update the partition of the distributed graph using all-to-all communication and subsequently improve it using a refinement algorithm. We repeat this process until we obtain a partition where each block contains roughly $C$ vertices. Note that if $k > |V(G_1)|/C$, the partition computed on the finest graph has not enough blocks. In this case, we distribute and partition the block-induced subgraphs once more to compute the missing blocks.

*Coarsening.* We use a similar parallelization of size-constrained label propagation as ParHIP [19] and KaMinPar [9] to cluster the graphs. The algorithm works by first assigning each vertex to its own cluster. In further iterations over the vertices (we use $\{3, 5\}$ iterations), they are then moved to adjacent clusters such that the weight of intra-cluster edges is maximized without violating the maximum cluster weight $W_i := \varepsilon \frac{c(V)}{k'_i}$, where $k'_i := \min\{k, |V(G_i)|/C\}$ [9] and $i$ is the current level of the graph hierarchy.

As noted in Ref. [1,18], the solution quality of label propagation is improved when iterating over vertices in increased degree order. Since this is not cache efficient and lacks diversification by randomization, we sort the vertices into exponentially spaced degree buckets, i.e., bucket $b$ contains all vertices with degree $2^b \leq d < 2^{b+1}$, and rearrange the input graph accordingly. This happens locally on each PE. Then, during label propagation, we split buckets into small chunks and randomize traversal on a inter-chunk and intra-chunk level analogous to the randomization of the matching algorithm used by Metis [12].

To communicate the current cluster assignment of interface vertices, we follow ParHIP and split each iteration into $\max\{\alpha, \beta/P\}$ (we use $\alpha = 8$, $\beta = 128$) batches. After each batch, we use a sparse all-to-all operation to notify adjacent PEs of interface vertices that were moved to a different cluster. Since clusters can span multiple PEs, enforcing the maximum cluster weight becomes more challenging than in a shared-memory setting. ParHIP relaxes the weight limit and only enforces it locally, consequently allowing clusters with weight up to $P \cdot W$. This can lead to very heavy coarse vertices, making it more difficult to compute balanced partitions. Instead, we track the global cluster weights by sending the change in cluster weight after each batch to the PE owning the initial vertex of the cluster, which accumulates the changes and replies with the total weight of the cluster. If a cluster becomes heavier than $W$, each PE reverts moves proportional to its part of the total cluster weight. Those vertices can then be moved to other clusters in subsequent iterations.

After clustering the graph, we contract the clusters to build the next graph in the hierarchy. We give more details on this operation in Sect. 5.

*Balancing.* Balance constraint violations during deep MGP can occur after initial partitioning or after projecting a coarse graph partition onto a finer level of the graph hierarchy [9]. Since these balance constraint violations are bounded by the weight of the heaviest vertex, we design the following balancing algorithm based

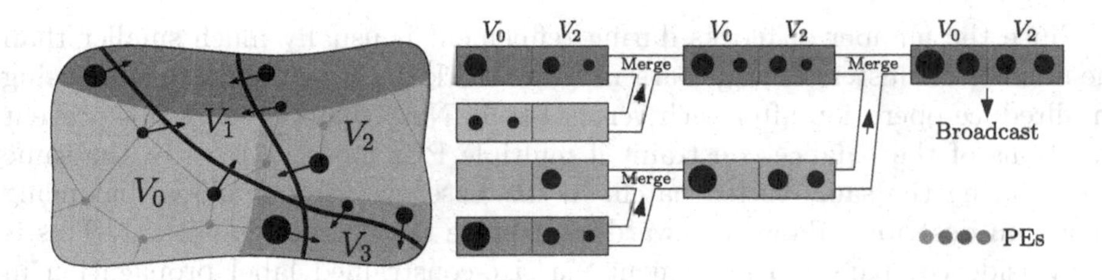


**Fig. 2.** Illustration of the rebalancing algorithm with $P = 4$ PEs (background color), two overloaded blocks $V_0$, $V_2$, and $\tau = 2$ vertices per overloaded block and round. Proposed moves are indicated by arrows, with their relative gains encoded by vertex size.

on the assumption that only few vertex moves are necessary to restore balance. Thus, it is feasible to invest a moderate amount of work per vertex move.

For each overloaded block $B$, each PE maintains a local priority queue $P_B$ of vertices in block $B$ ordered by their *relative gain* which we define as $g \cdot c(v)$ if $g \geq 0$ and $g/c(v)$ if $g < 0$. Here, $g$ is the largest reduction in edge cut when moving $v$ to a non-overloaded block. This rating function prefers moving few heavy vertices over many light vertices, supporting our assumption that few vertex moves are sufficient to balance the partition. To keep the priority queues small, we maintain the invariant that $P_B$ stores no more vertices than are necessary to remove all excess weight $o(B) := c(B) - L_{\max}$ from $B$. To this end, we initialize $P_B$ by iterating over all vertices $v$ in $B$ and inserting $v$ into $P_B$ if $c(P_B) < o(B)$. Otherwise, we only insert $v$ if it can replace another vertex with worse relative gain.

To choose which vertices to move, we then use a global reduction tree as illustrated in Fig. 2. Using the local PQs, each PE builds a sorted list per overloaded block containing up to $\tau$ (a tuning parameter) vertices. At each level of the reduction tree, the sorted lists are then merged and truncated to the prefix that is sufficient to remove all excess weight, but no more than $\tau$ vertices. Finally, the root PE selects a subset of the proposed vertices such that no other block becomes overloaded and broadcasts its decision to all PEs. Using this information, PEs update the current partition state, remove moved vertices from their PQs and update the relative gains of neighboring vertices. We repeat this process until the partition is balanced.

*Refinement.* We also use size-constrained label propagation to improve the current graph partition. In contrast to label propagation for clustering as described above, vertices are initially assigned to clusters representing the blocks of the partition, and the maximum block weight is used as weight constraint. We use the same iteration order and number of batches as during coarsening to move vertices to adjacent blocks such that the weight of intra-block edges is maximized without violating the balance constraint. Ties are broken in favor of the lighter block, or by coin flip if both blocks have the same weight.

Since the number of blocks during refinement is usually much smaller than the number of clusters during coarsening, we track the global block weights using an allreduce operation after each vertex batch. Note that this does not prevent violations of the balance constraint if multiple PEs move vertices to the same block during the same vertex batch. In this case, we use our global balancing algorithm described above afterwards to restore the balance constraint. This is a downside compared to refinement via size-constrained label propagation in shared-memory parallel graph partitioners, where the balance constraint can be strictly enforced using atomic compare-and-swap operations.

## 5 Implementation Details

*Vertex and Edge IDs.* To reduce the communication overheads, we distinguish between local- and global vertex- and edge identifiers. This allows us to use 64bit data types for global and 32bit data types for local IDs.

*Graph Contraction.* Contracting a clustering consisting of $n_C$ clusters and constructing the corresponding coarse graph works as follows. First, the clustering algorithm described above assigns a cluster ID to each vertex, which corresponds to some vertex ID in the distributed graph. We say that a cluster is *owned* by the PE owning the corresponding vertex. After contracting the local subgraphs (i.e., deduplicating edges between clusters and accumulating vertex- and edge weights), we map clusters to PEs such that each PE gets roughly the same number of coarse vertices while attempting to minimize the required communication amount. We assign $\leq \delta \cdot n_C/P$ clusters owned by each PE to the same PE (in our experiments, $\delta = 1.1$). If a PE owns more clusters, we redistribute the remaining clusters to PEs that have the smallest number of clusters assigned to them. Afterwards, each PE sends outgoing edges of coarse vertices to the respective PE using an all-to-all operation, then builds the coarse graph by deduplicating edges and accumulating vertex- and edge weights.

*Low-Latency Sparse All-to-All.* Many steps of dKaMinPar require communication along the cut edges of the distributed graph, which translates to (often very) sparse and irregular all-to-all communication. Since `MPI_Alltoallv` has relatively high latency, we instead use a two-level approach that arranges PEs in a grid [21]. Then, messages are first sent to the right row, then to the right column, reducing the total number of messages send through the network from $\mathcal{O}(P^2)$ to $\mathcal{O}(P)$.

## 6 Experiments

We implemented the proposed algorithm dKaMinPar in C++ and compiled it using g++-12.1 with flags `-O3 -march=native`. We use OpenMPI 4.0 as parallelization library and growt [17] for hash tables. Raw experimental results are available online[2].

[2] https://algo2.iti.kit.edu/seemaier/ddeep_mgp/.

*Setup.* We evaluate the solution quality of our algorithm on a shared-memory machine equipped with 1TB of main memory and one AMD EPYC 7702P processor with 64 cores (Machine A). Additionally, we perform scalability experiments on a high-performance cluster where each compute node is equipped with 256GB of main memory and two Intel Xeon Platinum 8368 processors (Machine B). The compute nodes are connected by an InfiniBand 4X HDR 200GBit/s network with approx. $1\mu$ s latency. We only use 64 out of the available 78 cores since some of the graph generators require the number of cores to be a power of two.

We compare dKaMinPar against the distributed versions of the algorithms included in Ref. [9], i.e., ParHIP [19] (v3.14) and ParMETIS [13] (v4.0.3). ParHIP offers two configurations, denoted ParHIP-Fast and ParHIP-Eco, which configure a trade-off between running time and partition quality. We do not include the distributed version PuLP [26] (XtraPuLP [25]) in our main comparison, since its quality is not competitive with multilevel partitioners. Instead, a comparison against XtraPuLP is available in the full version [23] of the paper. We evaluate two configurations of our algorithm: dKaMinPar-Fast uses $C = 2000$ as contraction limit (same as in Ref. [9]), KaMinPar [9] for initial partitioning and performs 3 iterations of label propagation during coarsening, whereas dKaMinPar-Strong uses $C = 5000$ (same as in Ref. [19]), Mt-KaHyPar [11] for initial partitioning and 5 iterations of label propagation during coarsening.

*Instances.* We evaluate our algorithm on the graphs from Benchmark Set B of Ref. [9] and the graphs used in Ref. [19]. Additionally, we use KaGen [8] to evaluate the scaling capabilities of our algorithm on huge randomly generated 2D and 3D geometric and hyperbolic graphs denoted $\mathsf{rgg}_{2D}N\mathrm{d}D$, $\mathsf{rgg}_{3D}N\mathrm{d}D$ and $\mathsf{rhg}_{3.0}N\mathrm{d}D$. These graphs have $2^N$ vertices per compute node (i.e., per 64 cores), average degree $D$ and power-law exponent 3 (hyperbolic graphs only).

*Methodology.* We call a combination of a graph and the number of blocks an *instance*. For each instance, we perform 5 repetitions with different seeds and aggregate the edge cuts and running times using the arithmetic mean. To aggregate over multiple instances, we use the geometric mean.

To compare the solution quality of different algorithms, we use *performance profiles* [7]. Let $\mathcal{A}$ be the set of algorithms we want to compare, $\mathcal{I}$ the set of instances, and $q_A(I)$ the quality of algorithm $A \in \mathcal{A}$ on instance $I \in \mathcal{I}$. For each algorithm $A$, we plot the fraction of instances $\frac{|\mathcal{I}_A(\tau)|}{|\mathcal{I}|}$ ($y$-axis) where $\mathcal{I}_A(\tau) := \{I \in \mathcal{I} \mid q_A(I) \leq \tau \cdot \min_{A' \in \mathcal{A}} q_{A'}(I)\}$ and $\tau$ is on the $x$-axis. Achieving higher fractions at lower $\tau$-values is considered better. For $\tau = 1$, the $y$-value indicates the percentage of instances for which an algorithm performs best.

*Solution Quality and Running Time.* To evaluate the quality and running time of dKaMinPar we partition all graphs of our benchmark set into $k \in \{2, 4, \ldots, 128\}$ blocks with $\varepsilon = 3\%$ using all 64 cores of Machine A and compare partition qualities and running times against competing distributed MGP algorithms. Additionally, we compare the results against KaMinPar to evaluate the penalties of dKaMinPar due to its distributed nature. Further experiments with larger values

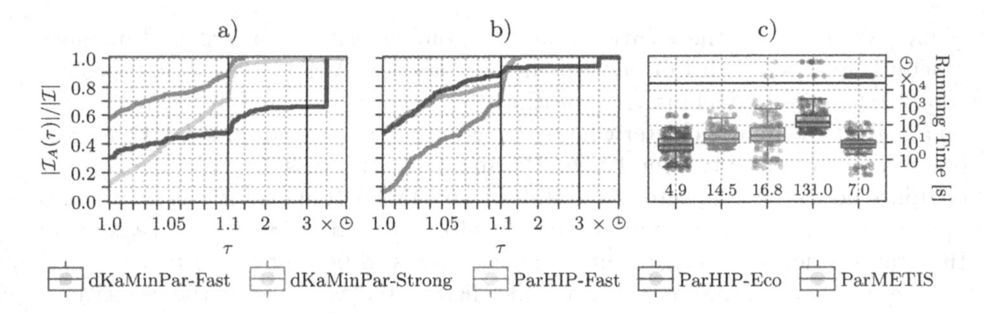


**Fig. 3.** Results for $k = \{2, 4, 8, 16, 32, 64, 128\}$ with $\varepsilon = 3\%$ on Machine A. From left to right: (a) edge cuts of dKaMinPar-Fast, ParHIP-Fast and ParMETIS, (b) edge cuts of dKaMinPar-Fast, dKaMinPar-Strong and ParHIP-Eco, (c) running times of all algorithms. The numbers above the x-axis are geometric mean running times [s] over all instances for which all algorithms produced a result. Timeouts are marked with ⏲, failed runs or infeasible results are marked with ×.

for $k$ are available in the full version [23] of the paper. We set the time limit for a single instance to one hour, which is approx. 10 times the running time of dKaMinPar-Fast on most instances[3].

The results are summarized in Fig. 3a–c. In Fig. 3a, we can see that dKaMinPar-Fast finds the lowest edge cuts on approx. 60% of all benchmark instances, whereas ParMETIS and ParHIP-Fast only find better edge cuts on approx. 30% resp. 10% of all instances. Moreover, both competing algorithms frequently fail to compute feasible partitions—in particular, ParMETIS is unable to partition most social networks, violating the balance constraint or crashing on 34% of all instances. When looking at running times (Fig. 3c), we therefore only average over instances for which all partitioners computed a feasible partition or ran into the timeout (145 out of 224 instances). dKaMinPar-Fast (4.93 s geometric mean running time) is 1.4 and 3.4 times faster than ParMETIS (6.98 s) and ParHIP-Fast (16.77 s), respectively. While ParHIP-Eco achieves higher partition quality than dKaMinPar-Fast, Fig. 3b shows that equipping dKaMinPar with a stronger algorithm for initial partitioning is sufficient to achieve similar partition quality, while still being faster than ParHIP-Fast.

We evaluate the weak scalability of dKaMinPar using families of randomly generated graphs, $k = 16$, and 64–8 192 cores (i.e., 1–128 compute nodes) of Machine B. Throughputs are shown in Fig. 4, where we observe weak scalability for dKaMinPar-Fast all the way to 8 192 cores on all three graph families. ParMETIS achieves similar and in cases slightly higher throughputs than dKaMinPar, but is unable to efficiently partition hyperbolic graphs. ParHIP-Fast shows a drop in scalability beyond 2 048 cores, which is most likely due to the extensive and inefficient communication that it performs during graph contraction. Moreover, we note that ParHIP-Fast was originally designed to overlap local work and global communication during label propagation through the use of nonblocking

[3] Only twitter-2010 takes 6min resp. 7min for $k = 64$ resp. $k = 128$.

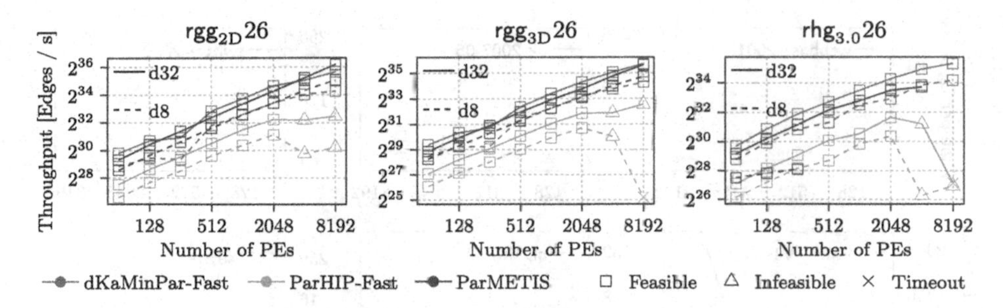


**Fig. 4.** Throughput of $\text{rgg}_{2D}$, $\text{rgg}_{3D}$ and rhg graphs with $2^{26}$ vertices per compute node, average degree $\in \{8, 32\}$, $k = 16$ and $\varepsilon = 3\%$ on 64–8 192 cores of Machine B.

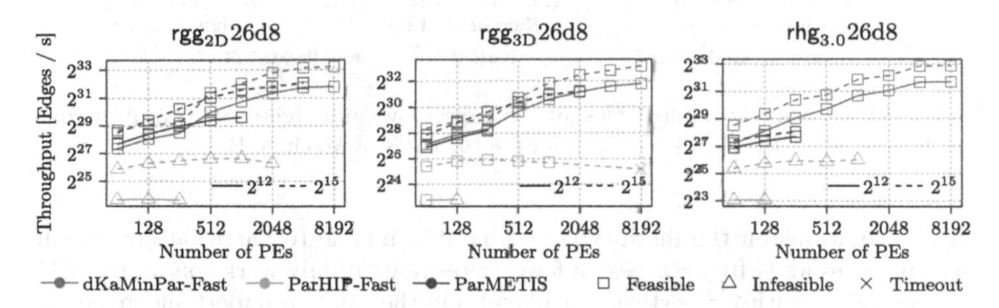


**Fig. 5.** Throughput of rgg2D, rgg3D and rhg graphs with $2^{26}$ vertices per compute node, average degree 8, and $\varepsilon = 3\%$ on 64–8 192 cores of Machine B. The number of blocks are scaled with the size of the graph such that each block contains $2^{12}$ or $2^{15}$ vertices.

MPI operations. This implementation relies on MPI progression threads, which seem to be unavailable in modern OpenMPI versions.

Per-instance edge cut results are available in the full version [23] of the paper. We observe that ParMETIS finds lower edge cuts than dKaMinPar-Fast on the dense $\text{rgg}_{2D}$26d32 graph and both $\text{rgg}_{3D}$ graphs by 5%–13%. However, on the sparser $\text{rgg}_{2D}$26d8 graph, dKaMinPar-Fast has 19% smaller cuts than ParMETIS which is already a considerable improvement. The gap gets much larger for the hyperbolic graph where ParMETIS only finds approx. 5.5–6.1 times larger cuts. Such solutions will be unsuitable for many applications.

We now evaluate weak scalability in terms of graph size *and* number of blocks by scaling $k$ with the number of compute nodes used. This implies that the number of blocks is large when using a large number of cores. The throughput of each algorithm in this setting is summarized in Fig. 5. Note that we only use the sparser graphs in this experiment, since ParMETIS and ParHIP are unable to partition the dense versions of the graphs even on few compute nodes.

ParHIP-Fast is unable to obtain a feasible partition on all but 6 instances, none of which uses more than 1 024 cores, and only shows increasing throughputs up to 256 cores. While ParMETIS achieves decent weak scalability and computes

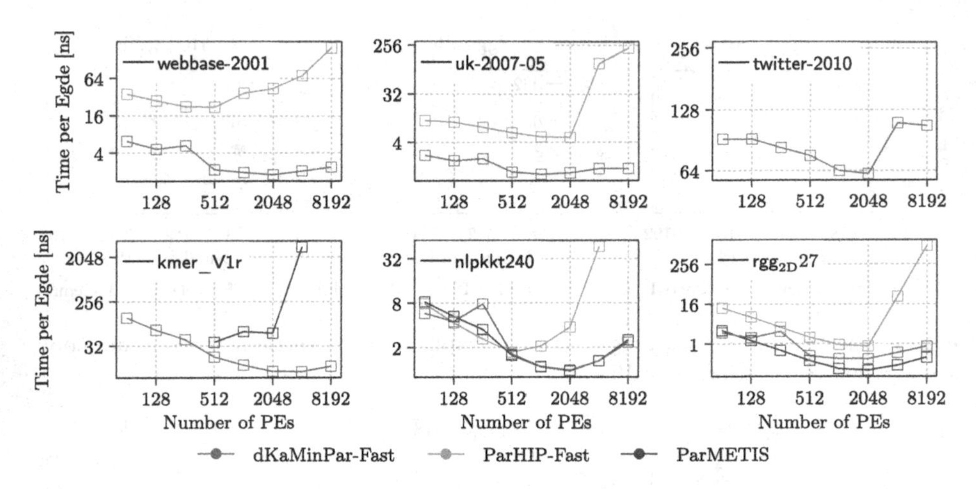


**Fig. 6.** Strong scaling running times for the largest low- and high-degree graphs in our benchmark set, with $k = 16$, $\varepsilon = 3\%$ on 64–8 192 cores of Machine B.

feasible solutions on the mesh-type graphs, it is unable to partition any graph on 8 192 cores and often crashes on fewer cores (e.g., it only works on up to 1 024 cores on $\mathsf{rgg}_{2D}$ with $2^{12}$ vertices per block). On the random hyperbolic graph, it only computes a feasible solution on 64 cores. Meanwhile, dKaMinPar-Fast shows weak scalability up to 8 192 cores on every graph family, although it should be noted that the throughput increase from 4 096 to 8 192 is rather small.

In terms of number of edges cut, we summarize that dKaMinPar finds on average 19.3% and 2.8% lower edge cuts than ParMETIS and ParHIP-Fast, respectively (only averaging over instances for which the respective partitioner computed a feasible partition), with improvements ranging from 0% on $\mathsf{rgg}_{3D}$26d8 to approx. 60% on $\mathsf{rhg}_8$3.0d26 ($2^{15}$ vertices per block). For detailed per-instance edge cut results, we refer to the full version [23] of the paper.

*Strong Scalability of* dKaMinPar. We partition three of the largest low- and high-degree graphs from our benchmark set into $k = 16$ blocks using 64–8 192 cores of Machine B and a time limit of 15min. The results are summarized in Fig. 6, where we can observe strong scalability for up to 1 024–2 048 cores on high-degree graphs. ParMETIS is unable to partition these graphs regardless of the number of cores used. While ParHIP-Fast scales up to 2 048 cores on uk-2007-05, we observe that its running time is still higher than dKaMinPar on just 64 cores. The twitter graph is difficult to coarsen due to its highly skewed degree distribution; here, we observe that only dKaMinPar can partition the graph within the time limit.

Turning towards graphs with small maximum degree, we observe strong scalability for up to 2 048, 2 048 and 1 024 cores on kmer_V1r, nlpkkt240 and $\mathsf{rgg}_{2D}$27, respectively. Similar to our weak scaling experiments, ParMETIS shows better scalability and throughput on the mesh-type graph $\mathsf{rgg}_{2D}$ as well as on nlpkkt240, but fails to partition kmer_V1r on 8 192 cores.

The edge cuts obtained remain relatively constant when scaling to large number of cores. Surprisingly, the geometric mean edge cut on 8 192 cores is slightly better than on 64 cores (by 2.0%).

## 7 Conclusion and Future Work

Our distributed-memory graph partitioner dKaMinPar successfully partitions a wide range of input graphs using many thousands of cores yielding high speed and good quality. Further improvements of the implementation might be possible, for example making better use of shared-memory on each compute node. Beyond that, one can explore the quality versus time trade off. By distributed implementations of more powerful local improvement algorithms like local search or flow-based techniques one could achieve better quality at the price of higher execution time. It then also makes sense to look at a portfolio of different partitioners variants that can be run in parallel achieving good quality for subsets of inputs. For example, matching based coarsening as in ParMETIS might help for mesh-like networks. On the other hand, more aggressive methods for handling high-degree nodes might help with some social networks.

**Acknowledgments.** This work was performed on the HoreKa supercomputer funded by the Ministry of Science, Research and the Arts Baden-Württemberg and by the Federal Ministry of Education and Research. This project has received funding from the European Research Council (ERC) under the European Union's Horizon 2020 research and innovation programme (grant agreement No. 882500).

## References

1. Akhremtsev, Y., Sanders, P., Schulz, C.: High-quality shared-memory graph partitioning. IEEE Trans. Parallel Distrib. Syst. **31**(11), 2710–2722 (2020)
2. Bichot, C., Siarry, P. (eds.): Graph Partitioning. Wiley, Hoboken (2011)
3. Buluç, A., Meyerhenke, H., Safro, I., Sanders, P., Schulz, C.: Recent advances in graph partitioning. In: Kliemann, L., Sanders, P. (eds.) Algorithm Engineering. LNCS, vol. 9220, pp. 117–158. Springer, Cham (2016). https://doi.org/10.1007/978-3-319-49487-6_4
4. Çatalyürek, U.V., et al.: More recent advances in (hyper)graph partitioning. ACM Comput. Surv. **55**, 1–38 (2022)
5. Chevalier, C., Pellegrini, F.: PT-scotch: a tool for efficient parallel graph ordering. Parallel Comput. **34**(6–8), 318–331 (2008)
6. Devine, K.D., et al.: Parallel hypergraph partitioning for scientific computing. In: 20th International Parallel and Distributed Processing Symposium (IPDPS 2006) (2006)
7. Dolan, E.D., Moré, J.J.: Benchmarking optimization software with performance profiles. Math. Program. **91**(2), 201–213 (2002)

8. Funke, D., et al.: Communication-free massively distributed graph generation. J. Parallel Distrib. Comput. **131**, 200–217 (2019)
9. Gottesbüren, L., et al.: Deep multilevel graph partitioning. In: 29th European Symposium on Algorithms (ESA). LIPIcs, vol. 204, pp. 48:1–48:17. Schloss Dagstuhl - Leibniz-Zentrum für Informatik (2021)
10. Gottesbüren, L., Heuer, T., Sanders, P.: Parallel flow-based hypergraph partitioning. In: 20th International Symposium on Experimental Algorithms (SEA 2022), vol. 233, pp. 5:1–5:21. LIPICS (2022)
11. Gottesbüren, L., Heuer, T., Sanders, P., Schlag, S.: Scalable shared-memory hypergraph partitioning. In: 23rd Workshop on Algorithm Engineering and Experiments (ALENEX 2021), pp. 16–30. SIAM (2021)
12. Karypis, G., Kumar, V.: A fast and high quality multilevel scheme for partitioning irregular graphs. SIAM J. Sci. Comput. **20**(1), 359–392 (1998)
13. Karypis, G., Kumar, V.: Multilevel $k$-way partitioning scheme for irregular graphs. J. Parallel Distrib. Comput. **48**(1), 96–129 (1998)
14. LaSalle, D., Karypis, G.: Multi-threaded graph partitioning. In: 27th IEEE International Parallel and Distributed Processing Symposium (IPDPS), pp. 225–236 (2013)
15. LaSalle, D., et al.: Improving graph partitioning for modern graphs and architectures. In: 5th Workshop on Irregular Applications - Architectures and Algorithms (IA3), pp. 14:1–14:4. ACM (2015)
16. von Looz, M., Tzovas, C., Meyerhenke, H.: Balanced k-means for parallel geometric partitioning. In: 47th International Conference on Parallel Processing (ICPP), pp. 52:1–52:10. ACM (2018)
17. Maier, T., Sanders, P., Dementiev, R.: Concurrent hash tables: fast and general(?)! ACM Trans. Parallel Comput. **5**(4), 16:1–16:32 (2019)
18. Meyerhenke, H., Sanders, P., Schulz, C.: Partitioning complex networks via size-constrained clustering. In: Gudmundsson, J., Katajainen, J. (eds.) SEA 2014. LNCS, vol. 8504, pp. 351–363. Springer, Cham (2014). https://doi.org/10.1007/978-3-319-07959-2_30
19. Meyerhenke, H., Sanders, P., Schulz, C.: Parallel graph partitioning for complex networks. IEEE Trans. Parallel Distrib. Syst. **28**(9), 2625–2638 (2017)
20. Raghavan, N., Albert, R., Kumara, S.: Near linear time algorithm to detect community structures in large-scale networks. Phys. Rev. E Stat. Nonlinear Soft Matter Phys. **76**, 36–106 (2007)
21. Sanders, P., Schimek, M.: Engineering massively parallel MST algorithms. In: 27th IEEE International Parallel and Distributed Processing Symposium (IPDPS) (2023)
22. Sanders, P., Schulz, C.: Think locally, act globally: highly balanced graph partitioning. In: Bonifaci, V., Demetrescu, C., Marchetti-Spaccamela, A. (eds.) SEA 2013. LNCS, vol. 7933, pp. 164–175. Springer, Heidelberg (2013). https://doi.org/10.1007/978-3-642-38527-8_16
23. Sanders, P., Seemaier, D.: Distributed deep multilevel graph partitioning (2023). https://arxiv.org/abs/2303.01417
24. Schulz, C., Strash, D.: Graph partitioning: formulations and applications to big data. In: Sakr, S., Zomaya, A. (eds.) Encyclopedia of Big Data Technologies, pp. 1–7. Springer, Cham (2018). https://doi.org/10.1007/978-3-319-63962-8_312-2
25. Slota, G.M., et al.: Scalable, multi-constraint, complex-objective graph partitioning. IEEE Trans. Parallel Distrib. Syst. **31**(12), 2789–2801 (2020)

26. Slota, G.M., Madduri, K., Rajamanickam, S.: PuLP: scalable multi-objective multi-constraint partitioning for small-world networks. In: 2014 IEEE International Conference on Big Data (IEEE BigData 2014), pp. 481–490 (2014)
27. Walshaw, C., Cross, M.: JOSTLE: parallel multilevel graph-partitioning software – an overview. Mesh Partitioning Tech. Domain Decomposition Tech. **10**, 27–58 (2007)

# TrainBF: High-Performance DNN Training Engine Using BFloat16 on AI Accelerators

Zhen Xie(✉), Siddhisanket Raskar, Murali Emani, and Venkatram Vishwanath

Argonne National Laboratory, Lemont, IL 60439, USA
{zhen.xie,sraskar,memani,venkat}@anl.gov

**Abstract.** Training deep neural networks (DNNs) with half-precision floating-point formats is widely supported on recent hardware and frameworks. However, current training approaches using half-precision formats neither obtain the optimal throughput due to the involvement of single-precision format nor achieve state-of-the-art model accuracy due to lower numerical digits. In this work, we present a new DNN training engine, named *TrainBF*, which leverages a typical half-precision format BFloat16 to maximize training throughput while ensuring sufficient model accuracy. TrainBF deploys BFloat16 across the entire training process for best throughput and improves model accuracy by introducing three proposed normalization techniques. TrainBF is also lightweight by only applying these normalization techniques to the layers that are most critical to model accuracy. Furthermore, TrainBF implements a parallel strategy that parallelizes the execution of operators in DNN training to make use of the spare memory space saved by half-precision for better throughput. Evaluating with six common DNN models and compared with the state-of-the-art mixed-precision approach, TrainBF achieves competitive model accuracy with an average throughput speedup of 1.21×, 1.74×, and 1.16× on NVIDIA A100 GPU, AMD MI100 GPU, and an emerging AI accelerator SambaNova, respectively.

## 1 Introduction

Recent advancements in Artificial Intelligence (AI) fueled by the resurgence of Deep Neural Networks (DNNs) have a spectacular success in widespread fields. Meanwhile, the increasingly complex DNN models require tremendous overhead for training. As a result, there has been broad interest in leveraging half-precision formats to reduce the training time [21]. A lot of DNN training frameworks support various half-precision formats to offer significant speedups [5,14,22].

Among them, `Float16` is a typical half-precision format, which consists of a sign bit, a 5-bit exponent, and a 10-bit fraction. Compared with the customized single-precision format TensorFloat-32 (TF32) that is used as the default format in NVIDIA Ampere architecture, Float16 has the same length of fraction bits, but shorter exponent bits, causing a narrower dynamic range of the representation than that of TF32. Thus, training DNN models with Float16 often


J. Cano et al. (Eds.): Euro-Par 2023, LNCS 14100, pp. 458–473, 2023.
https://doi.org/10.1007/978-3-031-39698-4_31

encounters *overflow* and *underflow* problems [15], which could degrade model accuracy or even lead to non-convergence.

To solve this problem, a training approach called *mixed-precision* training [14, 18, 20, 21] is proposed. However, the mixed-precision training with Float16 is far from achieving the theoretical performance improvement due to the involvement of single-precision format. Mixed-precision training introduces a master copy of the weights [21] in single-precision and a component called auto-casting [14] to avoid overflow problem. Also, a component called loss scaling [21] is presented to prevent underflow problem. These new components introduce a number of additional operations and incur considerable overhead. Experiments [16] show that, compared to TF32 training, mixed-precision training with Float16 brings an average throughput speedup of 1.34× using 12 common DNN models on an NVIDIA A100 GPU, which is lower than the theoretical performance speedup of 2×, because of the above three additional components.

Fortunately, such high overhead can be avoided by using another half-precision format, Brain Floating Point (BFloat16) [4], since it has the same length of exponent bits as TF32 and hence keeps the same dynamic range of representation. As a result, there is no overflow and underflow problems, and it becomes possible to avoid the involvement of single-precision and format conversions. In this paper, we will reintroduce BFloat16 format into DNN training. The motivation of this work is to achieve higher training throughput by applying BFloat16 format on all DNN operators. Thus, BFloat16 training, in nature, stores all the training data and model parameters, and performs all the computation operators in BFloat16 format entirely. However, current BFloat16 training cannot work well because of the following three challenges.

**Accuracy Challenge.** Recent studies [32] have shown that training DNN models in BFloat16 format alone can result in 17.3%–35.9% accuracy loss compared to training in single-precision format. The reason for accuracy loss is that, compared to single-precision, BFloat16 has only 7-bit fraction, which makes the stored data more inaccurate in numerical precision, resulting in the absence of partial model information. The more essential reason is that BFloat16 optimizes the overflow and underflow problems at the cost of sacrificing decimal precision, while the distribution of training data does not occupy the entire dynamic range of BFloat16, and therefore the exponent bits in BFloat16 is underutilized.

**Overhead Concern.** Even though there are some methods (will be described next) that can be applied to DNN layers to improve the bit utilization of BFloat16, these operations are accompanied by a certain overhead. For example, if we add such operations to each layer in DNN model to improve the floating-point bit utilization and amend model accuracy, the training throughput will be greatly affected and the performance advantage of half-precision will be lost. Thus, how to apply these operations to layers is another challenge.

**Parallel Efficiency.** Using BFloat16 format entirely in training will result in almost half of the memory (47.2% on average) being idle [2]. Traditional methods of improving memory usage by increasing batch size may lead to a compromise in model accuracy and numerical instability due to extra noise and unstable loss function. Thus, to utilize more memory and bring higher throughput, parallel execution strategy must be redesigned without changing batch size.

To address these first challenges, we introduce a DNN training engine using BFloat16 format, named TrainBF; TrainBF is accuracy-aware to training data by optimizing the offset of sign bit and maximizing the variance of data distribution; TrainBF is overhead-aware to training throughput by applying normalization selectively. TrainBF is parallel-aware to execution efficiency by parallelizing training operators on multiple execution streams. We also evaluate TrainBF with six typical DNN models, including three convolutional neural networks (CNNs), a recurrent neural network (RNN), a graph neural network (GNN), and a scientific model on three AI accelerators. TrainBF consistently outperforms the state-of-the-art mixed-precision training approach and leads to an average of 1.21× (up to 1.67×), 1.74× (up to 1.83×), and 1.16× (up to 1.18×) speedup on NVIDIA A100 GPU, AMD MI100 GPU, and an emerging AI accelerator SambaNova, respectively.

## 2 Preliminaries

We now establish important preliminaries and discuss work related to ours.

**Half-Precision Formats:** Half-precision formats have gathered significant interests in the industry and academia over the past few years [5,14,21,22].

Two formats namely `Float16` and `BFloat16` are the most popular half-precision formats and are supported by Google TPUs, NVIDIA GPUs, AMD Instinct MI GPUs, and the emerging AI accelerators, such as the next-generation dataflow processor SambaNova. Compared to single-precision format (Float32), Float16 has a 5-bit exponent and a 10-bit fraction thus resulting in a narrow dynamic range (from 65504 to $2e^{-14}$) due to fewer fraction bits, and BFloat16 retains the same number of exponent bits (8-bit) as Float32 and therefore covers the same dynamic range but at a lower numerical precision (7-bit fraction).

Both two half-precision formats have higher performance than single-precision on the existing AI accelerators. For example, Float16 and BFloat16 can provide 16× the theoretical performance of single-precision and 2× the theoretical performance of TensorFloat-32 (TF32, which has an 8-bit exponent and a 10-bit fraction, and it is a new optimized implementation for single-precision format in NVIDIA Ampere architecture) on NVIDIA A100 GPU. However, when training with Float16, many studies [16,17] have shown that lots of additional components are introduced to avoid underflow and overflow problems, thus resulting in unavoidable overhead. Thus, this paper selects BFloat16 as the basic half-precision format in DNN training engine to avoid such overhead.

**Various Training Data in DNN Training:** There are three kinds of training data involved in DNN training, namely, activations, weights, and gradients. Concretely, the intermediate result in CNN models, the hidden state in RNN models, and the activation matrix in GNN models are regarded as *activations.*

The weights in CNN models, the weights of the hidden state in RNN models, and the weight matrix in GNN models are considered as *weights*. The gradients of all the weights in DNN models is regarded as *gradients*. The computation between the three kinds of training data is the main numerical computation in DNN training. In addition, the distribution of these training data is not the same [7], therefore, we will give specific optimization techniques to improve the bit utilization of each training data in BFloat16.

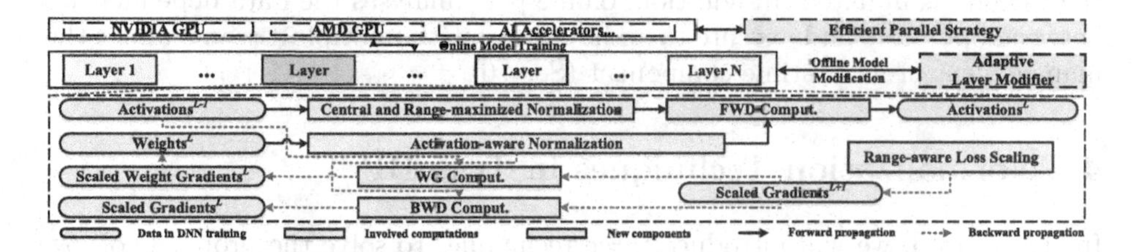


**Fig. 1.** Overview of TrainBF.

**Essential Reasons for Accuracy Loss with Bfloat16:** Besides, as per the floating-point computation theory, when adding or multiplying numbers with very different exponents can introduce a significant *floating-point error problem* [8,15]. For example, if we add $1.2 * 2^{45}$ and $3.4 * 2^{-5}$ in Float32 will yields the result of $1.2 * 2^{45}$, which drops the small one. Such error is even more pronounced when the distribution of these data is completely different and short fraction of Bfloat16 is used.

More seriously, the floating-point error caused by using low-precision format in the first few layers of DNN models will propagate to subsequent layers along with training proceeds, resulting in *error amplification problem*. The amplified computation error in the last layer can distort the main numerical information and greatly affect model accuracy.

Therefore, how to amend the information loss when converting from single-precision to Bfloat16 format, alleviate the floating-point error in computations, and avoid the error amplification problem will be the main focus in this paper.

## 3 Overview of TrainBF

We propose a high-performance DNN training engine using BFloat16 on AI Accelerators, called TrainBF. Figure 1 outlines its main components. TrainBF improves the training accuracy of DNN models in BFloat16 format by proposing *three normalization techniques* to optimize the data distribution of three kinds of training data. In addition, TrainBF introduces a lightweight module, *adaptive layer modifier*, to apply these normalization techniques with minimal overhead while ensuring model accuracy. Furthermore, TrainBF parallelizes the execution of training operators using an *efficient parallel strategy* on AI accelerators.

The workflow of TrainBF is divided into offline and online parts. Offline part starts from selecting the appropriate layers to apply normalization through adaptive layer modification (Sect. 5). In each selected layer, the activations is normalized to construct a bits utilization-friendly data distribution (Sect. 4.1). TrainBF normalizes its weights using the same mean and variance of the normalized activations (Sect. 4.2). During backward propagation, the training loss is amplified by a loss scaling factor provided by range-aware loss scaling to construct scaled gradients (Sect. 4.3). Next, the scaled gradients of weights is descaled and the weights is updated. In addition, online part analyses the data dependencies between operators and execute them in parallel with multiple streams under the management of its runtime component (Sect. 6).

## 4 Normalization Techniques in TrainBF

In this section, we will introduce three techniques to solve the problems of low bits utilization and inconsistent data distribution between different training data.

### 4.1 Central and Range-Maximized Normalization for Activations

As an important training data, activations are involved in all computations in forward and backward propagation to compute the gradients of previous layer and the weights. If the bits utilization of activations can be improved and the data distribution of weights and gradients can be shifted closer to it accordingly, the accuracy of numerical computations can be greatly improved, thereby amending model accuracy.

Based on our observations and existing work, the data distribution of activations is random and not centralized. Hence, the decentralized distribution cannot make full use of the sign bit in BFloat16 format due to unequal numbers of positive and negative values [1,15]. The most extreme case is when all the data is positive or negative, the sign bit is meaningless for storage. In addition, the activations are not evenly distributed across all numerical ranges in BFloat16, which makes it impossible to make full use of the exponential bits, thus resulting in very low bits utilization. For example, if all values are distributed from $2^k$ to $2^{k+1}$ in an extreme case, then the exponent bits are also meaningless.

Therefore, we propose a central and range-maximized normalization (CR_Norm) for activations, which is used to build a normalized data with zero-mean distribution and makes its values are evenly distributed in a wider data range to maximize the *number of exponent ranges* used by activations. We can apply CR_Norm after activations are generated, or replace the existing batch normalization layer [13], which is widely applied in almost all DNN models to ensure that the data is standardized over each mini-batch.

Maximizing the number of exponent ranges used by activations can improve the utilization of exponent bits, however, the disadvantage of training with such data is that it will lead to gradient explosion and oversensitive to input problems due to excessive variance. Therefore, CR_Norm designs a learnable parameter

$R_{max}$ and includes $R_{max}$ to loss function to trade-off between the maximum variance of normalized data and model accuracy.

The workflow of CR_Norm is shown in Algorithm 1. Algorithm 1 takes the activations over a mini-batch as input. Algorithm 1 includes two predetermined parameters $\phi$ and $\eta$ to adjust the weight in loss function and the learning rate of $R_{max}$, respectively. In Algorithm 1, $A$ represents the values of activations over a mini-batch, $\mu_A$ and $\sigma^2$ are the mean and variance of $A$. $\epsilon$ is the minimal amount (negligible) introduced to prevent division by zero. $O$ is the output of CR_Norm and its variance is controlled by the learnable parameter $R_{max}$. $L$ is the original loss function. In forward pass, the memorized statistics, including mean and variance of activations in $m$ mini-batches is calculated (Line 5 – 6). Then, the normalization of $A$ has two steps: step 1 standardizes the activations $A$ to a new distribution $\hat{A}$ with zero-mean and unit-variance (Line 7); step 2 scales $\hat{A}$ to a new distribution $O$ with zero-mean and a new variance of the learnable parameter $R_{max}$ (Line 8). In backward pass, $R_{max}$ is added to loss function with a predetermined learning rate $\phi$ (Line 10). Then, the gradients are calculated (Line 11) and $R_{max}$ is updated with a predetermined learning rate $\eta$ (Line 12).

**Algorithm 1.** Normalization for Activation

1: Input: Values of activation over a mini-batch ( $A = A^1, A^2, ..., A^m$ )
2: Input: Parameter to be learned: $R_{max}$. Predetermined parameters: $\phi$ in loss function and $\eta$ in $R_{max}$ update
3: Output: $O^i \leftarrow CR\_Norm(A^i)$
4: **Forward Propagation:**
5: $\mu_A \leftarrow \frac{1}{m}\sum_{i=1}^{m} A^i$ //memorized mean
6: $\sigma^2 \leftarrow \frac{1}{m}\sum_{i=1}^{m}(A^i - \mu_A)^2$ //memorized variance
7: $\hat{A}^i \leftarrow \frac{A^i - \mu_A}{\sqrt{\sigma^2 + \epsilon}}$ //step 1: standardization
8: $O^i \leftarrow R_{max} * \hat{A}^i$ //step 2: scaling function
9: **Backward Propagation:**
10: Loss with range-maximized: $L = L - \phi R_{max}$
11: Compute Gradients: $\frac{\partial \ell}{\partial O}$, $\frac{\partial O}{\partial R_{max}}$, and $\frac{\partial \ell}{\partial R_{max}}$
12: Update Parameter: $R_{max} := R_{max} - \eta \frac{\partial \ell}{\partial R_{max}}$

### 4.2 Activation-Aware Normalization for Weights

In the process of forward propagation, a large amount of computation occurs between the weights and activations. Increasing the numerical similarity between the two training data can alleviate the floating-point loss of numerical computation. Therefore, we normalize the weights according to the distribution of activations of the previous layer. Specifically, we normalize the weights with the same learnable parameter $R_{max}$. We call this normalization technique activation-aware normalization. The formula is as follows:

$$\hat{W} \leftarrow R_{max} * \frac{W - \mu_W}{\sqrt{\sigma_W^2 + \epsilon}}, \quad (1)$$

where $\mu_W$ and $\sigma_W^2$ are the mean and variance of weights $W$, $\epsilon$ is the minimal amount introduced to prevent division by zero, $\hat{W}$ is the normalized weights. Afterwards, the normalized weight will replace the original weights and participate in all forward and backward propagation.

### 4.3 Range-Aware Loss Scaling for Gradients

In backward propagation, the gradients of the previous layer and weights are computed by the gradients, activations, and weights of the current layer. Therefore, constructing a normalized gradients that has the same distribution as activations and weights is also another part to improve the numerical accuracy of computation. Therefore, this paper proposes a range-aware loss scaling and introduce a loss scaling factor $S$ to adjust the distribution of the gradients to match the distribution of activations and weights.

Figure 2 illustrates the process of range-aware loss scaling. First, the loss obtained from forward propagation can be scaled by multiplying by the loss scaling factor $S$. Then, the backward propagation deduces based on the scaled gradients and the scaled weight gradients. Weights are then updated by applying re-scaling to the scaled weight gradients. In addition, the variance of the scaled gradients is counted and compared with the learnable variance $R_{max}$ to adjust the loss scaling factor $S$.

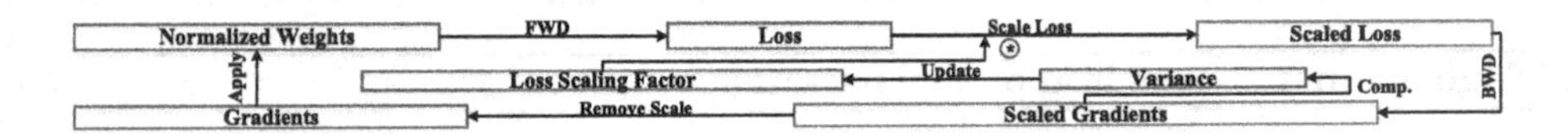


**Fig. 2.** Evaluation accuracy of four training approaches.

Specifically, the workflow of adjusting loss scaling factor $S$ consists of three steps: ❶ loss scaling factor $S$ starts from a relatively high value (e.g., $S \leftarrow 224$) because the gradient is generally small, and then the variance of the gradients is checked over iterations; ❷ If the variance of the gradients is close to $R_{max}$ within a threshold (e.g., 10% difference), the scaling factor will not be adjusted and training continues; if the variance of the gradients is much larger than $R_{max}$, the loss scaling factor $S$ will be halved to reduce the data distribution; Otherwise, the loss scaling factor $S$ will be doubled to build a wider data distribution; ❸ the adjustment process will go throughout the whole training process because its overhead is almost negligible due to only a few multiplications are added.

## 5 Adaptive Layer Modifier in TrainBF

In this section, we discuss the opportunity of applying these normalization techniques to few layers with acceptable overhead and sufficient accuracy.

### 5.1 Sensitivity Study

We use two data formats, ie, TF32 and BFloat16, and apply the normalization techniques to different layers to study its affects on model accuracy and overhead. We run eight models in Mlperf benchmark [19] on one NVIDIA A100 GPU using two data formats and apply normalization techniques to each layer separately. We use the exact same initialization values for both two data formats and treat the output of each layer of using TF32 as the ground-truth to calculate the computational error of using BFloat16. The computational error $\varepsilon_L$ of each activations $A_L$ in layer $L$ between TF32 and BFloat16 can be expressed as $\varepsilon_L = \sum(A_L^i\_TF32 - A_L^i\_BF16)^2 / \sum(A_L^i\_TF32)^2$, where $A_L^i\_TF32$ and $A_L^i\_BF16$ represent the activations in TF32 and BFloat16, respectively.

Results reveals that applying normalization to each layer always comes with overhead but not always bring the same benefit to computational error. For example, applying normalization to layer 7 in ResNet-50 model has a computational error of 0.926%, which is much better than not using normalization that has a computational error of 2.754%. While adding normalization to two more layers (e.g., layer 1 and 15) leads to a similar computational error of 0.927%. Nevertheless, adding more normalization operations incurs larger overhead. In this same example, the throughput of using normalization on three layers is 74.86% of that of using normalization on one layer. Hence, blindly applying normalization to all the layers in DNN models may result in unacceptable overhead.

We further analyze the collected results of throughput and computational error in all eight models and summarize some interesting observations.

- **Observation 1:** Using normalization to too many layers largely reduces the throughput of model training.
- **Observation 2:** Using normalization for each layer does not have the same effect on reducing computational error. It strongly depends on where does the normalization occur in the model.
- **Observation 3:** Inappropriate use of too many normalization operations may not be necessary. Applying a small number of normalization operations can also achieve the optimal throughput while meeting the accuracy requirement of numerical computation.
- **Observation 4:** Computational error gradually propagates backwards. There is no point in correcting error at the very beginning or at the end of the model.

### 5.2 Adaptive Layer Modifier

Driven by these observations, we introduce a lightweight and adaptive layer modifier to apply normalization and maximize training throughput. Algorithm 2 depicts its workflow. Layer modifier first avoids applying normalization to the first $f$ and last $l$ layers because of Observations 1 and 4 (Line 6), where $f$ and $l$ are predefined values and are typically 5% of the number of layers. Then, layer modifier collects activations of each layer using TF32/Float32 and BFloat16 formats to calculate the computational error between them (Line 8–12). Layer modifier chooses the layer with the largest computational error and applies normalization to it (Line 13–15). Next, the computational error of the last layer between in two formats is tested (Line 16), and new normalization operations continue to be added until the computational error is less than a threshold (Line 17–18). The algorithm happens only once before training, therefore, its overhead has a negligible impact on end-to-end training time.

**Algorithm 2.** Lightweight and Adaptive Layer Modifier

1: Input: DNN model with $N$ layers ( $L_1$, $L_2$, ... ,$L_N$ )
2: Input: A batch of testing dataset $B$, first layers $f$, last layers $l$
3: Output: A set of layers $S$ that need to be normalized
4: All layers in DNN model $M \leftarrow \{1, 2, ..., N\}$,
5: An empty set of errors $E \leftarrow \{\}$, An empty set of layers $S \leftarrow \{\}$
6: Remove the first $f$ and last $l$ layers from set $M$
7: **while** true **do**
8:   **for** $i \in$ set $M$ **do**
9:     Obtain activations $A_i^{FP32}$ of layer $L_i$ using data $B$ with TF32 format
10:     Obtain activations $A_i^{BF16}$ of layer $L_i$ using data $B$ with BFloat16 format
11:     Compute the computational error $E_i$ between $A_i^{FP32}$ and $A_i^{BF16}$
12:     Keep the computational error of each layer $E \leftarrow E + E_i$
13:   Choose the one with the greatest error in set $E$ with the index of $o$
14:   Remove $o$ from set $M$ and add $o$ to set $S$
15:   Apply normalization techniques to layer $o$
16:   Compute the final error $Final\_E$ between TF32 and BFloat16 format using data $B$
17:   **if** $Final\_E < threshold$ **then**
18:     Return a set of layers $S$

## 6 Efficient Parallel Strategy in TrainBF

TrainBF is also a work aiming at efficiently training DNN models on AI accelerators that have high parallelism and large memory. We propose an *efficient parallel strategy* to train DNN models using multiple execution streams. In addition, this strategy maintains the same batch size as single precision training to avoid the non-convergence and gradient explosion problem.

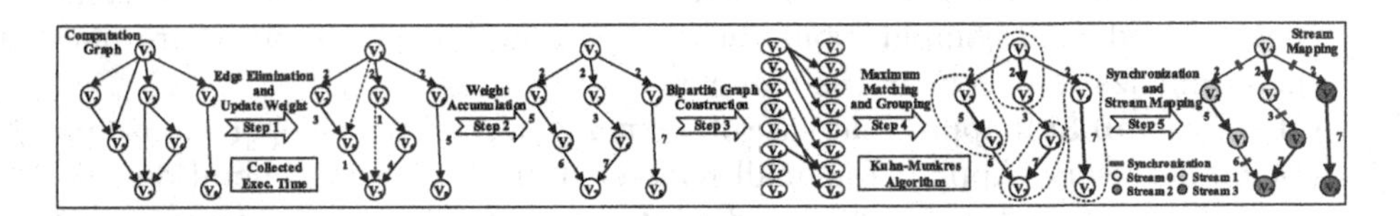


**Fig. 3.** Evaluation accuracy of four training approaches.

We propose an efficient parallel strategy to maximize memory usage, it is divided into two parts: the first one is an operator-to-stream mapping algorithm, where the input is the compiled computational graph of the model (such as TorchScript graph in PyTorch), and the output is the mapping between operators and execution streams; The second one is a runtime algorithm that collects the execution time of each operator and controls memory allocation of each stream.

Figure 3 describes the execution flow of the operator-to-stream mapping algorithm. At step ❶, we first eliminate the unnecessary edges with the minimum equivalent graph to avoid repeated and progressive data dependencies. For example, there are data dependencies from $V_1$ to $V_2$ and $V_2$ to $V_5$, so the data dependencies from $V_1$ to $V_5$ are repeated and can be removed. In addition, we collect the execution time of each operator in the previous iteration and use them as the weight of edges. Specifically, the weight of each edge is equal to the execution time of the outgoing node, because the incoming node must wait for all the incoming edges to complete before starting. At step ❷, the weight of each edge is accumulated with the weights of all the edges in the max-flow augmentation path to obtain the weight accumulation graph, which represents the minimum execution time for fully parallel execution. At steps ❸ and ❹, a weighted bipartite graph is constructed based on the weight accumulation graph, and its maximum matching is calculated by a typical graph algorithm, namely Kuhn-Munkres algorithm [33]. Then the grouping strategy minimizes the sum of weighted data dependence between groups, thereby minimizing the sum of the waiting time of each group. At step ❺, synchronization points are added to each edge between each group to ensure the correctness of the execution order, and each group is assigned to a different execution stream.

After getting the operator-to-stream mapping, we start all execution streams simultaneously at the beginning of training to maximize parallelism. However, each operation performed in a different execution stream consumes a certain amount of independent memory resources, and executing multiple memory-consuming operators in different streams simultaneously could lead to Out-of-Memory(OOM) issue. Therefore, we enable a memory table to check whether the memory overflows before each operator is launched. In addition, the execution time of each operator is recorded and passed to the operator-to-stream mapping algorithm to update the weight of the computational graph.

# 7 Evaluation

## 7.1 Experimental Setup

**Platforms and Formats:** We evaluate TrainBF on three architectures, as shown in Table 1. Two of them are GPU-based platforms equipped with NVIDIA A100 GPU (A100 in short) and AMD MI100 GPU (MI100 in short), respectively. The third is an AI accelerator-based platform, SambaNova SN10-8 (SambaNova in short). A100 and MI100 GPUs support Float32, Float16, and BFloat16 formats. A100 GPU also supports TF32 [3]. SambaNova supports Float32 and BFloat16 formats.

**Table 1.** Evaluated hardware

| | NVIDIA GPU | AMD GPU | AI accelerator |
|---|---|---|---|
| Core | Tesla A100 40 GB<br>56 SMs @1328 MHz | AMD Instinct MI100<br>120 Compute Units<br>@1502 MHz | SambaNova SN10-8<br>640 PCUs<br>640 PMUs |
| Caches | L2: 40 MB | L2: 8 MB | On-chip: 300MB |
| Memory | 40 GB HBM2 | 32 GB HBM2 | 12TB DDR4 |
| Bandwidth | 1555 GB/s | 1200 GB/s | 150TB/s |

**Table 2.** DNN models, datasets, and configurations

| DNN Model | Field | Dataset | Epoch | Throughput Unit |
|---|---|---|---|---|
| Resnet50 | Image Recognition | ILSVRC2012 | 90 | Images per second |
| VGG19 | Image Recognition | ILSVRC2012 | 100 | Images per second |
| U-Net | Image Segmentation | Brain MRI Kaggle3m | 30 | Images per second |
| Social-LSTM | Trajectory Prediction | Trajnet++ | 100 | Sequences per second |
| GCN | Graph Computation | Cora Dataset | 200 | Items per second |
| UNO | HPC model | CCLE Dataset | 50 | Items per second |

**Dataset and Models:** We use six DNN models with a public dataset that cover a wide range of CNN, RNN, GNN, and scientific models. The details of the models are summarized in Table 2. *Epoch* represents the number of epochs trained before obtaining the final model accuracy, *Throughput Unit* is the unit of throughput of each model during training. We use different batch sizes on different platforms to fill all available memory to maximize memory utilization.

**Implementation and Baselines:** This work is implemented based on PyTorch 1.11.0. We implement the three customized normalization techniques as three new modules in PyTorch. The statistics of modification of TrainBF given by git diff are 24 files changed, 1535 insertions (+), and 349 deletions (−).

We compare TrainBF with three solutions:

❶ A single-precision solution: pure Float32 or TF-32 training.

❷ A mixed-precision solution: Automatic Mixed Precision (AMP) with Float16 [23].

❸ A half-precision solution: pure BFloat16 training.

For a fair comparison, we compare TrainBF with AMP using Float16 on A100 since it provides the same theoretical performance for both Float16 and BFloat16. For MI100 and SambaNova, neither platform supports the same performance for Float16 and BFloat16, thus we compare the throughput and accuracy of TrainBF with the throughput of Float32 training and the accuracy of BFloat16 training, respectively. In addition, all six models are tested on A100 and MI100. For SambaNova, only two models (U-Net and UNO) are tested, because the support for LSTM and some kernels will not be released until Q4 2023.

### 7.2 Throughput and Accuracy

Figure 4 shows throughput and accuracy on all platforms. We run all models on A100 and MI100 and two models on SambaNova due to its limited support.

Figure 4 shows that TrainBF performs much better than the state-of-the-art training approaches. Specifically, for A100, TrainBF introduces 1.74×, 1.52×, 1.61×, 1.31×, 1.46×, 1.08× throughput improvement on six DNN models respectively, compared to TF32 training, with only 0.48% accuracy degradation on average, which is far below the accuracy loss of 1.5% that users can tolerate for training [25]. TrainBF also introduces 1.31×, 1.15×, 1.09×, 1.13×, 1.37×, 1.67× throughput improvement, compared to AMP with Float16, with almost the same accuracy. TrainBF improves the final accuracy by 15.7% on average and up to 45.8% on UNO model, compared to BFloat16 training.

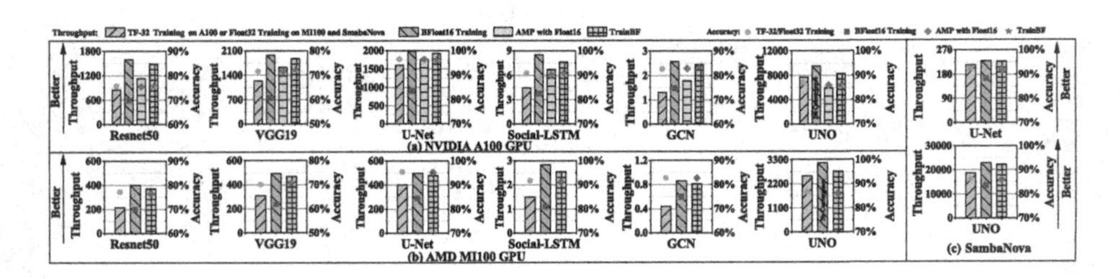


**Fig. 4.** Throughput and accuracy using four training methods on six models with three different hardware platforms.

For MI100, TrainBF introduces 1.63×, 1.40×, 1.83×, 1.42×, 1.53×, 1.04× throughput improvement on six DNN models respectively, compared to Float32 training, with only 0.52% accuracy loss on average. TrainBF improves the finial accuracy by 13.9% on average, compared to BFloat16 training.

For SambaNova platform, TrainBF introduces 1.15× and 1.18× throughput improvement on U-Net, UNO models, compared to Float32 training, with the accuracy loss of 0.32% on average. TrainBF improves the final accuracy by 3.59% on average, compared to BFloat16 training.

We have the following three observations: (1) TrainBF brings larger benefits to CNN models, because matrix multiplication as the main computation in CNN models can take full advantage of the high performance of BFloat16 format. (2) For RNN and GNN models, MI100 has higher speedup than A100, because these models are memory intensive. The amount of data accessed is greatly reduced by using BFloat16, which eliminates the bottleneck of lower memory bandwidth on MI100 compared to A100. (3) For SambaNova, TrainBF achieves almost the same throughput as BFloat16 training while maintaining the Float32 accuracy.

### 7.3 Breakdown for Accuracy Improvement

To quantify **the contribution of three normalization techniques to accuracy improvement**, i.e., (a) central and range-maximized normalization, (b) activation-aware normalization, and (c) range-aware loss scaling, we apply the three techniques one after another. The results in Fig. 5 are normalized by using the accuracy of applying all of the three techniques.

We have three observations. (1) The central and range-maximized normalization is very effective and accounts for 48.3% on average in improving model accuracy across all models, because this normalization is the cornerstone of reducing computational error, thus enabling more opportunities for all subsequent techniques. (2) The activation-aware normalization is very effective (52.7% on average) for the RNN model (e.g., social-LSTM) because a large number of small matrix multiplication are computed in RNN training, and the normalized weight could prevent the error of small matrix from propagating to the following computations, thereby avoiding greater accuracy loss. (3) The range-aware loss scaling contributes 33.1% on average to GNN and scientific models (e.g., GCN and UNO), because the loss in these models varies greatly, making the distribution range of gradients very unstable without scaling.

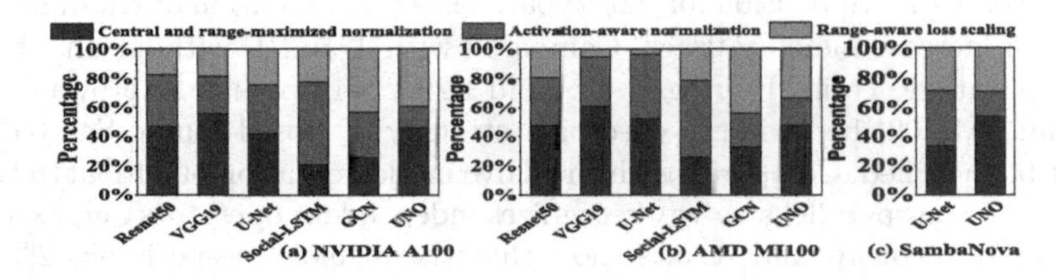


**Fig. 5.** Quantifying the contributions of three normalization to accuracy improvement.

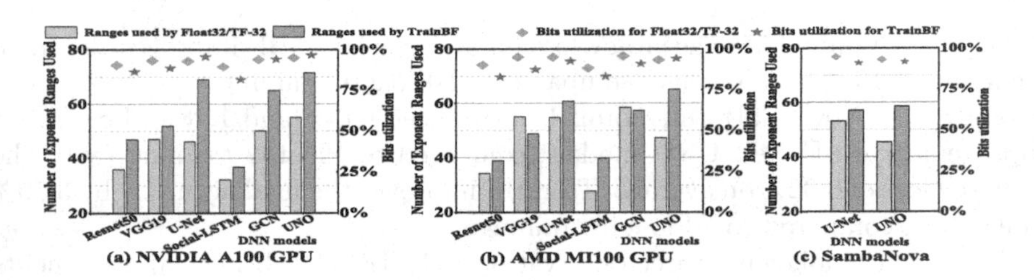


**Fig. 6.** Number of exponent ranges used and bits utilization on three platforms.

### 7.4 Effectiveness of Three Modules in TrainBF

**Quantifying Bits Utilization.** We use *number of exponent ranges used* to quantify the bits utilization. Results are shown in Fig. 6. With TrainBF, the average number of exponent ranges used on all models is improved from 41.4 to 57.6 on A100, 40.7 to 51.3 on MI100, and 49.7 to 57.6 on SambaNova. With TrainBF, the average bits utilization on all models is 92.7% on A100, 88.4% on MI100, and 91.5% on SambaNova. The bits utilization of BFloat16 in TrainBF is very close to the bits utilization of TF32/Float32 in single precision training and even exceeds by 1.7% and 3.5% on average on A100 and MI100 for GCN and UNO models. Based on the improvement of bits utilization, there is a large increase in computational accuracy, further improving model accuracy.

**Quantifying Learnable Parameter $R_{max}$.** TrainBF uses the learnable parameter $R_{max}$ to controls the variance of normalized output. In our experiments, $R_{max}$ is initialized to 1 and reaches 2.5 in the first 25% of the training process for most models, which implies that the primary (95%) data range of activations and weights are 1.45 times larger than the initial data range. Among the eight DNN models we evaluate, $R_{max}$ is stable for all three CNN models and three scientific models in the last 75% of the training process, while $R_{max}$ changes more drastically in the other two models, namely social-LSTM and GCN. The main reason is that the data distribution of gradients on social-LSTM and GCN differ greatly over epochs in model training, so $R_{max}$ is constantly tuned to find the optimal value that matches the distribution of activations.

**Quantifying Efficient Parallel Strategy.** TrainBF leverages the memory space saved by half-precision format to parallelize the execution of training operators and increase memory usage. Compared with TrainBF without an efficient parallel strategy, TrainBF brings 1.13× and 1.29× performance improvement on A100 and MI100, because the execution strategy of closed-source SambaNova cannot be modified. Compared with the naive implementation of BFloat16 training, our efficient parallel strategy recognizes independent operators and executes them simultaneously, and results show that the memory usage is 65.32% and 74.17% higher than naive implementation on A100 and MI100, respectively.

### 7.5 Overhead Analysis

We explore **the overhead of TrainBF** by comparing the throughput of TrainBF without the efficient parallel strategy and that of BFloat16 training in Fig. 4. The throughput of BFloat16 training represents the optimal training performance regardless of model accuracy in single-stream execution. After applying these normalization techniques to selected layers, the calculation of throughput will include all of the runtime overhead. Compared with the throughput of BFloat16 training, TrainBF introduces an average throughput degradation of 3.38%, 7.91%, and 9.67% on A100, MI100, and SambaNova, respectively. Obviously, A100 and MI100 have lower overhead, because the normalization operations can be merged by fusion optimization in GPU implementation.

## 8 Related Work

**Reduced Precision Training:** Using reduced precision for DNN training has been an active topic of research [6,9–12,28,34]. Seide et al. [24] were able to reduce the precision of gradients to one bit using Stochastic Gradient Descent. However, these works mainly focus on a small number of models and lack generality to apply to a wider range of DNN models.

**Mixed Precision Training:** Mixed precision training demonstrates a broad variety of DNN applications involving deep networks and larger datasets with minimal loss compared to baseline FP32 results. Micikevicius et al. [21] showed that Float16/Float32 mixed precision with autocasting and loss scaling can achieve near-SOTA accuracy. The only concern is about performance improvement by using Float16. TrainBF leverages BFloat16 format to avoid such overhead and maintain SOTA accuracy.

**Normalization:** Normalization techniques are essential for improving the generalization of DNN models [29–31]. Dmitry et al. [26] constructed instance normalization to prevent instance-specific mean and covariance shifts. Yuxin et al. [27] proposed group normalization to normalize features within each group. None of these are designed to eliminate computational error, which is the main goal of this paper.

## 9 Conclusion

BFloat16, as a typical half-precision format, has been neglected in recent AI accelerators. This paper designs a new training approach, which includes three normalization techniques, an adaptive layer modifier, and an efficient parallel strategy to avoid accuracy loss and improve hardware utilization. Results show that our approach yields better throughput than the state-of-the-art training approaches. We expect more data formats can be inspired by our approach.

**Acknowledgment.** This research was funded in part by and used resources at the Argonne Leadership Computing Facility, which is a DOE Office of Science User Facility supported under Contract DE-AC02-06CH11357.

## References

1. Blinn, J.F.: Floating-point tricks. IEEE Comput. Graphics Appl. **17**(4), 80–84 (1997)
2. Burgess, N., Milanovic, J., Stephens, N., Monachopoulos, K., Mansell, D.: BFloat16 processing for neural networks. In: 2019 IEEE 26th Symposium on Computer Arithmetic (ARITH), pp. 88–91. IEEE (2019)
3. Choquette, J., Gandhi, W., Giroux, O., Stam, N., Krashinsky, R.: NVIDIA A100 tensor core GPU: performance and innovation. IEEE Micro **41**(2), 29–35 (2021)
4. contributors, W.: BFloat16 floating-point format (2021). https://en.wikipedia.org/wiki/Bfloat16_floating-point_format
5. Das, D., et al.: Mixed precision training of convolutional neural networks using integer operations. arXiv preprint arXiv:1802.00930 (2018)
6. Emani, M., et al.: A comprehensive evaluation of novel AI accelerators for deep learning workloads. In: 2022 IEEE/ACM International Workshop on Performance Modeling, Benchmarking and Simulation of High Performance Computer Systems (PMBS), pp. 13–25. IEEE (2022)
7. Franchi, G., Bursuc, A., Aldea, E., Dubuisson, S., Bloch, I.: TRADI: tracking deep neural network weight distributions. In: Vedaldi, A., Bischof, H., Brox, T., Frahm, J.-M. (eds.) ECCV 2020. LNCS, vol. 12362, pp. 105–121. Springer, Cham (2020). https://doi.org/10.1007/978-3-030-58520-4_7
8. Gupta, S., Agrawal, A., Gopalakrishnan, K., Narayanan, P.: Deep learning with limited numerical precision. In: International Conference on Machine Learning, pp. 1737–1746. PMLR (2015)
9. He, X., Chen, Z., Sun, J., Chen, H., Li, D., Quan, Z.: Exploring synchronization in cache coherent manycore systems: a case study with xeon phi. In: 2017 IEEE 23rd International Conference on Parallel and Distributed Systems (ICPADS), pp. 232–239. IEEE (2017)
10. He, X., et al.: Enabling energy-efficient DNN training on hybrid GPU-FPGA accelerators. In: Proceedings of the ACM International Conference on Supercomputing, pp. 227–241 (2021)
11. He, X., Sun, J., Chen, H., Li, D.: Campo: {Cost-Aware} performance optimization for {Mixed-Precision} neural network training. In: 2022 USENIX Annual Technical Conference (USENIX ATC 22), pp. 505–518 (2022)
12. He, X., Yao, Y., Chen, Z., Sun, J., Chen, H.: Efficient parallel A* search on multi-GPU system. Futur. Gener. Comput. Syst. **123**, 35–47 (2021)
13. Ioffe, S., Szegedy, C.: Batch normalization: accelerating deep network training by reducing internal covariate shift. In: International Conference on Machine Learning, pp. 448–456. PMLR (2015)
14. Jia, X., et al.: Highly scalable deep learning training system with mixed-precision: training ImageNet in four minutes. arXiv preprint arXiv:1807.11205 (2018)
15. Johnson, J.: Rethinking floating point for deep learning. arXiv preprint arXiv:1811.01721 (2018)
16. Johnston, J.T., et al.: Fine-grained exploitation of mixed precision for faster CNN training. In: 2019 IEEE/ACM Workshop on Machine Learning in High Performance Computing Environments (MLHPC), pp. 9–18. IEEE (2019)
17. Kuchaiev, O., Ginsburg, B., Gitman, I., Lavrukhin, V., Case, C., Micikevicius, P.: OpenSeq2Seq: extensible toolkit for distributed and mixed precision training of sequence-to-sequence models. In: Proceedings of Workshop for NLP Open Source Software (NLP-OSS), pp. 41–46 (2018)

18. Kuchaiev, O., et al.: Mixed-precision training for NLP and speech recognition with openseq2seq. arXiv preprint arXiv:1805.10387 (2018)
19. Mattson, P., et al.: MLPerf training benchmark. Proc. Mach. Learn. Syst. **2**, 336–349 (2020)
20. Mellempudi, N., Srinivasan, S., Das, D., Kaul, B.: Mixed precision training with 8-bit floating point. arXiv preprint arXiv:1905.12334 (2019)
21. Micikevicius, P., et al.: Mixed precision training. arXiv preprint arXiv:1710.03740 (2017)
22. Mishra, A., Nurvitadhi, E., Cook, J.J., Marr, D.: WRPN: wide reduced-precision networks. arXiv preprint arXiv:1709.01134 (2017)
23. PyTorch: Automatic Mixed Precision package (2022). https://pytorch.org/docs/stable/amp.html. Accessed 1 Aug 2022
24. Seide, F., Fu, H., Droppo, J., Li, G., Yu, D.: 1-bit stochastic gradient descent and its application to data-parallel distributed training of speech DNNs. In: Fifteenth Annual Conference of the International Speech Communication Association. Citeseer (2014)
25. Sze, V., Chen, Y.H., Yang, T.J., Emer, J.S.: Efficient processing of deep neural networks: a tutorial and survey. Proc. IEEE **105**(12), 2295–2329 (2017)
26. Ulyanov, D., Vedaldi, A., Lempitsky, V.: Instance normalization: the missing ingredient for fast stylization. arXiv preprint arXiv:1607.08022 (2016)
27. Wu, Y., He, K.: Group normalization. In: Proceedings of the European conference on computer vision (ECCV), pp. 3–19 (2018)
28. Xie, Z., Dong, W., Liu, J., Liu, H., Li, D.: Tahoe: tree structure-aware high performance inference engine for decision tree ensemble on GPU. In: Proceedings of the Sixteenth European Conference on Computer Systems, pp. 426–440 (2021)
29. Xie, Z., Dong, W., Liu, J., Peng, I., Ma, Y., Li, D.: MD-HM: memoization-based molecular dynamics simulations on big memory system. In: Proceedings of the ACM International Conference on Supercomputing, pp. 215–226 (2021)
30. Xie, Z., Liu, J., Li, J., Li, D.: Merchandiser: data placement on heterogeneous memory for task-parallel HPC applications with load-balance awareness (2023)
31. Xie, Z., Tan, G., Liu, W., Sun, N.: IA-SpGEMM: an input-aware auto-tuning framework for parallel sparse matrix-matrix multiplication. In: Proceedings of the ACM International Conference on Supercomputing, pp. 94–105 (2019)
32. Zamirai, P., Zhang, J., Aberger, C.R., De Sa, C.: Revisiting BFloat16 training. arXiv preprint arXiv:2010.06192 (2020)
33. Zhu, H., Zhou, M., Alkins, R.: Group role assignment via a Kuhn-Munkres algorithm-based solution. IEEE Trans. Syst. Man Cybern.-Part A: Syst. Hum. **42**(3), 739–750 (2011)
34. Zvyagin, M., et al.: GenSLMs: genome-scale language models reveal SARS-CoV-2 evolutionary dynamics. bioRxiv, p. 2022–10 (2022)

# Distributed k-Means with Outliers in General Metrics

Enrico Dandolo, Andrea Pietracaprina, and Geppino Pucci(✉)

Department of Information Engineering, University of Padova, Padova, Italy
enrico.dandolo.1@studenti.unipd.it,
{andrea.pietracaprina,geppino.pucci}@unipd.it

**Abstract.** Center-based clustering is a pivotal primitive for unsupervised learning and data analysis. A popular variant is the $k$-means problem, which, given a set $P$ of points from a metric space and a parameter $k < |P|$, requires finding a subset $S \subset P$ of $k$ points, dubbed *centers*, which minimizes the sum of all squared distances of points in $P$ from their closest center. A more general formulation, introduced to deal with noisy datasets, features a further parameter $z$ and allows up to $z$ points of $P$ (outliers) to be disregarded when computing the aforementioned sum. We present a distributed coreset-based 3-round approximation algorithm for $k$-means with $z$ outliers for general metric spaces, using MapReduce as a computational model. Our distributed algorithm requires sublinear local memory per reducer, and yields a solution whose approximation ratio is an additive term $O(\gamma)$ away from the one achievable by the best known polynomial-time sequential (possibly bicriteria) approximation algorithm, where $\gamma$ can be made arbitrarily small. An important feature of our algorithm is that it obliviously adapts to the intrinsic complexity of the dataset, captured by its doubling dimension $D$. To the best of our knowledge, no previous distributed approaches were able to attain similar quality-performance tradeoffs for general metrics.

**Keywords:** Clustering · k-means · Outliers · MapReduce · Coreset

## 1 Introduction

Clustering is a fundamental primitive for data analysis and unsupervised learning, with applications to such diverse domains as pattern recognition, information retrieval, bioinformatics, social networks, and many more [19]. Among the many approaches to clustering, a prominent role is played by *center-based clustering*, which aims at partitioning a set of data items into $k$ groups, where $k$ is an input parameter, according to a notion of similarity modeled through a metric distance over the data. Different variants of center-based clustering aim at minimizing different objective functions. The *k-means* problem is possibly the most popular variant of center-based clustering. Given a set $P$ of points in a general metric space and a positive integer $k < |P|$, the discrete version of the problem requires to determine a subset $S \subset P$ of $k$ points, called *centers*, so that the sum


J. Cano et al. (Eds.): Euro-Par 2023, LNCS 14100, pp. 474–488, 2023.
https://doi.org/10.1007/978-3-031-39698-4_32

of all squared distances of the points of $P$ from their closest center is minimized. (In Euclidean spaces, centers may be chosen also outside the set $P$, giving rise to a wider spectrum of feasible solutions.)

Since the objective function of $k$-means involves squares of distances, the optimal solution is at risk of being impacted by few "distant" points, called *outliers*, which may severely bias the optimal center selection towards reducing such distances. In fact, the presence of outliers is inevitable in large datasets, due to the presence of points which are artifacts of data collection, either representing noisy measurements or simply erroneous information. To cope with this limitation, $k$-means admits a heavily studied robust formulation that takes into account outliers [8]: when computing the objective function for a set of $k$ centers, the $z$ largest squared distances from the centers are not included in the sum, where $z < |P|$ is an additional input parameter representing a tolerable level of noise. This formulation of the problem is known as *k-means with z outliers*.

There is an ample and well-established literature on sequential strategies for different instantiations of center-based clustering, with and without outliers. However, with the advent of big data, the high volumes that need to be processed often rule out the use of unscalable, sequential strategies. Therefore, it is of paramount importance to devise efficient clustering strategies tailored to typical distributed computational frameworks for big data processing (e.g., MapReduce [12]). The primary objective of this paper is to devise scalable, distributed strategies for discrete $k$-means with $z$ outliers for general metric spaces.

### 1.1 Related Work

The body of literature on solving $k$-means without outliers sequentially is huge. For brevity, we report only the results relative to the discrete case on general metrics, which is our target scenario. The best sequential algorithms to date for this scenario are the deterministic $(6.357 + \varepsilon)$-approximation algorithm of [1], or the randomized PTAS of [10] for spaces of constant doubling dimension. A simpler and faster randomized option is the $k$-`means++` algorithm of [2], whose approximation ratio, which is $O(\log k)$ in expectation, can be lowered to a constant by running the algorithm for $\rho k$ centers, with $\rho = O(1)$ [27]. For the distributed case, a 3-round MapReduce algorithm for $k$-means is presented in [23]. For arbitrarily small $\gamma > 0$, the algorithm attains an approximation ratio which is a mere $O(\gamma)$ term away from the best sequential approximation attainable for the weighted variant of the problem, where the weight $w_p$ of each point $p \in P$ multiplies the square-distance contribution of $p$ to the objective function.

A considerable number of sequential algorithms have also been proposed for $k$-means with $z$ outliers. Here, we report only on the works most relevant to our framework, and refer to [13] for a more detailed overview of the literature. In [16], a randomized local search strategy is described, which runs in time $O\left(|P|z + (1/\varepsilon)k^2(k+z)^2 \log(|P|\Delta)\right)$, yielding a 274-approximate bicriteria solution with $k$ centers and $O((1/\varepsilon)kz\log(|P|\Delta))$ outliers, where $\Delta$ is the ratio between the maximum and minimum pairwise distances. For spaces of doubling dimension $D$, [14] devises a different (deterministic) local search strategy yielding a bicriteria solution with $(1+\varepsilon)k$ centers and $z$ outliers, achieving an approximation $1+O(\varepsilon)$, in time $O\left((k/\varepsilon)|P|^{(D/\varepsilon)^{\Theta(D/\varepsilon)}}\log(|P|\Delta)\right)$. Finally, the LP-based approach of [21] yields the first non-bicriteria solution featuring an expected $53.002\cdot(1+\varepsilon)$-approximation in time $|P|^{O(1/\varepsilon^3)}$.

The literature on distributed approaches to $k$-means with outliers is more scant. The simple, sequential coreset-based strategy of [26] can be easily made into a 2-round MapReduce algorithm yielding a solution featuring a nonconstant $O(\log(k+z))$ approximation and local memory $\sqrt{|P|(k+z)}$. In [15], an LP-based algorithm is developed for the coordinator model, yielding a $O(1+1/\varepsilon)$-approximate bicriteria solution, with an excess factor $(1+\varepsilon)$ either in the number of outliers or in the number of centers, using $\tilde{O}(Lk+z)$ communication words, where $L$ is the number of available workers. In the coordinator model, better bounds have been obtained for the special case of Euclidean spaces in [9,22].

### 1.2 Our Contribution

We present a scalable coreset-based distributed MapReduce algorithm for $k$-means with $z$ outliers, targeting the solution of very large instances from general metrics. The algorithm first computes, distributedly, a coreset of suitably selected input points which act as representatives of the whole input, where each coreset point is weighted in accordance to the number of input points it represents. Then, the final solution is computed by running on the coreset an $\alpha$-approximate sequential algorithm for the weighted variant of the problem, defined similarly to the case without outliers. Our approach is flexible, in the sense that the final solution can also be extracted through a sequential bicriteria algorithm returning a larger number $\rho k$ of centers and/or excluding a larger number $\tau z$ of outliers. Our distributed algorithm features an approximation ratio of $\alpha+O(\gamma)$, where $\gamma$ is a user-provided accuracy parameter which can be made arbitrarily small. The algorithm requires 3 rounds and a local memory at each worker of size $O\left(\sqrt{|P|(\rho k+\tau z)}(c/\gamma)^{2D}\log^2|P|\right)$, where $c$ is a constant and $D$ is the doubling dimension of the input. For reasonable configurations of the parameters and, in particular, low doubling dimension, the local space is substantially smaller than the input size. It is important to remark that the algorithm is *oblivious* to $D$, in the sense that while the actual value of this parameter (which is hard to compute) influences the analysis, it is not needed for the algorithm to run. As a proof of concept, we describe how the sequential bicriteria algorithms by [16] and [14] can be extended to handle weighted instances, so that, when used within our MapReduce algorithm, allow us to get comparable distributed approximations.

We remark that the main contributions of our algorithm are: (i) its simplicity, since our coreset construction does not require multiple invocations of complex, time-consuming sequential algorithms for $k$-means with outliers (as is the case in [15]); and (ii) its versatility, since it is able to exploit any sequential algorithm for the weighted case (bicriteria or not) which can be run on a small coreset, with a minimal extra loss in accuracy. In fact, to the best of our knowledge, ours

**Table 1.** Notations used throughout the paper: $P$ is a set of $n$ points, $S$ is a subset of $P$, and $0 < z < |P|$ is an integer parameter.

| | | |
|---|---|---|
| $\text{cost}(P, S)$ | $=$ | $\sum_{p \in P} d(p, S)^2$ |
| $\text{OPT}_k(P)$ | $=$ | $\min_{S \subset P, \|S\|=k} \text{cost}(P, S)$ |
| $\text{out}_z(P, S)$ | $=$ | $z$ points of $P$ farthest from $S$ |
| $\text{OPT}_{k,z}(P)$ | $=$ | $\min_{S \subset P, \|S\|=k} \text{cost}(P \setminus \text{out}_z(P, S), S)$ |
| $\text{cost}(P, \mathbf{w}, S)$ | $=$ | $\sum_{p \in P} w_p d(p, S)^2$ |
| $\text{OPT}_k(P, \mathbf{w})$ | $=$ | $\min_{S \subset P, \|S\|=k} \text{cost}(P, \mathbf{w}, S)$ |
| $\text{OPT}_{k,z}(P, \mathbf{w})$ | $=$ | $\min_{S \subset P, \|S\|=k} \text{cost}(P, \hat{\mathbf{w}}, S)$, where $\hat{\mathbf{w}}$ is obtained from $\mathbf{w}$ by subtracting $z$ units from points of $P$ farthest from $S$ |

is the first distributed algorithm that can achieve an approximation arbitrarily close to the best one achievable by a (possibly bicriteria) polynomial sequential algorithm. Finally, we observe that our MapReduce algorithm can solve instances of the problem without outliers with similar approximation guarantees, and its memory requirements improve substantially upon those of [23].

**Organization of the Paper.** Section 2 contains the main definitions and some preliminary concepts. Section 3 describes a simplified coreset construction (Subsect. 3.1), the full algorithm (Subsect. 3.2), and a sketch of a more space-efficient coreset construction, which yields our main result (Subsect. 3.3). Finally, Sect. 4 discusses the extension of the algorithms in [16] and [14] to handle weighted instances. Section 5 provides some final remarks.

## 2 Preliminaries

Let $P$ be a set of points from a metric space with distance function $d(\cdot, \cdot)$. For any point $p \in P$ and subset $S \subseteq P$, define the distance between $p$ and $S$ as $d(p, S) = \min_{q \in S} d(p, q)$. Also, we let $p^S$ denote a point of $S$ closest to $p$, that is, a point such that $d(p, p^S) = d(p, S)$, with ties broken arbitrarily. The discrete *k-means* problem requires that, given $P$ and an integer $k < |P|$, a set $S \subset P$ of $k$ *centers* be determined, minimizing the cost function $\text{cost}(P, S) = \sum_{p \in P} d(p, S)^2$. We focus on a robust version of discrete $k$-means, known in the literature as *$k$-means with $z$ outliers*, where, given an additional integer parameter $z < |P|$, we seek a set $S \subset P$ of $k$ centers minimizing the cost function $\text{cost}(P \setminus \text{out}_z(P, S), S)$, where $\text{out}_z(P, S)$ denotes the set of $z$ points of $P$ farthest from $S$, with ties broken arbitrarily. We let $\text{OPT}_k(P)$ (resp., $\text{OPT}_{k,z}(P)$) denote the cost of the optimal solution of $k$-means (resp., $k$-means with $z$ outliers) on $P$. The following two facts state technical properties that will be needed in the analysis. (Proofs, omitted for brevity, can be found in the full version of this extended abstract [11].)

**Fact 1.** *For every $k, z > 0$ we have* $\text{OPT}_{k+z}(P) \leq \text{OPT}_{k,z}(P)$.

**Fact 2.** *For any $p, q, t \in P$, $S \subseteq P$, and $c > 0$, we have:*

$$d(p, S) \leq d(p, q) + d(q, S)$$
$$d(p, t)^2 \leq (1 + c)d(p, q)^2 + (1 + 1/c)d(q, t)^2.$$

In the *weighted* variant of $k$-means, each point $p \in P$ carries a positive integer weight $w_p$. Letting $\mathbf{w} : P \to \mathbb{Z}^+$ denote the weight function, the problem requires to determine a set $S \subset P$ of $k$ centers minimizing the cost function $\text{cost}(P, \mathbf{w}, S) = \sum_{p \in P} w_p \cdot d(p, S)^2$. Likewise, the weighted variant of $k$-means with $z$ outliers requires to determine $S \subset P$ which minimizes the cost function $\text{cost}(P, \hat{\mathbf{w}}, S)$, where $\hat{\mathbf{w}}$ is obtained from $\mathbf{w}$ by decrementing the weights associated with the points of $P$ farthest from $S$, progressively until exactly $z$ units of weights overall are subtracted (again, with ties broken arbitrarily). We let $\text{OPT}_k(P, \mathbf{w})$ and $\text{OPT}_{k,z}(P, \mathbf{w})$ denote the cost of the optimal solutions of the two weighted variants above, respectively. Table 1 summarizes the main notations used in the paper.

**Doubling Dimension.** The algorithms presented in this paper are designed for general metric spaces, and their performance is analyzed in terms of the dimensionality of the dataset $P$, as captured by the well-established notion of doubling dimension [18], extensively used in the analysis of clustering [6,10] and other primitives [5,7], and defined as follows. For any $p \in P$ and $r > 0$, let the *ball of radius $r$ centered at $p$* be the set of points of $P$ at distance at most $r$ from $p$. The *doubling dimension* of $P$ is the smallest value $D$ such that for every $p \in P$ and $r > 0$, the ball of radius $r$ centered at $p$ is contained in the union of at most $2^D$ balls of radius $r/2$, centered at suitable points of $P$. The doubling dimension can be regarded as a generalization of the Euclidean dimensionality to general spaces. In fact, it is easy to see that any $P \subset \mathbb{R}^{\text{dim}}$ under Euclidean distance has doubling dimension $O(\text{dim})$.

**Model of Computation.** We present and analyze our algorithms using the *MapReduce* model of computation [12,24], which is one of the reference models for the distributed processing of large datasets, and has been effectively used for clustering problems (e.g., see [3,6,25]). A MapReduce algorithm specifies a sequence of *rounds*, where in each round, a multiset $X$ of key-value pairs is first transformed into a new multiset $X'$ of pairs by applying a given *map function* in parallel to each individual pair, and then into a final multiset $Y$ of pairs by applying a given *reduce function* (referred to as *reducer*) in parallel to each subset of pairs of $X'$ having the same key. Key performance indicators are the number of rounds and the maximum local memory required by individual executions of the map and reduce functions. Efficient algorithms typically target few (possibly, constant) rounds and substantially sublinear local memory. We expect that our algorithms can be easily ported to the popular *Massively Parallel Computation* (MPC) model [4].

## 3 MapReduce Algorithm for $k$-Means with $z$ Outliers

In this section, we present a MapReduce algorithm for $k$-means with $z$ outliers running in $O(1)$ rounds with sublinear local memory. As typical of many efficient algorithms for clustering and related problems, our algorithm uses the following coreset-based approach. First, a suitably small weighted coreset $T$ is extracted from the input $P$, such that each point $p \in P$ has a "close" proxy $\pi(p) \in T$, and the weight $w_q$ of each $q \in T$ is the number of points of $P$ for which $q$ is proxy. Then, the final solution is obtained by running on $T$ the best (possibly slow) sequential approximation algorithm for weighted $k$-means with $z$ outliers. Essential to the success of this strategy is that $T$ can be computed efficiently in a distributed fashion, its size is much smaller than $|P|$, and it represents $P$ well, in the sense that: (i) the cost of any solution with respect to $P$ can be approximated well in $T$; and (ii) $T$ contains a good solution to $P$.

In Subsect. 3.1 we describe a coreset construction, building upon the one presented in [17,23] for the case without outliers, but with crucial modifications and a new analysis needed to handle the more general cost function, and to allow the use of bicriteria approximation algorithms on the coreset. In Subsect. 3.2 we present and analyze the final algorithm, while in Subsect. 3.3 we outline how a refined coreset construction can yield substantially lower local memory requirements.

### 3.1 Flexible Coreset Construction

We first formally define two properties that capture the quality of the coreset computed by our algorithm. Let $T$ be a subset of $P$ weighted according to a proxy function $\pi : P \to T$, where the weight of each $q \in T$ is $w_q = |\{p \in P : \pi(p) = q\}|$.

**Definition 1.** *For* $\gamma \in (0,1)$, $(T, \mathbf{w})$ *is a* $\gamma$-approximate coreset for $P$ with respect to $k$ and $z$ *if for every* $S, Z \subset P$, *with* $|S| \leq k$ *and* $|Z| \leq z$, *we have:*

$$|\text{cost}(P \backslash Z, S) - \text{cost}(T, \hat{\mathbf{w}}, S)| \leq \gamma \cdot \text{cost}(P \backslash Z, S),$$

*where* $\hat{\mathbf{w}}$ *is such that for each* $q \in T$, $\hat{w}_q = w_q - |\{p \in Z : \pi(p) = q\}|$.

**Definition 2.** *For* $\gamma \in (0,1)$, $(T, \mathbf{w})$ *is a* $\gamma$-centroid set for $P$ with respect to $k$ and $z$ *if there exists a set* $X \subseteq T$ *of at most* $k$ *points such that*

$$\text{cost}(P \backslash \text{out}_z(P, X), X) \leq (1+\gamma) \cdot \text{OPT}_{k,z}(P).$$

In other words, a $\gamma$-approximate coreset can faithfully estimate (within relative error $\gamma$) the cost of *any* solution with respect to the entire input dataset $P$, while a $\gamma$-centroid set is guaranteed to contain *one* good solution for $P$. The following technical lemma states a sufficient condition for a weighted set to be an approximate coreset.

**Lemma 1.** *Let* $(T, \mathbf{w})$ *be such that* $\sum_{p \in P} d(p, \pi(p))^2 \leq \delta \cdot \mathrm{OPT}_{k,z}(P)$. *Then,* $(T, \mathbf{w})$ *is a* $\gamma$*-approximate coreset for* $P$ *with respect to* $k$ *and* $z$*, with* $\gamma = \delta + 2\sqrt{\delta}$.

*Proof.* Consider two arbitrary subsets $S, Z \subset P$ with $|S| = k$ and $|Z| = z$, and let $\hat{\mathbf{w}}$ be obtained from $\mathbf{w}$ by subtracting the contributions of the elements in $Z$ from the weights of their proxies. We have:

$$
\begin{aligned}
|\mathrm{cost}(P \backslash Z, S) - \mathrm{cost}(T, \hat{\mathbf{w}}, S)| &= |\sum_{p \in P \backslash Z} d(p, S)^2 - \sum_{q \in T} \hat{w}_q d(q, S)^2| \\
&\leq \sum_{p \in P \backslash Z} \left| d(p, S)^2 - d(\pi(p), S)^2 \right| \\
&\leq \sum_{p \in P \backslash Z} (d(p, \pi(p)) + 2d(p, S)) d(p, \pi(p)) \\
&\quad \text{(since, by Fact 2, } -d(p, \pi(p) \leq d(p, S) - d(\pi(p), S) \leq d(p, \pi(p))) \\
&= \sum_{p \in P \backslash Z} d(p, \pi(p))^2 + 2 \sum_{p \in P \backslash Z} d(p, S) \cdot d(p, \pi(p)).
\end{aligned}
$$

By the hypothesis, we have that $\sum_{p \in P} d(p, \pi(p))^2 \leq \delta \cdot \mathrm{OPT}_{k,z}(P)$, and since $\mathrm{OPT}_{k,z}(P) \leq \mathrm{cost}(P \backslash Z, S)$, the first sum is upper bounded by $\delta \cdot \mathrm{cost}(P \backslash Z, S)$. Let us now concentrate on the second summation. It is easy to see that for any $a, b, c > 0$, we have that $2ab \leq ca^2 + (1/c)b^2$. Therefore,

$$
\begin{aligned}
2 \sum_{p \in P \backslash Z} d(p, S) \cdot d(p, \pi(p)) &\leq \sqrt{\delta} \sum_{p \in P \backslash Z} d(p, S)^2 + \left(1/\sqrt{\delta}\right) \sum_{p \in P \backslash Z} d(p, \pi(p))^2 \\
&\leq 2\sqrt{\delta} \cdot \mathrm{cost}(P \backslash Z, S).
\end{aligned}
$$

The lemma follows since $\gamma = \delta + 2\sqrt{\delta}$. □

The first ingredient of our coreset construction is a primitive, called `CoverWithBalls`, which, given any set $X \subset P$, a precision parameter $\delta$, and a distance threshold $R$, builds a weighted set $Y \subset P$ whose size is not much larger than $X$, such that for each $p \in P$, $d(p, Y) \leq \delta \max\{R, d(q, X)\}$. Specifically, the primitive identifies, for each $p \in P$, a *proxy* $\pi(p) \in Y$ such that $d(p, \pi(p)) \leq \delta \max\{R, d(p, X)\}$. For every $q \in Y$, the returned weight $w_q$ is set equal to the number of points of $P$ for which $q$ is proxy. Primitive `CoverWithBalls` has been originally introduced in [23] and is based on a simple greedy procedure. For completeness, we report the pseudocode below, as Algorithm 1. We wish to remark that the proxy function $\pi$ is not explicitly represented and is reflected only in the vector $\mathbf{w}$. In our coreset construction, `CoverWithBalls` will be invoked multiple times to compute coresets of increasingly higher quality.

The second ingredient of our distributed coreset construction is some sequential algorithm, referred to as `SeqkMeans` in the following, which, given in input a

**Algorithm 1:** CoverWithBalls$(P, X, \delta, R)$

```
1  Y ← ∅;
2  while P ≠ ∅ do
3      q ←— arbitrarily selected point in P;
4      Y ←— Y ∪ {q}; w_q ←— 1;
5      foreach p ∈ P do
6          if d(p,q) ≤ δ max{R, d(p,X)} then
7              remove p from P;
8              w_q ←— w_q + 1; {implicitly, q becomes the proxy π(p) of p}
9          end
10     end
11 end
12 return (Y, w)
```

dataset $Q$ and an integer $k$, computes a $\beta$-approximate solution to the standard $k$-means problem *without outliers* with respect to $Q$ and $k$.

We are ready to present a 2-round MapReduce algorithm, dubbed MRcoreset, that, on input a dataset $P$, the values $k$ and $z$, and a precision parameter $\gamma$, combines the two ingredients presented above to produce a weighted coreset which is both an $O(\gamma)$-approximate coreset and an $O(\gamma)$-centroid set with respect to $k$ and $z$. The computation performed by MRcoreset$(P, k, z, \gamma)$ in each round is described below.

**First Round.** The dataset $P$ is evenly partitioned into $L$ equally sized subsets, $P_1, P_2, \ldots, P_L$, through a suitable map function. Then, a reducer function comprising the following steps is run, in parallel, on each $P_i$, with $1 \leq i \leq L$:

1. SeqkMeans is invoked with input $(P_i, k')$, where $k'$ is a suitable function of $k$ and $z$ that will be fixed later in the analysis, returning a solution $S_i \subset P_i$.
2. Let $R_i = \sqrt{\text{cost}(P_i, S_i)/|P_i|}$. The primitive CoverWithBalls$(P_i, S_i, \gamma/\sqrt{2\beta}, R_i)$ is invoked, returning a weighted set of points $(C_i, \mathbf{w}^{C_i})$.

**Second Round.** The same partition of $P$ into $P_1, P_2, \ldots, P_L$ is used. A suitable map function is applied so that each reducer receives, as input, a distinct $P_i$ and the triplets ($|P_j|$, $R_j$, $C_j$) for all $1 \leq j \leq L$ from Round 1 (the weights $\mathbf{w}^{C_j}$ are ignored). Then, for $1 \leq i \leq L$, in parallel, the reducer in charge of $P_i$ sets $R = \sqrt{\sum_{j=1}^{L} |P_j| \cdot R_j^2/|P|}$, $C = \cup_{j=1}^{L} C_j$, and invokes CoverWithBalls$(P_i, C, \gamma/\sqrt{2\beta}, R)$. The invocation returns the weighted set $(T_i, \mathbf{w}^{T_i})$.
The final coreset returned by the algorithm is $(T, \mathbf{w}^T)$, where $T = \cup_{i=1}^{L} T_i$ and $\mathbf{w}^T$ is the weight function such that $\mathbf{w}^{T_i}$ is the projection of $\mathbf{w}^T$ on $P_i$, for $1 \leq i \leq L$.

We now analyze the main properties of the weighted coreset returned by MRcoreset, which will be exploited in the next subsection to derive the performance-accuracy tradeoffs featured by our distributed solution to $k$-means with $z$ outliers. Recall that we assumed that **SeqkMeans** is instantiated with an approximation algorithm that, when invoked on input $(P_i, k')$, returns a set $S_i \subset P_i$ of $k'$ centers such that $\text{cost}(P_i, S_i) \leq \beta \cdot \text{OPT}_{k'}(P_i)$, for some $\beta \geq 1$. Let $D$ denote the doubling dimension of $P$. The following lemma is a consequence of the analysis in [23] for the case without outliers, and its proof is a simple composition of the proofs of Lemmas 3.6, 3.11, and 3.12 in that paper.

**Lemma 2.** *Let* $(C, \mathbf{w}^C)$ *and* $(T, \mathbf{w}^T)$ *be the weighted coresets computed by* MRcoreset$(P, k, z, \gamma)$, *and let* $\pi^C, \pi^T$ *be the corresponding proxy functions. We have:*

$$\sum_{p \in P} d(p, \pi^X(p))^2 \leq 4\gamma^2 \cdot \text{OPT}_{k'}(P), \quad (\textit{with}\, X = C, T)$$

*and*

$$|C| = O\left(|L| \cdot k' \cdot (8\sqrt{2\beta}/\gamma)^D \cdot \log |P|\right),$$
$$|T| = O\left(|L|^2 \cdot k' \cdot (8\sqrt{2\beta}/\gamma)^{2D} \cdot \log^2 |P|\right).$$

As noted in the introduction, while the doubling dimension $D$ appears in the above bounds, the algorithm does not require the knowledge of this value, which would be hard to compute. The next theorem establishes the main result of this section regarding the quality of the coreset $(T, \mathbf{w}^T)$ with respect to the $k$-means problem with $z$ outliers.

**Theorem 1.** *Let* $\gamma$ *be such that* $0 < \gamma \leq \sqrt{3/8} - 1/2$. *By setting* $k' = k + z$ *in the first round,* MRcoreset$(P, k, z, \gamma)$ *returns a weighted coreset* $(T, \mathbf{w}^T)$ *which is a* $(4\gamma + 4\gamma^2)$*-approximate coreset and a* $27\gamma$*-centroid set for* $P$ *with respect to* $k$ *and* $z$.

*Proof.* Define $\sigma = 4\gamma + 4\gamma^2$ and, by the hypothesis on $\gamma$, note that $\sigma \leq 1/2$. The fact that $(T, \mathbf{w}^T)$ is a $\sigma$-approximate coreset for $P$ with respect to $k$ and $z$, follows directly from Fact 1, Lemma 1 (setting $\delta = 4\gamma^2$), and Lemma 2. We are left to show that $(T, \mathbf{w}^T)$ is a $27\gamma$-centroid set for $P$ with respect to $k$ and $z$. Let $S^* \subset P$ be the optimal set of $k$ centers and let $Z^* = \text{out}_z(P, S^*)$. Hence, $\text{cost}(P \backslash Z^*, S^*) = \text{OPT}_{k,z}(P)$. Define $X = \{p^T : p \in S^*\} \subset T$. We show that $X$ is a good solution for the $k$-means problem with $z$ outliers for $P$. Clearly, $\text{cost}(P \backslash \text{out}_z(P, X), X) \leq \text{cost}(P \backslash Z^*, X)$, hence it is sufficient to upper bound the latter term. To this purpose, consider the weighted set $(C, \mathbf{w}^C)$ computed at the end of Round 1, and let $\pi^C$ be the proxy function defining the weights $\mathbf{w}^C$. Arguing as before, we can conclude that $(C, \mathbf{w}^C)$ is also a $\sigma$-approximate coreset for $P$ with respect to $k$ and $z$. Therefore, since $\sigma \leq 1/2$,

$$\text{cost}(P \backslash Z^*, X) \leq \frac{1}{1 - \sigma} \text{cost}(C, \hat{\mathbf{w}}^C, X) \leq (1 + 2\sigma) \text{cost}(C, \hat{\mathbf{w}}^C, X),$$

where $\hat{\mathbf{w}}^C$ is obtained from $\mathbf{w}^C$ by subtracting the contributions of the elements in $Z^*$ from the weights of their proxies. Then, we have:

$$\begin{aligned}
\text{cost}(C, \hat{\mathbf{w}}^C, X) &= \sum_{q \in C} \hat{w}_q^C d(q, X)^2 \\
&\leq (1+\gamma) \sum_{q \in C} \hat{w}_q^C d(q, q^{S^*})^2 + (1 + (1/\gamma)) \sum_{q \in C} \hat{w}_q^C d(q^{S^*}, X)^2 \\
&\quad \text{(by Fact 2)} \\
&\leq (1+\gamma)(1+\sigma)\text{OPT}_{k,z}(P) + (1 + (1/\gamma)) \sum_{q \in C} \hat{w}_q^C d(q^{S^*}, X)^2 \\
&\quad \text{(since } (C, \mathbf{w}^T) \text{ is a } \sigma\text{-approximate coreset).}
\end{aligned}$$

We now concentrate on the term $\sum_{q \in C} \hat{w}_q^C d(q^{S^*}, X)^2$. First observe that, since $X \subset T$ contains the point in $T$ closest to $q^{S^*}$, we have $d(q^{S^*}, X) = d(q^{S^*}, T)$ and `CoverWithBalls` guarantees that $d(q^{S^*}, T) \leq (\gamma/\sqrt{2\beta}) \max\{R, d(q^{S^*}, C)\}$, where $R$ is the parameter used in `CoverWithBalls`. Also, for $q \in C$, $d(q^{S^*}, C) \leq d(q^{S^*}, q)$. Now,

$$\begin{aligned}
\sum_{q \in C} \hat{w}_q^C d(q^{S^*}, X)^2 &\leq (\gamma^2/(2\beta)) \sum_{q \in C} \hat{w}_q^C (R^2 + d(q, S^*)^2) \\
&\leq (\gamma^2/(2\beta)) \left( ((|P| - z)/|P|) \sum_{i=1}^{L} |P_i| \cdot R_i^2 + \sum_{q \in C} \hat{w}_q^C d(q, S^*)^2 \right) \\
&\leq (\gamma^2/(2\beta)) \left( \sum_{i=1}^{L} \text{cost}(P_i, S_i) + \sum_{q \in C} \hat{w}_q^C d(q, S^*)^2 \right) \\
&\leq (\gamma^2/(2\beta)) \left( \beta \sum_{i=1}^{L} \text{OPT}_{k+z}(P_i) + \text{cost}(C, \hat{\mathbf{w}}^C, S^*) \right) \\
&\leq (\gamma^2/2) \left( \sum_{i=1}^{L} \text{OPT}_{k+z}(P_i) + \text{cost}(C, \hat{\mathbf{w}}^C, S^*) \right) \quad \text{(since } \beta \geq 1\text{).}
\end{aligned}$$

Using the triangle inequality and Fact 1, it is easy to show that $\sum_{i=1}^{L} \text{OPT}_{k+z}(P_i) \leq 4 \cdot \text{OPT}_{k,z}(P)$. Moreover, since $(C, \mathbf{w}^C)$ is a $\sigma$-approximate coreset for $P$ with respect to $k$ and $z$, $\text{cost}(C, \hat{\mathbf{w}}^C, S^*) \leq (1+\sigma)\text{OPT}_{k,z}(P)$. Consequently, $\sum_{q \in C} \hat{w}_q^C d(q^{S^*}, X)^2 \leq (\gamma^2/2)(5+\sigma)\text{OPT}_{k,z}(P)$. Putting it all together and recalling that $\sigma = 4\gamma + 4\gamma^2 \leq 1/2$, tedious computations yield that $\text{cost}(P \backslash Z^*, X) \leq (1 + 27\gamma)\text{OPT}_{k,z}(P)$. □

### 3.2 Complete Algorithm

Let `SeqWeightedkMeansOut` be a sequential algorithm for weighted $k$-means with $z$ outliers, which, given in input a weighted set $(T, \mathbf{w}^T)$ returns a solution $S$ of

$\rho k$ centers such that $\text{cost}(T, \hat{\mathbf{w}}^T, S) \leq \alpha \cdot \text{OPT}_{k,z}(T, \mathbf{w})$, where $\rho \geq 1$ and $\hat{\mathbf{w}}^T$ is obtained from $\mathbf{w}$ by subtracting $\tau z$ units of weight from the points of $T$ farthest from $S$, for some $\tau \geq 1$. Observe that values of $\rho$ and $\tau$ greater than 1 allow for sequential *bicriteria algorithms*, that is, those requiring more centers or more outliers to achieve an approximation guarantee on $\text{OPT}_{k,z}(T, \mathbf{w})$.

For $\gamma > 0$, the complete algorithm first extracts a weighted coreset $(T, \mathbf{w}^T)$ by running the 2-round $\texttt{MRcoreset}(P, \rho k, \tau z, \gamma)$ algorithm, setting $k' = \rho k + \tau z$ in its first round. Then, in a third round, the coreset is gathered in a single reducer which runs $\texttt{SeqWeightedkMeansOut}(T, \mathbf{w}^T, k, z)$ to compute the final solution $S$. We have:

**Theorem 2.** *For $0 < \gamma \leq \sqrt{3/8} - 1/2$ and $\rho, \tau \geq 1$, the above 3-round MapReduce algorithm computes a solution $S$ of at most $\rho k$ centers such that*

$$\text{cost}(P \backslash \text{out}_{\tau z}(P, S), S) \leq (\alpha + O(\gamma)) \cdot \text{OPT}_{k,z}(P),$$

*and requires $O\left(|P|^{2/3} \cdot (\rho k + \tau z)^{1/3} \cdot (8\sqrt{2\beta}/\gamma)^{2D} \cdot \log^2 |P|\right)$ local memory.*

*Proof.* Let $T$ be the coreset computed at Round 2, and let $\hat{Z} \subseteq P$ be such that the weight function $\hat{\mathbf{w}}^T$, associated to the solution $S$ computed in Round 3, can be obtained from $\mathbf{w}^T$ by subtracting the contribution of each point in $\hat{Z}$ from the weight of its proxy in $T$. Clearly, $|\hat{Z}| \leq \tau z$ and $\text{cost}(P \backslash \text{out}_{\tau z}(P, S), S) \leq \text{cost}(P \backslash \hat{Z}, S)$. Now, let $\sigma = 4\gamma + 4\gamma^2 \leq 1/2$. We know from Theorem 1 that $(T, \mathbf{w}^T)$ is a $\sigma$-approximate coreset for $P$ with respect to $\rho k$ and $\tau z$. We have:

$$\begin{aligned} \text{cost}(P \backslash \hat{Z}, S) &\leq \frac{1}{1-\sigma} \text{cost}(T, \hat{\mathbf{w}}^T, S) \\ &\leq (1 + 2\sigma) \text{cost}(T, \hat{\mathbf{w}}^T, S) \leq (1 + O(\gamma)) \cdot \alpha \cdot \text{OPT}_{k,z}(T, \mathbf{w}). \end{aligned}$$

Since $\text{OPT}_{\rho k, \tau z}(P) \leq \text{OPT}_{k,z}(P)$, Fact 1 and Lemma 2 can be used to prove that both $(C, \mathbf{w}^C)$ (computed in Round 1) and $(T, \mathbf{w}^T)$ are $\sigma$-approximate coresets for $P$ with respect to $k$ and $z$. A simple adaptation of the proof of Theorem 1 shows that $(T, \mathbf{w}^T)$ is a $27\gamma$-centroid set for $P$ with respect to $k$ and $z$. Now, let $X \subseteq T$ be the set of at most $k$ points of Definition 2, and let $\overline{\mathbf{w}}^T$ be obtained from $\mathbf{w}^T$ by subtracting the contributions of the elements in $\text{out}_z(P, X)$ from the weights of their proxies. By the optimality of $\text{OPT}_{k,z}(T, \mathbf{w})$ we have that

$$\begin{aligned} \text{OPT}_{k,z}(T, \mathbf{w}) &\leq \text{cost}(T, \overline{\mathbf{w}}^T, X) \\ &\leq (1 + \sigma) \text{cost}(P \backslash \text{out}_z(P, X), X) \\ &\leq (1 + \sigma)(1 + 27\gamma) \cdot \text{OPT}_{k,z}(P) = (1 + O(\gamma)) \cdot \text{OPT}_{k,z}(P). \end{aligned}$$

Putting it all together, we conclude that

$$\text{cost}(P \backslash \text{out}_{\tau z}(P, S), S) \leq \text{cost}(P \backslash \hat{Z}, S) \leq (\alpha + O(\gamma)) \cdot \text{OPT}_{k,z}(P).$$

The local memory bound follows from Lemma 2, setting $L = (|P|/(\rho k + \tau z))^{1/3}$. □

### 3.3 Improved Local Memory

The local memory of the algorithm presented in the previous subsections can be substantially improved by modifying Round 2 of $\texttt{MRcoreset}(P, k, z, \gamma)$ as follows. Now, each reducer first determines a $\beta$-approximate solution $S_C$ to weighted $k$-means (without outliers) on $(C, \mathbf{w}^C)$, with $k' = k + z$ centers, and then runs $\texttt{CoverWithBalls}(C, S_C, \gamma/\sqrt{2\beta}, R)$, yielding a weighted set $C'$, whose size is a factor $|L|$ less than the size of $C$. Finally, the reducer runs $\texttt{CoverWithBalls}(P_i, C', \gamma/\sqrt{2\beta}, R)$. A small adaptation to CoverWithBalls is required in this case: when point $p \in C$ is mapped to a proxy $q \in C'$, the weight of $q$ is increased by $w_p^C$ rather than by one. With this modification, we get the result stated in the following theorem, whose proof follows the same lines as the one of Theorem 2, and is found in the full version of this extended abstract [11].

**Theorem 3.** *For $0 < \gamma \leq (\sqrt{3} - \sqrt{2})/6$ and $\rho, \tau \geq 1$, the modified 3-round MapReduce algorithm computes a solution $S$ of at most $\rho k$ centers such that*

$$\text{cost}(P \backslash \text{out}_{\tau z}(P, S), S) \leq (\alpha + O(\gamma)) \cdot \text{OPT}_{k,z}(P),$$

*and requires $O\left(|P|^{1/2} \cdot (\rho k + \tau z)^{1/2} \cdot (8\sqrt{2\beta}/\gamma)^{2D} \cdot \log^2 |P|\right)$ local memory.*

## 4 Instantiation with Different Sequential Algorithms for Weighted $k$-Means

We briefly outline how to adapt two state-of-the-art sequential algorithms for $k$-means with $z$ outliers in general metrics, namely, LS-Outlier by [16] and k-Means-Out by [14], to handle the weighted variant of the problem. Both these algorithms are bicriteria, in the sense that the approximation guarantee is obtained at the expense of a larger number of outliers (LS-Outlier), or a larger number of centers (k-Means-Out). Then, we assess the accuracy-resource trade-offs attained by the MapReduce algorithm of Sect. 3, when these algorithms are employed in its final round.

Given a set of points $P$ and parameters $k$ and $z$, LS-Outlier starts with a set $C \subset P$ of $k$ arbitrary centers and a corresponding set $Z = \text{out}_z(P, C)$ of outliers. Then, for a number of iterations, it refines the selection $(C, Z)$ to improve the value $\text{cost}(P \backslash Z, C)$ by a factor at least $1 - \varepsilon/k$, for a given $\varepsilon > 0$, until no such improvement is possible. In each iteration, first a new set $C'$ is computed through a standard local-search [20] on $P \backslash Z$, and then a new pair $(C_{\text{new}}, Z_{\text{new}})$ with minimal $\text{cost}(P \backslash Z_{\text{new}}, C_{\text{new}})$ is identified among the following ones: $(C', Z \cup \text{out}_z(P \backslash Z, C')$ and $(C'', Z \cup \text{out}_z(P, C'')$, where $C''$ is obtained from $C'$ with the most profitable swap between a point of $P$ and a point of $C'$.

It is shown in [16] that LS-Outlier returns a pair $(C, Z)$ such that $\text{cost}(P \backslash Z, C) \leq 274 \cdot \text{OPT}_{k,z}(P)$ and $|Z| = O\left((1/\varepsilon) kz \log(|P| \Delta)\right)$, where $\Delta$ is the ratio between the maximum and minimum pairwise distances in $P$. LS-Outlier can be adapted for the weighted variant of the problem as follows. Let $(P, \mathbf{w})$ denote the input pointset. In this weighted setting, the role of a set $Z$ of $m$

outliers is played by a weight function $\mathbf{w}^Z$ such that $0 \leq w_p^Z \leq w_p$, for each $p \in P$, and $\sum_{p \in P} w_p^Z = m$. The union of two sets of outliers in the original algorithm is replaced by the pointwise sum or pointwise maximum of the corresponding weight functions, depending on whether the two sets are disjoint (e.g., $Z$ and $\text{out}_z(P \backslash Z, C')$) or not (e.g., $Z$ and $\text{out}_z(P, C'')$). It can be proved that with this adaptation the algorithm returns a pair $(C, \mathbf{w}^Z)$ such that $\text{cost}(P, \mathbf{w} - \mathbf{w}^Z, C) \leq 274 \cdot \text{OPT}_{k,z}(P, \mathbf{w})$ and $\sum_{p \in P} w_p^Z = O\left((1/\varepsilon) kz \log(|P| \Delta)\right)$.

Algorithm `k-Means-Out` also implements a local search. For given $\rho, \varepsilon > 0$, the algorithm starts from an initial set $C \subset P$ of $k$ centers and performs a number of iterations, where $C$ is refined into a new set $C'$ by swapping a subset $Q \subset C$ with a subset $U \subset P \backslash C$ (possibly of different size), such that $|Q|, |U| \leq \rho$ and $|C'| \leq (1 + \varepsilon)k$, as long as $\text{cost}(P \backslash \text{out}_z(P, C'), C') < (1 - \varepsilon/k) \cdot \text{cost}(P \backslash \text{out}_z(P, C), C)$. It is argued in [14] that for $\rho = (D/\varepsilon)^{\Theta(D/\varepsilon)}$, `k-Means-Out` returns a set $C$ of at most $(1 + \varepsilon)k$ centers such that $\text{cost}(P \backslash \text{out}_z(P, C), C) \leq (1 + \varepsilon) \cdot \text{OPT}_{k,z}(P)$, where $D$ is the doubling dimension of $P$. The running time is exponential in $\rho$, so the algorithm is polynomial when $D$ is constant.

The adaptation of `k-Means-Out` for the weighted variant for an input $(P, \mathbf{w})$ is straightforward and concerns the cost function only. It is sufficient to substitute $\text{cost}(P \backslash \text{out}_z(P, C), C)$ with $\text{cost}(P, \hat{\mathbf{w}}, C)$, where $\hat{\mathbf{w}}$ is obtained from $\mathbf{w}$ by decrementing the weights associated with the points of $P$ farthest from $C$, progressively until exactly $z$ units of weights overall are subtracted. It can be proved that with this adaptation the algorithm returns a set $C$ of at most $(1+\varepsilon)k$ centers such that $\text{cost}(P, \hat{\mathbf{w}}, C) \leq (1 + \varepsilon) \cdot \text{OPT}_{k,z}(P)$.

By Theorems 2 and 3, these two sequential strategies can be invoked in Round 3 of our MapReduce algorithm to yield bicriteria solutions with an additive $O(\gamma)$ term in the approximation guarantee, for any sufficiently small $\gamma > 0$.

## 5 Conclusions

We presented a flexible, coreset-based framework able to yield a scalable, 3-round MapReduce algorithm for $k$-means with $z$ outliers, with an approximation quality which can be made arbitrarily close to the one of any sequential (bicriteria) algorithm for the weighted variant of the problem, and requiring local memory substantially sublinear in the size of the input dataset, when this dataset has bounded dimensionality. Future research will target the adaptation of the state-of-the-art non-bicriteria LP-based algorithm of [21] to the weighted case, and the generalization of our approach to other clustering problems.

**Acknowledgements.** This work was supported, in part, by MUR of Italy, under Projects PRIN 20174LF3T8 (AHeAD: Efficient Algorithms for HArnessing Networked Data), and PNRR CN00000013 (National Centre for HPC, Big Data and Quantum Computing), and by the University of Padova under Project SID 2020 (RATED-X: Resource-Allocation TradEoffs for Dynamic and eXtreme data).

## References


1. Ahmadian, S., Norouzi-Fard, A., Svensson, O., Ward, J.: Better guarantees for k-means and Euclidean k-median by primal-dual algorithms. SIAM J. Comput. **49**(4), 97–156 (2020)
2. Arthur, D., Vassilvitskii, S.: K-means++: the advantages of careful seeding. In: Proceedings of the ACM-SIAM SODA, pp. 1027–1035 (2007)
3. Bakhthemmat, A., Izadi, M.: Decreasing the execution time of reducers by revising clustering based on the futuristic greedy approach. J. Big Data **7**(1), 6 (2020)
4. Beame, P., Koutris, P., Suciu, D.: Communication steps for parallel query processing. In: Proceedings of the ACM PODS, pp. 273–284 (2013)
5. Ceccarello, M., Pietracaprina, A., Pucci, G.: Fast coreset-based diversity maximization under matroid constraints. In: Proceedings of the ACM WSDM, pp. 81–89 (2018)
6. Ceccarello, M., Pietracaprina, A., Pucci, G.: Solving k-center clustering (with outliers) in MapReduce and streaming, almost as accurately as sequentially. Proc. VLDB Endow. **12**(7), 766–778 (2019)
7. Ceccarello, M., Pietracaprina, A., Pucci, G., Upfal, E.: A practical parallel algorithm for diameter approximation of massive weighted graphs. In: Proceedings of the IEEE IPDPS, pp. 12–21 (2016)
8. Charikar, M., Khuller, S., Mount, D., Narasimhan, G.: Algorithms for facility location problems with outliers. In: Proceedings of the ACM-SIAM SODA, pp. 642–651 (2001)
9. Chen, J., Azer, E., Zhang, Q.: A practical algorithm for distributed clustering and outlier detection. In: Proceedings of the NeurIPS, pp. 2253–2262 (2018)
10. Cohen-Addad, V., Feldmann, A., Saulpic, D.: Near-linear time approximation schemes for clustering in doubling metrics. J. ACM **68**(6), 44:1–44:34 (2021)
11. Dandolo, E., Pietracaprina, A., Pucci, G.: Distributed k-means with outliers in general metrics. CoRR abs/2202.08173 (2022)
12. Dean, J., Ghemawat, S.: MapReduce: simplified data processing on large clusters. Commun. ACM **51**(1), 107–113 (2008)
13. Deshpande, A., Kacham, P., Pratap, R.: Robust k-means++. In: Proceedings of the UAI, pp. 799–808 (2020)
14. Friggstad, Z., Khodamoradi, K., Rezapour, M., Salavatipour, M.: Approximation schemes for clustering with outliers. ACM Trans. Algorithms **15**(2), 26:1–26:26 (2019)
15. Guha, S., Li, Y., Zhang, Q.: Distributed partial clustering. ACM Trans. Parallel Comput. **6**(3), 11:1–11:20 (2019)
16. Gupta, S., Kumar, R., Lu, K., Moseley, B., Vassilvitskii, S.: Local search methods for k-means with outliers. Proc. VLDB Endow. **10**(7), 757–768 (2017)
17. Har-Peled, S., Mazumdar, S.: On coresets for k-means and k-median clustering. In: Proceedings of the ACM STOC, pp. 291–300 (2004)
18. Heinonen, J.: Lectures on Analysis of Metric Spaces. Universitext. Springer, Berlin (2001)
19. Hennig, C., Meila, M., Murtagh, F., Rocci, R.: Handbook of Cluster Analysis. CRC Press, Boca Raton (2015)
20. Kanungo, T., Mount, D., Netanyahu, N., Piatko, C., Silverman, R., Wu, A.Y.: A local search approximation algorithm for k-means clustering. Comput. Geom. **28**(2–3), 89–112 (2004)

21. Krishnaswamy, R., Li, S., Sandeep, S.: Constant approximation for k-median and k-means with outliers via iterative rounding. In: Proceedings of the ACM STOC 2018, pp. 646–659 (2018)
22. Li, S., Guo, X.: Distributed k-clustering for data with heavy noise. In: Proceedings of the NeurIPS, pp. 7849–7857 (2018)
23. Mazzetto, A., Pietracaprina, A., Pucci, G.: Accurate MapReduce algorithms for k-median and k-means in general metric spaces. In: Proceedings of the ISAAC, pp. 34:1–34:16 (2019)
24. Pietracaprina, A., Pucci, G., Riondato, M., Silvestri, F., Upfal, E.: Space-round tradeoffs for MapReduce computations. In: Proceedings of the ACM ICS, pp. 235–244 (2012)
25. Sreedhar, C., Kasiviswanath, N., Chenna Reddy, P.: Clustering large datasets using k-means modified inter and intra clustering (KM-I2C) in Hadoop. J. Big Data **4**, 27 (2017)
26. Statman, A., Rozenberg, L., Feldman, D.: k-means: outliers-resistant clustering+++. MDPI Algorithms **13**(12), 311 (2020)
27. Wei, D.: A constant-factor bi-criteria approximation guarantee for k-means++. In: Proceedings of the NIPS, pp. 604–612 (2016)

# A Parallel Scan Algorithm in the Tensor Core Unit Model

Anastasios Zouzias(✉) and William F. McColl

Computing Systems Laboratory, Zurich Research Center, Huawei Technologies, Zürich, Switzerland
{anastasios.zouzias,bill.mccoll}@huawei.com

**Abstract.** We present a parallel scan (prefix sum) algorithm in the Tensor Core Unit (TCU) model of computation. The TCU model assumes that multiplication between two square matrices of constant size $s$ is a basic operation. In the $(s^2, \ell)$-TCU model, we show that for inputs of size $n$, the algorithm has depth at most $2\lfloor \log_s(n) \rfloor$ and runs in $\mathcal{O}(n(1+\ell/s^2)/p + (s^2+\ell)\log_s(n))$ assuming $p$ tensor core units. Equivalently, the algorithm performs $\mathcal{O}(n/s^2)$ multiplications of square matrices of size $s$.

**Keywords:** Prefix Sum · Scan · Matrix Multiplication · Tensor Core Unit Model

## 1 Introduction

Prefix sum (scan) is an important computational primitive in parallel computing with a plethora of applications [1,12]. An extensive literature on parallel scan algorithms provides trade-offs between the depth (length of the critical path of computation) and work (number of binary arithmetic operations) of several approaches in the Parallel Random-Access Machine (PRAM) model of computation. Prefix computation also occurs in carry-lookahead adders where several parallel scan algorithms have been (implicitly) designed (see [10,23] and references therein). Moreover, the depth and size trade-offs for parallel optimal prefix circuits are well-understood for binary operations [21,22]. In this work, we consider prefix sums in an emerging model of computation. Following the seminal work of [8], we present a parallel scan algorithm in a recently proposed Tensor Core Unit (TCU) model of computation [6,7].

The TCU model, denoted[1] by $(s^2, \ell)$-TCU, is a standard RAM model where there exists a circuit named tensor unit that performs matrix multiplication between a matrix of size $s \times s$ and $s \times m$ $(m \geq s)$ in time $\mathcal{O}(ms + \ell)$, where $s > 1$ and $\ell \geq 0$ are two model parameters [7]. The parameter $\ell$ corresponds to the latency of initiating a matrix multiplication operation on the tensor unit. Here,

[1] The first parameter $s^2$ of the TCU model is squared to avoid writing square roots on the matrix sizes.


J. Cano et al. (Eds.): Euro-Par 2023, LNCS 14100, pp. 489–502, 2023.
https://doi.org/10.1007/978-3-031-39698-4_33

in addition to the runtime analysis of the TCU model, we present a simplified analysis of the work/depth model by assuming that the multiplication of two square matrices of size $s$ is a basic operation and counting the matrix multiplications required by the algorithm. Then, we translate the bounds on the number of matrix multiplications to a time complexity bound of the TCU model.

The reader might wonder why the TCU model is currently an emerging domain-specific model of computation. The primary reason is that deep learning and High-Performance Computing (HPC) workloads have increased the demand for hardware that delivers more efficient matrix multiplication operations [14,16]. Hardware vendors have responded to such demand by manufacturing accelerators with specialized hardware units known as *tensor core units*. A representative list of specialized hardware units includes TPUs [13,14], Tensor Cores (TCs) [19] and Huawei's Ascend Cube Unit [17,18] to name a few. In short, today's high-performance hardware accelerators contain tensor core units that allow efficient multiplication of constant-sized square matrices. As advocated recently in [7], these tensor core units can be employed beyond deep learning and HPC applications to other essential computational primitives (matrix computations, graph algorithms, etc.). Here, we aim to advance this line of work by studying the computational primitive of parallel prefix sums.

The paper's main contribution is the analysis of a parallel scan algorithm (Algorithm 1) in the TCU model in terms of depth, number of matrix multiplications, work and time complexity. Interestingly enough, Algorithm 1 can be viewed as a generalization of the Brent-Kung scan algorithm [3]; Brent-Kung is a special case of Algorithm 1 where the matrices have size two, see Fig. 1 for examples.

Our motivation to study the parallel scan primitive in the TCU model is based on two applications: training gradient boosting trees models and parallel sorting. Indeed, an inspection of the binary tree split computation for training gradient boosting trees reveals that multiple prefix sum operations occur [5]. For the application of parallel sorting, following Blelloch's reduction of Radixsort to prefix sums [1], we resolve in the affirmative the open question "can TCU sort?" raised during the presentation of [6].

We conclude this section by introducing our notation. We use the terms *prefix sum* and *scan* interchangeably. By prefix sum, we always refer to *inclusive* prefix sum unless explicitly noted. All results are stated for the addition operator but can be extended to any arbitrary associative operator. Vectors are denoted by lower-case boldface font letters; vectors are always considered column vectors. $\mathbf{1}_s$ denotes the all-ones vector of size $s$. Let $\alpha$ be a scalar, and $\boldsymbol{q}$ be a vector of size $s-1$; we denote by $[\alpha; \boldsymbol{q}]$ the column vector of size $s$ whose first entry is $\alpha$ concatenated by $\boldsymbol{q}$. Matrices are denoted by upper-case bold-face letters. $\boldsymbol{L}_s$ is the lower triangular all-ones square matrix of size $s$, including ones on the diagonal. We use zero-based indexing for vectors and matrices. For a vector $\boldsymbol{x}$, we denote $\boldsymbol{x}[\text{start} :: \text{step}]$ the subvector of $\boldsymbol{x}$ starting from index *start* with a stride of size *step*. We frequently use the ceiling inequality: $\lceil \alpha \rceil + \lceil \beta \rceil \leq \lceil \alpha + \beta \rceil + 1$ for scalars $\alpha, \beta$.

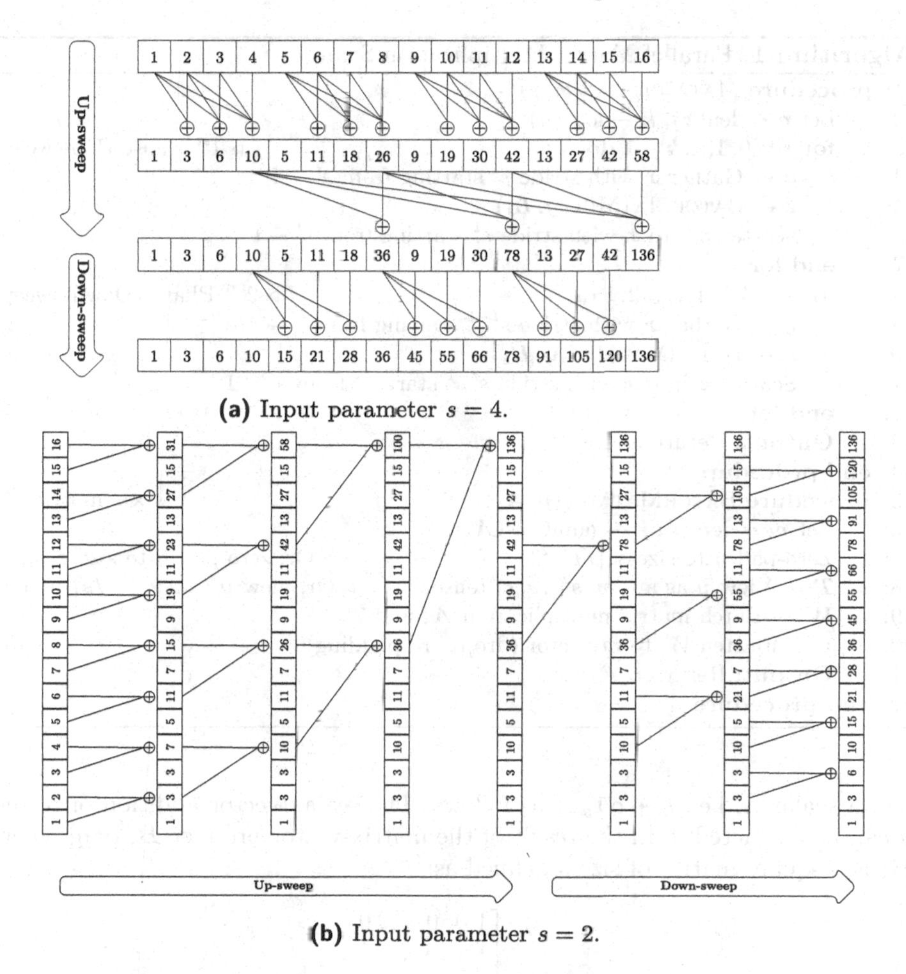


**(a)** Input parameter $s = 4$.

**(b)** Input parameter $s = 2$.

**Fig. 1.** Examples of Algorithm 1 for input $\boldsymbol{x} = [1, 2, \ldots, 16]$.

## 2 MatMulScan: Parallel Scan in the TCU Model

In this section, we present a parallel scan algorithm (Algorithm 1) designed to take advantage of the computational speedup offered by the matrix multiplication circuit of the TCU model. All numerical operations of Algorithm 1 are multiplications between two square matrices of size $s$. Surprisingly enough, only two special (constant) matrices take place as the left operand in all matrix multiplications. These two special matrices encode the computation of local prefix sums and a scalar/vector add operation.

Let's first define the matrix that encodes the (local) prefix sum operator. Given a vector $\boldsymbol{w}$ of size $s$, it is straightforward to verify that the prefix sum of $\boldsymbol{w}$ equals the matrix product $\boldsymbol{L}_s \boldsymbol{w}$ (recall $\boldsymbol{L}_s$ is the lower triangular all-ones square matrix). Next, we encode the addition between a vector $\boldsymbol{q}$ of size $s - 1$

**Algorithm 1.** Parallel Matrix Multiplication Scan

```
1: procedure MatMulScan(x, s)
2:     Let n ← len(x), k ← log_s(n)                                ▷ n := s^k
3:     for t = 0, 1, .., k − 1 do                        ▷ 1st Phase (Up-sweep)
4:         y ← Gather x with stride s^t starting from s^t − 1
5:         z ← BatchMatMul(y, L_s)
6:         Scatter z into x with stride s^t starting from s^t − 1
7:     end for
8:     for t = k − 1, . . . , 2, 1 do                  ▷ 2nd Phase (Down-sweep)
9:         y ← Gather x with stride s^(t−1) starting from s^t − 1
10:        z ← BatchMatMul(y, B_s)
11:        Scatter z into x with stride s^(t−1) starting from s^t − 1
12:    end for
13:    Output: Return x
14: end procedure
15: procedure BatchMatMul(y, A_s)                            ▷ s × s matrix A_s
16:    Let m ← len(y), s ← numCols(A_s)
17:    Zero-pad y to size s^2⌈m/s^2⌉              ▷ Or, zero-pad y to size s⌈m/s⌉
18:    T ← View y as a (⌈m/s^2⌉, s, s)-tensor     ▷ Or, view y as s × ⌈m/s⌉ matrix
19:    W ← Batch matrix multiplication A_s and T
20:    z ← Flatten W to m-vector (drop zero-padding)
21:    Output: Return z
22: end procedure
```

and a scalar $\alpha$, i.e., $\boldsymbol{q} + \alpha \mathbf{1}_{s-1}$ as follows. The scalar/vector addition of $\alpha$ and $\boldsymbol{q}$ can be extracted from the result of the matrix-vector product $\boldsymbol{B}_s[\alpha; \boldsymbol{q}]$ where $\boldsymbol{B}_s$ is a square matrix of size $s$ defined as:

$$\boldsymbol{B}_s := \begin{bmatrix} 1 & 0 & 0 & \dots & 0 \\ 1 & 1 & 0 & \dots & 0 \\ 1 & 0 & 1 & \dots & 0 \\ \vdots & 0 & 0 & \ddots & 0 \\ 1 & 0 & \dots & 0 & 1 \end{bmatrix}.$$

Now we are ready to define the main algorithm (MatMulScan). Algorithm 1 consists of two phases, as is typical in work-efficient parallel scan algorithms: the up-sweep phase (Lines 3–7) and the down-sweep (Lines 8–11) phase. In the first up-sweep phase, the prefix sums of the indices with exponentially increasing sizes are computed: $s, s^2, s^3, \dots$, etc. At the end of the first phase, the prefix sums are correct only on an exponentially increasing set of indices. The remaining indices contain a "local prefix sum", i.e., a prefix sum of $s$ contiguous indices that will be corrected in the second phase. The second down-sweep phase broadcasts and adds all the precedent prefix sums to the remaining local prefix sums. At each round of both phases, a strided subset of the input vector is viewed as a matrix/tensor and pre-multiplied with a constant matrix of size $s$ as is described in the procedure BatchMatMul (Lines 15–22).

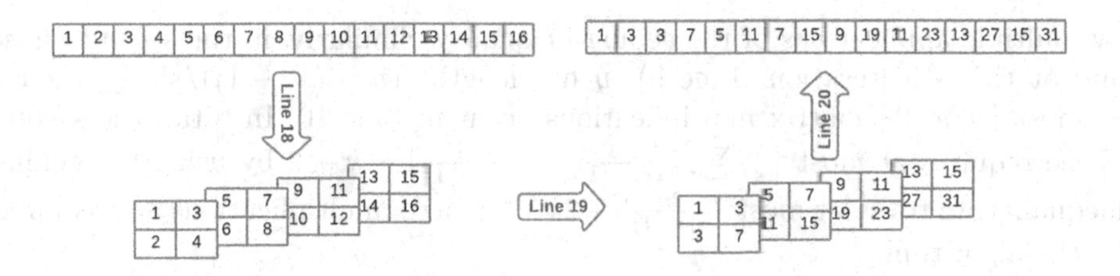


**Fig. 2.** Execution of BATCHMATMUL($\boldsymbol{y} = [1; 2; \ldots; 16], \boldsymbol{A}_2 = \boldsymbol{L}_2$).

The BATCHMATMUL procedure takes a vector $\boldsymbol{y}$ and a square matrix $\boldsymbol{A}_s$ of size $s$ as input. BATCHMATMUL performs a multiplication between $\boldsymbol{A}_s$ and a reshaped tensor view of $\boldsymbol{y}$. The vector/tensor reshaping operations of the BATCHMATMUL method (Lines 18 and 20) need more clarification. In Line 18, a vector is viewed as a three-dimensional tensor as follows. The zero-padded vector $\boldsymbol{y}$ (Line 17) is split into multiple chunks of size $s^2$, and each chunk is viewed as an $s \times s$ matrix in column-major layout. Each $s \times s$ matrix is stacked into a three-dimensional tensor of size $(\lceil n/s^2 \rceil, s, s)$ following the natural ordering, i.e., the first chunk is assigned to index zero of the first dimension of the tensor, the second chunk to index one, etc.

Figure 2 provides an illustrative example of the execution of BATCHMATMUL with inputs: a vector of size $n = 16$ and $\boldsymbol{A}_2 = \boldsymbol{L}_2$. In addition, we provide an end-to-end functional implementation of Algorithm 1 as a reference implementation in Appendix A.

### 2.1 Analysis

In this section, we analyse Algorithm 1 in terms of depth, the number of matrix multiplications required, work and time complexity in the TCU model. In the analysis, we ignore[2] the cost of the gather-scatter memory operations and the cost of vector/tensor reshaping operations. Recall that multiplication between two square matrices of size $s$ is a basic operation.

**Lemma 1.** *Fix an integer $s \geq 2$. Let $\boldsymbol{x}$ be a vector of size $n = s^k$ for some $k$. Algorithm 1 has depth $2k - 1$ in the TCU model and performs at most $\lceil \frac{2n}{s(s-1)} \rceil + 2k - 2$ matrix multiplications. Moreover, the number of scalar binary additions executed by Algorithm 1 is $\lceil n(1 + s/2) \rceil + \mathcal{O}(s^3 \log_s(n))$.*

*Proof.* The first phase takes $k$ steps, and the second takes $k - 1$ steps. In total, the depth is $2k - 1 = 2\log_s(n) - 1 = 2\log_2(n)/\log_2(s) - 1$ in the TCU model.

Let's calculate the number of matrix multiplications required per phase. In the first phase and at the $t$-th iteration (Line 4) $\boldsymbol{y}$ has length $\lfloor (n - (s^t - 1))/s^t \rfloor$. Hence, at most $\lceil n/s^{t+2} \rceil$ matrix multiplications occur in Line 5. In total, the first phase requires at most $\lceil \frac{n}{s^2} \sum_{t=0}^{k-1} \frac{1}{s^t} \rceil \leq \lceil \frac{n}{s(s-1)} \rceil + k - 1$ matrix multiplications

[2] That said, the cost of memory operations (memory coalescing, bank conflicts, etc.) is crucial to achieving high performance in an actual implementation.

by multiple applications of the ceiling inequality. Similarly, in the second phase and at the $t$-th iteration (Line 9), $\boldsymbol{y}$ has length $\lfloor (n - (s^t - 1))/s^{t-1} \rfloor$. Hence, at most $\lceil n/s^{t+1} \rceil$ matrix multiplications occur in Line 10. In total, the second phase requires at most $\lceil \frac{n}{s^2} \sum_{t=1}^{k-1} \frac{1}{s^{t-1}} \rceil \leq \lceil \frac{n}{s(s-1)} \rceil + k - 2$ by using the ceiling inequality. In total, at most $\lceil \frac{2n}{s(s-1)} \rceil + 2k - 2$ matrix multiplications are required by the algorithm.

Now, let's compute the work of the algorithm in terms of scalar binary additions when simulated in the RAM model, i.e., bound the number of arithmetic operations of the matrix multiplications. The number of scalar binary additions of matrix-vector multiplication between $\boldsymbol{L}_s$ and a vector of size $s$ takes $s(s-1)/2$ scalar additions. Therefore, the work of the first phase is

$$\left( \lceil \frac{n}{s(s-1)} \rceil + k - 1 \right) \cdot s \cdot \frac{s(s-1)}{2} = \lceil ns/2 \rceil + \mathcal{O}(ks^3).$$

Similarly, the work of the second phase is

$$\left( \lceil \frac{n}{s(s-1)} \rceil + k - 2 \right) \cdot s \cdot (s-1) = n + \mathcal{O}(ks^2),$$

since each matrix multiplication between $\boldsymbol{B}_s$ and a square matrix of size $s$ takes $s(s-1)$ scalar additions. In total, the work of the algorithm is $\lceil n(1 + s/2) \rceil + \mathcal{O}(s^3 \log_s(n))$.

We defer the correctness proof of Algorithm 1 to Appendix A.1.

Next, we translate the analysis of Lemma 1 into a time complexity bound in the $(s^2, \ell)$-TCU model with a minor modification of Algorithm 1. We view the tensor $\boldsymbol{T}$ (Line 18) into a single rectangular matrix of size $s \times \lceil m/s \rceil$ by stacking over its first dimension in Line 19. The stacking allows us to avoid excessive matrix multiplication invocations, i.e., increased latency cost.

**Theorem 1.** *Fix an integer $s \geq 2$. Let $\boldsymbol{x}$ be a vector of size $n = s^k$ for some $k$. Algorithm 1 takes $\mathcal{O}(n + \ell k)$ time in the $(s^2, \ell)$-TCU model.*

*Proof.* Let's bound the latency cost and the matrix multiplication cost separately. Recall that the depth of the computation is $2k - 1$. At each round, the batched matrix multiplication (Line 19) can be viewed as a multiplication invocation between an $s \times s$ and $s \times \lceil m/s \rceil$ matrix ($m$ is defined in Line 17). Hence, the latency cost is $(2k - 1)\ell$ since $2k - 1$ matrix multiplication invocations take place. Next, let's bound the time cost of matrix multiplications. For all matrix multiplications of the first phase, the time required is $\sum_{j=0}^{k-1} \lceil \frac{n}{s^j} \frac{1}{s} \rceil s \leq s \lceil \frac{n}{s} \sum_{j=0}^{k-1} \frac{1}{s^j} \rceil + sk - s = \mathcal{O}(n)$, where the first inequality follows by the ceiling inequality and the second inequality since $\sum_{j=0}^{k-1} \frac{1}{s^j} \leq 2$ provided that $s \geq 2$. Similarly, the time required for the matrix multiplications in the second phase is $\sum_{j=0}^{k-2} \lceil \frac{n}{s^j} \frac{1}{s} \rceil s = \mathcal{O}(n)$. In total, the time complexity of Algorithm 1 in the $(s^2, \ell)$-TCU model is $\mathcal{O}(n + \ell \log_s(n))$.

### 2.2 Extend Algorithm 1 to Arbitrary Input Length

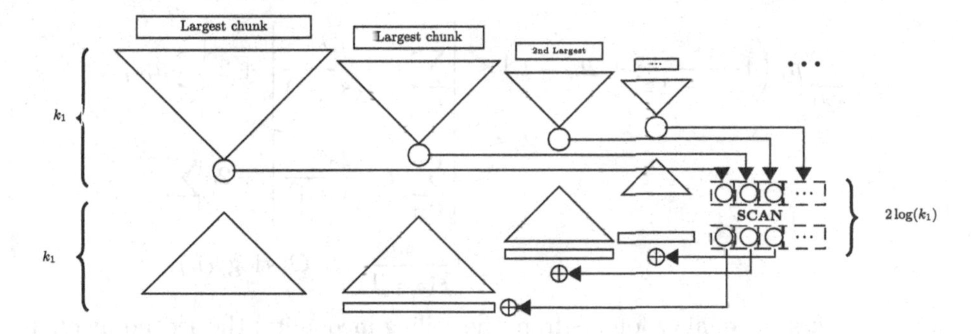


**Fig. 3.** Execution diagram of the general case leveraging Algorithm 1 as a building block. The diagram demonstrates that after the up-sweep phase of the first largest chunks of size $s^{k_1}$, the prefix sum computation of the maximum values of each chunk (excluding the first one) can be interleaved with the down-sweep computation of the largest chunks.

In this section, we extend Algorithm 1 for arbitrary input sizes (non-powers of $s$). The approach is based on a folklore approach, see for example [12, Chapter 11]. Let $n$ be an arbitrary positive number. Write $n$ in base $s$ as $n = \sum_i \mu_i s^{k_i}$ where $k_1 := \lfloor \log_s(n) \rfloor$, $0 \leq \mu_i < s$, and $k_1 > k_2 > \cdots \geq 0$. We assume that $n$ is given in base $s$.

The algorithm is depicted in Fig. 3 and consists of the following four steps:

1. Execute Algorithm 1 in parallel for each contiguous segment of sizes: $\mu_1$ times on chunks of size $s^{k_1}$, $\mu_2$ times on chunks of size $s^{k_2}$, ... etc.
2. Gather the maximum values of each segment after the corresponding $1^{\text{st}}$ phase of Algorithm 1 into a vector $\boldsymbol{w}$ of size at most $k_1(s-1)$. Indeed, there are at most $s-1$ multiples on each segment size and at most $k_1$ distinct segment sizes.
3. Zero-pad the vector of the maximum values to the smallest integer $q$ so that $k_1(s-1) \leq s^q$ holds. Run Algorithm 1 with the zero-padded input vector of length $s^q$, drop the zero-padding and write back the results on $\boldsymbol{w}$.
4. For each $i$-th entry of $\boldsymbol{w}$, in parallel, broadcast and add the value $w_i$ on the $i+1$ chunk of size $s^{k_{i+1}}$ using the BatchMatMul procedure of Algorithm 1.

Let us now analyse the above algorithm in terms of depth, number of matrix multiplications and runtime in the TCU model.

*Depth.* The first step has depth at most $2k_1 - 1$ since the largest chunks have size $s^{k_1}$ (Lemma 1). The execution of the second and third steps can be overlapped with the $2^{\text{nd}}$ phase of the execution of the first step for large enough $n$. The fourth step takes an extra round to perform a scalar/vector addition using matrix multiplications. In total, the depth is $2k_1 - 1 + 1 = 2\lfloor \log_2(n)/\log_2(s) \rfloor$.

*Matrix Multiplications.* Next, we upper bound the number of matrix multiplications. A direct application of Lemma 1 on the multiple segments of size $s^{k_1}, s^{k_2}, \ldots$ implies that the number of matrix multiplications is at most

$$\sum_{i\geq 1} \mu_i \left( \lceil \frac{2s^{k_i}}{s(s-1)} \rceil + 2k_i - 1 \right) \leq \left\lceil \sum_{i\geq 1} \mu_i \frac{2s^{k_i}}{s(s-1)} \right\rceil + 2 \sum_{i\geq 1} \mu_i k_i$$
$$\leq \left\lceil \sum_{i\geq 1} \mu_i \frac{2s^{k_i}}{s(s-1)} \right\rceil + 2s \sum_{i\geq 1} k_i$$
$$\leq \lceil \frac{2n}{s(s-1)} \rceil + \mathcal{O}(s \log_s^2(n))$$

where the first inequality follows from the ceiling inequality; the second inequality uses the fact that $\mu_i \leq s$; the third inequality follows since $k_i \leq k_1$, and there are at most $k_1$ terms in the sum. The number of matrix multiplications is negligible on steps 2 and 3 since the input size is $\mathcal{O}(sk_1)$. The fourth step performs a scalar/vector addition with matrix multiplications. Hence it takes at most

$$\sum_{i\geq 1} \mu_i \left\lceil \frac{s^{k_i}}{(s-1)^2} \right\rceil \leq \left\lceil \frac{2}{s(s-1)} \sum_{i\geq 1} \mu_i s^{k_i} \right\rceil + \sum_{i\geq 1} \mu_i = \lceil \frac{2n}{s(s-1)} \rceil + \mathcal{O}(s \log_s(n)),$$

where in the first inequality, we used the ceiling inequality and the fact that $\frac{1}{(s-1)^2} \leq \frac{2}{s(s-1)}$ for $s \geq 2$. In total, the number of matrix multiplications is $\lceil \frac{4n}{s(s-1)} \rceil + \mathcal{O}(s \log_s^2(n))$.

*Time Analysis in TCU Model.* Apply Theorem 1 on the $\mu_i$ segments of size $s^{k_i}$ implies that the time complexity is at most in the order of $\sum_i \mu_i \left(s^{k_i} + \ell k_i\right) = n + \ell \sum_i \mu_i k_i \leq n + \ell s \sum_i k_i \leq n + \ell s k_1^2$, where the first inequality holds since $\mu_i < s$ and the second inequality since $k_i \leq k_1$ and there are at most $k_1$ terms in the sum. In total, Step 1 takes $\mathcal{O}(n + \ell s \log_s^2(n))$ time.

Steps 2 and 3 are low-order terms and require $\mathcal{O}(s \log_s(n) + \ell \log_s \log_s(n))$ time. Next, we bound step 4. At each segment of size $s^{k_i}$, we view each segment as an $(s-1) \times \lceil s^{k_i}/(s-1) \rceil$ column-major matrix. Then, we prepend the constant row to this matrix that contains the broadcasted value of the previous segment, resulting in an $s \times \lceil s^{k_i}/(s-1) \rceil$ matrix. Similarly, the running time of step 4 in the TCU model is

$$\sum_{i>1} \mu_i \left( \lceil \frac{s^{k_i}}{(s-1)} \rceil + \ell \right) \leq \sum_{i\geq 1} \mu_i \lceil \frac{s^{k_i}}{(s-1)} \rceil + \ell \sum_{i\geq 1} \mu_i = \mathcal{O}(n/s + \ell s \log_s(n)).$$

The above discussion is summarized in the following corollary.

**Corollary 1.** *Fix an integer $s \geq 2$. Let $\boldsymbol{x}$ be a vector of size $n$. There is an algorithm in the $(s^2, \ell)$-TCU model that has depth at most $2\lfloor \log_s(n) \rfloor$, and takes $\mathcal{O}(n + s\ell \log_s^2(n))$ time. Equivalently, the algorithm performs $\mathcal{O}(n/s^2)$ matrix multiplications.*

Corollary 1 reveals that a single tensor core unit does not provide sufficient parallelism for prefix sum computation since the runtime has an additional $\mathcal{O}(s\ell \log_s^2(n))$ penalty. Therefore, an extension of the TCU model that consists of $p$ parallel tensor core units is essential to provide sufficient parallelism. Recall that the depth of the computation is at most $2\lfloor \log_s(n) \rfloor$ and $\mathcal{O}(n/s^2)$ matrix multiplications are required in total. Each matrix multiplication takes time $\mathcal{O}(s^2 + \ell)$. Hence an application of Brent's theorem [4] implies that the runtime is $\mathcal{O}(n(1 + \ell/s^2)/p + (s^2 + \ell) \log_s(n))$ when having $p$ parallel $(s^2, \ell)$-TCUs as advertised in the abstract.

### 2.3 Discussion

We shortly discuss some practical considerations of Algorithm 1. First, Algorithm 1 on the case where $s = 2$ corresponds to the Brent-Kung scan algorithm [2]. Moreover, for inputs of size $n$ that is a power of $s$, the fan-in[3] (and fan-out) on all the computations of Algorithm 1 viewed as a circuit with adder nodes are upper-bounded by $s$, see Fig. 1a. In a nutshell, there is a trade-off between the fan-in/-out and the depth of the computation in Algorithm 1. This trade-off is explicit in Lemma 1.

Next, we briefly discuss several implementation issues that could arise in an efficient implementation of Algorithm 1. Developing a high-performant implementation of parallel scan is a highly non-trivial task and requires a deep understanding of the underlying hardware [12]. As is evident by the definition of the matrices $\boldsymbol{L}_s$ and $\boldsymbol{B}_s$, the utilization of the tensor core unit is low due to the sparsity structure of these matrices. In the first phase, the tensor core unit could be at most 50% utilized due to the lower triangular operand $\boldsymbol{L}_s$. The utilization is extremely low in the second phase, roughly speaking $\mathcal{O}(1/s)$, since the tensor core unit is used for a scalar/vector add operation. However, in a practical implementation, the second phase's scalar/vector add operation can typically be efficiently performed using a vector unit if one exists in proximity to the tensor core unit. Last but not least, the scatter/gather memory operations of Algorithm 1 could be a critical bottleneck to achieving high performance if the tensor core units do not efficiently implement these operations.

## 3 Related Work

The study of accelerating the prefix sum (and reduction) operations using the tensor cores was first initiated in the seminal paper of [8] (to the best of our knowledge). The authors of [8] designed scan algorithms for the GPUs architecture, i.e., they proposed[4] a warp-level scan algorithm [8, Algorithm 6], and a block-level scan algorithm [8, Algorithm 7]. Moreover, they briefly mentioned

[3] Fan-in is the maximum number of inputs an adder can have. Similarly, fan-out is the maximum number of outputs.

[4] The main goal of the authors is to provide highly optimized kernels and, hence, use the terms of warp/block/grid of the CUDA programming model.

**Table 1.** Comparison of a few representative parallel prefix sum algorithms. Work is measured in terms of binary additions. (*) Depth is measured: in the PRAM model for prior work; and in the TCU model for Algorithm 1 and [8, Alg. 7].

| Method | Depth* | Work | Comments |
|---|---|---|---|
| Sklansky [20] | $\log_2(n)$ | $n\log_2(n)/2$ | Unbounded fan-out |
| Hillis-Steele [11] | $\log_2(n)$ | $n\log_2(n) - n + 1$ | a.k.a. Kogge-Stone [15] |
| Blelloch [1] | $2\log_2(n)$ | $2(n-1)$ | Exclusive Scan |
| Brent-Kung [2,3] | $2\log_2(n) - 1$ | $2n - \log_2(n) - 2$ | Inclusive Scan |
| [8, Alg. 7] | $5\lceil n/s^3\rceil$ | $\mathcal{O}(ns)$ | TCU/GEMMs |
| Algorithm 1 ($n = 2^k$) | $2\log_2(n) - 1$ | $2n + \mathcal{O}(\log_2(n))$ | TCU/(Fig. 1b) |
| Algorithm 1 ($n = 4^k$) | $\log_2(n) - 1$ | $3n + \mathcal{O}(\log_2(n))$ | TCU/$s = 4$ (Fig. 1a) |
| Algorithm 1 ($n = s^k$) | $2\log_s(n) - 1$ | $n(1 + s/2) + \mathcal{O}(s^3\log_s(n))$ | TCU/Lemma 1 |

that the device/grid level algorithm is based on the textbook approach, see Sect. 2.2. Here, we compare Algorithm 1 against Algorithm 7 of [8] in asymptotic analysis. A minor difference with our work is that GEneral Matrix Multiplication (GEMM) is considered as a basic operation in [8]. GEMM is, roughly speaking, a matrix multiplication followed by matrix addition on the output matrix product. Indeed, most tensor core units offer an efficient matrix multiplication and accumulation of the output result with no additional performance cost.

We should highlight that comparing the current work and [8] is not straightforward. The reason is that the goal of [8] was to improve the performance of the state-of-the-art GPU scan kernels (a very challenging task), whereas our focus is currently only limited to algorithmic design and analysis. Moreover, the authors mentioned that their approach works best for small segment sizes [8], whereas our approach might scale to larger input sizes. Nevertheless, we attempt to compare Algorithm 1 against Algorithm 7 of [8] below. In addition, we assume that GEMM operations are considered basic operation in the analysis below.

Algorithm 7 of [8] is expressed for the particular case $s = 16$, and it is assumed that each warp takes 256 elements, and each block has at most 16 warps. For comparison, we replace in [8, Alg. 7], the constants 16 and 256 with $s$ and $s^2$, respectively. If $n$ is large enough, Algorithm 7 of [8] serializes the processing on the block level (for loop in Lines 7–23 of [8, Alg. 7]) and, hence, the depth of the algorithm is at least $5\lceil n/s^3\rceil$ since at most $s$ warps exist per block and 3 GEMMS, an exclusive scan of size 16 and a broadcast is required. Regarding work, each warp gets $s^2$ elements, and each GEMM operation requires $\mathcal{O}(s^3)$ binary operations. Hence, the number of binary operations is $\mathcal{O}(ns)$.

From an implementation point of view, the authors of [8] demonstrated that by taking advantage of the additional computational power offered by the tensor core units, it is possible to improve the performance of the state-of-the-art and high-performance scan implementations for small segment sizes on GPUs. On the other hand, we haven't yet developed a high-performance implementation of Algorithm 1, but we plan to investigate such a direction in the near future.

Table 1 summarises several representative parallel scan algorithms from the literature. Prior work is evaluated on the PRAM model, whereas Algorithm 1 and [8, Alg. 7] are evaluated on the TCU model where we assume that multiplication of square matrices of constant size $s$ is a basic operation. As it is depicted in the table, for $s = 4$, Algorithm 1 has depth $\log_2(n) - 1$ in the TCU model. In this case, the work is $3n + \mathcal{O}(\log_2(n))$ when simulated in the PRAM model (to have a fair comparison in terms of work with prior work). It is not possible to make a fair comparison in terms of depth in the PRAM model since the fan-in/fan-out of Algorithm 1 is also increased from two to four. Algorithm 7 of [8] has linear depth in the TCU model, and its work is $\mathcal{O}(ns)$ when simulated in the PRAM model.

## 4 Conclusion and Future Work

We presented a parallel scan algorithm (MatMulScan) designed for the TCU model where matrix multiplication of square matrices of constant size is assumed to be a basic operation. A future research direction is to enlarge the applicability of the tensor core units to additional applications. Last but not least, we plan to design and develop a high-performant implementation based on MatMulScan using the Tensor Iterator Kernel (TIK) programming framework of the Ascend cube unit [17].

## A Appendix

We provide a functional end-to-end (but not high-performance) Python implementation of Algorithm 1 using NumPy (v1.24.1) [9]. The implementation demonstrates the memory layout operations required to orchestrate the batched matrix multiplications of Algorithm 1.

```
import numpy as np

def matmul_scan(x, s, k):
    L_s = np.tril(np.ones(s))
    B_s = np.eye(s)
    B_s[:, 0] = 1

    for t in range(k):
        start, step = s ** t - 1, s ** t
        y = x[start::step]
        z = batch_matmuls(y, L_s)
        x[start::step] = z

    for t in range(k - 1, 0, -1):
        start, step = s ** t - 1, s ** (t - 1)
        y = x[start::step]
        z = batch_matmuls(y, B_s)
        x[start::step] = z

def batch_matmuls(y, A_s):
    m, s = len(y), A_s.shape[0]
    y = y.flatten()
    extra_pad = int((s ** 2) * np.ceil(m / s ** 2))
    y.resize(extra_pad)

    T = y.reshape((-1, s, s)).transpose((0, 2, 1))
    W = A_s @ T # batched matrix multiplication
    z = np.reshape(W, (-1, s ** 2), order='F').flatten()
    return z[:m]
```

**Listing 1.1.** Reference implementation of Algorithm 1

### A.1 Correctness of Algorithm 1

In this section, we prove the correctness of Algorithm 1. We reformulate Algorithm 1 using recursion as stated in Algorithm 2. The recursive formulation will enable us to prove the correctness using strong induction. Indeed, we prove by induction that MatMulScanRecursive is correct for all inputs that are powers of $s$, given an arbitrary $s \geq 2$.

In particular, it suffices to show that the Recurse method with input $\boldsymbol{z}$ and $s$ has the following precondition/postcondition relation: given the precondition that on all consecutive chunks of size $s$ of $\boldsymbol{z}$, i.e., $(0, 1, \dots, s-1), (s, s+1, \dots, 2s-1), \dots$, the "local" prefix sums on each chunk is precomputed, Recurse returns the prefix sum of $\boldsymbol{z}$ (postcondition). Indeed, by the definition of MatMulScanRecursive in Line 2 the "local" prefix sums of size $s$ are computed and, in Line 3, the Recurse method is called with the precondition to be true.

**Algorithm 2.** Parallel Matrix Multiplication Scan (Recursive version)

1: **procedure** MATMULSCANRECURSIVE($\boldsymbol{x}$, $s$) ▷ $s \geq 2$
2: $\boldsymbol{z} \leftarrow$ BATCHMATMUL($\boldsymbol{x}, \boldsymbol{L}_s$) ▷ BATCHMATMUL() of Algorithm 1
3: **Output:** Return RECURSE($\boldsymbol{z}, s$)
4: **end procedure**
5: **procedure** RECURSE($\boldsymbol{z}$, $s$)
6: If len($\boldsymbol{z}$) $\leq s$, return $\boldsymbol{z}$ ▷ Termination criterion
7: start $\leftarrow s - 1$, step $\leftarrow s$
8: $\boldsymbol{z}$[start :: step] $\leftarrow$ BATCHMATMUL($\boldsymbol{z}$[start :: step], $\boldsymbol{L}_s$)
9: $\boldsymbol{z}$[start :: step] $\leftarrow$ RECURSE($\boldsymbol{z}$[start :: step], $s$)
10: $\boldsymbol{z}$[start :] $\leftarrow$ BATCHMATMUL($\boldsymbol{z}$[start :], $\boldsymbol{B}_s$)
11: **Output:** Return $\boldsymbol{z}$
12: **end procedure**

*Base Case.* For inputs of size less than $s$, the termination criterion of Line 6 is met, therefore the postcondition follows directly from the precondition since the input size is less than $s$.

*Inductive Step.* The inductive hypothesis is that RECURSE is correct for input sizes strictly less than $n$. We will show that RECURSE is correct for inputs of size $n$. Indeed, given an input $\boldsymbol{z}$ where all its "local" prefix sums are precomputed, we prove that RECURSE with input $\boldsymbol{z}$ returns the prefix sum of $\boldsymbol{z}$. Now, Line 8 computes the "local" prefix sums on the $s$-strided subvector $\boldsymbol{x}$[start :: step]. The prefix sum on $\boldsymbol{x}$[start :: step] is computed on Line 9 by the inductive hypothesis. Then, Line 11 broadcasts and add the correct prefix sum values of the $s$-strided subvector of $\boldsymbol{z}$ to the corresponding $s$ following indices of each subvector. Hence, the postcondition of RECURSE holds.

## References


1. Blelloch, G.E.: Prefix sums and their applications. In: Sythesis of Parallel Algorithms, pp. 35–60. Morgan Kaufmann (1990)
2. Brent, Kung: A regular layout for parallel adders. IEEE Trans. Comput. **C-31**(3), 260–264 (1982). https://doi.org/10.1109/TC.1982.1675982
3. Brent, R.P., Kung, H.T.: The chip complexity of binary arithmetic. In: Proceedings of the Symposium on Theory of Computing (STOC), pp. 190–200. ACM (1980). https://doi.org/10.1145/800141.804666
4. Brent, R.P.: The parallel evaluation of general arithmetic expressions. J. ACM **21**(2), 201–206 (1974). https://doi.org/10.1145/321812.321815
5. Chen, T., Guestrin, C.: XGBoost: a scalable tree boosting system. In: Proceedings of International Conference on Knowledge Discovery and Data Mining (KDD), pp. 785–794. ACM (2016). https://doi.org/10.1145/2939672.2939785
6. Chowdhury, R., Silvestri, F., Vella, F.: A computational model for tensor core units. In: Proceedings of Symposium on Parallelism in Algorithms and Architectures (SPAA), pp. 519–521. ACM (2020). https://doi.org/10.1145/3350755.3400252

7. Chowdhury, R., Silvestri, F., Vella, F.: Algorithm design for tensor units. In: Sousa, L., Roma, N., Tomás, P. (eds.) Euro-Par 2021. LNCS, vol. 12820, pp. 353–367. Springer, Cham (2021). https://doi.org/10.1007/978-3-030-85665-6_22
8. Dakkak, A., Li, C., Xiong, J., Gelado, I., Hwu, W.M.: Accelerating reduction and scan using tensor core units. In: Proceedings of the ACM International Conference on Supercomputing, ICS 2019, pp. 46–57. ACM (2019). https://doi.org/10.1145/3330345.3331057
9. Harris, C., et al.: Array programming with NumPy. Nature **585**(7825), 357–362 (2020). https://doi.org/10.1038/s41586-020-2649-2
10. Harris, D.: A taxonomy of parallel prefix networks. In: 2003 the Thirty-Seventh Asilomar Conference on Signals, Systems & Computers, vol. 2, pp. 2213–2217 (2003). https://doi.org/10.1109/ACSSC.2003.1292373
11. Hillis, W.D., Steele, G.L.: Data parallel algorithms. Commun. ACM **29**(12), 1170–1183 (1986). https://doi.org/10.1145/7902.7903
12. Hwu, W.W., Kirk, D.B., El Hajj, I.: Programming Massively Parallel Processors, 4th edn. Morgan Kaufmann (2023). https://doi.org/10.1016/B978-0-323-91231-0.00006-9
13. Jouppi, N.P., et al.: In-datacenter performance analysis of a tensor processing unit. In: Proceedings of International Symposium on Computer Architecture (ISCA), pp. 1–12. ACM (2017). https://doi.org/10.1145/3079856.3080246
14. Jouppi, N.P., et al.: Ten lessons from three generations shaped Google's TPUv4i: industrial product. In: Proceedings of International Symposium on Computer Architecture (ISCA), pp. 1–14 (2021). https://doi.org/10.1109/ISCA52012.2021.00010
15. Kogge, P.M., Stone, H.S.: A parallel algorithm for the efficient solution of a general class of recurrence equations. IEEE Trans. Comput. **C-22**(8), 786–793 (1973). https://doi.org/10.1109/TC.1973.5009159
16. Krizhevsky, A., Sutskever, I., Hinton, G.E.: ImageNet classification with deep convolutional neural networks. In: Advances in Neural Information Processing Systems (NIPS), pp. 1097–1105 (2012)
17. Liao, H., et al.: Ascend: a scalable and unified architecture for ubiquitous deep neural network computing: industry track paper. In: Proceedings of International Symposium on High-Performance Computer Architecture (HPCA), pp. 789–801. IEEE (2021). https://doi.org/10.1109/HPCA51647.2021.00071
18. Liao, H., Tu, J., Xia, J., Zhou, X.: DaVinci: a scalable architecture for neural network computing. In: Hot Chips Symposium on High-Performance Chips (HCS), pp. 1–44 (2019). https://doi.org/10.1109/HOTCHIPS.2019.8875654
19. NVIDIA Authors: NVIDIA DGX-1 with Tesla V100 system architecture. Technical report MSU-CSE-06-2, Nvidia Corporation (2017). https://images.nvidia.com/content/pdf/dgx1-v100-system-architecture-whitepaper.pdf
20. Sklansky, J.: Conditional-sum addition logic. IRE Trans. Electron. Comput. **EC-9**(2), 226–231 (1960). https://doi.org/10.1109/TEC.1960.5219822
21. Snir, M.: Depth-size trade-offs for parallel prefix computation. J. Algorithms **7**(2), 185–201 (1986). https://doi.org/10.1016/0196-6774(86)90003-9
22. Zhu, H., Cheng, C.K., Graham, R.: On the construction of zero-deficiency parallel prefix circuits with minimum depth. ACM Trans. Des. Autom. Electron. Syst. **11**(2), 387–409 (2006). https://doi.org/10.1145/1142155.1142162
23. Zimmermann, R.V.: Binary adder architectures for cell-based VLSI and their synthesis. Ph.D. thesis, Swiss Federal Institute of Technology Zurich, Zurich (1997)

# Improved Algorithms for Monotone Moldable Job Scheduling Using Compression and Convolution

Kilian Grage(✉), Klaus Jansen, and Felix Ohnesorge

Kiel University, Christian-Albrechts-Platz 4, 24118 Kiel, Germany
kilian-g@t-online.de, kj@informatik.uni-kiel.de, felix-eutin@gmx.de

**Abstract.** In the moldable job scheduling problem one has to assign a set of $n$ jobs to $m$ machines, in order to minimize the time it takes to process all jobs. Each job is moldable, so it can be assigned not only to one but any number of the identical machines. We assume that the work of each job is monotone and that jobs can be placed non-contiguously. In this work we present a $(\frac{3}{2}+\epsilon)$-approximation algorithm with a worst-case runtime of $O(n\log^2(\frac{1}{\epsilon}+\frac{\log(\epsilon m)}{\epsilon})+\frac{n}{\epsilon}\log(\frac{1}{\epsilon})\log(\epsilon m))$ when $m \leq 16n$. This is an improvement over the best known algorithm of the same quality by a factor of $\frac{1}{\epsilon}$ and several logarithmic dependencies. We complement this result with an improved FPTAS with running time $O(n\log^2(\frac{1}{\epsilon}+\frac{\log(\epsilon m)}{\epsilon}))$ for instances with many machines $m > 8\frac{n}{\epsilon}$. This yields a $\frac{3}{2}$-approximation with runtime $O(n\log^2(\log m))$ when $m > 16n$.

We achieve these results through one new core observation: In an approximation setting one does not need to consider all $m$ possible allotments for each job. We will show that we can reduce the number of relevant allotments for each job from $m$ to $O(\frac{1}{\epsilon}+\frac{\log(\epsilon m)}{\epsilon})$. Using this observation immediately yields the improved FPTAS. For the other result we use a reduction to the knapsack problem first introduced by Mounié, Rapine and Trystram. We use the reduced number of machines to give a new elaborate rounding scheme and define a modified version of this knapsack instance. This in turn allows for the application of a convolution based algorithm by Axiotis and Tzamos. We further back our theoretical results through a practical implementation and compare our algorithm to the previously known best result. These experiments show that our algorithm is faster and generates better solutions.

**Keywords:** machine scheduling · moldable · compression · convolution

## 1 Introduction

The machine scheduling problem, where one assigns jobs to machines in order to finish all jobs in a preferably short amount of time, has been a core problem

Supported by DFG-Project JA 612 /25-1.


J. Cano et al. (Eds.): Euro-Par 2023, LNCS 14100, pp. 503–517, 2023.
https://doi.org/10.1007/978-3-031-39698-4_34

of computer science. Its applications are not only limited to the usual context of executing programs on a range of processor cores but it also has many applications in the real world. For example one can view machines as workers and jobs as tasks or assignments that need to be done. In this setting we allow that multiple workers can work on one task together to solve it more quickly. This however gives rise to another layer of this problem, where one has to assign a number of machines to each job and a starting time. The resulting problem is called Parallel Task Scheduling with Moldable Jobs. Our goal is to minimize the time when the last job finishes, which is called the *makespan*.

In this problem the time necessary for a job to be processed is dependent on the number of assigned machines. The work of a job $j$ with $k$ machines is defined as $w(j,k) := t(j,k) \cdot k$, which intuitively is the area of the job. We further assume that this function for a fixed job $j$ is non-decreasing in the number of machines. This monotony assumption is natural since distributing the task on multiple machines will not reduce the amount of work but actually induce a bit of overhead due to communication among the machines.

Since finding an optimal solution to this problem is NP-hard [12] our goal is to present approximation algorithms. Such an algorithm has to guarantee for every instance $I$ with optimal makespan $OPT(I)$ to find a solution with a makespan of at most $c \cdot OPT(I)$ for some multiplicative approximation ratio $c > 1$. In this paper we introduce two algorithms that work with an accuracy $\epsilon > 0$: The first guarantees an approximation ratio of $c_1 = 1 + \epsilon$ in time $O(n \log^2(\frac{4}{\epsilon} + \frac{\log(\epsilon m)}{\epsilon}))$ under the additional premise that $m > 8\frac{n}{\epsilon}$. Our second algorithm achieves an approximation ratio of $c_2 = \frac{3}{2} + \epsilon$ with running time $O(n \log^2(\frac{1}{\epsilon} + \frac{\log(\epsilon m)}{\epsilon}) + \frac{n}{\epsilon} \log(\frac{1}{\epsilon}) \log(\epsilon m))$ when $16n \geq m$. If we apply the first algorithm for $\epsilon = \frac{1}{2}$ and combine both algorithms we get in total an efficient $(\frac{3}{2} + \epsilon)$-approximation.

We achieve our results through a new core observation: Although a job can be assigned to every possible number of machines, not all $m$ different allotments may be relevant when looking for an approximate solution. In fact we will show that if $m$ is large enough we can reduce the number of relevant machine allotments to $O(\frac{1}{\epsilon} + \frac{\log(\epsilon m)}{\epsilon})$. This overall assessment is based on the concept of *compression* introduced by Jansen and Land [11].

We use the reduced number of relevant allotments to schedule moldable jobs via an instance of the knapsack problem. This approach was initially introduced by Mounié, Rapine and Trystram [14]. We give a new rounding scheme to convert moldable jobs into knapsack items to define a modified version of their knapsack instance. We construct this knapsack instance in a way that the number of different sizes and profits is small. This allows for the efficient application of a knapsack algorithm introduced by Axiotis and Tzamos [1] using convolution. Their algorithm works well on such instances and thanks to our rounding we can even do the required pre-processing for their algorithm efficiently in linear time.

## 1.1 Problem Definitions and Notations

Two problems will play an important role in this paper: The first being parallel task scheduling with moldable jobs, which we will call moldable job scheduling in the following. In this problem one is given a set $J$ of $n$ jobs and a set $M$ of $m$ equal machines. We write $[l] = \{i \in \mathbb{N} \mid 1 \leq i \leq l\}$ for any $l \in \mathbb{N}$. The processing time of a job in the moldable setting is given through a function $t : J \times [m] \to \mathbb{R}_{\geq 0}$ where $t(j,k)$ denotes the processing time of job $j$ on $k$ machines. We denote with $\gamma(j,d) = \min\{i \in [m] \mid t(j,i) \leq d\}$ the minimal number of machines required for job $j$ to achieve processing time smaller than $d$. If $d$ is not achievable with $m$ machines, we say $\gamma(j,d)$ is undefined.

For a solution of this problem we require two things: First an allotment $\alpha : J \to [m]$ and an assignment of starting times $s : J \to \mathbb{R}_{\geq 0}$. For simplicity we denote $\alpha_j := \alpha(j)$ and $s_j = s(j)$ respectively. A feasible solution must now fulfill that at any time at most $m$ machines are in use. Denote with $U(t) := \{j \in J \mid t \in [s_j, s_j + t(j,\alpha_j)]\}$ the jobs that are processed at time $t$. If at all times $t \in \mathbb{R}_{\geq 0}$ we have that $\sum_{j \in U(t)} \alpha_j \leq m$ then the schedule defined by $\alpha$ and $s$ is feasible.

Finally we look to minimize the makespan of this schedule, which is the time when the last job finishes. Given an allotment $\alpha$ and starting times $s$ the makespan is defined by $\max_{j \in J}\{s_j + t(j,\alpha_j)\}$. As mentioned before the work of a job is defined as $w(j,k) = k \cdot t(j,k)$ and we assume the work for every job is non-decreasing. More precisely for all jobs $j$ and $k, k' \in [m]$ with $k \leq k'$ we have $w(j,k) \leq w(j,k')$.

The second main problem we will consider in this work is the knapsack problem[1]. For our scheduling algorithm we will require to solve a knapsack instance. In the knapsack problem one is given a knapsack with capacity $t \in \mathbb{N}$ and a set of $n$ items where each item $i$ is identified with a profit value $p_i \in \mathbb{R}_{>0}$ and a size or weight $w_i \in \mathbb{N}$. The task is to find a maximum profit subset of these items such that the total weight does not exceed the capacity $t$.

### 1.2 Related Work

The moldable job scheduling problem is known to be NP-hard [7] even with monotone work functions [12]. Further there is no polynomial time approximation algorithm with a guarantee less than $\frac{3}{2}$ unless P=NP [6]. Belkhale and Banerjee gave a 2-approximation for the problem with monotony [3], which was later improved to the non-monotone case by Turek et al. [16]. Ludwig and Tiwari improved the running time further [13] and achieved a running time polylogarithmic in $m$, which is especially important for compact input encoding, where the length of the input is dependent on $\log m$ and not $m$.

Mounié et al. gave a $(\frac{3}{2} + \epsilon)$-approximate algorithm with running time $O(nm \log \frac{1}{\epsilon})$ [14]. Jansen and Land later improved this result further by giving an FPTAS for instances with many machines and complementing this with an algorithm that guarantees a ratio of $(\frac{3}{2} + \epsilon)$ with polylogarithmic dependence on $m$. They picked up on the idea of Mounié et al. to use a knapsack instance to find a schedule distributing jobs in two shelves and modified the knapsack

[1] We mainly consider 0-1 Knapsack, though some items may appear multiple times.

problem to solve it more efficiently. In a recent result Wu et al. [17] gave a new $\frac{3}{2}$- approximation that works in time $O(nm\log(nm))$.

The Knapsack problem as a generalization from Subset Sum is another core problem of computer science that is NP-hard as well. For this problem pseudopolynomial algorithms have been considered starting with Bellmans classical dynamic programming approach in time $O(nt)$ [4]. Many new results with pseudopolynomial running times have recently been achieved in regards to various parameters such as largest item size or number of different items [1,2,8,15].

One interesting connection has come up between Knapsack and the $(\max,+)$-convolution problem. In this problem one is given two sequences of length $n$ $(a_i)_{0\leq i<n}, (b_i)_{0\leq i<n}$ and has to find the convolution $c = a \oplus b$ which is defined through $c_i = \max_{j\leq i}(a_j + b_{i-j})$ for all $i \in \mathbb{N}_{<n}$. This problem can be solved in quadratic time $O(n^2)$. Cygan et al. [5] conjecture that a subquadratic algorithm may not be possible and used this conjecture as a basis for many fine-grained complexity results for Knapsack and similar problems. Axiotis and Tzamos showed that with concave sequences, convolutions can be computed in linear time $O(n)$ and they used this to give a $O(Dt)$ time algorithm for Knapsack where $D$ is the number of different item sizes [1]. This approach has also been used by Polak et al. [15] in conjunction with proximity arguments from Eisenbrand and Weismantel [8] to gain fast algorithms for knapsack with small item sizes.

### 1.3 Our Results

We present a new algorithm, in particular a $(\frac{3}{2}+\epsilon)$-approximation algorithm, for any accuracy parameter $\epsilon > 0$, with a runtime polynomial in $n$, $\frac{1}{\epsilon}$ and in $\log m$. With a running time polynomial in $\log m$ our algorithm will be able to handle certain compact input encodings and will scale well into large $m$.

The main difficulty in moldable job scheduling is that for every job we need to choose between $m$ different allotments and then schedule jobs efficiently. We will however show that not all $m$ possible allotments have to be regarded. Since we look for an approximate solution and we have monotone jobs, it is sufficient to only consider $O(\frac{1}{\epsilon} + \frac{\log(\epsilon m)}{\epsilon}))$ different machine counts. This leads immediately to a fully polynomial time approximation scheme (FPTAS) for instances with many machines.

**Theorem 1.** *Let* $\epsilon > 0$. *For moldable job scheduling with instances where* $m > 8\frac{n}{\epsilon}$ *there exists a* $(1+\epsilon)$*-approximation that runs in time* $O(n\log^2(\frac{1}{\epsilon} + \frac{\log(\epsilon m)}{\epsilon}))$.

This result can be used for a $\frac{3}{2}$-approximation if we use $\epsilon = \frac{1}{2}$.

**Corollary 1.** *Consider moldable job scheduling on instances with* $m > 16n$. *There exists a* $\frac{3}{2}$*-approximation in time* $O(n\log^2(\log m))$.

We complement this result with an efficient $(\frac{3}{2}+\epsilon)$-approximation for the case where $m \leq 16n$. For this we follow the same approach as [11,14] and construct a knapsack instance. We will introduce a new rounding scheme for machine counts, processing times and job works and convert these modified jobs into knapsack items. The resulting knapsack instance will only have a small amount of different item sizes. We then apply an algorithm introduced by Axiotis and Tzamos [1] that works well on such instances. Thanks to our rounding we will be able to do the pre-processing of their algorithm in linear time as well.

**Theorem 2.** *For moldable job scheduling there exists an algorithm that for instances with* $m \leq 16n$ *and for any* $\epsilon > 0$ *yields a* $\frac{3}{2} + \epsilon$ *approximation in time:* $O(n \log^2(\frac{1}{\epsilon} + \frac{\log(\epsilon m)}{\epsilon}) + \frac{n}{\epsilon} \log(\frac{1}{\epsilon}) \log(\epsilon m))$

These two results make up one $(\frac{3}{2} + \epsilon)$-approximation that improves on the best known result by Jansen and Land [11] in multiple ways. For large $m$ we manage to reduce the dependency on $m$ even further. When $m$ is small we improve on their running time by reducing the dependency on $\epsilon$ by a factor of $\frac{1}{\epsilon}$ and several polylogarithmic factors. We also argue that our algorithm is overall simpler compared to theirs, as we do not require to solve knapsack with compressible items in a complicated manner. Instead our algorithm merely constructs the modified knapsack instance and delegates to a simple and elegant algorithm from Axiotis and Tzamos [1].

| Result | Jansen & Land [11] | This paper |
|---|---|---|
| $1 + \epsilon$, $(m > 8\frac{n}{\epsilon})$ | $O(n \log(m)(\log(m) + \log(\frac{1}{\epsilon})))$ | $O(n \log^2(\frac{1}{\epsilon} + \frac{\log(\epsilon m)}{\epsilon}))$ |
| $\frac{3}{2}$, $(m > 16n)$ | $O(n \log^2(m))$ | $O(n \log^2(\log m))$ |
| $\frac{3}{2} + \epsilon$, $(m \leq 16n)$ | $O(\frac{n}{\epsilon^2} \log m(\frac{\log m}{\epsilon} + \log^3(\epsilon m)))$ | $O(n \log^2(\frac{1}{\epsilon} + \frac{\log(\epsilon m)}{\epsilon}) + \frac{n}{\epsilon} \log(\frac{1}{\epsilon}) \log(\epsilon m))$ |

## 2 General Techniques and FPTAS for Many Machines

The core technique used in this paper is the concept of *compression* introduced by Jansen and Land [11]. Compression is the general idea of reducing the number of machines a job is assigned to. Due to monotony the resulting increase of processing time can be bound.

**Lemma 1** **([11]).** *Let* $\rho \in (0, 1/4]$ *be what we denote in the following as a compression factor. Consider now a job* $j$ *and a number of machines* $k \in \mathbb{N}$ *with* $\frac{1}{\rho} \leq k \leq m$*, then we have that* $t(j, \lfloor (1-\rho)k \rfloor) \leq (1 + 4\rho) t(j, k)$.

The intuitive interpretation of this lemma is that if a job uses $k \geq \frac{1}{\rho}$ machines then we can free up to $\lceil \rho k \rceil$ machines and the processing time increases by a factor of $1 + 4\rho$. We are going to use this lemma in the following by introducing a set of predetermined machine counts.

**Definition 1.** *Let* $\rho$ *be a compression factor and set* $b := \frac{1}{\rho}$*. We define* $S_\rho := [\lfloor b \rfloor] \cup \{\lfloor (1+\rho)^i b \rfloor \mid i \in [\lceil \log_{1+\rho}(\frac{m}{b}) \rceil]\}$ *as the set of* $\rho$*-compressed sizes.*

Note that reducing machine numbers to the next smaller size in $S_\rho$ corresponds to a compression and processing time may only increase by a factor of at most $1+4\rho$. We assume without loss of generality that $1/\epsilon$ is integral by modifying $\epsilon$. With this assumption $1/\rho$ is also integral.

**Corollary 2.** *Let $\epsilon \in (0,1)$ be an accuracy parameter then $\rho = \frac{\epsilon}{4}$ is a compression factor and $|S_\rho| \in O(\frac{1}{\epsilon} + \frac{\log(\epsilon m)}{\epsilon})$.*

Generally our algorithms will work on the set $S_\rho$ for $\rho = \frac{\epsilon}{4}$ and only assign machine counts in $S_\rho$. If $m \leq \frac{4}{\epsilon}$ we work with any machine number as $S_\rho = [m]$. The algorithms we present will work in a dual approximation framework.

A dual approximation framework is a classical approach for scheduling problems. The general idea is to use an approximation algorithm with constant ratio $c$ on a given instance and gain a solution with makespan $T$. While this is only an approximation we can conclude that the makespan $T^*$ of an optimal solution must be in the interval $[\frac{T}{c}, T]$ and we can search this space via binary search. We can then see a candidate $d \in [\frac{T}{c}, T]$ as a guess for the optimal makespan.

The approximation algorithm is then complemented with an estimation algorithm, that receives an instance $I$ and a guess for the makespan $d$ as input. This estimation algorithm then must be able to find a schedule with a makespan of at most $(1+\epsilon)d$ if such a schedule exists. If $d$ was chosen too small, i.e. $(1+\epsilon)d < OPT(I)$, our algorithm can reject the value $d$ and return false.

We continue to apply this algorithm for candidates, until we find $d$ such that the algorithm is successful for $d$ but not for $\frac{d}{1+\epsilon}$. Note that if the algorithm fails for $\frac{d}{1+\epsilon}$ we have that $d = (1+\epsilon)\frac{d}{1+\epsilon} < OPT(I)$. Therefore the solution generated for $d$ has a makespan of $(1+\epsilon)d < (1+\epsilon)OPT(I)$. Using binary search we can find such a candidate $d$ in $O(\log \frac{1}{\epsilon})$ iterations [11].

### 2.1 Constant Factor Approximation

Our constant factor approximation is going to work in two steps: First we compute an allotment and assign each job to a number of machines. Secondly we will use list scheduling in order to schedule our now fixed parallel jobs. For the first step we use an algorithm introduced by Ludwig and Tiwari [13].

**Lemma 2** ([13]). *Let there be an instance $I$ for moldable job scheduling with $n$ jobs and $m$ machines. For an allotment $\alpha : J \to [m]$ we denote with*

$$\omega_\alpha := \min(\frac{1}{m}\sum_{j \in J} w(j,\alpha(j)), \max_{j \in J} t(j,\alpha(j)))$$

*the trivial lower bound for any schedule that follows the allotment $\alpha$. Furthermore for $S \subseteq [m]$ we denote with $\omega_S := \min_{\alpha: J \to S} \omega_\alpha$ the trivial lower bound possible for any allotment, which allots any job to a number of machines in $S$.*

*For any $S \subseteq [m]$ we can compute an allotment $\alpha : J \to S$ with $\omega_\alpha = \omega_S$ in time $O(n \log^2 |S|)$.*

We apply this lemma but limit machine numbers to $\rho$-compressed sizes $S_\rho$ for $\rho = \frac{\epsilon}{4}$. With that we gain an approximate value of $\omega_{[m]}$.

**Lemma 3.** *Given an instance $I$ for moldable job scheduling with $n$ jobs, $m$ machines and accuracy $\epsilon < 1$. In time $O(n \log^2(\frac{4}{\epsilon} + \frac{\log(\epsilon m)}{\epsilon}))$ we can compute an allotment $\alpha : J \to [m]$ such that $\omega_\alpha \leq (1+\epsilon)\omega_{[m]}$.*

*Proof.* Let $\rho = \frac{\epsilon}{4}, b = \frac{1}{\rho}$ and $S_\rho$ be the set of $\rho$-compressed sizes by Definition 1. We now use Lemma 2 to compute an allotment $\alpha' : [n] \to S_\rho$ such that $\omega_{\alpha'} = \omega_{S_\rho}$ and note that the proposed running time follows from Corollary 2 and Lemma 2. It remains to show that $\omega_{\alpha'} \leq (1+\epsilon)\omega_{[m]}$.

For this let $\alpha$ be an allotment with $\omega_\alpha = \omega_{[m]}$. We now modify this allotment by rounding its assigned number of machines down to the next value in $S_\rho$. To be more precise let $\alpha'' : [n] \to S_\rho; j \mapsto \max\{s \in S_\rho | s \leq \alpha(j)\}$. Note that based on the definitions and Lemma 2 it follows immediately that $\omega_\alpha \leq \omega_{\alpha'} \leq \omega_{\alpha''}$. We will conclude the proof by showing that $\omega_{\alpha''} \leq (1+\epsilon)\omega_\alpha$.

We note that the rounding from $\alpha$ to $\alpha''$ is a compression. To see that consider two consecutive item sizes $\lfloor b(1+\rho)^{(i-1)} \rfloor, \lfloor b(1+\rho)^{(i)} \rfloor$ for some $i$ and note that:

$$\begin{aligned}
\lfloor b(1+\rho)^{(i)} \rfloor - \lfloor b(1+\rho)^{(i-1)} \rfloor &\leq b(1+\rho)^{(i)} - (b(1+\rho)^{(i-1)} - 1) \\
&= b(1+\rho)^{(i)} - b(1+\rho)^{(i-1)} + 1 \\
&= \rho b(1+\rho)^{(i-1)} + 1 \leq \rho b(1+\rho)^{(i)}
\end{aligned}$$

Since we only round a job down when $\alpha(j) < \lfloor b(1+\rho)^{(i)} \rfloor$ we get that $\alpha(j) - \alpha''(j) \leq \rho\alpha(j)$. According to Lemma 1 the processing time of the job may only increase by a factor of at most $1 + 4\rho = 1 + \epsilon$. Therefore we have

$$\max_{j \in J} t(j, \alpha''(j)) \leq \max_{j \in J}\{(1+\epsilon)t(j, \alpha(j))\} = (1+\epsilon)\max_{j \in J} t(j, \alpha(j)).$$

Since the work function is monotone $\omega_{\alpha''} \leq (1+\epsilon)\omega_\alpha$ follows directly. □

With this allotment we use list scheduling to achieve a constant factor approximation [9]. We use this in our dual-approximation framework. In the next sections we will assume that we are given a makespan guess $d$ and give the required estimation algorithms for the desired results.

**Corollary 3.** *The proposed algorithm is an approximation algorithm with a multiplicative ratio of 4 and requires time $O(n \log^2(\frac{4}{\epsilon} + \frac{\log(\epsilon m)}{\epsilon}))$.*

*Proof.* The running time results mainly from applying Lemma 3 to gain an allotment $\alpha$ with $\omega_\alpha \leq (1+\epsilon)\omega_{[m]}$. Applying list scheduling to our computed allotment yields a schedule with makespan $2\omega_\alpha \leq 2(1+\epsilon)\omega_{[m]} \leq 4OPT(I)$. □

## 3 FPTAS for Large Machine Counts

In the following we assume that for every instance we have $m > 8\frac{n}{\epsilon}$. Jansen and Land showed that an FPTAS can be achieved by simply scheduling all jobs $j$ with $\gamma(j, (1+\epsilon)d)$ machines at time 0. They consider all possible number of machines for each job. We argue that it is sufficient to consider assigning a number in $S_{\frac{\epsilon}{4}}$ to achieve a similar result. We will however require another compression to make sure our solution is feasible.

**Lemma 4.** *Given an instance $I$ with $n$ jobs, $m > 8\frac{n}{\epsilon}$ machines and a target makespan $d$, we can in time $O(n \log(\frac{4}{\epsilon} + \frac{\log(\epsilon m)}{\epsilon}))$ find a schedule with makespan $(1+3\epsilon)d$ if $d \geq OPT(I)$ or confirm that $d < OPT(I)$.*

*Proof.* Let $S_\rho$ be the set of $\rho$-compressed sizes for $\rho = \frac{\epsilon}{4}$ and $b = \frac{1}{\rho}$. Let $\gamma'(j,d) := \max\{s \in S_\rho | s \leq \gamma(j,d)\}$ and denote a job as *narrow* when $\gamma'(j,d) \leq b$ or *wide* when $\gamma'(j,d) > b$. The schedule we propose results from scheduling narrow jobs with $\gamma'(j,d)$ machines and wide jobs with a compressed number of machines, that is $\lfloor (1-\rho)\gamma'(j,d) \rfloor$. We schedule all jobs at time 0 next to each other. The running time results from finding $\gamma'(j,d)$ for all jobs via binary search. Note that if $\gamma(j,d)$ is undefined for some job, then $d$ was chosen too small.

Every job $j$ scheduled with $\gamma(j,d)$ machines has processing time of at most $d$. Rounding down the number of machines to $\gamma'(j,d)$ may increase the processing time by a factor of $1+4\rho$, as this process corresponds to a compression. We then apply another compression to wide jobs, which may increase the processing time again by the same factor. In total the new processing time of a job is bound by: $(1+4\rho)((1+4\rho)t(j,\gamma(j,d))) \leq (1+\epsilon)^2 d \leq (1+3\epsilon)d$.

It remains to show that our schedule uses at most $m$ machines in total. Jansen and Land showed [11] that $\sum_{j \in J} \gamma(j,d) \leq m+n$. We assume that $\sum_{j \in J} \gamma(j,d) > m$, since otherwise our schedule would be feasible already. Denote with $J_W$, $J_N$ the set of wide and narrow jobs. We can see that that $\sum_{j \in J_N} \gamma(j,d) \leq n \cdot b = 4\frac{n}{\epsilon} < \frac{1}{2}m$ and therefore $\sum_{j \in J_W} \gamma(j,d) > \frac{1}{2}m$.

Consider a wide job $j$ and write $\gamma(j,d) = \gamma'(j,d) + r$ for some $r$. Since $j$ was assigned to $\lfloor (1-\rho)\gamma'(j,d) \rfloor$ machines, the number of freed up machines is at least:

$$\begin{aligned} \gamma(j,d) - \lfloor (1-\rho)\gamma'(j,d) \rfloor &\geq \gamma'(j,d) + r - (1-\rho)\gamma'(j,d) \\ &= \rho\gamma'(j,d) + r \\ &\geq \rho(\gamma'(j,d) + r) = \rho(\gamma(j,d)) \end{aligned}$$

In total we free at least $\sum_{j \in J_W} (\rho\gamma(j,d)) > \rho\frac{1}{2}m > \frac{\epsilon}{4}4\frac{n}{\epsilon} = n$ machines. Our schedule therefore uses at most $\sum_{j \in J} \gamma(j,d) - n \leq m + n - n = m$ machines. □

Note that we can apply this lemma with $\epsilon' = \frac{\epsilon}{3}$ or an even more simplified algorithm that results by rounding down $\gamma(j, (1+\epsilon)d)$, which also allows a simple schedule with less than $m$ machines [11]. If we use this algorithm in our dual approximation framework we achieve the desired FPTAS.

*Proof (of Theorem 1).* We conclude for the runtime that we have to apply our dual approximation framework, meaning we apply the constant factor approximation and then for $\log(\frac{1}{\epsilon})$ makespan guesses we apply Lemma 4. Combining these running times we get a time of $O(n\log^2(\frac{1}{\epsilon}+\frac{\log(\epsilon m)}{\epsilon}))$. □

## 4 $(\frac{3}{2}+\epsilon)$-Approximation

We will now consider the goal of achieving a $\frac{3}{2}+\epsilon$ multiplicative approximation ratio. Our algorithm will operate again in the context of the dual approximation framework. Therefore we assume a makespan guess $d$ and give an estimation algorithm. Our estimation algorithm will reduce the scheduling problem to a knapsack instance in a way that was initially introduced by Mounié et al. [14]. This approach was also used by Jansen and Land [11] who gave a modified version of this knapsack instance. We however propose a new simpler rounding scheme that uses $\rho$-compressed sizes for $\rho=\frac{\epsilon}{4}$ and further modify item profit. In that way we do not need a complicated algorithm to solve the knapsack problem, but we can actually apply the result from Axiotis and Tzamos [1] in an efficient manner.

At the start we split the set of jobs in small and big jobs $J=J_S(d)\cup J_B(d)$ with $J_S(d):=\{j\in J\,|\,t(j,1)\leq\frac{d}{2}\}$ and $J_B(d)=J\backslash J_S(d)$. Since we can add small items greedily at the end in linear time [11], we only need to schedule large jobs. We give a short run-down on the most important results in regards to the knapsack instance introduced by Mounié et al. .

Their main idea was to distribute all jobs into two shelves with width $m$. The first shelf $S_1$ has height $d$ and the second shelf $S_2$ has height $\frac{d}{2}$. If a job $j$ was scheduled in either shelf with height $s\in\{d,\frac{d}{2}\}$ then $j$ would be allotted to $\gamma(j,s)$ machines. In order to assign jobs to a shelf, they use the following knapsack instance:

Consider for each job $j\in J_B(d)$ an item with size $s_j(d):=\gamma(j,d)$ and profit $p_j(d):=w(j,\gamma(j,d/2))-w(j,\gamma(j,d))$ and set the knapsack size to $t:=m$. Intuitively this knapsack instance chooses a set of jobs $J'$ to be scheduled in $S_1$. These jobs are chosen such that their work increase in $S_2$ would be large.

We will denote this problem as $KP(J_B(d),m,d)$ where the first two parameters declare the items and knapsack size and the third parameter is the target makespan, which then determines the size and profits of the items. Given a solution $J'\subseteq J$ we denote the total work of the resulting two-shelf schedule by $W(J',d)$ and note that:

$$\begin{aligned}W(J',d)&=\sum_{j\in J'}w(j,\gamma(j,d))+\sum_{j\in J_B(d)\backslash J'}w(j,\gamma(j,\frac{d}{2}))\\&=\sum_{j\in J_B(d)}w(j,\gamma(j,\frac{d}{2}))+\sum_{j\in J'}w(j,\gamma(j,d))-\sum_{j\in J'}w(j,\gamma(j,\frac{d}{2}))\\&=\sum_{j\in J_B(d)}w(j,\gamma(j,\frac{d}{2}))-\sum_{j\in J'}p_j(d)\end{aligned}$$

As the knapsack profit is maximized, the total work $W(J', d)$ is minimized. The result from Mounié et al. which we use is summarized in these two lemmas. We refer to either [11,14] for a detailed description of these results.

**Lemma 5** ([14]). *If there is a schedule for makespan $d$, then there is a solution $J' \subseteq J_B(d)$ to the knapsack instance with $W(J', d) \leq md - W(J_S(d), d)$.*

**Lemma 6** ([14]). *If there is a solution $J' \subseteq J_B(d)$ to the knapsack instance with $W(J', d) \leq md - W(J_S(d), d)$, then we can find a schedule for all jobs $J$ with makespan $\frac{3}{2}d$ in time $O(n \log n)$.*

Based on these lemmas we can easily reject a makespan guess $d$ if $W(J', d)$ is larger than $md - W(J_S(d), d)$. We note as well that Lemma 6 can be applied if we find a solution for a higher makespan.

**Corollary 4** ([11]). *Let $d' \geq d$ and $J' \subseteq J_B(d)$ be a feasible solution of the knapsack problem $KP(J_B(d), m, d')$ with $W(J', d') \leq md' - W(J_S(d), d)$. Then we can find a schedule with makespan at most $\frac{3}{2}d'$ in time $O(n \log n)$.*

We now construct a modified knapsack instance in order to apply this corollary for $d' = (1+4\epsilon)d$. First of all we reduce machine counts to $\rho$-compressed sizes for $\rho = \frac{\epsilon}{4}$ . Consider $S_\rho$ and $b := \frac{1}{\rho}$ and let $\gamma'(j, s) := \max\{k \in S_\rho | k \leq \gamma(j, s)\}$ for any job $j$ and $s \in \{\frac{d}{2}, d\}$. With $\widetilde{p_j}(d) := \gamma'(j, \frac{d}{2})t(j, \gamma'(j, \frac{d}{2})) - \gamma'(j, d)t(j, \gamma'(j, d))$ we denote the intermediary profit that is going to be further modified.

We further consider a job *wide* in a shelf if it uses more than $b$ machines in the respective shelf, that is if $\gamma'(j, s) \geq b$ for the respective $s \in \{\frac{d}{2}, d\}$. If a job is not wide we call it *narrow* instead, with respect to some shelf.

For jobs that are narrow in both shelves we will directly modify the profits. Let $j$ be a job with $\gamma'(j, s) < b$ for both $s \in \{\frac{d}{2}, d\}$, then we round the intermediary profit up to the next multiple of $\epsilon d$ by setting $p'_j(d) := \min\{i\epsilon d \mid i\epsilon d \geq \widetilde{p_j}(d) \text{ and } i \in \mathbb{N}^*_{\leq \frac{2}{\epsilon^2}}\}$. This is well defined since the original profit in this case is bounded by $w(j, \frac{d}{2}) < b\frac{d}{2} = \frac{2}{\epsilon^2}\epsilon d$. For later arguments denote the modified work with $w'(j, \frac{d}{2}) := w(j, \frac{d}{2})$ and $w'(j, d) := w'(j, \frac{d}{2}) - p'_j(d)$.

For jobs $j$ that are wide in both shelves, that is when $\gamma'(j, \frac{d}{2}) \geq \gamma'(j, d) \geq b$, we will modify the processing time. In particular we set $t'(j, s) := \frac{1}{1+4\rho}s$ for $s \in \{\frac{d}{2}, d\}$, which results in modified work values $w'(j, s) := t'(j, s)\gamma'(j, s)$. We then define the new profit based on the modified works as: $p'_j(d) := w'(j, \frac{d}{2}) - w'(j, d)$.

That leaves jobs that are narrow in one shelf and wide in the other. Consider such a job $j$ with $\gamma'(j, \frac{d}{2}) \geq b > \gamma'(j, d)$. For the wide version we round again the processing time $t'(j, \frac{d}{2}) := \frac{1}{1+4\rho}\frac{d}{2}$ and obtain $w'(j, \frac{d}{2}) := t'(j, \frac{d}{2})\gamma'(j, \frac{d}{2})$. As for the narrow job we round down the work $w(j, \gamma'(j, d))$ to the next multiple of $i\epsilon d$. To be precise we set $w'(j, d) := \max\{i\epsilon d \mid i\epsilon d \leq w(j, \gamma'(j, d)) \text{ and } i \in \mathbb{N}_{\leq \frac{4}{\epsilon^2}}\}$. Note that the unmodified work is bounded by $w(j, \frac{d}{2}) \leq w(j, d) < bd = \frac{4}{\epsilon}d = \frac{4}{\epsilon^2}\epsilon d$. We then obtain the modified profit value $p'_j(d) = w'(j, \frac{d}{2}) - w'(j, d)$.

With these modified profits and sizes $s'_j(d) = \gamma'(j, d)$ we then solve the resulting problem $KP'(J_B(d), m, d, \rho)$ to obtain an optimal item set $J'$. Due to spatial constraints we had to omit the proof for the following lemma, but note that it can be found in the full version [10].

**Lemma 7.** *Let $J'$ be a solution to $KP'(J_B(d), m, d, \rho)$ and $d' = (1+4\epsilon)d$, then with unmodified processing times and machine numbers $J'$ is also a solution to $KP(J_B(d), m, d')$. Furthermore if there is a schedule with makespan $d$, we have that $W(J', d') \leq md' - W(J_S(d), d)$.*

### 4.1 Solving the Knapsack Problems

As we already mentioned we intend to use an algorithm from Axiotis and Tzamos [1]. Their algorithm works in two main steps. In the first step the items of the knapsack instance are partitioned into sets containing items of equal size. The knapsack problem is then solved for each item set separately and for every item size $s$ with item set $I_s = \{i \in I \mid s_i = s\}$ a solution array $R_s$ is generated where $R_s[t']$ denotes the maximum profit achievable for a knapsack of size $t' \leq t$ using only items with size $s$. Note that by the nature of this problem $R_s[t']$ will always be given by the sum of profits of the $\lfloor \frac{t'}{s} \rfloor$ items with the highest profit in $I_s$.

These solution arrays $R_s$ have a special structure as $R_s[k \cdot s] = R_s[k \cdot s + s']$ for all $s' < s$ and $k \in \mathbb{N}$. Further considering the unique entries we have that $R_s[(k+1) \cdot s] - R_s[k \cdot s] \geq R_s[(k+2) \cdot s] - R_s[(k+1) \cdot s]$ for each $k$. This structure is also called *s-step concave* as the unique entries build a concave sequence. In the second step of their algorithm they combine the solution arrays in sequential order via convolution to generate a final solution array $R = R_1 \oplus R_2 \oplus \cdots \oplus R_{[s_{max}]}$.

A very important result from Axiotis and Tzamos is that if these convolutions are done in sequential order, then one sequence will always be $s$-concave for some respective $s$. They proved in their paper that convolution with one $s$-step-concave sequence can be done in linear time, opposed to the best known quadratic time.

**Lemma 8** ([1])**.** *Given any sequence $A$ and $R_h$ for some $h \in \mathbb{N}$, each with $t$ entries, we can compute the convolution $A \oplus R_h$ in time $O(t)$.*

In our setting the knapsack capacity is given by $t = m$. Thanks to our rounding we only have $|S_\rho|$ different item sizes, which defines the number of convolutions we have to calculate. We however must also compute the initial solutions that consist of the highest profit items for each size. Thanks to rounding item profits we can also sort these efficiently to generate the initial solutions arrays $R_h$.

**Lemma 9.** *Given a modified knapsack instance $KP'(J_B(d), m, d, \rho)$, we can compute for all $t' \leq t$ the entry $R_h[t']$ in time $O(n + m(\frac{1}{\epsilon} + \frac{\log(\epsilon m)}{\epsilon}))$.*

*Proof.* Our goal is to sort items by profits and subsequently add up the highest profits to fill the arrays $R_h$. We will sort items based on how they were rounded:

Consider jobs $j$ with $\gamma'(j, s) < b$ for both $s \in \{\frac{d}{2}, d\}$ and denote the number of these jobs with $n_1$. By scaling their profits with $\frac{1}{\epsilon}\frac{1}{d}$ we obtain profits of the form $\tilde{p}_j(d) = i$ for some $i \in \mathbb{N}_{\leq \frac{2}{\epsilon^2}}$. We can sort profits using radix sort in time $O(n_1 + \frac{1}{\epsilon})$ where we encode them using $O(1)$ digits ranging from 0 to $\frac{1}{\epsilon}$.

Consider now the $n_2$ jobs $j$ with $\gamma'(j, \frac{d}{2}) \geq \gamma'(j, d) \geq b$. If we scale the profit of these items with $\frac{1+4\rho}{d}$ then we have that $\tilde{p}_j(d) = \frac{1}{2}\gamma'(j, \frac{d}{2}) - \gamma'(j, d)$. These items can be sorted by profit using bucket sort in $O(n_2 + m)$.

For the remaining $n_3$ of the jobs $j$ with $\gamma'(j, \frac{d}{2}) \geq b > \gamma'(j, d)$ we have to consider the modified profits $p'_j(d) := \frac{d}{2(1+4\rho)}\gamma'(j, \frac{d}{2}) - i\epsilon d$ for some $i \in \mathbb{N}$. We scale these profits with $\frac{2(1+\epsilon)}{d\epsilon^2}$ to obtain $\tilde{p}_j(d) = \gamma'(j, \frac{d}{2})\frac{1}{\epsilon^2} - \frac{2i}{\epsilon} - 2i \leq \frac{m}{\epsilon^2}$. These items can be sorted with radix sort in time $O(n_3 + \frac{m}{\epsilon})$ by encoding profits with two digits ranging from 0 to $\frac{m}{\epsilon}$.

Putting these three steps together takes time $O(n_1 + n_2 + n_3 + \frac{1}{\epsilon} + m + \frac{m}{\epsilon}) = O(n + \frac{m}{\epsilon})$. We can additionally merge the three sorted lists via merge sort in $O(n)$ and iterate through all items to fill the actual solution arrays. The number of total entries we have to fill in is at most $m(\frac{4}{\epsilon} + \frac{\log(\epsilon m)}{\epsilon})$ since we have $m$ entries in each array, and one array for every item size. □

**Corollary 5.** *We can compute $R_1 \oplus R_2 \oplus \cdots \oplus R_{|S_\rho|}$ in time $O(m(|S_\rho|))$.*

With this knapsack solution we apply Corollary 4. We note that this final construction using the procedure from Mounié et al. [14] can be implemented in time $O(n)$ by using rounded processing times [11]. We note that combining these results proves Theorem 2. A proof can be found in the full version [10].

## 5 Implementation

We implemented all algorithms introduced and used in this paper, along with a version of the algorithm introduced by Jansen and Land [11]. We note that we did not implement the final version of their algorithm to solve Knapsack with compressible items, as it was very intricate and complicated. Instead our implementation computes their modified knapsack instance and solves it via their proposed dynamic programming approach.

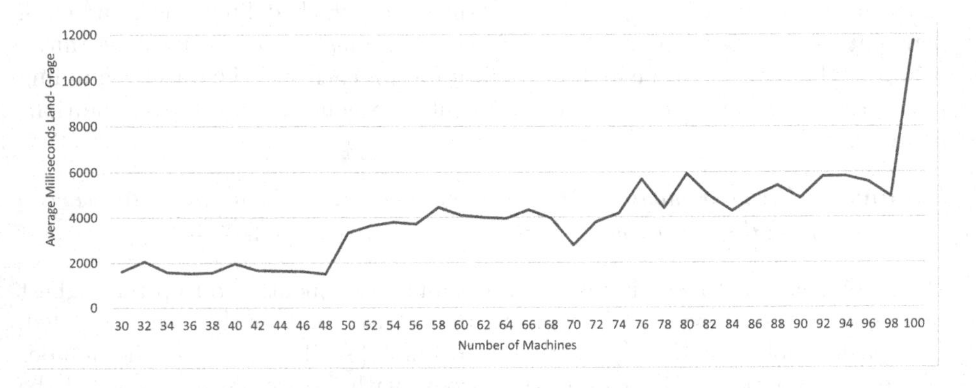


**Fig. 1.** Average runtime difference in relation to machine numbers.

The implementations and experiments were conducted on a Raspberry Pi 4 Model B and we limited the experiment to one CPU-core as we did not use any mean of parallelization. We uploaded a version of our implementation to GitHub (https://github.com/Felioh/MoldableJobScheduling). In the following we mainly tested for the part where $m \leq 16n$. We did not include all results due to spatial constraints and refer to the full version [10] for more graphs and comparisons.

We generated sets of randomized instances for moldable job scheduling. Machine numbers mainly range from 30 to 100 and jobs from 10 to 120. We tested on these instances for $\epsilon = \frac{1}{10}$. Figure 1 shows the difference of average runtime between our algorithm and the one by Jansen and Land. Note that the runtime of their algorithm is subtracted from ours. Hence we can see that our algorithm does slightly better for the analyzed number of jobs and machines and that our algorithm seems to scale better with growing numbers of machines.

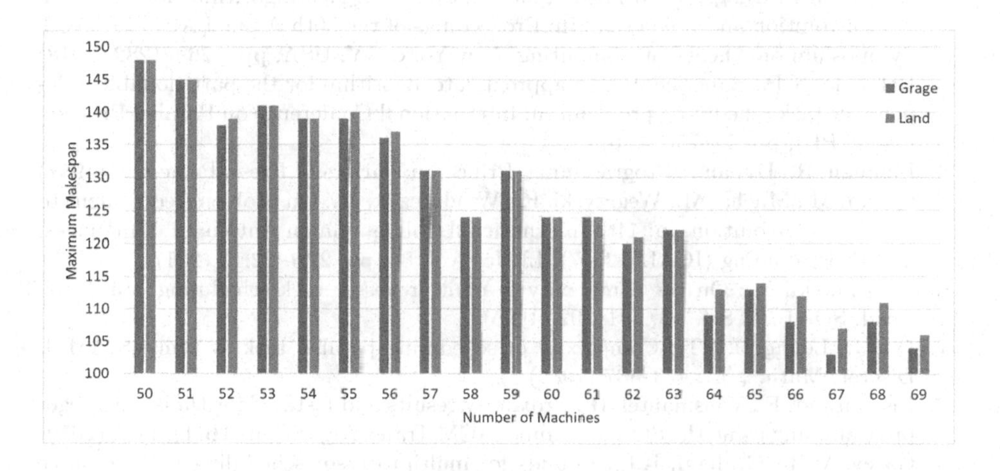


**Fig. 2.** Average makespan from both algorithms

In Fig. 2 we compare the makespans to compare solution quality. In most cases that solution quality is quite similar but in some cases generally better for our algorithm. We believe that is due to our rounding. For one our rounding of machine numbers to values in $S_\rho$ is in its core a compression but does not fully utilize the potential introduced in Lemma 1. Since we do not reduce the machine counts by the maximal possible amount, our effective error is smaller. In a similar manner do our knapsack modifications also induce a smaller error.

## 6 Conclusion and Open Questions

In this paper we presented our new $\frac{3}{2} + \epsilon$-approximation, that results from the combination of different techniques from moldable scheduling, knapsack and convolution. Not only do we achieve a theorical improvement on the runtime upper bound for this approximation ratio, but our algorithm also proves to be faster in practice as shown by our experiments.

For future research it remains open whether we can achieve even smaller approximation ratios, such as $\frac{4}{3}$ or $\frac{4}{3} + \epsilon$ by using monotone work. We believe that a concept such as $\rho$-compressed sizes may help with simplifying moldable job scheduling. Another interesting topic are lower bounds for running time and how much room for improvement the currently known results have.

## References


1. Axiotis, K., Tzamos, C.: Capacitated dynamic programming: faster knapsack and graph algorithms. In: 46th International Colloquium on Automata, Languages, and Programming (ICALP), Dagstuhl, Germany, vol. 132, pp. 19:1–19:13 (2019)
2. Bateni, M., Hajiaghayi, M., Seddighin, S., Stein, C.: Fast algorithms for knapsack via convolution and prediction. In: Proceedings of the 50th Annual ACM SIGACT Symposium on Theory of Computing, New York, NY, USA, pp. 1269–1282 (2018)
3. Belkhale, K.P., Banerjee, P.: An approximate algorithm for the partitionable independent task scheduling problem. In: International Conference on Parallel Processing (ICPP), pp. 72–75 (1990)
4. Bellman, R.: Dynamic Programming. Princeton University Press, Princeton (1957)
5. Cygan, M., Mucha, M., Wegrzycki, K., Wlodarczyk, M.: On problems equivalent to (min, +)-convolution. In: 44th International Colloquium on Automata, Languages, and Programming (ICALP 2017). LIPIcs, vol. 80, pp. 22:1–22:15 (2017)
6. Drozdowski, M.: On the complexity of multiprocessor task scheduling. Bull. Pol. Acad. Sci.-Tech. Sci. **43**, 381–392 (1995)
7. Du, J., Leung, J.Y.T.: Complexity of scheduling parallel task systems. SIAM J. Discret. Math. **2**(4), 473–487 (1989)
8. Eisenbrand, F., Weismantel, R.: Proximity results and faster algorithms for integer programming using the Steinitz lemma. ACM Trans. Algorithms **16**(1), 1–14 (2019)
9. Garey, M.R., Graham, R.L.: Bounds for multiprocessor scheduling with resource constraints. SIAM J. Comput. **4**, 187–200 (1975)
10. Grage, K., Jansen, K., Ohnesorge, F.: Improved algorithms for monotone moldable job scheduling using compression and convolution (2023). https://arxiv.org/abs/2303.01414
11. Jansen, K., Land, F.: Scheduling monotone moldable jobs in linear time. In: 2018 IEEE International Parallel and Distributed Processing Symposium (IPDPS), pp. 172–181. IEEE Computer Society, Los Alamitos (2018)
12. Jansen, K., Land, F., Land, K.: Bounding the running time of algorithms for scheduling and packing problems. Bericht des Instituts für Informatik, vol. 1302 (2013)
13. Ludwig, W., Tiwari, P.: Scheduling malleable and nonmalleable parallel tasks. In: Proceedings of the Fifth Annual ACM-SIAM Symposium on Discrete Algorithms, SODA 1994, pp. 167–176. Society for Industrial and Applied Mathematics, USA (1994)
14. Mounié, G., Rapine, C., Trystram, D.: A 3/2-dual approximation for scheduling independant monotonic malleable tasks. SIAM J. Comput. **37**, 401–412 (2007)

15. Polak, A., Rohwedder, L., Węgrzycki, K.: Knapsack and subset sum with small items. In: 48th International Colloquium on Automata, Languages, and Programming (ICALP 2021), vol. 198, pp. 106:1–106:19 (2021)
16. Turek, J., Wolf, J.L., Yu, P.S.: Approximate algorithms scheduling parallelizable tasks. In: Proceedings of the Fourth Annual ACM Symposium on Parallel Algorithms and Architectures, SPAA 1992, pp. 323–332. Association for Computing Machinery, New York (1992)
17. Wu, F., Zhang, X., Chen, B.: An improved approximation algorithm for scheduling monotonic moldable tasks. Eur. J. Oper. Res. **306**(2), 567–578 (2023)

# On Size Hiding Protocols in Beeping Model

Dominik Bojko[2], Marek Klonowski[1], Mateusz Marciniak[1](✉), and Piotr Syga[1]

[1] Department of Artificial Intelligence, Wrocław University of Science and Technology, Wrocław, Poland
{marek.klonowski,mateusz.marciniak,piotr.syga}@pwr.edu.pl
[2] Department of Fundamental Problems of Computer Science, Wrocław University of Science and Technology, Wrocław, Poland
dominik.bojko@pwr.edu.pl

**Abstract.** Execution of a protocol in a wireless sensor network may reveal some information about its size. For example, the time required to elect a leader or establish size approximation using the most popular protocols is strongly correlated with the number of participating stations. This property may be very undesirable in many natural scenarios, like e.g., the military area of applications.

This paper considers how much information about the network size a passive adversary eavesdropping on the communication channel can learn from the protocol execution. We formalize this problem in a general form (modeling the system as a multiple access channel with various feedbacks) and then present some practical results for the popular *beeping model*. In particular, we demonstrate how to construct a universal method that provably conceals the exact number of participating stations. Moreover, we explain the limitations of the presented approach. Finally, we show that in the case of some particular problems, the size-hiding property can be archived without any additional activities.

**Keywords:** Beeping model · Size hiding · Leader election

## 1 Introduction

We consider the problem of executing a distributed protocol in a multiple access channel model that reveals no substantial information about the size of the system (i.e., the number of stations). We focus on a popular single-hop radio network using the beeping model, wherein one can find plenty of prominent motivating examples to keep the number of stations secret (e.g., in a military area or industrial espionage protection).

In Sect. 2, we present the model and formalize a *size-hiding* problem using an approach analogous to differential privacy [5]. Section 3 is dedicated to a universal algorithm that may hide (to some extent) the size of the network in the

The paper is supported by Polish National Science Center NCN grants 2018/29/B/ST6/02969.


J. Cano et al. (Eds.): Euro-Par 2023, LNCS 14100, pp. 518–532, 2023.
https://doi.org/10.1007/978-3-031-39698-4_35

beeping model while executing any underlying protocol. We also show that our method can be combined with various fundamental algorithms to obtain desired properties for the price of a minor or moderate overhead of the time execution. Among others, we show size approximation protocols that are additionally size-hiding. These two properties are seemingly contradictory. Namely, on the one hand, we need to estimate the number of stations in the network precisely. On the other, we need to guarantee that this approximation is not too precise (to keep the adversary uncertain about the actual value of stations). Section 4 demonstrates that some classic protocols are size-hiding by design and do not reveal much information about the network size, even if we use a rigorous definition. The last part of this paper is devoted to the conclusion and the description of further extensions.

*Related Work.* The introduced measure of hiding the size of stations can be seen as an extended version of differential privacy from [3] that is currently considered a benchmark in privacy protection research and related problems. Most fundamental concepts related to differential privacy can be found in [5].

In [1,2], a similar problem of distributed protocol execution obfuscation in a similar model is considered. However, these papers assume that stations share a secret, established in advance, to simulate private channels and use standard cryptographic methods. As we avoid such a predefined assumption, our model requires a different approach, and hiding the information in it poses more challenges. Additionally, the approaches are not directly comparable as the protocol in [2] allows to conceal all the details of the protocol execution (not only the number of participating stations).

There is a well-developed body of literature devoted to communication hiding in distributed systems based on the idea of key predistribution introduced in [17], wherein devices have randomly assigned (*pre-deployed*) subset of keys from a large, fixed set and then try to establish a one-to-one secure connection (possibly via a path of secure connections of other devices) using shared keys. This idea has been extended in many directions ( [18–20]), recently in the context of IoT systems security. Note, however, that this line of research is somehow orthogonal to our approach, wherein the system cannot hide any information from the adversary using any shared secret due to the lack of a pre-deployment phase.

## 2 Formal Model

We consider a communication model with a single shared channel and $n$ participating stations. The parameter $n$ is unknown in advance to the stations, or, possibly, some limited knowledge about $n$ is available (e.g., a rough upper bound on $n$ is given). Stations are anonymous, i.e., initially, they do not have any individual identifiers. We assume that time is divided into separated and synchronized rounds, and all stations can determine the round of communication. In every round, stations can transmit or listen to the channel following the beeping model [12]. Depending on the number of transmitting stations in a given round, each station can recognize a present state amongst these in the set $\mathcal{S} = \{Beep, Silence\}$. The state of the channel is *Beep* in a given round if and only if at least one station transmits. Otherwise, the state is *Silence*.

*Adversary and Security Model.* In our work, we consider an outer *adversary* observing the channel while some protocol $\mathcal{P}$ (e.g., initialization, leader election, or size approximation) is executed. Thus, its input can be described as some $\mathbf{s} \in \mathcal{S}^*$, i.e., a finite sequence of states of the channel[1]. Even if $\mathcal{P}$ is randomized, its distribution may depend on the number of participating stations $n$. The adversary is passive and is limited to eavesdropping on the communication channel. The adversary aims to gain additional knowledge about $n$ given the sequence of states $\bar{\mathbf{s}}$. In other words, the adversary may have some *a priori* knowledge about $n$ before the execution of the protocol $\mathcal{P}$; however, his goal is to extend this by analyzing the observed execution. In contrast to previous work (e.g., [1,2]), we do **not** assume that the stations share any secret information, nor cryptographic key unknown to the adversary, that could be used to establish a secure communication channel inaccessible to the adversary. This assumption makes even passive adversaries very powerful, as they have the same information as any legitimate station. However, we assume that the adversary has no access to local sources of the randomness of stations.

*Size-hiding Definition.* Informally, we demand that protocols in networks with similar sizes result in (almost) indistinguishable channel states. Let $X_n^{\mathcal{P}} \in \mathcal{S}^*$ be a random variable denoting the states of the channel when executing the protocol $\mathcal{P}$ by exactly $n$ stations. For the sake of clarity, let us use a simplified notation: $p_{n,\mathcal{P}}(x) := \Pr[X_n^{\mathcal{P}} = x]$. Similarly, $p_{n,\mathcal{P}}(A) := \Pr[X_n^{\mathcal{P}} \in A]$. Moreover, whenever it is clear from the context, we skip the name of the protocol using just $p_n(x)$.

**Definition 1.** *We say that a protocol $\mathcal{P}$ is $(d, \varepsilon, \delta)$-size-hiding when for any possible set of channel states $A \subset S^*$:*

$$p_{n,\mathcal{P}}(A) \leq \exp(\varepsilon) p_{m,\mathcal{P}}(A) + \delta \tag{1}$$

*for $n, m \in \mathbb{N}_+$ such that $|n - m| \leq d$.*

**Lemma 1.** *If there exist parameters $\varepsilon$, $\delta$ and a set $A$ of channel states of protocol $\mathcal{P}$ that, for any $n$, $m$ such that $|n - m| \leq d$:*

1. $\Pr[X_n^{\mathcal{P}} \notin A] \leq \delta$ *and*
2. $(\forall\, x \in A)\ \Pr[X_n^{\mathcal{P}} = x] \leq \exp(\varepsilon) \Pr[X_m^{\mathcal{P}} = x]$,

*then $\mathcal{P}$ is $(d, \varepsilon, \delta)$-size-hiding.*

---

[1] Note that $\mathcal{S}$ can represent different sets of states. We are not limited to a two-state beeping model.

The above lemma is very intuitive, so we omit the proof. However, the reader can find the analogous proof for differential privacy property of probabilistic counters in [11].

Protocols with this property will yield similar results when performed by networks having similar sizes, resulting in the probability of distinguishing the network of size $n$ from any network of size $[n-d, n+d]$ negligible if $\varepsilon$ and $\delta$ are small.

In some cases, the definition is fulfilled only for $n$ greater than some $n_0$[2].

Let us note that Definition 1 can be seen as a counterpart of the very popular *differential privacy* introduced in [3]. The main difference is that we use the parameter $d$ instead of "neighboring" states. Note also that one cannot directly apply methods for preserving privacy in a distributed system (e.g., like the Laplace mechanism in [4]) since we cannot "add" negative values while mimicking the nodes.

*Need of Randomness.* First, let us note that any nontrivial protocol hiding the size needs to be randomized. Clearly, if $\mathcal{P}$ is deterministic w.r.t the size $n$, then $p_{n,\mathcal{P}}(x_n) = 1$ for a unique $x_n$. The deterministic protocol for a fixed network size generates a fixed sequence of the states on the channel $x_n$.

One can easily see that for any $\varepsilon \geq 0$, and any $n > 0$, the inequality 1 from the Definition 1 can be fulfilled for two consecutive sizes of networks $n$ and $n+1$ only if $x_n = x_{n+1}$. Inductively, this reasoning can be extended for all $n > 0$. Thus the Definition 1 can be fulfilled only if the algorithm returns trivially the same value for any size $n$.

## 3 Universal Algorithm for Beeping Model

This section presents a universal algorithm that can be used as a preprocessing for a broad class of algorithms. In a typical case, this approach moderately extends the execution time.

The presented approach is based on the following trick. Each station additionally mimics some random number of "virtual" stations (called *dummies*). This simple idea needs a precise calibration of parameters to be efficient. A careful analysis of security is presented below.

This approach is universal in the sense that it can be applied to various algorithms as a separate subroutine[3]. In particular, the stations do not need any extra knowledge about the system and do not require any substantial changes in the executed code. A station "virtually" executes a code of a regular protocol for itself and additionally in the name of dummies, so the number of mimicked stations is never zero. This approach does not require global knowledge and communication outside the shared channel.

[2] That is, it is more difficult to mask the difference between executions when comparing 2 with 22 stations than when comparing 102 with 122 stations.

[3] Note that it can be applied in many arrangements distinct from the beeping model as well.

On the other hand, one may need to notice some limitations of this approach, namely it can be applied only in the system, where a single station can imitate several stations.

It can be realized, for example, in the *beeping model* described in Sect. 2. If a given station or any dummy station is scheduled to be transmitted, the station transmits. Otherwise, it remains silent.

Moreover, this approach can be applied to some restricted classes of problems. We say that the randomized algorithm is *size determined* if its random output $\Xi$ has the same distribution while executed for any network of size given a priori. Many fundamental problems considered in distributed systems are size determined, including size approximation, leader election, waking-up, initialization or naming [8]. However, note that some natural problems are **not** size determined. One example is summing up all values kept by local stations.

Let us start with a fundamental observation:

**Fact 1.** *Let $\mathcal{A}(n)$ be a size-determined protocol executed by $n$ stations. Moreover, let $T$ be $(d, \varepsilon, \delta)$-size-hiding protocol in values in $\mathbb{N}$ (independent of $\mathcal{A}$). Then $\mathcal{A}(T)$ is $(d, \varepsilon, \delta)$-size-hiding.*

*Proof.* By the assumption about $T$, for any $n, m \in \mathbb{N}$ such that $|n - m| \leq d$, we have $\Pr(T(n) \in \mathbb{N}) \leq \exp(\varepsilon) \Pr(T(m) \in \mathbb{N}) + \delta$. Thus, for any $l \in \mathbb{N}$, one can find values $\delta_{n,m,l} \geq 0$, such that $\Pr(T(n) = l) \leq \exp(\varepsilon) \Pr(T(m) = l) + \delta_{n,m,l}$ and $\sum_{l \in \mathbb{N}} \delta_{n,m,l} = \delta$. Observe that

$$
\begin{aligned}
\Pr[\mathcal{A}(T)(n) \in S] &= \sum_{l \in \mathbf{N}} \Pr[\mathcal{A}(l) \in S] \Pr[T(n) = l] \\
&\leq \sum_{l \in \mathbf{N}} \Pr[\mathcal{A}(l) \in S] \left(\exp(\varepsilon) \Pr[T(m) = l] + \delta_{n,m,l}\right) \\
&\leq \exp(\varepsilon) \sum_{l \in \mathbf{N}} \Pr[\mathcal{A}(l) \in S] \Pr[T(m) = l] + \sum_{l \in \mathbf{N}} \delta_{n,m,l} \\
&= \exp(\varepsilon) \Pr[\mathcal{A}(T)(m) \in S] + \delta.
\end{aligned}
$$

□

Let us note that this fact is a straightforward extension of the post-processing theorem for differential privacy (e.g., [5]) changed in two aspects. Technically, we need to consider randomized algorithms $\mathcal{A}$ and adapt the formulation to the modified definition.

How many dummy stations a given real station shall mimic? As proved above, this number has to be randomized. We assumed that there are $n$ real stations. The $i$-th station mimics $X_i$ virtual stations, wherein $X_i$, for all $i \in \{1, \ldots, n\}$, are independently and identically distributed according to some fixed distribution $F$. In result, the whole system mimics $T(n) = n + \sum_{i=1}^{n} X_i$ stations.

A crucial decision is to choose the distribution $F$. Intuitively, $F$ with higher variance should have better size-hiding property; however, it may extend the expected time of protocol execution compared to the original protocol and worsens the precision of size approximation.

Here, we present a *binomial Strategy* $BS$, depending on a parameter $p \in [0, 1)$, wherein each station chooses if it represents just itself (with probability $1-p$) or also mimics one extra station (plays two stations) with probability $p$. Note that the analysis below assumes that the parameter $p$ can be known to the adversary.[4]

In the case of $BS$ Strategy, the total number of dummy stations has binomial distribution $\mathrm{Bin}(n, p)$.

*Analysis*

**Theorem 2.** *Let $T_{BS}(n)$ be the number of stations mimicked by $n$ stations applying binomial Strategy with parameter $p$. Let $\beta(n) < \frac{1}{2}$ be such that:*

$$[np(1-\beta(n)), np(1+\beta(n))] \cap \mathbb{N} \neq \emptyset ,$$

$$d(n) \leq \min\left\{(1-\beta(n))np - 1, (1-p(1+\beta(n)))\frac{n}{2} - \frac{1}{2}\right\}$$

*for any considered size of the system $n$. Then $T_{BS}(n)$ is $(\varepsilon(n), \delta(n), d(n))$-size hiding, where*

–

$$\begin{aligned}\varepsilon(n) = {} & \frac{d(n)(1+p)\beta(n)}{1-p} + d(n)\beta^2(n)\max\left\{\frac{1}{2}, \frac{p^2}{(1-p)^2}\right\} \\ & + \frac{\binom{2d(n)+1}{2}}{n(1-p)}\left(1 + \frac{p\beta(n)}{1-p}\right) + \frac{\binom{d(n)+1}{2}}{np}(1-p+\beta(n)) \\ & + \frac{d(n)\beta(n)}{n}\max\left\{\frac{1}{p}, \frac{2p}{(1-p)^2}\right\} + \frac{\binom{4d(n)+2}{3} + 8d(n)}{8n^2p^2(1-p)^2} ,\end{aligned}$$

– $\delta(n) = 2e^{-2np^2\beta(n)^2}$ .

Before we start a proof, we will introduce some auxiliary notation and a related lemma.

**Definition 2.** *For $x \in \mathbb{R}$, $m \in \mathbb{N}$ and $h \in \mathbb{R}$, we define a generalized shifted rising factorial*[5]

$$[x]_m^{(h)} := \prod_{i=1}^{m}(x + ih) .$$

*One can define a generalized shifted falling factorial as $(x)_m^{(h)} = [x]_m^{(-h)}$. We omit the upper index whenever $h = 1$.*

[4] Many other natural strategies can be considered. We have considered several of the most natural approaches, and however surprisingly, they give similar results to $BS$, so we have picked the most elegant one.

[5] An adjective "shifted" is due to a fact that product starts with $i = 1$ instead of $i = 0$ as it is usually defined (in both versions, the product has $m$ factors). Also predominantly, $h > 0$, however we allow $h \leq 0$.

**Lemma 2.** *If $|x-1\pm mh|<1$, then*

$$m(x-1)+h\binom{m+1}{2}-\frac{m(x-1)^2}{2}-h(x-1)\binom{m+1}{2}-\frac{h^2\binom{2m+2}{3}}{8}$$
$$\leq \ln\left([x]_m^{(h)}\right)\leq m(x-1)+h\binom{m+1}{2}.$$

*Proof.* Note that $\ln\left([x]_m^{(h)}\right)=\sum_{i=1}^{m}\ln(1+(x-1)+ih)$. Moreover, for $|y|<1$, $y-\frac{y^2}{2}\leq\ln(1+y)\leq y$ (simple application of Maclaurin series). Therefore

$$\sum_{i=1}^{m}(x-1)+ih-\frac{(x-1)+ih)^2}{2}\leq\ln\left([x]_m^{(h)}\right)\leq\sum_{i=1}^{m}(x-1)+ih\,.$$

Now, the thesis follows from two classical facts: $\sum_{i=1}^{m}i=\binom{m+1}{2}$ and

$$\sum_{i=1}^{m}i^2=\frac{m(m+1)(2m+1)}{6}=\frac{\binom{2m+2}{3}}{4}\,.$$

□

*Proof (of Theorem 2).* Assume that $f(n)$ is a sequence in $\mathbb{N}^{\mathbb{N}}$ and $f(n)\leqslant d(n)$. Further, we write shortly $f$ instead of $f(n)$ for convenience. One can see that $\Pr(T_{BS}(n)=n+k)=\binom{n}{k}p^k(1-p)^{n-k}$ , so

$$\Pr(T_{BS}(n\pm f)=n+k)=\binom{n\pm f}{k\mp f}p^{k\mp f}(1-p)^{n-k\pm 2f}\,.$$

Let us introduce $u_{\pm}$ as the following quotient of probabilities:

$$u_{\pm}:=\frac{\Pr(T_{BS}(n)=n+k)}{\Pr(T_{BS}(n\pm f)=n+k)}=\frac{n!(k\mp f)!(n-k\pm 2f)!p^{\pm f}}{k!(n-k)!(n\pm f)!(1-p)^{\pm 2f}}\,. \tag{2}$$

Note that $\mathbb{E}\left(T_{BS}(n)\right)=n+np$. A form of $k$ of our interest is, therefore, $np(1+b(n))$, where $|b(n)|\leq\beta(n)$ (roughly speaking, we want to consider the quotient only for the points in the vicinity of the mean). Let us consider the "plus sign" case of (2) first, using generalized shifted factorials:

$$u_+=\frac{[n-k]_{2f}p^f}{[n]_f(k+1)_f(1-p)^{2f}}=\frac{[n-np(1+b(n))]_{2f}p^f}{[n]_f(np(1+b(n))+1)_f(1-p)^{2f}}$$
$$=\frac{[1-p(1+b(n))]_{2f}^{(\frac{1}{n})}}{[1]_f^{(\frac{1}{n})}[1+b(n)+\frac{1}{np}]_f^{(-\frac{1}{np})}(1-p)^{2f}}=\frac{[1-\frac{pb(n)}{1-p}]_{2f}^{(\frac{1}{n(1-p)})}}{[1]_f^{(\frac{1}{n})}[1+b(n)+\frac{1}{np}]_f^{(-\frac{1}{np})}}\,.$$

Dually, one can get similar:

$$u_-=\frac{(n+1)_f[k]_f(1-p)^{2f}}{(n-k+1)_{2f}p^f}=\frac{[1+\frac{1}{n}]_f^{(-\frac{1}{n})}[1+b(n)]_f^{(\frac{1}{np})}}{[1-\frac{pb}{1-p}+\frac{1}{n(1-p)}]_{2f}^{(-\frac{1}{n(1-p)})}}\,.$$

By Lemma 1, one can realize that $\varepsilon$ parameter is related to upper bounds of $|\ln(u_\pm)|$. Namely, if

$$(\forall\, n \in \mathbb{N})(\exists\, A(n) \in \mathcal{P}(\mathbb{N}))(\forall\, k \in A)\ |\ln(u_\pm(n,k))| \leq \varepsilon(n)\ ,$$

then the 2.condition of Lemma 1 is satisfied. Here, the discrete interval $[np(1-\beta(n)), np(1+\beta(n))] \cap \mathbb{N}$ plays a role of the set $A(n)$. At this point, let us remark that the need for constraint on $d(n)$ in the formulation of Theorem 2 is dictated by the assumptions of Lemma 2. We are going to carefully analyze the aforementioned upper bounds by utilizing Lemma 2 as follows:

$$\begin{aligned}
\ln(u_+) \leq{} & \left(-\frac{2fpb(n)}{1-p} + \frac{\binom{2f+1}{2}}{n(1-p)}\right) - \frac{\binom{f+1}{2}}{n} - \left(f\left(b(n)+\frac{1}{np}\right) - \frac{\binom{f+1}{2}}{np}\right) \\
& + \frac{\binom{2f+2}{3}}{8n^2} + \left(\frac{f\left(b(n)+\frac{1}{np}\right)^2}{2} - \frac{\left(b(n)+\frac{1}{np}\right)\binom{f+1}{2}}{np} + \frac{\binom{2f+2}{3}}{8n^2p^2}\right) \\
\leq{} & \frac{d(n)(1+p)\beta(n)}{1-p} + \frac{d(n)\beta(n)^2}{2} + \frac{\binom{2d(n)+1}{2}}{n(1-p)} + \frac{\binom{d(n)+1}{2}(1-p)}{np} \\
& + \frac{\binom{d(n)+1}{2}\beta(n)}{np} + \frac{d(n)\beta(n)}{np} + \frac{\binom{2d(n)+2}{3}(1+p^2) + 4d(n)}{8n^2p^2}\ .
\end{aligned}$$

Remark that we tacitly used inequalities $0 \leq f(n) \leq d(n)$ and $|b(n)| \leq \beta(n)$ in the latter transformation. Analogously, we attain:

$$\begin{aligned}
\ln(u_-) \leq{} & \left(\frac{f}{n} - \frac{\binom{f+1}{2}}{n}\right) + \left(fb(n) + \frac{\binom{f+1}{2}}{np}\right) \\
& - \left(2f\left(\frac{-pb(n)}{1-p} + \frac{1}{n(1-p)}\right) - \frac{\binom{2f+1}{2}}{n(1-p)}\right) \\
& + \left(f\left(\frac{-pb(n)}{1-p} + \frac{1}{n(1-p)}\right)^2 - \frac{\binom{f+1}{2}\left(\frac{-pb(n)}{1-p} + \frac{1}{n(1-p)}\right)}{n(1-p)} + \frac{\binom{4f+2}{3}}{8n^2(1-p)^2}\right) \\
\leq{} & \frac{d(n)(1+p)\beta(n)}{1-p} + \frac{d(n)p^2\beta(n)^2}{(1-p)^2} + \frac{\binom{2d(n)+1}{2}}{n(1-p)} + \frac{\binom{d(n)+1}{2}(1-p)}{np} \\
& + \frac{\binom{2d(n)+1}{2}p\beta(n)}{n(1-p)^2} + \frac{d(n)}{n} + \frac{2d(n)p\beta(n)}{n(1-p)^2} + \frac{\binom{4d(n)+2}{3} + 8d(n)}{8n^2(1-p)^2}\ ,
\end{aligned}$$

with a similar upper bound. However, we are also interested in the lower bounds, so one can carefully use the same tricks and obtain the following:

$$\ln(u_+) \geq \left(-\frac{2fpb(n)}{1-p} + \frac{\binom{2f+1}{2}}{n(1-p)}\right) - \frac{\binom{f+1}{2}}{n} - \left(f\left(b(n)+\frac{1}{np}\right) - \frac{\binom{f+1}{2}}{np}\right)$$
$$- \left(\frac{fp^2b(n)^2}{(1-p)^2} - \frac{\binom{2f+1}{2}pb(n)}{n(1-p)^2} + \frac{\binom{4f+2}{3}}{8n^2(1-p)^2}\right)$$
$$\geq -\frac{d(n)(1+p)\beta(n)}{1-p} - \frac{d(n)p^2\beta(n)^2}{(1-p)^2} - \frac{d(n)}{np} - \frac{\binom{2d(n)+1}{2}p\beta(n)}{n(1-p)^2}$$
$$- \frac{\binom{4d(n)+2}{3}}{8n^2(1-p)^2},$$

$$\ln(u_-) \geq -\frac{d(n)(1+p)\beta(n)}{1-p} - \frac{d(n)\beta(n)^2}{2} - \frac{2d(n)}{n(1-p)}$$
$$- \frac{\binom{d(n)+1}{2}\beta(n)}{np} - \frac{\binom{2d(n)+2}{3}(1+p^2)+4d(n)p^2}{8n^2p^2}.$$

In the end, by Hoeffding's inequality, we get

$$\Pr\left[|T_{BS}(n) - n(1+p)| \geqslant \beta(n)np\right] \leq 2\exp\left\{-2\beta(n)^2np^2\right\}. \tag{3}$$

By Lemma 1, inequality (3) and the bunch of inequalities for $|\ln(u_\pm)|$, it emerges that we can put $\delta(n) = 2\exp\left\{-2\beta(n)^2np^2\right\}$ and

$$\varepsilon(n) = \frac{d(n)(1+p)\beta(n)}{1-p} + d(n)\beta(n)\max\left\{\frac{1}{2}, \frac{p^2}{(1-p)^2}\right\}$$
$$+ \frac{\binom{2d(n)+1}{2}}{n(1-p)}\left(1+\frac{p\beta(n)}{1-p}\right) + \frac{\binom{d(n)+1}{2}}{np}(1-p+\beta(n))$$
$$+ \frac{d(n)\beta(n)}{n}\max\left\{\frac{1}{p}, \frac{2p}{(1-p)^2}\right\} + \frac{\binom{4d(n)+2}{3}+8d(n)}{8n^2p^2(1-p)^2},$$

in order to attain $(\varepsilon(n), \delta(n), d(n))$-size-hiding property of the universal protocol. □

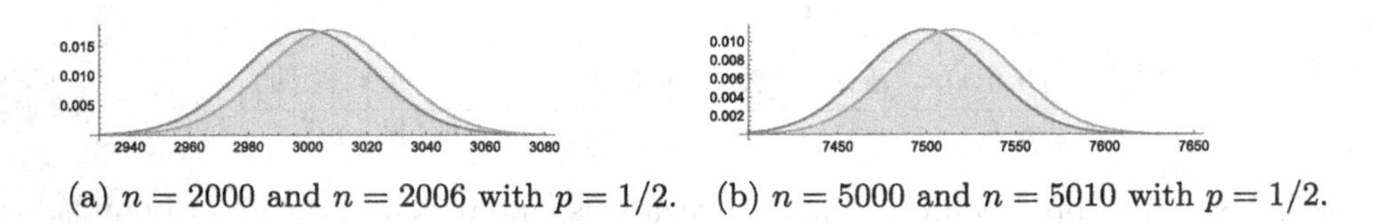


(a) $n = 2000$ and $n = 2006$ with $p = 1/2$. (b) $n = 5000$ and $n = 5010$ with $p = 1/2$.

**Fig. 1.** Examples of distributions for different stations with BS strategy. In the case of a relatively small difference in the number of stations (parameter $n$), the behaviors of networks are practically indistinguishable.

*Corollaries and Applications.* Theorem 2 is very general and can be used in various scenarios offering various tradeoffs between the hiding range $d$ and security hiding quality parameters $(\epsilon, \delta)$ . Let us mention three of them (Fig. 1).

**Corollary 1.** *Fix $p \in (0,1)$. Let $f_1(p) := \frac{1+p}{1-p} + \max\left\{\frac{1}{2}, \frac{p^2}{(1-p)^2}\right\}$ and $f_2(p) := \frac{2}{1-p} + \frac{1-p}{2p}$. Then there exists $n_0(p)$ such that, for any $n > n_0(p)$, $T_{BS}(n)$ is*

1. $\left(\varepsilon(n) = f_1(p) + \frac{f_2(p)}{(\ln(n))^2} + O\left(\frac{1}{\sqrt{n}\ln(n)}\right), \delta(n) = \frac{2}{n^{2p^2\ln(n)}}, d(n) = \frac{\sqrt{n}}{\ln(n)}\right)$ *-size hiding;*
2. $\left(\varepsilon(n) = \frac{f_1(p)}{p\sqrt{\ln(n)}} + \frac{f_2(p)}{(\ln(n))^2} + O\left(\frac{1}{\sqrt{n}\ln(n)}\right), \delta(n) = 2n^{-2}, d(n) = \frac{\sqrt{n}}{\ln(n)}\right)$ *-size hiding;*
3. $\left(\varepsilon(n) = \frac{f_1(p)}{p\sqrt[15]{n}} + \frac{f_2(p)}{\sqrt[3]{n}} + O\left(n^{-2/3}\right), \delta(n) = 2\exp(-2\sqrt[5]{n}), d(n) = \sqrt[3]{n}\right)$ *-size hiding;*

These results are obtained from Theorem 2 by substituting the pointed $d(n)$ and $\beta(n)$ equal respectively $\frac{\ln n}{\sqrt{n}}, \frac{1}{p}\sqrt{\frac{\ln(n)}{n}}$ and $\frac{1}{pn^{2/5}}$. Note that the $n_0(p)$ should be chosen concerning the chosen parameter $p \in (0,1)$ in such a way that the assumptions of Theorem 2 are true (for $n \le n_0(p)$ one can modify $d(n)$ and $\beta(n)$ to satisfy the assumptions in order to apply the Theorem). Note that in the two latter cases of Corollary 1, both security parameters tend to 0. On the other hand, the bound $\varepsilon(n) = \Theta(1)$ is acceptable and commonly used in differential privacy literature. Therefore, the first mentioned system of parameters is appropriate, especially when $p$ is relatively small (however, we do not recommend choosing very small $p$ because it occurs that then $f_2(p)$ may be uncomfortably big). Remark that $\varepsilon(n) = \Theta(1)$ may be obtained from Theorem 2 whenever $d(n)\beta(n) = \Theta(1)$. Also, note that, if $\beta(n) = O\left(n^{-1/2}\right)$, then we can only attain $\delta(n) = \Omega(1)$ from Theorem 2.

We demonstrate the power of Theorem 2 under application to some classic results in the beeping model. We apply Binomial Strategy as a preprocessing step before executing the algorithm.

**Corollary 2.** *There exists an explicit algorithm that returns $(1+\varepsilon)$ approximation of the size of the network in $O(\log\log n + \log f/\varepsilon^2)$ with probability at least $1 - 1/f$ that is $\left(\varepsilon(n) = 1 + o(1), \delta(n) = O(\frac{1}{n^2}), d(n) = \frac{\sqrt{n}}{\ln n}\right)$ size hiding.*

This fact follows from [7] (Theorem 1). Note that in [6], the optimality for this class of protocols has been proved.

**Corollary 3.** *There exists an explicit algorithm that names $n$ stations with running time $O(n\log n)$ that is correct with probability $1 - n^{-\alpha}$ and is:*

$$(\varepsilon(n) = o(1), \delta(n) = o(1), d(n) = \sqrt[3]{n}) - \textit{size-hiding} .$$

This fact follows from the analysis of the naming algorithm in [8]. From the energy-preserving perspective, a similar result appeared in [9].

In particular, the results listed below describe explicit algorithms as long as they extend explicit procedures.

Let us note that the chosen decision about mimicking some extra station can be kept for any number of executions of any algorithm. This approach protects from information leakage and security decay when the adversary observes the system from a longer perspective. In effect, there is no need to apply any composition-like theorems (cf. [5]).

*Limitations of the Universal Strategy.*

The $BS$ Strategy presented above is adequate when we hide an exact number of stations with excellent security parameters and negligible execution overhead. The adversary cannot distinguish between $n$ and $n \pm \sqrt{n}$ stations. This is a counterintuitive result since one may think that adding, say, a random number of virtual stations uniformly distributed from $\{1, 2, \ldots, n\}$ could improve the hiding effect and extend the approach for an arbitrary range of mimicked stations.

**Fact 3.** *Let us consider a strategy such that each station mimics independently $X$ stations, where $X$ has an expectation and variance $\mu$ and $\sigma$, respectively. No such strategy can hide the number of stations for general $n$ and $d = \omega(\sqrt{n})$ .*

The sketch of the proof would be as follows. Consider two cases for $n$ and $N$ real stations ($N > n$). If, according to the algorithm, all stations mimic $X$ other stations, the total number of mimicked stations would be close to $T_n \sim \mathcal{N}(n\mu, n\sigma^2)$ and $T_N \sim \mathcal{N}(N\mu, N\sigma^2)$ (Berry-Essen-type theorem). One can easily see that $T(n)$ and $T(N)$ can be distinguished with probability greater than 0.977 if $N\mu - 2\sqrt{N}\sigma > 2n\mu + \sqrt{n}\sigma$. The last relation is true even for $n, N$ of moderate size.

## 4 Size Hiding in Regular Protocols

Although the previous approach has clear merits, it is limited with respect to the number of stations that can be hidden in networks of realistic sizes. Moreover, as demonstrated in the previous chapter, this type of approach cannot be substantially improved when we insist on the assumption that the legitimate stations do not share any knowledge and execute the same code.

One may suspect, however, that there are particular problems that can be solved using some size-hiding algorithm offering better properties, in particular higher $d$.

In this section, we demonstrate that `GreenLeaderElection` protocol introduced in [15] by Jacquet et al. is size-hiding for parameter $d = \Theta(n)$ (comparing $d = O(\sqrt{n})$ for the universal algorithm) keeping parameters $\delta$ and $\varepsilon$ reasonably small. Explaining in application terms, the adversary cannot distinguish between, say, 1000 and 1300 stations, which is a substantial improvement compared to the previous approach. Moreover, we demonstrate that we do not need to modify the original algorithm by Jacquet et al. to get the size-hiding property. Note that this is a similar case as *noiseless* privacy (cf. [13,14]).

*Algorithm Description.* The `GreenLeaderElection` algorithm consists of two phases. In Phase I, stations transmit in consecutive slots with geometrically decreasing probability until the silence on the channel. Only the stations transmitting in the last slot with a beep (i.e., *survivors*) participate in Phase II. The aim of Phase I is to reduce the size of competing stations. Note that Phase II can be executed using any leader election protocol effectively since, with high probability, the number of survivors is very small. This fact is proved in [15,16]).

*Analysis.* One can see that the information revealed to the adversary consists of the time of the Phase I execution $T$ and observable of the execution of the leader election for the limited subset of stations. The latter, however, is entirely determined by $S$, the number of stations that survived Phase I.

```
Algorithm GreenLeaderElection(p)
  Phase I
    t ← Geo(p)
    for round ← 1,...,t do
      | Transmit()
    end
    channel = GetChannelState()
    if channel = Silence then
      | status ← Candidate
    else
    status ← NotCandidate
  Phase II
    if status = Candidate then
      | LeaderElection()
    end
```

**Algorithm 1:** Size-hiding leader election scheme for a single station.

Let the pair $(T_n, S_n)$ be the observed random variable by the adversary if the initial number of stations is $n$ .

The conclusion is based on two observations 1. The expected length of the Phase I, $T_n$ for $n$ stations, is logarithmic with respect to the network size $n$, and it is difficult to distinguish even cases with $n$ and $2n$ real stations. 2. Number of survivors $S_n$ that are promoted to Phase II is almost independent of $n$ and constant w.h.p. While the first observation is relatively intuitive, the second is based on a careful analysis from [15,16], wherein authors prove some other properties of this algorithm (mainly limited energy expenditure). This fact is depicted in Fig. 2.

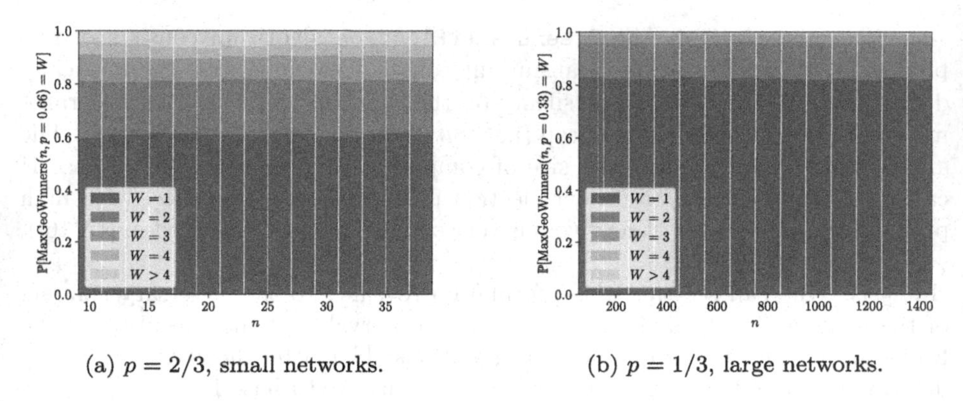


(a) $p = 2/3$, small networks. (b) $p = 1/3$, large networks.

**Fig. 2.** Distribution of the number of stations participating in Phase II for various network sizes (parameter $n$). This distribution is almost independent of $n$ (but depends on $p$).

Using the exact formulas from [15,16] for distribution of $S_n$ and a very straightforward analysis of $T_n$ we can numerically check that:

**Fact 4.** `GreenLeaderElection` *with parameter* $p = 1/2$ *with* $n$ *devices guarantees* $(\varepsilon, \delta, d(n))$*-size hiding for* $\varepsilon = 2, \delta = 0.0002$ *and* $d(n) = 0.25n$ *and for* $n > 10$ .

Due to space constraints, our presentation is limited to proving that the original algorithm hides a significant number of stations according to a rigorous definition. Note that its analysis can be subject to many extensions upon the needs of a particular scenario. In particular, accepting higher $\varepsilon$ can make $\delta$ completely negligible. Moreover, one can easily prove that the same observable execution may occur for very different sizes much exceeding 25% specified in Fact 4 with comparable probabilities. In effect, the adversary cannot be certain even about the order of magnitude of the network size (Fig. 3).

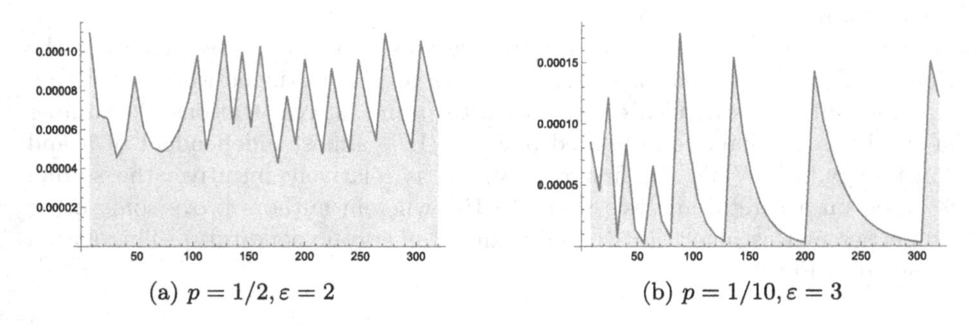

(a) $p = 1/2, \varepsilon = 2$ (b) $p = 1/10, \varepsilon = 3$

**Fig. 3.** Maximal parameter $\delta$ for $n$ in the range $[5, 320]$ when $d = 0.25n$. Two examples with different parameters $\varepsilon$, $p$.

## 5 Conclusions and Future Work

In future work, we aim to answer many natural questions. Even for the beeping model, it is still to be determined how to construct methods simulating the number of stations much higher than the actual number $n$ for a broader class of protocols. We learned from 3 that this might only be possible by introducing shared information between a subset of the stations. It is also unclear how to extend the results for other restricted communication models with different feedbacks, especially in the case of classic MAC with or without collision detection. Next, we may extend this problem to multi-hop networks. It requires a significant model extension and uses substantially different analytical methods. Finally, one can see that the results can be significantly improved if we assume sharing secrets between **some** of the stations (local cooperation). One may consider investigating an intermediate model wherein only a part of the devices knows the secret unknown to the outer adversary.

## References


1. Klonowski, M., Syga, P.: Enhancing privacy for ad hoc systems with predeployment key distribution. Ad Hoc Netw. **59**, 35–47 (2017)
2. Kardas, M., Klonowski, M., Syga, P.: How to obfuscate execution of protocols in an ad hoc radio network? Ad Hoc Netw. **84**, 90–106 (2019)
3. Dwork, C., McSherry, F., Nissim, K., Smith, A.D.: Calibrating noise to sensitivity in private data analysis. Theory Crypt. **3876**, 265–284 (2006)
4. Chan, T.-H.H., Shi, E., Song, D.: Privacy-preserving stream aggregation with fault tolerance. In: Keromytis, A.D. (ed.) FC 2012. LNCS, vol. 7397, pp. 200–214. Springer, Heidelberg (2012). https://doi.org/10.1007/978-3-642-32946-3_15
5. Dwork, C., Roth, A.: The algorithmic foundations of differential privacy. Found. Trends Theor. Comput. Sci. **9**, 211–407 (2014)
6. Brandes, P., Kardas, M., Klonowski, M., Pajak, D., Wattenhofer, R.: Fast size approximation of a radio network in beeping model. Theoret. Comput. Sci. **810**, 15–25 (2020)
7. Brandes, P., Kardas, M., Klonowski, M., Pająk, D., Wattenhofer, R.: Approximating the size of a radio network in beeping model. In: Suomela, J. (ed.) SIROCCO 2016. LNCS, vol. 9988, pp. 358–373. Springer, Cham (2016). https://doi.org/10.1007/978-3-319-48314-6_23
8. Chlebus, B.S., De Marco, G., Talo, M.: Naming a channel with beeps. Fund. Inform. **153**, 199–219 (2017)
9. Andriambolamalala, N.A., Ravelomanana, V.: Energy efficient naming in beeping networks. Ad-Hoc, Mobile, Wirel. Netw. **11803**, 355–369 (2019)
10. Altman, T., Aldawsari, L.S.: Naming processes in multichannels with beeps in the weak model. Intell. Comput. **283**, 118–132 (2022)
11. Bojko, D., Grining, K., Klonowski, M.: Probabilistic counters for privacy preserving data aggregation. In: CoRR, vol. 2003.11446 (2020)
12. Cornejo, A., Kuhn, F.: Deploying wireless networks with beeps. Distrib. Comput. **6343**, 148–162 (2010)

13. Bhaskar, R., Bhowmick, A., Goyal, V., Laxman, S., Thakurta, A.: Noiseless database privacy. In: Lee, D.H., Wang, X. (eds.) ASIACRYPT 2011. LNCS, vol. 7073, pp. 215–232. Springer, Heidelberg (2011). https://doi.org/10.1007/978-3-642-25385-0_12
14. Grining, K., Klonowski, M.: Towards extending noiseless privacy: dependent data and more practical approach. AsiaCCS **2017**, 546–560 (2017)
15. Jacquet, P., Milioris, D., Mühlethaler, P.: A novel energy efficient broadcast leader election. MASCOTS **2013**, 495–504 (2013)
16. Cichon, J., Kapelko, R., Markiewicz, D.: On leader green election. CoRR, vol. 1605.00137 (2016)
17. Eschenauer, L., Gligor, V.D.: A key-management scheme for distributed sensor networks. In: ACM CCS, pp. 41–47 (2002)
18. Li, L., et al.: A secure random key distribution scheme against node replication attacks in industrial wireless sensor systems. IEEE Trans. Ind. Inform. **16**, 2091–2101 (2020)
19. Klonowski, M., Kutyłowski, M., Ren, M., Rybarczyk, K.: Forward-secure key evolution in wireless sensor networks. In: Bao, F., Ling, S., Okamoto, T., Wang, H., Xing, C. (eds.) CANS 2007. LNCS, vol. 4856, pp. 102–120. Springer, Heidelberg (2007). https://doi.org/10.1007/978-3-540-76969-9_7
20. Li, L., et al.: Key pre-distribution scheme with join leave support for SCADA systems. Int. J. Crit. Infrastruct. Prot. **24**, 111–125 (2019)

# Efficient Protective Jamming in 2D SINR Networks

Dominik Bojko[1], Marek Klonowski[1], Dariusz R. Kowalski[2], and Mateusz Marciniak[1](✉)

[1] Wrocław University of Science and Technology, Wrocław, Poland
mateusz.marciniak@pwr.edu.pl
[2] Augusta University, Augusta, Georgia, USA

**Abstract.** This paper studies how intentional jamming can be used for selective hiding communication in the 2D Signal-to-Interference-plus-Noise-Ratio (SINR) model. We aim to place a set of additional jamming stations to generate interference that blocks all the signals in a specified restricted area, i.e., by making the SINR value of the genuine stations' signal below a pre-defined threshold. We aim to optimize the accuracy of the jamming strategy by minimizing the impact of the jamming stations on the area of desired genuine communication while jamming the signals in the given restricted zone. We present solutions in various network settings for uniform and non-uniform networks. As a secondary aim, we try to minimize the total energy of the jamming stations. Among others, we show that, surprisingly, it is possible to jam arbitrarily large areas by jammers using total energy arbitrarily close to zero. Our contribution is an extension of recent results for the same problem in the 1D SINR network. Let us stress, however, that a 2D environment is closer to real-life settings. Still, the 2D model turned out to be much more complex in analysis (even for the most uncomplicated cases) and required a different approach to constructing algorithms.

**Keywords:** SINR · information hiding · jamming

## 1 Introduction

This paper considers limiting genuine communication in two-dimensional SINR to protect it from eavesdropping selectively. We assume that there are some *restricted areas* where we expect that any entity should not successfully receive the genuine wireless communication signal. On the other hand, communication outside the restricted areas should be untouched. As a motivation, we can point to many scenarios, including military communication, preventing industrial espionage, privacy protection by hiding personal communication, or providing wireless services in selected workspaces without being overheard in other ones. Such

The paper is supported by Polish National Science Center NCN grant 2017/25/B/ST6/02553. The work of Dariusz R. Kowalski was partially supported by the NSF grant 2131538.


J. Cano et al. (Eds.): Euro-Par 2023, LNCS 14100, pp. 533–546, 2023.
https://doi.org/10.1007/978-3-031-39698-4_36

an approach is essential if it is not possible to use cryptographic mechanisms. A good example is an ad hoc network of computationally restricted devices without the possibility of pre-deployment of any cryptographic material. Finally, in some cases, one needs to hide not only the content of the message but also the fact that communication takes place (in systems providing anonymous communication).

Our paper assumes a standard SINR model (Signal to Interference plus Noise Ratio; model formulated in [1]). In the SINR model, it is assumed that the signal's power is fading with distance from the transmitting station and is impacted by interference from other network devices. It makes a model close to reality and acceptable from the technology perspective. On the other hand, analysis in this model can be challenging.

We consider two configurations of SINR networks - uniform and non-uniform in the 2D space. We construct algorithms for positioning the jamming stations under these configurations, drawing out the chosen restricted areas while reducing the unnecessary impact on the original reception zones outside the restricted areas. Below we recall the most important related work. We introduce the communication model in Sect. 2 and formalize the addressed Zone-restriction with the Max-coverage problem. Section 3 presents the algorithm for jamming network configuration for stations that can be heard only inside some area delimited by 2D convex geometric shapes in the uniform network model. Section 4 focuses on the non-uniform network and presents the 2D variant of *noisy dust* from [16]. It utilizes jamming stations with small power levels to cover arbitrary fragments of a 2D plane with interference high enough to block chosen station's signal. Notably, this approach allows the reduction of overall energy with the increase of jamming stations number, reducing its impact on protected station reception zone as well. Section 5 presents conclusions and the most important future directions.

*Related Work.* This contribution can be seen as an extension of [16], wherein a similar problem is considered in the 1D SINR model. The current paper uses the same notation, describing the problem statement similarly. Note, however, that the transition analysis of the 2D case is much more difficult. The class of topological regions in 2D Euclidean space is substantially richer than on the 1D line. Therefore, the presented analysis required a much more complex approach and could not be reduced to re-using the methods from [16], which relied on the interval-based representation of reception zones.

The approach taken in this paper, using jamming stations as a protective security mechanism (called *friendly jamming*, has been considered in [3,4,13,17] in the context of non-SINR models. Some similar approaches for other models were proved to be practically feasible [14]. Due to the complexity of the SINR model, our approach and the analysis needs to be completely different. Regarding the SINR, [3,15] consider a model similar to the one used in this paper, but with the additional assumption that some regions are restricted from positioning jamming stations (so-called *buffers*). In contrast, our solutions are designed to provide protection of arbitrary configurations without prior restrictions on their construction and target the optimization of the energy cost of the additional jamming stations. The directional antennas are also considered there, while this paper focuses solely on the omnidirectional antennas, what makes fitting the noising substantially more challenging. Compared to another similar model in [17], we target the reduction of the jamming network energy consumption rather than limit the number of jamming stations. Moreover, a scheme for positioning stations in a grid relies on the combined interference of adjacent stations, which do not scale well with some of the network parameters we assume. Let us also stress that the approach change (primarily focusing on energy usage rather than limiting the number of stations) led to entirely different jamming strategies. Some other proactive approaches to securing communication in similar models can be found in [12].

Our paper can be seen as a continuation of a long list of results about the SINR model motivated by many real-life wireless networks, including 5G [5]. Note that in [7] authors consider SINR in $D$-dimensional space for some $D > 3$. Although such an assumption seems unjustified in the physical sense, the analysis of such a case turned out to be beneficial in analyzing algorithms of lower-dimensional spaces. Geometrical properties of the SINR model were studied by Avin et al. [2], who analyzed the properties of reception zones under the uniform SINR model, showing, among others, their convexity. Non-uniform network properties were analyzed in [7], along with a new point location algorithm, and in [8], where non-uniform SINR network model, combined with Voronoi Diagrams, proved to retain some of the valuable properties of the uniform setting. There is also a large amount of work considering the fundamental problems under the SINR model, such as *broadcasting* [9], *link scheduling* [10] or *power control* [11].

## 2 Model and Problem Statement

*Notation.* In the following paper, we use the notation presented in [16] extended and adapted to the 2D model. Let us stress that the rest of the technical part of this contribution is completely different. Indeed, we failed to re-ruse the techniques from the previous paper, possibly because the topology of $2D$ case is much richer, and from the algorithmic point of view, one needs to use subtler methods to limit communication even in regular-shaped regions.

We consider $D$-dimensional Euclidean spaces. Since $D$ is always initially fixed, we indicate a metric simply by $d$. We denote points as $p = (p_1, \ldots, p_D)$, vectors as $\vec{v} = \overrightarrow{(v_1, \ldots, v_D)}$ and line segments between points $p_0$ and $p_1$ as $\overline{(p_0, p_1)}$. For some polygon $\mathcal{P}$, we will denote the set of its edges as $F_{\mathcal{P}} = \{\overline{(x, y)} : x, y \in \mathbb{R}\}$, where $x, y$ for each edge will be consecutive vertices of the polygon $\mathcal{P}$. Moreover, for $n \in \mathbb{N}$, we use the notation $[n] = \{1, \ldots, n\}$ and a *D-ball* of radius $r$ is denoted as $\mathcal{B}(r, p) = \{x \in \mathbb{R}^D : d(x, p) \leqslant r\}$.

*Model of* SINR *network*
The SINR **network** is a tuple $\mathcal{A} = \langle D, S, N, \beta, P, \alpha \rangle$, where:

- $D \in \mathbb{N}^+$ is the dimension of the network,
- $S = \{s_1, \ldots, s_n\}$ is a set of positions of stations in $\mathbb{R}^D$,
- $N > 0$ is an ambient background noise (fixed real number),

- $\beta \geqslant 1$ is the reception threshold (fixed real number),
- $P : S \rightarrow \mathbb{R}$ is a stations' power function; by $P_i = P(s_i)$ we denote the power of station $s_i$,
- $\alpha \geqslant 2$ is a path-loss parameter (fixed real number).

For a network $\mathcal{A}$, we define the SINR function for station $s_i \in S$ and a point $x \in \mathbb{R}^D \backslash S$ as:

$$\mathrm{SINR}_{\mathcal{A}}(s_i, x) = \frac{P_i \cdot d(s_i, x)^{-\alpha}}{N + \sum_{s_j \in S \backslash \{s_i\}} P_j \cdot d(s_j, x)^{-\alpha}} .$$

If a network $\mathcal{A}$ is known from a context, we simplify the notation to $\mathrm{SINR}(s, x)$ for any station $s$. For $x \in S \backslash \{s_i\}$ we put $\mathrm{SINR}(s, x) = 0$ and it is not defined for $x = s_i$. The model in which $N = 0$ is called SIR. Therefore we replace the SINR function/model with SIR whenever it is admissible.
We define a *reception zone* of some station $s$ in a network $\mathcal{A}$ as the space where communication of the station $s$ can be correctly received and we denote it as $H_s^{\mathcal{A}} = \{x \in \mathbb{R}^D : \mathrm{SINR}_{\mathcal{A}}(s, x) \geqslant \beta\}$. $H_i^{\mathcal{A}}$ will be equivalent to $H_{s_i}^{\mathcal{A}}$. Finally, we define a *range* of station $s$ for a network with positive noise value ($N > 0$) as $\mathrm{range}(s) = \left(P(N\beta)^{-1}\right)^{\frac{1}{\alpha}}$, which maximizes the radius of reception zone of $s$ in the network consisting of the single station $s$. This value is also an upper bound for the possible range of $s$ while other stations are present in the network. Due to the lack of the noise component in the SIR model, the range definition does not apply.

*Formulation of the Zone-restriction with Max-coverage Problem.* For a network $\mathcal{A}$, there is given a *restricted area* $\mathcal{R}$: a subset of the space, wherein no station should be heard. In other words, in all points in $\mathcal{R}$, the SINR function of all stations in the set $S$ has to be lowered below the threshold $\beta$. It can be done using two techniques. The first is to modify the network parameters – one can increase the threshold value $\beta$, decrease the stations' powers, or increase the path-loss parameter $\alpha$. Second, we can add special *jamming stations* to the network to generate interference and change the shapes of the reception zones of the original set of stations in the network $\mathcal{A}$. An illustration of such approaches for a single broadcasting station is presented in Fig. 1.

Assume that there is a network $\mathcal{A} = \langle D, S, N, \beta, P, \alpha \rangle$ and some subspace $\mathcal{R} \subset \mathbb{R}^D$ representing a *restricted area* to be excluded from any communication involving stations from $S$. The problem of Zone-restriction with Max-coverage is to find a set of *jamming stations* $\mathcal{J} = (S^{(J)}, P^{(J)})$ with positions in $S^{(J)}$ and powers defined by the function $P^{(J)}$ in such a way that the resulting network $\mathcal{A}^{\mathcal{J}} = \langle D, S^{(J)} \cup S, N, \beta, P \cup P^{(J)}, \alpha \rangle$ satisfies the following two conditions (1 and 2).

**Condition 1.** $S^{(J)}$ *correctly protects* $\mathcal{R}$, i.e. $(\forall\, s \in S)(\forall\, x \in \mathcal{R})\ \mathrm{SINR}(s, x) < \beta$.

Note that Condition 1 itself could be trivially solved by adding single stations with appropriately high transmission powers in every connected component of

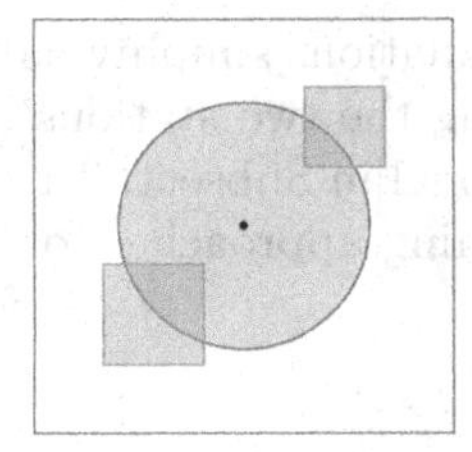

(a) Initial problem with one reception zone (blue) and two restricted zones (red rectangles).

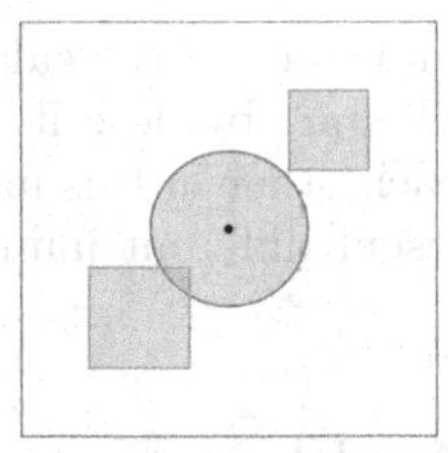

(b) Single zone problem solved (upper rectangle) by reducing station power.

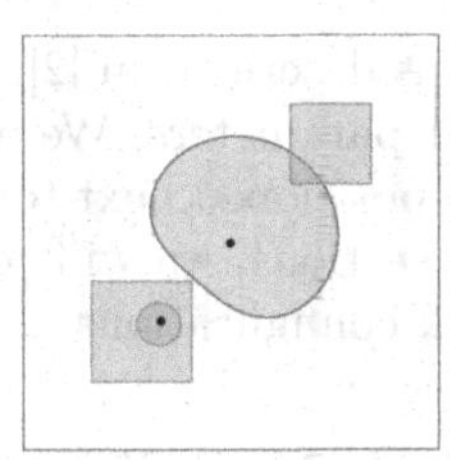

(c) Single zone problem solved (lower rectangle) by adding jamming station.

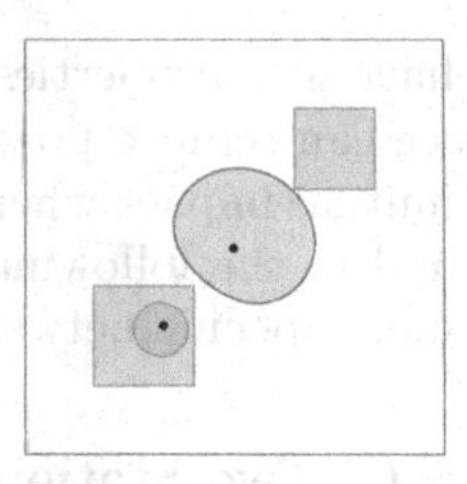

(d) Jamming station combined with a power reduction - both zones are protected.

**Fig. 1.** Sample problem for a single broadcasting station.

the restricted area within the ranges of broadcasting stations. It would, however, significantly suppress the desired communication in the reception zones of the genuine network. In order to control the above-undesired issue, we define a yardstick called a *coverage* – specifying how new reception areas correspond to their original sizes, excluding the restricted area.

**Condition 2.** $S^{(J)}$ *maximizes the following coverage (ratio) formula:*

$$\mathrm{Cover}(\mathcal{J},\mathcal{A}) = \left|\bigcup_{s_i\in S}\left(H_i^{\mathcal{A}^{\mathcal{J}}} \cap (H_i^{\mathcal{A}} \setminus \mathcal{R})\right)\right| \cdot \left|\bigcup_{s_i\in S} H_i^{\mathcal{A}} \setminus \mathcal{R}\right|^{-1},$$

where $|A|$ denotes the measure (volume) of a set $A$. The inverted part is the size of the maximal area in which the station's signal can be received, excluding the restricted areas. The first part is the size of the real reception area with jamming. Namely, for each station, we consider $H_i^{\mathcal{A}^{\mathcal{J}}}$, which is cropped to the maximal area where $s_i$ can be heard i.e. $(H_i^{\mathcal{A}} \setminus \mathcal{R})$. Note that $\mathrm{Cover}(\mathcal{J},\mathcal{A})$ is always properly defined, as long as $N > 0$. Moreover $0 \leqslant \mathrm{Cover}(\mathcal{J},\mathcal{A}) \leqslant 1$.
To summarize, the problem considered in this paper is specified as follows:

**Zone-restriction with Max-coverage problem:** *For a given network $\mathcal{A}$ and a restricted area $\mathcal{R}$, find a set of jamming stations and their powers, $\mathcal{J} = (S^{(J)}, P^{(J)})$, correctly protecting $\mathcal{R}$ and maximizing* $\mathrm{Cover}(\mathcal{J},\mathcal{A})$.

We also would like to minimize a *total (jamming) power*, defined as

$$\mathrm{Cost}(\mathcal{J}) = \sum_{s\in S^{(J)}} P^{(J)}(s) .$$

## 3 Uniform Networks Jamming

In this section, we consider networks of the form $\mathcal{A} = \langle D = 2, S, N, \beta, P \equiv 1, \alpha\rangle$, i.e., *uniform networks*, for which every station will have identical power. Without a loss of generality, this can be reduced to $((\forall s \in S)(P(s) = 1))$. Such networks have nice properties as described in [2], and some of the calculations simplify as we can remove power parameters. We will start by describing the two stations' mutual impact when positioned next to each other in this model in Subsect. 3.1, and in the following sections, we will present different jamming approaches for more specific network configurations.

### 3.1 Two Stations in the Uniform Model

In the following lemma, we describe how a single jamming station can split the plane into two half-planes, such that one is jammed.

**Lemma 1.** *For a network* $\mathcal{A} = \langle D = 2, S = \{s_0, s_1\}, N, \beta, P \equiv 1, \alpha\rangle$ *and some point* $b = (b_x, 0)$*, where* $s_0 = (0, 0)$ *and* $s_1 = \left(b_x\left(1 + \beta^{\frac{1}{\alpha}}\right), 0\right)$*, for any point* $p \in \{(a, b) \in \mathbb{R}^2 : a \geqslant b_x\}$*:*

- $\mathrm{SIR}(s_0, p) \leqslant \beta$*,*
- $\mathrm{SINR}(s_0, p) < \beta$*, for* $N > 0$*.*

*Proof.* At first, we are trying to find the distance $x = d(s_1, b)$, such that $\mathrm{SIR}(s_0, b) = d(s_0, b)^{-\alpha} d(s_1, b)^{\alpha} = b_x^{-\alpha} x^{\alpha} = \beta$. This will give us $x = b_x \beta^{\frac{1}{\alpha}}$. Now examine the point $b^* = (b_x, h)$, located on the line perpendicular to the segment $\overline{s_0 s_1}$ and crossing the point $b$. The distances from $b^*$ to stations $s_0$ and $s_1$ are equal to $d(s_0, b^*) = \sqrt{b_x^2 + h^2}$ and $d(s_1, b^*) = \sqrt{x^2 + h^2}$ respectively, for $h = d(b, b^*)$. A value of SIR for $s_0$ and such points take the form of:

$$\mathrm{SIR}(s_0, b^*) = \frac{d(s_0, b^*)^{-\alpha}}{d(s_1, b^*)^{-\alpha}} = \left(\frac{x^2 + h^2}{b_x^2 + h^2}\right)^{\frac{\alpha}{2}} = \left(\frac{b_x^2 \beta^{\frac{2}{\alpha}} + h^2}{b_x^2 + h^2}\right)^{\frac{\alpha}{2}} .$$

For $h = 0$ we get $b^* = b$ and $\mathrm{SIR}(s_0, b^*) = \beta$. On the other hand, for $h > 0$, we get:

$$\frac{\mathrm{SIR}(s_0, b^*)}{\beta} = \left(\frac{b_x^2 \beta^{\frac{2}{\alpha}} + h^2}{b_x^2 \beta^{\frac{2}{\alpha}} + h^2 \beta^{\frac{2}{\alpha}}}\right)^{\frac{\alpha}{2}} \leqslant 1 ,$$

as $\beta \geqslant 1$; and strict inequality for $\beta > 1$. Replacing SIR with SINR, where $N > 0$, also gives us strict inequality. Realize, that any point $(x^*, y^*)$, such that $x^* > b_x$, will be closer to $s_1$ and further away from $s_0$ than some point $b^* = (b_x, y^*)$, meaning that $\mathrm{SINR}(s_0, (x^*, y^*)) < \mathrm{SIR}(s_0, (x^*, y^*)) < \mathrm{SIR}(s_0, (b_x, y^*)) \leqslant \beta$. □

From Lemma 1, we immediately conclude that one can configure the position of jamming station $s_1$ for an arbitrary line and a given station $s_0$ in such a way that it guarantees the limitation of $s_0$'s reception zone to one side of this line.

### 3.2 Jamming the Enclosing Area

Let us define a class of *enclosing* restricted areas, which will surround one or more jamming stations. In this class, let us define two subclasses - *polygonal*, denoted as $\mathcal{R}_{\mathcal{P}}^{\mathrm{ep}} = \mathbb{R}^2 \setminus \mathcal{P}$, where $\mathcal{P}$ is a convex polygon and *circular*, denoted as $\mathcal{R}_{(x,y),r}^{\mathrm{ec}} = \mathbb{R}^2 \setminus \mathcal{B}(r, (x, y))$.

**Algorithm 1:** Assign 2D uniform jamming stations

```
Algorithm AssignUniformJammingStations(P, s)
    S^(J) ← {}
    for (x_j, y_j) ← F_P do
        l_j^d ← GetLine(x_j, y_j)
        l_j^p ← GetPerpendicularLine(l_j^d, s)
        b_j ← GetLinesCrossingPoint(l_j^d, l_j^p)
        s_j ← s + (b_j − s) · (1 + β^(1/α))
        S^(J) ← S^(J) ∪ {s_j}
    return S^(J)
```

Starting with the *enclosing polygonal* area, we will focus on the problem of a single station $s$ inside some polygon $\mathcal{P}$, and we want to block the station's signal outside the polygon's boundaries. The following functions are used in the algorithm:

- `GetLine`$(x, y)$ creates a line, which includes the segment $\overline{(x, y)}$,
- `GetPerpendicularLine`$(l, s)$ generates a line passing through the point $s$ and being perpendicular to the line $l$,
- `GetLinesCrossingPoint`$(l, l')$ calculates the position of the crossing point for the lines $l$ and $l'$.

The algorithm uses Lemma 1 on each of the polygon edges to position one station on the opposite side of the edge from the $s$ position and within the distance, which will provide enough interference along the edge to block a signal of $s$.

**Theorem 1.** *For a network $\mathcal{A} = \langle D = 2, S = \{s\}, N, \beta, P \equiv 1, \alpha\rangle$, a station $s \in \mathcal{P}$ and some restricted area $\mathcal{R}_{\mathcal{P}}^{ep} = \mathbb{R}^2 \setminus \mathcal{P}$, where $\mathcal{P}$ is a convex polygon, which encloses $s$, Algorithm 1 returns a set of jamming stations' positions $S^{(J)}$ such that the set of jamming stations $\mathcal{J} = \{S^{(J)}, P \equiv 1\}$ correctly protects restricted area $\mathcal{R}_{\mathcal{P}}^{ep}$.*

*Proof.* The algorithm constructs a straight line for each polygon segment, splitting space into two half-planes. Then the positioning of jamming station $s_j$ for such a segment is done according to the scheme presented in Lemma 1, which guarantees that all points on the half-plane at the opposite side of the line to station $s$, are outside its reception zone. Since we operate for all segments of the convex polygon, all of these half-planes could be united into the restricted area $\mathcal{R}_{\mathcal{P}}^{\mathrm{ep}}$. An additional interference introduced from other stations can only reduce the reception zone, so the restricted area will be correctly protected. □

This approach works well for the areas given as the convex polygon, but we cannot apply it directly when the restricted areas contain some curvy or circular fragments. Nevertheless, if we assume that some station $s$ is in the center of some circular enclosing area, it can be solved by applying the method from Fact 1.

**Fact 1.** *For a network $\mathcal{A} = \langle D = 2, S = \{s\}, N, \beta, P \equiv 1, \alpha\rangle$, a station $s$ and some restricted area $\mathcal{R}^{\mathrm{ec}}_{s,r} = \mathbb{R}^2 \setminus \mathcal{B}(r, s)$, Algorithm 1 with a regular polygon $\mathcal{P}$, inscribed into the disk $\mathcal{B}(r, s)$, as an input, returns a set of jamming stations' positions $S^{(J)}$ such that a set of jamming stations $\mathcal{J} = \{S^{(J)}, P \equiv 1\}$ correctly protects restricted area $\mathcal{R}^{\mathrm{ec}}_{s,r}$.*

By inscribing the polygon into the circular area, we can directly apply the Algorithm 1, and it will correctly block the signal outside the polygon. We can use different $n$-gons as the inscribed polygons. The choice of $n$ impacts the cost (i.e., $\mathrm{Cost}(\mathcal{J}) = n$) and the coverage. In Fig. 2, we present numerical results for some of the regular polygons. The coverage of a chosen regular polygon can be bounded using Lemma 2.

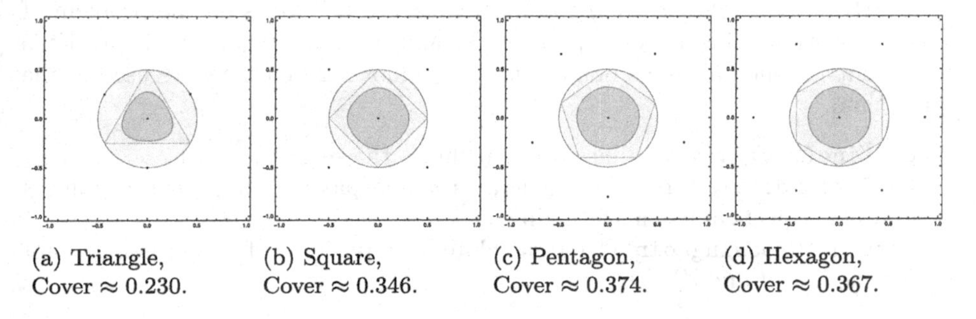

(a) Triangle, Cover ≈ 0.230. (b) Square, Cover ≈ 0.346. (c) Pentagon, Cover ≈ 0.374. (d) Hexagon, Cover ≈ 0.367.

**Fig. 2.** Approximations of different circular shapes. Red spaces represent the initial disks, green spaces – the polygons – and blue spaces are the final reception zones. (Color figure online)

**Lemma 2.** *Let $s$ be a single broadcasting station and $0 < r < \mathrm{range}(s)$. If a restricted area is given by $\mathcal{R}^{\mathrm{ec}}_{s,r} = \mathbb{R}^2 \setminus \mathcal{B}(r, s)$ and a jamming network $\mathcal{J}$ is created by Algorithm 1 for some regular $n$-gon $\mathcal{P}$, then coverage of the returned network with a set of jamming stations $\mathcal{J}$ satisfies:*

$$\frac{(b(\beta b^{\alpha} N + n)^{-\frac{1}{\alpha}})^2}{r^2} \leqslant \mathrm{Cover}(\mathcal{J}, \mathcal{A}) \leqslant \frac{|\mathcal{P}|}{\pi r^2},$$

*where $b$ is the length of the polygon's apothem (the distance between $s$ and sides of the polygon $\mathcal{P}$).*

The upper bound is obvious from Fact 1 — we limit the maximal reception zone by some polygon $\mathcal{P}$. The lower bound can be calculated by approximating the maximal range of station $s$ in a direction to one of the jamming stations $s_j$. It is realized by modifying the resulting network, which assumes that all jamming stations are placed in the same point $s_j$ (this trick effectively increases the power of $s_j$ $n$ times). It allows us to calculate the station range in this scenario. We skip the details of this proof due to space limitations.

# 4 Noisy Dust for Non-uniform Networks

This section considers non-uniform networks, wherein the reception zones can be concave, increasing the analytic complexity. We apply the *noisy dust* approach from [16] to flood the restricted area with jamming stations having small power levels. Note that despite the similarity of the problem and jamming strategy, the 2D case technically significantly differs from considerations in [16].

## 4.1 Single Station Effective Jamming Range

Consider a single station $s = (0,0)$ with power $P(s) = 1$ and some *border point* $b = (b_x, 0)$ such that $0 < b_x <$ range(s). Let us place a jamming station $s_j = (b_x(1+F_j), 0)$ where $F_j = (P_j\beta)^{\frac{1}{\alpha}}$ (from now on, we tacitly assume that $P(s_j) = P_j$) and $r = b_x F_j$ (see the arrangement in Fig. 3a). Note that we require $F_j < 1$, so we keep the $\alpha \geqslant 2$ and $P_j < \beta^{-1}$ (what also corresponds to the forementioned property $P_j \lll P$). Clearly the segment $\overline{(b_x, s_j)}$ is jammed. The disk $\mathcal{B}(s_j, r)$ could be used as an initial approximation of a space, where a single disturbing station can effectively jam the signal emitted by $s$ – however, it would be imprecise if we would compare it with the real effective jamming space (see Fig. 3b - blue space denotes $\mathcal{B}(r, s_j)$ and a green curve represents a boundary of the maximal region, where $s_j$ correctly jams $s$).

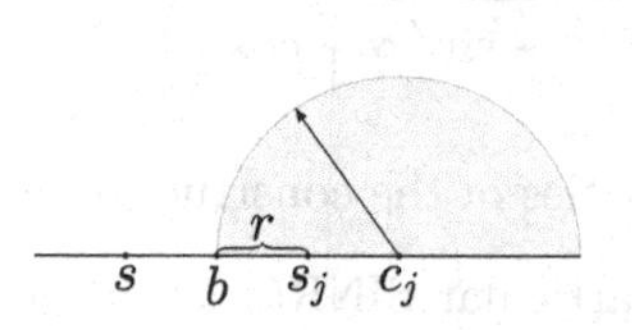


(a) Top half of the area where the single jamming station can effectively block signal of $s$.

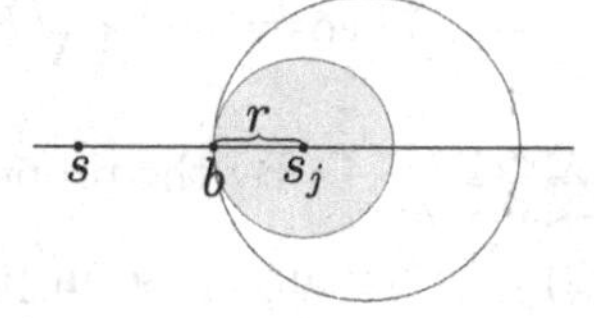


(b) Single station's jamming range.

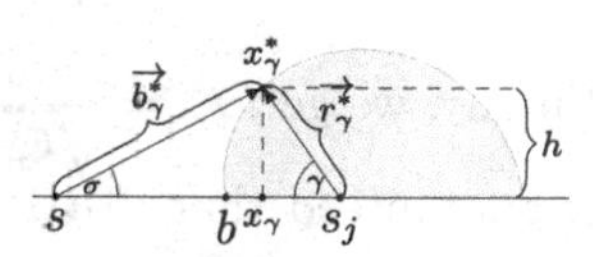


(c) Construction of radial based description of $\mathcal{B}\left(\frac{d(s,b)}{F_j^{-1}-1}, c_j\right)$ space.

**Fig. 3.** Effective jamming range construction.

In the SIR model, the shape of the space, where $s_j$ blocks the signal of $s$, is expected to form some oval, irregular shape. Surprisingly, it forms a circle, centered at $c_j = \left(b_x + \frac{d(s,b)}{F_j^{-1}-1}, 0\right)$.

**Theorem 2.** *Let* $\mathcal{A} = \langle D = 2, S = \{s, s_j\}, N, \beta, P, \alpha\rangle$ *be a network, then for any* $x \in \mathcal{B}\left(\frac{d(s,b)}{F_j^{-1}-1}, c_j\right)$, *the condition* $\mathrm{SINR}(s,x) \leqslant \beta$ *is satisfied.*

Fix $s_j$ and $s$. We are looking for such points $x$, that $\mathrm{SIR}(s,x) = \beta$. These points form the border of the area where the signal is blocked (by continuity of SIR with respect to the tested position). We are using the radial approach, i.e., we create a vector $\overrightarrow{r_\gamma^*}$ in some direction ($\gamma \in [0, \pi]$ is an angle between the segment $\overline{ss_j}$ and the vector), such that $x_\gamma^* = s_j + \overrightarrow{r_\gamma^*}$ and $\text{SIR}(s, x_\gamma^*) = \beta$ (note that SIR is monotonous in the direction of the vector, so there is exactly one appropriate $x_\gamma^*$). This method is presented in Lemma 3 with construction depicted in Fig. 3c. We must analyze only half of the reception zone, as the other half is symmetrical.

**Lemma 3.** *Let $\mathcal{A} = \langle D = 2, S = \{s, s_j\}, N, \beta, P, \alpha\rangle$ be a network. For $\gamma \in [0, \pi]$, we define $r_\gamma^* = d(s, s_j)((F_j^{-2} - \sin^2\gamma)^{\frac{1}{2}} + \cos\gamma)^{-1}$ and a point $x_\gamma^* = s_j + \overrightarrow{r_\gamma^*}$, where $\overrightarrow{r_\gamma^*} = \overrightarrow{(-r_\gamma^*\cos\gamma, r_\gamma^*\sin\gamma)}$. Then $\text{SIR}(s, x_\gamma^*) = \beta$ and $\text{SINR}(s, x_\gamma^*) \leqslant \beta$. Moreover, for any point $x \in \overline{s_j x_\gamma^*}$, we get $\text{SINR}(s, x) \leqslant \beta$.*

*Proof.* Let us define a base vector $\overrightarrow{r} = \overrightarrow{(b - s_j)}$. The vector $\overrightarrow{r_\gamma^*}$ is acquired by rotating $\overrightarrow{r}$ by angle $\gamma$ in clockwise direction. Obviously, if $r_\gamma^* = \|\overrightarrow{r_\gamma^*}\|$, then $\overrightarrow{r_\gamma^*} = \overrightarrow{(-r_\gamma^*\cos\gamma, r_\gamma^*\sin\gamma)}$. Let us define a new vector $\overrightarrow{b_\gamma^*} = \overrightarrow{x_\gamma^* - s}$ of length $b_\gamma^*$ and the angle between $\overrightarrow{b_\gamma^*}$ and $\overrightarrow{s_j - s}$ as $\sigma$ (see Fig. 3c). Note that $\sin\gamma = \frac{h}{r_\gamma^*}$, $\sin\sigma = \frac{h}{b_\gamma^*}$, $\frac{r_\gamma^*}{b_\gamma^*} = \frac{\sin\sigma}{\sin\gamma}$. Point $x_\gamma^*$ has to keep the property $\text{SIR}(s, x_\gamma^*) = \beta$, so $\frac{r_\gamma^*}{b_\gamma^*} = F_j = \frac{\sin\sigma}{\sin\gamma}$ and $\cos\sigma = \sqrt{1 - F_j^2\sin^2\gamma}$. By applying it to the $d(s, s_j) = b_\gamma^*\cos\sigma + r_\gamma^*\cos\gamma$, we get

$$d(s, s_j) = \frac{r_\gamma^*\sqrt{1 - F_j^2\sin^2\gamma}}{F_j} + r_\gamma^*\cos\gamma = r_\gamma^*\left(\sqrt{F_j^{-2} - \sin^2\gamma} + \cos\gamma\right) .$$

Finally, we get: $r_\gamma^* = \frac{d(s,s_j)}{\sqrt{F_j^{-2} - \sin^2\gamma} + \cos\gamma}$. By the properties of the construction it is guaranteed that $\text{SIR}(s, x_\gamma^*) = \beta$ for any $\gamma$, so in particular $\text{SINR}(s, x_\gamma^*) \leqslant \beta$. From monotonicity of $s$ and $s_j$ energy functions in the direction of $\overrightarrow{r_\gamma^*}$, for any point $p \in \overline{x_\gamma^* s_j}$, $\text{SINR}(s, x_\delta^*) \geqslant \text{SINR}(s, p)$, making all such $p$ correctly jammed. □

In the next step, we want to convert the vector representation of $\overrightarrow{r_\gamma^*}$ to a parametric one. In particular, we may specify $h$ component of $\overrightarrow{r_\gamma^*}$, basing on the $x_\gamma$ argument as $\overrightarrow{r_\gamma} = \overrightarrow{(x_\gamma, r^*(x))}$, via a function $r^*(x) = h$, where $x = d(b, x_\gamma) \in [0, d(b, x_\pi)]$. This transformation is presented in Lemma 4:

**Lemma 4.** *For every point $x_\gamma^*$ ($\gamma \in [0, \pi]$), there exists $x$ such that $x_\gamma^* = (b_x + x, r^*(x))$, where $r^*(x) = \left(-x^2 + \left(\frac{2d(s,b)}{F_j^{-1} - 1}\right)x\right)^{\frac{1}{2}}$ and $b = (b_x, 0)$. Moreover, $\{x_\gamma^* : \gamma \in [0, \pi]\}$ forms a half of a circle.*

*Proof.* Let $x_\gamma^* = (b_x + x, h)$, where $x \in [0, d(b, x_\pi)]$. We want to calculate $h$ in this formula. It depends on angle $\gamma$ as follows:

$$r_\gamma^*\cos\gamma = d(s_j, b) - x\ , \qquad r_\gamma^*\sin\gamma = \sqrt{\left(r_\gamma^*\right)^2 - (d(s_j, b) - x)^2}\ . \qquad (1)$$

Combining the previously calculated value of $d(s, s_j)$ with Eq. 1 brings

$$(r_\gamma^*)^2 = ((d(s,b)+x)^2 - (d(s_j,b)-x)^2)(F_j^{-2}-1)^{-1} .$$

This equation might have two real solutions for $(r_\gamma^*)^2$. However, we consider only the positive one, which under assumptions $d(s,b) \geqslant d(s_j,b)$ and $F_j^{-2} - 1 > 0$, satisfies: $r_\gamma^* = (((d(s,b)+x)^2 - (d(s_j,b)-x)^2)(F_j^{-2}-1)^{-1})^{\frac{1}{2}}$ . Finally, we can use this result to calculate the parametrization $r^*(x) = r_\gamma^* \sin\gamma$:

$$r^*(x) = r_\gamma^* \sin\gamma = \sqrt{(r_\gamma^*)^2 - (d(s_j,b)-x)^2} = \sqrt{-x^2 + \left(\frac{2b_x}{F_j^{-1}-1}\right)x} .$$

Moreover, the last formula is a geometric mean of $x$ and $\left(\frac{2b_x}{F_j^{-1}-1} - x\right)$, hence $\{x_\gamma^* : \gamma \in [0,\pi]\}$ is a half of a circle of diameter $\frac{2b_x}{F_j^{-1}-1}$. Therefore, the considered region is in fact $\mathcal{B}\left(\frac{d(s,b)}{F_j^{-1}-1}, c_j\right)$. □

Lemmas 3 and 4 conclude the proof of Theorem 2. If we know the point $b$ and the expected $r = \frac{d(s,b)}{F_j^{-1}-1}$, then we can calculate the power level of station $s_j$ as: $P_j = \beta^{-1}\left(1 + \frac{d(s,b)}{r}\right)^{-\alpha} = \beta^{-1} r^\alpha d(s,c_j)^{-\alpha}$. We will use this equation in the following sections to calculate power levels for stations with fixed positions and for predefined values of $r$.

### 4.2 Noisy Dust Algorithm

Using the effective jamming range of a single station, represented by some disk, we can approximate such the disk by inscribing some hexagon inside. We may use this fact to tile the 2D regions requiring the jamming. Let us define such a hexagonal grid by $\mathcal{H} = \{h_0, h_1 \dots\}$ where $h_i$ are central points of equally sized regular hexagons, each with radius $r$ and assume such grid fully covers the restricted zone inside the reception zone of some station $s$. Then the algorithm for positioning stations for each hexagon is defined in Algorithm 2.

The center of the hexagon can be treated as the $c_j$ from the Theorem 2. The algorithm will position the jamming station somewhere on the line going through the $h = c_j$ and the $s$ and assign enough power to cover the whole disk circumscribed on the hexagon with center $h$, providing correct protection. Correctness of the offset and power assignment comes directly from the Theorem 2 and related constructions.

One must create the hexagonal grid to use the algorithm - the process details are not part of this paper. For the algorithm to work, the grid must densely fill the restricted area region intersecting the reception zone of the protected station $s$ (note that details of the algorithm can be aligned to protect more than one station).

**Algorithm 2:** Create noisy dust for $s = (0, 0)$, restricted area $\mathcal{R}$ and hexagonal grid $\mathcal{H}$ with circumradius equal to $r$.

**Algorithm** GenerateNoisyDust($s, \mathcal{H}, r$)
- $J \leftarrow \{\}$
- **for** $h \leftarrow \mathcal{H}$ **do**
  - $P_j \leftarrow \left(\frac{1}{\beta}\right)\left(\frac{d(s,h)-r}{r}+1\right)^{-\alpha}$
  - $F_j \leftarrow (P_j\beta)^{1/\alpha}$
  - $s_j \leftarrow h + (r - F_j(d(s,h) - r))\left(\frac{\overrightarrow{s-h}}{d(s,h)}\right)$
  - $J \leftarrow J \cup \{s_j, P_j\}$
- **return** $J$

Let us consider the energy cost of Algorithm 2. We assume that the parts of the restricted area located outside of the range of $s$ are excluded and that the required number of hexagons of circumradii $r$ required to fill some restricted area $\mathcal{R}$ is defined as $n = (|\mathcal{R} \cap \mathcal{B}(\text{range}(s), s)| + o(A(r)))A(r)^{-1}$ , where $A(r) = \frac{3\sqrt{3}r^2}{2}$ is the area of a hexagon with circumradius $r$ (the assumption about the value of $n$ is fulfilled in all realistic scenarios). The area of the effectively restricted region $|\mathcal{R} \cap \mathcal{B}(\text{range}(s), s)|$ is a constant ($\mathcal{R}$ and $s$ are given a priori). It is naturally bounded by the area of the initial disk around the broadcasting station in SINR model: $|\mathcal{R} \cap \mathcal{B}(\text{range}(s), s)| \leqslant |\mathcal{B}(\text{range}(s), s)| \leqslant \pi \cdot \text{range}(s)^2$. Cumulative energy required to set up jamming stations for arbitrary $\mathcal{R}$ is given by $\sum_{i=0}^{n-1} \beta^{-1} r^{\alpha} d(s, c_i)^{-\alpha}$ , where the circumradius of every single hexagon equals $r$, and each jamming station $s_i$ is positioned in a unique hexagonal cell and vice versa. Each cell contains only one jamming station.

Observe that one can limit the value of $d(s, c_i)$ by a distance between $s$ and the closest single hex within the hexagonal grid — let us denote it by $d_s = \min\{d(s, c_j) : j = 1, 2, \ldots, n\}$. Since $d(s, c_i) \geqslant d_s$ for any hex cell:

$$\sum_{i=0}^{n-1} \beta^{-1} r^{\alpha} d(s, c_i)^{-\alpha} < \sum_{i=0}^{n-1} \beta^{-1} \left(\frac{r}{d_S}\right)^{\alpha} = \frac{nr^{\alpha}}{\beta d_S^{\alpha}} \approx \frac{2|\mathcal{R} \cap \mathcal{B}(\text{range}(s), s)|}{3\sqrt{3}\beta d_s^{\alpha}} r^{\alpha-2} .$$

Remark that for $\alpha = 2$, this upper bound is constant – $\frac{2|\mathcal{R}|}{3\sqrt{3}\beta d_s^{\alpha}}$ and one can similarly find a lower bound of cumulative energy required to set up jamming stations, by substitution of $d_s$ by its antipodal counterpart $\max\{d(s, c_j) : j = 1, 2, \ldots, n\}$ (which is also bounded by $\text{range}(s) + r$) and realizing that $n \geqslant \frac{|\mathcal{R} \cap \mathcal{B}(\text{range}(s), s)|}{A(r)}$, what shows that in this case (of $\alpha = 2$), the cumulative energy is $O(1)$ as $r \to 0^+$. On the other hand, for $\alpha > 2$, the upper bound converges to 0 as $r \to 0^+$, which upholds the zero-energy property from the 1D version of the noisy dust algorithm. When $\alpha < 2$, both upper and lower bounds are $O(r^{2-\alpha})$, as $r \to 0^+$, so in this case, the total energy usually rises along with the number of jamming stations.

We are going to check the actual coverage numerically. We consider four different scenarios for initial network configuration of $\mathcal{A} = \langle D = 2, S = \{s\}, N =$

$1.0, \beta = 1.0, P, \alpha = 3.0\rangle$. Each experiment is conducted for hexagons with radii $r \in \{0.125, 0.25, 0.5, 1\}$ and the coverage results, along with example visualization presented in Fig. 4. One can easily see that all cases hold the property that the coverage value increases as the sizes of hexagons decrease. We see that the method might not work very well for larger sizes of hexagons in some configurations (like, e.g., the one presented in Fig. 4a), but generally, the method is quite efficient in practice.

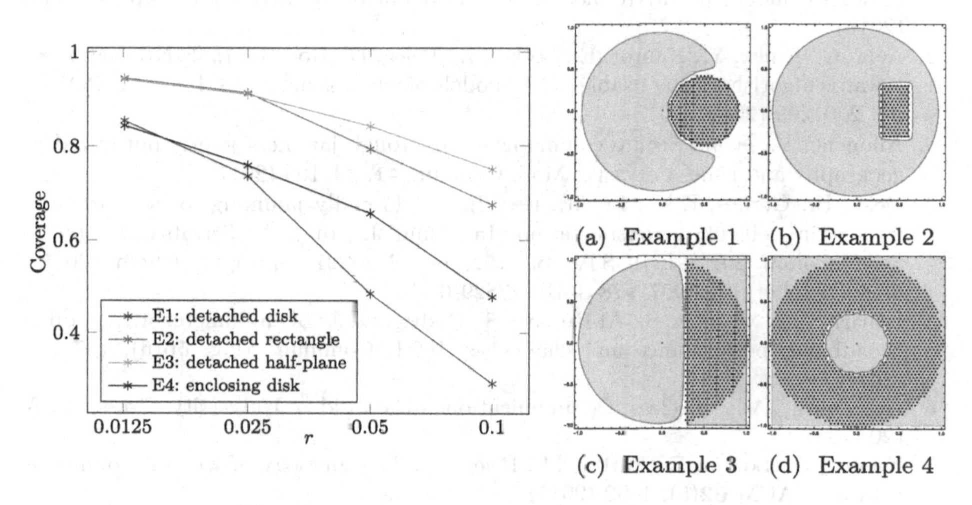


**Fig. 4.** Coverage obtained for four considered examples with respect to circumradius $r$ of each hexagon in the grid and illustration of examples with $r = 0.025$.

## 5 Conclusions and Future Work

In our paper, we study the problem of protecting communication in the 2D SINR network. We introduced a formal, realistic model and presented algorithms usable for uniform and non-uniform network settings. The idea for designing these algorithms is to limit communication by introducing a carefully prepared noise generated collectively by a set of stations.

Even though presented solutions are introduced only for some chosen, limited scenarios, they should be capable of generalization for more complex ones since more complicated (but still realistic) cases can be represented as combinations of regular-shaped areas investigated here.

There are multiple directions in future research that can extend these results. One such is the idea of dynamic environments, where stations and restricted areas are not static space objects but can change locations and parameters with time, modeling real-world scenarios like cars or drones. Another direction would be extending the solutions to 3D or creating generic versions for any number of dimensions. Finding the energy bounds for generic configurations or tighter coverage bounds for presented solutions is also challenging. The model can also be an object of modifications, e.g., assuming we have different receivers' sensitivity (e.g., like in [3], where adversary and legitimate receivers use different reception thresholds).

## References


1. Jurdzinski, T., Kowalski, D.R.: Distributed randomized broadcasting in wireless networks under the SINR model. In: Encyclopedia of Algorithms, pp. 577–580 (2016)
2. Avin, C., Emek, Y., Kantor, E., Lotker, Z., Peleg, D., Roditty, L.: SINR diagrams: towards algorithmically usable SINR models of wireless networks. In: ACM PODC, pp. 200–209 (2009)
3. Allouche, Y., et al.: Secure communication through jammers jointly optimized in geography and time. Pervasive Mob. Comput. **41**, 83–105 (2017)
4. Deka, B., Gerdes, R.M., Li, M., Heaslip, K.: Friendly jamming for secure localization in vehicular transportation. In: Tian, J., Jing, J., Srivatsa, M. (eds.) SecureComm 2014. LNICST, vol. 152, pp. 212–221. Springer, Cham (2015). https://doi.org/10.1007/978-3-319-23829-6_16
5. Busari, S.A., Mumtaz, S., Al-Rubaye, S., Rodriguez, J.: 5G millimeter-wave mobile broadband: performance and challenges. IEEE Commun. Mag. **56**(6), 137–143 (2018)
6. Goldsmith, A.: Wireless Communications. Cambridge University Press, USA (2005)
7. Kantor, E., Lotker, Z., Parter, M., Peleg, D.: The topology of wireless communication. J. ACM **62**(5), 1–32 (2015)
8. Kantor, E., Lotker, Z., Parter, M., Peleg, D.: Nonuniform SINR+Voronoi diagrams are effectively uniform. Theoret. Comput. Sci. **878–879**, 53–66 (2021)
9. Jurdzinski, T., Kowalski, D.R., Stachowiak, G.: Distributed deterministic broadcasting in wireless networks of weak devices. In: Fomin, F.V., Freivalds, R., Kwiatkowska, M., Peleg, D. (eds.) ICALP 2013. LNCS, vol. 7966, pp. 632–644. Springer, Heidelberg (2013). https://doi.org/10.1007/978-3-642-39212-2_55
10. Halldórsson, M.M., Mitra, P.: Nearly optimal bounds for distributed wireless scheduling in the SINR model. Distrib. Comput. **29**(2), 77–88 (2016)
11. Lotker, Z., Parter, M., Peleg, D., Pignolet, Y.A.: Distributed power control in the SINR model. In: IEEE INFOCOM, pp. 2525–2533 (2011)
12. Lashkari, A.H., Danesh, M.M.S., Samadi, B.: A survey on wireless security protocols (WEP, WPA and WPA2/802.11i). In: ICCSIT, pp. 48–52 (2009)
13. Martinovic, I., Pichota, P., Schmitt, J.B.: Jamming for good: a fresh approach to authentic communication in WSNs. In: WiSec, pp. 161–168 (2009)
14. Kim, Y.S., Tague, P., Lee, H., Kim, H.: Carving secure Wi-Fi zones with defensive jamming. In: ACM ASIACCS, pp. 53–54 (2012)
15. Sankararaman, S., et al.: Optimization schemes for protective jamming. In: MobiHoc, pp. 65–74 (2012)
16. Bojko, D., Klonowski, M., Kowalski, D.R., Marciniak, M.: Exact and efficient protective jamming in SINR-based wireless networks. MASCOTS **2021**, 1–8 (2021)
17. Commander, C.W., Pardalos, P., Ryabchenko, V., Shylo, O.V., Uryasev, S., Zrazhevsky, G.: Jamming communication networks under complete uncertainty. Optim. Lett. **2**, 53–70 (2008)

# Multidisciplinary, Domain-Specific and Applied Parallel and Distributed Computing

# GPU Code Generation of Cardiac Electrophysiology Simulation with MLIR

Tiago Trevisan Jost, Arun Thangamani, Raphaël Colin, Vincent Loechner(✉), Stéphane Genaud, and Bérenger Bramas

Inria Nancy Grand Est and ICube Lab., University of Strasbourg, Strasbourg, France
{arun.thangamani,berenger.bramas}@inria.fr,
{raphaelcolin,loechner,genaud}@unistra.fr

**Abstract.** We show the benefits of the novel MLIR compiler technology to the generation of code from a DSL, namely EasyML used in openCARP, a widely used simulator in the cardiac electrophysiology community. Building on an existing work that deeply modified openCARP's native DSL code generator to enable efficient vectorized CPU code, we extend the code generation for GPUs (Nvidia CUDA and AMD ROCm). Generating optimized code for different accelerators requires specific optimizations and we review how MLIR has been used to enable multi-target code generation from an integrated generator. Experiments conducted on the 48 ionic models provided by openCARP show that the GPU code executes 3.17× faster and delivers more than 7× FLOPS per watt than the vectorized CPU code, on an Nvidia A100 GPU versus a 36-cores AVX-512 Intel CPU.

**Keywords:** automatic GPU code generation · code transformation · MLIR · domain-specific languages · heterogeneous architectures

## 1 Introduction

Cardiac electrophysiology is a medical specialty in which the research community has long been using computational simulation. Understanding the heart's behavior (and in particular cardiac diseases) requires to model the ionic flows between the muscular cells of cardiac tissue. Such models, called *ionic models*, describe the way an electric current flows through the cell membranes. The widespread practice in this field is for experts to describe their ionic model in a domain-specific language (DSL), which essentially enables to model the current flow by ordinary differential equations. The openCARP[1] [15] simulation framework has been created to promote the sharing of the cardiac simulation efforts from the electrophysiology community. To describe ionic models, this framework offers a DSL named EasyML [20], from which a code generator can derive C/C++ code.

[1] https://opencarp.org.

T. T. Jost and A. Thangamani—Both authors contributed equally to the paper.


J. Cano et al. (Eds.): Euro-Par 2023, LNCS 14100, pp. 549–563, 2023.
https://doi.org/10.1007/978-3-031-39698-4_37

The next major advances in cardiac research will require to increase by several orders of magnitude the number of cardiac cells that are simulated. The ultimate goal is to simulate the whole human heart at the cell level [16], that will require to run several thousands of time steps on a mesh of several billions of elements.

In order to achieve such simulations involving exascale supercomputers, the generation of efficient code is a key challenge. This is the general purpose of our work. We propose to extend the original openCARP code generator using the state-of-the-art compiler technology MLIR (Multi-Level Intermediate Representation) [11] from LLVM [10].

MLIR offers a means to express code operations and types through an extensible set of *intermediate representations* (IR), called dialects, each dedicated to a specific concern, at different levels of abstractions. The code representation can use a mix of operations and types from different IRs. Representing the code at an appropriate level of abstraction enables transformation and optimizations that would be difficult to achieve with a single general purpose IR. An example of a high-level abstraction dialect is the `linalg` dialect which defines operations on matrices, and comes with a set of optimizations that can take advantage of some mathematical properties. The `linalg` operations can then be transformed into operations expressed in a less abstract IR (this is called *lowering*). An intermediate level of abstraction is the `scf` dialect to represent control flow operations like loops and conditional statements. Eventually the code is lowered in a dialect, such as `llvm`, that has the ability to generate machine code.

In a previous paper [18], we introduced architectural modifications to openCARP to enable the generation of CPU vectorized code using MLIR. We have shown that the MLIR generated vectorized code outperforms the original `C/C++` code compiled (and optimized) by standard compilers (`clang`, `gcc`, and `icc`).

In this paper, we present our work to take further advantage of the capabilities of MLIR, to extend the code generator to GPU code generation. This represents a stepping stone for the final objective of the MICROCARD[2] project to be able to combine instances of optimized CPU and GPU kernels, that will eventually be dynamically scheduled by a runtime on the varied computing resources of a supercomputer. The main contributions of this work are: (i) a code generator from a DSL to efficient heterogeneous code by leveraging MLIR; (ii) an integration of this code generator in the compilation flow of a cardiac electrophysiology simulator (openCARP); (iii) a performance improvement of openCARP beneficial to the electrophysiologists, paving the way to larger scale experiments.

The paper is organized as follows. Section 2 details the extension we propose for the openCARP compilation flow. Section 3 presents our GPU code generation using MLIR. A discussion about the challenges we faced and the reusability of our work is provided in Sect. 4. Performance and energy efficiency is evaluated on CPU and GPUs in Sect. 5 on all 48 ionic models available in openCARP. Related work is covered in Sect. 6, and finally Sect. 7 concludes the paper.

[2] https://microcard.eu.

```
Vm; .external(Vm); .nodal();
Iion; .external(); .nodal();
group { mu1 = 0.2; mu2 = 0.3; }.param();

t_norm = 12.9; vm_norm = 100; vm_rest = -80;
touAcm2=100/12.9;
V_init = 0; Vm_init=vm_rest; K = 8; epsilon = 0.002; a = 0.15;

U = (Vm-vm_rest)/vm_norm;
diff_V = -(epsilon+mu1*V/(mu2+U))*(V+K*U*(U-a-1))/t_norm;

Iion = (K*U*(U-a)*(U-1)+U*V)*touAcm2;
```

**Listing 1.** AlievPanfilov ionic model written in EasyML

## 2 Compilation Flow in OpenCARP

### 2.1 EasyML: Description of Ionic Models

In openCARP, biomedical mathematicians use EasyML [20] as a DSL to write ionic models (as mathematical equations) that represent the current that flows through a cell of cardiac tissue from a given cell state. Many other languages (e.g. CellML, SBML, MMT) used to write ionic models can be easily translated to/from EasyML through scripts available in openCARP and Myokit [7]. Some characteristics of EasyML are as follows:

1. SSA (static single assignment) [8] representation, so all variables are defined as mathematical equalities in an arbitrary order;
2. specific variables prefixes/suffixes (such as `_init`, `diff_`, etc.);
3. calls to *math* library functions;
4. *markup* statements to specify various variable properties, such as: which method to use for integrating differential equations (`.method(`*m*`)`), whether to pre-compute a lookup table of predefined values over a given interval (`.lookup`), which variables to output (`.trace`), etc.;
5. it is not Turing-complete since it cannot express loops, control flow, or sequence of elements—but there can be tests expressed as restricted `if/else` statements or as C-like ternary operators.

**Example.** Listing 1 shows the EasyML code for the very simple AlievPanfilov [1] ionic model. The variables `Vm` and `Iion` (voltage and current) are declared as external on lines 1–2 as they will be used by other parts of the openCARP simulator. Line 3 defines a group of runtime controllable parameters. Lines 5–7 initialize some variables. Line 10 calls the *Forward Euler (fe)* default integration method to recompute `V` by using the DSL `diff_` prefix, and line 12 computes the `Iion` (current) flow out of the cell.

### 2.2 Code Generation in OpenCARP

The openCARP simulation handles a mesh of elements, potentially containing many biological cells, but for simplification purposes we will refer to a mesh element as a *cell* in the following. A simulation step is composed of two stages:

```
void compute_AlievPanfilov(...) {
#pragma omp parallel for schedule(static)
for (int __i=start; __i<end; __i++) {
  AlievPanfilov_state *sv = sv_base+__i;
  //Initialize the ext vars to current values
  Iion = Iion_ext[__i], Vm = Vm_ext[__i];
  //Compute storevars and external modvars
  U = ((Vm-(vm_rest))/vm_norm);
  Iion = (((((K*U)*(U-(a)))*(U-(1.)))+(U*sv->V))*touAcm2);
  //Complete Forward Euler Update
  diff_V = (((-(0.002+((p->mu1*sv->V)/(p->mu2+U))))*(sv->V+((8.*U)*((U
     -(0.15))-(1.)))))/12.9);
  V_new = sv->V+diff_V*dt;
  //Finish the update
  Iion = Iion, sv->V = V_new;
  //Save all external vars
  Iion_ext[__i] = Iion, Vm_ext[__i] = Vm;
}
```

**Listing 2.** Baseline openCARP generated code snippet of the AlievPanfilov model from Listing 1

- a *compute stage*: the ionic model is used to compute the current (`Iion`) that flows in and out of each cell; all cells share read-only data and each one of them updates its private state variables;
- a *solver stage*: the computed current is passed to a linear solver to recompute each cell membrane electric potential (`V`). OpenCARP uses either PETSc [4] or Ginkgo [2] as a linear solver.

In this paper, we only discuss the first stage compilation flow, code generation, and optimization opportunities. The solver is out of the scope of this paper.

The upper part of Fig. 1 (so excluding the dashed line box) shows the original code generation flow in openCARP. A python code generator called `limpet_fe` takes an EasyML model description as input and generates an Abstract Syntax Tree (AST) from it. From the AST, `limpet_fe` emits `C/C++` output code with (i) functions to initialize parameters, lookup tables, and state variables, and (ii) a `compute` function that scans all cells in a *for* loop, to calculate the output `Iion` current and update the state variables. Finally, the generated code is compiled using a standard `C/C++` compiler and the object file is used for simulation. We call this original compilation flow of openCARP the *baseline*.

Listing 2 shows a snippet of the `compute` function emitted by the openCARP baseline version for the AlievPanfilov model. The `for` loop at line 3 iterates across all cells. Notice the preceding `omp parallel for` directive (line 2) as there is no loop-carried dependency between iterations. Line 4 retrieves the state variables pointer. Line 9 and 14 are the calculation of the new current (`Iion`) and its flow. Lines 11–12 integrate the potential with the *Forward Euler* method.

### 2.3 Vectorized CPU Code Generation Using *limpetMLIR*

The fact that the main loop independently computes the cell's states suggests that we can parallelize computations further using different types of parallel hardware. One possibility is to exploit the CPU SIMD units by vectorizing the code. While the current mainstream compilers try to automatically generate

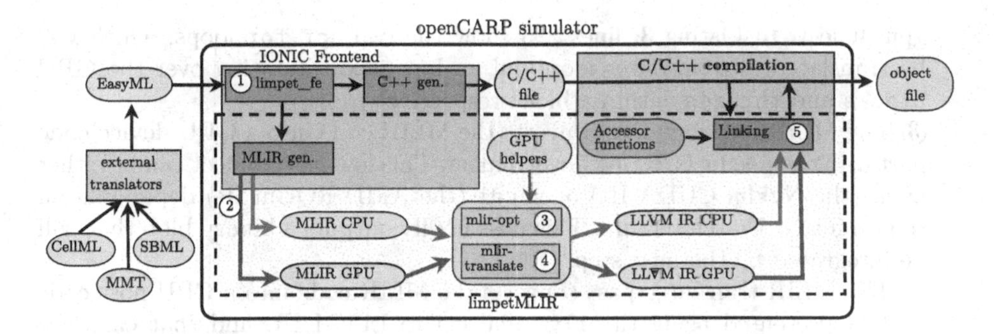


**Fig. 1.** Overview of the code generation, from the EasyML model to an object file. The dashed line box shows how *limpetMLIR* fits into the original code generation process, to emit optimized code for CPU and GPU.

vectorized code, they fail to do so in the presence of complex control-flow operations, external function calls, or pointer arithmetic used in complex stride-based memory accesses, which is the case in the openCARP generated code.

We have presented in a previous paper [18] how this limitation can be dealt with by generating code represented in specific intermediate representations (IR) suited to express vectorization. For that purpose, we used MLIR [11] from the LLVM [10] compiler infrastructure. Using some of the conventional MLIR dialects (namely `vector`, `scf`, `arith`, `math`, `memref`, and `openmp`) we have integrated an extension called *limpetMLIR* in the openCARP code generator. The most computationally intensive part of the code (the *compute* function's main loop) is generated in MLIR. The advantage of using MLIR lies in its abstraction with respect to the final target: for example, instructions in the `vector` dialect might be compiled for different hardware (`SSE`, `AVX2`, `AVX-512`, or even `SVE`, `NEON`, ...) while being on par regarding performance with the equivalent code using target specific intrinsics.

Another advantage is that MLIR can target completely different hardware, like GPUs. We present in the following the challenges that we faced to generate efficient GPU code from a real application DSL using the MLIR infrastructure.

## 3 Optimized GPU Code Generation

### 3.1 Overview of GPU Code Compilation Flow

Figure 1 shows the compilation flow of *limpetMLIR*. The process is as follows:

① From the EasyML description the `limpet_fe` python program creates an AST, which serves as a common entry point for the baseline openCARP and *limpetMLIR*.

② Using python bindings, our *limpetMLIR* code generator emits MLIR code using the `scf`, `arith`, `math` and `memref` dialects; the control flow expressed in `scf` allows the latter MLIR passes to lower it to a parallel control flow in the

`gpu` dialect. In Listing 3, lines 2–3 show the two `scf.for` loops, which will be translated into an outer loop and an inner loop iterating over the GPU `blocks` and `threads` within a block respectively.
③ The MLIR lowering pass converts the MLIR code into a GPU device code part using a specific GPU low-level dialect. This low-level dialect can be either `nvvm` (the Nvidia CUDA IR) or `rocdl` (the AMD ROCm IR) depending on the target GPU architecture. This pass finally outputs a binary blob that will be integrated by the next step.
④ The MLIR translator pass converts the MLIR code into a CPU host code part (represented using the `llvm` dialect) to LLVM IR, and that calls the kernel embedded in the binary blob.
⑤ Last is the linking phase, where `C/C++` and LLVM IR GPU files are linked together into an object file using LLVM.

### 3.2 *LimpetMLIR* for GPU

Some specific features of openCARP were adapted or extended by the CPU version of *limpetMLIR* for their integration with MLIR and optimized code generation: lookup tables (LUTs), integration methods, multi-model support, and data layout transformation. Similarly, the GPU version of *limpetMLIR* provides support for host/device memory management, integration methods, lookup tables, and multi-model support. They are provided as a set of GPU helper functions and as specific MLIR emitted code, and are described hereafter.

**Memory Management.** One well-known pitfall regarding performance is the data transfers between host and device because of the PCIe bus bottleneck. These necessary transfers are not part of the MLIR code generation process, but are inserted into the code that wraps the ionic model computation for the following reasons: (i) we want to keep the structure of the MLIR code as similar as possible for all types of devices, so we focus on generating MLIR for the compute function only, (ii) other openCARP software parts access this memory (e.g. solvers), and (iii) we want to precisely control the data movements behavior regarding performance. We implement the memory management preferably using unified memory with `cudaMallocManaged` or `hipMallocManaged`. As a side note, it happened on our AMD test platform that `hipMallocManaged` is not supported and falls back to inefficient data transfers. In that case, we could easily change it to explicit allocation and memory copies between host and device.

**Integration Methods.** The complex mathematical functions and equations in the integration methods are represented using MLIR. The MLIR code that we generate for GPU has the same structure as the one generated for the vectorized version. They differ in the data type they use (`vector<?xf64>` vs. `f64` data type) and their respective memory load/store primitives. We only need the `arith` and `math` dialects to represent the following methods: *Forward euler*, *Runge-Kutta* with 2 and 4 steps (*rk2* and *rk4*), *Rush-larsen*, *Sundnes*, and *Markov_be*. Brief information on these integration methods can be found in [18, Sect. 3.3.2] of our previous work. In Listing 3 lines 10–26 show the MLIR representation for

```
1  %7 = memref.load %6[%c0_3] : memref<?xf64>
2  scf.for %arg9 = %0 to %3 step %c1 { // iterate over blocks
3   scf.for %arg10 = %c0 to %c512 step %c1 { // iterate over threads
4   // ... code skipped for space
5    scf.execute_region {
6     %11 = arith.cmpi slt, %9, %1 : index
7     cf.cond_br %11, ^bb1, ^bb2
8    ^bb1:  // pred: ^bb0
9     // ... code skipped for space
10    %cst_11 = arith.constant 8.000000e+00 : f64
11    %cst_12 = arith.constant 1.500000e-01 : f64
12    %cst_13 = arith.constant 1.000000e+00 : f64
13    %cst_18 = arith.constant 2.000000e-03 : f64
14    %35 = arith.mulf %5, %31 : f64
15    %36 = arith.addf %7, %24 : f64
16    %37 = arith.divf %35, %36 : f64
17    %38 = arith.addf %cst_18, %37 : f64
18    %39 = arith.negf %38 : f64
19    %40 = arith.mulf %cst_11, %24 : f64
20    %41 = arith.subf %24, %cst_12 : f64
21    %42 = arith.subf %41, %cst_13 : f64
22    %43 = arith.mulf %40, %42 : f64
23    %44 = math.fma %40, %42, %31 : f64
24    %45 = arith.mulf %39, %44 : f64
25    %cst_19 = arith.constant 1.290000e+01 : f64
26    %46 = arith.divf %45, %cst_19 : f64
27    // ... code skipped for space
```

**Listing 3.** MLIR code snippet for GPU generated by *limpetMLIR* for the AlievPanfilov model from Listing 1

*Forward euler.* Line 10 in Listing 1 and lines 11–12 in Listing 2 represents the same *Forward euler* code in EasyML and in the baseline generated openCARP code, respectively. The *Rosenbrock* integration method using function calls was implemented using GPU helper functions.

**GPU Helper Functions.** During the compute stage, openCARP performs function calls to (i) lookup table based interpolation (to use pre-computed LUT values for complex mathematical functions), and (ii) the *Rosenbrock* integration method (to perform LU decomposition and integration). MLIR cannot inline a function call and it is very hard to automatically generate MLIR code for those function calls. So, we add those function calls during the MLIR code generation and we write their respective implementations in GPU device code such that they are called and executed on GPU without any call back to CPU. For example in Listing 4, lines 5 and 7 are the function calls. Also, we provide `accessor` functions that assist in loads and stores of external variables of ionic models and state variables of cells.

**Implementation Effort.** For our implementation, we wrote about 10k source lines of code (39% python, 26% MLIR, 23% C++, and some GPU kernel and CMake code). The total auto generated lines of code for all 48 ionic models are as follows: *baseline*: 39621; vectorized *limpetMLIR*: 111883; GPU: 78025.

```
// ... code skipped for space
scf.execute_region {
 // ... code skipped for space
 %147 = memref.view %146[%c0_127][] : memref<?xi8> to memref<1xi8>
 func.call LUT_interpRow(%144,%122,%147):(f64,i32,memref<1xi8>)->()
 // ... code skipped for space
 func.call rosenbrock_StepX(%814,%830,%c3):(memref<1xi8>,f32, i32)->()
 // ... code skipped for space
```

**Listing 4.** MLIR code snippet generated for GPU by *limpetMLIR* for the BONDARENKO model

# 4 Discussion

We have explained above the overall software architecture of openCARP and how we have fit into it our optimizations of the critical part concerning the ionic model computation. We now discuss in this section the general principles and caveats to consider when envisaging such an approach.

**Writing Abstract Optimizations.** The identification of a general pattern of optimization can be an incentive to use MLIR to describe this pattern. For instance in our case, the loop that carries no dependencies between iterations can trigger the idea that it can be represented as a parallel loop, whatever the available hardware to execute it in parallel. Generating only the loop control flow in a language-independent representation enables to later generate specialized code for different programming models or accelerators, as we do in our case for OpenMP, CPU vector processing units or GPUs. Although writing this representation still requires to precisely understand the code semantics and the optimization potential like an expert would do to optimize for a given device, MLIR offers a more abstract and therefore portable way of coding these optimizations. The programmer is indeed relieved from the burden of writing the eventual implementation for each specific target architecture as he/she can rely on the lowering passes included in MLIR. And as MLIR continues to evolve, relying on LLVM as a back-end, it is expected that optimization improvements and support for new targets will be integrated over time.

**Choosing Dialects.** One challenge lies in how to represent the input problem using the large number of available dialects in MLIR. In our example, the control flow expressed by the loop can be represented in the `scf` dialect or in the `affine` dialect. The `affine` dialect is more specific than `scf` as it represents the particular case of affine loops (which matches our case). As MLIR offers a transformation from `affine` into the `gpu` dialect it would be a possible choice. However, our objective to have the most abstract representation makes us choose `scf` because it allows to derive both GPU and vectorized CPU code. For the GPU code, we wrote a simple pass to transform `scf` to `affine` and rely afterwards on the `affine` to `gpu` pass provided by MLIR. For the vectorized version, we used the MLIR pass that lowers `scf` to the `cf` dialect, which represents the control flow using SSA blocks.

**A New Dialect?** MLIR can be extended by defining new dialects along with associated transformation passes. Hence, a legitimate question is to assess if the problem would be better expressed in a new dialect, especially if optimizations are more tractable using operations and types at this level. Some works [9,17] have proposed such higher level dialects while interacting with other domains. In this work, we have not felt the need for a new dialect as the set of existing ones is expressive enough to represent the statements and mathematical operations that we need to support heterogeneous code generation.

## 5 Experimental Results

We evaluate *limpetMLIR* on an A100 Nvidia GPU (9,700 GFLOP/s peak performance on *doubles*, 400 W), on an AMD Radeon Instinct MI50 GPU (6,600 GFLOP/s, 300 W), and on a 2× 18-core Cascade Lake Intel Xeon Gold 6240 @2.6 GHz (850 GFLOP/s, 2× 150 W), turbo boost and hyperthreading disabled, 192 GB of RAM @2933MT/s. On CPU we ran (i) the 36 OpenMP threads baseline openCARP, and (ii) the 36 OpenMP threads `AVX-512` *limpetMLIR* version.

We implemented *limpetMLIR* on top of the openCARP source from the git repository. We compiled them using the LLVM compiler infrastructure tag `15.0.2`, which has all necessary compilation tools including Clang and MLIR. We run all 48 ionic models available in the openCARP benchmarks, using the `bench` executable to run the compute step alone and get a trace every 100 steps. We used 819,200 cells with a 10,000 step simulation. Each model is run five times, the two extreme measures are eliminated and the remaining three are averaged.

The total number of floating point operations necessary to run each ionic model was measured with the hardware counters on the CPU. The GPU probably does less operations due to mathematical functions being optimized, but we used the same baseline value measured on CPU for a fair comparison.

For the GPU execution we chose a block and thread dimension of 1, a `number of threads per block` (CTA size) of 64, and a `number of blocks` of {number of cells/64}. We empirically determined that this provides the best performance results on our platforms for all models. This value can be easily adjusted if running on different hardware.

### 5.1 Performance

**Nvidia CUDA Performance.** Figure 2 shows the floating-point operations executed per second by the CPU baseline, *limpetMLIR* `AVX-512` vectorized, and A100 GPU versions of openCARP. The x-axis lists all 48 ionic models and the y-axis is the GFLOP/s performance. On the `x-axis`, we sorted the ionic models from the shortest to the longest execution time (of the baseline). We classified them into three categories: 17 ionic models executing in less than one minute into the *small* category, 19 ionic models executing in 1–5 min into the *medium* category and the remaining 12 with more than 5 min execution time into the

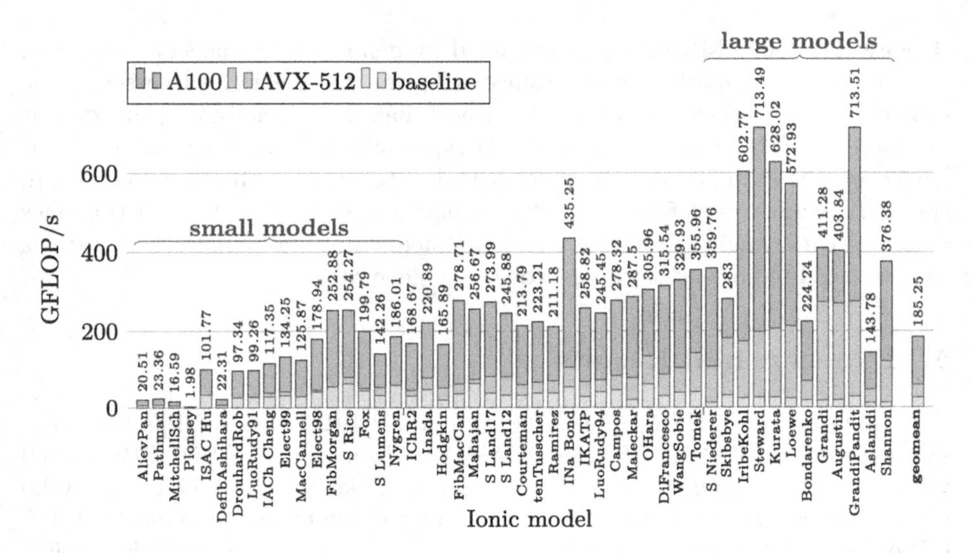


**Fig. 2.** Performance on Nvidia A100, in giga floating operations per second

*large* category. Note that the large models are usually also the most realistic ones (they are the closest to the physics) and are widely used in realistic physiological simulations.

From Fig. 2 we can observe with no surprise that the GPU code performs better than the CPU openCARP versions in all ionic models. GPU optimized codes report the highest GFLOP/s for the large models, that perform the most computations. Overall, considering the geometric mean, we reach 185 GFLOP/s on this platform, the GPU optimized code executes 3.17× faster than the vectorized CPU code, and 7.4× faster than the baseline openCARP.

However, the model that exhibits the best performance reaches 713 GFLOP/s, that is only 1/13 of the raw performance the A100 can deliver. Also, the A100 has 11.4x the raw performance of our test bed CPU (850 GFLOP/s) so the average gain of 3.17x seems pretty low. The reason is that those ionic models, taken from a real simulation application, have a pretty low compute intensity: a geomean of 0.35 flop/byte. This means that they execute many memory operations along with floating point calculations. Better performance on large models is explained by their greater compute intensity: a geomean of 3.02 flop/byte if we exclude Bondarenko and Aslanidi. Those two specific models have lower performance results than the other ones, as they have in common to call a memory intensive integration method (Rosenbrock). Overall, the low compute intensity explains that the GPU performance is far from the maximal hardware performance, and that the CPU with multiple levels of fast and large caches is better at this.

We also report that one of those best performing model (Steward) was manually written in CUDA by our HPC expert, using explicit memory copies.

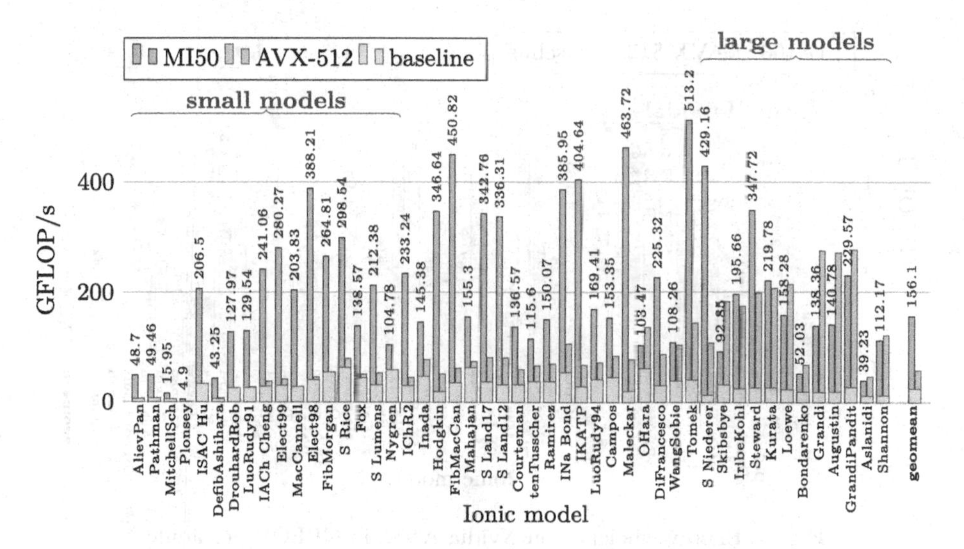


**Fig. 3.** Performance on AMD MI50, in giga floating operations per second

We measured very similar performance between this code and the *limpetMLIR* generated code (the handwritten code is less than 5% faster).

**AMD ROCm Performance.** We did the same experiments on the AMD MI50, as reported in Fig. 3. We reach a geomean performance of 156 GFLOP/s on this platform, and the overall results are pretty similar except for one point: the MI50 performs better than the A100 on small and medium ionic models while we can observe the opposite for the large models. The AMD version is sometimes even outperformed by the CPU vectorized version (for example on Grandi and Augustin). The difference in memory management (see Sect. 3.2) between the CUDA and ROCm implementations is the main reason for this lower performance on large models and better performance on small models.

Considering the geometric mean, the AMD ROCm *limpetMLIR* code executes 2.67× faster on MI50 than the vectorized CPU version. This number compares to 3.17× on A100, since the A100 has almost 50% more maximal raw performance than the MI50.

## 5.2 Energy Efficiency

We reported GFLOP/s raw performance results as it is good practice, but those numbers are not very meaningful when comparing completely different architectures with very different raw computing power. The FLOP per consumed Joule is a much better scale to compare them with the perspective of running on energy-aware supercomputers. We measured the total energy consumption by running the benchmarks on the CPU using the hardware counters, as the sum of package and RAM consumption; on the Nvidia GPU, we used the `nvidia-smi` command

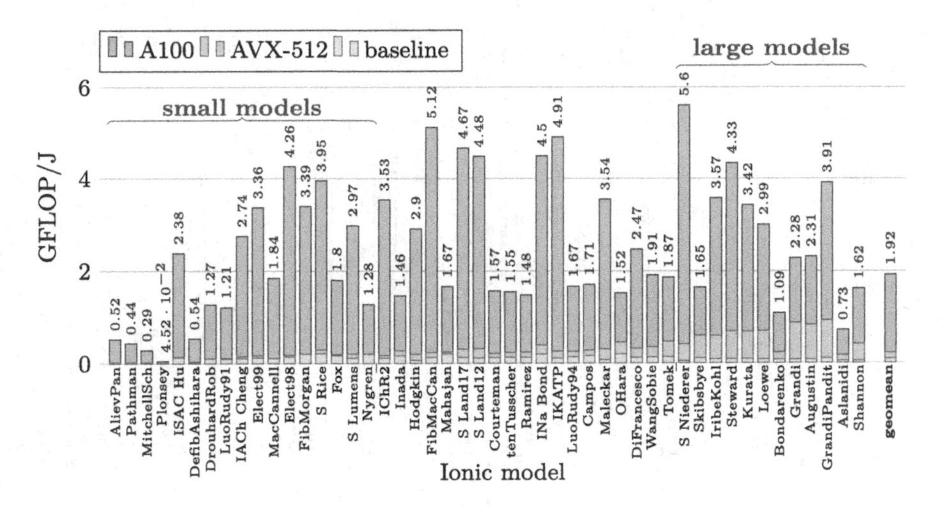


**Fig. 4.** Energy efficiency on Nvidia A100, in GFLOP per Joule

to regularly poll instant power consumption during the kernels execution, and averaged them; a similar command (`rocm-smi`) was used on AMD GPUs.

Figure 4 shows the energy efficiency (`y-axis`) of the *limpetMLIR* generated code on the A100 GPU compared to the CPU baseline and vectorized versions, for all 48 ionic models (`x-axis`). A first remark from this figure is that the difference between small, medium, and large models is much less significant than on the previous figure. Only the very small models performing very few floating point operations, and in general the ones that have a small compute-intensity (e.g., as already noticed, Bondarenko and Aslanidi), have a low efficiency on GPU. The numbers reported in this plot pretty closely relate to the compute-intensity of those different benchmarks. For example, ISAC Hu (col. 4) has an intensity of 1.6 flop/byte, while DefibAshihara (col. 5) has only 0.28 flop/byte and is much less power efficient.

Not reported in our previous work [18], the geomean energy gain of the CPU `AVX-512` vectorized version compared to the baseline openCARP CPU version is 2.3×, and it is especially significant on the large models (7.1×): on CPU, the largest benchmarks have the most energy gain when vectorized. On the other hand, for all benchmarks, the efficiency of the GPU is consistently higher than the best CPU version. Considering all ionic models the geomean energy gain of the A100 GPU over the vectorized CPU version is 8.72×.

We performed the same measurements (not shown in the plot) on the AMD MI50 GPU and obtained similar results: as reported before, the MI50 is faster and has also better energy efficiency than the A100 on small models, but worse efficiency on the medium and large ones. The geomean power efficiency of the MI50 is 1.54 GFLOP/J, a bit lower than the A100 1.92 GFLOP/J, but still much better than the vectorized CPU version 0.22 GFLOP/J.

## 6 Related Work

Since we integrated our GPU code generation in *limpetMLIR* on top of the vectorized code generator [18], it resembles our very close work and most of related work intersects.

Fried Lionetti et al. [12,13] generated CUDA kernels for electrophysiology simulations in cardiac modeling using *python* tools. With the help of python `sympy` [6] they represented mathematical equations of cell models and translated them into a `C` code. With python `pycparser` they build an AST from the emitted `C` code. Finally, they traverse the AST to emit equivalent CUDA kernels, and applied source-to-source optimizations on the CUDA kernels.

Myokit [7] is a python-based software used for the cardiac simulation of myocytes (cardiac muscular cells). Myokit accepts inputs in multiple formats and can generate heterogeneous source code (`C, python, Matlab, CUDA,` and `OpenCL`), relying on the standard compilers for optimizations. Though openCARP and Myokit share very similar characteristics for ionic cardiac simulation, their purpose is different, the first one targeting simulation of (parts of) the whole organ, the second one considering individual biological cells.

Campos et al. [5] used GPU technology to utilize the parallelism in Lattice Boltzmann method for cardiac simulations using the monodomain model, a different ionic model. Zhang et al. [21] developed a GPU system for cardiac simulation and visualization.

All these code generators rely on external systems or scripts to generate GPU code, and perform source-to-source translation or depend on standard compilers for optimizations. Our code generator differs from theirs, as we incorporate the cardiac simulation code into the compiler IR, and then give hints to the compiler for optimization and code generation for various architectures.

With respect to MLIR, there are works that generate GPU or heterogeneous optimized code. Polygeist [14] acts as a `C/C++` frontend to MLIR and generates `affine` dialect code to better utilize the polyhedral optimization and code generation available in MLIR. As said in previous work [18], Polygeist cannot handle complex codes (like ionic model descriptions) as input. Gysi et al. [9] propose a new dialect for GPU-based stencil computations in weather and climate domains. Both those works followed a similar approach to ours but we have different input requirements.

## 7 Conclusion

In this paper, we have presented how the quite recent *multi-level intermediate representation* concept that arose from the research community in compilation can be applied to a production-level scientific application, namely openCARP, a cardiac electrophysiology simulator. The challenge is to integrate into the existing code base the generation of highly optimized code both for CPU and GPU. We have explained the modifications we have brought to the code generation process which originally generated C/C++ code from models expressed with a

DSL. The paper discusses the design choices that arise when it comes to choose among the available dialects to represent the code structures and statements at the appropriate abstraction level. We show that we were able to factorize a large part of the MLIR generated code that was used for vectorization in CPU, and explain how the necessary additions to generate GPU code are implemented through the lowering passes. Finally, MLIR allows us to produce code that has the same level of performance as native code but in a more portable way. The evaluation of our GPU version is carried out on the full set of models shipped with openCARP and shows it brings a significant performance improvement over the CPU vectorized version both in terms of execution time and energy efficiency. As a perspective, we want to further extend this work by integrating the code generator with a task-based runtime system like StarPU [3], in order to exploit simultaneously CPU and GPU so able to run experiments at larger scales.

**Acknowledgments.** This work was supported by the European High-Performance Computing Joint Undertaking EuroHPC under grant agreement No 955495 (**MICROCARD**), co-funded by the Horizon 2020 programme of the European Union (EU), and France, Italy, Germany, Austria, Norway, and Switzerland (https://microcard.eu).

Some experiments presented in this paper were carried out using the **PlaFRIM** experimental test bed, supported by Inria, CNRS (LABRI and IMB), Université de Bordeaux, Bordeaux INP and Conseil Régional d'Aquitaine (https://plafrim.fr). Some experiments presented in this paper were carried out using the **Grid'5000** testbed, supported by a scientific interest group hosted by Inria and including CNRS, RENATER and several Universities as well as other organizations (https://www.grid5000.fr).

**Data Availibility Statement.** An artifact (docker image file) for reproducing the results presented in Figs. 2, 3 and 4 is provided [19].

## References

1. Aliev, R.R., Panfilov, A.V.: A simple two-variable model of cardiac excitation. Chaos Solitons Fractals **7**(3), 293–301 (1996). https://doi.org/10.1016/0960-0779(95)00089-5
2. Anzt, H., et al.: GINKGO: a modern linear operator algebra framework for high performance computing. ACM Trans. Math. Softw. **48**(1), 1–33 (2022). https://doi.org/10.1145/3480935
3. Augonnet, C., Thibault, S., Namyst, R., Wacrenier, P.A.: StarPU: a unified platform for task scheduling on heterogeneous multicore architectures. CCPE - Concurr. Comput.: Pract. Exp. Spec. Issue: Euro-Par 2009 **23**, 187–198 (2011). https://doi.org/10.1002/cpe.1631
4. Balay, S., et al.: PETSc Web page (2022). https://petsc.org/
5. Campos, J., Oliveira, R., dos Santos, R., Rocha, B.: Lattice Boltzmann method for parallel simulations of cardiac electrophysiology using GPUs. J. Comput. Appl. Math. **295**(C), 70–82 (2016). https://doi.org/10.1016/j.cam.2015.02.008
6. Certik, O.: SymPy python library for symbolic mathematics (2008)

7. Clerx, M., Collins, P., de Lange, E., Volders, P.G.: Myokit: a simple interface to cardiac cellular electrophysiology. Prog. Biophys. Mol. Biol. **120**(1), 100–114 (2016). https://doi.org/10.1016/j.pbiomolbio.2015.12.008
8. Cytron, R., Ferrante, J., Rosen, B.K., Wegman, M.N., Zadeck, F.K.: An efficient method of computing static single assignment form. In: Proceedings of the 16th ACM SIGPLAN-SIGACT Symposium on Principles of Programming Languages, POPL 1989, pp. 25–35. ACM (1989). https://doi.org/10.1145/75277.75280
9. Gysi, T., et al.: Domain-specific multi-level IR rewriting for GPU: the open earth compiler for GPU-accelerated climate simulation. ACM Trans. Archit. Code Optim. **18**(4), 1–23 (2021). https://doi.org/10.1145/3469030
10. Lattner, C., Adve, V.: LLVM: a compilation framework for lifelong program analysis & transformation. In: 2004 International Symposium on Code Generation and Optimization, pp. 75–86 (2004). https://doi.org/10.1109/CGO.2004.1281665
11. Lattner, C., et al.: MLIR: scaling compiler infrastructure for domain specific computation. In: 2021 IEEE/ACM International Symposium on Code Generation and Optimization (CGO), pp. 2–14 (2021). https://doi.org/10.1109/CGO51591.2021.9370308
12. Lionetti, F.V.: GPU accelerated cardiac electrophysiology. Masters thesis, University of California, San Diego (2010)
13. Lionetti, F.V., McCulloch, A.D., Baden, S.B.: Source-to-source optimization of CUDA C for GPU accelerated cardiac cell modeling. In: D'Ambra, P., Guarracino, M., Talia, D. (eds.) Euro-Par 2010. LNCS, vol. 6271, pp. 38–49. Springer, Heidelberg (2010). https://doi.org/10.1007/978-3-642-15277-1_5
14. Moses, W.S., Chelini, L., Zhao, R., Zinenko, O.: Polygeist: raising C to polyhedral MLIR. In: 30th International Conference on Parallel Architectures and Compilation Techniques (PACT), pp. 45–59 (2021). https://doi.org/10.1109/PACT52795.2021.00011
15. Plank, G., et al.: The openCARP simulation environment for cardiac electrophysiology. Comput. Methods Program. Biomed. **208**, 106223 (2021). https://doi.org/10.1016/j.cmpb.2021.106223
16. Potse, M., Saillard, E., Barthou, D., Coudière, Y.: Feasibility of whole-heart electrophysiological models with near-cellular resolution. In: 2020 Computing in Cardiology, pp. 1–4 (2020). https://doi.org/10.22489/CinC.2020.126
17. Sommer, L., Axenie, C., Koch, A.: SPNC: an open-source MLIR-based compiler for fast sum-product network inference on CPUs and GPUs. In: 2022 IEEE/ACM International Symposium on Code Generation and Optimization (CGO), pp. 1–11 (2022). https://doi.org/10.1109/CGO53902.2022.9741277
18. Thangamani, A., Trevisan, T., Loechner, V., Genaud, S., Bramas, B.: Lifting code generation of cardiac physiology simulation to novel compiler technology. In: 21st ACM/IEEE International Symposium on Code Generation and Optimization (CGO). ACM, Montréal Québec (2023). https://doi.org/10.1145/3579990.3580008
19. Trevisan Jost, T., Thangamani, A., Colin, R., Loechner, V., Genaud, S., Bramas, B.: Artifact for GPU code generation of cardiac electrophysiology simulation with MLIR (2023). https://doi.org/10.6084/m9.figshare.23546157
20. Vigmond, E.: EasyML (2021). https://opencarp.org/documentation/examples/01_ep_single_cell/05_easyml
21. Zhang, L., Wang, K., Zuo, W., Gai, C.: G-heart: a GPU-based system for electrophysiological simulation and multi-modality cardiac visualization. J. Comput. **9**(2), 360–367 (2014)

# SWSPH: A Massively Parallel SPH Implementation for Hundred-Billion-Particle Simulation on New Sunway Supercomputer

Ziyu Zhang, Junshi Chen(✉), Zhanming Wang, Yifan Luo, Jineng Yao, Shenghong Huang, and Hong An

University of Science and Technology of China, No.96, JinZhai Road Baohe District, Hefei 230026, Anhui, People's Republic of China
cjuns@mail.ustc.edu.cn

**Abstract.** Fluid instability plays a fundamental role in the research of astrophysics, energy power, chemical industry and new materials. The Smoothed Particle Hydrodynamics (SPH) method is a useful tool for simulating interfacial flows such as multiphase flow, high-velocity impact, explosion phenomenon. However, SPH method harnesses an enormous amount of particles for accuracy, which consumes a lot of computing power. In this paper, we present a massively parallel SPH scheme on the new Sunway supercomputer, SWSPH. In order to take full advantage of large-scale heterogeneous many-core computing system, we propose a series of parallel strategies and optimization methods. Experiments show that SWSPH has the capability of handling hundred-billion-particles simulations of fluid instability phenomenon on 39 million cores with a performance of 76% parallel efficiency.

**Keywords:** Smoothed Particle Hydrodynamics · Sunway Supercomputer · Manycore computing · Large-scale simulation

## 1 Introduction

Fluid instability plays a fundamental role in the research of astrophysics [12], energy power [17], chemical industry and new materials [11]. The macroscopic fluid dynamics method based on grid discretization requires high order precision algorithm to track the interface evolution accurately because of numerical diffusion, and it is inconvenience to capture moving features such as free surfaces, deformable boundaries and moving interfaces [18]. Smoothed Particle Hydrodynamics (SPH) method, which adopts pure Lagrangian algorithm is a useful tool for simulating interfacial flows such as multiphase flow, high-velocity impact, explosion phenomena.

In SPH simulation, fluid is represented by a large number of freely moving "particles" with physical properties such as density, velocity, pressure, and temperature. The motion and thermodynamic state of these "particles" are governed

National Natural Science Foundation of China (Grant No. 62102389).


J. Cano et al. (Eds.): Euro-Par 2023, LNCS 14100, pp. 564–577, 2023.
https://doi.org/10.1007/978-3-031-39698-4_38

by the conservation laws of mass, momentum, and energy in the Lagrangian form. Its core algorithm evolves a system of particles via a set of pairwise interactions. The interactions between particles are evaluated by calculating pairwise distance and checking whether they reside in each other's support domain, which is typically the most time-consuming part for the simulation.

With the development of modern architecture, the growth rate of computing power is faster than the speed of memory transfer. Therefore, memory access becomes the bottleneck for various applications. Each strive for performance portability, flexibility, and scalability across architecture with deep memory hierarchies by providing optimized data structure, data layout, and data movement. The New Sunway Supercomputer is the successor of the Sunway TaihuLight [9], which is equipped with over 600000 SW26010pro processes cores and provide a theoretical peak performance of 1 EFlops/s. The homegrown many-core SW26010pro is composed of 6 core-groups (CGs), each of which includes one management processing element (MPE), and one 64 computing processing elements (CPEs) cluster arranged in an 8 by 8 grid, a total of 390 cores. It would be a severe challenge for task partitioning and assignment strategies for 390-cores CPU to achieve high performance, and it will be of exemplary significance to study and evaluate how to optimize the performance of particle simulation applications. As compared to its predecessor, SW26010pro's 256 KB scratch pad memory (SPM) can be configured as eith user-controlled local data memory (LDM) or hardware cache for automatic data buffering. Compared with using a software-emulated cache adopted by early efforts [7,8], the highly coalesced global memory access can more naturally boost the memory access performance by enhancing both the temporal and the spatial locality.

In this paper, we propose an implementation of massively parallel SPH on New Sunway Supercomputer. Compared with GPU and other many-core accelerators, the unique master-slave architecture and deep memory hierarchical of SW26010pro make the design of parallel programs significantly challenging. The main contributions of this paper are summarized as follows:

- We implement SWSPH, a SPH package for simulating of fluid instability on new generation Sunway supercomputer and scale it to 39 million heterogeneous cores handling one hundred billion particles and evaluate its performance.
- We address a mesh refinement method towards large-scale distributed computing system and a volume adaptive scheme for modeling strongly-compressible multiphase flows. Aiming at the load balance in the simulation application, we have adopted corresponding methods in the design of multi-level parallelism.
- In the absence of a low overhead locking mechanism on the Sunway processor, we propose a fine-grained task partitioning and assignment strategies for 390-cores of the SW26010pro heterogeneous architecture. In the big sharing model, we adopt compute core grouping scheme that partitions both hardware resources and computing tasks, which achieves a trade-off between CPE task-level load balance and avoiding write conflicts.

The rest of this paper is organized as follows: Sect. 2 introduces the SPH method, SW26010pro processor and summarizes related work. Section 3 presents the optimization strategies and implementation details regarding SWSPH on the new Sunway TaihuLight. Section 4 gives the performance test result and analysis. Section 5 concludes this paper.

# 2 Background

## 2.1 Smooth Particle Hydrodynamic Method

Smoothed Particle Hydrodynamics (SPH) is a popular mesh-free method and has potential to be the next generation of more effective computational methods for more complicated problems [14,15]. In SPH simulation, the computational domain is filled with a great number of "SPH particles". These particles all possess physical properties we concerned like pressure, density, energy. During the simulation, an SPH particle moves and refreshes its physical properties in each time step following the conservation law of mass, momentum and energy in Lagrangian form and equation of state of the particle's material, based on a set of nearby particles which forms its support domain. This support domain is determined by each particle's location and volume, thus it always needs to be refreshed for each particle in each time step [13].

As for refreshing each particle's physical properties, the SPH method can be seen as replacing the Dirac delta function with a smoothed kernel $W$. Thus an SPH approximate scalar function $A$ can be defined as:

$$A(x) = \int A(x') W(x - x', h)\, dx'.$$

And the discretized form of smoothed variables A and its gradient vector can be written as

$$\begin{aligned} \langle A \rangle_i &= \sum_j^n A_j W_{ij} V_j \\ \langle \nabla A \rangle_i &= -\sum_j^n A_j \nabla_i W_{ij} V_j \end{aligned} \tag{1}$$

where $W_{ij}$ is $W(x_i - x_j, h_{ij})$, and in this progress we adopted a quintic spline function as kernel function. $h$ is the smoothing length of the particle pairs, $V$ is the volume, and the subscriptions $i$,$j$ represents particle $i$ and $j$.

## 2.2 Related Work and Analysis

The most time-consuming part of the SPH method is the pair-wise interaction during the calculation of particle forces, which can be accelerated by many-core devices. It is important for optimization to exploit the spatial locality and decompose the parallel domain reasonably, which can avoid invalid searches and is beneficial for vectorization. Considering the scalability, the synchronization operation induced by the neighborhood communication in each time integration step has a significant impact on the parallel efficiency. With the development of HPC system, there are many well-known SPH frameworks used in different scenarios simulation. For example, DualSPHysics [5], implemented in SPHysics [10] is validated for different problems of wave breaking, dam-break behavior and interaction with coastal structures. It can achieve efficiencies of 85.9% using 128 GPUs of the Barcelona Supercomputing Center [6]. However, for problems such as compressible explosion impact, it cannot effectively solve the problem of load-imbalance. SWIFT [3,16] is a hydrodynamics and gravity code for astrophysics and cosmology designed to run on hybrid shared/distributed-memory architectures using task-based parallelism. It can maintain 75% weak-scalability with a dynamic range of $10^4$ in time-step size. Moreover, SPH-EXA [4], SPHERA [1] and Gadget [2] etc. have used the SPH algorithm for gas dynamical cosmological simulations, and achieve good parallel efficiency. As far as we know, there is no large-scale fluid instability simulation involving complex material phase change and interface tracking using the SPH algorithm.

### 2.3 Overview of the New Sunway System and SW26010pro Many-Core Processor

The SW26010pro is composed of 6 core-groups (CGs), each of which includes one management processing element (MPE), and one 64 computing processing elements (CPEs) cluster arranged in an 8 by 8 grid, a total of 390 cores as shown in Fig. 1. Within the CPE cluster, every four neighboring CPEs share one local cluster management unit, with a router integrated for efficient message forwarding. In each CG, the MPE is in charge of spawning threads for the 64 CPEs and handle management and communication tasks. The CPE cluster is designed to provide high aggregated computing capability. The MPE support 256-bit vector instructions and CPEs adopt the SW64 instructions to support 512-bit SIMD. Each SW26010pro processor can provide a theoretical peak performance of around 14 Tflop/s in double precision.

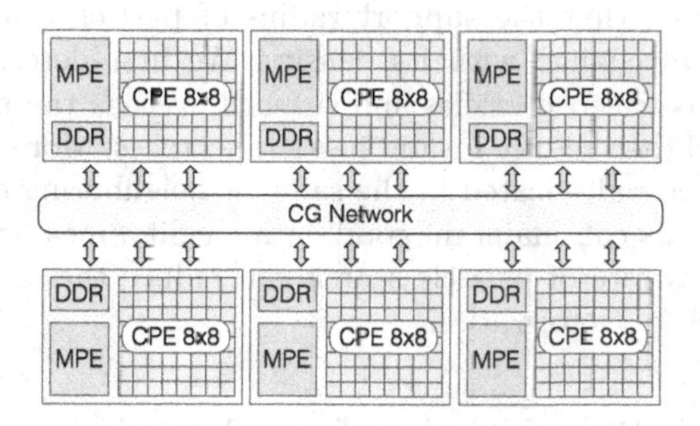


**Fig. 1.** Architecture of SW26010-pro many-core processor.

SW26016pro is relatively moderate in terms of memory capacity. Each CG has its own memory controller (MC), connecting to 16GB DDR4 memory, with a bandwidth of 51.2 GB/s. Both MPE and the CPE within the same CG share the same memory controlled by the MC. It is different from the heterogeneous host-device architecture CPU-GPU that supports address mapping for memory access, the MPE-CPE hybrid architecture can provide a unified address space for each CPE to access the main memory directly with a low latency of below 0.2µs. As compared to its predecessor, SW26010, the upgraded CPE in SW26010Pro has 256 KB scratch pad memory (SPM). The SPM on CPE can be configured as either user-controlled local data memory (LDM) or hardware cache for automatic data buffering. Data transfer between LDM and main memory can be realized by direct memory access (DMA). The data exchange between each two CPEs in the same CPE cluster is achieved by the Remote Memory Access (RMA) interface (an upgrade to the register communication feature in the previous generation).

## 3 Implementation and Optimization

### 3.1 Domain Decomposition Strategy

**Cell-List Based Pair-Wise Interactions.** The most time consuming kernels in SWSPH include particle force calculation and density summation method, both of them need pair-wise interactions. Due to the requirement for frequent access to neighbor particle data, this type of computation results in a large number of random memory accesses, resulting in low data reuse. We introduce an uniformed spatial mesh allocated in the simulation domain, which decomposes the space into cells of a certain size, and place the particles in the corresponding cell according to their spatial coordinates as shown in Fig. 3.

During particle-pair interaction, each particle only needs to perform computations with particles in the same cell and surrounding neighbor cells, as shown in Alg.1. The first loop iterates over the cell, and the second loop iterates its surrounding neighbor cells through the recorded index. The conventional way is to use the SPMD paradigm to achieve parallelism. We use MPI and OpenMP to achieve parallelism between CPUs and CGs within the CPU respectively and the third and fourth layer loops use the compute core grouping scheme for parallelism. Considering that the support radius of particles in the compressible SPH algorithm will change with its density, We first determine whether the shortest distance between particles and sub-cell exceeds the maximum support domain radius and then reduce invalid particle searches. More importantly, since adjacent particles are all located in the same or neighboring cell, cell-list based pair-wise interactions can maintain good data locality, meanwhile, the improvement of the success rate of particle search can reduce the number of branches, which is beneficial to vectorization.

**Adaptive Particle Partitioning for Load Balancing.** To achieve computational load balancing, we have applied two categories on SWSPH. One includes

**Algorithm 1:** Pair-wise interaction kernel

```
Data: Particle P is in the subcell of Cell C, C.neighbor is cell list of its
      neighbor, r^cut is radius of support domain
Function Dist(C_i, C_j); Dist(P, C); Dist(P_i, P_j):
    Output: Distance between Cells, between Cell and Particle, between
            Particles
for I ← 1, |C| do
    for J ← 1, |C_I.neighbor| do
        for i ← 1, |C_I.subcell| do
            for j ← 1, |C_J.subcell| do
                if Dist (C_I.subcell_i, C_J.subcell_j) > C_I.subcell_i.r^cut_max then
                    continue;
                for each P_m ∈ C_I.subcell_i do
                    if Dist (P_m, C_J.subcell_j) > P_m.r^cut then
                        continue;
                    for each P_n ∈ C_J.subcell_j do
                        if Dist (P_m, P_n) < P_m.r^cut then
                            Calculate particle force or density summation
```

adaptive domain decomposition for particle partitioning from the perspective of parallel techniques and the other is physics-based particle volume adaptive scheme. Due to the dynamics of massive particle migration and aggregation at the macroscopic scale, e.g., fluid instabilities under simulated converging shock wave, there will be serious load imbalance between node during the simulation. The strategy adopted in the traditional SPH framework is to assign a uniform number of particles to each node, however, it is not the most efficient strategy(the computational complexity is $O(N^2)$ within the support domain). We use the radius of the maximum support domain of the particles in each cell to estimate the calculation amount of each cell and this can be used as a more accurate measure of load. For the area where the particles converge, we use a tree-like adaptive grid to refine it until the calculation amount of each sub-cell is reduced below the average.

In the decomposition of the parallel domain, we use the Hilbert curve to traverse the cell, which can traverse the adjacent cells as much as possible and makes more of them reside on the same node. In addition, quite a few of invalid searches can be avoided during particle search by setting the edge length of the cell to be slightly than the radius of the support domain. After the spatial mesh refinement, we build the task allocation and mapping table. The allocation strategy is to ensure that the calculation amount of all nodes is close to the average, which can effectively alleviate the problem of load imbalance between processes.

**Volume Adaptive Scheme.** When it comes to shock simulation, compressed particles tend to clump together and increase local computing loads, while over-expanded particles require larger support domain to collect enough particles for SPH interpolation, which meanwhile requires higher zone length and increase the computational load in the zones where there is no expansion wave. The volume adaptive particle method is adopted to deal with this problem as shown in Figure 2. When particle volume becomes larger than a preset upper limit, mother particles are split into eight daughter particles. The physical quantities of daughter particles inherit those of mother particles. When a pair of daughter particles whose volumes are both less than a preset lower limit and center distance is less than preset maximum length, they are merged into one mother particle. The physical quantities of the mother particle is computed by mass weighted sum of the daughter particles.

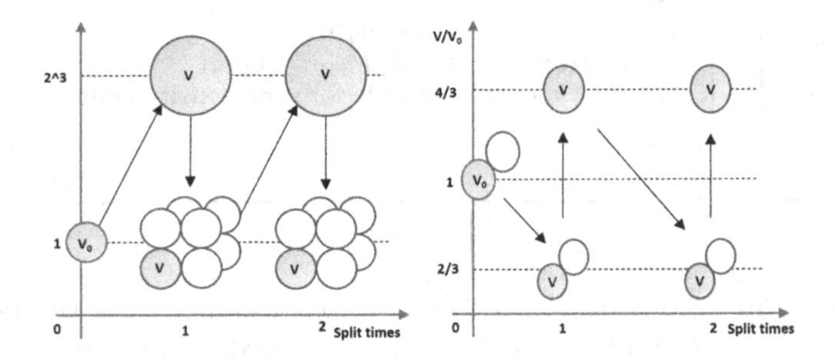


**Fig. 2.** When the mother particle expands to eight times volume of the initial volume, it will be split into eight daughter particles sharing the same volume; when the particle has a volume less than $\sqrt[3]{3V_0/2}$ of initial volume, it will merge with another particle below the same volume within a distance of $\sqrt[3]{3V_0/2}$

### 3.2 Point-to-Point Asynchronous Communication and Task Overlapping

Similar to other particle simulation applications, the process-level parallelism of SPH adopts the parallel paradigm of SPMD. Since it needs to update the neighborhood at each iteration, the inherent communication-intensive characteristics have an important impact on the scalability. Therefore, the optimization of communication inter-node and the balance of task division are crucial for the scalability and parallel efficiency of SPH simulation.

There are two kinds of communication in the SPH algorithm: 1. atom-migration: send displaced particles to the destination process; 2. halo-exchange: update the particle data in the ghost area. By using the non-blocking interfaces `MPI_Isend` and `MPI_IProbe` to accurately complete data transmission and reception, it can not only avoid invalid communication in the All-to-All mode, but also reduce the idle waiting time of the process. In addition, the non-blocking communication mode also provides the possibility of task overlap and delay concealment, which has a significant impact on the scaling efficiency of SPH applications that are inherently communication-intensive.

We can divide the cells stored on each node into three types by analyzing the data dependencies of cell-pair interactions: core cell, edge cell, ghost cell as shown in Fig. 3. Each node is only responsible for the calculation of the local cell (including the core cell and edge cell), while the data update of ghost cell is completed by MPI communication. The core cell does not depend on the data in the ghost cell, so we can achieve the overlap of communication and computation for atom-migration and halo-exchange, respectively, as shown in Fig. 3. For atom-migration, we can first find the displaced particles in the edge cell, and then send them asynchronously. At the same time, we start sorting the particles in each core cell, and then accept the displaced particles from neighbor node and complete the particle sorting in the edge cell. For halo-exchange, we can preferentially send data in edge cells asynchronously and start the pair-wise interactions of core cells and edge cells, after accepting the data and updating the ghost cell, we can proceed to complete the edge cell computation.

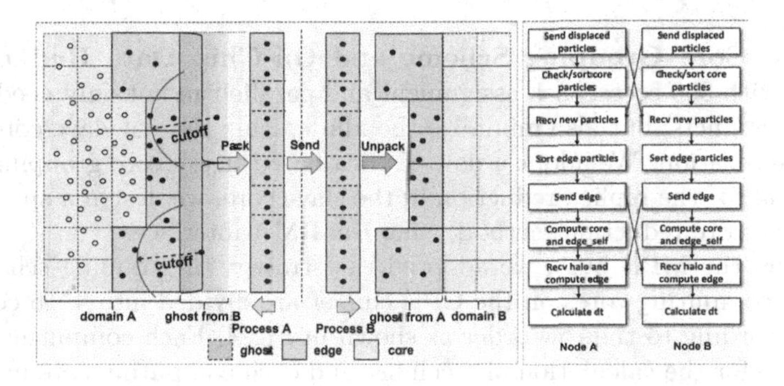


**Fig. 3.** Scheme of the communication:update of the ghost cell(neighbor particle support domain radius will not exceed the sub-cell range, so only sub-cells are packed to remove redundancy) communication and computation overlap.

The halo_exchange in most frameworks does not need to preprocess the data of the edge part, but directly packs and sends it to the neighbor process, which will have a lot of redundant data. In fact, some particles in the ghost cell are outside the range of the support domain, which not only increases the amount of data communicated, but also causes redundant calculations that are not conducive to the efficiency of vectorization. Using the refined sub-cell, by analyzing the effective radius of the support domain, the redundant particle data in edge cell can be eliminated before the communication, which not only reduces the data volume of communication, but also improves the performance of particle search,which is more conducive to the efficiency of vectorization.

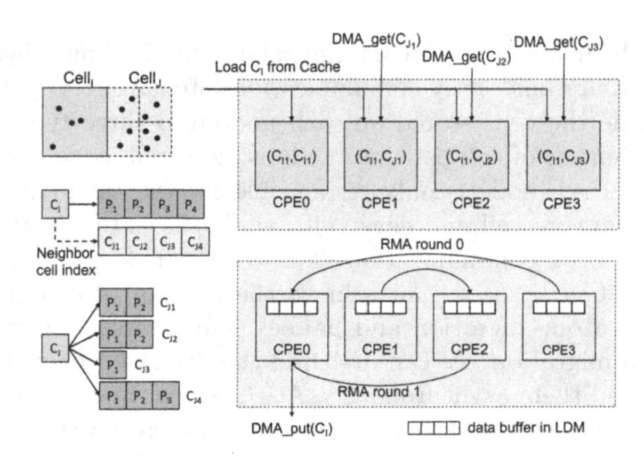


**Fig. 4.** Fine-grained CPE task mapping strategies.CPE group uses DMA to load the corresponding cell-pair as a calculation task according to the neighbor cell index, then uses RMA to reduce the data to the first cpe, and finally write back to the main memory.

**Compute Core Grouping Scheme and On-Chip Data Reduction.** In the node with 390 cores, task assignment and parallelism not only need to avoid the write conflicts, but also minimize the idle waiting time of slave cores caused by synchronization. We adopt a data-replica based many core grouping parallel scheme and for the replica reduction in the slave core, we design a special intra-group slave core reduction method using the RMA interface.

To keep the MPE busy, we adopted the strategy of grouping scheme, that is, the 64 computing cores on the CPE cluster are divided into 4*16 computing groups according to the row order as shown in Fig. 4. Each computing group is responsible for the calculation of a cell list and each computing core in the computing group is responsible for the calculation of a pair of cells. The grouping strategy allows each CPE have a more even number of tasks and it is conflict-free in each group because the same cell-pair does not exist in each group. However, write conflict still exists between CPE groups. For this purpose, it only needs to set up one data copy in the LDM of the column 0 CPE. When all of members of one group complete the cell list, each CPEs reduce data to the replica of the 0th column CPE, and then use DMA to update data in the memory. Data reduction on the CPE is implemented by the remote data transfer operation(RMA) between LDMs. Since the runtime system does not provide an interface for the specification of the CPE, we can only use the unilateral interface rma_get provided by CPE to obtain the data in the specified LDM. In each CPE cluster, every four adjacent CPEs share a local cluster management unit, which integrates a router for efficient message forwarding. We design different reduction methods for 4 and 8 CPEs respectively and test both B-tree and butterfly reduction methods for the row reduction. Since the B-tree reduction method is more suitable for the interconnection structure of the slave core array, it is more suitable. As for the reduction method of four CPE, our test shows that the tree structure is not the optimal way, but a corresponding design is adopted. As shown in Fig. 4, for the reduction method of 4 CPEs, our test shows that the tree-based reduction is not the optimal method, but the corresponding design is adopted. Due to the unique interconnection structure between the slave core arrays, we adopt special RMA reduction method to achieves better performance.

**Data-Layout Optimizations and Vectorization.** In the process of vectorization, we first sort the particles in each cell-pair by their relative positions and their own properties (The sorting is implemented in parallel by the CPEs) and then convert the data layout of the AoS format in LDM to AoSoA, so that we can use the simd_load instruction to read 8 consecutive double data from LDM and place them in the vector register, note that the AoSoA structure reserves high cache locality for all fields of a given particle. In addition, SW26010pro 512bit SIMD provides reciprocal and square root reciprocal vector instructions, which are useful for calculating particle spacing and solving physical values. In addition, the vselect instructions unique to Sunway provide a vectorization method for the ternary operation, which can make us very convenient to eliminate the branch.

# 4 Evaluation

## 4.1 Single Node Evaluation

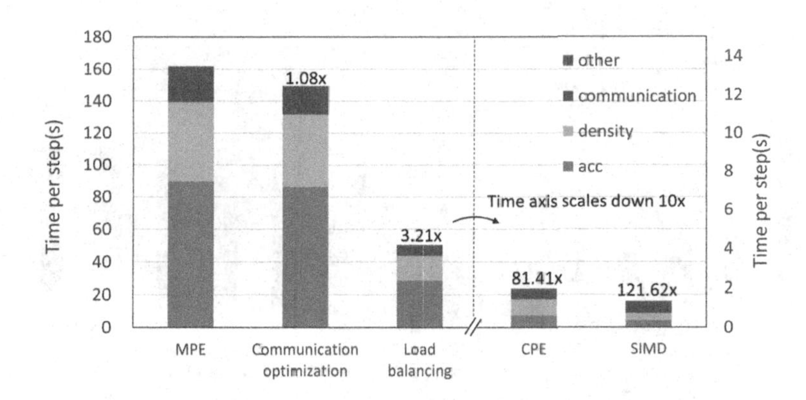


**Fig. 5.** The running time of different subroutine in each SPH iteration loop using 6 CGs. Here MPE, CPE and SIMD represent the MPE-only version, the CPE accelerated version and the 512 bit SIMD vectorized version, respectively.

Figure 5 shows the speedup of the most time-consuming kernels in the simulation of SPH. Due to the pair-wise interaction, the calculation of acceleration and sum of density occupy most (90%) of the integration time. In all-shared mode, a process can use 6 OpenMP threads to control 6 MPEs. We perform performance evaluation on a system with 2.5 billion particles using 5000 processes (CPUs) and each process handles 500,000 particles. The single-step simulation time is 161s when using MPEs and we take the performance of MPE-only version as baseline. After communication optimization, the communication time of each step is reduced by 20%, and the performance of each step is improved by 1.3 times. After applying adaptive particle partitioning and volume adaptive Scheme, the performance of each step can be improved by 3.21 times. After parallelization with CPE cluster, the calculation of acceleration and sum density can achieve 145 and 60 times of performance improvement respectively and each integration step can achieved 81.41× performance improvement. In addition, we evaluated the performance of CPE using DMA and Cache respectively and find that there is no difference as a result of the CPE can take full advantage of the locality of data. The peak bandwidth (DMA) utilization is 40.3/51.2GB/s=78.7%. After taking advantage of CPE's 512-bit vector floating-point instructions, it end up with a 121.62× performance boost and each integration time can be reduced to 1.33s. Considering that the high precision Riemann solver contains many square root and division operation (need ~30 cycles), the CPE pipeline cannot perform instruction-level parallelism, resulting in performance loss, and the FLOP rate on a single node is 134.2/1079.7Gflop/s(12%), the peak is 145.9/1079.7Gflop/s(14%) based on the sampled data of the PMU events.

## 4.2 Scalability

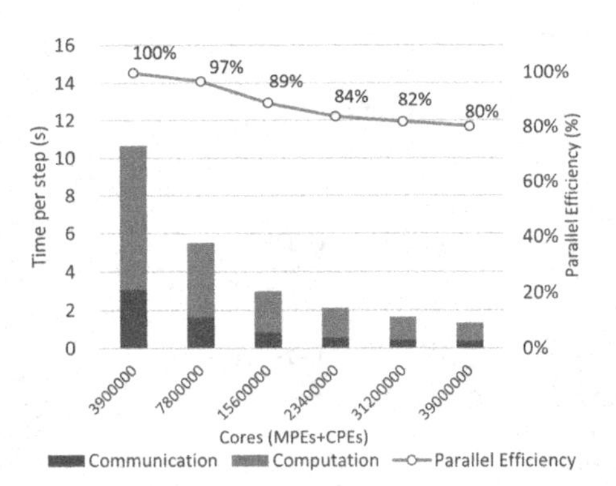


**Fig. 6.** Strong scalability for 100 billion particles

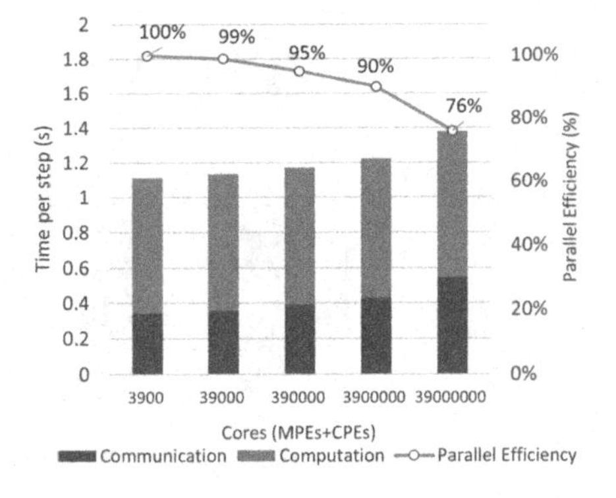


**Fig. 7.** Weak scalability for 333 thousand particles per process

This section shows the experiment results of the scalability of SWSPH on the new Sunway supercomputer. To achieve a balance between simulation size for strong scalability and the limited memory on SW26010pro (total 92 GB per node), we take the performance of 60000 CGs (60000 MPEs with 3840000 CPEs)

as a baseline, which simulates about 100 billion (1 x $10^{11}$) particles total and the example used is the converging RM instability at a three-dimensional cube air/SF6 interface. The weak scalability initializes the simulation from 60 CGs as a baseline, which simulates about 333 thousand particles per process (CPU). Fig. 6 shows the change in the iteration time of the test case when the number of cores scaled from 3,900,000 to 39,000,000. We can see that computation time occupies a larger proportion of the whole simulation, and both computation and communication time decrease with the number of cores. However, with the increase of the number of nodes, the proportion of the communication time also increases. As shown in Fig. 6, when the number of cores is increased to 39 million, the parallel efficiency reaches 80%, which shows that SWSPH has good scalability.

Figure 7 illustrates the weak scaling performance with a baseline of 60 CGs and each process handles 3.33x$10^5$ particles. It can be seen that it keeps a high parallel efficiency with growth of cores and ultimately reaches 600000 CGs(2x$10^{11}$ particles total) with 76% efficiency. It is worth noting that when the core count is less than 390000, almost all parallelization efficiency are close to 100%. This shows that SWSPH has the ability to simulate large-scale fluid dynamics with massive parallelism. From Fig. 7, it can be seen that the computation time remains almost the same under different core counts. But the communication time is slightly longer at 39 million cores, mainly due to the contention of communication.

### 4.3 Load-Balance Test

We evaluate the load-balance of each process by an RMI simulation problem of a 2.5 billion particles system. We extracted the most unbalance performance data of 16 processes, and analyzed the computation, communication, and synchronization wait times respectively. When the shock wave converges near the interface between the two fluids, the particle density near the shock wave can reach more than 1000 times the average value. If the adaptive method is not used, the process with the smallest amount of tasks spends nearly 69% of the time waiting idle, while the computing time of the process with the heaviest task is more than 3 times that of the most idle process shownas shown in Fig. 8a. By adopting our mesh refinement and volume adaptive particle method, the worst idle process waiting time ratio can be reduced from 69% to 32% as shown in Fig. 8b, and the iteration time of each step can be increased by more than 10 times due to the more even division of tasks.

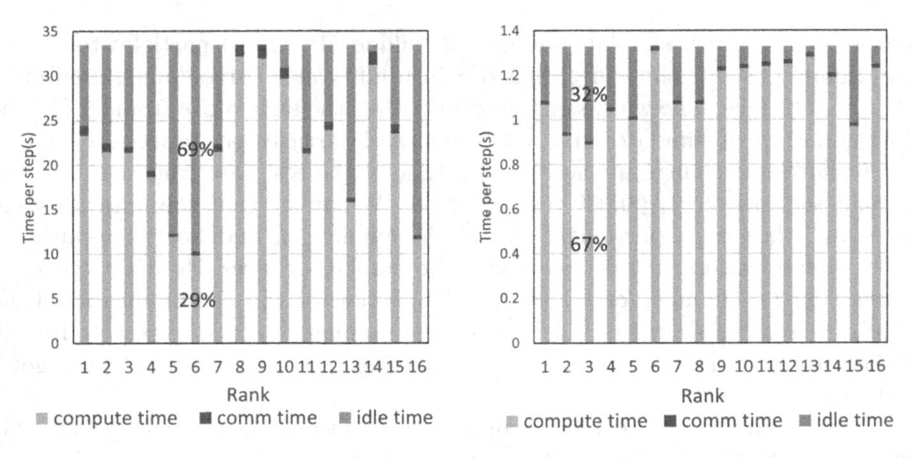


(a) result of not using the adaptive method (b) mesh refinement and volume adaptive

**Fig. 8.** Unbalance communication in SPH simulation with 2.5 billion particles using 5000 processes and extract the 16 most unbalanced processes for profiling.

# 5 Conclusion

In this paper, we present a massively multi-level parallel SPH scheme on the new Sunway supercomputer. To exploit the data locality, the tree-like multi-level cell division strategy is more suitable for Sunway's deep memory hierarchies. And the adaptive domain decomposition and particle volume adaptive scheme can solve non-uniform large scale SPH simulations by reducing the imbalance between nodes. In addition, the load-balancing strategy based on the amount of calculation is more effective than the method based on the number of particles. Considering the many-core architecture, the compute core grouping scheme and on-chip data reduction can not only avoid the problem of write conflicts, but also keep 64 CPEs busy. For communication-intensive behavioral features, the non-blocking Point-to-Point communication can not only reduce the idle waiting time of the process and it can also provides the possibility of task overlap and delay concealment, which has a significant impact on the scaling efficiency of SPH simulation.

# References

1. Amicarelli, A., et al.: SPHERA v.9.0.0: a computational fluid dynamics research code, based on the smoothed particle hydrodynamics mesh-less method. Comput. Phys. Commun. **250**, 107157 (2020). https://doi.org/10.1016/j.cpc.2020.107157
2. Bertschinger, E., Gelb, J.M.: Cosmological N-body simulations. Comput. Phys. **5**, 164–175 (1991). https://doi.org/10.1063/1.4822978

3. Borrow, J., Bower, R.G., Draper, P.W., Gonnet, P., Schaller, M.: SWIFT: maintaining weak-scalability with a dynamic range of $10^4$ in time-step size to harness extreme adaptivity. CoRR **abs/1807.01341** (2018). http://arxiv.org/abs/1807.01341
4. Cavelan, A., Cabezón, R.M., Grabarczyk, M., Ciorba, F.M.: A smoothed particle hydrodynamics mini-app for exascale. In: PASC '20: Platform for Advanced Scientific Computing Conference, Geneva, Switzerland, 29 June – 1 July 2020, pp. 11:1–11:11. ACM (2020). https://doi.org/10.1145/3394277.3401855
5. Crespo, A.J.C., et al.: Dualsphysics: open-source parallel CFD solver based on smoothed particle hydrodynamics (SPH). Comput. Phys. Commun. **187**, 204–216 (2015). https://doi.org/10.1016/j.cpc.2014.10.004
6. Domínguez, J.M., Crespo, A.J.C., Valdez-Balderas, D., Rogers, B.D., Gómez-Gesteira, M.: New multi-GPU implementation for smoothed particle hydrodynamics on heterogeneous clusters. Comput. Phys. Commun. **184**(8), 1848–1860 (2013). https://doi.org/10.1016/j.cpc.2013.03.008
7. Dong, W., Li, K., Kang, L., Quan, Z., Li, K.: Implementing molecular dynamics simulation on the Sunway TaihuLight system with heterogeneous many-core processors. Concurr. Comput. Practice Exp. **30**, e4468 (2018)
8. Duan, X., Gao, P., Zhang, T., Zhang, M., Yang, G.: Redesigning LAMMPS for peta-scale and hundred-billion-atom simulation on Sunway TaihuLight. In: SC18: International Conference for High Performance Computing, Networking, Storage and Analysis (2019)
9. Fu, H., et al.: The Sunway TaihuLight supercomputer: system and applications. Sci. China Inf. Sci. **59**(7), 072001:1–072001:16 (2016). https://doi.org/10.1007/s11432-016-5588-7
10. Gómez-Gesteira, M., Crespo, A.J.C., Rogers, B.D., Dalrymple, R.A., Domínguez, J.M., Barreiro, A.: SPHysics - development of a free-surface fluid solver - part 2: efficiency and test cases. Comput. Geosci. **48**, 300–307 (2012). https://doi.org/10.1016/j.cageo.2012.02.028
11. Kuranz, C.C., et al.: How high energy fluxes may affect Rayleigh-Taylor instability growth in young supernova remnants. Nat. Commun. **9**(1), 1564 (2018)
12. Lindl, J., Landen, O., Edwards, J., Moses, E.: Review of the national ignition campaign 2009–2012. Phys. Plasmas **21**(2), 339–566 (2014)
13. Liu, G.R., Liu, M.B.: Smoothed Particle Hydrodynamics: A Meshfree Particle Method. World Scientific (2003)
14. Lucy, L.B.: A numerical approach to the testing of the fission hypothesis. Astrophys. J. **8**(12), 1013–1024 (1977)
15. Gingold, R.A., Monaghan, J.J.: Smoothed particle hydrodynamics: theory and application to non-spherical stars. MNRAS **181**, 375–389 (1977)
16. Schaller, M., Gonnet, P., Chalk, A.B.G., Draper, P.W.: Swift: Using task-based parallelism, fully asynchronous communication, and graph partition-based domain decomposition for strong scaling on more than 100,000 cores. ACM (2016)
17. Yang, Q., Chang, J., Bao, W.: Richtmyer-Meshkov instability induced mixing enhancement in the scramjet combustor with a central strut. Adv. Mech. Eng. **6**, 614189 (2014)
18. Zukas, J.A.: High Velocity Impact Dynamics. Wiley-Interscience, Hoboken (1990)

# Transactional-Turn Causal Consistency

Benoît Martin(✉), Laurent Prosperi, and Marc Shapiro(✉)

Sorbonne-Université, CNRS, Inria, LIP6, Paris, France
{benoit.martin,laurent.prosperi,marc.shapiro}@lip6.fr

**Abstract.** Function-as-a-Service (FaaS, serverless) computing systems use an actor-like model that executes a function asynchronously, atomically and in an isolated context. However, a function must often also access state, e.g., memory or a database. This mixed model can break the actor guarantees, leading to bugs, crashes and data loss. To avoid this, we define Transactional-Turn Causal Consistency (TTCC). TTCC unifies the Turn of the actor model with the Transaction of the database model, under asynchronous, atomic and isolated execution, and guarantees mutual consistency of messages and memory. We define the model formally and present a reference implementation, along with preliminary experimental evaluation.

**Keywords:** causal consistency · actor model · message-passing · shared-memory · serverless

## 1 Introduction

This paper studies the issues that occur in a system that combines event- (or message-)based and shared-memory communication, and proposes a solution.

For instance, in Function-as-a-Service (FaaS, serverless) computing, a computation is a set of functions that execute following the actor model [2,10]. When an actor receives an event or a message, this triggers a computation called a *turn*, to run the function being called. A turn runs in parallel with other actors, executes in the actor's separate memory space, and is uninterrupted until it terminates. Its results become visible only by sending more messages. We say an actor is *asynchronous, isolated* and *atomic*. These features are pleasing for developers, who can leverage concurrency without having to worry about memory interference, locking or deadlocks.

However, business logic often requires state; examples include video encoding, file conversion or collaborative workspaces [1,16]. For instance, a turn may observe the memory state left by the previous turn in the same actor.[1]

Frameworks such as Orleans, Cloudflare Durable Objects, Lightbend Akka Serverless or Azure Durable Entities allow an actor to store application state in a database (Fig. 1). A database computation, called a transaction, runs in

[1] This may create consistency anomalies known as *glitches* [12]. Although not well known, they are an indication that the actor model is underspecified.


J. Cano et al. (Eds.): Euro-Par 2023, LNCS 14100, pp. 578–591, 2023.
https://doi.org/10.1007/978-3-031-39698-4_39

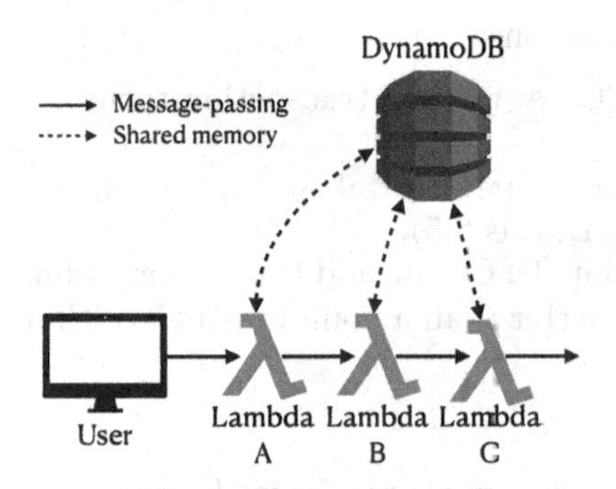


Fig. 1. A stateful serverless construct.

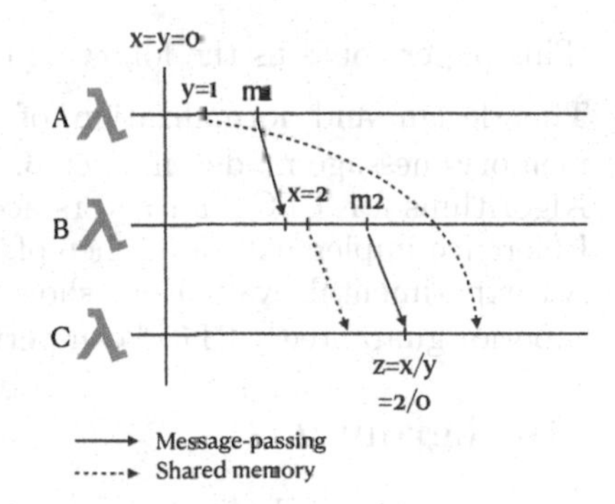


Fig. 2. An inconsistency leading to a crash.

isolation and is atomic, i.e., its results become visible at once when the transaction commits. Transactions may be or not be asynchronous, depending on the database's *isolation level* (a.k.a. consistency model): under *serializability,* transactions execute (logically) in lockstep; whereas under *snapshot isolation* (SI), a transaction does not block but operates upon a private snapshot of the database [4]. The lesser-known *Transactional Causal Consistency* (TCC) is fully asynchronous, as it also supports concurrent writes [3,14]. In summary, TCC is also asynchronous, isolated and atomic; developers may leverage concurrency without having to worry about memory interference, locking or deadlocks.

Unfortunately, even though the buzzwords align, actors and database remain different worlds. The guarantees of one do not extend to the other. For instance, despite a turn accessing isolated local memory, it can still suffer interference via the database; and conversely, messages between transactions can defeat the consistency guarantees of the database.

To illustrate, consider Fig. 2, the timeline representation of Fig. 1. Database data items $x$ and $y$ are initially set to 0, and replicated at all nodes. Node $A$ updates $y$ to 1, and notifies $B$ with message $m1$. Node $B$ updates $x$ to 2, notifies node $C$ with message $m2$. In response, $C$ computes $z = x/y$. Unfortunately, in existing systems, nothing stops $m2$ from being delivered before $y$ is replicated on node $C$. Because the message view and the database view are mutually inconsistent, $C$ computes $z = 2/0$, leading to a crash. Even if messages are delivered in order, and even if the database guarantees strong consistency, maintaining separate consistency guarantees fails to maintain mutual consistency and violates the fundamental *causality* assumption.

To avoid such anomalies, we unify the actor/message-passing and the database/shared-memory views of the world with *Transactional-Turn Causal Consistency* (TTCC). TTCC combines an actor-style execution model with shared-memory access, and identifies turns with transactions. A transactional turn is *isolated* and *atomic*, and executes *asynchronously.* TTCC ensures that information remains consistent, whether carried in messages or in shared memory.

This paper contains the following contributions:

- The design and formalization of TTCC, a unified transaction-turn and memory-message model, in Sect. 3.
- Algorithms for TTCC for actors accessing a shared database, in Sect. 4.
- Reference implementations thereof, in Akka (Sect. 5).
- An experimental evaluation, showing that TTCC in addition to providing superior guarantees, TTCC can perform better than a non-unified algorithm.

# 2 Background

In summary, existing FaaS environments provide a mixture of asynchronous, isolated computation execution models, and of inter-actor communication models. What is lacking is a unified, consistent view across them. Therefore, this work defines a common asynchronous and isolated execution model, and a common consistent communication model.

## 2.1 Groundwork

A (distributed) system consists of any number of sequential processes, called actors. Actors execute in parallel, and communicate via messages and shared memory. A message may be point-to-point (from one actor to another, or to itself) or multicast (from one actor to several). Our current treatment does not consider failures.

A system may become inconsistent if events are observed in the wrong order. Intuitively, *causal consistency* is the property that if some event $e$ might influence (cause) some event $f$, no actor could observe $f$ before observing $e$.[2] For instance, in Fig. 2, message $m2$ should not be delivered until after the update to $y$ is replicated to $C$.

Borrowing from Burckhardt [6] and Viotti and Vukolić [15], we model a system execution using a multi-graph $A = (\mathcal{E}, vis)$ built on a set $\mathcal{E}$ of *events*.[3] Events comprise send, receive, read and write operations. More specifically:

**Program-order** $\xrightarrow{PO}$ is a binary relation over $\mathcal{E}$ that expresses the natural execution order of operations by a process.

**Visibility** $vis$ is a binary relation over $\mathcal{E}$ that describes the propagation of information through the system. It satisfies the following rules:

① $\xrightarrow{vis}$ is acyclic.

② It is transitive: $\forall e, f, g \in \mathcal{E} : e \xrightarrow{vis} f \wedge f \xrightarrow{vis} g \implies e \xrightarrow{vis} g$

③ Program order implies visibility: $\xrightarrow{PO} \subseteq \xrightarrow{vis}$

For instance, $a$ is visible to $b$ (i.e., $a \xrightarrow{\text{vis}} b$) means that the effects of $a$ are visible to the process invoking $b$. Two operations are said *concurrent* if they are not ordered by $vis$.

[2] Lamport [11] calls the relation between $e$ and $f$ "happened-before;" recent literature uses the term "visible." [6,7,15].

[3] Burckhardt also defines a total arbitration order, but it is not necessary for our purpose.

### 2.2 Actor Execution Model

The classical actor model describes processes communicating only via messages. An actor alternates between being ready to accept a message, and busy processing a message. An actor responds to a message by doing local computation, creating actors, and sending messages. A *turn* is the processing of a single message. Actors conform to the following "Isolated-Turn Principle" of de Koster et al. [9]:

- Continuous message processing: An actor's turn terminates without interruption.
- Consecutive message processing: An actor processes messages from its own inbox, and processes them one by one. Within a single actor, turns do not interleave.
- Isolation: An actor can access its own memory only.

Thus, the actor is isolated, and the processing of a turn is free from low-level data races. The programmer can reason about the application as a sequence of isolated, functional turns.

### 2.3 Message-Based Communication Model and Causal Delivery

We note messages $m, n$ (messages are assumed unique); message-related events are send and receive, noted $send(m)$ and $recv(m)$ respectively. A message is *causally delivered* if and only if it satisfies the common rules ①–③, as well as the following:

④ A received message must be sent: $rcv(m) \in \mathcal{E} \implies send(m) \in \mathcal{E}$
⑤ A send precedes the corresponding receive: $send(m) \xrightarrow{vis} rcv(m)$
⑥ A message does not overtake another message:

$$send(m) \xrightarrow{vis} send(n) \implies \neg(rcv(n) \xrightarrow{PO} rcv(m))$$

Rule ⑤ states that $m$ is visible when it is received, which is after it was sent. Rule ⑥ defines the order in which messages $m$ and $n$ are made visible (delivered). If an actor sends $m$, and later an actor sends $n$, a destination actor must observe $m$ before $n$.[4]

### 2.4 Shared-Memory Transactional Execution Model

We borrow our shared-memory execution model from Cerone et al. [7]. They consider a database consisting of *objects* $Obj = \{x, y, \dots\}$. Events consist of $wr(x, v)$, writing version $v$ to object $x$, and $rd(x, v)$, reading $v$ from $x$; a write associates a new, unique version to the object being updated.

[4] We use negation ($\neg$) because a destination might receive only one of the messages.

Reads and writes are grouped into *transactions*. A transaction is a sequential and isolated execution. Its writes become visible, *atomically*, to other transactions only after it *commits*. Formally, we say transaction $T$ is atomic iff: $\forall e, f \in T \wedge g \in T' \neq T \implies (e \xrightarrow{\text{vis}} g \Leftrightarrow f \xrightarrow{\text{vis}} g)$, i.e., either all of $T$'s effects are visible ($T$ is committed), or none are ($T$ hasn't terminated yet or aborted). In what follows, we consider only committed transactions.

A transaction operates on its own *snapshot* [5], which is a copy of the state of the database at a given point in time. The snapshot ensures the transaction executes without interference from concurrent transactions.

To formalize this intuition, we define the predecessors for $x$ in transaction $T$ as $pred_T(x) = \{y \mid y \xrightarrow{\text{vis}} x \wedge y \notin T\}$. $T$ has the snapshot property iff: $x \in T \wedge y \in T \implies pred_T(x) = pred_T(y)$. In other words, all the reads of a transaction come from the same set of committed transactions.

### 2.5 Shared-Memory Communication and Causal Consistency

Transactions communicate through the shared memory. A transaction's committed updates can be transmitted asynchronously to another transaction's snapshot, without waiting; this might cause inconsistency. An execution is *causally consistent for shared memory* if and only if it satisfies the common rules ①–③, as well as the following:

⑦ A version read must be written: $rd(x, v) \in \mathcal{E} \implies wr(x, v) \in \mathcal{E}$
⑧ A write precedes the corresponding read: $wr(x, v) \xrightarrow{vis} rd(x, v)$
⑨ An update does not overtake another update:

$$wr(x, v_1) \xrightarrow{vis} wr(x, v_2) \xrightarrow{vis} wr(y, w) \implies \neg(rd(y, w) \xrightarrow{PO} rd(x, v_1))$$

Rule ⑧ states that an update to object $x$ with version $v$, is visible before reading $x$. Rule ⑨ states that once an update, tagged with version $v_2$, is visible, then no subsequent operation can see a version prior to $v_2$. In other words, only the latest version of an object is visible.

## 3 Transactional-Turn Causal Consistency: Unifying Messages and Shared Memory

To avoid the inconsistency in Fig. 2, while maintaining a familiar execution model, we propose to unify the asynchronous, isolated and causally consistent properties of the message and memory models. We call this model *Transactional-Turn Causal Consistency* (TTCC).

### 3.1 TTCC Unified Execution Model

Our execution model equates an (actor) turn with a (database) transaction. When an actor receives a message, this triggers a transactional turn. It reads from a snapshot that is causally consistent with the message received. When it terminates, its writes and its sends become visible atomically.

The model allows a transaction to send no more than a single message per destination actor. Otherwise, the result would not be atomic, as sending multiple messages to the same actor would cause multiple sequential turns, each one observing only a subset of the transaction's commit. If an actor must send multiple message to the same destination, it can do so in multiple sequential turns.

### 3.2 TTCC Unified Causally-Consistent Communication Model

In the unified model, actors communicate through any mixture of message-passing and shared-memory access. An execution is *causally consistent for shared memory and messages* if and only if it satisfies the common, message-passing, and memory rules above (1)–(9), as well as the following *interaction rules*:

(10) An update does not overtake a message:

$$send(m) \xrightarrow{vis} wr(x,v) \implies \neg(rd(m,v) \xrightarrow{PO} rcv(m))$$

(11) A message does not overtake an update:

$$wr(x,v_1) \xrightarrow{vis} wr(x,v_2) \xrightarrow{vis} send(m) \implies \neg(rcv(m) \xrightarrow{PO} rd(m,v_1))$$

These rules define visibility when messages interact with shared-memory operations. Rule (10) states that if an actor writes version $v$ to $x$ knowing $send(m)$, then the receiving actor must receive $m$ before observing version $v$ for key $x$. Conversely, Rule (11) states that if an actor sends $m$ while knowing $wr(x,v_2)$, then the destination actor must no longer observe the earlier $v_1$ after receiving $m$. Indeed, upon receiving $m$, the receiving actor sees the causal dependencies of $send(m)$, i.e., $wr(x,v_1) \xrightarrow{vis} wr(x,v_2)$. Hence, the read must return $v_2$, the freshest visible version of $x$.

# 4 Unified Message-Memory Protocol

In this section, we present a reference protocol that uses a unified version vector (with one entry per node) to track causal dependencies for both messages and shared objects. We present the causal delivery mechanism for messages as well as replication for shared objects.

Our protocol assumes that values in shared memory are conflict-free data structures (CRDTs) [13], which is helpful to resolve conflicts in concurrent updates without coordination.

### 4.1 Overview

Our protocol executes in two phases: in an actor (when a transaction is executed and when a message is received) and in a *replicator* actor that is unique per node. Replicators of different nodes communicate with each other and are responsible for maintaining transactions, snapshots and replication. A transaction operation (read, update, send message) runs inside an actor, and accesses an isolated snapshot version that is managed by the local replicator. The replicator provides the latest *local*, causally consistent snapshot to new transactions. A transaction originating from the local node is immediately visible to local actors when it commits, as local actors share the latest local snapshot. However, a transaction arriving from a remote node is visible to local actors only after the preceding transactions have committed locally.

*Causal Message Delivery.* To implement causal message delivery, TTCC delays messages until all its causal dependencies are satisfied. Conversely, sending a message is non-blocking. Causal dependencies are propagated by piggy-packing metadata to messages. For instance, if an actor sends $m$ then $n$, the metadata of $n$ indicates that $n$ causally depends on $m$.

*Causal Shared-Memory.* To maintain causal consistency for shared memory, TTCC maintains multiple versions of objects and exposes them through isolated snapshots. Write operations are non-blocking and replication is done asynchronously. When reading an object, TTCC materializes only the requested value for the given object, as opposed to all objects in the snapshot, to reduce compute and memory consumption.

*Memory-Message Interactions.* TTCC unifies causal consistency for shared memory and causal message delivery, by considering the interactions between the two memory models. Messages are delayed until causally dependent messages are delivered (Rule ⑥) *and* shared-memory is up-to-date (Rule ⑪). A snapshot is causally visible, when causally dependent snapshots are available (Rule ⑨). Visibility of a snapshot is not delayed by causally dependent messages as the reception of a message triggers an actor's turn, which exposes a causally consistent snapshot.

### 4.2 Notation and Definitions

Table 1 introduces the notation followed in this section to describe the execution of our protocols on an actor and on a replicator. We assume a singleton Replicator $R$ on each node. A snapshot $S$ is a tuple composed of a version vector $vv_S$ and a dataset $data_S$. The $GSS$ is a snapshot that is known to be available on all nodes at a given point in time. $LLSS$ stores a set of local snapshots that are committed. When the protocol updates $GSS$, snapshots from $LLSS$ are merged into $GSS$ using CRDT logic. An ongoing transaction $T$ is stored in *ongoing* at index $T$. $R$ stores its neighbor $n$'s version vector in $kvv$ at index $n$. When $kvv$ updates, the protocol recompute $GSS$. $lastVV$ stores the latest Version Vector seen by an actor.

**Table 1.** Notation used in the protocol description.

| | |
|---|---|
| $R$ | Local replicator actor |
| $T$ | Transaction |
| $q_T$ | Queue containing messages for transaction $T$ |
| $S$ | Snapshot |
| $vv_S$ | Version vector of $S$ |
| $data_S$ | Dataset of $S$ |
| $GSS$ | Globally Stable Snapshot |
| $LLSS$ | Set of Locally Latest Stable Snapshots |
| $ongoing[T]$ | Ongoing transaction is stored at index $T$ |
| $kvv[n]$ | Known Version Vector for neighbor is stored at index $n$ |
| $m$ | Message sent between a pair of actors |
| $from_m$ | Sender actor of $m$ |
| $vv_m$ | Version Vector of $m$ |
| $lastVV$ | Last seen Version Vector |
| $B$ | Buffer for delayed messages |
| $+=$ | CRDT merge operation |

### 4.3 Execution on an Actor

Algorithm 1 shows the pseudo-code of the protocol for executing transaction $T$ and the reception of message $m$ on a causal actor. Algorithm 1 is responsible for message delivery (and delay) and transaction operations (begin, read, update, commit, abort). A message is delayed if the local shared memory is not up-to-date.

A transaction begins by sending a synchronous *StartTransaction* message to the *local* replicator $R$, which contains a transaction id; we use a locally-generated UUID, as it is unique and does not require coordination. $R$ responds with an initialized transaction snapshot, which contains the latest locally available snapshot, which is stored in $LLSS$. $LLSS$ contains the latest *local* committed snapshots that are not yet merged into the $GSS$. If $LLSS$ is empty, we use $vv_{GSS}$. Finally, if $GSS$ is empty, we use an empty version vector.

Read and update operations send a *ReadObject* or *UpdateObject* message to $R$ respectively. $R$ returns the object's value in the transaction's snapshot.

A message sent in a transaction is stored in a buffer $q_T$ until $T$ commits or aborts (Algorithm 1, line 2). On commit, the actor sends a *Commit* message containing the transaction id and $q_T$ to $R$. On abort, $q_T$ is emptied, and no messages are sent.

When it receives a message (Algorithm 1, line 28), the actor checks if $m$ is causally deliverable. A message $m$ is causally deliverable if: (1) $vv_m \leq lastVV$; (2) $vv_m[from_m] < lastVV[from_m]$; and (3) $\forall d \in (vv_m - vv_m[from_m]), d == lastVV[d]$. (Algorithm 1, line 4 and 10). If $m$ is not deliverable, it is appended to buffer $B$. After the delivery of $m$, the protocol checks $B$ for any other deliverable messages. $lastVV$ is updated by being merged with the received message's version vector.

**Algorithm 1.** Execution of Actor a

```
1: function SEND_MSG(m, to)
2:     append m to q_T[to]
3: end function
4: function CHECK_DEPENDENCIES(m)
5:     deps ← (vv_m − from_m)
6:     for all d ∈ deps do
7:         return lastVV[d] == d
8:     end for
9: end function
10: function IS_DELIVERABLE(m)
11:     if vv_m ≤ lastVV &
12: vv_m[from_m] < lastVV[from_m] &
13: CHECK_DEPENDENCIES(m) then
14:         lastVV+ = vv_m
15:         return true
16:     else
17:         return false
18:     end if
19: end function
20: function DELIVER_CAUSAL_MESSAGES
21:     for all m ∈ B do
22:         if IS_DELIVERABLE(m) then
23:             deliver m
24:             remove m from B
25:         end if
26:     end for
27: end function
28: function ON_MESSAGE(m)
29:     if IS_DELIVERABLE(m) then
30:         deliver m
31:         DELIVER_CAUSAL_MESSAGES
32:     else
33:         B ← m
34:     end if
35: end function
```

### 4.4 Execution on Replication Actor

Algorithm 2 shows the pseudo-code of the protocol for executing transaction $T$ on $R$.

When $R$ receives a *StartTransaction* for $T$ and $T \notin$ *ongoing*, the protocol initializes the transaction context by appending the latest snapshot in $LLSS$ to *ongoing*$[T]$. $R$ replies with a message containing the latest $vv_{LLSS}$, which represents the latest locally available snapshot.

When $R$ receives *ReadObject*, the protocol materializes the requested data. The protocol requires that $T \in$ *ongoing*. Value $v$ for key $k$ is: (1) materialized from $GSS$, $v$ is initially set to $data_{GSS}$; (2) all values $\leq vv_T \in LLSS$ are merged into $v$, using the underlying CRDT merge operation. (3) finally, $data_{ongoing[T]}$ is merged into $v$. (See Algorithm 2, line 7). An update for key $k$ and value $v$ updates $data_{ongoing[T]}$ for $k$ with $v$. If $T$ aborts, $data_{ongoing[T]}$ is emptied and updates are ignored.

When $R$ receives *Commit* (Algorithm 2, line 16), commit version vector $cvv_T$ is initially set to the latest $vv_{LLSS}$. If *ongoing*$[T]$ contains update operations or $q_T$ is not empty, $cvv_T$ in incremented. The protocol then updates $kvv[self]$ with $cvv_T$ to maintain an updated version vector for the current node. Then, to terminate the commit and make the new snapshot visible to other actors, $data_T$ moves from *ongoing* into $LLSS$ at $cvv_T$. Finally, the resulting snapshot is broadcast to all nodes.

On reception of a snapshot broadcast update message (Algorithm 2, line 29), $R$ checks if $vv_S$ is concurrent with a snapshot contained in $LLSS$. This may be the case, as local transactions can commit without coordination with other nodes. If $vv_S$ is concurrent, we merge $vv_S$ and $data_S$ with $vv_{LLSS[vv_S]}$ and $data_{LLSS[vv_S]}$ respectively. Then, we update $LLSS$ with the resulting snapshot. If $vv_S$ is not concurrent, we update $LLSS$ with $S$. Finally, $kvv[from]$ is set to $vv_S$ before updating $GSS$.

The replicator leverages the $GSS$ mechanism that ensures progress by periodically broadcasting the latest local version vector to neighboring nodes [3]. This mechanism is useful to prune $LLSS$ by merging snapshots into $GSS$ for all $data_{LLSS} \leq vv_{GSS}$. Note that high frequency updates may result in a high network and compute overhead, while low frequency updates may result in longer buffering and slow visibility of remote committed snapshots.

**Algorithm 2.** Protocol executed on Replicator $R$

```
1: function ON_PREPARE(T)
2:    if ongoing[T] does not exist then
3:       ongoing[T] ← latest LLSS
4:          return latest vv_LLSS
5:    end if
6: end function
7: function ON_READ_OBJECT(T, key)
8:    value = data_GSS for key
9:    value+ = data_LLSS for key
10:   value+ = data_ongoing[T] for key
11:   return value
12: end function
13: function ON_UPD_OBJECT(T, k, v)
14:   put v in ongoing[T] at k
15: end function
16: function ON_COMMIT(T, vv_T)
17:   commitVv ← latest vv_LLSS
18:   if upd or msg ∈ ongoing[T], incr commitVv[self]
19:   kvv[self] ← commitVv
20:   LLSS[commitVv] ← ongoing[T]
21:   remove T from ongoing
22:   TRIGGER_BCAST(LLSS[commitVv])
23: end function
24: function TRIGGER_BCAST(S)
25:   for all n ∈ allNodes do
26:      send SnapshotUpdate(S) to n
27:   end for
28: end function
29: function ON_SNAP_UPD(from, S)
30:   if vv_S is concurrent then
31:      vv_S+ = vv_S, vv_LLSS
32:      data_S+ = data_S, data_LLSS
33:      update LLSS with vv_S and data_S
34:   else
35:      update LLSS with vv_S and data_S
36:   end if
37:   update kvv[from] with vv_S
38:   UPDATE_GSS
39: end function
40: function UPDATE_GSS
41:   for i = 1, 2, ..., size(kvv) do
42:      vv_GSS ← min(kvv[i])
43:   end for
44:   data_GSS = data from GSS
45:   data_GSS+ = data_LLSS from vv_LLSS until vv_GSS
46:   GSS ← (vv_GSS, data_GSS)
47:   remove merged data from LLSS
48: end function
```

## 5 Implementation

We implement our unified memory model on top of the Akka actor framework.[5] Akka is open source and enables actors to share data using eventual consistency guarantees. An actor accesses data in the shared store through a replicator actor that provides a key-value API and that handles data replication. Each node spawns a singleton instance per node of a replicator actor. The replicator actor spreads object updates to its neighbors via direct replication and gossip-based dissemination.

In Akka's key-value API, a key is a unique identifier of a CRDT data value. Our solution consists in applying TTCC next to the existing Akka key-value store

[5] https://akka.io/.

by including additional protocols for an actor (Algorithm 1) and replicator actor (Algorithm 2), and additional metadata to guarantee transitive causal delivery of messages and shared objects.

### 5.1 Causal Shared Memory

We add support for transactions by encapsulating an actor's data in a causally consistent snapshot. An actor sends a message and manipulates shared objects within a transaction. A transaction begins by querying the local replicator for the latest available snapshot from $LLSS$. Get and update operations affect only the transaction's snapshot. A get operation for a given key $k$, materializes the value associated to $k$ by reading from $GSS$, $LLSS$ and the ongoing transaction snapshot.

On commit, we compute a commit version vector and append the transaction's snapshot to $LLSS$ (Sect. 4.4). Then, the gossip-based replication mechanism is triggered, which asynchronously broadcasts the newly committed snapshot to other replicators.

### 5.2 Causal Message Delivery

A message sent in a transaction is associated with the transaction's snapshot and is causally sent to the recipient actor when the transaction commits. To ensure atomicity, messages remain in a private buffer until the transaction commits. If the transaction aborts, we delete the buffer.

On commit, we send the buffered messages, with an additional version vector that represents the transaction snapshot, to the destination actor. On reception of a message, the piggy-packed version vector is compared to the local replicator's version vector. Actors inherit the *CausalActor* class. This base class is responsible for delaying delivery of messages until the context is causally consistent.

## 6 Evaluation

Our experimental evaluation address the following questions: What is the overhead of *unified* causal consistency for messages and shared memory? How does TTCC scale on multiple nodes?

### 6.1 Experimental Protocol

We implement four protocols in a transactional key-value store (KVS) that supports messages. Protocol 1, which is our baseline that does not guarantee causal order. Protocol 2, our reference protocol that uses a single version vector (Sect. 4). Protocol 3, which adds a matrix to track causality with messages. Protocol 4, that ensures causality for messages and shared memory *independently*. In this protocol, inconsistencies between messages and shared memory may happen if a message is delivered before shared memory is up-to-date. We implement all four protocols using the Akka actor framework.

To conduct performance benchmarks, we modify YCSB [8] (version 0.17.0) to include messages and transactions[6] that we call YCSB+MT.

We provide a custom YCSB+MT workload that is similar to the original YCSB *workload* where read and write operations are run in equal proportion. Our transactional Workloads A and B executes read, update and message operations in the following proportions: 90%/5%/5% for Workload A and 5%/90%/5% for Workload B. We compare protocols 2 and 3 against protocol 4 to evaluate the overhead of mutual causal consistency.

We run the performance experiments on multiple nodes, each equipped with two Intel Xeon E5-2690v3 clocked at 2.60 GHz with 192 GB of memory.

We deploy up to ten instances (i.e., replicas) of our key-value service. Each KVS instance has its corresponding YCSB+MT client that we configure (16 threads each), to reach maximum throughput (ops/s) on each KVS. We measure the overall throughput and latency while increasing the number of nodes.

The size of a version vector is proportional to the number of nodes. In our experiment, we scale up to ten nodes. In Protocol 3, the size of the matrix is equal to the number of actor pairs, which in our experiment scales up to the number of concurrent YCSB+MT threads (16 threads).

### 6.2 Results

We measure the overhead of protocol 2 and protocol 3 by comparing them with protocol 4 (non-unified). Our results show that protocol 4 performs better in all workloads. We explain this by the lesser number of constraints that the protocol enforces (i.e., rules for interaction. Rules (10) and (11)).

Protocol 3 (extra matrix), performs the worst and does not scale past 4 nodes. We explain this by the cost of maintaining an extra matrix, which is both costly in transferred data and computation. For this reason, we exclude protocol 3 in the following result interpretation.

For read operations, protocol 2 (single unified version vector) performs with an overhead of up to 1.55× compared to protocol 4. We explain this by the required delay caused by our protocol to maintain *mutual* causal consistency. Furthermore, data is re-materialized for all requested values. Caching materialized data would greatly benefit read performance.

Write operations show a similar trend to read operations. Protocol 2 performs with an overhead of up to 1.14× compared to protocol 4. We explain this by the use of isolated snapshots, which enables concurrent writes without synchronization.

Our results show that message delivery also shows a similar trend compared to protocol 4 but is more dependent on write operations. Workload B (90% writes) shows a significant increase in message response time compared to workload A, where there are less write operations. This increase in message delay is explained by the addition of required causal dependencies due to more write operations. Protocol 2 performs with an overhead of up to 2.43× compared to protocol 4.

[6] GitHub link: https://github.com/benoitmartin88/YCSB.

Our experiments show that TTCC performs, in all workload conditions, similarly than a non-unified causally consistent implementation. More importantly, the overhead of maintaining *mutual* causal consistency scales up to ten nodes while providing a reasonable response time (Figs. 3 and 4).

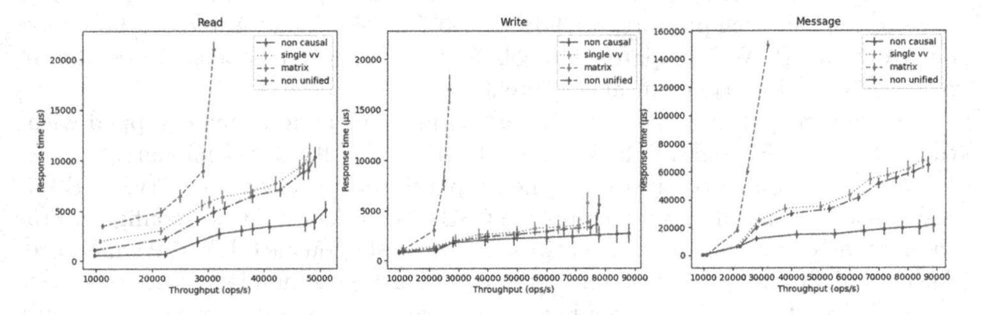


**Fig. 3.** Transactional workload A (90R/5W/5M)

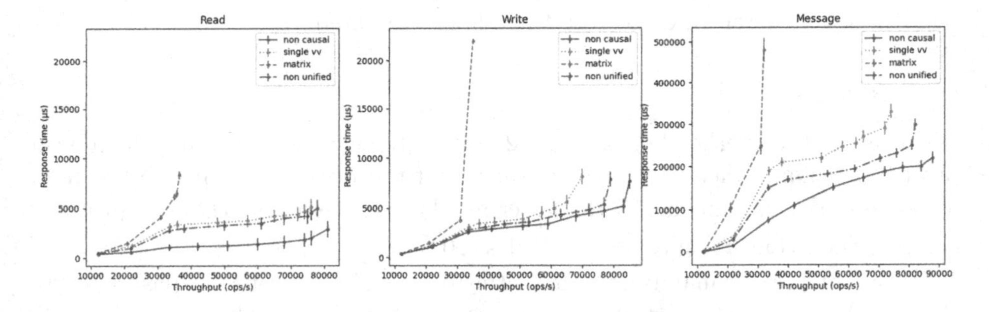


**Fig. 4.** Transactional workload B (5R/90W/5M)

## 7 Conclusion

In this paper we describe a transactional, causally consistent, unified model for message passing and shared memory, which supports asynchrony and isolated execution. TTCC is compatible with actor-based frameworks and provides an intuitive memory model that ensures that multiple pieces of information remain *mutually* consistent, whether sent using messages or shared in a distributed memory.

We presented our protocols and actor-based reference implementation. Our evaluation shows an overhead in response time of 1.55×, 1.14× and 2.43× for read, write and messages respectively, compared to two independent causally consistent memory models.

## References

1. Netflix & AWS Lambda case study. https://aws.amazon.com/solutions/case-studies/netflix-and-aws-lambda/

2. Agha, G.: ACTORS: A Model of Concurrent Computation in Distributed Systems (1985). https://dspace.mit.edu/handle/1721.1/6952. Accepted: 2004-10-20T20:10:20Z
3. Akkoorath, D.D., et al.: Cure: strong semantics meets high availability and low latency, pp. 405–414. Nara, Japan (2016). https://doi.org/10.1109/ICDCS.2016.98. http://doi.ieeecomputersociety.org/10.1109/ICDCS.2016.98
4. Berenson, H., Bernstein, P., Gray, J., Melton, J., O'Neil, E., O'Neil, P.: A critique of ANSI SQL isolation levels. SIGMOD Rec. **24**(2), 1–10 (1995). https://doi.org/10.1145/568271.223785
5. Bernstein, P.A., Goodman, N.: Multiversion concurrency control — theory and algorithms. ACM Trans. Database Syst. **8**(4), 465–483 (1983). https://doi.org/10.1145/319996.319998
6. Burckhardt, S.: Principles of Eventual Consistency, Foundations and Trends in Programming Languages, vol. 1. Now Publishers (2014). https://doi.org/10.1561/2500000011. http://research.microsoft.com/pubs/230852/final-printversion-10-5-14.pdf
7. Cerone, A., Bernardi, G., Gotsman, A.: A framework for transactional consistency models with atomic visibility, p. 14 (2015). https://doi.org/10.4230/LIPICS.CONCUR.2015.58
8. Cooper, B.F., Silberstein, A., Tam, E., Ramakrishnan, R., Sears, R.: Benchmarking cloud serving systems with YCSB. In: Proceedings of the 1st ACM Symposium on Cloud Computing, pp. 143–154. SoCC 2010, ACM (2010). https://doi.org/10.1145/1807128.1807152
9. De Koster, J., Van Cutsem, T., De Meuter, W.: 43 years of actors: a taxonomy of actor models and their key properties. In: Proceedings of the 6th International Workshop on Programming Based on Actors, Agents, and Decentralized Control, pp. 31–40. AGERE 2016, ACM (2016). https://doi.org/10.1145/3001886.3001890
10. Hewitt, C., Bishop, P., Steiger, R.: A universal modular ACTOR formalism for artificial intelligence. In: Proceedings of the 3rd International Joint Conference on Artificial Intelligence, Stanford, USA, pp. 235–245. IJCAI 1973, Morgan Kaufmann Publishers Inc. (1973)
11. Lamport, L.: Time, clocks, and the ordering of events in a distributed system. Commun. ACM **21**(7), 558–565 (1978). https://doi.org/10.1145/359545.359563
12. Mogk, R., Baumgärtner, L., Salvaneschi, G., Freisleben, B., Mezini, M.: Fault-tolerant distributed reactive programming. In: 32nd European Conference on Object-Oriented Programming, ECOOP 2018, July 16–21, 2018, Amsterdam, The Netherlands, pp. 1:1–1:26 (2018)
13. Shapiro, M., Preguiça, N., Baquero, C., Zawirski, M.: Conflict-free replicated data types. In: Défago, X., Petit, F., Villain, V. (eds.) SSS 2011. LNCS, vol. 6976, pp. 386–400. Springer, Heidelberg (2011). https://doi.org/10.1007/978-3-642-24550-3_29
14. Toumlilt, I., Sutra, P., Shapiro, M.: Highly-available and consistent group collaboration at the edge with Colony, pp. 336–351. ACM/IFIP, Québec, Canada (online) (2021). https://doi.org/10.1145/3464298.3493405
15. Viotti, P., Vukolić, M.: Consistency in non-transactional distributed storage systems (2016). http://arxiv.org/abs/1512.00168
16. Warden, J.: Large step function data – dealing with eventual consistency in S3 – software, fitness, and gaming. https://jessewarden.com/2020/09/large-step-function-data-dealing-with-eventual-consistency-in-s3.html

# Im2win: An Efficient Convolution Paradigm on GPU

Shuai Lu[1(✉)], Jun Chu[1], Luanzheng Guo[2], and Xu T. Liu[3]

[1] Nanchang Hangkong University, Nanchang, Jiangxi, China
2016085400101@stu.nchu.edu.cn, chuj@nchu.edu.cn
[2] University of California Merced, Merced, CA, USA
lguo4@ucmerced.edu
[3] University of Washington, Seattle, WA, USA
x0@uw.edu

**Abstract.** Convolution is the most time-consuming operation in deep neural network operations, so its performance is critical to the overall performance of the neural network. The commonly used methods for convolution on GPU include the general matrix multiplication (GEMM)-based convolution and the direct convolution. GEMM-based convolution relies on the im2col algorithm, which results in a large memory footprint and reduced performance. Direct convolution does not have the large memory footprint problem, but the performance is not on par with GEMM-based approach because of the discontinuous memory access. This paper proposes a window-order-based convolution paradigm on GPU, called `im2win`, which not only reduces memory footprint but also offers continuous memory accesses, resulting in improved performance. Furthermore, we apply a range of optimization techniques on the convolution CUDA kernel, including shared memory, tiling, micro-kernel, double buffer, and prefetching. We compare our implementation with the direct convolution, and PyTorch's GEMM-based convolution with cuBLAS and six cuDNN-based convolution implementations, with twelve state-of-the-art DNN benchmarks. The experimental results show that our implementation 1) uses less memory footprint by 23.1% and achieves 3.5× TFLOPS compared with cuBLAS, 2) uses less memory footprint by 32.8% and achieves up to 1.8× TFLOPS compared with the best performant convolutions in cuDNN, and 3) achieves up to 155× TFLOPS compared with the direct convolution. We further perform an ablation study on the applied optimization techniques and find that the micro-kernel has the greatest positive impact on performance.

**Keywords:** Convolution · CUDA · im2win · im2col · parallel computing · CNN

## 1 Introduction

Convolutional neural network (CNN) is an important network model widely used in computer vision, image processing, and scientific computing. CNN consists


J. Cano et al. (Eds.): Euro-Par 2023, LNCS 14100, pp. 592–607, 2023.
https://doi.org/10.1007/978-3-031-39698-4_40

of an input layer, an output layer, and convolutional layers between them [7]. Convolutional operations can take 50%–90% of the total inference operations of the neural network model [15]. Also, convolution operations often account for over 90% of the total execution time of many neural networks [20]. Therefore, it is critical to reduce the cost of convolutional operations to improve the overall performance of neural networks.

Graphics processing unit (GPU) has been used to accelerate tensor convolution operations. Popular deep learning frameworks, such as PyTorch [17] and TensorFlow [3], use GPU to accelerate convolution operations with cuBLAS [1] and cuDNN [5], both developed by NVIDIA. cuBLAS is a GPU-accelerated library for the basic linear algebra subroutines. cuDNN is a set of primitives for forward and backward convolution, pooling, normalization, and activation layers used by neural networks.

There are mainly two types of convolution methods on GPU in terms of data transformation: the im2col data transformation-based and no data transformation at all. The im2col-based convolution transforms the input tensor and the filter tensor into two matrices, known as *the im2col algorithm*, followed by the general matrix-matrix multiplication (GEMM) with cuBLAS or cuDNN, and finally transforms the resultant matrix back to the output tensor [4]. The problem with the im2col-based convolution is that 1) the im2col operation generates a high memory footprint and bandwidth overhead, which is exaggerated on GPU where the memory/cache capacity is highly limited; 2) its performance is significantly affected by the performance of the GEMM operation in cuBLAS, which takes the input im2col matrix and the filter im2col matrix as inputs while the two matrices are significantly different in size, leading to bad performance [9,22].

A typical direct convolution has no data transformation, and is implemented as seven nested for loops over the original input and filter tensors, with the scalar $a$ multiplied by $x$ plus $y$ (AXPY) computed in the innermost loop [22]. Compared to the im2col-based convolution, the direct convolution has no additional memory overhead. However, its AXPY operations suffer from discontinuous memory access, because of visiting distinct dimensions of the input tensor across the nested for loops. This results in low data reuse and low cache hit rate. This problem is seriously magnified on GPU.

To solve similar problems on CPU, we previously proposed a novel convolution algorithm, called `im2win` [14] (image to window), which rearranges the input tensor in the access order of the dot product windows. In this paper, we evolve the `im2win` algorithm and develop a memory-efficient and high-performance `im2win`-based convolution paradigm on GPU. The `im2win` convolution paradigm first transforms the input tensor into an `im2win` tensor using the `im2win` data transformation (see Sect. 3.1). Next, the convolution is implemented as a three-level nested loop structure akin to an implicit GEMM convolution, and the indices of input tensor, filter tensor and output tensor can be mapped to the three levels of for loops when performing an AXPY operation. Our `im2win` data transformation algorithm can significantly reduce memory consumption compared to the im2col data transformation. We implement the `im2win`-based convolution paradigm in CUDA and propose a range of optimization techniques, including tiling, micro-kernel, double buffer, and prefetching.

We compare our implementation with various convolution methods, including the direct convolution, PyTorch's GEMM-based convolution using cuBLAS, and six different cuDNN-based convolution implementations, using twelve different state-of-the-art deep neural network benchmarks. The results of our experiments indicate that our implementation outperforms the others in different aspects. Specifically, it uses less memory by 23.1% compared to cuBLAS and by 32.8% compared to the best-performing convolution implementations in cuDNN, while on average achieving 3.5× and 1.1× TFLOPS, respectively. Additionally, our implementation achieves up to 155× TFLOPS compared with the direct convolution. We also conduct an ablation study to understand which optimization technique has the greatest positive impact on performance, and find that the micro-kernel has the most significant effect. We make our code publicly available at https://github.com/seth-lu/Im2win under *cuda* branch.

To summarize, this paper makes the following **contributions**:

1) We propose an innovative convolution paradigm on GPU, called `im2win`-based convolution (Sect. 3.2), along with a set of optimizations that are specifically designed to improve its memory efficiency and performance (Sect. 3.3). Our proposed convolution paradigm is shown to be both high-performance and memory-efficient, offering a promising alternative to existing convolution methods on GPU.
2) We implement our `im2win`-based convolution in CUDA and compare it with the direct convolution, existing convolution algorithms in cuBLAS and cuDNN. We conduct an experimental evaluation using twelve DNN benchmarks of various dimensions that provides a comprehensive result of our proposed method (Sect. 4.2).
3) We conduct an ablation study on the optimization techniques applied to the proposed im2win-based convolution paradigm, which reveals that the micro-kernel optimization technique has the most significant impact on performance (see Sect. 4.4).

The rest of paper is organized as follow. Section 2 defines the notations used in this paper, reviews existing convolution techniques and related works. Section 3 presents our convolution paradigm on GPU along with a set of optimizations that are specifically designed to improve its memory efficiency and performance. We conduct an experimental evaluation, an ablation study and present the performance and memory usage of different convolution algorithms in Sect. 4. Finally, we conclude our work in Sect. 5.

## 2 Preliminaries and Related Work

In this section, we define the notations used in this paper, review the related works in the direct convolution, the GEMM-based convolution and other convolutions.

### 2.1 Notations

Three main tensor data in the convolution operation are the Input tensor ($\mathcal{I}$), the Filter tensor ($\mathcal{F}$), and the Output tensor ($\mathcal{O}$). These tensors in $NCHW$ layout are expressed as $\mathcal{I}[N_i][C_i][H_i][W_i]$, $\mathcal{F}[C_o][C_i][H_f][W_f]$ and $\mathcal{O}[N_i][C_o][H_o][W_o]$. The convolution is defined as:

$$\mathcal{O}_{(i,j,m,n)} = \sum_{j=0}^{C_i-1} \sum_{m=0}^{H_f-1} \sum_{n=0}^{W_f-1} \left( \mathcal{I}_{(i,j,m\times s+u,m\times s+v)} \times \mathcal{F}_{(j,r,u,v)} \right), \tag{1}$$

subject to

$$\begin{aligned} i &= 0,1,..,N_i-1, j=0,1,..,C_o-1, m=0,1,..,H_o-1,\\ n &= 0,1,..,W_o-1, u=0,1,..,H_f-1, v=0,1,..,W_f-1,\\ r &= 0,1,..,C_i-1. \end{aligned}$$

$N_i$ is the batch size, $s$ is the stride size, $C_i$ and $C_o$ are the number of input and output channels, $H_{i/f/o}$ and $W_{i/f/o}$ denote height and width in spatial dimensions.

### 2.2 The Direct Convolution

The direct convolution is one of the most naive implementations of convolutions. A basic direct convolution has seven nested for loops. The outer four loops iterate over the four dimensions of $\mathcal{O}$, and the inner three loops iterate over $\mathcal{F}$ and $\mathcal{I}$. Each element of $\mathcal{O}$ is computed with an AXPY operation in the innermost loop. These nested loops can be parallelized well on GPU. However, the larger $\mathcal{O}$ is, the less data can fit in the cache. In this case, the direct convolution accesses directly through the global memory. The data access is discontinuous and the latency is high, resulting in poor performance [22]. It has been shown that the performance of the direct convolution can be greatly improved by redesigning specific data layouts and data flows on the GPU [19].

### 2.3 The GEMM-Based Convolution

The GEMM-based convolution proposed by Chellapilla et al. [4] is the most commonly used convolution algorithm, and is widely used in existing deep learning frameworks [3,17]. Due to its fundamental and general nature, it is often used as a benchmark for performance comparison. The GEMM-based convolution unrolls the convolution operation into a GEMM operation. The $\mathcal{I}$ of size $N_i \times C_i \times H_i \times W_i$ is processed in $N_i$ batches, each batch contains data $\mathcal{I}'$ of size $C_i \times H_i \times W_i$ (i.e., a single image). As shown on the right in Fig. 1, the im2col algorithm transforms $\mathcal{I}'$ into a 2D matrix; and $\mathcal{F}$ is unfolded into a filter matrix. In im2col, the elements of each dot product window of $\mathcal{I}'$ is flattened and copied into a single row of a matrix (see Fig. 1). Denoting the im2col matrix as $M$ and the filter matrix as $N$, the im2col algorithm can be written as:

$M(mW_o+n,(rH_f+u)W_f+v)=\mathcal{I}'(r,m+u,n+v)$, $N((rH_f+u)W_f+v,j)=\mathcal{F}(j,r,u,v)$. Next, a GEMM operation in BLAS library performs the matrix product of the transformed input matrix and the transformed filter matrix to get the output matrix: $R'=M\times N$. The convolution result tensor $R$ is transformed from $R'$: $R(j,m,n)=R'(mW_o+n,j)$.

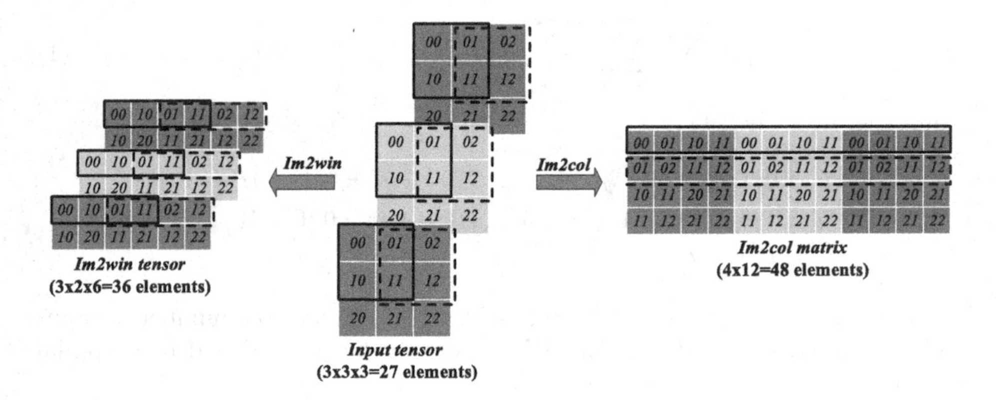


**Fig. 1.** The im2col and im2win data transformation examples with $C_i=H_i=W_i=3$, $H_f=W_f=2$, $s_h=s_w=1$. The solid and dashed boxes indicate the different dot product windows of the input tensor. We can see that the im2win tensor has less elements than the im2col matrix.

Dongarra et al. has demonstrated that the GEMM-based convolution benefits from the efficient implementation on GPU and the nature of GPU architectures [8]. Due to the highly optimized cuBLAS library, GEMM-based convolution has reliable performance and supports various input tensor sizes. However, this approach requires a large memory to store the im2col matrix transformed from the input tensor and the filter tensor. Because it has to store duplicated elements due to overlap of the filter positions in the convolution, the im2col matrix is much larger than the original tensor. What's worse, the im2col matrix is much larger than the filter matrix, this results the GEMM operation in significantly lower performance than the best achievable performance [9,22]. MEC proposes a compact lowering trick on the im2col matrix and splits a single GEMM into multiple small GEMMs to reduce the memory footprint [6]. The small GEMM operations are performed in parallel to complete the convolution. We intend to compare our convolution with MEC on GPU, unfortunately, MEC is not open-sourced.

## 2.4 The Convolution Algorithms Implemented in cuDNN

cuDNN is a GPU-accelerated deep learning library from NVIDIA, which implements six convolution algorithms including the *direct convolution*, the *GEMM-based convolution*, two *implicit GEMM-based convolutions*, the *Fast Fourier Transform (FFT) convolution*, and the *Winograd convolution*. The implicit

GEMM-based convolution is a variant of the direct convolution, which operates natively on the input tensors, converting the computation into a GEMM on the fly. During the computation, the im2col matrices are implicitly formed. There is another variant that precomputes offsets used in the implicit GEMM. The FFT convolution uses the fast Fourier transform to achieve convolution. It can achieve fast convolution with fewer operations the direct convolution, however, it requires more memory and is more difficult to implement as it works with complex numbers instead of real numbers. The Winograd convolution is based on the Winograd's minimal filtering algorithm [13], which is computationally efficient for some small convolution kernels.

cuDNN supports autotunning, which automatically selects an algorithm on a per-layer basis based on the layer dimensions. But even so, cuDNN still has some shortcomings. The cuDNN call parameter API is pre-defined, so it does not have the flexibility to build some special convolutions. cuDNN often resorts to a slower algorithm that fits the workspace size constraint. To alleviate this behavior of cuDNN, u-cuDNN divides layers' mini-batch computation into multiple micro-batches transparently by decreasing the workspace size requirements [16]. We refer the readers the performance evaluation of cuDNN convolution algorithms in [12].

## 3 The Im2win-Based Convolution Paradigm on GPU

To reduce the huge memory usage of the im2col-based convolution and avoid nonconsecutive memory access of the direct convolution, we use the `im2win` data transformation and propose a high-performance and memory efficient `im2win`-based convolution paradigm on GPU. Furthermore, we propose several optimization techniques for our `im2win`-based convolution.

### 3.1 Motivations

Now we present the `im2win` data transformation algorithm and the implicit GEMM-based convolution algorithm as the motivations of our `im2win`-based convolution.

**The `im2win` Data Transformation Algorithm.** As shown on the left in Fig. 1, our image to window algorithm (called `im2win`) rearranges the input tensor $\mathcal{I}$ in the access order of the dot product windows. It dramatically reduces memory overhead with more compact data arrangement compared with the im2col data transformation algorithm. For the dot product windows in the same row, each dot product operation reuses the elements of the previous loaded window except for the first one. Our im2win algorithm supports great data reusability, temporal and spatial data locality.

In the `im2win` algorithm, we divide each channel of $\mathcal{I}'$ into $H_o \times W_o$ windows of size $H_f \times W_f$, and copy $W_o$ windows in the same row to one row in our `im2win` tensor. Performing the above operation for all windows on a single channel of $\mathcal{I}'$, we obtain a tensor of size ($H_o$, $H_f \times W_i$) (see Fig. 1). This tensor is ordered by the dot product windows and has fewer redundant elements than what the im2col matrix has. Performing the above algorithm for the batch and channel dimensions in $\mathcal{I}$, we will get a tensor of size ($N_i$, $C_i$, $H_o$, $W_i \times H_f$) and call this tensor as an `im2win` tensor. Denoting the `im2win` tensor as $\hat{\mathcal{I}}$, the algorithm can be written as:

$$\hat{\mathcal{I}}(i, r, m, kH_f + u) = \mathcal{I}(i, r, m + u, n + v). \tag{2}$$

subject to

$$\begin{aligned} m &= 0, 1, .., H_o - 1, n = 0, 1, .., W_o - 1, u = 0, 1, .., H_f - 1, \\ v &= 0, 1, .., W_f - 1, i = 0, 1, .., N_i - 1, r = 0, 1, .., C_i - 1, \\ k &= 0, 1, .., W_i - 1. \end{aligned}$$

Recall in Fig. 1 $s = 1$, the im2col matrix has 48 elements, while in Fig. 1, the im2win tensor has 36 elements. The im2win tensor has 1/3 less elements than the im2col matrix in addition to provide better data locality and data reusability.

**The Implicit GEMM-Based Convolution Algorithm.** In addition to the GEMM-based convolution algorithm with explicit im2col data transformation, there is also an implicit GEMM-based convolution algorithm, shown in Algorithm 1. Instead of an explicit data transformation process, a three-level nested for loop structure is used in the algorithm to calculate the indices of $\mathcal{I}$ (Line 4 and Line 8 - Line 13), $\mathcal{F}$ (Line 2 and Line 8 - Line 11) and $\mathcal{O}$ (Line 2 - Line 6). In the innermost loop, the AXPY operation is performed to result in $\mathcal{O}$ (Line 14). Implicit GEMM-based convolution does not have the memory consumption of data transformation. The name of implicit GEMM-based convolution algorithm can be confusing. With no explicit input and filter matrices, it is impossible to call cuBLAS GEMM API. In addition, the indices to perform an AXPY must be computed on the fly. This algorithm is commonly viewed as a variant of the direct convolution. Since Algorithm 1 has the same three-level nested for loop structure as GEMM operation, the optimization techniques that are proposed for GEMM can also be applied to implicit GEMM-based convolution algorithm, such as shared memory, tiling, micro-kernel, vectorized load/store and prefetching.

**Algorithm 1:** Implicit GEMM-based Convolution Algorithm

**Input:** Input $\mathcal{I}$, Filter $\mathcal{F}$, Stride $s$
**Output:** Output $\mathcal{O}$
**Dimensions:** $\mathbf{M} = C_o, \mathbf{N} = N_o \times H_o \times W_o, \mathbf{K} = C_f \times H_f \times W_f$

1 **for** $m = 0$ **to** $M - 1$ **do**
2 $\quad o_c = f_n = m$
3 $\quad$ **for** $n = 0$ **to** $N - 1$ **do**
4 $\quad\quad o_n = i_n = n/(H_o \times W_o)$
5 $\quad\quad o_h = (n\%(H_o \times W_o))/W_o$
6 $\quad\quad o_w = (n\%(H_o \times W_o))\%W_o$
7 $\quad\quad$ **for** $k = 0$ **to** $K - 1$ **do**
8 $\quad\quad\quad f_c = i_c = k/(H_f \times W_f)$
9 $\quad\quad\quad k_{res} = k\%(H_f \times W_f)$
10 $\quad\quad\quad f_h = k_{res}/W_f$
11 $\quad\quad\quad f_w = k_{res}\%W_f$
12 $\quad\quad\quad i_h = o_h \times s + f_h$
13 $\quad\quad\quad i_w = o_w \times s + f_w$
14 $\quad\quad\quad \mathcal{O}(o_n, o_c, o_h, o_w) += \mathcal{I}(i_n, i_c, i_h, i_w) \times \mathcal{F}(f_n, f_c, f_h, f_w)$

**Algorithm 2:** Basic Im2win-based Convolution On GPU

**Input:** Input $\mathcal{I}$, Filter $\mathcal{F}$, Stride $s$
**Output:** Output $\mathcal{O}$
**Im2winTensor:** $\hat{\mathcal{I}} =$ **Function** IM2WIN($\mathcal{I}, \mathcal{F}, s$)
**Dimensions** : $\mathbf{M} = C_o, \mathbf{N} = N_o \times H_o \times W_o, \mathbf{K} = C_f \times H_f \times W_f$
**# of blocks** : $M/32 \times N/32$
**# of threads per block:** $32 \times 32$

1 $m = bx \times 32 + tx$, $n = by \times 32 + ty$
2 $o_c = m$, $o_n = i_n = n/(H_o \times W_o)$
3 $o_h = (n\%(H_o \times W_o))/W_o$
4 $o_w = (n\%(H_o \times W_o))\%W_o$
5 **for** $k = 0$ **to** $K - 1$ **do**
6 $\quad f_c = i_c = k/(H_f \times W_f)$
7 $\quad k_{res} = k\%(H_f \times W_f)$
8 $\quad f_h = k_{res}/W_f$, $f_w = k_{res}\%W_f$
9 $\quad i_h = o_h \times s + f_h$, $i_w = o_w \times s + f_w$
10 $\quad \mathcal{O}(o_n, o_c, o_h, o_w) += \hat{\mathcal{I}}(i_n, i_c, i_h, i_w) \times \mathcal{F}(f_n, f_c, f_h, f_w)$

### 3.2 The im2win-based convolution on GPU

We propose a basic `im2win`-based convolution on GPU shown in Algorithm 2 implemented in CUDA. The input tensor $\mathcal{I}$ is initially transformed into the `im2win` tensor $\hat{\mathcal{I}}$ based on Eq. (2). Next, the convolution is implemented as a three-level nested for loop structure same as the implicit GEMM-based convolution. In Algorithm 2, dimension M and dimension N are mapped to grid and block respectively, where each block includes $32 \times 32$ threads, i.e., grid = (M/32, N/32), block = (32, 32). The $bx$ and $by$ denote block indices in the x and y dimensions respectively, and $tx$ and $ty$ denote thread indices in the x and y dimensions respectively (Line 1). Within the kernel of each block, the three levels of for loops are $\mathbf{M} = C_o, \mathbf{N} = N_o \times H_o \times W_o$, and $\mathbf{K} = C_f \times H_f \times W_f$. The indices of $\hat{\mathcal{I}}$ (Line 2, Line 6 - Line 9), $\mathcal{F}$ (Line 6 - Line 8) and $\mathcal{O}$ (Line 2 - Line 4) tensor are computed on the fly within the kernel function. The innermost for loop performs an AXPY operation.

In the kernel function, we first compute indices m and n from dimension M and dimension N respectively from the global indices of the thread tx and ty (Line 1 in Algorithm 2). Next, the indices of the four dimensions of the output tensor required for the AXPY operation are calculated by performing division and remainder operations on m and n (Line 2 - Line 4). Finally, we compute the remaining indices of $\hat{\mathcal{I}}$ and $\mathcal{F}$ in a for loop in dimension K, and perform AXPY operations after obtaining all the indices of $\mathcal{O}$, $\hat{\mathcal{I}}$ and $\mathcal{F}$ (Line 5 - Line 10).

The most expensive computation in Algorithm 2 is the AXPY operation at Line 10, which requires three read operations and one write operation. On GPU, frequent read and write operations to the global memory have substantial

**Algorithm 3:** High Performance Im2win Convolution Algorithm On GPU

**Input:** Input tensor $\mathcal{I}$, Filter tensor $\mathcal{F}$, Stride $s$
**Output:** Output tensor $\mathcal{O}$
**Im2winTensor:** $\hat{\mathcal{I}}$ = **Function** IM2WIN($\mathcal{I}, \mathcal{F}, s$)
**Dimensions** : $\mathbf{M} = C_o, \mathbf{N} = N_o \times H_o \times W_o, \mathbf{K} = C_f \times H_f \times W_f$
**# of blocks** : $M/M_B \times N/N_B$
**# of threads per block:** $M_B/M_T \times N_B/N_T$

1 Registers: $R_{\hat{\mathcal{I}}}[2][N_T], R_{\mathcal{F}}[2][M_T], R_{\mathcal{O}}[M_T \times M_T]$ *//double buffer*
2 Shared memories: $S_{\hat{\mathcal{I}}}[2][K_B \times N_B], S_{\mathcal{F}}[2][M_B \times K_B]$ *//double buffer*
3 $S_{\hat{\mathcal{I}}}[0][k_B \times n_B]$ $\underleftarrow{\text{load}}$ $k_B \times n_B$ of $\hat{\mathcal{I}}(0, by)$
4 $S_{\mathcal{F}}[0][m_B \times k_B]$ $\underleftarrow{\text{load}}$ $m_B \times k_B$ of $\mathcal{F}(bx, 0)$
5 __syncthreads()
6 $R_{\hat{\mathcal{I}}}[0][n_T]$ $\underleftarrow{\text{vec\_load}}$ $n_T$ of $S_{\hat{\mathcal{I}}}[0][0 \times n_B]$
7 $R_{\mathcal{F}}[0][m_T]$ $\underleftarrow{\text{vec\_load}}$ $m_T$ of $S_{\mathcal{F}}[0][m_B \times 0]$
8 **for** $kk = 0$ **to** $C_f \times H_f \times W_f/K_{f,b} - 1$ **do**
9     **for** $k' = 1$ **to** $K_{f,b} - 1$ **do**
10         $R_{\hat{\mathcal{I}}}[load][n_T]$ $\underleftarrow{\text{vec\_load}}$ $n_T$ of $S_{\hat{\mathcal{I}}}[store][k' \times n_B]$ *//prefetching*
11         $R_{\mathcal{F}}[load][m_T]$ $\underleftarrow{\text{vec\_load}}$ $m_T$ of $S_{\mathcal{F}}[store][m_B \times k']$ *//prefetching*
12         $R_{\mathcal{O}}[m_T \times n_T]$ += $R_{\mathcal{F}}[store][m_T] \times R_{\hat{\mathcal{I}}}[store][n_T]$ *//micro-kernel*
13     **if** $kk \neq C_f \times H_f \times W_f/K_{f,b} - 1$ **then**
14         $S_{\hat{\mathcal{I}}}[load][k_B \times n_B]$ $\underleftarrow{\text{load}}$ $k_B \times n_B$ of $\hat{\mathcal{I}}(kk + 1, by)$ *//prefetching*
15         $S_{\mathcal{F}}[load][m_B \times k_B]$ $\underleftarrow{\text{load}}$ $m_B \times k_B$ of $\mathcal{F}(bx, kk + 1)$ *//prefetching*
16         __syncthreads()
17     $R_{\hat{\mathcal{I}}}[0][n_T]$ $\underleftarrow{\text{vec\_load}}$ $n_T$ of $S_{\hat{\mathcal{I}}}[store][0 \times n_B]$
18     $R_{\mathcal{F}}[0][m_T]$ $\underleftarrow{\text{vec\_load}}$ $m_T$ of $S_{\mathcal{F}}[store][m_B \times 0]$
19     $R_{\mathcal{O}}[m_T \times n_T]$ += $R_{\hat{\mathcal{I}}}[1][n_T] \times R_{\hat{\mathcal{I}}}[1][n_T]$ *//micro-kernel*
20 $\mathcal{O}(bx, by)$ $\underleftarrow{\text{store}}$ $R_{\mathcal{O}}[m_T \times n_T]$

latency. Therefore we need to cache as much data as possible used for AXPY operations into shared memory and registers per block, which have much lower latency. At Line 2 - Line 4 of the algorithm, we divide the index of outputs based on the global id of the thread so that each individual thread is responsible for a separate output. This data partition is obvious, but not computationally efficient. We can use the micro-kernel technique (elaborated shortly) to partition the $M_T \times N_T$ of $\mathcal{O}$ computation tasks for each individual thread, which will increase the data reusability. We propose in the next subsection a composition of optimizations making the best use of the `im2win`-based convolution on GPU.

### 3.3 Optimizations on GPU

Inspired by the optimization techniques used in GEMM on GPU, we apply the following optimizations to Algorithm 2, including tiling, shared memory, micro-kernel, vectorized load/store, double buffer, and prefetching. Those optimizations are especially important to maximize workload and data parallelism and reduce data access latency. We present our high-performance `im2win`-based convolution on GPU as Algorithm 3.

**Tiling.** Since Algorithm 2 has a similar implicit GEMM-based convolution implementation with three nested loops of M, N and K, the indices of the input tensor can be divided into small blocks called *tiles* [21]. We tile the sizes of $\hat{\mathcal{I}}$ and $\mathcal{F}$ into sizes of $M_B \times N_B \times K_B$ at the block level and $M_T \times N_T$ at the thread level in Algorithm 3. As the basic computational unit during computation, the main effect of tiling is to improve computational performance by reducing data accesses and improving data locality. For example, the size of the tile can be adapted to match the size of the shared memory or the registers, which has substantial lower latency, to improve the data reuse and to increase cache hit rate.

**Shared Memory and Register.** The memory on a GPU device consists of four levels of hierarchy: the global memory, the shared memory, the L1&L2 caches (not programmable in CUDA) and the registers. From the global memory to the shared memory, and to the registers, the access latency decreases and the size also decreases. After tiling the input tensor and the filter tensor, we allocate registers and shared memory blocks of size $M_B \times K_B$ and size $K_B \times N_B$ (Line 1 - Line 2), and we load $\hat{\mathcal{I}}$ and $\mathcal{F}$ located in global memory into the registers and shared memory (Line 3 - Line 7) in Algorithm 3. Because each dot product operation reuses the elements of the previous loaded dot product window from the same row in the `im2win` tensor. To take advantage of this, we load the data to the share memory of each block with as many dot product windows from the same row as possible, to achieve highest possible data reusability and data locality.

**Micro-kernel.** The micro-kernel technique can be used to increase the computational intensity. Without it, one AXPY operation in the innermost for loop of our `im2win`-based convolution computes one element of $\mathcal{O}$. Micro-kernel are typically implemented as outer product multiplications of vectors. With each micro-kernel used in each thread in a block, each thread is now responsible for computing multiple elements of $\mathcal{O}$. We tile the size of the micro-kernel at $M_T \times N_T$ divided at the thread level (Line 12 - Line 19 in Algorithm 3). The micro-kernel partitions the matrix multiplication among multiple threads, reducing the number of memory accesses and improving the parallelism and computational efficiency of the AXPY operations.

**Vectorized load/store.** The vectorized load/store are techniques to improve memory access efficiency by loading or storing multiple consecutive data elements from the shared memory into registers under single instruction (SIMD), thereby improving data IO efficiency and memory throughput. Data IO and memory throughput are often the performance bottlenecks when performing convolutional computation on the GPU. Our im2win tensor data structure is stored in a consecutive physical memory, with the dot product windows of the same row arranged continuously. Because each APXY operation loads consecutive dot product windows in the micro-kernel, loading $\hat{\mathcal{I}}$ and $\mathcal{F}$ from the shared memory of a block into the registers can be done using vectorized load (Line 6 - Line 7 in Algorithm 3).

**Double Buffer and Prefetching.** The double buffer optimization refers to the use of two buffers to store the input and filter tensors for pipelined concurrent computation. In Algorithm 3, we allocate two registers at Line 1 and two shared memories at Line 2. Typically, one buffer is used for the ongoing computation and the other is for prefetching the new data used into registers (or shared memory) in the next computation. It hides the latency and overhead of loading data. When the computation is completed, the roles of the two buffers are swapped, i.e., the original buffer becomes the new load buffer and the original load buffer becomes the new computation buffer. The prefetching technique is performed on $\hat{\mathcal{I}}$ and $\mathcal{F}$ (Line 10 - Line 11 and Line 14 - Line 15 in Algorithm 3), followed by a *__syncthread()* that synchronizes the data among all the threads of a block performing prefetching. The prefetching technique allows certain amount of data (we prefetch 128 elements for the shared memory, and 8 elements for the register in our implementation) to be prefetched before the computation, thus reducing data waiting time and improving computational efficiency [11].

# 4 Experimental Results

In this section, we compare our `im2win` convolution algorithm with a naive direct convolution, PyTorch's im2col-based algorithm using cuBLAS and cuDNN's convolution implementations, present the performance results and memory usages of them, and perform an ablation study of our proposed optimization techniques.

## 4.1 Experimental Setup

**Platform.** We perform our experiments on a NVIDIA GeForce RTX 3090 GPU which has 24GB memory and is connected to an Intel Xeon Silver 4214 CPU server.

**Software.** The APIs of cuBLAS and cuDNN are pre-defined and are not available for the `im2win`-based convolution, so we implement our `im2win` convolution paradigm using CUDA 11.1. We use the tensor data structure of PyTorch 1.10.0 [2] with the single 32bit precision. We list the algorithms we compared, theirs notations, and their descriptions in Table 1.

**Table 1.** The convolution algorithms used in the experimental evaluations, the notations used in figures, and their implementation details.

| Notation | Description |
|---|---|
| im2col+cuBLAS | the im2col-based convolution in PyTorch using cuBLAS 11.2 |
| direct | a naive direct convolution implemented in CUDA 11.1 |
| cuDNN | six convolutions in PyTorch using cuDNN 8.0.1 |
| im2winGPU | our im2win-based convolution implemented in CUDA 11.1 |

**Benchmarks.** We aim to check how well our convolution paradigm performs on various convolutional layers in terms of dimensions. However, it is not persuasive if we only benchmark with one neural network model. For example, all the filters in VGG-16 [18] are $3 \times 3$, and ResNet-50 [10] contains only three different filters in sizes. Hence we select twelve state-of-the-art DNN benchmarks [6] in our evalution, including twelve unique convolution layers, Conv1-Conv12 (the parameters are shown in Table 2).

**Table 2.** Parameters of the twelve DNN benchmarks.

| NAME | INPUT | FILTER, STRIDE | OUTPUT |
|---|---|---|---|
| | $C_i \times H_i \times W_i$ | $C_o \times H_f \times W_f, s_h(s_w)$ | $C_o \times H_o \times W_o$ |
| Conv1 | $3 \times 227 \times 227$ | $96 \times 11 \times 11, 4$ | $96 \times 55 \times 55$ |
| Conv2 | $3 \times 231 \times 231$ | $96 \times 11 \times 11, 4$ | $96 \times 56 \times 56$ |
| Conv3 | $3 \times 227 \times 227$ | $64 \times 7 \times 7, 2$ | $64 \times 111 \times 111$ |
| Conv4 | $64 \times 224 \times 224$ | $64 \times 7 \times 7, 2$ | $64 \times 109 \times 109$ |
| Conv5 | $96 \times 24 \times 24$ | $256 \times 5 \times 5, 1$ | $256 \times 20 \times 20$ |
| Conv6 | $256 \times 12 \times 12$ | $512 \times 3 \times 3, 1$ | $512 \times 10 \times 10$ |
| Conv7 | $3 \times 224 \times 224$ | $64 \times 3 \times 3, 1$ | $64 \times 222 \times 222$ |
| Conv8 | $64 \times 112 \times 112$ | $128 \times 3 \times 3, 1$ | $128 \times 110 \times 110$ |
| Conv9 | $64 \times 56 \times 56$ | $64 \times 3 \times 3, 1$ | $64 \times 54 \times 54$ |
| Conv10 | $128 \times 28 \times 28$ | $128 \times 3 \times 3, 1$ | $128 \times 26 \times 26$ |
| Conv11 | $256 \times 14 \times 14$ | $256 \times 3 \times 3, 1$ | $256 \times 12 \times 12$ |
| Conv12 | $512 \times 7 \times 7$ | $512 \times 3 \times 3, 1$ | $512 \times 5 \times 5$ |

**Table 3.** The fastest algorithms selected by cuDNN automatically on twelve benchmarks.

| cuDNN ALGORITHM |
|---|
| Fastest chosen |
| *IMPLICIT_GEMM* |
| *IMPLICIT_GEMM* |
| *IMPLICIT_GEMM* |
| *IMPLICIT_GEMM* |
| *WINOGRAD* |
| *IMPLICIT_GEMM* |
| *IMPLICIT_GEMM* |
| *FFT* |
| *WINOGRAD* |
| *WINOGRAD* |
| *WINOGRAD* |
| *IMPLICIT_GEMM* |

### 4.2 Performance

In the experiments, we use the wall-clock time in the standard C++ library to measure the runtime of different algorithms. We run each algorithm 100 times and record the best runtime among 100 runs. The batch size of each benchmark input data is 128.

Figure 2 shows the TFLOPS of different convolution algorithms of twelve different DNN benchmarks respectively on GPU. cuDNN has six convolution algorithms, with the fastest automatically chosen based on the input tensor dimensions. Table 3 shows the fastest algorithm automatically chosen by cuDNN at different benchmarks. Among the twelve benchmarks, our im2win-based convolution achieves about on average 3.5 × TFLOPS than that of im2col+cuBLAS convolution, and achieves 5× to 155× TFLOPS compared with the direct convolution Our im2win-based convolution has comparable performance with the cuDNN convolutions and achieves up to 1.8 × TFLOPS (the first benchmark) than that of the fastest algorithm chosen by cuDNN. Thanks to our customized optimizations tailored for our im2win-based convolution on GPU, we demonstrate better performance than the im2col-based convolution and the direct convolution of cuDNN, and show comparable performance with the implicit GEMM-based convolution, the FFT convolution, and the Winograd convolution in cuDNN.

### 4.3 Memory Usage

Figure 3 shows the memory usages of different convolution algorithms on twelve different DNN benchmarks respectively on GPU. Note that cuDNN auto-tunes itself to use the fastest algorithms among its six convolution algorithms based on the input tensor dimensions. The figure shows that our im2win-based convolution algorithm dominantly uses less memory footprint over all twelve benchmarks compared with the im2col-based convolution in cuBLAS and the fastest convolution among the six algorithms in cuDNN. On average, our algorithm uses 23.1% less memory than cuBLAS, and uses 32.8% less memory than cuDNN. Our algorithm has slightly higher memory usage than the direct convolution. Considering that the memory of a single GPU is usually not big (even Nvidia A100 has at most 80 GB of memory), our convolution paradigm supports substantially larger tensor to be processed on a single GPU over cuBLAS and cuDNN, which is much preferable.

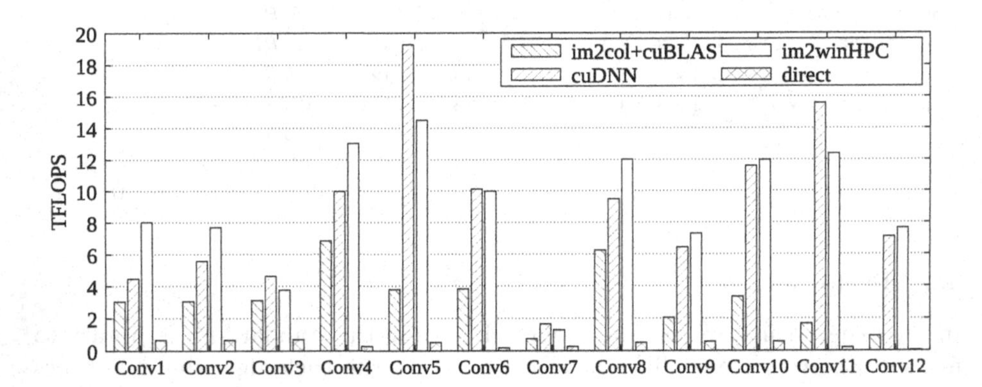


**Fig. 2.** Performance comparison of our im2win-based convolution with the direct convolution, the im2col-based convolution using cuBLAS and the convolutions in cuDNN (see Table 3).

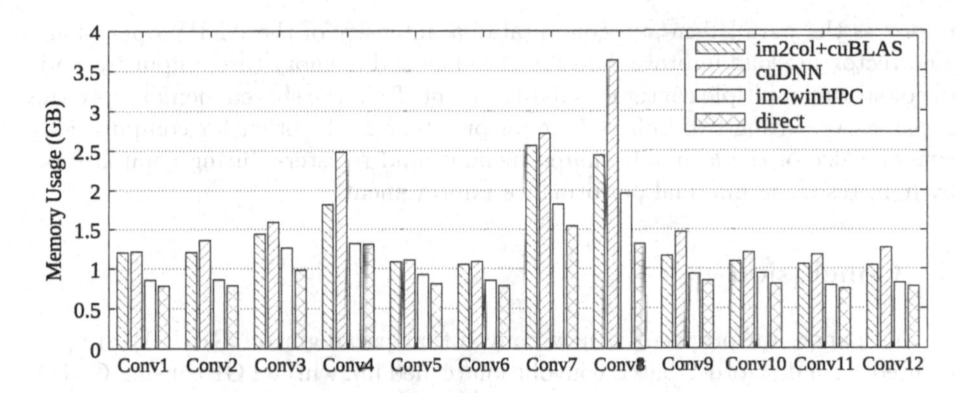


**Fig. 3.** Memory usages of our convolution compared to the direct convolution as well as PyTorch's im2col+cuBLAS convolution and cuDNN convolutions.

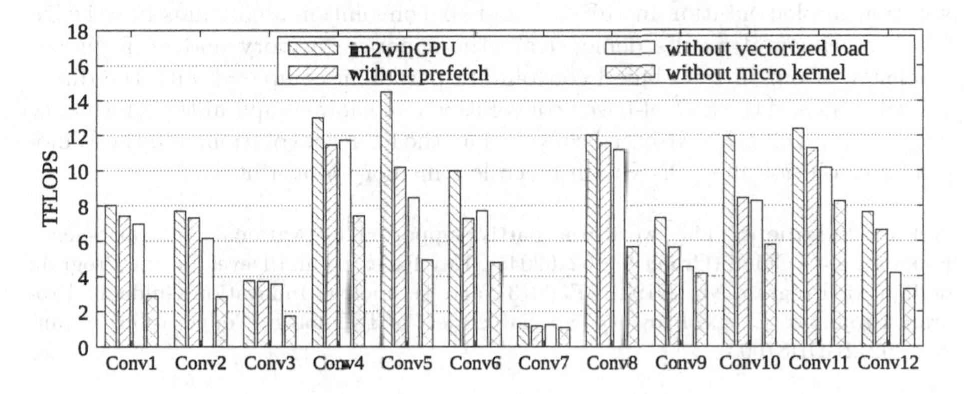


**Fig. 4.** Performance comparison of the ablation study on the prefetching, the vectorized load, and the micro-kernel optimization techniques. One technique is removed at a time.

### 4.4 Ablation Study

To explore the performance impact of the prefetching (along with double buffer), the vectorized load, and the micro-kernel techniques we apply in our kernel, we conduct an ablation study on our high-performance `im2win`-based convolution paradigm. We have im2winGPU as the baseline, which includes all the optimization techniques. For other three variants, we remove one technique at a time to study its effectiveness. Figure 4 shows the performance impact of different optimization techniques on our convolution paradigm in terms of the TFLOPS metric. Among the twelve benchmarks, the micro-kernel technique gives the greatest performance boost, followed by the vectorized load, and the prefetching gives the poorest performance boost for our paradigm.

With the micro-kernel implemented as outer product multiplications of vectors in a thread of a block, each thread computes multiple elements of the output tensor $\mathcal{O}$ instead of one. This reduces the number of memory accesses and improves the parallelism and computational intensity of the AXPY operations. The vectorized load improve data IO efficiency and memory throughput by loading or storing multiple contiguous data elements from the shared memory into the register. Allocating two buffers (one for prefetching, the other for computation) cuts the size of the available shared memory and registers during computation by half, resulting minimal performance improvement.

## 5 Conclusion

In this paper, we proposed a new convolution paradigm on GPU. We implemented a window-order-based convolution (called im2win) on GPU using CUDA along with a range of optimizations, including shared memory, tiling, micro-kernel, double buffer, and prefetching. Using twelve DNN benchmarks, we compared our algorithm with the direct convolution, PyTorch's GEMM-based convolution implementation in cuBLAS and six convolution algorithms in cuDNN. The experimental results demonstrate the superior memory and performance efficiency of our im2win-based convolution paradigm compared with the direct convolution and the im2col-based convolution and show comparable performance with the implicit GEMM-based convolution, the FFT convolution, and the Winograd convolution in cuDNN with much less memory footprint.

**Acknowledgment.** This work was partly supported by National Natural Science Foundation of China (Grant No. 62162045), Key Research and Development Program of Jiangxi (Program No. 20192BBE50073), and Technology Innovation Guidance Program Project of Jiangxi Province (Special Project of Technology Cooperation) (Grant No. 20212BDH81003).

## References

1. cuBLAS library (2023). https://docs.nvidia.com/cuda/cublas/
2. PyTorch (2023). https://github.com/pytorch/pytorch
3. Abadi, M., Barham, P., Chen, J., et al.: TensorFlow: a system for large-scale machine learning. In: Proceedings of the 12th USENIX Conference on Operating Systems Design and Implementation, OSDI 2016, pp. 265–283. USENIX Association, USA (2016)
4. Chellapilla, K., Puri, S., Simard, P.: High performance convolutional neural networks for document processing. In: 10th International Workshop on Frontiers in Handwriting Recognition (2006)
5. Chetlur, S., et al.: cuDNN: efficient primitives for deep learning. CoRR abs/1410.0759 (2014)
6. Cho, M., Brand, D.: MEC: memory-efficient convolution for deep neural network. In: International Conference on Machine Learning (ICML), pp. 815–824. PMLR (2017)
7. Crowley, E.J., Gray, G., Storkey, A.J.: Moonshine: distilling with cheap convolutions. In: Advances in Neural Information Processing Systems, vol. 31 (2018)

8. Dongarra, J., Hammarling, S., Higham, N.J., Relton, S.D., Valero-Lara, P., Zounon, M.: The design and performance of batched BLAS on modern high-performance computing systems. Procedia Comput. Sci. **108**, 495–504 (2017)
9. Gunnels, J.A., Henry, G.M., van de Geijn, R.A.: A family of high-performance matrix multiplication algorithms. In: Alexandrov, V.N., Dongarra, J.J., Juliano, B.A., Renner, R.S., Tan, C.J.K. (eds.) ICCS 2001. LNCS, vol. 2073, pp. 51–60. Springer, Heidelberg (2001). https://doi.org/10.1007/3-540-45545-0_15
10. He, K., Zhang, X., Ren, S., Sun, J.: Deep residual learning for image recognition. In: IEEE Conference on Computer Vision and Pattern Recognition (CVPR), pp. 770–778 (2016)
11. Huang, J., Yu, C.D., van de Geijn, R.A.: Implementing Strassen's algorithm with CUTLASS on NVIDIA volta GPUs. CoRR abs/1808.07984 (2018)
12. Jordà, M., Valero-Lara, P., Peña, A.J.: Performance evaluation of cuDNN convolution algorithms on NVIDIA Volta GPUs. IEEE Access **7**, 70461–70473 (2019)
13. Lavin, A., Gray, S.: Fast algorithms for convolutional neural networks. In: IEEE Conference on Computer Vision and Pattern Recognition (CVPR), pp. 4013–4021 (2016)
14. Lu, S., Chu, J., Liu, X.T.: Im2win: memory efficient convolution on SIMD architectures. In: 2022 IEEE High Performance Extreme Computing Conference (HPEC), pp. 1–7 (2022)
15. Ma, N., Zhang, X., Zheng, H.T., Sun, J.: ShuffleNet v2: practical guidelines for efficient CNN architecture design. In: Proceedings of the European conference on computer vision (ECCV), pp. 116–131 (2018)
16. Oyama, Y., Ben-Nun, T., Hoefler, T., Matsuoka, S.: Accelerating deep learning frameworks with micro-batches. In: 2018 IEEE International Conference on Cluster Computing (CLUSTER), pp. 402–412 (2018)
17. Paszke, A., Gross, S., Massa, F., et al.: PyTorch: an imperative style, high-performance deep learning library. In: Proceedings of the 33rd International Conference on Neural Information Processing Systems (NeurIPS), pp. 8024–8035 (2019)
18. Simonyan, K., Zisserman, A.: Very deep convolutional networks for large-scale image recognition. CoRR abs/1409.1556 (2015)
19. Song, Z., et al.: GPNPU: enabling efficient hardware-based direct convolution with multi-precision support in GPU tensor cores. In: 2020 57th ACM/IEEE Design Automation Conference (DAC), pp. 1–6. IEEE (2020)
20. Sze, V., Chen, Y.H., Yang, T.J., Emer, J.S.: Efficient processing of deep neural networks: a tutorial and survey. Proc. IEEE **105**(12), 2295–2329 (2017)
21. Wolfe, M.: Iteration space tiling for memory hierarchies. In: Proceedings of the Third SIAM Conference on Parallel Processing for Scientific Computing, pp. 357–361. SIAM, USA (1989)
22. Zhang, J., Franchetti, F., Low, T.M.: High performance zero-memory overhead direct convolutions. In: International Conference on Machine Learning, pp. 5776–5785. PMLR (2018)

# Accelerating Drug Discovery in AutoDock-GPU with Tensor Cores

Gabin Schieffer and Ivy Peng(✉)

KTH Royal Institute of Technology, Stockholm, Sweden
{gabins,ivybopeng}@kth.se

**Abstract.** In drug discovery, molecular docking aims at characterizing the binding of a drug-like molecule to a macromolecule. AutoDock-GPU, a state-of-the-art docking software, estimates the geometrical conformation of a docked ligand-protein complex by minimizing a scoring function. Our profiling results indicate that the current reduction operation that is heavily used in the scoring function is sub-optimal. Thus, we developed a method to accelerate the sum reduction of four-element vectors using matrix operations on NVIDIA Tensor Cores. We integrated the new reduction operation into AutoDock-GPU and evaluated it on multiple chemical complexes on three GPUs. Our results show that our method for reduction operation is 4–7 times faster than the AutoDock-GPU baseline. We also evaluated the impact of our method on the overall simulation time in the real-world docking simulation and achieved a 27% improvement on the average docking time.

**Keywords:** Molecular docking · AutoDock · GPU · Tensor Core · Drug Discovery

## 1 Introduction

The pharmacological effect of a drug is generally induced by the binding of a drug molecule to a specific protein target. Thus, characterizing the ability of binding is crucial for drug discovery. Once a target for a disease is identified, tens of millions of chemical compounds, or *ligands*, will go through high-throughput screening. For such vast search space, virtual screening that leverages computational approaches is becoming increasingly important for accelerating the process and reducing the high cost required in experimental screenings [5,12]. In particular, structure-based virtual screening software uses molecular docking tools to test a molecule drug candidate for binding a protein target (receptor). In recent COVID-19 research, high-performance virtual screening software has been used in combating the pandemic [5].

A typical molecular docking job consists of evaluating a large number of ligands, each as an independent docking task. Further distributing individual docking tasks onto high-performance computing (HPC) systems, with multi-core CPU or GPUs, can significantly accelerate docking, e.g., AutoDock-GPU reports


J. Cano et al. (Eds.): Euro-Par 2023, LNCS 14100, pp. 608–622, 2023.
https://doi.org/10.1007/978-3-031-39698-4_41

350-fold speedup over single-threaded implementation [8,12]. AutoDock is widely used in the pharmaceutical industry to characterize protein-ligand complexes. In recent efforts, AutoDock4 implements its search engine based on Lamarckian Genetic Algorithm (LGA) and is ported to GPUs. A CUDA implementation of AutoDock-GPU with enhanced workflow successfully scaled to leverage the Summit supercomputer [5].

In this work, we focus on the CUDA implementation of AutoDock-GPU as it represents the state-of-the-art of docking software on HPC systems. AutoDock-GPU predicts the geometrical conformation of a ligand-protein complex by minimizing an energy-based *scoring* function that quantifies the free energy of a given binding pose. A docking job typically have many LGA runs, each consisting of multiple iterations till reaching the max number of score evaluations or GA generations. Therefore, the scoring function is called many times, e.g., $10^6$ to $10^8$, in a docking job, dominating the runtime [12]. The scoring function parallelizes the computation of the energy and associated gradient values by distributing iterations across all threads in a block and computing the total energy in a block-level reduction operation. Our profiling results show that the current implementation of the reduction operation causes a significant proportion of the overall number of warp stalls in the local search kernel.

We propose a Tensor Core based reduction operation to accelerate the docking process – leveraging Tensor Core Units and reducing synchronization points. We designed a multi-dimensional reduction algorithm based on previous works [1,10]. Our design leverages compacted data layout in shared memory. By merging multiple matrix multiplications into a single one, we dramatically reduce the number of synchronization points. We implemented the new algorithm in CUDA using the Nvidia WMMA API and integrated it in the energy calculation function in AutoDock-GPU. We validated the implementation and then evaluated its performance in single kernel and overall docking time on three generations of NVIDIA GPUs, including T4, V100, and A100. The results show that our method consistently outperform the AutoDock-GPU baseline, achieving up to 6.7× and 4.7× speedup on A100 and V100, respectively. We summarize our contributions as follows:

- Our performance charaterization of the AutoDock-GPU identified the scalability bottleneck in reduction operation in scoring function
- We proposed a multi-dimension reduction operation leveraging the mixed-precision Tensor Core Units
- We provided an implementation in CUDA using WMMA API in AutoDock-GPU and validated the implementation
- We evaluated the performance within single kernel on three GPUs and achieved 4.1–6.7× speedup, and a 27% improvement on average docking time

## 2 Background

In this section, we introduce the computation method in molecular docking and the GPU implementation of AutoDock-GPU. We also introduce Tensor Core Unit and its programming interfaces on NVIDIA GPUs.

## 2.1 Computational Method in AutoDock-GPU

AutoDock [9] variants, e.g., AutoDock-Vina, AutoDock4, and AutoDock-GPU, use an energy-based scoring function to measure the quality of a given binding pose. The scoring function is a free-energy force field. It captures contributions from various physical interactions between atom pairs to associate an energy value to a ligand-receptor conformation. Recent development [12] introduces different search algorithms, such as the Solis-Wets and the ADADELTA methods, to accelerate the docking.

In the docking method in AutoDock-GPU, the target molecule is fixed. Thus, the ligand-receptor complex can be fully described by a set of variables related to the position, rotation, and internal conformation of the ligand. This set of variables, referred as *ligand pose* or *genotype*, is composed of seven dimensions, i.e., $x, y, z$ representing the ligand's position in space, $\phi, \theta, \alpha$ characterizing the rotation of the ligand, and $N_{rot}$ dimensions characterizing the torsion angles of rotatable bonds in the ligand by $\psi_1 \ldots \psi_{N_{rot}}$. These variables are the input to the scoring function.

AutoDock-GPU uses a parallelized version of the original LGA [12]. The LGA uses a genetic algorithm (GA) to perform a global search, which generates several genotypes (denoted as $\Omega$). Each genotype is then improved by a local search algorithm (LS) that minimizes the scoring function (free energy). Two commonly used local search algorithms are ADADELTA and Solis-Wets. ADADELTA [17] is a gradient-based optimization algorithm. It updates the genotype $\Omega$ at each iteration $t$ by $\Omega_{t+1} = \Omega_t + \eta_t g_t$, where $\eta_t$ depends on the history of previous update and gradient values, and $g_t$ is the gradient of the scoring function at the point $\Omega_t$. The computational cost of this method is dominated by the gradient calculation. AutoDock-GPU parallelizes computation of the energy value by distributing iterations across all threads in a block. Each thread computes a partial value of the total energy and a block-level reduction is used to compute the total energy value. Similarly, each thread computes a partial value of the gradient for each of the three geometrical dimensions $x, y, z$, as well as the torque generated by physical interactions on the ligand, which is required for the calculation of the rotation-related and torsion-related gradient values. In total, seven block-level reductions are required for each evaluation of the scoring function, during the local-search optimization process.

## 2.2 NVIDIA Tensor Cores

NVIDIA Tensor Cores were introduced in the Volta GPU microarchitecture, providing tremendous computing power in reduced precision [6]. NVIDIA V100 features 640 first-generation Tensor Cores and a theoretical peak performance of 125 Tflops/s in mixed precision. The Turing architecture extended Tensor Cores abilities by adding support for computation using more data types. The Tesla T4 offers 320 Tensor Cores, and provides a theoretical peak performance of 65 Tflops/s. In the Ampere architecture, the A100 GPU features 432 Tensor Cores, and provides a theoretical peak performance of 312 Tflops/s.

Tensor Core Units (TCU) are designed to perform matrix multiply-and-accumulate operations (i.e., $V \leftarrow A \cdot B + V$) in high throughput, while enforcing constraints on matrix sizes and precision. The operands of the multiplication operation must be of size $16 \times 16$ and contain half-precision elements [11]. The accumulator can use single-precision float representation.

Tensor Core operations use the *half-precision* data type, which relies on a 16-bit binary representation. This level of precision is generally sufficient for deep learning workloads, and scientific workloads resilient to precision loss can also benefit from it. However, the *half-precision* data type requires explicit conversion to the single-precision 32-bit float representation. Starting with the Ampere GPU architecture, NVIDIA added support for both *bfloat16* and *tf32* in Tensor Cores. While double-precision data type is also supported on Tensor Cores from the Ampere GPU architecture, the matrix size in this precision is limited to $8 \times 4$ for the multiplication operands, and $8 \times 8$ for the accumulator.

The WMMA API (*Warp Matrix Multiply-and-Add*) provides a limited set of functions for developers to use Tensor Cores. Codes using this API are portable across different NVIDIA GPU architecture. This API exposes functions to set up and perform multiply-and-accumulate operations on Tensor Cores. It defines a data structure named *fragment*. A fragment is an abstraction to represent a matrix. Each fragment holds the matrix metadata, i.e., the data type, the matrix size, and the type of matrix as either an operand or an accumulator. The actual matrix elements held by a fragment are spread across threads in the warp, this data-to-threads mapping is not known by the developer [1]. Instead, the WMMA API provides basic load and store functions to map generic CUDA data structures, such as arrays, to fragments. A multiply-and-accumulate operation is exposed as a function operating on fragments and requires the collaboration of all threads in a warp.

## 3 Performance Characterization on GPU

In this section, we first provide an overview of the runtime breakdown of a simulation and then focus on the GPU computation. We used the `7cpa` protein-ligand complex and ran with a block size of 64 threads on NVIDIA A100 GPU, using all default parameters. The profiling results were obtained with NVIDIA Nsight Systems. At high level, the runtime of a simulation is dominated by the docking time, which is GPU bound, and then I/O pre-processing [7]. In Fig. 1, NVIDIA Nsight Systems reports 90% time spent in docking.

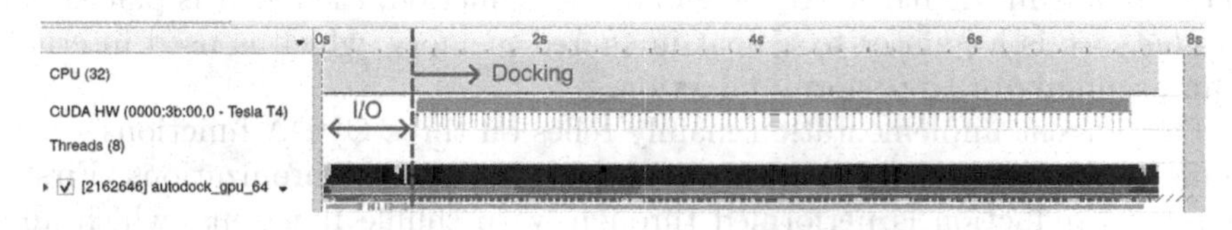


**Fig. 1.** Profiling results of a docking process of the `7cpa` protein-ligand complex.

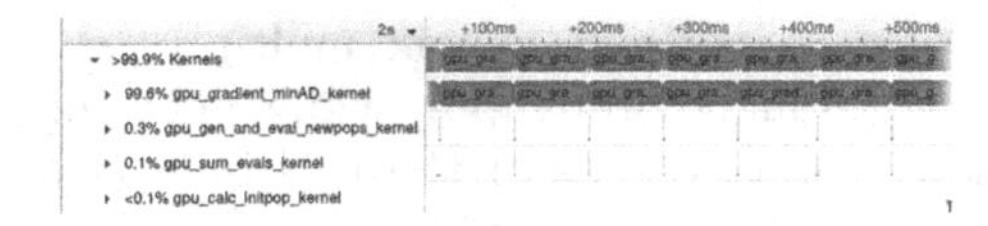


**Fig. 2.** The kernel launch timeline for iterations of the optimization process.

**Table 1.** Time breakdown in CUDA kernels

| kernel name | % of total kernel runtime |
|---|---|
| gpu_calc_initprop_kernel | <0.1% |
| gpu_sum_evals_kernel | 0.1% |
| gpu_gen_and_eval_newpops_kernel | 0.3% |
| gpu_gradient_minAD_kernel | 99.6% |

| # | Source | Live Registers | Warp Stall Sampling (All Cycles) | Warp Stall Sampling (Not-Issued Cycles) | Instructions Executed |
|---|---|---|---|---|---|
| 730 | REDUCEFLOATSUM(torque_rot.x, pFloatAccumulator); | 37 | 56,731 | 44,951 | 20,402,426 |
| 731 | REDUCEFLOATSUM(torque_rot.y, pFloatAccumulator); | 36 | 57,131 | 45,490 | 20,400,606 |
| 732 | REDUCEFLOATSUM(torque_rot.z, pFloatAccumulator); | 36 | 60,279 | 48,058 | 20,399,346 |
| 739 | REDUCEFLOATSUM(energy, pFloatAccumulator); | 36 | 57,268 | 45,362 | 20,401,641 |

**Fig. 3.** Profiling results of the gpu_gradient_minAD_kernel kernel.

In the docking process, the runtime is dominated by the local-search kernel, gpu_gradient_minAD. As shown in Fig. 2, the gradient-based local search dominates the docking time on GPU, i.e., 99.6% kernel time is spent in the gpu_gradient_minAD kernel (the details are described in [12]). The breakdown of GPU kernel runtime is reported in Table 1. In this kernel, seven reduction operations are performed to compute the value and gradient of the scoring function, which happens at every iteration of the gradient-descent algorithm. This reduction operation is defined as a C++ macro named REDUCEFLOATSUM (denoted as *ReduceFS* in the remainder of this paper).

We observe a large number of warp stalls in each execution of *ReduceFS* in Fig. 3, which reports four consecutive calls of *ReduceFS* macro. Moreover, these lines of code are identified among the top ten lines of code causing high numbers of warp stalls, indicating that the stalls could have a high impact on overall kernel performance. From the causes for these warp stalls returned by NVIDIA Nsight Compute, we observe that approximately 40% of warp stalls are caused by memory barriers ("membar"), related to the use of memory fence operations. Also, about 25% of warp stalls are caused by "short scoreboard", which is often caused by shared memory instruction latency.

The profiling results led us to investigate further the block-level reduction in AutoDock-GPU. We established that REDUCEFLOATSUM(value, acc) performs a block-level reduce-and-broadcast operation. Each thread provides one single-precision number *value*, which will be reduced with all other values for other threads in the block. At the end of the reduction, the result is placed back in *value*. *acc* is a pointer to a float in shared memory, which is used internally as an accumulator to perform reduction.

The current implementation mainly relies on three CUDA functions – warp shuffle functions, atomic operations, and block-level synchronizations. First, a warp-level reduction is performed through warp shuffle functions, which allow data exchange between threads within a warp without using shared memory. In particular, the __shfl_sync function allows a thread to read a value from another thread within the same warp, in a synchronized fashion.

In the warp-level reduction algorithm, this function is called multiple times by each thread. At each call, each thread adds the value received from another thread into its local copy. By organizing communication in a tree-like pattern, five consecutive calls to __shfl_sync are sufficient for each thread to have its own local copy of the total sum across all 32 threads (a warp). This warp-level reduction algorithm is state-of-the-art [1].

After the warp-level reduction is completed, the first thread of each warp performs an atomic add of the result to a shared memory accumulator. Finally, each thread in a thread block performs a read from the accumulator in shared memory to receive the reduction result, finishing the whole operation.

*Takeaway 1: Atomic operations are used for value accumulation, and could cause contention when a large number of warps is used.*

As described in Sect. 2, the scoring function implementation needs to perform reduction over seven dimensions – one for the global energy value, three for the gradient calculation, and three for the torque calculation. In the current AutoDock-GPU version, this is implemented by sequentially calling the *ReduceFS* macro seven times in the scoring function kernel.

*Takeaway 2: each evaluation of the scoring function repeats the block-level reduction operation seven times sequentially.*

For each use of *ReduceFS*, three explicit block-level thread synchronizations are performed, which results in a total of 21 synchronizations for the seven-dimensional reduction. This could drastically reduce the parallelism of the algorithm.

*Takeaway 3: Performing reduction operation on seven dimensions separately results in 21 block-level synchronizations, a potential bottleneck for scalability.*

## 4 Methodology

In this work, we leverage Tensor Core Units (TCU) to accelerate matrix-based reduction. In [1], scan and reduction operations on an array are expressed as matrix operations and accelerated on NVIDIA Tensor Cores. This method relies on placing the elements to be reduced in a matrix, which is then multiplied by a well-chosen matrix to perform summation on the rows. A similar operation is then applied to perform summation on the columns. This line-then-column summation process effectively sum up all elements, equivalent to performing a reduction operation.

We propose an approach to replace the reduction operation in AutoDock-GPU by an implementation of a reduction method which is able to leverage Tensor Core Units. We first list the requirements that our method must meet to be used in AutoDock-GPU code. Then, we describe how we adapt and optimize the general Tensor Core-based reduction operation to meet the specific requirements in AutoDock-GPU. It is worth noting here that even though the method and implementation proposed in this paper are tailored to a specific application, the performed operation is general. Therefore, our approach can be generalized to other applications, with reasonable adaptation efforts.

### 4.1 Requirements and Design Choices

The scoring function in AutoDock-GPU performs seven consecutive reductions, each time for one variable. Previous TCU-based reduction method only reduces one variable at a time. To improve the efficiency, we propose to merge the reduction operations of four variables. This change would bring two main benefits. First, the profiling results show that a single reduction operation inherently requires synchronization between threads. Thus, merging four reductions would ideally reduce the synchronization cost by four times, improving parallelism. Second, we can improve the efficiency of data movement by reducing the number of separate data transfers. As introduced in Sect. 2.2, data arrays needs to be transferred (and mapped) from shared memory to be used on TCUs. By transforming the data layout into one contiguous data layout in shared memory, this overhead can be reduced.

The mapping between matrix elements and thread registers is not consistent across different GPU architectures. For this reason, NVIDIA recommends using the exposed API functions, i.e., load_matrix_sync() to load matrices data. When this function is called, each thread copies a portion of shared memory array to its registers. The matrix data is hence spread across all threads in the warp. This process may be sub-optimal in applications where matrices elements are already initially stored in registers, since those elements would first need to be copied to shared memory and then loaded to registers while they only need to be read back from registers. For this reason, previous work [3] has reverse-engineered the memory mapping between matrix elements and corresponding thread registers. Previous TCU-based reduction method [1] chose to use this knowledge to manipulate matrix data directly in registers.

In AutoDock-GPU, matrix elements are initially stored in each thread's registers. Thus, the reverse engineered memory mapping technique could squeeze more performance. However, this technique also requires specific tuning for each architecture. Therefore, for portability across different GPUs, we chose to use the NVIDIA-recommended approach.

### 4.2 Matrix-Based Multi-dimensional Reduction Method

We design a method using matrix operations to perform sum reduction of a set of four-element vectors. Our method aims at computing the sum of $n$ four-element vectors $\boldsymbol{u_i} = (x_i, y_i, z_i, e_i)$. The result is also a four-element vector, which contains on each of its coordinates the sum for each corresponding dimension, i.e., $\boldsymbol{y_i} = (\sum_i x_i, \sum_i y_i, \sum_i z_i, \sum_i e_i)$. We represent our input data as a $16 \times 16$ matrix $A$, containing coordinates of the first 64 vectors, organized in a column-major fashion. We also declare two $16 \times 16$ matrices – $P$ and $Q$. $P$ is a matrix filled with ones. $Q$ is a block-matrix composed of $4 \times 4$ blocks, each being the $4 \times 4$ identity matrix $I_4$.

$$A = \begin{pmatrix} x_0 \; x_4 \ldots x_{60} \\ y_0 \; y_4 \ldots y_{60} \\ z_0 \; z_4 \ldots z_{60} \\ e_0 \; e_4 \ldots e_{60} \\ \vdots \;\; \vdots \;\;\;\; \vdots \end{pmatrix} \qquad P = \begin{pmatrix} 1 \ldots 1 \\ \vdots \ddots \vdots \\ 1 \ldots 1 \end{pmatrix} \qquad Q = \begin{pmatrix} I_4 \; I_4 \; I_4 \; I_4 \\ I_4 \; I_4 \; I_4 \; I_4 \\ I_4 \; I_4 \; I_4 \; I_4 \\ I_4 \; I_4 \; I_4 \; I_4 \end{pmatrix}$$

We first compute the matrix product $AP$ into $V$. This operation effectively performs summation on the rows. If more than 64 vectors need to be reduced, we iterate the same operation, each time with $A$ containing elements for a new set of 64 vectors in the input dataset and accumulating the results into $V$. We then perform sum on every $4^{th}$ column in $V$ with the matrix operation $QV$ and save the result into $W$. At this point, the matrix $W$ contains the desired result as the four first elements on the first column.

$$V \leftarrow AP = \begin{pmatrix} \sum x_{4i} & \sum x_{4i} & \ldots & \sum x_{4i} \\ \sum y_{4i} & \sum y_{4i} & \ldots & \sum y_{4i} \\ \sum z_{4i} & \sum z_{4i} & \ldots & \sum z_{4i} \\ \sum e_{4i} & \sum e_{4i} & \ldots & \sum e_{4i} \\ \sum x_{4i+1} & \sum x_{4i+1} & \ldots & \sum x_{4i+1} \\ \sum y_{4i+1} & \sum y_{4i+1} & \ldots & \sum y_{4i+1} \\ \sum z_{4i+1} & \sum z_{4i+1} & \ldots & \sum z_{4i+1} \\ \sum e_{4i+1} & \sum e_{4i+1} & \ldots & \sum e_{4i+1} \\ \vdots & \vdots & \vdots & \vdots \end{pmatrix} \qquad \begin{matrix} V \leftarrow AP + V \\ \\ W \leftarrow QV \\ \\ W = \begin{pmatrix} \sum x_i & \sum x_i & \ldots & \sum x_i \\ \sum y_i & \sum y_i & \ldots & \sum y_i \\ \sum z_i & \sum z_i & \ldots & \sum z_i \\ \sum e_i & \sum e_i & \ldots & \sum e_i \\ \vdots & \vdots & \vdots & \vdots \end{pmatrix} \end{matrix}$$

We implement our method as a CUDA __device__ function using the NVIDIA WMMA API to perform matrix operations. This function replaces four sequential uses of the *ReduceFS* macro in the energy-and-gradient calculation in AutoDock-GPU. The four elements to be reduced for each thread are first converted from float to half-precision using the CUDA half2float function, and then loaded into a contiguous data array in shared memory. The data loading is collectively performed by all threads in a block.

The accumulator $V$ is a product of matrices $A$ and $P$. Meanwhile, it is also an operand for the matrix multiplication calculating $W$. Then, in order to compute $W$ using TCUs, $V$ must be half-precision. Using single precision for accumulation in $V$ would require to convert it to half-precision before computing $W$, a casting back to single precision would then be necessary. This approach requires two non-trivial conversions between two levels of precision. Instead, we choose to use half-precision for both operations.

In our implementation, two block-level synchronizations are needed in total. A first one is performed before the first WMMA API call, to ensure that values for all threads are available in shared memory before starting the reduction process. The second synchronization is performed after the last WMMA API call, to ensure that all threads in the block can read the results. Compared to the 21 synchronizations in original AutoDock-GPU, our method significantly reduces synchronization points.

Our implementation requires no memory barriers and atomic operations, unlike the current AutoDock-GPU method. Note that those operations are responsible for a significant number of stalls (Sect. 3). In addition, the decreased amount of those contention-causing operations could improve scalability.

# 5 Evaluation

We evaluated our implementation on four testbeds, featuring three GPU architectures, i.e., T4, V100, and A100. We summarize their system specifications in Table 2. Docking experiments were performed using five protein-ligand complexes, referred by their four-character Protein Data Bank identifier. We used the following complexes: `1stp`, `7cpa`, `1ac8`, `3tmn`, `3ce3`. Those five complexes, which are real-world samples, are provided with AutoDock-GPU code as test samples. Three of them were chosen for their particular molecular characteristics, in order to validate various aspects of the docking implementation, in particular the gradient calculation.

## 5.1 Validation of the Scoring Function

Our first step is to validate the TCU-based implementation in AutoDock-GPU scoring function. For this, we leverage similar metrics defined in [12] to evaluate the correctness in LGA run and overall simulations. In particular, we compare simulation results to the baseline results to quantify the precision loss introduced by the half-precision operations on TCU.

Figure 4 presents box-and-whisker plots for the best energy value reached by the scoring function, as reported by AutoDock-GPU. As the initialization process is random, we repeat 1000 runs for each protein-ligand complexes to increase the statistical significance as in [12]. For each run, the pseudo-random number generator is initialized with the same arbitrary seed for both our code, and the original code.

Table 3 reports the absolute and relative errors in the energy value from our method and the AutoDock-GPU baseline. For both `1ac8` and `3tmn`, the best energy values show no significant variance between runs for both implementations. For `1stp`, `7cpa`, and `3ce3`, the statistical distribution produced by our code is similar to the one produced by the original code. We notice that for all tested complexes, the relative difference between the average best scores for each method is below 0.18%. This observation leads us to conclude that our method provides satisfactory results, and thus validates our approach to perform reduction in the context of AutoDock-GPU. The justification for this conclusion is two-fold. First, the result of the reduction process is used as the energy value,

**Table 2.** A summary of four testbeds used for evaluation

| Testbed | GPU | CPU | Interconnect | GPU Memory | CPU Memory |
|---|---|---|---|---|---|
| TB1 | NVIDIA Tesla T4 | 16 core Intel(R) Xeon(R) Gold | PCIe | 16 GB RAM | 576 GB DDR4 |
| TB2 | NVIDIA Tesla V100 SXM2 | 8 core Intel(R) Xeon(R) Gold | NVLink | 32 GB HBM2 | 768 GB DDR4 |
| TB3 | NVIDIA Tesla V100 SXM2 | 16 core Intel(R) Xeon(R) Gold | NVLink | 32 GB HBM2 | 768 GB DDR4 |
| TB4 | NVIDIA Tesla A100 | 32 core Intel(R) Xeon(R) Gold | NVLink | 40 GB HBM2 | 576 GB DDR4 |

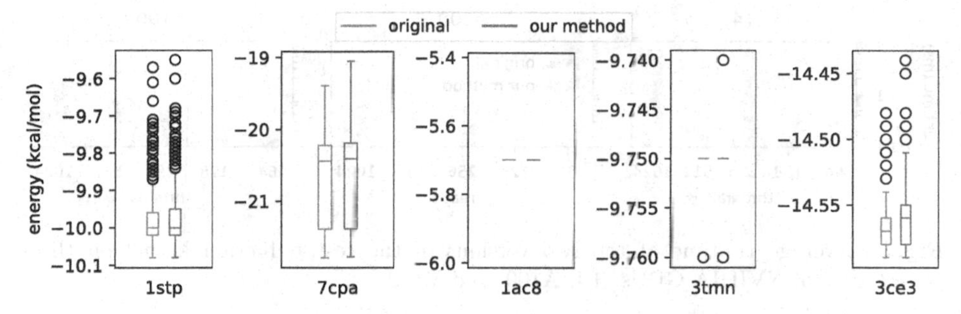


**Fig. 4.** Distribution of average best energy values for five protein-ligand complexes using the original code, and our method.

**Table 3.** Absolute difference and relative error in the best energy values and the speedup by our method compared with the baseline.

| Complex | 1stp | 7cpa | 1ac8 | 3tmn | 3ce3 |
|---|---|---|---|---|---|
| $\lvert E_{half} - E_{ref} \rvert$ | $2.00 \cdot 10^{-5}$ | $3.72 \cdot 10^{-2}$ | 0.0 | $1.92 \cdot 10^{-3}$ | $5.78 \cdot 10^{-3}$ |
| Relative Error | <0.01% | 0.2% | 0.00% | 0.02% | 0.04% |
| Speedup | ×1.16 | ×1.08 | ×1.22 | ×1.27 | ×1.20 |

thus a low difference with the reference value shows that our implementation provides a satisfactory level of accuracy for the application. Moreover, the result of the reduction process is used in further computations. Any detrimental error would thus accumulate, and the local-search algorithm would not yield satisfactory results, which is not the case in our tests.

### 5.2 Runtime Per Evaluation of the Scoring Function

Next, we evaluate the performance of a single evaluation function. To isolate the reduction process from the energy scoring function, we design a test kernel, where each thread in a block holds a single vector of four single-precision elements. The kernel performs a block-level reduce-and-broadcast operation over all threads. After the reduction operation, the final result is accessible by each thread in their respective local memory. We design two versions of the test kernel.

The first version uses the original AutoDock-GPU code. It first performs a warp-level reduction using warp shuffle functions, which allows to exchange data between threads without using shared memory. A block-level reduction is then performed, where the first thread of each warp adds the value it holds to a shared-memory accumulator, using an atomic operation. The value of the accumulator is then read back by all threads in the block. This three-step process is repeated for each variable that needs to be reduced. The second version of the test kernel uses our TCU-based method.

We measure the elapsed walltime for 1000 launches of each version using the CUDA Runtime API and report the average time. The only parameter

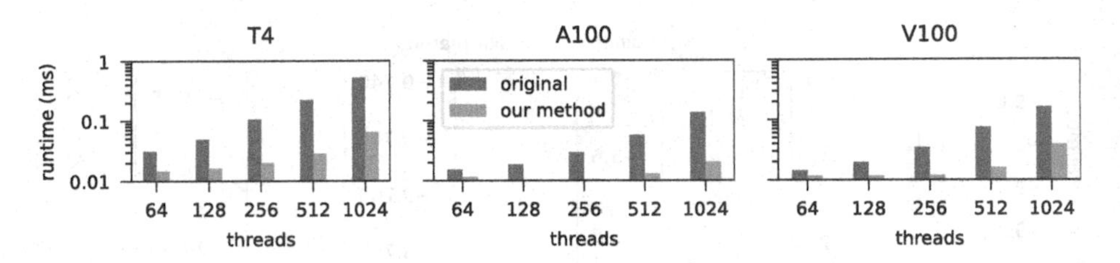


**Fig. 5.** Average runtime of the two versions of the test reduction kernel on three generations of NVIDIA GPUs: T4, A100, and V100.

influencing the runtime in both versions is the number of threads per block. 64 threads is the lower limit defined by our method – a 256-element matrix is used to store the values to be reduced, and each threads holds exactly four values, which results in a minimum of 64 threads to fill a single matrix. Future adaptation of the code may overcome this limitation. The upper limit of 1024 is defined by the CUDA platform [11].

Figure 5 shows the average runtime for both versions. The results show that our method consistently performs better than the AutoDock baseline for all block sizes and on all GPUs. This first observation validates the potential of our approach to perform faster block-level reduction in the context of the energy scoring function of AutoDock-GPU.

We notice that performance for both methods is significantly lower on T4 GPU than on A100 and V100. The lower performance for T4 can be explained by the lower performance Tensor Cores on T4. Performance on A100 and V100 are very similar utill the block size of 1024 threads. When using 1024 threads per block, a significant runtime difference is shown on the two GPUs – the runtime on A100 is 20 ms, which is half of the 39 ms runtime for V100. Our profiling results from NVIDIA Nsight Compute show that the test kernel achieved 100% occupancy on A100 but only 50% on V100. This low occupancy causes the device to be under-utilized. Such low theoretical occupancy indicates that the number of active threads per Streaming Multiprocessor is under the maximum achievable value because the resource requirements for the kernel are too high to be accommodated by the device. This could be, for example, the amount of available shared memory.

We evaluate the scalability of our method at increased threads per block. Figure 6 presents the speedup by our reduction method over the baseline on three GPU architectures. Figure 7 compares the execution times of local search kernel launches during a docking run, using our reduction method or the original method. We observe an increased speedup at an increased number of threads. For instance, the speedup increases from 2× at a block size of 64 on T4 to the maximum of 8.1× on 1024 threads. Overall, the speedup by our method increases linearly with the block size, up to 512 threads per block for all GPUs.

One interesting observation is that at the maximum block size of 1024 threads, the speedup on A100 increases to a maximum of 6.7× while the speedup on V100 decreases to 4.1×. Before reaching the maximum block size, speedup

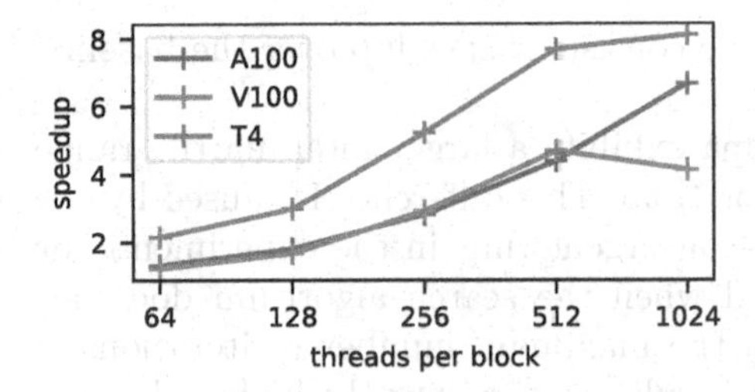


Fig. 6. Speedup of the reduction operation using our method over the AutoDock baseline on three GPUs.

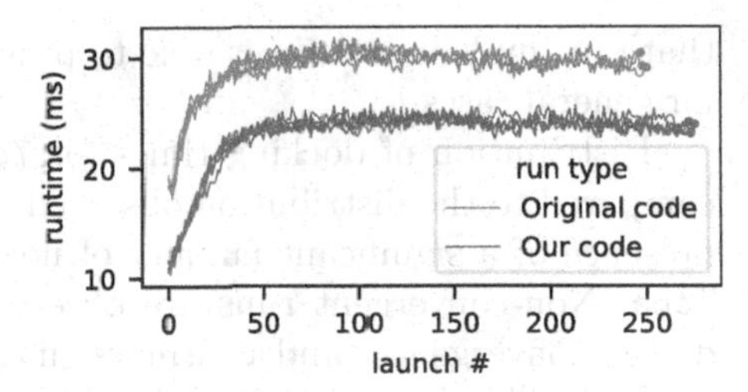


Fig. 7. Runtime of the local-search kernel, using our TCU-based method and AutoDock-GPU baseline.

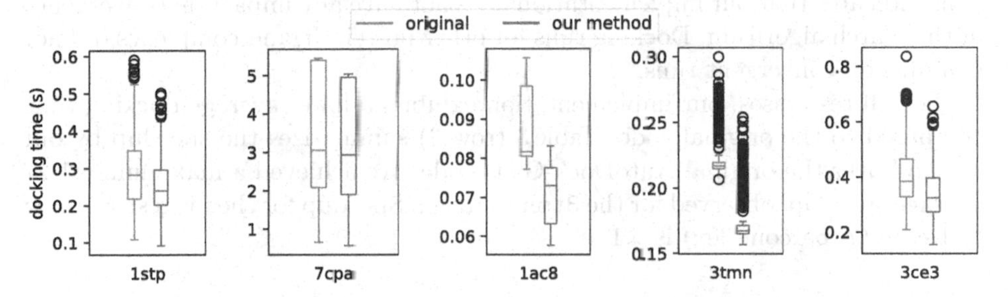


Fig. 8. Docking time on A100 for several protein-ligand complexes, using both the original code and our method.

on A100 and V100 GPUs show similar linear scalability. We investigate this and found from the runtime measurements that the amount of shared memory required when using 1024 threads per block exceeds the hardware limit on V100 GPU, thus resulting in a lower occupancy. Since the original method does not rely on shared memory, this bottleneck only affects our TCU-based method.

## 5.3 Impact on the Docking Time

We evaluate the contribution of our method on the overall simulation. For this, we integrated our block-level reduction method into the scoring function kernel in AutoDock-GPU. We use the docking time, a widely used figure of metric (FoM) in works on AutoDock-GPU [12,13]. The docking time is reported by AutoDock-GPU, including all docking executions and excluding the I/O operations.

Figure 8 shows the distribution of docking times for five protein-ligand complexes. Note that the docking time is significantly affected by the initial state, which is randomly chosen in AutoDock-GPU. Thus, for a fair comparison, we set the same random initialization seed for both methods. We also gather a large number of samples (1000 runs) to ensure statistical significance of the measurement. We observe that our method achieves a lower median, min, max, 25%, and 75% percentile docking time compared to the original version. This indicates that our implementation is able to provide consistent speedup over the baseline for general cases.

Distribution of docking times for 7cpa exhibits a larger interquartile range compared to the distribution observed for 1stp. This difference is caused by the presence of a significant number of non-convergent runs in the experiments for 7cpa. Non-convergent runs are observed when the search algorithm does not detect convergence, and continues until the maximum number of iterations is reached. This increased iteration count results in significantly higher docking time values for non-convergent runs when compared to convergent ones, for which the search algorithm is stopped earlier. We measured the proportion of non-convergent runs to be 61% for both versions, when using the 7cpa complex. This indicates that our implementation does not have any impact on convergence of the search algorithm. Docking runs for other protein-ligand complexes did not exhibit non-convergent runs.

For all test cases, our implementation exhibits a lower average docking time compared to the original code. Table 3 (row 3) summarizes the speedup by our method over the original AutoDock-GPU code. We achieved a maximum $\times 1.27$ average speedup, observed for the 3tmn complex. Speedup for the longest-running test case (7cpa complex) is $\times 1.08$.

## 6 Related Works

Molecular docking methods are widely used in drug discovery [4,9,14]. Various search techniques are used to find the best conformation between molecules [4], they rely on scoring functions that aim at evaluating the quality of a specific conformation [14]. AutoDock is a molecular docking program that relies on a genetic algorithm to find the docking conformation by minimizing a energy-based scoring function [9].

Several works have been conducted to accelerate the original AutoDock code. AutoDock Vina improved AutoDock's local-search method, and made use of multicore and multi-CPU systems to improve performance [16]. AutoDock-GPU added GPU acceleration to AutoDock by adapting the local-search method. Both OpenCL and CUDA versions have been developed. It provided up to a $\times 50$ speedup [12]. The recent addition of early stopping to AutoDock-GPU search algorithm allowed to further increase performance [13]. Once adapted for the Summit supercomputer, the CUDA version of AutoDock-GPU allowed to reach a $10\times$ speedup in a real-world docking pipeline [5]. Our work proposes a method to increase performance of the CUDA implementation of AutoDock-GPU, by using half-precision number representation in specific portions of the code.

Despite Tensor Cores being specialized in performing operations on small-size matrices, especially for deep learning applications, efforts have been made to make use of this hardware feature to accelerate other applications. For this purpose, algorithms to perform various widely-used operations on Tensor Cores have been developed, such as reduction and scan algorithms [1,10]. In our work, we adapted those methods in order to use them in AutoDock-GPU. Extensive study of Tensor Cores characteristics have also been conducted. Benchmarking allowed to evaluate Tensor Cores performances in details [15]. The impact of using half-precision numbers for computation using Tensor Cores, and the associated accuracy loss, have also been documented and precision-refinement techniques have been developed [2,6].

## 7 Conclusions

In this work, we investigate a state-of-the-art GPU-accelerated molecular docking software for drug discovery – AutoDock-GPU. Our profiling results identified a core reduction operation to be sub-optimal due to a large number of synchronization points. We analyzed the specific requirements in the docking process and propose a matrix-based multi-dimensional reduction algorithm for accelerating the local search in AutoDock-GPU. We implemented our method by leveraging NVIDIA Tensor Cores and integrated it in AutoDock-GPU code. We validated our implementation and evaluated its performance on three GPUs. The results show a 4–7× speedup of the reduction operation and a 27% improvement on the average docking time for a real-world docking scenario.

**Acknowledgments.** This research is supported by the European Commission under the Horizon project OpenCUBE (GA-101092984).

## References

1. Dakkak, A., Li, C., Xiong, J., Gelado, I., Hwu, W.M.: Accelerating reduction and scan using tensor core units. In: Proceedings of the ACM International Conference on Supercomputing, ICS 2019, pp. 46–57. Association for Computing Machinery, New York (2019). https://doi.org/10.1145/3330345.3331057
2. Haidar, A., Tomov, S., Dongarra, J., Higham, N.J.: Harnessing GPU tensor cores for fast FP16 arithmetic to speed up mixed-precision iterative refinement solvers. In: SC18: International Conference for High Performance Computing, Networking, Storage and Analysis, pp. 603–613. IEEE (2018)
3. Jia, Z., Maggioni, M., Staiger, B., Scarpazza, D.P.: Dissecting the NVIDIA volta GPU architecture via microbenchmarking (2018)
4. Kitchen, D.B., Decornez, H., Furr, J.R., Bajorath, J.: Docking and scoring in virtual screening for drug discovery: methods and applications. Nat. Rev. Drug Discov. **3**(11), 935–949 (2004)
5. LeGrand, S., et al.: GPU-accelerated drug discovery with docking on the summit supercomputer: porting, optimization, and application to COVID-19 research. In: Proceedings of the 11th ACM International Conference on Bioinformatics, Computational Biology and Health Informatics, BCB 2020, ACM (2020)
6. Markidis, S., Chien, S.W.D., Laure, E., Peng, I.B., Vetter, J.S.: NVIDIA tensor core programmability, performance & precision. In: IEEE International Parallel and Distributed Processing Symposium Workshops (IPDPSW), pp. 522–531 (2018)
7. Markidis, S., Gadioli, D., Vitali, E., Palermo, G.: Understanding the I/O impact on the performance of high-throughput molecular docking. In: 2021 IEEE/ACM Sixth International Parallel Data Systems Workshop (PDSW), pp. 9–14. IEEE (2021)

8. Mermelstein, D.J., Lin, C., Nelson, G., Kretsch, R., McCammon, J.A., Walker, R.C.: Fast and flexible GPU accelerated binding free energy calculations within the amber molecular dynamics package (2018)
9. Morris, G.M., et al.: Automated docking using a Lamarckian genetic algorithm and an empirical binding free energy function. J. Comput. Chem. **19**(14), 1639–1662 (1998)
10. Navarro, C.A., Carrasco, R., Barrientos, R.J., Riquelme, J.A., Vega, R.: GPU tensor cores for fast arithmetic reductions. IEEE Trans. Parallel Distrib. Syst. **32**(1), 72–84 (2021)
11. NVIDIA: CUDA C programming guide. https://docs.nvidia.com/cuda/cuda-c-programming-guide/element-types-and-matrix-sizes
12. Santos-Martins, D., Solis-Vasquez, L., Tillack, A.F., Sanner, M.F., Koch, A., Forli, S.: Accelerating AutoDock4 with GPUs and gradient-based local search. J. Chem. Theory Comput. **17**(2), 1060–1073 (2021)
13. Solis-Vasquez, L., Tillack, A.F., Santos-Martins, D., Koch, A., LeGrand, S., Forli, S.: Benchmarking the performance of irregular computations in AutoDock-GPU molecular docking. Parallel Comput. **109**, 102861 (2022)
14. Stanzione, F., Giangreco, I., Cole, J.C.: Use of molecular docking computational tools in drug discovery. Progr. Med. Chem. **60**, 273–343 (2021). https://doi.org/10.1016/bs.pmch.2021.01.004
15. Sun, W., Li, A., Geng, T., Stuijk, S., Corporaal, H.: Dissecting tensor cores via microbenchmarks: latency, throughput and numeric behaviors. IEEE Trans. Parallel Distrib. Syst. **34**(1), 246–261 (2022)
16. Trott, O., Olson, A.J.: AutoDock Vina: improving the speed and accuracy of docking with a new scoring function, efficient optimization, and multithreading. J. Comput. Chem. **31**, 455–461 (2009)
17. Zeiler, M.D.: ADADELTA: an adaptive learning rate method (2012). https://doi.org/10.48550/arXiv.1212.5701

# FedCML: Federated Clustering Mutual Learning with non-IID Data

Zekai Chen[1], Fuyi Wang[2], Shengxing Yu[3], Ximeng Liu[1(✉)], and Zhiwei Zheng[1]

[1] College of Mathematics and Computer Science, Fuzhou University, Fuzhou 350108, China
czzeekai@gmail.com, snbnix@gmail.com

[2] School of Information Technology, Deakin University, WaurnPonds, VIC 3216, Australia
wangfuyi@deakin.edu.au

[3] School of Electronics Engineering and Computer Science, Peking University, Beijing, China
ysxjames@126.com

**Abstract.** Federated learning (FL) enables multiple clients to collaboratively train deep learning models under the supervision of a centralized aggregator. Communicating or collecting the local private datasets from multiple edge clients is unauthorized and more vulnerable to training heterogeneity data threats. Despite the fact that numerous studies have been presented to solve this issue, we discover that deep learning models fail to attain good performance in specific tasks or scenarios. In this paper, we revisit the challenge and propose an efficient federated clustering mutual learning framework (FedCML) with an semi-supervised strategy that can avoid the need for the specific empirical parameter to be restricted. We conduct extensive experimental evaluations on two benchmark datasets, and thoroughly compare them to state-of-the-art studies. The results demonstrate the promising performance from FedCML, the accuracy of MNIST and CIFAR10 can be improved by 0.53% and 1.58% for non-IID to the utmost extent while ensuring optimal bandwidth efficiency (4.69× and 4.73× less than FedAvg/FeSem for the two datasets).

**Keywords:** Cosine similarity · Distributed computing · Federate learning · Inter-clustering learning · non-IID data

## 1 Introduction

Recently, the pervasiveness of mobile and Internet-of-Things (IoT) [18,24] has witnessed the number of clients has undergone a sharp increase, which presses ahead with many applications to develop, such as drug discovery [6,15], medical diagnosis [1,2], face recognition [19], etc. Instead of the traditional centralized learning paradigm [12] gathering massive data from clients for training purposes, Federated Learning (FL) [3,9] collaboratively trains in terms of uploaded local model updates from clients for the global model with superior performance. More


J. Cano et al. (Eds.): Euro-Par 2023, LNCS 14100, pp. 623–636, 2023.
https://doi.org/10.1007/978-3-031-39698-4_42

generally, FL is an emerging distributed learning for improving efficiency, privacy, and scalability by training locally in parallel and uploading model updates rather than datasets from each client. Despite its attractive advantages, it is more vulnerable to training heterogeneity data threats [14]. Largely, this is because datasets across multiple clients in practical application scenarios, particularly in different organizations/companies, usually have heterogeneous characteristics, called non-IID data. More concretely, FL is unauthorized to communicate or collect local sensitive datasets. There are serious accuracy concerns caused by the heterogeneity of training data. Hence, addressing the high statistical heterogeneity of local private dataset distribution [5] from multiple edge clients is a fundamental challenge in FL.

Concerning data heterogeneity for FL, the conventional workaround of limited performance trains a consensus global model upon incongruent data for responding to the non-IID challenge [4]. However, the problem is primarily the following points: (1) The accuracy of the model is sensitive to the distribution of labels. (2) The model robustness of the feature distribution is poor. (3) The unique model scalability of quantity distribution is limited. Instead of training a consensus global model, CFL divides clients into multiple clusters for optimizing several sub-objectives, which can maintain higher performance in non-IID scenarios. Sattler et al. [21] propose the CFL framework, which adopts a recursive bi-partitioning algorithm to separate clients with incongruent descent directions. Due to a lack of inter-cluster learning, CFL maintains unsatisfactory performance in various degrees of non-IID settings. To improve the efficiency of CFL, FeSem [16] introduces the Euclidean distance-based ($\ell_2$-based) stochastic expectation maximization to enhance inter-cluster learning, which needs to all clients participate in each round. However, in high dimensions, the Euclidean distance suffers in the HDLSS [20] situation, resulting in adverse effects on the performance of distance-based clustering algorithms. In addition, FeSem defines $\lambda$ to balance the trade-off between distance and loss, which is difficult to control. Furthermore, FlexCFL [7,8] utilizes $\eta$ to control inter-cluster learning, and a decomposed data-driven measure to improve the effectiveness of clustering.

In response to the above-identified challenge, we propose an efficient Federated Clustering Mutual Learning framework (FedCML). *Firstly*, we adopt a one-shot clustering approach, for intra-cluster learning over the first-round model updates from all clients. *Then*, we make each cluster aggregate uploaded model updates from selected clients in parallel for inter-cluster learning. *Finally*, the cosine distance for the similarity measurement is utilized to tailor an inter-cluster learning scheme for establishing dynamic inter-cluster weight, which will reduce divergences between the local models and the global model in each cluster. In this way, we can avoid the need for a specific empirical parameter to restrict inter-cluster learning through expertise and experience. Extensive experimental evaluations demonstrate that FedCML produces 98.98% and 87.47% accuracy for MNIST and CIFAR10 in non-IID (ratio = 0.8) while maintaining the best communication overhead from the prior art. In addition, FedCML performs progressively better with the gradual increase of the non-IID ratio.

Our contributions are summarized below.

- In this work, we propose an efficient federated clustering mutual learning framework (FedCML) against non-IID scenarios in FL. Instead of the empirical parameter to restrict inter-cluster learning, our FedCML maintains stronger capabilities and performance of the aggregated model in non-IID scenarios.
- Analyzing the type of non-IID distributions, we adopt one-shot clustering for grouping data distributions into multiple clusters. Furthermore, we present dynamic inter-cluster learning for compensating intra-cluster exclusive knowledge.
- Theoretically, we give a detailed convergence analysis for supporting FedCML. For fairness, experimental settings are consistent with prior work. Besides, we tune the non-IID data rate to simulate the real data distribution. Compared with state-of-the-art studies, the comprehensive experimental validation on benchmark datasets reveals FedCML is practical and applicable to complex scenarios.

The rest of this paper is organized as follows. In Sect. 2, we review the work of FL and CFL for tackling the data heterogeneity problem. In Sect. 3, we formulate the non-IID problem definition and optimization goal. In Sect. 4, we propose federated clustering mutual learning framework. Then we give the proof for convergence of FedCML in Sect. 5. Subsequently, performance evaluations are presented in Sect. 6. Finally, Sect. 7 concludes this paper.

## 2 Related Work

### 2.1 Federated Learning

Federated learning (FL) is a modern distributed learning for improving efficiency, privacy, and scalability, that intends to utilize clients' uploaded models for collaboratively training a remarkable global model. McMahan et al. [17] first present federated learning and the vanilla FL optimization framework FedAvg. In contrast to the traditional centralized learning paradigm, only each edge node's local model updates are uploaded, alleviating potential data privacy issues. In particular, the optimization in the FL is:

$$\min_{w} f(w) = \sum_{i=1}^{N} p_i F_i(w_i), \tag{1}$$

where $N$ is the number of clients, $\sum_i p_i = 1$, $F_i(w_i)$ is the $i$-th local loss function, and $w_i$ is the $i$-th clients' model parameter. Moreover, in a real-world scenario, datasets across multiple clients have inherently heterogeneous characteristics (i.e., non-IID) data. Despite the attractive advantages of FL, it is more vulnerable to potential unstable convergence and poor model performance threats in non-IID scenarios.

### 2.2 Clustering Federated Learning

At present, there are many methods to tackle the statistical heterogeneity problem. Li et al. [13] first completely demonstrate the typical non-IID data skew, including (1) label distribution skew, (2) feature distribution skew, and (3) quantity skew. To consider such non-IID concerns, McMahan et al. [17] propose a generic FL framework (FedAvg), and studies indicate that it can converge under non-IID conditions. Nevertheless, Sattler et al. [23] validate that the system heterogeneity is not considered. In practice, if some local clients fail to complete the training within the specified time, the server will discard these clients, thus losing the accuracy of the trained global model. Hence, Sattler et al. [21,22] provide Clustered Federated Learning (CFL) strategy to deal with the non-IID problem by adopting a cluster approach to group data distribution. The complement to CFL, Long et al. [16] design a novel framework (FeSem) by introducing stochastic expectation maximization to reduce inter-cluster learning differences. Additionally, they define a specific parameter $\lambda$ to balance the trade-off between distance and loss. Subsequently, Duan et al. [7,8] customize a novel semi-pluralistic architecture for CFL-based frameworks (FlexCFL) that adopt parameter $\eta$ to achieve stable equilibrium between accuracy and communication efficiency. In state-of-the-art methods, certain parameters must be set to limit inter-cluster learning and merely utilize a simple inter-cluster learning approach, which applies only to specific datasets or scenarios.

## 3 Problem Formulation

### 3.1 Problem Definition

Concerning heterogeneous scenarios, the degree of non-IID can map as a series of data distribution $\{\mathcal{X}_1, \cdots, \mathcal{X}_K\}$. For automatically dividing clients into multiple clusters of jointly trainable data distribution, CFL improves resilience and flexibility. More detailed, the global joint optimization in FL can be regarded as local joint optimization for clustering clients'$\mathcal{X}$ into multiple clusters, denoted as $c_1, \cdots, c_K$, and each cluster represents a group of clients with similar data distributions and models. The multi-cluster optimization in the FL problem can be formulated into $K$ distributed sub-problems aiming to solve:

$$\begin{aligned} \hat{G}_i^* &= \arg\min_{\hat{G}\in\Theta} \sum_{j=1, j\in c_i}^{N} \frac{|\mathcal{D}_j|}{\sum_{k\in c_i}^{N} |\mathcal{D}_k|} \mathcal{L}(\mathcal{D}_j; \hat{G}) \\ &\triangleq \mathbb{E}_{\mathcal{D}\sim\mathcal{X}_i}[\mathcal{P}(\mathcal{D}; \hat{G}) = \tau], \forall i \in [K] \end{aligned} \tag{2}$$

where $\Theta$ is the parameter space of the uploaded models in $i$-th clusters, $N$ is the total number of clients, $\tau$ is a set of the target in training data, $[r]$ denotes the set of integers $\{1, \cdots, r\}$, $\mathcal{X}$ is the training data distribution, each client-$i$ holds local datasets $\mathcal{D}_i$, $\forall i \in [N]$, $|\cdot|$ is size, $\mathcal{L}(\cdot)$ is a general definition of the loss function for supervised learning tasks, $\mathcal{P}(\cdot)$ is inference function for evaluating the uploaded model $\hat{G}$, and $\min \sum_{j=1,j\in c_i}^{N} \frac{|\mathcal{D}_j|}{\sum_{k\in c_i}^{N} |\mathcal{D}_k|} \mathcal{L}(\mathcal{D}_j; \hat{G})$ is to minimize the sum of loss from the same $c_i$ cluster.

### 3.2 Optimization Goal

Since client-wise weights are inconsistent, weight coefficients are crucial to robust FL aggregation. Generally, we establish weight coefficients for each cluster to constrain potentially consistent clusters. Therefore, in various degrees of non-IID scenarios, due to partial coherence between $\mathcal{X}_i$ and $\mathcal{X}_j$ ($i \neq j$), the problem can be approached by minimizing the distance between the goal clustering model and other proximity clustering models, which can be formulated as:

$$\min \frac{1}{K} \sum_{i=1}^{K} \sum_{j=1}^{K} \lambda_{i,j} \times Dist(\Delta w_i, \Delta w_j), \tag{3}$$

where $Dist(\cdot, \cdot)$ is distance metric, $w_i$ is the $i$-th clusters' model update and $\lambda_{i,j}$ is weight coefficient between $c_i$ and $c_j$.

## 4 Federated Clustering Mutual Learning

### 4.1 System Overview

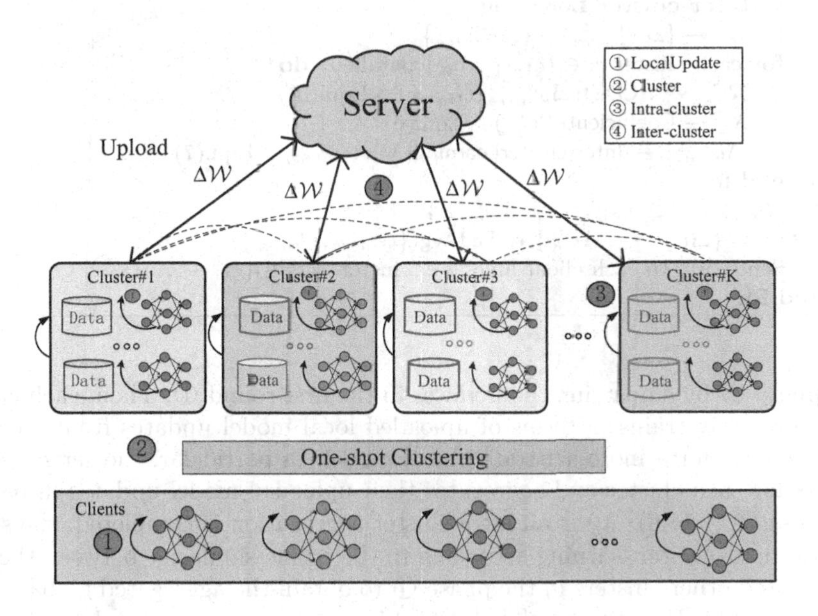


**Fig. 1.** A system overview of FedCML.

**Architecture.** FedCML targets a typical scenario of CFL for training non-IID data service. As shown in Fig. 1 and Algorithm 1, FedCML has four phases: ① local model update (line 2 ∼ 5), ② one-shot hierarchical clustering for all clients (line 8 ∼ 11), ③ intra-cluster aggregation, and ④ inter-cluster aggregation. Initially, the server determines the local joint optimization of each cluster through

**Algorithm 1.** FedCML Framework

**Input:** The number of clients $N$, the number of selected clients from each cluster per round $M$, the number of communication rounds $T$, and the number of clusters $K$.
**Output:** Global models update $G^t \leftarrow \{\Delta w_1^t, \cdots, \Delta w_K^t\}$

```
1: for each round t = {1, 2, ..., T} do
2:     for each client i = {1, 2, ..., N} do
3:         /* selected clients execute LocalUpdate*/
           Δw_i ← LocalUpdate(D_i, w_i^{t-1} + Δw_i^{t-1})
4:         Send Δw_i to the server. ▷ client-i is selected.
5:     end for
6:     Server selects M clients from each cluster or N clients.
7:     # One-shot Clustering
8:     if round t is 1 then
9:         G_cos ← CostDist({Δw_1, ..., Δw_N}) ▷ getting cosines distance.
10:        {c_1, ..., c_N} ← HierarchicalClustering(K, G_cos)
11:    end if
12:    # Intra-cluster Learning
13:    for each cluster c_i ∈ {c_1, ..., c_K} parallelly do
14:        S_i ← {Δw_{i,j} | j ∈ c_i} ▷ |S_i| = M.
15:        Δw^i_intra ← Intra-clusterLearning(S_i) ▷ Equ.(4)
16:    end for
17:    # Inter-cluster Learning
18:    G_intra ← {Δw^1_intra, ..., Δw^K_intra}
19:    for each cluster c_i ∈ {c_1, ..., c_K} parallelly do
20:        RC_{c_i} ← RCDist(Δw^i_intra, G_intra) ▷ Equ.(5)
21:        λ_{c_i} ← Coefficient(RC_{c_i}) ▷ Equ.(6)
22:        Δw^i_inter ← Inter-clusterLearning(λ_{c_i}, G_intra) ▷ Equ.(7)
23:    end for
24:    G_inter ← {Δw^1_inter, ..., Δw^K_inter}
25:    G^t = {Δw_1^t, ..., Δw_K^t} ← FedAvg({G_intra, G_inter})
26:    Send Δw_i^t to each client among c_i cluster. ▷ c_i ∈ {c_1, ..., c_K}.
27: end for
```

the phase ② by employing the updates in the first round ①. Then, each cluster collaboratively trains in terms of uploaded local model updates from a certain set of clients for a more accurate global model. In particular, the server selects clients for each cluster and aggregates their uploaded model updates in parallel in phase ③ (line 6). After all intra-cluster aggregation is completed, the server creates inter-cluster learning according to the cosine similarity between the goal cluster and other clusters in the phase ④ to obtain the aggregated global model (line 12 $\sim$ 26). Finally, the global model is sent to each client and continues to loop phases ③ and ④ until the model converges.

### 4.2 One-Shot Clustering

In various degrees of non-IID, the prior studies [16,21] focus on iterative clustering to distinguish clients from model updates in each communication round, such as FeSem. However, when faced with similar model parameters, FeSem is vulnerable to transform into FedAvg from CFL through clustering in each round. Obviously, the gap between data distribution $\mathcal{X}$ of each client can be measured from the divergence of model updates at the first round. Hence, FlexCFL and our FedCML leverage one-shot clustering at the first communication round for optimizing communication overhead, which avoids rescheduling clients for each round while maintaining performance. Besides, our one-shot clustering strategy is static cosines distance-based method, avoiding HDLSS [20] situation.

### 4.3 Intra-cluster Learning

In general, based on the similarity of data statistics, our FedCML separates all clients into $K$ clusters at the first round in the serve aggregation through one-shot clustering. For each subsequent round of aggregation, the server selects a certain amount of intra-cluster local models in each cluster. In brief, our intra-cluster aggregation is defined as follows:

$$\Delta w_{intra}^{i} = \frac{1}{M_{c_i}} \sum_{i \in c_i}^{M_{c_i}} \Delta w_{i,j}, \tag{4}$$

where $M_{c_i}$ is the number of selected clients in $c_i$, $\Delta w_{i,j}$ is the model update from client $i$ belonging to $c_i$, and $\Delta w_{intra}^{i}$ is intra-cluster model update of $c_i$.

### 4.4 Inter-cluster Learning

The prior CFL-related studies lack inter-cluster learning [16,23], failing to adequately address the non-IID data problem. Considering both magnitudes and directions of the goal clustering model and other clustering models, the heterogeneity inter-cluster learning problem can be avoided by dynamically determining other proximity clustering models for model updates. In addition, the Euclidean distance indicates an absolute discrepancy between the goal clustering model and other clustering models, and the cosine distance indicates a relative discrepancy. Hence, FedCML adopts dynamic formulation similarity $RC$ derived from the cosine distance. Note that $RC \leq 0$ represents this clustering model inevitably deviations from the target clustering model update. When the ReLU-clipped technique is introduced, $RC$ is defined as:

$$RC_{i,j} = ReLU(\frac{\langle \Delta w_i, \Delta w_j \rangle}{||\Delta w_i|| \cdot ||\Delta w_j||}), \tag{5}$$

where $RC_{i,j}$ is the clipped cosine distance between $c_i$ and $c_j$, $\langle \cdot, \cdot \rangle$ is the dot product, $\Delta w_i$ is an intra-cluster model update of $c_i$, and $ReLU(\cdot) = max(0, \cdot)$.

To compensate for intra-cluster exclusive knowledge from inter-cluster shared knowledge, we establish an inter-cluster coefficient formula as follows:

$$\lambda_{i,j} = \frac{RC_{i,j}}{\sum_{j=1 \ and \ i \neq j}^{K} RC_{i,j}}, \tag{6}$$

Then, considering the value of $\sum_{j=1 \ and \ i \neq j}^{K} \lambda_{i,j}$, $\Delta w_{inter}^{i}$ can be described as:

$$\Delta w_{inter}^{i} = \begin{cases} 0, & \sum_{j=1 \ and \ i \neq j}^{K} \lambda_{i,j} = 0 \\ \sum_{j=1 \ and \ i \neq j}^{K} \lambda_{i,j} \times \Delta w_i, & \sum_{j=1 \ and \ i \neq j}^{K} \lambda_{i,j} = 1 \end{cases}, \tag{7}$$

where $\lambda_{i,j}$ is weight coefficient between $c_i$ and $c_j$, and $\Delta w_{inter}^{i}$ is inter-cluster model update of $c_i$.

## 5 Convergence Analysis

We analyze convergence for FedCML in this section. And we follow prior works of assumptions [8,20,25].

**Assumption 1.** *For any client i in cluster c, the loss function $\mathcal{F}_{i,c}(w)$is convex.*

**Assumption 2.** *The loss function $\mathcal{F}_{i,c}(w)$is M-Lipschitz continuous: for $w_1$, $w_2$, $||\mathcal{F}_{i,c}(w_1) - \mathcal{F}_{i,c}(w_2)|| \leq M||w_1 - w_2||$.*

**Assumption 3.** *The loss function $\mathcal{F}_{i,c}(w)$is L-Lipschitz continuous: for $w_1$, $w_2$, $||\nabla\mathcal{F}_{i,c}(w_1) - \nabla\mathcal{F}_{i,c}(w_2)|| \leq L||w_1 - w_2||$.*

**Definition 1.** *For $\forall_c$ cluster $c \in \{c_1, c_2, \cdots, c_K\}$, the cluster loss function is $\mathcal{F}_c(\cdot) \triangleq \sum_{i,i \in c} p_i \mathcal{F}_{i,c}(\cdot)$, and $\sum_i p_i = 1$.*

**Definition 2.** *Given any client-i, and c ($c \in \{c_1, \cdots, c_K\}$), $\xi_{i,c}$ denotes divergence between the loss functions of client-i and c, which is expressed as: $\xi_{i,c} \triangleq \max_w ||\nabla\mathcal{F}_{i,c}(w) - \nabla\mathcal{F}_c(w)||$, and the intra-cluster divergence is defined as: $\xi_c \triangleq \sum_{c \in C} \sum_{i \in c} p_c p_i \xi_{i,c}$, where $\sum_c p_c = 1$, and $\sum_i p_i = 1$.*

**Lemma 1.** *According to Assumptions 1 to 3, the cluster loss function $\mathcal{F}_c(w)$ is convex, M-Lipschitz continuous, L-Lipschitz smooth for any c.*

*Proof.* Following the **Definition** 1, $\mathcal{F}_c(w) \triangleq \sum_{i,i \in c} p_i \mathcal{F}_{i,c}(w)$. According to **Assumption** 1 and **Assumption** 2, for any $w_1$ and $w_2$, we have:

$$||\mathcal{F}_c(w_1) - \mathcal{F}_c(w_2)|| = ||\sum_{i,i \in c} p_i \mathcal{F}_{i,c}(w_1) - \sum_{i,i \in c} p_i \mathcal{F}_{i,c}(w_2)|| \leq M||w_1 - w_2||$$

The proof of the $M$-Lipschitz continuous, $L$-Lipschitz smooth in $\mathcal{F}_c$ is similar, and we omit it for brevity.

**Lemma 2.** *Suppose **Assumption** 1 $\sim$ 3 hold, there is a virtual cluster model $\hat{w}_{t,e}^{c}$ that is centralized trained on the cluster c of clients' data and is synchronized with the federated model, and $w_{t,e}^{i,c}$ is c of client-i'model without inter-cluster aggregation in local training epoch e and the communication round t. The upper bound of divergence between $w_{t,e}^{i,c}$ and $\hat{w}_{t,e}^{c}$, for any t, e, and learning rate $\eta$ has:*

$$||w_{t,e}^{i,c} - \hat{w}_{t,e}^{c}|| \leq \frac{\xi_{i,c}}{L}((\eta L + 1)^e - 1)$$

*Proof.* For simplicity, the iterator of $w_{t,e}^{i,c}$ in FedCML can be introduced:

$$w_{t,e}^{i,c} = \begin{cases} w_t^c \triangleq \sum_i p_i w_{t,E}^{i,c}, & \text{e=0} \\ w_{t,e-1}^{i,c} - \eta \nabla \mathcal{F}_{i,c}(w_{t,e-1}^{i,c}), & e \in [1, E] \end{cases}$$

For similarity, the $\hat{w}_{t,e}^c$ as:

$$\hat{w}_{t,e}^{c} = \begin{cases} w_t^c \triangleq \sum_i p_i w_{t,E}^{i,c}, & \text{e=0} \\ \hat{w}_{t,e-1}^{c} - \eta \nabla \mathcal{F}_{c}(\hat{w}_{t,e-1}^{c}), & e \in [1, E] \end{cases}$$

Under **Assumption** 3 and **Definition** 2, the divergence between $w_{t,e}^{i,c}$ and $\hat{w}_{t,e}^c$ is bounded as follows in each iteration:

$$\begin{aligned} &||w_{t,e}^{i,c} - \hat{w}_{t,e}^c|| = ||w_{t,e-1}^{i,c} - \eta \nabla \mathcal{F}_{i,c}(w_{t,e-1}^{i,c}) - \hat{w}_{t,e-1}^c + \eta \nabla \mathcal{F}_c(\hat{w}_{t,e-1}^c)|| \\ &+ \nabla \mathcal{F}_{i,c}(\hat{w}_{t,e-1}^c) - \nabla \mathcal{F}_c(\hat{w}_{t,e-1}^c)|| \\ &\leq ||w_{t,e-1}^{i,c} - \hat{w}_{t,e-1}^c|| + \eta ||\nabla \mathcal{F}_{i,c}(w_{t,e-1}^{i,c}) - \nabla \mathcal{F}_{i,c}(\hat{w}_{t,e-1}^c)|| \\ &+ \eta ||\nabla \mathcal{F}_{i,c}(\hat{w}_{t,e-1}^c) - \nabla \mathcal{F}_c(\hat{w}_{t,e-1}^c)|| \leq (\eta L + 1)||w_{t,e-1}^{i,c} - \hat{w}_{t,e-1}^c|| + \eta \xi_{i,c} \end{aligned}$$

Let $h(e) = ||w_{t,e}^{i,c} - \hat{w}_{t,e}^c||$, we have:

$$\begin{aligned} &h(e) \leq (\eta L + 1) h(e-1) + \eta \xi_{i,c} \\ &\Rightarrow^{(a)} h(e) + \frac{\xi_{i,c}}{L} \leq (\eta L + 1)^e \xi_{i,c} \Rightarrow h(e) \leq \frac{\xi_{i,c}}{L}((\eta L + 1)^e - 1) \\ &\Rightarrow ||w_t^c - \hat{w}_t^c|| \leq \sum_i p_i ||w_{t,E}^{i,c} - \hat{w}_{t,e}^c|| \leq \frac{\xi_c}{L}((\eta L + 1)^E - 1) \end{aligned}$$

where $(a)$ is $h(0) = ||w_{t,0}^{i,c} - \hat{w}_{t,0}^c|| = 0$. Consider the continuous of $\mathcal{F}_c(\cdot)$ (**Lemma** 1 and **Assumption** 2), we have: $||\mathcal{F}_c(w_t) - \mathcal{F}_c(\hat{w}_{t,e}^c)|| \leq \frac{M\xi_c}{L}((\eta L + 1)^E - 1)$.

**Theorem 1.** *Support* **Assumption** *1* $\sim$ *3 hold. Let* $\tilde{w}_{t,e}^c$ *define the model parameter after inter-cluster learning. Combing* **Lemma** *1* $\sim$ *2, for* $\sum_i p_i = 1$, *we get convergence bound of FedCML as:*

$$||\mathcal{F}_c(\tilde{w}_t^c) - \mathcal{F}_c(\hat{w}_{t,e}^c))|| \leq \begin{cases} \frac{M\xi_c}{L}((\eta L + 1)^E - 1), & \sum_{i \in C, i \neq c} \lambda_i = 0 \\ \frac{M((\eta L+1)^E - 1)}{L}(p_1 \xi_c + p_2 \sum_{i \in C, i \neq c} \lambda_i \xi_i), & \sum_{i \in C, i \neq c} \lambda_i = 1 \end{cases}$$

*Proof.* The $\tilde{w}_{t,e}^c$ can be introduced as:

$$\tilde{w}_{t,e}^c = \sum_{i \in C} p_i \lambda_i w_{t,e}^c = p_1 w_{t,e}^c + p_2 \sum_{i \in C, i \neq c} \lambda_i w_{t,e}^i$$

**Analysis for** $\sum_{i \in C, i \neq c} \lambda_i = 0$, we have:

$$||\tilde{w}_{t,e}^c - \hat{w}_{t,e}^c|| = ||p_1 w_t^c - \hat{w}_{t,e}^c|| \leq^{(a)} \frac{\xi_c}{L}((\eta L + 1)^e - 1),$$

where (*a*) is $\sum_i p_i = 1$. Under **Lemma** 2, we have $||\mathcal{F}_c(\tilde{w}_t^c) - \mathcal{F}_c(\hat{w}_{t,e}^c))|| \leq \frac{M\xi_c}{L}((\eta L+1)^E - 1)$.

**Analysis for** $\sum_{i \in C, i \neq c} \lambda_i = 1$, we have:

$$
\begin{aligned}
||\tilde{w}_{t,e}^c - \hat{w}_{t,e}^c|| &= ||p_1 w_t^c - \hat{w}_{t,e}^c + p_2 \sum_{i \in C, i \neq c} \lambda_i w_{t,e}^i|| \\
&\leq p_1 ||w_{t,e}^c - \hat{w}_{t,e}|| + p_2 || \sum_{i \in C, i \neq c} \lambda_i w_{t,c}^i - \hat{w}_{t,e}^c|| \\
&=^{(b)} p_1 ||w_{t,e}^c - \hat{w}_{t,e}|| + p_2 || \sum_{i \in C, i \neq c} \lambda_i w_{t,c}^i - \sum_{i \in C, i \neq c} \lambda_i \hat{w}_{t,e}^c|| \\
&=^{(c)} p_1 ||w_{t,e}^c - \hat{w}_{t,e}|| + p_2 \sum_{i \in C, i \neq c} \lambda_i ||w_{t,c}^i - \hat{w}_{t,e}^c|| \\
&\leq^{(d)} \frac{(\eta L+1)^E - 1}{L} (p_1 \xi_c + p_2 \sum_{i \in C, i \neq c} \lambda_i \xi_i),
\end{aligned}
$$

where (*b*) is because $\sum_{i \in C, i \neq c} \lambda_i = 1$, (*c*) is because $\lambda_i \geq 0, \forall_i$, and (*d*) is because **Lemma** 2. Under **Lemma** 2, we have $||\mathcal{F}_c(\tilde{w}_t^c) - \mathcal{F}_c(\hat{w}_{t,e}^c))|| \leq \frac{M((\eta L+1)^E - 1)}{L}(p_1 \xi_c + p_2 \sum_{i \in C, i \neq c} \lambda_i \xi_i)$.

## 6 Experimental Evaluation

We implement a prototype of FedCML by PyTorch framework. All experiments are conducted on the server equipped with 64-core CPUs, 128GB RAM, and 2 NVIDIA GeForce RTX 2080Ti. We evaluate FedCML with two benchmarking datasets (MNIST [11] and CIFAR10 [10]) and compare it with three prior works as baselines. *For MNIST*, we construct the CNN with two 5×5 convolution layers, one 2 × 2 max pool layer, two fully connected layers, the ReLU function, and the final softmax output layer. *For CIFAR10*, we adopt LetNet5 [11], a CNN model with two 5 × 5 convolution layers, one 2 × 2 max pool layer, three fully connected layers, one ReLU function, and one final softmax output layer. The three baselines are introduced as follows in brevity.

- FedAvg: the SGD-based FL with model updates averaging.
- FlexCFL: semi-pluralistic architecture CFL-based that adopts the MADC-based Agglomerative Clustering method for one-shot clustering, and follows $\eta$ to limit inter-cluster learning.
- FeSem: the $\ell_2$-based CFL that adopts stochastic expectation maximization to minimize the discrepancies inter-cluster learning and specific $\lambda$ balance between loss and distance.

We follow most of the prior works. In our experiment, we set the local epoch $E = 2$, the number of all clients $N = 50$, the selected clients from each cluster $|c_i|$ per round $M = 0.2 \times |c_i|, i = [K]$, the number of clusters $K = 5$ and 10 for MNIST and CIFAR10 datasets, respectively. Besides, non-IID ratio reflects the degrees of non-IID distributed ratio. For example, when the non-IID ratio is 0.5, assigned data is consist of 50% images of one class and 50% images of the same number of images in different classes in each client. The specific parameters $\lambda$ and $\eta$ are set to 0.01 (FeSem) and 0.1 (FlexCFL), respectively.

### 6.1 Accuracy Comparison

We compare performance of FedCML in various degrees of non-IID ratio settings with notable prior works: FedAvg, FlexCFL, and FeSem, to demonstrate effectiveness of FedCML.

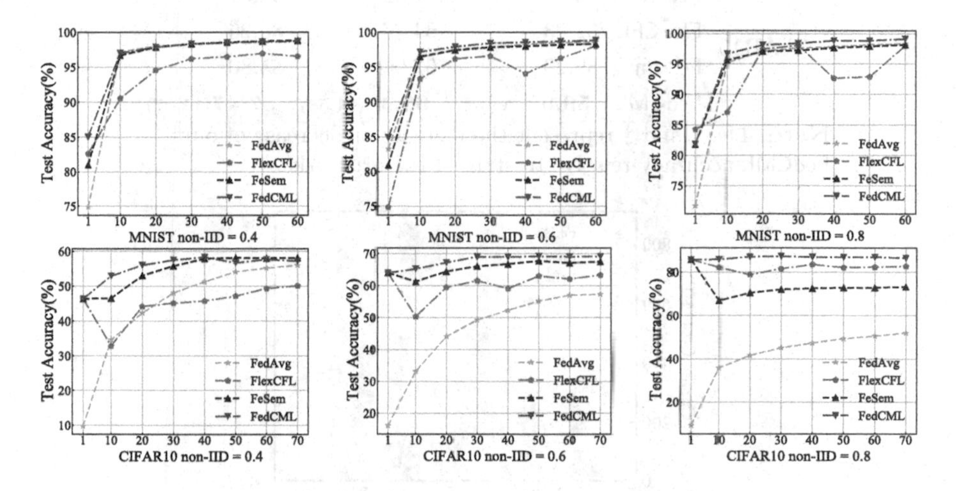


**Fig. 2.** Performance comparison of accuracy with different communication (comm.) rounds over MNIST and CIFAR10.

The comparison results from Fig. 2 and Table 1 show the performance of FedCML and 3 baselines on the MNIST dataset and the CIFAR10 dataset. As shown in Fig. 2, FedCML converges smoothly and quickly, and has greater accuracy than the baselines, owing to adaptive formulas in inter-cluster learning from other proximate clusters, while fixed $\eta$ in inter-cluster learning in FlexCFL is unstable on these two benchmark datasets. *For MNIST*, FedAvg and FeSem have similar efficiency performance for non-IID MNIST dataset. Besides, FlexCFL performs worst in non-IID distribution with different ratios. *For CIFAR10*, the accuracy derived from FedAvg drops with the increase in non-IID distribution ratio. FlexCFL has the opposite phenomenon of FedAvg, that is, FlexCFL performs progressively better as the ratio of non-IID distribution increases. Despite specific $\eta$ in FlexCFL for determining inter-cluster learning, this methodology cannot be applied to non-IID distributions or different datasets.

From Table 1, it is evident that FedCML has a significant advantage over FlexCFL when ratio = 0.8, which is increased by 0.53% compared to FlexCFL. In addition, FeSem has significant improvements over the non-IID CIFAR10 dataset

**Table 1.** Test accuracy (%) of FedAvg, FeSem, FlexCFL, and FedCML (ours) over MNIST, and CAFAR10 in different data distribution.

| Dataset | Method | non-IID | | |
|---|---|---|---|---|
| | | 0.4 | 0.6 | 0.8 |
| MNIST | FedAvg | 98.82 | 98.62 | 98.29 |
| | FlexCFL | 97.59 | 98.33 | 98.45 |
| | FeSem | 98.81 | 98.36 | 98.14 |
| | FedCML | **98.90** (↑0.08) | **98.95**(↑0.33) | **98.98**(↑0.53) |
| CIFAR10 | FedAvg | 56.28 | 57.32 | 52.01 |
| | FlexCFL | 52.03 | 64.77 | 86.26 |
| | FeSem | 59.20 | 67.90 | 85.80 |
| | FedCML | **59.52**(↑0.32) | **69.48**(↑1.58) | **87.47**(↑1.67) |

**Note.** The ↑ and ↓ represent the increase or decrease of ours FedCML accuracy relative to state-of-the-art works.

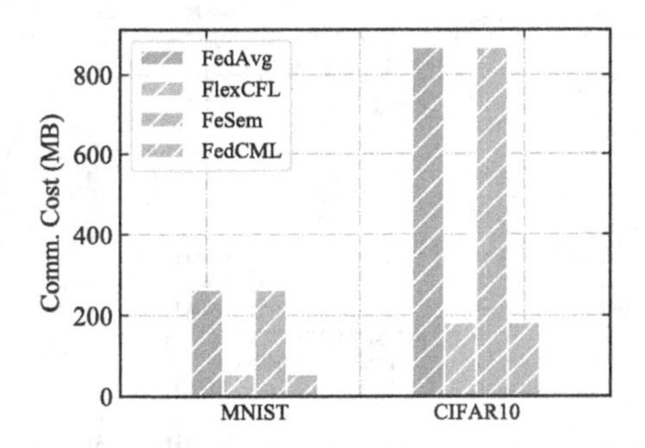


**Fig. 3.** Comm. costs of FedAvg, FlexCFL, FeSem and FedCML on benchmark datasets.

with ratio = 0.4, 2.92% ↑ and 7.17% ↑ in accuracy when compared with FedAvg and FlexCFL, respectively. Moreover, its accuracy is lower than our FedCML at ratios of 0.4, 0.6, and 0.8 by 0.32%, 1.58%, and 1.67%, respectively. Since FeSem utilizes stochastic expectation maximization to partition the model update of each client into balanced clusters based on $\ell_2$, each client can learn from the experience of another client who has a proximate model update. Consequently, FeSem is powerful and more expressive than FedAvg and FlexCFL for most scenarios. Nonetheless, FeSem is susceptible to transforming into FedAvg, and methods to reduce the loss are difficult to identify in different cases. With improvements of up to 0.08% $\sim$ 7.49%, our FedCML has been shown to be significantly more efficient and effective than both FeSem and FlexCFL. Because FedCML introduces dynamic inter-cluster formulas that prevent intra-cluster models from becoming stuck in local overfitting, it maintains a better balance between inter-cluster and intra-cluster shared knowledge. In a nutshell, our FedCML surpasses FedAvg, FlexCFL, and FeSem in all degrees of non-IID settings.

### 6.2 Communication Efficiency

In order to further measure the effectiveness of FedCML, we evaluate the efficiency of the scheme from the communication cost between the server and each client. The comparison of communication costs in FedCML, FedAvg, FeSem, and FlexCFL under the different datasets is shown in Fig. 3. There is a major advantage to FedCML in that it reduces the communication costs. The communication costs of FedAvg and FeSem obviously are relatively large as expected, since these two schemes upload model updates of all participants to get an accurate global model. Unlike the above two schemes,FlexCFL and FedCML merely need to upload model updates from selected clients within each cluster, resulting in the close communication costs. Figure 3 shows that the communication costs of FedAvg and FeSem is 4.69× (for MNIST) and 4.73× (for CIFAR) more than FedCML.

## 7 Conclusion

In this work, we present FedCML, an efficient federated clustering mutual learning framework aiming at performance improvement in the non-IID FL setting. Besides, our framework establishes an inter-cluster strategy to balance intra-cluster learning and inter-cluster learning, which can eliminate the need to restrict a specific empirical parameter for inter-cluster learning based on empirical or expert knowledge. In contrast to the widely known literature, FedCML uses a one-shot clustering approach, which has lower communication costs. Comprehensive experimental validation on benchmark datasets demonstrates FedCML practical and applicable for complex scenarios. Furthermore, we intend to apply the proposed framework to some privacy-critical applications in future work.

## References

1. Antunes, R.S., André da Costa, C., Küderle, A., Yari, I.A., Eskofier, B.: Federated learning for healthcare: systematic review and architecture proposal. ACM Trans. Intell. Syst. Technol. **13**(4), 1–23 (2022)
2. Bharati, S., Mondal, M.R.H., Podder, P., Prasath, V.S.: Federated learning: Applications, challenges and future directions. Int. J. Hybrid Intell. Syst. **18**(1–2), 19–35 (2022)
3. Bonawitz, K., et al.: Towards federated learning at scale: system design. Proc. Mach. Learn. Syst. **1**, 374–388 (2019)
4. Cao, L.: Beyond IID: non-IID thinking, informatics, and learning. IEEE Intell. Syst. **37**(4), 5–17 (2022)
5. Chai, Z., Fayyaz, H., Fayyaz, Z., Anwar, A., Zhou, Y., Baracaldo, N., Ludwig, H., Cheng, Y.: Towards taming the resource and data heterogeneity in federated learning. In: 2019 USENIX Conference on OpML 2019, pp. 19–21 (2019)
6. Chen, S., Xue, D., Chuai, G., Yang, Q., Liu, Q.: FL-QSAR: a federated learning-based QSAR prototype for collaborative drug discovery. Bioinformatics **36**(22–23), 5492–5498 (2021)

7. Duan, M., et al.: FedGroup: efficient federated learning via decomposed similarity-based clustering. In: 2021 IEEE International Conference on Parallel & Distributed Processing with Applications, Big Data & Cloud Computing, Sustainable Computing & Communications, Social Computing & Networking, pp. 228–237. IEEE (2021)
8. Duan, M., et al.: Flexible clustered federated learning for client-level data distribution shift. IEEE Trans. Parallel Distrib. Syst. **33**, 2661–2674 (2021)
9. Kairouz, P., McMahan, H.B., Avent, B., Bellet, A., Bennis, M., et al.: Advances and open problems in federated learning. Found. Trends® Mach. Learn. **14**(1–2), 1–210 (2021)
10. Krizhevsky, A., Nair, V., Hinton, G.: The cifar-10 dataset, vol. 55, no. 5 (2014). http://www.cs.toronto.edu/kriz/cifar.html
11. LeCun, Y., Bottou, L., Bengio, Y., Haffner, P.: Gradient-based learning applied to document recognition. Proc. IEEE **86**(11), 2278–2324 (1998)
12. Li, M., Andersen, D.G., Smola, A.J., Yu, K.: Communication efficient distributed machine learning with the parameter server. In: Advances in Neural Information Processing Systems vol. 27 (2014)
13. Li, Q., Diao, Y., Chen, Q., He, B.: Federated learning on non-IID data silos: an experimental study. In: ICDE, pp. 965–978. IEEE (2022)
14. Li, Z., et al.: Data heterogeneity-robust federated learning via group client selection in industrial IoT. IEEE Internet Things J. **9**(18), 17844–17857 (2022)
15. Liang, X., Bandara, E., Zhao, J., Shetty, S.: A blockchain-empowered federated learning system and the promising use in drug discovery. In: Charles, W. (eds.) Blockchain in Life Sciences. Blockchain Technologies, pp. 113–139. Springer (2022). https://doi.org/10.1007/978-981-19-2976-2_6
16. Long, G., Xie, M., Shen, T., Zhou, T., Wang, X., Jiang, J.: Multi-center federated learning: clients clustering for better personalization. World Wide Web **26**, 481–500 (2022)
17. McMahan, B., Moore, E., Ramage, D., Hampson, S., y Arcas, B.A.: Communication-efficient learning of deep networks from decentralized data. In: Artificial Intelligence and Statistics, pp. 1273–1282. PMLR (2017)
18. Nguyen, T.D., Marchal, S., Miettinen, M., Fereidooni, H., Asokan, N., Sadeghi, A.R.: Dïot: a federated self-learning anomaly detection system for IoT. In: ICDCS, pp. 756–767. IEEE (2019)
19. Niu, Y., Deng, W.: Federated learning for face recognition with gradient correction. In: Proceedings of the AAAI Conference on Artificial Intelligence, vol. 36, no. 2, pp. 1999–2007 (2022)
20. Sarkar, S., Ghosh, A.K.: On perfect clustering of high dimension, low sample size data. IEEE Trans. Pattern Anal. Mach. Intell. **42**(9), 2257–2272 (2019)
21. Sattler, F., Müller, K.R., Samek, W.: Clustered federated learning: model-agnostic distributed multitask optimization under privacy constraints. IEEE Trans. Neural Netw. Learn. Syst. **32**(8), 3710–3722 (2020)
22. Sattler, F., Müller, K.R., Wiegand, T., Samek, W.: On the byzantine robustness of clustered federated learning. In: ICASSP, pp. 8861–8865. IEEE (2020)
23. Sattler, F., Wiedemann, S., Müller, K.R., Samek, W.: Robust and communication-efficient federated learning from non-IID data. IEEE Trans. Neural Netw. Learn. Syst. **31**(9), 3400–3413 (2019)
24. Shih, C.S., Chuang, C.C., Yeh, H.Y.: Federating public and private intelligent services for IoT applications. In: IWCMC, pp. 558–563. IEEE (2017)
25. Wang, S., et al.: Adaptive federated learning in resource constrained edge computing systems. IEEE J. Sel. Areas Commun. **37**(6), 1205–1221 (2019)

# A Look at Performance and Scalability of the GPU Accelerated Sparse Linear System Solver Spliss

Jasmin Mohnke(✉) and Michael Wagner

German Aerospace Center (DLR), Institute of Software Methods for Product Virtualization, Dresden, Germany
jasmin.mohnke@dlr.de

**Abstract.** A significant part in computational fluid dynamics (CFD) simulations is the solving of large sparse systems of linear equations resulting from implicit time integration of the Reynolds-averaged Navier-Stokes (RANS) equations. The sparse linear system solver Spliss aims to provide a linear solver library that, on the one hand, is tailored to these requirements of CFD applications but, on the other hand, independent of the particular CFD solver. Spliss allows leveraging a range of available HPC technologies such as hybrid CPU parallelization and the possibility to offload the computationally intensive linear solver to GPU accelerators, while at the same time hiding this complexity from the CFD solver.

This work highlights the steps taken to establish multi-GPU capabilities for the Spliss solver allowing for efficient and scalable usage of large GPU systems. In addition, this work evaluates performance and scalability on CPU and GPU systems using a representative CODA test case as an example. CODA is the CFD software being developed as part of a collaboration between the French Aerospace Lab ONERA, the German Aerospace Center (DLR), Airbus, and their European research partners. CODA is jointly owned by ONERA, DLR and Airbus. The evaluation examines and compares performance and scalability in a strong scaling approach on Nvidia A100 GPUs and the AMD Rome architecture.

**Keywords:** sparse linear solver · computational fluid dynamics · CFD solver · high performance computing · heterogeneous computing · GPU

## 1 Introduction

Computational fluid dynamics (CFD) simulations for aircraft aerodynamics are a non-negotiable part in today's aircraft design process. They allow to reduce cost and time of aircraft development and help accelerating the introduction of progressive technologies and improvements. Moreover, high-precision CFD simulations are inevitable for the assessment of future aircraft designs by providing reliable insight into new aircraft technologies and reach best overall aircraft performance. They allow to design quieter, safer, and more fuel-efficient planes.


J. Cano et al. (Eds.): Euro-Par 2023, LNCS 14100, pp. 637–648, 2023.
https://doi.org/10.1007/978-3-031-39698-4_43

For CFD simulations in the aircraft design process, solving the large systems of linear equations that result from implicit time integration of the Reynolds-averaged Navier-Stokes (RANS) equations plays a significant role. Consequently, the utilized linear solver must be tailored to the requirements of the problems and efficiently complete these computations. The sparse linear system solver Spliss meets these requirements independently of a specific CFD solver while leveraging various available HPC technologies [1].

Many current HPC systems take advantage of GPU compute power, as can be seen in the current Top500 list [2]. Of the first ten systems on the list, six have a heterogeneous architecture with accelerators available on compute nodes. Spliss takes advantage of such architectures with the wide range of parallelization approaches it implements, including a hybrid CPU parallelization and offloading to GPU accelerators. Spliss provides CFD solvers the capabilities to efficiently and transparently execute the computationally intensive linear solver on new architectures and hardware accelerators such as GPUs. This way, the CFD solver can leverage new architectures and hardware accelerators without the necessity of any code adaptation in the CFD solver. One of the CFD solvers that utilize Spliss is CODA. CODA is the CFD software being developed as part of a collaboration between the French Aerospace Lab ONERA, the German Aerospace Center (DLR), Airbus, and their European research partners. CODA is jointly owned by ONERA, DLR and Airbus.

The contribution of this work is, first, a presentation of the improvements made to Spliss to allow an efficient scaling to a large number of GPUs and, second, an evaluation of the achieved performance and scalability using a test case with the CODA CFD software as an example. The evaluation includes a performance assessment of GPU accelerated Spliss with CODA on the JUWELS Booster system with Nvidia A100 GPUs in comparison to a CPU-only execution on German Aerospace Center's CARO HPC system based on AMD Rome CPUs.

This work starts by introducing the software ecosystem in Sect. 2, followed by discussing the improvements to enable acceleration distributed among multiple GPUs in Sect. 3 and their impact on overall performance. In Sect. 4, the evaluated HPC systems and the test case are described and performance and scalability results are presented and compared. Finally, Sect. 5 summarizes the presented work and draws conclusions.

## 2 Background

At the German Aerospace Center (DLR), the development of computational fluid dynamics software has a long history. Today, the *TAU* CFD package [3] has been in production in the European aircraft industry, research organizations and academia for more than 20 years and was, for instance, used for the Airbus A380 and A350 wing design. As state-of-the-art for its time, TAU implements a classical MPI parallelization to compute steady and unsteady external aerodynamic flows using a second order finite-volumes discretization.

In 2012 DLR began the development of a new, flexible, unstructured CFD solver called *Flucs* [4] from the ground up. The focus of this new development was set on, first, a flexible and comprehensive parallelization concept suited for current and future HPC systems and, second, on algorithmic efficiency using strong implicit solvers, higher-order spatial discretization via the Discontinuous Galerkin method featuring hp-adaptation in addition to finite volumes with maximum code share, and seamless integration into Python-based multi-disciplinary process chains via *FlowSimulator* [5,6]. While the development of Flucs had been started at DLR, it since has become part of a larger cooperation that is driven by Airbus, the French aerospace lab ONERA, and DLR. The joint development of the CFD software based on Flucs was named *CODA* (CFD for ONERA, DLR and Airbus) to honor the new collaboration and the involvement of all three partners pursuing the joint effort and co-development.

Similar to TAU, the CODA CFD software uses classical domain decomposition to utilize distributed-memory parallelism via MPI and, additionally, the GASPI [7] implementation GPI-2 as an alternative to MPI, which allows for efficient one-sided communication to reduce network traffic and latency. In addition, CODA supports the overlapping of halo-data communication with computation to hide network latency and further increase scalability. Besides classical domain decomposition, CODA employs a hybrid two-level parallelization to utilize shared-memory parallelism for multi- and many-core architectures [8]. CODA implements sub-domain decomposition, where each domain is further partitioned into sub-domains, each of which being processed by a dedicated software thread that is mapped one-to-one to a hardware thread to maximize data locality. The hybrid approach allows utilizing all layers of parallelism and providing a flexible adaption to different hardware architectures [9,10].

An integral part of the CODA software architecture is the integration of the before mentioned sparse linear system solver *Spliss* [1]. Spliss is used for solving linear equation systems for implicit time integration methods, e.g. for the test case used in this work and is a linear solver library that, on the one hand, is tailored to the requirements of CFD applications but, on the other hand, independent of the particular CFD solver. It is specialized to solve large sparse systems of linear equations, providing a sparse matrix structure with dense blocks of fixed or variable sizes and a range of different iterative solver components and preconditioners that can be stacked as needed. Spliss leverages available compute resources through mechanisms such as one-sided communication, hybrid parallelization and the use of accelerators, i.e. GPUs, to take advantage of heterogenous architectures while hiding the complexity of these hardware-specific optimizations from a CFD solver such as CODA.

## 3 Porting Spliss to GPU

This section takes a look at GPU acceleration for the sparse linear system solver Spliss. This can be taken advantage of from CPU-only codes such as CODA by simply linking against a version of Spliss compiled for GPU.

Porting the linear solver components to GPU consists of both the initial implementation enabling single GPU usage through computation kernels as well as ensuring that performance scales to multiple GPUs. The process was aided by the Nvidia performance analysis tools [11] NSight Systems (profiling the timeline of GPU usage) and NSight Compute (analysis on a GPU kernel level) for multiple iterations of improvements on general GPU usage and specific computation kernels. The focus of this work is to enable efficient multi-GPU usage including good scalability. This ensures that future improvements made on computation kernel level can also benefit at scale for distributed execution.

A baseline for all following changes and measurements is established as the initial GPU port with multi-GPU usage enabled in code. The computational load is expected to be close to balanced across all processes since this is provided by the according CFD solver. In addition, we assume that the targeted compute architectures are comprised of multiple of the same type of GPU, which is the case for most or all available systems. As a result, Spliss multi-GPU means each process is offloading to a single GPU, which stays consistent throughout the entire runtime. This baseline is displayed as the gray set of bars in Fig. 1, where the solid bar represents the runtime of the entire iteration phase and the shaded bar the time spent within the linear solver (including host to device and vice versa data transfers), which makes up about 75 % of the runtime.

### 3.1 Implementation Changes

By performing an initial analysis we found that the following steps need to be implemented to establish efficient multi-GPU capability and to enable the acceleration that can be achieved by offloading computation to a single GPU also to scale to a distributed use-case using multiple GPUs.

**Data Movement.** At the start, measurements showed an increased runtime for distributed GPU usage. An analysis of the runtime behavior with the Nvidia tools revealed redundant data copy operations from host to device as well as within host memory. We resolved all redundant transfers from host to device and all redundant copy operations in the host memory. The impact of these improvements is highlighted with the blue set of bars in Fig. 1. The improved version achieves a performance gain of about 20 % for the entire iteration phase and about 30 % for linear solver.

**CUDA-aware MPI.** In addition, we identified that when offloading data and computation to GPU the amount of time spent in point-to-point MPI communication needed for halo updates during the key computation of the matrix-vector multiplication was significant. By taking advantage of CUDA-aware MPI capabilities [12], we avoid the need to transfer notable amounts of data between host and device when the MPI communication is executed via the CPU host. We used this to improve the halo exchange by directly passing a pointer to GPU memory to MPI. As a result, an explicit data transfer from device to host on the sender and an explicit data transfer from host to device on the receiver is no longer needed. In order to facilitate this halo exchange we pack the non-contiguous

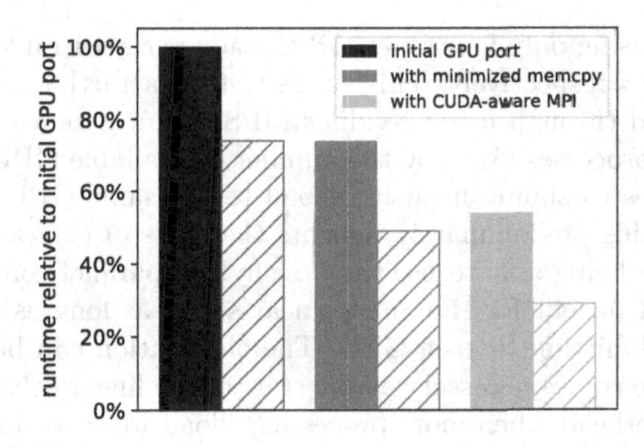


**Fig. 1.** Runtime of different improvements in relation to initial GPU port for a small test case on four A100 GPUs with the entire time integration iterate phase in solid colors and the linear solver within that in shaded colors.

halo data on the device to a contiguous GPU buffer that can be passed directly to the CUDA-aware MPI installation. This allows the MPI library and underlying frameworks to make the decision if and when to copy relevant chunks of data to host memory or communicate directly from and to device memory for best performance. Figure 1 shows that the improvements using CUDA-aware MPI reduce the runtime of the iteration phase to about 50 % of the baseline. In this case, the time spent in the linear solver, i.e. the part running on GPUs, is reduced to about half of the iteration time.

### 3.2 Adjustments at Runtime

Next to the above changes made to enable multi-GPU usage, we can take advantage of optimizations at runtime: GPUDirect Accelerations [12,13] and Nvidia Multi Process Service (MPS) [14]. While the former is automatically applied as deemed appropriate by the CUDA-aware MPI software stack, the latter can be enabled by the user when considered necessary.

**Nvidia Multi Process Service.** Generally, the goal for GPU acceleration is using the hardware as efficiently as algorithmically possible while maintaining little overhead. This favors having only one MPI process offload computation to one distinct GPU each. However, other components of the software framework for the CFD solver (except the linear solver) may benefit from not constricting the number of processes by the number of available GPU accelerators. For instance, with CODA when no GPU acceleration is used the time spent in the non-linear part of the iteration phase is about 5–10 % and the time in the linear solver about 90–95 %. With enabled GPU acceleration the ratio is closer to half and half. As a result, all computation outside of the accelerated linear solver needs to also be executed as efficiently as possible. As will be discussed in Sect. 4, for example, on the AMD Naples and Rome architecture best hybrid performance can be achieved using only four OpenMP threads per MPI rank, i.e. using 16 or 32 MPI processes, respectively. This suggests that a further performance gain could be achieved through using Nvidia's MPS to mitigate a restriction on the number of MPI processes given by the number of available GPUs. MPS enables multiple processes to simultaneously offload to the same GPU as efficiently as possible. While this predominately benefits the parts of computation that take place on CPU by being able to use the best hybrid parallel configuration, there is also a minimal benefit for the Spliss linear solver as long as there are only a few processes submitting to each GPU. The observation can be traced back to the host to device copies necessary at the start of the linear solver execution and is negated by overhead when more processes offload work to the same GPU.

# 4 Evaluation

This section, first, introduces the test systems and the test case, second, provides an assessment of the scalability of Spliss with CODA on the German Aerospace Center's CARO HPC production system and, third, compares the performance and scalability of CODA with Spliss executed on Nvidia A100 GPUs on the JUWELS Booster module at Jülich Supercomputing Center.

## 4.1 The Test Systems

The *Cluster for Advanced Research in Aerospace* CARO is one of the two German Aerospace Center's main HPC systems. It was ranked at 135 in the Top500 list of 11/2021 providing 3.5 TFlop/s out of 5.6 TFlop/s theoretical peak performance [2]. The system offers 1364 compute nodes, whereas each compute node consists of two AMD EPYC 7702 (64 cores at 2.0 GHz). In total, the system offers 174,592 compute cores.

Similar to the AMD Naples architecture, the AMD Rome architecture within this system includes 16 NUMA (non-uniform memory access) domains and three NUMA distances: first, to the memory of the seven other cores on the same die, second, to the memory on the 7 other dies on the same chiplet (socket) and, third, to the memory located on the other chiplet. In addition, only four of the eight cores on each die share a last level cache (L3 cache), which presents an additional difference in memory access latency depending on the locality of the data; whether it is in the shared L3 cache of the according core or in the adjoining L3 cache on the same die.

The second test system is the JUWELS Booster module at Jülich Supercomputing Center. The JUWELS Booster module was ranked at 7 in the Top500 list of 11/2020 providing 44.1 PFlop/s out of 71.0 PFlop/s theoretical peak performance; making it the most powerful system in Europe at that time. The system offers 936 compute nodes, whereas each compute node consists of two AMD EPYC 7402 and four Nvidia A100 GPUs with four-times InfiniBand HDR (Connect-X) interconnect. In total, the system offers 3744 GPUs.

### 4.2 The Test Case

The test case for the evaluation is based on the NASA 3D Onera M6 wing test case [15], which simulates the external airflow at transonic speed and computes typical characteristics like air velocity and direction, pressure and turbulence via a turbulence model. The NASA 3D Onera M6 wing test case is well studied and provides experimental data as well as numerical solutions by other CFD applications for comparison. For the test case, CODA solves the Reynolds-averaged Navier-Stokes equations (RANS) with a Spalart-Allmaras one-equation turbulence model in its negative form (SAneg). It uses a second-order finite-volume spatial discretization with an implicit Euler pseudo-time integration based on local (pseudo) time steps scaled via an up-ramping CFL number starting at 5.0. For the linear problem, a Block Inversion preconditioned Block-Jacobi Solver is applied to solve the linear system. The flow conditions are outlined by the following parameters: the Mach number is set to 0.84, the Reynolds number to 14.6e6, and a fixed 3.06° angle of attack is set.

For this case, the vast majority of the iteration phase is spent in the linear solver, which makes it ideal to offload the computationally intensive linear system solving to GPUs. Measuring the iteration time of CODA provides a very close estimation of the performance and scalability of Spliss within a real-world example. In addition, it highlights the performance of the entire simulation, i.e. it includes all time spent for data transfer between CPU and GPU, CPU-only sections as well as communication and synchronization; not just the time for the GPU kernels. While results may be biased by CODA, the measurements show the combined performance and scalability of CODA with Spliss since performance degrading effects accumulate. In this sense, CODA and Spliss may achieve better performance and scalability individually.

The test case operates with a medium-sized, unstructured mesh with 69.2 million volume elements. This way, it is large enough to achieve good performance per GPU with the chosen linear solver components but still small enough to allow for a reasonable strong scaling evaluation.

### 4.3 Measurement Setup

As a reference, we evaluated the scalability of CODA with the above test case on the CARO HPC system. For the scalability evaluation all software threads are bound to a hardware thread to ensure thread affinity and using one hardware thread per core. For the reference, we compared different hybrid-parallel setups suitable for the specific memory and NUMA layout of the AMD Rome architecture. The comparison showed that best hybrid-parallel performance is reached when using only four OpenMP threads per MPI process, so that these threads share the same last level cache. This is consistent with its predecessor, the AMD Naples architecture, and stands in contrast to other architectures, for instance, the Intel Cascade Lake architecture, where comparable performance for all hybrid setups was obtained [10,16]. Consequently, we chose the best hybrid setup, i.e. with 32 MPI ranks and 4 OpenMP threads per node, as a reference.

For the GPU measurements all software threads are bound to a hardware thread to ensure thread affinity and using one hardware thread per core, too. Similarly, we compared different hybrid-parallel setups that matched well with specific memory and NUMA layout of the AMD Rome architecture on the host as well as the number of installed GPUs, namely 4 MPI processes with 12 OpenMP threads each, 8 process with 6 threads, 16 processes with 3 threads and 48 processes MPI-only. Out of these, the setup with 8 MPI processes and 6 OpenMP threads each achieved the best overall performance and, as a result, was selected to represent the GPU measurements.

For all GPU measurements the linear systems solving via Spliss is offloaded to the Nvidia A100 GPUs, while the non-linear part in CODA is executed on the host CPU. The offloading is achieved by simply linking against the GPU-version of Spliss; without any modifications to the CODA source code or installation.

### 4.4 Comparing CPU and GPU Performance and Scalability

The CPU reference measurement runs the above described test case as strong scaling setup, i.e. the problem size is fixed for increasing core counts, and contains measurements from 2,048 to 12,288 cores or 16 to 96 nodes, respectively. This represents an appropriate range for the given mesh size, with on average about 5600 elements per thread at the largest core count. In this range, the test case achieves a near ideal speedup and a compute performance that matches experiences from previous measurements, which makes it a valid and strong reference to compare the GPU measurements against.

The GPU measurement runs the same strong-scaling test case from 8 to 128 GPUs or 2 to 32 nodes, respectively. This represents an appropriate range for the given mesh size, where two nodes is the minimum number of nodes to fit the simulation data into main memory and at 32 nodes the individual GPU utilization starts to decline. At 32 nodes and 128 GPUs, respectively, the given test case can theoretically achieve about 85 % of the maximum single GPU performance since there is simply not enough computational load to meet the massive demand of parallel load for the A100 GPUs. Since there is an additional decrement for running multiple processes via MPS (two in this case) the resulting utilization is about 70 % of the maximum single GPU performance. For further increasing numbers of GPUs the resulting individual GPU utilization declines faster than the parallel efficiency within Spliss or CODA, i.e. increasing the number of GPUs would necessitate larger input data to match the GPUs demand for computational load.

On the GPU system the test case achieves a scaling efficiency of 82 %, i.e. a speedup of 13.1 of ideally 16 for 128 GPUs, for the entire CODA iteration phase including the linear part in Spliss running on the GPUs, the non-linear part in CODA running on the CPUs and all transfers between host and device. Whereas, the linear part in Spliss makes up about 60 % for 8 GPUS up to 75 % for 128 GPUs of the iteration phase. The linear part in Spliss running on the GPUs on its own, achieves a scaling efficiency of 66 %, i.e. a speedup of 10.5, which is mainly due to the above described decreasing individual GPU utilization to about 70 %

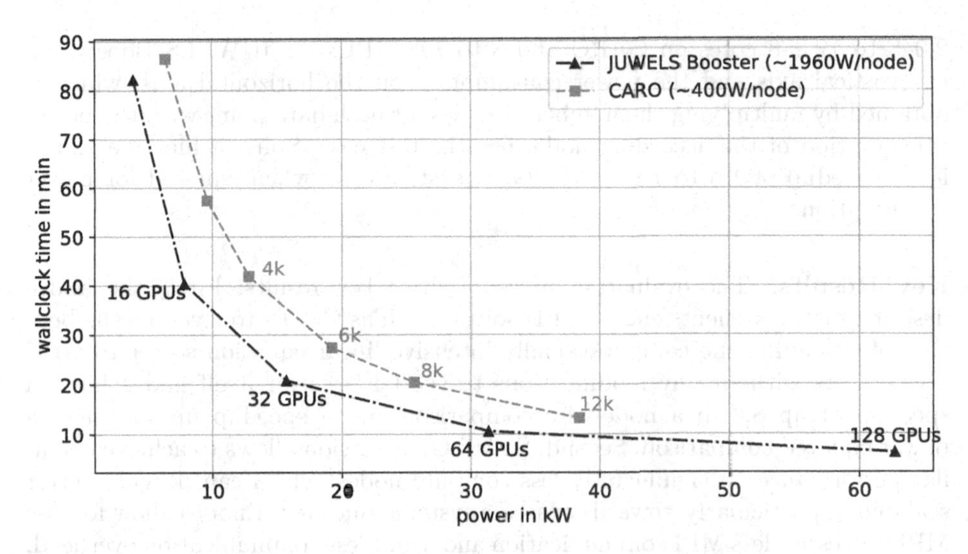


**Fig. 2.** Runtime comparison on CARO (AMD Rome) and JUWELS Booster (4x Nvidia A100) with the M6 wing testcase in relation to power consumption.

on 128 GPUs. The remaining efficiency decrease of about 4 % is due to increasing ratio of synchronization to computation, whereas the synchronization includes MPI communication between the GPUs and transfers between host and device.

When comparing the relative performance per node, i.e. 16 CARO nodes (128 cores AMD Rome each) versus 16 JUWELS Booster nodes (48 cores AMD Rome and 4 GPUs each), the GPU nodes outperform the CPU nodes by a factor of up to 8.4, whereas with increasing scale the factor declines to 6.7 due to the above described reduced GPU utilization for the given test case. While this node-wise comparison matches two high-end nodes that were both state-of-the-art for CPU and GPU systems at their similar installation time, it must be considered that the GPU nodes are significantly more costly in both acquisition and operation, the later due to their much higher power consumption.

To allow for a fairer assessment of both systems, we compare the runtime in relation to estimated power consumption using the Thermal Design Power (TDP) value, as well. A single CARO compute node has a power consumption of about 400 W, which is composed of the 2× 200 W of the AMD Epyc 7702 CPUs. In comparison, a single JUWELS Booster node has a power consumption of about 1960 W, which is made up of the 2× 180 W of the AMD Epyc 7402 CPUs and the 4× 400 W of the Nvidia A100 GPUs. Since both systems are production systems it is infeasible to retrieve the proportionate power consumption of further involved components such as network, storage or cooling. Nonetheless, their impact can be assumed to be insignificant in comparison to the nodes themselves.

Figure 2 shows the runtime comparison for the test case on CARO and JUWELS Booster in relation to power consumption. It depicts the runtime for

2,048 to 12,288 cores on CARO and 8 to 128 GPUs on JUWELS Booster on the vertical axis and the power consumption on the horizontal axis, which is obtained by multiplying the number of nodes for each data point with the power consumption of the according node. For the test case, Spliss achieves a significant speedup of 1.6 to 1.9 on the GPU system even when equated for power consumption.

**Key Results.** The evaluation presents three key results: First, the above described improvements enable CFD solvers such as CODA to leverage the benefits of offloading the computationally intensive linear equation solver to GPU accelerators without any modifications to the CFD solver itself and achieve a speedup of up 8.4 in a node-wise comparison and a speedup up to 1.9 in a power-equated comparison. Second, Spliss' GPU version allows to achieve a similar performance on significantly less compute nodes, which can provide better scalability, particularly, towards exascale systems since fewer nodes allow for less MPI processes, less MPI communication and, thus, less communication overhead. Third, due to the significant acceleration of the linear part on GPUs, the non-linear part that is executed on the CPU becomes more prominent: where it is typically about 5–10 % of the iteration phase it increases to about 40 %. Since the main purpose of the usage of Spliss is to hide the complexity of hardware-specific optimizations from the CFD solver, the non-linear part in the CFD solver might remain exclusive to CPUs by design. To further increase the performance in this case would require a) larger workloads at the given scale, which would be quite typical for industrial applications or b) move to systems that have more performant CPUs in the GPU nodes. For instance, a hypothetical node that replaces the CPU in the JUWELS Booster system with the state-of-the-art CPU from the CARO system would provide an additional speedup of about 20 %, i.e. a power-equated speedup of about 2.3 for the GPU version over the CPU version on CARO.

## 5 Conclusion

The sparse linear system solver Spliss efficiently solves the large sparse systems of linear equations that result from the time integration of the Reynolds-averaged Navier Stokes (RANS) equations. It takes advantage of various current HPC technologies while hiding the resulting complexity from the CFD solver. The heterogenous compute node architecture consisting of CPUs and GPUs that can be found on many current top HPC systems is one of them. In combination with an efficient, hybrid CPU parallelization, Spliss and the improvements of this work allow the performance gain achieved with a single GPU to scale to large distributed systems consisting of hundreds of GPUs. We outlined the steps taken to enable efficient multi-GPU usage for the Spliss linear solver reducing the runtime in a distributed set-up on Nvidia A100 GPUs by up to 50 %. Additionally, using the NASA 3D Onera M6 wing test case for Spliss with the CODA CFD software, we looked at performance in a strong scaling scenario on current

HPC systems. We showed that GPU acceleration of Spliss can yield a up to 8.6 times speedup over state-of-the-art CPU systems or a up to 1.9 times speedup when equated for power consumption.

**Acknowledgements.** Funded by the European Union. This work has received funding from the European High Performance Computing Joint Undertaking (JU) and Germany, Italy, Slovenia, Spain, Sweden, and France under grant agreement No 101092621.

## References

1. Krzikalla, O., Rempke, A., Bleh, A., Wagner, M., Gerhold, T.: Spliss: a sparse linear system solver for transparent integration of emerging HPC technologies into CFD solvers and applications. In: Dillmann, A., Heller, G., Krämer, E., Wagner, C. (eds.) STAB/DGLR Symposium 2020. NNFMMD, vol. 151, pp. 635–645. Springer, Cham (2021). https://doi.org/10.1007/978-3-030-79561-0_60
2. Strohmaier, E., Dongarra, J., Simon, H., Meuer, M.: The 60th Top500 list (2022). https://www.top500.org/lists/top500/2022/11/ Accessed 23 Feb 2023
3. Schwamborn, D., Gerhold, T., Heinrich, R.: The DLR TAU Code: recent applications in research and industry. In: Proceedings of the European Conference on Computational Fluid Dynamics, ECCOMAS CFD (2006). https://elib.dlr.de/22421
4. Leicht, T., et al.: DLR-project digital-X – next generation CFD solver 'Flucs'. Deutscher Luft- und Raumfahrtkongress (2016). https://elib.dlr.de/111205
5. Meinel, M., Einarsson, G.: The FlowSimulator Framework for Massively Parallel CFD Applications. In: PARA 2010 (2010).https://elib.dlr.de/67768
6. Huismann, I., et al.: Accelerating the FlowSimulator: profiling and scalability analysis of an industrial-grade CFD-CSM toolchain. In: 9th Edition of the International Conference on Computational Methods for Coupled Problems in Science and Engineering (COUPLED PROBLEMS 2021) (2021). https://doi.org/10.23967/coupled.2021.008
7. Alrutz, T., et al.: GASPI - a partitioned global address space programming interface. Facing Multicore-Challenge III, LNCS **7686**, 135–136 (2013). https://doi.org/10.1007/978-3-642-35893-7_18
8. Jägersküpper, J., Vollmer, D.: On highly scalable 2-level-parallel unstructured CFD. In: 8th European Congress on Computational Methods in Applied Sciences and Engineering (2022) https://doi.org/10.23967/eccomas.2022.208
9. Wagner, M., Jägersküpper, J., Molka, D., Gerhold, T.: Performance analysis of complex engineering frameworks. In: Mix, H., Niethammer, C., Zhou, H., Nagel, W.E., Resch, M.M. (eds.) Tools for High Performance Computing 2018 / 2019, pp. 123–138. Springer, Cham (2021). https://doi.org/10.1007/978-3-030-66057-4_6
10. Wagner, M.: Scalability evaluation of the CFD solver CODA on the AMD Naples architecture. In: Sustained Simulation Performance 2021, pp. 95–106 (2023). https://doi.org/10.1007/978-3-031-18046-0_7
11. Nvidia: Performance Analysis Tools. https://developer.nvidia.com/performance-analysis-tools. Accessed 20 Feb 2023
12. Kraus, J.: An introduction to CUDA-aware MPI (2013). https://developer.nvidia.com/blog/introduction-cuda-aware-mpi. Accessed 17 Feb 2023
13. Nvidia: GPUDirect. https://developer.nvidia.com/gpudirect. Accessed 20 Feb 2023

14. Nvidia: Multi-Process Service (2021). https://docs.nvidia.com/deploy/pdf/CUDA_Multi_Process_Service_Overview.pdf
15. Daniel Destarac, Antoine Dumont: ONERA M6 Wing Test-Case, Original and TMR (2016). https://turbmodels.larc.nasa.gov/onerawingnumerics_val.html. Accessed 17 Feb 2023
16. Wagner, M., Mohnke, J., Krzikalla, O., Rempke, A.: Evaluating performance and scalability of the sparse linear systems solver Spliss. In: Methods, Tools and Technologies for Design in Aviation (to be published)

# Parareal with a Physics-Informed Neural Network as Coarse Propagator

Abdul Qadir Ibrahim(✉), Sebastian Götschel, and Daniel Ruprecht

Chair Computational Mathematics,
Institute of Mathematics,
Hamburg University of Technology,
Hamburg, Germany
{abdul.ibrahim,sebastian.goetschel,
daniel.ruprecht}@tuhh.de

**Abstract.** Parallel-in-time algorithms provide an additional layer of concurrency for the numerical integration of models based on time-dependent differential equations. Methods like Parareal, which parallelize across multiple time steps, rely on a computationally cheap and coarse integrator to propagate information forward in time, while a parallelizable expensive fine propagator provides accuracy. Typically, the coarse method is a numerical integrator using lower resolution, reduced order or a simplified model. Our paper proposes to use a physics-informed neural network (PINN) instead. We demonstrate for the Black-Scholes equation, a partial differential equation from computational finance, that Parareal with a PINN coarse propagator provides better speedup than a numerical coarse propagator. Training and evaluating a neural network are both tasks whose computing patterns are well suited for GPUs. By contrast, mesh-based algorithms with their low computational intensity struggle to perform well. We show that moving the coarse propagator PINN to a GPU while running the numerical fine propagator on the CPU further improves Parareal's single-node performance. This suggests that integrating machine learning techniques into parallel-in-time integration methods and exploiting their differences in computing patterns might offer a way to better utilize heterogeneous architectures.

**Keywords:** Parareal · parallel-in-time integration · PINN · Machine learning · GPUs · heterogeneous architectures

## 1 Introduction

Models based on differential equations are ubiquitous in science and engineering. High-resolution requirements, often due to the multiscale nature of many prob-

This project has received funding from the European High-Performance Computing Joint Undertaking (JU) under grant agreement No 955701. The JU receives support from the European Union's Horizon 2020 research and innovation programme and Belgium, France, Germany, and Switzerland. This project also received funding from the German Federal Ministry of Education and Research (BMBF) grant 16HPC048. This project has also received funding from the German Federal Ministry of Education and Research (BMBF) under grant 16ME0679K.



J. Cano et al. (Eds.): Euro-Par 2023, LNCS 14100, pp. 649–663, 2023.
https://doi.org/10.1007/978-3-031-39698-4_44

lems, typically require that these models are run on high-performance computers to cope with memory demand and computational cost. Spatial parallelization is already a widely used and effective approach to parallelize numerical algorithms for partial differential equations but, on its own, will not deliver enough concurrency for extreme-scale parallel architectures. Parallel-in-time integration algorithms can help to increase the degree of parallelism in numerical models. Combined space-time parallelization can improve speedup over spatial parallelization alone on hundreds of thousands of cores [24].

Parallel-in-time methods like Parareal [14], PFASST [4] or MGRIT [5] rely on serial coarse level integrators to propagate information forward in time. These coarse propagators constitute an unavoidable serial bottleneck which limits achievable speedup. Therefore, the coarse-level integrators must be as fast as possible. However, these methods are iterative and speedup will also decrease as the number of iterations goes up. A coarse propagator that is too inaccurate, even when computationally cheap, will not provide good speedup because the number of required iterations will be too large. Hence, a good coarse propagator needs to be at least somewhat accurate but also needs to run as fast as possible. This trade-off suggests that using neural networks as coarse propagators could be promising: once trained, they are very fast to evaluate while still providing reasonable accuracy. Furthermore, neural networks are well suited for running on GPUs whereas mesh-based discretizations are harder to run efficiently because of their lower computational intensity. Therefore, algorithms featuring a combination of mesh-based components and neural network components would be well suited to run on heterogeneous systems combining CPUs and GPUs or other accelerators.

Our paper makes three novel contributions. It (i) provides the first study of using a PINN as a coarse propagator in Parareal, (ii) shows that a PINN as a coarse propagator can accelerate Parareal convergence and improve speedup and (iii) illustrates that moving the PINN coarse propagator to a GPUs improves speedup further. While we demonstrate our approach for the Black-Scholes equation, a model from computational finance, the idea is transferable to other types of partial differential equations where Parareal was shown to be effective. We only investigate performance on a single node with one GPU. Extending the approach to parallelize in time across multiple nodes and to work in combination with spatial parallelization left for future work.

## 2 Related Work

Using machine learning (ML) to solve differential equations has become an active field of research. Some papers aim to entirely replace the numerical solver by neural networks [21,25]. Physics-informed neural networks (PINNs) [20], which use the residual of a partial differential equation (PDE) as well as boundary- and initial conditions in the loss function, are used in many applications. This includes a demonstration for the Black Scholes equation (1), showing that a PINN is capable of accurately pricing a range of options with complex payoffs, and is significantly faster than traditional numerical methods [23]. However, solving differential equations with ML alone generally does not provide the high accuracy that can be achieved by numerical solvers. This has led to a range of ideas where ML is used as an ingredient of classical numerical methods instead and not as a replacement [9].

Specific to parallel-in-time integration methods, there are two research directions aiming to connect them with machine learning. On the one hand, there are attempts to use ML techniques to improve parallel-in-time algorithms. Our paper falls into this category. Using a neural network as coarse propagator for Parareal has been studied in two previous papers. Yalla and Enquist [26] were the first to explore this approach. They use a neural network with one hidden layer of size 1000 and demonstrate for a high dimensional oscillator that it helps Parareal converge faster compared to a numerical coarse propagator. However, no runtimes or speedups are reported. Agboh et al. [1] use a feed-forward deep neural network as a coarse propagator to integrate an ordinary differential equation modeling responses to a robot arm pushing multiple objects. They also observe that the trained coarse propagator improves Parareal convergence compared to a simplified analytical coarse model. Nguyen and Tsai [17] do not fully replace the numerical coarse propagator but use supervised learning to enhance its accuracy for wave propagation modeling. They observe that this enhances stability and accuracy of Parareal, provided the training data contains sufficiently representative examples. Gorynina et al. [6] study the use of a machine-learned spectral neighbor analysis potential in molecular dynamics simulations with Parareal.

A few papers go the opposite way and adopt ideas from parallel-in-time integration methods to parallelize and accelerate the process of training deep neural networks. Günther et al. [7] use a nonlinear multi-grid method to improve the training process of a deep residual network. They use MGRIT, a multi-level generalization of Parareal, to obtain layer-parallel training on CPUs, reporting a speedup of up to 8.5 on 128 cores. Kirby et al. [11] extend their approach to multiple GPUs, obtaining further performance gains. In a similar way, Meng et al. [16] use Parareal to generate starting values for a series of PINNs to help with the training process. Motivated by the observation that it becomes expensive to train PINNs that integrate over long time intervals, they concatenate multiple short-time PINNs instead. They use a cheap numerical coarse propagator and a Parareal iteration to connect these PINNs with each PINN inheriting the parameters from its predecessor. While they mention the possibility of using a PINN as coarse propagator, they do not pursue this idea further in their paper. Lorin [15] derives a parallel-in-time variant of neural ODEs to improve training of deep Residual Neural Networks. Finally, Lee et al. [13] use a Parareal-like procedure to train deep neural networks across multiple GPUs.

## 3 Algorithms and Benchmark Problem

The Black-Scholes equation is a widely used model to price options in financial markets [3]. It is based on the assumption that the price of an asset follows a geometric Brownian motion, so that the log-returns of the asset are normally distributed. Closed form solutions exist for the price of a European call or put option [12], but not for more complex options such as American options or options with multiple underlying assets. To be able to compute numerical errors, we thus focus on the European call option, a financial derivative that gives the buyer the right, but not the obligation, to buy an underlying asset at a predetermined price (the strike price) on or before the expiration date. The price $V$ of the option can be modeled by

$$f(V) = \frac{\partial V}{\partial t}(S,t) + \frac{1}{2}\sigma^2 S^2 \frac{\partial^2 V}{\partial S^2}(S,t) + rS\frac{\partial V}{\partial S}(S,t) - rV(S,t) = 0, \quad (1)$$

where $S$ denotes the current value of the underlying asset, $t$ is time, $r$ denotes the no-risk interest rate (for example saving rates in a bank) and $\sigma$ denotes the volatility of the underlying asset. To fully determine the solution to (1), we impose a final state at expiry time $t = T$ and two boundary conditions with respect to $S$, motivated by the behaviour of the option at $S = 0$ and as $S \to \infty$. For the call option, the expiry time condition is

$$V(T,S) = \max(S - K, 0) \text{ for all } S. \quad (2)$$

If the underlying asset becomes worthless, then it will remain worthless, so the option will also be worthless. Thus,

$$V(t,0) = 0 \text{ for all } t. \quad (3)$$

On the other hand, if $S$ becomes very large, then the option will almost certainly be exercised, and the exercise price is negligible compared to $S$. Thus, the option will have essentially the same value as the underlying asset itself and

$$V(t,S) \sim 0 \text{ as } S \to \infty, \text{ for fixed } t. \quad (4)$$

For the European call option, we select an interval of $t = 0$ and $T = 1$ and an artificial bound for the asset of $S = 5000$€.

### 3.1 Parareal

Parareal is an iterative algorithm to solve an initial value problem of the form

$$V'(t) = \phi(V(t)), \ t \in [0,T], \ V(0) = V_0, \quad (5)$$

where in our case the right hand side function $\phi$ stems from the discretization of the spatial derivatives in (1). Note that the coefficients in (1) do not depend on time, so we can restrict our exposition to the autonomous case. Decompose the time domain $[0,T]$ into $N$ time-slices $[T^n, T^{n+1}]$, $n = 0, \ldots, N-1$. Denote as $\mathcal{F}$ a numerical time stepping algorithm with constant step size $\delta t$ and high accuracy and as

$$V_{n+1} = \mathcal{F}(V_n) \quad (6)$$

the result of integrating from some initial value $V_n$ at the start time $T^n$ of a time slice until the end time $T^{n+1}$. Classical time stepping corresponds to evaluating (6) for $n = 0, \ldots, N-1$ in serial. Parareal replaces this serial procedure with the iteration

$$V_{n+1}^{k+1} = \mathcal{G}(V_n^{k+1}) + \mathcal{F}(V_n^k) - \mathcal{G}(V_n^k) \tag{7}$$

where $k = 1, \ldots, K$ counts the iterations. The key in (7) is that the computationally expensive evaluation of $\mathcal{F}$ can be parallelized across all $N$ time slices. Here, we always assume that $P = N$ many processes are used and each process holds a single time slice. A visualization of the Parareal workflow as well as pseudocode can be found in the literature [22]. As $k \to N$, $V_n^k$ converges to the same solution generated by serial evaluation of (6). However, to achieve speedup, we require convergence in $K \ll N$ iterations. An upper bound for speedup achievable with Parareal using $P$ processors to integrate over $N = P$ time slices is given by

$$s_{\text{bound}}(P) = \frac{1}{\left(1 + \frac{K}{P}\right)\frac{c_c}{c_f} + \frac{K}{P}} \tag{8}$$

where $K$ is the number of iterations, $c_c$ the runtime of $\mathcal{G}$ and $c_f$ the runtime of $\mathcal{F}$ [22]. Since (8) neglects overhead and communication, it is an upper bound on achievable speedups and measured speedups will be lower.

### 3.2 Numerical Solution of the Black-Scholes Equation

We approximate the spatial derivatives in (1) by second order centered finite differences on an equidistant mesh

$$0 = S_0 < S_1 < \ldots < S_N = L \tag{9}$$

with $S_{i+1} - S_i = \Delta S$ for $i = 0, \ldots, N-1$. For the inner nodes, we obtain the semi-discrete initial value problem

$$V_j'(t) = -\frac{1}{2}\sigma^2 S_j^2 \frac{V_{j+1} - 2V_j + V_{j-1}}{\Delta S^2} - rS_j \frac{V_{j+1} - V_{j-1}}{2\Delta S} + rV_j \tag{10}$$

with $j = 1, \ldots,$. This is complemented by the boundary condition $V_0 = 0$ for a zero asset value. We also impose the asymptotic boundary condition (4) at finite distance $L$ so that $V_N = 0$. In time, we use a second order Crank-Nicolson method for $\mathcal{F}$ and a first order implicit Euler method as numerical $\mathcal{G}$. Since we have a final condition instead of an initial condition, we start at time $T = 1$ and solve the problem backwards. We use 200 steps for the fine method and 100 steps for the coarse.

### 3.3 Physics Informed Neural Network (PINN)

The PINN we use as coarse propagator gets a time slice $[t_{\text{start}}, t_{\text{end}}] \subset [0, T]$, the asset price $V$ at $t_{\text{start}}$ and stock values $S$, and outputs the predicted state of the asset price $\tilde{V}$ at $t_{\text{end}}$. To train it, we define three sets of collocation points in time and stock price: $(S_i, t_i), i = 1, \dots N_f$ in the interior of the space-time domain for evaluating the residual $f(V)$ of the Black-Scholes eqation (1), $(S_i, t_i), i = 1, \dots N_b$ collocation points on the boundary to evaluate (2), and $S_i, i = 1, \dots N_{\text{exp}}$ for the final state conditions (3), (4). The loss function to be minimized is given by

$$\text{MSE}_{\text{total}} = \text{MSE}_f + \text{MSE}_{\text{exp}} + \text{MSE}_b, \tag{11}$$

consisting of a term to minimize the PDE residual $f(V)$

$$\text{MSE}_{\text{f}} = \frac{1}{N_f} \sum_{i=1}^{N_f} |f(\tilde{V}(t_i, S_i))|^2, \tag{12}$$

the boundary loss term

$$\text{MSE}_{\text{b}} = \frac{1}{N_b} \sum_{i=1}^{N_b} \left| \tilde{V}(t_i, S_i) - V(t_i, S_i) \right|^2, \tag{13}$$

and the loss at expiration

$$\text{MSE}_{\text{exp}} = \frac{1}{N_{\text{exp}}} \sum_{i=1}^{N_{\text{exp}}} \left| \tilde{V}(T, S_i) - \max(S_i - K, 0) \right|^2, \tag{14}$$

For our setup, we randomly generate $N_f = 100,000$ collocation points within the domain $[0, 5000] \times [0, 1]$, $N_b = 10,000$ collocation points at the boundary $[0, 1]$ and $N_{\text{exp}} = 10,000$ collocation points to sample the expiration condition over $[0, 5000]$. The derivatives that are required to compute the PDE loss are calculated by automatic differentiation [2]. We compute the PDE residual (12) over the points inside the domain, the boundary condition loss (13) over the spatial boundary and the expiration loss (14) over the end points. The sum of the three forms the total loss function (11). Figure 1 shows a subset of the generated collocation points to illustrate the approach.

The neural network consists of 10 fully connected layers with 50 neurons in each and was implemented using Pytorch [18]. Figure 2 shows the principle of a PINN but for a smaller network for the sake of readability. Every linear layer, excluding the output layer, is followed by the ReLU activation function. The weights for the neural network are initialized using Kaiming [8]. We focus here on a proof-of-concept and have not undertaken a systematic effort to optimize the network architecture but this would be an interesting avenue for future research.

We used the Adam optimizer [10] with a learning rate of $10^{-2}$ for the initial round of training for 5000 epochs, followed by a second round of training with a learning rate of $10^{-3}$ for 800 epochs. The training data (collocation points) was shuffled during every epoch to prevent the model from improving predictions based on data order rather than the underlying patterns in the data. Table 1 shows the behavior of the three loss function terms. The total training time for this model was around 30 min.

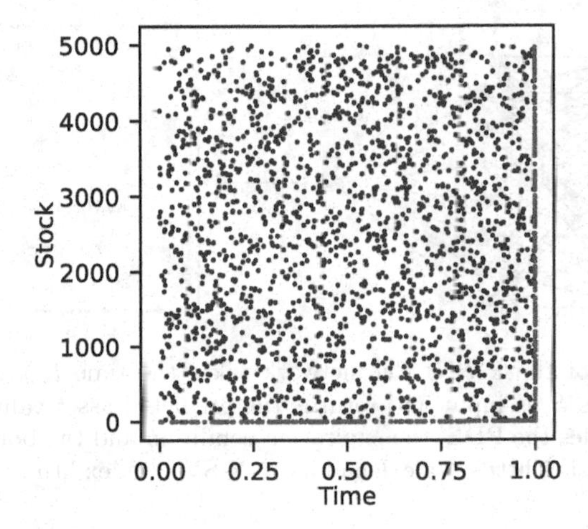


**Fig. 1.** Subset of the randomly generated collocation nodes. The solution is forced to satisfy the PDE at the inner nodes by minimizing the PDE residual, to satisfy the boundary condition at the green nodes via the boundary loss and the expiration condition at the red nodes via the expiration loss. (Color figure online)

# 4 Results

The numerical experiments were conducted on OpenSUSE Leap 15.4 running an Intel Core 24 × 12th Gen Intel i9-12900K with a base clock speed of 3.2 GHz and a maximum turbo frequency of 5.2 GHz, with 62.6 GiB of RAM and an NVIDIA GeForce RTX 3060/PCIe/SSE2 GPU. Implementations were done using Python 3.10, pytorch1.13.1+cu117, mpi4py3.1.4, as well as numba0.55.1 for the GPU runs. All results shown in this paper are reproducible using the code and instructions available in the figshare or GitHub repository [19].

*Parareal Convergence.* Figure 3 shows the normalized $\ell_2$ error for the serial fine, numerical coarse and PINN-coarse propagator over time (left). As expected, the fine propagator is the most accurate with an $\ell_2$ error of around $10^{-3}$ at the end of the simulation. The numerical coarse propagator is noticeably less accurate. The PINN coarse propagator is more accurate than the numerical coarse propagator but also does not reach the accuracy of the fine. To illustrate the importance of encoding the differential equation in the loss function, we also show a neural network (NN) trained only on data produced with the fine propagator but without the terms encoding the differential equation. The neural network without PDE residual is somewhat more accurate than the numerical coarse method but not as good as the PINN. Note that the PINN used here does not need numerically generated trajectories as training data, as the loss function (11) only consists of PDE residual, boundary and expiration conditions and does not include a data mismatch term.

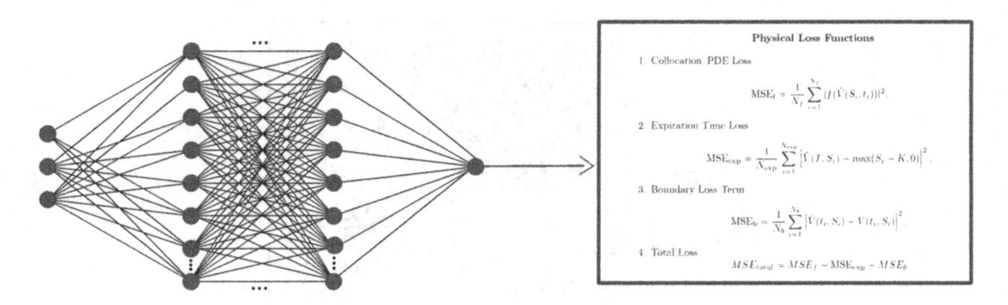


**Fig. 2.** Structure of the PINN. The network takes the time $t_{\mathtt{start}}, t_{\mathtt{end}}$, asset values $V$ and stock values $S$ as input and returns the predicted asset values $\tilde{V}$ at $t_{\mathtt{end}}$. The loss function encodes the PDE, the expiration condition and the boundary conditions. Figure produced using https://alexlenail.me/NN-SVG/index.html.

Figure 3 (right) shows the normalized $\ell_2$ error of Parareal against the number of iterations. For all three coarse propagators, numerical, NN and PINN, Parareal converges very quickly. Although PINN and NN are slightly more accurate than the numerical coarse propagator, the impact on convergence is small. After one iteration, the iteration error of Parareal is smaller than the discretization error of the fine method. After $K = 3$ iterations, Parareal has reproduced the fine solution up to round-off error. Below, we report runtimes and speedup for $K = 3$. With only a single iteration, the $K/P$ term in (8) is less important and reducing the runtime of the coarse propagator increases overall speedup even more. Therefore, the case with $K = 3$ is the case where switching to the coarse propagator will yield less improvement.

*Generalization.* Figure 4 shows how Parareal with a PINN coarse propagator converges if applied to (1) with parameters different from those for which the PINN was trained. As parameters become increasingly different from the training values, the coarse propagator will become less accurate. However, if Parareal converges, it will produce the correct solution since the numerical fine propagator always uses the correct parameters. The combination of Parareal + PINN generalizes fairly well. Even for parameters more than ten times larger than the training values it only requires one additional iteration to converge. While the additional iteration will somewhat reduce achievable speedup as given by (8), the performance results presented below should not be overly sensitive to changes in the model parameters.

*Parareal Runtimes and Speedup.* Reported runtimes are measured using the `time` command in Linux and include the time required for setup, computation and data movement. Table 2 shows the runtime in milliseconds of Parareal using $P = 16$ cores for four different coarse propagator configurations. Shown are averages over five runs as well as the standard deviation. Replacing the numerical

**Table 1.** Evolution of the loss function during network training. The three columns show the MSE for the three terms of the loss function related to the end condition (2), boundary conditions (3) and (4) and residual (1). After 5000 epochs with training rate $10^{-2}$, another 800 epochs of training with a reduced training rate of $10^{-3}$ were performed.

| Epoch | Expiration | Boundary | Residual |
|---|---|---|---|
| 0 | $9.21 \times 10^{2}$ | $9.21 \times 10^{2}$ | $7.33 \times 10^{3}$ |
| 2000 | $5.58 \times 10^{-1}$ | $3.45 \times 10^{-2}$ | $2.50 \times 10^{-2}$ |
| 4000 | $4.11 \times 10^{-2}$ | $2.34 \times 10^{-2}$ | $5.00 \times 10^{-3}$ |
| 5000 | $5.92 \times 10^{-1}$ | $1.34 \times 10^{-2}$ | $4.22 \times 10^{-3}$ |
| 5300 | $4.19 \times 10^{-2}$ | $3.22 \times 10^{-3}$ | $1.94 \times 10^{-4}$ |
| 5500 | $6.46 \times 10^{-4}$ | $1.96 \times 10^{-4}$ | $5.73 \times 10^{-5}$ |
| 5800 | $2.92 \times 10^{-5}$ | $1.14 \times 10^{-5}$ | $3.19 \times 10^{-4}$ |

coarse propagator with a PINN on a CPU reduces Parareal execution time by a factor of 2.4, increasing to 2.9 if the PINN is run on a GPU. For the numerical coarse propagator, using the GPU offers no performance gain because the resolution and thus computational intensity is not high enough. The much faster coarse propagator provided by the PINN significantly reduces the serial bottleneck in Parareal and will, as demonstrated below, yield a marked improvement in speedup.

**Table 2.** Runtime $c_c$ in milliseconds of the coarse propagator $\mathcal{C}$ averaged over five runs plus/minus standard deviation.

| | Numerical | PINN | Speedup over CPU-Numerical |
|---|---|---|---|
| CPU | $3.48 \pm 0.056$ | $1.47 \pm 0.073$ | 2.4 |
| GPU | $3.99 \pm 0.651$ | $1.21 \pm 0.041$ | 2.9 |
| Speedup | – | 1.21 | |

Table 3 shows runtimes for the full Parareal iteration averaged over five runs. The fastest configuration is the one that runs the numerical fine propagator on the CPU and the PINN coarse propagator on the GPU. Executing both fine and coarse propagator on the CPU takes about a factor of three longer. Importantly, moving both to the GPU, while somewhat faster than running all on the CPU, is slower than the mixed version by a factor of about two. The full GPU variant will eventually be faster if the resolution of the fine and coarse propagator are both extremely high. However, the current resolution already produces an error of around $10^{-3}$ which will be sufficient in most situations. This illustrates how a combination of numerical method and PINN within Parareal

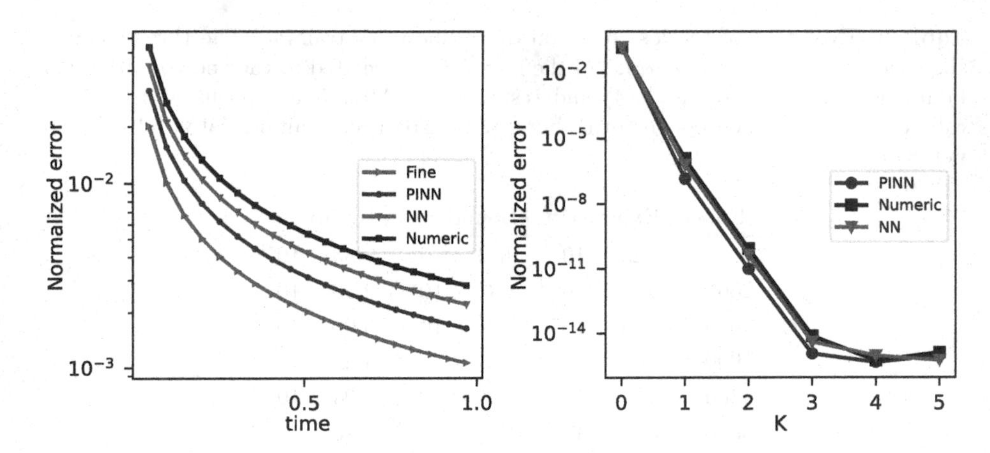


**Fig. 3.** Normalized $\ell_2$-error over time of coarse and fine propagator against the analytical solution (left). Normalized $\ell_2$-error against the serial fine solution versus number of iterations for three different variants of Parareal (right). The black line (squares) is Parareal with a numerical coarse propagator, the green line (diamonds) is Parareal with a neural network as coarse propagator that is trained only on data while the blue line (circles) is Parareal with a PINN as coarse propagator that also uses the terms of the differential equation in the loss function. Parareal uses $P = 16$ time slices in all cases. (Color figure online)

can not only improve performance due to the lower cost of the PINN but also help to better utilize a node that features both CPUs and GPUs or even neural network accelerators. Thus, the different computing patters in finite difference numerical methods and neural networks can be turned into an advantage.

**Table 3.** Runtimes in milliseconds for Parareal averaged over five runs plus/minus standard deviation.

| | CPU-Coarse | GPU-Coarse |
|---|---|---|
| CPU-Fine | $128.48 \pm 0.715$ | $41.241970 \pm 0.334$ |
| GPU-Fine | $83.2545 \pm 0.356$ | $87.45234 \pm 0.253$ |

Figure 5 shows runtimes for Parareal with both a PINN and numerical coarse propagator on a CPU (left) and GPU (right) against the number of cores/time slices $P$. The numerical fine propagator is always run on the CPU. In both cases, runtimes decrease at a similar rate as the number of time slices/cores $P$ increases. The numerical coarse propagator is consistently slower than the PINN and the gap is similar on the CPU and GPU. Finally, Fig. 6 shows the speedup (left) and parallel efficiency (right) for Parareal with a numerical, PINN-CPU and PINN-GPU coarse propagator. The speedup bounds (8) are shown as lines. Moving from a numerical coarse propagator to a PINN and moving the

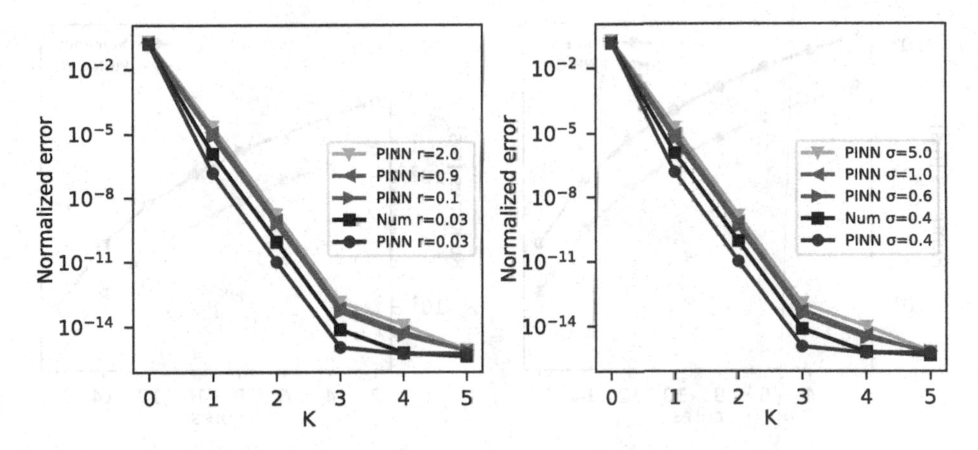


**Fig. 4.** Convergence of Parareal for different interest rates $r$ (left) and volatilities $\sigma$ (right). In all cases, the coarse propagator is the PINN trained for values of $r = 0.03$ and $\sigma = 0.4$. Even for parameter values more than ten times larger than the ones for which the PINN was trained, Parareal requires only one additional iteration to converge to within machine precision of the fine integrator.

PINN from the CPU to a GPU each improves speedup significantly. For the numerical coarse propagator, Parareal achieves a speedup of around $S(16) \approx 2$. Replacing the numerical integrator with a PINN improves speedup to $S(16) \approx 3$. Running this PINN on a GPU again improves speedup to $S(16) \approx 4.5$, more than double what we achieved with the numerical coarse propagator on a CPU. The improvements in speedup translate into increased parallel efficiency, which improves from around 30% for the numerical coarse propagator to around 60% for the PINN-GPU coarse method. For smaller numbers of processors, the gains in speedup are less pronounced, because the $K/P$ term in (8) is more dominant. But gains in parallel efficiency are fairly consistent from $P = 2$ cores to $P = 16$ cores. In summary, this demonstrates that replacing a CPU-run numerical coarse propagator with a GPU-run PINN can greatly improve the performance of Parareal by minimizing the serial bottleneck from the coarse propagator.

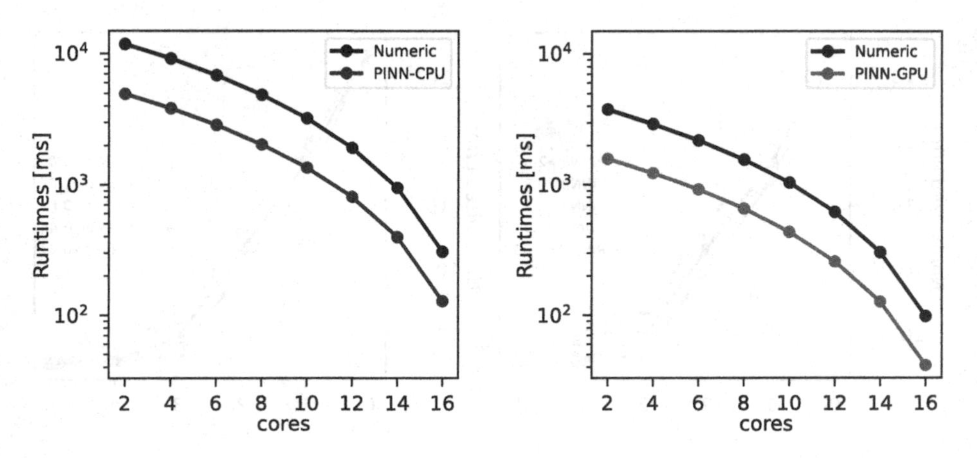


**Fig. 5.** Runtimes in milliseconds for Parareal (dots) and the serial numerical fine propagator (horizontal lines) on a CPU (left) and GPU (right)

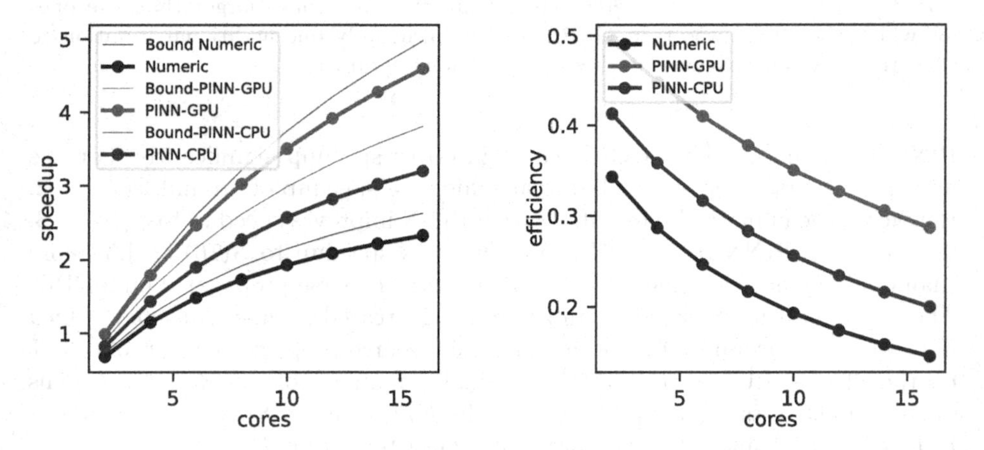


**Fig. 6.** Speedup (left) and parallel efficiency (right) of Parareal over the serial numerical fine propagator on a CPU. Because the PINN-GPU coarse propagator is faster, it reduces the serial bottleneck of Parareal and allows for better speedup and parallel efficiency.

## 5 Discussion

Parareal is a parallel-in-time method that iterates between a cheap coarse and a parallel expensive fine integrator. To maintain causality, the coarse propagator needs to run in serial and therefore reflects a bottleneck that limits achievable speedup. Mostly, coarse propagators are similar to fine propagators and build using numerical methods but with lower order, lower resolution or, in some cases, models of reduced complexity. We investigate the use of a physics-informed neural network (PINN) instead. The PINN is shown to be slightly more accurate than a numerical coarse propagator but a factor of three faster. Using it does not affect convergence speed of Parareal but greatly reduces the serial bottleneck from the coarse propagator.

We show that, on a single node with one GPU, a combination of a numerical fine propagator run on a CPU with a PINN coarse propagator run on a GPU provides more than twice the speedup than vanilla Parareal using a numerical coarse propagator run on the CPU. Also, we demonstrate that moving both fine and coarse propagator to the GPU is slower than moving just the PINN coarse method to the GPU and keeping the numerical fine method on the CPU. The reason is that unless the resolution of the fine propagator is extremely high, its low computational intensity means there is little gain from computing on a GPU and so overheads from data movement are dominant. By contrast, evaluating PINNs is well suited for GPU computation. Our results demonstrate that using PINNs to build coarse level models for parallel-in-time methods is a promising approach to reduce the serial bottleneck imposed by causality. They also suggest that parallel-in-time methods featuring a combination of numerical algorithms and neural networks might be useful to better utilize heterogeneous systems.

## References

1. Agboh, W., Grainger, O., Ruprecht, D., Dogar, M.: Parareal with a learned coarse model for robotic manipulation. Comput. Vis. Sci. **23**(8), 1–10 (2020)
2. Baydin, A.G., Pearlmutter, B.A., Radul, A.A., Siskind, J.M.: Automatic differentiation in machine learning: a survey. J. March. Learn. Res. **18**, 1–43 (2018)
3. Black, F., Scholes, M.: The pricing of options and corporate liabilities. J. Polit. Econ. **81**(3), 637–654 (1973)
4. Emmett, M., Minion, M.L.: Toward an efficient parallel in time method for partial differential equations. Commun. Appl. Math. Comput. Sci. **7**, 105–132 (2012). https://doi.org/10.2140/camcos.2012.7.105
5. Falgout, R.D., Friedhoff, S., Kolev, T.V., MacLachlan, S.P., Schroder, J.B.: Parallel time integration with multigrid. SIAM J. Sci. Comput. **36**, C635–C661 (2014). https://doi.org/10.1137/130944230
6. Gorynina, O., Legoll, F., Lelievre, T., Perez, D.: Combining machine-learned and empirical force fields with the parareal algorithm: application to the diffusion of atomistic defects (2022)
7. Günther, S., Ruthotto, L., Schroder, J.B., Cyr, E.C., Gauger, N.R.: Layer-parallel training of deep residual neural networks. SIAM J. Math. Data Sci. **2**(1), 1–23 (2020). https://doi.org/10.1137/19M1247620
8. He, K., Zhang, X., Ren, S., Sun, J.: Delving deep into rectifiers: surpassing human-level performance on ImageNet classification. In: Proceedings of the IEEE International Conference on Computer Vision, pp. 1026–1034 (2015)
9. Huang, R., Li, R., Xi, Y.: Learning optimal multigrid smoothers via neural networks. SIAM J. Sci. Comput. S199–S225 (2022). https://doi.org/10.1137/21M1430030
10. Kingma, D.P., Ba, J.: Adam: a method for stochastic optimization (2014). https://doi.org/10.48550/arxiv.1412.6980
11. Kirby, A., Samsi, S., Jones, M., Reuther, A., Kepner, J., Gadepally, V.: Layer-parallel training with GPU concurrency of deep residual neural networks via non-linear multigrid. In: 2020 IEEE High Performance Extreme Computing Conference (HPEC). IEEE (2020). https://doi.org/10.1109/hpec43674.2020.9286180

12. Kumar, S., Yildirim, A., Khan, Y., Jafari, H., Sayevand, K., Wei, L.: Analytical solution of fractional Black-Scholes European option pricing equation by using Laplace transform. J. Fractional Calculus Appl. **2**(8), 1–9 (2012)
13. Lee, Y., Park, J., Lee, C.O.: Parareal neural networks emulating a parallel-in-time algorithm. IEEE Trans. Neural Netw. Learn. Syst. 1–12 (2022). https://doi.org/10.1109/tnnls.2022.3206797
14. Lions, J.L., Maday, Y., Turinici, G.: A "parareal" in time discretization of PDE's. Compt. Rendus l'Acad. Sci. - Ser. I - Math. **332**, 661–668 (2001). https://doi.org/10.1016/S0764-4442(00)01793-6
15. Lorin, E.: Derivation and analysis of parallel-in-time neural ordinary differential equations. Ann. Math. Artif. Intell. **88**(10), 1035–1059 (2020). https://doi.org/10.1007/s10472-020-09702-6
16. Meng, X., Li, Z., Zhang, D., Karniadakis, G.E.: PPINN: parareal physics-informed neural network for time-dependent PDEs. Comput. Methods Appl. Mech. Eng. **370**, 113250 (2020). https://doi.org/10.1016/j.cma.2020.113250
17. Nguyen, H., Tsai, R.: Numerical wave propagation aided by deep learning. J. Comput. Phys. **475**, 111828 (2023). https://doi.org/10.1016/j.jcp.2022.111828
18. Paszke, A., et al.: PyTorch: an imperative style, high-performance deep learning library (2019). https://doi.org/10.48550/arXiv.1912.01703
19. Qadir, I.A., Götschel, S., Ruprecht, D.: Parareal with a physics-informed neural network as coarse propagator (2023). https://doi.org/10.6084/m9.figshare.23544636
20. Raissi, M., Perdikaris, P., Karniadakis, G.E.: Physics informed deep learning (part I): Data-driven solutions of nonlinear partial differential equations (2017). https://doi.org/10.48550/arXiv.1711.10561
21. Ranade, R., Hill, C., Pathak, J.: DiscretizationNet: a machine-learning based solver for Navier-Stokes equations using finite volume discretization. Comput. Methods Appl. Mech. Eng. **378**, 113722 (2021). https://doi.org/10.1016/j.cma.2021.113722
22. Ruprecht, D.: Shared memory pipelined parareal. In: Rivera, F.F., Pena, T.F., Cabaleiro, J.C. (eds.) Euro-Par 2017. LNCS, vol. 10417, pp. 669–681. Springer, Cham (2017). https://doi.org/10.1007/978-3-319-64203-1_48
23. Sirignano, J., Spiliopoulos, K.: DGM: a deep learning algorithm for solving partial differential equations. J. Comput. Phys. **375**, 1339–1364 (2018)
24. Speck, R., et al.: A massively space-time parallel N-body solver. In: Proceedings of the International Conference on High Performance Computing, Networking, Storage and Analysis, SC 2012, pp. 92:1–92:11. IEEE Computer Society Press, Los Alamitos (2012). https://doi.org/10.1109/SC.2012.6
25. Stender, M., Ohlsen, J., Geisler, H., Chabchoub, A., Hoffmann, N., Schlaefer, A.: Up-Net: a generic deep learning-based time stepper for parameterized spatio-temporal dynamics. Available at SSRN 4053304 (2022)
26. Yalla, G.R., Engquist, B.: Parallel in time algorithms for multiscale dynamical systems using interpolation and neural networks. In: Proceedings of the High Performance Computing Symposium, HPC 2018, pp. 9:1–9:12. Society for Computer Simulation International (2018)

# Faster Segmented Sort on GPUs

Robin Kobus, Johannes Nelgen, Valentin Henkys, and Bertil Schmidt(✉)

Institute of Computer Science,
Johannes Gutenberg University,
55128 Mainz, Germany
{kobus,henkys,bertil.schmidt}@uni-mainz.de

Euro-Par Artifact Evaluated AEC

**Abstract.** Efficient parallel implementations of various sorting algorithms on modern hardware platforms are essential to numerous application areas. In this paper, we first measure the performance of the leading segmented sort implementation on CUDA-enabled GPUs and determine optimal setups using the resulting runtimes. Subsequently, we propose a number of changes that improve efficiency for segments of specific lengths. Furthermore, an alternative key-only version is introduced, that is specifically optimized to just sort keys instead of key-value pairs, which allows for further optimization. Performance is evaluated by comparing runtimes of the original algorithm with our improved version for segments of different lengths resulting in average speedups between 1.26 and 1.35 on four GPUs of different generations (Pascal, Volta, Ampere, Ada Lovelace). Furthermore, comparison to alternative segmented sort implementations from CUB and ModernGPU results in average speedups of at least 2.2 and 2.5, respectively, across all tested architectures. To illustrate how our improved sorting algorithm can be beneficial in a practical application, we have integrated it into the MetaCache-GPU pipeline for metagenomic DNA classification resulting in speedups of up to 25.6% for the sorting step. Code is publicly available at
https://gitlab.rlp.net/pararch/faster-segmented-sort-on-gpus.

**Keywords:** GPUs · Sorting · Massively Parallel Algorithms · CUDA · Bioinformatics

## 1 Introduction

Sorting is one of the most commonly discussed algorithmic problems in computer science. Almost anyone in the discipline will have implemented a sorting algorithm at one point and calculating their computational complexity is a common task for students of the field. Although the task of "putting elements of a list into an order" is fairly simple, new research regarding the sorting problem remains relevant. This is partly due to a large variety of different approaches aiming to solve the problem efficiently and partly due to the need for sorted data in a plethora of other algorithms and applications. Efficient sorting algorithms are, for example, used in database systems [6], 3D computer graphics [7] and bioinformatics [3].


J. Cano et al. (Eds.): Euro-Par 2023, LNCS 14100, pp. 664–678, 2023.
https://doi.org/10.1007/978-3-031-39698-4_45

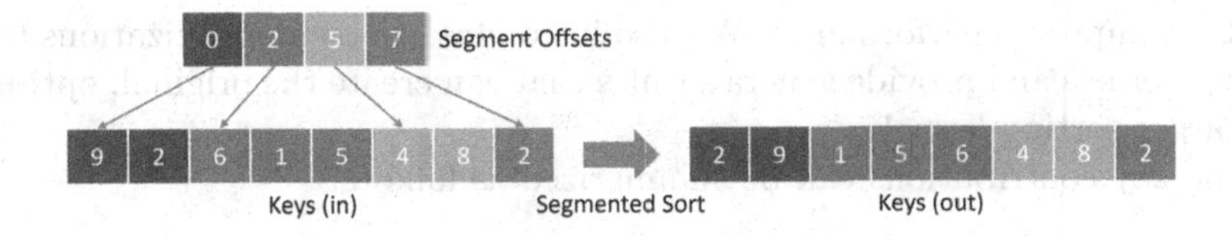


**Fig. 1.** Segmented sort example.

Using parallel platforms to implement sorting algorithms has become a popular approach. For more than a decade now, a lot of research has been focused on implementing parallel sorting algorithms on GPUs [1,8,11,14]. This coincides with a drastic improvement in computational power of new processors, especially GPUs. GPUs have seen an increased use in big data processing and high performance computing. Algorithms in both of these fields often have a need to sort many independent arrays at the same time. Examples of this include processing data warehousing queries [17], sparse matrix multiplication [12] and DNA sequencing [9]. Because many of these tasks are now commonly performed on GPUs, there is a need for efficient segmented sort algorithms, which can sort many independent arrays on a GPU.

Segmented sort (see Fig. 1 for an illustrative example) corresponds to the problem of sorting multiple independent lists (segments) of keys or key-value-pairs of arbitrary sizes. In a sequential approach a single thread could simply sort one segment after the other. However, in a parallel implementation load-balancing problems may emerge from the varying number of elements per segment when distributing work among multiple threads. Different from CPUs, GPUs employ a large number of execution units, making them well suited for an implementation of segmented sort which not only processes a large number of segments simultaneously, but also utilizes multiple cores to sort each individual segment. A simple approach to implementing a segmented sort algorithm on a GPU would be to handle each segment in the same manner. However, different segments can drastically vary in length, which may lead to an uneven load distribution. Handling every segment identically would waste resources on small segments, while not assigning enough resources to large ones.

Hou et al. [8] addressed this problem by generating several different GPU kernels each designed for a specific range of segment sizes. Depending on the size these kernels utilize different memory resources (registers, shared memory, global memory) for intermediate results and map a certain number of to-be-sorted elements to each thread. Their approach focused on key-value segmented sort and ignored the key-only case, which differs in memory requirements and likely favors a different data to thread mapping. Since their publication a number of new CUDA-enabled GPU generations have been released. One of the contributions of this work is to determine the optimal sorting kernels for different segment lengths on modern graphic devices. Additionally we provide an alternative to the original algorithm, designed to sort key-value pairs. Our key-only version of segmented sort efficiently utilizes the additional memory available by omitting the values and thus improves performance. We also introduce our own optimizations to the sorting kernels and provide generator files that can create the original, optimized and larger sorting kernels.

The key contributions can be summarized as follows:

- Improving the original fast segmented sort algorithm [8] by introducing a "coarser" way of handling short segments
- Determining optimal sorting kernels on four different GPU architectures: Pascal (GeForce 1080 GTX Ti), Volta (Quadro GV100), Ampere (A100), and Ada Lovelace (GeForce RTX 4090).
- Adding sorting kernels that utilize more shared memory to sort longer segments.
- Offering a key-only algorithm, that only sorts keys while omitting the values to achieve better performance.
- Providing kernel-generators that allow users to create and modify the sorting kernels used by the fast segmented sort algorithm.
- Performance comparison of our optimized version to the original implementation and to current alternative segmented sort implementations from CUB [13] and ModernGPU [2].

Our code with the improved algorithm, kernel generators and benchmark programs is available on Gitlab[1], and figshare [10].

The remainder of the paper is organized as follows. Section 2 provides an overview of related work. Section 3 explains our approach in detail and highlights changes to the original algorithm. Performance is evaluated and compared in Sect. 4. Finally, Sect. 5 concludes.

## 2 Related Work

There have been a number of prior approaches to address segmented sort problems on GPUs. A simple solution is to transform the problem into a global sort of a single list. In order to achieve this, the input data is augmented by adding a segment ID to each element. Then a global sort primitive can be called which respects the IDs as well as the original keys [4,5]. This not only adds memory overhead but also increases computational complexity. A similar approach is used by other GPU programs [12,18] which reformulate their problems to be able to call global sort from support libraries.

Fix sort [15] follows a hybrid approach by grouping segments into larger chunks and sorting these chunks as a whole. Instead of adding separate segment IDs to each element, individual offsets are applied per segment in order to ensure that every element in a given segment is larger than every element in the previous segments. After sorting the whole group of segments, the elements of each segment have been sorted while the order of the segments is still preserved. Finally, the offsets have to be subtracted to regain the original values. This

[1] https://gitlab.rlp.net/parach/faster-segmented-sort-on-gpus.

strategy does not require additional memory to store segment IDs, because offsets are combined with the actual values of the elements. However, the pre- and post-processing steps of calculating and applying offsets cause a non-negligible runtime overhead and the strategy can only be applied if the values are in a certain range to avoid overflows.

Another strategy, employed by ModernGPU [2], is to use a merge sort algorithm which respects segment boundaries. It first assigns a fixed number of elements to each thread which are then rearranged using a sorting network without crossing segments. Subsequently, neighboring blocks of elements are merged as long as they contain elements from a common segment. The merge steps continue until even the largest segments are completely sorted.

The CUB library [13] which is included in the CUDA toolkit uses radix sort for global and segmented sort primitives. For segmented sort as many thread blocks as there are segments are spawned. Each block is responsible for sorting a designated segment regardless of segment size. This may waste resources on small segments while larger segments could benefit from the use of more parallel processing power than a single block can provide. CUB's documentation states that this strategy was suited for larger segment sizes ("tens of thousands of items and more"[2]).

Since version 1.15 CUB also provides an alternative segmented sort algorithm which improves runtimes for smaller or imbalanced segment sizes. Segments are partitioned according to their size into different groups which are then processed by different sorting strategies. Large segments are still sorted using radix sort while smaller segments are sorted by a separate kernel using a merge sort implementation.

Hou et al. [8] try to take advantage of the data distribution by treating segments of different size separately. Their segmented sort consists of multiple kernels, each tailored to a specific range of segment sizes. In each CUDA kernel, threads operate conjointly sorting the elements of a segment using bitonic sort. The corresponding sorting networks can be implemented efficiently exploiting fast register accesses and warp shuffles. For larger segments with more than 2048 elements they first sort chunks of elements with bitonic sort and subsequently merge the partial results until the whole segments are sorted. Their implementation has been shown to outperform other libraries like CUB (radix sort version) and ModernGPU. A recent paper [16] has compared these different approaches on a variety of array dimensions and number of segments on different GPUs.

## 3 Improved Segmented Sort on GPUs

In 2017 Hou et al. introduced their "Fast Segmented Sort on GPUs" [8] algorithm. At its core, the algorithm tries to fully utilize GPU resources by handling segments differently according to their lengths. As bitonic sorting networks naturally map to segment lengths of powers of two, the algorithm begins by categorizing all segments into bins depending on their segment lengths. All segment

[2] https://nvlabs.github.io/cub/struct_device_segmented_sort.html.

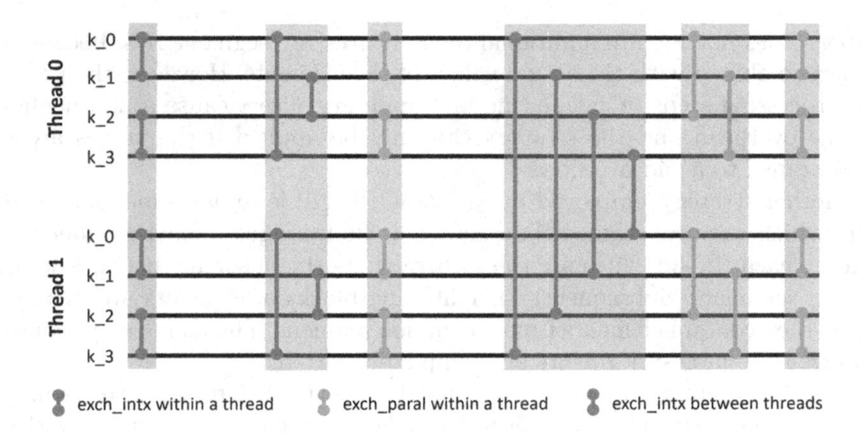


**Fig. 2.** Register sort example sorting 8 keys in 2 threads.

lengths between two powers of two are assigned to the same bin. The authors chose to use 12 bins for sizes from $2^0$ to $2^{11}$ and an additional bin for all segments of larger size. Segments in the same bin will be sorted in an identical manner, optimized to exploit the resources for a given range of segment sizes.

Short segments are handled by a small group of up to 32 threads within a single warp using only registers to store intermediate results. Communication within the same warp can be performed efficiently using shuffle operations, which allows short segments to be sorted extremely quickly using a bitonic sorting network (see Fig. 2). Segments of medium lengths are processed by larger groups of threads. First, they are sorted partially in a similar manner to short segments. Then the sorted parts are merged by utilizing shared memory. Finally, the longest segments are sorted using techniques from both short and medium segments until the merged chunks become too large to fit into shared memory. Then the sorted parts need to be merged by utilizing comparatively slow global memory. This differentiated approach to sorting segments ensures to employ the fastest possible type of memory for each segment length. Additionally, it forces every segment to only use as many threads as needed for sorting, increasing the number of segments the GPU can sort simultaneously.

A segment will consequently be sorted by a specific GPU kernel, according to the bin the segment length falls into. For each range of segment sizes Hou et al. tested a number of kernels, differing in terms of the amount of threads used and the choice and size of utilized memory. During testing they found that the best kernel for a specific segment length depends on the choice of GPU. This resulted in two different optimal segmented sort algorithms for the two tested GPUs, namely K80 (Kepler) and Titan X (Pascal).

In the following, we discuss common features and differences that we implemented using the same three strategies (register-based sorting, shared memory merging, and global memory merging) in order to improve performance on modern GPUs.

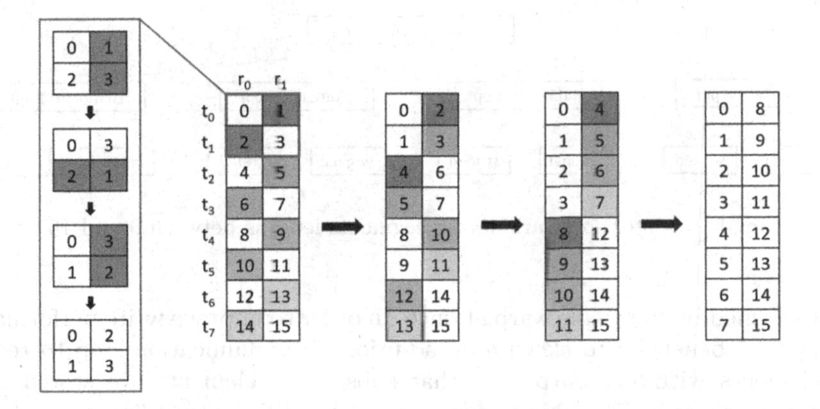


**Fig. 3.** Example element transposition for strided kernels. A 16 element long segment is distributed across 8 threads after sorting (2ppt). In each step elements of the same colors are swapped between both threads. After three shuffle steps all elements are distributed across all threads ready for coalesced memory writes.

### 3.1 Register Sort Kernels

Registers are the fastest form of memory available on GPUs. However, the numbers of registers per thread and per multiprocessor are limited. Solely register-based kernels can thus be used to sort smaller segments, where all of the data fit into registers of the 32 threads of a single warp. Threads within the same warp are able to communicate through warp-level primitives, avoiding costly data exchange through shared or global memory, which makes them the fastest of the discussed sorting strategies.

Register sort kernels use bitonic sorting networks to sort segments in a certain size range. Here, different choices of how many elements of a segment are assigned to each individual thread are possible and lead to different performance. The segment range 5–8, for instance, could be sorted using a group of 2 threads and 4 pairs per thread (*ppt*), 4 threads and 2 ppt, or 8 threads and 1 ppt. All of these choices achieve the same task of sorting 8 elements. For group sizes of less than 32 threads, each warp is divided into multiple groups, which each sort a separate segment in the same size range.

Depending on the mapping of ppt, different communication steps are required to perform sorting. Keys within the same thread can simply be compared by using the respective registers. For comparisons of keys from different threads, data needs to be exchanged via warp shuffle operations. Due to the layout of the bitonic sorting network, different patterns emerge which can be used to generate sorting networks for each ppt mapping and for arbitrary segment sizes. Figure 2 illustrates an example of a network for 2 threads with 4 ppt. For an in-depth explanation of respective code generation we refer the inclined reader to the original paper by Hou et al. [8].

After sorting a segment, results must be written to memory. Each thread contains a number of consecutively sorted elements, however, memory accesses

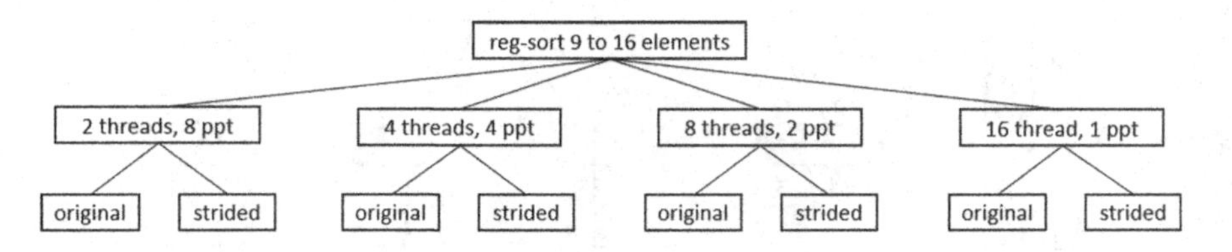


**Fig. 4.** Register sort variants for segments lengths between 9 and 16.

are performed by the whole warp at once. In order to improve write performance, it might be beneficial to execute an additional communication step to reorder the elements within a warp such that subsequent elements are stored along subsequent threads. To achieve this in a quick fashion we utilize warp shuffles over multiple steps. In each step, pairs of threads are selected with an increasing offset, as shown in Fig. 3. Each thread pair performs a diagonal swap of two elements, as depicted by the red box in Fig. 3. In practice this operation does not only shuffle around elements of each individual segment, but across all segments within the same warp to optimize the memory access pattern.

This strategy is denoted as *strided* kernels in our benchmarks which we used to find the best performing kernel for each GPU. As an example, Fig. 4 shows the different variants for sorting segments of lengths between 9 and 16. Since each warp in the register sort kernels performs independent work, these kernels can be executed with an arbitrary number of warps. When deciding whether to use a strided kernel, we noticed that with a ppt of 8 or higher the strided kernels are faster than their non-strided counterparts.

### 3.2 Shared Memory Sort Kernels

Shared memory is attached to each multiprocessor of the GPU and can be accessed by all threads within the same CUDA thread block. Its size depends on the employed GPU architecture and ranges in the tens to hundreds of kilobytes. Shared memory kernels begin by sorting chunks of (up to) 128 elements using a warp of 32 threads and 4 pairs per thread in the same manner as register sort kernels. Once each warp has finished sorting its chunk of 128 elements and stored the result in shared memory, threads in a block cooperatively merge chunks until the whole segment is sorted. Similar to merge sort, each merge step combines two chunks into a larger sorted chunk. A 512-element segment, for example, would be merged in two steps. First a total of four pre-sorted 128-element chunks are merged together, resulting in two 256-element chunks, which are then merged together in a second step.

If a segment's size is small enough, Hou et al. assign some warps only 64 elements instead of 128 to reduce the number of bitonic sorting steps. This continues in the merging phase where the warps either handle 64 or 128 elements. We investigated a different strategy, where some warps skip the sorting and merge phases if a segment can be handled by a lower number of warps. This approach reduces code complexity while active warps can do more work in registers, which improves runtime.

Similar to register kernels, shared memory kernels can either write the final results to global memory in strided or unstrided fashion. Since the kernels are already using shared memory, they can simply read the elements from shared memory accordingly.

Because different GPU architectures feature different shared memory capacities, the maximum segment size which fits into shared memory depends on the employed GPU. To fully exploit shared memory, it is necessary to adapt the segmented sort algorithm to the utilized GPU architecture. Avoiding slower global memory as much as possible leads to significant speedup.

### 3.3 Global Memory Sort Kernels

All segments with sizes too large to fit into shared memory have to be sorted using slower global memory for intermediate results. However, similar to the shared memory approach partial results can be calculated using faster memory. Thus, shared memory kernels are used to partially sort the segments up to a certain chunk size. After that, a global merge kernel is executed multiple times, each call merging two chunks into a larger one until even the largest segments are sorted completely. Because every single merge step has to read from and write to global memory, global sort is fairly slow when compared to previous methods.

### 3.4 Kernel Selection

The original segmented sort algorithm uses a total of 13 unique kernels to sort segments. Each kernel is responsible for all segments in a certain range of segment lengths. Hou et al. employ register kernels for each power of two up to 256 elements and shared memory kernels for segment sizes between 257 and 2048 elements.

Based on our experiments we determined optimal kernels for four GPUs, namely GeForce GTX 1080 Ti (Pascal), Quadro GV100 (Volta), A100 (Ampere), and GeForce RTX 4090 (Ada Lovelace). Note, that the optimal kernel choices differ noticeably between graphics cards. Additionally, our optimized versions feature coarser bins for small segment lengths, using only two kernels (coarse register kernel): one for segments of length 0–2 and another for lengths 3–16. Using fewer kernels reduces code complexity and reduces kernel call overhead. Furthermore, the larger shared memory available on V100, A100 and RTX 4090 GPUs allows us to use shared memory kernels for larger segment lengths. Table 1 shows an overview of employed kernels for the different GPUs.

**Table 1.** Optimal segmented sort kernels for different segment sizes.

| Segment Size | Hou et al. | Opt. Key-Value Segsort | | | | Opt. Key-Only | |
|---|---|---|---|---|---|---|---|
| | | 1080 Ti | GV100 | A100 | 4090 | 1080 Ti[a] | 1080 Ti[b] |
| 0 – 1 | C | CR | CR | CR | CR | CR | CR |
| 2 | R | | | | | | |
| 3 – 4 | R | CR | CR | CR | CR | CR | CR |
| 5 – 8 | R | | | | | | |
| 9 – 16 | R | | | | | | |
| 17 – 32 | R | R | R | R | R | R | R |
| 33 – 64 | R | R | R | R | R | R | R |
| 65 – 128 | R | R | R | R | R | R | R |
| 129 – 256 | R | R | R | R | R | R | R |
| 257 – 512 | S | S | S | S | S | R | R |
| 513 – 1024 | S | S | S | S | S | R | S |
| 1025 – 2048 | S | S | S | S | S | S | S |
| 2049 – 4096 | G | S | S | S | S | S | S |
| 4097 – 8192 | | G | S | S | S | S | G |
| 8193 – 16384 | | | G | S | G | G | |
| $\geq$ 16385 | | | | G | | | |

C = copy kernel, R = register kernel, CR = coarse register kernel,
S = shared merge kernel, G = global merge kernel
[a] 32-bit keys [b] 64-bit keys

### 3.5 Key-Only Segmented Sort

Key-only segmented sort has reduced memory requirements because values are omitted. Thus, more registers and shared memory are available for keys and larger segments can be sorted by register kernels and shared memory kernels while the general approach from Sects. 3.1–3.3 stays the same. The two rightmost columns in Table 1 show the optimal kernel selection for key-only segmented sort on a GTX 1080 Ti for sorting 32-bit and 64-bit keys. Note, that compared to the key-value segmented sort, segment sizes of up to 1024 elements can be sorted in registers and only segments larger than 8192 elements (4096 for 64-bit keys) need to be sorted with the global memory kernel.

## 4 Performance Evaluation

Our experiments have been conducted using the CUDA-enabled GPUs listed in Table 2 and nvcc 11.8. Benchmarks are performed on $n = 2^{28}$ random integer keys, with segment lengths randomly drawn from a uniform distribution between a minimum segment length of 1 and various maximum lengths. In the key-value

**Table 2.** Properties of utilized GPUs.

| | GTX 1080 Ti | Quadro GV100 | A100 | RTX 4090 |
|---|---|---|---|---|
| CUDA Cores | 3584 | 5120 | 6912 | 16384 |
| Boost Clock | 1582 MHz | 1627 MHz | 1410 MHz | 2520 MHz |
| Shared Memory per SM | 48 KB | 128 KB | 192 KB | 128 KB |
| Global memory | 11 GB | 32 GB | 80 GB | 24 GB |
| Memory Bandwidth | 484 GB/s | 870 GB/s | 2039 GB/s | 1008 GB/s |

benchmarks the 32-bit keys are accompanied by 64-bit values stored in a separate array. The key-only benchmarks have been performed on 32-bit as well as on 64-bit keys. All data resides in device memory. Kernels are executed concurrently using CUDA streams in order to better utilize the GPU resources. We compare our implementation to Hou's segmented sort as well as the segmented sort primitives from CUB v. 1.17 and ModernGPU v. 2.13. Temporary memory allocations required for binning the segments prior to sorting are excluded from runtime measurements. CUB's temporary memory allocations were also excluded, while ModernGPU's interface did not allow to do so. The reported runtimes are average values of twenty executions of the entire sort algorithm for each range of segment lengths.

### 4.1 Key-Value Segmented Sort

Figure 5 shows that the throughput of our algorithm scales proportionally with the memory bandwidth, with the A100 beating the newer RTX 4090 slightly. Although it is interesting to note that their respective peak performances are at a different max segment size, with the A100 peaking at a max segment size of 128 compared to the RTX 4090 peaking at 2048, showing the impact of higher CUDA core count of the RTX 4090.

To evaluate the impact of our coarse register kernel we now focus at max segment sizes of $\leq 16$. Across all four GPUs Hou's implementation is beaten with speedups of 2 to 2.5$\times$, peaking for the smallest segment size of 2 and the largest maximum size 16. At the smallest segment sizes of 2–3 our implementation beats all other algorithms on all GPUs except for the A100, where CUB's SegSort prevails. It is also the only algorithm having a higher throughput on these GPUs for max segment sizes between 4 and 16. The newer the GPU the bigger the discrepancy in this region, except for the A100, where CUB SegSort is only faster until a max segment size of 8, where its throughput drops drastically.

Approaching higher max segment sizes we can see the impact of our coarse register kernel diminish, as Hou's algorithm closes the performance gap on all four GPUs, reaching a similar performance at around size 128 for all GPUs, again except for the A100. By using the strategy of active and inactive warps described in Sect. 3.2, our implementation regains a performance advantage for segment sizes between 513 and 2048 elements. For larger segments the biggest improvement can be seen where our algorithm keeps using shared merge kernels,

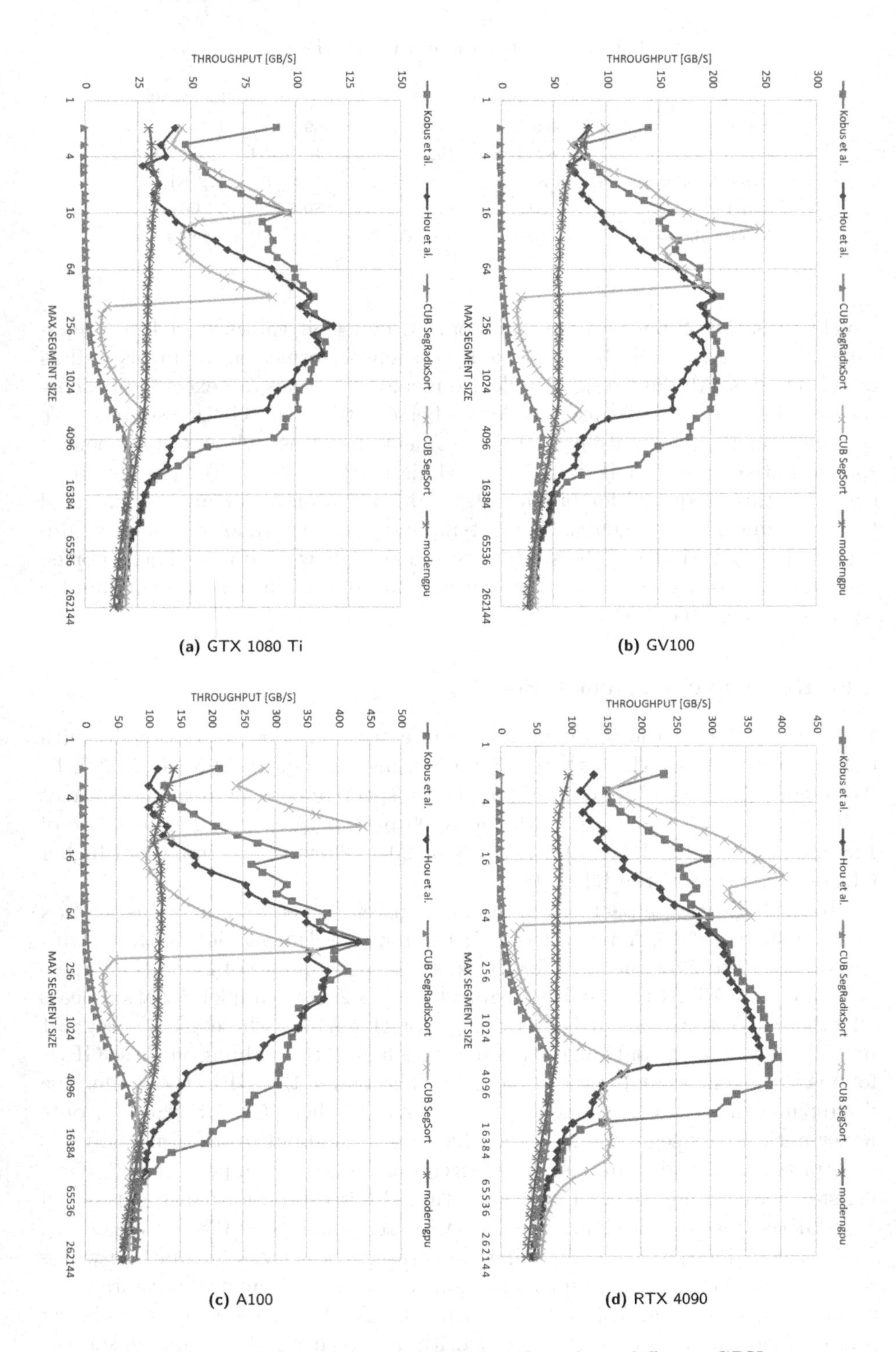


**Fig. 5.** Key-Value Segmented Sort Benchmark on different GPUs.

**Table 3.** Geometric Mean Speedup. Max segment sizes between 2 and 16384.

| | Key-Value Segsort | | | | Key-Only Segsort | |
|---|---|---|---|---|---|---|
| | 1080 Ti | GV100 | A100 | 4090 | 1080 Ti[a] | 1080 Ti[b] |
| Hou et al. | 1.35 | 1.32 | 1.34 | 1.32 | 1.35 | 1.26 |
| CUB SegRadixSort | 59.28 | 44.58 | 59.00 | 36.64 | 110.18 | 135.34 |
| CUB SegSort | 2.82 | 2.33 | 2.72 | 2.27 | 2.95 | 4.1 |
| moderngpu | 2.77 | 2.73 | 2.53 | 3.52 | 2.59 | 2.53 |

[a] 32-bit keys [b] 64-bit keys

while Hou et al. move to the global merge kernel, slowing down drastically by losing more than a third of their throughput across all GPUs. As expected, we see a similar drop for our implementation later, since we only delay the switch to global memory based on shared memory sizes.

Across the board our algorithm is faster than all competitors except CUB SegSort, which is generally faster for small segment sizes but drops drastically at a max segment size of 128. Subsequently, CUB SegSort is only able to outpace our algorithm again for max segment sizes beyond 10000. Although it has huge performance spikes in the beginning, CUB is on average outperformed by our algorithm with a speedup of $> 2.2\times$ over all GPUs as shown in Table 3. Hou's algorithm performs better and more consistent for larger segment sizes than CUB SegSort, however, it is consistently surpassed by our algorithm with speedups of $> 1.3\times$. ModernGPU has a relatively consistent performance with no visible spikes, but is generally slower, resulting in mean speedups of 2.53 to $3.52\times$ in favor of our algorithm. While these speedups are measured for segment sizes smaller than 16384, CUB's algorithms become faster beyond a certain segment size, depending on the GPU used. The earliest being the RTX 4090, where CUB SegSort is faster for max segment sizes $> 10240$.

### 4.2 Key-Only Segmented Sort

The key-Only version helps us observe the impact of the element sizes on performance, as can be seen in Fig. 6. In general, using smaller element sizes, here the key size, allows us to stay in a faster memory type for bigger segment sizes. This results in a shift of the peak performance towards bigger segment sizes, from 128 to 256 for 64 and 32-bit keys, respectively. These peaks are not happening at the switch from register to shared memory, showing that memory bandwidth is the bottleneck for our algorithm here.

Comparing our algorithm to the version from Hou et al. we notice the same relative behaviour as in the key-value benchmarks. Both algorithms scale similar over the key sizes, resulting in a similar speedup to the key-value version of $1.35\times$ for 32-bit keys, as seen in Table 3. CUB SegSort behaves similarly as well for 64-bit key sizes, but with a bigger discrepancy in throughput, resulting in a mean speedup of $4.1\times$ for segment sizes $\leq 16384$. However, looking at smaller

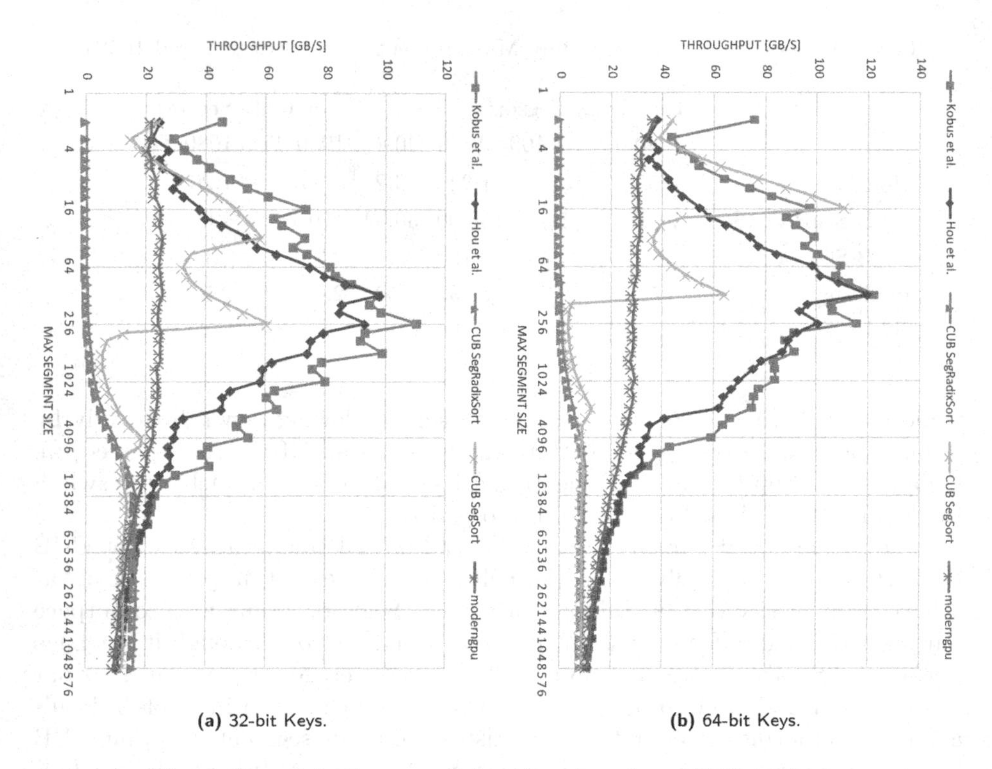


**(a)** 32-bit Keys.

**(b)** 64-bit Keys.

**Fig. 6.** Key-Only Segmented Sort Benchmark on GTX 1080 Ti.

key size we only have a speedup of 2.95× over CUB SegSort, even though it performs worse than our algorithm across all segment sizes. As for ModernGPU the relative performance stays the same across key sizes and the Key-Value version, resulting in a similar mean speedup of 2.59 for 32-bit keys and 2.53× for 64-bit keys.

### 4.3 MetaCache

In the MetaCache GPU pipeline for metagenomic classification [9], sorting the lists of potential target locations resulting from database queries is a time-consuming step. For each batch of queries an adapted version of Hou's segmented sort algorithm is employed to efficiently sort multiple location lists in parallel, where each location is stored as a 64-bit value. The results are then processed further to perform the classification. Segmented sort takes the biggest share of the pipeline and is responsible for about halve of the total runtime.

In order to investigate performance improvements by replacing Hou's algorithm by our segmented sort implementation decoupled from the complete MetaCache pipeline, we extracted the segment sizes for all batches of four example queries and stored them on disk. The statistical properties of the distribution of segments sizes generated by querying two metagenomic read data sets (D1

**Table 4.** Statistical properties of segment sizes generated by different metagenomic dataset queries and corresponding speedups achieved on a GTX 1080 Ti for the sorting step. Stddev = standard deviation.

| Dataset | Min | Max | Mean | Stddev | Skewness | Total items | Speedup |
|---|---|---|---|---|---|---|---|
| D1A | 0 | 4064 | 591.5 | 588.3 | −1.739 | 11.829 bn | 9.1% |
| D1B | 0 | 4064 | 576.5 | 568.5 | −1.584 | 11,529 bn | 6.6% |
| D2A | 0 | 9846 | 1411.5 | 1133.7 | −4.812 | 28.230 bn | 25.6% |
| D2B | 0 | 9866 | 1386.1 | 1110.9 | −4.788 | 27.721 bn | 25.5% |

and D2) against the two different databases (A and B) are shown in Table 4. In total all batches of D1 encompassed more than 11 billion items, while all batches of D2 add up more than 27 billion items due to longer read lengths. The last column of Table 4 presents the achieved speedup when performing a segmented sort for all batches of a data set using our improved implementation instead of the one by Hou et al. D1A and D1B contain smaller segments with mean lengths of 591.5 and 576.5 elements, respectively, resulting in a speedup of 9.1 and 6.6%. For larger segments in D2A and D2B we were able to achieve a speedup of 25.6% and 25.5%, respectively.

## 5 Conclusion

We have introduced improvements of the algorithm of Hou et al. [8] and have shown their performance impact in comparison to several modern segmented sort implementations. Our improvements include a "coarser" way of treating small segment sizes and a more efficient use of shared memory, resulting in bigger segment sizes processed in the faster memory. We have also provided optimal sorting kernels for four different GPU architectures and compared the performance of our algorithm with other state-of-the-art algorithms. Here we have shown that our algorithm outperforms on average all other algorithms across all tested GPUs for segment sizes $< 16384$. Furthermore, we have implemented our algorithm in the MetaCache-GPU pipeline for metagenomic classification showing a speedup of up to 25.6% for the sorting step.

Possible future improvements of segmented sort could include the usage of (bigger) distributed shared memory on Hopper architectures and named streams for improving asynchronous kernel execution.

## References

1. Arkhipov, D.I., Wu, D., Li, K., Regan, A.C.: Sorting with GPUs: a survey. arXiv preprint arXiv:1709.02520 (2017)
2. Baxter, S.: ModernGPU: Patterns and behaviors for GPU computing (2016). https://github.com/moderngpu/moderngpu

3. Büren, F., Jünger, D., Kobus, R., Hundt, C., Schmidt, B.: Suffix array construction on multi-GPU systems. In: Proceedings of the 28th International Symposium on High-Performance Parallel and Distributed Computing, pp. 183–194 (2019)
4. Dalton, S., Bell, N., Olson, L., Garland, M.: CUSP: A C++ Templated Sparse Matrix Library (2015). http://cusplibrary.github.io/
5. Flick, P., Aluru, S.: Parallel distributed memory construction of suffix and longest common prefix arrays. In: International Conference for High Performance Computing, Networking, Storage and Analysis, SC 2015, Austin, TX, USA, pp. 16:1–16:10 (2015)
6. Graefe, G.: Implementing sorting in database systems. ACM Comput. Surv. (CSUR) **38**(3), 10-es (2006)
7. Gu, Y., He, Y., Fatahalian, K., Blelloch, G.: Efficient BVH construction via approximate agglomerative clustering. In: Proceedings of the 5th High-Performance Graphics Conference, pp. 81–88 (2013)
8. Hou, K., Liu, W., Wang, H., Feng, W.C.: Fast Segmented sort on GPUs. In: Proceedings of the International Conference on Supercomputing, pp. 1–10 (2017)
9. Kobus, R., Müller, A., Jünger, D., Hundt, C., Schmidt, B.: MetaCache-GPU: ultra-fast metagenomic classification. In: 50th International Conference on Parallel Processing, pp. 1–11 (2021)
10. Kobus, R., Nelgen, J., Henkys, V., Schmidt, B.: Artifact for euro-par 2023 paper: "faster segmented sort on GPUs". Figshare (2023). https://doi.org/10.6084/m9.figshare.23540553
11. Leischner, N., Osipov, V., Sanders, P.: GPU sample sort. In: 2010 IEEE International Symposium on Parallel & Distributed Processing (IPDPS), pp. 1–10. IEEE (2010)
12. Liu, W., Vinter, B.: A framework for general sparse matrix-matrix multiplication on GPUs and heterogeneous processors. J. Parallel Distrib. Comput. **85**, 47–61 (2015)
13. NVIDIA: CUB: Cooperative primitives for CUDA C++ (2021). https://nvlabs.github.io/cub/
14. Satish, N., Harris, M., Garland, M.: Designing efficient sorting algorithms for manycore GPUs. In: 2009 IEEE International Symposium on Parallel & Distributed Processing, pp. 1–10. IEEE (2009)
15. Schmid, R., Pisani, F., Borin, E., Cáceres, E.: An evaluation of segmented sorting strategies on GPUs. In: 2016 IEEE HPCC/SmartCity/DSS, pp. 1123–1130. IEEE (2016)
16. Schmid, R.F., Pisani, F., Cáceres, E.N., Borin, E.: An evaluation of fast segmented sorting implementations on GPUs. Parallel Comput. **110**, 102889 (2022)
17. Yuan, Y., Lee, R., Zhang, X.: The Yin and Yang of processing data warehousing queries on GPU devices. Proc. VLDB Endowment **6**(10), 817–828 (2013)
18. Zhang, J., Wang, H., Feng, W.C.: cuBLASTP: fine-grained parallelization of protein sequence search on CPU+GPU. IEEE/ACM Trans. Comput. Biol. Bioinf. **14**(4), 830–843 (2015)

# Hercules: Scalable and Network Portable In-Memory Ad-Hoc File System for Data-Centric and High-Performance Applications

Javier Garcia-Blas[1](✉), Genaro Sanchez-Gallegos[1], Cosmin Petre[1], Alberto Riccardo Martinelli[2], Marco Aldinucci[2], and Jesus Carretero[1]

[1] University Carlos III of Madrid, Leganes, Spain
{fjblas,jcarrete}@inf.uc3m.es, {gesanche,cpetre}@pa.uc3m.es
[2] University of Torino, Turin, Italy
aldinuc@di.unito.it, albertoriccardo.martinelli@unito.it

**Abstract.** The growing demands for data processing by new data-intensive applications are putting pressure on the performance and capacity of HPC storage systems. The advancement in storage technologies, such as NVMe and persistent memory, are aimed at meeting these demands. However, relying solely on ultra-fast storage devices is not cost-effective, leading to the need for multi-tier storage hierarchies to move data based on its usage. To address this issue, ad-hoc file systems have been proposed as a solution. They utilise the available storage of compute nodes, such as memory and persistent storage, to create a temporary file system that adapts to the application behaviour in the HPC environment. This work presents the design, implementation, and evaluation of a distributed ad-hoc in-memory storage system (Hercules), highlighting the new communication model included in Hercules. This communication model takes advantage of the Unified Communication X framework (UCX). This solution leverages the capabilities of RDMA protocols, including Infiniband, Onmipath, shared memory, and zero-copy transfers. The preliminary evaluation results show excellent network utilisation compared with other existing technologies.

**Keywords:** HPC · Data intensive · In-memory storage

This work was partially supported by the European Union's Horizon 2020 under the ADMIRE project, grant Agreement number 956748-ADMIRE-H2020-JTI-EuroHPC-2019-1 and by the Agencia Española de Investigación under Grant PCI2021-121966. This research was partially supported by Madrid regional Government (Spain) under the grant "Convergencia Big Data-HPC: de los sensores a las Aplicaciones. (CABAHLA-CM)". Finally, this work was partially supported by the Spanish Ministry of Science and Innovation Project "New Data Intensive Computing Methods for High-End and Edge Computing Platforms (DECIDE)" Ref. PID2019-107858GB-I00.


J. Cano et al. (Eds.): Euro-Par 2023, LNCS 14100, pp. 679–693, 2023.
https://doi.org/10.1007/978-3-031-39698-4_46

## 1 Introduction

Current scientific and engineering applications running on today's large-scale supercomputers are usually characterised by a data-intensive nature. A single application's workflow easily generates tens of terabytes of data, mostly produced by on-line operations. As M. Radulovic *et al.* [17] stated, from the performance point of view, a set of tested applications behave as data intensive ones when they spent a significant portion of time with a memory bandwidth utilisation above 60% or even 80%. Due to the appearance of these data-demanding high-performance applications, multiple software solutions have been introduced in an attempt to cope with challenges along the entire I/O software stack [10], such as high-level I/O libraries, parallel file systems, and I/O middleware, with a final objective consisting on reducing the amount of file system calls and offloading I/O functionalities from compute nodes, respectively. Those optimisations are even more important for data-intensive workflows, consisting of interdependent data processing tasks often connected in a DAG-style sequence, which communicate through intermediate storage abstractions, typically files. While workflow management systems deployed on HPC systems (*e.g.*, parallel machines) typically exploit a monolithic parallel file system that ensures a high efficiency in data access [21], workflow systems implemented on distributed infrastructures (most often, a public Cloud) must borrow techniques from the Big Data computing field [11].

For several years, I/O-intensive HPC-based applications have been primarily based on distributed object-based file systems, which separate data from metadata management and allow each client to communicate in parallel directly with multiple storage servers. Exascale I/O raises the throughput and storage capacity requirements by several orders of magnitude. Therefore, developing methods that can manage the network and storage resources accordingly is a must [13]. It is assumed that the systems already developed for data analytics are not directly applicable to HPC due to the fine-granularity I/O involved in scientific applications. Another weakness of existing HPC I/O systems is the semantic gap between the application requests and the way they are managed by the storage backend at the block level.

Nowadays, many emerging data workloads are driven by machine learning and other data analytics techniques that rely on workflow frameworks (*e.g.*, Apache Spark), analytics packages (*e.g.*, Horovod and TensorFlow [15]), and domain-specific libraries that traditionally have not been used in HPC. As demonstrated by Chowdhury *et al.* [5], machine learning applications are mainly dominated by a large number of small files and read and seek POSIX operations. Those I/O patterns do not perform well in current HPC I/O systems, that have been designed for applications accessing a few very large files mostly sequentially.

Our hypothesis is that those applications can be accelerated by reducing the I/O bottleneck induced by the file system, and that facilitating the storage of temporal data in an ad-hoc file system can significantly impact the overall performance. This work presents the design, implementation, and evaluation of a distributed ad-hoc in-memory storage system (Hercules[1]), a proposal to enhance I/O in both traditional HPC and High-Performance Data Analytics (HPDA) systems. The architectural design follows a client-server design model, where the client itself will be responsible for the server entities deployment. The client layer is in charge of dealing with data locality exploitation alongside the implementation of multiple I/O patterns providing diverse data distribution policies.

In a previous work, we presented a preliminary work of our ad-hoc file system [8], where we propose two kind of deployments: an application-attached deployment constrained to application's nodes, and an application-detached considering offshore nodes. We identified some limitations in this past implementation: first, it used ZeroMQ for communication, which offers various transports such as in-process, inter-process, TCP, and multicast. However, it lacks of high-performance network support and portability; second, that IMSS version offered a library-based API, not offering a POSIX compliant interface, which still is fairly used by the HPC community, but only an object-oriented interface. In the version presented in this paper, we have solved both weaknesses by replacing the communication layer to UCX and by providing a POSIX compliant library for IMSS. Compared with the related work, the strengths of this new version of Hercules are the use of main memory resources, full POSIX support and network portability.

The rest of the paper is organised as follows. Section 2 shows related works with Hercules. Section 3 describes the Hercules architecture. In Sect. 4, we depict the design of our parallel file system based on POSIX. Section 5 focus on the integration of Hercules and UCX. Section 6 shows the performance results obtained in the evaluation phase. Finally, Sect. 7 concludes the paper and lists future works.

## 2 Related Work

General-purpose parallel file systems such as GPFS [19] and Lustre [2] have been providing for a long time well-known solutions for long term persistent storage in HPC systems. However, they are very rigid and cannot be modified or suited to an application once they are deployed. Current HPC systems and applications are not well suited to that kind of systems and intensive workloads.

Moreover, the growing complexity of the HPC I/O stack by adding new I/O layers and devices, generates an increasing in I/O operations latency that hampers applications' performance. Thus, nowadays use cases have empowered the proliferation of low-latency storage systems using local or remote in-memory storage devices as a feasible approach to the problem [24]. Such has been the impact of these storage systems [25] that multiple solutions, such as in-memory relational databases, in-memory NoSQL databases, in-memory cache systems, and in-memory data processing systems, have been implemented in the last years.

[1] Available at https://gitlab.arcos.inf.uc3m.es/admire/hercules.git.

Another alternative that has been explored in order to approach the data challenge is ad-hoc file systems [3]. Ad-hoc file systems provide a customised data resource at application level, taking advantage of internal storage devices while acting as a middleware between persistent storage entities and the application itself. Major features are: (i) negligible deployment overhead, to be deployed either on an HPC cluster for lifetimes as small as the runtime of a single job; (ii) global name space for all nodes linked to the same ad-hoc file system; and (iii) interaction with the backend storage system through data staging.

GekkoFS [22] is a high-performance, parallel, and distributed file system designed to handle large scale data-intensive workloads in HPC environments. It is a tier-based file system, meaning it can move data between different levels of storage based on its usage, or "hotness". This allows to balance performance and cost-efficiency. GekkoFS supports parallel I/O operations, which enables it to read and write data from multiple nodes at the same time, increasing the overall performance of the file system. BurstFS [23] is a burst buffer file system that provides I/O capabilities for HPC environments. BurstFS acts as a cache between the compute nodes and the storage system, providing temporary storage area for the data that is being generated. This buffer allows the compute nodes to write data at high speeds, improving the overall performance of the system. BurstFS system makes use of persistent storage devices while, in contrast, Hercules backend makes use primarily of main memory resources. As a result, the benefits of the data-locality exploitation will be achieved more easily using the Hercules tool.

In a previous work, we presented a hierarchical parallel storage system based on distributed memory [7]. In this work, we present a new version that differs in the following aspects. First, Hercules was based on Memcached [14] in terms of front and backend layers. This approach suffers from the limitation of the Memcached protocol for data transferring modes, such as inter-process communication and inter-thread communication. Second, it only provided a key-value interface, while the new version also includes a POSIX compliant file system, while keeping the previous object store features. To cope with the first limitation we evolved the system to use ZeroMQ for communication, which offers various transports such as in-process, inter-process, TCP, and multicast. However ZeroMQ has evolved more towards distributed systems with short messages, and it was not able to cover the needs of HPC applications.

As an alternative, there are many communication frameworks available. GASNet-EX [1] is a high-performance communication framework for Exascale. This framework supports collective operations and many network devices such as Infiniband, Omni-path, and ethernet. GASNet-EX also enables communications over other well-known frameworks such as MPI or UPC. However, it lacks support for intra-node shared memory communication, useful for coupled deployments. A similar solution is UCX, a framework designed for HPC networks [6,20]. This library supports many programming models (*i.e.*, MPI, OpenSHMEM, PGAS), network devices (Infiniband, Omni-Path, Ethernet), as well as CUDA and shared memory for intra-node communications. UCX offers two network APIs: UCT and UCP. UCT is a low-level transport layer that offers access to hardware network resources efficiently. UCP is a high-level API that implements several communication interfaces. We ultimately chose UCX as the backbone of Hercules.

## 3 Hercules Architecture Design

As shown in Fig. 1, the architectural design of Hercules follows a client-server design model. Hercules is an ad-hoc file system that can be deployed by each application and it is responsible for the metadata and data server entities deployment. Each application process will be connected to Hercules through a frontend layer. This way, each application can adjust the dimensions of each Hercules deployment to fit its I/O needs. That means that there could be many deployments of Hercules in the same computer system, as we are going to show, but they will be independent to protect data isolation.

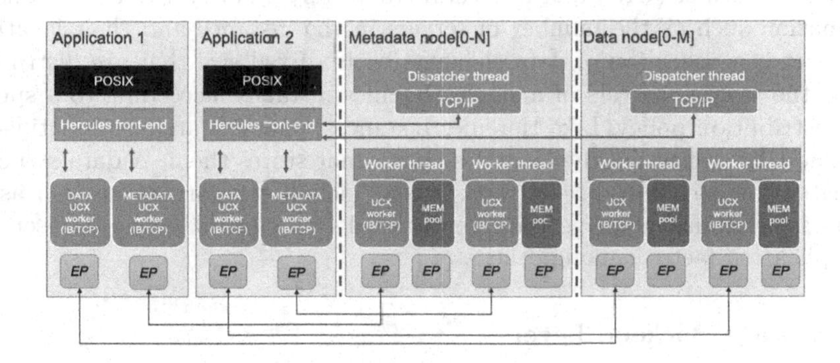


**Fig. 1.** Architecture of an Hercules deployment.

The development of the present work was strictly conditioned by a set of well-defined objectives. Firstly, Hercules provides flexibility in terms of deployment. To achieve this, the Hercules API provides a set of deployment methods where the number of servers conforming the instance, as well as their locations, buffer sizes, and their coupled or decoupled nature, can be tuned. Second, parallelism should be maximised. To achieve this, Hercules follows a multi-threaded design architecture. Each server conforming an instance counts with a dispatcher thread and a pool of worker threads. The dispatcher thread distributes the incoming workload between the worker threads with the aim of balancing the workload in a multi-threaded scenario. Main entities conforming the architectural design are Hercules clients (frontend), Hercules data (1 to M) and metadata (1 to N) servers (backend). Addressing the interaction between these components, the Hercules frontend exclusively communicates with the Hercules metadata servers whenever a metadata-related operation is performed, such as *create* and *open*. Data-related operations (*get* and *set*) will be handled directly by the corresponding storage server calculated in the frontend side. Thus, global data mapping is not needed at all levels. Finally, Hercules offers to the application a set of data distribution policies at dataset level, increasing the application's awareness about the location of the data. As a result, the storage system will increase awareness in terms of data distribution at the client side, providing benefits such as data locality exploitation and load balancing.

### 3.1 Frontend Layer

The client application will handle Hercules and dataset instances through a Hercules client library. The API provides a set of operations to *create*, *release*, *get*, and *set* data, datasets, and Hercules instances.

Throughout a session, clients create and join multiple instances of Hercules. A Hercules instance refers to an ad-hoc temporary storage entity composed of multiple servers spread across a set of user-specified machines, using main memory to store datasets. Each Hercules instance is assigned a unique Uniform Resource Identifier (URI) and it is characterised by a data structure that stores information such as the number of servers in the instance and their locations. A dataset is a collection of data elements with a fixed size that are distributed among the storage servers of a single Hercules instance, according to a specific data distribution policy. Like Hercules instances, datasets are also identified by a unique URI, reflecting the Hercules entity that stores them. A data structure is created for each instance of the dataset, including information such as the assigned distribution policy, the number of data elements in the dataset, and the replication factor, among others.

### 3.2 Storage Backend Layer

In order to handle *get* and *set* requests, each worker thread provides direct access to the data block location in the in-memory data container. In case of a *get* operation, the requested data block is wrapped into a message and sent back to the client. If the operation is a *set*, the worker thread overwrites the concerned data block if it was already stored. Otherwise, the data block is written and a new key-value pair representing the previous block is added to the map (implemented as a C++ map). Thus, as may be seen, Hercules backends provide a key-value based object store based on *GLib* balanced binary trees, boosting both insertions and queries.

Hercules can use NVMe as a final persistent storage layer. If applications require to store in a lower layer of the storage hierarchy, data persistence is provided through periodic flushing operations that replicate all data blocks (data and metadata) to persistence disks. The period can be different for each Hercules instance and it is defined when that instance of Hercules is created. In the future, we plan to use burst buffer modules that will enable Hercules to mostly coordinate massive asynchronously data transfers to dump datasets [12].

In the current version, nodes list in the backend storage layer is static, defined during the initial deployment. However, we are already working to dynamically update the backend nodes of a Hercules deployment with the aim of providing storage malleability, shrinking and increasing the number of data and metadata backend on run time.

# 4 File System Design

Figure 2 depicts the different abstraction designed in Hercules, from the application perspective to the final in-memory layout. As shown in the Figure, a UNIX-like file path is translated to a dataset entity, mapping the mounted path to a global space URI (dataset view).

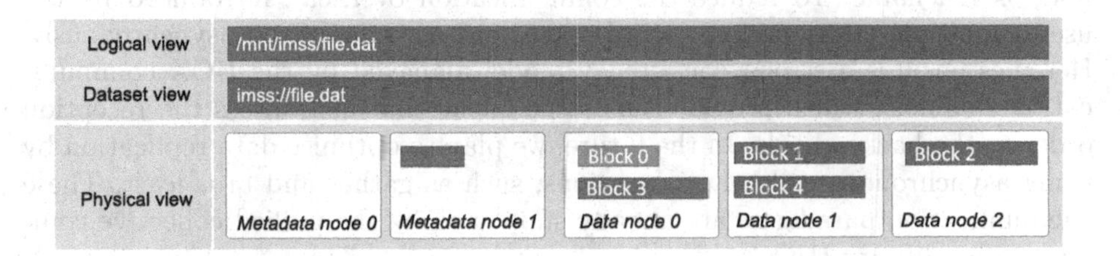


**Fig. 2.** Logical, dataset, and physical representation of a file in Hercules. Data path is translated from logical to dataset shape. Later, file is divided into multiple blocks under three data nodes. Inter-node metadata information is stored at the Metadata node 0.

Each file or directory is mapped into a Hercules dataset composed of a list of fixed-size blocks (physical view). Hercules allows block access by offset. Thus, the frontend layer can request access to a particular block at a specific offset. Sent requests contain the desired operation (read/write), dataset URI, block to access, and the offset. In case of write operations, the request also contains the size to write. This optimises data transfers by reducing the amount of data transmitted.

The current version fully supports the entire POSIX standard (*i.e.*, *open*, *close*, *write*, *rm*, *mkdir*, etc.) and also libc library calls suc has *fopen* and *fwrite*. In the next subsections, we will cover the following aspects of the file system running on top of Hercules: memory pool, data replication, and metadata management.

## 4.1 Memory Pool

In order to eliminate the overhead of intensive dynamic memory allocations, Hercules provides a memory pool per listening thread. This memory pool is based on a lock-free solution. This pool is allocated at backend initialisation and it offers memory aligned fixed-size blocks. In case the memory pool is fully utilised, we implement an LRU block replacement policy, which forwards blocks to persistent storage. Blocks are initially allocated under huge pages with the aim of reducing the TLB table size and therefore to reduce the memory access latency.

### 4.2 Data Replication

Hercules offers a client-side replica manager. This replication mechanism is mainly handled at client-side. When a dataset is created, the application can specify the replication factor required for data. As Hercules's dataset object exposes the list of available data and metadata backends, at write and read operations, data requests are sent to a subset of backend determined by the replication factor. This subset is created applying sparsity polices based on maximum distance between the replicas. Once Hercules detects a failure in one or more backends, it marks this specific backend as down/broken and uses the following in the list. Eventually, the broken copy will be restored if the data node is reachable. To reduce the communication overhead introduced by the use of multiple transmissions, write operations are committed asynchronously. Hercules ensures a strong consistency model managed by the UCX communication channels, which provide a message queue that guarantees the reception order at the backend side. In the future, we plan to optimise data replication by using asynchronous collective operations, such as gather and broadcast. These communication paradigms are already supported by the unified collective communication library (UCC).

### 4.3 Metadata

Hercules is based on two metadata tiers. The first tier is composed by multiple distributed metadata entities to manage inter-node information related to each dataset (*i.e.*, dataset type, block distribution policy, replication factor). The frontend layer selects the most adequate inter-node metadata server given the data distribution policy (*i.e.*, round-robin, CRC, bucket). This mechanism aims to alleviate the overhead of metadata management, especially in applications with a huge number of small files. It is important to highlight that a mix of co-allocated and distributed metadata servers is feasible.

The second tier is composed by each file/folder metadata, that is stored at *Block 0* on each dataset including traditional POSIX-like metadata (*struct stat*). First blocks are distributed like any other data node and accessed applying hash functions to the dataset URI, thus avoiding the need of a new layer of metadata servers and maximising parallelism. If replication is applied, in order to guarantee data consistency, replication of *Block 0* is orchestrated in the frontend layer.

First tier metadata is internally stored as an opaque data structure representing a balanced binary tree provided by the *GLib* library. The tree is automatically balanced as key/value pairs are added, key lookup is $O(\log_n)$, where $n$ is the number of key/value pairs in the tree. Therefore, given our distributed approach of metadata management, we can assume that the $O(\log_n /meta)$, where $meta$ is the number of metadata servers. It is important to note that the metadata server is calculated at the frontend using our configurable distribution policies, so there is a margin of optimisation in this aspect.

## 5 Communication Layer

This section describes the communication model provided by Hercules, based on Unified Communication X (UCX). The main components of the communication layer are the UCX workers. A UCX worker abstracts an instance of network resources such as a host, network interface, or multiple resources such as multiple network interfaces. UCX workers also represent virtual communication resources that can aggregate multiple devices, allowing Hercules to take advantage of cross-transport multi-rail communications by delivering data in multiple network interfaces in parallel (network bounding), without the need for any special tuning. The frontend layer relies on two independent UCX workers to enable point to point communication [16] with data and metadata servers. This mechanism guaranties isolated transmission by using different communication queues. The data consistency is managed by UCX, and by using UCX/UCP, the appropriate transfer protocol is chosen and the fragmentation of the message is doing when it is necessary. As future work, we are planning to work in the consistency between data and metadata servers.

When the frontend layer is initialised, the client library requests to the backend dispatcher thread the UCX worker address. This address is employed for the creation of endpoints at both sides that represent a connection from a local worker to a remote worker (see Sect. 3). All *get* and *set* requests are sent through these endpoints.

Metadata and data backends deploy a pool of worker threads and a single dispatcher thread. First, the goal of the pool of worker threads is to overlap data transfers and the internal memory management (*i.e.*, seek, memory staging, garbage collection), exploiting the network utilisation by allowing a larger number of concurrent clients. Second, a dispatcher thread listens for connection requests from clients. Given this process is not network demanding, communication between clients and dispatchers is established by using TCP/IP protocol.

The storage backend maintains a list of active endpoints. This list is updated at first request arrival and destroyed once the client library releases and finalised the application execution. These end-points are cached and utilised for future requests, reducing the creation cost. Finally, this mechanism eliminates the necessity of dealing with a global ID, given that, UCX generates universally unique identifiers (UUID) for each UCX worker.

Similarly to MPI, Hercules exploits tag-based message passing in multiple ways. First, both request and raw data messages are tagged with different values, facilitating the message order at reception. UCX ensures the order in the reception of messages, emulating the POSIX consistency model. Second, usage of tag-based messages eliminates the need of dealing with a costly list of endpoints, as UCX offers a similar approach to *MPI_Probe*. Finally, this mechanism offers a feasible alternative to RPC given that the tags identifies the message operation as well.

## 6 Experimental Evaluation

In this section we describe the experiments conducted to evaluate Hercules performance, the evaluation environment setup, and the results obtained from the tests made.

### 6.1 Experimental Setup

The hardware used to carry out the experiments consists of a 64-nodes cluster running Ubuntu 20.04.5 LTS. Each node is equipped with two Intel Xeon CPU E5-2697 v4 16-Core processors with a total of 32 physical cores and a clock speed per core of 2.6 GHz. Network topology is created with three switches conforming a fat-tree network of two levels. All the compute nodes are connected through Intel Omni-path network reaching a peak performance of 100 Gbps. The software employed is UCX 1.15, OpenMPI 4.1 and *glib*. UCX exposed OPA network using *ibverbs* library, reaching a similar bandwidth comparing with the native OpenMPI installation. The backend storage is provided by a BeeGFS installation deployed as a single I/O server with 32 SSD organised as a RAID, with 8 SSD per controller channel. It uses 64 I/O workers. BeeGFS runs under *buffered mode* as the default cache type.

Experimental results were obtained using the IOR benchmark, a widely-used solution for measuring I/O performance at scale, and IO500 [4], a benchmark suite bundled with execution rules targeting throughput and metadata performance. The evaluation metrics shown in this paper correspond with the average value of 10 consecutive executions.

We evaluated five configurations of Hercules, where the main differences between them are the number of data nodes (labelled as DN) launched (1 to 16), and for these experiments we only tested the application-detached deployment (labelled as *dis*). For example, *Hercules 16DN/dis* is the configuration of 16 data nodes and every client processes deployment on different nodes.

### 6.2 Strong Scalability

The first experimental evaluation consists of running an IOR strong scalability test comparing the performance between Hercules and BeeGFS. In this evaluation, the total write/read size has been set at 1,024 MBytes, and as the number of clients increases this valued is distributed between them as follows: $File\_Size\_Per\_Client = 1,024/Number\_of\_Clients$.

As can be seen in Fig. 3, the Hercules configuration with 16 data nodes (*Hercules 16DN/dis*) reaches the best averages throughput for write operations. For 8 processes, this solution gets a performance gain of 80.22% compared with BeeGFS. On the other hand, for 16 processes reading the data, the same configuration got a performance gain of 69.35% compared with BeeGFS.

Compared with the *Hercules 1DN/dis* (the slower solution in all cases for write operations), *Hercules 16DN/dis* get an average speedup of 7.04$x$. In contrast, for read operations, we notice that *Hercules 1DN/dis* works fine for 1,

2 and 4 processes, but it remains with almost the same throughput for 8 and 16 processes. We can observe that BeeGFS is competitive for 1 and 2 process, having a performance gain of 18.59% and 6.74% respectively against *Hercules 16DN/dis*, but for 4 to 16 processes this trend changes, and *Hercules 16DN/dis* performance increases, resulting in a performance enhancement from $1.25x$ to $3.25x$.

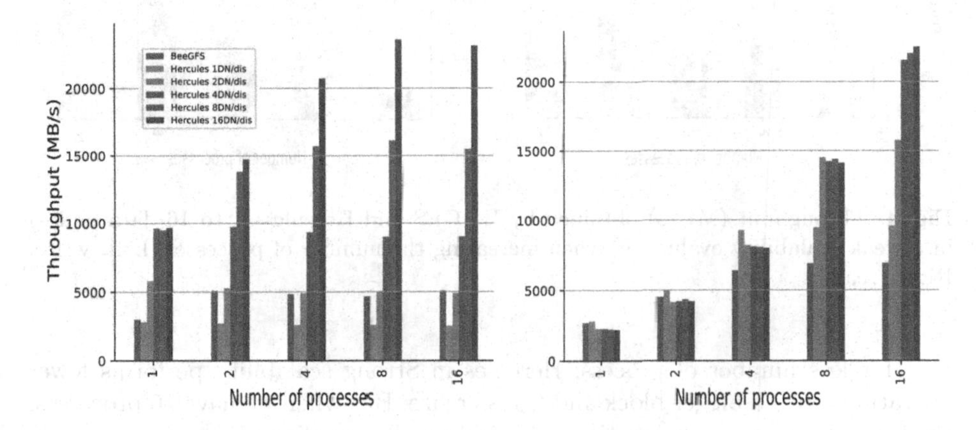


**Fig. 3.** Throughput (MB/s) obtained by BeeGFS and Hercules (1, 2, 4, 8 and 16 data nodes) in a strong scalability evaluation when increasing the number of processes. Left: write. Right: read.

### 6.3 Weak Scalability

We run an IOR weak scalability tests to assess Hercules performance compared to BeeGFS. In this configuration, we increase the number of clients for 1 to 16, varying also the numbers of data servers in Hercules from 1 to 16. Each client write a single shared file of 100 MBytes, up to a total of 1.6 GBytes in the largest configuration. Figure 4 plots the results of this experiment. As may be seen, Hercules outperforms BeeGFS when we have more than 4 processes. It also shows a very good scalability for both read and write operations. Reaching the maximum bandwidth available in the network switch when deploying 16 clients and 16 servers.

We can also observe that Hercules weak scalability is worse than strong scalability with a small number of data node servers (from 1 to 8). The reason could be because of the block size and transfer size that we used in every test. Independently of the block size used by Hercules to store every dataset, the IOR benchmark allows specifying its own block size and transfer size, and for the result shown, we use the same value for both parameters. As you can see in the Table 1, for Strong scalability evaluation these values decrease when there is more number of processes available, but for the Weak scalability evaluation we used the same value in all cases. Taking this under consideration, we assume

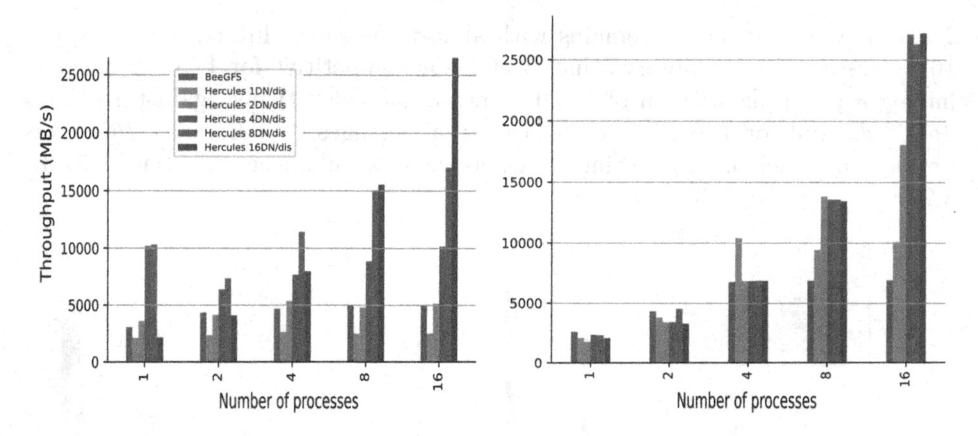


**Fig. 4.** Throughput (MB/s) obtained by BeeGFS and Hercules (1 to 16 data nodes) in a weak scalability evaluation when increasing the number of processes. Left: write. Right: read.

that for less number of process, Hercules in Strong scalability performs fewer operations with a bigger block and transfer size. But when we have 16 processes, these values decrease, generating more but small operations.

**Table 1.** Block size and Transfer Size used in Weak and Strong scalability evaluations.

| Processes | Weak (MBytes) | Strong (MBytes) |
|---|---|---|
| 1 | 100 | 1024 |
| 2 | 100 | 512 |
| 4 | 100 | 256 |
| 8 | 100 | 128 |
| 16 | 100 | 64 |

Figure 5 plots the write throughput when using 16 processes per compute node. This experiment aims to demonstrate the feasibility of Hercules in presence of I/O stress on the compute node. We demonstrate that Hercules reaches the aggregated throughput limit for an increasing number of I/O processes. Although BeeGFS reaches the achievable peak performance with a single I/O node, Hercules allows to overcome the application needs (*i.e.*, temporal data, check-pointing).

### 6.4 Metadata

The objective of this experiment is to evaluate the metadata access performance using the well-known benchmark suite IO500. The stonewall timer has been set

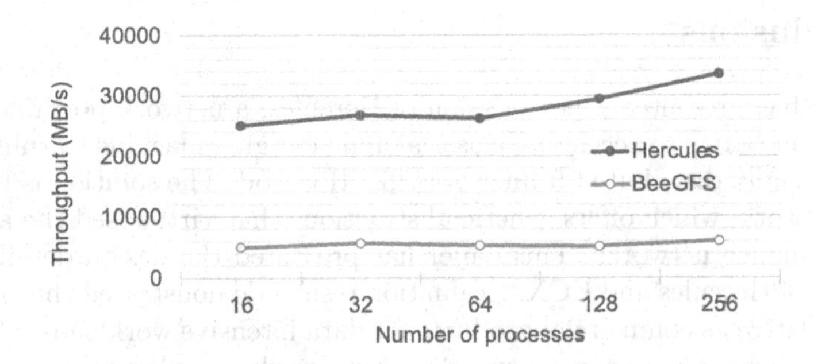


**Fig. 5.** Write throughput (MB/s). Weak scalability evaluation when fixing 16 data nodes and 16 processes per compute node. In case of Hercules 16, data nodes are employed.

up to 30 and 90 s. Table 2 shows the results obtained comparing BeeGFS and Hercules. Hercules is deployed on distributed compute nodes with remote metadata and data nodes. This setup aims to emulate the current BeeGFS deployment. Results denotes that Hercules reached a similar performance. We observe a small performance degradation in *find* case, mainly motivated by the use of *GLib* binary tree as index. In the future, this component can be replaced by applying bulk namespace insertion for the creation of intensive workloads and stateless consistent metadata caching at frontend layer [18].

**Table 2.** Results of IO500 benchmark comparing BeeGFS with Hercules using one single data/metadata node in different compute nodes.

| | BeeGFS (30) | Hercules (30) | BeeGFS (90) | Hercules (90) |
|---|---|---|---|---|
| find | 1.056 | 8.120 | 8.088 | 23.538 |
| mdtest-hard-write | 31.062 | 34.565 | 92.322 | 73.179 |
| mdtest-easy-stat | 16.162 | 24.667 | 40.760 | 25.439 |
| mdtest-hard-stat | 9.860 | 8.332 | 32.482 | 22.165 |
| mdtest-easy-delete | 23.052 | 10.329 | 59.737 | 50.579 |
| mdtest-hard-read | 23.953 | 18.432 | 77.337 | 53.956 |
| mdtest-hard-delete | 14.648 | 19.887 | 48.321 | 60.104 |

As results depict, Hercules outperforms BeeGFS in the evaluated cluster. Those results are very important, as we plan to use also Hercules for AI applications using millions of small files that have to be created/open and closed. The results obtained are due to the two tier metadata structure provided in Hercules.

## 7 Conclusions

This paper has presented a new version of Hercules, a network portable ad-hoc file system that aims to accelerate classical and emerging machine learning applications, specially distributed frameworks like Horovod. The solution is based on UCX framework, which offers generic abstractions that virtualised the access to high performance networks. This paper has presented the design details of the integration of Hercules and UCX. Evaluation results demonstrated that Hercules is as competitive as commercial products for data intensive workloads, obtaining 2x to 3x performance enhancement. As future work, we plan to exploit intra-node shared memory capabilities of UCX in the context of data staging. Current preliminary results demonstrate that UCX's transports such as *sysv* and *POSIX* expose a negative impact in Hercules performance. More efficient shared-memory accelerator like KNEM and XPMEM [9] should be considered.

## References

1. Bonachea, D., Hargrove, P.H.: GASNet-EX: a high-performance, portable communication library for exascale. In: Hall, M., Sundar, H. (eds.) LCPC 2018. LNCS, vol. 11882, pp. 138–158. Springer, Cham (2019). https://doi.org/10.1007/978-3-030-34627-0_11
2. Braam, P.J., Schwan, P.: Lustre: the intergalactic file system. In: Ottawa Linux Symposium, pp. 3429–3441 (2002)
3. Brinkmann, A., et al.: Ad hoc file systems for high-performance computing. Comput. Sci. Technol. **35**(1), 4–26 (2020)
4. Chasapis, K., Vet, J.Y., Acquaviva, J.T.: Benchmarking parallel file system sensitiveness to I/O patterns. In: 2019 IEEE 27th International Symposium on Modeling, Analysis, and Simulation of Computer and Telecommunication Systems (MASCOTS), pp. 427–428. IEEE (2019)
5. Chowdhury, F., et al.: I/O characterization and performance evaluation of BeeGFS for deep learning. In: Proceedings of the 48th International Conference on Parallel Processing, ICPP 2019. Association for Computing Machinery (2019)
6. Czarnul, P., Proficz, J., Drypczewski, K.: Survey of methodologies, approaches, and challenges in parallel programming using high-performance computing systems. Sci. Program. **2020** (2020)
7. Duro, F.R., Garcia-Blas, J., Carretero, J.: A hierarchical parallel storage system based on distributed memory for large scale systems. In: Proceedings of the 20th European MPI Users' Group Meeting, pp. 139–140 (2013)
8. Garcia-Blas, J., Singh, D.E., Carretero, J.: IMSS: in-memory storage system for data intensive applications. In: Anzt, H., Bienz, A., Luszczek, P., Baboulin, M. (eds.) High Performance Computing. ISC High Performance 2022 International Workshops. ISC High Performance 2022. LNCS, vol. 13387, pp. 190–205. Springer, Cham (2022). https://doi.org/10.1007/978-3-031-23220-6_13
9. Hori, A., Ouyang, K., Gerofi, B., Ishikawa, Y.: On the difference between shared memory and shared address space in HPC communication. In: Panda, D.K., Sullivan, M. (eds.) SCFA 2022. LNCS, vol. 13214, pp. 59–78. Springer, Cham (2022). https://doi.org/10.1007/978-3-031-10419-0_5

10. Isaila, F., Garcia, J., Carretero, J., Ross, R., Kimpe, D.: Making the case for reforming the I/O software stack of extreme-scale systems. Adv. Eng. Softw. **111**, 26–31 (2017). Advances in High Performance Computing: on the Path to Exascale Software
11. Kune, R., Konugurthi, P.K., Agarwal, A., Chillarige, R.R., Buyya, R.: The anatomy of big data computing. Softw. Pract.: Experience **46**(1), 79–105 (2016)
12. Lockwood, G.K., et al.: Storage 2020: a vision for the future of HPC storage. Technical report, Lawrence Berkeley National Lab. (2023)
13. Narasimhamurthy, S., et al.: Sage: percipient storage for exascale data centric computing. Parallel Comput. **83**, 22–33 (2019)
14. Nishtala, R., et al.: Scaling memcache at Facebook. In: Presented as Part of the 10th USENIX Symposium on Networked Systems Design and Implementation (NSDI 2013), pp. 385–398 (2013)
15. Pang, B., Nijkamp, E., Wu, Y.N.: Deep learning with TensorFlow: a review. J. Educ. Behav. Stat. **45**(2), 227–248 (2020)
16. Papadopoulou, N., Oden, L., Balaji, P.: A performance study of UCX over InfiniBand. In: 2017 17th IEEE/ACM International Symposium on Cluster, Cloud and Grid Computing (CCGRID), pp. 345–354. IEEE (2017)
17. Radulovic, M., Asifuzzaman, K., Carpenter, P., Radojković, P., Ayguadé, E.: HPC benchmarking: scaling right and looking beyond the average. In: Aldinucci, M., Padovani, L., Torquati, M. (eds.) Euro-Par 2018. LNCS, vol. 11014, pp. 135–146. Springer, Cham (2018). https://doi.org/10.1007/978-3-319-96983-1_10
18. Ren, K., Zheng, Q., Patil, S., Gibson, G.: IndexFS: scaling file system metadata performance with stateless caching and bulk insertion. In: Proceedings of the International Conference for High Performance Computing, Networking, Storage and Analysis, SC 2014, pp. 237–248 (2014)
19. Schmuck, F., Haskin, R.: GPFS: a shared-disk file system for large computing clusters. In: Proceedings of the 1st USENIX Conference on File and Storage Technologies, FAST 2002, USA, p. 19-es. USENIX Association (2002)
20. Shamis, P., et al.: UCX: an open source framework for HPC network APIs and beyond. In: IEEE 23rd Annual Symposium on High-Performance Interconnects, pp. 40–43 (2015)
21. Vahi, K., Rynge, M., Juve, G., Mayani, R., Deelman, E.: Rethinking data management for big data scientific workflows. In: 2013 IEEE International Conference on Big Data, pp. 27–35. IEEE (2013)
22. Vef, M., et al.: GekkoFS - a temporary distributed file system for HPC applications. In: 2018 IEEE International Conference on Cluster Computing, pp. 319–324 (2018)
23. Wang, T., Mohror, K., Moody, A., Sato, K., Yu, W.: An ephemeral burst-buffer file system for scientific applications. In: Proceedings of the International Conference for High Performance Computing, Networking, Storage and Analysis, SC 2016, pp. 807–818 (2016)
24. Yang, J., Izraelevitz, J., Swanson, S.: Orion: a distributed file system for non-volatile main memory and RDMA-capable networks. In: 17th USENIX Conference on File and Storage Technologies (FAST 2019), pp. 221–234 (2019)
25. Zhang, H., Chen, G., Ooi, B.C., Tan, K.L., Zhang, M.: In-memory big data management and processing: a survey. IEEE Trans. Knowl. Data Eng. **27**(7), 1920–1948 (2015)

# An Efficient Parallel Adaptive GMG Solver for Large-Scale Stokes Problems

S. Saberi[1(✉)], G. Meschke[2], and A. Vogel[1]

[1] High Performance Computing, Ruhr University Bochum, Universitätsstr. 150, 44801 Bochum, Germany
{seyed.saberi,a.vogel}@rub.de

[2] Institute for Structural Mechanics, Ruhr University Bochum, Universitätsstr. 150, 44801 Bochum, Germany
guenther.meschke@rub.de

**Abstract.** We study the performance and scalability of the adaptive geometric multigrid method with the recently developed restricted additive Vanka (`RAV`) smoother for the finite element solution of large-scale Stokes problems on distributed-memory clusters. A comparison of the `RAV` smoother and the classical multiplicative and additive Vanka smoothers is presented. We present three cache policies for the smoother operators that provide a balance between cached and on-the-fly computation and discuss their memory footprint and computational cost. It is shown that the restricted additive smoother with the most efficient cache policy has the smallest memory footprint and is computationally cheaper in comparison with the other smoothers and can, therefore, be used for large-scale problems even when the available main memory is constrained. We discuss the parallelization aspects of the smoother operators and show that the `RAV` operator can be replicated exactly in parallel with a very small communication overhead. We present strong and weak scaling of the GMG solver for 2D and 3D examples with up to roughly 540 million degrees of freedom on up to 2048 MPI processes. The GMG solver with the restricted additive smoother is shown to achieve rapid convergence rates and scale well in both the strong and weak scaling studies, making it an attractive choice for the solution of large-scale Stokes problems on HPC systems.

**Keywords:** Multigrid · Stokes flow · Finite element method · Massively parallel

## 1 Introduction

The scalable solution of the Stokes equations is a challenging task and is relevant to both scientific and industrial applications. While direct solvers can handle the saddle-point systems that arise from the discretization of the Stokes problem effectively, it is well known that their scalability typically suffers from their computational complexity on the one hand and lack of sufficient concurrency


J. Cano et al. (Eds.): Euro-Par 2023, LNCS 14100, pp. 694–709, 2023.
https://doi.org/10.1007/978-3-031-39698-4_47

on the other. Iterative methods seek to circumvent such algorithmic bottlenecks and solvers based on Krylov methods [26], multigrid methods [15] and the Uzawa method [21] have been proposed for the Stokes problem. Geometric multigrid methods are among the most efficient iterative solvers and can achieve optimal convergence, independent of the problem size [15]. The smoother operator, in this regard, plays a decisive role insofar as determining the convergence and scalability of the solver, rendering its choice indispensable to successful multigrid methods. In this work, we consider a finite element discretization of the Stokes equations and focus on adaptive geometric multigrid (GMG) methods based on the recently developed restricted additive Vanka (`RAV`) smoother [27]. We employ space tree data structures [5,28] for the adaptive resolution of the spatial domain. We extend the work in [27] to the solution of large-scale problems on massively parallel systems, propose three cache policies for the smoother operators and discuss the parallelization aspects of the GMG solver. The performance of the solver in terms of convergence, scalability and memory footprint are studied and its suitability for the solution of large-scale problems on parallel machines is evaluated. The contributions of this work can be summarized as follows:

- We present a parallel adaptive GMG solver with the recently developed `RAV` smoother [27] for the Stokes equations and discuss its convergence and weak and strong scaling for large-scale problems on distributed-memory clusters using 2D and 3D benchmarks with up to roughly 540 million degrees of freedom and on up to 2048 MPI processes
- We compare the `RAV` smoother with the classical multiplicative and additive Vanka smoothers [31] and discuss their performance, parallel application and memory requirements
- We propose three cache policies for the smoother operators that provide a balance between cached and on-the-fly computation and discuss their implementation details and memory footprint
- We show that the GMG solver based on the `RAV` smoother is favorable in terms of convergence, communication overhead, computational cost and memory footprint compared with the classical and additive Vanka smoothers and is, therefore, attractive in high-performance computing environments

The remainder of this work is organized into the following sections. Related works are discussed in Sect. 2. In Sect. 3, we briefly present the finite element discretization of the model problem. In Sect. 4, we present the parallel adaptive geometric multigrid solver for the model problem as well as the proposed cache policies and discuss the memory requirements and parallelization aspects of the smoother operators. We present the numerical benchmarks and scaling studies in Sect. 5 and discuss the findings. Finally, we draw some conclusions based on the obtained results in Sect. 6.

## 2 Related Work

A wide variety of solvers, including Uzawa methods, Krylov subspace solvers and multigrid methods have been employed for the solution of saddle-point problems.

A parallel solver based on the prediction-projection method for the finite difference formulation of fluid flow problems, for instance, was studied in [33], and a parallel pressure Schur complement solver based on uniform mesh multiplication for flow problems was presented in [17]. Multigrid methods are among the most efficient iterative solvers, see, e.g., [15] and have been successfully used for the solution of saddle-point systems, see, e.g., [9,29,32,34]. A multigrid solver based on incomplete LU factorization was proposed in [34]. The classical Vanka smoother for the solution of the finite difference discretization of the Navier-Stokes equation was proposed in [31]. Semi-implicit method for pressure-linked equations (SIMPLE) pressure correction schemes as smoothers were studies in [13]. The parallel performance of the Braess-Sarazin smoother [3] and the classical Vanka smoother were studied in [18]. Inexact Uzawa methods as smoothers have also been used for the Stokes equations, see, e.g., [8,12,20,22]. An early scalability study of multigrid algorithms on parallel computers was presented in [23], and a survey of techniques for the parallelization of multigrid methods can be found in [6], see also [7,25,28] for more recent scalability studies of multigrid methods. A matrix-free multigrid method based on the Chebyshev smoother was studied in [24], and a matrix-free multigrid method with the inexact Uzawa smoother for the Stokes system based on hierarchical hybrid grids (HHG) was studied in [20]. In [14], a parallel multigrid method based on HHG is applied to the velocity block of the Stokes system within a pressure correction scheme. A space-time multigrid solver for time-periodic incompressible flow was presented in [2], and parallel multigrid methods based on Gauss-Seidel relaxation were studied in [4,16]. The `RAV` smoother was recently proposed in [27] and shown to achieve competitive convergence rates in comparison to the classical Vanka smoother.

## 3 Model Problem

We consider the incompressible Stokes equations for a viscous fluid which can be written in strong form as

$$\begin{aligned} -\eta\nabla^2 \boldsymbol{u} + \nabla p = \boldsymbol{f} & \qquad \text{in } \Omega, \\ \nabla \cdot \boldsymbol{u} = 0 & \qquad \text{in } \Omega, \\ \boldsymbol{u} = \boldsymbol{w} & \qquad \text{on } \Gamma_D \subset \partial\Omega, \\ \eta \frac{\partial \boldsymbol{u}}{\partial \boldsymbol{n}} - \boldsymbol{n} p = \boldsymbol{h} & \qquad \text{on } \Gamma_N = \partial\Omega \setminus \Gamma_D, \end{aligned} \tag{1}$$

where $\boldsymbol{u}$ is the fluid velocity, $p$ is the fluid pressure, $\boldsymbol{f}$ is the body force, $\Omega$ is the flow domain, $\partial\Omega$ denotes the boundary of the domain, $\boldsymbol{w}$ and $\boldsymbol{h}$ are prescribed functions on the Dirichlet, $\Gamma_D$, and Neumann, $\Gamma_N$, parts of the boundary, respectively, and $\boldsymbol{n}$ is the unit-length outer normal vector to the boundary. $\eta$ is the fluid viscosity. Following the standard finite element formulation, see, e.g., [10], and denoting by $(\cdot,\cdot)$ the scalar $L^2$ product, the discrete weak form of the model problem can be written as seeking $(\boldsymbol{u}_h, p_h) \in (\boldsymbol{V}_h, Q_h)$ such that

$$\begin{aligned} a(\boldsymbol{v}_h, \boldsymbol{u}_h) + b(\boldsymbol{v}_h, p_h) = f(\boldsymbol{v}_h) & \qquad \forall \boldsymbol{v}_h \in \boldsymbol{V}_{h,0}, \\ b(q_h, \boldsymbol{u}_h) + c(q_h, p_h) = 0, & \qquad \forall q_h \in Q_h, \end{aligned} \tag{2}$$

where $\boldsymbol{V}_h$, $\boldsymbol{V}_{h,0}$ and $Q_h$ are the appropriate finite-dimensional trial and test spaces, $\boldsymbol{V}_{h,0}$ is the restriction of $\boldsymbol{V}_h$ with zero Dirichlet boundary conditions, $\boldsymbol{v}_h$ and $q_h$ are the velocity and pressure test functions, respectively, and the bilinear and linear forms are defined as

$$\begin{aligned} a(\boldsymbol{v}_h, \boldsymbol{u}_h) &:= (\eta \nabla \boldsymbol{v}_h, \nabla \boldsymbol{u}_h)_{\Omega_h}, \\ b(\boldsymbol{v}_h, p_h) &:= -(\nabla \cdot \boldsymbol{v}_h, p_h)_{\Omega_h}, \\ f(\boldsymbol{v}_h) &:= (\boldsymbol{v}_h, \boldsymbol{f}_h)_{\Omega_h} + (\boldsymbol{v}_h, \boldsymbol{h}_h)_{\Gamma_{N_h}}, \end{aligned} \tag{3}$$

where $\Omega_h$ defines an approximation of the domain $\Omega$ such that $\overline{\Omega}_h := \cup_{i=1}^{n_K} K_i$, where $\mathcal{T}_h := \{K_i\}_{i=1}^{n_K}$ is a tessalation of $\Omega$ into compact, connected, Lipschitz sets. $\Gamma_{N_h}$ is the discretization of the Neumann part of the boundary and $\boldsymbol{h}_h := \boldsymbol{n} \cdot (\eta \nabla \boldsymbol{u}_h - p_h \boldsymbol{I})$. It is well known that either the pair $(\boldsymbol{V}_h, Q_h)$ must satisfy the inf-sup condition or the formulation must be stabilized. We employ a stabilized $Q1$-$Q1$ discretization, see, e.g., [19], where the stabilization term is defined as

$$c(q_h, p_h) := -\beta \sum_{K_i \in \mathcal{T}_h} h_{K_i}^2 (\nabla q_h, \nabla p_h)_{K_i}, \tag{4}$$

where the stabilization parameter $\beta$ is a sufficiently large constant, and $h_{K_i}$ is the diameter of $K_i$. We note that the equal-order pair $Q1$-$Q1$ is an attractive choice compared to its higher order counterparts in terms of ease of implementation. Equation (2) leads to a system of equations of the form

$$\begin{bmatrix} \mathbf{A} & \mathbf{B} \\ \mathbf{B}^T & \mathbf{C} \end{bmatrix} \begin{bmatrix} \mathbf{u} \\ \mathbf{p} \end{bmatrix} = \begin{bmatrix} \mathbf{f} \\ \mathbf{0} \end{bmatrix}, \tag{5}$$

where the matrices $\mathbf{A}$, $\mathbf{B}$, and $\mathbf{C}$ are defined according to the bilinear forms in Eqs. (3) and (4), and the vector $\mathbf{f}$ is defined according to the linear form in Eq. (3). The vectors $\mathbf{u}$ and $\mathbf{p}$ are the coefficients of expansion of the velocity and pressure basis functions, respectively.

## 4 Parallel Adaptive Geometric Multigrid

We start by briefly presenting the geometric multigrid solver. We employ a monolithic geometric multigrid method for the solution of the Stokes equations and employ adaptive mesh refinement (AMR) using space tree data structures, see, e.g., [5,28], whereby a flexible framework for the adaptive resolution of the solution in spatial regions of interest is provided, which in flow applications, for instance, often includes the boundary layer. We treat hanging nodes as constraints and remove them from the global system of equations. A 2:1 balance is imposed on the mesh, i.e., the difference between the refinement level of neighbor elements is at most one. The nested grid hierarchy $\Omega_h^i, i = 1, \ldots, n$ is constructed top down, where $\Omega_h^1$ and $\Omega_h^n$ are the coarsest and finest grids, respectively. In order to maintain load balancing, each grid is distributed across the processes such as to keep the number of elements per process roughly equal. In the presence

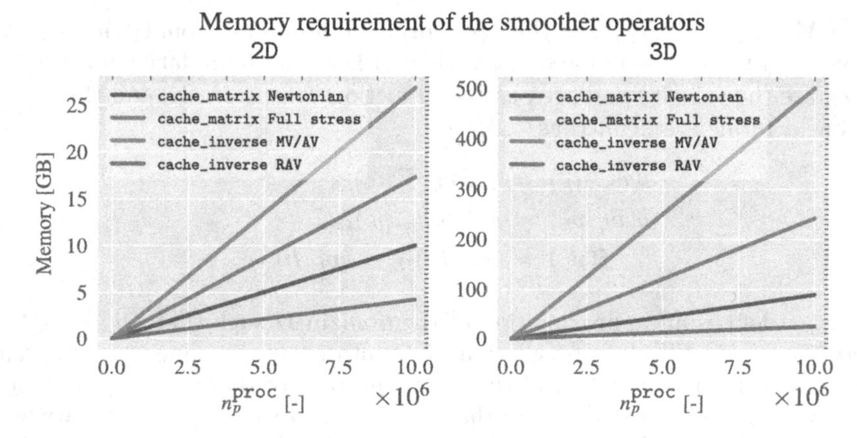


**Fig. 1.** The memory requirement of the smoother operators with the `cache_matrix` and `cache_inverse` policies, assuming a regular neighborhood. Off-process subdomains are neglected. Note that the `cache_matrix` policy has the same memory requirement for all smoother operators, and a distinction between Newtonian/non-Newtonian formulation is not necessary for the `cache_inverse` policy as the block inverse is in general dense. It is assumed that the size of double is 8 Bytes

of AMR, refined child nodes are not guaranteed to remain on the same process as their parent nodes, and data transfer between grids is consequently carried out in two steps. Given a vector $\mathbf{v}^i$ on $\Omega_h^i$, the restriction operator $\mathcal{R}_i^{i-1} : \Omega_h^i \rightarrow \Omega_h^{i-1}$ can be expressed as

$$\mathcal{R}_i^{i-1} := \mathcal{T}^{i-1}\tilde{\mathcal{R}}_i^{i-1}, \tag{6}$$

where $\tilde{\mathcal{R}}_i^{i-1} : \Omega_h^i \rightarrow \tilde{\Omega}_h^{i-1}$ first transfers $\mathbf{v}^i$ to $\tilde{\mathbf{v}}^{i-1}$ on an intermediate process-local coarse grid $\tilde{\Omega}_e^{i-1}$, followed by $\mathcal{T}^{i-1} : \tilde{\Omega}_h^{i-1} \rightarrow \Omega_h^{i-1}$ that transfers $\tilde{\mathbf{v}}^{i-1}$ to $\mathbf{v}^{i-1}$ on the coarse grid $\Omega_h^{i-1}$. The intermediate coarse grid $\tilde{\Omega}_h^{i-1}$ is constructed from the fine grid $\Omega_h^i$ such as to guarantee that the parent of refined child nodes are on the same process as $\Omega_h^i$, and $\tilde{\mathcal{R}}_i^{i-1}$ is, therefore, a process local operator. $\mathcal{T}^{i-1}$ is then responsible for transferring data between $\tilde{\Omega}_h^{i-1}$ and the distributed coarse grid $\Omega_h^{i-1}$. Similarly, the prolongation operator $\mathcal{P}_{i-1}^i : \Omega_h^{i-1} \rightarrow \Omega_h^i$, which can be expressed as $\mathcal{P}_{i-1}^i := \mathcal{R}_i^{i-1^T}$ transfers $\mathbf{v}^{i-1}$ first to an intermediate grid and then to the fine grid.

### 4.1 Smoother Operators

We discuss the `RAV` smoother as well as the classical multiplicative and additive Vanka smoothers in the following. Note that the grid level index is dropped in favor of legibility. Given a grid $\Omega_h$ with $n_p$ pressure nodes, the iterative correction is defined as $\mathbf{c} := \mathbf{S}\mathbf{r}$, where $\mathbf{r}$ is the residual vector, and the smoother operator $\mathbf{S}$ can be written as follows

$$\mathbf{S}_{\mathtt{MV}} = \Big[\mathbf{I} - \prod_{i=1}^{n_p}(\mathbf{I} - \mathbf{R}_i^T\omega_i\mathbf{L}_i^{-1}\mathbf{R}_i\mathbf{L})\Big]\mathbf{L}^{-1}, \tag{7}$$

**Table 1.** The number of cached values in the `cache_none`, `cache_matrix` and `cache_inverse` policies for the `MV`, `AV` and `RAV` smoothers in $d$ dimensions, assuming a regular neighborhood. $n_p^{\texttt{proc}}$ is the number of locally owned pressure DoFs and $n_{\mathcal{S}}^{\texttt{offp}}$ is the number of off-process subdomains. We note that $n_{\mathcal{S}}^{\texttt{offp}}$ is contained within $n_p^{\texttt{proc}}$, and the $n_{\mathcal{S}}^{\texttt{offp}}$ term, therefore, does not appear under the `cache_inverse` policy. $a$ and $b$ are the number of subdomain DoFs and the number of non-zero entries in the subdomain block in the regular neighborhood, respectively. Note that $n_{\mathcal{S}}^{\texttt{offp}} \ll n_p^{\texttt{proc}}$ and the $n_p^{\texttt{proc}}$ terms are, therefore, dominant, as indicated by black and grey.

| Smoother/ Cache policy | `cache_none` | `cache_matrix` | `cache_inverse` |
|---|---|---|---|
| `MV` | $n_{\mathcal{S}}^{\texttt{offp}} \cdot a^2$ | $(n_p^{\texttt{proc}} - n_{\mathcal{S}}^{\texttt{offp}}) \cdot b + n_{\mathcal{S}}^{\texttt{offp}} \cdot a^2$ | $n_p^{\texttt{proc}} \cdot a^2$ |
| `AV` | $n_{\mathcal{S}}^{\texttt{offp}} \cdot a^2$ | $(n_p^{\texttt{proc}} - n_{\mathcal{S}}^{\texttt{offp}}) \cdot b + n_{\mathcal{S}}^{\texttt{offp}} \cdot a^2$ | $n_p^{\texttt{proc}} \cdot a^2$ |
| `RAV` | $n_{\mathcal{S}}^{\texttt{offp}} \cdot (d+1)a$ | $(n_p^{\texttt{proc}} - n_{\mathcal{S}}^{\texttt{offp}}) \cdot b + n_{\mathcal{S}}^{\texttt{offp}} \cdot (d+1)a$ | $n_p^{\texttt{proc}} \cdot (d+1)a$ |

$$a := 3^d d + 1$$
$$b := l[2^d(2^d c + 1) + 4 \cdot 3^{d-2}(2^{d-1} \cdot 3c + 1) + e + (3^d c + 1)l] \cdot d + (3^d d + 1)$$
$$c := \begin{cases} 1 & \text{Newtonian fluids} \\ d & \text{Full stress} \end{cases} \quad e := \begin{cases} 0 & d = 2 \\ 2d(6dc + 1) & d = 3 \end{cases}$$

$$\mathbf{S}_{\texttt{AV}} = \sum_{i=1}^{n_p} (\mathbf{R}_i^T \boldsymbol{\omega}_i \mathbf{L}_i^{-1} \mathbf{R}_i), \tag{8}$$

$$\mathbf{S}_{\texttt{RAV}} = \sum_{i=1}^{n_p} (\tilde{\mathbf{R}}_i^T \boldsymbol{\omega}_i \mathbf{L}_i^{-1} \mathbf{R}_i), \tag{9}$$

where $\mathbf{S}_{\texttt{MV}}$, $\mathbf{S}_{\texttt{AV}}$ and $\mathbf{S}_{\texttt{RAV}}$ denote the multiplicative Vanka (`MV`) [31], additive Vanka (`AV`) and restricted additive Vanka (`RAV`) [27] smoother operators, respectively. The smoother operators, understood as Schwarz domain decomposition methods [11], consist in the application of a set of subdomains $\mathcal{S}_i, i = 1, \ldots, n_p$, where $\mathcal{S}_i$ is composed of the pressure degree of freedom $p_i$ and all the velocity degrees of freedom that are connected to it, see [27]. $\mathbf{L}$ is the matrix corresponding to the global system of equations, defined according to Equation (5). Given a subdomain $\mathcal{S}_i$, $\mathbf{R}_i$ is the subdomain restriction operator, $\mathbf{L}_i$ is the subdomain block and $\boldsymbol{\omega}_i$ is a diagonal damping matrix. The `RAV` restriction operator $\tilde{\mathbf{R}}_i$ restricts a given vector to the DoFs in a subset $\tilde{\mathcal{S}}_i \subset \mathcal{S}_i$, where $\tilde{\mathcal{S}}_i$ only consists of the pressure degree of freedom $p_i$ and the velocity degrees of freedom on the same pressure node. We refer to [27] for more details.

### 4.2 Cache Policies

The application of each subdomain $\mathcal{S}_i$ corresponds to the solution of a local saddle-point problem that algebraically corresponds to the local block $\mathbf{L}_i$. Therefore, the necessary operations for the application of $\mathcal{S}_i$ can be summarized as retrieving the local block and solving the local problem. Note that in the general case, where viscosity is spatially dependent, the local problem would be similarly spatially dependent. Even for Newtonian fluids, where the viscosity is constant, the local problem is dependent on the configuration of the elements to which the corresponding pressure node is connected. Therefore, in order to remain relevant to the general case, the subdomains are assumed to be spatially dependent in the following. We assume that the global system is stored in a sparse matrix format, and the retrieving of the local problem, thereby, involves the lookup of its associated entries, an operation most sparse formats are not optimized for and, therefore, entails a noticeable computational cost. Given the relatively small size of the local blocks, we solve the subdomain problems down to machine accuracy using a direct solver. Hence, the solution step can be further divided into computing the inverse and applying it to the subdomain residual. As the smoother operator must typically be applied several times until convergence is achieved, and given that the local systems remain constant during linear iterations, there is a clear incentive to eliminate as much as possible the computations associated with the first two steps outlined above, namely the retrieving of the local block and computing its inverse. Therefore, we present three caching policies in the following, each offering a different balance between caching and on-the-fly computation and discuss their memory footprint and computational cost.

Given a subdomain $\mathcal{S}_i$ with $n_i$ degrees of freedom, the most aggressive policy, denoted as `cache_inverse` is to cache the inverse of the local system for each subdomain, computed only once during the initialization of the system. As the inverse of the local block is in general a dense matrix, such policy requires the storage of $n_i^2$ values per subdomain for the `MV` and `AV` smoothers. On the other hand, as the prolongation operator of the `RAV` smoother $\tilde{\mathbf{R}}_i^T$ in Equation (9) effectively acts only on a subset of the degrees of freedom in $\tilde{\mathcal{S}}_i \subset \mathcal{S}_i$, padding the rest with zeros, it is sufficient to store only those rows of the local inverse that belong to $\tilde{\mathcal{S}}_i$, see [27] for a detailed description of the `RAV` smoother. Given that $\tilde{\mathcal{S}}_i$ only consists of the pressure degree of freedom $p_i$ and the velocity degrees of freedom on the same pressure node, amounting to a total of $1 + d$ DoFs in $d$ dimensions, the `RAV` smoother with the `cache_inverse` policy requires the storage of $(1 + d) \cdot n_i$ values, and there exists a marked difference between the memory footprint of the `RAV` smoother and the `MV` and `AV` smoothers. An alternative approach, denoted as `cache_matrix` is to only store the entries of the local block, which being sparse, can be stored using a sparse matrix format and compute the inverse of the block on the fly at each iteration of the smoother. The `cache_matrix` policy, therefore, requires the storage of $\texttt{nnz}(\mathbf{L}_i)$ values per subdomain, where `nnz` indicates the number of non-zero entries. Finally, denoted as the `cache_none` policy, both the retrieving of the local block and the computation of its inverse can be performed on the fly. Such policy is the most computationally demanding of the three but offers the smallest memory footprint as no extra matrices need to be stored. Given that the global system is stored in a sparse matrix format and the local problems are solved using LU factorization, the `cache_inverse` policy is expected to be virtually always more efficient than both the `cache_none` and `cache_matrix` policies as it eliminates the costly solution of the local block.

### 4.3 Parallelization and Computational Aspects

A further distinction between the smoother operators is marked by their application in parallel. The ownership of the subdomains follows the distribution of the mesh such that $\mathcal{S}_i$ is owned by the process that owns the pressure DoF $p_i$. As the degrees of freedom are uniquely owned, each subdomain is owned by exactly one process, leading to $n_p^{\texttt{proc}}$ subdomains on a given process, where $n_p^{\texttt{proc}}$ is the number of owned pressure DoFs. $\mathcal{S}_i$ is process local if all of its DoFs are locally owned, or off process, otherwise. The additive smoothers, `AV` and `RAV`, entail the application of the subdomains in any arbitrary order without intermediate updates to the residual. We note that the application of process-local subdomains is then a process-local operation and does not require any communication as both the local system as well as the subdomain residual are stored process locally. Therefore, the `AV` and `RAV` operators can be replicated exactly in parallel without any communication, except for the communication necessary for the off-process subdomains and the update of the residual after the application of all subdomains. Note that such communication is nevertheless small since $n_{\mathcal{S}}^{\texttt{offp}} \ll n_p^{\texttt{proc}}$. On the other hand, the `MV` operator in Eq. 7 requires the sequential application of the subdomains and updating the residual after each subdomain correction. Replication of the `MV` operator in parallel is, therefore, a non-trivial task that entails substantial orchestration and communication. Furthermore, regardless of the communication cost, the operator is not agnostic to the order in which the subdomains are applied. Therefore, the exact replication of Eq. (7) in parallel would be essentially serial. We implement the parallel version of the `MV` operator by relaxing the conditions outlined above, namely we apply Eq. (7) multiplicatively process locally and additively on process interfaces, leading to the `inexact MV` operator in parallel, which is, nevertheless, denoted as `MV` in the following in favor of brevity. The repercussion of such relaxations is the dependence of the parallel version of the `MV` operator on the number of processes, while the `AV` and `RAV` operators are process independent. Furthermore, the application of the subdomain correction in the `RAV` operator consists in the application of the $1 + d$ rows of the local inverse that appear in $\tilde{\mathcal{S}}_i$, as opposed to the application of the entire local inverse, which is the case for the `MV` and `AV` smoother operators. Therefore, the `RAV` smoother, by merit of its prolongation operator $\tilde{\mathbf{R}}_i^T$, presents an optimization opportunity that can be exploited not only in terms of memory footprint, as discussed in Sect. 4.2, but also computational cost.

Assuming a regular neighborhood in $d$ dimensions where each vertex is connected to $2^d$ elements, we present the memory requirement of each cache policy in Table 1. We note that the terms $a$, $b$ and $c$ in Table 1 are derived by counting the DoF connectivities in such a regular neighborhood. The velocity block $\mathbf{A}$ in Eq. (5) is block diagonal for Newtonian fluids and fully coupled otherwise, as reflected in the estimates. The number of off-process subdomains $n_{\mathcal{S}}^{\texttt{offp}}$

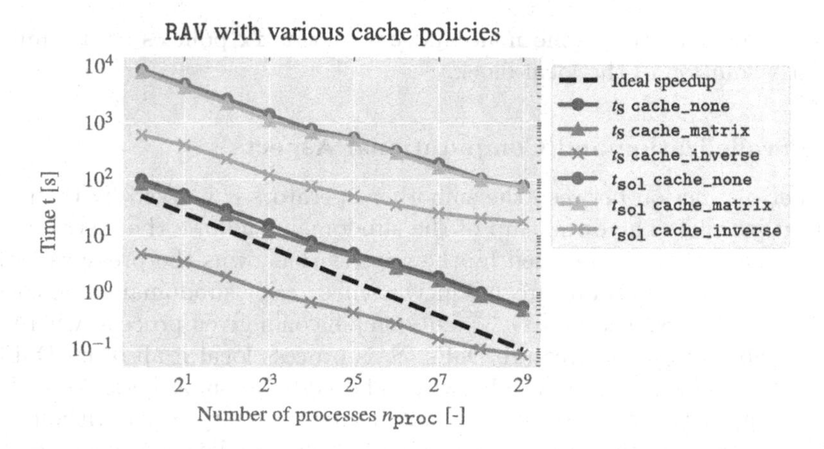


**Fig. 2.** Strong scaling of the GMG solver with the `RAV` smoother using different cache policies in the channel flow benchmark with $\Omega_h^9$ as the fine grid, see Table 2 with $n_{\mathrm{proc}} = 1, \ldots, 512$. $t_S$ and $t_{\mathrm{sol}}$ denote the runtime of the smoother per iteration on the fine grid and the total solver runtime including the setup time, respectively. The GMG solver converges in 9 iterations

is typically much smaller than their process-local counterparts, as they only occur on process interfaces; therefore, we always use the `cache_inverse` policy for off-process subdomains in order to minimize the communication overhead without incurring substantial penalty in terms of memory footprint. The memory requirement of the `cache_matrix` and `cache_inverse` policies is shown in Fig. 1. It can be observed that the required memory for the `MV` and `AV` smoothers with the `cache_inverse` policy quickly surges past the `cache_matrix` policy which provides a more moderate alternative. It is important to note that the `cache_inverse` policy for the `RAV` smoother requires the least amount of main memory even compared to the `cache_matrix` policy, which highlights an attractive aspect of the `RAV` smoother given that the `cache_inverse` policy is the most efficient of the three policies. We further discuss the performance of each cache policy in Sect. 5.

## 5 Numerical Experiments

We present a number of numerical experiments in this section in order to investigate the performance and scalability of the GMG solver for large-scale Stokes problems on distributed-memory clusters. Two well-known benchmarks for flow applications, namely the channel flow benchmark [29] and the lid-driven cavity benchmark [30] are employed. We present both strong and weak scaling of the `RAV`, `AV` and `MV` smoothers and discuss the different cache policies. We note that geometric multigrid method can be used as a preconditioner within Krylov accelerator methods; nevertheless, in order to exclude such external effects, we use GMG with a V cycle as a solver in the following benchmarks, where the

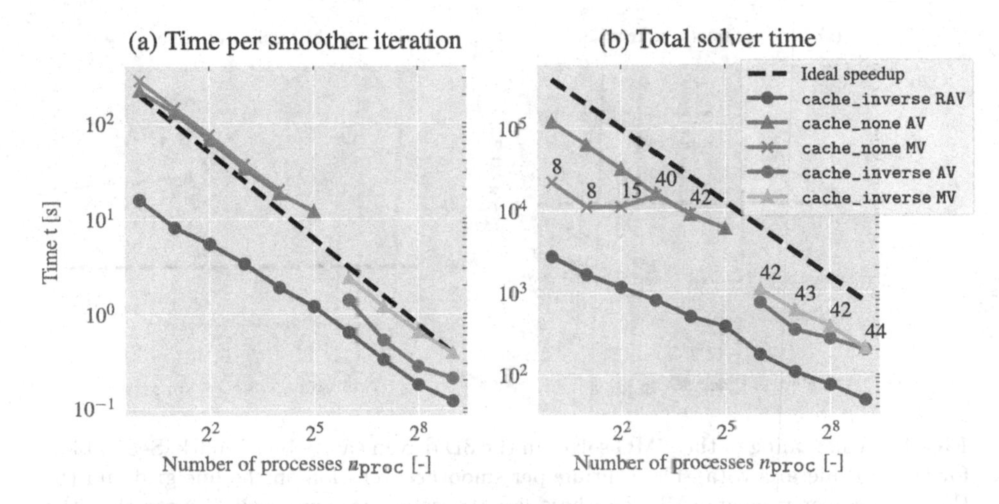


**Fig. 3.** Strong scaling of the GMG solver with different smoothers in the channel flow benchmark with $\Omega_h^{10}$ as the fine grid, see Table 2 with $n_{\text{proc}} = 1, \ldots, 512$. (a) The runtime per smoother iteration on the fine grid and (b) the total solver runtime. In each case, the most efficient applicable cache policy in terms of runtime is reported. The numbers above the MV smoother in (b) indicate the iteration count of the solver. We note that the solver with the MV smoother does not converge for $n_{\text{proc}} = 32$. The GMG solver with the AV and RAV smoothers converges in 48 and 19 iterations, respectively

convergence criterion is the reduction of the relative residual by $10^8$. We do not observe any difference in the converged solution between the smoother operators. The coarse grid is solved using a direct solver down to machine accuracy. Three pre- and post-smoothing steps are used. We note that MV in parallel is the inexact operator described in Sect. 4.3. Furthermore, since the subdomains on the process interfaces are applied additively in the parallel version of the MV operator, the MV smoother uses the damping factor of the AV smoother for the off-process subdomains in parallel. The runtime per smoother operation includes the application of the smoother operator as well as the synchronization of the residual vector at each smoothing step.

The numerical experiments are carried out on a distributed-memory CPU cluster where each node is equipped with double-socket Intel Xeon Skylake Gold 6148 CPUs each with 20 cores at 2.4GHz, 27.5MB of L3 cache and 64kB of L1 cache per core and 180GB of DDR4 main memory, and a 100GBit/s Intel Omni-Path Interconnect via PCIe x16 Gen 3 connects the nodes. The following studies are carried out in pure MPI mode, i.e., without shared-memory parallelization, where each node is filled with up to 32 MPI processes, and for a given number of processes, always the smallest possible number of nodes is employed. An in-house C++ implementation is used for the benchmarks. p4est [5] and PETSc [1] are used for space tree and some linear algebra functionalities, respectively.

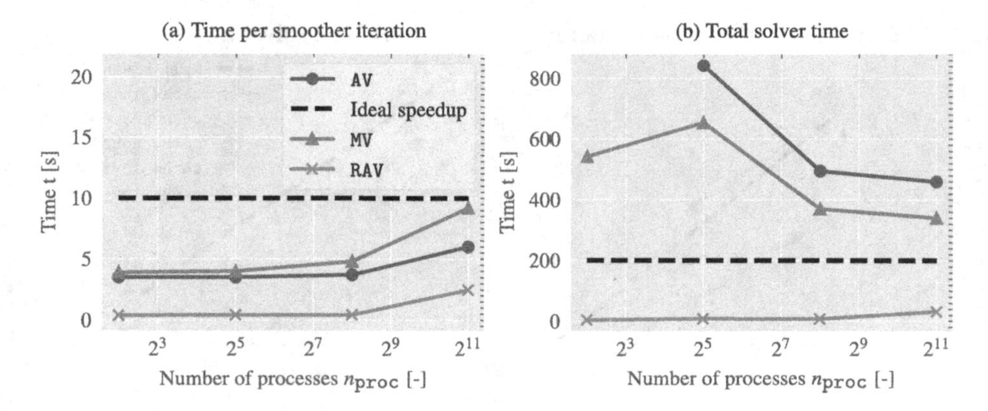


**Fig. 4.** Weak scaling of the GMG solver in the 3D driven cavity benchmark. See Table 3 for the grid hierarchy. (a) The runtime per smoother iteration on the fine grid and (b) the total solver runtime. All smoothers use the `cache_inverse` policy. Note that the solver with the `AV` smoother does not converge with $\Omega_h^2$ as the fine problem

**Table 2.** The grid hierarchy for the strong scaling study of the channel flow benchmark. $n_e$ and $n_{\text{DoF}}$ denote the number of elements and degrees of freedom, respectively. The adaptive refinement of the channel is shown on the right

| Grid | $n_e$ | $n_{\text{DoF}}$ | $n^i_{\text{DoF}}/n^{i-1}_{\text{DoF}}$ |
|---|---|---|---|
| $\Omega_h^1$ | 3,032 | 9,600 | - |
| $\Omega_h^2$ | 12,128 | 37,392 | 3.89 |
| $\Omega_h^3$ | 48,512 | 147,552 | 3.95 |
| $\Omega_h^4$ | 114,206 | 344,574 | 2.33 |
| $\Omega_h^5$ | 318,239 | 956,658 | 2.78 |
| $\Omega_h^6$ | 573,914 | 1,723,824 | 1.80 |
| $\Omega_h^7$ | 1,389,698 | 4,171,404 | 2.42 |
| $\Omega_h^8$ | 3,837,605 | 11,515,464 | 2.76 |
| $\Omega_h^9$ | 10,377,365 | 31,135,200 | 2.70 |
| $\Omega_h^{10}$ | 23,510,378 | 70,534,695 | 2.26 |

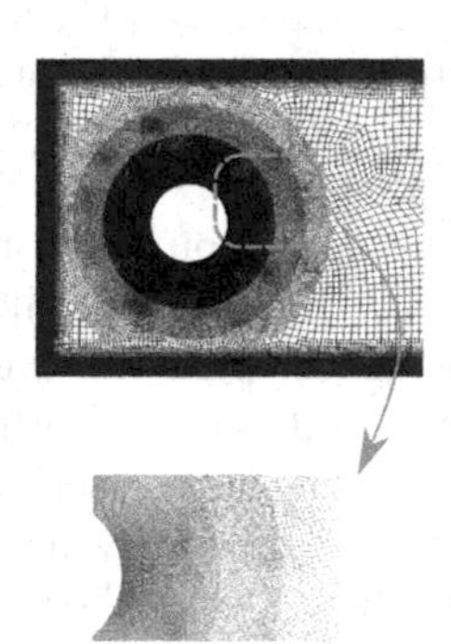

## 5.1 Strong Scaling

We first examine the strong scaling of the GMG solver using the channel flow benchmark, where the fluid with a prescribed velocity flows through a 2D channel with a cylindrical obstacle towards the inflow of the domain, see [27] for a detailed description of the problem. Therefore, a grid hierarchy, as shown in Table 2, is effected through adaptive refinement of the domain towards the channel walls and the cylinder. A damping factor of 0.66 for the `RAV` and `MV` smoothers and a damping factor of 0.1 for the `AV` smoother are used, which were observed to be necessary for convergence. In order to provide a comparison between the performance of the cache policies, the strong scaling of the GMG solver with the `RAV` smoother for the problem with $\Omega_h^9$ as the fine grid and $\Omega_h^1$ as the coarse grid, see Table 2, is shown in Fig. 2. We note that the fine grid $\Omega_h^9$ is chosen such that

**Table 3.** The grid hierarchy used for the weak scaling study of the 3D lid-driven cavity benchmark. $n_e$ and $n_{\text{DoF}}$ denote the number of elements and degrees of freedom, respectively. $n_{\text{proc}}$ is the number of processes. $n_{\text{it}}$ denotes the iteration count of the GMG solver with a given smoother operator. Note that the solver with the `AV` smoother does not converge with $\Omega_h^2$ as the fine problem

| Grid | $n_e$ | $n_{\text{DoF}}$ | $n^i_{\text{DoF}}/n^{i-1}_{\text{DoF}}$ | $n_{\text{proc}}$ | $n^{\text{MV}}_{\text{it}}$ | $n^{\text{AV}}_{\text{it}}$ | $n^{\text{RAV}}_{\text{it}}$ |
|---|---|---|---|---|---|---|---|
| $\Omega_h^1$ | 32,768 | 143,748 | – | – | – | – | – |
| $\Omega_h^2$ | 262,144 | 1,098,500 | 7.64 | 4 | 41 | – | 4 |
| $\Omega_h^3$ | 2,097,152 | 8,586,756 | 7.82 | 32 | 24 | 36 | 3 |
| $\Omega_h^4$ | 16,777,216 | 67,898,372 | 7.91 | 256 | 11 | 19 | 2 |
| $\Omega_h^5$ | 134,217,728 | 540,022,788 | 7.95 | 2,048 | 4 | 7 | 2 |

all three cache policies can be used throughout the entire range of the scaling study, including the most restricted configurations in terms of the available main memory, namely $n_{\text{proc}} = 1, \ldots, 32$ which are executed on a single node. It can be seen that the `cache_inverse` policy is, as expected, by far the fastest policy per smoother iteration, and consequently, also in terms of the total solver runtime. Likewise, the `cache_matrix` policy is more efficient than the `cache_none` policy—up to more than 25% in this benchmark. However, its relative advantage is overshadowed by the large gap between the `cache_inverse` policy and the `cache_matrix` and `cache_none` policies—up to well above 1000% in this benchmark. Furthermore, it is important to note that because of the efficiency of the `cache_inverse` policy, the effect of the parallelization of other GMG operations such as restriction, prolongation and the update of the residual at the end of each smoother iteration can be felt sooner compared to the `cache_matrix` and `cache_none` policies; as a result, it can be observed that while all cache policies scale relatively well compared to the ideal speedup, the speedup of the `cache_inverse` policy, especially in terms of the total solver runtime slows down towards the higher range of $n_{\text{proc}}$. Similarly, given the deep multigrid hierarchy and the stark contrast between the size of the grids, the micro-parallelization of vector operations on coarser grids is increasingly manifest in the scaling of the total solver runtime as the number of processes increase for all cache policies.

The strong scaling of the GMG solver with the different smoother operators is presented in Fig. 3, where $\Omega_h^{10}$ and $\Omega_h^1$ are used as the fine and coarse grids, respectively. In each case, the most efficient applicable cache policy is employed. The `MV` and `AV` smoothers must use the `cache_none` policy for $n_{\text{proc}} \leq 32$ as the memory requirement of the other cache policies exceeds the available main memory on a single node. On the other hand, the `RAV` smoother can employ the `cache_inverse` policy throughout the entire range of the scaling study, see Sect. 4.2, which highlights the advantage of the `RAV` smoother in terms of its memory footprint. Furthermore, while the GMG with the `RAV` and `AV` smoothers require 19 and 48 iterations, respectively, independent of $n_{\text{proc}}$, the iteration count with the `MV` smoother heavily depends on $n_{\text{proc}}$, as shown in Fig. 3. Consequently, although the MV operator scales well per smoother iteration, the scaling of the solver suffers in the presence of significant jumps in the iteration count. On the contrary, the exact replication of the additive smoother operators in parallel guarantees the iteration count to be independent of $n_{\mathtt{proc}}$. Given the lower computational cost of the RAV smoother in addition to its higher convergence rate compared to the MV and AV smoothers, the RAV smoother is by far the fastest both per smoother iteration and in terms of the total solver runtime.

### 5.2 Weak Scaling

We present the weak scaling of the GMG solver in this section. In order to study the scalability of the solver also in the 3D case, a second benchmark, namely the 3D lid-driven cavity benchmark is used. The grid hierarchy, the number of processes and the iteration count of the solver with different smoother operators are shown in Table 3, where the number of elements per process is kept roughly constant. $\Omega_h^1$ is used as the coarse grid in all cases, i.e., finer problems use a deeper grid hierarchy. Note that the coarse grid problem is relatively small, and hence its solution is not a bottleneck for the scaling of the solver. A damping factor of 0.66 for the MV smoother, 0.6 for the RAV smoother and 0.04 for the AV smoother is observed to be necessary for convergence, see [27]. The weak scaling of the solver is shown in Fig. 4. It can be observed that all of the smoother operators scale well in terms of the runtime per smoother iteration. The slight deviation from ideal speedup in Fig. 4(a) can be attributed to the overhead associated with the synchronization of the residual vector and potentially suboptimal network topology, especially when larger number of nodes are employed. On the other hand, as the iteration count of the solver with the MV and AV smoothers fluctuates significantly with problem size, the total solver runtime similarly varies, while the iteration count and, as a result, the total solver runtime with the RAV smoother remain roughly constant independent of the problem size and the number of processes. We note that the slight deviation from the ideal speedup that is observed on the largest problems is due to the same coarse grid overhead discussed in Sect. 5.1.

## 6 Conclusions

We presented a parallel adaptive GMG solver based on the RAV smoother for the solution of large-scale Stokes problems. We proposed three cache policies and discussed the memory footprint and parallelization aspects of the smoother operators. The convergence and scalability of the solver were evaluated using numerical benchmarks on a distributed-memory cluster and a comparison between the RAV smoother and the classical multiplicative and additive Vanka smoothers was presented. The GMG solver with the RAV smoother was shown to have favorable properties in terms of convergence, communication overhead, computational cost and memory footprint, especially in high-performance computing environments. It achieves rapid convergence rates and the iteration count of the solver remains bounded. Unlike the MV smoother, the RAV operator can be replicated exactly in parallel with a very small communication overhead, meaning that the smoother operator, and hence the GMG solver is independent of the number of processes. The RAV smoother provides significant optimization opportunities both in terms of computational cost and memory footprint compared to the MV and AV operators. One the one hand, the RAV smoother with the `cache_inverse` policy has a small memory footprint and allows for the accommodation of large problems even when the available main memory is limited. On the other hand, the RAV is considerably cheaper per iteration in terms of computational cost compared to the MV and AV smoothers. As a result, the GMG solver with the RAV smoother showed excellent scalability and achieved by far the fastest time to solution compared to the MV and AV smoothers in both strong and weak scaling studies. Therefore, the presented GMG solver with the RAV smoother is an attractive choice for the solution of large-scale Stokes problems on HPC systems.

**Acknowledgements.** Financial support was provided by the German Research Foundation (DFG), grant number 77309832. This support and the cluster computing time at Ruhr University Bochum is gratefully acknowledged.

## References

1. Balay, S., Gropp, W.D., McInnes, L.C., Smith, B.F.: Efficient management of parallelism in object oriented numerical software libraries. In: Arge, E., Bruaset, A.M., Langtangen, H.P. (eds.) Modern Software Tools in Scientific Computing, pp. 163–202. Birkhäuser Press (1997)
2. Benedusi, P., Hupp, D., Arbenz, P., Krause, R.: A parallel multigrid solver for time-periodic incompressible Navier–Stokes equations in 3D. In: Karasözen, B., Manguoğlu, M., Tezer-Sezgin, M., Göktepe, S., Uğur, Ö. (eds.) Numerical Mathematics and Advanced Applications ENUMATH 2015. LNCSE, vol. 112, pp. 265–273. Springer, Cham (2016). https://doi.org/10.1007/978-3-319-39929-4_26
3. Braess, D., Sarazin, R.: An efficient smoother for the Stokes problem. Appl. Num. Math. **23**(1), 3–19 (1997)
4. Bruneau, C.H., Khadra, K.: Highly parallel computing of a multigrid solver for 3d Navier-Stokes equations. J. Comput. Sci. **17**, 35–46 (2016)
5. Burstedde, C., Wilcox, L.C., Ghattas, O.: p4est: scalable algorithms for parallel adaptive mesh refinement on forests of octrees. SIAM J. Sci. Comput. **33**(3), 1103–1133 (2011)
6. Chow, E., Falgout, R.D., Hu, J.J., Tuminaro, R.S., Yang, U.M.: A survey of parallelization techniques for multigrid solvers. Parallel Process. Sci. Comput., 179–201 (2006)
7. Clevenger, T.C., Heister, T., Kanschat, G., Kronbichler, M.: A flexible, parallel, adaptive geometric multigrid method for FEM. ACM Trans. Math. Softw. (TOMS) **47**(1), 1–27 (2020)
8. Drzisga, D., John, L., Rude, U., Wohlmuth, B., Zulehner, W.: On the analysis of block smoothers for saddle point problems. SIAM J. Matrix Anal. Appl. **39**(2), 932–960 (2018)
9. Elman, H.C.: Multigrid and Krylov subspace methods for the discrete Stokes equations. Int. J. Num. Methods Fluids **22**(8), 755–770 (1996)

10. Ern, A., Guermond, J.L.: Theory and Practice of Finite Elements. Springer, Cham (2004). https://doi.org/10.1007/978-1-4757-4355-5
11. Gander, M.J.: Schwarz methods over the course of time. Electr. Trans. Num. Anal. **31**, 228–255 (2008)
12. Gaspar, F.J., Notay, Y., Oosterlee, C.W., Rodrigo, C.: A simple and efficient segregated smoother for the discrete Stokes equations. SIAM J. Sci. Comput. **36**(3), A1187–A1206 (2014)
13. Gjesdal, T., Lossius, M.E.H.: Comparison of pressure correction smoothers for multigrid solution of incompressible flow. Int. J. Num. Methods Fluids **25**(4), 393–405 (1997)
14. Gmeiner, B., Rüde, U., Stengel, H., Waluga, C., Wohlmuth, B.: Performance and scalability of hierarchical hybrid multigrid solvers for Stokes systems. SIAM J. Sci. Comput. **37**(2), C143–C168 (2015)
15. Hackbusch, W.: Multi-Grid Methods and Applications. Springer Series in Computational Mathematics, 1st edn. Springer, Heidelberg (1985). https://doi.org/10.1007/978-3-662-02427-0
16. Henniger, R., Obrist, D., Kleiser, L.: High-order accurate solution of the incompressible Navier-Stokes equations on massively parallel computers. J. Comput. Phys. **229**(10), 3543–3572 (2010)
17. Houzeaux, G., de la Cruz, R., Owen, H., Vázquez, M.: Parallel uniform mesh multiplication applied to a Navier-Stokes solver. Comput. Fluids **80**, 142–151 (2013)
18. John, V., Tobiska, L.: Numerical performance of smoothers in coupled multigrid methods for the parallel solution of the incompressible Navier-Stokes equations. Int. J. Num. Methods Fluids **33**(4), 453–473 (2000)
19. Knobloch, P., Tobiska, L.: Stabilization methods of bubble type for the q1/q1-element applied to the incompressible Navier-Stokes equations. ESAIM: Math. Model. Num. Anal. **34**(1), 85–107 (2000)
20. Kohl, N., Rüde, U.: Textbook efficiency: massively parallel matrix-free multigrid for the Stokes system. SIAM J. Sci. Comput. **44**(2), C124–C155 (2022)
21. Maday, Y., Meiron, D., Patera, A.T., Rønquist, E.M.: Analysis of iterative methods for the steady and unsteady Stokes problem: application to spectral element discretizations. SIAM J. Sci. Comput. **14**(2), 310–337 (1993)
22. Maitre, J., Musy, F., Nigon, P.: A fast solver for the Stokes equations using multigrid with a Uzawa smoother. In: Braess, D., Hackbusch, W., Trottenberg, U. (eds.) Advances in Multi-Grid Methods. Notes on Numerical Fluid Mechanics, vol. 11, pp. 77–83. Springer, Cham (1985). https://doi.org/10.1007/978-3-663-14245-4_8
23. Matheson, L.R., Tarjan, R.E.: Analysis of multigrid algorithms on massively parallel computers: architectural implications. J. Parallel Distrib. Comput. **33**(1), 33–43 (1996)
24. May, D.A., Brown, J., Le Pourhiet, L.: A scalable, matrix-free multigrid preconditioner for finite element discretizations of heterogeneous Stokes flow. Comput. Methods Appl. Mech. Eng. **290**, 496–523 (2015)
25. Reiter, S., Vogel, A., Heppner, I., Rupp, M., Wittum, G.: A massively parallel geometric multigrid solver on hierarchically distributed grids. Comput. Vis. Sci. **16**, 151–164 (2013)
26. Saad, Y.: Iterative Methods for Sparse Linear Systems, vol. 82. SIAM, Philadelphia (2003)
27. Saberi, S., Meschke, G., Vogel, A.: A restricted additive Vanka smoother for geometric multigrid. J. Comput. Phys. **459**, 111123 (2022)
28. Sampath, R.S., Biros, G.: A parallel geometric multigrid method for finite elements on octree meshes. SIAM J. Sci. Comput. **32**(3), 1361–1392 (2010)

29. Schäfer, M., Turek, S., Durst, F., Krause, E., Rannacher, R.: Benchmark computations of laminar flow around a cylinder. In: Hirschel, E.H. (ed.) Flow simulation with high-performance computers II. NNFM, vol. 48, pp. 547–566. Springer, Cham (1996). https://doi.org/10.1007/978-3-322-89849-4_39
30. Shankar, P., Deshpande, M.: Fluid mechanics in the driven cavity. Ann. Rev. Fluid Mech. **32**(1), 93–136 (2000)
31. Vanka, S.P.: Block-implicit multigrid solution of Navier-Stokes equations in primitive variables. J. Comput. Phys. **65**(1), 138–158 (1986)
32. Verfürth, R.: A multilevel algorithm for mixed problems. SIAM J. Num. Anal. **21**(2), 264–271 (1984)
33. Wang, Y., Baboulin, M., Dongarra, J., Falcou, J., Fraigneau, Y., Le Maître, O.: A parallel solver for incompressible fluid flows. Procedia Comput. Sci. **18**, 439–448 (2013)
34. Wittum, G.: Multi-grid methods for Stokes and Navier-Stokes equations. Numer. Math. **54**(5), 543–563 (1989)

# Optimizing Distributed Tensor Contractions Using Node-Aware Processor Grids

Andreas Irmler[1(✉)], Raghavendra Kanakagiri[3], Sebastian T. Ohlmann[2], Edgar Solomonik[3], and Andreas Grüneis[1]

[1] Institute for Theoretical Physics, TU Wien, Vienna, Austria
andreas.irmler@tuwien.ac.at
[2] Max Planck Computing and Data Facility, Garching, Germany
[3] University of Illinois at Urbana-Champaign, Champaign, USA

**Abstract.** We propose an algorithm that aims at minimizing the inter-node communication volume for distributed and memory-efficient tensor contraction schemes on modern multi-core compute nodes. The key idea is to define processor grids that optimize intra-/inter-node communication volume in the employed contraction algorithms. We present an implementation of the proposed node-aware communication algorithm into the Cyclops Tensor Framework (CTF). We demonstrate that this implementation achieves a significantly improved performance for matrix-matrix-multiplication and tensor-contractions on up to several hundreds modern compute nodes compared to conventional implementations without using node-aware processor grids. Our implementation shows good performance when compared with existing state-of-the-art parallel matrix multiplication libraries (COSMA and ScaLAPACK). In addition to the discussion of the performance for matrix-matrix-multiplication, we also investigate the performance of our node-aware communication algorithm for tensor contractions as they occur in quantum chemical coupled-cluster methods. To this end we employ a modified version of CTF in combination with a coupled-cluster code (Cc4s). Our findings show that the node-aware communication algorithm is also able to improve the performance of coupled-cluster theory calculations for real-world problems running on tens to hundreds of compute nodes.

## 1 Introduction

Matrix-matrix multiplication (MMM) is ubiquitous in the field of scientific computing, computational physics, machine learning and many other areas of significant technological and scientific relevance. One important area of application of MMM in physics includes electronic structure theory, which is part of the motivation for the present work. We note that electronic structure theory calculations often involve operations on large matrices that need to be distributed over many tens to hundreds of modern compute nodes in order to satisfy memory requirements. Therefore, electronic structure theory calculations have evolved in


J. Cano et al. (Eds.): Euro-Par 2023, LNCS 14100, pp. 710–724, 2023.
https://doi.org/10.1007/978-3-031-39698-4_48

parallel to hardware improvements and newly developed efficient linear algebra libraries over the past few decades. In this paper, we seek to compare and improve algorithms employed in popular MMM libraries including ScaLAPACK [9], COSMA [13] and CTF [18]. In particular, we focus on the effect of network contention and inter-node communication within CTF.

In addition to MMM, the present work seeks to extend the presented development to more general tensor algebraic operations. We note that tensor algebra is yet another important technique widely-used in electronic structure theory, especially for highly accurate and computationally expensive many-electron methods. With the development of more sophisticated distributed tensor algebra libraries, however, their implementation becomes simpler and allows for efficient calculations of increasingly large problems on modern HPC clusters.

We also demonstrate a real-world application that involves coupled-cluster theory calculations. Coupled-cluster theory is a many-electron perturbation theory, which is widely-used in the field of computational chemistry and many-body physics. The solution of the underlying set of nonlinear equations involves tensor contractions. Already for the study of relatively few atoms, the memory footprint of the required tensors typically exceeds even the main memory of modern nodes. Furthermore, the computational cost required by these calculations also grows rapidly with the number of atoms. This necessitates implementations of coupled-cluster methods employing massively parallel tensor contraction libraries. Our node-aware CTF implementation shows speed-ups of up to 3X relative to the prior node-oblivious implementation for real-world coupled-cluster calculations.

Overall, our paper introduces the following contributions:

- node-aware parallel algorithms for matrix multiplication and tensor contraction, which minimize the inter-node communication volume,
- an implementation of these algorithms as part of the Cyclops library,
- an experimental evaluation comparing the implementation to other codes on two supercomputers and as part of a quantum chemistry method.

## 2 Node-Aware Multiplication and Contraction

Distributed-memory algorithms for matrix multiplication generally aim to minimize communication cost (in terms of latency, i.e., the number of messages, and bandwidth cost, i.e., the amount of data sent). Communication cost in this setting is often measured by the amount of matrix entries (words) sent and received by each processor, with matching sends and receives assumed to execute concurrently. In the memory-constrained setting, for multiplication of $n \times n$ matrices, Cannon's algorithm [7] achieves a communication cost of $O(n^2/\sqrt{p})$ when running with $p$ processors. This cost is optimal according to known lower bounds [12]. In practice, the SUMMA algorithm [2,20] or variants thereof are most often implemented in libraries (e.g., ScaLAPACK and CTF both use SUMMA). The SUMMA algorithm leverages broadcasts and reductions, which have a slightly higher latency (require $O(\log p)$ messages) than the point-to-point messages used in Cannon's algorithm. However, large-message broadcasts and reductions can be done with the same asymptotic bandwidth cost as sends, $O(n)$ for a message of size $n$, so long as $n = \Omega(p)$ [8,19]. Further, the SUMMA algorithm is easier to extend to non-square matrices than Cannon's approach, and use of similar collective communication also allows for implementation of 3D algorithms, which minimize communication cost when additional memory is available [2,3,16,17].

On modern supercomputers and clusters, each node contains many CPUs and/or GPUs. Even with the use of threading, most MPI-based codes achieve highest efficiency when executed with multiple MPI processes per node (e.g., one per GPU or one per NUMA region). Given the presence of multiple communicating processes per node, the performance of collective communication operations, such as broadcast and reduction, become dependent on the number of distinct nodes in the subcommunicator used for the operation. In particular, while we have mentioned that the per-processor communication-cost is largely independent of $p$, the communication volume (total number of words sent or received by any processor) for a broadcast of a message of $n$ words to $p$ nodes is $n(p-1)$. Unlike the per-processor communication cost, the communication volume does not directly model runtime, but a higher communication volume entails increased contention for network and injection bandwidth. We propose an algorithm to select an MPI-process-to-node mapping that minimizes the inter-node communication volume for dense matrix multiplication (and later tensor contractions) executed on any given initial processor grid. Similarly motivated node-aware optimizations have previously been presented for accelerating point-to-point communication in sparse matrix vector products [5,6,14,15].

### 2.1 Node-Aware Matrix Multiplication

We first propose a scheme to map processes to nodes for matrix multiplication, aiming to accelerate 2D (SUMMA) and 3D matrix multiplication algorithms used by CTF [18]. CTF generally selects a 3D processor grid $p_1 \times p_2 \times p_3$ (1D or 2D processor grids may be obtained by setting of $p_1$, $p_2$, and $p_3$ to 1) at runtime so as to minimize cost (based on not just communication, but a more detailed performance model that includes predicted cost of local work and redistribution). All communication within the matrix multiplication algorithm is performed by concurrent broadcasts and reductions among fibers of the 3D processor grid (e.g., $p_1p_2$ concurrent broadcasts with $p_3$ processors involved in each). Once a processor grid mapping is selected, the counts of words communicated along each fiber $W_1$, $W_2$, and $W_3$ are known. When executing with $m$ processors per node, we consider the best choice of an $m_1 \times m_2 \times m_3$ intra-node processor grid with $m_1m_2m_3 = m$ and $p_i \equiv 0 \bmod m_i$, for all $i$. The $p/m$ nodes are then arranged in a 3D processor grid of dimensions $p_1/m_1 \times p_2/m_2 \times p_3/m_3$, so that each original fiber of size $p_i$ stretches across $p_i/m_i$ physical nodes. We choose the intra-node processor grid, so as to minimize the communication volume,

$$V = W_1(p_1/m_1 - 1) + W_2(p_2/m_2 - 1) + W_3(p_3/m_3 - 1).$$

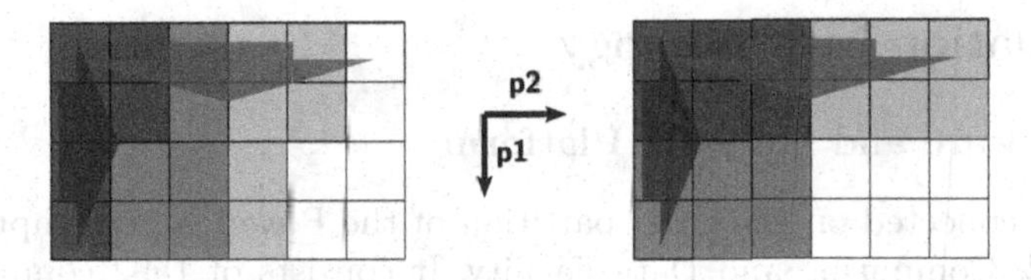


**Fig. 1.** Communication pattern of the SUMMA algorithm. A series of broadcast is performed within each row/column. Boxes represent different ranks, color indicates the resident node. Example shows 4 nodes with 6 ranks each. For each SUMMA block row/column broadcast, default topology (left) yields 2 inter-node messages vertically and 12 horizontally, while the node-aware topology (right) yields 6 and 4, respectively.

Once the mapping is chosen, we redistribute the matrix data, which can be done with a single round of concurrent point-to-point messages (each processor sends all of its matrix data to a single other processor in the new mapping). For a given node-aware mapping, the SUMMA algorithm is unchanged, except that the MPI communicators span different processor ranks, resulting in different amounts of inter-node communication. Figure 1 provides an example of a default and a node-aware mapping.

## 2.2 Node-Aware Tensor Contractions

CTF leverages nested SUMMA, in combination with 1D replication/reduction, to generalize 2D and 3D algorithms for matrix multiplication to tensor contraction [18]. Processor grids $p_1 \times \cdots \times p_d$ with $d > 3$ are used to accommodate nested SUMMA and to support symmetric-packed tensor formats efficiently (only unique entries of a symmetric tensor are stored by CTF, e.g., only the lower triangular part of a symmetric matrix). Each of these matrix multiplication variants results in some amount of words broadcast or reduced along each processor grid fiber, say $W_i$ along fiber $p_i$. Our node-aware mapping algorithm proceeds analogously to the matrix multiplication case. We select the best choice of $m_1 \times \cdots \times m_d$ intra-node processor grid and combine it with a $p_1/m_1 \times \cdots \times p_d/m_d$ inter-node processor grid, so that the $i$th fiber of the grid spans $p_i/m_i$ distinct nodes. Again, we select the processor grid to minimize the communication volume, $V = \sum_{i=1}^{d} W_i(p_i/m_i - 1)$.

CTF chooses a processor grid and an associated plan for a nested SUMMA algorithm based on a cost model of the cost of its nested SUMMA algorithm, local products, and data redistribution. Our node-aware algorithm first allows CTF to perform this search, then determines the cost-optimal factorization of the chosen processor grid into inter-node and intra-node processor grids. We use exhaustive search to enumerate all distinct factorizations of $m = m_1 \cdots m_d$ such that $p_i \equiv 0 \bmod m_i$. Provided a model of the affect of communication volume on runtime, this search could be done together with the selection of the best processor grid $p_1 \times \cdots \times p_d$ and the tensor mapping. However, if $K$ plans are considered, each having $L$ different inter-node grids, the combined search space is of size $O(KL)$ instead of $O(K + L)$.

# 3 Evaluation Methodology

## 3.1 Hardware and Software Platform

Results are collected on the CPU partition of the Raven supercomputer at the Max Planck Computing and Data Facility. It consists of 1592 compute nodes; each node has an Intel Xeon IceLake-SP Platinum 8360Y processor with 72 cores and 256 GB RAM per node. As interconnect, it uses Mellanox HDR InfiniBand network (100 Gbit/s) with a pruned fat-tree topology and non-blocking islands of 720 nodes; all jobs run inside one island. To demonstrate the robustness of our approach, we also collect results (for a subset of the experiments) on the Stampede2 supercomputer. Each node has an Intel Xeon Phi 7250 CPU with 68 cores and 96 GB of DDR4 RAM. We stress the fact that Stampede2 has a distinct configuration when compared to that of Raven.

We evaluate our node-aware version of CTF (CTF-na) by comparing against the default CTF (CTF-def) [18][1], ScaLAPACK [9], and COSMA [13][2]. We use ScaLAPACK as provided by Intel MKL (version 2022.0). All codes were compiled using the Intel compiler (version 2021.5) with Intel MPI (version 2021.5). In all our calculations, we use one core per MPI rank. All codes would in principle allow a hybrid OpenMP/MPI approach. Our tests show that CTF performs equally good with one to four cores per rank. In COSMA, the authors note that their strategy performs best with one core per rank [13].

COSMA allows for communication-computation overlap. Our tests show that for the chosen matrix dimensions the results with and without overlap strategy are very similar. The differences are at most in the order of 5%. For a more expressive comparison against CTF and ScaLAPACK, both of which do not offer overlapping strategies, we do not use computation-communication overlap in any of our COSMA calculations. Furthermore, it is possible to adjust the used memory in a COSMA calculation. More memory possibly allows to employ more efficient parallelization strategies, viz. a higher performance. In this work, we use two values for the allowed memory. The lower limit is chosen to be 2.5-times the size of storing the three matrices. The upper limit is chosen to be such that the full memory of the machine can be utilized. In the following, we will label these schemes as COSMA-lim and COSMA-unl.

## 3.2 Matrix-Multiplication Benchmarks

In this section, we present details about the dataset used for our main results, which is collected from the Raven cluster. We investigate four cases of products of an $m \times k$ matrix with a $k \times n$ matrix, namely, square ($m = n = k$), large $K$ ($m = n \ll k$), large $M$ ($m \gg n = k$), and small $K$ ($m = n \gg k$). The ratio between small and large edge is chosen to be 10 for all systems. We exploit results for different number of nodes ranging from 1 to 288 nodes using all node

[1] CTF-def and CTF-na can be run with https://github.com/airmler/ctf, branch node-awareness, commit ID 2f32bd6.

[2] https://github.com/eth-cscs/COSMA.git commit ID fe98d3eb.

numbers which fulfill the following equation $n = j \cdot 2^i$, with: $j \in [1, 3, 9]$, to obtain results from an adequately large number of different ranks/nodes. We consider both strong and weak scaling in our experiments. For strong scaling, we choose the dataset size such that it is just large enough to be stored (and contracted) on a single node which is approximately 150 GB. For weak scaling, we use two different matrix dimensions (sizes), such that the matrices occupy either 0.5% or 5% of the overall system memory. In subsequent sections, we denote the strong scaling results as "strong", while the weak scaling datasets are referred to as "weak18" and "weak180", corresponding to the 0.5% and 5% memory occupation, respectively.

### 3.3 Experimental Methodology

For each combination of parameters considered, we perform five contractions (runs) using each of the five strategies (CTF-def, CTF-na, ScaLAPACK, COSMA-lim and COSMA-unlim) on the same node allocation (i.e. via a single job submission to the cluster). We exclude the two slowest runs and compute the average based on the remaining three runs. We submit each job twice in order to have two random node allocations. Consequently, all presented data points are mean values averaged from 6 calculations, each. Typically, the standard deviation of the mean value is below 1 GFLOPS/core, so we do not include any error bars.

In the individual MMM and tensor contractions we employ the node-aware mapping whenever an advantageous topology is found. This allows to study possible situations where the required tensor redistribution time exceeds the gain due to the favorable processor grid. In the CCSD calculations we asses the performance of a variety of individual tensor contractions. Thus, we are interested in an optimal overall performance. Therefore the redistribution time was included in the cost model to optimize the overall performance.

## 4 Performance Results/Evaluation

### 4.1 Memory Footprint

Prior to comparing the performance of the various implementations, we analyze their memory requirements. We refer to the maximum memory consumption by the implementation (when executing the contraction) as high-water mark (HWM). In Fig. 2, we present HWM for weak180 calculations for all considered matrices, representing the maximum memory consumption. If we exclude the results for one to three nodes, we observe that ScaLAPACK maintains a nearly constant ratio of HWM over storage size, averaging around 1.66. This is true for all type of matrix contractions. For CTF, the ratio is between 2.5 and 5, depending on the number of nodes and the contraction type. The additional memory overhead compared to ScaLAPACK is explained by the extra redistribution buffers and the 2.5D algorithm. COSMA-lim shows a very similar

HWM as CTF with values between 4 and 7 for the ratio HWM over storage size. This enables a fair comparison between CTF and COSMA in the case of similar memory constraints. Disregarding a handful of outliers COSMA-unl shows a ratio between 10 and 18. We recall that for these calculations the storage size is 5% of the main memory, implying that the COSMA calculation utilizes a large fraction of the total main memory. We note that CTF-na has the same memory footprint as CTF-def.

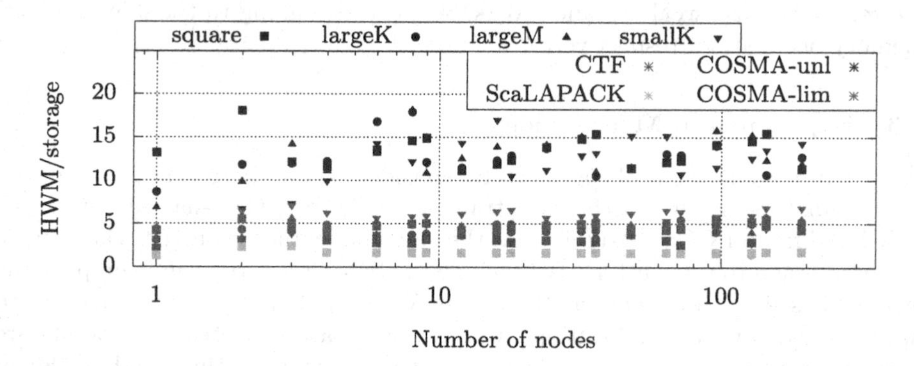


**Fig. 2.** Ratio of computation's HWM over storage size for different node counts.

### 4.2 Matrix Multiplication

In this section, we present one of the primary results of this work. Figure 3 shows the performance results for all the matrix sizes and implementations considered (see Sect. 3.3). We first note that for all contraction types and all scaling scenarios, COSMA-unl achieves the best performance. The improvement over the second best method is very pronounced for situations where the operations per core are low, i.e. large node numbers in strong scaling scenario and for the weak scaling scenario with 18 MB. For the weak scaling scenario with 180 MB, the improvements are much smaller. We note, however, that the memory footprint of COSMA-unl is relatively high in all calculations as depicted in the previous sections. The goal of the present work is to advance memory efficient tensor contraction algorithms with high scalability on multi-core nodes.

Square: The performance for the square contractions is shown in the top panels of Fig. 3. When employing more than ten nodes, CTF-na shows the second best performance followed by COSMA-lim. ScaLAPACK and CTF-def perform similarly and show the worst performance. For small node numbers the same trend is generally present, however, the results are noisier here. We note that CTF-na is particularly efficient for the large memory weak scaling scenario (180MB). Large square MMM present one of the best application regimes of CTF-na compared to the even more efficient but memory intense COSMA-unl implementation.

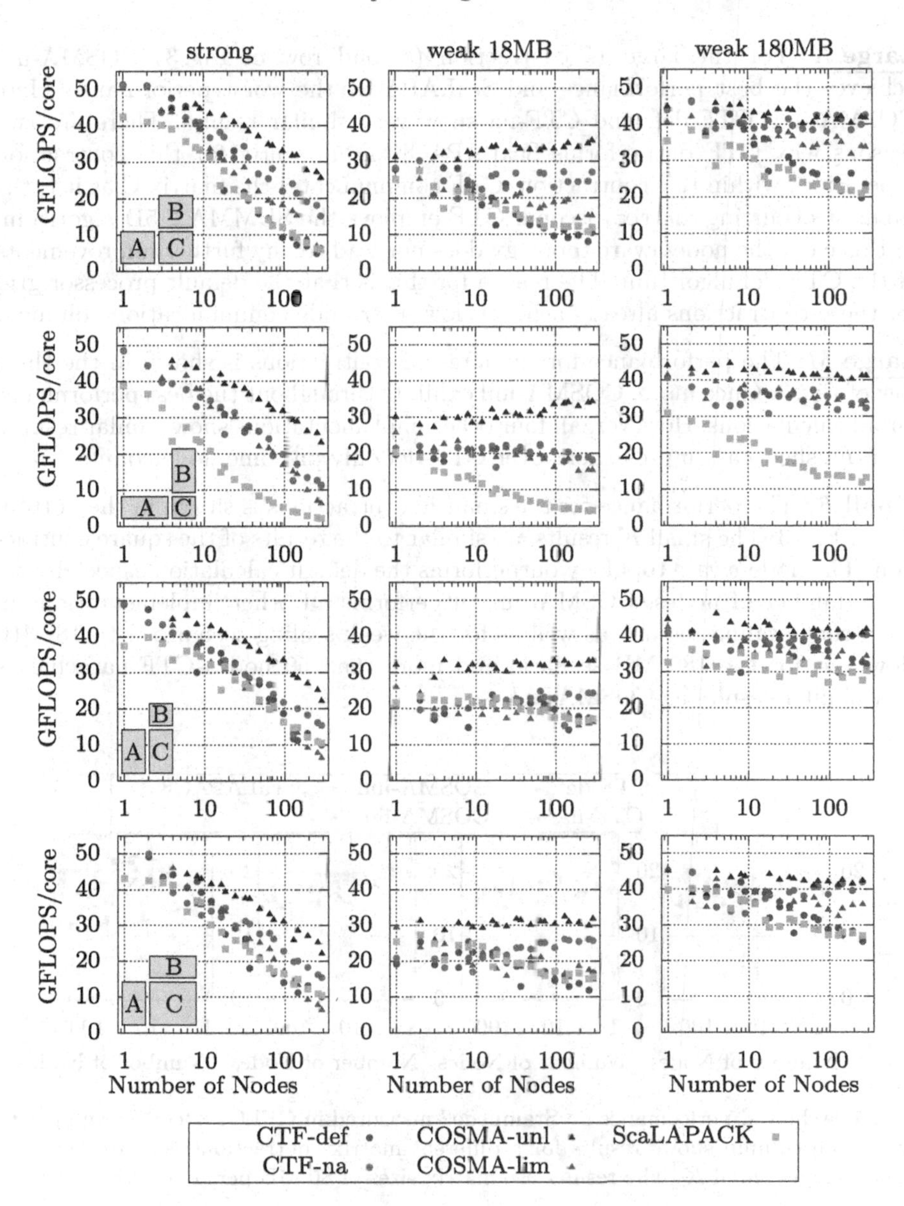


**Fig. 3.** Performance in GFLOPS/core on Raven. From top to bottom, rows show results for different matrix-matrix products: square, large $K$, large $M$, and small $K$.

The node-aware algorithm significantly improves the results compared to the results with CTF in default topology. For more than 50 nodes the performance improves by a factor of 1.5–5.5X in weak and strong scaling scenarios. Further, CTF-na outperforms COSMA-lim when using more than ten nodes.

**Large $K$**: For the large $K$ contraction (second row of Fig. 3) COSMA-unl achieves the best performance and ScaLAPACK the worst performance. Here COSMA-lim, CTF-def, and CTF-na show very similar results. There are two reasons why CTF outperforms ScaLAPACK significantly for this contraction type. First, within this contraction, CTF communicates the matrix C as it is the smallest occurring matrix. Second, CTF employs the SUMMA 2.5D algorithm. In this case, the node-aware topology does not lead to any further improvements of the CTF-def algorithm. The reason for this is that the default processor grid for these contractions already achieves low inter-node communication volume.

**Large $M$**: The performance for the large M contractions is shown in the third row of Fig. 3. Once more, COSMA-unl exhibits throughout the best performance for all calculations. However, all four other implementations show similar results. CTF-na shows an improvement over CTF-def only on some node counts.

**Small $K$**: The performance for the small $K$ contractions is shown in the bottom row of Fig. 3. The small $K$ results are similar to the results of the square contraction. The node-aware topology outperforms the default calculation especially for large number of nodes. COSMA-unl outperforms all other implementations in the strong scaling regime, as well as for the weak scaling scenario with 18 MB. However, for the 180 MB scenario and more than 50 nodes CTF-na achieves very similar results as COSMA-unl.

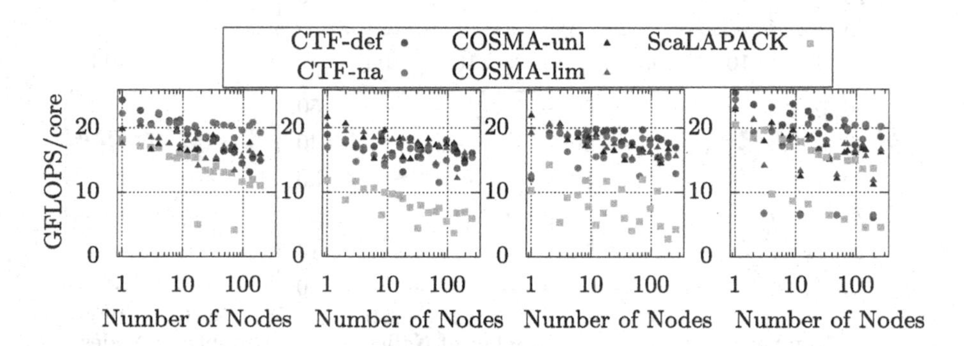


**Fig. 4.** Achieved performance on Stampede2 measured in GFLOPS/core. From left to right each column shows results for a different matrix contractions: square, large $K$, large $M$, and small $K$. The results use matrix sizes of 80 MB per processor.

**Weak Scaling Performance on Stampede2**: In addition to the results obtained on Raven, we have also investigated the performance of the different MMM libraries on Stampede2. The Stampede2 compute nodes are equipped with significantly less main memory than Raven nodes, making it more difficult to perform calculations with implementations that exhibit a large memory footprint such as COSMA. Figure 4 depicts performance results for weak scaling.

**Table 1.** Measured speedup of CTF-na compared to the other algorithms for the results obtained on the Raven system. Average values are carried out for calculations with more than 50 nodes.

| | | strong | weak 18 | weak 180 | | strong | weak 18 | weak 180 |
|---|---|---|---|---|---|---|---|---|
| CTF-def | square | 2.6 | 2.5 | 1.7 | large $K$ | 1.0 | 1.0 | 1.0 |
| ScaLAPACK | | 2.3 | 2.1 | 1.8 | | 4.1 | 3.9 | 2.5 |
| COSMA-unl | | 0.7 | 0.8 | 1.0 | | 0.6 | 0.6 | 0.8 |
| COSMA-lim | | 1.8 | 1.5 | 1.2 | | 1.3 | 1.2 | 1.0 |
| CTF-def | large $M$ | 1.3 | 1.3 | 1.2 | small $K$ | 1.6 | 1.7 | 1.4 |
| ScaLAPACK | | 1.3 | 1.3 | 1.3 | | 1.5 | 1.6 | 1.4 |
| COSMA-unl | | 0.7 | 0.7 | 0.9 | | 0.7 | 0.8 | 1.0 |
| COSMA-lim | | 1.6 | 1.3 | 1.1 | | 1.7 | 1.5 | 1.2 |

**Square and Small $K$:** The results obtained are similar to those obtained for Raven. ScaLAPACK exhibits the worst performance. CTF-na improves significantly over CTF-def for large numbers of nodes. COSMA-unl and COSMA-lim perform slightly worse than CTF-na for large numbers of nodes. While COSMA-unl exceeded available memory in some cases, it outperforms COSMA-lim in most cases. We also note that some node counts exhibit a much poorer performance for all employed libraries. A performance analysis of these outliers reveals that this reduction is not caused by increased communication volume, but by performance drops in the GEMMs.

**Large $K$:** Here CTF-na shows no improvement over CTF-def and ScaLAPACK yields the lowest performance. Interestingly the performance of COSMA is very similar, whereas on the Raven system COSMA clearly outperformed CTF.

**Large $M$:** The large $M$ contractions on Stampede2 show similar patterns to Raven. CTF-na is not improving over CTF-def for large node counts due to efficiency of the default mapping of CTF-def.

**Summary**

We now summarize the most important findings for the performance analysis. Table 1 lists mean values of the achieved speedups for CTF-na compared to the four other implementations. Averaged results are provided for calculations employing more than 50 nodes. The values are smaller or equal than 1 only for the case of COSMA-unl, indicating that COSMA-unl achieves in all scenarios the best performance compared to the other methods at the price of a larger memory footprint. All other reported values are equal to 1.0 or larger than 1.0, implying that CTF-na achieves the same or better performance than CTF-def, COSMA-lim and ScaLAPACK most cases. Compared to ScaLAPACK the speedup is on average between 1.4 and 4.1 for square, large $K$ and small $K$ for all scenarios when using more than 50 nodes. The speedup compared to ScaLAPACK is only about 1.3 in the case of large $M$. Compared to COSMA-lim, CTF-na achieves on average a speedup between 1.2 and 1.8 for more than 50 nodes in the cases of square and small $K$ MMMs. This speedup reduces to about 1.0 to 1.6 in the

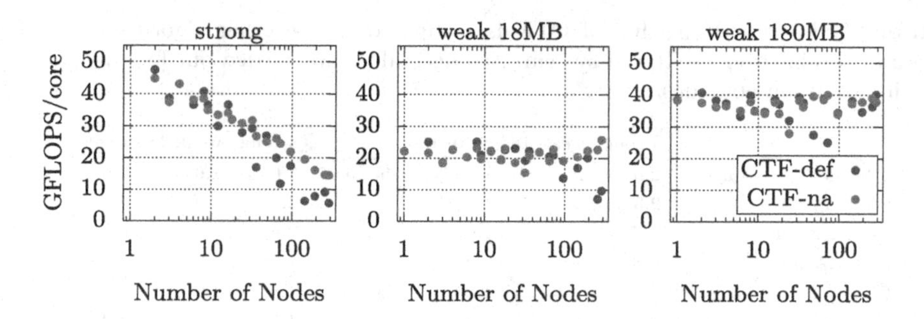


**Fig. 5.** Results for the drCCD contraction on Raven.

cases of large $K$ and large $M$. Similarly, compared to CTF-def, which disregards node-awareness, we see significant speedups for square and small $K$ contractions.

## 5 Performance of Coupled-Cluster Calculations

We now present results for more general tensor contractions, going beyond matrix multiplications. This section presents performance results obtained for coupled cluster (CC) calculations as implemented in the Cc4s code [1], which employs the CTF library. CC methods are widely used in the field of electronic structure theory to study many-electron systems [4]. From a computational perspective, CC methods involve high order tensor contractions. The CC method, which employs single and double particle-hole excitation operators, is called CCSD. The computational cost of a CCSD calculation is dominated by solving the nonlinear doubles amplitude equations given by

$$D_{ij}^{ab} t_{ij}^{ab} = v_{ij}^{ab} + 2\sum_{ck} v_{ic}^{ak} t_{kj}^{cb} + \sum_{klcd} t_{il}^{ad} v_{dc}^{lk} t_{kj}^{cb} + \sum_{cd} v_{cd}^{ab} t_{ij}^{cd} - \sum_{ck} v_{ic}^{ak} t_{kj}^{bc} + ..., \quad (1)$$

where the dimensions are chosen such that $\dim(i) = \dim(j) = \dim(k) = \dim(l)$ and $\dim(a) = \dim(b) = \dim(c) = \dim(d)$. The amplitude equations are solved iteratively employing a Jacobi method such that most of the computational cost originates from tensor contractions as defined by terms on the right-hand-side of the above equation. CCSD exhibits a memory footprint and computational cost that scales as $\mathcal{O}(N^4)$ and $\mathcal{O}(N^6)$, respectively. $N$ is proportional to the number of electrons in the system. The dimension of the indices $i, j, k, ...$ and $a, b, c, ...$ corresponds to the number of occupied orbitals and the number of virtual orbitals, respectively. In a typical calculation, the number of virtual orbitals is 10–30 times larger than the number of occupied orbitals. As a result the so-called particle-particle-ladder (ppl) term, $r_{ij}^{ab} = \sum_{cd} v_{cd}^{ab} t_{ij}^{cd}$, is treated in a special way to avoid storing the tensor $v_{cd}^{ab}$ in main memory. This is achieved by computing slices of $v_{cd}^{ab}$ on-the-fly and contracting them consecutively.

In addition to the CCSD method, we also investigate the performance of drCCD, which is a popular approximation to the CCSD method. The drCCD

**Table 2.** Performance given in GFLOPS/core from different coupled-cluster calculations for three different node counts.

| Method | 32 nodes<br>$\dim(i) = 116$<br>$\dim(a) = 1161$ | | 72 nodes<br>$\dim(i) = 142$<br>$\dim(a) = 1422$ | | 128 nodes<br>$\dim(i) = 164$<br>$\dim(a) = 1642$ | |
|---|---|---|---|---|---|---|
| | default | node-aware | default | node-aware | default | node-aware |
| CCSD | 19.4 | 21.0 | 20.5 | 24.0 | 25.0 | 25.0 |
| CCSD no ppl | 26.6 | 32.6 | 25.1 | 37.0 | 37.3 | 37.5 |
| drCCD | 37.4 | 37.9 | 24.7 | 39.0 | 38.6 | 38.5 |

method only includes so-called ring diagrams in the amplitude equations, corresponding to terms given by $r_{ij}^{ab} = \sum_{ck} v_{ic}^{ak} t_{kj}^{cb}$.

We now seek to discuss the performance of the following types of CC calculations: drCCD, CCSD and CCSD excluding the ppl-term. Performance results have been obtained using the default CTF version and the node-aware CTF version. Figure 5 depicts the performance of drCCD calculations in strong and weak scaling scenarios. Our findings show that the improvements are not as pronounced as for the case of MMMs. Only for the strong scaling case we observe significant improvements when comparing CTF-na to CTF-def for about 100 nodes. For the weak scaling case with smaller problem sizes, CTF-na achieves no significant improvements compared to CTF-def. For weak scaling with large problem sizes, CTF-na improves the performance of CTF-def for a few cases. We find that higher-order tensors are more often already distributed in an communication efficient manner using the default topology, which is why the node-aware distribution often has a negligible effect. However, improvements of up to 3X are achieved on some node counts, and overall the performance of CTF-na is more robust with respect to the choice of the node count than CTF-def. We also explore the performance of CCSD calculations. These calculations are computationally even more expensive than drCCD. Table 2 lists results for a selected number of nodes, including special cases described above for drCCD. In addition to CCSD calculations, we also measure the performance of CCSD excluding the ppl-term (CCSD no ppl). The presented results imply that the evaluation of the ppl-term is performed at lower efficiency than the other tensor contractions. The cause for the bad performance can be attributed to unsatisfactorily slow slicing and redistribution operation of $v_{cd}^{ab}$ and is therefore unrelated to this work. Consequently, we will restrict the following discussion on CCSD calculation excluding the ppl-term.

Similar to drCCD, we observe performance improvements of CCSD calculations when using CTF-na instead of CTF-def only for some node numbers. There are cases where a drCCD calculation is not improved by node-awareness, whereas the CCSD calculation improves by 10–20%. This is because the processor grid for every single contraction is determined on runtime and generally differs for different contractions as they appear in the CCSD equations.

## 6 Related Work

There have been several works that derive communication-optimal algorithms for matrix-matrix multiplication [10,13,17]. CARMA [10] has provided the first approach to minimize communication for any $M$, $N$, $K$ and any number of processors/available memory. COSMA [13] provides a theoretically optimal distributed dense matrix-matrix algorithm as well as the current best known implementation. Similar to CTF, COSMA finds the best layout via a cost model subject to memory constraints. It leverages RDMA, and a custom implementation of a binary tree collective. It also proposes to overlap communication with computation. Both CTF and COSMA rely on an analytical model and minimize the communication cost. In this work, we explore a cost model that goes beyond what is considered in CTF and COSMA. We take into account the communication cost not just between MPI processes but also across nodes in the network. Further, we are able to obtain nearly the same performance and in some cases better, without low-level optimizations that may be less portable.

In [5], the authors propose a node-aware sparse matrix-vector multiply, where values are gathered in processes local to each node before being sent across the network, followed by a redistribution at the receiving node. This optimized point-to-point communication leads to reduction in communication cost. A similar technique is used in [14] when using enlarged conjugate gradient methods.

## 7 Conclusion

In this work we have presented a modification to the Cyclops Tensor Framework that employs node-aware processor grids. We have shown that the achieved performance improvements due to the node-aware topology in CTF are most strongly pronounced in the case of square and small $K$ matrix-matrix products. In the case of large $K$ and large $M$ matrix multiplication, the default processor grids employed by CTF are already efficient. Although the memory-unlimited version COSMA achieves overall the best performance for matrix multiplication, CTF with node-awareness is competitive and often more performant when the same memory limit is imposed on COSMA.

In addition to the results for MMMs, we have also investigated the performance of the modified version of CTF for tensor contractions in coupled-cluster theory calculations. Our findings show that the improvements due to node-aware topologies are less significant, but allow for more consistent performance across different node counts. As the number of cores per node continues to grow on modern architectures, the benefit of node-aware mapping is likely to be more pronounced in the future.

## 8 Acknowledgments and Data Availability Statement

Instructions to install and reproduce our results are available in a Figshare repository [11]. A full list of matrix dimensions, as well as the corresponding raw data, can be found there.

Andreas Irmler and Andreas Grüneis acknowledge support from the European Union's Horizon 2020 research and innovation program under Grant Agreement No. 951786 (The NOMAD CoE). Raghavendra Kanakagiri and Edgar Solomonik received support from the US NSF OAC SSI program, via award No. 1931258. The authors acknowledge application support and computing time of the MPCDF.

## References

1. cc4s. https://manuals.cc4s.org
2. Agarwal, R.C., Balle, S.M., Gustavson, F.G., Joshi, M., Palkar, P.: A three-dimensional approach to parallel matrix multiplication. IBM J. Res. Dev. **39**(5), 575–582 (1995)
3. Aggarwal, A., Chandra, A.K., Snir, M.: On communication latency in PRAM computations. In: Proceedings of the First Annual ACM Symposium on Parallel Algorithms and Architectures, pp. 11–21 (1989)
4. Bartlett, R.J., Musiał, M.: Coupled-cluster theory in quantum chemistry. Rev. Mod. Phys. **79**, 291–352 (2007)
5. Bienz, A., Gropp, W.D., Olson, L.N.: Node aware sparse matrix-vector multiplication. J. Parallel Distrib. Comput. **130**, 166–178 (2019)
6. Bienz, A., Gropp, W.D., Olson, L.N.: Reducing communication in algebraic multigrid with multi-step node aware communication. Int. J. High Perform. Comput. Appl. **34**(5), 547–561 (2020)
7. Cannon, L.E.: A cellular computer to implement the Kalman filter algorithm. Ph.D. thesis, Montana State University, Bozeman, MT, USA (1969)
8. Chan, E., Heimlich, M., Purkayastha, A., Van De Geijn, R.: Collective communication: theory, practice, and experience. Concurr. Comput.: Pract. Experience **19**(13), 1749–1783 (2007)
9. Choi, J., Dongarra, J., Pozo, R., Walker, D.: ScaLAPACK: a scalable linear algebra library for distributed memory concurrent computers. In: The Fourth Symposium on the Frontiers of Massively Parallel Computation, pp. 120–127 (1992)
10. Demmel, J., et al.: Communication-optimal parallel recursive rectangular matrix multiplication. In: 2013 IEEE 27th International Symposium on Parallel and Distributed Processing, pp. 261–272 (2013)
11. Irmler, A., Kanakagiri, R., Ohlmann, S.T., Solomonik, E., Grüneis, A.: Artifact overview document for Euro-Par 2023 paper: Optimizing distributed tensor contractions using node-aware processor grids. https://doi.org/10.6084/m9.figshare.23548113
12. Irony, D., Toledo, S., Tiskin, A.: Communication lower bounds for distributed-memory matrix multiplication. J. Parallel Distrib. Comput. **64**(9), 1017–1026 (2004)
13. Kwasniewski, G., Kabić, M., Besta, M., VandeVondele, J., Solcà, R., Hoefler, T.: Red-blue pebbling revisited: near optimal parallel matrix-matrix multiplication. In: Proceedings of the International Conference for High Performance Computing, Networking, Storage and Analysis, SC 2019. Association for Computing Machinery, New York (2019)
14. Lockhart, S., Bienz, A., Gropp, W., Olson, L.: Performance analysis and optimal node-aware communication for enlarged conjugate gradient methods. ACM Trans. Parallel Comput. **10**, 1–25 (2023)

15. Lockhart, S., Bienz, A., Gropp, W.D., Olson, L.N.: Characterizing the performance of node-aware strategies for irregular point-to-point communication on heterogeneous architectures. Parallel Comput. **116**, 103021 (2023)
16. McColl, W.F., Tiskin, A.: Memory-efficient matrix multiplication in the BSP model. Algorithmica **24**, 287–297 (1999)
17. Solomonik, E., Demmel, J.: Communication-optimal parallel 2.5D matrix multiplication and LU factorization algorithms. In: Jeannot, E., Namyst, R., Roman, J. (eds.) Euro-Par 2011. LNCS, vol. 6853, pp. 90–109. Springer, Heidelberg (2011). https://doi.org/10.1007/978-3-642-23397-5_10
18. Solomonik, E., Matthews, D., Hammond, J.R., Stanton, J.F., Demmel, J.: A massively parallel tensor contraction framework for coupled-cluster computations. J. Parallel Distrib. Comput. **74**, 3176–3190 (2014)
19. Thakur, R., Gropp, W.D.: Improving the performance of collective operations in MPICH. In: Dongarra, J., Laforenza, D., Orlando, S. (eds.) EuroPVM/MPI 2003. LNCS, vol. 2840, pp. 257–267. Springer, Heidelberg (2003). https://doi.org/10.1007/978-3-540-39924-7_38
20. Van De Geijn, R.A., Watts, J.: Summa: scalable universal matrix multiplication algorithm. Concurr. Pract. Experience **9**(4), 255–274 (1997)

# Parallel Cholesky Factorization for Banded Matrices Using OpenMP Tasks

Felix Liu[1,2](✉), Albin Fredriksson[2], and Stefano Markidis[1]

[1] KTH Royal Institute of Technology, Stockholm, Sweden
felixliu@kth.se
[2] RaySearch Laboratories, Stockholm, Sweden

**Abstract.** Cholesky factorization is a method for solving linear systems involving symmetric, positive-definite matrices, and can be an attractive choice in applications where a high degree of numerical stability is needed. One such application is mathematical optimization, where direct methods for solving linear systems are widely used and often a significant performance bottleneck. An example where this is the case, and the specific type of optimization problem motivating this work, is radiation therapy treatment planning, where mathematical optimization is used to create individual treatment plans for patients. To address this bottleneck, we propose a task-based multi-threaded method for Cholesky factorization of banded matrices with medium-sized bands. We implement our algorithm using OpenMP tasks and compare our performance with state-of-the-art libraries such as Intel MKL. Our performance measurements show a performance that is on par or better than Intel MKL (up to ∼26% on a single CPU socket) for a wide range of matrix bandwidths on two different Intel CPU systems.

**Keywords:** Cholesky factorization · Task-Based Parallelism · Linear Solver

## 1 Introduction

Cholesky factorization is a well known method for solving linear equations where the matrix is symmetric and positive-definite and belongs to a class of algorithms often referred to as *direct* methods for solving linear systems of equations [6]. While iterative methods are often considered the state-of-the-art for solving large systems of linear equations, there are still applications where the use of direct methods is the standard, due to issues with ill-conditioning of the linear systems, for instance. Examples of such fields include mathematical optimization, where in some algorithms, the systems become increasingly ill-conditioned as the algorithm progresses [14]. In many applications, matrices involved are not dense, but rather have some structure. A common example of structure that arises is banded matrices, where all non-zero elements are located no more than $k$ rows and columns from the main diagonal. In the context of banded matrices, the


J. Cano et al. (Eds.): Euro-Par 2023, LNCS 14100, pp. 725–739, 2023.
https://doi.org/10.1007/978-3-031-39698-4_49

number $k$ is often referred to as the *bandwidth* of the matrix. With this definition, a diagonal matrix is a banded matrix with bandwidth zero. We emphasize that this use of the term bandwidth is not to be confused with bandwidth when referring to e.g. throughput of memory channels in computer hardware.

The specific problem motivating this work is mathematical optimization for radiation therapy treatment planning (see e.g. [2,24] and references therein for a background on optimization in radiation oncology), where mathematical optimization is used to create specialized treatment plans (control parameters for the treatment machine) for individual patients. In such problems, we have observed certain cases which require factorization of banded matrices with bandwidths in the hundreds. Furthermore, we have seen this be a significant computational bottleneck, with banded matrix factorization representing more than 50% of the total time spent in treatment plan optimization.

Of course, optimization problems also arise from a wide range of different application domains, such as operations research, model predictive control among many others. An example from model predictive control is the work of Wang and Boyd [26], where they devise a computational method involving the factorization of matrices with bandwidths up to about 100. We refer readers interested in more details on algorithms for optimization to the review found in [11]. For a more high-level overview on optimization methods and High-Performance Computing (HPC) we refer the interested reader to the review found in [19].

In this paper, we develop a task-based method for parallelizing Cholesky factorization for banded matrices. We show that our method performs well compared to state-of-the-art libraries on matrices with large bands and further give some discussion and analysis of the performance. We summarize our claimed contributions as follows:

- We design and implement a task-based parallel method for Cholesky factorization of banded matrices using OpenMP.
- We assess the performance of our method compared to state-of-the-art libraries for matrices with bandwidths between 50–2000, which can be found in optimization problems from radiation therapy.
- We demonstrate an up to 26% performance improvement, on average, compared to state-of-the-art libraries such as Intel MKL.

## 2 Related Work

Previous research on parallel Cholesky factorization for banded matrices with similar ideas as ours include work by Quintana-Ortí et al. [22], which was implemented in the SuperMatrix [4] framework. Our work differs from the work by Quintana-Ortí et al. in that we use the standard packed LAPACK storage format for banded matrices and OpenMP for tasking (OpenMP task implementations were in their infancy at the time the work by Quintana-Ortí et al. was published). We believe this lowers the barrier for adoption in existing codes, and removes the need for potential overhead in converting the matrix into an internal storage format.

The topic of multithreaded Cholesky factorization is one which has been studied extensively in the literature previously. For example, Remon et al. [23] studied multithreaded performance for Cholesky factorization of band matrices. In their work, they propose some performance optimization by slightly modifying the storage scheme for band matrices used in LAPACK to allow merging some computational steps described in Sect. 3.1 into single calls to BLAS-3 kernels, increasing available parallelism for each BLAS kernel invocation. Similar work on small modifications to the LAPACK storage scheme to merge kernels and improve efficiency was also studied by Gustavson et al. [16].

Task parallel banded Cholesky factorization has also been previously studied as part of more extensive efforts to utilize task-based parallelism for different computational kernels in for instance the FLAME [25] and PLASMA [8] projects. A part of this effort was the previously mentioned work by Quintana-Ortí et al. in [22]. On the distributed computing side, parallel algorithms for banded Cholesky has also been studied by e.g. Gupta et al. [15]. For general dense matrices, the topic has been studied by Dorris et al. [9], where different variants of Cholesky factorization algorithms and their suitability for task-based parallelism were considered. For sparse matrices, task-based parallel Cholesky factorization has been studied in the 1980s by Liu [20], as well as Geist and Ng [13], and more recently by Hogg et al. [17]. Many recent works in the area of task-parallel Cholesky factorization are for general sparse matrices, see for instance [18].

## 3 Background

Cholesky factorization is a well-known method for solving systems of linear equations with symmetric, positive-definite matrices. The method works based on the observation that every symmetric positive-definite matrix $A$ admits a factorization of the form $A = LL^T$ where $L$ is a lower triangular matrix. This factorization is called the *Cholesky factorization* and is unique [7, Ch. 2.7 p. 77].

One application where banded systems with very large bandwidth can occur is mathematical optimization (see e.g. [26,27]), where many algorithms rely on solving a block-structured linear system of equations in each iteration. The current state-of-the-art in optimization solvers often rely on matrix factorization algorithms to perform this solution step. As an example, in interior point methods [11] – a popular choice of algorithm for many constrained optimization problems – the linear systems to solve will have specific structure depending on the structure of the objective and constraints of the optimization problem. This structure is often exploited in certain cases by, for instance, block-elimination, which may result in the need to solve linear systems with specific structure, where banded structures is one possibility [26].

### 3.1 Cholesky Factorization

The implementation that provided the initial inspiration for our method is the one proposed by Du Croz et al. in [5]. The key idea is to organize the computations in the factorization into operations on dense sub-blocks, such that the use of level-3 BLAS kernels is enabled. The method of Du Croz et al. divides the current active window in the non-zero band of the matrix into a $3 \times 3$ *block grid*, as illustrated in Fig. 1a. To note is that only the upper triangular part of the $A_{31}$ block lies within the band of the matrix. This is dealt with in the implementation by using an internal square work array with the same dimensions as $A_{31}$, but with the lower triangular part set to zero. A basic outline of the method is:

1. Factorize $A_{11}$ into $L_{11}L_{11}^T$ using dense Cholesky
2. Compute $L_{21} = A_{21}(L_{11}^T)^{-1}$ using DTRSM
3. Compute $A'_{22} = A_{22} - L_{21}L_{21}^T$ using DSYRK
4. Copy the upper triangular part of $A_{31}$ into the square work array
5. Compute $L_{31} = A_{31}(L_{11}^T)^{-1}$ using DTRSM (store $L_{31}$ in the work array, overwriting $A_{31}$)
6. Compute $A'_{32} = A_{32} - L_{31}L_{21}^T$ using DGEMM
7. Compute $A'_{33} = A_{33} - L_{31}L_{31}^T$ using DSYRK
8. Copy the upper triangular part of $L_{31}$ into the main matrix.

Here, we have used the BLAS routines DTRSM, DSYRK and DGEMM, which are double precision routines for solving linear systems of equations with triangular matrices, symmetric rank-k updates and general matrix-matrix multiplication respectively. More detailed description of these routines can be found in, for example, the Netlib website[1].

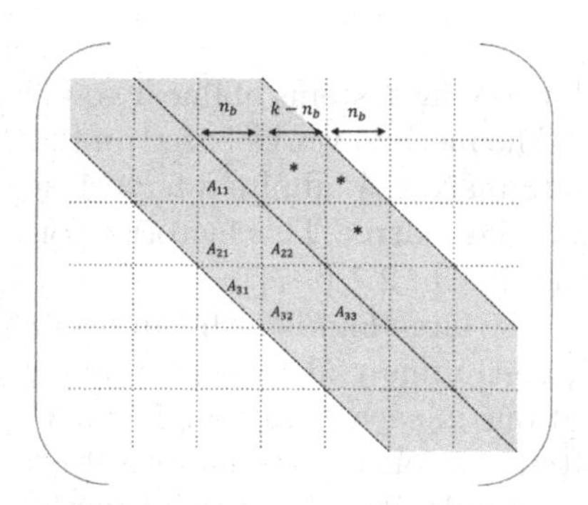


(a) Figure illustrating the block-algorithm for banded matrices from Du Croz et al. [5].

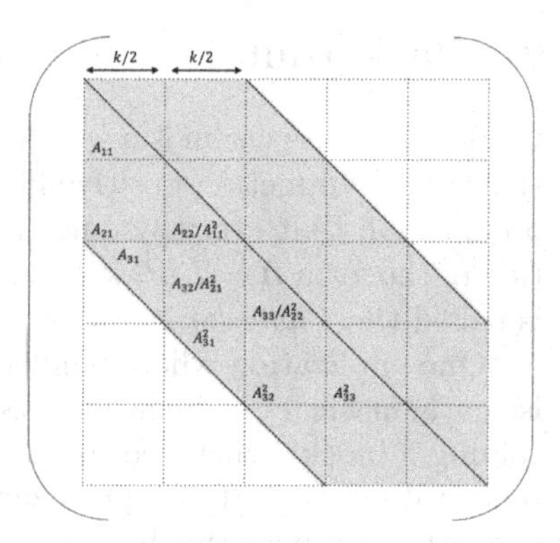


(b) Illustration of two iterations of our parallel algorithm for $3 \times 3$ sub-windows.

**Fig. 1.** Illustrations of block-algorithms.

## 4 Method

The computational scheme outlined in the previous section lends itself naturally to a task-based parallel formulation by inspection of the dependencies between

[1] https://www.netlib.org/lapack/explore-html/.

**Algorithm 1** Fine-grained Cholesky factorization

**Require:** $n \geq 0$. {*n is the dimension of the $n \times n$ grid in each iteration*}

1: **for** each active window in the matrix **do**
2: Factorize $A_{11}$ into $L_{11}L_{11}^T$ using dense Cholesky
3: **for** $i \leftarrow 2$ to $n-1$ **do**
4: Compute $L_{i1} = A_{i1}(L_{11}^T)^{-1}$ using DTRSM
5: **for** $j \leftarrow 2$ to $i-1$ **do**
6: Compute $A'_{ij} = A_{ij} - L_{i1}L_{j1}^T$ using DGEMM
7: **end for**
8: Compute $A'_{ii} = A_{ii} - L_{i1}L_{i1}^T$ using DSYRK
9: **end for**
{*The last row requires special handling, since the bottom-left block is cut off by the banded structure of the matrix.*}
10: Copy $A_{n1}$ to the work array (a square matrix with bottom left triangle explicitly set to zero).
11: Compute $L_{n1} = A_{i1}(L_{11}^T)^{-1}$ using DTRSM (overwriting the value in the work array).
12: **for** $k \leftarrow 2$ to $n-1$ **do**
13: Compute $A'_{nk} = A_{nk} - L_{n1}L_{k1}^T$ using DGEMM (with $L_{n1}$ stored in the work array)
14: **end for**
15: Compute $A'_{nn} = A_{nn} - L_{n1}L_{n1}^T$ using DSYRK (with $L_{n1}$ stored in the work array)
16: **end for**

the different steps. For instance, we see that step (2) depends on step (1) for $L_{11}^T$ and step (3) depends on step (2) for $L_{21}$, and so forth. One major drawback of this parallelization scheme is that the $3 \times 3$ active windows may not yield enough parallelism to exploit the hardware to its fullest.

In this work, we extend the $3 \times 3$ block-based algorithm to be able to handle more fine subdivisions of the active block into $n \times n$ sub-blocks. The benefit of this is a finer task-granularity when parallelizing the algorithm (since each task comprises an operation on a single cell in the grid). One advantage of our method is the use of the standard LAPACK storage format, which lowers the barrier for adoption of our method in existing codes, and avoids possible overhead in converting the matrix to a specialized internal storage format. To note is that we do not use any explicit barriers in our code, but rather all the task dependencies and scheduling is handled by the OpenMP runtime. A pseudocode implementation of our algorithm is shown in Algorithm 1.

The dependency analysis between the different steps shown in Algorithm 1 is relatively straightforward when only considering the operations within one *outer iteration* (one iteration of the loop on line 1 in Algorithm 1). Each DTRSM operation on the $A_{i1}$ blocks depends on the factorization of the $A_{11}$ block (and the copying to the work array in the case of the bottom left block), the DGEMM operations depend on two of the updates using DTRSM, and the DSYRK operation on the $A_{ii}$ block depends on the DTRSM of the leftmost block on the same block-row. Some special care is required for the bottom block row, due to the use of a temporary array to hold the upper right triangle of the $A_{n1}$ block. To further decrease the amount of synchronization needed, we further extend the analysis of task dependencies to include multiple outer iterations as well. This is made possible by ensuring that the block-grid of the current iteration partially overlaps the block grid from the previous outer iteration, see Fig. 1b for an illustration of the $n = 3$ case. Thus, the updates on each $A_{ij}$ block that overlaps the previous iteration also depends on the operations on the $A_{i+1,j+1}$ block *from the previous iteration*. This overlapping does however come with the assumption that the dimension $n-1$ of each $n \times n$ sub-grid evenly divides the bandwidth $k$ in our current implementation.

Finally, the question of how to select the number of sub-blocks to divide each $n \times n$ active window into in the algorithm remains. Recall that we have the requirement that $n-1$ must divide the bandwidth $k$ of the matrix. As a first prototype, we have implemented a heuristic that tries to select an appropriate value $n$ that fulfills the divisibility requirement while giving the algorithm sufficient parallelism and suitable block sizes to work with. Our heuristic works by selecting a value $n$ that balances the following requirements:

- $n-1$ divides the bandwidth $k$ of the matrix
- $n$ is selected such that the block size for the level-3 BLAS operations is approximately 50 by 50.
- $n$ is not greater than the number of physical cores of the system.

These criteria were selected based on our experimental experience with tuning the performance on our systems. However, this heuristic is still rather crude and may not give optimal performance for all configurations and sizes. As such, users with *a priori* knowledge of the approximate matrix bandwidths and hardware configurations for their use case may tune the number of blocks separately to achieve greater performance.

### 4.1 Implementation Using OpenMP Tasks

We implement a prototype for our method in C++, where we rely on BLAS libraries to perform the block computations in Algorithm 1. To implement the task-based parallel Cholesky factorization for banded matrices, we use OpenMP tasks with task dependencies, a feature from OpenMP 4.0. The motivation for using OpenMP is mainly one of availability and portability. OpenMP implementations are available for a number of the most widely used C/C++ compiler suites, making our implementation accessible on a range of platforms. To specify data-dependencies between tasks, OpenMP provides `in`, `inout` and `out` clauses to the task pragma, which we use to define the task dependencies described in the previous section. As seen in Listing 1.1, we use a dummy array to specify the task dependencies, which is not directly accessed by the actual tasks. This works since the OpenMP implementation is agnostic to whether the task dependencies are actually accessed and modified by the tasks, but simply builds the dependency graphs *as if* the data was modified. Thus, the entry at index $(i, j)$ in our dummy array logically represents the block at row index $i$ and column index $j$ in the current active window. For readers interested in other task-based parallel programming frameworks, we refer to the study in [21]. The remainder of our implementation also depends on some BLAS implementation for the level-3 BLAS kernels used (DTRSM, DSYRK and DGEMM, see Sect. 3.1), as well as an implementation of `dpotrf` from LAPACK (for step (1)). One important point to note is that our implementation assumes that the bandwidth $k$, defined as the number of super- and sub-diagonals of the matrix, is divisible by $n - 1$, where $n$ is the dimension of the $n \times n$ block grid in each iteration. Our heuristic for selecting $n$ (described in Sect. 4) selects such a value when possible. Of course, this requirement is impossible to fulfill in certain cases (the bandwidth may for instance be prime). Thus, we have a minimum requirement that the bandwidth of the input matrix is, at least, even such that a division into $3 \times 3$ blocks is valid, which can be ensured by the user by zero-padding their matrix during allocation. Our implementation is available as open source on GitHub[2].

```
1   char task_dep[BLOCK_DIM][BLOCK_DIM];
2   #pragma omp parallel
3   #pragma omp single
4   {
5       for (int i = 0; i < mat_dim; i += nb) {
6           #pragma omp task depend(out:task_dep[0][0]) depend(in: task_dep[1][1])
7           dpotrf(...);
8
9           for (int blk_i = 1; blk_i < block_dim-1; ++block_i) {
10              #pragma omp task depend(in: task_dep[0][0], task_dep[block_i + 1][1]) \
11                                   depend(out: task_dep[block_i][0])
12              cblas_dtrsm(...);
13              for (int block_j = 1; block_j <= block_i; ++block_j) {
14                  #pragma omp task depend(in: task_dep[block_i][0], task_dep[block_j][0]) \
15                                       depend(out: task_dep[block_i][block_j])
16                  cblas_dgemm(...);
17              }
18              #pragma omp task depend(in: task_dep[block_i][0], \
19                                   task_dep[block_i + 1][block_i + 1]) \
20                                   depend(out: task_dep[block_i][block_i])
21              cblas_dsyrk(...);
22          }
23      }
24  }
```

**Listing 1.1.** Skeletonized C++ code snippet illustrating the implementation of the tasking using OpenMP. Function arguments are omitted for clarity.

---
[2] https://github.com/felliu/BandCholesky.

**Algorithm 2** Left-looking Cholesky for banded matrices

**Input:** Matrix $A$ with dimension $N$ and bandwidth $k$
**Output:** Factorized matrix $L$

1: **for** $i \leftarrow 1$ to $N$ **do**
2: **for** $j \leftarrow \max(1, i-k)$ to $i$ **do**
3: $t \leftarrow 0$
4: **for** $l \leftarrow \max(1, i-k)$ to $j$ **do**
5: $t \leftarrow t + L(i,l) * L(j,l)$
6: **end for**
7: **if** $i == j$ **then**
8: $L(i,i) \leftarrow \sqrt{A(i,i) - t}$
9: **else**
10: $L(i,j) \leftarrow (A(i,j) - t)/L(j,j)$
11: **end if**
12: **end for**
13: **end for**

### 4.2 Performance Model

The algorithm for Cholesky factorization for banded matrices discussed in this paper mainly comprises calls to level-3 BLAS kernels, which are typically highly compute-bound operations. A simple way to judge the performance of a compute-bound algorithm's implementation is to consider the number of floating point operations required to factorize a matrix with given dimensions and (matrix) bandwidth. Since Cholesky factorization is stable without pivoting, the minimum number of floating point operations required to factorize any symmetric positive definite matrix with given dimensions is constant and can be computed relatively exactly. The number of floating point operations required can be computed by considering a left-looking algorithm for Cholesky decomposition, where some loops are truncated from the dense algorithm by the banded structure. Pseudocode for the algorithm is shown in Algorithm 2. Computing the number of floating point operation required for the factorization can be done in a straightforward way by simply replacing the computational statements in the algorithm with their number of floating point operations and summing for the total value. Let $r = \max(1, i-k)$, then the resulting sum is

$$\sum_{i=1}^{N} \sum_{j=r}^{i} \sum_{l=r}^{j} 2 + \sum_{i=1}^{N} \sum_{j=r}^{i} 2, \tag{1}$$

if we consider the square root to be a single floating point operation. While this sum can be evaluated exactly on a computer (which is how we derive the exact FLOP-counts used for the benchmarks), one may also get an approximate value on the order of the number of operations required. We have

$$\sum_{i=1}^{N}\sum_{j=r}^{i}\sum_{l=r}^{j} 2 + \sum_{i=1}^{N}\sum_{j=r}^{i} 2 \approx \sum_{j=i-k}^{i}\sum_{l=i-k}^{j} 2N + 2Nk =$$
$$\sum_{j=i-k}^{i} 2N(j-(i-k)+1) + 2Nk = 2N\sum_{l=1}^{k} l + 2Nk$$
$$\approx Nk^2 + 2Nk = \mathcal{O}(Nk^2),$$

where the first approximation is disregarding the truncation in $\max(1, i-k)$, and the second approximation (in the second to last step) uses the observation that the first term is an arithmetic progression.

## 5 Experimental Setup

We evaluate our methods on randomly generated positive-definite (which is ensured by making the matrices diagonally dominant) banded matrices, since the values of the entries do not matter for the number of operations required for Cholesky decomposition (so long as the matrix remains symmetric positive-definite). In all of the experiments below, we fix the dimension of the matrices (the number of rows and columns) to 100,000, and vary the matrix bandwidth.

### 5.1 Benchmarking Systems

In the following, we list the benchmarking systems used in this work.

- **Coffee Lake Workstation** is a workstation laptop with a six-core Intel Xeon E-2186M (Coffee Lake) CPU, running Ubuntu 22.04 LTS.
- **Kebnekaise** is an HPC cluster at HPC2N in Umeå, Sweden. Kebnekaise with two Intel Xeon E5-2690v4 (Broadwell) per node. The nodes are running Ubuntu 20.04 LTS.

For running benchmarks, we use the Google Benchmark[3] suite, a C++ library providing different utilities for running (micro)benchmarks. We let the benchmark suite decide the number of iterations to run the benchmark (typically around 10) and then we repeat each run 10 times to gather statistics and estimate noise, all done using the built-in functionality in Google Benchmark. In all the plots below, the median time is reported, to exclude influence from outliers affected by system noise and similar.

For our tasking implementation, we use Intel's OpenMP runtime library, linked with code compiled with GCC (Intel's OpenMP runtime library has a compatibility layer with GNU OpenMP symbols). We compiled our code using GCC 11.2.0 and CMake, with the CMake build set to `Release` mode (implying optimization level `-O3` for GCC). The following software versions were used in the experiments:

[3] https://github.com/google/benchmark.

- Intel MKL version 2022.1.0 on Coffee Lake Workstation and 2022.2.0 on Kebnekaise
- BLIS version 0.9.0
- OpenBLAS version 0.3.20
- PLASMA version 21.8.29

# 6 Results

**Table 1.** Summary of *average* performance of the different implementations *in GFLOP/s* over the different matrix bandwidth ranges, test systems and implementations. The specific matrix bandwidths benchmarked are the same as in Fig. 2 and 3. The best performing implementation is shown in bold, with the improvements over the best performing baseline (which are sequential and multithreaded MKL and PLASMA), are shown in the bottom row.

| Implementation | Kebnekaise | | | Coffee Lake Workstation | |
|---|---|---|---|---|---|
| Problem setup | Low BW (50–200) | High BW (200–2000) Full node | High BW (200–2000) Single socket | Low BW (50–200) | High BW (200–2000) |
| Task Parallel + MKL | **22.544** | **218.574** | **269.133** | **32.158** | **168.402** |
| Task Parallel + BLIS | 12.224 | 176.513 | 186.601 | 17.9 | 139.82 |
| MKL Multithread | 17.256 | 161.078 | 249.022 | 25.089 | 162.2 |
| MKL Sequential | 17.852 | – | – | 25.731 | – |
| PLASMA | – | 127.361 | 128.636 | – | 88.705 |
| **Improvement over best baseline** | **26.283%** | **35.694%** | **8.076%** | **24.978%** | **3.824%** |

In the following section, we present performance results comparing our parallel Cholesky factorization with different state-of-the art libraries (Intel MKL and PLASMA) and settings. Note that our implementation depends on a BLAS implementation as well as an implementation of `dpotrf` from LAPACK. In some results we will use Intel MKL for these dependencies in our algorithm. These are not to be confused with the stand-alone MKL results, where MKL's `dpbtrf` (LAPACK kernel for Cholesky factorization of banded matrices) is used. In all of the experiments involving our task-based implementation below, we use the heuristic described in Sect. 4 to decide the dimension $n$ of the block grid in each iteration. In all plots, the performance is shown in GFLOP/s, with the number of floating point operations required computed as described in Sect. 4.2 (in particular, the floating point operation count used to calculate the FLOP/s is the same for all benchmarks). The plots also show the peak performance of the CPU (or node for some Kebnekaise benchmarks) in terms of GFLOP/s in double precision. The values for the peak performance is retrieved from the export compliance metrics provided by Intel for their CPUs (available online[4]).

[4] https://www.intel.com/content/www/us/en/support/articles/000005755/processors.html).

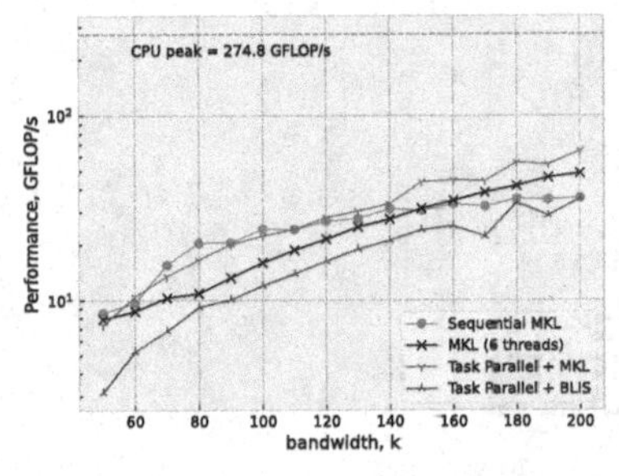


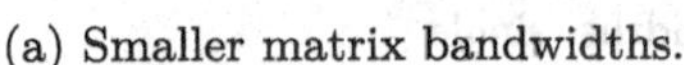
(a) Smaller matrix bandwidths.

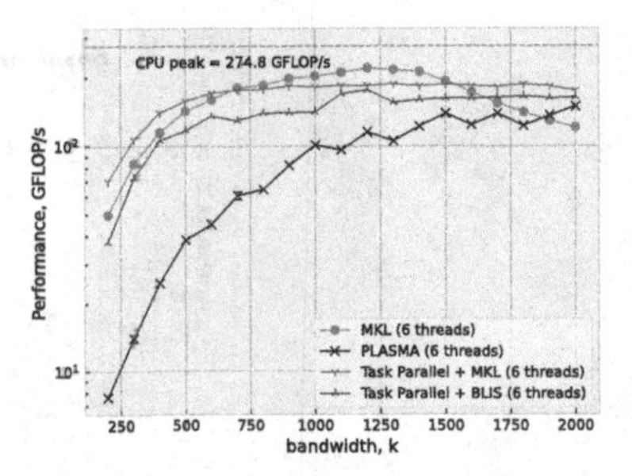


(b) Larger matrix bandwidths.

**Fig. 2.** Performance comparison of different Cholesky factorizations on the Coffee Lake Workstation. The performance is shown in GFLOP/s. The left plot shows the performance for smaller matrix bandwidths, and the right for larger matrix bandwidths. Note the log scale on the y-axes.

The performance plots on the Coffee Lake Workstation are shown in Fig. 2 and the results on Kebnekaise are shown in Fig. 3. On Kebnekaise, the compute nodes have two CPU sockets on different NUMA domains. For the larger matrix bandwidths, we show results using both a single CPU socket (thus avoiding NUMA effects) in Fig. 3b, and results using the full node in Fig. 3c. In cases where the standard deviation in runtime as reported by Google Benchmark exceeds 5% (which was only the case for the results in Fig. 3b), we show a (symmetric) offset of the sample standard deviation as the shaded areas in the plot. The average performance in GFLOP/s over the different matrix bandwidth ranges (50–200 for the low range and 200–2000 for the high range) is summarized in Table 1.

We find that our task-based implementation using MKL's BLAS backend is the best performing when considering the average performance across the range of matrix bandwidths, with Intel MKL's `dpbtrf` being the second best performing in most cases. However, Intel MKL performs better in certain configurations and at certain bandwidths, as we can see in the plots. The difference in performance at different matrix bandwidths for our task-based implementation may be affected by the heuristic used to select sub-block sizes (described in Sect. 4), which is still rather crude. Furthermore, we see that the performance of our task-based approach using BLIS for the BLAS backend has a rather significant drop in performance compared to using MKL for BLAS. One possible reason for this is that MKL's BLAS level-3 kernels may be better tuned for small matrices (the matrix sizes in each BLAS call will often be approximately $50 \times 50$). This performance difference for smaller matrices has also been observed in previous work [12]. PLASMA's performance is lower than MKL in our experiments, which we believe to be caused by overhead in converting the matrix format to PLASMA's internal storage format from the standard LAPACK format used in our benchmarks. On average, we find that our performance improvement relative to Intel MKL is larger for the smaller matrix bandwidth. The average performance across the range of matrix bandwidths is far from the peak performance

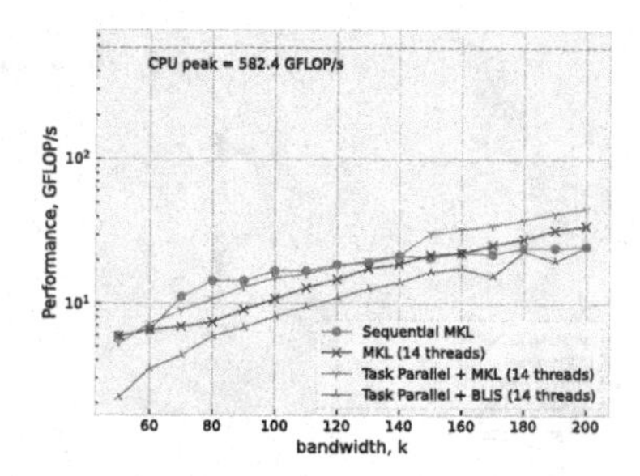


(a) Smaller matrix bandwidths, single CPU socket

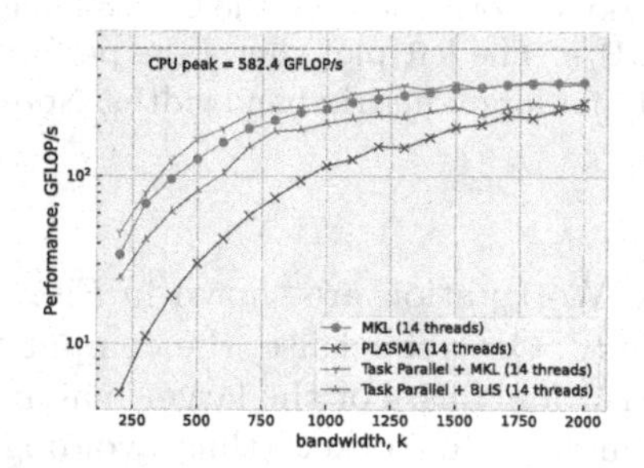


(b) Larger matrix bandwidths, single CPU socket.

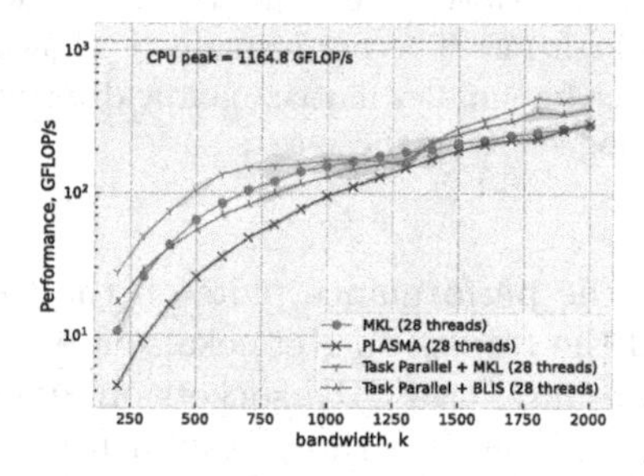


(c) Larger matrix bandwidths, full node.

**Fig. 3.** Performance comparison of different Cholesky factorization implementations on Kebnekaise. The performance is shown in GFLOP/s (higher is better). Two types of runs are shown, one using the full node with two Intel Xeon E2690v4 CPUs (28 physical cores) and two corresponding NUMA domains, and two using a single socket (14 physical cores) and a single NUMA domain.

of the CPUs in all cases, with the size of the gap increasing significantly as the bandwidths of the matrix decreases. For the largest bandwidths, the best performing implementations achieve approximately 70% of the peak performance of the CPUs.

## 7 Conclusions and Future Work

In this paper, we have presented our work on evaluating the performance of a task-based parallel algorithm for Cholesky factorization of banded matrices. Our results demonstrate that our method performs, on average, better than state-of-the-art libraries such as Intel MKL for matrices with dimensions and bandwidths similar to those that may arise from our aforementioned optimization problems. However, achieving the optimal performance may depend on a number of factors, including the specific CPU hardware used, the dimensions of the input matrix, among other things.

Furthermore, the rapid rise in utilization of GPUs in HPC motivates an investigation of the suitability of our algorithm for GPUs. Implementation wise, using task based parallel programming models to target GPUs is possible, for example using the OmpSS programming model [3, 10]. Another possible approach is to use the CUDA Graph functionality introduced in CUDA 10, whereby graphs consisting of kernels and their dependencies can be built explicitly and executed on the GPU. Regardless of the specific implementation used, one of the main challenges we see is the limited amount of parallelism available in the Cholesky factorization of banded matrices when the size of the bands is modest (our results show that the performance is far from the peak performance of even CPUs at smaller matrix bandwidths). GPUs often require a large amount of available parallelism to run at their peak performance. Thus, the performance benefit of porting to GPUs may be modest, but this is a question we leave for future research.

In conclusion, our implementation performs competitively compared to Intel MKL for our use case, all while keeping a LAPACK-compatible storage scheme for the matrices. Finally, we hope to be able to evaluate our algorithm in a real optimization pipeline for radiation therapy problems in the future to assess the performance improvement in such cases.

**Acknowledgments and Data Availability.** The computations were enabled by resources provided by the Swedish National Infrastructure for Computing (SNIC) at HPC2N, partially funded by the Swedish Research Council through grant agreement no. 2018-05973.

The datasets and code generated during and/or analysed during the current study are available in the Figshare repository https://doi.org/10.6084/m9.figshare.23537259 [1].

## References

1. Liu, F., Fredriksson, A., Markidis, S.: Reproducibility artifact for: Parallel Cholesky factorization for banded matrices using OpenMP tasks (2023). https://doi.org/10.6084/m9.figshare.23537259
2. Baumann, M., et al.: Radiation oncology in the era of precision medicine. Nat. Rev. Cancer **16**(4), 234–249 (2016)
3. Bueno, J., et al.: Productive programming of GPU clusters with OmpSs. In: 2012 IEEE 26th International Parallel and Distributed Processing Symposium, pp. 557–568. IEEE (2012)
4. Chan, E., Van Zee, F.G., Bientinesi, P., Quintana-Orti, E.S., Quintana-Orti, G., Van de Geijn, R.: SuperMatrix: a multithreaded runtime scheduling system for algorithms-by-blocks. In: Proceedings of the 13th ACM SIGPLAN Symposium on Principles and Practice of Parallel Programming, pp. 123–132 (2008)
5. Du Croz, J., Mayes, P., Radicati, G.: Factorizations of band matrices using level 3 BLAS. In: Burkhart, H. (ed.) CONPAR/VAPP -1990. LNCS, vol. 457, pp. 222–231. Springer, Heidelberg (1990). https://doi.org/10.1007/3-540-53065-7_102
6. Davis, T.A., Rajamanickam, S., Sid-Lakhdar, W.M.: A survey of direct methods for sparse linear systems. Acta Numer **25**, 383–566 (2016)

7. Demmel, J.W.: Applied Numerical Linear Algebra. SIAM (1997)
8. Dongarra, J., et al.: PLASMA: parallel linear algebra software for multicore using OpenMP. ACM Trans. Math. Softw. (TOMS) **45**(2), 1–35 (2019)
9. Dorris, J., Kurzak, J., Luszczek, P., YarKhan, A., Dongarra, J.: Task-based Cholesky decomposition on knights corner using OpenMP. In: Taufer, M., Mohr, B., Kunkel, J.M. (eds.) ISC High Performance 2016. LNCS, vol. 9945, pp. 544–562. Springer, Cham (2016). https://doi.org/10.1007/978-3-319-46079-6_37
10. Duran, A., et al.: OmpSs: a proposal for programming heterogeneous multi-core architectures. Parallel Process. Lett. **21**(02), 173–193 (2011)
11. Forsgren, A., Gill, P.E., Wright, M.H.: Interior methods for nonlinear optimization. SIAM Rev. **44**(4), 525–597 (2002)
12. Frison, G., Sartor, T., Zanelli, A., Diehl, M.: The BLAS API of BLASFEO: optimizing performance for small matrices. ACM Trans. Math. Softw. (TOMS) **46**(2), 1–36 (2020)
13. Geist, G., Ng, E.: Task scheduling for parallel sparse Cholesky factorization. Int. J. Parallel Program. **18**(4), 291–314 (1989). https://doi.org/10.1007/BF01407861
14. Gondzio, J.: Interior point methods 25 years later. Eur. J. Oper. Res. **218**(3), 587–601 (2012)
15. Gupta, A., Gustavson, F.G., Joshi, M., Toledo, S.: The design, implementation, and evaluation of a symmetric banded linear solver for distributed-memory parallel computers. ACM Trans. Math. Softw. (TOMS) **24**(1), 74–101 (1998)
16. Gustavson, F.G., Quintana-Ortı, E.S., Quintana-Ortı, G., Remón, A., Wasniewski, J.: Clearer, simpler and more efficient LAPACK routines for symmetric positive definite band factorization (2008)
17. Hogg, J.D., Reid, J.K., Scott, J.A.: Design of a multicore sparse Cholesky factorization using DAGs. SIAM J. Sci. Comput. **32**(6), 3627–3649 (2010)
18. Le Fèvre, V., Usui, T., Casas, M.: A selective nesting approach for the sparse multi-threaded Cholesky factorization. In: 2022 IEEE/ACM 7th International Workshop on Extreme Scale Programming Models and Middleware (ESPM2), pp. 1–9. IEEE (2022)
19. Liu, F., Fredriksson, A., Markidis, S.: A survey of HPC algorithms and frameworks for large-scale gradient-based nonlinear optimization. J. Supercomput. **78**(16), 17513–17542 (2022). https://doi.org/10.1007/s11227-022-04555-8
20. Liu, J.W.: Computational models and task scheduling for parallel sparse Cholesky factorization. Parallel Comput. **3**(4), 327–342 (1986)
21. Podobas, A., Brorsson, M., Faxén, K.F.: A comparative performance study of common and popular task-centric programming frameworks. Concurr. Comput. Pract. Exp. **27**(1), 1–28 (2015)
22. Quintana-Ortí, G., Quintana-Ortí, E.S., Remón, A., van de Geijn, R.A.: An algorithm-by-blocks for SuperMatrix band Cholesky factorization. In: Palma, J.M.L.M., Amestoy, P.R., Daydé, M., Mattoso, M., Lopes, J.C. (eds.) VECPAR 2008. LNCS, vol. 5336, pp. 228–239. Springer, Heidelberg (2008). https://doi.org/10.1007/978-3-540-92859-1_21
23. Remón, A., Quintana-Ortí, E.S., Quintana-Ortí, G.: Cholesky factorization of band matrices using multithreaded BLAS. In: Kågström, B., Elmroth, E., Dongarra, J., Waśniewski, J. (eds.) PARA 2006. LNCS, vol. 4699, pp. 608–616. Springer, Heidelberg (2007). https://doi.org/10.1007/978-3-540-75755-9_73
24. Unkelbach, J., et al.: Optimization approaches to volumetric modulated arc therapy planning. Med. Phys. **42**(3), 1367–1377 (2015)

25. Van Zee, F.G., Chan, E., Van de Geijn, R.A., Quintana-Orti, E.S., Quintana-Orti, G.: The libflame library for dense matrix computations. Comput. Sci. Eng. **11**(6), 56–63 (2009)
26. Wang, Y., Boyd, S.: Fast model predictive control using online optimization. IEEE Trans. Control Syst. Technol. **18**(2), 267–278 (2009)
27. Wright, S.J.: Applying new optimization algorithms to more predictive control. Technical report, Argonne National Lab. (ANL), Argonne, IL, United States (1996)

# Author Index




J. Cano et al. (Eds.): Euro-Par 2023, LNCS 14100, pp. 741–743, 2023.
https://doi.org/10.1007/978-3-031-39698-4

Printed in the United States
by Baker & Taylor Publisher Services